The Tribes *and* Castes *of* Bengal

by

Herbert Hope Risley

INDIAN CIVIL SERVICE, COMPANION OF THE INDIAN EMPIRE,
OFFICER D'ACADÉMIE FRANÇAISE

ETHNOGRAPHIC GLOSSARY

Vol. 1

(In Two Volumes)

τίς πόθεν εἷς ἀνδρῶν; πόθι τοι πόλις ἠδὲ τοκῆες;

ODYSSEY i, 170.

Low Price Publications
2017

First Published 1892
Reprinted in **LPP** 2017

ISBN 10: 81-7536-560-9 (Set)
ISBN 13: 978-81-7536-560-5 (Set)

ISBN 10: 81-7536-561-7 (Vol. 1)
ISBN 13: 978-81-7536-561-2 (Vol. 1)

Published by
Low Price Publications
A-6, 2nd Floor, Nimri Commercial Centre,
Ashok Vihar Phase 4, Delhi 110052 (INDIA)
tel.: +91-11-27302453 fax.: +91-11-47061936
url: www.LPPindia.com e-mail: info@LPPindia.com

Printed at
D.K. Fine Art Press Pvt. Ltd.
Delhi

PRINTED IN INDIA

Official edition, circulated for criticism.

THE

TRIBES AND CASTES OF BENGAL.

By H. H. RISLEY,

INDIAN CIVIL SERVICE, COMPANION OF THE INDIAN EMPIRE,
OFFICIER D'ACADÉMIE FRANÇAISE.

ETHNOGRAPHIC GLOSSARY.

Vol. I.

τίς πόθεν εἰς ἀνδρῶν ; πόθι τοι πόλις ἠδὲ τοκῆες ;

ODYSSEY i, 170.

CALCUTTA:

Printed at the Bengal Secretariat Press.

1892.

TO THE MEMORY OF

Dr. James Wise,

SOME TIME CIVIL SURGEON OF DACCA,

THIS VOLUME,

EMBODYING IN PART THE RESULTS OF HIS RESEARCHES DURING THIRTEEN YEARS' RESIDENCE IN EASTERN BENGAL,

IS DEDICATED.

PREFACE.

The following volumes contain the results of what is, I believe, the first attempt to apply to Indian ethnography the methods of systematic research sanctioned by the authority of European anthropologists.

I am painfully aware that in many respects the work is exceedingly imperfect, and can hardly claim to do more than map out and define in view of further inquiry the large field of research which had to be covered. In attempting within a given time to draw up an ethnographic description of the various castes and tribes found among the seventy millions of people inhabiting the territory administered by the Lieutenant-Governor of Bengal, it is difficult, on the one hand, to secure complete information regarding all the groups which have to be dealt with, and on the other to avoid making general statements concerning castes as a whole, which are only true of particular sections of those castes. For this reason it has been decided to bring out at first an official edition, and to invite criticism with the object of supplying omissions and correcting mistakes. All suggestions will be carefully considered, and the conclusions to which they give rise embodied in a second edition. It is hoped that criticisms may be sent in promptly enough for this second edition to be brought out within eighteen months' or two years' time. All communications on this subject should be addressed to me at the Bengal Secretariat, Calcutta.

INTRODUCTORY ESSAY:

CASTE IN RELATION TO MARRIAGE.

CONTENTS.

INTRODUCTORY ESSAY:

CASTE IN RELATION TO MARRIAGE.

On a stone panel forming part of one of the grandest Buddhist monuments in India—the great tope at Sanchi—a carving in low relief depicts a strange religious ceremony. Under trees with conventional foliage and fruits, three women, attired in tight clothing without skirts, kneel in prayer before a small shrine or altar. In the foreground, the leader of a procession of monkeys bears in both hands a bowl of liquid and stoops to offer it at the shrine. His solemn countenance and the grotesquely adoring gestures of his comrades seem intended to express reverence and humility. In the background four stately figures—two men and two women—of tall stature and regular features, clothed in flowing robes and wearing most elaborate turbans, look on with folded hands and apparent approval at this remarkable act of worship. Antiquarian speculation has for the most part passed the panel by unnoticed, or has sought to associate it with some pious legend of the life of Buddha. A larger interest, however, attaches to the scene, if it is regarded as the sculptured expression of the race sentiment of the Aryans towards the Dravidians, which runs through the whole course of Indian tradition and survives in scarcely abated strength at the present day. On this view the relief would belong to the same order of ideas as the story in the Ramayana of the army of apes who assisted Rama in the invasion of Ceylon. It shows us the higher race on friendly terms with the lower, but keenly conscious of the essential difference of type and not taking part in the ceremony at which they appear as patronising spectators. An attempt is made in the following pages to show that the race sentiment, which this

The race basis of caste.

curious sculpture represents, so far from being a figment of the intolerant pride of the Brahman, rests upon a foundation of fact which scientific methods confirm, that it has shaped the intricate groupings of the caste system, and has preserved the Aryan type in comparative purity throughout Northern India.

Some nine years ago, when the vast array of figures called up by the last census of India was being gradually worked into shape, it occurred to the Census Commissioner that this costly statistical material might be made the basis of an attempt to extend and systematise our knowledge of the customs, beliefs, and occupations of the Indian people. In August 1882, while the statistics of the census of 1881 were still under compilation, Sir William Plowden reported that the local census officers throughout India had been directed not only to show the major castes and the occupations under large general heads in their statistical tables, but also to give in the body of their report the numbers of all castes recorded, and the names of all occupations followed by 10,000 persons or more in each province. He then suggested that lists should be drawn up for each district, showing separately the castes and occupations found in each, with their vernacular designations, to be followed by an abstract showing clearly to what larger head, if any, each caste or occupation had been attached. Finally, he proposed that when these lists had been made out, detailed enquiries should be instituted locally regarding any special caste or occupation about which further information might seem desirable, and that the result of these enquiries should be embodied in a memorandum to be appended to the district lists in question. In a subsequent letter he drew attention to Mr. Denzil Ibbetson's Memorandum on Ethnological Enquiry in the Panjáb,[1] and

Origin of ethnographic inquiry in Bengal.

[1] This admirable paper is reprinted with Mr. Ibbetson's permission as Appendix III to the second volume.

suggested that copies of it should be circulated to the district officials in other provinces, in order to assist them in collecting information regarding the castes and occupations of the people. The Census Commissioner's proposals were generally approved by the Government of India and commended to the consideration of the Local Governments and Administrations in India, but in no Province besides Bengal was it found possible to initiate any large scheme of enquiry. Early in 1884 the Government of Bengal recommended to the Government of India the appointment of the present writer for a period of two years to conduct an enquiry into castes and occupations throughout Bengal. "The results of the enquiry," it was said, "would be of great value in connection with the next census; but it is still more important to observe that, if the enquiry is postponed till after the next census, it will be impossible to make it so complete as it can now be made. The late census showed how rapidly the old aboriginal faiths are being effaced, and what progress is being made in the absorption of the primitive races in the great system of Hinduism. At the same time the opening of communications, the increase in the facilities for travel, and the spread of education, are tending to obliterate the land-marks of the Hindu faith, to slacken the bonds of caste, and to provide occupations unknown to the ancient polity. There is nothing to be gained, and much to be lost, by postponing this important work. If it is not undertaken now, a mass of information of unsurpassed interest will be lost to the world." While thus laying stress on the importance of the work, the Lieutenant-Governor considered that the officers of the regular staff had not sufficient leisure to prosecute ethnographic enquiries in addition to their ordinary duties; while many of them had no special taste for such enquiries. Moreover, as the chief value of the work would consist in the comparative treatment of the customs of the same or different castes in different districts of these provinces, it was essential that this comparison should be made by a single officer, who would have before him a large body of facts, and would not be confined to the data obtainable within a single district. The scheme was sanctioned by the Government of India and the Secretary of State; but, owing to administrative reasons, effect was not given to the appointment till early in February 1885.

After making some experimental enquiries in Behar and North-Eastern Bengal, and preparing a scheme for collecting information regarding the castes and occupations of the people in a systematic manner, I visited Lahore in March 1885 for the purpose of conferring with Mr. Denzil Ibbetson, Director of Public Instruction in the Panjáb, and Mr. J. C. Nesfield, Inspector of Schools in Oudh, both of whom had considerable experience in similar enquiries, and were in a position to offer valuable advice on the subject. The Conference sat from the 18th to the 22nd March, and drew up proceedings which will be found in Appendix II to the second volume. One chief object of our deliberations was to secure, so far as might be possible, that ethnographic researches carried on in different Provinces of the Bengal Presidency should proceed on the same general lines in order that their results might be of some service to students of comparative ethnology in Europe. We considered the question as to the best means to be adopted to collect original data in addition to those already on record in books, reports, and publications of learned societies. For this purpose two sets of questions were drawn up, which form annexures B and C to the proceedings. The general series (annexure B) was framed with the object of bringing out by as few and as simple questions as possible the leading characteristics of any particular caste. The special series (annexure C) goes into more minute detail, and attempts to cover the main heads of ethnographic enquiry in India. The former represents the amount of original enquiry which we considered might fairly be imposed upon the district staff, while the

Ethnographic Conference at Lahore: their scheme.

latter was intended for use only by those whom inclination might lead to pursue the subject further. In order to guard against the confusion which may arise from the ambiguous use of words, we also prepared a note upon certain doubtful points of ethnographic nomenclature, in which we attempted to define, for the purpose of the proposed inquiries, the principal terms ordinarily used to denote the various forms of social organization prevalent in India. The endeavour throughout was not so much to strike out new lines of inquiry as to adapt the methods already sanctioned by the approval of European men of science to the special conditions which have to be taken account of in India. Considerable use was made of the series of questions or heads of enquiry prepared by a committee of the Anthropological Institute of Great Britain and Ireland in 1874, and to this doubtless is owing the fact that when the proceedings of the Conference were submitted for criticism to a number of scientific experts and learned societies in Europe, we received comparatively few complaints that subjects had been omitted or inadequately dealt with. Use was also made of the set of questions given in Mr. C. L. Tupper's volumes on the Customary Law of the Panjáb.

Its scientific objects.

The scheme of inquiry sketched by the Conference may seem at first sight to cover a far wider range than can have been contemplated by the Census Commissioner and the Government of India. But this apparent extension was found to be unavoidable directly the attempt was made to give effect to the general idea thrown out by Mr. Plowden. In dealing with the intricate fabric of social usage, it is difficult to define the component parts of the main subject closely enough to distinguish minutely the point where administrative utility fades away into scientific interest. Most of all in the East, where religion, law, custom, and morality are all inextricably mixed and jumbled up together, would the attempt to attain such precision be futile and misleading. It was understood, therefore, from the first that the objects to be aimed at in the enquiry were partly scientific and partly administrative. From the standpoint of the modern science of anthropology, it was hoped that it might be possible, by careful observation and record of the social practices now prevailing in Bengal, to arrive at fresh data throwing light on the ethnological problems which scientific men, such as Sir John Lubbock, Sir Henry Maine, Mr. E. B. Tylor, Herr Bachofen, M. Fustel de Coulanges, and Herr Adolf Bastian, have discussed in Europe. The principal points, which it was supposed a record of Indian custom might help to clear up, are the early history of marriage, the development of the family, modes of relationship, the early history of inheritance, and the growth of property in land. These are some of the questions which European ethnologists are interested in, and a distinct hope has already been expressed by Sir Henry Maine that something may be done to render available, for the use of scientific men in Europe, the large body of barbarous or semi-barbarous custom, both Aryan and non-Aryan, which still survives in India. It was felt that many of the ethnological speculations of recent years have been based too exclusively upon comparatively unverified accounts of the customs of savages of the lowest type; that the unrivalled opportunities for observation which European officials in India possess have hitherto been imperfectly utilised; and that such results as have been obtained have been recorded in publications not readily accessible, and without sufficient regard to the lines of investigation pursued by ethnologists in Europe. It was also apprehended that the rapid spread of education, and the growth of practical intelligence in India, may lead, within the next generation, to the abandonment of many practices which are of special interest to ethnologists. Besides the general problems enumerated above, there are various questions of special interest to students of Indian history and literature, which may be rendered more intelligible by an accurate record of the actual facts existing at the present day in respect of caste arrangements.

From the administrative point of view, on the other hand, many persons will set down the enquiry as practically useless. Indian administration, it will be said, is not made any more efficient by the elucidation of historical or pre-historic problems. Such researches are in the nature of luxuries. Government may countenance them in the same way and to the same extent as it patronizes learned societies; but they have no direct bearing upon the actual work of administration. This view is, at first sight, plausible enough, but it ignores the important fact that native society is made up of a network of subdivisions governed by rules which affect every department of life, and that, in Bengal at any rate, next to nothing is known about the system upon which the whole native population regulates its domestic and social relations. If legislation, or even executive action, is ever to touch these relations in a satisfactory manner, an ethnographic survey of Bengal, and a record of the customs of the people, is as necessary an incident of good administration as a cadastral survey of the land and a record of the rights of its tenants. The census provides the necessary statistics. It remains to bring out the facts which lie behind the statistics. The relations of different castes to the land, their privileges in respect of rent, their relations to trade, their social status, their internal organization, their rules as to marriage and divorce,—all these are matters intimately concerned with practical administration. For instance, the marriage and divorce customs of the lower castes are constantly coming into the criminal courts, and it would be a decided advantage to judicial officers if accurate information could be made available on the subject. Again, the distribution of the various castes in each district has a direct and important bearing on the relief of distress, as different classes of the population may require

Its administrative objects.

Its bearing on famine relief.

different modes of relief. In order to deal effectively with a famine, we want to know what is the characteristic occupation of each caste in the distressed area, what is their social status, and from whose hands they can take cooked food or sweetmeats, respectively, without losing caste. To our ignorance of these peculiarities is due the loss of life which so often results from the reluctance of people to come to relief camps where they think their notions of purity of diet are likely to be disregarded, or their caste endangered by work which to them is degrading. There exists now in Orissa a caste, called Chattar-khai, recorded in the lists of 1881, which is made up of people who lost their caste in 1866 for eating in relief-kitchens (*chattras*). The caste is divided into an upper and a lower sub-caste—the former comprising Brahmans, Karans, Khandaits and Gop-Goalas, the latter consisting of the castes ranking below these in the social scale. Members of each sub-caste marry within that group, irrespective of the caste to which they originally belonged; but no intermarriage is possible between members of the two sub-castes. All Chattar-khais are entirely cut off from their original castes. It can hardly be doubted that much social misery must have been endured before these people adopted a solution so entirely at variance with the principles in which they had been brought up, and that for one who became a *Chattar-khái*, many died of want. The same argument applies to the working of primary village schools, and to some kinds of land questions. Thus, the Mundas in Lohardugga and the Santáls in the Santál Parganás and elsewhere put forward apparently fantastic claims to privileges in respect of land, the clue to which is probably to be sought in some traditional customary law peculiar to the Dravidian races of Central India. Under the head of marriage, again, an accurate knowledge of the practices actually prevailing among the main body of the people, as distinguished from the literate castes, could hardly fail to be an important factor

On land questions and marriage.

in any influence that Government or unofficial bodies might, at any time, bring to bear with the object of discouraging infant-marriage or promoting the remarriage of widows Social reforms are beginning to be discussed by the leader of native society, and a time may come when Government will be invited to exercise its influence in such matters. It is clear, at any rate, that the more Government officers know about the religious and social customs of the people of their districts, the better able they will be to deal either with the possible social problems of the future, or with the practical questions referred to above.

Its administrative machinery.

For these reasons it was decided by the Government of Bengal to publish and circulate the questions framed by the members of the Conference, and to enlist the aid of the district officers and of others who were in a position to help in obtaining answers to them. Experience had shown that a single person can do very little towards collecting the requisite information within a given time. To elicit facts by oral inquiry is necessarily a lengthy process, and accuracy can only be secured by testing the statements of particular individuals or groups of individuals by numerous independent observations. On the other hand, it was essential that no more labour than was absolutely necessary should be thrown upon the regular administrative staff, and particularly upon the district officers. Every district officer was therefore requested to nominate from among his subordinates one or more officers who were qualified and willing to assist, in addition to their ordinary work, in collecting information for their respective districts or subdivisions. The names of the officers selected were reported to Government. They corresponded direct with the officer in charge of the enquiry, who supplied them with copies in English and vernacular of the general series of ethnographic questions (enclosure B to the proceedings of the Conference), and indicated what use should be made of these questions in each district. The functions of the district officer in the matter were limited to seeing that the selected officers did what was required of them within a reasonable time.

Through the agency of the district officers, supplemented by a good deal of personal enquiry and correspondence, were secured the services of 190 correspondents scattered over every district of Bengal, and communicating in their turn with an indefinite number of representatives of the tribes and castes which formed the subjects of enquiry.[1] Operations were based in the outset on a series of statistical memoranda prepared by the Census Office, showing for every thana (police circle), subdivision, and district the strength of each caste, the number of Mahomedans (who in theory, at any rate, do not recognize caste), and the occupations of both Hindus and Mahomedans. Copies of these memoranda were sent to the correspondents in each district, and they were asked to obtain by

Based on Census statistics.

[1] The names of these gentlemen are shown in Appendix IV to the second volume. The work entrusted to them was, with few exceptions, admirably done, and to them, more than to any efforts of my own, is due whatever measure of success may have been attained. I may be permitted to take this opportunity of specially acknowledging the very valuable assistance and advice which I received from Dr. D. D. Cunningham, F.R.S., Professor of Physiology, Medical College, Calcutta; from Messrs. W. B. Oldham and Denzil Ibbetson, of the Bengal Civil Service; Mr. J. C. Nesfield, Inspector of Schools, Oudh; Mr. A. H. Giles, of the Bengal Police; the Revd. L. Skrefsrud and Revd. A. Campbell, missionaries to the Santáls; Mr. W. H. P. Driver, Emigration Agent, Ránchi; Babu Protab Chandra Ghosha, Registrar of Calcutta; Babu Sarat Chandra Das, C.I.E., Deputy Inspector of Schools; Mr. James Taylor, Tahsildar of Khandmals; Lala Sheo Nandan Lal Ray, Deputy Collector, Patna; Babu Bepin Behary Mukherji, Deputy Collector, Kandi; Babu Haris Chandra Rai, Assistant Superintendent of Ghatwali Survey, Bankura; Babu Adya Nath Banerji, Head Assistant, Statistical Department, Bengal Secretariat; and most of all from the late Babu Rakhal Das Háldár, Manager of the Chutiá Nágpur Ráj. My most cordial acknowledgments are also due to Babu Tara Pada Mukharji, of the Bengal Secretariat, who has acted as my clerk throughout; and has done me invaluable service in revising proofs and arranging matter; to Babu Kumud Behari Sámanta, Civil Hospital Assistant, who took nearly all of the measurements in Bengal, and made some useful ethnographic inquiries; to Chandi Singh, who, under Mr. Nesfield's supervision, took the measurements in the North-Western Provinces and Oudh; and to Civil Hospital Assistant Alá-ud-din, who did similar work in the Panjáb, in addition to his ordinary duties and without extra pay.

personal enquiry, or by any means that seemed likely to yield accurate results, replies to the shorter series of questions for certain specified castes, and to elucidate, as briefly as possible, the numerous obscure and unintelligible entries in the memoranda which purported to be caste designations, but could not readily be recognized as referable to any known caste. Correspondents were also invited, if disposed to travel beyond the range of the shorter questions, to make use of the special questions annexed to the proceedings of the Lahore Conference. With regard to the obscure entries, it should perhaps be explained that all of them were originally written in the local vernacular by the Census enumerators, were then transliterated into English by temporary clerks, who often wrote from dictation instead of reading the entries themselves, and were set up in type from manuscript copied from this transliteration. In this way the process of compilation of itself opened the door to all kinds of mistakes. An unusual caste appellation misunderstood and misspelled by an ignorant enumerator might be misread by a clerk of small local experience, and finally be transformed past all recognition by a printer's error. For instance, in one of the police circles of the Patna district a number of persons were entered under the name *tijra*. No such caste or sub-caste as *tijra* exists, and the word was therefore taken to be a misprint for *hijra*, a eunuch or hermaphrodite. It being, however, *primâ facie* unlikely that so many as 139 persons of both sexes in one *thánd* should come under this category, I made further enquiry into the matter, and ascertained that the people in question were Dosádhs, who had described themselves by the common *padabi* (title) of *Hájra*. What seems to have happened is this: The enumerator who filled in the schedule wrote *Hájra* in Urdu, possibly omitting the *alif*. This was transliterated as *Hijra*, and eventually printed as *Tijra*. The case is worth quoting as an instance of the transformation which perfectly simple words may undergo

Obscure entries.

when the process of transliteration has to be performed by a temporary establishment of clerks on a large scale and under great pressure as to time. But actual errors and misprints, though they form a large proportion of the unintelligible entries in the schedules of an Indian census, by no means account for the whole. Names of small castes, of religious sects, of sections or septs, titles, family names, names of occupations, trades, etc., are, in our present stage of knowledge regarding the internal structure of Indian social groups, almost equally difficult to identify, even when no clerical error has occurred in the triple process of writing in the local vernacular, transliterating, and finally printing them. Before such names are finally banished in the Census Report to the large group set down as "unknown," elaborate attempts have to be made to elucidate them, and the correspondence carried on with this object between the Deputy Superintendent of Census and the district officers adds materially to the cost of the census, as the work of tabulation is delayed and an expensive establishment maintained while enquiries are being carried on. It was therefore for sound administrative reasons that Mr. J. A. Bourdillon, Deputy Superintendent of Census for Bengal, expressed a hope that "something would be done before the next census comes round to prepare a dictionary of castes and a proper classification of occupations. Hundreds of names of castes, clans, or families (containing, however, very few members in most cases) have been unavoidably relegated to the 'unknown' group, because no one could say to what main caste they belong. As to occupations, as has been explained long since, the English system of classification is utterly unsuited to this country and completely destroys all sense of proportion between the different groups, as may be judged from the fact that, according to it, 'tenant-cultivator,' 'farmer's daughter,' 'hangman,' and 'crocodile-catcher' are all placed upon the same level, and are all considered as principal occupations of the people of these provinces."

In organizing the enquiry the object kept in view throughout was to multiply independent observations and to give as much play as possible to the working of the comparative method. The local correspondents were instructed to extend their inquiries over a wide field, to mistrust accounts published in books, to deal with the people direct, and to go for their information to the persons most likely to be well informed on questions of custom, such as priests, marriage brokers, genealogists, headmen of caste *panchâyats*, and the like. When reports were received, they were tested by comparison with notes on the same caste collected by myself, with reports by other correspondents in the same or different districts, with accounts already published, and with Dr. Wise's unpublished notes. Correspondents were invited to clear up discrepancies thus brought to notice, and frequently an entire report was sent back, with marginal annotations, for further inquiry upon points which appeared to be doubtful. As the inquiry proceeded, several special subjects were taken up and examined in circular letters addressed to all correspondents with the object of summarising the general results ascertained up to a certain stage, and thus indicating lines of inquiry which might lead to fuller results.

Method of working.

An elaborate study of the castes of Eastern Bengal was made by the late Dr. James Wise, who was for ten years Civil Surgeon of Dacca, and in that capacity had great opportunities of observing the social life of the people. I quote from a letter written to me by him in July 1885, not long before his death, a description of the admirable method which he adopted for the collection of evidence of custom :—"My system was as follows: Mr. H. M. Weathrall, District Superintendent of Police at Dacca in my day, who spoke rural Bengali as well as any native, accompanied me whenever I started on a tour. Having ascertained where any caste predominated, we went there, and invited the Purohit and headmen to meet us. Having

Dr. James Wise.

wrung from them every particular and written down the result at once, we did the same wherever another settlement of the caste was found. On comparing the records, we arrived at the conclusion given in my notes. If still in doubt, we tested the facts by a third or even a fourth visit. I know of no plan so likely to elicit truth as this." Working on these lines, Dr. Wise collected during his residence at Dacca a very considerable mass of original information concerning the religion, customs, and occupations of the population of Eastern Bengal as represented by the inhabitants of the Dacca district. His notes also contain copious references to the special literature of the subject, and indicate very wide reading. It seems to have been his intention to prepare an exhaustive illustrated monograph on the ethnography of that part of Bengal; and with this view he employed a professional photographer to take a series of nearly two hundred photographs of representative types and groups of all classes of the people. The greater portion of his materials was provisionally worked up by him into a volume, which he modestly designated "Notes on the Races, Castes, and Trades of Eastern Bengal," but only a dozen copies of this appear to have been printed, and Dr. Wise declined to publish any part of it until it had been tested by further and fuller enquiry. In the cold weather of 1884-85 he visited India, and made a tour in Dacca with this object; but even then, from mistaken diffidence as to his literary capacity, he deferred the commencement of his systematic work, and it is impossible to gather from his papers what form he had intended it to take. In the course of this visit to India, Dr. Wise discussed with me the scheme of an ethnographic survey of Bengal, which was then under consideration, and made over to me the printed portion of his notes for any use that I might think fit to make of them. At the time of his death, which occurred suddenly on the 11th of July 1886, he had before him, and was, I believe, inclined to accept, a proposal which I made to him, that we should collaborate for the production of a book on the ethnography of the territories under the Lieutenant-Governor of Bengal. Some months later the whole of his papers were made over to me by Mrs. Wise on the understanding that after testing the data contained in them as far as possible in the manner contemplated by Dr. Wise himself, I should incorporate the results in the ethnographic volumes of the present work, and, by dedicating those volumes to Dr. Wise, should endeavour to preserve some record, however imperfect, of the admirable work done by him during his service in India. Mrs. Wise also sent me the negatives taken under her husband's supervision in or about 1874 in the belief that these could be used for the purpose of illustration. For several reasons this has been found impossible. Not only would the expense of reproducing them by any permanent process be greater than the Government of Bengal could properly be asked to incur, but the introduction of photographs of the types of one (and that by no means the most interesting) part of Bengal would necessarily have involved the preparation of similar illustrations for the other parts—an undertaking which would have cost a very large sum, and would have indefinitely delayed the completion of the present work.

The advance of Brahmanism at the present time.

During several years of district work in Chota Nagpore, and again while organizing the recent inquiry, some special opportunities have come in my way of observing the progress of the great religious and social movement described by Sir Alfred Lyall as "the gradual Brahmanising of the aboriginal, non-Aryan, or casteless tribes."[1] That this movement is progressing on a large scale is beyond doubt; but it by no means maintains a uniform character throughout its sphere of action, and it includes in Bengal

---

[1] *Asiatic Studies*, p. 102.

at least four distinct processes, which may be analysed as follows:—

1. The leading men of an aboriginal tribe, having somehow got on in the world and become independent landed proprietors, manage to enrol themselves in one of the leading castes. They usually set up as Rajputs; their first step being to start a Brahman priest, who invents for them a mythical ancestor, supplies them with a family miracle connected with the locality where their tribe are settled, and discovers that they belong to some hitherto unheard-of clan of the great Rajput community. In the earlier stages of their advancement they generally find great difficulty in getting their daughters married, as they will not marry within their own tribe, and Rajputs of their adopted caste will of course not intermarry with them. But after a generation or two their persistency obtains its reward, and they intermarry, if not with pure Rajputs, at least with a superior order of manufactured Rajputs, whose promotion into the Brahmanical system dates far enough back for the steps by which it was gained to have been forgotten. Thus a real change of blood may take place; while in any caste the tribal name is completely lost, and with it all possibility of accurately separating this class of people from the Hindus of purer blood, and of assigning them to any particular non-Aryan tribe. They have been absorbed in the fullest sense of the word, and henceforth pose, and are locally accepted, as high-caste Hindus. All stages of the process, family miracle and all, can be illustrated by actual instances taken from the leading families in Chota Nagpore.

2. A number of aborigines embrace the tenets of a Hindu religious sect, losing thereby their tribal name and becoming ' shnabs, Ramayats, and the like. Whether there is any ıixture of blood or not will depend upon local circumstances and the rules of the sect regarding intermarriage. Anyhow the identity of the converts as aborigines

is usually, though not invariably, lost, and this also may therefore be regarded as a case of true absorption.

3. A whole tribe of aborigines, or a large section of a tribe, enrol themselves in the ranks of Hinduism under the style of a new caste, which, though claiming an origin of remote antiquity, is readily distinguishable by its name from any of the standard and recognized castes. Thus the great majority of the Kochh inhabitants of Rungpore now invariably describe themselves as Rajbansis or Bhanga Kshatriyas—a designation which enables them to represent themselves as an outlying branch of the Kshatriyas who fled to North-Eastern Bengal in order to escape from the wrath of Parasu-Ráma. They claim descent from Raja Dasarath, father of Ráma; they keep Brahmans, imitate the Brahmanical ritual in their marriage ceremony, and have begun to adopt the Brahmanical system of *gotras*. In respect of this last point they are now in a curious state of transition, as they have all hit upon the same *gotra* (Kasyapa), and thus habitually transgress the primary rule of the Brahmanical system, which absolutely prohibits marriage within the *gotra*. But for this defect in their connubial arrangements—a defect which will probably be corrected in a generation or two as they and their *purohits* rise in intelligence—there would be nothing in their customs to distinguish them from Aryan Hindus, although there has been no mixture of blood, and they remain thoroughly Kochh under the name of Rajbansi.

4. A whole tribe of aborigines, or a section of a tribe, become gradually converted to Hinduism without, like the Rajbansis, abandoning their tribal designation. This is what is happening among the Bhumij of Western Bengal. Here a pure Dravidian race have lost their original language, and now speak only Bengali: they worship Hindu gods in addition to their own (the tendency being to relegate the tribal gods to the women), and the more advanced among them employ Brahmans as family priests. They

still retain a set of totemistic exogamous subdivisions closely resembling those of the Mundas and the Santáls, but they are beginning to forget the totems which the names of the subdivisions denote, and the names themselves will probably soon be abandoned in favour of more aristocratic designations. The tribe will then have become a caste, and will go on stripping itself of all customs likely to betray its true descent. The physical characteristics of its members will alone survive. After their transformation into a caste, the Bhumij will be more strictly endogamous than they were as a tribe, and even less likely to modify their physical type by intermarriage with other races.

Probably typical of its advance in the past.

There is every reason to suppose that the movement, of which certain phases are roughly sketched above, has been going on for many centuries, and that, although at the present day its working can probably be most readily observed in Chota Nagpore, the Orissa hills, and parts of Eastern and Northern Bengal, it must formerly have operated on a similar scale in Bengal Proper and Behar. The well-known tenth chapter of Manu, which endeavours to account for the existence of the non-Aryan castes by representing them as the offspring of marriages between the four original castes, gives clear indications that in Manu's time, fixed by Burnell at 500 A.D., some of the non-Aryan races had already begun to intrude upon the Brahmanical caste system, while others were still in the tribal stage. Arguing from facts now observable, it seems likely that some of the castes alleged by Manu to be the result of more or less complicated crosses are really tribes which had lost their identity like the Rajbansis; for at the present day, if we look merely to customs, ceremonies, and the like, we find in the majority of cases that the admission of a tribe into the Hindu community results after a generation or two in the practical disappearance of the tribe as such. Its identity can no longer be traced by direct enquiry from its members, or inferred from observation of their usages. The Rajbansi and the Bhumij are instances of tribes in an early stage of transition, whose antecedents can be accurately determined. Later on not only do distinctive customs fall into disuse, but the tribe itself, after its promotion to the rank of a caste, breaks up into a number of endogamous groups, each of which practically forms a separate caste. But even in this extreme case the physical characteristics which distinguished the tribe tend on the whole to be preserved; and it is this persistence of the type which accounts for the differences of feature, which, though only definable by scientific methods, are marked enough to render it possible within certain limits to make a fair guess at a man's caste from his personal appearance.

Resort to anthropometry.

These general impressions regarding the differences of physical type observable within the range of the recognized caste organization, coupled with the difficulty of throwing much light upon the true origin of the lower and intermediate castes by collating customs and ceremonies which they have borrowed in the most liberal fashion from the higher castes, suggested to me the possibility of applying to the leading tribes and castes of Bengal the methods of recording and comparing typical physical characteristics which have yielded valuable results in other parts of the world. Those methods might, it seemed, enable us to detach considerable masses of non-Aryans from the general body of Hindus, and to refer them, if not to the individual tribes to which they originally belonged, at least to the general category of non-Aryans, and perhaps to such specific stocks as Dravidian, Lohitic, Tibetan, and the like. If, for example, in Europe, where the crossing of races constantly obscures their true affinities, the examination of statistics drawn from physical measurements has been found to throw light upon the distribution of different race stocks in the population, a similar analysis of the leading tribes and castes in Bengal, where crossing operates only on a comparatively small scale, would *primâ facie* appear likely to enable us to determine the divergence of each of these aggregates from known Aryan or non-Aryan types. Such an analysis would, it was thought, be regarded with approval by the leaders of the Hindu community in all parts of Bengal, among whom both the orthodox and the advanced lay considerable stress upon the purity of their Aryan descent: it would appeal in some measure to scientific men in Europe, and the results would command whatever political value may attach to the demonstration that a given population either is or is not composed of homogeneous ethnic elements.

Mr. Nesfield's theory of caste.

The necessity of applying some exact method was strengthened by the publication of Mr. J. C. Nesfield's "*Brief View of the Caste System of the North-Western Provinces and Oudh.*" In this remarkable work, which bears throughout the impress of Comte's historical and philosophical speculations, the view is put forward that "the bond of sympathy or interest which first drew together the families or tribal fragments, of which a caste is composed, and formed them into a new social unit, was not, as some writers have alleged, community of creed or community of kinship, but community of function. Function, and function only, as I think, was the foundation upon which the whole caste system of India was built up." In introducing his theory Mr. Nesfield points out in language which leaves little to be desired on the score of clearness and emphasis, that it is incompatible "with the modern doctrine which divides the population of India into Aryan and aboriginal. It presupposes an unbroken continuity in the national life from one stage of culture to another, analogous to what has taken place in every other country in the world whose inhabitants have emerged from the savage state. It assumes, therefore, as its necessary basis, *the unity of the Indian race.* While it does not deny that a race of 'white-complexioned foreigners,' who called themselves by the name of Arya, invaded the Indus valley *viâ* Kabul and Kashmir some four thousand years ago and imposed their language and religion on the indigenous races by whom they found themselves surrounded, it nevertheless maintains that the blood imported by this foreign race became gradually absorbed into the indigenous, the less yielding to the greater, so that almost all traces of the conquering race eventually disappeared, just as the Lombard became absorbed into the Italian, the Frank into the Gaul, the Roman (of Roumania) into the Slav, the Greek (of Alexandria) into the Egyptian, the Norman into the Frenchman, the Moor (of Spain) into the Spaniard; and as the Norwegians, Germans, etc., are at this day becoming absorbed into Englishmen in North America, or as the Portuguese (of India) have already become absorbed into Indians. I hold that for the last three thousand years at least no real difference of blood between Aryan and aboriginal (except perhaps in a few isolated tracts, such as Ráj-putana, where special causes may have occurred to prevent the complete amalgamation of race) has existed; and the physiological resemblance observable between the various classes of the population, from the highest to the lowest, is an irrefragable proof that no clearly defined racial distinction has survived—a kind of evidence which ought to carry much greater weight than that of language, on which so many fanciful theories of ethnology have been lately founded. Language is no test of race; and the question of caste is not one of race at all, but of culture. Nothing has tended to complicate the subject of caste so much as this intrusion of a philological theory, which within its own province is one of the most interesting discoveries of modern times, into a field of enquiry with which it has no connection. The 'Aryan brother' is indeed a much more mythical being than Ráma or Krishna, or any other of the popular heroes of Hindu tradition whom writers of the Aryan school have vainly striven to attenuate into solar myths. The amalgamation of the two races (the Aryan and the Indian) had been completed in the Panjáb as we may gather from the Institutes of Manu) before the Hindu, who is the result of this amalgamation, began to extend his influence into the Ganges valley, where by slow and sure degrees he disseminated among the indigenous races those social and religious maxims which have been spreading wider and wider ever since throughout the continent of India, absorbing one after another, and to some extent civilizing, every indigenous race with whom they are brought into contact, raising the choice spirits of the various tribes into the rank of Brahman or Chhatri, and leaving the rest to rise or fall in the social scale according to their capacities and opportunities."

Necessity for testing it.

A theory which assumed so scientific a form and led up to such important social and political conclusions was obviously entitled to be tried by a more precise test than the vague personal impressions concerning the physical type and race affinities of particular castes or tribes which figure so largely in Indian ethnological literature. Evidence showing resemblances or differences of custom, religion, social status, culture and profession would clearly afford no sure grounds for criticizing an hypothesis based on the assumption of the substantial identity in physical type of the numberless distinct aggregates which make up the population of India. Once concede this identity of type, and the question of the real origin of Indian caste recedes into a dim pre-historic distance, where it would be waste of labour to attempt to follow it. If it were really true, as Mr. Nesfield supposes, that "the great majority of Brahmans are not of lighter complexion or of finer and better bred features than any other caste:" if, to quote another passage, a stranger walking through the class-rooms of the Sanskrit College at Benares "would never dream of supposing that the students seated before him were distinct in race and blood from the scavengers who swept the roads," we might either accept Mr. Nesfield's hypothesis on the ground that it is as likely to be true as any other, or might put the problem aside altogether for the sufficient reason that no data would be available for its solution. If, on the other hand, as many competent observers hold, marked differences of type may be traced within the limits of the caste system, the modern system of anthropometry might, it seemed, be relied upon, if applied on a sufficiently large scale, to distinguish some of the leading types, and perhaps even to furnish a clue to their origin. It would at any rate form an effective, if not a conclusive, test of the validity of the assumption on which Mr. Nesfield's theory rests, while it might, at the same time, contribute materially to the solution of other problems concerning the true affinities of particular tribes or groups of tribes.

Starting with this general idea, I wrote to Professor Flower, F.R.S., Director of the Natural History Department of the British Museum, explaining the nature of the enquiry on which I was engaged and the particular difficulty which I desired to overcome, and asked for his advice as to the character and number of the measurements to be taken, the apparatus which should be used, and the form in which the results should be recorded. In a long letter, discussing the subject very thoroughly, Professor Flower observed: —"I entirely agree with you that physical characters are the best—in fact, I may say the only true—tests of race, that is, of real affinity. Language, customs, etc., may help or give indications, but they are often misleading. Therefore the physical examination which you propose to make of the tribes of the Indian empire will be most important. The difficulty, however, is to define and test these characters. I have endeavoured, in my last address to the Anthropological Institute, to formulate what

Professor Flower's opinion.

is known of the differences between the great divisions of the human race, and these are easy enough when we meet with pure examples. There is of course no mistaking a Mongol Tartar, a pure Caucasian, or a Negro. But the differences you will meet with among the different tribes of India are much more difficult of discrimination; for although you may have a Mongolic element along the northern and eastern frontier, and possibly a Negro or Negrito element forming a substratum of the population in the southern part of the Peninsula, I take it that the great mass of the people of India Proper belong to the great division of the human species, which (for want of a better name) may still be called Caucasian, and whether Aryan, Dravidian, or whatever else, will be found to agree in their main physical characteristics, although they may possibly be separated by slight characters, which would be elucidated by such an investigation as that you have in hand. Such characters will in my opinion be found chiefly in the features and not in the proportions of the cranium: the shape of the nose, mouth, and cheeks, though so difficult of definition, are wonderfully characteristic of sub-races. Of course they vary individually, but averages can be obtained from large numbers which should be pretty constant. The nasal index (height and breadth of nose compared) is perhaps the most valuable means of distinguishing races in the skull, and I should think it ought also to be the same in the living. As far as I have been able to observe, the proportions of the cranium (when a sufficient number are observed) are pretty constant throughout the whole Indian peninsula, ranging between dolicho and meso-cephaly, the only tendency to brachycephaly being where the Mongolic element has been introduced in the north."

Anthropometric scheme.

For fuller instructions concerning the mode of operations to be followed, Professor Flower referred me to the exhaustive work "*Les Éléments d'Anthropologie Générale*," by

Dr. Paul Topinard, Professor of the School of Anthropology and Secretary to the Anthropological Society of Paris. Having satisfied myself that Professor Topinard's instructions for dealing with living subjects, and the instruments prescribed by him, were applicable to Indian conditions, I proceeded, after making some experimental measurements in Rangpur, to frame a complete scheme for giving effect to his system in Bengal. This scheme was submitted to Professors Flower and Topinard for criticism, and, after having received their approval, was sanctioned by the Government of Bengal, the services of Civil Hospital Assistant Babu Kumud Behari Sámanta, then attached to the Tibet Mission, being placed at my disposal for the purpose of taking measurements. After some experience had been gained in the working of the system in Bengal, proposals were drawn up for extending it to other parts of India. In the North-West Provinces Sir Alfred Lyall sanctioned a special grant of Rs. 1,000 for instruments, measuring agency, etc., and a fine series of measurements were taken by Chandi Singh, an ex-pupil of the Balrampur Medical School, under the supervision of Mr. J. C. Nesfield, Inspector of Schools for Oudh, himself a high authority upon the castes of that part of India. A small but interesting set of measurements was also taken in the Panjáb by Civil Hospital Assistant Alá-ud-din under the supervision of Deputy Surgeon-General Stephen. In every case the measurers were taught the use of the instruments by me, and were supplied with printed instructions, defining the procedure with extreme minuteness of detail, and discussing at length a variety of difficulties which experience had suggested to me.

Before attempting to sketch the main results of the Bengal inquiries we may pause for a moment to take stock of our terminology. Thanks to Sir John Lubbock and Dr. E. B. Tylor, the study of ethnography has of late years begun to be understood in England. "It embraces," says M. Elisee Reclus, "the

Ethnography defined.

descriptive details, and ethnology the rational exposition, of the human aggregates and organizations known as hordes, clans, tribes, and nations, especially in the earlier, the savage, and barbarous stages of their progress." In other words, ethnography collects and arranges large masses of social data; ethnology applies the comparative method of investigation, and frames by this means hypotheses concerning the origin of the tribes themselves.

The less familiar anthropometry has an ancient and curious history. By its aid the Egyptian sculptors of Carnac and Memphis worked out an artistic canon of the ideal proportions of the human figure, the influence of which may be traced in Greek art, which was studied by Da Vinci and Dürer, and which has descended to French studies in the form given to it by their contemporary Jean Cousin. Its latest application may be witnessed in a branch of the Prefecture of Police at Paris, where the features and limbs of convicted criminals are measured under scientific supervision, and the results recorded with a view to tracing their identity in future. For our present purpose anthropometry may be defined as the science which seeks, by measuring certain leading physical characters, such as the stature and the proportions of the head, features, and limbs, to ascertain and classify the chief types of mankind, and eventually by analysing their points of agreement and difference to work back to the probable origin of the various race-stocks now traceable. Like ethnography and ethnology, it forms part of the circle of studies grouped together under the head of anthropology.

Anthropometry.

Looked at merely as a scientific experiment, an anthropometric examination of even a small fraction of the people of India promised to yield results of no ordinary interest. Nowhere else in the world do we find the population of a large continent broken up into an infinite number of mutually exclusive aggregates, the members of which are forbidden by an inexorable social law to marry outside of the group to which they themselves belong. Whatever may have been the origin and the earlier developments of the caste system, this absolute prohibition of mixed marriages stands forth at the present day as its essential and most prominent characteristic, and the feeling against such unions is so deeply engrained in the people that even the Theistic and reforming sect of the Brahmo Samaj has found a difficulty in freeing itself from the ancient prejudices. In a society thus organized, a society sacrificing everything to pride of blood and the idea of social purity, it seemed that differences of physical type, however produced in past time, might be expected to manifest a high degree of persistence, and that the science which seeks to trace and express such differences would find a peculiarly favourable field for its operations. In Europe anthropometry has to confess itself hindered, if not baffled, by the constant intermixture of races which tends to obscure and confuse the data arrived at by measurement. In a country where such intermixture is to a large extent eliminated, there were grounds for believing that divergent types would reveal themselves more clearly, and that their characteristics would furnish some clue to their original race affinities.

Indian conditions favour anthropometry.

Apart from these special conditions, the necessity of having recourse to methods of research more exact in their character and less misleading in their results than the mere collation of customs and beliefs is brought into prominence by the transformation which religion is gradually bringing about in Indian society. At the risk of driving patient analogy too hard, we may perhaps venture to compare the social gradations of the Indian caste system to a series of geological deposits. The successive strata in each series occupy a definite position determined by the manner of their formation, and the varying customs in the one may be said to represent the fossils in the other. The lowest castes preserve

Stratification of caste.

the most primitive customs, just as the oldest geological formations contain the simplest forms of organic life. Thus the totems or animal-names, by which the Mundas and Oraons regulate their matrimonial arrangements, give place, as we travel upwards in the social scale, to group-names based upon local and territorial distinctions, while in the highest castes kinship is reckoned by descent from personages closely resembling the eponymous heroes of early Greek tradition. Even the destructive agencies to which the imperfection of the geological record is attributed have their parallel in the transforming influence by which the two great religions of modern India, Brahmanism and Islam, have modified the social order. A curious contrast may be discerned in their methods of working and in the results which they produce.

Hinduism and Islam.

Islam is a force of the volcanic sort, a burning and integrating force, which, under favourable conditions, may even make a nation. It melts and fuses together a whole series of tribes, and reduces their internal structure to one uniform pattern, in which no survivals of pre-existing usage can be detected. The separate strata disappear; their characteristic fossils are crushed out of recognition, and a solid mass of law and tradition occupies their place. Brahmanism knows nothing of open proselytism or forcible conversion, and attains its end in a different and more subtle fashion, for which no precise analogue can be found in the physical world. It leaves existing aggregates very much as they were, and so far from welding them together, after the manner of Islam, into larger cohesive aggregates, tends rather to create an indefinite number of fresh groups; but every tribe that passes within the charmed circle of Hinduism inclines sooner or later to abandon its more primitive usages or to clothe them in some Brahmanical disguise. The strata, indeed, remain, or are multiplied; their relative positions are, on the whole, unaltered; only their fossils are metamorphosed into more advanced forms. One by one the ancient totems drop off, or are converted by a variety of ingenious devices into respectable personages of the standard mythology; the fetish gets a new name, and is promoted to the Hindu Pantheon in the guise of a special incarnation of one of the greater gods; the tribal chief sets up a family priest, starts a more or less romantic family legend, and in course of time blossoms forth as a new variety of Rajput. His people follow his lead, and make haste to sacrifice their women at the shrine of social distinction. Infant-marriage with all its attendant horrors is introduced; widows are forbidden to marry again; and divorce, which plays a great and, on the whole, a useful part in tribal society, is summarily abolished. Throughout all these changes, which strike deep into the domestic life of the people, the fiction is maintained that no real change has taken place, and every one believes, or affects to believe, that things are with them as they have been since the beginning of time.

It is curious to observe that the operation of these tendencies has been quickened, and the sphere of their action enlarged, by the great extension of railways which has taken place in India during the last few years. Both Benares and Manchester have been brought nearer to their customers, and have profited by the increased demand for their characteristic wares. Siva and Krishna drive out the tribal gods as surely as grey shirtings displace the more durable hand-woven cloth. Pilgrimages become more pleasant and more popular, and the touts, who sally forth from the great religious centres to promote these pious excursions, find their task easier and their clients more open to persuasion than was the case even twenty years ago. A trip to Jagannáth or Gya is no longer the formidable and costly undertaking that it was. The Hindu peasant who is pressed to kiss the footprints of Vishnu, or to taste the hallowed rice that has been offered to the Lord of the World, may now reckon the journey by days instead of months. He need no longer sacrifice the savings

Railways and religion.

of a lifetime to this pious object, and he has a reasonable prospect of returning home none the worse for a week's indulgence of religious enthusiasm. Even the distant Mecca has been brought, by means of Messrs. Cook's steamers and return-tickets, within the reach of the faithful in India; and the influence of Mahomedan missionaries and return pilgrims has made itself felt in a quiet but steady revival of orthodox usage in Eastern Bengal.

Rapidly as the levelling and centralising forces do their work, a considerable residue of really primitive usage still resists their transforming influence. The race element remains, for the most part, untouched. Diversity of type is still the rule, and identity the exception among the manifold groupings of the Indian people. To a practised eye the personal appearance of most Hindus gives a fairly accurate clue to their caste; and within certain limits it is even possible to determine the strata of the population to which given sections of Mahomedans must have belonged before their conversion to Islam.

Race in relation to caste.

The scientific methods which anthropometry prescribes attempt to fix vague personal impressions by reducing them to statistical formulas. No one could mistake a Brahman for a Kol, but the most minute verbal description of their characteristic differences of feature falls far short of the numerical analysis that can be arrived at by measuring specific dimensions of the head, nose, cheekbones, orbits, forehead, and zygomatic arches, and working out their proportions by the system of indices invented by the Swedish anthropologist, Anders Retzius, in 1842. Add to these weight, stature, and the facial angle devised by Cuvier, extend the observations to about a hundred specimens of each group, and it will be found that the averages calculated from this mass of figures bring out a uniform tribal type to which all individuals tend to conform. The data thus obtained from nearly

The method of anthropometry.

6,000 persons, representing 89 of the leading castes and tribes in Northern India, from the Bay of Bengal to the frontiers of Afghanistan, enable us to distinguish two extreme types of feature and physique, which may be provisionally described as Aryan and Dravidian. A third type which in some respects may be looked upon as intermediate between these two, while in other, and perhaps the most important, points it can hardly be deemed Indian at all, is found along the northern and eastern borders of Bengal. Its most prominent characters are a relatively short (brachycephalic) head; a broad face; a short, wide nose, very low in the bridge, and in extreme cases almost bridgeless; high and projecting cheekbones,. and eyelids peculiarly formed so as to give the impression that the eyes are obliquely set in the head. With this type, which may conveniently be described as Mongoloid, we have for our present purpose no immediate concern. Except in the districts of Assam and North-Eastern Bengal, it has contributed comparatively little to the evolution of caste as it now exists in India, and may be left out of consideration in the attempt to trace the stages of growth by which the prevailing state of things has been arrived at.

Three types: Aryan, Dravidian, and Mongoloid.

In adopting, even tentatively, the designations Aryan and Dravidian I am aware that I am disregarding advice which Professor Max Müller was good enough to give me, about three years ago, in a letter since published (I believe) in an Appendix to his latest work. He warned me against the confusion which might arise from using philological terms to denote ethnological conclusions. I am entirely sensible of the value and the necessity of the warning, and fully recognize his right to speak with authority on such questions. But we must have some general names for our types: it is a thankless task to invent new names; and I trust to justify my invasion of the domain of philology by the universal practice of the Indians themselves, and by the example of Professor Sayce, who did not hesitate, on a recent occasion to speak of the Aryan race as an established ethnic aggregate.

The Aryan type.

The Aryan type, as we find it in India at the present day, is marked by a relatively long (dolichocephalic) head; a straight, finely cut (lepto-rhine) nose; a long, symmetrically narrow face; a well-developed forehead, regular features, and a high facial angle. The stature is fairly high, ranging from 171·6 centimeters in the Sikhs of the Panjáb to 165·6 in the Brahmans of Bengal; and the general build of the figure is well proportioned, and slender rather than massive. In the castes which exhibit these characteristics the complexion is a very light transparent brown—"wheat-coloured" is the common vernacular description—noticeably fairer than that of the mass of the population. Colour, however, is a character which eludes all attempts to record or define its gradations, and even the extreme varieties can only be described in very general terms. As representative Aryan groups we may name the Sikhs and Khatris of the Panjáb, and the Brahmans, Kayasths, Babhans, and Chattris of Bengal and the North-West Provinces. A larger series of measurements would probably add several more castes to the list, especially in the Panjáb, where the observations were greatly restricted by financial difficulties.

The Dravidian type.

In the Dravidian type the form of the head usually inclines to be dolichocephalic, but all other characters present a marked contrast to the Aryan. The nose is thick and broad, and the formula expressing its proportionate dimensions is higher than in any known race, except the Negro. The facial angle is comparatively low; the lips are thick; the face wide and fleshy; the features coarse and irregular. The average stature ranges in a long series of tribes from 156·2 to 162·1 centimeters; the figure is squat, and the limbs sturdy. The colour of the skin varies from very dark brown to a shade closely approaching black. The most characteristic Dravidian tribes are the Málé Pahárias of the Rajmahal hills, and the Mundas and Oraons of the Chota Nagpur plateau. The two latter are better known under the general name of Kol, which, according to Herr Jellinghaus, a good authority on this subject, means "pig-killer" or "pig-eater," and belongs to the large class of epithets by which, since Vedic times, the Aryans have expressed their contempt for the voracious and promiscuous appetite of the Dravidian. Others, however, and this is perhaps the better opinion, regard Kol as a corruption of Hor or Horo, the Mundari word for 'man,' which has been adopted as the name of the tribes in question.

Between these extreme types, which may fairly be regarded as representing two distinct races, we find a large number of intermediate groups, each of which forms for matrimonial purposes a sharply defined circle, beyond which none of its members can pass. By applying to the entire series the nasal index or formula of the proportions of the nose, which Professors Flower and Topinard agree in regarding as the best test of race distinctions, some remarkable results are arrived at. The average nasal proportions of the Málé Pahária tribe are expressed by the figure 94·5, while the pastoral Gujars of the Panjáb have an index of 66·9, the Sikhs of 68·8, and the Bengal Brahmans and Kayasths of 70·4. In other words, the typical Dravidian, as represented by the Málé Pahária, has a nose as broad in proportion to its length as the Negro, while this feature in the Aryan group can fairly bear comparison with the noses of sixty-eight Parisians, measured by Topinard, which gave an average of 69·4. Even more striking is the curiously close correspondence between the gradations of racial type indicated by the nasal index and certain of the social data ascertained by independent inquiry. If we take a series of castes in Bengal, Behar, or the North-Western Provinces, and arrange them in the order of the average nasal index, so that the caste with the finest nose shall be at the top, and that with

The nasal index.

the coarsest at the bottom of the list, it will be found that this order substantially corresponds with the accepted order of social precedence. The casteless tribes, Kols, Korwas, Mundas, and the like, who have not yet entered the Brahmanical system, occupy the lowest place in both series. Then come the vermin-eating Musahars and the leather-dressing Chamárs. The fisher castes of Bauri, Bind, and Kewat are a trifle higher in the scale; the pastoral Goala, the cultivating Kurmi, and a group of cognate castes from whose hands a Brahman may take water, follow in due order, and from them we pass to the trading Khatris, the landholding Bábhans, and the upper crust of Hindu society. Thus, it is scarcely a paradox to lay down as a law of the caste organization in Eastern India that a man's social status varies in inverse ratio to the width of his nose. Nor is this the only point in which the two sets of observations—the social and the physical—bear out and illustrate each other. The character of the curious matrimonial groupings for which the late Mr. J. F. McLennan devised the happy term exogamous, also varies in a definite relation to the gradations of physical type. Within a certain range of nasal proportions, these subdivisions are based almost exclusively on the totem. Along with a somewhat finer form of nose, groups called after villages and larger territorial areas, or bearing the name of certain tribal or communal officials, begin to appear, and above these again we reach the eponymous saints and heroes, who in India, as in Greece and Rome, are associated with a certain stage of Aryan progress.

It would be vain to attempt within the compass of this essay to analyse and compare the large mass of figures which has been collected, or to develop at length the inferences which they may be thought to suggest. I can only glance at a few of their more important bearings. In the first place, it deserves notice that the data obtained by the most modern anthropological method agree in the main

The literary theory of caste.

not only with the long chain of Indian tradition, beginning with the Vedas and ending with the latest vernacular treatise on the theory and practice of caste, but also with the rationalised and critical story of the making of the Indian peoples, as it has been told by Sir William Hunter in the *Imperial Gazetteer.* Here the historian shows how, through the veil of fable and miracle in which pre-historic India is shrouded, traces may be discerned of a protracted struggle between a lower and a higher race, which would have tended to produce much the same results as our statistics bring out. Studied in the light of these statistics it would seem that the standard Indian theory of caste may deserve more respectful consideration than has been accorded to it of late years.

The division of the people into four classes corresponding roughly to the chief professions or modes of life of the time is in itself plausible enough, and is supported by parallel cases in the history of ancient societies. It is nowhere stated that these groups were rigidly exclusive, like modern castes, and the rules laid down to regulate their intermarriage show a general resemblance to those observed by the Kulin classes of to-day. So far as anthropological considerations are concerned, there would be no great difficulty in our recognizing the Brahmans, Rajputs and higher trading castes as descendants of the three upper classes—Brahmans, Kshatriyas, and Vaisyas—of the ancient Aryan Commonwealth. The Sudras alone have no compact aggregate as their modern representative. But the fourth caste in the ancient system was apparently not of pure Aryan descent, and it is a plausible conjecture that it may have been constantly recruited by the admission of Dravidian elements.

Modern representatives of the four original castes.

The dominant Aryan society must have exercised a strong attraction on the Dravidians, but the only caste into which the latter could ordinarily expect to be received would be the Sudra. Their admission into this group would doubtless have been facilitated by resort to the fiction, characteristic of all early societies, that they had belonged to it all along. But such accretions must have swelled the caste to unwieldy dimensions, and thus have introduced the tendency to disintegration or fission, which affects all social aggregates in India. In course of time, as new groups split off, and took to themselves new names, the original caste would have been, so to speak, lost in the crowd, and only a small nucleus would have retained its original designation. In support of the hypothesis that the survivors of the ancient Sudras are to be sought among the higher strata of the so-called mixed castes, we may point to the fact that a group of castes, whose physical characters approach more closely to the Aryan than to the Dravidian type, still cling to the name Sudra, and regard themselves as descendants of the classical fourth caste.

Theory of the 'mixed castes.'

Modern criticism has been especially active in its attacks on that portion of the traditional theory which derives the multitude of mixed or inferior castes from an intricate series of crosses between members of the original four. No one can examine the long lists which purport to illustrate the working of this process without being struck by much that is absurd and inconsistent. But in India it does not necessarily follow that, because the individual applications of a principle are ridiculous, the principle itself can have no foundation in fact. The last thing that would occur to the literary theorists of those times, or to their successors, the *pandits* of to-day, would be to go back upon actual facts, and to seek by analysis and comparison to work out the true stages of evolution. They found, as I infer from troublesome experience among some of my Indian coadjutors, the *à priori* method simpler and more congenial. That at least did not compel them to pollute their souls by the study of plebeian usage. Having once got hold of a formula, they insisted, like Thales and his contemporaries, in making it account for the entire order of things. Thus, castes which had been developed out of corporations like the mediæval trade guilds, or which expressed the distinction between fishing and hunting, agriculture and handicrafts, were all supposed to have been evolved by interbreeding.

But the initial principle, though it could not be stretched to explain everything, was in the main correct. It happens that we can still observe its workings among a number of Dravidian tribes, which, though not yet drawn into the vortex of Brahmanism, have been in some degree affected by the example of Hindu organization. As regards inter-tribal marriages, they seem to be in a stage of development through which the Hindus themselves have passed. A man may marry a woman of another tribe, but the offspring of such unions do not become members of either the paternal or maternal groups, but belong to a distinct endogamous aggregate, the name of which often denotes the precise cross by which it was started. Among the large tribe of Mundas we find, for instance, nine such groups—Khangar-Munda, Kharia-Munda, Konkpat-Munda, Karanga-Munda, Mahili-Munda, Nágbansi-Munda, Oraon-Munda, Sad-Munda, Savar-Munda—descended from intermarriages between Munda men and women of other tribes. The Mahilis, again, have five sub-tribes of this kind, and themselves trace their descent to the union of a Munda with a Santál woman. Illustrations of this sort might be multiplied almost indefinitely. The point to be observed is that the sub-tribes formed by inter-tribal crossing are from an early stage complete endogamous units, and that they tend continually to sever their slender connection with the parent group, and stand forth as independent tribes. As soon as this comes to pass, and a functional or territorial name disguises their mixed descent, the process by which they have been formed is seen to resemble closely that by which the standard Indian tradition seeks to explain the appearance of other castes alongside of the classical four.

From the literary theory of caste we are led on to speculate regarding the origin of caste itself. How comes it that the Aryan race, which in South Europe, as Herr Penka has shown, has modified its physical type by free intermixture with Turanian elements, displayed in India a marked antipathy to marriage with persons of alien race, and devised an elaborate system of taboo for the prevention of such unions? An explanation may, perhaps, be found in the fact that in India alone were the Aryans brought into close contact with an unequivocally black race. The sense of differences of colour, which, for all our talk of common humanity, still plays a great, and, politically, often an inconvenient, part in the history of the world, finds forcible expression in the Vedic descriptions of the people whom the Aryans found in possession of the plains of India. In a well-known passage the god Indra is praised for having protected the Aryan colour, and the word meaning colour (*varna*) is used down to the present day as the equivalent of caste, more especially with reference to the castes believed to be of Aryan descent. Another text depicts the Dasyus or Dravidians as noseless; others dwell on their low stature, their coarse features, and their voracious appetite. It is hardly an exaggeration to say that from these sources there might be compiled a fairly accurate anthropological definition of the Dravidian tribes of to-day. When it is added that the aggregates which would be included in the definition represent the lower end of a long series of social gradations, which in their turn correspond not only to varieties of physical type, but also to peculiarities of custom and tribal structure, it is obviously but a short step to the conclusion that the motive principle of Indian caste is to be sought in the antipathy of the higher race for the lower, of the fair-skinned Aryan for the black Dravidian.

The origin of caste.

It will be said, reasonably enough, that this hypothesis, however applicable to certain larger groups, fails to account for the vast network of intricate divisions which the caste system now presents. The differences of type which distinguish the various trading, agricultural, pastoral, and fishing castes from each other are, it may be argued, not sharp enough to have brought the sentiment of race antipathy into play. On what principle, then, were these multifarious groups separated from the larger aggregates of which they formed part? I would reply, by the influence of fiction—a factor which Sir Henry Maine has shown to have contributed largely to the development of early societies. For illustrations of the working of this principle we need not travel far. The caste-making impulse has by no means spent its force, and its operation can be studied in most Indian districts at the present day. In Bengal, where the Aryan and Dravidian elements are in continual contact, it has created a series of endogamous groups, which may be roughly classified as *Ethnic*, *Provincial* or *Linguistic*, *Territorial* or *Local*, *Functional* or *Occupational*, *Sectarian*, and *Social*. In the first of these classes the race basis is palpable and acknowledged. The others have been generated by the fiction that men who speak a different language, who dwell in a different district, who worship different gods, who observe different social customs, who follow a different profession, or practise the same profession in a slightly different way, must be of a fundamentally different race. Usually, and in the case of sub-castes invariably, the fact is that there is no appreciable difference of race between the newly formed group and the aggregate from which it has been broken off.

Influence of fiction.

If, then, caste was an institution evolved by the Aryans in the attempt to preserve the purity of their own stock, and afterwards expanded and adapted, by the influence of a series of fictions, to fit an endless variety of social, religious, and industrial conditions, we may expect that the physical data recently collected will have some bearing on Herr Karl Penka's speculations concerning the origin of the Aryans themselves. Clearly the Indian Aryans represent the furthest extension of the race towards the East. All along the eastern and

Penka's Herkunft der Arier.

northern frontier of Bengal we meet with a fringe of compact tribes of the short-headed or brachycephalic type, who are beyond question Mongolian. Starting from this area, and travelling up the plains of India north-westward towards the frontier of the Panjáb, we observe a gradual but steady increase of the dolichocephalic type of head, which Herr Penka claims as one of the chief characteristics of the original Aryans. Bengal itself is mostly mesaticephalic, and dolichocephaly only appears in some of the Dravidian tribes. In Behar dolichocephalic averages are more numerous; in Oudh and the North-West Provinces this type is universal, and it reaches its maximum in the Panjáb. Assuming that Herr Penka has correctly determined the original Aryan type to be dolichocephalic, and that the theory of caste propounded above is the true one, these are just the results which might be looked for. According to the French anthropologists, the shape of the head is the most persistent of race characters, and the one which offers the greatest resistance to the levelling influence of crossing. That the Aryans should have retained this more durable character while undergoing a change in the more fugitive character of colour is in keeping with what we know of the conditions, social and climatic, to which they were exposed. In point of colour, indeed, the Aryan castes are by no means so dark as Europeans are apt to suppose. The complexion, moreover, tends to grow lighter the further north-west we go, and survivals of reddish-blonde complexion and auburn hair are met with beyond the frontier.

Prevalence of dolichocephaly in Northern India.

A possible objection may be disposed of here. It may be argued that if the Dravidians are dolichocephalic, the prevalence of this character in North-Western India may be accounted for by the assumption of an intermixture of Dravidian blood. But if this were so, the proportion and degree of dolichocephaly would increase as we approach the Dravidian area, instead of diminishing, as is actually the case. Moreover, it is impossible to suppose that the races of the North-West, if originally brachycephalic, could have acquired their dolichocephalic form of head from the Dravidians, without at the same time acquiring the characteristic Dravidian nose and the distinctive Dravidian colour.

Owing in the main to the labours of Broca and the French anthropologists, it is no longer necessary to challenge the assumption of the elder generation of philologists that affinity of language implies affinity of race. That view has now been abandoned by most, if not all, of the leading authorities on the subject, and the best opinion of the present day seems to regard the fact that races speak the same language as proving little more than that at some time or other they must have been in close local contact. Abundant illustrations of the working of this process can be given from tribes all along the frontier of Bengal. In the first place it is clear that the hitherto recognized distinction between Dravidian and Kolarian stocks, concerning which so much has been written during the last twenty years, rests solely upon linguistic peculiarities, and does not correspond to any differences of physical type. The Málé of the Rajmahal hills and the Oraons of Chota Nagpore, both of whom speak languages classed as Dravidian, are identical in point of physique with the Mundas and Santáls, who are classed on linguistic grounds as Kolarian. Secondly, a number of tribes concerning whose non-Aryan origin there can be no manner of doubt, have within recent times adopted Aryan dialects and abandoned their original languages. Thus the Dravidian Bhumij, Kurmi, and Mahili of Western Bengal now speak only Bengali, the most Aryan of the Indian vernaculars, while the Mongoloid Khambus and Murmis of the Darjiling hills have taken to Hindi, and the Maghs and Tipperahs of the Eastern frontier have adopted, or are on the way to adopt, Bengali.

Language and race.

It is now nearly thirty years since the late Mr. J. F. McLennan introduced to the scientific world, in his well-known essay on *Primitive Marriage*, the terms exogamy and endogamy. The laws governing marriage which these terms denote were, when Mr. McLennan wrote, unnamed. He was, I believe, the first to draw attention to them, and the terms devised by him have been adopted by all who have since written on the same subjects. In the preface to the latest edition of *Studies in Ancient History*, Mr. D. McLennan, brother of the author, complains that both terms have in some cases been misunderstood, and gives a definition of each which may conveniently be quoted here. Exogamy, he says, "is prohibition of marriage between all persons recognized as being of the same blood, because of their common blood,—whether they form one community or part only of a community, or parts of several communities; and accordingly it may prevent marriage between persons who (though of the same blood) are of different local tribes, while it frequently happens that it leaves persons of the same local tribe (but who are not of the same blood) free to marry one another." Endogamy, on the other hand, "allows marriage only between persons who are recognized as being of the same blood-connection or kindred; and if, where it occurs, it confines marriage to the tribe or community, it is because the tribe regards itself as comprising a kindred."

Exogamy and endogamy.

Seeing, then, that caste is mainly a matter of marriage, special attention has been paid throughout the inquiry to the marriage usages of the tribes and castes concerned. Following up a suggestion made by Sir Henry Maine[1] questions were framed tending to elucidate the practice of every caste in respect of the outer or endogamous limit within which a man *must* marry, and the inner or exogamous limit within which he *may not* marry. Taking the exogamous limit first, we find

Exogamy in Bengal: Totems of Santáls and Oraons.

[1] *Early Law and Customs*, p. 223.

the non-Mahomedan races of Bengal at the present time regulating their matrimonial arrangements by several different kinds of exogamous subdivisions. At the bottom of the social system, as understood by the average Hindu, stands a large body of non-Aryan tribes and castes, each of which is broken up into a number of what may be called *totemistic* exogamous septs. Each sept bears the name of an animal, a tree, a plant, or of some material object, natural or artificial, which the members of that sept are prohibited from killing, eating, cutting, burning, carrying, using, etc. Well-defined groups of this type are found among the Dravidian Santáls and Oraons, both of whom still retain their original language, worship non-Aryan gods, and have a fairly compact tribal organization. The following are specimens selected from among the seventy-three Oraon and the ninety-one Santál septs:—

Oraon.		Santal.	
Name of Sept.	*Totem.*	*Name of Sept.*	*Totem.*
Tirki.	Young mice.	Murmu.	Nilgái.
Ekka.	Tortoise.	Hánsdá.	Wild goose.
Kispotta.	Pig's entrails.	Márndi.	A kind of grass.
Lakrá.	Hyena.	Besrá.	Hawk.
Bagh.	Tiger.	Hemron.	Betel palm.
Kurjrár.	Oil from *Kujrár* tree.	Saren.	The constellation Pleiades.
Gede.	Duck.		
Khoepa.	Wild dog.	Sankh.	Conch shell.
Minji.	Eel.	Guá.	Areca nut.
Chirra.	Squirrel.	Kárá.	Buffalo.
Ergo.	Rat.		

The Hos of Singbhum and the Mundas of the Chota Nagpore plateau have also exogamous septs of the same type as the Oraons and Santáls, with similar rules as to the totem being taboo to the members of the group. The lists given in Appendix I contain the names of 323 Munda septs and 46 Ho septs. Six of the latter are found also among the Santáls. The other Ho septs appear to be mostly of the local or communal type, such as are in use among the Kandhs, but this is not quite certain, and the point needs looking into by some one well acquainted with the Ho dialects, who would probably find little difficulty in identifying the names, as the tribe is well known to be in the habit of giving to places descriptive names having reference to their natural characteristics. Nearly all the Munda sept names are of the totem type, and the characteristic taboos appear to be recognized. The Tarwár or Talwár sept, for example, may not touch a sword, the Udbaru may not use the oil of a particular tree, the Sindur may not use vermilion, the Baghala may not kill or eat a quail, and, strangest of all, rice is taboo to the Dhán sept, the members of which must supply its place with *gondli* or millet.

A step higher in the social scale, according to Hindu estimation, the Bhumij of Western Bengal and Orissa mark an early stage in the course of development by which a non-Aryan tribe transforms itself into a full-blown caste, claiming a definite rank in the Brahmanical system. With the exception of a few residents of outlying villages bordering on the Munda country of Chota Nagpore Proper, the Bhumij have lost their original language (Mundári), and now speak only Bengali. They worship Hindu gods in addition to the fetishistic deities more or less common to them and the other Kolarians, but the tendency is to keep the latter rather in the background and to relegate the less formidable among them to the women and children to be worshipped in a hole-and-corner kind of way, with the assistance of a tribal hedge-priest (*Láyá*), who is supposed to be specially acquainted with their ways. Some of the leading men of the tribe, who call themselves Bhuinhárs, and hold large landed tenures on terms of police service, have set up as Rajputs, and keep a low class of Brahmans as their family priests. They have, as a rule, borrowed the Rajput class titles, but cannot conform with the

Totems of the Bhumij of Western Bengal.

Rajput rules of intermarriage, and marry within a narrow circle of pseudo-Rajputs like themselves. The rest of the tribe, numbering at the last Census 226,167, are divided into a number of exogamous groups, of which the following are examples. It is curious to observe, in a tribe still in a state of transition, that one of the Brahmanical gotras, Sándilya, has been borrowed from the higher castes, and in the process of borrowing has been transformed from a Vedic saint into a bird:—

BHUMIJ.

Name of Sept.	*Totem.*
Sálrisi.	*Sál* fish.
Hánsda.	Wild goose.
Leng.	Mushroom.
Sándilya.	A bird.
Hemron.	Betel palm.
Tumarung.	Pumpkin.
Nág.	Snake.

At a further stage in the same process of evolution, and on a slightly superior social level, we find the Mahilis, Koras, and Kurmis, all of whom claim to be members of the Hindu community. They have totemistic exogamous sections, of which the following are fairly representative:—

MAHILI.		KORA.		KURMI.	
Name of Section.	*Totem.*	*Name of Section.*	*Totem.*	*Name of Section.*	*Totem.*
Dungri.	*Dumur* fig.	Kasyab.	Tortoise.	Kesariá.	*Kesar* grass.
Turu.	*Turu* grass.	Saulá.	*Sál* fish.	Karár.	Buffalo.
Kánti.	Ear of any animal.	Kásibak.	Heron.	Dumuriá.	*Dumur* fig.
Hánsda.	Wild goose.	Hánsda.	Wild goose.	Chonchmutruár.	Spider.
Murmu.	Nilgái.	Butku.	Pig.	Hastowár.	Tortoise.
		Sánpu.	Bull.	Jalbanuár.	Net.
				Sankhowár.	Shell ornaments.
				Bághbanuár.	Tiger.
				Katiár.	Silk cloth.

Of these three castes the Mahilis appear to have broken off most recently from the tribe. They still worship some of the Santál gods in addition to the standard Hindu deities; they will eat food cooked by a Santál; their caste organization is supervised, like that of the Santáls, by an official bearing the title of Parganait; they permit the marriage of adults and tolerate sexual intercourse before marriage within the limits of the caste; and they have not yet attained to the dignity of employing Brahmans for ceremonial purposes. If I may hazard a conjecture on so obscure a question, I should be inclined to class them as Santáls who took to the degraded occupation of basket-making, and thus lost the *jus connubii* within the tribe. In the case of the Korás there is no clue to warrant their affiliation to any particular tribe, but their traditions say that they came from the Chota Nagpore plateau, while their name suggests a Dravidian origin, and it seems possible that they may be an offshoot of the Mundas, who somehow sank from the status of independent cultivators to their present position of earth-cutting and tank-digging labourers. They allow adult marriage, their standard of feminine chastity is low, and they have not yet fitted themselves out with Brahmans. In the customary rules of inheritance which their *panchayát* or caste council administers, it is curious to find the usage known in the Panjáb as *chundávand*, by which the sons, however few, of one wife take a share equal to that of the sons, however many, of another. The Kurmis may perhaps be a Hinduised branch of the Santáls. The latter, who are more particular about food, or rather about whom they eat with, than is commonly supposed, will eat cooked rice with the Kurmis, and according to one tradition regard them as elder brothers of their own. However this may be, the totemism of the Kurmis of Western Bengal stamps them as of Dravidian descent, and clearly distinguishes them from the Kurmis of Behar and the North-West Provinces. They show signs of a leaning toward orthodox Hinduism, and employ Brahmans for the worship of Hindu gods, but not in the propitiation

Totems of the Mahili, Korá and Kurmi of Chota Nagpore.

of their family and rural deities, or in their marriage ceremonies.

One more instance of totemism deserves special notice here, as it shows the usage maintaining its ground among people of far higher social standing than any of the castes already mentioned. The Kumhárs of Orissa take rank immediately below the Karan or writer-caste, and thus have only two or three large castes above them. They are divided into two endogamous sub-castes—Jagannáthi or Uria Kumhárs, who work standing and make large earthen pots, and Khattya Kumhárs, who turn the wheel sitting and make small earthen pots, cups, toys, etc. The latter are immigrants from Upper India, whose number is comparatively insignificant. For matrimonial purposes the Jagannáthi Kumhárs are subdivided into the following exogamous sections:—

Totems of the Kumhárs of Orissa.

JAGANNATHI KUMHAR.

Name of section.	*Totem.*
Kaundinyá.	Tiger.
Sarpa.	Snake.
Neul.	Weasel.
Goru.	Cow.
Mudir.	Frog.
Bhadbhadriá.	Sparrow.
Kurmmá.	Tortoise.

The members of each section express their respect for the animal whose name the section bears, by refraining from killing or injuring it, and by bowing when they meet it. The entire caste also abstain from eating, and even go so far as to worship, the *sál* fish, because the rings on its scales resemble the wheel which is the symbol of the craft. The Ḳhattya Kumhárs have only one section (Kásyapa), and thus, like the Rájbansis of Rungpore, are really endogamous in spite of themselves. The reason, no doubt, is that there are too few of them in Orissa to fit up a proper exogamous system, and they content themselves with the pretence of one. Both sub-castes appear to be conscious that the names of their sections are open to misconception, and explain that they are really the names of certain saints who, being present at Daksha's horse sacrifice, transformed themselves into animals to escape the wrath of Siva, whom Daksha, like Peleus in the Greek myth, had neglected to invite.* It may well be that we owe the preservation of these interesting totemistic groups to the ingenuity of the person who devised this respectable means of accounting for a series of names so likely to compromise the reputation of the caste. In the case of the Khattya Kumhárs. the fact that their single section bears the name of Kásyapa, while they venerate the tortoise (Kachhap), and tell an odd story by way of apology for the practice, may perhaps lend weight to the conjecture, in itself a fairly plausible one, that many of the lower castes in Bengal, who are beginning to set up as pure Hindus, have taken advantage of the resemblance in sound between *Kachhap* and *Kasyap* (*chh* and *s* both become *sh* in colloquial Bengali) to convert a totemistic title into an eponymous one, and have gone on to borrow such other Brahmanical *gotras* as seemed to them desirable. If, for example, we analyse the matrimonial arrangements of the Bhars of Manbhum, many of whom are the hereditary personal servants of the pseudo-Rajput Raja of Pachete, we find the foregoing conjecture borne out by the fact that two out of the seven sections which they recognize are called after the peacock and the *bel* fruit, while the rest are eponymous. But this is an exceptionally clear case of survival, and I fear it is hardly possible to simplify the diagnosis of non-Aryan castes by laying down a general rule, that all castes with a section bearing the name Kásyapa, who have not demonstrably

---

* Muir, *Sanskrit Texts*, iv, p. 372.

borrowed that appellation from the Brahmans, are probably offshoots from some non-Aryan tribe.

Among all the castes noticed above, the exogamous rule is one-sided in its operation. In no case may a man marry into his own section, but the name of the section goes by the male side, and consequently, *so far as the rule of exogamy is concerned*, there is nothing to prevent him from marrying his sister's daughter, his maternal aunt, or even his maternal grandmother. To bar alliances of this kind, a separate set of rules is required, which usually overlap the exogamous rule to some extent. Marriage with any person descended in a direct line from the same parents is universally forbidden. To simplify the calculation of collateral relationship—a complicated business which severely taxes the rural intellect—the following formula is in use throughout Behar:—"*Chacherá, mamerá, phupherá, maserá ye chár nátá bacháke shádi hotá hai*" ("The line of paternal uncle, maternal uncle, paternal aunt, maternal aunt—these four relationships are to be avoided in marriage"). The first point to notice in this is, that in the first generation the whole of the paternal uncle's descendants, both male and female, would be excluded by the rule prohibiting marriage within the section. In the second and subsequent generations, agnates would be barred, but descendants through females would not. For the paternal uncle's daughters having necessarily married out of the section, their children would belong to some other section, and thus second cousins would be able to marry. Another point is that the formula does not state the number of generations to which the prohibition extends, and that different castes supply this omission in different ways. Non-Aryan races generally incline to laxity. The Santáls, for example, in the Santál Parganás, are said to make up for their sweeping prohibition on the father's side by allowing very near alliance on the mother's side—a fact pointedly exemplified in their proverb 'No man heeds a cow-track, or regards his

Calculation of prohibited degrees.

mother's sept.' Many castes, again, exclude a smaller number of generations on the female side, while others profess to prohibit intermarriage so long as any relationship, however remote, can be traced between the parties.

Exogamy among the Brahmans.

In the foregoing paragraphs I have attempted to follow the totemistic system of exogamy upwards from the well-defined non-Aryan tribes of Western Bengal, through a series of castes formed from the detritus of the tribe, and now undergoing a process of gradual stratification and upheaval into the Hindu system, to the highly respectable Kumhárs of priest-ridden Orissa. A fresh starting point may now be taken at the top of Hindu society. Here we find the Brahmans, and the large body of castes which ape Brahmanical customs, divided into exogamous sections (*gotras*), the members of which profess to be descended from the mythical *rishi* or inspired saint whose name the *gotra* bears. So a man belonging to the Bharadwáj *gotra* may not marry a woman of the same *gotra*, as both are supposed to be descended from the *rishi* Bharadwája. Exogamous sections of this kind may conveniently be styled *eponymous*. Within the main class of eponymous sections we may further distinguish two sub-classes—one tracing its descent to a wholly mythical eponym, and the other deriving its name from a historic or semi-historic personage who is believed to have been the chief or founder of the clan. Many, if not most, of the Rajput septs are of the latter type, and were the materials for the history of India more abundant than they are, there would probably be no great difficulty in identifying the eponyms. As it is, we can trace some of them in books like Tod's *Rájasthán* and in local traditions of various kinds. In any case, the theoretical distinction between the two sub-classes is clear. I do not propose to discuss the Brahmanical marriage system at length. Its leading features are well known, and have been described in several standard text-books on Hindu law. It deserves notice that in the eponymous as in the totemistic type of section the exogamous rule is often, though not invariably, one-sided, and that intermarriage with the mother's relations is guarded against by what Sir Henry Maine calls "a most extensive table of prohibited degrees."

Strictly speaking, as the eponyms of the Brahmanical *gotras* were necessarily Brahmans themselves, the Kshatryas and Vaisyas could have no *gotras* of their own. By a sort of authorised fiction, however, these castes were permitted to adopt the *gotras* of the family priests of their ancestors, and this practice has now spread by imitation to other castes in Bengal. Thus the physician and writer-castes (Baidyas and Káyasths), the Naba-Sákha or nine castes (actually now thirteen) from whose hands a Brahman may take water, and many castes ranking even lower than these in the social scale, have exogamous sections bearing the same name as the Brahmanical *gotras*, and based upon similar traditions. The wide diffusion of these names is doubtless due in great measure to the influence of the *Patit* (fallen) or Varna Brahmans, who act as family priests to the lower castes, and gradually raise their standard of ceremonial purity. How clumsily these reforms are introduced, and how little their theoretical object is understood by the reformers or their clients, may be gathered from the fact that the Rájbansi, a very numerous Dravidian caste of Rungpore and Kuch or Kochh Behar, the Kámárs of Bengal, and several other castes, have only one eponymous section which includes the entire caste; and thus while professing to practise exogamy of the Brahmanical type, necessarily and habitually transgress the exogamous rule which forms the essence of the *gotra* system.

Diffusion of Brahmanical section-names.

Among several other castes, the exogamous sections belong to a different type. Their names denote neither mythical eponyms, nor historic founders of clans, but appear to refer to the original habitation of the members

e 2

or of some leader under whom they branched off from their parent tribe. Instances of this, which may perhaps be called the *territorial* class of names, are the Sesodia and Bhadauria septs of the Rajputs of Upper India, the Banodhia and Ujjaini sections of the Rajputs of Behar, and perhaps the Agarwálá and Agrahri Baniyas. It is rarely, however, that the members of a section can give an intelligible account of the meaning of its name, or can quote any tradition distinct enough to enable a particular place to be identified. All one can say is that a particular name is certainly not the name of a man, and is therefore probably the name of a place. Moreover, the names preserved in these section-titles are as often as not compressed and mangled renderings of the names of obscure or abandoned villages, or of those colloquial rustic names of particular tracts of country which are shown on no map, and can only be picked up, mostly by accident, from the people themselves. Until some scholar who knows both books and people as Mr. Beames knows them finds time to reconstruct the tribal geography of India on the basis of an etymological and antiquarian analysis of these *territorial* names, we can hardly expect to get much beyond conjecture as to the manner in which the castes arose among whom such names are found. Among the higher castes territorial names for exogamous sections or septs are curiously mixed up with names preserving the memory of a chief who founded or led the sept within historic times, and with the mythical eponyms of the Brahmans. This is the case with the Rajputs and Babhans of Behar, both of whom prohibit marriage within the section of *either* father or mother, and thus practise what might be called *bi-lateral* exogamy. In connexion with this rule, a curious case has recently come to my notice illustrating the way in which a tribal series of sections—territorial or eponymous—comes to be overlaid by the Brahmanical system of *gotras*. Bábu Ajodhiá Singh, of Hájipur in Tirhut, being himself a Sulank

Territorial sections.

Rajput, married a wife from the Chandel section, and his son, Bábu Baijnáth Singh, has married into the same section. At the time of the latter's betrothal a question was raised as to the correctness of the procedure, and the Brahmans held that as the son's betrothed, though of the same *tribal sept* as his mother, belonged to a different Puránic *gotra*, the rule of exogamy would not be infringed by the marriage. The formula of prohibited degrees previously quoted is also recognized by the Tirhut Rajputs, who in theory consider it binding down to seven generations on the father's and five on the mother's side.

Classification of exogamous groups.

It would seem, then, from the facts sketched above, that we may trace in Bengal at the present time three district classes of exogamous septs or sections—(1) Totemistic; (2) Eponymous; (3) Territorial. The number may be raised to four if we choose to distinguish the mythical eponym of the Brahmanical or Puránic *gotra* from the more or less historic eponym of the Rajput sept. All three classes are based upon a fiction far removed from fact, and have certain characteristics in common which mark them off from other exogamous groups which I have still to describe. In the first place, the circle of affinity which each section encloses is an absurdly wide one, including persons between whom there exists no relationship whatever in the ordinary sense of the word, who live hundreds of miles apart, and have no personal acquaintance with each other. Secondly, the centre from which the circle is drawn—be it totem, eponym, or birth-place—is lost in a period of remote antiquity, and cannot be identified by any process of genealogical or historical research. You could as soon bring back the Mastodon as the Murmu, and the most ingenious Euhemorist would be baffled by figures such as Bharadwája and Kásyapa. Thirdly, the vitality of these groups is remarkable, while their number is small in relation to the tribes and castes whose marriages they control. Three years ago I came across a small colony of seventeen families of Oraons in the east of Rungpore who regulate their marriages by the totemistic septs already described. These people had long ago settled down as *Bunas* or clearers of jungle, and had no intention of returning to Chota Nagpore. Their neighbours in their new home were non-Aryan Mahomedans and Rájbansis, both of whom know nothing of exogamy, and rarely marry beyond the narrow circle of their own village and its immediate vicinity. For all this the Oraons showed no signs of relaxing their strictness, and three families of Christians among them, while free from prejudice in the matter of food and drink, still observed the totemistic rules of intermarriage which govern the main body of the tribe on the distant plateau of Chota Nagpore. Fourthly, the distribution of the groups has nothing to do with locality. In none of the castes or tribes hitherto mentioned do we find the members of a particular section dwelling in a particular village or tract of country: on the contrary, representatives of the various sections are scattered about through all the villages where the tribe or caste is found.

There seem to be indications in the history of the Rajputs that in former times a Rajput sept occupied a distinct area of country from which its members emerged on predatory excursions to capture wives and lift cattle. In Rájputana, however, this state of things has long passed away, and with it has passed the opportunity of enquiring more closely into an organization which has been believed by several authorities to be the primitive unit of human society. The local sept dwelling together as a group of blood relations in its own territory has everywhere been so completely broken up and scattered that critics of Mr. McLennan's theory of primitive society have questioned whether it ever existed, and Mr. McLennan himself was driven to account for the dispersion of these groups and their diffusion among a number of local tribes by assuming the universal prevalence of female kinship.

Rajput exogamy.

A fortunate combination of circumstances has preserved for us in the Kandhs of the secluded tract, known as the Kandhmals in Orissa, a singularly perfect specimen of a tribe divided into local septs, each inhabiting the area from which it derives its name. The Kandhs are divided into fifty *gochis* or exogamous septs, each of which traces its descent from a common ancestor, and takes its name from the *muta* or circle of villages in which its members live. A man may not marry a woman of his own *gochi* or *muta*—the two words denoting the same set of facts regarded from different points of view. Until comparatively recent times the Kandhs of the Kandhmals dwelled apart in that state of nature which Hobbes teaches us to regard as a state of war. Contiguous septs were always at war with each other; wives were captured, female infants were slain, and all the incidents of primitive society as sketched by Mr. McLennan were in full force. The *gochi* or exogamous sept is regarded by the Kandhs themselves as one of their most ancient and treasured institutions. Its members claim to be descended from a common parent, but the names of these ancestors have not been preserved, and the name of the *muta* or group of villages in which the members of the *gochi* actually reside takes the place of the eponym in use among the higher Aryan castes. Every *gochi* again is divided into a number of sub-septs or *klambus*, each of which is called after one of the villages included in the *muta*, and the members of which profess to trace their descent from an ancestor of much more recent date than the progenitor of the *gochi*, who is supposed to have founded the village from which the *klambu* takes its name. The *gochi* name descends in the male line, and there are no indications of the tribe having at any time been acquainted with the practice of reckoning kinship through females. As a man may not marry in his own *gochi*, still less may he marry within the limits of the *klambu*. The latter, however is by no means a useless or ornamental appendage, nor,

Kandh exogamy.

on the other hand, does it take the place of the *gochi*, as is the case among many castes which have found their original exogamous groupings inconveniently large. It serves a distinct purpose, and seems to have been consciously adopted in comparatively recent times to supplement the defects of simple exogamy by providing against consanguineous marriages on the mother's side. Not only is a man forbidden to marry within his mother's *klambu*, but this prohibition is observed always for four and often for five generations in the descending line. It may fairly be inferred from these facts that the Kandh tribe has been organized from the earliest times on the sole basis of male kinship, and has only recently begun to recognize the idea of relationship on the mother's side. A similar arrangement exists among the Santáls, with whom the *khunt* or sub-sept serves the same purpose as the *klambu* among the Kandhs. The prohibition of intermarriage is not, however, observed for so many generations, nor are the septs and sub-septs localised as with the Kandhs.

Among the numerous castes whose marriage system is *not* regulated by the large sections already described, we find what may be called *family* and *local* sections of a much more fluid and variable type. Instances of the former are the *thar* of the Darjiling hills, and the *kul*, *múl* or *párich* of Behar. All these terms express a circle of agnatic descent, but the ancestor from whom the members of the *kul* are supposed to be descended is much less remote in point of time than the mythic progenitor of the Brahmanical gotra, or the semi-historic eponym of the Rajput clan. They are, in fact, very much what a Hindu joint family or a South Slavonic House community would be if it cast off the bond of community of goods and dwelling, and were held together by no stronger link than the rule of exogamy. Thus the Sribástab sub-caste of the Káyasths of Patna is divided for marriage purposes into a number of *kuls*, one of which—the Akhauri—can be traced to the village of Churámanpur in Sháhabád, where the family, which has

Family groups.

now expanded into the Akhauri *kul*, is said to have been settled a few centuries ago. Similar groups exist under the name of *múl* among the Báis, a cultivating caste of North Bhágalpur, who claim to be the descendants of the Vaisyas of early Aryan tradition. These groups are small and very numerous in relation to the size of the caste. A panjiár or marriage referee of the Báis, who claims to have in his possession registers recording the alliances of three hundred families for the last hundred years, informs me that in applying the rule of exogamy regard is had to the following considerations: First, a man may not marry a woman who belongs to the same *múl* as himself, his mother, or his paternal grandmother. Secondly, he may not marry a woman whose mother or maternal grandmother belonged to any of the *múls* prohibited to him. For instance (*vide* table below), the question is whether Propositus may marry Proposita. The capital letters show the *múls*. Proposita herself does not belong to any of the three *múls* A, B, D, which are barred on the man's side. But her maternal grandmother belonged to D *múl*, which is barred for Propositus; consequently the marriage cannot take place. The *múl* of Proposita's maternal grandfather is not taken into account.

Paternal Grandfather = Paternal Grandmother (D)	Maternal Grandfather (E) = Maternal Grandmother (D)
Father (A) = Mother (B)	Father (P) = Mother (E)
Propositus (A)	Proposita (P)

The *local* type of exogamous section, usually called *dih*, seems to be based on the assumption that all the members of a caste residing in the same village must be more or less related, and that therefore intermarriages between them should be prohibited. In some cases these prohibitions are singularly cumbrous and intricate. The Bargwár Goálás in Bhágalpur exclude seven *dihs* on each side; that is to say, if the proposed bride's *dih* is found within seven degrees of the bridegroom, or *vice versâ*, no marriage can take place between the parties. Still more curious are the prohibitions on intermarriage arising from *mith*, friendship, or fictitious brotherhood, among the Murmi, Mangar, Gurung, Limbu, Lepcha, and other hill races in Darjiling.* Two men contract friendship by a special ritual, at which a Brahman, or, when the parties are Buddhists, a Lama, officiates, and reads *mantras* or mystic formulæ, while the two friends exchange rupees, handkerchiefs, or scarves, and bedaub each other between the eyebrows with the paste made of rice and curds which is used in the marriage ceremony. The effect of the union is that the friends are reckoned as brothers, and not only is intermarriage between the two families prohibited for several generations, but the members of each family may not marry with the *thar* or exogamous section to which the other belongs. Any breach of the rule is punished in British territory by exclusion from caste. In Nepal, I am informed, more severe punishments, such as death or slavery, are inflicted. It is difficult to test the accuracy of a statement of this kind; but the fact that it was made to me in perfect good faith by a number of Murmis living in British territory is of itself enough to show how thoroughly the fictitious kinship arising from *mith* was identified by my informants with the real kinship which it imitates.

Local groups.

A fifth class of sept-names is found among the Tibetans and Limbus of the Darjiling hills and the Chakmas of the Chittagong Hill Tracts. These names are neither the personal names of the supposed ancestors of the group, nor the names of the village where he lived or the territory which he conquered. They are a sort of nicknames, having

* Compare the Slavonian confraternity mentioned by Sir Henry Maine at p. 258 of *Early Law and Custom*.

reference to some personal adventure or individual peculiarity of the ancestor himself, which now serves as the designation of the group of kindred who trace their descent from him. Many of them are of unflattering and indelicate character. Thus among the Limbus we find Lechenche, the dissolute one; Serling, the thief; Yungám, the idler; Inglamphe, the liar; Lekhogma, the man with swollen testicles; Thobukya, the man with skin disease: and among the Chakmas, Ichapocha, the man who ate rotten shrimps; Pirábhanga, the fat man who broke the stool; Aruyá, the skeleton; Kurjya, the lazy one, and so forth. It is important to observe that side by side with these singular names, concerning the origin of which members of the tribe will often tell long and elaborate stories, there are also found names of the totemistic type. Thus the Limbus have Khema, the pheasant, as the name of one of their groups, and explain that the ancestor who bore this name went out to shoot pheasants in a fir copse, but found none, or missed what he found, and vowed on his return home never to eat a pheasant again. A similar story is told of the Sangma or buffalo sept of the same tribe. Among the Chakmas the plantain tree and several rivers appear as sept-names. In this class may also be included certain exogamous groups which bear the names of village or communal officials, such as Mánjhi, village headman; Naiya or Láyá, village priest; Mánki, head of a group of villages, and the like. These names are commonly found in castes in a state of transition from animism to Hinduism, which have, as Mr. Andrew Lang expresses it, 'sloughed off the totem,' but have not yet adopted the full-blown eponym characteristic of those castes which are organized on a Brahmanical model. The theory of course is that the original progenitor of the septs held the office of which the sept bears the name, but I have never succeeded in verifying this in a particular case, and I believe the names to have been for the most part adopted at random. In the

Nickname groups.

Official groups.

case of the nickname septs of the Limbus and Tibetans, there are grounds for believing that the account given of the origin of the names is in the main true.

As distinguished from the larger exogamous groups, the sections known as *thar*, *múl*, *kul*, or *dih*, enclose a much narrower circle of relations, and, as has been remarked above, seem to be little more than somewhat expanded joint families, kept together solely for the purpose of controlling matrimonial relations, and having no common interests in respect of property. Most of them are comparatively modern, and their origin can in many cases be ascertained. To complete the contrast with the larger groups it should be added that the *thars* are much more numerous in relation to the strength of the caste, and that their number admits of being added to. The hill Brahmans, for instance, by no means a very large caste, are said to have more than 1,400 *thars*. Similar statistics could, I believe, be procured for many of the lower castes, were it not for the extreme ignorance of the people themselves.

Summing up the facts sketched, we find the following types of exogamous groups existing in Bengal:—

I. *Totemistic.* Confined for the most part to tribes and castes of Dravidian descent.

II. *Eponymous,* the eponym being either a Vedic saint (as with the Brahmans and the castes who imitate them), or a chief of comparatively modern date, as with the Rajputs and others.

III. *Territorial,* referring either to some very early settlement of a section or to the birthplace of its founder: prevalent among the Rajputs and the trading castes supposed to be allied with them and found also among the Kandhs of Orissa in a very primitive form, the sept there residing in the local area whose name it bears.

IV. *Local, communal,* or *family* sections of small size and comparatively recent origin.

V. *Titular*, or *nickname* groups referring to some personal adventure of the founder of the sept or to some office which he is supposed to have held.

Besides these we also find castes which have no sections of any kind, or, which comes to the same thing, have only one section and habitually marry within it, and simply reckon up prohibited degrees in much the same way as we do ourselves. Castes of this type are more numerous in Bengal Proper, particularly in Eastern and Northern Bengal than in Behar, Orissa, and Chota Nagpore. For this there seem to be two reasons. On the one hand, the tendency to imitate Brahmanical institutions has been stronger in the former area, so that people have adopted one or two of the standard *gotras*, and abandoned their original section names; while on the other hand the influence of Islam in districts where a large proportion of the population has recently become Mahomedan, and social intercourse goes on freely between votaries of the rival creeds, may be expected to lead to sept-names dropping out of use even among non-Mahomedan groups.

On the question of the origin of exogamy itself I may be allowed to make a few general remarks. The first point to notice in the custom of exogamy is that in some form or other it is practically universal: it is observed *semper ubique et ab omnibus*. Any cause therefore that is adequately to account for it must be also of universal operation. This disposes of a theory derived from the Aryan advance into India which I put forward in the *Asiatic Quarterly Review* for July 1886, and which was discussed in the Academy shortly afterwards by Mr. Andrew Lang. Mr. Lang's own view has since been briefly stated in a note to one of the early chapters of *Myth Ritual and Religion*. He there explains exogamy as being an application to marriage of the principle of taboo of the totem. A man may not use his totem for food and so forth, and he may not use (in the Greek sense of χρῆσθαι γύναικι) a woman

The origin of exogamy.

who bears the totem name. But granting that this is the form which the prohibition ultimately assumes, we may fairly ask how it got started. The analogy of the animal world, of which savages are keen observers, and which they regard as closely akin to themselves, so far from suggesting objections to the marriage of a Swan man with a Swan woman, would rather encourage such intercourse. From the animal point of view, the union of a swan with a mongoose, or of either with a snake, would appear to be unnatural and illicit. We must look therefore for some wider cause, and it seems worth while to consider whether the habit of exogamy may not have arisen at a stage of social development antecedent to, and incapable of anything like, the conscious adaptation of means to ends and quite apart from the action of any influence save that of natural selection. We know that changes of habits often occur in certain individuals or in whole species, and that useful variations, or those which are beneficial to the organism or species under the conditions to which it is exposed, tend to be preserved. Finally, the hereditary transmission of such variations leads, as Mr. Wallace expresses it in his recent work on Darwinism, "to the preservation of favoured races in the struggle for life." Now let us take a community, such as the local sept or *gochi* of the Kandh tribe, in a very rudimentary stage of evolution, when the proceedings of individuals are determined, not by deliberate calculation, but by so-called instinct—when, in other words, they are comparatively simple reflex acts. Suppose that in such a community certain individuals, as the result of the inherent tendency to vary present in all organisms, varied physiologically so as to find the women of other communities more attractive than their own. They would naturally tend to marry according to their instinctive attractions, and the community would thus come to consist of an aggregate composed of families derived from one stock and of families

Exogamy and natural selection.

derived from the crossing of two stocks. Next suppose—which we have certainly some good ground to do—that the individuals belonging to the crossed families were at an advantage in the struggle for existence as compared with those of the pure families. As a result of the survival of the fittest they would tend more and more to replace the latter, and would at the same time tend to become more and more exogamic in habits, simply as the result of the cumulative hereditary strengthening of the original instinct. It would further appear that the element of sexual selection might also be brought into play, as an exogamous family or group would have a larger range of selection than an endogamous one, and would thus get better women, who again, in the course of the primitive struggle for wives, would be appropriated by the strongest and most warlike men.

It will of course be objected to this hypothesis that inter-breeding is not necessarily injurious. To this I would reply, first, that the question is one of degree. Savages would probably inter-breed very closely and freely, and we are not in a position to argue, from the comparatively limited amount of inter-breeding observed among civilized races in modern times, what might have been the practice of an earlier generation of mankind. We can say that a limited amount of inter-breeding is not necessarily injurious, but our instances are only occasional, and their influence is continually being counteracted by the effect of recurring crosses. Secondly, it may be answered that the question is one of conditions. The amount of inter-breeding that is innocuous, or apparently innocuous, in civilized life might have been fatal in savage life, where the struggle for existence is infinitely greater, and where talents and brain power generally do less to mitigate the effects of congenital weakness.

Is inter-breeding injurious?

This attempt to bring the phenomena of exogamy within the operation of a known general law is, I need hardly say, put forward with the utmost diffidence, and

I am entirely conscious of the difficulties which surround the subject. But it does not seem unreasonable to suppose that here and there some half-accidental circumstance, such as the transmission of a physical defect or an hereditary disease, might have given primitive man a sort of warning, and thus have induced the particular kind of variation we want, or at any rate have stimulated the general tendency to variation of habit which we are justified in assuming. We are also, it would seem, entitled to contrast the remarkable stability of the habit of exogamy with the known instability of non-adaptive characters, and to conclude from this that exogamy is to be regarded as an adaptive character. Lastly, it may be claimed for this hypothesis that it excludes the element of deliberate calculation on the part of the members of the exogamous aggregate, thus escaping the criticism which has assailed those theories which impute to primitive man a power of foretelling remote possibilities out of all proportion to his known improvidence. So far from doing this, the theory now presented goes rather into the opposite extreme, and places primitive man on much the same level as orchids and many other plants having most elaborate exogamic arrangements which no one dreams of ascribing to calculation. If, then, an elaborate system of exogamy has been evolved in plants by the action of natural selection, there can be nothing to prevent its having arisen in the earliest stages of human society by the same means.

One more objection may be noticed. It will be said, with truth, that the earlier forms of exogamy are always unilateral; that is to say, that the totem or class name goes either by the male side only or by the female side only, and that the system as known to savages makes no attempt to deal with both paternal and maternal relations. Here I would reply that, though unilateral exogamy is not a complete escape from the objections to consanguineous unions, it represents at any rate a considerable advance on promiscuity which in very small communities would probably have disastrous cumulative results. The idea that parentage can be reckoned on the side of both parents is one of comparatively late development. Even the Athenians of the time of Aeschylus seem to have been hazy—witness the famous trial in the Eumenides—on this point. But certainly an imperfect check on promiscuity must have been better than none.

Finally, the hypothesis set forth above would tend to clear up one of the vexed questions of ethnology—the question of female infanticide and its relation to the custom of exogamy. Mr. J. F. McLennan saw that the two usages often existed side by side, and in the theory of exogamy put forward in his essay on Primitive Marriage, he argued that female infanticide as practised by savages disturbed the balance of the sexes and drove men to capture their wives from other tribes—a practice which in course of time resolved itself into the systematic observance of exogamy.

Female infanticide and exogamy.

This view was open to the obvious rejoinder that if all tribes killed their female infants at an equal rate, there would soon be no women to capture, and the race would die out. Even without pressing this point, it was difficult to see why primitive man should prefer the dangerous and inconvenient process of capturing a wife from a hostile tribe to the simpler method of marrying a girl belonging to his own local community. Given, however, an adequate cause inducing people to practise exogamy—a force as effective as the influence of natural selection would unquestionably be—and it is easy to understand that in certain states of society a tendency to female infanticide would be a natural consequence—not as McLennan supposed a *cause*—of the custom of exogamy. For if men were restrained by inexorable usage from marrying the girls born in the sept or local group of blood kindred, which we may assume to be the unit of early society, the temptation to kill these *bouches inutiles* would probably be very strong. Not only would girls be useless to the men of the tribe as wives, but the more of them there were, the more would the tribe be preyed upon by neighbours in quest of wives. As a matter of fact, this was very much the view that the Kandhs took of the question. In 1842 they told Major Macpherson in so many words that it was better to destroy girls in their infancy than to allow them to grow up and become causes of strife afterwards. I am indebted to Sir John Edgar for a parallel instance from the Nága tribe. It seems that on a tour through the Nága country, Colonel McCulloch, Political Agent for Manipur, came across a village which struck him as singularly destitute of female children. On making inquiries he found that there was not a single girl in the place, for the simple reason that the people killed all that were born in order to save themselves from the annoyance of being harried by wife-hunting parties from a stronger tribe. Colonel McCulloch got hold of the mothers and managed to induce them to promise to spare their girls in future on the understanding that their neighbours should stop raiding and adopt a more peaceable method of wooing. By a judicious mixture of threats and persuasion, the other tribe was led to agree to the arrangement, and many years after, while staying in Manipur, Sir John Edgar was present when a troop of Nága girls from the weaker tribe paid a visit of ceremony to Colonel McCulloch, bearing presents of cloth of their own weaving in token of their gratitude to the man who had saved their lives.

Instances of this sort, vouched for by competent observers, and drawn from tribes dwelling so far apart and belonging to such widely different stocks as the Dravidian Kandhs of Orissa and the Mongoloid Nágas of Assam, may be regarded as crucial in their bearing on the question of the relation of female infanticide to the custom of exogamy. They seem to show that the practice of killing female infants is a consequence, not a cause—and assuredly not *the* cause—of the rule that a man may not marry a woman of his own tribe

This consequence, moreover, ensues only so long as society is in a savage state, and tends to die out, as it has died out among both Kandhs and Nágas, directly a *régime* of violence is succeeded by a *régime* of law. As soon as this change has been effected, the value of women tends to rise. They become a saleable commodity, which neighbouring tribes will buy with a price, and the inducement to kill them in infancy ceases to exist: in other words, savage infanticide is an incident of the primitive struggle for bare existence which disappears when the severity of the struggle is alleviated by peace. There is, however, another form of infanticide which arises from wholly different causes and requires to be carefully distinguished from the savage type. Given a tribe like the Rajputs of Northern India, divided into a number of exogamous septs, and strongly impressed with the ideas of purity of blood and the importance of correct ceremonial observances, it follows of necessity that in course of time some septs will drop behind the others and will come to be regarded as socially inferior to the rest. Members of such septs will find difficulty in marrying their daughters, and will be obliged to buy husbands for them. This custom will spread, and the bridegroom price will tend to rise until it presses severely on the means of families unfortunate enough to have several daughters to marry. Family pride and the necessity of avoiding scandals render it impossible to let girls grow up with the prospect of remaining old maids; convents and sisterhoods are unknown; and the only way out of the difficulty, as it presents itself to the Rajput father, is to permit no more girls to arrive at maturity than can certainly be provided with husbands. The ultimate result no doubt is much the same as is witnessed among savage people like Nágas and Kandhs, but it is arrived at in a different way and springs from a different principle. It may be added that this refined form of infanticide is far more difficult to suppress than the savage form. The one

The two kinds of infanticide.

dies out of itself as the forcible capture of wives falls into disuse, and life generally becomes easier; the other tends to spread with the growth of family pride and personal luxury, and may even offer substantial resistance to attempts made to stamp it out by penal legislation.

In the closing paragraphs of his work on *totemism*, Mr. J. G. Frazer observes: —"No satisfactory explanation of the origin of totemism has yet been given. Mr. Herbert Spencer finds the origin of totemism in a 'misinterpretation of nicknames.' Savages first named themselves after natural objects, and then, confusing these objects with their ancestors of the same names, reverenced them as they already reverenced their ancestors.[1] The objection to this view is that it attributes to verbal misunderstandings far more influence than, in spite of the so-called comparative mythology, they ever seem to have exercised. Sir John Lubbock also

Origin of totemism.

thinks that totemism arose from the habit of naming persons and families after animals; but in dropping the intermediate links of ancestor worship and verbal misunderstanding, he has stripped the theory of all that lent it even an air of plausibility." In the face of this finding by so high an authority, it would be almost presumptuous for me to approach the subject at all, were it not that the novel facts elicited by the Bengal inquiry seem to throw some fresh light upon the question. In all the discussions that have hitherto taken place, it has been assumed that the totem is a thing *sui generis*, an isolated survival which stands by itself and cannot be compared with similar institutions for the sufficient reason that no similar institutions exist. This is not the view which an examination of the Indian evidence seems to suggest. The totem comes before us in India as only one class out of a number of different classes or types of sept-names, all of which serve the same purpose, that of providing the machinery

---

[1] Spencer, *Principles of Sociology*, i, 367.

for giving effect to the rule of exogamy. None of the denominations are now used as personal names, and but for the fact of their discharging special functions in respect of marriage, they would doubtless have fallen long ago into disuse. All of them are, in fact, survivals which do for the people who use them precisely what is done for ourselves by the table of prohibited degrees at the end of the Book of Common Prayer. Now among these various classes of sept-names we find the Tibetans and Limbus of the Eastern Himalayas and the people of the Hill Tracts of Chittagong using names which profess to be, and in fact are, nothing more nor less than nicknames of the original ancestors of septs. Other castes use names which are the names of certain village or communal offices which the ancestor of the sept is supposed to have held. Others, again, use names of villages, groups of villages, or tracts of country which are similarly explained to be the names of settlements founded by the common progenitor. What can be simpler than to apply the same principle to the animal-names which are also used to regulate exogamy, and to assume that these also are the names of founders of septs? This, in fact, is the explanation which the Limbus do give of the names of this type which are used by them along with the unmistakeable nicknames instanced above. I can see no reason for doubting its correctness, and I think we are justified in defining the totem as we find it in India as an ancient nick-name, usually derived from some animal, of the supposed founder of an exogamous sept, now stripped of its personal associations and remembered solely in virtue of the part which it plays in giving effect to the rule of exogamy. To any one who deems it incredible that men should be called after animals, I would reply that if savages are capable of believing, as we know they are, that men can transform themselves into animals at will, or can be so transformed by the agency of witchcraft, nothing would seem to them more natural and reasonable than to call a man by the name of an animal to which he bears some fancied resemblance. If the man so named were the head of a sept, the name would be perpetuated by its use in connexion with the rule of exogamy long after the man who originally bore it had been forgotten; and in a large tribe where new septs are continually being formed, the practice of naming them after animals would be kept alive by fiction and the force of habit after the fashion of giving such names to individuals had died out. Moreover, when sept names came to be adopted without reference to any particular individual, but merely as symbols marking off a particular group for the purpose of the rule of exogamy, any sort of distinctive designation would do as well as the name of an animal. This would account for the number of queer totems found among the Mundas, with regard to some of which it is difficult to see how, from any point of view, they can ever have been looked upon as appropriate personal names.

This hypothesis, it seems to me, explains in a simple and intelligible fashion all that needs explanation in the phenomena of totemism. It puts the totem on the same footing as the nicknames we find among the Mongoloid races, the eponyms of the Brahmanical system, and the territorial and local sept-names of the Rajputs and Kandhs, and it accounts for all of these on the well-known principle of survival. Upon the religious aspects of totemism I do not propose to enter here. They are not very prominent in India, and the data requisite for full treatment of the subject are not yet available. But if the view put forward above is accepted, it would clearly account for the reverence with which the totem is regarded, and would explain why on occasion it receives divine honours. A man who is looked upon as a tiger during life clearly stands a fair chance of being worshipped as a tiger after he is dead. Some tribes, indeed, regard the sacrifices offered to ancestors as a sort of black-mail paid to the spirits of the dead for fear lest, if left unappeased. they should enter into the bodies of wild beasts and in that form make themselves unpleasant to the living.

Working of endogamy.

Reference has been made above to the influence of fiction in bringing about within the limits of the caste system the formation of endogamous aggregates, each of which is regarded by its members as in some sense a collection of relatives, although in fact no relationship may be traceable. Such groups are extremely numerous, and fresh ones are continually being formed, so that it seems worth while to attempt to classify them with reference to the principles upon which they are based. The following are the main classes which may be distinguished:—

I. *Ethnic* groups, composed of the higher grades of Aryans or of non-Aryan tribes, like the Rajbansi-Kocch, who have adopted Hinduism, and transformed themselves into a caste. In the case of the latter the assumption of a common origin is borne out by what is known of the history and affinities of the tribe, but after having become a caste, its members set to work to strip themselves of all customs likely to betray their true descent. At the same time the substantial landholders, if there are any among the tribe, usually break off from the rest and convert themselves into Rajputs.

II. *Linguistic* or *Provincial* groups, such as Bengali, Uriya, and Pachimá, or Behári Brahmans, Káyasths, Kumhárs, etc. These classes are very large, and include whole castes, which in their turn are broken up into endogamous sub-castes. These groups arise partly from the fiction which assumes that men who live in a different part of the country and speak a different language must be of a different race, and probably also in some measure to the inclusion of different stocks under a single caste-name.

III. *Territorial* or *local* groups, not corresponding to any distinction of language, such as the Rárhi and Barendra Brahmans, the Uttariya and Dakshini (north and south of the Ganges) Doms of Behar, Tamária and Sikharbhumi Bhumij of Mánbhum, and numerous others. It is curious to observe that in some cases these groups are called after ancient territorial divisions, such as Rárh, Bárendra, Sikharbhum, etc., which appear on no map, and the names of which may possibly throw some light upon the early history of Bengal.

IV. *Functional* or *occupational* groups, such as the Mecho and Helo sub-castes of Kaibarttas, of whom the former sell fish, while the latter confine themselves to cultivation; the Dulia, Máchhuá, and Mátiál sub-castes of Bágdi who are distinguished by carrying palanquins, fishing, and labouring as tank-diggers and earth-workers generally.

V. *Sectarian* groups like the Kherwár or Safáhor revivalists among the Santáls, and the Vaishnava divisions of some of the Orissa castes. It is doubtful, however, whether any groups based upon religious differences within the range of Hinduism are really endogamous.

VI. *Social* groups marked off by abstaining from or practising some particular social or ceremonial usage. Thus the Sagáhut sub-caste of Sunris (traders and liquor-sellers) of Behar allow their widows to remarry by the maimed rite of *sagai*, while another sub-caste of Sunris forbid widow marriage, and designate themselves Biyáhut, "the married ones," from *biyah*, the full-blown wedding ceremony which no woman can go through twice.

Illustrations of these groupings might be multiplied almost indefinitely, and it might be shown how the fact of such separations having taken place has given rise to a variety of curious legends and traditions which seek to furnish a mythological explanation of existing facts. Thus in the district of Bankura, where the original structure of the caste seems to have been singularly well-preserved, we find the Bágdis divided into the following endogamous sub-castes:—(1) Tentulia, called after the tamarind tree; (2) Kasaikuliá, named from the Kasai river. These two groups work as masons, and also prepare the lime which is mixed with the betel

Endogamous groupings of the Bágdi caste.

leaves and areca nut chewed by all classes of natives of India. (3) Duliá Bágdis carry palanquins or *dulis*, and in common with the other sub-castes, earn their livelihood by fishing, making gunny-bags, weaving cotton, and preparing the red powder (*abir*) used in the Holi festival. The Bágdi fisherman uses the ordinary circular cast-net, but swings the net round his head before casting it, a practice which is supposed by the regular fishing castes of Bengal—Tiyar, Mál and Kaibartta—to be peculiarly dishonourable. Of the other sub-castes—there are fourteen in all—the Máchhuá derive their name from fishing, the Mátiál from earth-working, the Kusmetea are called after the *Kusa* grass; the Ojha are, or are supposed to have been, the priests of the tribe. Among the Bágdis of Orissa the grotesque tale is told how, once upon a time, the gods being assembled in council, a goddess suddenly gave birth to three sons, and feeling embarrassed by the situation, hid the first under a heap of tamarind (*tentul*) pods, the second in an iron pan, and the third under a hermit's staff. From these vicissitudes of their infancy the children got the names—Tentulia, Guli-mánjhi and Danda-mánjhi—which the sub-castes descended from them still bear. To us this apparently foolish story is of interest as marking the transition from the tribe to the caste. It can only have arisen when the Bágdis had in some measure cast in their lot with Hinduism, and had begun to feel the want of a mythical pedigree of the orthodox type. The mention of the tamarind pods in particular furnishes an excellent example of a myth devised for the purpose of giving a respectable explanation of the totemistic name Tentulia.

Widow and infant marriage.

But of all the factors which have contributed to shape the internal structure of tribes and castes in Bengal, none has exercised so searching an effect as the custom prohibiting the second marriage of widows and the parallel usage enjoining the marriage of a daughter before she attains physical maturity. Both customs appear to have been developed in the form which they now assume at a comparatively recent date under the pressure of peculiar social conditions. Both, again, are looked upon by the people who observe them as badges of social distinction, and to the fact that they are regarded in this light is mainly due their rapid extension within the last two or three generations. No excuse therefore is needed for examining their prevalence and its causes in some detail.

For the ultimate origin of the prohibition of widow marriage among the higher castes we must look back, far beyond the comparative civilization of the Vedas, to the really primitive belief that the dead chief or head of the family will need human companionship and service in that other world which savage fancy pictures as a shadowy copy of this. To this belief is due the practice of burning the widow on the funeral pile of her dead husband, which is referred to as an "ancient custom" (*dharma purána*) in the "Atharva Veda."* The directions given in the Rig Veda for placing the widow on the pile with her husband's corpse, and then calling her back to the world of life, appear, as Tylor† has pointed out, to represent "a reform and a reaction against a yet more ancient savage rite of widow sacrifice, which they prohibited in fact, but yet kept up in symbol." The bow of the warrior and the sacrificial instruments of the priests were thrown back upon the pile to be consumed; the wife, after passing through the mere form of sacrifice, was held to have fulfilled her duties to her husband, and was free to marry again. A passage in the Rig Veda quoted by Zimmer‡ shows that in some cases, at any rate, the widow married her husband's younger brother (*devar*); and it is not unreasonable to suppose that her obligations in this respect were very much what we now find among the castes which permit widow marriage.

Prohibition of widow marriage.

---

* "Atharva Veda," 18, 3, 1, quoted by Zimmer, *Altindisches Leben*, p. 331.

† *Primitive Culture*, i, 466.

‡ *Altindisches Leben*, p. 329.

At this point the historical record, such as it is, breaks off, and conjecture alone can divine the precise motives which induced the Brahmans of a later age to revive that custom of primitive savagery which their ancestors had expressly condemned. Closer contact with more barbarous races, the growth of the sacerdotal spirit, the desire, as Sir Henry Maine has suggested, to get rid of the inconvenient lien which the widow held over her husband's property, may all have contributed to this result. But when widow sacrifice had been thus reintroduced, it is *primâ facie* unlikely that it should have been enforced with that rigid consistency which distinguishes the true savage; and, in fact, the texts prescribe for the widow the milder alternative of a life of ascetic self-denial and patient waiting to join the husband who has gone before. According to some authorities, they also recognize, though as a less excellent path than the two former, the alternative of remarriage.

Causes of its revival.

I will not attempt to enter upon the controversy as to the precise meaning of the passage in Parásara's Institutes, on which the modern advocates of widow marriage rely, still less to discuss its applicability to the present age of the world. It seems more profitable to state the causes which, irrespective of isolated texts, would in any case have favoured the growth of the modern custom which forbids the widows of the highest castes to marry again, and which shows signs of extending itself far beyond its present limits, and finally of suppressing widow marriage throughout the entire Hindu community of Bengal. Some, at any rate, of these causes are not far to seek. In the first place, the anxiety of the early Hindu law-givers to circumscribe a woman's rights to property would unquestionably tend to forbid her to join her lot to a man whose interest it would be to assert and extend those rights as against the members of her husband's family. At the same time the growth of the

Considerations of property, of spiritual benefit, of sacramental doctrine.

doctrine of spiritual benefit would require her to devote her life to the annual performance of her husband's* *sráddh.* Technical obstacles to her remarriage also arise from the Brahmanical theory of marriage itself. That ceremony being regarded as a sacrament ordained for the purification of women, and its essential portion being the gift of the woman by her father to her husband, the effect of the gift is to transfer her from her own *gotra* or exogamous group into that of her husband's. The bearing of this transfer on the question of her remarriage is thus stated by an orthodox Hindoo at pp. 276-77 of the *Papers relating to Infant Marriage and Enforced Widowhood* published by the Government of India:—

> "Her father being thus out of the question, it may be said that she may give herself in marriage. But this she cannot do, because she never had anything like disposal of herself. When young she was given away, so the ownership over her (if I may be permitted to use the phrase), vested then in the father, was transferred by a solemn religious act to the husband, and he being no more, there is no one to give her away; and since Hindu marriage must take the form of a religious gift, her marriage becomes impossible."

A powerful influence must also have been exerted by a cause which, so far as I am aware, has not hitherto been noticed in this connection. This is the custom which Mr. Ibbetson† has called "*hypergamy*, or the law of superior marriage"—the rule which compels a man to wed his daughter with a member of a group which shall be equal or superior in rank to his own, while he himself may take his wife, or at any rate his second wife, from a group of inferior standing. The Kulinism of Bengal is perhaps the best known illustration of this law; but instances of its

---

* *Tagore Law Lectures*, 1879, pp. 187, 188.

† *Panjáb Census Report*, p. 356. Mr. Ibbetson adds in a note:—"I am indebted to Mr. Coldstream for these two words [hypergamy and isogamy]." Hypergamy, indeed, would appear rather to mean "too much marriage" than "marriage in a higher rank," but the highest classical authority in India prefers it to anoterogamy, the only alternative which suggested itself.

working are found all over India, and it clearly may have arisen wherever great pride of blood co-existed with a mode of life demanding the continual maintenance of a high standard of ceremonial purity. In a society so organized it must needs be that offences come, and that they affect the matrimonial status of the family by whom they come. The tribe or caste would then be broken up, like the Jews in modern Germany, into divisions of varying social position and purity of lineage, and intermarriage between these would in India be regulated by the law stated above, which appears to owe its form to the passages in the early texts which admit of the marriage of a man of a higher caste to a woman of a lower caste, but condemn the converse practice in the strongest terms. The first consequence of this restriction would be a surplus of marriageable women in the superior groups; for the men of a given superior group might, and presumably in some instances would, marry women of an inferior group, while men of this group would be barred for the women of the superior group. Competition for husbands would follow; the bride-price of early usage would disappear, and would be replaced by the *bridegroom-price* now paid among most of the higher castes in India; and in extreme cases female infanticide would be resorted to. Widows certainly would be the first to be excluded from the marriage market, for in their case the interests of the individual families would be identical with those of the group. The family would already have paid a bridegroom-price to get their daughter or sister married, and would naturally be indisposed to pay a second, and probably higher, price to get her married again. The group, in its turn, would be equally adverse to an arrangement which tended to increase the number of marriageable women. Members of the higher castes, indeed, have frequently told me that these reasons of themselves were sufficient to make them regard with disfavour the

The law of hypergamy.

modern movement in favour of widow marriage. For, they said, we find it hard enough already to get our daughters married into families of our own rank, and things will be worse still if widows enter the competition with all the advantages they derive from having got over their first shyness, and acquired some experience of the ways of men. The sentiments of Mr. Weller sounded strange in the mouth of a Kulin Brahman, but the argument was used in entire good faith, and was backed up by much lamentation over the speaker's ill-luck in being the father of four daughters, all unmarried.

The considerations stated above are entitled to whatever support they may derive from the fact that the castes which permit widows to remarry know nothing of the custom of hypergamy, and as a rule pay for brides, not for bridegrooms. Among these groups the normal proportion of the sexes, whatever that may be, at the age of marriage has not been affected by any artificial divisions, and there is every reason to believe that widows who are in other respects eligible have no particular difficulty in finding husbands. Polygamy prevails on a limited scale, and a large proportion of the men have two wives, the second wife being often a young widow chosen by the man himself for her personal attractions, after the first wife, whom his parents selected for him, has lost her looks and become little more than a household drudge. Another point is that the lower castes seem to have a greater capacity than the higher for throwing off sub-castes. Deviations from caste usage, trivial changes of occupation, settlement outside the traditional habitat of the caste, and a variety of similar causes which in the higher castes would, as a rule, merely affect the standing of certain families in the scale of hypergamy, tend in the lower castes to form endogamous groups, the members of which intermarry only among themselves. The difference is important, as the latter process does not disturb the balance of the sexes, and the former does.

Let me now state as concisely as possible the actual practice which rules in respect of widow marriage in the four great Provinces—Behar, Bengal Proper, Orissa, and Chota Nagpore—which make up the Lieutenant-Governorship of Bengal. In Behar a fairly liberal tendency seems to prevail. All castes except Brahmans, Rajputs, Bábhans, Káyasths, and certain castes belonging to the Baniyá class, which are not properly native to Behar, permit widows to marry again by the form known as *sagai.* The etymology of the word *sagai* is obscure. It has been supposed to be a corruption of *sa-gotra* or *sva-gotra;* the idea being that as a woman passes by marriage into her husband's *gotra* or exogamous group, if she marries again *within that gotra* (as she usually does), she constitutes an exception to the ordinary rule of exogamy. The Bengal term (*sanga* or *senga*) does not, however, bear out this view, and it seems probable that the word simply denotes cohabitation (*sanga*), and has reference to the fact that a widow marriage is established by the parties living together, and is accompanied by a very meagre ceremony, or none at all. The *phera* or pacing round the sacred fire is never practised on such occasions: the husband merely smears some vermilion on the woman's forehead and takes her to live with him.

Widow marriage in Behar.

Widow marriages in Behar are usually brought about by the relatives of the widow. In some cases she may herself take the initiative, "but," as one of my Behar correspondents writes to me, "public opinion is against love marriages." The *sardár* or head of the caste council (*pancháyat*) has also to be consulted, but this is mostly a matter of form, as he rarely withholds his consent. Although by marriage every woman is supposed to pass into her husband's *gotra*, no regard is paid to that *gotra* in arranging for the remarriage of a widow. Whether her husband's death is supposed to dissolve the *gotra* tie or not is a point I am unable to

Its limits.

clear up. Certain it is that the persons whom she may not marry as a widow are the persons who would have been barred for her as a maiden. She may marry her late husband's younger brother, or younger cousin, and in some castes she is under a sort of obligation to do so. Marriage, however, with her late husband's elder brother or elder cousin, or with any of his direct or collateral ascendants, is strictly prohibited. To this extent her table of prohibited degrees is enlarged.

The ceremony varies in certain respects according as the bridegroom is himself a widower or a bachelor. If he is a widower, he goes at nightfall to the bride's house in his ordinary dress with a few of his friends. There they are feasted during the night. Towards daybreak the bridegroom, dressed in a new suit of clothes presented by the bride's relations, meets the bride, who wears a new cloth (*sari*) given her by the bridegroom, in one of the inner rooms of the house. There in the presence of her female relations he smears powdered vermilion (*sindur*) on her forehead and the parting of her hair. This completes the ceremony. Some castes add to it the form of throwing a sheet (*chadur*) over both parties, and under this sheet the smearing of vermilion is gone through. Brahmans take no part in the ritual, nor are any calculations entered into to find out an auspicious day. Early next morning the married couple go home to the husband's house without the final ceremony (*rukhsati*) which is used in bringing home a virgin bride. Even in the case of a virgin widow no *rukhsati* is performed; but as a child-widow is never married again until she has attained puberty, there is no necessity for a ceremony designed to celebrate that event.

Its ritual.

When a bachelor marries a widow, the ritual is more elaborate. Astrologers are called in to fix a lucky day; a bridal canopy (*marwa*) is erected in the bridegroom's house, and his ancestors are solemnly propitiated by Brahmans. In none of these ceremonies, however, does the bride take part, nor does she approach the *marwa*. She is brought to the house by night, and towards daybreak is conducted to an inner room, where the bridegroom puts vermilion on her forehead in the presence of the females of the family.

Such marriages are not considered disreputable. The *sagai* bride has all the rights and position of a wife married by the full-blown Brahmanical ceremony. Her children by her second husband inherit equally with any children whom he may have had by a former virgin bride; they offer sacrifices to their father and his ancestors; they are received as members of his *gotra*, and they marry among the women of the caste. In these respects their position differs materially from that of the widow's children by her late husband, who properly belong to his family and are usually taken care of by his relations. Should they decline the charge, the children follow the widow; but they are not deemed members of the family into which she has married, and they are not allowed to join in the domestic worship or to share in the inheritance.

Status of children.

So far, it may be said, the question of widow marriage in Behar seems to rest upon a reasonable footing. Symptoms of a tendency in the opposite direction are, however, not wanting. The Kurmis are a case in point. Some months ago I had a large body of them before me, and was asking "what sort of Kurmis" they were. One group answered promptly, "We are Ayodhya Kurmis: we do not allow widows to marry again." Another group, of Jeswar Kurmis, admitted with considerable reluctance that their widows did remarry. In fact, the tone in which both sets spoke on the subject made it clear that the Ayodhya had adopted this restriction in comparatively recent times, and were very proud of the distinction. The Jeswars, on the other hand, were rather ashamed of themselves, and were particularly anxious to explain that they did not allow the widow to marry any

Tendency towards prohibition of widow marriage in Behar.

one she chose, but expected her to marry her deceased husband's younger brother. If she married an outsider, she forfeited all claim not only to her husband's property, but also to the custody of her children. It is possible that remarriage restricted by these conditions may represent an advance from the promiscuous remarriage practised by the lower castes towards the total prohibition in vogue among the higher castes. It should be mentioned that the Kurmis of Behar are a perfectly distinct race from the aboriginal Kurmis of Chota Nagpore and parts of Orissa, whose totemistic usages have been referred to above. Both Jeswar and Ayodhya Kurmis approach closely to the Aryan type of feature, and some of them are very fine-looking men.

Other Behar castes in a state of transition as regards widow marriage are the Sonars, Sunris, Koiris, and Telis. Among the Sonar, the Bhojpuria and Kanaujia allow widows to remarry, while the Kamarkalla, Mairh and Ayodhiabasi do not. All five sub-castes are endogamous, and are subdivided into smaller exogamous sections, called *múls*. In Durbhunga, the Biyahut Sunris prohibit widow marriage; the Sagáhut and Darchua allow it. In Gya, the Koiris belong for the most part to three sub-castes—the Barkidángi, Chutki-dángi, and Jaruhár, of whom the last-mentioned practise widow remarriage; the former do not. So also the Telis of Saran have five sub-castes, four permitting widow remarriage, and one, the Behuta (corruption of Biyahuta, "the married ones") forbidding it.

In Chota Nagpore the castes which are, or pretend to be, of Behar origin follow the Behar rules in the matter of widow marriage. The aboriginal tribes—Santáls, Bhumij, Mundas, Oraons, and Hos—permit widows to marry again without imposing any restrictions on their selection of a second husband, except that the prohibited degrees must be avoided. They also sanction considerable liberty of divorce at the instance of either husband or wife, and permit divorced wives to marry again. A step higher in the social scale, the transition to orthodox habits is well marked by the Koiris of Mánbhum. These people, while retaining exogamous groups which stamp them as of aboriginal descent, forbid, at least in theory, the remarriage of widows, though they allow them to live in a sort of licensed concubinage not preceded by any kind of ceremony. Even this concession is unknown to the Lohars and Dhobis, who though occupying a very low social position in relation to the higher castes, have completely thrown off a practice which they regard as a badge of social degradation. They absolutely prohibit the remarriage of widows and divorced wives.

In Chota Nagpore.

The tendency to imitate the usages of the higher castes, which has been remarked in Behar and Chota Nagpore, operates much more strongly in Bengal Proper and Orissa. In Orissa, for instance, the Goálás take a higher position than in Behar, and rigorously prohibit widow remarriage. Throughout Bengal the Kaibarttas, though ranking below the Nabasakh or group of thirteen (formerly nine) castes from whose hands an orthodox Brahman can take water, marry their daughters as infants, and forbid their widows to remarry. In Dacca the gunny-weaving and mat-making Kapalis, and the Chandals, spoken of in Manu as 'the vilest of mankind,' have given up widow remarriage, and the practice appears to be confined to the Gareri, Rishi, Koch-Mandai, and other aboriginal and semi-aboriginal castes. Similar evidence of the gradual spread of practices prevalent among the higher castes comes to us from Northern Bengal. The Rájbansis of Rungpore, people of distinctly non-Aryan type, who have abandoned their tribal name of Koch in quite recent times, now pose as high-caste Hindus, and affect great indignation if asked whether their widows can remarry. The Paliyas of Dinagepore, also demonstrably Koch, fall into two sections—Rájbansi Paliyas and Byabahári, or

In Bengal Proper and Orissa.

'common' Paliyas. The latter practise widow marriage, but are beginning to be ashamed of it, and in this and other matters show signs of a leaning towards orthodox usage. The former are as strict as the extreme ignorance of the 'fallen' Brahmans who act as their family priests admits; and as education spreads among them, they will go on continually raising their standard of ceremonial purity.

The present attitude of the Hindu community towards the recent proposals to recognize and extend the practice of widow marriage may, I think, be briefly stated somewhat to the following effect:—The most advanced class of educated men sympathise in a general way with the movement, but their sympathy is clouded by the apprehension that any considerable addition to the number of marriageable women would add to the existing difficulty and expense of getting their daughters married. Below these we find a very numerous class of men who are educated enough to appreciate the prohibition of widow marriage supposed to be contained in certain texts, and who have no desire to go behind that or any similar injunction in support of which tolerably ancient authority can be quoted. Then come the great mass of the uneducated working classes, with rather vague notions as to the Shastras, but strong in their reverence for Brahmans and keen to appreciate points of social precedence. To them widow marriage is a badge of social degradation, a link which connects those who practise it with Doms, Boonas, Bagdis and 'low people' of various kinds. Lastly, at the bottom of society, as understood by the average Hindu, we find a large group of castes and tribes of which the lower section is represented by pure aborigines practising adult marriage and widow remarriage, while the upper section consists of castes of doubtful origin, most of whom, retaining widow marriage, have taken to infant marriage, while some have got so far as to throw off

Feeling of the people as to extension of widow marriage.

sub-castes distinguished by their abstention from widow marriage.

It is not suggested that the groups indicated above can be marked off with absolute accuracy. But without insisting upon this, it is clear that the tendency of the lower strata of Hindu society is continually towards closer and closer conformity with the usages of the higher castes. These alone present a definite pattern which admits, up to a certain point, of ready imitation, and the whole Brahmanical system works in this direction. Of late years, moreover, the strength of the Hinduising movement has been greatly augmented by the improvement of communications. People travel more, pilgrimages can be more easily made, and the influence of the orthodox section of society is thus much more widely diffused. The case of the Rájbansis—the fourth largest caste in Bengal—is an excellent illustration of the scale on which this force does its work.

The practice of infant marriage has spread much further and taken root more deeply among the lower castes than its social complement, the prohibition of widow marriage. Both customs, the positive as well as the negative, have been borrowed from the higher castes, and are now regarded as paths leading towards social distinction. But the one is much easier to follow than the other. A man must get his daughter married at latest when she is fourteen or fifteen years old. To marry her five or six years earlier causes him no particular inconvenience, and confers on him whatever consideration may attach to religious orthodoxy and social propriety. On the other hand, to stop the remarriage of widows, in castes where the balance of the sexes has not been disturbed by hypergamy, must at starting cause some practical inconvenience. Among the lower castes women are much more of a power than they are among the higher; they assert themselves freely on a variety of public occasions, and in many cases they have secured for themselves the

Prevalence of infant marriage.

right to initiate proceedings for divorce. One can hardly doubt that their influence would be exercised in favour of widow marriage, and that it would tend on the whole towards keeping that institution alive. Some allowance must also be made for the fact that the lower castes do not keep their women in seclusion. A good-looking widow shut up in the family zenana can be more easily sacrificed to notions of social propriety than a woman who goes out and meets possible suitors every day of her life. To whatever cause the difference may be due, it is certain that of two customs, both adopted under pressure of the same motives, the one—infant marriage—is almost universal, while the other——the prohibition of widow marriage—has only the comparatively limited currency already explained. Infant marriage in fact is now so widely diffused as to have almost entirely displaced adult marriage within the limits of the caste system proper. The aboriginal races of Chota Nagpore and the Orissa hills, the semi-Mongolian tribes of the Himalayan region and the Indo-Chinese people of the Chittagong Hill Tracts still maintain a system of courtship and marriage between full-grown youths and maidens which has been minutely described by several sympathetic observers. Directly we leave these tolerably compact tribes, and pass on to the less definite groups which form a debateable land between the tribe and the caste, we find either infant marriage in undisputed possession, or a mixed system which tolerates adult marriage as a resource open to those who cannot afford to do anything better for their children, but at the same time enjoins the more respectable custom of infant marriage for all parents whose circumstances admit of it.

In the case of the lower castes there is little room for doubt but that the custom of infant marriage has been consciously borrowed from the higher castes in obedience to that tendency to imitation which we may almost describe as an ultimate law of the caste system. But how did the higher castes come by a custom which is without a parallel (at any rate on so large a scale) elsewhere in the world, and which cannot be referred to any of those primitive instincts which have usually determined the relations of the sexes? Neither sexual passion nor the desire for companionship and service can be called in to account for a man marrying a girl at an age when she is physically incapable of fulfilling any of the duties of a wife.

Origin of infant marriage.

Primitive man knows nothing of infant marriage, nor is it easy to conceive how such an institution could have arisen in the struggle for existence out of which society has been evolved. The modern savage woos in a summary and not over delicate fashion a sturdy young woman who can cook his food, carry his baggage, collect edible grubs, and make herself generally useful. To his untutored mind the Hindu child-bride would seem about as suitable a helpmate as an American professional beauty. If, then, infant marriage is in no way a normal product of social evolution, and in fact is met with only in India, to what causes shall we look for its origin? The standard Brahmanical explanation is palpably inadequate. It represents marriage as a sort of sacrament, of which every maiden must partake in order that she may cleanse her own being from the taint of original sin, that she may accomplish the salvation of her father and his ancestors, and that she may bring forth a son to carry on the domestic worship (*sacra privata*) of her husband's family. So far as marriage itself goes, all this is intelligible enough as a highly specialised development of certain well-known ancient ideas. But it does not touch the question of age. Granted that the begetting of a son is essential for the continuance of the *sacra privata*, as Greek and Roman examples teach us, why should the householder, on whom this solemn duty devolves, go out of his way to defer its fulfilment by marrying a girl who has not yet attained the age of child-bearing? The Brahmans reply that the earlier in a girl's life she accomplishes her mystical functions, the better. But this clearly belongs to the large class of *ex post facto* explanations of which sacerdotal and legal literature is in all ages and countries so full. The priests and lawyers who compile the text-books find certain customs in force, and feel bound to invent reasons for their existence. Being unfettered by the historical sense, and disposed to give free play to their inner consciousness, it is hardly surprising that their reasons should be as often false as true. An ingenious explanation of a more scientific character has been given by Mr. John Nesfield in an article* on the Thárus and Bogshas of Upper India. Mr. Nesfield says:—

"In the oldest type of society a woman was exposed to a double evil —the stain of communism within her own clan so long as she remained there, and the risk of forcible abduction into an alien clan, where she became the wife-slave of the man who captured her. And herein, I think, lies the secret of the seemingly irrational and certainly unnatural customs of Hindus, by which a girl is betrothed at six or eight and married at ten or eleven. The betrothal ceremony is considered by all classes of the Hindu community to be of immense importance. The force of public opinion has made it as binding as marriage itself. If the boy dies before the marriage is performed, the child who has been betrothed remains a widow for life. A father is publicly disgraced in the eyes of his countrymen if he neglects to get his daughter finally married before she has completed the age of twelve. There are few points in which the social customs of the Hindus have been more severely condemned. But though it may be granted that the time has long passed when any good could be gained from their retention, it may yet be contended that they have been of some use in their day, and that customs so opposed to the plain dictates of nature could not have been accepted by a rational people without some rational purpose. It must be remembered that the natives of Hindustan, at the time when they first appear in history as antagonists to the invading Aryans, were in the savage stage, and that they have owed their subsequent reclamation, imperfect as it is, to the subtle and ever-widening influence of Hinduism—a composite and very elastic creed, made up of the fusion of Aryan with native or aboriginal elements.

Mr. Nesfield's theory.

* *Calcutta Review*, January 1885.

I conceive, then, that the customs, to which so much exception has been taken, were the restraints imposed by this creed upon the rough matrimonial usages of the races amongst whom its lot was cast, some of which usages were formerly countenanced even by Hinduism itself as a concession to the prevailing savagery. Marriage by stealth, marriage by capture, and marriage by the simple act of voluntary reciprocal intercourse, were all recognized by the ancient Hindu lawgivers as permissible to certain castes; and even Brahmans, the holy priests, and teachers of Hinduism were allowed to indulge in the kind last named. It is no wonder, then, that a religion which was forced to concede so much to existing custom should have sought to provide safeguards for the protection of the weaker sex through some counter-teaching of its own. By ruling, as it did, that a girl must be betrothed and married at a tender age to a youth of some outside clan, and by making this rule binding for life on pain of the severest penalties, it protected her both from the stain of communism within her own clan, and from the risk of forcible abduction into another. This explains, too, how it has come to pass that amongst Hindus, and Hindus only, the larger price is paid for the youth, and the smaller one for the maid—an exact inversion of the rule which prevails everywhere else. The Hindi word for betrothal is *mangni*, that is, 'begging' for a boy, for until the boy had been secured, the girl was not safe."

I have quoted Mr. Nesfield's views at length in order to guard against the danger of misstating an argument which I think inapplicable to the particular society with which we are concerned. The motives to which his theory appeals are no doubt highly intelligible, and in certain states of society would possibly be sufficient to account for the institution of infant marriage. It seems to me, however, that the society depicted in the Rig and Atharva Vedas must have got far beyond, if indeed they ever passed through, the stage of communal marriage and forcible abduction of wives. Courtship of a very modern type was fully recognized, and the consent of the girl's father or brother was sought only after the young people had themselves come to an understanding. As an additional and conclusive indication that the kind of marriage contemplated

His view discussed.

by the Vedas was the *individual* marriage of comparatively advanced civilization, I may refer to a remarkable custom, traces of which have survived in modern Italy—the lustration of the bride's night-dress after the wedding night.* This custom is clearly incompatible with communal marriage, and could only have arisen in a society which set a high value on female chastity and had left primitive communism ages behind.

For these reasons I prefer to seek the origin of infant marriage in the custom of hypergamy described above. In further illustration of the working of that custom, I invite reference to the following diagram:—

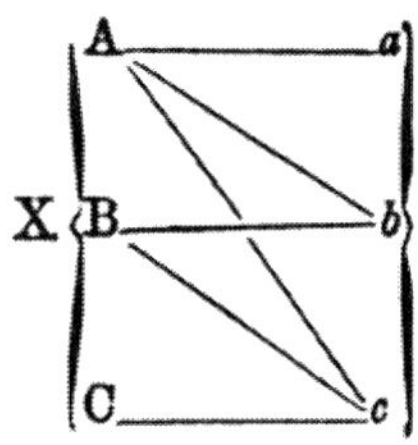

Let X represent a caste divided into the three hypergamous groups A, B, and C. Within each group the capital letters stand for the marriageable men, and the small letters for the marriageable women of the group. The horizontal and diagonal lines connecting the capitals with the small letters show what classes of men and women can intermarry. It will be seen that a man of the A group can marry a woman of his own or of the two lower groups; a man of B can marry into B or C, while a man of C is confined to his own class, and cannot marry a woman from either of the classes above him. Conversely, a woman of the C class can get a husband from A, B, or C, and a woman of the B class from A or B; but a woman of the A class cannot find a husband outside of her own group. Excluding polygamy or polyandry, and supposing the women of each group to be evenly distributed

Influence of hypergamy.

* Zimmer, *Altindisches Leben*, p. 314; Gubernati's *Usi Nuziali*, p. 234.

among the groups they are entitled to marry into, the result of the first series of marriages would be to leave two-thirds of the women in the A group without husbands, and two-thirds of the men in the C group without wives. The women of all the groups, and especially those of A, will compete for husbands, and the men of C group for wives. But the fact that the social status of a family is determined not so much by the class from which it takes its wives as by the class from which it gets its husbands, would put the men of the lowest class and the women of the highest at a great comparative disadvantage, and would thus tend to produce infant marriage; for the number of possible husbands being limited, the natural tendency is to endeavour to secure them as soon as possible. That this motive operates strongly at the present day is plainly stated by one of the writers in the official publication already referred to,* who says:—

> "Under these circumstances, when, in the case of a daughter, parents see that, unless they marry her at once, the one or two bridegrooms that there are open for their selection would be availed of by others, and that they would be disabled from marrying her before the eleventh year, and that they would thereby incur a religious sin and social degradation as regards the caste, they would seize that opportunity to marry their daughter, quite disregardful of the evil effects of infant marriages."

Again, when the custom of infant marriage had once been started, under pressure of social necessity, by the families of the highest group, who had the largest surplus of marriageable daughters, a sort of fashion would have been set and would be blindly followed through all the grades.

Two forces are thus at work in the same direction, both tending to disturb the balance of the sexes and to produce abnormal matrimonial relations between the members of different social groups. Enforced competition for husbands on the part of the higher groups, and the desire to imitate

---

* *Papers relating to Infant Marriage and Enforced Widowhood in India*, p. 178.

their superiors which animates the lower groups, combine to run up the price of husbands in the upper classes; while the demand for wives by the men of the lowest class, which ought by rights to produce equilibrium, is artificially restricted in its operation by the rule that they can under no circumstances marry a woman of the classes above their own. These men, therefore, are left very much out in the cold, and often do not get wives until late in life. An unmarried son does not disgrace the family, but there is no greater reproach than to have a daughter unmarried at the age of puberty. Husbands are bought for the girls, and the family gets its money's worth in social estimation. Bargains, however, must be taken when they are to be had; and no father dares run the risk of waiting till his daughter is physically mature. He is bound to be on the safe side, and therefore he marries her, child as she may be, whenever a good match offers.

Many hard things have been said of infant marriage, and the modern tendency is to assume that a population which countenances such a practice must be in a fair way towards great moral degradation, if not to ultimate extinction. Much of this criticism seems to me to be greatly exaggerated, and to be founded on considerable ignorance of the present conditions and future possibilities of Oriental life. In truth, excluding the poetical view, that marriages are made in heaven, two working theories of the institution are at present in existence—one which leaves marriages to make themselves by the process of unrestricted courtship, and another which requires them to be made by the parents or guardians of the persons who are to be married. The first, which we may perhaps call the method of natural selection, is accepted and more or less acted up to by all Western nations, except those who follow the French custom of *mariages de convenance*. The second, a system of avowedly artificial selection, is in force, with few exceptions, throughout the East. For all Hindus, except the handful of *déclassés* who have adopted more or less completely European ideas on the subject of marriage, and seem now to be on the high road to form a new caste, the bare idea that a girl can have any voice in the selection of her husband is excluded by the operation of three inexorable sanctions—by the ordinances of the Hindu religion, by the internal structure of the caste system, and by the general tone and conditions of social life in India. Religion prescribes that, like the Roman bride of early days, a Hindu girl shall be given (*tradita in manum*) by her father into the power of her husband; caste complications demand that the ceremonial portion of the transfer shall be effected while she is still a child; while the character of society, the moral tone of the men, the seclusion of the women, the immemorial taboos and conventions of family etiquette, render it impossible that she should be wooed and won like her European sister. To persons of a romantic turn of mind the admission that infant marriage in some shape must be accepted as an ultimate fact of the Hindu social system will sound like a final abandonment of all hope of reform. But there is more to be said for the custom than appears at first sight. A moment's dispassionate consideration will show that if any sort of controlling authority is to make people's marriages for them, the earlier it commences and completes its operations, the better. Where the choice of a husband must in any case be undertaken by the parents, it is clearly tempting Providence for them to defer it until their daughter has grown up, and may have formed an embarrassing attachment on her own account. As for love, that may come—and, from all one hears of Hindu unions, usually does come—as readily after marriage as before, provided that opportunities for falling in love with the wrong man are judiciously withheld. This may seem a cynical way of handling the matter, but it is the only way that accords with the lines of oriental life as at present ordered, and it were folly to dream of making all things new.

The case for infant-marriage.

A

Abadhut, one who has 'shaken off' the infirmities of humanity, the title used among themselves by a sect of Saiva ascetics, which is divided into four classes—Brahma, Saiba, Bhakta, and Hánsa or Turiyá—of which the first three may be either householders or mendicants, while the fourth lead a pure ascetic life. Abadhuts are said to be distinguished from Dandis by not observing the practice, strictly enjoined by the latter, of shaving the head on the day of new moon.

Abadhutáni, *Abadhuti*, a member of a sect of female ascetics said to have been founded by a woman named Gangágiri: hence in Upper India the term Abadhuti is commonly applied to all female religious mendicants. Abadhutánis smear themselves with the ashes of burnt cowdung and wander about begging their way on the great pilgrim routes. With few exceptions, they lead an immoral life. It should be observed, however, that they are excluded from the *pangats* or societies of the male Abadhuts, and that an Abadhutáni can only be initiated by a woman.

Abar, a sub-sept of the Kisku sept of Santáls.

Abasakti, a title of Bangaja Káyasths.

Abbaye, a village or communal headman among the Kandh (Khond) tribe in Orissa.

Abdál, a group of low Mahomedans, believed to have been originally a subdivision of the Bediyás, whom the orthodox do not recognise as members of the brotherhood of Islam. For this reason the Abdál marry among themselves, and the community is virtually a caste. The characteristic occupation of the men is to castrate bullocks, and their females act as midwives.

Ábdár, a servant whose office it is to prepare water for domestic use or for drinking, a title occasionally used by Kahárs and other castes of similar social standing who belong to the *jal-ácharani* group, from whose hands a Brahman may take water.

Abhepur, a *mul* or section of the Majraut sub-caste of Goálás in Behar.

A'bhir, a synonym for Goálá.

Abhirám, a sub-caste of Telis in Orissa.

Abhyágat, a sect of devotees who live alone, and subsist by begging. They are sometimes found dwelling together in small communities, somewhat resembling the minor monastic associations of mediæval Europe.

Abkahilá, a *mul* or section of the Kesarwáni Baniás in Behar; a section of the Biyáhut and Kharidáhá Kalwárs in Behar.

Abkahon, a *kul* or section of Bábhans in Behar.

Ábkár, a manufacturer or retailer of spirituous liquors, a title of Kalwárs in Behar.

Abya, a section of Brahmans.

Achal, a hypergamous group of the Bangaja Káyasths.

Achambitá, a *mel* or hypergamous sub-group of Rárhi Brahmans in Bengal.

Achámi, a *thar* or sept of Mangars in Darjiling.

Achárj, *Achári*, *Achárya*, a religious teacher; properly, the Brahman who instructs the religious student of the two next castes—the Kshatriya and the Vaisya—as well as the Brahmans, in the Vedas. In modern use it is applied to any religious instructor, or to any Brahman or religious mendicant professing to be qualified to give spiritual instruction or to supervise and direct religious ceremonies. The term has thus come to be a title or family name of high-caste Smriti Brahmans in Bengal. In the North-West Provinces it has been selected by the Educational Department as the title to be given to those students who pass the most difficult examination in the Benares Sanskrit College. A title signifying an instructor, given by the Gayawals of Gya to Brahmans employed to lead the pilgrims in their devotions. It is to be carefully distinguished from *Achárji*, the designation of the despised sub-caste of astrologers.

Achárji, "the teacher," ironical designation of a sub-caste of Brahmans in Bengal; also known as Lagan-Achárji, Ganak, Daivajna, and in Purneah as Upádhyáya. The members of this sub-caste prepare and decipher horoscopes, draw up almanacs, tell fortunes by palmistry and by astrological methods, draw pictures of Hindu deities, make idols, manufacture *solá* or pith, and decorate houses by painting rough designs of flowers and animals on the walls. They also attend at *annaprásan* and *upanayan* ceremonies of the higher castes. According to some authorities they rank socially below the Agradáni Brahmans, from whom they will receive alms. On the other hand, Patit or Sudra Brahmans will eat with the Achárji, but not with the Agradáni.

Achárwálá, a maker or vendor of pickles, preserves, etc., usually a Mahomedan.

Achárya, a group of the Srotriya sub-caste of Utkal Brahmans in Orissa; a *thar* of the Kaundin *gotra* of Nepáli Brahmans; a title of Brahmans.

Acháryasekhari, a *mel* or hypergamous sub-group of Rárhi Brahmans in Bengal.

Achut, a sept of Bairágis.

Adaki, a title of Kaibarttas in Bengal.

Adampur, a section of the Ariár sub-caste of Bais Baniyás in Behar.

Adarki, a sub-caste of Baniyás in Behar, most of whom make their living by selling vegetables: others trade in grain, and some cultivate land. They permit widows to marry again, and eat flesh—practices condemned by the more orthodox members of the trading group of castes. They abstain, however, from wine, and in other respects conform to the standard rules of Hinduism.

Addádár, the owner of a stand or station (*addá*) where porters, bearers, carters, and the like wait to be hired, paying the proprietor a percentage on their earnings for the accommodation.

Adeb, a sept of the Santál tribe in Western Bengal.

Adhama, a sub-caste of Káyasths in Behar.

Adhárpur, a section of the Pachainyá sub-caste of Doms in Behar.

Adhiá, a section of Kurmis; a title of Nápits in Maldah.

Adhiár, (i) a cultivator who holds land on a sort of metayer tenure, paying his landlord half the produce as rent; (ii) a cultivator who spends half his time in one village, half in another, cultivating lands in both.

Adhikári, (i) a title of Brahmans, Jugis, and Vaishnabs who officiate at religious ceremonies, serve as priests and spiritual guides of Vaishnabs and lower castes, and deal in charms, especially in use among Vaishnavas; (ii) a title of Sadgops, of Rajbansis in Jalpaiguri, and of Paliyás in Dinajpur; (iii) a manager of theatrical performances; (iv) a *thar* of the Kasya *gotra* of Nepáli Brahmans.

Adhkurmi or *Madhyam Kurmi*, a sub-caste of Kurmis in Western Bengal.

Adhya, a title of Bangaja Káyasths and Subarnabaniks in Bengal.

Adi, a section of Jugis.

Adi Gaura, a group of Gaura Brahmans.

Adinpuso, a sept of Lepchas in Darjiling.

Adi Sri-Gaura, a group of the Sri-Gaura sub-caste of Gaura Brahmans.

Aditi or *Aditiya*, a mercantile correspondent or agent: the word is probably a corruption of *Adat*, *Arhat*, or *Arhatiá*.

Aditya, a title of Dakshin-Rárhi and Bangaja Káyasths.

Adra, a section of Goráits in Chota Nagpur.

Adrakhiá, a *mul* or section of the Banodhiá sub-caste of Kalwárs in Behar.

Adriár, a *pur* or section of Sákadwipi Brahmans in Behar.

Adya, a *gotra* or section of the Baidya caste in Bengal.

Adyeb, a section of the Sárák caste in Mánbhum.

Afang, a sept of Tipperahs in the Chittagong Hill Tracts.

Afin-wálá, *Afin-farosh*, a seller of opium. The Arabic word *afiún* is usually corrupted to *afin* or *afim* in the Indian vernaculars.

Aganpuriá, a *mul* or section of the Majraut sub-caste of Goálás in Behar.

Agariá, a sub-tribe of Asuras in Chota Nagpur; a class of beggars wandering about with tame monkeys, whose antics they exhibit.

Agariá, *Anguwar*, a cultivating caste found in the Tributary Mahals of Chota Nagpur. They claim to be the descendants of certain Kshatriya immigrants from the neighbourhood of Agra, who put off the sacred thread when they settled in a new country and took to holding the plough. Dalton describes them as tall and well-made, with high Aryan features and tawny complexions. Ágariás betroth their daughters as infants, but do not marry them until they are full-grown. They allow widows to marry again. The caste employ Brahmans from the North-West Provinces, and will not accept the services of the Uṭkal Brahmans, who ordinarily serve as priests in the Southern Tributary Mahals. In one point they depart remarkably from orthodox Hindu practice: they bury their dead, and, after the bones have got dry, dig up the skull and the chief joints and convey them to the Ganges. This may perhaps be thought to suggest a connexion with some religious sect.

In Gangpur, where every one believes in witchcraft, Ágariá women are supposed to be the most potent witches in the country.

The following statement shows the number and distribution of Ágariás in 1872 and 1881:—

District.	1872.	1881.
Hazaribagh ...	1,966	1,146
Lohardága ...	1,678	66
Singbhum ...	7	...
Manbhum ...	885	...
Tributary States ...	3,448	6,278

Agaria-Binjhiá, a sub-tribe of Binjhiás in Chota Nagpur.

Agaria-Korwa, a sub-tribe of Korwas.

Agarwál, *Agarwálá*, a wealthy trading caste of Behar and Upper India, who deal in grain and jewellery, and are also bankers and usurers. Authorities differ regarding their origin and the etymology of the name they bear. Following a tradition communicated to him by the *chaudhri* or headman of the caste in Benares, Mr. Sherring traces the Agarwáls to the banks of the Godavery, in Madras, and derives their name from one Agar Náth or Agar Sen, who is believed to have preserved the customs of the caste inviolate when all his brethren joined themselves to the Súdras. Agar Sen is supposed to have lived at Agroha, a small town on the borders of the Ráj-putana desert, where his family expanded into the Agarwál caste. Another and more common version of the story describes Agar Sen as the Vaisya Rájá of Agroha, and adds that the Agarwál caste spread over Hindustan after the taking of their original home by Shaháb-ud-din Ghori in 1195. This is the view favoured by Sir Henry Elliot, who points out that the association of the Agarwáls throughout the North-West Provinces with the worship of Guga Pir, the snake-king of Agroha, bears testimony to the historical accuracy of the tradition. Mr. Nesfield prefers to derive the name, both of this caste and of the cognate caste of Agrahri, from *agari* or *agar* (Sansk. *aguru*), the aromatic wood of the eagle wood tree (*Aquilaria agallocha*, Roxb.), which is sold as a perfume. There seems, however, to be no evidence to connect either caste with the production or sale of this scent; and the fact that the best kind is extracted from the leguminous tree *Alŏexylon agallochum*, Loureiro, growing in Camboja and South Cochin China, may perhaps be thought to support this view.

Traditions of origin.

The Agarwáls of Behar are divided into the following seventeen sections (*gotras*) :—

Internal structure.

(1) Garg, (2) Goil, (3) Gáwál, (4) Bátsil, (5) Kásil, (6) Singhal, (7) Mangal, (8) Bhaddal, (9) Tingal, (10) Airan, (11) Tairan, (12) Thingal, (13) Tittal, (14) Mittal, (15) Tundal, (16) Táyal, (17) Gobhil, (17½) Goin.

The section-names are said to refer to eighteen sacrifices performed by Rájá Agar Náth in honour of Lakshmi. By these sacrifices, so says the legend current in Behar, he won from the goddess the boon that his descendants by Mádhavi, a daughter of the Nága Rájá Kumud, should bear the name of Agarwál, should never be in want, and should enjoy the protection of Lakshmi so long as they kept the *diwáli* festival. When the eighteenth sacrifice was half over, the Rájá was struck with horror at the slaughter of animals involved, broke off the ceremony, and enjoined his descendants never to take life. The last, or "half-*gotra*" Goin, represents this incomplete sacrifice. Another explanation is that some member of the caste by oversight married a woman of his own *gotra*, and that the *gotra* in question was divided into two by the heads of the caste in order to cover this breach of the rule of exogamy. There is nothing in the names themselves to throw light on their origin. The first certainly, and possibly the third and fourth, are names of Vedic saints. The second occurs among the Rajputs.

With the Agarwáls, as with all castes at the present day, the section-names go by the male side. In other words, a son belongs to the same *gotra* as his father—not to the same *gotra* as his mother, and kinship is no longer reckoned through females alone. Traces of an earlier matriarchal system may perhaps be discerned in the legend already referred to, which represented Rájá Agar Náth as successfully contending with Indra for the hand of the daughters of two Nága Rájás, and obtaining from Lakshmi the special favour that his children by one of them should bear *their father's name*. The memory of this Nága Princess is still held in honour. "Our mother's house is of the race of the snake" (*ját ká nánihál Nágbansi hai*), say the Agarwáls of Behar; and for this reason no Agarwál, whether Hindu or Jain, will kill or molest a snake. In Delhi, Vaishnava Agarwáls paint pictures of snakes on either side of the outside doors of their houses, and make offerings of fruit and flowers before them. Jain Agarwáls do not practise any form of snake-worship.

Read in the light of Bachofen's researches[1] into archaic forms of kinship, the legend and the prohibition arising from it seem to take us back to the prehistoric time when the Nága race still maintained a separate national existence, and had not been absorbed by the conquering Aryans; when Nága women were eagerly sought in marriage by Aryan chiefs; and when the offspring of such unions belonged by Nága custom to their mother's family. In this view the boon granted by Lakshmi to Rájá Agar Náth, that his children should be called after his name, marks a transition

[1] *Antiquarische Briefe*, vol. i, pp. 41–92.

from the system of female kinship, characteristic of the Nágas, to the new order of male parentage introduced by the Brahmans, while the Behar saying about the *Nánihál* is merely a survival of those matriarchal ideas according to which the snake-totem of the race would necessarily descend in the female line.

In the last of the six letters, entitled "Orestes-Astika, Eine Griechisch-Indische Parallele," Bachofen has the following remarks on the importance of the part played by the Nága race in the development of the Brahmanical polity:—

"The connexion of Brahmans with Nága women is a significant historical fact. Wherever a conquering race allies itself with the women of the land, indigenous manners and customs come to be respected, and their maintenance is deemed the function of the female sex. Countless examples of all ages and countries bear witness to the fact. A long series of traditions corroborate it in connexion with the autochthonous Nága race. The respect paid to Nága women, the influence which they exercised, not merely on their own people, but also in no less degree on the rulers of the country, the fame of their beauty, the praise of their wisdom—all this finds manifold expression in the tales of the Kashmir chronicle and in many other legends based upon the facts of real life."

All the sections are strictly exogamous, but the rule of unilateral exogamy is supplemented by provisions forbidding marriage with certain classes of relations. Thus a man may not marry a woman—(*a*) belonging to his own *gotra;* (*b*) descended from his own paternal or maternal grandfather, great-grandfather, or great-great-grandfather; (*c*) descended from his own paternal or maternal aunt; (*d*) belonging to the grand-maternal family (*nánihál*) of his own father or mother. He may marry the younger sister of his deceased wife, but not the elder sister, nor may he marry two sisters at the same time. As is usual in such cases, the classes of relations barred are not mutually exclusive. All the agnatic descendants of a man's three nearest male ascendants are necessarily members of his own *gotra*, and therefore come within class (*a*) as well as class (*b*). Again, the paternal and maternal aunt and their descendants are included among the descendants of the paternal and maternal grandfathers, while some of the members of the *nánihál* must also come under class (*b*). The *gotra* rule is undoubtedly the oldest; and it seems probable that the other prohibited classes may have been added from time to time as experience and the growing sense of the true nature of kinship demonstrated the incompleteness of the primitive rule of exogamy.

It is certainly remarkable that a caste so widely diffused as the Agarwáls should not have broken up into endogamous divisions, based upon differences of locality, of the type so common in Bengal. In the North-West Provinces, indeed, it is stated that the Pachhainya or Western branch of the caste cannot intermarry with the Purbiya or Eastern Agarwáls. Members of these groups, however, may eat together, and the prohibition on intermarriage is said to have arisen from a comparatively recent quarrel, which is now likely to be made up. In Behar the tendency is to ignore these distinctions and to represent restrictions on intermarriage between Purbiyas and Pachhainyas as matters of family prejudice rather than of caste custom. This, however, may be due to the fact that most of the Behar Agarwáls belong to the Purbiya branch, and are regarded as socially inferior to the Pachhainyas. Both intermarriage and community of food are prohibited to the Dasá sub-caste, who are illegitimate descendants of an Agarwál named Basu, and to the Birádari Rájá, or Bisá, who are said to be descended from one Ratan Chand, who was made a Rájá by the Emperor Farokhsir in the early part of last century.

Marriage.

Agarwáls usually marry their daughters after they have reached their ninth year, but if no suitable match offers in infancy, it often happens that a girl is not married until she is grown up. In the latter case she goes to live with her husband at once. When married as an infant, the final ceremony (*rukhsati*), by which she is made over to her husband, may take place one year, three years, or five years after the regular marriage ceremony. That is to say, if the husband does not claim his wife at the expiration of one year, he must wait three; and if he does not come forward then, he must wait five years. This custom prevails among most of the higher castes in Northern India, and is believed to rest upon some obscure superstition regarding lucky numbers. Whatever may be the origin of the practice, it contrasts favourably with the custom in force among many families of the higher castes in Lower Bengal, in so far as it tends on the whole to defer child-bearing to years of comparative maturity.

Polygamy is prohibited on pain of expulsion from caste, unless the first wife is barren. The Agarwáls of Sahâranpur, however, disregard the rule, and are nevertheless admitted to intermarriage with the Jain Agarwáls of Delhi. A widower may marry again: a widow may not. Divorce is not recognised. If a woman goes wrong, she is turned out of the caste, and must either join some religious sect of dubious morality or become a regular prostitute.

Religion.

The bulk of the Agarwáls belong to the Vaishnava form of Hinduism, but a large proportion follow the tenets of the Digambara sect of Jains, and are stigmatised by orthodox Hindus as *nástik* or infidels. A few Saivas and Śáktas are met with among the caste; but in deference to the prejudices of the majority, these depart from their ordinary custom by abstaining from sacrificing animals and partaking of flesh or wine. Owing, perhaps, to this uniformity of practice in matters of diet, these differences of religious belief do not operate as a bar to intermarriage; and when a marriage takes place between persons of different religions, the standard Hindu ritual is used. When husband and wife belong to different sects, the wife is formally admitted into her husband's sect, and must in future have her own food cooked separately when staying in her mother's house.

In matters of ritual the Agarwáls do not differ materially from the average orthodox Hindus of Upper India. Their special goddess is Lakshmi, to whose favour they attribute the general prosperity of the caste. Gaur Brahmans act as their priests, and do not forfeit their position by doing so. The dead are burned in the ordinary Hindu fashion, and the ashes thrown into the Ganges. The bodies of children under seven years are buried. Among the Agarwáls of Behar it is thought right for a man's descendants to perform his *srádh* at Gyá. On such occasions a separate cake, called *bikrá ká pind*, is presented before the propitiation of the other ancestors begins, for the benefit of those ancestors who may have died a violent death. The spiritual interests of the childless dead are supposed to be cared for by their heirs; but where these are distant relatives or merely members of the same *gotra*, the obligation comes to be very lightly regarded.

Occupation.

The Agarwáls claim to be the modern representatives of the Aryan Vaisyas, and profess to trace their descent from a mythical ancestor, Dhanpál, who was the recognised chief of the Vaisyas, and whose daughter, Mukuta, was married to Yajnavalkya. Their occupations have throughout been in keeping with these traditions. After the dispersion of the caste by Shaháb-ud-din their talent for business brought individual members to the front under the Mahommedan Emperors of Delhi. Two of Akbár's ministers—Madhu Sáh and Todar Mal—are said to have been Agarwáls. To the latter was entrusted the settlement of the land revenue: the former held high financial office, and a variety of pice still bears his name. Among the Agarwáls of Behar we find the largest proportion engaged in banking, trade, petty money-lending, and similar pursuits. A few are zemindars and holders of large tenures, but in most cases their connexion with the land may be traced to a profitable mortgage on the estate of an hereditary landholder, so that landholding cannot properly be reckoned among the characteristic pursuits of the caste. The poorer members of the caste find employment as brokers, book-keepers, touts, workers in gold and silver embroidery, and servants, and take to any respectable pursuit except cultivation.

Social status.

In the Hindu social system Agarwáls stand at the head of the group of castes included in the term Baniya. Colonel Tod classes them among the "eighty-four mercantile tribes, chiefly of Rájput origin," enumerated by him, and their features and complexion stamp them as of tolerably pure Aryan descent. All Pachhainya and most Purbiya Agarwáls wear the sacred thread. In Behar they rank immediately below Brahmans and Káyasths, and the former can take water and certain kinds of sweetmeats from their hands. According to their own account, they can take cooked food only from Brahmans of the Gaur, Tailanga, Gujráti, and Sanáth sub-castes: water and sweetmeats they can take from any Brahmans, except the degraded classes of Ojha and Mahabrahman, from Rájputs, Báis-Baniyas, and Khatris (usually reckoned as Vaisyas), and from the superior members of the class of so-called mixed castes from whose hands Brahmans will take water. Some Agarwáls, however, affect a still higher standard of ceremonial purity in the matter of cooked food, and carry their prejudices to such lengths that a mother-in-law will not eat food prepared by her daughter-in-law. All kinds of animal food are strictly prohibited, and the members of the caste also abstain from *jowándá* rice, which has been parboiled before husking. Jain Agarwáls will not eat after dark for fear of swallowing minute insects. Smoking is governed by the rules in force for water and sweetmeats. It is noticed as remarkable that the purohits of the caste will smoke out of the same hookah as their clients.

The following table illustrates the distribution of the Agarwáls in Bengal in 1872 and 1881 :—

District.	1872.	1881.	District.	1872.	1881.
Bardwan	2,674	125	Patna	1,139	1,714
Bankura	79	8	Gya	2,472	5,242
Birbhum	203	201	Shahabad	1,069	1,310
Midnapur	13	63	Tirhut { Darbhanga ...	995	2,474
Hughli with Howrah ...	84	92	Tirhut { Mozufferpur ...		1,191
24-Parganas	791	218	Saran	617	1,084
Nadiya	39	144	Champaran	272	556
Jessore	13	461	Monghyr	1,011	2,947
Khulna	......	1	Bhágalpur	728	2,456
Murshedabad	347	408	Purniah	74	3,899
Dinajpur	246	331	Maldah	50	97
Rajshahye	......	989	Santál Parganas	721	1,046
Rangpur	67	51	Cuttack	200	216
Bogra	6	11	Puri	17	3
Pabna	......	4	Balasore	......	220
Darjiling	28	608	Tributary States	15	25
Jalpigori	44	35	Hazaribagh	276	1,051
Kuch Behar	......	323	Lohardága	977	1,096
Faridpur	143	75	Singbhum	......	7
Bakarganj	76	46	Manbhum	187	368
Maimansinh	7	142	Tributary States	533	90

Agarwáni, a small caste, only found in the Supul subdivision of Bhágalpur, whither they are believed to have immigrated from Nepal. They work as sawyers, and also collect the sap of *kath* (*Acacia catechu*).

Agasti, a title of Kanaujiá Brahmans; a *gotra* or section of Nepáli Brahmans.

Agastya, a section of Brahmans.

Agastya-Rishi, a section of Tántis in Bengal.

Aggechal, a section of Bábhans in Behar.

Aghariá, one of the six subdivisions of the Lohar caste, who manufacture and smelt iron ore, while the Lohondia manufacture pig-iron from it.

Aghor, a low and despised class of men in the Supul subdivision of Bhágalpur, who are said to have no caste and to eat food cooked by either Hindus or Mahomedans. Their number is small (43 in 1881), and most of them live by begging, though of late years a few have taken to cultivation. It is surmised that they may be Aghoris who have abandoned the distinctive practices of their sect. In support of this view it may be noticed that Aghori ascetics eat the *jhutá* or leavings of all Hindu castes, and that the practice ascribed to the Aghors of Supul only goes a step further.

Aghori, *Aghorapanthi,* the lowest class of Saivite religious mendicants, who eat human ordure, bones, and filth of all kinds, and extort alms by threatening to exhibit these practices or to pollute the bystanders. They sometimes carry staves set with human bones, and use the upper half of a skull as a water-pot. In 1881 one of these wretches was caught at Rohtak, in the Panjab, in the act of devouring the body of a newly-buried child, which he had dug out. According to Lassen (*Ind. Alt.* III, 881, and IV, 629) the Aghoris of the present day are closely related to the *Kápálika* or *Kápáladhárin* sect of the middle ages, who wore crowns and necklaces of skulls and offered human sacrifices to Chámundá, a horrible form of Devi or Párvati. In support of this view it is observed that in Bhavabhuti's drama of Málati Mádhava, written in the eighth century, the Kapáliká sorcerer, from whom Málati is rescued as she is about to be sacrificed to Chámundá, is euphemistically described as an Aghorakantha, from *aghora*, 'not terrible.' The Aghoris of the present day represent their filthy habits as merely giving practical expression to the abstract doctrine of the Paramahansa sect of Saivites, that "the whole universe is full of Brahma," and consequently that one thing is as pure as another. The *mantra* or mystic formula by which Aghoris are initiated is believed by other ascetics to be very powerful, and to be capable of restoring to life the human victims offered to Devi and eaten by the officiating priest. The sect is regarded with disgust by all respectable Hindus, and is believed to be dying out. In 1881 it numbered 565 votaries in Bengal (all but two in Behar), 316 in the Panjab, and 93 in the Central Provinces.

Aghorpanthi, a religious group of Jugis.

Aghráit, a section of the Kámar sub-caste of Dosádhs in Behar.

Agiyári, a *pangat* or section of Dosádhs in Behar.

Aglidin Chauri, pichhlirát jeonár Baniáke put jor le háth, "the day before parched barley, the next night the wedding feast, sons of the Baniyá join your hands"—a formula or shibboleth denoting a *mul* or section of Kesarwáni Baniyás in Behar. The leading idea of the formula seems to be that people who live frugally enough in ordinary times spend their money freely in the Baniyá's shop when they have a wedding on hand. For *chauri* and *jeonár*, see Grierson's *Peasant Life in Behar*, *s.v.*

Agni, a section of the Bhar caste in Mánbhum. The term appears to have been borrowed from the Brahmanical system in comparatively recent times, as the caste has also a set of the totemistic sections characteristic of the non-Aryan races.

Agniá, a sub-tribe of Dhimáls in the Darjiling Terai.

Agniá-Mech, a sub-tribe of Meches in Darjiling and Assam.

Agnibesma, a section of the Páschátya Baidik Brahmans in Bengal; a Kshatra-peta *gotra* or section of Brahmans; a section of Káyasths in Bengal.

Agni-brahman, a Brahman who officiates as priest at the burning of dead bodies.

Agnidhaut, a section of Bábhans in Behar.

Agnihotri: according to Wilson a Brahman who maintains a perpetual fire in his house. Sherring interprets the term as denoting "one who possesses the materials for the *hom* or burnt sacrifice." He adds—"All Brahmans are directed to perform this ceremony; nevertheless, it is usual to employ an Agnihotri, who lives on alms and receives fees and presents." *Agnihotri* is a title of Brahmans in Behar, and one of the sections of the Bábhan caste is called *Agnihotra*.

Agoriá, a synonym for Asura, a small caste of wild people in Chota Nagpur who smelt iron and make rude iron utensils and implements of agriculture.

Agradána, *Agradáni*, *Agrasráddhí*, a degraded sub-caste of Brahmans, ranking slightly above the *Achárji*. They read *mantras* at the cremation of Brahmans and members of the Nava-Sákha, and take gifts (*dán*) at the first *sráddh* on the eleventh or thirty-first day after death, and at the subsequent monthly *sráddhas* for a year, after which time no more presents are given. Pure Brahmans will eat sweetmeats with the Agradáni, but not rice. In Bengal they bear the ironical designations of Mahá-Bráhman, Mahá-purohit, Mahá-sráddhi, Mahá-puttra, Marui-porá Brahman and, in the rare instances when they have a smattering of Sanskrit, Pandit. In Behar they are called Mahá-Bráhman and Kántáha.

Agrahari, *Agrahri*, a trading and cultivating caste of Behar and Upper India, who are probably closely related to the Agarwáls. Mr. Nesfield thinks that the two groups must originally have been "sections of one and the same caste, which quarrelled on some trifling question connected with cooking or eating and have remained separate ever since." Agraharis marry their daughters as infants, forbid widows to marry again, and do not recognise divorce. Unlike the Agarwáls, they allow polygamy; and on this account, says Mr. Sherring, they are believed to have lost the high position they formerly held. Should this opinion be correct, it may supply the explanation of the divergence of the Agraharis from the Agarwáls, whom they closely resemble in physical type. It is curious to observe that the higher mercantile castes, such as Agarwáls, Khatris, and Oswáls, have a stronger repugnance to polygamy than Brahmans and Rajputs, both of whom incur no social reproach for their polygamous habits. In matters of food, Agraharis follow the regular practice of orthodox Hindus, and spirit-drinking is strictly forbidden. It deserves notice that their women are not secluded, as among the Agarwáls, but take part in the business of their husbands by selling rice-flour, etc. In point of social standing the caste, though reckoned among the Vaisyas and wearing the sacred thread, ranks below the Agarwáls, and their business is generally on a smaller scale. They are, in fact, tradesmen rather than bankers. The proper home of the caste is in Hindustan, and their numbers in the

Lower Provinces of Bengal are comparatively small. The following table shows their distribution in 1872 and 1881 :—

District.	1872.	1881.	District.	1872.	1881.
Patna	833	363	Bhágalpur	196	83
Gya	223	11	Purniah	2	......
Shahabad	1,181	1,244	Hazaribagh	......	176
Mozufferpur	1,066	571	Tributary States	......	541
Saran	1,060	659	Puri	......	1
Champaran	1,315	16	Balasore	......	39
Monghyr	113	104			

Agrahri, a synonym for Agrahari.

Agraja, a synonym for Brahman.

Agri, a *thar* or sept of Mangars in Darjiling, the members of which work in mines.

Aguri, a cultivating and trading caste, very numerous in Western Bengal. They are popularly believed to be the modern representatives of the Ugra or Ugra Kshatriyas mentioned in *Manu*, x, 9: "From a Kshatriya by a Súdra girl is born a creature called an Ugra (cruel), which has a nature partaking both of Kshatriya and of Súdra, and finds its pleasure in savage conduct." In verse 49 of the same chapter their occupation is said to be "catching and killing animals that live in holes." At the present day the Aguris are divided into seven sub-castes, viz. (1) **Bardwaniya**, (2) **Kasipuriya**, (3) **Bagha**, (4) **Sátcháki** or **Sátsaikiya**, (5) **Chagnaya** or **Changa**, (6) **Jana**, (7) **Suta**. Each of these is subdivided into Kulins and Mauliks, the former being distinguished by the titles Kesh, Pai, Shyám, and Pál. A Kulin is not positively forbidden to marry a Maulik, but to do so brings a certain amount of discredit on the Kulin bridegroom, and a series of such marriages would reduce the entire family to the rank of Maulik. Intermarriage between members of different sub-castes is prohibited, and the Jáná and Suta sub-castes, both of whom profess to be descended from a mythical ancestor named Dakshin Rai, taunt one another with being bastards. The entire caste claims to be twice-born (dwija), but the sacred thread is worn only by members of the Jáná sub-caste, who assume it on marriage. Those, however, who work as cultivators and drive the plough with their own hands usually discard the thread.

Internal structure.

Each sub-caste contains a number of sections, bearing names—Kásyap, Sandilya and Bharadwaja and others—which appear to show that they have been borrowed from the Brahmans. Marriage is forbidden within the section, and the supplementary rules defining the prohibited degrees are substantially the same as among Brahmans and Kayasths. Aguris marry their daughters as infants, forbid widows to marry again, and do not recognise divorce. A woman of proved unchastity is turned out of the caste, and usually takes refuge among the Bairági Vaishnavas or some similar religious sect. Polygamy is permitted, but is not practised on a large scale, and it is rare to find men with more than two wives.

Religion.

In their religious and ceremonial observances Aguris differ little from the higher castes of Hindus in Bengal. They belong for the most part to the Vaishnava and Sákta sects, and there are comparatively few Saivas among them. Their religious ceremonies are performed by Brahmans, who incur no degradation by serving them. It deserves notice that the first *sráddh* is performed by them on the thirtieth day after death, and not, as is the case with Brahmans, on the eleventh day.

Social status.

The social position of the Aguris differs in different parts of Bengal. The scattered members of the caste found in Eastern Bengal are classed with the hunting and fishing castes—a fact which suggests that there may be an element of historical truth in the functions assigned to them by Manu. In Bardwan and Western Bengal, where Aguris are numerous, they take rank with the Nava-Sákha, and Brahmans will take water and certain kinds of sweetmeats from their hands. Many of them hold estates and tenures of various grades, and the bulk of the caste are fairly prosperous cultivators. If popular rumour may be trusted, they still, as in the days of Manu, "find pleasure in savage conduct," for they are said to be extraordinarily short-tempered and irascible, and the criminal records of the districts where they are most numerous seem to show that, in proportion to the numbers of the caste, an unusual number of crimes of violence were laid to their charge.

The following table shows the distribution of Aguris in Bengal in 1872 and 1881:—

District.	1872.	1881.	District.	1872.	1881.
Bardwan	59,887	51,292	Maimansinh	1	......
Bankura	9,283	13,108	Chittagong	......	113
Birbhum	2,993	2,517	Noakháli	38	25
Midnapur	1,026	1,403	Tipperah	10	324
Hughli with Howrah	1,141	3,938	Bhágalpur	......	974
24-Parganas	1,846	177	Purniah	......	543
Nadiya	118	124	Santál Parganas	......	1,270
Jessore	63	149	Maldah	68	183
Murshedabad	249	153	Patna	......	80
Dinajpur	57	134	Gya	......	60
Rajshahye	55	78	Champaran	......	392
Bogra	......	44	Cuttack	381	315
Rangpur	9	22	Puri	6	......
Pabna	36	21	Balasore	806	197
Darjiling	15	......	Tributary Mehals	3	......
Jalpiguri	4	132	Hazaribagh	......	179
Kuch Behar	......	1	Lohardága	......	898
Dacca	313	......	Singbhum	......	2
Faridpur	1	13	Manbhum	......	443

Agwá, a village servant, who acts as a guide to travellers.

Ah, a sub-sept of the Kisku sept of Santáls.

Ahar, a sub-caste of Goálás in the North-Western Provinces.

Ahdadar, *Ahadar*, an officer; a functionary, whether military or civil; a title given by the former Rájás of Rámgarh to some of their servants without distinction of caste, whose duty it was to superintend the expenditure of the household. The title is now borne by one Dambar Ahadar, of Ichak, who is a Bania of the Nichondia sub-caste.

Aheriá, a sportsman, a fowler.

Ahilásariár, a *pur* or section of Sákadwipi Brahmans in Behar.

Ahir, *Ahiri, Abhir, Abhiri*, the cowherd caste of Behar and Upper India. The name also is sometimes used to denote a sub-caste of Goálás. See **Goálá**.

Ahir, a section of Ghásis in Chota Nagpur.

Ahir-Páik, a sept of Rájputs in Behar.

Ahitágni, a Brahman householder who maintains a perpetual family-fire, hence a title of Brahmans.

Ahriti, hunters, a sept of the Málé or Mál Paháriá tribe in the Santál Parganas.

Ahtharai, a sub-tribe of Limbus in Darjiling.

Aialong, a sept of Tipperahs in the Chittagong Hill Tracts.

Aich, a title of Dakshin-Rárhi and Bangaja Káyasths.

Aichá, a group of Bárendra Sunris in Eastern Bengal.

Aichittra, a so-called *gotra* in which all members of the Rámávat sect of religious ascetics are enrolled when initiated. As the Rámávats profess celibacy, and the *gotra* includes the entire sect, it differs from the *gotras* of most Hindu castes in having no bearing upon marriage.

Aidhar, an agricultural day-labourer in Western Bengal, usually paid in kind.

Ailwár, a section of Bábhans in Behar.

Ainak-sáz, an optician. The ordinary *ainak-sás* merely frames glasses, which he procures from *bisátis*; but in most large cities manufacturers of lenses are found.

Ainá-sáz, a looking-glass maker.

Aind, the eel, a totemistic section or sept of Rautiás, Asuras, Goálás, Santáls, Mundas, Páns, and Kharwars in Chota Nagpur.

Ainduár, eel, a totemistic sept of Korwas.

Aindwár, a section of Goráits; of Goálás in Behar.

Ainiá, a section of Sonárs in Behar.

Air, a section of Ghásis.

Airan, a *gotra* or section of Agarwáls.

Aithána, a sub-caste of Káyasths in Behar.

Aiyár, a *pur* or section of Sákadwipi Brahmans in Behar.

Ajá-ásram, a sub-caste of Mayarás in Central Bengal.

Ajagyak Brahman, a Brahman who does not offer sacrifices or receive presents; a synonym for Bábhan, having reference to the tradition that the Bábhans are merely landholding Brahmans.

Ajaidápál, a section of the Karan Káyasths in Behar.

Ajaitiá, a *kul* or section of the Bábhan caste in Behar.

Aján, a *mul* or section of the Kanaujiá sub-caste of Sonárs in Behar.

Ajner, a *mul* or section of the Chhamuliá Madhesiá sub-caste of Halwáis in Behar.

Ajodhyábási, a sub-caste of Kewats, Kumhárs, and Sonárs in Behar.

Ajodhyápuri, a sub-caste of Sonárs in Behar.

Akán, a section of the Maghayá sub-caste of Kándus in Behar.

Akás, a *gáin* of the Sándilya *gotra* of Rárhi Brahmans in Bengal.

Akasaria, a section of the Bábhan caste in Behar.

Akásmukhi, a class of ascetics of the Saiva sect, who keep their faces always turned to the sky until the muscles of the neck become rigid and the head is fixed in that position.

Akhanbári, a *mul* or section of the Tinmuliá-Madhesiá, Chhamuliá-Madhesiá, and Bhojpuriá sub-castes of Halwáis in Behar.

Akhará, a *samáj* or local group of the Sándilya *gotra* of the Páschátya Baidik Brahmans in Bengal.

Akhaur, a section of the Sribástab sub-caste of Káyasths and of the Magahiyá sub-caste of Doms in Behar.

Akhgáon, a section of the Magahiyá sub-caste of Kándus in Behar.

Akhutiá, a sub-caste of Doms in Bengal. An opprobrious expression, generally applied to a spendthrift.

Akhwáni, a title of Bábhans in Behar.

Akrur-Paramánanda, a sub-caste of Sutradhars in Murshedabad.

Akshagrámi, a *gáin* of the Bátsya *gotra* of Bárendra Brahmans in Bengal.

Aktenhang, name of a domestic demi-god, a sept of the Chárkhola sub-tribe of Limbus in Darjiling.

Aladási, a section of Tántis in Bengal and of Kaibarttas in Murshedabad.

Aládhi, a *samáj* or local group of the Basishtha *gotra* of Páschátya Baidik Brahmans in Bengal.

Aladoshi, a section of Kumhárs in Jessore.

Alakjáridárhuá, a *mul* or section of tne Kishnaut sub-caste of Goálás in Behar.

Alamalaka, Almalak, an exogamous section of Baidyas in Bengal.

Alam-rishi, a section of Kámárs in Singbhum and the Santál Parganás; a section of Sutradhars in Bengal.

Alamyán, an eponymous section of Brahmans, Gandhabaniks, Pods, Bágdis, Kámárs, Káyasthas, Kumhárs, Madhunápits, Mális, Mayarás, Nápits, and Tántis in Bengal; a section of the Paschim Kuliyá Sadgops; of Suklis in Midnapur; of Sutradhars and

Kaibarttas in Murshedabad and Sunris in Maldah.

Alarishi, a section of Jugis in Bengal.

Alchárá, a section of the Baranwár sub-caste of Baniyás in Behar.

Alekhiá, a sect of Saiva ascetics having their head-quarters near Girnár and Poona, in Western India, whence they visit the chief places of pilgrimage. They collect alms for the purpose of feeding other ascetics, and proclaim their mission by repeating the word *alakh* ('awake'?), from which their name is derived. Alekhiás profess profound respect for their alms-bag (*jhuli*), and are divided into three classes, the members of which dedicate the *jhuli* to Ganesa, Bhairab, and Káli respectively. Ganesa-Alekhiás beg in the morning, Bhairab-Alekhiás in the afternoon and evening, and Káli-Alekhiás only at midnight. Members of the first class beg from house to house, and may even stay for some time in a house where they are hospitably received: ascetics of the other two classes may not enter a door, and merely walk along the road shouting '*alakh*' to attract the attention of the pious.

This appears to be the sect referred to by Wilson, *s.v. Alakhnámi*, from Sanskrit *alakshya*, 'undefinable,' 'invisible.'

Alemba, hailstones, a totemistic sept of Juángs in Orissa.

Alepkháni, a *pathi* or hypergamous sub-group of the Bárendra sub-caste of Brahmans in Bengal.

Aliákháni, a *pathi* or hypergamous sub-group of Bárendra Brahmans in Bengal.

Aliman, Alimán, a section of Báruis, Bauris, Chásádhobás, Báitis, Bhuinmalis, Kahárs, of Bárendra Sunris and of Subarnabaniks and Telis in Bengal, a *gotra* or section of Káyasths, Nápits, of Málos in Eastern Bengal, and the group of castes (*Nava-Sákha*) from whose hands a Bengal Brahman can take water.

Alimmán, a section of Sudras in Eastern Bengal.

Allay, Alliá, Aleh, a *thar* or sept of Mangars in Darjiling.

Almál, a section of the Bangál sub-caste of Baniyás in Behar; of Kaibarttas in Central Bengal.

Almasi or **Alamyán**, a section of Goálás in Bengal.

Almas-Tarásh, a diamond-cutter. The term is also incorrectly applied to the *begri*, *nayinásás* and others, all of whom perform different operations and are really distinct artisans.

Almisi, a section of Kaibarttas in Murshedabad.

Alru, a sept of Hos in Singbhum.

Alu, a section of Korás in Chota Nagpur.

Aluná, a title of ascetics of the Saiva sect, who abstain from taking salt with their food.

Alyamán, an eponymous section of Pátnis and Sánkháris.

Am, Amba, mango, a totemistic sept of Goálás, Nageswars, Korwas, and Mundas in Chota Nagpur.

Amal-dár, a manager, an agent.

Amam, a section of the Kamár sub-caste of Dosádhs in Behar.

Aman, a class of Nepalese liquor-sellers found only in the Supul subdivision of Bhágalpur.

Amar, a class of Nepalese cultivators found only in the Supul subdivision of Bhágalpur.

Amarábádi, a sub-caste of Bhuinmális found in Noakháli.

Amarnáth, an up-country religious sect who live on alms.

Amashta, a sub-caste of Káyasths in Behar.

Amát, *Amáth*, a cultivating caste of Behar, many of whom are employed as personal servants by the higher classes of Hindus. This circumstance has led to the formation of two sub-castes (*pangats*): **Gharbáit** or "householder" and **Bahiot** or "bearer," the members of which do not intermarry. Gharbáit Amáts, who also style themselves Ráut, live solely by cultivation, and cannot take service except at the risk of exclusion from their *pangat*; Bahiot Amáts, who bear the significant titles of Khawás, "servant," Ghibihár, "ghi-eater," and Saghár, or "vegetable-eater," regard service as their characteristic occupation, but many of them work as cultivators without, however, thereby qualifying themselves for membership in the more respectable sub-caste of Gharbáit. Within the Bahiot class, men who serve Rájás are held in special esteem, and an extra bride-price is paid for their daughters. That the Gharbáit sub-caste is the more ancient of the two, and represents the original nucleus of the entire caste, may be inferred from the fact that it is divided into exogamous sections (*dihs*), such as Larwár, Narhan, Pataiwár, Parabwár, and others; while the Bahiots have no such sections, and regulate their marriages by the less archaic system of prohibited degrees. Marriage between persons descended in a direct line from the same parents is of course forbidden; and in addition to this the descendants of the paternal and maternal uncles and aunts, and of the maternal grandmother, are barred ordinarily for seven generations, and even beyond that, so long as they reside in the same place and the practice of *asoch* or mutual ceremonial impurity on the occurrence of death is kept up. These rules are also observed by Gharbáit Amáts, so far as they are not included in the rule of exogamy, which with them, as with many other castes, is one-sided in its operation, the name of the section following the male line. There is no definite rule to prevent a man from marrying two sisters, both living, but no instance of this is known to have occurred. A man may marry the younger sister of his deceased wife, but not her elder sister. It is unusual for Amáts to marry outside the district in which they reside; and with them, as with other Behar castes, the fact of a family having emigrated to Bengal puts a certain slur upon its members, and renders it difficult for them to procure wives from their original home.

Origin and internal structure.

Amáts practise both infant and adult-marriage according to their means, infant-marriage being deemed the more respectable, and adult-marriages being

Marriage.

confined to those whose parents cannot afford to get them married earlier in life. Widows are allowed to marry again. It is considered right, if possible, for the widow to marry her late husband's younger brother or younger cousin; and, in the case of Gharbáits, for her to marry within the *dih* or section to which her husband belonged; but there is no positive rule against her marrying an outsider, and she incurs no social penalty by doing so. Under no circumstances can she mary her husband's elder brother. The ritual in use at the marriage of a widow is far less elaborate than at that of a spinster. Brahmans are not employed; only the simplest *mantras* are recited; a small present of cloth, sweetmeats, and cash is given to the woman; and the bridegroom completes the ceremony by smearing vermilion (*sindur*) on her forehead with his left hand.

Polygamy is permitted, but the conditions are not strictly defined, and, so far as rules go, there is nothing to prevent a man from marrying as many wives as he can maintain. Custom, however, and the normal standard of living among the caste, combine in practice to limit the number of wives to two, and it is unusual for a man to take a second wife unless the first is barren. In cases of proved infidelity a man may put away his wife with the sanction of the panchâyat or council of elders, and may marry again. There seems, however, to be no regular ceremony appointed for the purpose of divorce, and resort to it is far less frequent than among the lower castes. Many Amáts, indeed, deny that they allow divorce in any form, and the caste, as a whole, sets a high value on female chastity.

Religion.

The religious observances of Amáts do not differ materially from those in vogue among orthodox Hindus of about the same social standing. Most of them belong to the Sakta sect, and worship Kali with the usual sacrifice of a he-goat. Maithil Brahmans are empolyed as priests, and incur no special degradation by serving in this capacity. Among the *dî minores* so numerous in Behar, the Amáts worship the five goddesses (*panch devati*), a form of Bhaváni, with offerings of betel, areca-nut, *arwa* rice boiled in milk with sugar, cakes boiled in ghi, plantains, etc.; Goraiyá is propitiated with a pig; Sokhá with *pithá*, "a kind of boiled pudding made of *sattu* or meal;" and Bandi with unleavened bread and sweetmeats. No special days are set apart for this worship. It is conducted by the members of the household without the intervention of Brahmans, and the worshippers eat the offerings with the exception of the pig sacrified to Goraiyá, which is carefully buried. Bahiot Amáts have also a special ancestral deity of their own, called Pheku Ram, to whom kids, goats, sweetmeats, and betel-nut are offered, and afterwards distributed among the members of the sub-caste who happen to be present.

Disposal of the dead.

The dead are burned in the ordinary Hindu fashion, the ashes being thrown into the Ganges or into any sacred river that may happen to be handy. In the case of persons who die at a distance from a river, this duty is usually neglected, and the ashes are collected under a small platform (*chabutra*), upon which a *tulsi*-tree is planted. Infants under eight months are buried. *Sráddh* is performed according to the standard ritual on the fourteenth day after death. Ancestors are propitiated in the first half of Asin (September–October) by offerings of water poured from the palms of the hands.

Social status and occupation.

The social standing of Amáts is much the same as that of Kurmis, Koiris, and Goálás, and they belong to the group of castes from whom a Brahman can take water. This indeed is a matter of necessity for a caste largely employed in personal service. They will eat sweetmeats with, and take water from, members of the *acharani* group of castes and of the higher castes. Cooked food they will eat only with men of their own caste, and some Amáts are so particular that they will eat only with members of their own sub-caste. Formerly they would smoke with members of the *acharani* group, but of late years they have become more strict, and the question is governed by the rule applicable in the matter of cooked food. They indulge in all kinds of clean animal food, such as goats, both male and female, deer, hares, pigeons, wild fowl, and fish, with the exception of some scaleless varieties, which are supposed to bear a resemblance to snakes; but some of them abstain wholly from meat and fish, and are held in special respect for this abstinence. Spirituous liquors are not forbidden. Some Amáts say that they have no objection to eating the leavings of Brahmans, while others resent the suggestion. The point is an obscure one, on which accurate information is not readily to be had; but it seems likely that Bahiot Amáts, serving high-class Brahmans, would in practice eat what was left of their master's food, while Gharbáit Amáts would of course not be exposed to this temptation, and would therefore deny the possibility of such a thing taking place. In Purneah cultivating Amáts take credit to themselves for not ploughing with cows—a practice common in some parts of that district. Their status as agriculturists appears to vary somewhat in different districts, but the bulk of the caste appear to be fairly prosperous rayats, usually possessed of occupancy rights; some have sunk to the position of landless day-labourers, receiving wages in kind, while a very few have risen to be tenure-holders and proprietors of small estates.

The following table shows the distribution of Amáts in 1872 and 1881:—

DISTRICT.	1872.	1881.	DISTRICT.	1872.	1881.
Patna	61	......	Bhágalpur	6,872	8,438
Tirhut—			Purniah	7,153	7,906
Darbhanga	} 31,614	{ 26,067	Santal Parganas	......	12
Mozufferpur		2,315	Balasore	10	271
Saran	120	......	Tributary St	1,548	1,293
Champaran	241	214	Dinajpur	......	1
Monghyr	......	27	Rajshahye	......	2

Amátia, a *mul* or sept of the Suryabansi sub-tribe of Rájputs in Behar.

Amáut, a title of Khandáits in Chota Nagpur.

Amáyat, a title of Sudhás in Orissa.

Ambahlá, a section of the Karan sub-caste of Káyasths in Behar.

Ambariá, a section of Bábhans in Behar.

Ambastha, a synonym for Baidya in Bengal. In *Manu* (x. 13, 47) the Ambasthas are described as the offspring of a Brahman by a Vaisya girl, and are said to follow the practice of medicine.

Ambras, a fruit, a totemistic sept of Mundas in Chota Nagpur.

Ambuli, a *gáin* of the Kásyapa *gotra* of Rárhi Brahmans in Bengal.

Amethi, a sub-caste of Rástogis in Behar.

Amghát, a section of Bhojpuriá Halwáis in Behar.

Ami, a *mul* or section of the Chhamuliá-Madhesiá sub-caste of Halwáis and of the Biyáhut and Kharidáhá Kalwárs in Behar.

Aminápur, a section of Báis Sonárs in Behar.

Amol, a section of the Kamár sub-caste of Dosádhs in Behar.

Ampur, a *mul* or section of the Kanaujia sub-caste of Sonárs in Behar.

Amraut, a section of Awadhiá Hajáms in Behar.

Amri, a totemistic sept of Oraons, who are prohibited from drinking rice gruel.

Amrot, a section of the Magbayá sub-caste of Koiris in Behar.

Amu, a sept of Chakmás in the Hill Tracts of Chittagong.

Anábrikaksha, a section of Brahmans.

Anádi, a section of Jugis in Bengal.

Anaet, a sept of Bairágis in Chota Nagpur.

Anal, a section of Bháts.

Ananta, a section of the Sárák caste in Chota Nagpur.

Anar, a *mul* or section of the Chhamuliá-Madhesiá sub-caste of Halwáis in Behar.

Anarai, Anraya, a section of Bábhans in Behar.

Anarpuri, Anwarpuri, a sub-caste of Kámárs, Nápits, and Telis in the 24-Parganas.

Anchit, tiger, a totemistic sept of Bairágis in Chota Nagpur.

Andarie-Nehra, a *mul* of the Sándil section of Maithil Brahmans in Behar.

Andarie-Laguniá, a *mul* of the Sándil section of Maithil Bráhmans in Behar.

Andarie-Pirápur, a *mul* of the Sándil section of Maithil Bráhmans in Behar.

Andhachábár, a section of Kurmis in Chota Nagpur and Orissa.

Andhachipá panaria, a section of Kurmis in Chota Nagpur and Orissa.

Andhigot, a totemistic section of Nuniás in Behar.

Andhra, see **Tailangi**.

Andrish, a rope of untanned hide with which the yoke is fastened to the plough, a totemistic section of Sunris in the Santál Parganas and Manbhum.

Angariá, a sub-caste of Lohárs in Chota Nagpur; charcoal-burners, a sub-sept of the Tudu sept of Santáls and a sept of Hos.

Angbohang, king of the fir wood, a sept of the Ahtharai sub-tribe of Limbus.

Angbu, the forest-dweller, a sub-sept of the Thekim sept of Limbus in Darjiling.

Angdenba, lord of the forest, a sept of the Pánthar sub-tribe of Limbus in Darjiling.

Angira, a *gotra* or section of the Baidya caste in Bengal.

Angirasa, a *gotra* or section of Brahmans professing to be descended from the Vedic Rishi or sage Angira; a Brahmanical section of Khatris.

Angláh, a sept of Limbus in Darjiling.

Angrok or **Angwár**, a sub-caste of Rajwárs.

Angwár, a section of Turi or Dakhiná Doms in Behar, who perform their domestic worship inside the *angan* or court-yard of their houses.

Ankur, a title of Dakshin-Rárhi and Bangaja Káyasths.

Ankuri, a section of the Sátmuliá Maghayá sub-caste of Kándus in Behar.

Ankuriá, a sub-caste of Doms in Bengal who are basket-makers.

Anlábáng, a sept of Limbus in Darjiling.

Anmár, a section of the Bangál sub-caste of Baniyás in Behar.

Annásani, a *gáin* of the Sábarna *gotra* of the Uttar-Bárendra Brahmans in Bengal.

Anokánwár, a *mul* or section of the Chhamuliá-Madhesiá sub-caste of Halwáis in Behar.

Anraiwár-Anrai, a *mul* of the Bátsa section of Maithil Brahmans in Behar.

Anraiwár-Usrauli, a *mul* of the Bátsa section of Maithil Brahmans in Behar.

Anraiwár-Jhauá, a *mul* of the Bátsa section of Maithil Brahmans in Behar.

Anraiwár-Baingni, a *mul* of the Bátsa section of Maithil Brahmans in Behar.

Anril, a section of Sonárs in Behar.

Anrráhi, a *mul* or section of the Majraut sub-caste of Goálás in Behar.

Anruá, a *mul* or section of the Chhamuliá-Madhesiá sub-caste of Halwáis in Behar.

Antahriá, a section of Bháts.

Antáiya, a *mul* or section of Sonárs in Behar.

Antarvedi or **Kanaujiá**, one of the three main divisions of Kanaujiá Brahmans found in Behar. They are said to have come from the country between the Ganges and Jamna.

Anulomaj (from *anu*, 'according to,' *loma*, 'the hair of the body,' and *ja*, 'born,'—born with the hair or grain, *i.e.*, in due order), the offspring of two persons of different classes, of whom the father is of the superior caste in social standing, as of a Brahman father and Kshatriya mother. If the woman be of the Brahman and the man of the Kshatriya caste, the order is inverted, and the progeny is termed *Pratilomaj*, born against the hair.

Anwár, a section of Bábhans in Behar.

Anyapurba, a woman who has been previously married.

Aoghar, a sect of Saiva ascetics founded in Guzerat by a Dasnámi mendicant, named Brahmagiri, through the favour of Gorakhnáth, a religious reformer, who flourished early in the fifteenth century, and is now recognised in the Himalayan districts as an incarnation of Siva and the special protector of the Gorkhális. They have not the custom of making proselytes. On the death of a chief of the *math*, one of the mendicants is promoted to his place with certain ceremonies. It is said that Gorakhnáth invested Brahmagiri with his ear-ring and certain other symbols, which the latter afterwards distributed among five mendicants, each of whom formed a separate group of the sect—Gudar, Sukhar, Rukhar, Bhukhar, and Kukar. Members of the first three groups dress themselves in a long yellow overcoat. The Gudar wear a ring in one ear, and in the other a flat copper plate with the footprint of Aoghar or Gorakhnáth. The Sukhar and Rukhar wear rings of copper or pewter on both the ears. These ornaments are said to be a sort of masonic signs, by means of which the members of each group may recognise each other. Ascetics belonging to the Bhukhar and Kukar divisions are rarely met with in Bengal. The main distinction between them and the first three groups lies in that they do not burn incense in their alms-pot, while the others do. The Kukar group collect alms with a new earthen-pot, called *káli hándi*, in which they also cook their food. Mention is made of a sixth group, called Ukhar, concerning whom no precise information is available. Some say, indeed, that the name is merely a title of those members of the first three groups who are given to indulgence in flesh and strong drink.

Apa, a title of Bangaja Káyasths.

Aphariá, a section of the Ahir or Goálá caste in the North-Western Provinces.

Ar, a sept of the Chandrabansi division of Rájputs in Behar.

Arad-farosh, a flour-vendor.

Araich, a section of Bábhans in Behar.

Aráishwálá, a trader who makes and sells *takhts*, *tásiás*, toys, artificial flowers, fruits, and festal decorations, such as paper or talc lanterns, and horses and other figures of paper pulp.

Aráit, a *kul* or section of Bábhans in Behar.

Aráiyá, Areá, Arre, a sub-caste of Telis in Behar, who claim to intermarry with the Maghayá sub-caste. The latter, however, do not admit the claim.

Arajpuria, a section of Maghayá Dhobis in Behar.

Arak-kash, a distiller of extracts and essences of flowers, etc., which are used as beverages and as medicinal draughts.

Aráp, a section of the Sátmuliá Maghayá sub-caste of Kándus in Behar.

Arápe, a title of Bábhans in Behar.

Arash, a title of Kaibarttas in Bengal.

Arath, a *gáin* or sub-section of Saptasati Brahmans in Bengal.

Archnáni, a *thar* of the Atrái *gotra* of Nepáli Brahmans.

Arddhá lakhiá, a section of the Banodhiá and Jaiswár Kalwárs in Behar.

Ardhauti, a sub-caste of Kumhárs in Behar.

Ardi (fish), a totemistic section of Bágdis in Bengal.

Areá, a sub-caste of Gareris in Behar.

Area, fish, a totemistic sept of Mundas in Chota Nagpur.

Arewár, a *kul* or section of Bábhans in Behar.

Argariá, a section of the Ghosin sub-caste of Goálás in Behar.

Arghaunle, a *thar* or sept of Mangars in Darjiling.

Arhá, a title of Khandáits in Chota Nagpur.

Arhái-ghar, a hypergamous group of the Chárjáti sub-caste of Khatris in Bengal.

Arhatiyá, a broker or middle man, especially one who has a shop, sometimes with considerable storage accommodation, in a *ganj* or emporium for the sale of grain. Hence, more generally, a business agent or correspondent.

Ari, a sub-caste of Sutradhars in Western Bengal.

Ari, a title of Kámárs and a section of Káyasths in Bengal.

Ariár, a sub-caste of Bais Baniyás in Behar.

Ariyár, a sub-caste of Sunris in Mánbhum.

Arjel, a *thar* of the Atrái *gotra* of Nepáli Brahmans.

Arkasiya, a sawyer, a title usually applied to the Maghayá sub-caste of Barhis in Behar.

Arkáti, (i) a pilot; (ii) an unlicensed purveyor of labourers for the tea districts, who collects emigrants in small batches within their native districts and makes them over for the purpose of transport to recruiters licensed under the Inland Emigration Act or formally authorised by their employers to collect free emigrants.

Arna, a sect of Dasnámi Sannyásis.

Arnab, a title of Dakshin-Rárhi and Bangaja Káyasths.

Arnwait, a section of Bábhans in Behar.

Arrai or **Arákash**, *ari*, a saw, a title of Chandáls or Namasudras who are sawyers.

Arriár, a sub-caste of Thatherá or brass-chaser in Behar.

Arthi, *Arthiá*, a broker, an agent, a salesman, a commercial correspondent, one who conducts business on commission for a principal at a distance; a banker who grants and accepts bills on other bankers or correspondents.

Aru, yam, a totemistic sept of Mundas in Chota Nagpur.

Arul, a sept of Mundas in Chota Nagpur.

Aruyá, a sept of the Tungjainya sub-tribe of Chakmás in the Chittagong Hill Tracts.

Áryajáti, "Aryan caste;" a pedantic designation adopted by nine persons, probably Brahman Pandits, in the 24-Parganas in the census of 1881.

Ás, Ásh, a title of Dakshin-Rárhi Káyasths and of Báruis and Mayarás in Bengal.

Ásan, *Asin-Tánti*, *Aswini-Tánti*, the highest sub-caste of weavers in Bengal, who claim to be the original stock from which the other sub-castes have diverged. Asin-Tánti women do not wear nose-rings, and this peculiarity is regarded as the chief distinction of the sub-caste. See **Tánti**.

Asarhi, a *mul* or section of the Kanaujiá sub-caste of Sonárs in Behar.

Asármállá, Asarmaurá, a *mul* or section of the Chhamuliá-Madhesiá sub-caste of Halwáis in Behar.

Asesmeghrám, a section of Kanaujiá Lohárs in Behar.

Ashár, a month—June, a totemistic sept of Mundas in Chota Nagpur.

Ashtagrámi or *Kataki*, a sub-caste of Támbulis in Bengal.

Ashtalai, a sub-caste of Kámárs in the Santál Parganas.

Asiswár, a section of the Kamár sub-caste of Dosádhs in Behar.

Asmait, a section of the Magahayá sub-caste of Kumhárs in Behar.

Asotoar, a sept of Korwas in Chota Nagpur.

Asraur, a sect of Dasnámi Sannyásis, properly belonging to the Panjáb, but sometimes found in Bengal.

Asrháf, *Asráph*, noblemen, persons of rank. In Behar the designation is assumed by the more respectable classes of both Mahomedans and Hindus, and in particular by high-caste cultivators, who receive in virtue of their social status a remission of rent, variously known as *máfi*, *chhuti*, *kamsare*, *reáet*, *marawati*, *kami*, and *inám*. The word is the plural of Ar. *sharif*, 'noble,' but, like many similar forms, is used in the Indian vernaculars as a singular.

Asrukoti, a *gáin* of the Kásyapa *gotra* of Bárendra Brahmans in Bengal.

Assam-Mech, a sub-tribe of Meches in Assam.

Assampá, a *rui* or sept of Dejong Lhoris, the members of which are of a mixed, low origin.

Asur-Agariá, a sub-tribe of Agariás in Chota Nagpur.

Asur-Brijiá, a sub-tribe of Binjhiás in Chota Nagpur.

Asura, *Agoriá*, *Lohrá*, a small non-Aryan tribe of Lohardagá and the eastern portion of Sargujá, who live almost entirely by iron smelting. Colonel Dalton seems inclined to connect them with the Asuras, who, according to Munda tradition, were destroyed by Singbonga; and, judging from the present position of the tribe, it is likely enough that the Asuras may be the remnant of a race of earlier settlers who were driven out by the Mundas. Herr Jellinghaus, however, suggests[1] that the Asúra legend may refer to the more civilised mining and temple-building people of whom traces are found throughout Chota Nagpur. The legend is discussed at length in the article Munda.

Origin.

The Asuras have thirteen totemistic sections, which are shown in Appendix I. Two of these—**Basriár** (the bamboo) and **Mukruár** (the spider)—occur also among the Kurmis. A man may not marry a woman belonging to the same section as himself, nor may he eat, cut, or injure the plant or animal whose name his section bears. Marriage is usually adult, though a tendency towards the adoption of infant-marriage is traceable. Polygamy is permitted, and great license of divorce prevails. The women of the tribe indeed are notorious for their lax morality, and many of them earn their living as *Khelris* or dancing-girls in the towns and larger villages of Chota Nagpur.

Marriage.

Little is known about the religion of the Asúras. According to Dalton, they worship Singbonga, the supreme deity of most Kolarian tribes, but know nothing of Marang Buru, though they worship the great hills near them under other names. The name Agoriá or Angoriá appears in Hazáribágh as the appellation of a sub-caste of the non-Aryan Lohars, whose special function is the smelting of iron ore, from which rough pig-iron is manufactured by members of the Lohondia sub-caste.

Religion.

The following table gives the number and distribution of Asuras in 1872 and 1881:—

District.	1872.	1881.	District.	1872.	1881.
Santál Parganas	......	538	Singbhum	......	1
Hazáribágh	31	173	Manbhum	61	223
Lohardagá	897	67	Tributary States	1,578	1,204

Asur Lohara, a sept of Mundas in Chota Nagpur.

Aswariá, a section of Bábhans and Sonárs in Behar.

Aswini, see **Asan**.

Atá-farosh, a seller of *átá* or wheat flour.

Ataiá, a sept of Rájputs in Behar.

Atai Baidya, a doctor who defrauds the ignorant; a title of Baidyas used by outsiders.

[1] *Zeitschrift für Ethnologie*, iv, 237.

Atari, a section of the Karan sub-caste of Káyasths in Behar.

Atashbaz, a maker of fire-works.

Atghariá, a group of Phulkátá Mális in Bengal.

Athárachurá, a group of the Bárendra Sunris in Tipperah.

Athárah Panth, a sub-tribe of Mangars in Darjiling.

Atharb, an eponymous section of Bábhans.

Atharva, a low group of Brahmans in Behar.

Athisá, a sub-caste of Dhobás in Central Bengal.

Ath-pahari, one who is always on duty (an eight-watch man), applied specially to a servant employed to collect rents; or, in Bengal, to one who is set to watch the crop and acts as a messenger for the rest of the villagers.

Athral, Athrol, a sept of Rájputs, a section of Bábhans in Behar.

Athwárá, *Athryára*, a money-lender who advances money on condition that the borrower shall pay by weekly instalments a larger sum than he receives; a cultivator who, for the use of agricultural implements on his own account for eight days, works the rest of the month for the benefit of the lender.

Atit, *Atith*, from Sansk. *atit*, one who has passed away from worldly interests, or from *atithi*, a guest, a temporary dweller upon earth, a title of religious mendicants, practically synonymous with **Sannyási**, *q.v.* The term is applied to both Vaishnavas and Saivas, and does not appear to be capable of very precise definition. As used in Behar, it includes two classes of persons—**Sannyási Atits**, who adopt a purely ascetic and celebate life, and transmit their property to their pupils (*chelás*) by a sort of spiritual succession, and **Gharbári Atits**, whose manner of life is that of ordinary householders. The latter group, indeed, whatever may have been its original mode of formation, whether by descent from Sannyási Atits, who broke their vows and married, or otherwise, does not now differ materially from any ordinary occupational caste. The term is also colloquially applied to a person going on a journey who puts up on the way either at a shop or house of some resident, whose guest he becomes. Sannyási Atits are divided into four classes bearing different titles :—(1) **Bhárati**, from Bhárat or Hardwár, (2) **Giri**, (3) **Puri**, and (4) **Arun**. They are distinguished by wearing a head gear of an ochre colour dyed in *geru* (red ochre), and a necklace of *rudráksha*, called *kanthi*. They abstain from animal food and wine, and wander about from one *chelá* or disciple to another, teaching *mantras*. The Gharbári Atits do not admit outsiders into their groups, follow the Hindu law of inheritance, and perform the *sráddh*. They are sometimes cultivators, holding from zemindars rent-free *jágirs*, many of which were not improbably granted to their ancestors on the ground of their being Sannyásis.

Atpárá, a sub-caste of Kotáls in Western Bengal.

Atrab, a territorial section of Bábhans in Behar.

Atrái, Atri, a *gotra* or section of Nepáli Brahmans.

Atreya, a *gotra* or section of Brahmans; of the Srotriya sub-caste of Utkal Brahmans; of Baidyas and Káyasths in Bengal; and of Karans in Orissa.

Attár, a maker of perfumes and essences.

Attri-rishi, a section of Tántis in Bengal.

Atul-rishi, a section of Chásá-dhobás in Bengal.

Aturá, a section of Doms in Western Bengal, who officiate as the priests of the caste.

Atur-Sannyási, a sect of religious mendicants, joined by persons who suppose themselves to be at the point of death. It is said to have been popularised by Tulsi Das, a Dakshinatya Brahman, who accepted the *mantra* of the sect when he was seriously ill, and afterwards recovering became a conspicuous adherent of the Vedánta school of philosophy at Benares. Persons who enter the sect *in extremis* and afterwards get well must remain Sannyásis for the rest of their lives.

Aturthi, a *gáin* of the Bharadwája *gotra* of Bárendra Brahmans in Bengal.

Auigh Baid, a section of Bábhans in Behar.

Aujana, a sept of Chiks in Chota Nagpur.

Aunria, a *mul* or section of the Majraut sub-caste of Goálás in Behar.

Aura, fruit, a totemistic sept of Mundas in Chota Nagpur.

Austhi, a title of Kanaujiá Brahmans in Behar.

Aut-Asram, a sub-caste of Gandhabaniks in Bengal.

Awadhiár, a *pur* or section of Sákadwipi Brahmans in Behar.

Awadhiá, Ayodhiá, or *Ayodhiábasiá*, literally those who live in Ayodhyá or Oudh—members of different sub-castes, who trace their origin from Ayodhyá. Also a sub-caste of Nuniyás in Behar, who practise infant-marriage and observe a curious custom, called *demáni shádi*, which requires that the bride and bridegroom shall be held off the ground during the marriage ceremony. A sub-caste of Beldars, Binds, Dhobis, Hajáms, Kalwárs, Kumhárs, Kurmis and Sonárs in Behar. Sonárs of this sub-caste affect a high standard of orthodoxy, and do not permit widows to marry again. Ayodhiá Kurmis affect superiority over the other members of the caste, and do not permit widows to marry again.

Azghalla, a totemistic sept of Chamárs and Doms in Chota Nagpur.

B

Baba, rice, a totemistic sept of Mundas in Chota Nagpur.

Bábáji, a synonym for Brahman and of members of religious sects affecting to practise asceticism.

Babangá, a sept of Hos in Singbhum.

Babbaliá, a hanger-on about courts of law, ready to give false testimony or to bring false or malicious charges against a person for hire.

Bábhániame Katma, a *mul* of the Bátsya section of Maithil Brahmans in Behar.

Bábhan, *Bhuinhár, Zamindár Brahman, Girhasth Brahman, Pachhimá Brahman, Magahayá Brahman, Ajagyak Brahman, Zamindár, Chaudhriji*, a large and influential caste which counts among its members some of the chief landholders of Behar. Regarding the origin of the Bábhans, a variety of traditions are current. One story represents them as the descendants of the Brahman rulers whom Parasu Ram set up in the place of the Kshatriyas slain by him, and who in course of time abandoned their Brahmanical duties and took to the profession of landholding. Another tells how a certain king of Ayodhya, being childless, sought to remove his reproach by the sacrifice of a Brahman, and bought for this purpose the second son of the Rishi Jamadagni, the father of Parasu Ram. By the intervention of Viswámitra, the maternal uncle of the victim, the Rájá was enabled to get a child without bloodshed; but the young Brahman was held to have been degraded by the sale, and was called upon to settle down on the land and become the forefather of the Bábhan caste.[1] A third legend, perhaps the best known of all, traces the Bábhans back to a sacrifice offered by Jarásandha, King of Magadha, at which a very large number of Brahmans, some say a lakh and a quarter, were required to be present. Jarásandha's Dewán, a Káyasth of the Amasht or Karan sub-caste, did his best to meet the demand, but was driven to eke out the local supply by distributing sacred threads among members of the lower castes and palming them off on the king as genuine Brahmans. Jarásandha's suspicions being roused by the odd appearance of some of the guests, the Dewan was compelled to guarantee their respectability by eating the food which they had cooked; while the Brahmans thus manufactured, failing to gain admission into their supposed caste, had to set up a caste of their own, the name of which (Bábhan or Báhman) is popularly supposed to mean a *sham* Brahman; "just as in some districts an inferior Rájput is called a Ráut, the corruption of the name betokening the corruption of the caste."

Traditions of origin: what are Bábhans?

The last theory is at once refuted by the appearance and demeanour of the caste. "They are," says Mr. Beames, "a fine manly race, with the delicate Aryan type of feature in full perfection."

Not promoted Non-Aryans.

[1] The legend referred to is that of Sunah Sephas, told in the *Aitareya Brahmana* and in a slightly different form in the *Ramayana*.

This type, I may add, is singularly uniform and persistent among the Bábhans, which would not be the case if they were descended from a crowd of low-caste men promoted by the exigencies of a particular occasion; for brevet rank thus acquired would in no case carry with it the right of intermarriage with pure Brahmans or Rajputs, and the artificially-formed group, being compelled to marry within its own limits, would necessarily perpetuate the low-caste type of features and complexion. As a matter of fact, this is what happens with the sham Rajputs whom we find in most of the outlying districts of Bengal. They marry among themselves, never among the true Rajputs, and their features reproduce those of the particular aboriginal tribe from which they may happen to have sprung.

If, then, the hypothesis of a low-caste origin breaks down, there remains the question—Are the Bábhans Brahmans who have somehow been degraded and dropped out of the ranks of their original caste? There seems to be no *primâ facie* improbability in this theory. Within the Brahman caste itself we find plenty of instances of inferior sub-castes being formed owing to the adoption of practices deemed inconsistent with the dignity of a Brahman. The Agradáni, Acharji, and Varna Brahmans are cases in point. There is no reason therefore in the nature of the caste system why the Bábhans should not be Brahmans who, having lost status for some reason now forgotten, broke off entirely from the parent caste instead of accepting the position of an inferior sub-caste. The suggestion that they were degraded by taking to agriculture must of course be put aside, for, as Mr. Beames has pointed out, "there are many thousands of Brahmans in the same part of the country who are engaged in agricultural pursuits, but without losing caste, such as Tiwáris, Upádhyas, Ojhás or Jhás, and others."

Nor degraded Brahmans

An examination of the sections or exogamous groups into which the Bábhans are divided appears, however, to tell strongly against the hypothesis that they are degraded Brahmans. These groups are usually the oldest and most durable element in the internal organization of a caste or tribe, and may therefore be expected to offer the clearest indications as to its origin. Now we find among the Bábhans section-names of two distinct types,—the one *territorial*, referring either to some very early settlement of the section, or to the birthplace of its founder, and the other *eponymous*, the eponym being in most cases a Vedic *rishi* or inspired saint. The names of the former class correspond to or closely resemble those current among Rajputs; the names of the latter are those of the standard Brahmanical *gotras*. Lists of both are given in Appendix I, *s.v.* Bábhan. Where the matrimonial prohibitions based on these two classes of sections conflict, as must obviously often happen where every member of the caste necessarily belongs to both sets, the authority of the territorial class overrides that of the eponymous or Brahmanical class. Suppose, for instance, that a man of the Karánch territorial section and of the Sándilya eponymous section wishes to marry a woman of the Sakarwár territorial section, the fact that she also belongs to the Sándilya eponymous section will not operate as a bar to the marriage. Whatever may be the theory of the purohits of the caste, the Brahmanical *gotra* is disregarded in practice, and doubtful cases are decided in accordance with the *mul* or territorial section to which the parties belong. This circumstance seems to indicate that the *territorial* sections are the older of the two, and are probably the original sections of the caste; while the eponymous sections have been borrowed from the Brahmans in comparatively recent times. It would follow that the Bábhans are an offshoot, not from the Brahmans, but from the Rájputs. If Bábhans had originally been Brahmans, they would at the time of their separation from the parent caste have been already fitted up with a complete set of Brahmanical *gotras*, and it is difficult to imagine any reason which could have induced them to borrow a strange and much more elaborate set of sections from a tribe of inferior status, and to relegate their own sections to an entirely subordinate position. Territorial sections, moreover, do not lend themselves to the process of borrowing. They are as a rule exceedingly numerous; the meanings of their names are obscure and difficult to trace; and, with the exception of a few names borne by famous Rajput clans, they are wanting in the note of social distinction. The Brahmanical *gotras*, on the other hand, form a clearly-defined and not inconveniently-numerous group to which well-known and honourable traditions attach; they can be borrowed *en masse* without any particular trouble; and the influence of Brahman *purohits* is sufficient to diffuse them throughout any caste which affects a high standard of ceremonial purity and wishes to rise in the social scale. Numerous examples of the process of borrowing the Brahmanical eponymous *gotras* can be found among most of the lower castes at the present day: I know of no instance of a caste adopting sections of another type. To take a familiar illustration: it is as unlikely that a rising caste would borrow territorial sections when the Brahmanical *gotras* were to be had for the asking, as it is that an English manufacturer who has got on in the world and is about to change his name would select Billing, Wace, or one of the earlier English patronymics instead of some more high-sounding name which may have come in with the Conquest. Kasyapa, Sandilya, and the other Brahmanical section names do for the rising castes of Bengal what Vavasour, Bracy, and Montresor are supposed to do for the wealthy *parvenu* in England.

It should be added here that alongside of the clearly territorial section names we find a few names of another type, such as Bághauchhiá, Belauriá, Kastuár, which are said to have reference to the tiger, the *bel* tree (*ægle marmelos*), and the *kas* grass, and Harárìá, Kodária, Bhusbarát, Domkatar (foundling, spade-wielder, husk-picker, Dom's knife), which seem to be nicknames of the same kind as we meet among some of the Himalayan tribes. In the absence of evidence that the members of the first three sections regard with veneration the animal and plants whose names they bear, we are hardly justified in pronouncing the names to be survivals from the totemistic stage. Some suggestion of inferiority does, however, seem to attach to the last four sections, and this point is more fully discussed below. For the purpose of controlling connubial arrangements, both of these classes seem to possess the same value as the territorial section, so that the argument stated above is not affected.

Probably a branch of the Rajputs.

The considerations set forth above appear to me to render it highly probable that the Bábhans are a branch of the Rajputs. It must, however, be admitted that evidence in favour of a Brahmanical origin is not wanting. Mr. Sherring lays stress on the fact that the Bhuinhárs of Benares "call themselves Brahmans; have the *gotras*, titles, and family names of Brahmans, and practise for the most part the usages of Brahmans." In Behar, though the claim to be Brahmans is not invariably put forward, Brahmanical titles, such as Misr, Pánre, and Tewári, are used along with the Rajput titles of Singh, Rái, and Thákur. In Shahabad and in parts of the North-Western Provinces members of other castes accord to a Bábhan the salutation *pranám* ordinarily reserved for Brahmans; while the Bábhan responds with the benediction *asirbad*. Further south, however, this practice is unknown; and in Patna a Bábhan would give the first greeting to a Káyasth, thereby implicitly recognising the superior status of that caste in the social system.

Marriage: exogamy.

Like the Rajputs, the Bábhans exclude the section of both father and mother, or, in other words, forbid a man to marry a woman who belongs to the same section as he himself or his mother. The operation of this rule is further extended by the manner in which it is applied. Account is taken, not merely of the section to which the proposed bride herself belongs (*i.e.*, her father's section), but also of her mother's section; so that the marriage will be barred if the bride's mother belonged to the same section as the bridegroom's mother, though of course neither bride nor bridegroom can be members of that section. In respect of prohibited degrees, they follow the rules current among the Káyasths and explained in the article on that caste.

Endogamy.

Among the Bábhans of Behar, as among the Rajputs, no endogamous divisions exist, and they also intermarry on terms of equality with the Bábhans of the North-Western Provinces. Some sections, however, are reckoned inferior to the rest, notably the HArária, Kodária, and Bhusbarát mentioned above, regarding whom there is a saying in Behar—

"Harárià, Kodária, Bhusbarát mare, to Tirhut ka páp hare."

In the north of Manbhum the Rámpai and Domkatár sections are in such low repute that members of the other sections will not give their daughters in marriage to Rámpai or Domkatár men, although they have no objection to taking wives from those sections themselves. Consequently in that part of the country Rámpai and Domkatár Bábhans can only get wives from each other, though their women can obtain husbands from all sections except their own. If the restrictions were carried a step further, and Bábhans belonging to other sections interdicted from taking Rámpai and Domkatár women to wife, those sections would be wholly cut off from the *jus connubii*, and would in fact, if not in name, have hardened into a sub-caste. I have no evidence to show that this is at all likely to take place—the Manbhum practice indeed appears to be quite exceptional—but the point deserves notice as tending to throw light on the obscure problem of the formation of sub-castes.

Age at marriage.

All Bábhans who can afford to do so marry their daughters as infants, the bride's age being often no more than four or five years. The same rule holds good for boys, only they are married comparatively later in life, and a son unmarried at the age of puberty does not bring the same sort of reproach on the family as a daughter is supposed to do. Instances, however, are not wanting where for special reasons the daughters of wealthy families have been married after they were grown up, as was the case with the late Maharani of Tikari; and it seems to be clear that even the most orthodox members of the caste do not take the extreme sacerdotal view of the necessity of infant-marriage. Ordinarily a price is paid for a bridegroom, but the purchase of brides is by no means uncommon. A man may marry two sisters, and the number of wives he may have is subject to no limit except his ability to maintain them. Some say, however, that a second wife is only permissible if the first proves barren, is convicted of unchastity, or suffers from an incurable disease. Whatever may be the rule on the subject, it is rare to find a man with more than two wives. Widows are not allowed to marry again. Divorce is unknown: a faithless wife is simply turned out of the caste and left to shift for herself by becoming a prostitute, turning Mahomedan, or joining some of the less reputable religious sects.

Marriage ceremony.

The marriage ceremony of the Bábhans does not appear to differ materially from the standard type of a Behar marriage, which has been very fully described by Mr. Grierson at page 362 of *Behar Peasant Life*. It should perhaps be noted that a Bábhan *marhwa* or marriage shed had six posts, not four, and that the bride is held throughout the ceremony by a woman of the Kahár caste. I may further observe that whereas according to Hindu law the completion of the seventh step by the bride renders the marriage final and irrevocable, a number of Bábhans in Patna assured me with much particularity of statement that in their opinion *sindurdán*, or the smearing of vermilion on the parting of the bride's hair, formed the binding portion of the ceremony—not the circumambulation of the sacrificial fire (*bhánwar* or *bedi ghumaeh*), which in Behar takes the place of the Vedic *saptapadi*. My informants emphasised their statement by adding that if the bridegroom were to die after *bhánwar* and before *sindurdán*, the bride would not be deemed a widow, and would be permitted to marry another man. In the article on Kumhár below, I have endeavoured to trace the origin of *sindurdán*, and have ventured to put forward the theory that it has probably been borrowed from the marriage service of the non-Aryan races.

Disposal of the dead.

Bábhans burn their dead and perform the *sráddh* ceremony on the eleventh day after death in the fashion described by Mr. Grierson (*Behar Peasant Life*, page 391). Bairagi Bábhans are buried. In cases of extreme poverty the corpse is thrown into a river after the nearest relative has touched the mouth with a burning torch. At the *sráddh* ceremony, as in all other acts of domestic worship for which the services of a *purohit* are required, Kanaujiá Brahmans officiate without thereby incurring any degradation in comparison with the Brahmans who serve the higher castes. In some parts of Eastern Behar Maithil Brahmans are employed by the Bábhans. These rank below Kanaujiás, and are looked down upon by the Srotriya Brahmans, not because they serve in Bábhans' houses, but because their own origin is believed to be of doubtful purity.

Religion.

The religion of the Bábhan, like that of the ordinary high-caste Hindu, conforms in its details to the ritual of whatever recognised sect he happens to belong to. Representatives of all sects are found amongst the caste in much the same proportion as in the population at large. Vaishnavism, however, is said to have been only recently introduced among them, and in North Behar most Bábhans are either Saivas or Saktas. No social consequences are involved by professing the tenets of any of the regular sects, and intermarriage between their members goes on freely within the limits of the caste. Besides the standard worship which a Bábhan performs in virtue of belonging to a particular sect, all householders offer he-goats and rams to Káli on the 24th or 25th of Kuar (September-October), sweetmeats, sandal-paste, flowers to Sitalá on the 24th Chait (March-April), and sugared cakes to Hanumán on every Tuesday. On the 1st of Chait these three deities are propitiated with *púá* (wheat-flour and molasses cooked in oil), *bárá* (cakes of *urid* fried in oil), and *kachwaniá* (round balls of rice-flour, sugar, and butter). These offerings are presented by the men of the family without the aid of a Brahman, and are afterwards divided among the members of the household. To the women is relegated the task of appeasing a lower order of gods—Bandi Mai, Sokha, and Goraiya—with molasses and *pithá*, a sort of boiled pudding made of *sattu* or meal.

Social status.

Owing probably to the controversy about their origin, the social standing of the Bábhans is not altogether easy to determine precisely, and varies slightly in different parts of the area which they inhabit. In South-Eastern Behar they rank immediately below Káyasths, but in Shahabad, Sáran, and the North-Western Provinces they appear to stand on much the same level as Rájputs. The fact that in Patna and Gya the Amashtha or Karan Káyasths will eat *kachchi* food which has been cooked by a Bábhan, while the other sub-castes of Káyasths will not, may perhaps be a survival from times when Bábhans occupied a higher position than they do at the present day. In Champáran, according to Mr. Beames, Bábhans are not permitted to drink and smoke with Bráhmans, "and only under some restrictions with "Rájputs. Thus, a Rájput may eat rice with them only when it is "without condiments; he may not eat bread, and he may drink water "only from an earthen vessel, not from a brass *lota*. Similarly, when "he eats with them his food must be placed on a dish made of "leaves, and not on the usual brass *thali*. The meaning of these "apparently trifling distinctions is that the Rájput, on an emergency, "may eat hastily prepared food with them, but nothing that implies "a long preparation or deliberate intention." Bábhans themselves claim to observe a higher standard of ceremonial purity than Rájputs, in that they will not touch the handle (*parihath or lagna*) of the plough, and that they use the full *upanayan* ritual when investing their children with the *janeo* or sacred thread. In the matter of food they profess to take cooked food only with Brahmans, and sweetmeats, curds, parched rice, etc. (*pakki*), from Rájputs and the group of castes from whose hands a Brahman can take water. As regards the latter class, they are careful to explain that, although they will take sweetmeats, &c., as guests in their houses, they will not sit down and eat with them. The Bábhan's own diet is the same as that of all orthodox Hindus, and, like theirs, depends in some respects on considerations of sect. Thus Saivas and Saktas eat flesh, while Vaishnavas are restricted to vegetable food. Spirituous liquors are strictly forbidden, and can only be indulged in secretly.

Occupation.

The characteristic occupation of the Bábhan caste, as indeed is indicated by the title Bhuinhár, is that of settled agriculturists; but they will under no circumstances drive the plough with their own hands. Apart from this special prohibition, they do not appear to be unreasonably fastidious as to how they get their living, and will take service as soldiers, constables, durwans, nagdis or láthiáls, cut wood, work as coolies, and do anything that is not specifically unclean. Many of them trade in grain, but it is considered derogatory to deal in miscellaneous articles or to go in for general shop-keeping. Some Bábhans hold great estates in Behar and the North-Western Provinces, among whom may be mentioned the Maharajas of Benares, of Bettiah in Champáran, Tikari in Gya, Hatwa in Sáran, and Tamakhi in Gorakhpur, the Raja of Sheohar, and the Rájkumár Babu of Madhoban in Champáran. They are found as tenure-holders of all grades, and occupancy and non-occupancy raiyats, while a very few have sunk to the position of landless day-labourers. According to their own account, although ranking as *ashráf* or high caste cultivators, they enjoy no special privileges in respect of rent, and are not particularly sought after as tenants, because, in common with Brahmans, Rájputs and Káyasths, they cannot be called upon for forced labour (*begári*) or for specific services in addition to the money-rent. The fact seems to be that, as they will not plough themselves, and therefore must employ labourers (*kamiyás*) for this purpose, they cannot pay so high a rent as men who work with their own hands; while their bold and overbearing character, and their tendency to mass themselves in "strong and pugnacious brotherhoods," render them comparatively undesirable tenants in the eyes of an exacting landlord. It is said, indeed, that the title Bhuinhár, a term which Bábhans never apply to themselves, has passed into a by-word for sharpness and cunning.

The following statement shows the number and distribution of Bábhans as ascertained in the census of 1872 and 1881:—

District.	1872.	1881.	District.	1872.	1881.
Howrah	......	33	Tirhut { Darbhanga ...	{ 318,597	{ 127,424
24-Parganas	......	14	Tirhut { Mozufferpur ...		190,625
Jessore	......	4	Saran	97,064	93,231
Murshidabad...	......	160	Champaran	49,298	52,415
Rajshahye	......	1	Monghyr	160,973	176,958
Rangpur	......	4	Bhagalpur	39,764	42,358
Pabna	......	119	Purniah	6,585	11,843
Darjiling	......	11	Santál Parganas	102	6,089
Kuch Behar	......	15	Maldah	......	96
Patna	116,714	121,496	Hazaribagh	6,369	29,596
Gya	140,244	152,697	Lohardaga	5,786	11,648
Shahabad	72,038	76,339	Singbhum	......	3
			Tributary States	......	13,250

Babhaniáme-Karráin, a *mul* of the Bátsa section of Maithil Brahmans in Behar.

Bábhaunchha, a *thar* or sept of Khambus in Darjiling.

Bábri, a synonym for Bhar-bhunja.

Bábu, also called Bábu Paliyá, a group of the Paliyá sub-caste of Kochhs in Northern Bengal. A title of Rájputs in Behar and Chota Nagpur, importing descent from one of the leading families of the locality, and not unfrequently carrying with it the right to hold land on favourable terms by the privileged tenure known as *bábuán*. Colonel Yule gives the following note on the word in his *Anglo-Indian Glossary*:—"Properly a term of respect attached to a name, like *Master* or *Mr.*, and formerly applied in some parts of Hindustan to certain persons of distinction. Its application as a term of respect is now almost or altogether confined to Lower Bengal (though C. P. Brown states that it is also used in Southern India for 'Sir, My Lord, Your Honour'). In Bengal and elsewhere, among Anglo-Indians, it is often used with a slight savour of disparagement, as characterising a superficially-cultivated, but too often effeminate, Bengali; and from the extensive employment of the class, to which the term was applied as a title, in the capacity of clerks in English offices, the word has come often to signify 'a native clerk who writes English.'"

Bábuán, a title of Cheros in Chota Nagpur, probably referring to the peculiar landed tenure noticed under Bábu.

Babunhathia, a sept of Páns in Chota Nagpur.

Bachá, calf, a sept of Goálás in Chota Nagpur.

Bachás, a section of Goálás in the North-Western Provinces.

Bachberait, a territorial section of the Maghayá sub-caste of Barhis in Behar.

Báchgotiá, a section of Bábhans in Behar.

Bachgotra, a section of the Chaubhán sub-caste of Nuniás in Behar.

Bachh, a *gotra* or section of Nepáli Brahmans.

Báchhil, a sept of Rajputs in Behar.

Bachhraián, a section of the Banodhiá and Jaiswár Kalwárs.

Bachhwaliá, a section of Goálás in the North-Western Provinces.

Bádál, a sept of the Tungjainya sub-tribe of Chakmás in the Chittagong Hill Tracts.

Bádámbasti, a *mul* or section of the Chhamuliá-Madhesiá sub-caste of Halwáis in Behar.

Bádámiá, a sub-caste of Korás in Western Bengal.

Baddá Kurkutiá, a sept of Bhumij in Manbhum.

Badgar, a section of Goálás in the North-Western Provinces.

Badhariyá, see **Bathawa**.

Badhik, a sept of Rajputs in Gorakhpur.

Badhiria, a section of Ghásis in Chota Nagpur.

Badhwadiá, a section of Goálás in the North-Western Provinces.

Badisámá, a section of the Karan sub-caste of Káyasths in Behar.

Bádlá-gar, a wire drawer. The trade of wire-drawing, or Tár-kash, is followed by Hindus of all castes, and sometimes by Muhammadans, in a very primitive manner. Silver wire is heated and merely passed through apertures in a steel plate, according to the fineness wanted. In gilding silver, China gold leaf wrapped round the silver is put over a charcoal fire and slowly heated. When partially fused, it is withdrawn and burnished with 'Lahsan patthar,' perhaps soapstone, after which it is drawn into wire and sold to workers in embroidered muslin and brocade. The Bádlágar also manufacture chamki, or spangles, and Gokhru-gota, or filigree ankle bells.

Badoniá, a section of Bábhans in Behar.

Badraka or *Badrika*, a guide, a guard, an escort.

Badramiá, a section of Bábhans in Behar.

Bádsháhi, a section of the Pailwár sub-caste of Dosádhs in Behar.

Báduriá, an eater of the flying fox (*Vespertilis vampyrus*), a title of Doms, Háris, Mallas, and other low castes in Behar.

Bádyakar, a musician, a sub-caste of Pátnis who play on drums on ceremonial and festive occasions. The term is also a title denoting the occupation of the following castes:—Báiti and Muchi, who use the *dhák* or big drum; Hári or Kaora, who use the *dhol* or small drum.

Báergoá, a *mul* or section of the Naomulia or Majraut sub-caste of Goálás in Behar.

Bág, a sept of Parheyas in Chota Nagpur.

Bagáiya, a *mul* or section of Sonárs in Behar.

Bágál, a cowherd, *occ*.

Bágáli, *Bágáni*, a title of Ekádas Telis—agriculturists and traders.

Bagályа, a *thar* or sept of Gurungs and of the Bharadwája *gotra* of Nepáli Brahmans.

Bágande, a sub-caste of Pods in Bengal.

Bágauchiá, a section of Bábhans in Behar.

Bágchhi, a *gáin* of the Sándilya *gotra* of the Uttar-Bárendra Brahmans in Bengal.

Bágchi, a title of Bárendra Brahmans in Bengal.

Bágdi, *Bágtit*, *Mudi*, a cultivating, fishing, and menial caste of Central and Western Bengal, who appear from their features and complexion to be of Dravidian descent, and closely akin to the tribes whom, for convenience of description, we may call aboriginal. A variety of more or less indelicate legends are current regarding the origin of the caste. One story tells how Parvati disguised herself as a fisherwoman and made advances to Siva with the object of testing his fidelity to herself. When the god had yielded to the temptation, Parvati revealed her identity, and Siva, out of pique at her triumph, ordained that the child to be born from her should be a Bágdi and live by fishing. Another account lays the scene of this adventure in Kochh Behar, where Siva is represented as living with a number of concubines of the Kochh tribe. Parvati was moved by jealousy to come in the disguise of a fisherwoman and destroy the standing crops of the Kochhnis, and Siva could only induce her to depart by begetting on her a son and a daughter. These twins were afterwards married, and gave birth to Hamvir, King of Bishanpur in Bankura, from whose four daughters—Sántu, Netu, Mantu, and Kshetu—the four sub-castes Tentuliá, Duliá, Kusmetiá, and Mátiá are descended.

Traditions of origin.

According to a third tradition, the first Bágdi was accidentally begotten by Ráma on a widow maid-servant in attendance on Sita, and, after undergoing some persecution at the hands of his reputed father, was recompensed by the promise that he and his descendants should be palanquin-bearers, and in that capacity should be trusted to carry females of the highest classes. From Orissa comes the still more grotesque tale how once upon a time the gods being assembled in council, a goddess suddenly gave birth to three sons, and feeling embarrassed by the situation, hid the first under a heap of tamarind (*tentul*) pods, the second in an iron pan, and the third under a hermit's staff (*danda*). From these vicissitudes of their infancy the children got the names of Tentuliá Bágdi, Lohár Mánjhi, and Dandachhatra Mánjhi. It will, of course, be understood that these traditions are quoted here, not for any light that they may throw upon the origin of the Bágdis, but as contributions to the modern science of folklore. Apart from any value they may possess as illustrations of the working of the myth-making faculty among primitive folk, I may point out that all of them must have grown up after the Bágdis had ceased to be a compact tribe. Such traditions could only have been invented by people who had already in some measure attorned to Hinduism and felt the want of a mythical pedigree of the orthodox type. The last in particular furnishes an excellent example of a myth devised for the purpose of giving a respectable explanation of the totemistic name Tentuliá. A parallel case will be found among the Kumhárs of Orissa.

Internal structure.

In the district of Bankura, where the original structure of the caste seems to have been singularly well preserved, we find the Bágdis divided into the following sub-castes:—(1) **Tentuliá**, bearing the titles Bágh, Sántrá, Rái, Khán, Puilá; (2) **Kasáikuliá**, with the titles Mánjhi, Masálchi, Palankhái, Pherká; (3) **Duliá**, with titles Sardár and Dhárá; (4) **Ujhá** or **Ojhá**; (5) **Máchhuá**, **Mechhuá**, or **Mecho**; (6) **Guli-mánjhi**; (7) **Dandamánjhi**; (8) **Kusmetiá**, **Kusmátiá**, or **Kusputra**; (9) **Mallametiá**, **Mátiá**, or **Mátiál**. Within these again are a number of exogamous sections, among which may be mentioned *Kásbak*, the heron; *Ponkrishi*, the jungle cock; *Sálrishi* or Sálmách, the sál fish; *Pátrishi*, the bean; and *Kachchhap*, the tortoise. The totem is taboo to the members of the section; that is to say, a Kásbak Bágdi may not kill or eat a heron; a Pátrishi, like the Pythagoreans according to Lucian, may not touch a bean.

A Bágdi cannot marry outside the sub-caste, nor inside the section to which he belongs. Thus a Tentuliá must marry a Tentuliá, but a man of the Sálrishi section, to whatever sub-caste he may belong, cannot marry a woman of that section. The section names go by the male side, and the rule prohibiting marriage within the section requires therefore to be helped out by a separate set of rules, which to some extent overlap the rule of exogamy. Marriage with any person descended in a direct line from the same parents is forbidden as long as any relationship can be traced. To simplify the calculation of collateral relationship, the formula "Paternal uncle, maternal uncle, paternal aunt, maternal aunt—these four relationships are to be avoided in marriage," is in use. Ordinarily the prohibition extends only to three generations in the descending line; but if *bhaiyádi* or mutual recognition of relationship is kept up, intermarriage is barred for five or, as some say, seven generations. In counting generations the person under consideration is included.

In the more eastern districts the organization of the caste seems to be less elaborate, and has clearly been affected by closer contact with Hinduism, inducing the adoption of Brahmanical customs. In the 24-Parganas only five sub-castes are found—**Tentuliá**, **Kusmetiá**, **Trayodas**, **Mánjhi**, **Noda**; while the sections are reduced to three—Kásyapa, Káncho, and Dásya—the members of which profess to be descended from Vedic Rishis, and have abandoned the totemistic observances which are common further west. Traces of totemism, however, still survive in the names of sub-castes. Tentuliás admit that they are called after the tamarind tree, and Kusmetiás that they take their name from the kusá grass, but neither show any reverence for the plants in question. The system of exogamy has also been developed in the direction of closer conformity with the usages of the higher castes. The mother's section is excluded in addition to the father's, and marriage with *Sapindas* is prohibited.

Marriage.

In Bankura, Manbhum, and the north of Orissa, where the example of the aboriginal races is prominent, Bágdis practise both infant and adult marriage indifferently. In the case of girls who are not married in infancy, sexual license before marriage is virtually tolerated, it being understood that if a girl becomes pregnant she will find some one to marry her. Further east, infant-marriage is the rule and adult the exception, while the Bágdis of the 24-Parganas, Jessore, and Nadiya pretend entire ignorance of the custom of adult-marriage. Polygamy is permitted. In theory, a man may marry as many wives as he can afford to maintain: practically, however, the standard of living of the caste limits him to two. He may also marry two sisters at the same time.

Marriage ceremony.

Among a mass of ritual borrowed from the Brahmanical system, the marriage ceremony (*bibáha* or *byáh* as opposed to *sángá*) of the Bágdis of Western Bengal has preserved some interesting usages, which appear to belong to a different, and perhaps more primitive, order of symbolism. Early on the wedding morning, before the bridegroom starts in procession for the bride's house, he goes through a mock marriage to a *mahuá* tree (*Bassia latifolia*). He embraces the tree and bedaubs it with vermilion; his right wrist is bound to it with thread, and after he is released from the tree this same thread is used to attach a bunch of *mahuá* leaves to his wrist. The *barát* or procession of the bridegroom's party is usually timed so as to reach the bride's house about sunset. On arrival, the inner courtyard of the house is defended by the bride's friends, and a mimic conflict takes place, which ends in the victory of the *barát*. Symbolic capture having been thus effected, the bridegroom himself is seated with his face to the east on a wooden stool (*pirá*) placed under a bower of *sál* leaves, having pots of oil, grain, and turmeric at the four corners, and a small pool of water in the centre. When the bride enters, she marches seven times round the bower, keeping it always on her right hand, and seats herself opposite to the bridegroom, the pool of water being between the pair. The right hands of the bride, the bridegroom, and the bride's eldest relative are tied together with thread by the officiating Brahman, who at the same time recites sacred texts (*mantras*), the purport of which is that the bride has been given by her people to the bridegroom and has been accepted by him. The priest then claims his fee, and, after receiving it, unties the thread and knots together the scarves worn by the married couple. This part of the ceremony is called *gotrántar*, 'the change of *gotra*,' and is supposed to transfer the bride from her own section or exogamous group into that of her husband. It is followed by *sindurdán*, when the bridegroom takes a small cup of vermilion in his left hand and with his right hand smears the colour on the parting of the bride's hair. By the Bágdis, as by most of the aboriginal tribes of Western Bengal, *sindurdán* is deemed to be the essential and binding portion of the marriage ceremony, and they know nothing of the "seven steps" of the Brahmanical rite. Garlands of flowers are then exchanged by the parties, and the rest of the night is spent in feasting, the married couple leaving for the bridegroom's house early next morning. The knotted scarves are not untied until the fourth day after the wedding.

Widows.

All sub-castes, except the Tentuliá Bágdis, allow widows to marry again by the ceremony known as *Sángá*,—a maimed rite, at which no Brahman officiates,[1] no *mantras* or Vedic texts are recited, and the sacred fire, which from the days of the Rig-Veda has formed the distinguishing feature of the marriage ritual, is not kindled. In the Sángá ceremony as practised by the Bágdis of Central Bengal, the bride and bridegroom sit face to face on a mat, and each daubs the other's forehead with a paste of powdered turmeric and water. A sheet (*chádar*) is then thrown over the heads of the pair, so as to cover them entirely, and under this the bridegroom puts an iron bracelet (*lohár kháru*) on the left wrist of the bride. The proceedings are finished by a feast to the caste brethren of the village. If the newly-married couple are too poor to afford a feast, they pay a fee of Re. 1-4. A widow may marry her late husband's younger brother, but she is not compelled to do so.

Divorce.

In the matter of divorce, the practice of the caste seems to vary in different parts of Bengal. Hinduised Bágdis follow the example of the higher castes in denying that such a thing is possible. The general opinion, however, seems to be that a wife may be divorced for barrenness, unchastity, or disobedience, duly proved to the satisfaction of a council of elders of the caste. When the council have given their assent, the husband closes the proceedings by the symbolical act of breaking a straw in two, or by taking away the iron bracelet which every married woman wears on her left wrist. A divorced wife is entitled to claim maintenance from her late husband for a period of six months after the divorce. She may marry again by the *Sángá* form, and in some districts such marriages are exceedingly common. Cases, indeed, have come to my notice in which a wife has taken steps to get a divorce with the avowed object of marrying another man. As a rule, however, the initiative is supposed to be taken by the husband.

Admission of outsiders.

Like the Bauris, all sub-castes of Bágdis, except the Tentuliá, admit into their circle members of any caste higher than themselves in social standing. No regular ceremony is appointed for such occasions: the new member merely pays to the caste panchayat a sum of money, varying from Rs. 10 to Rs. 15, to be spent on a feast, in which for the first time he openly eats with his adopted caste brethren. When admitted into the Dulia sub-caste, he is made to take the palanquin on his shoulder to signify his acceptance of the characteristic occupation of the body to which he has joined himself. The origin of this singular practice, which is entirely out of accord with the spirit of the caste system at the present day, is apparently

[1] Among the Bágdis of the Tributary States of Orissa, I am informed that Brahmans do attend at the Sángá ceremony for the purpose of chanting *mantras* and sanctifying by their touch the new cloth and iron bracelet which the bridegroom presents to the bride.

to be sought in the lax views of the Bágdis and Bauris on the subject of sexual morality. In every other caste a woman who has an intrigue with an outsider is punished by expulsion from the caste; but Bágdis and Bauris not only allow their women to live openly with men of other castes, but receive those men into their own community when, as frequently happens, they are outcasted by their own people for eating rice cooked by their mistresses.

Religion.

The religion of the Bágdis is compounded of elements borrowed from orthodox Hinduism and survivals from the mingled Animism and Nature-worship which prevails among the aborigines of Western Bengal. Siva, Vishnu, Dharmaráj (Yama), Durgá, the Saktis, and the myriad names of the modern Hindu Pantheon, are worshipped in a more or less intelligent fashion under the guidance of the degraded (*patit*) Brahmans who look after the spiritual welfare of the lower castes. Alongside of these greater gods we find the Santáli goddess Gosáin Erá and Barpahár, the "great mountain" god (Marang Buru) of the same tribe. According to the Bágdis themselves, their favourite and characteristic deity is Manasá, the sister of the Snake-king Vasuki, the wife of Jaratkáru and mother of Astiká, whose intervention saved the snake race from destruction by Janmejaya.

Manasá is worshipped by the caste with great pomp and circumstance. On the 5th and 20th of the four rainy months—Asár, Srában, Bhádra, and Aswin (middle of June to middle of October)—rams and he-goats are sacrified, rice, sweetmeats, fruit, and flowers are offered; and on the Nagpanchami (5th of the light half of Srában = end of August) a four-armed effigy of the goddess, crowned by a tiara of snakes, grasping a cobra in each hand, and with her feet resting on a goose, is carried round the village with much discordant music, and finally thrown into a tank. The cult of Manasá is of course by no means confined to the Bágdis. In Eastern Bengal all castes, from the Brahman to the Chandál, adore her, and no class is more strict in attending to the details of her worship than the Kulin Brahmans of Bikrampur in Dacca. Bágdis, however, regard her with peculiar respect, and say that they alone among her votaries make images in her honour. Some add that the *puja* has the effect of securing the worshippers from snake-bite, which is naturally more frequent during the rains; and this notion finds a curious echo in the promise given by Vásuki to Astiká in the Mahábhárata, that those who call upon his name, be they Brahmans or common folk, shall be safe from the attacks of the snake race.

On the last day of Bhadra (middle of September) the Bágdis of Manbhum and Bankura carry in procession the effigy of a female saint named Bhádu, who is said to have been the favourite daughter of a former Rájá of Pachete, and to have died a virgin for the good of the people. The worship consists of songs and wild dances, in which men, women, and children take part. The story of its origin may well have some foundation in fact, it being notorious that the Rájás of Pachete, like most of the pseudo-Rajput families of Chota Nagpur, find great difficulty in arranging suitable alliances for their daughters, and often have to keep them at home unmarried until they have long passed the age of puberty. Regarded from this point of view, the legend adds one more to the numerous instances which may be cited in support of the theory propounded by Sir Alfred Lyall in his essay on the origin of Divine Myths in India.[1]

Disposal of the dead.

Bágdis burn their dead and throw the ashes into a stream or tank. The bodies of persons who die of small-pox or cholera are either buried or exposed. Infants under three years are buried. In parts of Orissa the universal practice is to bury the dead on the left side with the head towards the north. The *sráddh* ceremony is performed a month after death under the supervision of a Brahman and in general conformity with the standard Hindu ritual.

Inheritance.

Bágdis profess to follow the Hindu law of inheritance, but their legal business, as with most of the lower castes, is of a very simple character, and is generally disposed of by their own caste councils (pancháyats) without the intervention of the Courts. In making a division of property the eldest son gets an extra share (*jeth-angs*), which seems to be intended to enable him to support the female members of the family, who remain under his care. A similar provision was recognised by early Hindu law, but it has since become obsolete, and entire equality of division is now the rule among all the higher castes, unless perhaps where some special family custom can be proved.

Occupation.

Opinions differ regarding the original occupation of the caste. Some say fishing, others personal service, but the question clearly is not one on which we can hope to arrive at any definite conclusion. At the present day the Tentuliá and Kasáikuliá Bágdis work as masons, and also prepare the lime which is mixed with betel and areca nut. Duliá Bágdis carry palanquins or *dulis*, and, in common with the other sub-castes, earn their livelihood by fishing, making gunny-bags, weaving cotton, and preparing the red powder (*abir*) used in the Holi festival. The Bágdi fisherman uses the ordinary circular cast-net described in the article on Málo, but swings the net round his head before casting it —a practice which is supposed by the regular fishing castes of Bengal—Tiyar, Málo, and Kaibartta—to be peculiarly dishonourable. Most of the Bágdis are also to some extent engaged in agriculture, usually as *kurfa* or under-raiyats, and comparatively few have attained the more respectable position of occupancy tenants. In Western Bengal we find large numbers of them working as landless day-labourers, paid in cash or kind, or as nomadic cultivators, tilling other men's lands on the *bhág-jot* system, under which they are remunerated by a definite share of the produce—sometimes one-half, sometimes less, as may be arranged with their immediate landlord. I can recall no instance of a Bágdi holding a zemindari, or even a superior tenure, such as *patni* or *mukarari*, of any importance; but some of the Manbhum zemindars, who now claim to be Rajputs, are said by Colonel Dalton to be really Bágdis, and the conjecture is likely enough to be true. In the neighbouring district of Bankura, Bágdis

[1] *Asiatic Studies*, p. 30.

must have been among the earliest settlers, if not the actual aborigines, of that part of the country, for at the present time there are 14 Bágdis holding the tenure of *sardár ghatwál*, 6 are *sadiáls*, 2 are village *sardárs*, 178 *tábidárs*, and 117 *chákrán chaukidars*. In Mánbhum one Bágdi holds a village *sardár's* tenure, and four are employed as *tábidárs*. In Central Bengal, Bágdis are frequently met with as chaukidárs.

Social status.

Their social rank is very low. They are usually classed with Bauris and Bhuiyás as dwellers on the outskirts of Hinduism. Some Bágdis eat beef and pork, and all indulge freely in flesh of other kinds, and are greatly addicted to drink. Tentuliá Bágdis, however, will not eat beef, and many members of this sub-caste have become Vaishnavas and abstain from all sorts of flesh. By abstaining from beef they consider themselves to be raised above the Bauri, Muchi, and Oraon, and the beef-eating members of their own caste.

Duliá Bágdis eat tortoises. In Western Bengal the Bágdis eat and drink with the Mál; in Orissa they eat rice with the Lohár Mánjhi and sweetmeats with the Bhuiyá.

The following statement shows the number and distribution of Bágdis in 1872 and 1881:—

District.	1872.	1881.	District.	1872.	1881.
Bardwan	206,074	169,242	Faridpur	1,460	2,239
Bankura	18,632	105,741	Bakarganj	76	941
Birbhum	56,094	73,297	Maimansinh	1,326	3,823
Midnapur	76,285	114,700	Chittagong	39	485
Hughli	} 152,618	{ 179,761	Noakhali	86	38
Howrah		60,628	Tipperah	101	66
24-Parganas	93,833	84,533	Patna	5	......
Nadiya	35,576	42,048	Shahabad	2	......
Jessore	6,126	18,224	Monghyr	19	16
Khulna	......	4,614	Purniah	86	......
Murshedabad	23,929	33,197	Santál Parganas	3,507	4,078
Dinajpur	182	1,921	Maldah	706	3,344
Rajshahye	1,990	2,055	Cuttack	3,896	4,802
Rangpur	63	527	Puri	7	262
Bogra	573	1,489	Balasore	497	410
Pabna	1,540	6,115	Tributary States	11,757	4,850
Darjiling	......	46	Hazaribagh	64	6
Jalpigori	146	34,527	Lohardaga	8,540	2,896
Kuch Behar	......	14,289	Singbhum	263	102
Dacca	1,505	2,485	Manbhum	9,843	7,067
			Tributary States	......	137

Bágdi-Lohár, a sub-caste of Lohárs in Manbhum.

Bage, anything forbidden, a sept of Mundas and Khariás in Chota Nagpur.

Bagehár, a section of Turis in Chota Nagpur.

Bágh, tiger, a totemistic sept or section of Goálás, Kharwars, Lohárs, Oraons, Páns, Ghásis, Goráits, and Gonds; a title of Bágdis and Kaibarttas in Bengal.

Bághá, a sub-caste of Aguris in Western Bengal; tiger, a title of Khandáits in Orissa.

Bághái or **Bághál**, a sub-caste of Rájus in Midnapur.

Baghail or **Baghel**, a sept of the Suryabansi Rájputs in Behar; tiger, a totemistic sept of Páns, Gonds, and Rautiás in Chota Nagpur.

Bágháir, a sept of the Suryabansi sub-tribe of Rajputs in Behar.

Bághákol, a section of the Sátmuliá Maghayá sub-caste of Kándus in Behar.

Bághbán or *Bágwan*, a gardener, or a vendor of vegetables, fruits, and flowers.

Bághbanuár, tiger, a totemistic section of Kurmis in Western Bengal and Chota Nagpur, the members of which will not touch or kill a tiger.

Baghela, quail, a totemistic sept of Mundas in Chota Nagpur.

Bagher, tiger, a totemistic sept of Korwas in Chota Nagpur.

Bághiá, a section of Goálás in the North-Western Provinces.

Baghoar, tiger, a sept of Mundas in Chota Nagpur.

Bághgot, tiger, a totemistic section of Nuniás in Behar.

Baghot, a title of the Ghosi sub-caste of Goálás in Behar.

Bághrishi (the tiger), a totemistic section of Bágdis, Chásádhobás, and of Kámárs in Singbhum and the Santál Parganas.

Baghtuar, a devotee, a sept of Mundas in Chota Nagpur.

Baghuár, a section of Goráits in Chota Nagpur.

Bághwár, tiger, a section of Kurmis in Chota Nagpur and Orissa; a *pur* or section of Sákadwipi Brahmans and Goálás in Behar.

Bágre or **Ujaini**, a sub-caste of Goálás in Bengal.

Bagri, a section of Bágdis in Bengal.

Bágri, a section of Bábhans in Behar; a sub-caste of Kaibarttas in Murshedabad.

Bágsariá, a sub-caste and a section of Kurmis in Chota Nagpur and Orissa.

Bágti, a sub-caste of Bauris in Western Bengal; a sept of Mundas and Páns in Chota Nagpur.

Bágtit, a synonym for Bágdi.

Báguan, a section of Sonárs in Behar.

Baguli, a title of Brahmans.

Báguri, a *gáin* or sub-section of Saptasati Brahmans in Bengal.

Bagwe, a section of the Banapár sub-caste of Koiris in Behar.

Báhak, a title of palki-bearers; a synonym for Behara, *q.v.*

Bahál, a *gáin* of the Bharadwája *gotra* of Bárendra Brahmans in Bengal.

Bahánnajáti, a sub-caste of Khatris in Bengal.

Báhattarghari, a sub-caste of Suklis in Midnapur.

Bahelá, a title assumed by the Dosádhs who have come as immigrant labourers to the Terai from Behar.

Baheliá, a sub-caste of Dosádhs in Behar, also called Bhula, who are employed as labourers and bird-catchers. Although closely allied to Dosadhs, the Baheliás will not eat or drink with them; and when serving as policemen, they call themselves Hazaras. Many pursue agriculture, while some serve as grooms in Bengal. There is a caste of the same name in Bengal who are professional hunters, and are thus allied to Bediyas.

Bahera, a jungle fruit, a totemistic sept of Kharwars and Mundas in Chota Nagpur.

Baheriá, a class of Rájputs in Jaunpur and Chunar.

Baherwár, a fruit, a section of Kurmis in Chota Nagpur and Orissa; a totemistic sept of Agarias and Kharwars.

Bahiá or *Bahiot*, the 'water-carrier,' the 'bearer,' a title of Dhánuks and Kahárs in Behar, who are personal servants in the houses of the higher castes. The term also denotes a sub-caste of Kewats in Bhágalpur, who are said to have been outcasted for eating the *jhutá*, or leavings, of their masters.

Bahiáwak, *Bahiot*, or *Ghibihár*, a sub-caste of Kewats in Behar.

Bahio, a sub-caste of Khatwes in Behar.

Bahiot, a sub-caste of Amáts in Behar. The name implies personal service—bearer of water.

Bahirarwár-Parhat, a *mul* of the Bátsya section of Maithil Brahmans in Behar.

Bahirarwár-Punách, a *mul* of the Bátsa section of Maithil Brahmans in Behar.

Bahirarwár-Párkhand, a *mul* of the Bátsa section of Maithil Brahmans in Behar.

Bahirarwár-Kasiám, a *mul* of the Bátsa section of Maithil Brahmans in Behar.

Bahomar, a sept of Mundas in Chota Nagpur.

Bahra, a title of Dhobis in Behar.

Báhubalendra, strong as the god Indra, a title of Khandáits in Orissa.

Bahudaka, a mendicant who lives in a strange town and begs his food from house to house. The name is said to be derived from *bahu*, 'many,' and *udaka*, 'water,' drinking water from various sources.

Báhuja, a synonym for Rajput.

Bahurupiá, a mimic, an actor, a person assuming various characters and disguises. Bahurupiás are believed to have been originally low-caste Hindus, who on their conversion to Islam affected to trace their descent from Umar-i-yár, the court jester of Naushirwan. They often appear in the guise of a decrepit old woman, her face puckered with *gáb* juice, who calls herself Akbar's nurse. Another popular rôle is that of Siv-Gauri, in which the Bahurupiá gets up one side of his person as Siva and the other as Gauri, and conducts a humorous dialogue between the two.

Bái, Mahomedan dancing-girls and prostitutes.

Baiághrapad, an eponymous section of Rájputs in Behar.

Báibá, a section of Murmis in Darjiling.

Baid, a section of Maghayá Kumhárs in Behar; a corrupted form of Baidya or Vaidya; a title of the barber caste in Hazaribagh, where they practise surgery and prescribe for the sick; a section of Oswáls.

Baidha, a title of Dhobis in Behar.

Baidik, a sub-caste of Brahmans and Jugis in Bengal.

Baidmota, a section of Oswáls.

Baidohang, a sept of Limbus in Darjiling.

Baidsáin, a section of the Amashta Káyasths in Behar.

Baidya,[1] *Vaidya* (from Sansk. *vid*, to know) *Ambastha, Bhisak, Chikitsak*, a well-known and highly respected caste, found only in Bengal Proper, whose features and complexion seem to warrant their claim to tolerably pure Aryan descent. There has been much controversy regarding their origin. The name Vaidya does not occur in Manu, but the Ambasthas are there said to be the offspring of a Brahman father and a Vaisya mother, and their profession to be the practice of medicine. According to this account the Baidyas are *anulomaj* (born *with* the hair or grain, *i.e.*, in due order), the father being of higher caste than the mother. Another tradition describes them as begotten on a Brahman woman by one of the Aswini Kumáras, the light-bringing and healing twin-horsemen of Vedic mythology; and then, oddly enough, goes on to say that they were reckoned as Sudras because their mother was of superior rank to their father, and their generation was consequently *pratilomaja*, "against the hair," or in the inverse order according to the succession of the castes. It would appear from this that the Aswini Kumáras were classed as Kshatriyas, and that, according to Brahmanical ideas, even the gods were not equal mates for a Brahman maiden.

Traditions of origin.

An expanded version of the pedigree given by Manu is found in the Skanda Purana. This legend tells how Gálava Muni, a pupil or son of Viswámitra, being greatly distressed by thirst while on a pilgrimage, was given a draught of water by a Vaisya girl named Birbhadrá. The grateful sage blessed the maiden that she should soon have a son. Birbhadrá demurred to this boon, on the ground that she was unmarried; but the rash oath, so characteristic of Indian mythology, could not be recalled, nor could Gálava himself put matters straight by marrying the virgin whose kindness had involved her in so strange a difficulty. For, so it is explained, she had saved his life by the draught of water, and therefore he looked upon her in the light of a mother. A miracle was clearly in request. By the

[1] The term Baidya is not distinctive, and may denote either a member of the Baidya caste properly so called, or a man who practises medicine, whether a Brahman or a member of some lower caste. In Behar, where the Baidya caste is unknown, Sakadwipi Brahmans are the regular physicians.

word of power of a Vedic *mantra* a wisp of *kusa* grass (*Poa Cynosuroides*) was transformed into a male child, variously known as Dhanvantari, Amrita Ácharya, and Ambastha. He was the first of the Vaidyas, because to a Vedic (*Vaidik*) text he owed his birth. He was also Ambastha because he had no father, and therefore belonged to the family of his mother (*Ambá*). A number of analogous myths have been collected by Bachofen in his two letters on "Pueri juncini," and his method of interpretation, if applied to the present case, would lead to the conclusion that the tradition given in the Skanda Purana records an instance of female kinship.

Internal structure.

The Baidyas are now divided into the following four sub-castes:—(1) Rárhi, (2) Banga, (3) Bárendra, (4) Panchakoti, according to the parts of Bengal in which their ancestors resided. All of these are endogamous. A fifth endogamous group, which, however, bears no distinctive name, comprises those Baidya families of the districts of Sylhet, Chittagong, and Tipperah who intermarry with Káyasths and Sunris, the children in each case following the caste of the father. This practice appears to be the only modern instance of intermarriage between members of different castes. It is said to have arisen from the reluctance of the Baidyas farther west to give their daughters to men who had settled in the country east of the Brahmaputra. Failing women of their own caste, the latter were compelled not only to marry the daughters of Káyasths, but to give their own daughters in return. This interchange of women is said to extend even to the comparatively degraded caste of Sunri, and it may be for this reason that the Chittagong, Tipperah, and Sylhet Baidyas are cut off from community of food with the other sub-castes. The sections or exogamous groups in use among the Baidyas will be found in Appendix I. All of them appear to be eponymous, the eponyms being Vedic Rishis or saints. The restrictions on intermarriage are the same as among Brahmans.

Legend of Ballál Sen.

The evidence of inscriptions shows that a dynasty of Baidya kings ruled over at least a portion of Bengal from 1010 to 1200 A.D. To the most famous of these, Ballál Sen, is ascribed the separation of the Baidyas into two divisions, one of which wore the sacred thread and observed fifteen days as the prescribed period of mourning, while with the other investiture with the thread was optional and mourning lasted for a month. Before his time, it is said, all Baidyas formed a single group, the members of which intermarried with one another, as all were equal in rank. All wore the thread and observed the term of mourning characteristic of the Vaisyas. Ballál Sen, however, insisted on marrying a ferryman's daughter, named Padmavati, of the Patni or Dom-Patni caste. His son, Lakshan Sen, followed by a majority of the caste, protested against the legality of the marriage, and, finding their remonstrances unheeded, tore off the sacred cord which all Baidyas then wore, and retired into a distant part of the country. These were the ancestors of the Banga and Bárendra sub-castes of the present day, while the Rárhi Baidyas represent the remnant who condoned Ballál Sen's offence. It is difficult to reconcile this legend with the accepted tradition that in the course of his social reforms Ballál Sen separated the Baidyas into three classes—Rárhi, Bárendra, and Banga—according to the place of their abode, and introduced the hypergamous divisions of

Hypergamous groups.

Kulin, Bangsaj, and **Maulik.** A Kulin must marry his daughter to a Kulin, but he himself may marry either a Kulin or a Bangsaj woman. If he marries a Maulik woman, his family is to a certain extent dishonoured, but the stain may be wiped out by marrying his sister or daughter to a Kulin. Hence the saying, "Rising and falling is the Baidya's lot, provided the original stock remains sound." Ballál Sen is said to have distributed the Baidyas of his time into twenty-seven *sthâns* or communes, beyond which no one could reside without losing caste. The principal settlements were at Senhati, Chandam Mahál, Daspárá, Puigrám, Karoria, Shendiá, Itna, and Bhattapratáp in Jessore; Poragáchha in Bikrámpur; and Dásora and Chánd-prátáp in Dacca. To him also is attributed the institution of the three classes—*Siddha*, *Sádhya*, and *Kashta*, which, like the Kulinistic groups, have reference to social esteem or purity of lineage. They differ from the latter in being more rigid. Thus, a Siddha Baidya who takes a wife from the Sádhya or Kashta class sinks at once to their level, and his descendants cannot recover their status by marrying into a higher class.

The Samáj-pati, or presidency of the Banga Baidyas, has for several generations been vested in the family of Rájá Ráj Ballabh of Rájnagar, who reside on the south bank of the Padma river, and though now poor and dependent, the members are still consulted on matters affecting the caste. In the middle of last century the influence of the family was still stronger, and a Rájá of that time induced many of the Banga and Barendra Baidyas to resume the sacred thread which their ancestors had discarded. With reference to this tradition, Ward writes as if the entire caste had then for the first time obtained the right to wear thread by means of Ráj Ballabh's influence. He says:—"Raj Ballabh, a person of this [Baidya] class, steward to the Nawáb of Murshedábád, about a hundred years ago first procured for Baidyas the honour of wearing the *paitá*: he invited the Brahmans to a feast, and persuaded them to invest his son; from which time many Baidyas wear this badge of distinction."

Marriage.

Infant-marriage is the rule of the caste, rare exceptions being met with in highly-educated families, which have come under the influence of European ideas. Polygamy is permitted, but is not practised on a large scale. Divorce is unknown: a woman taken in adultery is simply turned adrift, and ceases to be a member of respectable Hindu society. Widows are not allowed to marry again, and the practice of *sati* was formerly very common. On this point Ward, writing in 1811, says:—"Many Baidya widows ascend the funeral pile. At Sonakhali, in Jessore, which contains many families of this order, almost all the widows are regularly burnt alive with the corpses of their husbands."

The Baidya marriage ceremony does not differ materially from that in vogue among Brahmans, except that sometimes the *Kusundiká* ceremony is performed on the marriage night. When equals marry a curious custom is observed. A bond is executed certifying that the bridegroom has received twelve rupees; should a second son marry, he executes a bond for twenty-four; and in the case of a third son the acknowledgment is for thirty-six. Beyond this it never goes, however many brothers the bridegroom may have older than himself.

Religion.

The religion of the Baidyas is that of the orthodox high caste Hindu. All old Baidya families are Sakti worshippers, but among the poorer classes Vaishnavas are occasionally found. Of late years many of the caste have joined the Bráhma Samáj. Brahmans are employed for religious and ceremonial purposes; but it is doubtful whether these are of the highest rank, as they also officiate for the Nava-sákha. They have also ghataks of their own, who were formerly Brahmans, but for many years past members of their own caste have discharged this important social function. The innovation is ascribed to one Viswarath of Jessore, who is said to have been the first regular Baidya ghatak.

Occupation.

The practice of medicine, according to the traditional Hindu method, was no doubt the original profession of the Baidya caste. From the time of the Sen kings, however, the tendency has been towards the adoption of other pursuits, and at the present day hardly one-third of the caste are believed to be engaged in their traditional avocation. These latter are still in pretty general request. Certain passages of the Shástras regard the taking of medicine from a Baidya as a sort of sacramental act, and forbid resort to any one not of that caste, so that some orthodox Hindus when at the point of death call in a Baidya to prescribe for them in the belief that by swallowing the drugs he orders for them they obtain absolution for their sins. Many Baidyas have distinguished themselves at the Bar, and as agents, managers, and school-masters, whilst others have taken to the study of English medicine and have entered Government service or engaged in private practice as medical men. Many again are found among the higher grades of land-holders, as zemindars, tenure-holders, and a few are occupancy raiyats. They will on no account hold the plough, or engage in any form of manual labour, and thus necessarily carry on their cultivation by means of hired servants paid in cash or by a share of the crop.

Social status.

In point of social standing, Baidyas rank next to Brahmans and above Káyasths. Strictly speaking, they are inferior to Rajputs, but this point cannot be insisted on in practice, as there are comparatively few Rajputs in the area inhabited by Baidyas, and those are mostly immigrants from Upper India, who belong to a different social system from Bengalis. There has been some controversy between Baidyas and Káyasths regarding their relative rank, the leading points of which will be found in the article on Káyasths. Putting aside the manifest futility of the discussion, we may fairly sum it up by saying that in point of general culture there is probably little to choose between the two castes, and that the Baidyas have distinctly the best of the technical claim to precedence. On the other hand, it would, I think, strike most observers that the Káyasths are the more pliant and adaptive of the two, and have thereby drawn to themselves a larger share of official preferment than the more conservative Baidyas.

Baidyas eat boiled rice and food coming under that category only with members of their own caste. They will drink and smoke with the Nava Sákha and with castes ranking higher than that group, but will not use the same drinking vessel or the same hookah. Brahmans will eat sweetmeats in a Baidya's house, and will drink and smoke in their company, subject to the restriction noticed in last sentence as to not using the same vessel or pipe.

The following statement illustrates the distribution of Baidyas in 1872 and 1881:—

DISTRICT.	1872.	1881.	DISTRICT.	1872.	1881.
Bardwan	8,004	3,320	Bakarganj	12,960	11,810
Bankura	2,366	3,881	Maimansinh	2,067	4,615
Birbhum	1,352	1,834	Chittagong	4,016	4,667
Midnapur	2,490	3,763	Noakhali	833	1,297
Hughli	3,023	2,463	Tipperah	3,251	6,470
Howrah		778	Chittagong Hill Tracts ...	10	61
24-Parganas	4,556	1,960	Patna	17	......
Nadiya	2,337	1,747	Monghyr	14	......
Jessore	3,259	1,972	Bhagalpur	30	......
Khulna	......	1,895	Purniah	457	564
Murshedabad	2,258	1,474	Santál Parganas	349	208
Dinajpur	583	656	Maldah	403	611
Rajshahye	1,179	852	Cuttack	234	88
Rangpur	886	2,163	Puri	9	184
Bogra	147	213	Balasore	88	60
Pabna	1,206	1,216	Tributary States	......	3
Darjiling	10	20	Hazaribagh	70	50
Jalpigori	82	201	Lohardaga	729	564
Kuch Behar	......	289	Singbhum	25	102
Dacca	8,420	10,031	Manbhum	2,394	1,552
Faridpur	2,032	4,983	Tributary States	......	33

Baidya, a title of Pods, and of Nápits in Bengal who practise medicine. A synonym for Doái.

Baidya-nidhi, a title or popular designation of Baidyas practising medicine, used by themselves.

Baiga, a sorcerer; a sept of Dhenuárs in Chota Nagpur. Also a synonym for, or title of, the Kharwár tribe of Chota Nagpur, possibly having reference to the idea that they being among the original inhabitants of the country are best qualified to play the part of sorcerer and propitiate the local gods.

Baijahmapadya or **Baiyághrapadya**, a section of Brahmans and Káyasths in Bengal.

Baikar, a synonym for Goráit in Chota Nagpur.

Bail, fruit, a totemistic sept of Kharwars and Páns in Chota Nagpur.

Báilhar, Báilhor, a section of the Kumhár caste in Western Bengal. The members of the caste say that the term denotes one of the Rishis or Vedic seers. The last syllable of the word, however, seems to be the Santali for man (*hor* or *horo*), and to suggest a Kolarian eponym for this section of the caste.

Bainá, a sub-caste of Rájus in Midnapur.

Baini, a section of Majhraut Goálás in Behar.

Bainipati, a group of the Srotriya sub-caste of Utkal Brahmans.

Bair, plums, a totemistic sept of Binjhiás and Kharwars in Chota Nagpur.

Bairági, 'one who is free from all worldly desires, one devoid of passion:' a class of Hindu religious mendicants who worship Vishnu, to be distinguished from the Sannyási, who are usually Saivites; but the term is indiscriminately applied to different classes of vagrants professing a religious life. In Chota Nagpur there exists a group bearing the name Bairagi, which appears closely to resemble a true caste. The exogamous sections of this group are shown in appendix I. Some of them are totemistic and some have reference to divisions of the Bairagi sect based upon differences of ascetic practice.

Bairiá, a sub-caste of Lohárs in Behar.

Bais, a trading caste of North Bhágalpur, who claim to be the lineal descendants of the Vaisyas of early Aryan tradition, goes by this name. They disown all connexion with the Bais Baniyás mentioned below, and keep up elaborate genealogies for the purpose of preserving the purity of the stock and guarding against consanguineous marriages. They observe an intricate system of exogamy, in which regard is had to the following considerations:—First, a man may not marry a woman who belongs to the same *mul* as he himself, his mother, or his paternal grandmother. Secondly, he may not marry a woman whose mother or paternal grandmother belonged to any of the *muls* prohibited to him. For instance (*vide* table below), the question is whether Propositus may marry Proposita. The capital letters show the *muls*. Proposita herself does not belong to any of the three *muls* A, B, D, which are barred on the man's side. But her maternal grandmother belonged to D *mul*, which is barred for Propositus. Consequently the marriage cannot take place. The *mul* of Proposita's maternal grandfather is not taken into account:—

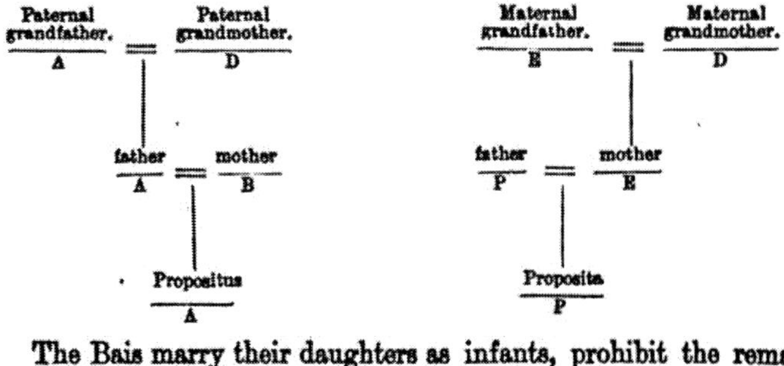

The Bais marry their daughters as infants, prohibit the remarriage of widows, and do not recognise divorce. They rank high socially, and their physical appearance lends some support to their claims to be of comparatively pure Aryan descent.

Báis, a sub-caste of Sonárs and a sept of the Chandrabansi division of Rájputs in Behar.

Baisák, *Basákh*, a title of Tántis in Bengal.

Báis-Baniyá, a sub-caste of Baniyás in Behar, some of whom claim to be the modern representatives of the ancient Vaisyas. It is, however, equally likely that they may be an offshoot from the Báis sub-tribe of Rajputs, which was separated from the parent group by reason of its members taking to trade. They have three sections—**Morwait**, **Karnait**, and **Gothman**, supplemented by the usual rules regarding prohibited degrees. Marriage is either infant or adult, the former custom being deemed the more respectable. The standard ceremony is followed, and *tilak* is paid to the parents of the bridegroom. Widow-marriage and divorce are prohibited, and polygamy is permitted only in the event of the first wife being barren. They burn their dead and perform the *sráddh* on the thirty-first day after death. Trade and agriculture are their regular occupations.

Baiswánar, a *gotra* or section of the Baidya caste in Bengal.

Baiswara, a sub-caste of Tántis in Behar.

Baisya, a synonym for Vaisya, *q.v.*

Baitál, a sub-caste of Muchis in Bengal.

Baithá, a synonym for Dhobi in Behar. Also a title of Dhobis and a *pangat* or section of Bánsphor Doms in Behar.

Báiti, *Báoti*, a small caste of Central and Eastern Bengal, usually called **Chunári** or **Chuniyá**, from being engaged in the manufacture of lime from shells. They are also mat-makers, weavers, dancers, and beggars.

Internal structure.

Regarding the internal structure of the caste very little is known. The Báitis of Dacca all belong to one section, **Aliman**, and thus, like several other castes of Eastern Bengal, habitually transgress the rule of exogamy implied in the recognition of a section-name. A degraded sub-caste is found in Faridpur, under the name of **Magi**, the members of which do not intermarry with the Báitis of Dacca. In the 24-Parganas, Musalmán Báitis are found. These, of course, do not intermarry with Hindu Báitis, nor do they follow the characteristic occupation of making lime.

The Purohit of the Báiti is a Patit Bráhman, and the caste consists mainly of Vaishnavas. The only titles met with are Rái, Bhuya, and Sen.

Occupation.

The Báiti do not gather shells themselves, but Bediyás occasionally do, and fishermen from the Murshedabad district come annually in March and April to collect them. The best fishing ground is the Kamargangá river in

Faridpur, and the only shells calcined by the Báiti are the Ghonghá, Sípí, and Shámuk, the molluscs (*gita*) being extracted by an iron hook. A maund of shells, costing from fourteen to twenty annas, produces, when calcined, about four maunds of lime, which sells for about an anna a seer. The Káthuria Sutárs and Bágdis are the only other classes of Bengalis engaged in lime-burning.

Social status.

Although the Báiti is one of the most impure of Bengali castes, their water-vessels defiling any pure Hindu, no one will refuse to chew lime moistened with water from these very same vessels. Kabírájs purchase unslaked lime (gúra-chún) from the Báiti for medicinal purposes, while the finest and most expensive lime for chewing, pan-chún, is prepared with the ashes of tamarind wood.

The Súdra barber and washerman work for the Báiti, but the Bhúinmálí, owing to some party grudge, will not, and the Muhammadan Beldár has to be engaged whenever the Báiti has a house to build or a ditch to dig.

The following statement shows the number and distribution of Báitis in 1872 and 1881:—

DISTRICT.	1872.	1881.	DISTRICT.	1872.	1881.
Bardwan	4,691	2,930	Bogra	170	43
Bankura	337	1,983	Pabna	1,433	496
Birbhum	660	1,036	Darjiling	67	......
Midnapur	2,627	646	Jalpigori	27	18
Hughli	} 3,001	2,539	Kuch Behar	......	1,684
Howrah		813	Dacca	1,408	1,278
24-Parganas	1,543	709	Faridpur	1,133	427
Nadiya	2,619	2,151	Bakarganj	634	41
Jessore	2,493	1,296	Maimansinh	2,099	651
Khulna	......	925	Chittagong	123	2
Murshedabad	1,584	1,210	Noakhali	223	......
Dinajpur	801	83	Tipperah	906	197
Rajshahye	821	145	Maldah	19,323	1,121
Rangpur	1,091	104	Santál Parganas	......	200

Baitiriba, buffalo, a totemistic sept of Juángs in Orissa.

Baitosh, Baittash, a title of Dakshin-Rárhi and Bangaja Káyasths.

Baiyághrapadya or **Baijahmapadya**, a section of Brahmans and Kayasths in Bengal.

Bájándariá, a sub-caste of Bágdis found in Jessore.

Bájaniá, players on musical instruments, whether Hindus or Mahomedans; if the latter, usually barbers or the husbands of midwives (dái); a title of Ghásis in Chota Nagpur.

Bájapeyi, a title of Kanaujiá and Sáraswat Brahmans in Behar.

Bajar, Bajarpuriji, a sept of Chiks or Páns in Chota Nagpur.

Bajgáin, a *thar* or section of Nepáli Brahmans.

Bájikar, *Básigar*, a sub-caste of Bediyas, the common name applied to wandering jugglers; some of them profess to be Hindus, others are Mahomedans.

Bajitpur, a *mul* or section of the Naomulia or Majraut sub-caste of Goálás in Behar.

Bájná, a synonym for Bádyakar, *q.v.*

Bájpai (corruption of Bájapeyi), a title of Kanaujiá Brahmans; also a section of Doms who are employed as drummers in Behar.

Baju, a section of Murmis in Darjiling.

Bajua, a variant of Daibayna, an astrologer, *q.v.*

Bájuniá, a sub-caste of Doms in Bengal who are musicians.

Bakál, Bakkál, a grocer, a chandler, a grain-merchant, a cloth-dealer; a shopkeeper in general, hence a title of Banias. See Baqqál below.

Bakáli, a title of Baniás.

Bakat, pánre ke pánre, a section of the Biyáhut and Kharidáhá Kalwárs in Behar.

Bákhim, a sept of Limbus in Darjiling.

Bakho, a profession followed by both Hindus and Mahomedans, who go about singing on the occasion of the birth of a child, the husband carrying a *khanjri* to play on and the wife (Bakháin) a *machiá* or stool, on which she sits at the door and sings.

Bakholá, a section of the Karan Káyasths in Behar.

Bakriyár, a title of Maithil Brahmans in Behar.

Baksár, a *mul* or section of the Chhamuliá-Madhesiá sub-caste of Halwáis in Behar.

Baksar Chausá, a *mul* or section of the Kanaujia sub-caste of Hajáms in Behar.

Baksariá, belonging to Buxar, a section of the Biyáhut and Kharidáhá Kalwárs and of Bábhans in Behar.

Bakshi, a paymaster; a subordinate in the Treasury Department of a Collector's Office; a section of the Sribástab Káyasths in Behar; an honorary title of Brahmans and Káyasths in Bengal.

Bakulári, a *mul* or section of the Chhamuliá-Madhesiá sub-caste of Halwáis in Behar.

Bákuli, a title of Goálás.

Bákundi, a title of Sadgops in Bengal.

Bakurá or *Bakulá*, paddy bird, a totemistic sept of Chiks and Oraons in Chota Nagpur.

Bal, a section of Murmis; a title of Dakshin-Rárhi and Bangaja Káyasths.

Bála, a *gáin* of the Bharadwája *gotra* of Bárendra Brahmans in Bengal.

Bálágachpargaria, a *mul* or section of the Naomulia or Majraut sub-caste of Goálás in Behar.

Bálágachpokhrám, a *mul* or section of the Naomulia or Majraut sub-caste of Goálás in Behar.

Baláhar, *Baládhar*, a low-caste servant, a village guide or messenger, a village watchman, inferior to the ordinary chaukidár; he is also employed as a sweeper.

Baláhi, a man of low caste; a *Chamár* or worker in hides and leather, sometimes employed to measure land.

Baláiár, a section of Bábhans in Behar.

Baláin, a section of the Karan Káyasths in Behar.

Balamdár, spearman, a totemistic sept of Mundas in Chota Nagpur.

Balamtiriá, *Bállamtiriá*, a sub-caste of Halwáis and Kándus in Behar.

Balarám or **Balabhadriá**, a section of the Mahasthán sub-caste of Utkal Brahmans.

Balarámi, a sub-caste of Tántis in Bengal.

Bálayashthi, a *gáin* of the Kásyapa *gotra* of Bárendra Brahmans in Bengal.

Balbandhi, a sept of Páns in Chota Nagpur.

Balbandhiá, a section of Bháts.

Balbandhiya, a sept of Chiks who tie up the hair.

Balbheráit, a section of the Maghayá sub-caste of Barhis in Behar.

Baldev, a cowherd.

Baldiá, a herdsman or drover.

Bálgori, a sub-tribe of Rajputs in Western Bengal.

Balháti, a territorial section of Barhis in Behar.

Balhava, a title of Chásádhobás in Bengal.

Báli, a *gáin* of the Sábarna *gotra* and a *mel* or hypergamous sub-group of Rárhi Brahmans in Bengal.

Baliáse-Narsam, a *mul* of the Kásyapa section of Maithil Brahmans in Behar.

Baliáse-Balha, a *mul* of the Kásyap section of Maithil Brahmans in Behar.

Baliáse-Asi, a *mul* of the Kásyap section of Maithil Brahmans in Behar.

Baliáse-Sakuri, a *mul* of the Kásyap section of Maithil Brahmans in Behar.

Baliáse-Dharaurá, a *mul* of the Kásyap section of Maithil Brahmans in Behar.

Baliáse-Suket, a *mul* of the Kásyap section of Maithil Brahmans in Behar.

Baliáse-Baghánt, a *mul* of the Kásyap section of Maithil Brahmans in Behar.

Balihári, a *gáin* of the Kásyapa *gotra* of Bárendra Brahmans in Bengal.

Bálimba, mosquito, a totemistic sept of Juángs in Orissa.

Bálká, a young follower of a religious Hindu mendicant.

Balkharya, a sept of Rajputs in Behar.

Ballabhi, a *mel* or hypergamous sub-group of Rárhi Brahmans in Bengal.

Balliati, a *mul* or section of the Maghayá sub-caste of Barhis in Behar.

Ballisor, a sept of Páns in Chota Nagpur.

Balliwálá, a trader in beams of undressed wood, used for scaffolding by masons and others, and also as rafters in thatched and tiled roofing.

Bálmik, a sub-caste of Káyasths in Behar.

Bálmus, a kind of insect which lives in river sand, a totemistic sept of Mundas in Chota Nagpur.

Bálthabi, a *gáin* or sub-section of Saptasati Brahmans in Bengal.

Baltong, a section of Murmis in Darjiling.

Balum, salt, a totemistic sept of Mundas in Chota Nagpur.

Bálwán, a section of Goálás in the North-Western Provinces.

Báman, a totemistic sept of Mundas, the members of which may not touch or be touched by a Brahman. Also a synonym for Brahman.

Bámanbane, a sub-caste of Nápits in Bengal.

Bámanjagya, a hypergamous division of Tiyars found by Buchanan in Bhagalpur.

Bambai, a kind of eel, a totemistic sept of Kaurs in Chota Nagpur.

Bámboriá, a section of Goálás in the North-Western Provinces.

Bamhangaur, a class of the Gaur Rajputs.

Bámhaniá, a subdivision of the Káchhi tribe, a class of cultivators in Behar and the North-Western Provinces.

Bamnia, salt, a sept of Kharwars in Chota Nagpur.

Bámo, a title of Kaibarttas in Bengal.

Bamodá, a sept of the Agniá sub-tribe of Meches in Darjiling.

Bamu, a sept of Chakmás in the Hill Tracts of Chittagong.

Bámuniá, a section of Kámárs in Singbhum and the Santál Parganas.

Bán, eel, a totemistic sept of Lohars; a title of Dakshin-Rárhi and Bangaja Káyasths; a section of Goálás in the North-Western Provinces.

Banadhiá, see **Banaudhiá**.

Banáfar or **Banáphar**, a sept of Yadubansi Rájputs, chiefly settled in Oudh, but also found in small numbers in Behar.

Bánaiba, bear, a totemistic sept of Juángs in Orissa.

Banámpur, a sept of Rajputs in Behar.

Banapár, *Banáphar*, a sub-caste of Koiris in Behar.

Bánaprasth (from *ban*, 'a solitude,' *prasth*, 'who proceeds to'), the Hindu of the third order, who has discharged the duty of a householder and has become a hermit.

Bánarási, a section of Málos in Eastern Bengal.

Banárasiá, a section of the Biyáhut and Kharidáhá Kalwárs in Behar.

Banari, a class of up-country *mánjhis* or boatmen, probably members of the Gonrhi caste, who are met with occasionally on the rivers of Bengal.

Banasil, a title of Subarnabaniks in Bengal.

Banaudhiá, a sub-caste of Baniyas, Kurmis, Kumhárs, Dhánuks, Tántis, Suuris, and Kalwárs in Behar; also a sept of the Chandrabansi division of Rájputs and a section of Kaserás in Behar.

Banáut, a variant for Bandáwat, *q.v.*

Ban-char, a forester, a woodman.

Bánda, a kind of leaf, a totemistic sept of Mundas in Chota Nagpur.

Bandáwat, a respectable cultivating caste in Hazaribagh, who wear the sacred thread and claim to be Rajputs.

Bandarbikretá, monkey-seller, title of Birhors and other non-Aryan hunting castes.

Bandáwat Sombansi, a branch of the Bandáwat caste in Hazaribagh, who claim descent from the moon.

Bandh, a sept of Oraons in Chota Nagpur.

Bándhalgoti, a sept of Rájputs of Chauhán descent occupying part of Bundelkhand.

Bandhiá, a sept of Kharwars in Chota Nagpur.

Bandhu, Bandhur, a title of Dakshin-Rárhi and Bangaja Káyasths and of Sánkháris in Bengal.

Bandi, a title of Bháts, said to be derived from the laudatory verses recited by them; a sept of Hos in Singbhum.

Bandigwár, a forest guard; a title of Bhumij in Manbhum.

Bandihá, a section of Bábhans in Behar.

Bandijan or Suta, a division of Brahmans in Behar.

Bando, a wild cat that barks at night, a totemistic sept of Lohárs, Mundas, Oraons, and Páns in Chota Nagpur; a section of Kahárs.

Bandrishi, fish, a totemistic section of the Paripál sub-caste of Sunris in Manbhum.

Bandya, a *gáin* of the Sándilya *gotra* of Rárhi Brahmans in Bengal.

Bánebenáras, a *mul* or section of the Chhamuliá-Madhesiá sub-caste of Halwáis in Behar.

Bán-farosh, *Bán-sás*, a rope-maker, chiefly of the Kahár and Malláh castes, who make twine and rope from *munj*, *san*, *káns*, and *háthi chingár*.

Banga, *Bangaja*, a sub-caste of Baidyas, Káyasths, Jugis, Subarnabaniks, and Sunris in Bengal.

Bangál, a sub-caste of Baniyás in Behar, who immigrated from Bengal some generations ago and have now forgotten their original language; a sept of the Tungjainya sub-tribe of Chakmás, who are said to be descended from a Bengali father.

Bángál, a *mel* or hypergamous sub-group of Rárhi Brahmans and of Jugis and Kaibarttas in Bengal.

Bangáli, a sub-caste of Hajjáms or barbers in Behar, whose ancestors immigrated into that province from Bengal; a sub-caste of Bhars in Western Bengal, comprising the two sections of Agni and Rishi, both of which seem to have been borrowed from the Brahmans. A sub-caste of Dhobás in Western Bengal, of Dhobis in Mánbhum, of Kaibarttas in Behar, and Kumhárs in Western Bengal.

Bangáli or **Rárhi**, a sub-caste of Kumhárs in Behar.

Bangareri, a sub-caste of Gareris in Hazaribagh.

Bangas-rási, a section of Málos in Eastern Bengal.

Bángdel, a *thar* or sept of Khambus in Darjiling.

Banger Rárhi, a sub-caste of Sunris in Eastern Bengal.

Banglá, a sub-caste of Dhobis, Pods, and Sunris in Behar, who are probably immigrants from Bengal.

Bangrongpá, a *rui* or sept of the Bed tshan-gye sub-tribe of Dejong Lhoris or Bhotias of the south.

Banhor, "jungle-man," the same as Birhor ('ho,' or 'hor,' being the Kolarian for man), a name by which some of the primitive people of Chota Nagpur who emigrate to the tea gardens, who are generally known as Dhángars, occasionally call themselves.

Báni, a sub-caste of Sutradhars in Noakhali.

Baniá, Baniyá, a synonym for Gandhabanik and Subarnabanik.

Bania, a sept of Kharwars and Telis in Chota Nagpur.

Baniápáthar, a *mul* or section of the Chhamulia-Madhesiá sub-caste of Halwáis and Kándus in Behar.

Banichar, a sept of Chiks in Chota Nagpur.

Banik, *Baniya*, *Banika*, *Banikar*, a generic term including most of the banking and trading castes, and specially denoiting those who deal in money as distinguished from commodities.

Banika, a synonym for Subarnabanik.

Bánikarnauti, a *mul* or section of the Sátmulia or Kishnaut sub-caste of Goálás in Behar.

Baniya, *Banik*, *Barnik*, *Banikar*, a generic name, derived from Sansk. *vanij*, 'a merchant,' applied to almost all of the trading castes throughout India. In Bengal *Baniya* is not, strictly speaking, a caste name at all; that is to say, there is no endogamous group exactly co-extensive with the title of Baniya, although that name includes a large number of groups, some of which are endogamous within a circle defined more or less by their trading functions, while others belong to castes or sub-castes which follow other pursuits, such as agriculture or service. There is nothing, for instance, to prevent Bábhans, Chhatris, or Káyasths from keeping grain-shops or engaging in money-lending, and they might in this way come to be designated by the vague term Baniyá, although their occupation would not debar them from intermarriage within their original caste. In order to define the term more closely, it should be remarked that it appears to connote the idea of a rather general trade, and to exclude special forms of shopkeeping, such as that of the Halwai and the Kandu. It is also more or less associated with the sale of some kind of food-grain. If a man trades in money rather than in commodities, he is commonly known by the more dignified title of *mahájan*, or banker. One of the variants of the word is used colloquially in Bengal as a synonym for Gandhabanik, a dealer in medicinal drugs and spices. An Anglicised form, 'banian,' is specially applied to the native brokers attached to European houses of business in Calcutta. These brokers have most of the bazar transactions in their hands, and usually give substantial security to the firm. In the early part of this century high officials used to keep banians to transact their private business; and the intrigues of "Kanto Baboo," Warren Hastings' banian, are mentioned by Burke in several of his speeches on Indian affairs.

Baniyá, a section of the Banodhiá and Jaiswár Kalwárs in Behar.

Banjar, a sept of Kaurs.

Banjára, a *thar* or section of Nepáli Brahmans.

Banjárá, Banjári: the term is most usually applied to a grain and cattle merchant, who, with a more or less numerous party of the same calling, moves about to different markets, and specially accompanies bodies of troops to supply them with corn. It is specially applicable also to a numerous tribe spread along the foot of the mountains from Haridwar to Gorakhpur, and forming various subdivisions, many of whom are stationary and follow agriculture. They comprise both Hindus and Mahomedans, acknowledging a common origin and affinity. The most migratory are the Bahurupa Banjárás, of whom there are five branches, four of whom assume the well-known appellations of the chief Rajput tribes, or Ráhtor, Chauhán, Powar, and Tumár. The fifth, called Barka, is said to be descended from a Gaur Brahman. Each of these is infinitely subdivided. The Ráhtor branch, for instance, splits into four families, and these comprehend 138 sub-branches. Some of these Banjárás have the privileges of the Cháran and Bhát, *q.v.*, their persons being sacred and accepted in guarantee of engagements. The origin of these people is obscure. If they were primarily a distinct race, they are now much intermixed.

Banjir, a sub-caste of Bhuiyás in Hazaribagh who make baskets.

Banjor, a section of Páns in Chota Nagpur.

Bank, a sub-caste of Khatris in Bengal.

Banni or *Baniháр*, a ploughman or labourer, whose services are paid in kind.

Banodhiá, see **Banaudhiá**.

Banpar, a sub-caste of Malláhs and Gonrhis in Behar, probably of Dravidian descent. Their original occupation seems to be that of boatmen and fishermen, but away from the big rivers they till the soil and sometimes engage in trade. They are skilful sportsmen, entrapping the alligator (*magar*) and *ghariyal* in strong rope nets and eating their flesh. They marry their daughters as infants or adults, according to their means. Widow-marriage is permitted, but the widow may not marry her husband's younger brother, as is usual among the lower castes of Hindus. Socially the Banpar rank low, but it is a curious circumstance that, like the Máls of Bengal, tradition ascribes their inferior position, not to their use of unclean food, but to their habit of passing the netting needle from above downwards in making nets, whereas the other fishing castes of Behar work from below upwards. Banpar is the name of a nomadic subcaste of Goálás in Behar, whose special function it is to take charge of the large herds of cattle which are driven into Chota Nagpur, Sirgujá, Mirzápur, and other jungle-clad tracts for grazing during the hot weather. This sub-caste is also found in Nepal.

Banráhá, a section of the Biyáhut and Kharidáhá Kalwárs in Behar.

Banreit, a *mul* or section of the Ghosin sub-caste of Goálás in Behar.

Banriá, a section of Bábhans in Behar.

Bánrishi, a section of Sutradhars in Bengal.

Báns, bamboo, a totemistic sept of Lohars; a section of Kurmis in Chota Nagpur and Orissa.

Bansa, a sept of Hos in Singbhum.

Bansahr, a *mul* or section of the Chhamuliá-Madhesiá subcaste of Halwáis in Behar.

Bansáin, Bausáin, a class of Mahomedan religious mendicants, who are also weavers.

Bansaja, a hypergamous group of Rárhi Brahmans and Baidyas in Bengal.

Báns-árá, a title of the Kochh caste in Northern Bengal.

Bansari, a sub-caste of Baniyás in Behar.

Bánsbatti, a synonym for Dom in Behar.

Bánsdeo, a sept of Santáls.

Bánsdih, a section of the Maghayá sub-caste of Barhis in Behar.

Bansetti, a sept of Binjhiás in Chota Nagpur who are not permitted to touch bamboo at a wedding.

Bansil, a section of the Agarwál caste in Behar.

Bánskhori, a synonym for Dom in Behar.

Bánsmáli, a synonym for Hári who work in bamboo; a sub-caste of Doms who make bamboo baskets, etc.

Bánsphor, *Baspurawá*, *Bánsbakurá*, "bamboo-splitter," a subcaste of Pátnis in Bengal; a subcaste of Doms in Behar who are mat and basket-makers and do not remove filth. They have nothing to do with funerals, and do not eat beef, offal, or other people's leavings. The Bánsphors of Banka in Bhagalpur have a number of exogamous sections (*pangats*), which have been entered in their proper places. Other Bánsphors on the Nepal frontier regulate their marriages by local sections (*dihs*); while others in the town of Bhagalpur have neither *pangat* nor *dih*. Bánsphors work with a peculiarly curved knife (*kattár*), with a heavy back, which they regard as characteristic of their sub-caste, and which is used by them in their domestic sacrifices.

Bánsphor-Mahili, "bamboo-splitter," a sub-caste of Mahilis in Western Bengal, who work in bamboos.

Bánsriár, a section of the Kurmis in Mánbhum, the members of which may not play the *bánsi* or bamboo flute used by the Kolarian tribes throughout Chota Nagpur and Orissa.

Bánsrishi, a totemistic section of Bhars in Mánbhum.

Bánswálá, a dealer in bamboos.

Banswár, a sub-caste of Rajwárs in Western Bengal.

Bánt, a section of the Játhot division of the Parbatti-Kurin sub-caste of Gonrhis in Behar.

Bantar, a sub-tribe of Thárus in Behar.

Bántar, *Bánt*, *Bátor*, a small Dravidian caste of Behar who make baskets and work at thatching houses. They keep and eat pigs, practise widow-marriage, and rank socially somewhat lower than Dosádhs.

Bantari, a sub-caste of Gulguliás in Gya and Hazaribagh.

Bantariá, a sub-caste of Kándus in Behar.

Bánth, a sept of the Rautár sub-tribe of Thárus in Behar.

Bantiriá, a sub-caste of Halwáis or confectioners in Behar who have departed from the original occupation of the caste and now find employment as servants and petty shopkeepers dealing in miscellaneous articles.

Bantor, a cultivating caste of the Nepal Terai.

Banuár, a section of Kurmis in Chota Nagpur and Orissa.

Bánukiá, a sub-caste of Doms who breed silkworms and work in silk filatures in Murshedabad and Rajshahye.

Bánwar, *Banwár*, a small caste, probably of Dravidian descent, found in the Santál Parganas. They have no traditions of their own, and nothing seems to be known regarding their origin. The fact that they have no exogamous sections may perhaps indicate that they are an offshoot from some of the compact aboriginal tribes of the neighbourhood, who, by embracing Hinduism, cut themselves off from their parent tribe, but were not numerous enough to secure for themselves a recognised position in the caste system.

Origin.

Banwárs practise both adult and infant-marriage, but sexual intercourse before marriage is strongly reprobated, and the tendency is for all persons who can afford to do so to marry their daughters as infants. Polygamy is permitted, and in theory there is no limit to the number of wives a man may have. It is rare, however, in actual life to find more than two. Divorce is permitted; the form consists in the couple expressing their wishes in the presence of their assembled relatives and tearing a sál leaf in two as a symbol of separation. Widows and divorced wives are allowed to marry again by the *sanga* ritual. A widow may marry her husband's younger brother, but is not compelled to do so. She may on no account marry his elder brother.

Marriage.

They follow the Hindu religion, Kali and Satya Narain being the favourite objects of worship. For the worship of these deities, and for the *sráddh*

Religion.

ceremony, Brahmans are employed, who, however, do not associate on equal terms with the Brahmans who serve the higher castes.

Disposal of the dead.

Banwárs either burn their dead or bury them in a recumbent position. In either case the propitiatory rite of *sráddh* is performed, in general accordance with orthodox usage, on the thirteenth day after death. It is not, however, followed by periodical offerings for the benefit of ancestors in general, as is common among the higher castes.

Social status.

The social rank of the Banwárs may best be defined by stating that the Khetauri, Pergha, Bhuiya, and Rajwar will take water and sweetmeats from their hands. They stand therefore below the castes from whom Brahmans and the members of the upper castes generally can take water. Agriculture is their usual occupation; a few are found as occupancy raiyats, but the majority are under-raiyats or landless day-labourers.

Banwár, a sub-caste of Baniyás in Behar.

Báoti, a synonym for Báiti; a section of Mahesris.

Bápuli, a *gáin* of the Bátsya *gotra* of Rárhi Brahmans in Bengal.

Baqqál (Arabic), a grocer, chandler, grain-merchant, cloth-dealer, also generally a shopkeeper; a title of Baniyás which ordinarily has no bearing upon questions of caste.

In Eastern Bengal the term denotes a small sub-caste of Chandals, who neither eat nor intermarry with the parent stock, although their Brahman is the same. The Baqqáls are wandering traders, who retail turmeric, bay-leaves, rice, ginger, and other condiments in inland villages and markets. They are numerous in the Ja'farganj and Manikganj parganas of Dacca. They will not cultivate the soil, but, possessing cargo-boats of their own, navigate them without any hired servants. All belong to one *gotra*, the Kasyapa, and the majority follow the Krishna Mantra. In the belief that by engaging in trade they have attained a higher and more respectable position than the Chandáls, they have renounced the drinking of spirits and the eating of pork.

Bar, *Ficus Indica*, a totemistic sept or section of Kumhárs, Khariás, Goráits, Turis, Bediyás, Chiks, Oraons, Goálás, Kharwárs, Mundas, and Páns, in Chota Nagpur.

Bara, a sept of Chiks in Chota Nagpur.

Bárabátia, a section of the Dhaprá sub-caste of Doms in Behar.

Bara-bhág, a sub-caste of Bhuinmális and Háris in Bengal.

Barabhágiya, a sub-caste of Kumhárs in Bengal.

Bara-Bhágiya or *Bikrampur Sánkhári*, a sub-caste of Sánkháris in Eastern Bengal.

Bará-bhágiyá, a sub-caste of Muchis in Bengal.

Bárabhalá, twelve brothers whose families cannot intermarry, a sept of Chiks and Mundas in Chota Nagpur.

Barabháiyá, a sub-caste of Suklis in Midnapur.

Barábhumiá, a sub-tribe of the Bhumij in Mánbhum who claim to be connected with the zamindars of pargana Barabhum. The zamindars, on the other hand, affect to be Rajputs, and disown all affinity with the Bhumij tribe.

Barabihá, a section of Páns in Chota Nagpur.

Bará-Bráhman, an ironical synonym for Agradáni Brahman, *q.v.*

Barachain, a respectable division of the Chain caste in Behar and the North-Western Provinces, who claim to be somewhat superior to ordinary Chains. They are agriculturists, and their women prepare and sell vegetables. It is not clear that the Barachain have as yet formed themselves into an endogamous group, but they appear to be on the way to do so.

Baradái, a sub-tribe of Rajputs in Western Bengal.

Barágáin, a sept of the Suryabansi sub-tribe of Rajputs in Behar.

Báráhake Máhto, a section of the Biyáhut and Kharidáhá Kalwárs in Behar.

Bára-Hazár, a sub-caste of Cheros in Palamau.

Báraházari, a sub-caste of Telis and Kaibarttas in Bengal.

Bárah-Gurung, a sub-tribe of Gurungs in Darjiling.

Baráhi, a sept of the Surajbansi division of Rajputs in Behar; a *thar* or sept of Gurungs in Darjiling.

Baráhil, a zamindári servant, employed generally in the collection of rent and on the duties of a bailiff.

Barai, a synonym for Bárui.

Baráiá, Baraihiá, a sept of the Suryabans sub-tribe of Rajputs in Behar.

Baraij, a synonym for Barai, *q.v.*

Baráik, a title (signifying *great*) of Jadubansi Rajputs; of Binjhiás, Rautias, Chiks or Páns, and of Khandáits in Chota Nagpur.

Baráik or **Chik-Baráik**, a sub-caste of Páns in Chota Nagpur.

Baráili, a section of Kámis in Darjiling.

Bárajáti, a sub-caste of Khatris in Bengal.

Baraji, *Barajibi*, a synonym for Barui.

Barákar, a sub-caste of Koiris.

Bará-kharak, a section of the Pailwár sub-caste of Dosádhs in Behar.

Barál, a *gáin* of the Sándilya *gotra* of Rárhi Brahmans in Bengal; a *thar* of the Dhartá-Kausik *gotra* of Nepáli Brahmans; a title of Subarnabaniks in Bengal. In the case of the latter intermarriage is prohibited within the title, which has therefore developed into a section.

Barál, *Bhariál*, a title of Brahmans, said to be a corruption of Batabyál.

Barambhát, *Barnabhát*, *Birmbhát*, a sub-caste of Bháts in Behar.

Bará-mián, a term of address, originally Persian, used in speaking to an elderly and respectable or venerable person, or to the head of a village. The term is properly a Mahomedan one, and is only used by those Hindus who have come a good deal into contact with Mahomedans.

Barandiá, a section of *grihasth* or householding Bairágis in Chota Nagpur.

Baranwár, *Baranwál*, *Banwár*, a sub-caste of Baniyas in Behar, divided into the following sections:—**Alchárá, Barbigahiá, Bariá, Bhawániá, Dhekh, Mirchaiá, Malhán, Tiliá.** A man may not marry a woman of his own section or of the section to which his mother belonged before her marriage. As a woman changes her section on marriage, this rule is usually expressed by saying that the section of the maternal grandfather is excluded. Beyond the operation of the rule of exogamy, prohibited degrees are reckoned by the usual formula. Baranwárs marry their daughters as infants, forbid widows to marry again, and do not recognise divorce. Their marriage ceremony is of the standard type, with this peculiarity that *pánigrahan*, or the formal gift of the bride to the bridegroom, is omitted when, owing to the poverty of the bride's parents, the wedding takes place in the bridegroom's house. They are orthodox Hindus, usually of the Vaishnava sect, and affect to employ only Gaur Brahmans as their priests. If, however, these are not to be had, they will content themselves with members of the Maithil and Srotri groups. Baranwárs are mostly shopkeepers, and only a small proportion of them have taken to agriculture.

Barapatti, a sub-caste of Telis in Bengal.

Barar, a sub-section of the Levátiá section of Majhraut Goálás in Behar.

Bararási, a section of Tántis in Bengal.

Bara-Samáj, a sub-caste of Dhobás in Hughli.

Barásh, a title of Tántis in Bengal.

Bara-Sudhá, a sub-caste of Sudhás in Orissa.

Barát, a title of Baidyas and Mayarás in Bengal.

Bárátaba, boar, a totemistic sept of Juángs in Orissa.

Barbáik, a *pangat* or section of Dosádhs in Behar.

Barbariá, a *mul* or section of the Ghosin sub-caste of Goálás in Behar.

Barbattá, a section of the Tirhutiyá sub-caste of Doms in Behar.

Barbigahiá, a section of the Baranwár sub-caste of Baniyás in Behar.

Barbora, a sept of Chakmás in the Hill Tracts of Chittagong.

Bárchain, a section of the Chain sub-caste of Nuniás in Behar.

Barchi, spearman, a sub-sept of the Saren sept of Santáls.

Bard, a sept of Dhenuárs in Chota Nagpur.

Bárdá, a totemistic sept of the Bhumij tribe in Western Bengal, the members of which do not touch or eat the yam or sweet potato; a section of Korás in Chota Nagpur.

Bardarhá, a section of the Banodhiá and Jaiswár Kalwárs in Behar.

Barddhamáni, a sub-caste of Támbulis in Bengal.

Barddhan, a title of Dakshin-Rárhi and Bangaja Káyasths, and of Kaibarttas and Subarnabaniks in Bengal.

Bardhiá, a sub-caste of Kumhárs in Behar; also a sept of Rajputs in Behar.

Bardi, a section of Páns in Chota Nagpur.

Bardiá, a sept of Rajputs in Behar.

Bardiár, a section of the Amashta Káyasths in Behar.

Bardwáná, a group of the Áswini Tántis and Dwádas Telis in Bengal.

Bardwániyá, a sub-caste of Águris and Sutradhars in Western Bengal.

Báre, a section of the Kádar caste in Behar which intermarries only with the Mirdáha, Kampti, and Ráut sections.

Bárendra, *Várendra*, a sub-caste of Brahmans in Bengal, who allege that their ancestors were brought by Adisur from Kanauj in order to perform certain sacrifices, the local Brahmans having degenerated and lost their ceremonial purity. For a fuller account of the Barendra sub-caste, see the article Brahman. A sub-caste of Kumhárs, Tántis, Telis, Baidyas, Báruis, Jugis, Chásádhobás, and Káyasths in Bengal; of Kámárs in Murshedabad, who in Pabna are also called Panch Samáj; of Goálás and Sunris in Bengal; of Kaibarttas in Murshedabad; of Nápits and the group of Phulkátá Mális in Bengal.

Bareya, a *thar* or sept of Mangars in Darjiling.

Bargahá or *Bargáhi*, a title of Rajputs who are domestic servants of the Rájás of Chota Nagpur.

Bargáin, a *mul* or section of the Kanaujiá sub-caste of Sonárs in Behar.

Bargáir, a sept of the Suryabansi Rajputs in Behar.

Bargáit, one who cultivates the land on an agreement by which the cultivator engages to pay the landlord half the produce, the latter providing half the seed and paying the whole revenue.

Bargamáet, a section of the Dhaprá and Pachainyá sub-castes of Doms in Behar.

Bargharri, the twelve brethren, a sept of the Chhothar sub-tribe of Limbus in Darjiling.

Bargoár, Bargwár, a sub-caste of Goálás in Behar, who are believed to have separated from the parent caste by reason of their taking service (*khawási*) in the houses of the higher castes. They also keep cattle, sell milk, and cultivate land. Bargoárs rank with Kurmis, Koiris, etc., and Brahmans can take water from their hands. They ordinarily marry their daughters as infants, adult-marriage being looked upon as exceptional and not quite respectable. Widows are allowed to marry again, but divorce is not recognised. It deserves notice that Bargoárs have none of the exogamous sections so numerous among the Goálas, and regulate their marriages by the formula of prohibited degrees explained in the introductory essay.

Bar-gohri, a sub-caste of Khandáits, Rajwárs, and Rautiás in Chota Nagpur.

Bargwál, the title of a class of Srotriya Brahmans who act as servants to the Maharaja of Darbhanga.

Barhá, hog, a totemistic sept of Mundas in Chota Nagpur.

Barhadagiá, a section of Goálás in Behar.

Barhai, a synonym for Barhi.

Barhambiá, a section of Bábhans in Behár.

Barhampurái-Barhampur, a *mul* of the Gautam section of Maithil Brahmans in Behar.

Barhampuriá, a section of Bábhans in Behar.

Barhari, a section of the Karan sub-caste of Káyasths in Behar.

Barháriá, a sub-caste of Telis in Behar.

Barhariá ke pánre, a section of the Biyáhut and Kharidáhá Kalwárs in Behar.

Barharoa, a wild fruit, a sept of Telis in Chota Nagpur.

Barhi, *Barhai*, the carpenter caste of Behar, claiming descent from the celestial architect and artificer Viswakarmá. The word *barhi* seems to be a corruption of the Sanskrit *Badhik*, from *bardh*, 'to bore,' and the caste may probably be regarded as a functional group composed of members of several intermediate castes, who have been drawn together by the attraction of a common occupation.

Internal structure.

The Barhis of Behar are divided into six sub-castes, as shown in Appendix I, the members of which do not intermarry. I cannot ascertain the precise basis of these divisions. According to some, the distinction between the Kanaujiá and Maghayá depends on the former working in wood only and the latter in both wood and iron; while others say that the Maghayá are house-carpenters and work on a larger and coarser scale than the Kanaujiá, who are turners, cabinet-makers, and the like. Again, the Lohár sub-caste in Bhágalpur work only in iron, but disclaim all connexion with the Lohárs, whom they regard as people of a different race. The Kamar-Kalla sub-caste have no settled homes, but wander about, exhibiting marionettes (*kát-putli*) and doing odd jobs like gypsies. Their sections (*mul* or *dih*) are mostly of the territorial type, but a few of the Brahmanical *gotras* have been borrowed of late years. Usually the prohibition of intermarriage extends only to women belonging to a man's own *mul*, and the rule is supplemented by the standard formula of degrees; but among Maghayá Barhis seven, or according to some accounts nine, *muls* are excluded. In the same sub-caste we also find the hypergamous divisions **Thákur, Rái,** and **Kuar.** The Thákur can take wives from the other two groups as well as their own, but will not give their daughters to men of a lower group. So also a man of the Rái group will marry a Kuar woman, while a man of the Kuar group cannot aspire to marry a Rái woman. Wherever the custom of hypergamy prevails, the preponderance of women in the higher groups and the consequent demand for husbands have necessarily led to the introduction of infant-marriage, which, again, has spread by imitation. Among the Maghayá Barhis of Darbhanga girls are married between the ages of three and five; and so firmly has the fashion established itself, that it is difficult to find a husband for a girl who is more than five years old.

Marriage.

Adult-marriage, however, is not entirely unknown among the other sub-castes, although all aver that infant-marriage is the rule. The marriage ceremony differs little from the standard form for middle-class Hindus in Behar, which has been described by Mr. Grierson in *Behar Peasant Life*, pages 362-73, except that instead of the parents of the parties exchanging paddy (*dhánbatti*) when the marriage has been agreed upon, they exchange betel-nut. This ceremony is called *pánbatti*. Polygamy is permitted in the event of the first wife being barren or suffering from some serious physical defect. A widow may marry again by the *sagai* form. Although such marriages are supposed to be arranged entirely by the parents of the widow, she appears to have some liberty of choice in the matter, and may marry any one outside the prohibited degrees. As is the case with other castes, it often happens that she marries her deceased husband's younger brother; and this is considered a proper thing to do, but no special pressure appears to be exercised in order to compel her to do so. Divorce is effected with the sanction of the caste council (*pancháyat*) on the complaint of the husband in case of adultery, or on the application of both husband and wife on the ground of inability to agree. Divorced women may marry again by the *sagai* form. This privilege, however, does not extend to a woman taken in adultery with a man of another caste. In that case no question of formal divorce arises: she is simply turned out of the caste, and usually ends by becoming a regular prostitute.

Religion.

The religion of the Barhis is simply the average Hinduism of the middle classes of Behar, and calls for no special remark. The caste employ Tirhutiá Brahmans for the worship of the greater gods, and these Brahmans are not held to incur any social degradation by performing these functions. Their special god is Viswakarmá, who is worshipped once a year, on the seventh of Sráwan, and when a son is apprenticed to the trade. On these occasions homage is done to the tools of the craft,—the adze (*basúla*), chisel (*rukháni*), and saw (*ára*), and a goat whose right ear has been slit, and a new waist-cloth, are offered to the god and afterwards presented to a Brahman. In addition to Bandi, Goraiya, the Pánch Pir, and the other village gods common in Behar, Barhis also offer sweetmeats and *ganja* to Ugri Mahráj, a sort of patron saint, whose origin and functions I have not been able to ascertain. They also worship the standard yard (*káni* or *gaj*).

In point of social standing Barhis rank with Goálás, Hajams, Koiris, etc., and Brahmans will take water from their hands. Their practice in the matter of diet does not differ from that of other orthodox Hindus of the same class. They will smoke with Lohárs. They believe carpentry to be their original occupation, but outside the larger towns many of them are now engaged in agriculture, and hold lands as occupancy and non-occupancy raiyats.

Social status.

The following statement shows the number and distribution of Barhis in 1872 and 1881:—

DISTRICT.	1872.	1881.	DISTRICT.	1872.	1881.
Patna	23,660	26,253	Santál Parganas	3,456	4,357
Gya	35,701	36,182	Cuttack	17,184	18,149
Shahabad	13,093	14,702	Puri	9,875	11,202
Tirhut { Darbhanga ...	39,730	38,343	Balasore	5,876	7,385
Tirhut { Mozufferpur ...		15,678	Tributary States	4,945	3,736
Saran	16,714	16,939	Hazaribagh	16,100	25,070
Champaran	6,745	9,114	Lohardaga	6,366	11,747
Monghyr	29,152	29,835	Singbhum	342	89
Bhagalpur	4,596	9,733	Manbhum	2,027	......
Purniah	12,703	14,632	Tributary States	114	2,067

Bárhi, a section of the Sátmuliá Maghayá sub-caste of Kándus in Behar.

Barhioth, a territorial section of Barhis in Behar.

Barhwatiá, a sept of Rajputs in Behar.

Bari, flower, a totemistic sept of Mundas in Chota Nagpur.

Bári, a small caste of Behar, who are supposed to have come from the North-West Provinces or Oude. They are employed as makers of the leaf-platters (*doná, khoná, khadoná, pattal, patri, patta, patrauri, panmárá*[1]) used at Hindu entertainments and festivals. They also make and carry torches, and sometimes sell betel-leaves. Their social rank is about the same as that of the Hajjám. Mr. Nesfield regards the Bári as "merely an offshoot from the semi-savage tribes known as Baumánush and Musahar. He still associates with them at times; and if the demand for plates and cups (owing to some temporary cause, such as a local fair or an unusual multitude of marriages) happens to become larger than he can at once supply, he gets them secretly made by his ruder kinsfolk and retails them at a higher rate, passing them off as his own production." If this view is correct, the Bári are a branch of a non-Áryan tribe who have been given a fairly respectable position in the Hindu system in consequence of the demand for leaf-plates, which are largely used by the highest as well as by the lowest caste. Instances of this sort, in which a non-Aryan or mixed group is promoted on grounds of necessity or convenience to a higher status than their antecedents would entitle them to claim, are not unknown in other castes, and must have occurred frequently in outlying parts of the country,

[1] *Behar Peasant Life*, p. 721.

where the Aryan settlements were scanty and imperfectly supplied with the social apparatus demanded by the theory of ceremonial purity. Thus the undoubtedly non-Aryan Bhuiyás have in parts of Chota Nagpur been recognised as *jal-ácharani;* and it may be conjectured that the Kahárs themselves only attained this privilege in virtue of their employment as palanquin-bearers. Of course in any case there is no breach of continuity and nothing resembling the sudden elevation of a social group. But a gradual upheaval takes place; the social levels are altered, and the fiction is maintained that things have been so all along.

The following statement shows the number and distribution of the Bári caste in 1872 and 1881:—

District.	1872.	1881.	District.	1872.	1881.
Patna	928	661	Bhagalpur	305	571
Gya	1,361	2,180	Purniah	......	2,428
Shahabad	4,609	5,234	Santál Parganas	118	20
Tirhut { Darbhanga ...	2,328	1,611	Hazaribagh	......	421
Tirhut { Mozufferpur ...		2,322	Lohardaga	......	428
Saran	5,044	4,521	Manbhum	......	194
Champaran	2,940	3,758	Tributary States	......	141
Monghyr	1,863	1,010	Darjiling	......	358

Bariá, a section of the Barnawár sub-caste of Baniyás in Behar.

Bariaro, a sept of Tántis in Chota Nagpur.

Bárik, a *pangat* or section of Dosádhs in Behar; a section of the Kádar caste in Behar which intermarries with the Kápar, Marik, Darbe, Mánjhi, Hazári, Naiyá, and Kampti sections, but not with the Mandar, Mirdáha, Ráut, and Báre; a section of Maghayá Kumhárs in Behar. A title of Goálás, Kaibarttas and Nápits in Bengal, and of Bhandáris in Orissa.

Bariswár, a *pur* or section of Sákadwipi Brahmans in Behar.

Báriya, a knife-grinder, razor-setter, etc.

Barjo, name of ancestor's village, a sept of Mundas in Chota Nagpur.

Barjoki, fig-tree roots, a totemistic sept of Mundas in Chota Nagpur.

Barkádeswári, a sub-caste of Kharwárs, who are also called Deswári; it is contradistinguished from Chotka Deswári.

Barkandáz (P. *bark*, 'lightning,' and *andáz*, 'who casts'), properly a matchlock-man, but commonly an armed retainer, an armed unmounted employé of a civil department. The term was especially used to denote the old zemindari police, and jail warders at the present day are often spoken as *barkandáz*.

Barki-dángi, a sub-caste of Koiris in Behar who do not permit widows to remarry.

Barla, *Ficus Indica*, a totemistic sept of Nágeswars and Mundas in Chota Nagpur.

Bárlá, a section of Khariás in Chota Nagpur.

Barlos, a *thar* or sept of Khambus in Darjiling.

Barmá, a title of Dakshin-Rárhi and Bangaja Káyasths.

Barmáit, a section of Sonárs in Behar.

Barman, (i) "wearer of armour," a title of Rajputs, Khatris, and Káyasths; (ii) a native of Burma.

Barmosiá, a section of the Kasarwáni sub-caste of Baniyás in Behar.

Barna or Patita Brahman, a sub-caste, or rather an aggregate of sub-castes, of Brahmans in Bengal, formed of as many endogamous groups as there are numbers of Hindu Sudra castes, whom they serve as priests.

Barnait, a section of Bábhans and of the Maghayá sub-caste of Barhis in Behar.

Barna-Kul, a sub-caste of Tántis in Bengal.

Barnakule, a sub-caste of Sunris in Western Bengal, who are vegetable-sellers.

Barnár, a sept of the Chandrabansi division of Rajputs in Behar.

Barnasankar (Sansk. *barna*, 'caste,' and *sankar*, 'mixed'), a mixed caste, properly the designation of the large class of castes supposed to have been formed by intermarriage between members of the four original castes. The term is also used to denote the offspring of illicit intercourse between members of different castes, and bears the same meaning as Bidurá, Chhokar, Doglá or Dográ, Járaj, Krishnapakshi, Málzadá, Ságarpeshá, and Surathwala.

Barna-sil, a title of barbers who shave the Chandáls in Eastern Bengal.

Barna Sreni, an indefinite term, probably denoting either members of the *barna sankar*, mixed castes, or the Brahmans, colloquially known as Barna-Brahmans, who serve those castes.

Barni, a section of Sonárs in Behar.

Barniá, a sept of Rajputs in Behar.

Barnawár, Barnwár, *Banwár*, a sub-caste of Baniyás engaged in trade, agriculture, and service in Behar. They abstain from spirits and forbid widows to marry again.

Baroá, a sept of Khariás and Asuras in Chota Nagpur.

Baroár, a section of Goráits in Chota Nagpur.

Baroha, a sept of Lohars in Chota Nagpur.

Barpai, a sept of Hos in Chota Nagpur.

Barpárá, a sub-caste of Sunris in Behar.

Barpaserá, a section of the Banodhiá and Jaiswár Kalwárs in Behar.

Barphungpuso, a sept of Lepchas in Darjiling.

Barra, a section of Newars in Darjiling.

Barsái, a *pur* or section of Sákadwipi Brahmans in Behar.

Barsam, a section of the Majraut sub-caste of Goálás in Behar holding the title of Marar, whose profession is to make curd.

Barthoár, a section of Awadhiá Hajáms in Behar.

Baruá, a mixed caste in Chittagong who are descendants of Magh fathers and Bengali mothers.

Baruá, (i) a title of certain castes in Assam; (ii) a title of village headmen exercising police functions in Midnapur and Orissa; (iii) a group of the Aswini Tántis in Bengal.

Baruár, a section of the Biyáhut and Kharidáhá Kalwárs in Behar.

Bárui, "**Barai**," the names of the two castes engaged in Bengal and Behar, respectively, in the cultivation of *piper betel*, ordinarily known as *pán* (Sansk. *parna*), *the* leaf *par excellence*. Although their occupation is the same, provincial and linguistic distinctions separate the Bengali-speaking Bárui of Bengal and the Hindi-speaking Barai of Behar into two entirely distinct castes, who do not intermarry or eat together, and whose domestic usages differ in important particulars. They will therefore be separately treated here.

Origin and internal structure.

Regarding the origin of the Báruis of Bengal several traditions are current. The popular legend represents them as specially created by Brahma in order to relieve the Brahmans from the labour of growing betel, which was found to interfere with their religious duties. The Játi-Málá makes them the offspring of a Tánti woman by a man of the Goálá caste, while the Brihadharma Purana describes their father as a Brahman and their mother as a Sudra. Other traditions assign to them a Kshatriya or Káyasth father and a Sudra mother. At the present day the Báruis are divided into four endogamous sub-castes:—(1) Rárhi, (2) Bárendra, (3) Náthán, (4) Kotá. Within these again we find a number of the standard Brahmanical *gotras*. The latter groups, however, appear to be mainly ornamental, for marriage in most places is allowed with persons belonging to the same *gotra*, provided they are not *Samanodakas*. As the fact of their belonging to this class would in any case have been a conclusive bar to marriage, it follows that the sections are exogamous only in theory, and we may assume that they were borrowed *dignitatis causâ* from the system of the higher castes. It may further be surmised that the Bárui caste is made up of members of various respectable castes, who were drawn together by the common occupation of betel-growing, and is not, as many castes undoubtedly are, a homogeneous offshoot from a single caste or tribe. The contradictory character of the legends regarding its origin, in which several different castes figure, tends on the whole to bear out this view.

Marriage.

Báruis marry their daughters as infants, forbid widows to marry again, and do not allow divorce. Polygamy is admitted only in the sense that a man may marry a second wife when the first proves barren. Hypergamy is unknown, and a bride-price is paid to the parents of the bride. Certain families enjoy the hereditary rank of Gostipati, or head of a clique or party within the caste; but this involves no restrictions on marriage, and the members of such families give their daughters in marriage to ordinary Báruis. The marriage ceremony of the Bárui differs little from that in use among Brahmans, except that the rite of *Kusandiká* is not always insisted upon. After the gift and acceptance of the bride, the bridegroom stands behind her, and, taking her hands in his, lifts an earthen vessel containing parched paddy, ghee, plantains, and betel leaves, and pours the contents on a fire kindled with straw. The couple then make obeisance to Agni, and the ceremony is held to be complete.

Religion.

In matters of religion the Báruis follow the usages of all orthodox Hindus. Most of them belong to the Sákta sect, and a few are Vaishnavas. Saivism is said to be unknown among them. For all the standard offices of religion they employ Brahmans, who stand on an equal footing with the Brahmans who serve the other members of the Navasák group. In some places they have also special ceremonies of their own. On the 4th of Baisakh (April–May) the patroness of betel cultivation is worshipped in some places in Bengal with offerings of flowers, rice, sweetmeats, and sandal-wood paste. Along the banks of the Lakhya in Eastern Bengal the Baruis celebrate, without a Brahman, the *Navami Puja* in honour of Ushas ('Ἠώς, Aurora) on the ninth of the waxing moon in Ásin (September–October). Plantains, sugar, rice, and sweetmeats are placed in the centre of the pân garden, from which the worshippers retire, but after a little return, and, carrying out the offerings, distribute them among the village children. In Bikrampúr the deity invoked on the above date is Sungáí, one of the many forms of Bhagabatí. The reason given by the Báruis for not engaging the services of a Brahman is the following:—A Brahman was the first cultivator of the betel. Through neglect the plant grew so high that he used his sacred thread to fasten up its tendrils, but as it still shot up faster than he could supply thread, its charge was given to a Káyasth. Hence it is that a Brahman cannot enter a pân garden without defilement.

Occupation.

At the present day some Báruis have taken to trade, while others are found in Government service or as members of the learned professions. The bulk of the caste, however, follow their traditional occupation. Betel cultivation is a highly specialised business, demanding considerable knowledge and extreme care to rear so delicate a plant. The pân garden (*bara*, *barej*) is regarded, says Dr. Wise, as an almost sacred spot. Its greatest length is always north and south, while the entrances must be east and west. The enclosure, generally eight feet high, is supported by hijul (Sansk. ijjala, *Barringtonia acutangula*) trees or betel-nut palms. The former are cut down periodically, but the palms are allowed to grow, as they cast little shade and add materially to the profits of the garden. The sides are closely matted with reeds, jute stalks, or leaves of the date or Palmyra palm, while *nal* grass is often grown outside to protect the interior from wind and the sun's rays. The top is not so carefully covered in, wisps of grass being merely tied along the trellis work over the plants. A sloping footpath leads down the centre of the enclosure, towards which the furrows between the plants trend, and serves to drain off rain as it falls, it being essential for the healthy growth of the plant that the ground be kept dry.

The pân plant is propagated by cuttings, and the only manures used are pák-matí, or decomposed vegetable mould excavated from tanks, and *khali*, the refuse of oil-mills. The plant being a fast growing one, its shoots are loosely tied with grass to upright poles, while thrice a year it is drawn down and coiled at the root. As a low temperature injures the plant by discolouring the leaves, special care must be taken during the cold season that the enclosure and its valuable contents are properly sheltered. Against vermin no trouble is required, as caterpillars and insects avoid the plant on account of its pungency. Weeds are carefully eradicated, but certain culinary vegetables, such as pepper, varieties of pumpkins, and cucumbers, *palwal* (*Trichosanthes dioeca*), and *baigun* (egg-plant, *Solanum melongena*), are permitted to be grown. Pân leaves are plucked throughout the year, but in July and August are most abundant, and therefore cheapest; while a garden, if properly looked after, continues productive from five to ten years. Four pân leaves make one *ganda*, and the *bira*, or measure by which they are sold, now-a-days contains in Eastern Bengal twenty *gandas*, although formerly it contained twenty-four. In the *Bháti* country (Bakarganj), thirty-six *gandas* go to the *bira*. Pân leaves are never retailed by the Bárui himself, but are sold wholesale to agents (*paikárs*), or directly to the pân-sellers.

The varieties of the piper betel are numerous, but it is probable that in different districts distinct names are given to the same species. The *kafúri* or camphor-scented pân, allowed by all natives to be the most delicately flavoured, is only grown at Sunárgaon in Dacca and Mandalghát in Midnapur for export to Calcutta, where it fetches a fancy price. The next best is the *sánchi*, which often sells for four annas a bíra. This is of a pale green colour, and if kept for a fortnight loses in pungency and gains flavour. The commoner sorts are the *desi*, *bangala*, *bhátiál*, *dháldogga*, *ghás pân*, grown best in Bakarganj, and a very large-leaved variety called *babná*. The usual market price of the inferior kinds is from one to two pice a bíra.

It has been mentioned that the *bara* is regarded as almost sacred, and the superstitious practices in vogue resemble those of the silk-worm breeder. The Bárui will not enter it until he has bathed and washed his clothes, while the low-caste man employed in digging is required to bathe before he commences work. Animals found inside are driven out, while women ceremonially unclean dare not enter within the gate. A Brahman never sets foot inside, and old men have a prejudice against entering it. It has, however, been known to be used for assignations. At the present day individuals belonging to the Dhobá, Chandál, Kaibartta, Sunri, and many higher and lower castes, as well as Muhammadans, manage pân gardens, but they omit the ceremonies necessary for preserving the *bara* clean and unpolluted.

Social status.

The social standing of the Báruis is sufficiently defined by stating that they belong to the Nabasák. They eat goats, deer, pigeons, fish, and the leavings of Brahmans, and drink country spirits. They will drink with

Kaibarttas, and smoke in their company, but will not use the same *hookah*. In respect of their relations to the land their position is fairly high. Some have risen to be zamindars, others are tenure-holders or substantial occupancy raiyats. Instances of their having come to be day-labourers or nomadic cultivators are so rare as to be practically unknown.

The following statement shows the numbers and distribution of the Báruis in 1872 and 1881 :—

District.	1872.	1881.	District.	1872.	1881.
Bardwan	11,508	3,007	Bogra	671	933
Bankura	979	2,749	Pabna	2,577	2,104
Birbhum	2,269	2,059	Darjiling	343	319
Midnapur	7,001	5,995	Jalpigori	405	377
Hughli	7,400	3,607	Kuch Behar	......	106
Howrah		4,219	Dacca	15,931	17,524
24-Parganas	6,931	4,733	Faridpur	6,120	8,357
Nadiya	4,279	3,329	Bakarganj	14,453	9,401
Jessore	18,794	9,512	Maimansinh	6,435	8,440
Khulna	......	11,983	Chittagong	12,448	343
Murshedabad	3,683	3,014	Noakhali	3,465	2,187
Dinajpur	2,606	1,370	Tipperah	8,982	4,804
Rajshahye	831	419	Hill Tracts of Chittagong...	......	6
Rangpur	1,374	1,525			

The **Barai** of Behar bear the title Ráut, and are divided into the following sub-castes :—(1) Maghayá, (2) Jaiswár, (3) Chaurasia, (4) Semeryá, (5) Sokhwá. They have only two sections, Kásyapa and Nág, and regulate their marriages by the formula of prohibited degrees already quoted. Marriage is both infant and adult, the former being deemed more respectable. Widow-marriage is permitted by the *sagai* form. The widow may marry her late husband's younger brother, but is not compelled to do so. If, however, she marries an outsider, she forfeits all claim to share in her deceased husband's property, and the custody of her children usually rests with his family. A man may marry two wives, but not more. Divorce is not recognised : indiscretions within the caste are winked at ; but a woman who goes wrong with an outsider is turned out of the caste, and probably ends by becoming a regular prostitute. It will be observed that the practice of widow-marriage and the recognition of adult-marriage for females sharply distinguish the Barai from the Bárui, and are sufficient of themselves to form a conclusive bar to intermarriage between the two groups. Curiously enough, the standard tradition regarding the origin of the Barai alleges that they were formerly Brahmans, who were turned out of the sacred caste because they allowed widows to marry again.

Marriage.

Most Barais are Hindus of the Sákta sect. Their minor gods are Mahabirji (Hanumán), Bandi, Goraiyá and Sokhá. The last mentioned is held in special reverence and awe, and it is believed that when his worship is neglected great disasters come upon the pân garden. Maithil, Kanojiá, and Srotri Brahmans are employed by the Barai in the

Religion.

worship of the greater gods; the *di minores* being usually propitiated by the members of the family without the intervention of Brahmans.

Occupation.

Betel cultivation is the main business of the Barai, to which they add the preparation of lime and *khair* or *kath*,ʳ an astringent extract from the wood of several species of acacia (*Acacia catechu*, Willd., the *khair*; *Acacia suma*, Kurz, *acsundra*, D.C., and probably more).[1] For a description of the methods of betel-growing followed in Behar, I may refer to Grierson's *Behar Peasant Life*, pages 248–49. The statement on page 249, that "the betel-nut, which is the fruit of the *areca catechu*, is called *supári* or *sopári*," seems to require correction. The following extracts from Colonel Yule's *Glossary* put the matter in a clear light:—

"**Betel**, *s.* The leaf of the *piper betel*, L., chewed with the dried **areca**-nut (which is thence improperly called *betel-nut*, a mistake as old as Fryer—1673—see page 40), *chunam*, etc., by the natives of India and the Indo-Chinese countries. The word is Malayál. *vettila*, *i.e. veru* + *ila* = 'simple or mere leaf,' and comes to us through the Port. *betre* and *betle*."

"**Pawn**, *s.* The **betel-leaf**. Hind. *pan*, from the Sansk. *parna*, 'a leaf.' It is a North-Indian term, and is generally used for the combination of betel, areca-nut, lime, etc., which is politely offered (along with otto of roses) to visitors, and which intimates the termination of the visit. This is more fully termed **pawn-sooparie** (*supári* is Hind. for areca)."

"**Areca**, *s.* The seed (in common parlance the nut) of the palm, *Areca catechu*. L., commonly, though somewhat improperly, called 'betel-nut'; the term *betel* (*q.v.*) belonging in reality to the *leaf*, which is chewed along with the *areca*. Though so widely cultivated, the palm is unknown in a truly indigenous state. The word is Malayálan *adakka*, and comes to us through the Portuguese."

In Beames' edition of Elliot's *Glossary*, vol. ii, p. 231 *s.v.* **Bírá**, the ingredients of *pán-supári* are stated, on the authority of the Kánun-i-Islám, to be "betel leaves, areca or betel-nut, catechu, quick-lime, aniseed, coriander seed, cardamoms, and cloves."

Social status.

Barais rank with the *ácharani* castes of Behar, and Brahmans can take water and sweetmeats from their hands. Their diet is that of the average orthodox Hindu. Unlike the Bárui of Bengal, they will not eat the leavings of Brahmans, nor will they drink spirituous liquors. The Barhi and Lohár are the lowest castes from whom a Barai will take water or sweetmeats. Cooked food, of course, they will only eat with people of their own caste and sub-caste. As regards their agricultural position, few of them appear to have risen above the status of occupancy raiyat.

The following table gives the number and distribution of the Baṛais and Támbulis or Támolis in 1872 and 1881. In the former year the figures of both castes are included, and in the latter they

---

[1] Yule's *Glossary*, *s.v.* Catechu.

are shown separately, so that absolutely accurate statistics cannot be prepared :—

District.	1872.	1881.		District.	1872.	1881.	
		Barai.	Tamoli.			Barai.	Tamoli.
Patna	8,675	4,431	5,024	Santál Parganas ...	7,320	2,287	3,186
Gya	8,141	5,863	3,890	Cuttack...	4,416	1,746	4,188
Shahabad	7,189	2,573	5,456	Puri	1,002	374	79
Tirhut { Darbhanga	32,014	11,187	3,966	Balasore	7,112	3,122	2,193
Tirhut { Mozufferpur		12,963	4,660	Tributary States ...	1,593	172	969
Saran	10,963	7,526	1,980	Hazaribagh	1,578	811	1,221
Champaran	9,714	10,455	1,031	Lohardaga	4,416	1,967	1,585
Monghyr	12,848	14,087	4,517	Singbhum	560	32	45
Bhagalpur	7,270	6,381	1,312	Manbhum	12,610	7,590	3,465
Purniah	8,297	4,802	1,484	Tributary States ...	48	54	115
Maldah	2,256	1,541	422				

Barui, a section of Báis Sonárs in Behar.

Barukandal, a totemistic sept of Mundas in Chota Nagpur who cannot touch the kusum-tree.

Barunda, a big frog, a totemistic sept of Mundas in Chota Nagpur.

Barupendil, kusum-tree, a totemistic sept of Mundas in Chota Nagpur.

Baruwa, a sept of Chakmás in the Hill Tracts of Chittagong.

Barwa, small cocoon, a totemistic sept of Mundas and Oraons in Chota Nagpur.

Barwáik, a title of Thárus in Champaran.

Barwár, a *pur* or section of Sákadwipi Brahmans in Behar; a sub-sept of the Hansda sept of Santáls; a section of Rájputs in Behar.

Basa, a tree, a totemistic sept of Oraons in Chota Nagpur.

Basáithi, a *mul* or section of the Naomuliá or Majraut subcaste of Goálás in Behar.

Basaiyá, a section of Kaserás in Behar.

Basák, a title of Tántis in Bengal.

Basárh, a *mul* or section of the Naomuliá or Majraut subcaste of Goálás in Behar.

Básáriá, a *mul* or section of the Tinmuliá Madhesiá and Bhojpuria sub-castes of Halwáis in Behar.

Basaroar, a small hawk, a totemistic sept of Mundas in Chota Nagpur.

Basbáit, Baswait, a *kul* or section of Bábhans in Behar.

Bás-baniya, a dealer in fragrant articles, a perfumer.

Basbariá, a sept of Rajputs in Behar.

Básdebpur, a section of Bhojpuria Halwáis in Behar.

Bashariá, a sept of Rajputs in Behar.

Basahe, a *mul* of the Garg section of Maithil Brahmans in Behar.

Basisht, *Vasishtha*, a section of Bábhans in Behar. The name, which denotes one of the Vedic Rishis or sages, appears to have been borrowed from the Brahmanical system in comparatively recent times. Most of the Bábhan section names belong to the territorial type.

Basiari, a synonym for Vaisya, *q.v.*

Basiniá, the headman of a village in Rangpur.

Basishtha, a *gotra* or section of Brahmans, Baidyas, and Káyasths in Bengal, and of Sudras in Eastern Bengal.

Báski, a sept of Santáls.

Basmait, a section of Bábhans in Behar.

Basriár, a sept of Asuras in Chota Nagpur.

Bastibarhoná, a *mul* or section of the Naomuliá or Majraut sub-caste of Goálás in Behar.

Basu, a titular adjunct to names borne by the Dakshin-Rárhi and Bangaja families of Káyasths or writer caste in Bengal, commonly pronounced as Bose; a sub-section of the Bharadwája section of Utkal Brahmans.

Basuári, a *gáin* of the Sándilya *gotra* of Rárhi Brahmans in Bengal.

Básudeo, an eponymous section of Rautiás in Chota Nagpur.

Básuki, a section of Brahmans and of Káyasths in Bengal.

Basuná, a sub-caste of Kámárs in Western Bengal.

Básundár, a section of the Biyáhut and Kharidáhá Kalwárs in Behar.

Baswariá, a section of Kanaujiá Lohárs in Behar.

Batabyál, Barál, a title of Brahmans in Bengal.

Batái-dár, a cultivator who shares the crop with the proprietor.

Batáli, a title of Kaibarttas and Chhutárs (carpenters) in Bengal. The word may perhaps be connected with *batáli*, a small chisel.

Batalya, a sept of Chakmás in the Hill Tracts of Chittagong.

Batásewálá, a maker of the small round sweetmeats of sugar offered up to deities at shrines and temples.

Batewár, a sub-tribe of Thárus in Behar.

Bátham, a sub-caste of Dhobis in Behar.

Bathawa or **Badhariyá**, a sub-caste of Malláhs in Behar.

Báthotiá, a section of Goálás in the North-Western Provinces.

Bathuá, *Betái*, *Betbansi*, or *Betuá*, a title of Muchis and of Chandáls whose occupation is to make baskets of *bet* or rattan, and who are recognised in some districts as a separate caste. Some of them eat pork, fowls, and beef. Certain Musalmans are called so who deal in cane-work.

Bathuait, a section of Lohárs in Behar.

Bathuáke Máhto, a section of the Biyáhut and Kharidáhá Kalwárs in Behar.

Bathuáke Ráut, a section of the Biyáhut and Kharidáhá Kalwárs in Behar.

Báthudi, a small aboriginal tribe of uncertain origin found in the Tributary States of Orissa.

Bathuet, a section of Kamárkalla Sonárs in Behar.

Bati, a sept of Chiks in Chota Nagpur.

Bátke, a labourer in the salt-works of Orissa, an assistant malangi.

Batkuar, a bird, a sept of Mundas in Chota Nagpur.

Bátor, a section of Madhesia Halwáis in Behar.

Bat-rassi, a rope-maker, chiefly of the Kahar or Malláh castes, who make twine and rope from *munj*, *san*, *káns*, and *háthi chingár*.

Batsagrámi, a *gáin* of the Bátsya *gotra* of Bárendra Brahmans in Bengal.

Batsas, a section of the Srotriya sub-caste of Utkal Brahmans in Orissa.

Batsauriark, a *pur* or section of Sákadwipi Brahmans in Behar.

Bátsil, a *gotra* or section of Agarwáls.

Bátsa, Bátsya, a *gotra* or section of Brahmans, Baidyas, Báruis, Káyasths, and Tántis in Bengal; and of Maithil Brahmans, Babhans, Khatris and Rajputs in Behar.

Battikbál, a section of the Karan sub-caste of Káyasths in Behar.

Batti-sáz, a chandler.

Battisi, a section of the Biyáhut and Kharidáhá Kalwárs in Behar.

Batu, a synonym for Brahman in Bengal.

Batuk, a section of Jugis.

Batwákariar, a *pur* or section of Sákadwipi Brahmans in Behar.

Bául, *Báolá*, *Báhul*, 'mad in love of God,' (i) a low class of mendicant Vaishnavas; (ii) a title of Káyasths and Telis in Bengal.

Baundihá, a *kul* or section of Bábhans in Behar.

Baurám, a *mul* or section of the Naomuliá or Majraut sub-caste of Goálás in Behar.

Bauri, a cultivating, earth-working, and palanquin-bearing caste of Western Bengal, whose features and complexion stamp them as of non-Aryan descent, although evidence is wanting to affiliate them to any particular tribe now in existence. Their meagre folk-lore throws no light on their origin. According to one story they were degraded for attempting to steal food from the banquet of the gods; another professes to trace them back to a mythical ancestor named Báhak Rishi (the bearer of burdens), and tells how, while returning from a marriage procession, they sold the palanquin they had been hired to carry, got drunk on the proceeds, and assaulted their *guru*, who cursed them for the sacrilege, and condemned them to rank thenceforward among the lowest castes of the community. Another name of this ancestor is Rik Muni, the same as the eponym of the Musahars or Bhuiyás, but it would be straining conjecture to infer from this any connexion between the Bauris and the Bhuiyas.

Traditions.

The Bauris are divided into the following nine sub-castes:—(1) **Mallabhumiá**, (2) **Sikhariá** or **Gobariá**, (3) **Panchakoti**, (4) **Molá** or **Mulo**, (5) **Dhuliá** or **Dhulo**, (6) **Maluá** or **Máluá**, (7) **Jhátiá** or **Jhetiá**, (8) **Káthuriá**, (9) **Páthuriá**. Some of these may perhaps be nothing more than different local names for what was originally the same sub-caste, but this point is not really very material, by reason of the marked reluctance of the lower castes to intermarry families living at a

Internal structure.

distance. Assuming, for example, that Mola or Mulo and Mallabhumia, two sub-castes of Bauris found in the 24-Parganas and Murshedabad, are really the same as the Maluá or Máluá sub-caste common in Manbhum, it would by no means follow that the eastern and western members of this sub-caste would be willing to intermarry. And if there were no intermarriage, the groups would rightly be treated as true sub-castes. On the whole therefore, in spite of the suspicious similarity of some of the names, I incline to think that the nine groups enumerated above are really distinct at the present day, whatever may have been the case some generations back. As for the origin of the sub-castes, the names Mallabhumiá, Maluá, and perhaps Molá, denote a group originally resident in pergunnah Manbhum or in the country south of the Kasái; the Dhuliá sub-caste is supposed to have come from Dhalbhum; and the Sikhariá from Sikharbhum, the tract between the Kasái and Barákar rivers, which includes the Pachete estate. Panchakoti again denotes the central portion of the Pachete estate. Gobariá is said to refer to a domestic custom of cleaning up the remnants of meals with cowdung, which has somehow come to be deemed a characteristic of the Sikhariá sub-caste; while Jhátiá is explained as denoting a group who simply sweep away the fragments of a meal without washing the place where it had been spread.

Exogamy.

The few exogamous subdivisions which we find among the Bauris have clearly been borrowed *dignitatis causâ* from the higher castes, and are inoperative for matrimonial purposes, as marriage between members of the same *gotra* is not forbidden. They profess to observe the standard formula mamerá, chacherá, etc., and in addition to prohibit marriage between persons descended from the same ancestors within seven degrees on the male and three degrees on the female side; but the caste is extremely illiterate: there is no machinery among them for maintaining genealogies, and thus guarding against consanguineous marriages, and in actual practice such marriages are believed to be far from uncommon.

The absence of compact exogamous groups, such as we find among tribes apparently closely akin to the Bauris, may possibly be due to the latter having adopted the profession of palanquin-bearing, and thus having been brought into closer contact with Hindus than was the case with their more independent congeners. Traces of totemism, however, still survive in their reverence for the red-backed heron and the dog, and perhaps in their strong objection to touching horse-dung. The heron is looked upon as the emblem of the tribe, and may not be killed or molested on pain of expulsion from the caste. Dogs also are sacred. A Bauri will on no account kill a dog or touch a dead dog's body, and the water of a tank in which a dog has been drowned cannot be used until an entire rainy season has washed the impurity away. "In regard to dogs," says Colonel Dalton, "I was gravely informed by some of their elders that as they killed and ate cows and most other animals, they deemed it right to fix on some beast which should be as sacred to them as the cow to the Bráhman, and they selected the dog, because it was a useful animal while alive, and not very nice to eat when dead—a neat reconciliation of the twinges of conscience and cravings of appetite." This ingenious explanation, however valueless in itself, shows that their own customs had become unintelligible to the Bauris themselves, and serves to illustrate the tendency to imitate Brahmanical usages.

Admission of outsiders.

Like the Bágdis, Bauris admit into their caste members of any caste higher than themselves in social standing. No regular ceremony is appointed for such occasions: the new member merely pays to the caste panchâyat a sum of money, varying from Rs. 10 to Rs. 15, to be spent on a feast, in which for the first time he openly eats with his adopted caste brethren. The origin of this singular practice, which is entirely out of accord with the spirit of the caste system at the present day, is apparently to be sought in the lax views of the Bauris and Bágdis on the subject of sexual morality. In every other caste a woman who has an intrigue with an outsider is punished by expulsion from the caste; but Bágdis and Bauris not only allow their women to live openly with men of other castes, but receive those men into their own community when, as frequently happens, they are outcasted by their own people for eating rice cooked by their mistresses.

Marriage.

Marriage among the Bauris is either infant or adult, the tendency being for those who can afford it to marry their daughters as infants. Polygamy is permitted: a man is allowed to have as many wives as he can afford to maintain. Widows may marry again, and are usually expected to marry their deceased husband's younger brother. No ceremony is gone through; the bridegroom pays Re. 1-4 to the bride's father, and gives a feast to the members of the caste. Divorce is recognised. It is effected by the husband taking away from his wife the iron ring which every married woman wears, and proclaiming to the *parámánik* and panchâyat the fact of his having divorced her. In some districts a wife may divorce her husband for ill-treatment, desertion, or adultery. Divorced wives may always marry again. The marriage ceremony in use among the Bauris of Western Bengal differs little from that of the Bágdis, except that there is no pool of water in the middle of the marriage bower, and the bride sits on the left of the bridegroom instead of facing him. In districts further east an attempt is made to follow the standard Hindu ritual, and the interchange of garlands is held to be the binding portion of the procedure.

Religion.

Bauris profess to be Hindus of the Sákta sect, but in Western Bengal, at any rate, their connexion with Hinduism is of the slenderest kind, and their favourite objects of worship are Manasá, Bhádu, Mánsingh, Barpahári, Dharmaráj, and Kudrasini. The cult of the two former deities has been described in the article on the Bagdis. Goats are sacrificed to Mánsingh, and fowls to Barpahári, which is merely another name for the "great mountain" (Marang Buru) of the Santáls. Pigs, fowls, rice, sugar, and ghee are offered to

Kudrasini on Saturdays and Sundays at the ákhra or dancing place of the village through the medium of a Bauri priest, who abstains from flesh or fish on the day preceding the sacrifice. The priest gets as his fee the fowls that are offered and the head or leg of the pig; the worshippers eat the rest. It should be mentioned here that in Western Bengal Bauris have not yet attained to the dignity of having Brahmans of their own. Their priests are men of their own caste, termed Lává or Deghariá, some of whom hold *láyáli* land rent-free or at a nominal rent as remuneration for their services. The headman of the village (*parámánik*) may also officiate as priest. The Bauris of Eastern Bengal employ a low class of Barna Brahmans. Káli and Visvakarmá are their favourite deities. In most districts Bauris have adopted the Hindu practice of burning their dead; but in Bankura corpses are buried with the head to the north and face downward, the object of this attitude being to prevent the spirit from getting out and giving trouble to the living. A rude funeral ceremony is performed on the eleventh day after death, when the relations feast together and the nearest relative of the deceased has his head shaved.

Occupation.

Agricultural labour and palanquin-bearing are supposed to be the original occupations of the caste, and this tradition corresponds pretty closely to the facts as we now find them. They work also as wood-cutters and masons, and in Bardwan a few have risen to be traders and money-lenders. In some respects they are more particular than would be expected, considering the low social position they hold. A Bauri who takes to curing leather, works as a syce, or keeps a liquor-shop, is turned out of the caste. Comparatively few Bauris are raiyats with occupancy rights, but the majority may probably be put down as under-raiyats or landless day-labourers. They were well known as indigo-cultivators and workers in the vats in the prosperous days of Bengal indgo, and nomadic tillage of *char* lands is one of their characteristic pursuits. In Manbhum and Bankura many of them hold substantial tenures on terms of police service—a fact which lends colour to the view that they are among the earliest settlers in that part of the country. Thus in Manbhum we find two *sadiáls*, one *digwár*, two *náib digwárs*, 17 village *sardárs*, and 49 *tábidárs* of the caste; while in Bankura the Bauris are represented by 14 *sardár ghatwáls*, 16 *sadiáls*, 8 *digwárs*, 375 *tábidárs*, and 554 *chákrán chaukidárs*.

Social status.

The social rank of Bauris is very low. Members of the higher castes will not take water from their hands, and they themselves eat with Bágdis, Kewats, Lohars, and the non-Aryan Kurmis of Western Bengal. They are, in fact, hardly distinguishable from the Háris of Bengal and the Ghásis of Chota Nagpur, and are despised everywhere except in Manbhum and Birbhum, where they are allowed by the Hindus to do certain menial offices which are usually done by people of higher castes. With few exceptions, they are entirely indifferent to the nice scruples regarding food, which have so important a bearing on the status of the average Hindu, for they eat beef, pork, fowls, all kinds of fish, and rats, and are much addicted to strong drink. Nevertheless they pique themselves on not eating snakes and lizards, like the Oraons.

The following statement shows the number of Bauris in 1872 and 1881 :—

District.	1872.	1881.	District.	1872.	1881.
Bardwan	70,596	77,381	Bakarganj	......	87
Bankura	76,915	117,548	Maimansinh	1	76
Birbhum	24,569	27,759	Chittagong	3	4,461
Midnapur	14,946	12,770	Tipperah	......	9
Hughli	} 780	{ 1,861	Shahabad	334	......
Howrah		4	Saran	9	......
24-Parganas	654	519	Monghyr	4	......
Nadiya	2,016	1,877	Purniah	3,188	514
Jessore	829	871	Maldah	383	509
Murshedabad	6,536	4,512	Santál Parganas	14,976	18,534
Dinajpur	384	1,099	Cuttack	45,391	59,925
Rajshahye	82	162	Puri	56,118	69,657
Rangpur	45	146	Balasore	5,872	7,376
Bogra	......	65	Tributary States	4,221	4,002
Pabna	25	255	Hazaribagh	392	382
Darjiling	100	1	Lohardaga	67	495
Jalpigori	2	30	Singhbhum	825	1,055
Dacca	14	808	Manbhum	82,938	70,211
Faridpur	......	229	Tributary States	2	1,445

Bauriha, a section of Bábhans in Behar.

Bawál, a title of Báruis in Bengal.

Báwan gali, tirpan bázár, chhatis láhá, battis parkár, "fifty-two lanes, fifty-three bazars, thirty-six profits, thirty-two ways of making money," a formula or shibboleth distinguishing a section of the Jaiswár sub-caste of Kalwárs in Behar. In the Glossary forming part of his Monograph on the Trade and Manufactures of Northern India, Mr. Hoey writes (*s.v. mandi*, 'a market'):—"They say of Lucknow in Saádat Ali's time that the city consisted of *báwan mandi, tirpan bázár*." The close correspondence between this phrase and the opening words of the shibboleth quoted above may perhaps deserve notice.

Bázárgasht, a wanderer in a *bázár*, a kind of broker who spies out customers and guides them to shops.

Bazigar, *Bájikar*, a juggler or conjuror, a synonym for Nat, *q.v.* See *Bediyá*.

Bazzáz, a cloth merchant, a draper.

Beanh, a large fish with thorns on its back, a totemistic sept of Oraons in Chota Nagpur.

Beár, a *pangat* or section of Dosádhs and a title of Chamárs in Behar.

Beauran, a section of Awadhiá Hajáms in Behar.

Bebarttu, the title of the head officer of a Rájá in the Tributary States of Orissa.

Bed-báf, a weaver of cane-work.

Bedbangsi, probably a synonym for Baidya, the physician caste, or for the group of vagrant castes generically known as Bediyá, from the Sanskrit vyádha, 'a hunter.' Both words are colloquially contracted into Bed.

Bed (*d* silent) or **Beh tshangye,** a sub-tribe of Dejong Lhoris or Bhotias of the south.

Bed, Bid, a title of Dakshin-Rárhi and Bangaja Káyasths.

Bedeá, a synonym for Bediá.

Bedi, a group of the Srotriya sub-caste of Utkal Brahmans.

Bediá, *Bedeá, Bejeá,* a small agricultural Dravidian tribe of Chota Nagpur, supposed to be *másiaut bhái,* or cousins through the maternal aunt, of the Kurmis. Formerly, it is said, Bediás and Kurmis intermarried, but a split occurred 'when it was discovered that the former ate beef,' or more probably, when the latter gave up eating it. They do not claim any connexion with the Mundas, nor do the Mundas recognise them as cognates. Their septs are totemistic. In their marriages a barber officiates as priest. Bediás take *kachchi* food from Kurmis only, and Khanghár Mundas take similar food from them. The twelfth sept of the Santáls, which is supposed to have been left behind in Champa, and has long been separated from the parent tribe, bears the name of Bediá, and it seems not improbable that the Bediás of Chota Nagpur may be actually a branch of the Santáls who did not follow the main tribe in their wanderings eastward. The connexion of the Bediás with the Kurmis tells rather for this view. The tribe has certainly nothing to do with the Bediyás of Eastern Bengal.

Bediya, the generic name of a number of vagrant gipsy-like groups, of whom it is difficult to say whether they can properly be described as castes. The following groups are included under the name (1) Babajiya, Lava, or Patwa, pedlars and mountebanks professing to be Mahomedans, but singing songs in praise of Rama and Lakshmana, and exhibiting painted scrolls representing the exploits of Hanumán. Their women have the reputation of being skilful in the treatment of children's diseases and the removal of nervous and rheumatic pains. They also tattoo, but are not so expert in this art as the Nat women. (2) Bázigar, Kabutari, Bhanumati, Dorábáz, acrobats and conjurors, probably closely akin to the Nats and Kanjars of Hindustan. As acrobats the women and girls are the chief performers : the men play tricks with balls and knives. The women also dabble in medicine, prescribe for children suffering from fever or indigestion, practise *massage* for rheumatism and affect to cure toothache. (3) Mál, also called Ponkwah from their dexterity in extracting worms from the teeth. They appear to be a vagrant group of the Máls of Western Bengal, who in their turn are possibly a Hinduised offshoot of the Malé. It seems at any rate more reasonable to suppose that the tribal name Mál may be a variant of Malé, a man, than to derive it from Mála, a hillman, or Malla, a wrestler. Máls do not now intermarry with other Bediyás, and repudiate any connexion with them : for further particulars, see the article Mál. (4) Mir-shikár or Chirimár, hunters and fowlers, takes birds with bird-lime or horse-hair nooses and the *Sátnali* or light lance divided into sections like a fishing rod. Some of the animals which the Mir-shikár catches are highly prized for medicinal purposes or for charms. The flesh of the scaly ant-eater,

Banrahu or Bajrakit (*Manis pentadactyla*), is believed to restore virile energy, its scales bound on the arm cure palpitations of the heart, and worn on the finger in the form of a ring are a sovereign prophylactic against venereal diseases. The flesh of the crow pheasant (*mahokha* or *pán-kori*), if killed on a Tuesday or Saturday, cures enlargement of the spleen and puerperal disorders. The claws and droppings of the spotted owlet (*penchá*) if pounded up with betel-nut are a powerful and certain love-philtre, and the dried flesh of the dáuk (*Gallinula phœnicura*) is very beneficial in rheumatism. (5) Sámperia, snake-charmers, hawkers of miscellaneous goods, and makers of fish-hooks and such like articles. According to Dr. Wise, the snakes usually exhibited are the cobra; the light and dark varieties of the Ophiophagus Elaps, named by them Dudh-raj and Mani-raj; the python; a whip-snake, with red, black, and yellow spots, called Udaya Sámp; and a large brown snake with black stripes on its neck, known as Ghár-bánká, from the singular way it bends before striking.

The Sámperia catches a snake by pinning it to the ground with a forked stick, and seizing it by the neck, the thumb being held over the first vertebra. If the snake be a poisonous one, the fangs are torn out, but the poison bag is carefully preserved. Snake poison is highly valued by Hindu physicians for the treatment of diseases, and fetches in the market from fifteen to sixteen rupees per bhari or 179 grains. Another valuable prize is the tick (kilní), occasionally found on the hood of the black cobra, about which many fabulous stories are told. One of these parasites is worth a large sum, as it is popularly believed to be a certain preservative against snake-bites and poisons in general.

The Sámperia feeds his snakes on fish, frogs, and mice. Sámperias have no specific for snake-bite, but each man carries, as a charm, the root of the Bhatráj, a forest creeper. The popular idea is that the bud (málatí) of the Bhatráj is a specific, but the Sámperias deny this. When any one is bitten by a poisonous animal, the Sámperia ties a string round the limb, sucks the wound, bathes the extremity in hot water, and covers the bite with the leaves of the Bhatráj. One of the company then recites Hindustání *matras* or incantations, which are usually utter gibberish.

Members of this caste are in great request at the festival of Manasá Devi, their patron deity in the month of Srávan (July-August), being engaged by Brahmans to exhibit their collection and make the snakes crawl in front of the idol. On such occasions the Sámperia plays on a pipe, while his wife or child chants a monotonous Hindustání song, and irritates the reptile to strike.

The Sámperia also tames jungle cocks to entrap wild ones, and the Kora (*Gallicrex cristatus*), a bird famous for its pugnacity. When he is in want of food he tethers the decoy near a marsh, arranging a low screen with three movable leaves from which horsehair nooses hang. The wild bird advancing to test the courage of the captive, gets entangled and falls an easy prey to the Sámperia, who is lying concealed close by. Like other Bediyás, the Sámperias keep tame cormorants to drive fish into the net, but they do not sell what they catch. They are keen sportsmen, and when an opportunity offers they stalk deer, and shoot partridges, paddy-birds, and egrets.

(6) The Shándárs have the reputation of being the most orderly and industrious of the Bediyá divisions. Their name is derived from the Persian Shánah, a comb. This comb, or more correctly reed, through which the warp threads pass, is in great demand by Tántís and Juláhas for their looms, and no one can make them so cheaply and neatly as the Shándár. The frame-work of the comb (*dhangi*) is made of split bamboo, and the teeth (*gaibi*) of well-seasoned wood. The latter are fixed at equal distances apart by strong cotton thread. The Shándár is also a Manihár, or pedlar, retailing in the villages beads and trinkets; waist-strings (*Kardhani*) bought from the Patwá; and needles, thread, and tape, procured from Mughuliyá shops.

Shándárs are expert divers, and, when anchored in suitable localities, gather the common bivalve shells (sípí), and sell them to the Chunári, or lime-burner. They also use the *sát-nali*, or bamboo rod of seven joints, tipped with bird-lime, catching bulbuls and other small birds. Like the Sámperia, they keep tame koras, jungle cocks, and cormorants, and, if they can afford to do so, take out a gun license to shoot game.

Of late years they have all become converts to Islam, but Mahomedans do not admit them into their society, and refuse to intermarry, to eat, and to pray with them.

(7) Rasia Bediyas use boats of curious construction, only half covered over, while the tilt is cocoon, or bottle-shaped, tapering gradually towards the stern, where there is a small round opening, through which a man can with difficulty crawl. These Bediyas work with zinc, which is bought in pigs, melted, and run into moulds. From the similarity in colour of zinc and mercury (*rasa*), the division has derived its distinctive name from the latter metal. The Rasias make anklets, bracelets, and collars for the neck (*hansli*), which are worn by all Hindu and Mahomedan females of the lower orders. At their homes they are cultivators, and being strict Farazís are accepted as members of the Mahomedan community. Their social standing, however, is so precarious that prolonged absence from home, or a manifest partiality for boat life, is punished by expulsion from society.

Begampuriá, a section of Bábhans in Behar.

Begra-Oraon, a sub-tribe of Oraons in Chota Nagpur.

Begri, a cutter of precious stones other than diamond.

Begsariá, a section of Kanaujiá Lohárs in Behar.

Behal, a section of the Bahánnajáti sub-caste of Khatris in Bengal.

Behárá, *Bahara*, a title of Hindu castes, such as Bágdis, Bauris, Chandals, Rawani Kahars, Orhs, and others who are employed as palanquin-bearers; also of Dhawas or low Mahomedans who follow the same occupation. Wilson derives the word from Sansk. *vyavahár*, 'business,' 'profession'; but it seems equally possible that the word 'bearer' may have been adopted into Bengali like many other English words. The word is also used as an honorific title of Gonds and of some Uriyá Brahmans; of the headmen of Jharuá, Kumhár, Bhuiya, and Kewat castes.

Behári, Bihári, a *mul* or section of the Kanaujiá sub-caste of Sonárs in Behar.

Beherá, a title of Sudhás in Orissa.

Behna, a cotton-vendor. Occ.

Behnáhán, a section of the Banodhiá and Jaiswár Kalwárs in Behar.

Bejeá, a synonym for Bediá.

Bekh, a totemistic sept of Oraons who cannot eat earth-salt.

Bel, a fruit, a sept of Páns; a totemistic section of the Bhar caste in Western Bengal, the members of which will not touch or eat the *bel* fruit.

Belálai, a sub-caste of Kámárs in the Santál Parganas.

Belási, a sub-caste of Kámárs in Bardwan.

Belaunche-Káko, a *mul* of the Bharadwája section of Maithil Brahmans in Behar.

Belaunche-Ghaul, a *mul* of the Bharadwáj section of Maithil Brahmans in Behar.

Belaunche-Sudai, a *mul* of the Bharadwáj section of Maithil Brahmans in Behar.

Belaunche-Ratpár, a *mul* of the Bharadwáj section of Maithil Brahmans in Behar.

Belaunche-Garh, a *mul* of the Bharadwáj section of Maithil Brahmans in Behar.

Belaunche-Dih, a *mul* of the Bharadwáj section of Maithil Brahmans in Behar.

Belawahari, a section of Mauliks in Chota Nagpur.

Beldár, 'one who works with a *bél*, or hoe.' A wandering Dravidian caste of earth-workers and navvies in Behar and Western Bengal, many of whom are employed in the coal-mines of Raniganj and Barakar. Both men and women labour, the former digging the earth and the latter removing it in baskets carried on the head. The Beldárs regard this mode of carrying earth as distinctive of themselves, and will on no account carry earth in baskets slung from the shoulders. They work very hard when paid by the piece, and are notorious for their skill in manipulating the pillars (*sákhi*, 'witness') left to mark work done, so as to exaggerate the measurement. On one occasion, while working for me on a large lake at Govindpur, in the north of the Manbhum district, a number of Beldárs transplanted an entire pillar during the night and claimed payment for several thousand feet of imaginary earthwork. The fraud was most skilfully carried out, and was only detected by accident. In Western Bengal they rank with Koras and Bauris, and, like them, are terribly addicted to drink. They profess to marry their daughters as infants, but the practice of adult-marriage still survives among them; while they certainly allow widows to remarry, and recognise considerable license of divorce. Divorced women may marry again.

Origin and internal structure.

The origin of the caste is obscure. They are certainly closely akin to the Binds and Nuniás, and it seems probable that the former represent the remnant of a compact aboriginal tribe, from which the Nuniás broke off by taking to the manufacture of saltpetre, and the Beldárs by going in for earthwork. The functions of the Binds are less specialised; and this circumstance, coupled with the fact that they reckon hunting and fishing among their characteristic occupations, leads me to regard them as the oldest of the three groups, and probably the parent of both Nuniás and Beldárs. The internal structure of the Beldárs throws little light upon their tribal affinities. In Behar they have two sub-castes:—**Chauhán** and **Kathautiá** or **Katháwá**, and one section, **Kásyapa**. Their marriages are regulated by the standard formula *mamerá*, *chacherá*, etc. Infant-marriage is in vogue, and the marriage ceremony is of the standard type. A second wife may be taken if the first is barren. Widows marry by *sagai*. Divorce by the caste panchâyat is recognised, and divorced women may marry again.

Religion.

Beldárs employ Maithil Brahmans as their priests, and conform in matters of religion, funeral rites, etc., to the average Hinduism of the lower castes. On the Tilá Sankránt festival, in Mágh, they worship the *Larha*, a pointed iron instrument used in pounding bricks—one of their standard occupations. A few of them are cultivators with occupancy rights: most, however, earn their living as navvies or as agricultural day-labourers. Their social rank is much the same as that of Nuniás.

In treating of the Beldárs much confusion is caused by the fact that the term Beldár, 'mattock-bearer,' besides denoting a distinct endogamous group, is also used as a generic title common to the low castes of Hindus employed on earthwork. This use of the word in its proper etymological sense, as denoting merely an occupation, comes out even more clearly in Eastern Bengal, where we find Mahomedan Beldárs, who act as scavengers in their own villages, removing carcasses or cutting brushwood, and serve as torch-bearers (*masalchi*) at Hindu and Mahomedan weddings.

The following statement shows the number and distribution of Beldárs in 1872 and 1881, but the statistics are worthless by reason of the confusion in the use of the name explained in the last paragraph:—

DISTRICT.	1872.	1881.	DISTRICT.	1872.	1881.
Bardwan	161	183	Tipperah	154	3
Bankura	26	......	Patna	18,461	18,460
Birbhum	102	......	Gya	16,185	18,461
Midnapur	102	34	Shahabad	9,003	222
Hughli with Howrah ...	2	......	Tirhut { Darbhanga ...	} 10,092	{ 8,643
24-Parganas	53	......	Tirhut { Mozufferpur ...		2,296
Nadiya	65	......	Saran	799	831
Jessore	4	8	Champaran	500	956
Murshedabad	538	195	Monghyr	16,676	17,411
Dinajpur	1,449	277	Bhagalpur	11,238	15,361
Rajshahye	68	49	Purniah	7,332	11,885
Rangpur	139	......	Santál Parganas	683	497
Bogra	88	......	Maldah	......	400
Jalpigori	298	375	Hazaribagh	955	1,065
Dacca	172	15	Lohardaga	818	258
Bakarganj	98	......	Singbhum	156	99
Maimansinh	781	308	Manbhum	103	110
Chittagong	100	2	Tributary States	......	6
Noakhali	66	......			

Beldár, a title of Nuniás in Behar.

Belgáchi, a sub-caste of Kumhárs in Jessore.

Belgrámi, a *gáin* of the Kásyapa *gotra* of Bárendra Brahmans in Bengal.

Belha, a section of Sonárs in Behar.

Beliár, a sept of Asuras in Chota Nagpur.

Belkhariyá, *Belkhari*, *Bilkhari*, a section of Bábhans in Behar.

Belkuar, a section of Bábhans in Behar.

Bella, a section of Goálás in Behar.

Beloar, fruit, a totemistic sept of Lohars in Chota Nagpur.

Belonchá, a section of Bábhans in Behar.

Belontiá, a division of Brahmans in Behar.

Belsandi, a section of the Magahiyá, Pachainyá, and Tirhutiyá sub-castes of Doms in Behar.

Beluri, a *gáin* of the Sándilya *gotra* of Bárendra Brahmans in Bengal.

Belwadhiya, a sub-tribe of Thárus in Nepal.

Belwár, a sub-caste of Dhobis in Behar, a *mul* or section of the Naomuliá or Majraut sub-caste of Goálás in Behar.

Bemwár, a section of Bábhans in Behar.

Benátiyá, a sub-caste of Chásás in Orissa.

Bendah, a *rui* or sept of Dejong Lhoris in Darjiling whose ancestor had emigrated from Bhotan.

Bendiár, a section of Kurmis in Chota Nagpur and Orissa.

Bendkar, a sub-tribe of Savars, *q.v.*

Beng, frog, a totemistic sept of Bhuiyas and Mundas in Chota Nagpur.

Beni, a *pathi* or hypergamous sub-group of Bárendra Brahmans in Bengal; a variant of Baniyá, *q.v.*

Beniah-Kandh, a sub-tribe of Kandhs in Orissa.

Beniaro, frog, a totemistic sept of Páns in Chota Nagpur.

Benk, a section of the Karan Káyasths in Behar.

Benkurá, a section of Páns in Chota Nagpur.

Benrá, a synonym for Páttar, a class of fishermen in Eastern Bengal.

Beopári, *bepári*, an importer of grain and a wholesale dealer, who frequently supplies goods on trust to retail shopkeepers to sell at a minimum price fixed by the *beopári*. If the goods are not sold within a month after delivery, the *beopári* charges interest at one per cent. per mensem on their value.

Bepári, a title of Málos in Eastern Bengal.

Berá, a title of Kaibarttas in Bengal.

Berar, a *mul* or section of the Maghayá sub-caste of Kándus in Behar.

Beraut, a section of Awadhiá Hajáms in Behar.

Bere, a section of the Sátmuliá Maghayá sub-caste of Kándus in Behar.

Berga-Khariá, a sub-caste of Khariás in Chota Nagpur.

Beri, a section of the Panch-játi sub-caste of Khatris in Bengal.

Bermán, a section of Kanaujiá Lohárs in Behar.

Berrá-Rajwár, a sub-caste of Rajwárs in Lohardagá.

Beruá, *Pátra-Beruá*, a small cultivating and fishing caste of Eastern Bengal, probably an offshoot of the Chandál tribe, with the members of which they still eat and drink, but do not intermarry. Their name is derived from *berá*, a weir of bamboos or reeds used for catching mullet. It is the well-known habit of this fish to jump over any obstacle it meets with in water. The Beruas at full tide throw a weir across a creek, and on the surface of the water below it they moor a broad raft. As soon as the mullet encounters the weir and finds no opening, it leaps over and is caught on the raft. The fish are sold in the market, but no Beruá will cast a net or earn a livelihood as the Kaibarttas do.

The whole of the Beruá caste belongs to the Kásyapa *gotra*, and they therefore practise exogamy only in name. Their headman is called Pátra. The intimacy of their connexion with the Chandáls is attested by the fact that the same purohits officiate for both.

Beruár, a sept of Rajputs in Behar.

Beruká Kisán, a *mul* or section of the Biyáhut sub-caste of Kalwárs in Behar.

Beru ke Máhto, a section of the Biyáhut and Kharidáhá Kalwárs in Behar.

Beru ke pánre, a section of the Biyáhut and Kharidáhá Kalwárs in Behar.

Besáti, *Bisáti*, a vendor of small wares, generally Mahomedans.

Beserwár, a sept of Kharwars in Chota Nagpur.

Beşra, small hawk, a totemistic sept or section of Lohárs, Mundas, Santáls, Cheros, and Gonds.

Besyá putra, the son of a prostitute, a bastard.

Betiah-Kandh, a sub-tribe of Kandhs in Orissa.

Betra Pán or **Raj-Pán**, a sub-caste of Páns in Orissa.

Betuá, a sub-caste of Muchis in Bengal.

Bhabánipuri, a *pathi* or hypergamous sub-group of Bárendra Brahmans in Bengal.

Bhabániswar, a section of the Kamár sub-caste of Dosádhs in Behar.

Bhabhut or **Bibhuti**, the ashes of burnt cow-dung, with which mendicants, of the Saiva orders chiefly, besmear their bodies: hence a title of such mendicants.

Bhadáiya, a *pangat* or section of Dosádhs in Behar.

Bhadaniá, a sept of Rajputs in Behar.

Bhádar, a *gáin* of the Bharadwája *gotra* of Bárendra Brahmans in Bengal.

Bhadariá or **Bhareri**, a sect of mendicants of Brahmanical descent, professors of astrology in Behar; a sub-caste of the Kraunchdwipi Brahmans in Behar.

Bhadauriá, a sept of the Suryabansi sub-tribe of Rajputs and of Kewats in Behar.

Bhad-bhadriá, sparrow, a totemistic section of the Jagannáthi sub-caste of Kumhárs in Orissa.

Bhaddal, a *gotra* or section of the Agarwál caste.

Bhádisawár, a *mul* or section of the Ghosin sub-caste of Goálás in Behar.

Bhadpá, a *rui* or sept of the Bed tshan-gye sub-tribe of Dejong Lhoris or Bhotias of the south.

Bhadra, a title of Dakshin-Rárhi and Bangaja Káyasths, and of Sánkháris in Bengal.

Bhadraghát, a section of Pátnis in Bengal.

Bhadraj, a *mul* or section of the Naomuliá or Goriá sub-caste of Goálás in Behar.

Bhadsuhiá, a section of Bábhans in Behar.

Bhádua or **Bhánruá**, a title of Nápits, from the *bhánr* or bag in which they carry their shaving implements.

Bháduri, a *gáin* of the Kásyapa *gotra* of Bárendra Brahmans; also a title of Sadgops in Bengal.

Bhadwariá, a *mul* or section of the Biyáhut sub-caste of Kalwárs in Behar.

Bhádya-bau, a title of Tántis in Bengal.

Bhagabán, a section of the Mahmudábáz sub-caste of Nápits in Bengal.

Bhágái, a *gáin* or sub-section of Saptasati Brahmans in Bengal.

Bhagan Bhájan, a family of the Grihasth group of Jugis in Bengal.

Bhagat, a title of the Jaiswár and Biyáhut sub-castes of Kalwárs in Behar; a title of those members of the Kasodhan sub-caste of Baniyás in Behar who refrain from eating fish. The same title is also used by Kasarwáni Baniyás without this distinction.

Bhagwat, *Bhakat*, literally a worshipper of Vishnu—a class of Baniyás who strictly observe the rules of the Hindu religion and abstain from meat and intoxicating drinks.

Bhainsá, buffalo, a totemistic sept of Gonds, Páns, and Korwas in Chota Nagpur.

Bhainsu, a section of Goálás in Behar.

Bhair, a section of Binjhiás in Chota Nagpur.

Bhairab Ghataki, a *mel* or hypergamous sub-group of Rárhi Brahmans in Bengal.

Bhaiskayári, a section of the Banodhiá and Jaiswár Kalwárs in Behar.

Bhaji Sag, vegetable, a totemistic sept of Mundas in Chota Nagpur.

Bháju, a section of Newars in Darjiling; also a pet name for a Newar child.

Bhaju Chakwar, a section of Bábhans in Behar.

Bhákar, Bhákur, a section of Kanaujiá Lohárs in Behar.

Bhakat, *Bhagat*. This term properly denotes a worshipper, and particularly Vaishnavas of the middle and lower castes, who from religious motives abstain from meat, fish, and spirituous liquors. It is used as a title of Vaishnavas generally, of the Jaiswár and Biyáhut sub-castes of Kalwárs, and of Támbulis in Behar, of Kasarwáni Baniyás, and of those members of the Kasodhan sub-caste of Baniyás who refrain from eating fish. In Manbhum and Hazaribagh Bhakats are very numerous, and have in their hands most of the business of the *chattis* or halting places along the Grand Trunk Road.

Bhakat-Oraon.

The word Bhakat also denotes a sub-tribe of the Oraons, which has been formed on the same basis of religious asceticism as the Kharwar or Safa-hor division of the Santáls. These Bhakats acknowledge themselves to be Oraons, and admit disciples from the tribe, which indeed forms their only source of recruits, but they will not intermarry with their unconverted brethren, nor take cooked food or water from their hands. They abstain from all flesh except that of goats which have been sacrificed to one of the Hindu gods, nor do they drink spirits. Fish, however, is not prohibited, and sweetmeats may be eaten with Oraons, Mundas, and Telis. Tobacco they will only smoke among themselves or out of the *hukka* of their own *guru* or spiritual guide.

Religion.

The favourite deities of the Bhakat-Oraons, as of most recently Hinduised aborigines, are Mahádeva and Káli, to whom goats, *ghi*, sweetmeats, etc., are offered on Wednesdays and Sundays, the offerings being eaten by the worshippers and their families. They employ Brahmans as *gurus*, but these Brahmans do not officiate as their priests, and the sacrificial victims are slain by any influential person among themselves who happens to be acquainted with the ritual. In marriages again, while the attempt is to imitate the Hindu ceremony, the purohit who officiates is not a Brahman, but a Bhakat, and the binding portion of the ceremony is the payment of the bride-price, which consists of a pair of bullocks, or Rs. 5 to Rs. 10 in cash.

Marriage.

Along with this striving after conformity with the externals of Hinduism, we find the Bhakats retaining in their entirety the totemistic exogamous sections characteristic of the Oraons, and observing the same prohibited degrees. They show at present no signs of carrying their asceticism into the domain of marriage. Like the Oraons, they marry their girls as adults, usually between the ages of twelve and sixteen. Unrestricted courtship is permitted before marriage, and sexual intercourse is tolerated, it being understood that if a girl becomes pregnant she will name the father of her child, and the two will get married. Polygamy is permitted, but is not usually resorted to unless the first wife is barren. Widows are allowed to marry again, but no ceremony is performed on such occasions, and the transaction is deemed to be complete when a few maunds of grain have been paid to the relatives of the woman. Divorce is easy and very common; a woman runs away from her husband with any man who suits her fancy, a man turns out his wife and takes up with another woman. In either case the parties may marry again and thus render the divorce final, but this may also be effected without remarriage by refunding to the husband the bride-price which he paid in the first instance for his wife.

Disposal of dead.

In the disposal of the dead the usages of the Bhakats do not differ materially from those of the Oraons. The rule is to burn the body, preserving some of the ashes and bones for burial, at the time of the *haddiphor* festival, in the *bhuinhári* village of the deceased, that is to say in the village from the first founders of which he believes himself to be descended. At this festival pigs and great quantities of rice are offered for the benefit of departed ancestors, who are also held in continual remembrance by fragments of rice or *dál* cast on the ground at every meal, and by a pinch of tobacco sprinkled whenever a man prepares his pipe. The bodies of women who die within fifteen days after child-birth are buried, and fowls offered over the grave. People who die during the rainy season are also buried, but the remains are exhumed and burned when the dry season sets in.

Bhakla, animal, a totemistic sept of Oraons in Chota Nagpur.

Bháklun, a section of Goálás in the North-Western Provinces.

Bhakta, a title of Kaibarttas and Sunris in Bengal; a sect of Vaishnavas in Behar.

Bhalauniár, a *pur* or section of Sákadwipi Brahmans in Behar.

Bhale, a section of the Chhajáti sub-caste of Khatris in Behar.

Bhálkiá, a section of Goálás in the North-Western Provinces and Behar.

Bhalráit, a *kul* or section of Bábhans in Behar.

Bhal Sultán, a sept of Rajputs in Behar.

Bhámbasrá, a section of Goálás in the North-Western Provinces and Behar.

Origin and internal structure.

Bhandári, *Nápit*, *Hajám*, the barber caste of Orissa. The name Bhandári or store-keeper is supposed to have reference to the position of trust and influence which the barber often occupies in the household of a Hindu landholder. In Orissa the caste claim to be the modern representatives of the Sudras of early Indian tradition; but they are usually classed among the mixed castes, and believed to be the offspring of a Kshatriya father and a Sudra mother. There are seven sub-castes—**Bangáli**, **Dakhini**, **Desi**, **Khariá**, **Khurda**, **Golá**, and **Hátuá**. Of these, the Bangáli and Dakhini are immigrants from Bengal and Madras respectively, the Desi are indigenous to Orissa, and Khurdá are supposed to have come from the estate of that name in Puri district. The Khariá and Hátuá sub-castes are found in Cuttack, the former being barbers who have for the most part given up their traditional occupation and taken to making salt and letting out pack-bullocks for hire; while the latter are an itinerant class of barbers who are attached to no particular village, but wander about plying their trade wherever they can find customers. The sections of the caste, which are shown in the Appendix, appear to have been borrowed from the Brahmanical system.

Marriage.

Bhandáris marry their daughters as infants, and regard it as a breach of a distinct religious obligation if a girl remains unmarried at the age of puberty. Such cases, however, do occur sometimes, when a girl's parents are poor or when some personal blemish renders it difficult to procure a husband for her. The ceremony is supposed to be identical with the *prajápatya* form referred to by Manu. Its essential portion is *hastagánthi*, or binding together the hands of the bride and bridegroom with a wisp of *kusa* grass. Polygamy is permitted to the extent that a man may take a second wife if the first is barren, suffers from an incurable disease, or has certain specified physical defects. A widow is allowed to marry again, and is generally expected to marry her late husband's younger brother if there is one. She may, however, marry any member of the caste outside the prohibited degrees of kinship. The ceremony in use at the marriage of a widow is called *thai*, 'change of place,' and is performed under the supervision of the bridegroom's family priest, who receives *dakshiná* for his services. It commences with the worship of an earthen vessel filled with water, and is completed by putting shell and brass bracelets (*sankha* and *katuri*) on the bride's wrists and smearing vermilion on her forehead. The status of a widow thus married, though clearly distinguished from that of a mere concubine, is deemed inferior to that of a woman who has been married as a virgin by the full *prajápatya* ritual. The caste council (panchâyat) may grant a divorce (*chharda-patra*) to a husband if it be proved before them that his wife has committed adultery. Pending the decision of the case the husband is held to be unclean, and he must burn a *kusa* grass figure of his wife and give a feast to the pancháyat before he can be again admitted to social intercourse. Divorced wives get alimony for six months, and may marry again by the form used at the remarriage of a widow, but they must first perform an expiatory ceremony of the same general character as that demanded from a husband who applies for a divorce.

Religion.

All Bhandáris are Vaishnavas, and conform in the course of their regular worship to the precepts of that sect. They also regard Visvakarmá as the patron of their craft, and on the fourth day of the Durgá Pujá the razors, scissors, and the mirror, which they deem the special emblem of their caste, are laid before his image with offerings of sweetmeats and flowers, while for three days all members of the caste rest from their usual avocations. In this, as in other religious offices performed in honour of the regular Hindu gods, Bhandáris employ Brahmans, who are received on equal terms by other members of the sacred order. The village goddess, **Grám-devati**, on the other hand, is worshipped by the heads of households, unassisted by Brahmans, with offerings of fruits, sweetmeats, and parched grain. No special day is set apart for these sacrifices, but Sundays, Tuesdays, Saturdays, and the first day of every month are believed to be auspicious times for approaching the goddess. Some Bhandáris are *sebáyats* or secular priests of **Grám-devati**, and in this capacity hold small grants of rent-free land.

Disposal of the dead.

The dead are usually burned, but the bodies of children and women who die in child-birth are buried. When a pregnant woman dies before delivery, her body is cut open and the child taken out, both corpses being then buried in the same grave. *Sráddh* is performed in the regular fashion on the eleventh day after death. Offerings are also made on the anniversary of the death of near relatives, and a *sráddh* is performed for remote ancestors at the Mahálaya festival and on the night of the Káli Pujá.

Social status.

The social standing of the caste is respectable. A Brahman will not only take water from the hands of a Bhandári, but will go to his house as a guest and partake there of any food that has been cooked by a Brahman. Their own practice in matters of diet is in accordance with that of orthodox Hindus. They eat *pakki* food with members of the Nabasákh only, and will only take the leavings of their own spiritual guide (*guru*). As a rule they practise their hereditary profession, and hold their homestead lands rent-free in consideration of the services rendered by them to the village community. Others, again, have special tenures (*hajámi jágir*) created by the former rulers of the country. Comparatively few have regularly taken to agriculture, and most of these are *thâni raiyats* with rights of occupancy. *Zemindárs*, however, and *lákhirájdárs*, are occasionally met with among them.

The following statement shows the number and distribution of Bhandáris in 1872 and 1881 :—

DISTRICT.	1872.	1881.
Cuttack	29,494	35,955
Puri	17,867	21,761
Balasore	13,733	15,859
Tributary States	14,372	16,286

Bhandári, a treasurer, a store-keeper. In Sylhet, a servant, an outdoor servant: in other parts of Bengal, a steward: in Orissa, a barber; an honorary title of Káyasths and Nápits in Bengal; a title of Sudras in Eastern Bengal; a title of Kahárs, Kewats, and of Ganjwár Sunris in Behar; a section of Mális, and a sept of Rajputs in Behar.

Bhándi, a synonym for Bhát, *q.v.*

Bhandsáli, a grain-storer.

Bhandsár, see **Arhativá**.

Bhanduwál, a *mul* of the Kásyapa section of Maithil Brahmans in Behar.

Bhanga Kshatriya, *Bhanga*, a title assumed by the Paliyas and Rajbansis of Northern and Eastern Bengal which has reference to the legend of the Kochh tribe that they are an outlying branch of the Kshatriyas who took refuge in Kochh Behar when the caste was destroyed by Parasu Rám.

Bhanga-Kulin, a hypergamous group of Rárhi Brahmans in Bengal.

Bhángar, a section of Goálás in the North-Western Provinces and Behar.

Bhangerá, a sub-caste of Sunris in Behar.

Bháng-farosh, a seller of *bháng (cannabis sativus)*, generally a Brahman.

Bhanj, a sub-caste of so-called Rajputs in Singbhum and the Tributary States of Orissa.

Bhanja, a title of Dakshin-Rárhi and Bangaja Káyasths.

Bhanja-Khandait, a sub-caste of Khandáits in Puri.

Bhanjor, a sept of Páns in Chota Nagpur.

Bhánr, a generic name of mimics, buffoons, and jesters, mostly Mahomedans, who attend at births and marriages to amuse the guests with their jokes; a sept of the Rautár sub-tribe of Thárus in Behar.

Bhansriá, a section of Goálás in the North-Western Provinces and Behar.

Bhant, a section of Goálás in Behar.

Bhaonrá, a large black bee, supposed to be enamoured of the lotus, a totemistic sept of Mundas in Chota Nagpur.

Bháonroá, a *mul* or section of the Naomulia or Majraut sub-caste of Goálás in Behar.

Bhar, a small Dravidian caste of Western Bengal and Chota Nagpur, most of whom are cultivators, while a few occupy the position of hereditary personal servants to the Rájás of Pachete. The Bhars are divided into two sub-castes, **Maghayá** and **Bangáli**, the members of which do not intermarry. Their sections show a curious mixture of the totemistic and eponymous types, which may perhaps indicate that the caste is undergoing the process of gradual conversion to Hinduism and incorporation into the regular caste system. This view is borne out, on the whole, by their domestic institutions, which appear to be in a similar state of transition. Thus the remarriage of widows has been discarded, and the license of divorce, conceded so freely by the non-Aryan races, entirely done away with; while adult-marriage still survives as a relic of the past, side by side with the growing usage of infant-marriage. It deserves notice that in this respect the Bhars form an exception to the usual course of development. It may be laid down as a general rule that the adoption of infant-marriage is the first step taken in the direction of conformity to orthodox usage, while the prohibition of widow-marriage usually follows as a later stage. The Bhars, however, have completely given up widow-marriage, while still recognizing the marriage of adults as permissible for those who cannot afford to marry their daughters as infants.

For the rest they appear in all respects to follow the usages of orthodox Hindus: professing the Hindu religion, employing Brahmans, burning their dead, and performing their *sráddh* on the thirtieth day after death. In the matter of inheritance they deviate slightly from the standard school, in that they give the eldest son an extra share (*jeth-angs*) of the property. This, however, is not uncommon in Western Bengal, and we may hazard the conjecture that it has some connexion with the custom of primogeniture which governs the succession to many of the large estates in that part of the country. The connexion of the Bhars with the Pachete family has probably tended to raise their general social position. They rank in Manbhum with Tamolis and Mairas, and the higher castes can take water from their hands.

The following statement shows the number and distribution of Bhars in the Lower Provinces in 1872 and 1881. It includes the Bhars of Behar, a Hinduised branch of the original stock, who disown all connexion with the Bhars of Western Bengal, and claim affinity with the Bhars of the North-Western Provinces. A full account of the latter is given in Mr. Crooke's Ethnographical Hand-book

District.	1872.	1881.	District.	1872.	1881.
Bardwan	......	39	Gya	28	11
Birbhum	......	2	Shahabad	5,679	2,593
24-Parganas	......	6	Tirhut { Darbhanga	} 252	{ ......
Nadiya	......	332	Tirhut { Mozufferpur		128
Jessore	......	11	Saran	7,647	8,397
Murshedabad	......	41	Champaran	4,845	2,115
Dinajpur	......	45	Monghyr	2	18
Rangpur	......	7	Bhagalpur	......	332
Bogra	......	10	Purniah	......	22
Pabna	......	8	Maldah	......	165
Darjiling	......	12	Santál Parganas	2,670	2,463
Kuch Behar	......	97	Hazaribagh	5,838	18
Dacca	......	11	Lohardagá	1,046	44
Faridpur	......	14	Singbhum	10	......
Maimansinh	......	357	Manbhum	10,917	1,232
Patna	28	8	Tributary States	......	120

Bhar, a title of Tántis in Bengal.

Bharadwája, a Brahmanical section of Khatris and Rajputs in Behar; of Káyasths in Bengal; and of Karans and Khandáits in Orissa; a *gotra* or section of Bábhans in Behar, borrowed from the Brahmanical system and superadded to the original exogamous groups (*kuls*) characteristic of the caste; a *gotra* or section of Brahmans, Baidyas, Aguris, Bháts, Gandhabaniks, Goálás, Kámárs, Madhunápíts, Mayarás, and Tántis in Bengal.

Bharadwáji, a section of Cháins in Behar.

Bharáit, a *mul* or section of the Kamarkalla sub-caste of Sonárs and of the Maghayá sub-caste of Barhis in Behar.

Bharan-rási, a section of Málos in Eastern Bengal.

Bharari, a title of the Ghosin sub-caste of Goálás in Behar.

Bharári, a *thar* of the Basishtha *gotra* of Nepáli Brahmans.

Bhárata, a title of Brahmans and of Bháts.

Bhárath, a section of the Sátmuliá Maghayá sub-caste of Kándus in Behar.

Bhárathi, Bhárati, (i) a worshipper of Siva; a title of Mahants: (ii) a name of Saraswati, Goddess of Learning, used as a title by Káyasths: (iii) a name of one of the ten orders of Dasnámi ascetics.

Bhárátiá, a tenant, a renter.

Bhárauli, a *mul* or section of the Tinmuliá Madhesiá sub-caste of Halwáis in Behar.

Bhar-Bhunjá, grain-parcher or fryer. The name of a sub-caste of Kándus who are employed in parching and frying different sorts of grain, pulse, etc. They are said to spring from a Kahár father and Sudra mother, and pretend to be divided into seven tribes, which do not intermarry. There is also a class of Káyasths in Behar, distinct from these, who follow the same business. A synonym for Kándu in Behar.

Bhar-Chhutár, a sub-caste of Sutradhars in the Santál Parganas.

Bharchuihá, a sept of Rajputs in Behar.

Bharduár, a *mul* or section of the Sátmuliá or Kishnaut sub-caste of Goálás in Behar.

Bhardwár, a *mul* or section of the Ayodhiábási sub-caste of Sonárs in Behar.

Bhárgava, a section of Brahmans.

Bharhe, a *mul* of the Kásyapa section of Maithil Brahmans in Behar.

Bhariyá, a metal-caster, a brazier, foundryman.

Bharotat, a section of the Ariár sub-caste of Bais Baniyás in Behar.

Bharpáik, a section of Kanaujiá Hajáms in Behar.

Bharsahr, a section of Bhojpuriá Halwáis in Behar.

Bharsárwala, *Bhandárwálá*, a grain-storer or corn-factor.

Bharsi-Misr, a title of Bábhans in Behar.

Bharsuriá, a sept of the Suryabansi Rajputs in Behar.

Bharthari, Bhartari, a sub-sect of Saivite religious mendicants who go about begging, singing, and playing on the *saringi*, said to be descendants of Rájá Bharthari of Dháránagar.

Bharthi, a synonym for Bhárati, *q.v.*

Bhartkul, one of the branches of the Gaur-Brahmans.

Bhartri-Hari-Jogi, an order of Hindu mendicants who profess to have been instituted by Bhartrihari, the brother of Vikramáditya, in the century before Christ.

Bharwe, a section of Sunris in Behar.

Bháskar, a small caste of stone-cutters, who make idols of stone, wood, or metal, and occupy about the same social position as the Dhobis.

Bhát (Sansk. *bhatta*, a title of respect, probably connected with *bhartri*, a 'supporter or master'), a caste of genealogists and family bards, usually supposed to have sprung from the intercourse of a Kshatriya with a Brahman widow. Others believe them to be the modern representatives of the Mágadha spoken of in Manu, x, 17, as the offspring of a Vaisya father and a Kshatriya mother. Lassen regards this mythical pedigree as merely a theoretical explanation of the fact that the professional singers of the praises of great men had come by Manu's time to be looked upon as a distinct class.[1] Zimmer, on the other hand, seems to take the tradition more seriously, and speaks of the Mágadha as a "mixed caste, out of which, as we learn from numerous passages in later writings, a guild of singers arose, who, devoting themselves to the deeds of the Kosala-Videha and Kuru-Panchála, may have laid the foundation of the epic poems."[2] Other authorities say that they were produced to amuse Párvati from the drops of sweat on Siva's brow, but as they chose to sing his praises rather than hers, they were expelled from heaven and condemned to live a wandering life as bards on earth. Sir John Malcolm, *Central India*, vol. ii, p. 132, says:—"According to the fable of their origin, Mahádeva first created Bháts to attend his lion and bull; but the former killing the latter every day gave him infinite vexation and trouble in creating new ones. He therefore formed the Cháran, equally devout as the Bhát, but of bolder spirit, and gave him in charge these favourite animals. From that period no bull was ever destroyed by the lion."[3] In his brief view of the caste system of the North-Western Provinces and Oudh, Mr. J. C. Nesfield propounds the original view that the Bháts are an offshoot "from those secularised Brahmans who frequented the courts of princes and the camps of warriors, recited their praises in public, and kept records of their genealogies. Such, without much variation, is the function of the Bhát at the present day. The ancient epic known as the Mahábhárata speaks of a band of bards and eulogists marching in front of Yudhishthira as he made his progress from the field of Kuru-Kshetra towards Hastinápur. But these very men are spoken of in the same poem as Brahmans. Nothing could be more natural than that, as time went on, these courtier priests should have become hereditary bards, who receded from the parent stem and founded a new caste bound together by mutual interests and sympathies." In support of this theory of the origin of the caste Mr. Nesfield refers to the facts that one of the sub-castes is called Baram-Bhát; that some Gaur-Brahmans still act as bards and genealogists; that the Bhát still wears the sacred thread, and is addressed by the lower classes as Maháráj—an honour generally only accorded to Brahmans; and lastly, that by an obvious survival of

Traditions of origin.

Mr. Nesfield's theory.

---

[1] Lassen, *Ind. Alt.* i, 777.
[2] Zimmer, *Alt-Indisches Leben*, 35, quoting Weber, *Ind. Stud.* i, 185.
[3] Elliot's *Glossary*, vol. i, p. 18.

Brahmanical titles the Bhát's employer is called *jajmán*, 'he who gives the sacrifice,' while the Bhát himself is called *jagwá*, *jájak*, or *jáchak*, 'the priest by whom the sacrifice is performed.'

Supported by Dr. Wise.

Strong testimony in favour of Mr. Nesfield's view comes to us from Eastern Bengal, where, according to Dr. Wise, the Bháts repudiate the traditional descent from a Kshatriya and a Brahman widow, and claim to be the offspring of the aboriginal Brahmans employed as ghataks or marriage-brokers by the other members of the sacred order. They say that they retired or were driven to the borders of Bengal for refusing to accept the reforms of Ballál Sen. In Silhet the Rárhi Brahmans still eat with the Bháts, but in Dacca the latter are reckoned unclean; and in Tipperah, having fallen in rank, they earn a precarious livelihood by making umbrellas. It is a curious fact that the Bhát would consider himself dishonoured by acting as a *pujári* or priest of a temple, or as a purohit.

Further discussed.

Admitting the force of this evidence, and fully recognising how great an advance Mr. Nesfield has made on the traditional methods of dealing with such questions, I find some difficulty in reconciling his theory as stated above with the internal structure of the Bhát caste. If the Bháts of the present day are descended solely from a class of degraded Brahmans—if, in other words, they are a homogeneous offshoot from the priestly caste—how do they come to have a number of sections, which are certainly not Brahmanical, and which appear rather to resemble the territorial exogamous groups common among the Rajputs? Brahmans, however degraded, hold fast to their characteristic series of eponymous sections, and I know of no case in which it can be shown that they have adopted section-names of a different type. On the other hand, there is nothing specially improbable in the conjecture that Rajputs may have taken up the profession of bard to the chiefs of their tribe, and thus may in course of time have become incorporated in the Bhát caste. It will be seen that this solution of the difficulty in no way conflicts with Mr. Nesfield's view, but merely modifies it by introducing a second factor into the formation of the caste. Mr. Nesfield regards the Bháts as a homogeneous functional group thrown off by the Brahmans. I look upon them as a heterogeneous group made up of Brahmans and Rajputs welded together into one caste in virtue of their exercising similar functions. I may add, however, that the inviolability of the Bhát's person, which was admitted in Western India towards the end of the last century, makes rather for Mr. Nesfield's view than for mine; while the theory of Roth and Zimmer, that the first germ of the Brahman caste is to be sought in the singers of Vedic times, may perhaps be deemed to tell in the same direction.[1]

Internal structure.

The sections of the caste are shown in Appendix I. A man may not marry a woman of his own section, nor any one descended from his sister, paternal

---

[1] Zimmer, *Alt-Indisches Leben*, p. 168. See also art. Brahman below.

aunt, paternal grandmother, maternal aunt, maternal grandfather, and maternal great-grandfather (mother's mother's father) as long as any relationship can be traced. The endogamous divisions of the caste are somewhat obscure. Two sub-castes appear to be known in Behar—**Rájbhát** and **Baram-Bhát**. To these may be added the **Turk-Bhát**, who are converts to Islám and perform the same functions in Mahomedan households as the Hindu Bháts for men of their own religion. The wives of Mahomedan Bháts sing in public on certain occasions. There seems to be no marked difference of occupation between the Rájbháts and Baram-Bháts, but I understand that they do not intermarry. Regarding the Bháts of the North-West Provinces Sir Henry Elliot says:—"By some tribes the Bhát and Jága are considered synonymous; but those who pretend to greater accuracy distinguish them by calling the former Birmbhát or Badí, and the latter Jágabhát. The former recite the deeds of ancestors at weddings and other festive occasions; the latter keep the family record, particularly of Rajputs, and are entitled by right of succession to retain the office, whereas the Birmbháts are hired and paid for the particular occasion. Jágabháts pay visits to their constituents every two or three years, and receive the perquisites to which they are entitled. After having recorded all the births which have taken place since their last tour, they are remunerated with rupees, cattle, or clothes, according to the ability of the registering party." In another place Sir Henry Elliot mentions a number of subdivisions of the caste, which are shown in a note in Appendix I.

Marriage.

Bháts usually marry their daughters between the ages of nine and twelve; but in exceptional cases, where a girl's parents are poor, it may happen that she is not married until after the age of puberty. The marriage ceremony is of the orthodox type, and *kanyádán*, or the presentation of the bride to the bridegroom and his acceptance of the gift, is reckoned to be the essential and binding portion of the ritual. Polygamy is not supposed to be allowed, but a man may take a second wife if the first is barren or suffers from an incurable disease. Widows are not allowed to marry again, nor is divorce recognised. An adulterous wife is turned out of the caste and ceases thenceforth to be a member of respectable society.

Succession.

In questions concerning the devolution of property, the caste are guided for the most part by the standard Hindu law recognised in the area where they live; that is to say, in Bengal they follow the Dáyabhága, and in Behar the Mitákshará Code. In one point, however, they observe a peculiar usage of their own. Where under the ordinary law a daughter's son would succeed, Bhát custom holds him to be excluded by the nearest male relative of the same section. It is the more remarkable that this custom should have survived, as the Bháts are not governed by pancháyat or caste councils to the same extent as the lower castes, and thus lack the most effective machinery for preserving peculiar usages, which the courts tend on the whole to destroy.

Religion.

The religion of the Bháts of Behar differs little from that of the average middle-class Hindu. Representatives of all the regular sects are found among their numbers, and the caste cannot be said to favour the tenets of any particular body. In Eastern Bengal, on the other hand, they are said to be mostly Sakti worshippers, and to be greatly addicted to intemperance. They employ Brahmans for religious and ceremonial purposes, who are received on equal terms by other members of the sacred order. Their minor gods are Bandi or Sanverdhir and Bariji, who are worshipped on the 22nd Srávan and the 24th Chait with offerings of he-goats, wheaten cakes, *tilchauri* made of rice and molasses, coloured cloths, and vermilion. The eatable portion of the offerings is divided among the members of the household. The dead are burned, and the ceremony of *sráddh* is performed on the thirteenth day after death.

Social status.

In point of social precedence Bháts rank immediately below Káyasths. They wear the sacred thread (*janeo*), and Brahmans take water from their hands. Their own rules concerning diet are the same as are observed by the higher castes, and, like them, they will take water and certain sweetmeats from Kurmis, Kahars, and castes of corresponding status.

Occupation.

The characteristic profession of the Bháts has an ancient and distinguished history. The literature of both Greece and India owes the preservation of its oldest treasures to the singers, who recited poems in the households of the chief, and doubtless helped in some measure to shape the masterpieces which they handed down. Their place was one of marked distinction. In the days when writing was unknown, the man who could remember many verses was held in high honour by the tribal chief, who depended upon the memory of his bard for his personal amusement, for the record of his own and his ancestors' prowess, and for the maintenance of the genealogy which established the purity of his descent. The bard, like the herald, was not lightly to be slain, and even Odysseus, in the heat of his vengeance, spares the ἀοιδὸς Phemius, "who sang among the wooers of necessity."[1] Possibly the duties of bard and herald may often have been discharged by the same person. However this may be, it is curious to find that about the middle of the sixteenth century the person of a Bhát was deemed inviolable by highway robbers in Rajputana and Guzerat, so that a member of that caste could protect a caravan of traders from attack by threatening to kill himself if they were molested; while as late as 1775 many of them made their living by pledging themselves as hostages for the payment of revenue, the performance of treaties and bonds, and the general good behaviour of princes or private individuals.[2]

---

[1] *Odyssey*, xxii, 331.

[2] Yule, *Anglo-Indian Glossary*, *s.v.* Bhát.

In most parts of modern India, except perhaps in Rajputana, the Bháts have fallen from their former state, and are now the tawdriest parody on the Homeric ἀοιδὸς. Mr. Nesfield describes them as "rapacious and conceited mendicants, too proud to work, but not too proud to beg." Mr. Sherring says they "are notorious for their rapacity as beggars, and are much dreaded by their employers on account of the power they have of distorting family history at public recitations if they choose to do so, and of subjecting any member to general ridicule." Dr. Wise's notes contain a telling sketch of the Bháts of Eastern Bengal:—"In January they leave their homes, travelling to all parts of Eastern Bengal, and, being in great request, are fully engaged during the subsequent Hindu matrimonial season. Each company receives a fixed yearly sum from every Hindu household within a definite area, amounting usually to eight annas. In return they are expected to visit the house and recite Kavitás, or songs extolling the worth and renown of the family. Satirical songs are great favourites with Hindus, and none win more applause than those laying bare the foibles and well-intentioned vagaries of the English rule or the eccentricities and irascibility of some local magnate. Very few bards can sing extemporary songs, their effusions, usually composed by one and learned off by heart by the others, being always metrical, often humorous, and generally seasoned with puns and equivocal words. Their sole occupation is the recital of verses, unaccompanied by instrumental music. They are met with everywhere when Hindu families celebrate a festival or domestic event, appearing on such occasions uninvited, and exacting by their noisy importunity a share of the food and charity that is being doled to the poor. Their shamelessness in this respect is incredible. During the Durgá Púja they force their way into respectable houses and make such a horrid uproar by shouting and singing that the inmates gladly pay something to be rid of them. Should this persecution have no effect on the rich man inside, they by means of a brass *lotá* and an iron rod madden the most phlegmatic Bábu, who pays liberally for their departure. The Bengali Bhát is as a rule uneducated, and very few know Sanskrit."

At weddings in Behar it is one of the duties of the Bhát to march out several miles to meet the bridegroom's procession, bearing with him a letter of welcome from the bride's father, and to conduct them to the bride's house. For these services, and for reciting verses and making himself generally useful, he receives presents of money and clothes. In some Behar districts and in parts of Chota Nagpur Bháts hold small parcels of land, usually about three or four *bighás* in extent, rent-free under the tenure known as *bhátottar*. Such grants are mostly of rather ancient date, and are regarded with disfavour by the landholders of to-day, who look more to Government as the fountain of honour, and do not make much account of the Bháts. A few Bháts have risen to be zamindars or tenure-holders, but the bulk of the caste are occupancy raiyats, cultivating by means of hired labourers and disdaining to touch the plough themselves.

The following statement shows the number and distribution of the Bháts in 1872 and 1881 :—

District.	1872.	1881.	District.	1872.	1881.
Bardwan	369	35	Patna	1,968	3,665
Bankura	17	74	Gya	4,763	4,996
Birbhum	146	1,381	Shahabad	7,101	12,000
Midnapur	1,484	1,151	Tirbut { Darbhanga ...	5,288	1,199
Hughli	72	103	Tirbut { Mozufferpur ..		3,936
Howrah		53	Saran	16,633	11,344
24-Parganas	176	227	Champaran	2,133	6,696
Nadiya	117	55	Monghyr	1,705	2,041
Jessore	113	5	Bhagalpur	2,975	4,346
Khulna	......	6	Purniah	1,179	1,968
Murshedabad	165	59	Maldah	152	16
Dinajpur	......	17	Santál Parganas	759	879
Rajshahye	2	5	Cuttack	469	1,015
Rangpur	21	175	Purí	106	131
Bogra	......	1	Balasore	375	295
Pabna	......	24	Tributary States	351	249
Darjiling	......	7	Hazaribagh	1,734	975
Jalpigori	......	370	Lohardagá	1,334	2,993
Kuch Behar	......	4	Singbhum	68	28
Maimansinh	135	48	Manbhum	678	1,148
Chittagong	87	522	Tributary States	489	1,515
Noakhali	......	31			

Bhát, a section of Ghásis in Chota Nagpur.

Bhatá, brinjal, a totemistic sept of Páns in Chota Nagpur.

Bhatan, a section of Bábhans in Behar.

Bhátásan, a *mul* or section of the Naomuliá or Goriá sub-caste of Goálás in Behar.

Bháter, Bhátes, a section of the Sátmuliá Maghayá sub-caste of Kándus in Behar.

Bhatgaián, a sept of Rajputs in Behar.

Bháthidár, a manufacturer or seller of spirituous liquor; a title of Kalwárs in Behar.

Bhatiárá, probably from *bhát*, 'boiled rice,' a class of Mahomedans who keep inns or eating-houses and also sell tobacco. Their female relatives are often of indifferent character.

Bhátiya, a low mendicant caste in Bengal who live by dancing, juggling, and singing.

Bhátnágar, a sub-caste of Káyasths and of Nágars in Behar.

Bhatore, a *mul* of the Sándil section of Maithil Brahmans in Behar.

Bhátpárá, a *samáj* or local group of the Páschátya Baidik Brahmans in the 24-Parganas.

Bhatrihari, a religious group of Jugis.

Bhatt or *Bhatta*, a learned Brahman. In some parts of India it specially designates a Brahman who professes a knowledge of the Vedas or belongs to a family in which they have been taught.

Bhatta, a *gáin* of the Kásyapa *gotra* of Rárhi Brahmans in Bengal. A title of Brahmans who officiate as priests for the Sukli caste.

Bhattáchárj, Bhattáchárji, a learned Brahman who teaches any branch of Sanskrit literature. In Bengal it is also applied to any respectable Brahman performing the functions of a priest.

Bhatta Misra, a group of the Srotriya sub-caste of Utkal Brahmans in Orissa.

Bhatta Rái, a *thar* of the Basishtha *gotra* of Nepáli Brahmans.

Bhattasáli, a *gáin* of the Bátsya *gotra* of Bárendra Brahmans in Bengal.

Bhattvál, a *thar* or section of Nepáli Brahmans.

Bhatuntara, a sub-caste of Karans in Orissa.

Bhaumik, a title of Brahmans and Kochhs; also conferred on petty landholders by the Nawabs of Dacca.

Bhaunrájpuri, a section of Sonárs in Behar.

Bhawániá, a section of the Baranwár sub-caste of Baniyás in Behar.

Bhedbakárár, a *pur* or section of Sákadwipi Brahmans

Bhekh, a *mul* or section of the Kanaujiá sub-caste of Sonárs in Behar.

Bheloriá, a section of Bábhans in Behar.

Bheludih, a *mul* or section of the Naomuliá or Majraut sub-caste of Goálás in Behar.

Bhengra, a horse, a totemistic sept of Mundas in Chota Nagpur.

Bherápákri, a *pur* or section of Sákadwipi Brahmans in Behar.

Bherihar, *Bheriál*, a synonym for Gareri, the shepherd caste of Behar, who also weave and sell blankets.

Bhikhári, a mendicant, a beggar.

Bhilár, a section of Kamárkalla Sonárs in Behar.

Bhimkáli, a *gáin* of the Bátsya *gotra* of Bárendra Brahmans in Bengal.

Bhin, a section of Murmis in Darjiling.

Bhinása, S. *binása*, destroyed, occupier of a deserted village, a sub-sept of the Nah-pá sept of Sherpa Bhotias of Nepal.

Bhind, a synonym for Bind.

Bhindhini, a synonym for Kámár in Singbhum.

Bhindowár, a *mul* or section of the Ghosin sub-caste of Goálás in Behar.

Bhingraj, king crow, a totemistic sept of Chiks, Lohars, Mundas, and Pátors in Chota Nagpur.

Bhinjo, a yellow bird, a totemistic sept of Mundas in Chota Nagpur.

Bhishak, a synonym for Baidya in Bengal.

Bhogá, a sub-caste of Goálás in Bengal who castrate bulls.

Bhogta, Bhogtá, a sub-caste of Bhuiyás in Behar, engaged in service and agriculture. They worship Masán, Dák, and other inferior gods. In Chota Nagpur, a sub-caste of Goálás; a title of Goálás in Behar. A sub-tribe of Kharwárs in Southern Lohardagá; a title and a sept of Kharwars and a section of Rajwárs in Chota Nagpur.

Bhojpuran, a section of Oraons in the North-Western Provinces and Behar.

Bhojpuriá, a sub-caste of Beldárs, Dosádhs, Halwáis, Nuniyás, Sonárs, Rajputs, and Támbulis in Behar; also a group of the Ráut Mehtar sub-caste of Doms; a section of the Biyáhut and Kharidáhá Kalwárs, and of Pachainya Doms in Behar.

Bhojraj, a kind of medicine, a sept of Chiks in Chota Nagpur.

Bhojyak, a synonym for Sákadwipi Brahmans.

Bhokwár, a section of Kurmis in Chota Nagpur and Orissa.

Bholark, a *pur* or section of Sákadwipi Brahmans in Behar.

Bhomápoli, a *kul* or section of Bábhans in Behar.

Bhora, a sept of Rajputs in Behar.

Bhotiet, a *mul* or section of the Naomuliá or Majraut sub-caste of Goálás in Behar.

Bhownrá, a hornet, a totemistic sept of Mundas in Chota Nagpur.

Bhritta, a hired servant or labourer.

Bhuá, a title of Kaibarttas in Bengal.

Bhuana, a section of Ghásis in Chota Nagpur.

Bhubankuri, a hypergamous group of Kaibarttas in Bakarganj.

Bhudeva, a synonym for Brahman.

Bhughi, a *mul* or section of the Maghayá sub-caste of Kándus in Behar.

Bhui, Bhuin, a title of Dakshin-Rárhi and Bangaja Káyasths.

Bhuiá, a title of Kewats in Orissa.

Bhuian, a tribe, a sept of Mundas in Chota Nagpur.

Bhuidhar, *Bhuisundar*, a synonym for Bhuinmáli, *q.v.*

Bhuihara, a title of Maithil Brahmans in Behar.

Bhui Kaibarta, a synonym for Haliá Kaibartta, a sub-caste of Kaibarttas who have taken to agriculture.

Bhuinhár, a synonym for Bábhan.

Bhuinhár, *Bhuinyá*, a title of the Bhumij tribe in Manbhum, and of Mundas and Oraons in Chota Nagpur, denoting their status as tenants of *bhuinhari* lands.

Bhuinhar-Munda, a sub-tribe of Mundas in Chota Nagpur.

Bhuinkora, a section of Ghásis in Chota Nagpur.

Bhuinmáli, *Bhusundar*, a cultivating, palanquin-bearing, and menial caste of Eastern Bengal, generally considered to be the remnant of an aboriginal tribe which embraced Hinduism, and accepted a servile position in relation to the Hindus of Eastern Bengal. This is likely enough, as instances are not wanting where it can be shown that the demand for labour in servile occupations, such as palanquin-bearing, was met by admitting aborigines to limited participation in the privileges of Hindus. In Dinájpur the names Hári and Bhúínmálí are used as synonyms, and it seems probable that the Bhúínmálís of the east are really the Háris of other parts of Bengal disguised under a more high-sounding name. According to Dr. Wise, the Dacca Bhúínmálís assert that they were originally Súdras, degraded in consequence of the following absurd incident: Párvatí obtained permission from her husband, Siva, to give a feast to her worshippers on earth. All castes were assembled at the entertainment, and in the midst of the enjoyment a luckless Bhúínmálí was overheard saying, "If I had such a beautiful woman in my house, I would cheerfully perform the most menial offices for her." Siva did not allow the speaker to retract what he had said, but gave him a beautiful wife and made him her sweeper. In confirmation of this legend a Bengali proverb defines the Bhúínmálí as the only Hindu ever degraded for love of garbage.

Origin.

The Bhúínmálí caste has two main sub-castes, the **Bara-bhágiyá** and **Chhotta-bhágiyá**, who never intermarry or hold social intercourse with each other. The former are chiefly cultivators, musicians, and palkí-bearers; the latter scavengers, looking down with contempt on the Dôm, Mehtar, and Halálkhors, who, after work, enter their houses without bathing, and allow their females to labour at the same offensive trade. At Saráil, in Tipperah, Bhúínmálís keep swine, but these recreants are not acknowledged as brethren. In certain villages the Bhúínmálí has ceased to be a professional musician and become a *chaukídár*, or watchman. No member of the caste ever keeps a shop, as he would have no customers, while want of capital precludes him from engaging in trade. A third division of the Bhúínmálí caste is known as Mitra Sení Behéras, tracing their descent from Mitra Sen, the reputed son or relative of Ballál Sen, and claiming to be the original bearers of Bengal. They cultivate the soil, and are in great request as household servants by Hindu families. Although the same Brahman officiates, the cultivating Bará-bhágiyá despises the cultivating Mitra Sení, and declines to eat with them. These palanquin-bearers, again, will not carry torches, and look down upon those who do.

Internal structure.

Although the caste has split up into divisions, following special occupations, the Bhúínmálí is properly one of the village servants employed in cutting down brushwood, repairing footpaths, sweeping the outside of the zamíndár's house, removing carcasses from the village, and preparing the *marocha* or marriage area, for doing which he receives one rupee, if the marriage is that of a village boy, and eight annas if that of a girl. He is likewise the masálchí engaged to carry the torch at Hindu weddings. A Bhúínmálí sweeper never enters a Hindu house to pollute it; but a maiden, called dásí or chhokrí, is engaged to sweep the floors of rooms and passages. Bhúínmálí women are sometimes employed as midwives or domestic servants.

Occupation.

The Bhúínmálí levels the space where the *sráddha* is held, constructs the small shed in which the votive offerings are placed, and, when a sacrifice is to be made, smears the ground with cowdung.

If the victim is killed in the morning, the flesh is distributed among Brahmans and clean Súdras; but if it is a *sandhyá* or evening sacrifice, everything, including the cloth by which the animal is bound, becomes the perquisite of the Bhúínmálí. He also prepares and plasters the mound on which the Vastú Puja is celebrated, receiving the ram as his remuneration, and, whenever a new house is built, he smears cowdung over the sides only, as he would lose caste if he touched the interior. Hindus of all castes smear the inside and steps of their own houses, but never those of others. The Bhúínmálí is the only native who will bedaub a strange house.

Marriage and religion.

The *gotras* among the Bhúínmálí of Dacca are Parásara and Áliman, the latter being only found along the banks of the old Brahmaputra. Both have clearly been borrowed from the higher castes. Marriage within the *gotra* is not prohibited. The caste has a degraded Brahman as purohit, and their washermen and barbers are members of the caste. The Bhúínmálí generally worship Krishna, and celebrate all the popular Hindu festivals. Along the Lakhya "Káwaj," who is probably the same as Kwájah Khizr, is invoked, as is also Pír Badr. Like the Hindu and Muhammadan peasantry generally, the Bhúínmálí abstains from work during the three days known as "Ambuváchí," which last from the tenth to the thirteenth of the waning moon of Ásharh (June–July), when the earth is believed to be impure and no Hindu can dig, plough, or even touch it.

Social status.

Although most anxious to represent themselves as Súdras, by aping the prejudices of the higher ranks, the Bhúínmálí are contemned, and obliged to live on the outskirts of villages apart from the Hindus, and to perform any menial work that is required of them. Like other low castes, the Bhúínmálí now-a-days have abjured pork. Until the last twenty years they associated on friendly terms with the Chandals, and would eat in a Chandal's house. They now decline to eat with, or even to work for, members of this caste, although they serve others quite as low.

The following statement shows the number and distribution of Bhúínmálís in 1872 and 1881 :—

District.	1872.	1881.	District.	1872.	1881.
Bardwan	......		Jalpigori	178	453
Bankura	......	84	Kuch Behar	......	381
Midnapur	......	93	Dacca	7,267	12,681
24-Parganas	14	91	Faridpur	1,836	8,263
Nadiya	1,866	1,382	Bakarganj	38	4,236
Jessore	1	413	Maimansinh	653	19,495
Khulna	......	59	Chittagong	......	1,412
Murshedabad	1	2,426	Noakhali	1,943	3,354
Dinajpur	792	3,194	Tipperah	5,522	12,490
Rajshahye	1,260	1,235	Maldah	2,109	2,975
Rangpur	3,771	5,083	Santál Parganas	......	8
Bogra	696	624	Manbhum	......	168
Pabna	......	6,408			

Bhuipurán, a title of Purans or Bhuiyás in Moharbhanj.

Bhuinputra, a title of Kaibarttas in Bengal.

Bhuist, a synonym for Sákadwipi Brahmans.

Bhuiyá, *Bhuinyá, Bhuiyán, Bhuinhár, Bhumiyá, Mushar, Náik Khandáyat, Khandáyat-Páik, Ghatwál, Ghatwár, Tikáyat, Purán, Rajwár, Rai, Rai-Bhuiyá, Ber-Bhuiyá, Sardár.* The bewildering array of synonyms which stands at the head of this article suggests a problem of great importance to ethnological research in India—the question what value can properly be attached to the names of tribes and castes as we find them at the present day. Are such names mainly fortuitous, deriving their origin from such accidents as locality, occupation, habit, and the like; or do they take us back to periods of remote antiquity and furnish clues that may safely be followed to the actual descent and true affinities of the human aggregates which they now serve to distinguish? Take, for example, the name Bhuiyá. Are we to regard this as the original designation of a tribe, once compact, which has now spread into the ends of the earth and disguised itself—πολλῶν ὀνομάτων ἐπώνυμος—under a variety of titles, which in course of time have come to be the badges of distinct endogamous groups; or, should we rather say, that the word Bhuiyá is itself no tribal name at all, but a mere title conferred on or assumed by many groups of men in different parts of India, on the strength in each case of their real or supposed claim to be deemed the original settlers and first clearers of the soil? If we adopt the former view, we are led to infer that all tribes or castes calling themselves Bhuiyá are offshoots from one original stock; while the latter theory points to no such general conclusion, and leaves us to account as we may for the various groups which use this title in a more or less pronounced and exclusive fashion. Most of the authorities who have written about the Bhuiyás have assumed at starting that the name must be a genuine tribal designation of very ancient date, and have thus been led into speculations which in my judgment rest on a very scanty foundation of ascertained fact. Thus Buchanan, finding in Bhágalpur, Behar, and Dinájpur a number of people calling themselves Bhuinyás,[1] seems to take it for granted that they all come of one stock. His line of argument on this point is not free from obscurity, but it certainly goes perilously near to identifying the distinctly non-Aryan Bhuinyás of North Bhágalpur and Dinájpur with the highly Aryan Bábhans of Behar, who assume the title Bhuinyá or Bhuinhár with reference to their claims upon the land. Sir George Campbell travels still further afield, and suggests that the Bhuiyás of Bengal are connected with the Buis of Madras and the Central Provinces. Colonel Dalton thinks this opinion probable, adding that the Bhuiyá features are on the whole of a Tamulian cast, and that the tribe is found in its greatest strength and purity on the southern frontier of Bengal.[2] The reference to the Bárah Bhuiyás of Assam, which

Tradition of origin.

---

[1] *Eastern India*, vol. ii, p. 426. Buchanan spells the name Bhungiyas, but this is obviously an attempt to transliterate the nasal *n* with which the word is usually written.

[2] *Ethnology*, p. 139.

follows, leaves it uncertain whether Colonel Dalton looked upon them also as an offshoot of the same stock as the Bhuiyás of Bengal; but it is clear from several passages in his account of the latter that he regarded them as a distinct tribe extending from Eastern and Northern Bengal to the southern borders of Chota Nagpur. His remark that "there are grounds for supposing that some of the noblest families in Bengal are sprung from this race, and they still hold high positions in the Jungle and Tributary Maháls" may even be taken to imply acceptance of Buchanan's identification of Bhuiyás and Bhuinhár-Bábhans, but this point is not entirely clear.

It seems to me that the history of the Bárah Bhuiyás of Assam and Eastern Bengal should of itself be sufficient to throw suspicion on a theory which admittedly rests on the basis of a mere resemblance of names. In an article published in the *Journal of the Asiatic Society of Bengal*, the late Dr. James Wise worked out with the patience and thoroughness which mark all his researches the obscure history of these twelve Bhuiyás or landlords, and showed that their designation had so little of a tribal character about it that at least one of them was a Mahomedan. They were in fact merely territorial chiefs of portions of Eastern Bengal or Assam. Nor is this state of things confined to the twelve historical Bhuiyás. The title survives in Assam at the present day as the designation of several forms of landholding rights. So in Chota Nagpur the Bhumij of Manbhum and the Oraons and Mundas of Lohardagá habitually use the term to denote a certain class of tenants who claim to hold large areas of land at privileged rates of rent in consideration of their being the descendants of the first clearers of the soil. In the Tributary States of Gángpur and Bonai the leading vassals of the chief are called Bhuiyás, both as members of a distinct tribe and in virtue of their status in connexion with the land; in Behar we find the high-caste Bábhan and the despised Musahar alike styling themselves Bhuinyá or Bhuinhár, though the latter have at the present day no special status in relation to the land. Lastly, in Rajputáná the term Bhumiá or Bhuiyá denotes Rajputs who hold land on a tribal tenure in virtue of their descent through a particular line.

Seeing, then, how wide is the area over which the term Bhuiyá is distributed; that it ranges from Assam to Rajputáná and from Behar to Madras; and that its use is elastic enough to include Rajputs and Bhumij, Mahomedans and Oraons, we should, I think, hesitate and demand some independent evidence of affinity before we pronounce it to be an original tribal designation, and accept the conclusion that all tribes which bear the name at the present day are sprung from a common stock. Further doubt is thrown upon this inference by the fact that the word Bhuiyá is itself a Sanskrit derivative, and is always associated with some sort of claim to the privileged tenure of land. Were it a genuine tribal name, we might expect that its etymology would be traceable to one of the non-Aryan languages, and that it would attach to groups defined rather by descent than by territorial status.

Although, however, the evidence, taken as a whole, goes to show that the title Bhuiyá does not necessarily denote a large original circle of tribal affinity, embracing all manner of men who now belong to separate groups, it by no means follows that there are no distinct tribes bearing the name. Among the Dravidian races of Western Bengal and Chota Nagpur large endogamous groups are certainly found who call themselves Bhuiyá and believe this to be their original designation. It may well be doubted whether their belief is correct, but the point is not very material for our present purpose. Among a considerable proportion of the non-Aryan tribes of Bengal a Sanskrit derivative has displaced the original tribal name so completely that in some cases no trace of the latter can now be discerned; and as often as not it happens that the name now sanctioned by actual usage may plausibly be referred to locality or to supposed rights in respect of the land. It is easy to see how this might happen. The advanced guard of the Aryan immigrants pressing forward in quest of land, and seeking a name for the alien races whom they found in possession of scanty clearings in the forest-clad tract of Central India, whither they had themselves been driven, would naturally ignore the tribal names of the groups with which they came in contact, and would call the strangers Bhuiyás or children of the soil. In course of time, as the Aryan domination grew, the name conferred by the conquering race would abide, and the older savage designations would pass away and be forgotten. But wherever the title of Bhuiyá, conferred in this rough general fashion by the new settlers on all the non-Aryans whom they came across, chanced to be adopted by a compact tribe, it would become the tribal name of that aggregate, and would be used by them for the purpose of describing themselves collectively. Thus, it would seem, may have arisen the distinction, well known in most parts of Chota Nagpur, between a 'Bhuiyá by tribe' and a 'Bhuiyá by title.' The Bhuiyás of Bonai and Keunjhar described by Colonel Dalton belong to the former category; the Bhumij, Mundas, and Oraons to the latter. The distinction will be made somewhat clearer if it is explained that every 'tribal Bhuiyá' will as a matter of course describe himself as Bhuiyá, while a member of the other tribes mentioned in the last sentence will only call himself Bhuiyá if he is speaking with reference to a question of land, or desires for some special reason to lay stress on his status as a landholder or agriculturist.

It is a plausible conjecture that the tribal Bhuiyás, properly so called, as distinguished from the titular Bhuiyás of other tribes or castes, may have had their origiual settlements in the Tributary States to the south of the Chota Nagpur plateau. In Gangpur. Bonai, Keunjhar, and Bamra the organisation of the tribe is more complete than elsewhere, and the name Bhuiyá is unequivocally recognised as the tribal designation. They form also a substantial proportion of the population of Singbhum, but their position there is less assured than in the Tributary States, and tradition avers that in the western and southern parts of the district they were subjugated by the Hos. Further north they seem to have been displaced in Lohardagá by the Mundas and Oraons, and in Manbhum by the Bhumij, for in those districts their settlements are scattered and weak. In Hazaribagh the tribe again gathers strength, and in Southern Behar we meet with Bhuiyás in large numbers bearing the opprobrious name of Musahar or rat-eater, but invariably calling themselves by their original tribal designation, which in Behar at any rate is not associated with any claim to hold land on privileged terms. The present distribution of the tribe seems in fact to accord fairly well with the hypothesis that the south of the Chota Nagpur country may have been their original centre of distribution. Spreading from that point, their social fortunes seem to have been determined by the character of the people with whom they came in contact. The stronger non-Aryan tribes—Mundas, Hos, and Santáls —cut like a wedge through the line of the Bhuiyá advance towards the north; a small number successfully established themselves in Hazaribagh beyond the range of Mundas, while those who travelled furthest in this direction fell under the domination of Hindus in Behar, and were reduced to the servile status which the Musahars now occupy. Travelling southward from the assumed centre, the conditions appear to have been more favourable, and the tendency has been for the Bhuiyás to rise rather than to decline in social status. Some of their leading families have come to be chiefs of the petty States of Orissa, and have merged their identity in the claim to quasi-Rajput descent. The main body of the southern colonists furnished the tribal militia of Orissa, and have now sunk the Bhuiyá in the Khandait or Swordsman—a caste of admitted respectability in Orissa, and likely in course of time to transform itself into some variety of Rajput.

Writing of the Bhuiyás of Gangpur and Bonai, Colonel Dalton says:—

Physical characteristics.

"They are a dark-brown, well-proportioned race, with black straight hair, plentiful on the head, but scant on the face; of middle height, figures well-knit and capable of enduring great fatigue, but light-framed like the Hindu, rather than presenting the usual muscular development of a hill-man. The features are very much of the same cast throughout. The cheek and jaw-bones are projecting, so as to give a breadth and squareness to the face. The nose is but slightly elevated, still neither so depressed nor so broad at the root as the generality of Turanian noses, and rather of a retroussé type; mouths and teeth well formed, and the facial angle generally good. The eyes well shaped and straight, but never very large or deep set." The Keunjhar Hill Bhuiyás, on the other hand, "are rather of an exaggerated Turanian type; very large mouths, thick and somewhat projecting lips, foreheads narrow and low but not receding, eyes dark, but well-shaped, hair plentiful on the head, though rather frizzly and generally scanty on face, but to this there are notable exceptions; short of stature, averaging about five feet two inches, round shouldered, and many of them with the lump that is produced by the displacement of the muscles in carrying loads banghy fashion. The colour of the skin varies from a deep chocolate, the predominating tint, to tawny." Further north, again, in the country round Párasnáth Hill, the landholders, though pretending to be Kshatriyas, are believed by Colonel Dalton to be Bhuiyás, and are described as swarthy, almost black in complexion, and with coarse, Negro-like features.

The traditions of the tribe vary greatly in different parts of the country, and in many cases refer merely to local migrations of recent date, which give no clue to their real affinities. Colonel Dalton says that the Bhuiyás to the south of Singbhum call themselves *Pawan bans*, 'the children of the wind,' to this day; and connecting this with Hanumán's title *Pawan-ka-put*, 'son of the wind,' suggests that the Bhuiyás are the veritable apes of the Rámáyana. The coincidence no doubt is curious, but can hardly be pressed to the point of associating a particular tribe with the epithet by which the early Aryans indicated their sense of the marked racial difference between themselves and the non-Aryans of Central India. With a single exception, their other traditions are valueless. This is the fact that all Bhuiyás, from the Musahars of Behar to the Khandait-Paiks of Southern Lohardagá, affect great reverence for the memory of Rikhmun or Rikhiásan, whom they regard, some as a patron deity, others as a mythical ancestor, whose name distinguishes one of the divisions of the tribe. It seems probable that in the earliest stage of belief Rikhmun was the bear-totem of a sept of the tribe, that later on he was transformed into an ancestral hero, and finally promoted to the rank of a tribal god. However this may be, his cult is peculiar to the Bhuiyás, and serves to link together the scattered branches of the tribe.

Internal structure.

The internal structure of the Bhuiyás is intricate and confusing, and illustrates the disorganisation which sets in when a tribe becomes scattered over a wide range of country, and is exposed to different religious and social influences. An examination of the groups into which they have now been broken up may throw some light upon the causes which work towards the disintegration of tribes and the formation of castes out of their fragments. The Bhuiyás of the Tributary States may be taken to represent the original nucleus of the tribe. They form at present a compact body, marrying among themselves, and secure in the possession of the ancestral landed tenures. Some of the chiefs have transformed themselves into Rajputs, but the memory of the tribal bond between them and their Bhuiyá vassal is preserved by the usage, described in detail below, which requires the former to seek investiture at the hands of the principal Bhuiyá. In Orissa and parts of Lohardagá the practice of military service paid for in land has become the distinctive characteristic, and an offshoot of the Bhuiyá tribe has parted from the parent body and assumed an independent existence as the Khandait caste. The social conditions of Orissa and the comparative weakness of its caste system seem to have favoured this development, so that the Khandaits now occupy rather a high place in the scale of precedence, and many of them look down upon the original stock and disown the tribal name.

In Behar the converse process has been at work. The Bhuiyá colonists of that part of the country fell under the domination of people stronger than themselves. Unlike their brethren in Orissa, they were in no demand as soldiers, while the swords of Rajputs and Bábhans were to be had for the asking. So the Bhuiyás found their level as landless workers in the fields; serving the men of the sword, who would not touch the plough; and their Hindu masters named them Musahars, from their non-Aryan practice of eating field-mice. Cut off geographically from the original nucleus of the tribe, and socially degraded by their unclean habits of food, they have now finally taken rank among the low castes of Behar. Known to the Hindus as Musahar or mouse-eater, they still treasure among themselves, as a sort of distinction, the old tribal name of Bhuiyá, which, as we have seen above, the Khandaits of Orissa are eager to cast off. These two groups—the Musahar caste of Behar and the Khandait caste of Orissa —mark for the Bhuiyá tribe the extremes of geographical and social displacement. Both are castes in the strict sense of the word, occupying a definite place in the systems to which they belong. One ranks high in the Orissa system, and tends on the whole to rise; the other is near the bottom of the social scale in Behar, and its prospects are not likely to improve.

"The Bhuiyás in Keonjhur," says Colonel Dalton, "are divided into four clans—the Mál or Desh Bhuiyás (they call themselves, and are called, the Desh-lok, or the people of the country), the Dandsena, the Khatti, and the Rájkúli Bhuiyás. The latter, as connected with the royal line, I should have placed first, but I give them in the order assigned to them by my informants. The Bhuiyás, it is said, twenty-seven generations ago stole a child of the Mohurbhanj Rájá's family, brought it up amongst them, and made it their Rájá. He was freely admitted to intercourse with Bhuiyá girls, and the children of this intimacy are the progenitors of the Rájkúli. But they are not considered first among Bhuiyás, because they are not of pure Bhuiyá descent."

The other divisions of the Bhuiyás need only be briefly noticed. The Ghatwál-Bhuiyás of Hazaribagh and the Santál Parganas hold service tenures, and the Tikait-Bhuiyás are usually small zamindars. Both affect to be endogamous, reject the name Bhuiyá, and represent themselves as belonging to independent landholding castes, and both will probably sooner or later gain admission into the large and miscellaneous community of local Rajputs. In the Santál Parganas Rai-Bhuiyá and Ber or Bhar-Bhuiyá and Deswáli-Bhuiyá are mentioned as sub-castes; but it is not clear that these are anything more than titular distinctions, which may or may not have an occasional bearing upon marriage. In Manbhum, on the other hand, the Kátrás-Bhuiyá, Musahar-Bhuiyá, and Dhorá-Bhuiyá seem to be true sub-castes.

Our information regarding the exogamous system of the tribe is unfortunately rather incomplete. We know nothing of the rules followed by the Bhuiyás of the Tributary States, where we might look for the closest adherence to primitive usage. In Singbhum a number of exogamous groups are recognised, and a man may not marry a woman belonging to his own group. Beyond this circle marriage is regulated by the ordinary method of counting prohibited degrees from the generation of the parents. The Musahar-Bhuiyás, too, who are shown in Appendix I as a distinct caste under the heading Musahar, have a long list of exogamous sections to which the ordinary rules apply. But among the Bhuiyás of Lohardagá and Hazaribagh the common tribal system of exogamy appears to be falling into disuse, and many groups which were at one time exogamous now admit of marriage within the group. I have endeavoured to represent the complex and obscure relations of the various divisions of the tribe in the Table given under the heading Bhuiyá in Appendix I, but the data available were in many cases far from perfect.

Marriage.

Among the Bhuiyás of the Tributary States, a girl rarely marries before she is fully grown up. Great freedom of courtship is allowed, and "slips of morality, so long as they are confined to the tribe, are not much heeded."[1] Colonel Dalton describes a curious and graceful custom by which the young men of one village pay a visit of courtship to the maidens of another, offering presents and receiving a meal, after which they spend the night in dancing and singing. He also mentions the fact that the bachelors always sleep together in a large house set apart for that purpose, and that in some villages the girls also have a house to themselves, where they spend the night with no one to look after them. In Singbhum these Arcadian habits seem to have died out, and infant-marriage, though by no means universal, is said to be gaining ground among the tribe. Khandaits, Tikaits, Ghatwals, and for the most part all landholding Bhuiyás in Hindu surroundings, marry their daughters as infants when they can get husbands for them. The two latter groups, however, are comparatively small, and their members are put to some difficulty in finding husbands within their own class; so that with them, as with the pseudo-Rajputs of Chota Nagpur, girls often remain unmarried until they have long passed the age of puberty. Musahars, on the other hand, still hold to adult-marriage.

Polygamy is allowed, and, in theory at least, a man may have as many wives as he can maintain. Few, however, can afford the luxury of more than one, and custom does not favour the taking of a second wife except when the first is barren. A widow may marry again by the *sagai* form, and it is usual, though not compulsory, for her to marry her late husband's younger brother. If she marries an outsider, her children by her late husband belong as of right to his family, though children at the breast are usually left in her charge till they are big enough to be independent of their mother. Marriage with an elder brother is strictly forbidden.

Divorce is permitted, with the sanction of the panchâyat of the tribe, if the wife be proved unchaste, if the husband neglect to maintain her, or if either party suffer from an incurable disease, such as leprosy or impotence. A divorced woman may marry again by the *sagai* form, unless she has been guilty of a *liaison* with a man of a lower caste, in which case any Bhuiyá who married her would render himself liable to expulsion from the community. An intrigue

---

[1] Dalton's *Ethnology*, p. 142.

within the tribe or with a man of respectable caste admits of being condoned by a fine, and does not operate as a bar to remarriage.

Colonel Dalton has the following remarks on the religion of the Bhuiyás in the Tributary State of Bonai :—

Religion.

"They have their own priests, called deoris, and their sacred groves, called 'deota sara,' dedicated to four deities—Dásum Pát, Bámoni Pát, Koisar Pát, and Borám. The three first are brethren, but there was some difference of opinion as to whether Bamoni was male or female. Borám is the sun, also worshipped under the name of Dharm Deota, as with the Oráons. The three minor deities are represented by stones in the sara, but Borám has no representation. Borám, as the first and greatest of gods and as the creator, is invoked at the sowing season with the offering of a white cock. In cases of sickness goats are offered to Dásum Pát and his brethren. On such occasions the goat is given by the owner of the house in which the sick person resides. On other occasions the victim is provided by the community. The sacrifices are all offered at the foot of trees in the sara; only men partake of the meat. The deori gets the head."

The Bhuiyás of Southern Lohardagá have advanced somewhat further on the path of orthodox Hinduism, but do not regularly employ Brahmans, except, as has been stated above, at the marriage ceremony. On certain occasions, however, Brahmans are called in to recite *mantras*, and the tendency towards conformity with Hindu usage will doubtless go on spreading as the country is opened up by the gradual improvement of communications. Already Thakuráni Mái, the 'bloodthirsty tutelary goddess' to whom, only twenty years ago,[1] the Hill Bhuiyás of Keonjhar offered the head of the obnoxious Dewan of their chief, has been transformed, in Singbhum and Lohardagá, into the Hindu Durgá, to whom a Bhuiyá priest makes offerings of goats, sheep, etc., which are afterwards partaken of by the worshippers. Changes of this sort raise an impassable barrier against researches into the origin of things, so that vestiges of the earlier beliefs of the people must be sought rather among the gods of the village and of the family than among the recognised *di majores* of popular worship. Thus the communal ghosts Darhá, Kudrá, Kudri, Dáno, Pacheriá, Haserwár, Pakáhi, with their ill-defined functions and general capacity for mischief and malevolence, are clearly akin to the host of evil spirits which people the world of the Munda and Oraon. To appease these ghosts by occasional offerings of fowls and rice, and thus to guarantee the community against the consequences of their ill-will, is the special function of the village Pahan, who levies small subscriptions for this sort of spiritual insurance. The tribal deities Rikhmun and Tulsibir belong to a different and less primitive type. Rikhmun, as has been mentioned above, is believed to be the original ancestor of the tribe; while Tulsibir was a restless and valorous Bhuiyá, who made war upon the gods until they appeased his wrath by admitting him to divine honours. I venture the conjecture that both Rikhmun and Tulsibir are merely transmuted

[1] 1st May 1868. Dalton's *Ethnology*, p. 147.

totems, in the hope that further enquiries among the more primitive Bhuiyás may bring out evidence on this point. Neither of these gods has special priests; their worship is conducted by any elder of the tribe. Sheep, goats, pigs, sweetmeats, and wine are the usual offerings, which afterwards furnish a feast for the assembled votaries. Snakes are only worshipped by those families which have lost one of their members by snake-bite. A certain herb, known as *gandhari ság*, and used as condiment, must be worshipped once a year, and can only be eaten if this rule is complied with. The custom suggests that the herb must once have been a totem of the tribe, but this cannot be certainly ascertained to be the case.

The following table shows the number and distribution of Bhuiyás in 1872 and 1881:—

District.	1872.	1881.	District.	1872.	1881.
Bardwan	1,625	1,197	Shahabad	234	......
Bankura	278	2,061	Tirhut	1,908	......
Birbhum	970	700	Saran	63	......
Midnapur	11,336	7,263	Champaran	113	227
Hughli	9	18	Monghyr	6,936	4,288
24-Parganas	817	8	Bhagalpur	33,163	29,887
Nadiyá	786	701	Purniah	41	177
Jessore	338	78	Maldah	194	292
Murshedabad	949	153	Santál Parganas	81,548	71,725
Dinajpur	......	46	Cuttack	5	3
Rajshahye	77	358	Puri	12	......
Rangpur	191	18	Balasore	61	153
Pabna	3	138	Tributary States	30,724	36,285
Darjiling	6	2	Hazaribagh	73,894	131,003
Kuch Behar	......	5	Lohardagá	45,008	58,159
Maimansinh	7	......	Singbhum	12,078	9,023
Chittagong	......	73	Manbhum	31,661	23,399
Patna	70	......	Tributary States	21,458	34,274
Gya	90,666	3,735			

Bhuiyá, a synonym for Kádar, a title of Báitis, Kapális, and Sunris in Bengal; a sept of Bhumijs.

Bhuiyá-Páik, a synonym for Khandáit.

Bhujál, a *thar* or sept of Mangars in Darjiling.

Bhujári, a synonym for Kándu.

Bhukhar, a group of the Aoghar sect of Saiva ascetics founded in Guzerat by a Dasnámi mendicant named Brahmagiri. *See* Aogar.

Bhuktuár, a section of the Mahili-Munda sub-caste of Mahilis in Chota Nagpur.

Bhulá, a *mul* or section of the Naiyá caste in Behar.

Bhuluá, a sub-caste of Bhuinmális, Dhobás, Jugis, Nápits, and of Kumhárs found in Noakháli.

Bhuluái, a sub-caste of Kaibarttas in Noakháli.

Bhumar, a sept of the Tungjainya sub-tribe of Chakmás in the Hill Tracts of Chittagong.

Bhumiá, a landlord, a proprietor of the soil; descendant of the founder of a village.

Bhumij, a non-Aryan tribe of Manbhum, Singbhum, and Western Bengal, classed by Dalton and others, mainly on linguistic grounds, as Kolarian. There can be no doubt that the Bhumij are closely allied to, if not identical with, the Mundas; but there is little to show that they ever had a distinct language of their own. In 1850 Hodgson published a short vocabulary[1] prepared by Captain Haughton, then in political charge of Singbhum; but most of the words in this appear to be merely Ho. The most recent observer, Herr Nottrott, of Gossner's Mission, says[2] that the Bhumij resemble the Mundas most closely in speech and manners, but gives no specimens of their language, and does not say whether it differs sufficiently from Mundári to be regarded as a separate dialect. I am inclined myself to believe that the Bhumij are nothing more than a branch of the Mundas, who have spread to the eastward, mingled with the Hindus, and thus for the most part severed their connexion with the parent tribe. This hypothesis seems on the whole to be borne out by the facts observable at the present day. The Bhumij of Western Manbhum are beyond doubt pure Mundas. They inhabit the tract of the country which lies on both sides of the Subarnarekhá river, bounded on the west by the edge of the Chota Nagpur plateau, on the east by the hill range of which Ajodhyá is the crowning peak, on the south by the Singbhum hills, and on the north by the hills forming the boundary between Lohardagá, Hazaribagh, and Manbhum districts. This region contains an enormous number of Mundári graveyards, and may fairly be considered one of the very earliest settlements of the Munda race. The present inhabitants use the Mundári language, call themselves Mundas, or, as the name is usually pronounced in Manbhum, Muras, and observe all the customs current among their brethren on the plateau of Chota Nagpur proper. Thus, like all the Kolarians, they build no temples, but worship Buru in the form of a stone smeared with vermilion, which is set up in a *sarna* or sacred grove near the village. A *sarna* is invariably composed of purely jungle trees, such as *sál* and others, and can therefore be recognised with certainty as a fragment of the primeval forest, left standing to form an abiding place for the aboriginal deities. They observe the *sarhul* festival at the same time and in the same way as their kindred in Lohardagá and Singbhum, and the *láyá* or priest is a recognised village official. Marriages take place when both parties are of mature age, and the betrothal of children is unknown. Like the Mundas of the plateau, they first burn their dead and then bury the remains under gravestones, some of which are of enormous size. On certain feast days small supplies of food and money are placed under these big stones to regale the dead, and are abstracted early the next morning by low-caste Hindus.

Origin.

On the eastern side of the Ajodhya range, which forms a complete barrier to ordinary communication, all is changed. Both the Mundári language and the title of Munda have dropped out of use, and the aborigines of this eastern tract call themselves

---

[1] *Bengal Journal*, vol. xviii, part II, p. 967; *Essays*, vol. ii, p. 97.
[2] *Grammatik der Kolh-Sprache*, p. 4.

Bhumij or Sardár, and talk Bengali. The physical characteristics of the race, however, remain the same; and although they have adopted Hindu customs and are fast becoming Hindus, there can be no doubt that they are the descendants of the Mundas who first settled in the country, and were given the name of Bhumij (autochthon) by the Hindu immigrants who found them in possession of the soil.

The early history of the tribe and its general characteristics are sketched by Colonel Dalton[1] in the following passages:—

Early history.

"The Bhúmij of the Jungle Maháls were once, under the nickname of *chuár* (robbers), the terror of the surrounding districts, and their various outbreaks were called *chuáris*. On several occasions since they came under the British rule they have shown how readily a *chuári* may be improvised on very slight provocation. I do not know that on any occasion they rose, like the Mundáris, simply to redress their own wrongs. It was sometimes in support of a turbulent chief ambitious of obtaining power to which, according to the courts of law, he was not entitled; and it was sometimes to oppose the Government in a policy which they did not approve, though they may have had very little personal interest in the matter. Thus, in the year A.D. 1798, when the Pánchet estate was sold for arrears of revenue, they rose and violently disturbed the peace of the country till the sale was cancelled. After hostilities had continued for some time, in reply to a very pacific message sent to them by the officer commanding the troops, they asked if the Government were going to sell any more estates. I do not think that the settlement of any one of the Bhúmij Jungle Maháls was effected without a fight. In Dhalbhúm the Rájá resisted the interference of the British power, and the Government set up a rival; but after various failures to establish his authority they set him aside and made terms with the rebel. In Barábhúm there was at one time a disputed succession. The courts decided that the eldest born of Rájá Viviká Náráyan, though the son of the second wife, should succeed in preference to the son of the first wife, the Pát Ráni. The Bhúmij did not approve of the decision, and it was found necessary to send a military force to carry it out. This was the origin of the last disturbance, known as Gangá Náráyan's rebellion, which broke out in 1832. Lakshman, the son of the Pát Ráni alluded to above, continuing to oppose his brother, was arrested, and died in jail, leaving a son, Gangá Náráyan. On the death of Rájá Raghunáth Sinh he also was succeeded by the son of his second Ráni, who was declared by the Supreme Court to be heir, in opposition to a claim again set up by Mádhab Sinh, the younger son, but the son of the Pát Ráni; but failing in his suit, Mádhab Sinh resigned himself to his fate, and was consoled by being appointed *díwán*, or prime minister, to his brother. In this capacity he made himself thoroughly unpopular, more especially by becoming an usurious money-lender and extortionate grain-dealer, and soon Gangá Náráyan found that, in opposing a man so detested, a majority of the people

[1] *Ethnology of Bengal*, p. 174.

would side with him. Accordingly, in the month of April 1832 he, at the head of a large force of *ghátwáls*, made an attack on Mádhab Sinh and slew him. This foul crime was committed with great deliberation, cunning, and cruelty. Mádhab was seized and carried off to the hills to be sacrificed. Gangá Náráyan himself first smote him with his battle-axe, then each *sardár ghátwál* was compelled to discharge an arrow at him, and thus all the leading *ghátwáls* became implicated in the plot. A system of plundering was then commenced, which soon drew to his standard all the *chuárs*—that is, all the Bhúmij of Barábhúm and adjoining estates. He attacked Barábázár, where the Rájá lived, burned the Munsif's *káchári* and the police station, from which the police had fled, but three unfortunate peons (runners) of the Munsif's court were caught and killed. The officials and the police fell back on Bardwan, and for some time Gangá Náráyan had the country at his mercy. He sacked every place worth plundering; but in November following a force was collected, consisting of three regiments of Native Infantry and eight guns, and military operations against the insurgents commenced. They were soon driven to take refuge in the hills, but being pressed there also Gangá Náráyan fled into Singbhúm, and endeavoured to enlist in his favour the reputed invincible and irrepressible Larkás. They were just then at issue with one of the chiefs, who claimed supremacy over a portion of them, the Thákur of Kharsáwán; and though they were not unwilling to join in the row, they wished, before they committed themselves to Gangá Náráyan's leadership, to test his capacity to lead. They therefore demanded that he should in the first place make an attack on the fort of the Thákur of Kharsáwán. In complying with this request he was killed, and the Thákur had the pleasure of sending his head to Captain Wilkinson with a letter quite in the style of Falstaff.

"I have not been able to discover that the Bhúmij possess any independent traditions of migrations. Those who live in proximity to Chutiá Nágpur recognise no distinction between themselves and the Mundas. They intermarry and associate and coalesce in all matters indicating identity of race; for, though it may be said that they are not much troubled with caste prejudices, there is no portion of the old Indian population which is quite free from it. The Bhúmij farther east have become too Hinduised to acknowledge the relationship. The Dhalbhúm Bhúmij consider themselves autochthones, and will not admit that they are in any way connected with the Mundas, Hos, or Santáls. It is pretty certain that the *zamindárs* of all these estates are of the same race as their people, though the only man among them whom I found sensible enough to acknowledge this was the Rájá of Bághmúndí; the others all call themselves Kshattriyas or Rajputs. but they are not acknowledged as such by any true scion of that illustrious stock. In claiming to be Rajputs they do not attempt to connect themselves with any of the recognised families of the tribe, but each family has its own special legend of miraculous production. The family legend of the Rájá of Barábhúm may be given as a specimen of their skill in making pedigrees:—'Nath Varáha and Kes Varáha, two brothers, quarrelled with their father, the Rájá of Virát, and settled at the Court of Vikramáditya. (This has some connection with the tradition of the adjoining estate of Pátkum, the Rájá of which claims descent from Vikramáditya.) Kes, the younger brother, was sawn into two pieces; and with his blood Vikram gave a *tiká* or mark on the forehead to the elder brother, and a pair of umbrellas, and told him that all the country he could ride round in a day and night should be his. Nath mounted his steed and accomplished a circuit of eight *yojanas* within the time specified in what is now Barábhúm; and this must be all true, as the prints of his horse's hoofs are still visible on the southern slopes of the hills.' With one or two exceptions all the *ghátwáls* (captains of the border and their men) of the Bhúmij part of Mánbhúm and Singbhúm districts are Bhúmij, which is a sure indication of their being the earliest settlers. They were the people (like the Mundárí Bhúinhárs in Chutiá Nágpur, the Bhuiyás in Bonái, Gángpur, Keunjhar, etc., and Gonds in Sargújá and Udaipur) to whom the defence of the country was entrusted. The Bhúmij *ghátwáls* in Mánbhúm have now, after all their escapades, settled down steadily to work as guardians of the peace. The Rájá of the extensive *samíndári* of Dhalbhúm is no doubt of Bhúmij extraction, but for him the Heralds' College of the period failed to manipulate a Rájput descent. His ancestor was a washerman, who afforded refuge to the goddess Kálí when, as Rankíní, she fled from a demon in Pánchet. The goddess, in gratitude, gave the washerman a young Bráhmaní, a ward of her own, to wife, and the Rájás of Dhalbhúm are the descendants of this union. The origin of the story appears to be that a Bhúmij chief of Dhalbhúm, probably at the instigation of a Bráhman, stole from its shrine in Pánchet an image of Rankíní and set it up as his own tutelary deity. The shrine from which the image was abstracted is shown at the village of Pára, near Puruliá in Mánbhúm, and it became the popular object of worship in Dhalbhúm for all classes of people there. Rankíní especially rejoiced in human sacrifices. It is freely admitted that in former years children were frequently kidnapped and sacrificed at her shrine; and it cannot be very positively asserted that the practice of offering such victims has long been discontinued. At the shrine of this goddess a very cruel scene was enacted every year till 1865, when, with the concurrence of the *samíndár*, it was put a stop to. It was called the *Bindaparab*; and Gangá Náráyan probably had it in his mind when he so cruelly disposed of Mádhab Sinh. At this *parab* two male buffaloes are driven into a small enclosure, and on a raised stage adjoining and overlooking it the Rájá and suite take up their position. After some ceremonies the Rájá and his *purohit* or family priest discharge arrows at the buffaloes, others follow their example, and the tormented and enraged beasts fall to and gore each other, whilst arrow after arrow is discharged. When the animals are past doing very much mischief, the people rush in and hack at them with battle-axes till they are dead. The Santáls and wild Kharriás, it is said, took delight in this festival; but I have not heard a murmur at its discontinuance, and this shows it had no great hold on the minds of the people. Many of the Bhúmij tribe are well off. Some of them, who are *sardár ghátwáls*, are in virtue of their office proprietors of estates, comprising each from one to twenty manors; but as the most substantial tenants under them are also hereditary *ghátwáls* rendering service and paying besides but a very low fixed rent, these *ghátwálí* estates are not so valuable to the proprietor as villages on the ordinary tenure would be. The Bhúmij live in commodious, well-built houses, and have all about them the comforts to which the better class of cultivators in Bengal are accustomed. Those who live quite amongst the Bengalis have retained few of their ancient customs; none, perhaps, except the great national amusement, the gay meetings for dance and song both at their villages and at *játras*, which are characteristic of all Kols. In appearance they are inferior to the Hos of Singbhúm and to the best of the Mundas of Chutiá Nágpur. They are short of stature, but strongly built, and, like the Santáls, rather inclined to fleshiness. In complexion they are variable, like the Mundas, ranging from a dark chocolate to a light brown colour; they observe many of the Hindu festivals, but retain their sacred groves, in which they still sacrifice to the old gods. They have generally left off eating cow's flesh, in which their unreformed brethren in Singbhúm and Chutia Nágpur indulge, but eat fowls. The Bhúmij have in a great degree lost the simplicity and truthfulness of character for which their cognates are generally distinguished. They have acquired from the Bengalí Hindus the propensity to lie, but they have not the same assurance or powers of invention, and their lies are so transparent that they are easily detected."

Internal structure.

The internal structure of the Bhumij tribe is shown in Appendix I. The sub-tribes are numerous, and vary greatly in different districts. With the possible exception of the iron-smelting Shelo in Manbhum, the names of these groups seem to have reference to their supposed original settlements. It deserves notice that the tendency to form endogamous divisions seems to be stronger in outlying districts than it is at the recognised head-quarters of the tribe. Thus in Manbhum and Singbhum we find only one sub-tribe Shelo, which obviously got detached from the parent group by reason of its members adopting, or perhaps declining to abandon, the comparatively degraded occupation of iron-smelting. In Midnapur, on the other hand, where the Bhumij settlements are of comparatively recent date, we find five territorial sub-tribes in addition to the functional group of Shelo. The reason seems to be that when the stream of emigration is not absolutely continuous, successive sections of immigrants into distant parts of the country are affected in various degrees by the novel social influences to which they are exposed. Some groups become more rapidly Hinduised than others, and thus there arise divergences of usage in matters of food and drink, which constitute a bar to intermarriage, and in time lead to the formation of sub-tribes. These divisions often outlast the differences of custom and ritual from which they took their origin, and in some cases the prohibition of intermarriage comes to be withdrawn, and the names alone remain to show that such a prohibition was once in force. The exogamous divisions of the tribe are totemistic, and closely resemble those met with among the Mundas. The rule of exogamy is simple.

Marriage.

A man may not marry a woman of his own sept, nor a woman who comes within the standard formula for reckoning prohibited degrees, calculated as a rule to three generations in the descending line, but sometimes extended to five where *bhaiyádi* or mutual recognition of kinship has been maintained between the families.

The aboriginal usage of adult-marriage still holds its ground among the Bhumij, though the wealthier members of the tribe prefer to marry their daughters as infants. The extreme view of the urgent necessity of early marriage is unknown among them, and it is thought no shame for a man to have a grown-up daughter unmarried in his house. Sexual intercourse before marriage is more or less recognised, it being understood that if a girl becomes pregnant arrangements will at once be made to marry her to the father of her child. Brides are bought for a price ranging usually from Rs. 3 to Rs. 12, and the wedding may take place, according to arrangement, at the house of either party. When, as is more usual, it is celebrated at the bride's house, a square space (*marwa*) is prepared in the court-yard (*angan*) by daubing the ground with rice-water. In the centre of this space branches of *mahuá* and *sidha* trees are planted, bound together with five cowrie shells (*Cypræa moneta*) and five pieces of turmeric, and at the corners are set four earthen water-vessels connected by a cotton thread, which marks the boundary of the square. Each vessel is half filled with pulse, and covered with a concave lid, in which a small lamp burns. On the arrival of the bridegroom with his following of friends, he is led at once to the *marwa* and made to sit on a bit of board (*pira*). The bride is then brought in and given a similar seat on his left hand. A sort of mimic resistance to the introduction of the bride is often offered by her more distant female relatives and friends, who receive trifling presents for allowing her to pass.

After the bride has taken her seat and certain *mantras* or mystic formulæ have been pronounced by the priest, usually a Bengal Brahman, the bridegroom proceeds to light the lamps at the corners of the square. As fast as each lamp is lighted the bride blows it out, and this is repeated three, five, or seven times, as the case may be. The couple then return to their seats, and the bride is formally given to the bridegroom, appropriate *mantras* being recited at the time, and their right hands being joined together by the officiating priest. Last of all, the bridegroom smears vermilion on the bride's forehead, and his clothes are knotted to hers, the knot being kept intact for three, four, five, seven, or ten days, according to the custom of the family. At the end of that time they must rub themselves with turmeric and bathe, and the knot is solemnly untied in the presence of the bridegroom's relations. No priest is present on this occasion.

The Bhumij recognise polygamy, and in theory at least impose no limitation on the number of wives a man may have. The tribe, however, are for the most part poor, and their meagre standard of living proves an effectual bar to excessive indulgence in the luxury of polygamy. When a man has no children by his first wife, he usually marries again if he can afford to do so; and it frequently happens that the second wife is a young widow, whom he marries by the *sanga* ritual, paying a nominal bride-price and incurring far less expenditure than would be necessary in the event of his marrying a virgin. Widow-marriage is freely permitted by the *sanga* ritual, in which a widow smears on the bride's forehead vermilion which the bridegroom has previously touched with his great toe. It is deemed right for a widow to marry her late husband's younger brother or cousin, if such an arrangement be feasible; and in the event of her marrying an outsider, she forfeits all claim to a share in her late husband's property and to the custody of any children she may have had by him. Traces of the growth of a sentiment adverse to the practice of widow-marriages may perhaps be discerned in the fact that the children of widows by their second husbands experience some difficulty in getting married, and tend rather to form a class by themselves.

Widow-marriage.

The Bhumij of Manbhum allow divorce only when a woman has been guilty of adultery. A council of relations is called, who hear the evidence and determine whether the charge has been proved. If their finding is against the woman, her husband solemnly draws from her wrist the iron ring, which is the visible sign of wedlock. Water is then poured on a *sál* leaf, and the husband tears the wet leaf in two to symbolise separation. This ceremony is called *pát páni chirá*, 'the wet leaf rent,' and besides making the divorce absolute, relieves the husband from any claim by the wife for maintenance. He is himself socially impure after the ceremony until he has shaved and performed certain expiatory rites, the most important of which appears to be giving a feast to the relatives who came together to adjudicate on the case. A woman has no right to divorce her husband, and if neglected or ill-treated her only remedy is to run away with another man. Divorced wives may marry again by the *sanga* ritual, but their offspring by their second husbands are at the same social disadvantage in respect of marriage as has been noticed above in referring to the children of widows. In both cases the sentiment is unquestionably due to the influence of Hinduism in modifying the original usages of the tribe.

Divorce.

In matters of inheritance and succession the tribe usually affect to follow the school of Hindu law in vogue in their neighbourhood, and hardly any vestiges of special tribal custom can now be traced. Almost all Bhumij, however, give the eldest son an extra share (*jethangs* or *bara angs*) when the property is divided; and the *ghatwáli* members of the tribe follow the local custom of primogeniture, the younger sons being provided for by small maintenance grants.

Succession.

If a man leaves no children, his widow takes a life-interest on the property.

Religion.

The religion of the Bhumij varies, within certain limits, according to the social position and territorial status of the individuals concerned. Zamindars and well-to-do tenure-holders employ Brahmans as their family priests, and offer sacrifices to Kali or Mahámáyá. The mass of the people revere the sun under the names of Sing-Bonga and Dharm, as the giver of harvests to men and the cause of all changes of seasons affecting their agricultural fortunes. They also worship a host of minor gods, among whom the following deserve special mention:—(1) Jáhir-Buru, worshipped in the sacred grove of the village (*jáhir-thán*) with offerings of goats, fowls, rice, and ghee at the Sarhul festival in the months of Baisakh (April–May) and Phálgun (January–February). The láyá presides at the sacrifice, and the offerings are divided between him and the worshippers. Jáhir-Buru is supposed to be capable of blasting the crops if not duly propitiated, and her worship is a necessary preliminary to the commencement of the agricultural operations of the year. (2) Kárákátá, (*Kárá* = 'buffalo,' and *Kátá* = 'to cut') another agricultural deity, to whom buffaloes and goats are offered towards the commencement of the rains. The skin of the buffalo is taken by the worshippers; the horns form the perquisite of the láyá; while the Doms, who make music at the sacrifice, are allowed to carry off the flesh. In the case of goats, the láyá's share is one-third of the flesh. If Kárákátá is neglected, it is believed there will be a failure of the rains. The cult of this deity, however, is not so universal as that of Jáhir-Buru. (3) Bághut or Bágh-Bhut, who protects his votaries from tigers, is worshipped in Kartick (October–November) on the night of the Amábasyá or the day preceding it. The offerings are goats, fowls, ghee, rice, etc., which may be presented either in the homestead or on the high land (*tánr*) close to the village. In the former case the head of the family officiates as priest; in the latter the láyá's services are enlisted, and he can claim a share of the offerings. (4) Grám-Deota and Deosháli, gods of village life, who ward off sickness and watch over the supply of water for drinking and irrigation of the crops. They are propitiated in Ashár (July–August) with offerings of goats, fowls, and rice, at which láyás preside. (5) Buru, a mountain deity associated with many different hills throughout the Bhumij country, and worshipped for recovery from sickness and general prosperity on the first or second Mágh. The head of the family or a láyá serves as priest. (6) Kudra and Bisaychandi are malignant ghosts of cannibalistic propensities, whom the láyás propitiate in the interests of the community. Private individuals do not worship them. (7) Pánchbahini and Báradelá are local deities worshipped by the Baukura Bhumij in much the same fashion as Jahir-Buru, the chief difference being that the offerings to Pánchbahini are she-goats and a kind of scent called *máthághashá*, while only fowls are presented to Báradelá.

Festivals.

With the Bhumij, as with other non-Aryan tribes of Chota Nagpur, the Karam festival, Colonel Dalton's description of which is quoted in the article

Oraon, seems to be especially popular. The Bhumij of Bankura district celebrate this feast in the latter half of the mouth Bhádra, corresponding roughly to the first half of September. A branch of the karam-tree (*Nauclea parvifolia*) is planted by the láyá in the centre of the village dancing ground (*ákhrá*). At the foot of this branch is a vessel partly filled with earth, into which, on the first day of the festival, the unmarried girls of the village throw various kinds of seed grain. These are carefully tended and watered from time to time so as to germinate by the Sankránti, or last day of the month, when the girls give the sprouting blades to each other, and wear them in their hair at the dance, which usually lasts the whole of that night.

Priests.

The sacerdotal arrangements of the tribe have already been incidentally referred to. The upper classes employ Brahmans of their own, and ignore the cult of the earlier gods; while the mass of the tribe are guided in their regular observances by the teachings of the láyás or priests of the forest gods, and only call in the assistance of Brahmans on the comparatively rare occasions when it is deemed necessary to propitiate one of the standard Hindu deities. But the Brahman who serves the Bhumij zamindar or tenure-holder as a family priest takes a higher place in the local community of Brahmans than the casual Brahman who ministers to the spiritual needs of the ordinary cultivator. The former will call himself a Rarhi Kulin, and will be received on equal terms by all other members of the sacred order; while the latter belongs to a much lower class, and associates with the comparatively degraded Brahmans who work for Kurmis and Dhobas.

Disposal of the dead.

The funeral rites of the Bhumij are characteristic, and lend strong support to the opinion that the tribe is merely a branch of the Mundas. On the death of a Bhumij his body is laid with the head to the south on a funeral pyre, which is kindled by his male relatives. When the pyre is well alight, the males go home, and the wife, sister, or other female relative of the deceased comes to the burning-place, carrying an earthen vessel of water. There she waits till the fire has burned down, quenches the ashes with water, and picks out and places in the vessel the fragments of bone left unconsumed. Some of these fragments are interred at the foot of a *tulsi* plant (*Ocymum sanctum*) in the courtyard of the dead man's house, others are taken in the vessel to the original cemetery of his family.[1] There a hole is dug and the vessel of bones placed

[1] The theory is that the bones should be taken to the village in which the ancestors of the deceased had the status of *bhuinhárs* or first clearers of the soil; but this is not invariably acted up to, and the rule is held to be sufficiently complied with if a man's bones are buried in a village where he or his ancestors have been settled for a tolerably long time. It deserves notice that the Tamárhiá Bhumij of Midnapur transport the bones of their dead to the great Munda cemetery at Chokahatu, the place of mourning in pargana Tamárh of Lohardagá. No stronger proof could well be given of the identity of the Bhumij with the Mundas. The Desi Bhumij of Midnapur go to Kuchong, in Singbhum, and some of the Singbhum Bhumij to Suisa, in Bagmundi of Manbhum.

inside, supported by three stones. The earth is then filled in, and a large flat stone laid over all, on which a fowl is sacrificed to ensure the repose of the dead. The spirits of those whose bones rest in the same place are solemnly informed that another has been added to their number, and are enjoined not to quarrel, but to abide peacefully in the land of the dead. The survivors then partake of a feast of rice, *dál*, and other vegetables prepared by the more distant relatives of the deceased. This strictly non-Aryan ritual has of late years been to some extent overlaid by observances borrowed from the regular Hindu *sráddh*. On the tenth day the mourners are shaved, and on the eleventh balls (*pinda*) of rice, sesamum, molasses, and plantain are offered to ancestors under the supervision of a Brahman, who receives such presents as the means of the family permit them to give. A more primitive mode of appeasing the departed spirit is met with among the Shelo Bhumij. On the eleventh day after death the chief mourner beats a bell-metal drinking-vessel with a stick, while another relation, standing by his side, calls loudly on the name of the dead. After a while a third man, unconnected with the family, and often a láyá, comes forward to personate the deceased, by whose name he is addressed, and asked what he wants to eat. Acting thus as the dead man's proxy, he mentions various articles of food, which are put before him. After making a regular meal he goes away, and the spirit of the deceased is believed to go with him. The relatives then finish the food prepared for the occasion.

Mention is made in the article on the Mundas of the custom by which the graves of the *bhuinhárs*, or representatives of those who first cleared the soil and founded the village, are marked by an upright stone pillar in addition to the horizontal slab which covers the bones of an ordinary raiyat not descended with one of these pioneer families. Precisely the same distinction is made among the Bhumij *ghatwáls* of Manbhum between village *sardárs*, or holders of entire *ghatwáli* tenures, and the *tábidárs*, or rural constables, who make up the rank and file of the *ghatwáli* force. The graves of the former are invariably distinguished by an upright monolith, sometimes bearing traces of rude attempts at ornamental shaping, while the tombs of the latter consist merely of a slab laid flush with the ground. This singular correspondence of funeral usage, coupled with the fact that many of the Manbhum *ghatwáls* call themselves by the title *bhuinhár* or *bhuinyá*, suggests the conjecture that the *ghatwáli* tenures in the south of that district are a survival under different names and changed conditions of the ancient tribal holdings known in Lohardagá as *bhuinhári*. Personal service of various kinds is one of the oldest incidents of the *bhuinhári* tenure, and it is not difficult to see how in a border district like Manbhum the character of this service might gradually be changed in accordance with local necessities until it came to take the form of the petty police functions which the *ghatwáls* perform, or are supposed to perform, at the present day. Their duties, it is true, are now discharged under the orders of Government, and not at the will of the zamindar, but this change

Police service.

has been brought about gradually, and is due partly to local disturbances, in which the Bhumij took the lead, and partly to the fact that the zamindars of Barabhum, originally the heads of the Bhumij community, have within the last hundred years assumed the style of Rajputs, and have spared no effort to sever their connexion with their own tribe. The antagonism thus set up between the chief and his retainers showed itself on his side by constant endeavours to resume their privileged tenures, and on theirs by steady resistance to his authority and assertion of their direct subordination to the Magistrate of the district. Thus in course of time it has come about that a number of very ancient tenures, representing in their inception the tribal rights of the first clearers of the soil, have been transformed into police *jágirs*, and have recently been surveyed and demarcated at the cost of Government in the interest of the executive administration of the Manbhum district.

Occupation.

The original occupation of the Manbhum Bhumij is believed by themselves to have been military service, and there can be little doubt that the bands of Chuárs or plunderers, who repeatedly overran the Midnapur district towards the end of last century, were largely recruited from this tribe. The circumstance, however, that they took a more or less prominent part in a series of marauding attacks on an unarmed and unwarlike population affords no ground for a belief in the existence among them of any real military instinct; and in fact they are conspicuous for the dislike of discipline, which is one of the prominent characteristics of the Kolarian races. For many years past agriculture has been the sole profession of all the sub-tribes except the iron-smelting Shelo. A few have engaged in petty trade, and some have emigrated to the tea districts of Assam. Their relations to the land are various. The zamindars of Barabhum, Dhalbhum, Manbhum, Patkum, and Bagmundi probably belong to the Bhumij tribe, though they now call themselves Rajputs. Next to them rank the sardar ghatwals of the large service-tenures known in Manbhum as *tarafs*. Three of these admit themselves to be Bhumij, while the fourth, Manmohan Singh, of Taraf Satarakháni, now claims to be a Rajput, regardless of the fact that a few years ago his grandfather wrote himself down in public documents as Bhumij. I mention this instance as an illustration of the facility with which brevet rank as a self-made Rajput may be obtained. Manmohan Singh keeps a Brahman to support his pretensions, and professes to be very particular in all matters of ceremonial observance. His descendants will doubtless obtain unquestioning recognition as local Rajputs, and will intermarry with families who have undergone the same process of transformation as themselves. The great bulk of the Bhumij, who are simple cultivators and labourers, stand on a far lower social level than the landholding members of the tribe. They rank somewhat below the Kurmi, and members of the higher castes will not take water from their hands. In their turn the Bhumij, though eating fowls and drinking spirituous liquors, look down upon Bauris, Bagdis, Doms, and Ghasis as more unclean feeders than themselves.

The following statement shows the number and distribution of the Bhumij tribe in 1872 and 1881 :—

District.	1872.	1881.	District.	1872.	1881.
Bardwan	293	7	Darjiling	......	31
Bankura	1,466	18,052	Dacca	11	66
Birbhum	49	58	Faridpur	4	194
Midnapur	35,344	25,639	Chittagong	......	376
Hughli with Howrah ...	13	383	Maldah	38	......
24-Parganas	660	5,551	Santál Parganas	......	7,969
Nadiya	159	37	Cuttack	2,169	2,425
Jessore	106	459	Balasore	1,676	2,591
Khulna	......	49	Tributary Mehals	29,596	10,081
Murshedabad	43	152	Hazaribagh	86	3
Dinajpur	......	6,819	Lohardaga	......	154
Rajshahye	91	667	Singbhum	37,353	43,894
Rangpur	3	......	Manbhum	90,261	104,358
Pabna	124	286	Tributary States	689	12,686

Bhumik, a title of Kaibarttas and Bangaja Káyasths in Bengal.

Bhumiká, a title of Korás in Western Bengal.

Bhumjan, a *thar* or sept of Gurungs in Darjiling.

Bhumphor, a title of the Mál sub-caste of Mauliks in Chota Nagpur.

Bhunángali, 'plougher of the soil,' a title of the cultivating castes; a title of Kaibarttas.

Bhunári, *Bhuniá*, *Bhuniwálá*, a grain-parcher. See **Kándu**.

Bhunasware, a section of Bábhans in Behar.

Bhunáwalá, *Bhunári*, up-country men who sell parched grain. In Behar the profession is followed by the Dhanuk and Kándu castes.

Bhuniá, the head of a village. In Cuttack, one of the former petty chiefs holding lands by tenure of military service.

Bhunjá, a synonym for Kándu.

Bhunja, *Bhujá*, a dealer in fried grain. See **Bharbhunja**.

Bhunjá-Teli, a sub-caste of Telis in Eastern Bengal.

Bhupál, a synonym for Rajput.

Bhupati, a prince, a sovereign, a landholder; a synonym for Rajput.

Bhuputra, *Bhubuta*, a title of Brahmans.

Bhuri, a *gáin* of the Kásyapa *gotra* of Rárhi Brahmans in Bengal.

Bhurji, a synonym for Kándu, a castor-oil maker.

Bhurswa, a sept of the Suryabansi sub-tribe of Rajputs in Behar.

Bhurtyál, a *thar* or section of Nepáli Brahmans.

Bhusáwálá or **Bhusiwálá**, a dealer in chaff—chopped straw—and bran of gram and pulses, who goes to villages and buys up the chaff at the threshing floors by the *khárá* or *kut*. *Khárá* is a net-like basket, containing from a maund to a maund and five seers; *kut* is 'valuation' or 'guess.'

Bhusbarát, a section of Bábhans in Behar, which may possibly be of totemistic origin.

Bhusbare, a *kul* or section of Bábhans in Behar.

Bhushná, a sub-caste of Kumhárs in Jessore; a *pathi* or hypergamous sub-group of Bárendra Brahmans in Bengal.

Bhusiwár, a sub-group of Maghaiyá Telis in Behar.

Bhuskuliá, a *mul* or section of the Ghosin sub-caste of Goálás in Behar.

Bhusnápati, a sub-caste of Kámárs in Eastern Bengal.

Bhusundar, a synonym for Bhuinmáli.

Bhusur, a synonym for Brahman and Rajput.

Bhusuwal, a *thar* or sept of Dámis in Darjiling, whose chief profession is sewing.

Bhu-swámi, a landholder, proprietor, prince, sovereign.

Bhuswáre, a *mul* of the Krishnan section of Maithil Brahmans in Behar.

Bhut, a title of Dakshin-Rárhi and Bangaja Káyasths.

Bhutáne, a section of the Biyáhut and Kharidáhá Kalwárs.

Bhutáni, a native of Bhután.

Bhuthá, a sept of Rajputs in Behar.

Bhutkuar, a sept of Lohars and Mundas in Chota Nagpur.

Biáhot, Biáhut, a sub-caste of Kalwárs in Behar who do not sell liquor and do not permit widows to remarry; a sub-caste of Kumhárs and Telis in Behar. See Biyáhut.

Biállisgrámi, a sub-caste of Támbulis in Bengal.

Biár, a section of Sunris in Behar.

Bibarhiá, a section of Sonárs in Behar.

Bich, a group of the Sundi sub-caste of Sunris in Western Bengal, who are distillers.

Bichhu, a section of Sunris in Behar.

Bichila, a sept of Rajputs in Behar.

Bichwar, a centipede, a totemistic sept of Chiks in Chota Nagpur.

Bid, a title of Baniyás.

Bidhiyá, a workman who perforates precious stones, pearls, coral, etc.

Bidrisáz, a maker of *bidri* or inlaid work in silver on a basis of inferior metal.

Bidyábágis, a literary title of Brahmans in Bengal.

Bidyadhari, a *mel* or hypergamous sub-group of Rárhi Brahmans in Bengal.

Bidyáratna, a literary title of Brahmans in Bengal.

Bidyárthi, a seeker after learning, a student.

Bidyasulokhi, a seeker after knowledge.

Bigahiá, a section of Bábhans in Behar.

Biha or **Binjha**, a fish, a totemistic sept of Bedyás in Chota Nagpur.

Bihan, a sept of Mundas in Chota Nagpur.

Bihiá, a section of the Biyáhut and Kharidáhá Kalwárs in Behar.

Bihishti, a water-bearer, generally Mahomedans.

Bijái, a *mul* or section of the Chhamuliá-Madhesiá sub-caste of Halwáis in Behar.

Bijaibanáras, a *mul* or section of the Tinmuliá Madhesiá and of Bhojpuriá Halwáis and Kándus in Behar.

Bijalpuriá, a section of Bábhans in Behar.

Bijayapanditi, a *mel* or hypergamous sub-group of Rárhi Brahmans in Bengal.

Bijhuniá, a sept of Rajputs in Behar.

Bijkunja, a *gáin* of the Kásyapa *gotra* of Bárendra Brahmans in Bengal.

Bikauwá, a class of Maithil or Tirhutiya Brahmans in Behar who derive their name from the practice of selling themselves or their sons in marriage to the daughters of the lower classes of Maithil Brahmans. Some Bikauwá Brahmans have as many as forty or fifty wives under this system. The wives live with their own parents, and are visited at intervals by their husbands. Bikauwá Brahmans who have married into the lower classes are not received on equal terms by the members of their own class, but the women whom they marry consider themselves raised by the alliance.

Bikrál, a *thar* or section of Nepáli Brahmans.

Bikrampur, a sub-caste of Telis in Eastern Bengal; a section of the Pachainyá sub-caste of Doms.

Bilar, a section of Sonárs in Behar.

Bilár, cat, a section of Kurmis in Chota Nagpur and Orissa.

Bilauriá, a section of Ayodhiábási Sonárs in Behar.

Bilkharia, a sept of Rajputs of the Bachgoti Chauhan sub-tribe, so named from Bilkhar, in Oudh.

Bilsar, a *mul* or section of the Ayodhiá sub-caste of Hajjáms in Behar.

Bilung, earth-salt, a totemistic section of Khariás in Chota Nagpur.

Bilwár, a section of the Amashta Káyasths in Behar.

Bilwár or *Bahalwár*, a sub-caste of Dosádhs in Behar.

Bin, a sub-caste of Malláhs in Behar; a sub-caste of Binds in Eastern Bengal.

Bind, *Bin*, *Bhind*, *Bindu*, a large non-Aryan caste of Behar an Upper India, employed in agriculture, earthwork, fishing, hunting, making saltpetre, and collecting indigenous drugs. Traditions current among the caste profess to trace their origin to the Vindhya Hills of Central India; and one of these legends tells how a traveller passing by the foot of the hills heard a strange flute-like sound coming out of a clump of bamboos. He cut a shoot and took from it a fleshy substance, which afterwards grew into a man, the supposed ancestor of the Binds. The myth seems to be of a totemistic character, but other traces of totemism are not forthcoming. Another story says that the Binds and Nuniás were formerly all Binds, and that the present Nuniás are the descendants of a Bind who consented to dig a grave for a Mahomedan king and was outcasted for doing so. Mr. Sherring treats the Binds as a branch of the Nuniás; others regard the Nuniás as a sub-caste of the Binds. The two castes are probably related in some way, but the evidence at present available does not enable us to determine with any approach to certainty which should be considered the parent group. It seems not improbable that the Binds may be a true aboriginal tribe, and the Nuniás a functional group differentiated by taking to the manufacture of earth-salt. But this is mainly conjecture.

Origin.

The Binds of Behar are divided into two sub-castes—**Khariát** and **Gondh**. These again are broken up into the *muls* or sections shown in the Appendix. The sections go by the male side, and the rule which forbids a man to marry a woman of his own section is supplemented by the standard formula *mamerá*, *chacherá*, etc., prohibiting intermarriage within certain degrees of collateral relationship. Binds admit both infant and adult-marriage, but the former is deemed more respectable, and all who can afford to do so endeavour to get their daughters married before they attain the age of puberty. Polygamy is permitted, but only to the limited extent that a man may marry a second wife in the event of the first proving barren. A widow is allowed to marry again by the *sagai* form, but is expected to marry her deceased husband's younger brother or younger cousin, should such a relative exist. Under no circumstances may she marry her late husband's elder brother or elder cousin. For the rest she is subject to the same table of prohibited degrees that would have regulated her marriage as a virgin. Divorce is not allowed. If a woman goes wrong with a man of another caste, she is summarily turned adrift and becomes a prostitute, turns Mahomedan, or joins some religious sect of dubious morality. Indiscretions within the caste are, however, more leniently dealt with, and admit of being atoned for by certain modes of penance. In such cases the woman, after having made amends for her offence, returns to her husband. It should be added that the morals of the Bind woman are said to be by no means above reproach.

Marriage.

The marriage ceremony of the Binds presents no features of special interest, and has obviously been modelled in most points on the orthodox Hindu ritual. After the first negotiations have passed between the parents of the bride and bridegroom, the headman (*manjan*) and the caste council (panchâyat) are consulted on the important question of prohibited degrees. This being settled, the next step is *ghardekhi*, an exchange of visits, at which the bridegroom's people see the bride, and *vice versâ*. In the course of the *ghardekhi* a date is fixed for *tilak*, when the bride's relatives come to the bridegroom's house and present to him a rupee, a new cloth, some cooking utensils, some betel leaves and areca-nut, and fix in the presence of the headman and some representatives of the caste council an auspicious date for the celebration of the marriage. The ceremony itself is substantially the same as that described by Mr. Grierson at pages 362 *seq.* of *Bihár Peasant Life.*

Religion.

The religion of the Binds, so far at least as it is concerned with the greater gods of the Hindu pantheon, is equally wanting in individual character, and differs in no material particulars from the vulgar Hinduism of the lower castes of Behar. The external observances of Brahmanism have been copied more or less accurately, while the esoteric doctrine, on which the whole body of symbolism depends, is entirely unknown to the votaries of the popular religion. Brahmans of the Maithil sub-caste preside at the worship of Siva as Bhagavat and of his consort as Jagadamba. Hanumán and the Narsingh avatár of Vishnu are also held in reverence. But these greater gods are worshipped at comparatively rare intervals, and far greater attention is paid to rural godlings, such as Bandi, Sokhá and Goraiyá, to whom goats, boiled rice, cakes, and sweetmeats of various kinds are offered every Wednesday by the men of each household; the offerings being eaten afterwards by the members of the family and the *deodi* relatives who are connected with the family by reason of their sharing in the same domestic worship. On Mondays and Fridays, in the months of Baisakh and Asár, the earth-god Bhuia is appeased with sacrifices of goats, sheep, and rice boiled in milk. In Srávan the Pánch Pir receive cakes and rice from the men, women, and children of the caste. Widows, however, may take no part in this rite. Mirá Sáhib, a Mahomedan saint, and Lukmáyi, a vengeful goddess, who burns men's houses with fire, are also worshipped in due season. Twice a year the entire caste make offerings to Tarturwárá of *achchhat* rice, flowers, betel leaves, and sweetmeats, which are afterwards divided among the caste brethren. The *kul devatá*, or patron deity of all Binds, is Kási Bába, about whom the following story is told:—A mysterious epidemic was carrying off the herds on the banks of the Ganges, and the ordinary expiatory sacrifices were ineffectual. One evening a clownish Ahír on going to the river saw a figure rinsing its mouth from time to time and making an unearthly sound with a conch shell. The lout, concluding that this must be the demon causing the epidemic, crept up and clubbed the unsuspecting bather. Kási Náth was the name of the murdered Brahman; and as the cessation of the murrain coincided with his death, the low Hindustani castes have ever since regarded Kási Bába as the maleficent spirit that sends disease among their cattle. Now-a-days he is propitiated by the following curious ceremony:—As soon as an infectious disease breaks forth, the village cattle are massed together and cotton seed sprinkled over them. The fattest and sleekest animal being singled out is severely beaten with rods. The herd, scared by the noise, scamper off to the nearest shelter, followed by the scape bull; and by this means it is thought the murrain is stayed. In ordinary times the Binds worship Kási Bába in a simpler fashion, each man in his own house, by presenting flowers, perfumes, and sweetmeats. The latter, after having done duty before the god, are eaten by his votary. Kási Bábá no doubt was an actual person who came by his end, if not exactly as told in the legend, at least in some tragic fashion which led to his being elevated to the rank of a god. In some of the other objects of the rural worship we may perhaps see survivals of the primitive animism which formed the religion of the aborigines of India before their insensible conversion to Brahmanism. Some of the tribal deities were, as we know, promoted to seats in the Hindu pantheon; others, whose position was less prominent and whose hold on the mind of the people was weaker, got thrust into the background as patrons of various rural events.

Occupation.

Some of the Binds in Behar possess occupancy holdings, but for the most part they are non-occupancy raiyats or landless day-labourers paid in cash or kind. Fishing, well-sinking, building mud walls, mat and basket-making, preparing saltpetre, and doing earthwork on roads and tanks, are among their chief occupations. A few of the more enterprising members of the caste have risen to be traders, and visit Bengal during the cold season with boat-loads of wheat, pulse, and gram. Binds, or Ráwats as they are commonly addressed, rank socially with Koiris, Gangotas, etc., and have Maithil Brahmans for their priests. In Ghazipur, says Dr. Wise, they are considered a pure caste, and in Sháhábád they are employed by Brahmans as water-carriers. Their status, however, in relation to Brahmans as regards water and *pakki* articles of food seems to vary in different districts. In Champáran and Chota Nagpur, for example, I am informed that Brahmans will take water and sweetmeats from the hands of a Bind, while in Sháhábád and Gya this appears not to be the case. In view of the fact that Binds freely indulge in spirit-drinking, eat crocodiles and field-rats like the Musahars, and are very fond of pork when they can get it, I think it likely that the rule is for them to be deemed impure.

Binds in Eastern Bengal.

Scattered colonies of Binds are also found along the great rivers of Central and Eastern Bengal. In Dacca they recognise three subdivisions—Jutaut Binds, Nún Binds, and Bin. The first is the most aristocratic, while those belonging to the second are degraded from working as palanquin-bearers, manufacturers of salt (nún), diggers, and, it is said, grave-diggers. Representatives of the Bin division are rarely met with, and I am inclined to doubt its existence. These settlers, who are distinguished by the title Chaudhri, lead an irregular life, eating pork and drinking spirits freely. Being debarred by reason of having settled in Bengal from intermarriage with the Binds of Behar and Upper India, they often find it difficult to procure wives from the small expatriated communities along the Padma. Some cultivate the soil, others kill mullet with the harpoon or catch them with *sirki* screens, like the *beruá*. Another occupation is cutting tamarisk (*jháu*) on the sandbanks of the Padma and selling it for fire-wood. By Binds, too, are made the best mud brasiers or *chúlhás*, used on board all native boats for cooking. Many are cunning sportsmen, and during December and January net great numbers of wild fowl and snipe. After the rice harvest the Binds wander about the country, digging up the stores of rice accumulated by field-rats in their burrows. From four to six pounds of grain are usually found, but even this quantity is sometimes exceeded. It is said that the Binds feast on the rats; but this they deny, explaining that to do so would be to reduce the next year's find of grain.

A Dasnámi Gosáin periodically visits the Dacca Binds, acting as their Guru, while a degraded Kanaujia Brahman officiates as purohit. Many of the Bengali Binds belong to the Panch Piriya sect, others worship Siva, and at the Mahábalí festival sacrifice a ram instead of the usual he-goat. At the Ganga Púja a swine is offered to Jalka Devi, the popular goddess of the Chamárs. Kárámat Ali and the Farazí Maulavís have of late years converted many of these outcaste Binds, but the village Muhammadans will not as yet associate with them. These converts are usually styled by the peasantry Chayli, from the Bengali word for the *berá*, or fish-trap.

The following statement shows the number and distribution of the Bind caste in 1872 and 1881:—

DISTRICT.	1872.	1881.	DISTRICT.	1872.	1881.
Bardwan	76	14	Maimansinh	37	57
Bankura	112	3	Chittagong	3	......
Birbhum	......	130	Tipperah	7	......
Midnapur	41	28	Patna	3,400	3,870
Hughli	} 38	{ 16	Gya	358	396
Howrah		9	Shahabad	21,383	24,582
24-Parganas	44	14	Tirhut { Darbhanga ...	} 19,323	{ 5,830
Nadiya	1,017	1,081	Tirhut { Mozufferpur ...		21,577
Jessore	47	4	Saran	18,429	19,127
Khulna	......	31	Champaran	21,730	23,569
Murshedabad	787	887	Monghyr	13,106	10,060
Dinajpur	117	29	Bhagalpur	2,531	3,822
Rajshahye	719	876	Purneah	7,580	8,750
Rangpur	......	4	Maldah	6,002	7,347
Bogra	100	91	Santál Parganas	2,934	2,377
Pabna	1,100	1,006	Hazaribagh	......	134
Kuch Behar	......	6	Lohardagá	......	1,524
Dacca	153	167	Singbhum	......	12
Faridpur	151	275	Manbhum	......	13
Bakarganj	......	22	Tributary States	......	62

Bindu, a synonym for Bind.

Bindu, a title of Dakshin-Rárhi and Bangaja Káyasths.

Bindumbo, a *rui* or sept of Dejong Lhoris, whose ancestor had emigrated from Bhotan.

Bindya, a resident of Brindában.

Binha, a sept of Mundas in Chota Nagpur.

Binjhiá, *Birjiá, Brijiá, Binjhwár*, an agricultural and landholding tribe found in the south of the Lohardagá district, in Palámau, and in the Tributary States of Gángpur and Sargujá in Bengal and Patna in the Central Provinces. The Binjhiás of the south are peculiar in that within their own households they speak

Uriya, their language for ordinary purposes being the jargon of Hindi current in Chota Nagpur. Mr. W. H. P. Driver describes them as a quiet, unwarlike people, flat-faced and black, but of good physique, and wearing their hair in matted locks. He considers them nearly allied to the Asuras or Agarias. Like many similar tribes, they are divided into two sub-tribes—the **Paháriya Binjhiás** and **Dánd-Binjhiás**, so called from living respectively in the hills and in the plains. Their traditions, like those of the Binds, associate them with the Vindhya Hills, where the god Mahadeo is supposed to have created them by breathing life into a scare-crow, and the present representatives of the caste in Chota Nagpur say that Ratanpur, in the Central Provinces, was their original habitat. From Ratanpur they moved eastward to Borásomar, thence to Keonjhar, and thence to Nagra in Gángpur. From this place a branch of them found their way, some twenty generations ago, to the plateau of Chota Nagpur, where they are now settled, the bulk of them as occupancy raiyats, and the chief men of the caste as tenure-holders of the second or third degree claiming *khunt káti* rights under the Maharaja of Chota Nagpur.

Internal structure.

The Ránd-Binjhiás have four exogamous septs:—**Nág**, the snake; **Dádul**; **Bhair**, supposed to be short for Bhairava; and **Kási**. The first two are clearly totemistic, and the members of these septs reverence the animals whose names they bear. The sept name goes by the male side. The prohibited degrees are the same as in the case of the Rautias. The hill Binjhiás have no septs, or rather the village takes the place of the sept; the rule being that a man must get his wife from a strange village. A man may marry two sisters, provided he marries the elder of the two first, but not otherwise; a wife's elder sister (*jeth sás*) being regarded by the husband in the light of a mother. Among the Dánd-Binjhiás, girls are married either as infants or after they have attained the age of puberty, the marriage being arranged between the parents by a male broker or *bisut;* but the Paháriya-Binjhiás still adhere to adult-marriage. The usual bride-price is Rs. 4. Polygamy is permitted without any theoretical limit on the number of wives. It is unusual, however, to find a man with more than two wives, and the largest number ever heard of is six. Mr. Driver says three is the outside limit, but I suspect this statement represents little more than the improvised reply of his informants to a question which they had never considered. At all events one would be curious to know on what principle this particular number was fixed. With the Binjhiás, as with all polygamous castes, the standard of living sets impassable bounds to the indulgence of caprice in the matter of wives. Widows are allowed to marry again by the *sagai* form. It is considered the right thing for a widow to marry her husband's younger brother (*dewar*) if there is one; but she may marry any one outside of her father's section and her original circle of prohibited degrees. Divorce is permitted on the ground of adultery by the wife or the inability of the parties to get on together. Either husband or wife may take

Marriage.

the initiative, and the bride-price and marriage expenses are supposed to be repaid.

The marriage ceremony of the Dánd-Binjhiás differs little from that in vogue among the Rautias. *Sindurdán*, or the smearing of vermilion on the bride's forehead, and knotting the clothes of the bride and bridegroom together, are the essential portions of the rite. Sometimes the parties are married first to a mango-tree, but this practice is not universal or necessary. The hill Binjhiás use oil instead of vermilion.

Religion.

In matters of religion the more civilised Dánd-Binjhias of the south profess to be orthodox Hindus, and worship Devi under the name Vindhu-básini, 'the dweller in the Vindhyas,' as the *ishtadevatá* or patron goddess of the caste. They also reverence Jagannáth. Their minor deities are Chadri Devi and Grám-sri, the goddesses who preside over villages. To both goats are sacrificed, but those offered to the former must be black. The gods of the Paháriyá-Binjhiás are Debi, Sing-Bonga or the Sun, Nind-Bongá or the Moon, and Mahadeo, who are worshipped by a Binjhiá priest called the Baigá-Páhan and his assistant the Dewar, who offer the sacrifices, while the Pujári or consulting priest determines what the sacrifice should be. Brahmans are employed in the worship of the greater gods and in the propitiation of dead ancestors, whom they call *muá*. These Brahmans incur no social degradation by serving Binjhiás. The dead are burned or buried. In the latter case the grave is dug deep and a cairn of large stones set with thorn bushes made up to keep off jackals and hyenas. Wealthy men make a merit of taking some of the ashes from the funeral pyre and casting them into the Ganges at Benares; but in fact this is rarely done, and the pretence of doing it is a mere imitation of the customs of the higher castes. *Sráddh* is performed by those who wish to make a parade of their orthodoxy; but even in these cases I am informed that some of the essential portions of the standard ceremony are omitted. The festivals of the tribe are the Phaguá in February, the Sarhul in April, the Chiná-parab or sowing-feast in June or July, the Karmá in October, and the Arwá or Kharway (harvest-home) in November, when a sacrifice is offered to Mahadeo.

Succession.

Binjhiás do not follow the Mitákshará, which is the personal law of most Hindus residing in Lohardagá. Inheritance among them is governed by a tribal custom of their own, which gives the bulk of a man's estate to his eldest son, subject to the obligation to make life-grants from the property for the maintenance of his younger brothers. Daughters do not share in the inheritance; but the eldest son is expected to maintain them in the paternal house and to get them married. In the order of succession a younger son by a wife who was married by the full marriage ceremony (*byáh*) excludes an elder son by a *sagai* wife, but the latter is entitled to maintenance—a right which is denied to the son of a concubine. These customs are recognised by the courts.

For the decision of questions of caste usage, the Binjhiás have a representative assembly consisting of delegates from every household in the community. The president, whose office is hereditary, is called *kartáhá*. The rules of debate are, as might be supposed, highly primitive. After enough talking has been done to enable the president to gather the sense of the assembly, he states his own view, and the decision, as in Homeric times, goes by acclamation.

Social status.

Notwithstanding that they eat fowls and wild pig, both abominable in the eyes of the orthodox, the Dánd-Binjhiás of the south are deemed to be Hindus, and enjoy much the same social rank as the Rautias. They will take cooked food only from the hands of known Brahmans; sweetmeats, etc., from Rajputs; and water from Rautias, Orhs, Kumhárs, Ahirs, Khandaits, and Zamindar-Jhorás, but not Kharwárs or Bhogtás. The hill Binjhiás, according to Mr. Driver, eat buffaloes, cows, and the *dháman* snake, but monkeys, frogs, and ordinary snakes are forbidden food.

The following statement shows the number and distribution of Binjhiás in 1872 and 1881:—

District.	1872.	1881.
Lohardagá	2,665	1,043
Tributary States	2,705	2,615

Binjhwár, a synonym for Binjhiá.

Binjoar, a sept of Kharwars in Chota Nagpur.

Binjuar, an eel, a totemistic sept of Mundas in Chota Nagpur.

Binriá, a sept of Rajputs in Behar.

Binsaiyá, a *pur* or section of Sákadwipi Brahmans in Behar.

Bipra, a synonym for Brahman in Bengal.

Biráji, a *mul* or section of the Ghosin sub-caste of Goálás in Behar.

Birar, cat, a totemistic sept of Tántis in Chota Nagpur.

Birbansa, a title of Doms.

Birbhairab, a section of Jugis.

Birbhumiá, a sub-caste of Lohárs in the Santál Parganas.

Bireri, a section of Maghayá Kándus in Behar.

Birho or **Birhor**, a sept of Mundas in Chota Nagpur.

Birhor, 'wood-man,' a small Dravidian tribe of Chota Nagpur, who live in the jungle in tiny huts made of branches of trees and leaves, and eke out a miserable living by snaring hares and monkeys, and collecting jungle products, especially the bark of the *chob* creeper (*Banhinia scandens*), from which a coarse kind of rope is made. They claim to be of the same race as the Kharwárs, and to come from

Khairagarh in the Kaimur hills, but this legend, like similar stories told by the Santáls and Oraons, can hardly be deemed to possess any historical value, and probably refers to a migration of comparatively recent date. A list of the Birhor septs is given in Appendix I. Two at least are totemistic; the others appear to be local or territorial. One of them, Hemrom, is found also among the Santáls, but with them it means a horse, while the Birhors say it is a kind of fish.

Origin.

Primitive as the habits of the Birhors are, they seem to have been to some extent affected by the influence of Hindu ideas. Marriage is a case in point. The free courtship in vogue among the compact Dravidian tribes has fallen into disuse, and parents arrange the marriage of their daughters at an early age. Three rupees is the standard bride-price. The tribe does not employ Brahmans, nor have they any special priests of their own. The marriage ceremony is therefore very simple, its essential and binding portion consisting in the process of drawing blood from the little fingers of the bride and bridegroom and smearing it on each of them. The bride stays two days in her husband's hut, and then goes back to her father's until she is grown up.

Marriage.

The Birhor religion is, as might be expected, a mixture of Animism and Hinduism. If questioned on the subject, the Birhors themselves will endeavour in their replies to give prominence to the Hindu elements, and to make themselves out more orthodox than they are, and with singular ingenuity they seek to harmonize the two systems by assigning to Devi the chief place in their Pantheon, and making out the animistic godlings, to borrow Mr. Ibbetson's expressive word, to be her daughters and granddaughters. Thus, according to Colonel Dalton, an oblong piece of wood, painted red, stands for Mahá Máyá, Devi's daughter; a small piece of white stone daubed with vermilion for her granddaughter, Buria Mái, and an arrow head for Dudha Mái, Buriá's daughter. A trident, painted red, represents Hanumán, who carries out Devi's orders. The minor gods, whose animistic character has not as yet been disguised by any veneer of Hinduism, are Biru Bhut, worshipped in the form of a raised semi-globe of earth, and Darhá, a Mundári-Oraon deity, represented by a piece of split bamboo some three feet high, stuck slantwise in the ground. The latter is also known as the sipahi or sentry, a term not uncommonly applied to minor gods of this type, and is supposed to be the immediate guardian of the place. A small round piece of wood about a foot long, with the upper part painted red, is called Banhi, goddess of the jungles. Another similar emblem stands for Sugu, a big hill in the south of the Hazaribagh district. Sets of these symbols are placed on either side of their huts to scare off evil spirits, snakes, tigers, and misfortune generally. When a Birhor dies, his body is burned and the remnant thrown, as Birhors say, into the Ganges, but really into any stream that may happen to be handy. For ten days the relatives show their grief by not shaving. On the eleventh they shave and have a feast. Birhors have been accused of eating their dead relations, but the evidence on this point is not convincing, and Colonel Dalton says he has no faith in the story.

Religion.

Birhorichopdár, a title of those members of the Birhor caste who make string (*chop*) from the bark of trees, as distinguished from Birhors proper, who collect honey and wax from the jungle and make *sikas* for carrying burdens.

Birinjári, a variant of Banjárá, *q.v.*

Birj, a section of the Panchjáti sub-caste of Khatris in Bengal.

Birjiá, a sub-tribe of Asuras and Goálás in Chota Nagpur.

Birnáwar, a section of the Amashta Káyasths in Behar.

Birtiá, a Brahman who lives on a grant made to him for religious service or as a Kathak or reciter of sacred poems.

Biruá, a sept of Hos in Singbhum.

Birwá, a sept of the Suryabansi sub-tribe of Rajputs in Behar.

Birwál, a sub-caste of Bhuiyás in Singbhum.

Birwár, a sept of the Chandrabansi sub-tribe of Rajputs in Behar.

Bisá or **Birádari Rájá**, a sub-caste of Agarwáls who hold a degraded position on account of their alleged illegitimate descent.

Bisáin, a sept of the Surajbansi sub-tribe of Rajputs in Behar. They cannot intermarry with persons of the Chaubhan and Mahraur septs, being supposed to be descended from the same ancestor.

Bisaiwár-Nánhpur, a *mul* of the Kásyap section of Maithil Brahmans in Behar.

Bisaiwár-Bisphi, a *mul* of the Kásyap section of Maithil Brahmans in Behar.

Bisariá, a sub-caste of Kahárs.

Bisáti, a pedlar, a hawker, a vendor of miscellaneous goods, whose stock embraces stationery, hardware, china, twines, thread, etc.; a trader not keeping a shop, but exposing his wares on a carpet or mat spread on the ground.

Bisdeliá a sub-caste of Doms in Bengal who make baskets and palm-leaf mats.

Bishdharí, holder of poison; a title of snake-charmers, usually Máls or Sámperiyas by caste.

Bishnbrit-dár, a Brahman holding lands granted in honour of Vishnu.

Bishnu, a *gotra* or section of Brahmans and Baidyas in Bengal; a title of Dakshin-Rárhi and Bangaja Káyasths; a sept of Bairágis in Chota Nagpur.

Bishnupur, a *samáj* or local group of the Páschátya Baidik Brahmans in Bengal.

Bishoi, a title of Karangás.

Bishtwár, a sub-caste of Sunris in Behár.

Bisishta Sakti, a *thar* of the Basishtha *gotra* of Nepáli Brahmans.

Biskarmá (*Viswakarmá*), a *gotra* or section of the Kanaujiá Lohárs in Behar. This designation has been borrowed from the Brahmanical system in comparatively recent times; and, as the sub-caste has only one other section (Kasyapa) of the same type, operates only to a limited extent as a bar to intermarriage. In fact, no systematic use appears to be made of these Brahmanical exogamous designations; for the sub-caste has no less than 360 sections (*muls* and *dihs*) of the ancestral or local type. The adoption of the tutelary god of the caste as the eponym of a section is an instance of a practice noticed by Professor W. Robertson Smith as common among the early Arabs. A *gotra* bearing the name Viswakarmá is also found among the Maghayá Barhis of Behar.

Bisokia, a sept of Rajputs in Behar.

Bisra, hawk, a totemistic sept of Kharwars in Chota Nagpur. The word is apparently a variant of Besra, *q.v.*

Bisrot, a sept of Mundas in Chota Nagpur.

Bisru, a bird, a totemistic sept of Mundas in Chota Nagpur.

Bissoi or *Bishayi*, the chief of a district in Orissa collecting the Government revenue and exercising police and judicial authority.

Biswál, a title of Uriyá Brahmans.

Biswámitra, a section of Brahmans, Káyasths, and of Tántis in Bengal.

Biswás, a title of Báruis, Chásádhobás, Jugis, Kaibarttas, Kewats, Kumhars, Nápits, and Pods, and an honorary title of Káyasths in Bengal; a section of the Maghayá sub-caste of Kumhárs, and a title of Nágars in Behar.

Biswás-Madak, a sub-caste of Madhunápits in Bengal.

Bit, a title of Tántis in Bengal.

Bitál, a sub-sept of the Murmu sept of Santáls.

Bitár, a title of Doms in Behar.

Bitwár, a sub-caste of Sunris in Behar.

Biyáhot, Biyahutá, a sub-caste of Hajjáms in Behar who do not permit the marriage of widows.

Biyáhut, a sub-caste of Sunris in Behar who do not allow widow marriage: they are grain-dealers and shopkeepers; a sub-caste of Kurmis in Behar who do not permit widows to marry again. It is often used in contradistinction to Sagáhut.

Biyáhut or **Bhojpuri,** a sub-caste of Kalwárs in Behar.

Biyáhuta, a sub-caste of Baniyás who sell grain and do not allow widows to remarry.

Boár, fish, a sub-sept of the Murmu sept of Santáls.

Bocho, a bird, a totemistic sept of Mundas in Chota Nagpur.

Bod, a sept of Gonds in Chota Nagpur.

Bodo, a sub-tribe of the Kochh tribe in Northern and Eastern Bengal.

Bodra, a sept of Mundas in Chota Nagpur whose ancestors neglected to wash their mouths after eating.

Bodrá, a sept of Lohars in Chota Nagpur.

Bodru, a sept of Hos in Singbhum.

Boga, a sept of Chakmás in the Hill Tracts of Chittagong.

Bohandiá, a cultivator who has not a plough of his own and either works with a hoe or a borrowed plough.

Bohit, a title of the Dhusiá sub-caste of Chamárs in Behar.

Bojra, a kind of grass, a totemistic sept of Mundas in Chota Nagpur.

Bokhime, a *thar* or sept of Khambus in Darjiling.

Bolá, a sept of the Tungjainya sub-tribe of Chakmás in the Hill Tracts of Chittagong.

Bomjan, a section of Murmis in Darjiling.

Bon-Gonju, a title of Nágeswars in Chota Nagpur.

Bonthárua, a *thar* or sept of Khambus in Darjiling.

Bora, a kind of snake, a totemistic sept of Chiks in Chota Nagpur.

Borál, a title of Kaibarttas in Bengal.

Bordi, a section of Tántis in Chota Nagpur.

Borhá, a section of Sonárs in Behar.

Borhgrámi, a *gáin* of the Bátsya *gotra* of Bárendra Brahmans in Bengal.

Boriá, a group of Maghaiyá Telis in Behar.

Borosánp, a section of Mauliks in Chota Nagpur.

Borsege, a sept of Chakmás in the Hill Tracts of Chittagong.

Bosmáthá, a sept of the Agniá sub-tribe of Meches in the Darjiling Terai.

Bot, a sub-tribe of Thárus in Behar.

Boyong, a *thar* or sept of Khambus in Darjiling.

Brahma, a title of Dakshin-Rárhi and Bangaja Káyasths.

Brahmachári, a youth of either of the three first pure classes during his pupilage and while studying the Vedas. A mendicant who professes to have prolonged the period of studentship and to observe through life the practice of study, poverty, and continence. In general, however, an ignorant vagrant; a Brahman recluse; a title of Brahmans.

Traditions of origin.

Bráhman, *Báman, Bipra, Dwija, Thákur, Sarmá, Deva-Sarmá, Bhudeva, Bhusur, Agraja, Mahárájji, Bábáji, Gosáinji*, the highest of the three twice-born castes, originally the priests of the Aryan community, and now engaged in various professions and following all respectable means of livelihood, except those involving personal or ceremonial pollution. Concerning the origin of the caste there has been much discussion, and it is hardly possible to speak of it without to some extent touching upon the vexed question of the origin and development of the caste system itself. Orthodox tradition as expressed in the so-called Institutes of Manu, in the Mahábhárata, in the Puránas, and in the Játimála or Garland of Castes, refers the evolution of the four original castes to a special act of creation, whereby from the mouth of the Supreme Being proceeded the Bráhman, from his arms the

Kshatriya, from his thighs the Vaisya, and from his foot the Sudra. Each of these orders had their special function in life assigned to them according to their natural aptitudes. To the Bráhman the knowledge and teaching of things divine; to the Kshatriya defence of the land from its enemies; to the Vaisya pasture and tillage of the soil; and to the Sudra the duty of doing willing service to the higher ranks. In the Purusha-Súkta hymn of the Rig Veda we find a more fanciful and mystic variant of the same legend. The gods drag the primeval man (*purusha*), regarded apparently as the microcosm or type of all mankind, to the sacrifice, and hew him into four pieces, which, according to the dignity of the members as in the former legend, become the four castes. Another account of the matter is given in the Mahábhárata:—In the beginning, says Bhrigu, there was no distinction of castes or colour. All men were Bráhmans. Created by Brahmá on one model, their own actions served to divide them. Bráhmans who yielded to the desires of the senses, who gave themselves up to anger and pride,—these, reddened by anger, became Kshatriyas; others who followed after pasture and agriculture grew yellow and were Vaisyas; others again, hasty, mendacious, and immoral, wholly lost their pristine purity, became black, and were turned into Sudras. A third legend seeks to bring the rise of the caste system into some sort of genealogical relation with the heads of ancient tribes and families of the Vedic era. This story represents the mythical Manu as the father of all mankind, and ascribes to his sons or grandsons the formation of the four castes. Members of the race of the Sun are mentioned, who became Bráhmans—"Kshatriya by birth, Bráhman by profession"—as the legend puts it; while the Saunaka of the race of the Moon, the descendants of Pururavas, became Bráhmans, Kshatriyas, or Vaisyas, according to their degree of personal merit. In another place we hear of a mighty king, named Bali, to whom Brahmá delegated authority to found the caste system.

These and similar legends, however destitute of historical accuracy, serve nevertheless to throw some light upon the probable origin of the caste system generally, and of the Bráhman caste in particular. They make it clear that early Indian tradition assumes the substantial unity of the Aryan race; that it looks upon kings and priests as men fashioned of the same substance, and on the distinctions of caste as having been gradually evolved rather than created before the beginning of time.

Caste then, at least in the rigid form in which we now know it, is an institution of comparatively late origin. During Vedic times, though the germ of Bráhmanism may be traced in the relations between the *purohita* and the *maghaván*, the separation of classes was no sharper than naturally arose from differences of occupation; and with the exception of a single hymn of later origin, the testimony of the whole body of Vedic literature as interpreted by modern scholars is adverse to the existence of a clearly-defined hierarchy of endogamous castes. Even in the Epic era the system had not hardened into its later form. Marriages between members of different castes were possible. We hear of Vidura the Kshattar, son of a Bráhman father and Sudra mother, of Yuyutsu the Karan, son of Dhritaráshtra by a Vaisya wife, and we are told that the former took a prominent part in public business, while the latter was conspicuous in battle. Finally, in the statement that among the impious Aryans of the Panjab only the eldest son of a Bráhman becomes a Bráhman, we may surely find a survival of an earlier order of ideas, of the belief that all Aryans are of one blood, and that Bráhmanhood is a matter of personal qualities and aptitudes rather than of descent.

The best modern opinion seems disposed to find the germ of the Bráhman caste in the bards, ministers, and family priests who were attached to the king's household in Vedic times. Different stages of this institution may be observed. In the earliest ages the head of every Aryan household was his own priest, and even a king would himself perform the sacrifices which were appropriate to his rank. By degrees families or guilds of priestly singers arose, who sought service under the kings, and were rewarded by rich presents for the hymns of praise and prayer recited and sacrifices offered by them on behalf of their masters. As time went on, the sacrifices became more numerous and more elaborate, and the mass of ritual grew to such an extent that the king could no longer cope with it unaided. The employment of *purohits* or family priests, formerly optional, now became a sacred duty if the sacrifices were not to fall into disuse. The Bráhman obtained a monopoly of priestly functions, and a race of sacerdotal specialists arose which tended continually to close its ranks against the intrusion of outsiders. The idea that virtue made the Bráhman gave place to the belief in the efficacy of birth. Intermarriage with other ranks of the Aryan community was first discouraged and then wholly prohibited, and thus by degrees was developed the rigid law of endogamy which distinguishes the Indian caste system from other apparently similar forms of social gradation.

Internal structure.

The Bráhman caste is commonly divided into ten large classes, according to their locality: five on the north and five on the south of the Vindhyá range. The classes are thus arranged in a Sanskrit mnemonic stanza quoted by Dr. Wilson—

(I) The five Drávidas, south of the Vindhyá range:—

(1) The *Maháráshtras*, of the country of the Marathi language.
(2) The *Andhrar* or *Tailangas*, of the country of the Telugu language.
(3) The *Drávidas*, of the country of the Drávidián or Tamil language.
(4) The *Kárnátas*, of the Karnátika, the country of the Canarese language.
(5) The *Gurjaras*, of Gurjaráshtra, or the country of the Gujaráti language.

(II) The five Gauras, north of the Vyndhyá range :—

(1) The *Sáraswatas*, so called from the country watered by the river Saraswati.
(2) The *Kányakubjas*, so called from the Kánwakubja or Kanauj country.
(3) The *Gauras*, so called from Gaur, or the country of the Lower Ganges.[1]
(4) The *Utkalas*, of the province of Utkala or Odra (Orissa).
(5) The *Maithilas*, of the province of Mithila (Tirhut).

The Bráhmans found in the Lower Provinces of Bengal belong to one or other of the Gaura groups. A tabular scheme of their subdivisions, which are extremely intricate, will be found in the Appendix. In the following brief description it will be convenient to deal first with the Bráhmans of Bengal Proper, then with those of Behar, and lastly with the Utkal or Orissa Bráhmans. The Bengal Bráhmans are divided into five main sub-castes—RARHI, BARENDRA, VAIDIK, SAPTASATI, and MADHYASRENI.

Rárhi.

The Rárhi Bráhmans derive their name from the Rárh, or the high-lying alluvial tract on the west bank of the river Bhagirathi. Their claim to be of comparatively pure Aryan descent is to some extent borne out by the results of the anthropometric inquiries recorded in another volume of this work. The current tradition is that early in the eleventh century A.D., Adisura or Adisvara, King of Bengal, finding the Bráhmans then settled in Bengal too ignorant to perform for him certain Vedic ceremonies, applied to the Rájá of Kanauj for priests thoroughly conversant with the sacred ritual of the Aryans. In answer to this request five Bráhmans of Kanauj were sent to him—Bhatta Náráyana of the Sándilya section or *gotra ;* Daksha of the Kasyapa *gotra;* Vedagarva or Vidagarbha of the Vatsa *gotra*, or, as other accounts say, from the family of Bhrigu ; Chandra or Chhándara of the Sávarna *gotra* ; and Sriharsa of the Bharadwája *gotra*. They brought with them their wives, their sacred fire, and their sacrificial implements. It is said that Adisura was at first disposed to treat them with scanty respect, but he was soon compelled to acknowledge his mistake and to beg the Bráhmans to forgive him. He then made over to them five populous villages, where they lived for a year. Meanwhile the king was so impressed with the superhuman virtue of Bhatta Náráyana, who was a son of Kshitisa, King of Kanauj, that he offered him several more villages. The Bráhman, however, declined to take these as a gift, but bought them, as the story goes, at a low price. They were annexed to the village already in Bhatta Náráyana's possession, and the whole area was relieved from payment of revenue for twenty-four years. Thus tradition chronicles an early *Brahmottar* grant, the first it may be of the long series of similar transactions which have played so important a part in the history of land

[1] This statement seems doubtful, see p. 157 below.

tenures, in the development of castes, and in promoting the spread of orthodox Hinduism throughout Bengal. Adisura did what the Rájás of outlying tracts of country have constantly done since and are doing still. A local chief, far removed from the great centres of Bráhmanical lore, somehow becomes aware of his ceremonial shortcomings. Probably, as is narrated of Adisura himself, a wandering Bráhman brings home to him that his local ritual is not up to the orthodox standard. He sends for Bráhmans, gives them grants of land near his own residence, and proceeds with their assistance to reform his ways on the model of the devout kings whom Bráhmanical literature holds up as the ideal for a Rájá to follow after. The Bráhmans find for him a pedigree of respectable antiquity or provide him with a family legend, and in course of time he succeeds in getting himself recognised as a member of some branch of the great Rajput community.

Although the immigrant Bráhmans brought their wives with them, tradition says that they contracted second marriages with the women of Bengal, and that their children by the latter were the ancestors of the Barendra Brahmans. The Barendra, on the other hand, claim to represent the offspring from the original Hindustani wives, and allege that the Rárhi Bráhmans themselves spring from the *mésalliance* contracted in Bengal.

By the middle of the eleventh century, when Ballál Sen, the second of the Sen kings of Bengal, instituted his famous inquiry into the personal endowments of the Rárhi Bráhmans, their numbers seem to have increased greatly. They are represented as divided into 56 *gáins* or headships of villages, which were reserved for them, and might not be encroached upon by Bráhmans of other orders.

It is interesting to trace in Ballál Sen's inquiry the survival or reassertion of the principle referred to above as recognised in ancient times, that the Bráhmanhood of the Bráhman depends not merely on birth, but also upon personal endowments. It is a question of virtue, not a question of descent. Ballál Sen, of course, could not go so far as this. The time had long passed when a Kshatriya could transform himself into a Bráhman by penance and self-denial. But the Sen monarch sought to reaffirm the ancient principle, so far as was then possible, by testing the qualifications of each Rárhi family for the priestly office, and classifying them, in the order of their virtue, according to the results of this examination. The following nine qualities were selected to serve as the touchstone of sacerdotal purity:—*Áchár*, ceremonial purity; *vinaya*, discipline; *vidyá*, learning; *pratishtha*, reputation for purity; *tirthadarsana*, zeal in pilgrimage; *nishtha*, piety; *ávritti*, observance of legal marriages; *tapa*, ascetic self-devotion; *dána*, liberality.

Tradition is silent concerning the precise method in which Ballál Sen carried out his somewhat inquisitorial measures. It seems, however, to be certain that some kind of inquiry into the nine characteristic Bráhmanical qualities was held under his orders, and that the *kul* or social and ceremonial standing of each family was determined accordingly. Some say that twenty-two *gáins* were raised to the highest distinction. Lakshmana Sen discarded fourteen *gáins* on account of their misconduct, and they became *gauna Kulins*, an order which has now disappeared. Nineteen families belonging to the other eight *gáins* were made Kulins. The other families of these eight *gáins* were lost sight of. Thus two classes or grades of sacerdotal virtue were formed :—(1) the Kulin, being those who had observed the entire nine counsels of perfection ; (2) the Srotriya, who, though regular students of the Vedas, had lost *avritti* by intermarrying with families of inferior birth. The Srotriya were again subdivided into Siddha or perfect, Sádhya or capable of attaining purity, and Kashta or difficult. The last-named group was also called Ari or enemy, because a Kulin marrying a daughter of that group was disgraced.

Marriage.

The relations of these three classes in respect of marriage were regulated by the principle laid down in the Institutes of Manu for members of the three twice-born castes, a principle for which Mr. Denzil Ibbetson has adopted the convenient and expressive name of *hypergamy*. The rule was that a man of the Kulin class could marry a woman of his own class or of the two higher Srotriya classes ; a Siddha Srotriya could marry in his own group or in the Sádhya Srotriya group ; while the Sádhya and Kashta Srotriyas might take wives only within the limits of their own classes. Conversely, women of the Sádhya Srotriya class could marry in their own class or the two classes above them ; Siddha Srotriya women in their own class or in the Kulin class ; while Kulin women at one end of the scale and Kashta women at the other were restricted in their choice of husbands to the Kulin and Kashta groups. Unequal or irregular marriages involved loss of reputation and forfeiture of rank. On the other hand, the marriage of a girl into a good Kulin house conferred a sort of reflected honour on her own family, and in course of time this idea was developed into the doctrine known as *kula-gotra*, whereby the reputation of a family depended upon the character of the marriages made by its female members.

This singular and artificial organization deranged the natural balance of the sexes, and set up a vigorous competition for husbands among the women of the higher groups. The Bansajas are those Kulins who lost their distinction on account of misconduct, *i.e.*, their want of charity, discipline, and due observance of marriage law, three qualities which in later times constituted Kulinism.

The growth of the Bansaja class introduced a further element of complication. In the struggle for husbands, Kulin girls who had no brothers or whose mothers were widows were often given to the sons of Bansaja parents ; but families resorting to this device were excluded from the recognised cadre. Thus the brothers of a girl who married beneath her at once became Bansaja, but this degradation did not extend to her uncles. If an original Kulin married a Bansaja maiden, he himself became a Swakrita Bhanga or broken Bráhman. His descendants in the second generation were known as Dwipurusha, in the third as Tripurusha, and in the fourth as Chaturthapurusha. After this stage special designations were dropped, and the branch was merged in the Bansaja class. Although in theory these lower branches were completely cut off from the original hierarchy formed by Ballál Sen, natural instincts could not be wholly eradicated from a number of closely related families, and girls of the Bhanga and Bansaja groups used to marry their cousins of the elder branch. It might perhaps have been expected that these groups would have been admitted to the same privileges as the Srotriya, but this was not the case.

The invasion of Bengal by the Muhammadans in 1203 and the instant collapse of the Hindu kingdom was not without its effect upon the matrimonial organization of the Rárhi Bráhmans. Ballál Sen's reforms had been imposed upon the caste by the order of a Hindu ruler, and their observance depended upon the maintenance of his supervising authority. When this check was removed, the system could no longer hold together, and soon showed signs of breaking up completely. Artificial restrictions had been introduced; the natural balance of the sexes had been disturbed, and a disastrous competition for husbands had set in among the three original groups. New and inferior groups had sprung up, and their natural ambitions still further swelled the demand for Kulin husbands. The pressure of necessity soon showed itself too strong for the rules. Poor Kulins sold their family rank and honour for the bridegroom-price, which had taken the place of the bride-price of earlier times; they added to the number of their wives without regard to the respectability of the families from which they came; and they raised their prices as the supply of suitable husbands diminished and competition ran higher for a Kulin bridegroom.

The reforms undertaken in the fourteenth century by Devi Vara, a ghatak or genealogist of Jessore, extended only to the Kulins. These were divided into three grades—(i) Swabháva or original Kulins, (ii) Bhanga, (iii) Bansaja. The Swabháva grade was further subdivided into 36 *mels* or endogamous groups,* each bearing the name of the original ancestor of the clan or of his village. This restriction of the marriages of Kulins to their own *mel* was the leading feature of Devi Vara's reform. Its principle was adopted and extended, it is believed, by the Kulins themselves, in the singular arrangement known as Pálti-Prakriti, or preservation of the type, by which families of equal rank were formed into triple groups as it were, for matrimonial purposes, and bound to observe a sort of reciprocity. Thus Mukhuti families were bound to marry their sons to the daughters of the Chatterji and Banerji families, and *vice versâ*. All kinds of complications are said to have arisen

* The names of the *mels* are as follows:—Phuliya, Khardaha, Sarvvanandi, Ballabhi, Surai, Ácharya Sekhari, Pandit Ratni, Bangala, Gopala Ghataki, Cháyanarendri, Pramadani, Dasaratha Ghataki, Subharajakháni, Nariya, Raya, Bhattarághavi, Deháti, Chayi, Vijáya Pandit, Chádái, Madhái, Bidyádhari, Párihal, Sri Rangabhatti, Máladkara Kháni, Kákumvi, Hari Majumdári, Sri Bandhani, Bhairava Ghataki, Achambita, Dharádhari, Vále, Rághava Ghosáli, Sungo Sarvvanandi, Sadananda Kháni, Chandravati.

from this understanding. If, for example, the Mukhuti had only one marriageable son and the Chatterji or Banerji ten daughters approaching puberty, the former must marry all ten or all must remain spinsters. Meantime the rush of competition for Kulin husbands on the part of Bhanga, Bansaja, and Srotriya classes was as strong as before, while the proportionate number of pure Kulins had been reduced by the loss of those who had become Bhangas and Bansajas. In order to dispose of the surplus of women in the higher groups polygamy was introduced, and was resorted to on a very large scale. It was popular with the Kulins because it enabled them to make a handsome income by the accident of their birth; and it was accepted by the parents of the girls concerned as offering the only means of complying with the requirements of the Hindu religion. Tempted by a *pan* or premium, which often reached the sum of two thousand rupees, Swabháva Kulins made light of their *kul* and its obligations, and married Bansaja girls, whom they left after the ceremony to be taken care of by their parents. Matrimony became a sort of profession, and the honour of marrying a daughter to a Bhanga Kulin is said to have been so highly valued in Eastern Bengal that as soon as a boy was ten years old his friends began to discuss his matrimonial prospects, and before he was twenty he had become the husband of many wives of ages varying from five to fifty.

With the spread of education among the upper classes of Bengal an advance in social morality has been made and the grosser forms of polygamy have fallen into disrepute. But the artificial organization of the caste still presses hard on a Kulin father who is unlucky enough to have a large family of daughters. These must be married before they attain puberty, or disgrace will fall on the family, and three generations of ancestors will be dishonoured. But a Kulin bridegroom can only be obtained by paying a heavy premium, many of the *mels* instituted by Devi Vara have died out, and in such cases, reciprocal marriage being no longer possible, the son of a family left without a corresponding *mel* must marry the only daughter of a widow; while the daughter of a Kulin widow, for whom no husband of equal birth can be procured, may be married to a Srotriya, and a premium accepted without endangering the family prestige. According to Dr. Wise, a Kulin father in Eastern Bengal could only preserve his kul intact in one of three ways:—By giving her to a Kulin of equal rank; by making an effigy (*kusa-kanya*) of her with *kusa* grass and giving it in symbolical marriage to a Kulin; by saying to a Kulin in the presence of ghatak witnesses:—"I would give my daughter, if I had one, to you," and putting on his forehead the tilak or distinguishing mark which a married woman wears.

The marriage ceremonies of the Bengal Brahmans comprise five important stages, viz.—

Marriage ceremony.

I. *Purba-bibáha*, consisting of—(1) The anointment, called *tel halud*. After preliminaries have been settled, and the *patra karan*, or formal intimation of the consent of the parties, or rather of their guardians on both sides, has been drawn up, an auspicious day is fixed for anointing both the bridegroom and the bride with turmeric. The process must be undergone by both on the same day—the bride a little while after the bridegroom, each in their own house. Usually a part of the turmeric prepared for the bridegroom is sent by his guardian for the use of the bride, but if the couple live at a distance, this is not deemed essential. In any case the time at which the ceremony should be performed is fixed by letter. Those who can afford to do so distribute oil and turmeric among their neighbours on this occasion.

(2) The entertainment, *thubará* or *áyubriddhánna*. From the day of the anointment until the day of the marriage the betrothed couple are daily entertained by their friends and neighbours, a piece of new cloth being presented at the same time. Presents of sweetmeats and cloth are sent to their houses by friends, and well-to-do people with a large circle of acquaintances often prolong the interval between the anointing with turmeric and the wedding from two or three days to a month. The rule is that after the anointing the first entertainment is given by the parents, and after that neither the bride nor the bridegroom should again eat in their own homes until they are married.

(3) The divine invocation or *adhibás*. On the night before the wedding some married ladies, the neighbours and relations of the bride and bridegroom are entertained with a repast, and given presents of betel leaves and areca nuts. This is supposed to render the occasion auspicious, and to draw down the blessing of the gods through the goodwill of the ladies entertained, who are looked upon as a sort of fairy god-mothers.

(4) The propitiation of ancestors, *Nándimukh* or *briddhi sráddh*, is an ordinary *sráddh* performed at noon on the wedding day in order to procure the blessing of the deceased ancestors on the couple. Four ancestors on the father's and three on the mother's side of both parties are thus invoked: if the father and grandfather of the intended bride or bridegroom be living, then only their two immediate (deceased) predecessors, and if only the father be living, then his three immediate predecessors only. The *sráddh* is performed by the father, or in his absence by the brother, or failing him again by a *gyáti* (agnate) of the bride or the bridegroom as the case may be. If a *gyáti* be not procurable, then the family priest may officiate.

(5) The bridal procession (*bar-játri*). In the evening or, if he lives at a distance, earlier, the bridegroom goes in procession accompanied by a *kolbar*, or best man, who is usually his younger brother, and by a number of his relations, friends and neighbours to the house of the bride, where he is received as in a *durbar*, his approach being welcomed by the cry of *ulu-ulu* from the females of the bride's family. He sits on a *masnad* set apart for him in the centre of the hall, and there surrounded by those who accompanied him and by the bride's people (*kanyájátri*), he awaits the moment fixed by the astrologers as auspicious for the performance of the actual ceremony.

(6) *Jámatá-baran*, or the bridegroom's welcome by the bride's father. When the proper time has come, the bridegroom is taken by the bride's father into the inner apartments of the house, and is made to stand on a piece of board painted with pounded or powdered rice stirred up with water. The bride's father then offers him water for washing his feet (*pádya argha*) and also *modhuparkya*, a concoction of honey, in a small copper cup. These the bridegroom touches in token of acceptance.

(7) *Stri-áchár*, or woman's usage, commences with the welcome given to the bridegroom by the bride's mother by pouring some curds on his feet. This is followed by—

(*a*) *Satusi* or the seven lights of Hymen. Seven married ladies (including the bride's mother or, if she be a widow, one of the bride's aunts) in their best attire, each with a small torch made of *chita* twig and cotton steeped in oil, go round the bridegroom in procession, led by the bride's mother, who carries on her head a *kulá*, or flat bamboo basket, on which are placed 21 small lights made of *dhaturá* fruits. As they go round, they sprinkle libations of water, one of them blows a shell trumpet, and all vociferate the hymeneal cry of *ulu-ulu*. After going seven times round the bridegroom, the lights are thrown one by one over his head, so that they fall behind him. The *kulá* is then picked up and placed in front of the bridegroom, and the bride's mother takes her stand upon it and touches (*baran*) the forehead of the bridegroom with water, paddy and *durba* grass, betel and areca nut, white mustard seed, curds, white sandal paste, vermilion, a looking-glass, a comb, a bit of clay from the bed of the Ganges, a yak's tail, shells, a cluster of plantains, and certain other odds and ends, while the rest of the women keep up the cry of *ulu-ulu*. The bridegroom's height is measured with a thin thread which the bride's mother eats in a bit of plantain. She then places a weaver's shuttle (*máku*) between his folded hands and ties them together with thread, and calls upon him, now that he has been bound hand and foot, to bleat once like a sheep to signify his humility and subjection. Last of all, she touches his breast with a padlock and turns the key, whereby the door of speech is closed to the passage of hard words against the bride.

(*b*) *Sátpák*, or the seven rounds of the bride. The bride is now brought out attired in a red silk cloth, and seated on a painted board is carried by two men seven times round the bridegroom, who remains standing and then placed in front of him. As they face each other, a cloth or cover is thrown over them, and their natural shyness being thus for the moment hidden, they are supposed to snatch the *subhadrishti* or auspicious glance, which will secure their mutual happiness during their married life. Then follows—

(*c*) *Málydán*, or the exchange of garlands, when the bride and bridegroom give each other garlands of flowers.

II. *Sampradán*, or the gift and acceptance. The bride and bridegroom are next brought to a place set apart in the outer apartment or courtyard of the house, where the bride's party and the bridegroom's party can witness the formal gift of the bride and her formal acceptance by the bridegroom. The bride's father or guardian repeats the *mantras* recited by the family priest, and the bridegroom accepts the gift in these words:—"Who gave her? To whom did he give her? Love gave her. To love he gave her. Love is the giver. Love is the taker. Love pervades the ocean. With love I accept her. Love! may this be thine."

At the same time wedding presents (*dán* or *dán sámagri*) are given to the bridegroom, and after this the father or guardian is required to bear witness to the contract entered into by the bridegroom by accepting the bride, and as a token of his assent to the marriage accepts a present of five *haritaki* fruits and a piece of cloth. This present is called the *parihar*.

III. *Básara* or the bridal wake. The bridegroom is next conducted along with the bride to a room in the inner apartment of the house, a corner of his *chádar* being tied to a corner of her cloth. The pair are there received by a bevy of young ladies, who make it their business to tease the bridegroom and try to keep him awake for the rest of the night.

IV. *Kusandiká* includes the *saptapadi gaman*, or pacing of the seven steps, which may be deemed the essential and binding portion of the marriage ritual observed by the higher castes. A sacred fire is prepared and worshipped with oblations of ghí. On the north side of the fire seven points are marked off, and the bride setting her face westward walks along these points, placing her foot on each in turn. As she walks, her husband follows close behind her, touching her heel with his toe and reciting at each step *mantras* or sacred texts.

Saptapadi gaman is followed by *gotra paribarttan*, or the changing of the bride's *gotra* for that of the bridegroom, and the *sindur-dán*, or the smearing of vermilion on the bride's forehead and the parting of her hair. The latter ceremony is performed by the husband with his own hand.

Properly speaking, *kusandiká* ought to take place on the day following the marriage, but Tuesdays and Saturdays are considered unlucky days for the ceremony; and if the day after the wedding is Tuesday or Saturday, *kusandiká* is deferred till the day following that. It is usually performed at the house of the bridegroom, but if he lives a long way off, the ceremony is performed at the bride's father's house. The marriage proper ends with *kusandiká*, but certain minor ceremonies follow which may be briefly mentioned here.

V. The concluding ceremonies—

(*a*) *Phul-sajyá*, or the bed of flowers. On the third night after the marriage, the married couple are laid together in a bed decorated with flowers.

(*b*) *Ashta-mangala*. On the eighth day the pair are made to enact with toys and cowrie shells a sort of pantomimic drama of their married life, playing the part of a faithful husband

and wife, and affecting to bear with resignation the vicissitudes of fortunes.

(c) *Baubhát* or *Páka-sparsa*. All the *gyátis*, relations and friends of the bridegroom are entertained at his house. Their acceptance of the invitation is deemed an admission on their part that the marriage has been duly performed, and that the ceremonial purity of the bridegroom has in no wise been affected. In token of their recognition of this fact, they are supposed to eat rice prepared by the bride herself.

After the *Páka-sparsa* ceremony, the bride is sent back to her father's house until she attains puberty. When this time arrives it is the custom of some families to perform the ceremony known as *garbhádhán* (purification of the womb) or *punarbibáha*. This rite, to which some Hindu writers have attributed a sort of sacramental character, seems to be closely analogous to the practices observed by a number of savage races on a similar occasion. The idea seems to be, as Mr. J. G. Frazer[1] has pointed out, that dangerous influences emanate from a girl when passing through this physical change, and it is considered necessary to seclude her from the rest of the community, and subject her to a sort of penance which varies greatly in severity. Thus the Macusi tribe of British Guiana hang a girl in this state in a hammock at the top of the hut, and make her fast rigorously so long as the symptoms are at their height. When she gets well the pots and drinking vessels which she has used are broken; and after her first bath she must submit to be beaten by her mother with thin rods without uttering a cry. Another tribe, instead of beating girls who have just recovered from this state, expose them to certain large ants whose bite is very painful. The usage followed by the Rárhi Brahmans of Bengal is less severe, but of the same general character as the savage observances. Like the Australian blacks and the African Bushmen, they require a girl to live alone, and do not allow her to see the face of any male. During three days she is shut up in a dark room and is made to undergo certain penances. She must lead the life of a Brahmachári, that is, she must live upon *átap* rice and ghee, fish and flesh being strictly interdicted, and she may not eat any sweetmeats. Where this ceremony is observed, it is held to be a necessary preliminary to the commencement of marital intercourse. By a recent change in the law it has been made criminal to have intercourse with a girl under twelve years of age.

Barendra.

It has been mentioned above that the Barendra Brahmans claim to be descended from the five Kanaujiya Brahmans imported by Adisura by their original or Hindustani wives. General tradition, however, rejects the latter portion of the claim, and holds that the Barendra are the offspring, not of the original wives, but of Bengali women whom the Kanaujiyas married after their settlement in Bengal. The sub-caste takes its name from the tract of country known as Barendra lying

---

[1] *The Golden Bough*, pp. 228–42.

north of the river Padma between the Karatoya and Mahánanda rivers, and corresponding roughly to the districts of Pabna, Rajshahi, and Bogra. Ballál Sen reorganised the Barendra at the same time as the Rárhi Brahmans, and divided them into three hypergamous classes: (1) Kulin, (2) Suddha or pure Srotriya, (3) Kashta or bad Srotriya. The first class was subdivided into eight *gáins* or communes: Bhadra, Bhádri, Bhima, Lahari, Maitra, Rudra-Vágisi, Sádhu-Vágisi, and Santámani or Sándilya; the second into seven groups of the same kind; Atharthi, Bhattasali, Champati, Kámadevta, Karanjan, Nandánavási, and Navsi; and the third into eighty-four families, the names of which need not be enumerated here. In addition to the *gáins* we find among the Kulins a further division into eight *páti* or social grades: Atub-Kahni, Baini, Bosnah, Janail, Kutb-Kahni, Nirabhil, Panchuria, Rahala. The object of this grouping is not very clear. Every *gáin* belongs to a *páti*, but the *páti* is not always identical with the *gáin*, for members of the same *gáin* sometimes marry into different *pátis*. The *gáins* appear to be in theory endogamous. The system of reciprocal marriage (pálti-prakriti) which prevails among Rárhi Brahmans is unknown in the Barendra group. The rules governing the three main classes permit a Kulin to marry a Suddha-Srotriya girl, and the children of such a marriage rank as Kulins. Should he marry a Kashta-Srotriya, he loses his kul and becomes a Káp, an irregular group occupying much the same position as the Bansaja among Rárhi Brahmans. If a Barendra Kulin marries the daughter of a Káp, he himself is degraded to the group to which his wife belongs, but his children hold somewhat higher rank, and are deemed eligible for marriage to Kulins. No Kulin girl may marry below her own class. If a suitable husband cannot be found, she goes through the form of symbolical marriage to a figure of *kusa* grass, and has red lead smeared upon her forehead to show that she is really a wife. The *gotras* of the Barendra sub-caste are the same as those of the Rárhi, viz., Bharadwaja, Kasyapa, Sándilya, Savarna and Vatsya. Their commonest titles are Bhattacharya, Bhumik, Chakravartti, Chaudhari, Majumdár, Parihal, and Sikhdár.

Vaidik.

Concerning the origin of the Vaidik Brahmans some differences of opinion exist. All agree in honouring them for their adherence to Vedic rites, their zeal for Vedic studies, their social independence, and their rejection of polygamy. From the fact that some of the most important settlements of the sub-caste are found in the outlying districts of Orissa and Sylhet, some authorities have been led to describe them as descendants of the original Brahmans of Bengal who refused to accept the reforms of Ballál Sen, and took refuge in regions beyond his jurisdiction. Genealogists of rival sub-castes maintain that Ballál Sen excluded them from his scheme on the ground that they did not come up to his standard of purity of descent. Buchanan mentions a tradition lingering among the Vaidik Brahmans of Dinájpur that they had been introduced into that district by Advaita Subuddhi Narayana, Rájá of Sylhet. In Orissa, on the other hand, the representatives of this sub-caste are said to have come direct from Kanauj, and to have made their first settlement in Puri about the twelfth century A.D. This opinion derives support from Mr. Sherring's statement that the Kanaujiya Brahmans of Benares recognise the Vaidik as a branch of their own tribe who have settled in Bengal.

There are two main divisions of Vaidik Brahmans—(1) Páschátya or western, claiming to have come from Kanauj, and (2) Dákshinátya or southern, tracing their origin to the original Bengal stock. The Páschátya had originally eleven *gotras*, divided into two groups, known as the *pancha* and *shash*. The former included Bharadwája, Sándilya, Saunaka Savarna, and Vasishtha; the latter, Gautama, Kasyapa, Krishnátreya, Rathikara, Sunaka, and Vachyara. The Bharadwája *gotra*, however, became extinct, its place being taken by the Sunaka *gotra* of the Shash group. In course of time other *gotras*, Ghrita Kausiki, Maitráyali, Tuthíkara, and Upamanya, came to be formed, but the relations of these to the original eleven are not very precisely defined.

Vaidik Brahmans have no Kulins, and their *ghataks* or genealogists are Brahmans of other sub-castes. Their titles are the same as those of other Bengal Brahmans: Bhattacharya, Chakravartti, and Thákur, are common designations among them. The Páschátya branch is said to have been formerly distributed in fourteen *sthâns* or settlements. Three of these—Dadhichigrám, Marichigrám, and Sántali—have now disappeared, and even their sites are unknown. Of the remaining eleven, Chandradwip, Kotálipáda, Sámanta Sára, are in Backergunge; Alambi, Brahma Paraka, Jayári in Rajshahi; Akhará, Gaurâli, Pani Kantaka in Faridpur; Madhyadesa in Jessore; and Navadvipa in Nuddea. In theory, these settlements seem to have been of the same character as the *mels* created for the Rárhi Brahmans by Devi Vara. It was intended that all Vaidik Brahmans should reside in one of these villages, and that marriage should be restricted to the local limits laid down. At the present day, however, many families live elsewhere and intermarry with families similarly situated. They can, however, rejoin the original *Samáj* or association of communes on payment of a heavy fine.

Saptasati.

According to popular tradition, the Saptasati Brahmans are descended from the seven hundred ignorant Brahmans sent by Adisura to the Court of Kanauj for the purpose of learning their priestly duties. Others trace their origin to certain Brahmans who were exiled beyond the Brahmaputra river for resisting the innovations of Ballál Sen. It seems to be certain that they are peculiar to Bengal, and that they cannot claim connexion with any of the ten standard Brahmanical tribes. This view is borne out by the names of their *gotras*, which, as will be seen from the list given in the Appendix, differ entirely from the standard Brahmanical series, and appear to be of a local or territorial rather than of an eponymous type. The Saptasati themselves virtually admit their inferiority to the other orders of Brahmans. Men of education and respectability are reluctant to admit that they belong to this sub-caste, all distinctive practices are being abandoned, and the entire group seems likely to be absorbed in the Srotriya grade of Rarhi

Brahmans. The Saptasati have no Kulins, nor do they keep ghataks for the purpose of maintaining genealogies. Notwithstanding this, they give their daughters in marriage to Kulins of the Rárhi sub-caste, and by paying a heavy dowry, often amounting to as much as one thousand rupees, may even obtain brides from families of the Srotriya class. It is further said that a Rárhi Kulin will eat and drink with the Saptasati, while a Bansaja, though of lower rank than a Kulin, would consider this a degradation. The ordinary title of the Saptasati is Sarma, not Dev-Sarmma, as among the ten recognised tribes. Chakravartti, Chaudhuri, Rái, and Sarkár are also common appellations.

Madhyasreni.

The Madhyasreni Brahmans profess to derive their name from the fact of their original settlements being in the district of Midnapur, lying midway (*Madhya-desa*) between Bengal and Orissa. They say that their ancestors were Rárhi Brahmans who settled early in Ballál Sen's reign in pargana Mayna in Midnapur. When Ballál Sen was engaged in classifying the Brahmans of the rest of Bengal according to their degree of virtue, he sent a *ghatak* or genealogist to the Brahmans settled in Mayna to include them in the scheme. They declined, however, to have anything to say to the institution of Kulinism, and there are no Kulins among them to this day. For their resistance to his orders, Ballál Sen ordered them to be cut off from the rest of the caste, and all intercourse between them and the Brahmans of Bengal Proper was strictly forbidden. The Rárhi Brahmans of the present day, with whom the Madhyasreni thus claim kinship, are by no means inclined to accept this legend as true. They point out that it is *primâ facie* most unlikely that a colony of Rárhi Brahmans should have left their original seats for no particular reason, and have settled in an out-of-the-way place like pargana Mayna. Again, it is said, if the Madhyasreni were really Rárhi Brahmans, how is it that they have eight *gotras*, including Parásara, Gautama and Ghrita Kausika, while the true Rárhi have only five? Gautama and Ghrita Kausika are found among the Brahmans of Orissa, and Parásara is said to be characteristic of the Saptasati Brahmans of Bengal, whose ignorance of correct ritual compelled Adisura to import the ancestors of the Rárhi Brahmans from Kanauj. On these grounds it is conjectured that the Madhyasreni Brahmans may be a composite group made up of members of the Rárhi, Utkal and Saptasati sub-castes, who for some reason broke off from their own classes, settled in an outlying district, and in course of time formed a new sub-caste. Some go so far as to suggest that the original Madhyasreni were expelled from their own sub-castes, and quote a local tradition attaching to them the name *Madyadoshi*, 'guilty of drunkenness,' in support of this view. Although the standard form of Kulinism is not recognised by the Madhyasreni, those families among them who bear the Rárhi Kulin names of Mukharji, Chatterji, Banerji, are specially sought after in marriage, which practically comes to much the same thing. Another curious form of hypergamy is also in force among them. People who live in the four villages (Bhamua in pargana Mayna

Gokulnagar in Chetua, and Mahárájpur and Bhogdanda in Kedar) supposed to be the original seats of the caste are held in great honour, and residents of other villages who marry their daughters to them are expected to pay a heavy bridegroom-price.

Most of the Madhyasreni are worshippers of the Saktis, but in the matter of religion and ceremonial observances generally they do not depart materially from the practices of other Brahmans. It should be observed, however, that widows among them are allowed to eat uncooked food on the eleventh day of either fortnight of the moon, while the widows of other Brahmanical sub-castes are not allowed to touch even water on that day. Some Madhyasrenis again serve the Goalás or Gops as their family priests, and others are said to eat uncooked food at religious ceremonies performed by members of the Kaibartta caste, and to accept gifts from them on those occasions.

The most striking features in the organization of the Brahman caste in Behar are the great number of sub-castes and sections and the complexity of the system of exogamy which prevails among them. All recognise the classical traditions concerning the origin of Brahmans in general, and to these are superadded a number of more or less credible legends designed to account for the separation of particular groups from the main body.

Sáraswat.

The few SARASWATA Brahmans who are found in Behar claim descent from the Aryan tribe of the Sáraswatas, who inhabited the banks of the Saraswati river in the Panjab. They rank as the first of the five Gauras living north of the Vindhya range. The Sáraswatas of the Panjab have a very large number of subdivisions, deriving their names from the places in which their ancestors had settled, or from nicknames given to individuals. Lists of these were collected by Pandit Radha Krishna for Dr. John Wilson, and are given in the second volume of the latter's work on Indian castes. No attempt, however, is made to distinguish the endogamous, exogamous, and hypergamous groups, and it is clear from an examination of the lists that sub-castes, sections, and titles denoting hypergamous classes have been mixed up together. The Sáraswat Brahmans of Behar, a comparatively small community living at a great distance from the main body of their tribe, have been unable to maintain the elaborate endogamous organization which is found among their brethren in the Panjab. They have no sub-castes, and the titles Sukul, Bájpai, Awasthi, etc., which are found among them, do not appear to have any bearing upon marriage. Within the last few years they have begun to intermarry with the Gaur Brahmans.

Kanaujia.

The KANYA KUBJA or KANAUJIA Brahmans are counted among the five Gauras. Three main divisions of them are found in Behar: (1) ANTARVEDI or KANAUJIA proper, coming from the country between the Ganges and Jamna: (2) SARJUPARI or SARWARIA, who are said to have settled on the east of the Sarju or Gogra in the time of Rájá Aja, grandfather of Ráma. Another story of the origin of the Sarwaria group is worth telling here for the light that it throws upon the part which misunderstood names may play in the growth of popular tradition:—Once upon a time there were two brothers, Kanha and Kubja. They lived at Kanauj, and their descendants were called Kanaujia Brahmans. Now Ram Chandra, King of Ajodhya, wished to perform the great sacrifice of a horse, and sent for the Kanaujia Brahmans to help him. When they were starting, their father made them promise not to take any present for what they were going to do. But it seems that the sacrifice was of no effect unless the Brahmans were duly rewarded. The Rájá knew this, and caused diamonds to be hidden in the packets of betel which he gave to the Brahmans. When they got home their father asked if they had taken any presents, and they said they had not. But when the packets of betel were opened the diamonds were found, and those Brahmans were at once turned out of their caste. So they went back to the king, ready to curse him for his treachery. But he appeased them with smooth words and with grants of land to dwell on, and the grants were made in this way. The king shot an arrow as far as he could, and the place where it fell was the boundary of the land. Now the name of an arrow is *sar*: so these Brahmans were called Sarwaria. (3) Sanádhia or Sanaudhiá, a group of inferior status, concerning whom the following legend is told. It is said that Rama, King of Ajodhya, celebrated a sacrifice and made a great feast, to which he invited all the Kanaujia Brahmans. In order to test their orthodoxy he desired them to perform the sacrifice, and afterwards to partake of the feast fully clothed and not merely with a loin-cloth on, as is the custom of Brahmans. The Sarwaria and the Antarvedi declined to agree to this departure from established usage, but the Sanaudhia attended the feast and did as the king suggested. For this breach of Brahmanical etiquette they were cut off from communion with the orthodox, and degraded to a lower level of social and ceremonial purity. The Kanaujias as a class are tall and athletic, though wanting in the peculiar fineness of feature and intellectual cast of countenance which distinguishes the higher grades of Brahmans in other parts of India. Those of them who enlist in the Native Army are known as Purbiyas, or men of the east, in contradistinction to the people of the Panjab, and one of their titles, Pánre or Pánde, being originally a corruption of the word *pandit*, a learned man, became, under the form of Pandy, the generic designation of the mutineers of 1857. Their immoderate scruples concerning ceremonial purity in matters of food and drink are held up to ridicule in the well-known proverb *Tin Kanaujiá tera chulhá*—"Three Kanaujias want thirteen fireplaces."

Gaur.

The Gaur Brahmans of Behar, like their brethren of the Delhi district, insist that their designation is derived from the ruined city of Gaur or Lakhnauti in Maldah, once the capital of Bengal. They say that their ancestors left Gaur in the days of the Pándavas at the commencement of the Kali Yuga, and settled in the country round Delhi. Another version of the same story is that Rájá Agar, the eponym of the Agarwal caste, sent for these Brahmans from Bengal, in the same way as Adisur summoned Brahmans from Kanauj. This tradition, reversing as it does the usual direction of the advance of the Brahmanical tribes, has been received with doubt by all writers on the subject of caste. General Cunningham's opinion, that the Gaura Brahmans must have belonged originally to the district of Gonda and not to the mediæval city of Gaur in Bengal seems to offer the best solution of the difficulty. The Gaur Brahmans serve the Agarwals as priests—a fact which is in keeping with, and may have given rise to, the legend noticed above. In Behar they recognise two sub-castes, ADI GAUR and MADHA GAUR. Many observers have remarked on the liberal spirit displayed by the Gaur Brahmans and on their freedom from that pedantry which the Kanaujias show in caste questions. We may perhaps claim as an illustration of these qualities the fact that within the last few years intermarriage between Gaur and Sáraswata Brahmans has come to be recognised in Behar. On the other hand, it is equally probable that this relaxation of the strict rule of exogamy may have been the result of the numerical weakness of the two groups. The members of a small sub-caste, broken up, as such a group necessarily is, into a number of exogamous groups and scattered over a large area of country, are bound to find considerable difficulty in getting their daughters married. Whenever this difficulty occurs, the tendency will be to enlarge the matrimonial circle so as to increase the number of husbands available at a given time. The Gaur and Sáraswata Brahmans, both immigrants into Behar from a distant part of India and separated from their original home by a number of intervening tribes, would be in much the same position as the Káyasths and Baidyas in the outlying districts of Eastern Bengal, and would, like them, be driven to modify the strict rules of caste in accordance with the dictates of social necessity.

Maithil.

The MAITHIL or TIRHUTIA Brahmans rank among the Panch Gaur. Their name is derived from Mithila, an ancient division of India, comprising the modern districts of Sáran, Mozufferpur, Darbhanga, Purniah, and part of Nepal. Dr. Wilson, following Colebrooke, observes that fewer distinctions are recognised among the Maithil Brahmans than among any other of the great divisions of Brahmans in India. This statement needs to be qualified. It is true that the Maithil have no endogamous divisions, but their exogamous groups are peculiarly numerous and complex, and they have a complete hypergamous system. For the latter purpose the caste is divided into five groups—SROTRIYA or SOTE, JOG, PANJIBADDH, NAGAR, and JAIWAR—which take rank in this order. A man of the Srotriya group may take a wife from the lower groups and is usually paid a considerable sum of money for doing so, but he loses in social estimation by the match, and the children of such unions, though higher than the class from which their mothers came, are nevertheless not deemed to be socially equal to the members of their father's class. The same rule applies to the other classes in descending order: each may take wives from the groups below it. The principle of this rule is the same as that followed by

Manu in laying down the matrimonial relations of the four original castes, and in its earliest form it seems to have gone the full length of forbidding a woman of a higher group to marry a man of a lower group. It is important, however, to notice that in Behar the rule is now much less stringent and rigid than in Bengal. Although it is admitted to be the right thing for a girl to marry within her own group or in a higher group, it is not absolutely obligatory for her to do so, and cases do occur in which a girl of a higher class marries a man of a lower class in consideration of a substantial bride-price being paid to her parents. The comparative laxity of Behar usage in this respect may be due partly to the character of the people and partly to the fact that caste observances in that part of the country have never been laid down by a superior authority, such as Ballál Sen, but have been settled by the people themselves at regular meetings held with that object. It is well known that the leading members of the Maithil sub-caste with their pandits, their *panjiárás* or genealogists, and their *ghataks* or marriage-brokers, come together at many places in Tirhut for the purpose of settling disputed questions of caste custom and of arranging marriages. A community which has five hypergamous classes and a double series of exogamous groups—one based on locality and the other on mythical ancestry—and at the same time attaches great importance to purity of blood, may well find it necessary to take stock of its arrangements from time to time and to see whether the rules are being observed.

Among the Maithil Brahmans of Behar, as among the Kulins of Bengal, the bride-price familiar to students of early tradition has given place to the bridegroom-price, which hypergamy necessarily tends to develop. Polygamy, formerly characteristic of the Bengal Kulin, is practised in Behar in much the same form by the Bikauwá or 'vendor,' a class of Maithil Brahmans who derive their name from the practice of selling themselves, or more rarely their minor sons, to the daughter of the lower groups of the series given above. Usually the Bikauwás belong to the Jog and Panjibaddh classes, and comparatively few of them are found among the Srotriya and Nagar groups. Some have as many as forty or fifty wives, who live with their own parents and are visited at intervals by their husbands. Bikauwá Brahmans who have married into the lower classes are not received on equal terms by the members of their own class, but the women whom they marry consider themselves raised by the alliance. The price paid for a Bikauwá varies according to the class to which he belongs and the means of the family of the girl whom he is to marry. It may be as little as Rs. 20: it has been known to rise as high as Rs. 6,000.

Sákadwipi.

The Sákadwipi or Sakaldwipi Brahmans are supposed to have been brought by Rama from Ceylon for the purpose of practising medicine. According to another opinion they were the indigenous Brahmans of the ancient country of Magadha. Some say that it is for this reason that they were formerly called Magas. The name, however, has dropped into disuse, and the Sákadwipi themselves prefer the legend associating them with Rama's famous invasion to that connecting them with a part of the country proverbial among Hindus for its ceremonial impurity. At the present day the bulk of the sub-caste are employed as priests in Rajput families; some are landholders, some practise Hindu medicine. It is a curious fact that, although the Sákadwipi have the standard eponymous *gotras* of the Brahman caste, their marriages are regulated not by these, but by ninety-five *purs* or divisions of the local or territorial type; that is to say, a Sákadwipi man may marry a woman of his own *gotra* who in theory is descended from the same mythical ancestor (*rishi*) as himself, but may not marry a woman whose forefathers are shown by the name of her *pur* to have come from the same village or the same tract of country as his own. To abandon the *gotra* altogether and to substitute for it exogamous divisions based on a wholly different order of facts involves so serious a departure from orthodox usage that one is inclined to doubt whether the Sakadwipi can ever have been organized on the regular lines. This doubt is borne out by the statement made by Mr. Sherring,* that "the test applied to a stranger pretending to be a Sákadwipi is to offer him what is called *jhuthá páni*, or water from a vessel from which another person has drunk—a custom prohibited by all strict sects of Hindus. Should the stranger not be a Sakadwipi, he will refuse the water, probably with some indignation, as, by drinking it, his caste, whatever it was, would be broken. If a Sákadwipi, however, he will take it readily."

Utkal.

According to Mr. John Beames, the best living authority on all questions touching the history of Orissa:—"Tradition relates that the original Brahmans of Orissa were all extinct at the time of the rise of the Gangá Vansa line of kings, but that 10,000 Brahmans were induced to come from Kanauj and settle in Jájpur, the sacred city on the Baitarani river. The date of this immigration is not stated, but the fact is probably historical, and may have been synchronous with the well-known introduction of Kanaujia Brahmans into the neighbouring province of Bengal by King Adisura in the tenth century. When the worship of the idol Jagannáth began to be revived at Puri, the Kings of Orissa induced many of the Jájpur Brahmans to settle round the new temple and conduct the ceremonies. Thus there sprang up a division among the Brahmans; those who settled in Puri being called the *Dakhinátya Sreni*, or southern class, and those who remained at Jájpur the *Uttara Sreni*, or northern class. This latter spread all over Northern Orissa. Many of the southern Bráhmans, however, are also found in Balasor; and the divisions of the two classes are fairly represented in most parts of the district, though the southern class is less numerous than the northern. The former are held in greater esteem for learning and purity of race than the latter." Mr. Beames goes on to explain how these two sub-castes are further broken up into functional divisions according

---

* *Hindu Tribes and Castes*, vol. i, p. 102.

to the Veda whose ritual they profess to observe, and into *gotras* or exogamous groups. In addition to this, certain titles or *upádhis* are appropriated to particular *gotras*, for which they serve, as Mr. Beames points out, the purpose of surnames. It is perhaps due to this connexion with the *gotra* that the titles themselves are frequently used as exogamous divisions. The scheme of *srenis*, *gotras*, *upádhis*, and Vedic classes worked out by Mr. Beames is shown in the Appendix. Concerning the *gotra* names, he observes that they "are for the most part patronymics from well-known Rishis, and are identical with many of those still in use in the North-Western Provinces. This circumstance seems to add confirmation to the legend of the origin of this caste from Kanauj. A Rishi's name occurs also among *upádhis* in one instance; Sárangi being from Sanksrit Sárangi, patronymic from Sringa Rishi."

The entire series of names offers an interesting illustration of the curious complexity of the internal structure of the Bráhman caste. Starting with the two groups, DAKHINATYA and UTTARA, based upon territorial habitat, we find each of these broken up into smaller groups, taking their names from certain specialised functions, and also into groups tracing their descent from a mythical ancestor; while through the whole runs a fourth series of distinctive titles, indicating some form of personal merit, whether proficiency in religious knowledge, fullness of ascetic virtue, or it may be merely descent from famous ancestry. By making it possible to classify families in order as it were of hereditary merit, such titles are specially adapted to give rise to a system of hypergamy. Once let it be admitted and placed on record that a particular family has attained to a high degree of ceremonial purity, and it follows that marriages with members of that family will acquire a special value, which in course of time will take the form of a bride or bridegroom-price. But besides this, titular groups can also be used for exogamous purposes, and this is the case in Orissa, though it is extremely unusual among the higher castes. Lastly, I may draw attention to the remarkable fact that among the Brahmans of this part of the country unquestionable traces may be found of a survival of the totemistic beliefs which are common among the Dravidian and semi-Dravidian groups. Thus the Brahmans of the Batsasa *gotra* revere the calf as their original ancestor; the Bharadwaja claim descent not from the Vedic Rishi, but from a bird bearing the same name; the Atreya are the offspring of a deer, and will not eat that animal or sit upon its hide; the Kauchhasa trace their lineage to a tortoise; and the Kaundinya commemorate their descent from the tiger by refusing to sit upon a tiger skin. No attempt can be made here to account for the prevalence of these superstitions. They may be a survival of ancient Aryan totemism; they may be due to the adoption by the immigrant Bráhmans of Dravidian beliefs and observances; or, lastly, they may show that the Bráhmans of Orissa are themselves Dravidians or have undergone a considerable infusion of Dravidian blood.

An attempt is made in the Appendix to reconcile Mr. Beames' account of the divisions of the Northern Orissa Bráhmans with the structural divisions of the caste in Orissa generally.

The following statement shows the number and distribution of Bráhmans in 1872 and 1881:—

District.	1872.	1881.	District.	1872.	1881.
Bardwan	160,824	107,684	Noakhali	7,652	10,963
Bankura	49,473	84,322	Tipperah	31,020	31,502
Birbhum	48,287	89,724	Chittagong Hill Tracts ...	15	191
Midnapur	118,700	117,414	Patna	39,878	47,041
Hughli	107,534	76,271	Gya	64,319	59,570
Howrah		39,141	Shahabad	196,631	213,306
24-Parganas	120,102	114,911	Mozufferpur	183,777	96,206
Nadiya	60,024	59,894	Darbhanga		179,263
Jessore	51,999	37,752	Saran	149,490	175,362
Khulna	...	28,654	Champaran	65,315	76,284
Murshedabad	38,749	33,935	Monghyr	43,402	57,291
Dinajpur	6,269	8,913	Bhagalpur	50,443	71,420
Rajshahye	15,660	16,523	Purniah	29,137	34,822
Rangpur	10,623	12,075	Maldah	8,507	12,001
Bogra	4,263	4,614	Santhál Parganas	29,330	36,975
Pabna	20,553	20,970	Cuttack	163,679	177,193
Darjiling	1,002	3,882	Puri	86,580	88,692
Jalpigori	1,275	3,909	Balasore	106,192	110,373
Kuch Behar	...	3,530	Tributary States	66,480	80,426
Dacca	51,638	60,542	Hazaribagh	21,740	26,421
Faridpur	23,294	46,915	Lohardagá	27,326	41,439
Bakarganj	65,254	44,736	Singbhum	4,098	2,886
Maimansinh	33,414	50,152	Manbhum	53,701	49,190
Chittagong	22,657	21,355	Tributary States	2,756	8,462

Bráhman, a synonym for Bábhan; a religious group of Jugis in Bengal.

Brahmapur, a *samáj* or local group of the Sábarna *gotra* of Páschátya Baidik Brahmans in Bengal.

Bráhmarshi, a section of the Bhar caste in Western Bengal. The term appears to have been borrowed from the Brahmanical system in comparatively recent times, as the caste has also a set of the totemistic sections characteristic of the Kolarian races. An eponymous section of Sánkháris and Tántis in Bengal.

Brahma-vádi, a title of Brahmans, meaning one who asserts that Brahma—the one spirit—really exists, and nothing else.

Bráhmilchá, a *thar* or sept of Sunuwárs in Darjiling.

Brahmimá Dhán, a *thar* of the Basishtha *gotra* of Nepáli Brahmans.

Braili, a *thar* or sept of Mangars in Darjiling.

Brajabási, (i) residents of Braj, the tract of country round Brindaban, in the North-Western Provinces; (ii) the warlike character of the Braj people has led to the term Brajabási being used to denote an armed attendant, one carrying arms, as a sword and shield, or sometimes a matchlock, and employed as a door-keeper, a guard, or an escort; (iii) a synonym for Bediyá, *q.v.*

Brangplagi, a *thar* or sept of Mangars in Darjiling.

Briddha, a section of Brahmans.

Brihaspati, a section of Brahmans.

Brihatbat, a section of Chásá-dhobás in Bengal.

Brijiá, a synonym for Binjhiá.

Brijiá-Agariá, a sub-tribe of Agariás in Chota Nagpur.

Brikhan, a section of the Korá caste in Western Bengal.

Bud or **Budwar**, Wednesday, a sept of Mundas in Chota Nagpur.

Budhaure, a *mul* of the Kásyapa section of Maithil Brahmans in Behar.

Budhbansi, a sept of the Chandrabansi division of Rajputs in Behar.

Budhware-Mahesi, a *mul* of the Bátsya section of Maithil Brahmans in Behar.

Budhwáre-Sakuri, a *mul* of the Bátsa section of Maithil Brahmans in Behar.

Budhwáre-Dumrá, a *mul* of the Bátsa section of Maithil Brahmans in Behar.

Budhwáre-Balhá, a *mul* of the Bátsa section of Maithil Brahmans in Behar.

Budhwárk, a *pur* or section of Sákadwipi Brahmans in Behar.

Buim, a worm, a totemistic sept of Mundas in Chota Nagpur.

Bukhariá, a title of Bábhans in Behar.

Bukru, a sept of Lohars and Mundas in Chota Nagpur.

Bulun, a section of Murmis in Darjiling.

Bulung, a *thar* or sept of Gurungs in Darjiling.

Bumákámchhá, a *thar* or sept of Khambus in Darjiling.

Buná, *Banuá*, *Buno*, the vague popular designation of a number of castes and tribes in Central and Eastern Bengal, who are believed to have immigrated into that part of the country from Western and Northern Bengal and from Chota Nagpur. The term does not lend itself to precise definition, but, I believe, the following to be a fairly accurate list of the castes which it ordinarily includes:—(1) Bhuiya, (2) Bhumij, (3) Bágdi, (4) Bauri, (5) Ghási, (6) Kharwár, (7) Korá, (8) Munda, (9) Oraon, (10) Rájbansi, (11) Rajwár, (12) Santál. Of these all but the Rájbansi are natives of Western Bengal or Chota Nagpur, where the undulating nature of the country and the system of terracing for rice render the area available for cold weather crops, such as wheat, millets, and the like, exceedingly small. The result is that from the end of November to about the middle of April the classes who live by field labour have practically nothing to do, and wander eastwards in large number in search of work. Many if not most of them are employed in gathering in the rice harvest of Central and Eastern Bengal; some clear the *chars* of the Megna and Brahmaputra, or sow indigo for the planters of Rajshahye, while others find employment nearer home under the municipalities of Calcutta and its suburbs. Towards the middle of March this stream of labour again sets westward, and long lines of men may be met returning to plough their own fields with the first showers of April. Some, however, stay behind and settle in a more or less nomadic fashion in the districts east of the Hughli. To these scattered colonists, whose freedom from scruples in the matter of food cuts them off from their more orthodox neighbours, who repel the Hindu by eating fowls, and the Mahomedan by their partiality for pork, the natives of Central and Eastern Bengal have given the name of Buna. The etymology of the word is obscure, but I suspect it to be a corrupted form of *ban* or jungle, having reference either to the fact that the castes and tribes in question hail from the jungles of Western Bengal, or to the aptitude that they show for clearing and bringing under cultivation waste lands covered with jungle. In either case it is closely analogous to the word "jungly," which is used by persons concerned with emigration to the tea districts as a general designation for all coolies who come from Chota Nagpur.

The aggregate denoted by the word Buna has some points of resemblance to a caste in the popular sense of the word. Its members bear a common descriptive name, perform very similar functions, and, I believe, eat certain kinds of food and smoke tobacco together. They do not, however, intermarry, and the various castes and tribes grouped together in Eastern Bengal under the name of Buna regard themselves in their own country as perfectly distinct. It is of course difficult to define precisely the extent of the *rapprochement* that has taken place between them in their new homes; but it is at least conceivable that the bonds which now unite them may hereafter be drawn closer, and that the different members of the Buna group may in course of time intermarry without regard to the caste to which they originally belonged. Should this be the case, it will serve to illustrate a process which I believe very rarely occurs—the formation of a caste by the re-integration of units already differentiated from a common stock. It is tolerably certain that most of the castes included among the Bunas are offshoots from the great aboriginal race whom the Aryans found in possession of the plains of India. They have, however, long ago parted into separate marriage groups, and it will be curious to see whether their comparative isolation as settlers in Central and Eastern Bengal causes them to re-unite. The only analogous instance that I know of is that of the Chattarkhai caste in Orissa.

The following statement shows the number and distribution of the Buna group in 1872 and 1881. The statistics are not very valuable, as many Bunas would probably have described themselves by the name of their own caste instead of by the less definite generic term Buna.

District.	1872.	1881.	District.	1872.	1881.
Bardwan	876	25	Rangpur	193	178
Bankura	2,175	477	Bogra	2,346	4,511
Birbhum	43	15	Pabna	5,234	2,129
Midnapur	6	262	Darjiling	......	49
Hughli with Howrah ...	945	......	Dacca	840	15
24-Parganas	11,032	6,321	Faridpur	2,412	2,375
Nadiya	16,028	9,294	Bakarganj	175	......
Jessore	8,315	4,392	Maimansinh	492	845
Khulna	......	1,622	Maldah	617	215
Murshedabad	2,320	397	Santál Parganas	......	211
Dinajpur	3,139	3,333	Singbhum	......	22
Rajshahye	1,116	4,804	Manbhum	......	2,900

Buná-Pán, a sub-caste of Páns in Orissa.

Buna-Rajwár, a designation of Rajwars who have emigrated from their original home in Chota Nagpur and settled as *bunas*, or clearers of jungle, in Bengal or Behar.

Bundelá, a sept of Rajputs in Behar, possibly connected with the spurious tribe of Rajputs who give the name to the province of Bundelkhand. The latter are descended from the Garhwárs of Kantit and Khairagarh, and first settled in Bundelkhand in the thirteenth or fourteenth century.

Bundra, a sub-sept of the Besrá sept of Santáls.

Bunduar, a section of Ghásis in Chota Nagpur.

Bung or **Bungza**, a sept of Chakmás in the Hill Tracts of Chittagong.

Bunichhor, a section of Kanaujiá Lohárs in Behar.

Buráthoki, a sub-tribe of Mangars in Darjiling.

Burdewá, a *thar* or sept of Dámis in Darjiling whose chief profession is sewing.

Buriali Kálundiá, a sept of Hos in Singbhum.

Buri Sámat, a sept of Hos in Singbhum.

Buru, a sept of Páns in Chota Nagpur.

Buru-birit, of the hills, a sub-sept of the Márndi sept of Santáls.

Busgarait, a section of the Kámár sub-caste of Dosadhs in Behar.

Butepáchhá, a *thar* or sept of Khambus in Darjiling.

Buthuja, a *thar* or sept of the Bárah Gurung sub-tribe of Gurungs in Darjiling.

Butká-Sudhá, a sub-caste of Sudhás in Orissa.

Butku, a section of the Korá caste in Chota Nagpur, the members of which will not touch or kill a pig.

Byábahári, a sub-caste of the Kochh tribe in Dinajpur.

Byádh, Sansk. *Vyádhá*, a synonym for Bediyá, *q.v.*

Byádhá, a sub-caste of Pasis in Behar, whose original occupation was to gather and sell *singhárá*, the water-chestnut (*Trapa bispinosa*). Most of them have now abandoned this and taken to extracting and selling the juice of the toddy-palm.

Byangnási, a *thar* or sept of Mangars in Darjiling.

Byápri, a *thar* or sept of Gurungs in Darjiling.

C

Cháb or *Chábi*, a sub-caste of Gonrhis in Behar. Some of them disown all connexion with the Gonrhis and claim to be a separate caste. Their houses are often circular.

Chabdiá, a section of Goálás in the North-Western Provinces.

Chábuksawár, a rough rider, a groom, a jockey—an occupation usually followed by Mahomedans.

Chachet, a small bird, a totemistic sept of Chiks in Chota Nagpur.

Chadchák, a *pur* or section of Sákadwipi Brahmans in Behar.

Chadu, a bird, a totemistic sept of Mundas in Chota Nagpur.

Chaencháir, a bird, a totemistic sept of Chiks in Chota Nagpur.

Chah-ba, a *rui* or sept of Sherpa Bhotias of Nepal.

Cháhil or **Cháhirá**, a sub-tribe of Rajputs, properly natives of Hissar, mostly converts to Mahomedanism. They nevertheless retain charge of the tomb of Goga Chauhán, a Hindu prince, now esteemed a saint.

Chahraitá, a section of the Pachainyá sub-caste of Doms in Behar.

Chahubar, a section of Ghásis in Chota Nagpur.

Chái, a title of Kaibarttas in Bengal; a synonym for Cháin.

Chaián, a hypergamous group of Karans in Orissa.

Chaibisá, a sub-tribe of Limbus in Darjiling and the Eastern Himalayas.

Chail, a title of Támbulis in Bengal.

Chailáhá, a section of the Banodhiá and Jaiswár Kalwárs in Behar.

Chaimarar, a title of the Chain sub-caste of Nuniás in Behar.

Cháin, a sub-caste of Nuniás in Behar; also a title of Bangaja Káyasths.

Cháin, *Chái*, *Barcháin*, a cultivating and fishing caste of Behar and Central Bengal, probably an offshoot from some non-Aryan tribe. The Cháins are found in Oudh, where Mr. Carnegy connects them with the Tháru, Raji, Nat, and other broken and gypsy-like tribes inhabiting the base of the Himalayas, and traces in their physiognomy features peculiar to Mongolian races. Mr. Sherring, again, in one place speaks of them as a sub-caste of Malláhs, in another as a class of 'jugglers, thimble-riggers, and adventurers, who attend fairs and other festivals like men of the same profession in England.' A sub-caste of the Nunias bears the name Chain, but the Nunias do not admit any

Origin.

affinity. Mr. C. F. Magrath, in his *Memorandum on the Tribes and Castes of Behar*, published in the *Bengal Census Report of* 1872, says they closely resemble Binds in their occupations, being chiefly boatmen, who also engage in fishing. Cháins are thickest south of the Ganges, while Binds are most numerous in North Behar. Mr. Magrath adds that their reputation as thieves, impostors, and swindlers is in his experience not altogether deserved, as the men whom the common people, and even the police of Behar, describe as Cháins usually turned out on inquiry to be Maghayá Doms, Nats, or Rajwárs. The term *Chái-paná*, however, is a common expression for stealing among Hindi-speaking natives, while throughout Bengal individuals belonging to the caste are watched with great suspicion.

Internal structure and marriage.

The *muls* or exogamous sections of the Cháins in Behar throw no light on the origin of the caste, as with one exception they appear to have been borrowed from the Brahmanical. Cháins practise adult as well as infant-marriage, but the latter is considered more respectable. Polygamy is permitted if the first wife is barren or suffers from an incurable disease or any serious bodily defect. A widow may marry again. Though not compelled to marry her deceased husband's younger brother, it is deemed right and proper for her to do so if such a relative exists. The standard of female morality appears to be lax, and sexual indiscretions are leniently dealt with provided that they occur within the limit of the caste. If a woman gives rise to scandal by an intrigue with a member of the caste, she may either obtain absolution by giving a feast to the brethren, or her husband may apply to the caste council for a divorce. In the latter case she may marry her lover. For offences outside the circle of the caste, no mode of atonement is appointed; and a woman who goes wrong with a member of either a higher or a lower caste is turned out of the Cháin community, and generally becomes a public prostitute.

Religion.

As among other impure castes, a Dasnami Gosain acts as guru, a degraded Maithil Brahman as purohit. In Oudh the Cháins worship Mahábira, the monkey-god, Sat Naráyana, and Devi Pátan, while they drink spirits and feast on pork. Those whom we find in Behar, like other fisher tribes, are followers of the Pánch Piríya creed, while the Bengal members of the caste worship Koila Bába. Both freely indulge in spirits whenever a favourable opportunity presents itself.

Social status and occupation.

In point of social standing Cháins rank with Binds, Nuniás, and Pasis; but nowhere do they rise to the distinction, which Binds and Nuniás sometimes attain, of giving water and certain kinds of sweetmeats to Brahmans. In Behar and Central Bengal they are cultivators holding lands as occupancy or, more frequently, non-occupancy raiyats. Others, again, are landless day-labourers or boatmen and fishermen, catching mullet with weirs of *sirki* mat, as the Binds do. In Oudh and the North-Western Provinces they are cutivators, and prepare *khair* or catechu. In Eastern Bengal they appear as traders in grain and pulse.

The following statement shows the number and distribution of Cháins in 1872 and 1881 :—

District.	1872.	1881.	District.	1872.	1881.
Bardwan	63	19	Maimansinh	13	3
Birbhum	2	17	Tipperah	......	314
Midnapur	801	......	Noakhali	......	6
Hughli with Howrah ...	21	......	Patna	6,780	4,670
24-Parganas	8	116	Gya	19	18
Nadiya	655	419	Shahabad	360	......
Khulna	......	171	Tirhut { Darbhanga ...	} 1,872	{ 95
Jessore	104	161	Tirhut { Mozufferpur ...		960
Murshedabad	26,133	20,649	Saran	905	879
Dinajpur	337	271	Champaran	1,148	306
Rajshahye	8,802	8,009	Monghyr	5,889	3,233
Rangpur	22	231	Bhagalpur	2,611	5,546
Pabna	120	12	Purneah	4,526	3,558
Darjiling	......	3	Maldah	30,082	33,639
Dacca	1	391	Santál Parganas	17,576	10,272
Faridpur	436	5			

Chaini, Chain or Chai, a sub-caste of Malláhs in Behar.

Chákar, a servant.

Chákarán, properly the plural of *chákar*, 'a servant,' ordinarily used to denote revenue-free or rent-free land appropriated to the support of persons performing public or *quasi*-public services, such as village watchmen, messengers, accountants, and the like. The term has thus come to be used in the Census papers as a designation of the holders of such land.

Cháki, a title of Barendra Brahmans and Káyasths in Bengal.

Cháki Dukri, a sept of Hos in Singbhum.

Chakkiwálá, a flour-grinder or miller, usually a Kurmi, who employs the women of his house or neighbourhood to grind singly.

Chakledár, the superintendent, or proprietor or renter, of a *chaklá*, a large division of a country comprehending a number of *parganás*.

Chakmá, *Tsakmá, Tsak, Thek* (Burm.), a Lohitic[1] tribe of the Chittagong Hill Tracts. Major Lewin groups them with the **Khyoungtha,** or tribes who live along the river courses, as distinguished from the **Toungtha,** whose settlements are confined to the hills. Concerning this division into river and hill peoples, which is believed to have originated with the Arakanese, Herr A. Grünwedel[2] remarks that it "not only supplies a good outward distinction, but is moreover fully justified, inasmuch as it at the same time preserves intact the division according to descent." Herr Virchow, however, observes that "these divisions, based as they are on the localities of the tribes along the rivers or on the hills, must by no means be supposed to represent either genetic or *de facto* homogeneous groups." The traditions regarding the origin of the Chakmás are conflicting, and allege (I)

Tradition of origin.

[1] From *lohita*, 'red,' a name of the Brahmaputra, believed by Lassen to have reference to the east and the rising sun. (*Ind. Alt.* i, 667, *note.*) F. Müller (*Allgemeine Ethnographie*, p. 405) includes the Burmese and the tribes of the Chittagong Hill Tracts and Arakan under the term *Lohita-Völker*.

[2] Summary Notice of the Hill Tribes, in Riebeck's *Chittagong Hill Tribes*, translated by Keane.

that they originally came from the Malay Peninsula, (2) that their ancestors were Chaus-bansi Kshatriyas of Champanagar in Hindustan, who invaded the Hill Tracts about the end of the 14th century, settled there, and intermarried with the people of the country; (3) that they are the descendants of the survivors of a Mogul army sent by the Vazir of Chittagong to attack the King of Arakan. Owing, it is said, to the Vazir declining the food offered to him by a Buddhist Phoongyee whom he met on the way, his army was defeated by art magic and his soldiers became slaves to the King of Arakan, who gave them land and wives in the Hill Tracts. In support of this tradition Major Lewin refers to the fact that the Chakmá Rájás from 1715 to 1830 bore the title Khán. This, however, clearly proves little, as the title is borne by many Hindus, and nothing is more probable than that the Rájá of a wild tribe should have borrowed it from the Mahomedan rulers of Chittagong.

The evidence at present available does not appear to warrant any more definite conclusion than that the Chakmás are probably a people of Arakanese origin, whose physical type has been to some extent modified by intermarriage with Bengali settlers. This view, though deriving some support from the fact that the tribe have only lately abandoned the use of an Arakanese dialect, possesses no scientific value, as for all we know the settlement in Arakan may be of very recent date, and the true affinities of the tribe can only be determined by a thorough examination of their physical characteristics. Dr. Riebeck's measurements comprised only three subjects—a number insufficient, as Herr Virchow points out, to admit of the calculation of an average which shall represent an approximation to the true physical type of the tribe.[1]

Internal structure.

The Chakmás are divided into three sub-tribes—Chakma, Doingnak, and Tungjainya or Tangjangya. The Doingnaks are believed to have broken off from the parent tribe about a century ago, when Jaun Baksh Khán was Chief, in consequence of his having ordered them to intermarry with the other branches of the tribe. This innovation was violently disapproved of, and many Doingnaks abandoned their homes on the Karnaphuli river and fled to Arakan. Of late years some of them have returned and settled in the hills of the Cox's Bazar subdivision. When Captain Lewin wrote, the Doingnaks spoke an Arakanese dialect, and had not yet acquired the corrupt form of Bengali which is spoken by the rest of the Chakmás. The Tungjainyá sub-tribe are said to have come into the Chittagong Hills from Arakan as late as 1819, when Dharm Baksh Khán was Chief. A number of them, however, soon returned to Arakan in consequence of the Chief's refusal to recognise the claims of their leader, Phapru, to the headship of the sub-tribe. About twenty years ago the elders of the Tungjainyá sub-tribe still spoke Arakanese, while the younger generation were following the example

[1] Since this was written one hundred specimens of the Chakma tribe have been measured under my supervision. The average cephalic index deduced from this large number of subjects is 84·5, and the average naso-malar index 106·4. A tribe so markedly brachy-cephalic and platyopic must clearly be classed as Mongoloid.

of the Chakmás and taking to Bengali. Outsiders are admitted into the tribe. They must spend seven days in the priest's house, and then give a feast to the tribe, at which certain *mantras* are repeated to sanctify the occasion, and fowls and pigs are killed. Persons so admitted are almost invariably natives of the plains who have become attached to Chakmá women. Although fully recognised as members of the tribe for social purposes, they would be distinguished by the designation Bangáli, but their offspring will rank in every respect as Chakmás.

A list of the exogamous septs (*gosa*) of the Chakmás and Tungjainiyás will be found in Appendix I. I have been unable to obtain a list of the septs of the Doingnaks. It will be observed that many of the septs are of the same type as those found among the Limbus and Tibetans; that is, the names record some curious adventure or personal peculiarity of the supposed ancestor of the sept. Others, again, are territorial; only, instead of taking their names from a village or a tract of country, they follow the names of rivers. The sept name descends in the male line, and the rule of exogamy based upon it is unilateral; that is, while a man is forbidden to marry a woman belonging to his own sept, there is nothing, so far as the rule of exogamy goes, to prevent him from marrying a woman belonging to his mother's sept. The prohibition arising from the sept name is therefore supplemented by forbidding men to marry the following relatives and their descendants:—Step-mother, mother's sister, sister, sister's daughter, mother's brother's daughter, father's sister's daughter, wife's elder sister. After his wife's death a man may marry her younger sister.

Among the Chakmás, as perhaps among the Greeks and Romans in the beginning of their history, the sept is the unit of the tribal organization for certain public purposes. Each sept is presided over by an hereditary dewán (among the Tungjainiyás called ahún), who represents the family of the founder. This officer collects the poll-tax, keeps a certain proportion himself, and pays the remainder with a yearly offering of first fruits to the Chief of the tribe. When a wild animal fit for food is killed, he has a right to a share in the carcass. He also decides the disputes, mostly matrimonial or more or less connected with women, which make up most of the litigation within the tribe, and divides the fines with the Chief. Where the sept is large and scattered, the dewán has subordinate headmen (*khejá*) to assist him. These are exempt from poll-tax and *begári* or compulsory labour, but must make to the dewán a yearly offering of one measure of rice, one bamboo vessel (*chungá*) of spirits, and a fowl.

I quote at length Major Lewin's[1] graphic and sympathetic description of the marriage customs of the Chakmás:—

Marriage.

"Child-marriages among the Chakmás, or indeed among the hill people in general, are unknown. There is no fixed time for getting married. Some of the young men indeed do not marry until they reach the age of 24 or 25: after that age, however, it is rare to see a man unmarried.

[1] *Hill Tracts of Chittagong*, pp. 70 *et seq.*

Marriage is after this fashion: Father, mother, and son first look about them and fix upon a bride. This indispensable preliminary accomplished, the parents go to the house where their intended daughter-in-law resides. They take with them a bottle of spirits (this is an absolute necessary in every hill palaver). The matter will at first be opened cautiously. The lad's father will say, 'That is a fine tree growing near your house; I would fain plant in its shadow.' Should all go well, they retire after mutual civilities. Both in going and coming omens are carefully observed, and many a promising match has been put a stop to by unfavourable auguries. A man or woman carrying fowls, water, fruit, or milk, if passed on the right hand, is a good omen and pleasant to meet with; but it is unfavourable to see a kite or a vulture, or to see one crow all by himself croaking on the left hand. If they are unfortunate enough to come upon the dead body of any animal on their road, they will go no further, but at once return home and stop all proceedings. Old people quote numerous stories to show that the disregard of unfavourable omens has in former times been productive of the most ruinous consequences.

"By the time a second visit is due the relatives on both sides have been consulted; and if all has progressed satisfactorily and there are no dissentient voices, they go accompanied by some of the girls of the village, taking with them presents of curds and *birní* grain, and *jográ*, a sweet fermented liquor made from rice. Then a day is settled (after the harvest is a favourite time), and a ring of betrothal is given to the bride. Now, also, is arranged what price the young man is to pay for his wife; for the Chakmás, in contradistinction to all our other tribes, buy their wives. The ordinary price is Rs. 100 to Rs. 150. On the marriage day a large stock of provisions is laid in by both houses. A procession of men and women start from the bridegroom's village with drums and music to fetch home the bride. The parents of the bridegroom present their intended daughter with her marriage dress. No ceremony, however, is performed; and the bride, after a short interval, is taken away, accompanied by all her relatives, to her new home.

"On arriving all enter the house, and the bride and the bridegroom sit down together at a small table—the bride on the left hand of her husband. On the table are eggs, sweetmeats, rice, and plantains, all laid out on leaf platters. The best man (*sowalla*) sits behind the bridegroom, and the bride has a representative bridesmaid (*sowalli*) behind her. These two then bind around the couple a muslin scarf, asking 'Are all willing, and shall this be accomplished.' Then all cry out, 'Bind them, Bind them,' so they are bound. The married pair have now to eat together, the wife feeding the husband and the husband the wife; and as at this stage of the ceremony a great deal of bashfulness is evinced, the bridesmaid and best man raise the hands of their respective charges to and from each other's mouths, to the intense enjoyment and hilarity of every one present. After they have thus eaten and drunken, an elder of the village sprinkles them with river-water, pronounces them man and wife, and says a charm used for fruitfulness. The couple then retire, and the guests keep it up until an early hour on the following morning. The next day, at the morning meal, the newly married come hand in hand and salute the elders of the families. The father of the bride generally improves this occasion by addressing a short lecture to his son-in-law on the subject of marital duties. 'Take her,' he says; 'I have given her to you; but she is young and not acquainted with her household duties. If therefore at any time you come back from the *jhum* and find the rice burnt, or anything else wrong, teach her: do not beat her. But at the end of three years, if she still continues ignorant, then beat her, but do not take her life; for if you do, I shall demand the price of blood at your hands, but for beating her I shall not hold you responsible or interfere.'

"All marriages, however, do not go on in this happy fashion: it often happens that the lad and the lass have made up their minds to couple, but the parents will not hear of the match. In such a case the lovers generally elope together; but should the girl's parents be very much set against the match, they have the right to demand back and take their daughter from the hands of her lover. If, notwithstanding this opposition, the lovers' intentions still remain unaltered and they elope a second time, no one has then the right to interfere with them. The young husband makes a present to his father-in-law according to his means, gives a feast to his new relatives, and is formally admitted into kinship."

Sexual indiscretions before marriage are not severely dealt with, and usually end in marriage. But a man who carries off a young girl against her will is fined Rs. 60, and "also receives a good beating from the lads of the village to which a girl belongs." Incest is punished by a fine of Rs. 50 and corporal punishment. Once married, the Chakmá women are said to be good and faithful wives, and it is unusual for the village council to be called upon to exercise its power of granting a divorce. Such cases, however, do occur occasionally. The offender has to repay to the husband the bride-price and the expenses incurred in the marriage, and in addition a fine of Rs. 50 or Rs. 60, which is divided between the dewán or ahún of the sept and the Chief of the tribe. Divorced women can marry again.

A widow is allowed to marry a second time. She may marry her husband's younger brother, but is not obliged to do so. The ceremony is simple, consisting mainly of a feast.

Religion.

The Chakmás profess to be Buddhists, but during the last generation or so their practice in matters of religion has been noticeably coloured by contact with the gross Hinduism of Eastern Bengal. This tendency was encouraged by the example of Rájá Dharm Baksh Khán and his wife Kálindi Rání, who observed the Hindu festivals, consulted Hindu astrologers, kept a Chittagong Brahman to supervise the daily worship of the goddess Káli, and persuaded themselves that they were lineal representatives of the Kshatriya caste. Some years ago, however, a celebrated Phoongyee came over from Arakan after the Rájá's death to endeavour to strengthen the cause of Buddhism and to take the

Ráni to task for her leanings towards idolatry. His efforts are said to have met with some success, and the Ráni is believed to have formally proclaimed her adhesion to Buddhism.

Lakhsmi is worshipped by the Tungjainyá sub-tribe as the goddess of harvest in a small bamboo hut set apart for this purpose. She is represented by a rude block of stone with seven skeins of cotton bound seven times round it. The offerings are pigs and fowls, which are afterwards eaten by the votaries. Chakmás observe the same worship with a few differences of detail, which need not be noticed here.

Vestiges of the primitive animism, which we may believe to have been the religion of the Chakmás before their conversion to Buddhism, still survive in the festival called Shongbásá, when *nats*, or the spirits of wood and stream, are worshipped, either by the votary himself or by an exorcist (*ojhá* or *naichhurá*), who is called in to perform the necessary ceremonies. The demons of cholera, fever, and other diseases are propitiated in a river-bed or in the thick jungle, where spirits delight to dwell, with offerings of goats, fowls, ducks, pigeons, and flowers. The regular priests have nothing to do with this ritual, which has been condemned as unorthodox.

"At a Chakmá village," says Major Lewin, "I was present when sacrifice was thus offered up by the headman. The occasion was a thank-offering for the recovery of his wife from child-birth. The offering consisted of a suckling pig and a fowl. The altar was of bamboo, decorated with young plantain shoots and leaves. On this raised platform were placed small cups containing rice, vegetables, and a spirit distilled from rice. Round the whole from the house-mother's distaff had been spun a long white thread, which encircled the altar, and then, carried into the house, was held at its two ends by the good man's wife. The sacrifice commenced by a long invocation uttered by the husband, who stood opposite to his altar, and between each snatch of his charm he tapped the small platform with his hill knife and uttered a long wailing cry. This was for the purpose of attracting the numerous wandering spirits who go up and down upon the earth and calling them to the feast. When a sufficient number of these invisible guests were believed to be assembled, he cut the throats of the victims with his *dao* and poured a libation of blood upon the altar and over the thread. The flesh of the things sacrificed was afterwards cooked and eaten at the household meal, of which I was invited to partake."

Of late years Bairági Vaishnavas have taken to visiting the Hill Tracts, and have made a few disciples among the Chakmás. The outward signs of conversion to Vaishnavism are wearing a necklace of *tulsi* beads (*Ocymum sanctum*), which is used to repeat the *mantra* or mystic formula of the sect. Abstinence from animal food and strong drink is also enjoined. I understand, however, that very few Chakmás have been found to submit to this degree of austerity.

Funeral.

Chakmás burn their dead. The body of a man is burned with the head to the west on a pyre composed of five layers of wood; that of a woman on a pyre of seven layers, the head being turned to the east. The ashes are thrown into the river. A bamboo post, or some other portion of a dead man's house, is usually burned with him—probably in order to provide him with shelter in the next world. At the burning place the relatives set up a pole with a streamer of coarse cloth. Infants and persons who die of small-pox or cholera or by a violent death are buried. If a man is supposed to have died from witchcraft, his body when half-burned is split in two down the chest—a practice curiously analogous to the ancient treatment of suicides in Europe. Seven days after death priests are sent for to read prayers for the dead, and the relatives give alms. It is optional to repeat this ceremony at the end of a month. At the end of the year, or at the festival of *navánna* (eating of new rice), rice cooked with various kinds of curry, meat, honey, wine, are offered to departed ancestors in a separate room and afterwards thrown into a river. Should a flea, or, better still, a number of fleas, be attracted by the repast, this is looked upon as a sign that the dead are pleased with the offerings laid before them.

Occupation.

Like the rest of the Hill Tribes, the Chakmás live by *jhum* cultivation, which they carry on in the method described below in the article **Magh.** In spite of the necessarily shifting character of their husbandry, they show remarkable attachment to the sites of their villages, and do not change these like most of the other tribes. Their bamboo houses, built upon high piles, are constructed with great care. An excellent sketch of one of these is given by Dr. Riebeck in the book already referred to.

The Census statistics of the Chakma tribe show an extraordinary fluctuation in their numbers, which I am wholly unable to account for. In 1872 there were 28,097 Chakmas in the Chittagong Hill Tracts, while the Census of 1881 shows only eleven! No attempt is made to clear up this singular *Völkerwanderung* in the text of the Census Report of 1881.

Chakravartti, a title borne by some families of Brahmans in Bengal.

Chakri, a synonym for Teli in Bengal.

Chaksiár, a section of Bábhans in Behar.

Chakwán, a sept of Rajputs in Behar.

Chakwár, a *mul* or section of the Ayodhiá sub-caste of Sonárs and Bábhans in Behar.

Chal-agge, a section of the Bahánnajáti sub-caste of Khatris in Bengal.

Chálak, a title of Kaibarttas in Bengal.

Chalaniá, a *mul* or section of Kesarwani Baniás in Behar.

Chalanta, a synonym for Doai.

Chalenga, a kind of vegetable, a totemistic sept of Korwas in Chota Nagpur.

Chalhaká, a section of Sonárs in Behar.

Chálhásan, a *mul* or section of the Naomuliá or Goriá sub-caste of Goálás in Behar.

Chálhásinhi, a *mul* or section of the Goriá and Kishnaut sub-castes of Goálás in Behar, whose title is Mandar.

Chálhuk, a sept of Rajputs in Behar.

Chali, rice soup, a totemistic sept of Mundas in Chota Nagpur.

Chálisa, Chelisya, a *thar* of the Basishtha *gotra* of Nepáli Brahmans.

Chalita-Sau, a synonym for Sunri in Bengal.

Challisghariá, a sub-caste of Sutradhars in Noakháli.

Chaluti, a sub-caste of Sunris in Western Bengal.

Chamagrámi, a *gáin* of the Kásyaps *gotra* of Bárendra Brahmans in Bengal.

Chamagu, a *thar* or sept of Newars in Darjiling.

Chamár, the tanner caste of Behar and Upper India, found also in all parts of Bengal as tanners and workers in leather under the name **Chámár** or **Charmakár**. According to the Puránas, the Chamárs are descended from a boatman and a Chandál woman; but if we are to identify them with the Kárávara or leather-worker mentioned in the tenth chapter of Manu, the father of the caste was a Nisháda and the mother a Vaideha. The Nisháda, again, is said to be the offspring of a Bráhman and a Súdra mother, and the Vaideha of a Vaisya father and Bráhman mother. In one place, indeed, Mr. Sherring seems to take this mythical genealogy seriously, and argues that the "rigidity and exclusiveness of caste prejudices among the Chamárs are highly favourable to the supposition" that Manu's account of them is the true one, and consequently that the Chamárs being "one-half of Brahmanical, one-fourth of Vaisya, and one-fourth of Súdra descent," may "hold up their heads boldly in the presence of the superior castes." Stated in this form, the argument verges on the grotesque; but it appears from other passages that Mr. Sherring was strongly impressed with the high-caste appearance of the Chamár caste, and thought it possible that in this particular instance the traditional pedigree might contain an element of historical truth. Similar testimony to the good looks of the Chamárs in certain parts of India comes to us from the Central Provinces, where they are said to be lighter in colour than the members of other cultivating castes, while some of the men and many of the women are remarkably handsome. In Eastern Bengal, again, Dr. Wise describes the caste as less swarthy than the average Chandál, and infinitely fairer, with a more delicate and intellectual cast of features than many Srotriya Bráhmans. On the other hand, Sir Henry Elliot, writing of the North-West Provinces, says:—"Chamárs are reputed to be a dark race, and a fair Chamár is said to be as rare an object as a black Bráhman.

Traditions of origin.

Kariá Brahman gor Chamár
Inke sáth na utariye pár,

—that is, do not cross a river in the same boat with a black Bráhman or a fair Chamár; both objects being considered of evil omen." Mr. Nesfield thinks the Chamár "may have sprung out of several different tribes, like the Dom, Kanjar, Habura Cheru, etc., the last remains of whom are still outside the pale of Hindu society.

Originally he appears to have been an impressed labourer or *begár*, who was made to hold the plough for his master and received in return space for building his mud hovel near the village, a fixed allowance of grain for every working day, the free use of wood and grass on the village lands, and the skins and bodies of all the animals that died. This is very much the status of the Chamár at the present day. He is still the field slave, the grass-cutter, the remover of dead animals, the hide-skinner, and the carrion-eater of the Indian village." Lastly, it should be observed that Mr. Hewitt, whose report on the settlement of the Ráipur district is the *locus classicus* for the Chamárs of the Central Provinces, clearly regards them as to some extent an exceptional type, and lays stress on the fact that they do not present the same degraded appearance as their brethren in other parts of India.

Chamárs trace their own pedigree to Raví or Ruí Dás, the famous disciple of Rámánanda at the end of the fourteenth century, and whenever a Chamár is asked what he is, he replies a Raví Dás. Another tradition current among them alleges that their original ancestor was the youngest of four Bráhman brethren who went to bathe in a river and found a cow struggling in a quicksand. They sent the youngest brother in to rescue the animal, but before he could get to the spot it had been drowned. He was compelled therefore by his brothers to remove the carcass, and after he had done this they turned him out of their caste and gave him the name of Chamár.

Looking at the evidence as a whole, and allowing that there are points in it which seem to favour the conjecture that the Chamárs may be in part a degraded section of a higher race, I do not consider these indications clear enough to override the presumption that a caste engaged in a filthy and menial occupation must on the whole have been recruited from among the non-Aryan races. It may be urged, indeed, that the early Aryans were well acquainted with the use of leather, and were free from those prejudices which lead the modern Hindu to condemn the art of the tanner as unclean. The degradation of the *Chármamná* of Vedic times into the outcaste Chamár of to-day may thus have been a slow process, carried out gradually as Brahmanical ideas gained strength, and the 'fair Chamár' whom the proverb warns men to beware of may be simply an instance of reversion to an earlier Aryan type, which at one time formed an appreciable proportion of the caste. All this, however, is pure conjecture, and counts for little in face of the fact that the average Chamár is hardly distinguishable in point of features, stature, and complexion from the members of those non-Aryan races from whose ranks we should *primâ facie* expect the profession of leather-dresser to be filled. Occasional deviations from this standard type may be due either to *liaisons* with members of the higher castes or to some cause which cannot now be traced.

Internal structure.

Like all large castes, the Chamárs are broken up into a number of endogamous groups. These are shown in Appendix I, but I am doubtful whether the enumeration is complete. The Dhusiá sub-caste alone appears to have exogamous divisions of the territorial or local type, while in the other sub-castes marriages are regulated by the usual formula for reckoning prohibited degrees calculated to seven generations in the descending line. Chamárs profess to marry their daughters as infants; but in practice the age at which a girl is married depends mainly upon the ability of her parents to defray the expenses of the wedding, and no social penalty is inflicted upon a man who allows his daughter to grow up unmarried. Polygamy is permitted, and no limit appears to be set to the number of wives a man may have.

Marriage.

Like the Doms, and unlike most other castes, Chamárs forbid the marriage of two sisters to the same husband. In the marriage ceremony an elder of the caste presides, but a Brahman is usually consulted to fix an auspicious day for the event. The father of the bride receives a sum of money for his daughter, but this is usually insufficient to meet the expenses of the wedding. During the marriage service the bridegroom sits on the knee of the bride's father, and the bridegroom's father receives a few ornaments and a cup of spirits, after which each of the guests is offered a cup. No *marwa* or wedding bower is made, but a barber prepares and whitewashes a space (*chauk*), within which the couple sit. He also stains the feet of the bride and bridegroom with cotton soaked in lac dye (*álta*), and is responsible that all the relatives and friends are invited to the marriage. The caste elder, who officiates as priest, binds mango leaves on the wrists of the wedded pair, and chants *mantras* or mystic verses; while the bridegroom performs *sindurdán* by smearing vermilion on the bride's forehead and the parting of her hair. This is deemed the valid and binding portion of the ceremony. Widows are permitted to marry again. Usually when an elder brother dies childless the younger brother must marry the widow within a year or eighteen months, unless they mutually agree not to do so, in which case she returns to her father's house, where she is free to remarry with any one. If there are children by the first marriage, it is deemed the more incumbent on the widow to marry the younger brother; but even in this case she is not compelled to do so. The custody of the children, however, remains with their paternal uncle, and the widow forfeits all claim to share in her late husband's estate. On her remarriage the family of her first husband cannot claim any compensation for the bride-price which they paid for her on her marriage. Before a widow marries again her relatives go through the form of consulting the pancháyat, with the object, it is said, of deciding whether the marriage is well-timed or not. Divorce is permitted with the sanction of the pancháyat of the caste. Divorced wives may marry again.

Religion in Bengal.

By far the most interesting features of the Chamár caste, says Dr. Wise, are their religious and social customs. They have no purohit; their religious ceremonies, like those of the Doms, being directed by one of the elders of the caste. But gurus, who give *mantras* to children, are found, and a Hindustani Brahman is often consulted regarding a lucky day for a wedding. Chamárs have always exhibited a remarkable dislike to Brahmans and to the Hindu ritual. They nevertheless observe many rites popularly supposed to be of Hindu origin, but which are more probably survivals of the worship paid to the village gods for ages before the Aryan invasion. The large majority of Bengali Chamárs profess the deistic Sri-Nárâyani creed. Sants, or professed devotees, are common among them, and the Mahant of that sect is always regarded as the religious head of the whole tribe. A few Dacca Chamárs belong to the Kabir-Panth, but none have joined any of the Vaishnava sects.

Festivals.

The principal annual festival of the Chamárs is the Srípanchamí, celebrated on the fifth day of the lunar month of Mágh (January–February), when they abstain from work for two days, spending them in alternate devotion at the Dhámghar, or conventicle of the Sri-Nárâyani sect, and in intoxication at home. The Dhámghar is usually a thatched house consisting of one large room with verandahs on all sides. At one end is a raised earthen platform, on which the open Grantha[1] garlanded with flowers is laid, and before this each disciple makes obeisance as he enters. The congregation squats all round the room, the women in one corner, listening to a few musicians chanting religious hymns and smoking tobacco and gánja, indifferent to the heat, smoke, and stench of the crowded room. The Mahant, escorted by the Sants carrying their parwánas or certificates of membership, enters about 1 A.M., when the service begins. It is of the simplest form. The Mahant, after reading a few sentences in Nágarí, unintelligible to most of his hearers, receives offerings of money and fruit. The congregation then disperses, but the majority seat themselves in the verandahs and drink spirits. If the physical endurance of the worshippers be not exhausted, similar services are held for several successive nights, but the ordinary one only lasts two nights.

On the "Nauamí," or ninth lunar day of Áswin (September–October), the day preceding the Dashará, the worship of Deví is observed, and offerings of swine, goats, and spirits made to the dread goddess. On this day the old Dravidian system of demonolatry, or Shamanism, is exhibited, when one of their number, working himself up into a frenzy, becomes possessed by the demon and reveals futurity. The Chamárs place great value on the answers given, and very few are so contented with their lot in life as not to desire an insight into the future. A few days before the Dashará the Chámaíns perambulate the streets, playing and singing, with

[1] The Grantha or scriptures of the Sri-Nárâyani or Siva-Nárâyani sect are believed by them to have existed for eleven hundred and forty-five years, but to have been unintelligible until Sítala, an inspired Sannyási, translated it in compliance with a divine command. The translation, consisting of several works in the Devanágarí character, is the undoubted composition of the Rajput Sivanárâyana of Ghazípúr, who wrote it about A.D. 1735.

The most important of these works are the Guru-nyása and Sánta-vilása. The former, compiled from the Puránas, gives an account of the ten Avatárs of Vishnu, or Nárâyana, and is subdivided into fourteen chapters, of which the first six treat of the author, of faith, of the punishment of sinners, of virtue, of a future state, and of discipline. The latter is a treatise on moral sentiments. The opening lines are,—"The love of God, and His knowledge is the only true understanding."

a pot of water in the left hand, a sprig of *nim* in the right, soliciting alms for the approaching Deví festival. Money or grain must be got by begging, for they believe the worship would be ineffectual if the offerings had to be paid for. Another of their festivals is the Rámanauamí, or birth-day of Ráma, held on the ninth lunar day of Chaitra (March–April), when they offer flowers, betel-nut, and sweetmeats to their ancestor, Ravi Dás.

When sickness or epidemic diseases invade their homes, the women fasten a piece of plantain leaf round their necks and go about begging. Should their wishes be fulfilled, a vow is taken to celebrate the worship of Deví, Sítalá, or Jalka Deví, whichever goddess is supposed to cause the outbreak. The worship is held on a piece of ground marked off and smeared with cowdung. A fire being lighted, and *ghí* and spirits thrown on it, the worshipper makes obeisance, bowing his forehead to the ground and muttering certain incantations. A swine is then sacrificed, and the bones and offal being buried, the flesh is roasted and eaten, but no one must take home with him any scrap of the victim. Jalka Deví seems identical with the Rakshyá Kálí of Bengali villagers, and is said to have seven sisters, who are worshipped on special occasions.

Religion in Behar.

The Chamárs of Behar are more orthodox in matters of religion than their brethren of Eastern Bengal, and appear to conform in the main to the popular Hinduism practised by their neighbours. Some of them indeed have advanced so far in this direction as to employ Maithil Brahmans for the worship of the regular Hindu gods, while others content themselves with priests of their own caste. In the Sautál Parganas such priests go by the name of *puri*, and the story is that they are Kanaujia Brahmans, who were somehow degraded to be Chamárs. Lokesari, Rakat Málá, Mansarám, Lálá, Káru Dáná, Masná, Mamiá, and Jalpait are the special minor gods of the caste, but Bandi, Goraiyá, and Káli are also held in reverence. Some hold that Ravi Dás ranks highest of all, but he seems to be looked upon as a sort of deity, and not as the preacher of a deistic religion. The offerings to all of these gods consist of sheep, goats, milk, fruit, and sweetmeats, of which the members of the household afterwards partake. According to Mr. Nesfield, the caste also worship the *rápi*, or tanner's knife, at the Diwáli festival. It is a curious circumstance, illustrating the queer reputation borne by the Chamárs, that throughout Hindustan parents frighten naughty children by telling them that Nona Chamáin will carry them off. This redoubtable old witch is said by the Chamárs to have been the mother or grandmother of Raví Dás; but why she acquired such unenviable notoriety is unknown. In Bengal her name is never heard of, but a domestic bogey haunts each household. In one it is the Burhí, or old woman; in another, Bhúta, a ghost; in a third, Pretní, a witch; and in a fourth, Galá-Kátá Káfir, literally, the 'infidel with his throat gashed.'

Funerals.

In Behar the dead are burned in the ordinary fashion, and *sráddh* performed on the tenth or, according to some, the thirteenth day after death. Libations of water (*tarpan*) and balls of rice (*pinda*) are offered to the spirit of ancestors in general in the month of Áswin. In Eastern Bengal Chamárs usually bury their dead, and if the husband is buried his widow will be laid beside him if she had been taught the same *mantra*, otherwise her body is burned. Sants of the Sri-Náráyani sect are objects of special reverence, and whenever one dies in a strange place the Sants on the spot subscribe and bury him. The funeral procession is impressive, but very noisy. The corpse, wrapped in a sheet with a roll of cloth wound round the head, is deposited on a covered litter. Red flags flutter from the four corners, and a white cloth acts as a pall. With discordant music the body is carried to the grave, dug in some waste place, where it is laid flat, not sitting, as with the Jugis.

Social status.

By virtue of his occupation, his habits, and his traditional descent, the Chamár stands condemned to rank at the very bottom of the Hindu social system; and even the non-Aryan tribes who have of recent years sought admission into the Hindu communion are speedily promoted over his head. His ideas on the subject of diet are in keeping with his degraded position. He eats beef, pork, and fowls, all unclean to the average Hindu, and, like the gypsies of Europe, has no repugnance to cooking the flesh of animals which have died a natural death. Some say that they only eat cattle which have died a natural death, but this may be merely a device to avert the suspicion of killing cattle by poison, which naturally attaches to people who deal in hides and horns. Despised, however, as he is by all classes of orthodox Hindus, the Chamár is proud and punctilious on certain special points, never touching the leavings of a Brahman's meal, nor eating anything cooked by a Bengali Brahman, though he has no objection to take food from a Brahman of Hindustan. Chamars are, says Dr. Wise, inconceivably dirty in their habits, and offend others besides the Hindu by their neglect of all sanitary laws. Large droves of pigs are bred by them, and it is no uncommon sight to witness children and pigs wallowing together in the mire. Hides in various stages of preparation hang about their huts, yet, strange to say, the women are very prolific, and, except in a fisher settlement, nowhere are so many healthy-looking children to be seen as in a filthy Chamár village. Mr. Beames, however, mentions in a note to his edition of Sir Henry Elliot's *Glossary* that Chamárs, from their dirty habits, are peculiarly liable to leprosy, and that the name of the Kori or Korhi sub-caste probably refers to this fact.

Occupation.

Chamárs are employed in tanning leather, making shoes and saddlery, and grooming horses. In Eastern Bengal the Chamrá-farosh hire them to preserve hides, but there is such bitter enmity between them and the allied caste of Muchi or Rishí, that they are rarely engaged to skin animals, lest the perquisites of the latter group should seem to have been interfered with. To some extent the distinctions between the various sub-castes seem to be based upon differences of occupation. Thus the Dhusia sub-caste adhere to the original occupation of leather-dressing, and also make shoes and serve as musicians at wedding and other domestic festivities, their favourite instruments being the *dhol* or drum, the cymbals (*jhánjh*), the harp (*ektára*), and the tambourine (*khanjari*). Most of these occupations are also followed by the Dhárh, who besides carry palanquins and eat the flesh of animals that have died a natural death, except only the horse. The Guria are cultivators; some few holding occupancy rights, and others being landless day-labourers, who wander about and work for hire at harvest time. The Jaiswára work as syces; the Dohar are cobblers, using only leather string, and not cotton thread, to mend rents; the Sikhariá are cultivators and shoemakers; the Chamár Tanti work as weavers, and will not touch carrion; and the Sárki, many of whom have emigrated from Nepal into Chumparan, are both butchers and hide-dressers. Some Chamárs burn lime, but this occupation has not become the badge of a sub-caste, though those who follow it call themselves Chunihárá. In Behar the Chamár is a village functionary like the Chaukidar or Gorait. He holds a small portion of village land, and is invariably called to post up official notices, and to go round with his drum proclaiming public announcements.

The Chamáins, or female Chámars, says Dr. Wise, are distinguished throughout Bengal by their huge inelegant anklets (*páirí*) and bracelets (*bangrí*), made of bell-metal. The former often weigh from eight to ten pounds, the latter from two to four, and both closely resemble the corresponding ornaments worn by Santál women. They also wear the *tikli*, or spangle, on the forehead, although in Bengal it is regarded as a tawdry ornament of the lowest and most immoral women. Chamáins consider it a great attraction to have their bodies tattooed; consequently their chests, foreheads, arms, and legs are disfigured with patterns of fantastic shape. In Hindustan the Natní is the great tattooer; but as members of this caste are seldom met with in Eastern Bengal, the Chamáins are often put to great straits, being frequently obliged to pay a visit to their original homes for the purpose of having the fashionable decoration indelibly stained on their bodies.

Chamár women are ceremonially unclean for ten days subsequent to childbirth, when after bathing, casting away all old cooking utensils, and buying new ones, a feast, called *Bárahiya*, is celebrated, upon which she resumes her usual household duties. They still observe the pleasing custom of *Bháìphotá* on the last day of the Hindu year, when sisters present their brothers with a new suit of clothes and sweetmeats, and make with a paste of red sandal wood a dot on their foreheads; a similar usage, known as *Bhrátrí-dvitíyá*, is practised by Bengalis on the second day after the new moon of Kártik.

Chamáins are the midwives of India, and are generally believed, though erroneously, to be skilled in all the mysteries of parturition. They have no scruples about cutting the navel string, as other Hindus have; but in the villages of the interior, where no Chamáins reside, the females of the Bhúinmálí, Chandál, and Ghulám Káyath castes act as midwives, and are equally unscrupulous. It is a proverbial saying among Hindus that a household becomes unclean if a Chamár woman has not attended at the birth of any child belonging to it.

The following statement shows the number and distribution of Chamárs in 1872 and 1881. The figures of the former year include, and those of the latter exclude, the Muchis in Bengal Proper.

DISTRICT.	1872.	1881.	DISTRICT.	1872.	1881.
Bardwan	53,477	631	Tipperah	4,256	1,740
Bankura	3,117	398	Noakhali	397	344
Birbhum	30,153	7,711	Hill Tracts	31	4
Midnapur	8,544	1,533	Patna	47,067	56,867
Hughli	} 24,457	......	Gya	70,937	78,552
Howrah		2,438	Shahabad	91,777	119,010
24-Parganas	70,463	11,800	Tirhut { Mozufferpur	} 171,793	122,837
Nadiya	57,375	11,314	Tirhut { Darbhanga		88,641
Khulna	......	3,807	Saran	94,844	111,144
Jessore	42,992	11,855	Champaran	89,061	112,789
Murshedabad	33,366	20,374	Monghyr	46,126	54,014
Dinajpur	4,179	1,175	Bhagalpur	63,085	76,294
Rajshahye	6,888	3,391	Purniah	13,571	22,035
Rangpur	9,103	842	Maldah	4,929	4,288
Bogra	1,873	1,908	Santál Parganas	23,460	27,740
Pabna	5,477	893	Cuttack	12,267	13,465
Darjiling	85	380	Puri	2,355	2,690
Jalpigori	436	81	Balasore	4,383	19,353
Kuch Behar	......	1,284	Tributary States	1,432	2,574
Dacca	24,063	8,560	Hazaribagh	26,112	40,981
Faridpur	3,721	1,519	Lohardaga	18,966	27,276
Bakarganj	3,991	1,033	Singbhum	591	429
Maimansinh	5,934	4,391	Manbhum	7,344	2,537
Chittagong	781	527	Tributary States	2,933	6,393

Chámar, a sub-caste of Tántis in Behar.

Chámár, a synonym for Chamár.

Chamár-gaur, a division of the Gaur Rajputs,—the highest class, although from their name liable to the suspicion of intercourse with Chamárs. They affect to call themselves Chaunhar-gaur, from a Rájá named Chaunhar; or sometimes Chiman-gaur, from a Muni called Chiman.

Chamár Gaura, a sub-caste of Gaura Brahmans.

Chamártali, a section of Tántis in Behar.

Chamár-Tánti, a sub-caste of Chamárs.

Chámkasaini, a *thar* or section of Nepáli Brahmans.

Chamlingeh, a *thar* or sept of Khambus in Darjiling.

Champa, a *gáin* of the Sándilya *gotra* of Bárendra Brahmans in Bengal.

Champágáin, a *thar* of the Atri *gotra* of Nepáli Brahmans.

Champati, a *gáin* of the Sándilya *gotra* of Bárendra Brahmans in Bengal.

Champia, a bird, a totemistic sept of Mundas in Chota Nagpur.

Champiá Tubir, a sept of Hos in Singbhum.

Chamrá-farosh, a leather-dealer, usually a Kuti Mahomedan.

Chamrauliá, a section of the Banodhiá and Jaiswár Kalwárs in Behar.

Chámuár, a *mul* or section of the Naomuliá or Majraut sub-caste of Goálás in Behar.

Chámuk Sápurdih, a *mul* or section of the Naomuliá or Majraut sub-caste of Goálás in Behar.

Chan, a title of Telis in Bengal.

Chána, a section of Kumhárs in Singbhum.

Chanamiá, a sub-tribe of Chandrabansi Rajputs in Jaunpur, Azimgarh, Gorakpur, and North-Western Behar.

Chanauli, a section of the Tirhutiyá sub-caste of Doms in Behar.

Chanaur, a sub-caste of Kurmis in Behar.

Chánchar Chhaurári, a *mul* or section of the Naomuliá or Majraut sub-caste of Goálás in Behar.

Chanchmatriár, a totemistic section of the Kurmi caste in Chota Nagpur, the members of which will not touch or kill a kind of spider.

Chand, a title of Gandhabaniks and Tántis in Bengal.

Chánd, moon, a totemistic sept of Chiks in Chota Nagpur; a title of Báruis in Bengal and of the Oswal Baniyás in Behar.

Chándái, a *mel* or hypergamous sub-group of Rárhi Brahmans in Bengal.

Chandail, a sept of the Surajbansi division of Rajputs in Behar.

Chandál, a synonym for Dom.

Chandál,[1] *Chánrál, Chang,*[2] *Nama-Sudra,*[3] *Nama, Nishád,* a non-Aryan caste of Eastern Bengal, engaged for the most part in boating and cultivation.

Traditions of origin.

The derivation of the name Chandál is uncertain, and it is a plausible conjecture that it may have been, like Sudra, the tribal name of one of the aboriginal races whom the Aryans found in possession of the soil. Unlike the Sudras, however, the Chandáls were debarred from entering even the outer circles of the Aryan system, and from the earliest times they are depicted by Sanskrit writers as an outcast and helot people, performing menial duties for the Brahmans, and living on the outskirts of cities (antebási) apart from the dwellings of the dominant race. Iron ornaments,

[1] The following synonyms are given by Amara Sinha:—Plava (the wanderer), Mátanga (elephant), Janmaghana (life-taker), Svapácha (dog-eater), Antevási (the dweller on the confines of the village), Divakirtti, and Pukkasa. None of these are in common use at the present day.

[2] Chang or Changa, says Dr. Wise, signifies handsome in Sanskrit, "and was most likely used in irony by the early Hindus."

[3] The derivation of this name is uncertain. Dr. Wise thinks it may be from "the Sanskrit *Namas*, adoration, which is always used as a vocative when praying, or the Bengali *Námate*, below, underneath." The latter suggestion seems the more plausible. The Pundits' interpretation of the former is understood to be that the Chandál is bound to do obeisance even to a Sudra. It would be promotion for the Chandáls of Manu to get themselves recognised as a lower grade of Sudras. The name may also be referred to Namasa or Lomasa Muni, whom some Chandáls regard as their mythical ancestor. On the other hand, Namasa Muni himself may have been evolved from the attempt to explain away the suggestion of inferiority implied in the name Nama-Sudra.

dogs, and monkeys, are their chief wealth, and they clothe themselves in the raiment of the dead. Manu brands them as "the lowest of mankind," sprung from the illicit intercourse of a Sudra man with a Brahman woman, whose touch defiles the pure and who have no ancestral rites. In the Mahabharata they are introduced as hired assassins, whose humanity, however, revolts against putting an innocent boy to death. In the Rámáyana they are described as ill-formed and terrible in aspect, dressing in blue or yellow garments with a red cloth over the shoulders, a bear's skin around the loins, and iron ornaments on the wrists. Even the liberal-minded Abúl Fazl speaks of the Chandáls of the sixteenth century as "vile wretches who eat carrion." At the present day the term Chandál is throughout India used only in abuse, and is not acknowledged by any race or caste as its peculiar designation. The Chandáls of Bengal invariably call themselves Nama-Sudra, and with characteristic jealousy the higher divisions of the caste apply the name Chandál to the lower, who in their turn pass it on to the Dom.

The legends of the Chandáls give no clue to their early history, and appear to have been invented in recent times with the object of glorifying the caste and establishing its claim to a recognised position in the Hindu system. Thus, according to a tradition of the Dacca Chandáls, they were formerly Bráhmans, who became degraded by eating with Súdras, while others assert that in days of yore they were the domestic servants of Bráhmans, for which reason they have perpetuated many of the religious observances of their masters. For instance, the Chandál celebrates the *sráddha* on the eleventh day as Bráhmans do, and the Gayáwál priests conduct the obsequial ceremonies of the Bengali Chandáls without any compunction. Another story gives them for ancestor Bamdeb, son of the Brahman Vasishtha, who was degraded by his father and turned into a Chandál as punishment for a ceremonial mistake committed by him when granting absolution to Dasarath, King of Oudh, for killing a Brahman by misadventure while hunting. The Dacca Chandáls retain an obscure tradition of having originally migrated from Gayá, and make mention of a certain Govardhan Chandál as an ancestor of theirs.

Mr. Wells[1] quotes a tradition of Hindu invention, current among the Chandáls of Faridpur, to the effect "that they were originally a complete Hindu community, consisting of persons of all castes, from the Bráhman downwards, who, on having the misfortune to be cursed in a body by a vengeful Bráhman of unutterable sanctity in Dacca, quitted their ancestral homes and emigrated bodily to the southern wastes of Faridpúr, Jessore, and Báqirganj."

Dr. Buchanan considered the Chandál of Bengal to be identical with the Dosádh of Behár. Although both are equally low in the scale of caste, and characterised by an unusual amount of independence and self-reliance, very great differences actually exist. The Dosádh worships deified heroes belonging to his tribe; the Chandál

---

[1] *Appendix to Census Report of* 1872, p. vi.

never does. The Dosádh invokes Ráhu and Ketu, the former being his tutelary deity, while we find no such divinity reverenced by the Chandál. Finally, the *sruddha* of the Dosádh is celebrated on the thirtieth day, as with the Súdras; that of the Chandál on the eleventh, as with Bráhmans.

Mr. Beverley, again, is of opinion that Chandál is merely a generic title, and the tribe identical with the Mals of the Rájmahal Hills, an undoubted Dravidian clan, and demonstrates from the Census figures that in many districts the number of Chandáls is in the inverse ratio to the Mals. There appear to be some grounds for this supposition, but an obvious error occurs in the return of 4,663 Mals in Dacca, where none exist, and the omission of any Málos, who are numerous. The latter, though undoubtedly a remnant of some aboriginal race, have not as yet been identified with the Mals.

It may perhaps be inferred from the present geographical position of the Chandáls that they came into contact with the Aryans at a comparatively late period, when the caste system had already been fully developed and alien races were regarded with peculiar detestation. This would account in some measure for the curious violence of the condemnation passed on a tribe in no way conspicuous for qualities calculated to arouse the feeling of physical repulsion with which the early writers appear to regard the Chandáls. It is possible, again, that they may have offered a specially stubborn resistance to the Aryan advance. Dr. Wise refers to the facts that they alone among the population of Lower Bengal use the Káyathí Nágarí, the common written language of Dinájpúr, and that a Chandál Rájá ruled from the fort, whose ruins are still shown in the Bhowál jungle, to prove that they were in early times a strongly-organized commonwealth driven forth from their homes in the north in search of freedom and security of religious worship.

Internal structure.

The internal structure of the caste is shown at length in Appendix I. It will be observed that only four exogamous groups are known, and that the main body of Chandáls in Eastern Bengal have only one section, Kasyapa, which is necessarily inoperative for the purpose of regulating marriage. In Bardwan the mythical ancestor Lomasa or Namasa, referred to in the note on page 183, appears as a section, but here, again, the system is incomplete. In two sections they are said to be recognised, but which have clearly been borrowed from the Brahmanical system with the object of exalting the social standing of the caste. Titles, on the other hand, are very numerous, and in different parts of the country a host of sub-castes have been formed, having reference for the most part to real or supposed differences of occupation. Thus, according to Dr. Wise, the Chandáls of Eastern Bengal have separated into the following eight classes, the members of which never eat, and seldom intermarry, with each other:—

(1) Hálwah, from *hál*, 'a plough,' are cultivators; (2) Ghási are grass-cutters; (3) Kandho, from *skandha*, 'the shoulder,' are palanquin-bearers; (4) Karrál are fishmongers; (5) Bári, probably a corruption of *barhái*, are carpenters; (6) Berua, from *byada ber*, 'an inclosure,' fishermen; (7) Pod; (8) Baqqál traders and hucksters.

The Hálwah claim precedence over all the others, not only as being of purer descent, but as preserving the old tribal customs unchanged. They associate with and marry into Karrál families, but repel the other classes. The Pôd, numerous in Hughli and Jessore, but unknown in Dacca, are cultivators, potters, and fishermen, and are also employed as club-men (*láthiyals*) in squabbles about landed property.

The question naturally arises whether some at any rate of these groups are not really independent castes whose members would now disown all connexion with the Chandáls. The Pôds, for example, at any rate in the 24-Parganas, affect to be a separate caste, and would probably resent the suggestion that they were merely a variety of Chandáls. This fact, however, does not necessarily affect the accuracy of Dr. Wise's observations, which were made nearly twenty years ago, in the district of Dacca. The subdivisions of the lower castes are always on the look-out for chances of promoting themselves, and the claims set up by the Pôds in the 24-Parganas are quite compatible with the theory that they were originally an offshoot from the Chandáls further east. The tendency towards separation is usually strongest among groups which have settled at a distance from the parent caste.

In Central and Western Bengal the sub-castes appear to have reference solely to occupation. Thus in Murshedabad we find the Helo or Háliyá Chandáls confining themselves to agriculture, and the Jelo or Jáliyá making their livelihood as fishermen. The Nolo group make mats and work in reeds (*nal*), and the Kesar-Kalo manufacture reed-pens. Of the Hughli sub-castes, the Saro are agriculturists, the Siuli extract the juice of date and palm-trees, the Kotál serve as *chaukidárs* and *darwáns*, while the Nuniá deal in vegetables and fish. The name of the Saralyá sub-caste of Noakháli suggests a possible connexion with the Saro of Hughli, but the former are fishermen, sellers of betel-nut, and palanquin bearers, while the latter deem any occupation but agriculture degrading. The Amarabádi are also fishermen, but do not carry palanquins. The Báchhári are cultivators, who deal also in *hoglá* leaves and mats. The Sandwipá appear to be a local group, who live in the island of Sandip and grow betel for sale. A man or woman of a higher caste living with and marrying a Chandál may be taken into the caste by going through certain ceremonies and feeding the caste men.

Marriage.

Chandáls marry their daughters as infants and observe the same ceremony as most of the higher castes: in this, as in other matters, the tendency to arrogate social importance may be observed. Dr. Wise remarks that "the Chandálni bride, who in old days walked, is now carried in state in a palanquin," from which it may perhaps be inferred that infant-marriage has been introduced in comparatively recent times in imitation of the usages of the upper classes of Hindus. In the case of the Chandáls it is not due to hypergamy, for no hypergamous groups have been formed, and the ancient custom of demanding a bride-price has not yet given place to the bridegroom-price insisted on by the higher castes. In Western Bengal, indeed, there would seem to be some scarcity of women, for the usual bride-price is from Rs. 100 to Rs. 150, and as much as Rs. 250 is sometimes paid. A similar inference may perhaps be drawn from a statement made to me by a good observer in Eastern Bengal, that marriages are usually celebrated in great haste, as soon as possible after the contract has been entered into by the parents. The rice harvest, when people meet daily in the fields, is the great time for discussing such matters; and the month of Phalgun, when agricultural work is slack, is set apart for the celebration of marriages. Polygamy is permitted in theory, but the extent to which it is practised depends on the means of the individuals concerned. Widow-marriage, once universally practised, has within the last generation been prohibited. Divorce is under no circumstances allowed.

Birth customs.

After the birth of a male child the Chandál mother is ceremonially unclean for ten days, but for a female child the period varies from seven to nine days. Should the child die within eighteen months, a *sraddha* is observed after three nights; but should it live longer, the obsequial ceremony is held at the expiration of ten days. On the sixth day after the birth of a boy the Sashṭhí Púja is performed, but omitted if the child be a girl. Whenever a Chamáín, or Ghulám Káyasth female, is not at hand, the Chandální acts as midwife, but she never takes to this occupation as a means of livelihood.

Religion.

Although the majority of the caste profess the tenets of the Vaishnava sect of Hindus, they still retain many peculiar religious customs, survivals of an earlier animistic cult. At the Bástu Púja on the Paus Sankránt, when the earth goddess is worshipped, the Chandáls celebrate an immemorial rite, at which the caste Bráhman does not officiate. They pound rice, work it up into a thin paste, and, colouring it red or yellow, dip a reversed cup into the mess, and stamp circular marks with it on the ground in front of their houses and on the flanks of the village cattle. This observance, which, according to Dr. Wise, is not practised by any other caste, has for its object the preservation of the village and its property from the enmity of malignant spirits.

In Central Bengal a river god called Bansura is peculiar to the fishing sub-castes of Chandáls. His function is supposed to be to protect fish from evil spirits who are on the watch to destroy them, and if he is not propitiated by the blood of goats and offerings of rice, sweetmeats, fruit and flowers, the popular belief is that the fishing season will be a bad one.

"Throughout Bengal," says Dr. Wise, "the month of Sravan (July-August) is sacred to the goddess of serpents, Manasa Deví, and on the thirtieth day the Chandáls in Eastern Bengal celebrate the *Náo-Ka-Púja*, literally boat worship, or, as it is more generally called, *Chandál Kúdní*, the Chandáls' rejoicing. As its name imports, the occasion is a very festive one, in Silhet being observed as the great holiday of the year. The gods and goddesses of the Hindu mythology are paraded, but the queen of the day is the great snake goddess, Manasa Deví. A kid, milk, plantains, and sweetmeats are offered to her, and the day is wound up with processions of boats, boat races, feasting and drinking. On the Dacca river the sight is singularly interesting. Boats manned by twenty or more men, and decked out with triangular flags, are paddled by short rapid strokes to the sound of a monotonous chant, and as the goal is neared, loud cries and yells excite the contending crews to fresh exertions. The Kutí Mahomedans compete with the Chandáls for prizes contributed by wealthy Hindu gentlemen."

Occupation.

Although subdivided according to trades, Chandáls actually work at anything. They are the only Hindus employed in the boats (bajrá) hired by Europeans; they form a large proportion of the peasantry; and they are shopkeepers, goldsmiths, blacksmiths, carpenters, oilmen, as well as successful traders. They are, however, debarred from becoming fishermen, although fishing for domestic use is sanctioned. In Northern Bengal they catch fish for sale.

Social status.

Chandáls have Brahmans of their own, who preside at religious and social ceremonies; but they are popularly called Barna-Brahman or Chandáler Brahman, and in Eastern Bengal are not received on equal terms by other members of the priestly caste. Their washermen and barbers are of necessity Chandáls, as the ordinary Dhobá and Napit decline to serve them. In Western Bengal, on the other hand, Chandáls have their clothes washed by the Dhobá, who works for other castes. The Bhúinmálí also is reluctant to work for them, and there is much secret jealousy between the castes, which in some places has broken out into open feuds. At village festivals the Chandál is treated as no higher in rank than the Bhúinmálí and Chamár, and is obliged to put off his shoes before he sits down in the assembly. Although he has adopted many Hindu ideas, the Chandál still retains his partiality for spirits and swine's flesh. In the Pirozpur thána of Bakarganj the Chandáls have recently started a combined movement to call themselves Namas, to wear shoes, and not to take rice from Káyasths or Sudras. This departure from the customs of their ancestors was vehemently disapproved of by the Mahomedan zamindars of the neighbourhood, and a breach of the peace was considered imminent. The clean Súdra castes occasionally, and the unclean tribes always, sit with the Chandál, and at times will accept his dry pipe. Nevertheless, vile as he is according to Hindu notions, the Chandál holds himself polluted if he touches the stool on which a Súnrí is sitting.

Chandáls are very particular as regards caste prejudices. They never allow a European to stand or walk over their cooking place on board a boat, and if any one inadvertently does so while the food is being prepared, it is at once thrown away. They are also very scrupulous about bathing before meals, and about the cleanliness of their pots and pans. Still more, they take a pride in their boat, and the tidy state in which they keep it contrasts forcibly with the appearance of one manned by Mahomedan boatmen.

On the whole, Dr. Wise regards the Chandál as "one of the most lovable of Bengalis. He is a merry, careless fellow, very patient and hard-working, but always ready, when his work is done, to enjoy himself. Chandáls are generally of very dark complexion, nearer black than brown, of short muscular figures and deep expanded chests. Few are handsome, but their dark sparkling eyes and merry laugh make ample amends for their generally plain features. In the 24-Parganas many members of the caste are said to be of a noticeably fair complexion. Singing is a favourite amusement, and a Chandál crew is rarely without some musical instrument with which to enliven the evening after the toils of the day. When young, the Chandál is very vain of his personal appearance, always wearing his hair long, and when in holiday attire combing, oiling, and arranging it in the most winsome fashion known. Many individuals among them are tall and muscular, famed as clubmen and watchmen. During the anarchy that accompanied the downfall of Moghal power, the rivers of Bengal swarmed with river thugs or dakaits, who made travelling unsafe and inland trade impossible. The Chandáls furnished the majority of these miscreants, but since their dispersion the Chandál has become a peaceful and exemplary subject of the English Government."

The following statement shows the number and distribution of Chandáls in 1872 and 1881. The figures for Kotál are included in the column of 1872 and excluded from that of 1881.

District.	1872.	1881.	District.	1872.	1881.
Bardwan	33,326	16,873	Jalpigori	1,980	1,895
Bankura	507	1,326	Kuch Behar	......	5,108
Birbhum	890	2,112	Dacca	191,162	204,953
Midnapur	34,805	38,123	Faridpur	156,223	244,948
Hughli	21,568	12,238	Bakarganj	326,775	281,606
Howrah		9,765	Maimansinh	123,262	151,495
24-Parganas	46,056	21,277	Chittagong	1,585	5,278
Nadiya	42,062	38,510	Noakhali	12,947	19,967
Khulna	......	149,677	Tipperah	81,156	63,199
Jessore	271,325	166,966	Hill Tracts	......	13
Murshedabad	21,764	18,854	Purniah	4,027	3,336
Dinajpur	7,371	7,217	Maldah	1,216	1,226
Rajshahye	28,762	31,128	Santál Parganas	547	849
Rangpur	36,148	36,809	Cuttack	......	42
Bogra	7,647	9,947	Lohardaga	......	41
Pabna	50,126	53,313	Manbhum	......	1,221
Darjiling	292	308	Tributary States	......	2

Chandana, a sub-caste of Mauliks in Chota Nagpur.

Chandan-sára, a sub-caste of Kumhárs in Pabna.

Chandaulyár, a section of the Pachainyá sub-caste of Doms in Behar.

Chandel, a section of the Dhengar sub-caste of Gareris in Behar.

Chandel or *Chandan*, a sub-caste of Kurmis in Behar.

Chandghos, a *mul* or section of the Ayodhia sub-caste of Hajjáms in Behar.

Chándil, place of worship of a headman, a local sept of Bhumij and Mundas in Chota Nagpur.

Chándinadár, a person paying ground-rent and holding his house and garden by that payment in Orissa.

Chánd-Kámár, a sub-caste of Kámárs in Midnapur.

Chándkatorá, a *mul* or section of the Naomuliá or Majraut sub-caste of Goálás in Behar.

Chandra, a family title of Kashta Baidyas, Mayarás, and Sánkháris; of Dakshin Rárhi and Bangaja Káyasths and of Subarnabaniks in Bengal. Intermarriage is prohibited within the title, which, though not one of the recognised *gotras* or eponymous sections by which marriage is regulated, has thus come to be virtually exogamous.

Chandra-baidya, a title of Nápits in Tipperah, who practise medicine.

Chandrabansi, a sub-tribe of Rajputs in Behar.

Chandrábat or **Chandrawát**, a *kul* or section of Bábhans in Behar.

Chandradwip, a sub-caste of Telis in Eastern Bengal; a *samáj* or local group of the Bharadwája *gotra* of Páschátya Baidik Brahmans in Bengal; a hypergamous group of Kaibarttas in Bakarganj.

Chandramani, a section of Rautiás in Chota Nagpur.

Chandramási, a section of Báruis in Bengal.

Chandrapati, a *mel* or hypergamous sub-group of Rárhi Brahmans in Bengal.

Chandrarishi, a section of Mayarás and Telis in Bengal.

Chandratiár, a *pur* or section of Sákadwipi Brahmans in Behar.

Chandrorh, a *pur* or section of Sákadwipi Brahmans in Behar.

Chandu, a *thar* or sept of Gurungs in Darjiling.

Chanduwálá, a vendor of *chandu*, a preparation of opium, on whose premises it is usually smoked. To make *chandu* the opium is steeped in water till it becomes soft, and it is then placed on a fire and boiled. When it is at boiling point it is strained and boiled again, till it is reduced to a syrup.

Chang, a synonym for Limbu in Darjiling, supposed to have reference to the tribe having immigrated from the Tibetan province of Tsang.

Changa, a synonym for Chandál, intended according to some authorities to conceal the fact that persons so describing themselves are really Chandáls.

Changáin, a *mul* or section of the Biyáhut sub-caste of Kalwárs in Behar.

Chángnáya or **Chánga**, a sub-caste of Aguris in Western Bengal.

Channankath Kathauliá, a *mul* or section of Kesarwáni Baniás in Behar.

Chanoár or **Cháowar**, a *mul* or section of the Chhamuliá Madhesiá sub-caste of Halwáis in Behar.

Chanpadda, a sub-caste of Joláhas in Behar.

Chánre ke ráut, a section of the Biyáhut and Kharidáhá Kalwárs in Behar.

Chansawár, a *mul* or section of Kesarwáni Baniás in Behar.

Chánti, a sub-tribe of Kaurs in Chota Nagpur.

Chápá, a section, originally totemistic, of the Rajwár caste in Western Bengal.

Chapariyá, a sub-caste of Doms in Behar who make baskets and build the bamboo framework which supports the thatched roof of a house.

Chapen Khor, a section of Murmis in Behar.

Chapotá, a sub-caste of Hindu Joláhas in Behar who have given up weaving and now work as labourers.

Chaprási, a messenger or courier wearing a *chaprás*, most usually a public servant.

Chápuá, a sub-caste of Kumhárs in Behar.

Chapwár, a sub-caste of Rajwárs.

Charak, festival, a sept of Pátors in Chota Nagpur.

Charanbansi, a section of Cháins in Behar.

Charchágiyá, a section of Turis in Chota Nagpur.

Chardhagia, a section of Mahilis in Chota Nagpur.

Chardhiár, a section of Mahilis in Chota Nagpur.

Chardiar, pineapple, a totemistic sept of Kharwars in Chota Nagpur.

Charhad, tiger, a totemistic section of Turis in Chota Nagpur.

Charhar, a section of Mahilis in Chota Nagpur, probably a variant of Charhad, and therefore originally totemistic. It is doubtful, however, whether the Mahilis belonging to this section believe themselves to be under any special obligation to worship or reverence the tiger.

Chári-ghar, a hypergamous group of the Chárjáti sub-caste of Khatris in Bengal.

Chárjáti, a sub-caste of Khatris in Bengal.

Charkhiá, a section of Goálás in the North-Western Provinces and Behar.

Charkholá, a sub-tribe of Limbus in Darjiling.

Charmakár, a synonym for Chamár in Bengal.

Cháran, the name of a caste analogous to, or identical with, the Bhát, following the profession of bards, heralds, and genealogists, and held in like estimation; so that their personal security is considered sufficient for engagements of the most important description, the breach of which involves the death of the surety or of some of his family. They also subsist by carrying grain, salt, groceries, and the like.

Charas-farosh, a synonym for *Sagin.*

Charban-farosh, a grain-parcher, who buys grain, stores it, and sells it again.

Charbeár, a *mul* or section of the Maghayá sub-caste of Barhis in Behar.

Charchain, a section of the Cháin sub-caste of Nuniás in Behar.

Chár Gotra or **Das Gurung,** a sub-tribe of Gurungs in Darjiling.

Charkházán, a cotton-spinner, usually a female.

Chárki, a *thar* or sept of Gurungs in Darjiling.

Charmanái Ráy, a hypergamous group of Kaibarttas in Bakarganj.

Charmi, Chermi, a *thar* or sept of Mangars in Darjiling.

Charnetah, a section of Maghayá Dhobis in Behar.

Charwá, a section of the Maghayá sub-caste of Barhis in Behar.

Charwáha, a herdsman, a grazier.

Chár-yár (from *chár*, 'four,' and *yar*, 'a friend'), a Mahomedan of the Sunni sect, one who maintains the rightful succession of the first four Khalifs, Abubakr, Omar, Osman, and Ali.

Chásá, a common title of cultivating Sadgops; also an epithet of contempt, applied to a rough and illiterate man; a synonym for Sadgop.

Chásá, the chief cultivating caste of Orissa, probably for the most part of non-Aryan descent. Chásás are divided into the following sub-castes:—**Orhchásá** or **Mundi-Chásá, Benátiyá, Chukuliyá**, and **Sukuliyá**. The last-named group is a small one found along the sea-coast and mainly engaged in the manufacture of salt. The sections are shown in Appendix I. A man may not marry a woman belonging to his own section, or one who falls within the standard formula for reckoning prohibited degrees calculated to three generations in the descending line. He may marry two sisters, but may not take to wife an elder sister after being already married to her younger sister.

Origin and internal structure.

The Chásá caste is an exceedingly numerous one, and is probably made up in great measure of non-Aryan elements. In Orissa the caste system is said to be more loosely organised than in Bengal, and this makes it possible on the one hand for outsiders to be admitted into the Chásá caste, and on the other hand for wealthy Chásás, who give up ploughing with their own hands and assume the respectable title of Mahanti, to raise themselves to membership in the lower classes of Káyasths.

Marriage.

Both adult and infant-marriage are recognised by the caste; but the latter is deemed the more respectable, and no one who could get his daughter married at the age of eight or nine years would allow her to remain without a husband until she reached years of puberty. The marriage ceremony is based upon the standard Hindu ritual, the binding portion being *hátganthi* or the tying together of the right hands of the couple with a wisp of *kusá* grass. There appears to be no positive rule either forbidding polygamy or setting any limit to the number of wives a man may have. Most Chásás, however, are too poor to keep more than one wife, and a man only takes a second wife when the first is barren. A widow may marry again, and it is usual for her to marry one of the younger brothers of her late husband. Failing these, she may marry any one not within the prohibited degrees. The ceremony differs from that used at the marriage of a virgin, in that the purely religious portion is omitted and the *left* hands of the couple (not the right) bound together with *kusá* grass. A woman may be divorced for unchastity, barrenness, or ill-temper. In all such cases she must be brought before a pancháyat, at which her own relatives are called upon to be present, and the charge against her must be publicly discussed. If a divorce is granted, the husband is required to pay the woman a year's alimony in advance. Divorced wives may marry again by the form in use at the remarriage of widows.

Religion. Chásás are orthodox Hindus, and most of them belong to the Vaishnava sect. They employ Brahmans for religious and ceremonial purposes, but these priests are not received on equal terms by the Sádani Brahmans, who serve the Khandait and Karan castes. The dead are usually burned, but recourse is sometimes had to what seems to be the older rite of burial. In such cases the corpse is laid on its back, and offerings of boiled rice and fruit are placed with it in the grave. When a body is burned, the ashes are sometimes buried on the spot, and sometimes kept in an earthen vessel in order that they may be thrown into the Ganges when occasion serves. The *sráddh* ceremony is performed in the orthodox fashion.

Occupation. The great majority of the Chásás are engaged in agriculture, which they regard as the characteristic occupation of their caste, and only a few have taken to trade or service. Some of them hold service tenures, the rest being *tháni* or *páhi* raiyats and landless day-labourers. Socially they rank next to the Máli caste, and Brahmans will take water from their hands. The Goálá and Bhandári are the lowest castes from whom Chásás will take sweetmeats. Cooked food they may eat only in Brahmans' houses, and they will also eat the leavings of members of that caste. There is nothing peculiar about their own diet, except that, like many other castes of aboriginal extraction, they eat the flesh of the wild boar. All fish, whether scaly or scaleless, are lawful food, except the *sál* fish, which is one of the totems of the caste.

The following statement shows the number and distribution of the Chásá caste in 1872 and 1881:—

District.	1872.	1881.
Cuttack	156,308	204,335
Puri	130,436	254,103
Balasore	24,278	12,673
Tributary States	172,471	154,599

Chásá or Hálwáha Kaibartta, a sub-caste of Kaibarttas in Central Bengal.

Chásá or *Orh-Khandait*, a sub-caste of Khandáits in Balasore and Cuttack.

Chásá Baidya, 'plough-doctor,' a title of Baidyas used by outsiders.

Chásádhobá, *Chásádhopá*, a cultivating and trading caste of

Origin. Bengal Proper, some of whose members are employed as artisans and builders. According to their own account, they are the modern representatives of the Vaidehas spoken of in Manu x, 11, as the offspring of a Vaisya rather and a Vaideha mother, the second half of their name being a corruption of the Sansk. *dhava* 'husband,' so that Chásádhobá means the husband or owner of cultivated fields (*chás*), and not, as is ordinarily supposed, a washerman who has taken to cultivation. Another story is that once upon a time Brahmá's washerwoman came with her son to fetch the dirty clothes. The god was busy and asked the woman to let her son wait till he was ready. After a bit the boy got tired of waiting and went home: meanwhile Brahmá brought out his dirty linen, and finding the boy not there concluded that a demon (*Asura*) had eaten him. To console the mother he created a new boy exactly like the first; but no sooner had he done so than the mother herself returned, bringing the original boy with her. Embarrassed by the confusion he had caused, Brahmá called upon the washerwoman to adopt the second boy, but stipulated that as he was of divine origin he should not follow the profession of his adoptive mother, but should set up as an agriculturist and dealer in food-grains. In spite of these exalted traditions it may be inferred from the social status of the Chásádhobás, and the apparently totemistic character of some of their *gotras* or exogamous groups, that they are really of Dravidian descent, and probably a branch of Dhobás who have taken to cultivation, and thus raised themselves so far above the parent caste that they now disown all connexion with it.

Internal structure.

The Chásádhobás are divided into three sub-castes—**Uttar-Rárhi**, **Dakshin-Rárhi**, and **Bárendra**, which indicate the chief settlements of the caste and are common to them and to some of the higher castes. Members of these groups cannot intermarry, but may eat together and may smoke from the same *hookah*. Their sections are shown in Appendix I. Two of them, **Bághrishi** and **Brihatbat**, seem to be totemistic, and to refer to the tiger and the banyan tree; but neither the tree nor the animal is worshipped by the caste, which has now become thoroughly Hinduised. A man may not marry a woman of his own *gotra*, but marriage with a woman belonging to his mother's *gotra* is not forbidden, provided such an alliance is not barred by the table of prohibited degrees, which is the same as is generally recognised by orthodox Hindus. Chásádhobás have two hypergamous divisions, **Kulin** and **Maulik**, which affect marriage in the ordinary way; that is to say, a **Kulin** man may marry a Maulik woman, while a Maulik man can only get a wife from his own group.

Marriage.

Chásádhobás marry their daughters as infants at ages ranging from two to twelve years. Eight or nine years may be taken as the usual age for the marriage. Boys, however, are not married under five, and the husband is usually a few years older than the wife. In the Maulik group, where there may often be a surplus of males owing to the constant endeavour to get the females married to Kulins, it sometimes happens that a youth is not married before twenty-five owing to the difficulty of procuring a wife within the circle of selection open to a particular family. In all cases the standard Brahmanical ritual is used. Special importance seems to be attached to *ásirbád*, or the ceremony of blessing the bride and bridegroom, and to the exchange of presents. These are represented as the essential and binding portions of the rite.

Polygamy is supposed to be forbidden, but the rule is subject to the usual exception that a man may marry a second wife when the first is barren or suffers from an incurable disease. The remarriage of widows is strictly prohibited. In respect of divorce Chásádhobás follow the higher castes in holding the practice to be incompatible with the orthodox theory of marriage among the Hindus. In cases of proved unchastity, the offending wife is turned out to shift for herself and ceases to be a member of respectable society. In order to clear himself and his household from the stain of impurity, the husband makes a straw effigy of the wife, which is solemnly burned, while rice cakes (*pindas*) are offered to her and a sort of *sráddh* is performed, as if she were literally dead. Brahmans and relations are feasted, and *pujá* is done to Satya Náráyan.

Religion.

The religion of the Chásádhobás differs little from that of the orthodox middle-class Hindus of Bengal. Most of them belong to the Vaishnava sect: only a few are Sáktas, and there are said to be no Saivas among them. The Vaishnavas abstain from flesh and wine, but may eat fish. Cultivators show special reverence to Lakshmi as the goddess of harvest, while artisans worship Viswakarma. Brahmans are employed for religious and ceremonial purposes; but they rank with the Barna Brahmans, who serve the lower castes and are looked down on by the higher classes of the priestly order.

Social status.

It will be seen from the Tables of Precedence for Bengal that the pretensions of the Chásádhobá to rank above the Dhobá are not generally recognised, and that both stand on about the same level in popular estimation. This fact, coupled with the numerical smallness of the caste, seems to suggest that it may be of comparatively recent formation. If the caste were an old one, we might expect that by abandoning the specially impure practices of the Dhobás and adopting the respectable occupation of agriculture they would have attained a higher social position than is actually conceded to them. Chásádhobás are generally classed along with the Chandál, the fishing Kaibarttas, and the Sunris, and Brahmans will not take water from their hands. The cultivating members of the caste are mostly occupancy or non-occupancy raiyats, and some have risen to the position of tenure-holders. So far as I have been able to ascertain, none of them are zamindars. Prosperous grain-merchants and money-lenders are found among them, and many follow the business of carpenters, builders, and artisans working in wood or metal.

The following statement shows the number and distribution of the Chásádhobá caste in 1872 and 1881:—

District.	1872.	1881.	District.	1872.	1881.
Bardwan	1,014	276	Rajshahye	304	......
Bankura	......	1,003	Rangpur	15	......
Birbhum	430	1,244	Bogra	4	2
Midnapur	67	28	Pabna	1,160	790
Hughli	} 6,436	1,244	Darjiling	......	9
Howrah		3,362	Dacca	2,409	......
24-Parganas	17,766	10,329	Faridpur	561	......
Nadiya	9,027	3,774	Bakarganj	7	......
Jessore	6,411	3,665	Maimansinh	1	......
Khulna	......	40	Tipperah	145	......
Murshedabad	6,320	4,812	Santál Parganas	......	873
Dinajpur	23	......	Maldah	......	41

Chásaduli, a sub-caste of Bágdis in Bengal who were originally palanquin-bearers, but have recently taken to cultivation and claim a certain measure of social superiority for that reason.

Cháságailá, a synonym for Sadgop in Bengal.

Chásá-karur or *Chásá-kolai*, a sub-caste of Muchis in Bengal.

Chásati, a small caste nearly allied to the Chásádhoba. They till land and rear silk-worm.

Chási, a synonym for Pod.

Chási, a section of Koránch Kándus in Behar.

Chasiár, a section of Bábhans in Behar.

Chási-Dás, a synonym for Háliá Dás or Kaibartta in Bengal.

Chási Pod, a sub-caste of Pods in the Presidency districts who have given up their profession of fishing and taken to cultivation. They do not intermarry with the ordinary Pod.

Chásiwár, a section of Bábháns in Behar.

Chata, umbrella, a totemistic sept of Mundas in Chota Nagpur.

Chátgáinyá, a sub-caste of Kumhárs in Noakháli.

Chatra Tuin, a sept of Hos in Singbhum.

Chatta, a *gáin* of the Kásyapa *gotra* of Rárhi Brahmans in Bengal.

Chattarághabi, a *mel* or hypergamous sub-group of Rárhi Brahmans in Bengal.

Chattarkhai, a social group in Orissa made up of people who lost their caste in 1866 for eating in relief-kitchens (*chattras*). The Chattarkhai caste, as it may properly be called, is divided into an upper and a lower sub-caste—the former comprising Brahmans, Karans, Khandaits, and Gop-Goalas; the latter of the castes ranking below these in the social scale. Members of each sub-caste marry within that group, irrespective of the caste to which they originally belonged; but no intermarriage is possible between members of the two sub-castes. All Chattarkháis are entirely cut off from their original castes.

Chaturábandi, a *gáin* of the Bátsya *gotra* of Bárendra Brahmans in Bengal.

Chaturan-Khán, a sub-caste of Sutradhars in Murshedabad.

Chaturásram or **Chaturthán,** a sub-caste of Sunris in Western Bengal.

Chattopádhyáya, the name of a family of Rárhi Brahmans in Bengal; commonly pronounced Chaturjia or Chaturji.

Chaturthán, a sub-caste of Sunris in Bengal.

Chaturvedi, a Brahman professing to have studied the four Vedas. In the abbreviated form of Chaube it is a common title of Brahmans in Behar.

Chauán, a sub-caste of Rájus in Midnapur.

Chau-aniá, a sub-caste of Goálás in Behar and Chota Nagpur.

Chauarsá, a section of Kaserás in Behar.

Chaubahán, a *mul* or section of the Banodhiá sub-caste of Kalwárs in Behar.

Chaubáriá, a sept of Surajbansi Rajputs in Behar.

Chauberiá, a *mul* or section of the Tinmuliá Madhesiá sub-caste of Halwáis in Behar.

Chaubhaiá, a section of the Banodhiá and Jaiswár Kalwárs, and of Bábhans in Behar.

Chaubhán, a sub-caste of Nuniyás in Behar.

Chaubhán, Chohán, a sept of the Suryabansi Rajputs in Behar. They cannot intermarry with persons of the Besáin and Mahraur septs, who are supposed to be descended from a common ancestor.

Chaubi, Chaube or **Chobe** (abbreviated from Chaturvedi), a Brahman learned in the four Vedas; a title now applied to a class of Brahmans who are not always men of literary habits. In the North-Western Provinces they are often boxers, wrestlers, and the like.

Chauddagrámi, a sub-caste of Támbulis in Bengal.

Chauddapárá Rárhibindu, a sub-caste of Kaibarttas in Central Bengal.

Chaudhari, a title of Maithil Brahmans in Behar.

Chaudhrána, a section of the Maghayá sub-caste of Barhis in Behar.

Chaudhri (a holder of four, perhaps, shares or profits), the headman of a profession, trade, or occupation in towns; the headman of a village, of a bazar, or of a caste pancháyat; a lessee of a *ganj* or grain emporium; a holder of landed property, classed with the zamindár or talukdár. In Cuttack the Chaudhari was the revenue officer of a district, corresponding with the Desmukh. The Chaudhari tálukdar, or head revenue officer, was there treated by the British Government as a proprietor or zamindár. The term Chaudhari is an honorific title of the Ariár sub-caste of Bais Baniyás; of the Banpár sub-caste of Gonrhis; of Halwáis; of the Ját and Majraut sub-castes of Ahirs or Goálás; of Ganjwar Sunris; of the Jeswár and Banodhiá sub-castes of Kalwárs; of Kurmis in Western Bengal, used both by members of the caste and by outsiders; of Nágars; of the Pacháiya sub-caste of Nuniyás; of Sonárs and Tiors in Behar; of Kochhs in Northern Bengal; and of Brahmans, Kaibarttas, Káyasths, Kewats, Támbulis, and Telis in Bengal. It also denotes a section of the Kanaujiá sub-caste of Goálás, and of Maghayá Doms in Behar, and a sept of Thárus.

Chaudhriá, a sept of the Malwe Rajputs in Chota Nagpur.

Chaudhrián, a section of Maghaiyá Kumhars in Behar.

Chaudhriji, a synonym for, and title of Bábhans.

Chaudihá, a section of Bantariá Kándus in Behar.

Chaudorti, a *mul* or section of the Kanaujiá sub-caste of Sonárs in Behar.

Chaugáin, a section of Kalwárs in Behar.

Chaugáin ke pánre, a section of the Biyáhut and Kharidáhá Kalwárs in Behar.

Chauhán, a sub-caste of Beldars in Behar.

Chauhán, a section of the Chandrabansi Rajputs and of the Maghaiyá sub-caste of Doms in Behar.

Chaukidár or *chokidar*, a village watchman, a police or customs peon.

Cháulwálá, a dealer in rice.

Chaumasiá, a ploughman hired for the four months of the rainy season.

Chaumukhdih, a section of Majraut Goálás in Behar.

Chaunriwálá, a maker of fly-flaps and besoms from strips of date-palm leaves, usually a Mahomedan.

Chaupre, a section of the Bárajáti sub-caste of Khatris in Bengal.

Chaurahá, a section of the Banodhiá and Jaiswár Kalwárs in Behar.

Chaurási, a sub-caste of Kumhárs in Central Bengal; a *thar* or sept of Khambus in Darjiling.

Chaurásiá, a sub-caste of Barais in Behar.

Chaurla, rat, a sept of Mundas in Chota Nagpur.

Chauriár, a section of Bábhans in Behar.

Chaurthán, a sub-caste of Sunris in Behar who deal in liquor.

Chausá, a section of the Biyáhut and Kharidáhá Kalwárs, a *kul* or section of Bábhans; a *mul* or section of the Chhamuliá Madhesiá sub-caste of Halwáis in Behar.

Chausáhá, a section of Kanaujiá Lohárs in Behar.

Chausar, a section of Awadhiá Hajáms in Behar.

Chauswár, a section of Sonárs in Behar.

Chautariá, a sept of the Rautár sub-tribe of Thárus in Behar.

Chauthá, a sub-caste of Goálás in Behar.

Chauthi, Haldiá, a sub-caste of Telis in Orissa.

Chautkhandi, a *gáin* of the Bátsya *gotra* of Rárhi Brahmans in Bengal.

Chavala Gáin, a *thar* or section of Nepáli Brahmans.

Chedi, a class of inferior Rajputs in Western Bengal.

Chehmjom, a native of Chehm, a sept of the Pánthar sub-tribe of Limbus in Darjiling.

Chelekchela, a small bird, a totemistic sept of Mundas in Chota Nagpur.

Chempajong, a sept of Limbus in Darjiling.

Cher, a section of Goálás in Behar.

Cherabesari, a section of Páns in Chota Nagpur.

Cherchete, a kind of jungle wood, a totemistic sept of Páns in Chota Nagpur.

Cherengtsa, a sept of Maghs in the Hill Tracts of Chittagong.

Chero, *Cheru*, a landholding and cultivating caste of Behar and Chota Nagpur. Found also in Benares and Mirzapur. Sir Henry Elliot, while mentioning the opinions that the Cheros are a branch of the Bhars or are connected with the Kols, appears himself to have considered them to be the aboriginal inhabitants of the provinces on the skirts of which they are now found, driven from their proper seats by Rajput races. It was Colonel Dalton's opinion that the Gangetic provinces were once occupied by peoples speaking a Kolarian language closely allied to the present Munda dialect, among whom the Cheros were the latest dominant race. If, however, the Cheros and Kols originally formed one nation, the Kols must have parted from the parent stock and settled in Chota Nagpur before the former tribe embraced Hinduism and erected the various temples of which the ruins are still referred by local tradition to their rule in Behar; for all of these are dedicated to the worship of idols, and it is a distinctive feature in the religion of the Kols of the present day, as of most races in the animistic stage of belief, that they never attempt to represent their deities or to build any sort of habitation for them. Convincing proof of the non-Aryan affinities of the Cheros is derived from the fact that the Chota Nagpur members of the caste, whose poverty and social insignificance have held them aloof from Hinduising influences, still retain totemistic section-names similar to those in use among the Khariás, who are beyond doubt closely akin to the Mundas. The landholding Cheros of Palamau have borrowed the Brahmanical *gotras* in support of their claim to be Rajputs, and have thus successfully obliterated all trace of their true antecedents. These Cheros are divided into two sub-castes, **Bára-hazár** and **Tera-hazár** or **Birbandhi**. The former is the higher in rank, and includes most of the descendants of former ruling families, who assume the title **Bábuán**. The Tera-hazár are supposed to be the illegitimate offspring of the Bára-hazár. Some of the wealthier members of the latter group who have married into local Rajput houses call themselves Chohan-bansi Rajputs, and decline alliances with the Bára-hazár Cheros. For the most part, however, the Cheros of Palamau are looked down upon by the Cheros of Bhojpur by reason of their engaging in the degrading occupations of rearing *tasar* cocoons and collecting catechu and lac.

Origin.

Colonel Dalton has the following remarks on the physical characteristics of the Cheros and their traditions of origin :—

"The distinctive physical traits of the Cheros have been considerably softened by the alliances with pure Hindu families, which their ancient power and large possessions enabled them to secure; but they appear to me still to exhibit an unmistakable Mongolian[1] physiognomy. They vary in colour, but are usually of a light brown. They have, as a rule, high cheek-bones, small eyes obliquely set, and

---

[1] It has been shown in the Introductory essay that the theory of the Mongolian origin of the Kols and cognate tribes is untenable, and that the distinction between Kolarian and Dravidian rests purely on linguistic grounds. In describing the Chero features as 'Mongolian,' Colonel Dalton meant that they resembled the ordinary Kol type.

eyebrows to correspond, low broad noses, and large mouths with protuberant lips. It appears from Buchanan that the old Cheros, like the dominant Kolarian family of Chota Nagpur, claimed to be Nágbansis, and had the same tradition regarding their origin from the great 'Nág,' or dragon, that has been adopted by the Chota Nagpur family. The latter were it seems, even in Gorakhpur and Behar, allowed to be the heads of the Nágbansi family, and Buchanan considered them to be Cheros; but they are, no doubt, originally of the same race as their Kol subjects, though frequent alliances with Rajput families have obliterated the aboriginal lineaments. The western part of Kosala, that is, Gorakhpur, continued some time under the Cheros after other portions of that territory had fallen into the hands of the people called Gurkha, who were in their turn expelled by the Thárus, also from the north. In Shahábád, also, the most numerous of the ancient monuments are ascribed to the Cheros, and it is traditionally asserted that the whole country belonged to them in sovereignty. Buchanan suggests they were princes of the Sunaka family, who flourished in the time of Gautama, about the sixth or seventh century before the Christian era. An inscription at Buddh Gyá mentions one Phudi Chandra, who is traditionally said to have been a Chero. The Cheros were expelled from Shahábád, some say, by the Savars or Suars, some say by a tribe called Hariha. The date of their expulsion is conjectured to have been between the fifth and sixth centuries of the Christian era. Both Cheros and Savars were considered by the Brahmans of Shahábád as impure or Mlechhas, but the Harihas are reputed good Kshatriyas.

"The overthrow of the Cheros in Mithila and Magadha seems to have been complete. Once lords of the Gangetic provinces, they are now found in Shahábád and other Behar districts only holding the meanest offices or concealing themselves in the woods skirting the hills occupied by their cousins, the Kharwárs; but in Palamau they retained till a recent period the position they had lost elsewhere. A Chero family maintained almost an independent rule in that *parganá* till the accession of the British Government; they even attempted to hold their castles and strong places against that power, but were speedily subjugated, forced to pay revenue and submit to the laws. They were, however, allowed to retain their estates; and though the rights of the last Rájá of the race were purchased by Government in 1813, in consequence of his falling into arrears, the collateral branches of the family have extensive estates in Palamau still. According to their own traditions (they have no trustworthy annals) they have not been many generations in the *parganá*. They invaded that country from Rohtás, and with the aid of Rajput Chiefs, the ancestors of the Thákurais of Ranká and Cháinpur drove out and supplanted a Rajput Rájá of the Ráksel family, who retreated into Sargujá and established himself there. It is said that the Palamau population then consisted of Kharwárs, Gonds, Márs, Korwás, Parheyás, and Nágeswars. Of these, the Kharwárs were the people of most consideration; the Cheros conciliated them, and allowed them to remain in peaceful possession of the hill tracts bordering on Sargujá. All the Cheros of note who assisted in the expedition obtained military service grants of land, which they still retain. It is popularly asserted that at the commencement of the Chero rule in Palamau they numbered twelve thousand families, and the Kharwárs eighteen thousand; and if an individual of one or the other is asked to what tribe he belongs, he will say, not that he is a Chero or a Kharwár, but that he belongs to the twelve thousand or to the eighteen thousand, as the case may be. The Palamau Cheros now live strictly as Rajputs, and wear the *paitá* or caste thread. They do not, however, intermarry with really good Rajput families. I do not think they cling to this method of elevating themselves in the social scale so tenaciously as do the Kharwárs. But intermarriages between Chero and Kharwár families have taken place. A relative of the Palamau Rájá married a sister of Manináth Sinh, Rájá of Rámgarh, and this is amongst themselves an admission of identity of origin. As both claimed to be Rajputs, they could not intermarry till it was proved to the satisfaction of the family priests that the parties belonged to the same class. But the Palamau Cheros, and I suppose all Cheros, claim to be descendants of Chain Muni, one of the Rishis, a monk of Kumáon. Some say the Rishi took to wife the daughter of a Rájá, and that the Cheros are the offspring of their union; others, that the Cheros are sprung in a mysterious manner from the *áshan*, or seat of Cháin Muni. They have also a tradition that they came from the Morang.'

Marriage.

Cheros profess to marry their daughters as infants, but it seems doubtful whether this practice has yet become fully established among them. The poorer members of the caste, particularly the totemistic Cheros of Chota Nagpur, have not yet completely cut themselves loose from the non-Aryan custom of adult-marriage; while the landholding Cheros find the same difficulties in getting husbands for their daughters which hamper all pseudo-Rajput families in the earlier stages of their promotion to the lower grades of the great Rajput group. The marriage service conforms on the whole to the orthodox pattern, but retains a few peculiar practices which may perhaps belong to a more ancient ritual. At the close of the *bhanwar* ceremony, when the couple march round an earthen vessel set up under the bridal canopy of boughs, the bridegroom, stooping, touches the toe of the bride and swears to be faithful to her through life. Again, after the binding rite of *sindurdán* has been completed, the bridegroom's elder brother washes the feet of the bride, lays the wedding jewellery in her joined hands, and then, taking the *patmauri* from the *maur* or pith head-dress worn by the bridegroom, places it on the bride's head. The practice known as *amlo* also deserves notice. This is performed by the bridegroom's mother before the bridal procession (*barát*) starts for the bride's house, and by the bride's mother after the procession has arrived. It consists of putting a mango leaf into the mouth and then bursting out into tears and loud lamentation: the maternal uncle of the bride or bridegroom meanwhile pours water on the leaf.

Polygamy is permitted, but is not very common. There is said to be no theoretical limit to the number of wives a man may have.

Widows may marry again, and among the less Hinduised members of the caste they usually do so. Widow-marriage, however, is regarded with disfavour by the wealthier Cheros, who affect orthodoxy, and within a generation or so we may expect that the practice will be abandoned. Where it is still recognised, the widow is expected, on grounds of family convenience, to marry her late husband's younger brother or cousin. She may, however, marry any one else provided that she does not infringe the prohibited degrees which were binding on her before her marriage, and does not select a man whose sister could not have been taken in marriage by her late husband. Divorce is not allowed. A woman found in adultery is turned out of the caste, and can under no circumstances marry again.

Religion.

The religion of the Cheros is still in a state of transition, and they observe a sort of dual worship, which discloses unmistakable traces of their non-Aryan descent. For the worship of the Hindu gods they employ Kanaujiá or Sakadwipi Brahmans, who are received on terms of equality by other members of the sacred order. Their spiritual guides *(gurus)* are either Brahmans or Gharbári Gosains. They also reverence animistic deities of the type known to the Khariás and Mundas—Bághaut, Chenri, Darhá, Dharti, Dukhnáhi, Dwarpar, and others, to whom goats, fowls, sweetmeats, and wine are offered in the month of Aghan so as to secure a good harvest. In these sacrifices Brahmans take no part, and they are conducted by a priest (*baigá*) belonging to one of the aboriginal races. Cheros also, like the Kols, observe triennial sacrifices. "Every three years," says Colonel Dalton, "a buffalo and other animals are offered in the sacred grove of *sarna*, or on a rock near the village. They also have, like some of the Kols, a priest for each village, called *páhn*. He is always one of the impure tribes, a Bhuiyá, or Kharwár, or a Parheyá, and is also called *baigá*. He alone can offer this great sacrifice. No Brahmanical priests are allowed on these occasions to interfere. The deity honoured is the tutelary god of the village, sometimes called Duár Pahár, sometimes Dharti, sometimes Purgahaili, or Daknai, a female, or Dura, a sylvan god—the same perhaps as the Darhá of the Kols. I found that the above were all worshipped in the village of Munka, in Palamau, which belongs to a typical Chero, Kunwar Bhikári Sinh."

Social status.

The Cheros of Palamau affect the ceremonial purity characteristic of the higher castes of Hindus, and the connexion of their leading families with the land secures to them a fairly high social position. Many of them wear the sacred thread with which they are invested by a Brahman at the time of their marriage. Brahmans will take water from their hands, and eat anything but rice that has been cooked by them. They are held, in fact, in much the same estimation as any of the local Rajputs. In Chota Nagpur, on the other hand, the status of the caste is by no means so high, and the Bhogtás, while admitting the Cheros to be a sub-caste of their community, decline to eat with them, and regard them as socially their inferiors. Agriculture is supposed to be the original occupation of the caste, and in Palamau many of them still hold various kinds of *jágir* tenures. Some have taken to shopkeeping and petty trade, while others live by cartage, working on roads or in coal-mines, and by collecting *tasar* cocoons, catechu, and lac. For all this, says Mr. Forbes, "the Cheros are a proud race, and exceedingly jealous of their national honour. They have never forgotten that they were once a great people, and that their descent was an honourable one. Only the very poorest among them will hold the plough, and none of them will carry earth upon their heads."[1]

The following statement shows the number and distribution of the Cheros in 1872 and 1881:—

District.	1872.	1881.
Shahabad	373	453
Saran	2,004	......
Champaran	......	270
Hazaribagh	11	......
Lohardagá	9,756	10,813
Tributary States	7,865	11,448

Chera, Cheru a synonym for Chero.

Cherui, a *mul* or section of the Kanaujiá sub-caste of Sonárs in Behar.

Cheruka, a fish, a totemistic sept of Binjhiás in Chota Nagpur.

Cherviyár, a title of Maithil Brahmans in Behar.

Cherwa, a sub-tribe of Kaurs in Chota Nagpur.

Chesiá, a section of Bábhans in Behar.

Cheswár, a section of the Kesarwáni sub-caste of Baniyás in Behar.

Chhaghariá Kápa, a hypergamous group of Bárendra Brahmans in Bengal.

Chhagri, goat, a title of Tántis in Bengal.

Chhágullá, a sub-caste of Telis in Bengal.

Chhajáti, a sub-caste of Khatris in Bengal

Chhalor, a sub-section of the Levátiá section of Majraut Goálás in Behar.

Chhamuliá, *Madhesiá*, a sub-caste of Halwáis in Behar.

Chhaparband, Chayál, a maker of bamboo frame-works for thatched roofs, an occupation usually followed by Mahomedans.

Chhápátichá, a *thar* or sept of Sunuwárs in Darjiling.

Chhaphuliá, a group of the Bárendra Sunris in Tipperah.

Chharidár, 'stick-bearer,' the title of the messenger who serves under the *manjhan* or headman of the Tior caste in Behar.

Chhariyár, a *pur* or section of Sákadwipi Brahmans in Behar.

[1] *Palamau Settlement Report*, p. 38.

Chhathwárk, a *pur* or section of Sákadwipi Brahmans in Behar.

Chhatimane-Chhatman, a *mul* of the Sándil section of Maithil Brahmans in Behar.

Chhatrawár, a *pur* or section of Sákadwipi Brahmans in Behar.

Chhatri or *Chhetri*, a man of the second or regal and military caste; a synonym for Rajput.

Chhatris-Asram, a sub-caste of Gandhabaniks in Bengal.

Chhayi, a *mel* or hypergamous sub-group of Rárhi Brahmans in Bengal.

Chhenilama, a *thar* or sept of the Das-Gurung sub-tribe of Gurungs. The founder of this *thar*, who became very powerful, defeated the chief of Ghaleh, married his daughter, and built a fort at Peun, on the Káligangá. He bored a hole in a sheep's horn and with its aid employed art magic to slay his enemies; hence his name was Loho Chheni, the borer with iron pin; and the *thar* is called *Chheni* to this day.

Chhilatiá or *Silhotia*, a sub-caste of Dhánuks in Behar.

Chhipi, Chhipigar, a calico-printer and a printer of patterns on cotton cloth, a chintz-stamper. The term seems also to include the making of dies.

Chhitni, a section of the Sát-muliá Maghayá sub-caste of Kándus in Behar.

Chhongphtháng, a sept of the Agniá sub-tribe of Meches in the Darjiling Terai.

Chhotá-bhág, a sub-caste of Bhuinmalis, Haris, and Muchis in Bengal.

Chhota-bhágiya, a sub-caste of Kumhárs in Dacca.

Chhota-bhágiyá or **Káyath-Tanti**, a sub-caste of Tántis in Eastern Bengal.

Chhota-Kurmi or **Sikhariá**, a sub-caste of Kurmis in Chota Nagpur.

Chhotapatti, a sub-caste of Telis in Bengal.

Chhota-Samáj, a sub-caste of Dhobás in Hughli.

Chhot-gohri, a sub-caste of Khandáits and Rautiás in Chota Nagpur.

Chhotgohri Deswari, a sub-caste of Kharwárs in Chota Nagpur.

Chhothar, a sub-tribe of Limbus in Darjiling.

Chhotki-dángi, a sub-caste of Koiris in Behar.

Chhumbipá, a *rui* or sept of Dejong Lhoris, whose ancestor had emigrated from North Bhotan.

Chhungpá, a sub-sept of the Pon-po sept of Dejong Lhoris or Bhotias of the south.

Chhutár, a sub-caste of, and synonym for, Sutradhar in Bengal.

Chidra or **Cherrá**, squirrel, a section of Bedyas and Binjhias in Chota Nagpur.

Chigah, jackal, a totemistic sept of Oraons in Chota Nagpur.

Chigi, Chiki, a sub-sept of the Tudu sept of Santáls.

Chik, a class of Mahomedan butchers. See **Chikwá**.

Chik or **Chik-Baraik**, a sub-caste of Páns in Chota Nagpur.

Chikaná, a section of Goálás in the North-Western Provinces and Behar.

Chikan-doz, an embroiderer of flowered muslin, who usually works for a Chikanwálá.

Chikanjari, a sept of Chiks in Chota Nagpur.

Chikanwálá, a dealer in hand-worked flowered muslin, usually a Mahomedan.

Chikbarikin, a sub-caste of Doms in Hazaribagh who make screens or blinds of thin slips of bamboo.

Chikchábá, a sept of the Pánthar sub-tribe of Limbus in Darjiling.

Chikitsak, a synonym for Baidya.

Chikkophung, he who planted the *brihati*, a thorny plant with a bitter berry used for medical purposes, a sept of the Phedáb sub-tribe of Limbus.

Chikni-daliwálá, a dealer in *supári* or betel-nut.

Chiksári, a section of Majraut Goálás in Behar.

Chiksoria, a section of Bábhans in Behar.

Chikwá, a butcher and fell-monger, a dealer in small slaughter animals—goats and sheep—as opposed to the *qassáb*, who deals in large cattle.

Chilbindhá, eagle-slayer, a sub-sept of the Hansda sept of Santáls.

Chilbindhá panariá, a section of Kurmis in Chota Nagpur and Orissa.

Chilbinuár, kite, a section of Kurmis in Chota Nagpur and Orissa.

Chilhár, a *mul* or section of the Chhamuliá Madhesiá sub-caste of Halwáis in Behar.

Chilhiá, kite, a totemistic sept of Mundas in Chota Nagpur.

Chilimár, a section of Bábhans in Behar.

Chilkhor, 'kite-eater?,' a *mul* or section of the Naiyá caste in Behar.

Chiluár, kite, a section of Kurmis in Chota Nagpur and Orissa.

Chinear, a section of Ghásis in Chota Nagpur.

Chingala, a group of the Sanádhya sub-caste of Gaura Brahmans.

Chingri, a section of Binjhiás in Chota Nagpur.

Chingrisha, a sept of Maghs in the Hill Tracts of Chittagong.

Chinpuriá, a group of the Ekádas Telis in Bengal.

Chírá-Kash, an engraver in gold, silver or copper. The pattern is traced in wax with a sharp style and afterwards cut out with a chisel. Patterns in relief are made by beating thin metal on wooden blocks placed underneath. The Chírá-Kash are usually Mahomedans, but some belong to the Káyasth, Tánti, and Sunri castes.

Chiranjiá, a section of the Bánsphor sub-caste of Doms in Western Behar.

Chiriyámár, *Chedimár, Chodimár*, bird-killer, (i) a title of Bediyás; (ii) in Behar a class of Mahomedans, possibly converted Bediyas, who catch and sell parrots, *mainás*, and the like.

Chirko, mushroom, a totemistic sept of Mundas in Chota Nagpur.

Chirkut or **Chirákut,** a title of Bágdis, Chandáls, and other castes who prepare *chira*, or rice parched and flattened.

Chirkuttá, a title of Khandaits in Orissa who make *churá*.

Chirme or *Chirmáit*, a sub-caste of Koiris in Behar, which, though endogamous as regards the rest of the caste, intermarries with the Maghayá sub-caste.

Chirra, a squirrel, a totemistic section of Binjhiás, Bhuiyás, Kharwars, Rajwárs, and Oraons in Chota Nagpur.

Chisim, a *dugu* or section of the Kochh-Mandai in Eastern Bengal. The name indicates the original habitat of the group, probably a village or hill in Assam, and at the present day has no bearing upon marriage.

Chitári, a painter.

Chitauriá, a *thar* or sept of Mangars in Darjiling.

Chitauriár, a *pur* or section of Sákadwipi Brahmans in Behar.

Chiterah, an engraver on metal.

Chithá, a section of Sonárs in Behar.

Chitosiá, a section of the Ját sub-caste of Goálás in Behar and the North-Western Provinces, whose titles are Chaudhri, Singh, and Marár.

Chitrakar, a painter, synonym for Patuá, *q.v.*

Chitrakar, painter—a profession followed by Acharji, Ganak, Sutradhar, and other low castes.

Chitti, a kind of snake, a totemistic sept of Mundas in Chota Nagpur.

Chitwaniá or *Chitauniá*, a sub-tribe of Thárus in Nepal; a sept of Rautár Thárus.

Chiwár, a section of Bábhans in Behar.

Chobdár, *Chopdar*, an attendant carrying a staff or mace, who accompanies rájás and wealthy zemindars on ceremonial occasions. His functions are purely ornamental.

Chobegu, a sub-sept of the Thekim sept and a sept of the Pánthar sub-tribe of Limbus in Darjiling.

Chocha, a bird, a totemistic sept of Mundas in Chota Nagpur.

Chokarhadi, a synonym for Chik in Chota Nagpur.

Chomar, a title of Goálás in Bengal.

Chonchwár, a *pur* or section of Sákadwipi Brahmans in Behar.

Chongá, a sept of Dhimáls in the Darjiling Terai.

Chongphrán, a sept of the Agniá sub-tribe of Meches in the Darjiling Terai.

Chonre, a sept of Santáls.

Chonrhá, a section of Sonárs in Behar.

Chopeár, a sub-sept of the Murmu sept of Santáls.

Chorá, a section of Goálás in the North-Western Provinces.

Chorál, a sept of Hos and Santáls.

Chorant, grass, a totemistic sept of Kharwars in Chota Nagpur.

Chorharuá, a section of Kurmis in Chota Nagpur and Orissa.

Chorka, a section of Binjhiás in Chota Nagpur.

Chorwar, a *mul* or section of the Kamar Kalla sub-caste of Sonárs in Behar.

Chota, a kind of bird, a totemistic sept of Mundas in Chota Nagpur.

Chota-Bhágiya or *Sunargáon Sánkhári*, a sub-caste of Sánkháris in Bengal.

Chotchain, a section of the Cháin sub-caste of Nunias in Behar.

Chouria, a sept of Lohárs in Chota Nagpur.

Chouria Musa, field-rat, a totemistic sept of Oraons in Chota Nagpur.

Chowniá, a totemistic sept of Goálás in Chota Nagpur who may not eat field-rats.

Chownr, a badge of office, a sept of Páns in Chota Nagpur.

Choyndai, a *thar* or sept of Chhatris in Nepal.

Chuár, a title of the Bhumij tribe.

Chuhrá, the lowest description of village servants, the same as the Bhangi, Halálkhor, Mehtar, etc.

Chuiráchhá, a *thar* or sept of Khambus in Darjiling.

Chukáni, an under-tenant in Rangpur and Jalpaiguri.

Chukuliyá, a sub-caste of Chásás in Orissa.

Chuliá, a salt boiler in Cuttack.

Chuliá-malangi, the head salt-maker in Orissa, who makes engagements with the Government.

Chumi, a section of Murmis; a *thar* or sept of Mangars in Darjiling.

Chunáru or *Chunári*, *Chunafarosh*, lime-burners, or workers in lime, as plasterers; a vendor of lime; also a synonym for Báiti, *q.v.*

Chundiar, a top-knot, a sept of Kharwars in Chota Nagpur.

Chungbang, a sept of Limbus in Darjiling.

Chungyepá, a *rui* or sept of Dejong Lhoris, the members of which are of a mixed low origin.

Chuniá, *Chuniyá*, a synonym for Báiti; a sub-caste of Jugis in Northern Bengal who deal in lime.

Chuniár, a sept of Kharwars in Chota Nagpur.

Chunihára, a title of Dohar Chamárs in Behar who burn lime.

Chunipárá, a title of Chamárs in Behar.

Churá-kuti, a sub-caste of Sutradhars in Dacca.

Churálai, a sub-caste of Kámárs in the Santál Parganas.

Churáliye, a section of Oswáls.

Churihár, *Churiwálá*, a maker of the glass bracelets worn by Mahomedan women. Churihárs are invariably Mahomedans, and the persons engaged in this occupation form an endogamous group.

Churihara, a title of Goálás.

Churuar, a sept of Lohárs in Chota Nagpur.

Chutiá, small rat, a totemistic sept of Mundas; a section of Binjhiás in Chota Nagpur.

Chutkádeswári, a sub-caste of Kharwárs who often call themselves Deswári. It is contradistinguished from Barká Deswári.

D

Dabgár, a subdivision of the Chamár or Muchi caste in Behar, who manufacture skin or leather vessels used for ghi and oil, country saddles, and the like.

Dabhauchwár, Dabhinchhwár, a *kul* or section of Bábhans in Behar.

Dabhreit, a *mul* or section of the Naomuliá or Majraut subcaste of Goálás in Behar.

Dadhi, a *gáin* of the Sábarna *gotra* of Bárendra Brahmans in Bengal.

Dadhichi, a *samáj* or local group of the Basishtha *gotra* of the Páschátya Baidik Brahmans in Bengal.

Dadhiyál, a *gáin* of the Bharadwája *gotra* of Bárendra Brahmans in Bengal.

Dadhpuriárk, a *pur* or section of Sákadwipi Brahmans in Behar.

Dadhraut, a *mul* or section of the Sátmuliá or Kishnaut subcaste of Goálás in Behar.

Dádukli, a *mul* or section of the Chhamuliá Madhesiá subcaste of Halwáis in Behar.

Dádul, bull-frog, a section of Binjhiás in Chota Nagpur.

Dafadár, a low class of Mahomedans in Eastern Bengal; also known as Nalwah from their using the *nal* grass to make baskets. They are said to be an offshoot of the Hajjam, but they claim a higher position than the parent stock by reason of their having adopted a different occupation. Hajjams eat with the Dafadárs, but the latter decline to deal with the Hajjam on terms of equality. No such class exists in Behar.

Dafáli, a class of Mahomedan weavers who sell trinkets, beads, etc., and also make drums.

Daftri, a book-binder; a servant who looks after stationery and the like in public offices.

Dágániá, a group of the Bárendra Goálás in Bengal.

Dágar, a section of Goálás in the North-Western Provinces.

Dágará, a sub-caste of Pátnis in Bengal.

Dághtá, those who brand cattle; generally Mahomedans.

Daginkairi, a sub-caste of Koiris who grow vegetables and fruits.

Dágri, a *pangat* or section of Bánsphor Doms in Behar.

Dáhá, a title of Dakshin-Rárhi and Bangaja Káyasths.

Dahait, a sept of Thárus in Behar.

Dahál, a section of Brahmans and Chhatris in the Eastern Himalayas.

Dahanga, torch-bearer, a sept of Mundas in Chota Nagpur.

Dáhárák, a *mul* or section of the Chhamuliá Madhesiá subcaste of Halwáis in Behar.

Dahiara, dealers in milk and curds, a sub-caste of Goálás in Behar, somewhat superior to ordinary Goálás. Their usual occupations are—service, shop-keeping, and agriculture.

Dahiet, a *mul* or section of the Naomuliá or Majraut sub-caste of Goálás in Behar.

Dah Láma, a *thar* or sept of Gurungs in Darjiling.

Dahmá, a section of Goálás in the North-Western Provinces and Behar.

Dái, a midwife, usually a Mahomedan or a Hindu of the Chamar caste. Among Hindus of all other castes there is a strong prejudice against cutting the navel cord, and a common term of abuse applied to a midwife is *narkátá* or cord-cutter. The male relatives of these women are usually tailors or musicians; while in villages they often work as weavers, and sometimes sell betel-leaves.

"In Dacca," says Dr. Wise, who had special opportunities for learning the truth on this subject, "the midwives are invariably ignorant and generally consequential, while, being few in number, they are very independent, extorting money in proportion to the anxieties of their patients. A midwife forms an important part of a household, and no family of note is without one. Like the Purohit and barber, the Dái is a privileged person, and has freedom of access to the female apartments at any hour. Her post is usually hereditary, but, if childless, the Dái adopts a young woman and educates her in the mysteries of the profession. Mahomedan ladies have no objection to be attended by a Hindu or Christian woman, but one of their own creed is preferred. The poorer classes attend on each other, and only in cases of difficulty is the European doctor, or the professional *accoucheuse*, called in. Parturition is in most instances easy, and the poor have seldom any need of skilled attendance; but among the listless inmates of zanánas, who never lead a healthy or invigorating life, labour is often tedious and exhausting.

"When a woman, either Hindu or Mahomedan, approaches the term of her pregnancy, an outhouse, or detached room, is prepared for her, to which, when labour begins, she retires with the Dái and a servant. This den, to which the highest as well as the lowest is condemned, is known as the *Asaucha-ghar*, or *Chhaṭhí-ghar*. The duty of the midwife is to rub and roll about the patient so as to increase the pains, and when the child is born to cut the cord with a piece of bamboo (tarlá-ka-chhalti), and to give immediate warning for the 'Azán,' or call to prayers.

"Of the mechanism of parturition, of the dangers to be avoided and provided against, midwives are profoundly ignorant; a woman being satisfied if she is attended by the family Dái, or by the pupil of the Dái, who aided her mother or sister under similar circumstances. Being obliged to observe many customs, without the due performance of which her own and her child's life would be endangered, the mother resigns herself to the hands of the midwife, assured that all will go well. To cause the uterus to contract they use an embrocation of the juice of the Nág-dauná leaf (*Artimisia vulgaris*) with spirit. When it is wished to stay the flow of milk, the dried bark of the Pání-kudú (*Cucurbita*) mixed with pease-meal (*Ervum hirsutum*) and rubbed up in water is used as a plaster.

"The midwife is expected to pay frequent visits until all danger has passed; but should the lady be rich, she is not allowed to leave the house for days. It devolves on her to anoint the infant daily, for in India babies are not bathed daily. Lampblack must be smeared along the eyelashes, and a mash of warm aromatics (ghuṭṭí) given daily. For two days after birth the mother is only allowed to take turmeric, molasses, and infusion of ajwain, while on the third and up to the fortieth day she may eat pulse (masúr) and rice.

"After the birth of a child many strange rites are performed. A bonfire (aláwa) is kept smouldering at the door of the Chhaṭhí-ghar for six days in the hot, for twenty-one in the cold season, and an oil lamp, placed within the room, must never be permitted to go out, an attendant being always on the watch to trim it, as darkness favours the entrance of evil spirits. A horse-shoe is placed beneath the bedding, as iron is most distasteful to all kinds of devils; and an earthen vessel, on which the name of God is written, is hung over the door. No one can leave the room before midday, and on no account must the baby's clothes be washed or dried anywhere but inside the room. If the husband or doctor has to visit the mother, his clothes are fumigated with the smoke of mustard seed thrown on the fire, and when the visitor leaves any food, milk, or drinking water standing in the room must be flung away. For six days the Hindu mother is confined in this den, her Muhammadan sister remaining for ten.

"On the sixth or Chhaṭhí day the barber and washerman are sent for; the former cutting the hair and paring the nails of the infant, the latter taking away the puerperal garments. It is from performing this menial work that the Dhobá belongs to a very unclean class.

"On the twenty-first or ikkísí day the barber and washerman again attend, when similar duties are discharged.

"On the fortieth day after the birth of a boy impurity ceases, as among the Jews, but several rites must be first of all performed. There is the "Kua-Jhánkna," or peeping into the well, which is identical with the worship of Subháchaní among Hindus, after which the mother resumes her household duties.

"If a child be stillborn, the mother is given an infusion of bamboo leaves in which a copper coin has been soaked. The draught is believed to decompose the poison which caused the death of the child. Should a woman give birth to several stillborn children in succession, the popular belief is that the same child reappears on each occasion, when, to frustrate the designs of the evil spirit that has taken possession of the child, the nose, or a portion of an ear, is cut off, and the body is cast away on a dunghill.

"Dáis have many secret remedies which they puff with unblushing assurance. Several are innocuous, a few useful, but in all cases they consist of so many and such heterogeneous substances that their action must be extremely doubtful. Their favourite remedy is called Mastúrí, or Battísá, from its being composed of thirty-two ingredients. Among other things it contains syrup, galls, litharge, sandal-wood, rock salt, and *gokhrú* (*Tribulus lanuginosus*), and is applied on balls of cotton soaked in Champá oil in all diseases peculiar to women."

Daibak, *Daibajna*, *Diwak*, *Daivajna*, an astrologer, calculator of nativities, almanac-maker, etc. He is usually an Achárji Brahman, and the name is therefore used as a synonym for Achárji.

Daibaki, a section of the Mahmudábáz sub-caste of Nápits in Murshedabad.

Dai-Dom, a sub-caste of Doms in Bengal whose men are day-labourers and women serve as midwives.

Dáikurar, a title of Muchis whose women practise midwifery.

Dáiná Ráju or **Chauán**, a sub-caste of Rájus in Midnapur, who derive their name from their women fastening their *sáris* on the right side.

Dáji, a *thar* or section of Nepáli Brahmans.

Dakhiná or *Turi*, a sub-caste of Doms in Behar.

Dakhinhá, a sub-caste of Láheris in Behar.

Dakhini, a sub-caste of Bhandáris in Orissa and of Telis in Chota Nagpur.

Dakhin-Kabát, south gate, a title of Khandáits in Orissa.

Dakhin-Rárhi, a sub-caste of Kámárs in the 24-Parganas; a sub-caste of Nápits; a group of the Barábhágiyá Muchis.

Dakráhi, a *pur* or section of Sákadwipi Brahmans in Behar.

Dákshinátya, an endogamous division of the Vaidik sub-caste of Brahmans in Bengal.

Dakshiná Uriyá, **Dakhinatya**, a sub-caste of Utkal Brahmans in Orissa.

Dakshini, a sub-caste of Kaibarttas in Murshedabad.

Dakshin-Rárhi, a group of the Hele Kaibarttas in Central Bengal; a sub-caste of Chásádhobás and Káyasths in Bengal.

Dákutiá, a sub-caste of the Kraunchdwipi Brahmans in Behar.

Dalai, a title of Kewats in Orissa.

Dalai or **Tiar**, a group of the Rájbansi sub-caste of Kochhs in Northern Bengal.

Dalál, broker, a title of Jugis and Tántis in Bengal.

Dálihará, a title of the castes who sell *dál* or pulses.

Dalihare, *Dullihará*, a section of Bábhans in Behar.

Dalui, a title of Karangás.

Dám, a title of Bangaja and Bárendra Káyasths in Bengal.

Damarwár, a sept of the Chandrabansi division of Rajputs in Behar.

Dámboriá, a section of Goálás in the North-Western Provinces and Behar.

Damdariá, a section of Kanaujiá Lohárs in Behar.

Dámi, *Damyi*, *Támi*, *Kotwál*, *Nágarchi*, *Darzi*, a Nepalese caste, by occupation tailors.

Damma Pariwár, a *thar* or sept of Dámis in Darjiling whose chief profession is sewing.

Dámu, a sub-section of the Levátiá section of Majraut Goálás in Behar.

Dán, a title of Káyasths, Mayarás, Gandhabaniks, and Subarnabaniks in Bengal.

Dáná, a title of Dakshin-Rárhi and Bangaja Káyasths.

Dandamáli, a title of Brahmans.

Dandá Mánjhi, a sub-caste of Lohárs and Bágdis in Western Bengal.

Dandapat, a section of Utkal or Orissa Bráhmans.

Dandapátdhári, *Dandapát*, a title of Suvarnabaniks in Bengal.

Dánd-Binjhiá, a sub-tribe of Binjhiás, so called from living in the plains.

Dandi, a religious group of Jugis; a staff-bearer, an order of Saivite religious mendicants said to have been founded in Malabar by Sankara Ácharya in the eighth or ninth century. See **Dasnámi.**

Dandiá, a title of Binjhiás in Chota Nagpur.

Dand-Korwa, a sub-tribe of Korwas in Chota Nagpur.

Dandpati, a section of Páns in Chota Nagpur.

Dándwar, a section of Bábhans; a sept of the Suryabansi sub-tribe of Rajputs in Behar.

Dáng, big stick, a totemistic sept of Mundas in Chota Nagpur.

Dángar, a sept of the Chandrabansi division of Rájputs in Behar.

Dangarwar, a sept of Mundas in Chota Nagpur.

Dángbe, a sub-caste of Koiris in Behar.

Dangwariá, a sept of the Rautár sub-tribe of Thárus in Behar.

Danjál, a *thar* or section of Nepáli Brahmans.

Danrehá or *Gaunhá*, a sept of the Rautár sub-tribe of Thárus in Behar.

Dánri, a title of Bangaja Káyasths.

Dánrsuriá, a section of Sonárs in Behar.

Dántela, a sub-sept of the Hemrom and Tudu septs of Santáls, said to be so called from their breeding pigs with very large tusks for sacrificial purposes.

Dántrái, a group of the Karaléi sub-caste of Kaibarttas in Noakháli.

Danwar, *Danuar*, a cultivating caste of the Nepal Terai.

Dáosri, a section of Agarwáls.

Daraha, a grain-splitter—an occupation followed by women of the labouring castes in Behar.

Darang, a *dugu* or section of the Kochh-Mandai in Dacca. The name indicates the original habitat of the group, probably a hill or village in Assam, and at the present day has no bearing upon marriage.

Darang-Chiachi, a section of the Kochh-Mandai in Dacca.

Darang-Saudana, a section of the Kochh-Mandai in Dacca.

Darang-Dakal, a section of the Kochh-Mandai in Dacca.

Darang-Dambak, a section of the Kochh-Mandai in Dacca.

Darátiá, a sub-caste of Bágdis found in Nadiya.

Darbe, a section of the Banapár sub-caste of Koiris; a *pangat* or section of Bánsphor Doms and of Dosádhs in Behar; a section of the Kádar caste in Behar which intermarries with all the other sections except the **Marik** and Báre.

Darchuá, a sub-caste of Sunris in Behar who distil and sell country spirits. By reason of their occupation they hold an inferior social position to the Biyáhut and Sagáhut Sunris, who are grain-dealers and shopkeepers.

Dárhibárhi, a *mul* or section of the Chhamuliá Madhesiá sub-caste of Halwáis in Behar.

Dariápár, *Dhariápár*, a *mul* or section of the Chhamuliá Madhesiá sub-caste of Halwáis in Behar.

Darihare, probably a variant of Dalihare; a section of Bábhans in Behar.

Darihare-Dih, a *mul* of the Kásyap section of Maithil Brahmans in Behar.

Darihare-Rájanpurá, a *mul* of the Kásyap section of Maithil Brahmans in Behar.

Darihare-Bargamiá, a *mul* of the Kásyap section of Maithil Brahmans in Behar.

Darihare-Ratauli, a *mul* of the Kásyap section of Maithil Brahmans in Behar.

Darihare-Sahasrám, a *mul* of the Kásyap section of Maithil Bráhmans in Behar.

Darjea, a sept of Chakmás in the Hill Tracts of Chittagong.

Darka, a sept of Chiks in Chota Nagpur who are said to have been born out of a rent in the earth.

Dárkhuriá, a *mul* or section of the Ghosin sub-caste of Goálás in Behar.

Darnal, a *thar* or sept of Dámis in Darjiling whose first ancestor is said to have sprung from a Brahman by a Dámi wife; a sept of Mangars.

Darnál, a section of Kámis in Darjiling.

Darrá Lámi, a *thar* or sept of Mangars in Darjiling.

Darshan, a title of Muchis in Bengal.

Darsuriá, a section of Lohárs in Behar.

Daryesh, a Mahomedan religious mendicant. The term is also incorrectly applied to Hindi ascetics. In the case of Mahomedans it includes the following classes—(1) Chishtia, (2) Kádiriá, (3) Nakshbandi, (4) Rafá'i, (5) Madáriá.

Darwán, a door-keeper. In Calcutta this post is usually held by up-country Brahmans and Rajputs.

Darzi, a tailor. Usually tailors are Mahomedans, but Dhobis and Ghulám Káyasths have been known to take up the business. A synonym for the Dámi tribe in Darjiling.

Dás, Jalwah Kaibartta, a sub-caste of Kewats in Western Bengal, and of Kaibarttas in Dacca.

Dás, a family title of Siddha Baidyas; of Halwáis and the Kathbaniá sub-caste of Baniás in Behar; a title of Káyasths and all Sudras of the Navasákh group in Bengal, also assumed by members of non-Aryan castes in

Bengal like the Kochhs, who become Vaishnavas with a view to be considered Hindus; a title of the Oswál Baniyás; a sept of Thárus; a section of Utkal or Orissa Brahmans and Karans; a title of Kaibarttas and Sunris in Bengal.

Dasá, an endogamous sub-caste of Agarwáls, Mahesris and Oswáls.

Dásabigha, a section of Páns in Chota Nagpur.

Dasáonth, a section of Barhis in Behar.

Dasarath Ghataki, a *mel* or hypergamous sub-group of Rárhi Brahmans in Bengal.

Dasásai, a sub-caste of Suklis in Midnapur.

Dasaundhi, a title of Bháts or genealogists. They also call themselves Rájbhát.

Dasbiha, a sept of Páns, in Chota Nagpur.

Das-ghariá, a group of the Bar-gohri sub-caste of Khandáits in Saranda of Singbhum.

Das-Gurung or **Chár Gotra**, a sub-tribe of Gurungs in Darjiling.

Dási, a maid-servant.

Dasika, a *dugu* or section of the Kochh-Mandai in Dacca. The name indicates the original habitat of the group, probably a hill or village in Assam, and at the present day has no bearing upon marriage.

Dásil, a *mul* or section of the Goriá sub-caste of Goálás in Behar.

Daskariá, wild fowl, a totemistic sept of Páns in Chota Nagpur.

Das Limbu, a synonym for Limbu, referring to the ten divisions of the tribe.

Dasnámi, the collective name of ten classes of Saivite religious mendicants, followers of Sankara Ácharya, each of which bears a peculiar name, as Tirtha, Asrama, Saraswati, Vana, Bharati, Áranya, Giri or Gir, Parvata, Puri, and Ságara which is added to the proper names of the members. According to Professor H. H. Wilson only the first three, and part of Bhárati, are now considered pure Dandis or bearers of the mendicant staff; the others are of a more secular character, and are usually called *Atits*.

Dáspárá, **Dáspáriá**, a sub-caste of Kumhárs and Telis in Bengal.

Daspuria, a section of Ghásis in Chota Nagpur.

Dastá-dár, an honorary title of Káyasths in Bengal.

Dastarband or **Pagriband**, a turban-maker, a purely Mahomedan trade, never engaged in by Hindus.

Dast-farosh, an old-clothesman, collecting old clothes and rags, which he sells to the naichaband to make hookah snakes; to the masalchi for torches; and to the jildgar for binding books.

Daswáni, a title of Bháts in Behar.

Dásya, a section of Bágdis in Bengal.

Datiyán, a section of Maghayá Kándus in Behar.

Datkiliár, a section of the Amashta Káyasths in Behar.

Datt, a *thar* or sept of Mangars in Darjiling.

Datta, a family title of Sádhya Baidyas, Káyasths, Mayarás, Sánkháris, Támbulis; of Baruis, of the Áut sub-caste of Gandhabaniks, Tántis, Sutradhars, and of Subarnabaniks in Bengal. Intermarriage is prohibited within the title.

Datta ke ráut, a section of the Biyáhut and Kharidáhá Kalwárs in Behar.

Dattamánjhi, a title of Kaibarttas in Bengal.

Dáturiá, a sub-caste of Sutradhars in Noakháli.

Daubárik, messenger or sentinel, a title of Khandáits in Orissa.

Daulbandh, a sub-tribe of Kharwárs in Palámau.

Daultá ke ráut, a section of the Biyáhut and Kharidáhá Kalwárs in Behar.

Dauru, a sept of Mundas in Chota Nagpur.

Dauwá, a sept of Dhimáls in the Darjiling Terai.

Dawári, a *thar* of the Basishtha *gotra* of Nepáli Brahmans.

Dawin, a sept of Chakmás in the Hill Tracts of Chittagong.

Dáyi, a *gáin* of the Sábarna *gotra* of Rárhi Brahmans in Bengal.

Dáymia, a group of the Sanadhya sub-caste of Gaura Brahmans.

De, a family name of Káyasths in Bengal; of the Áut sub-caste of Gandhabaniks; of Kámárs, Mayarás, Támbulis, Tantis, Telis, and Subarnabaniks in Bengal. Intermarriage is prohibited within the title.

Deási, a synonym for Lohár Mánjhi, *q.v.*

Deb, a family title of Sádhya Baidyas and of Bangaja and Bárendra Káyasths in Bengal.

Debangsi, a title of up-country and Uriya Brahmans.

Debansi, a sub-tribe of Rajputs in Chota Nagpur, to which the Rájás of Bishanpur, in Bankura, profess to belong.

Debánsi, a class of Tiyars who are fishermen.

Debkuliár, a *pur* or section of Sákadwipi Brahmans in Behar.

Debrishi, a section of Mayarás in Bengal.

Dedhgawe, a section of Káyasths in Behar.

Dehádbenáras, a *mul* or section of the Chhamuliá Madhesiá sub-caste of Halwáis in Behar.

Deháti, a *mel* or hypergamous sub-group of Rárhi Brahmans in Bengal.

Deháti Baidya, village doctor, a title of Baidyas used by outsiders.

Dehlásariár, a *pur* or section of Sákadwipi Brahmans in Behar.

Dehri, a section of Koránch Kándus in Behar.

Dehriti, priests, a sept of Mal Pahariás in the Santál Parganas.

Dehuri, a title of Sudhás in Orissa.

Dejong Lhori, Dejongpa (people of the fruit-district or

Sikkim); Lhopá Bhotia (Tibetans of the south), the common designation of the Tibetans who are settled in Sikkim. A list of their sub-tribes and septs will be found in Appendix I.

Demta, red tree-ant, a totemistic sept of Goálás, Khariás, Lohárs, Mundas, Páns, and Kharwars in Chota Nagpur.

Denrgamiá, a section of Awadhiá Hajáms in Behar.

Deo, a title of Báruis in Bengal.

Deobansi, a sub-caste of Mauliks in Chota Nagpur.

Deodhiár, a *pur* or section of Sákadwipi Brahmans in Behar.

Deoghát, a *mul* or section of the Chhamuliá Madhesiá sub-caste of Halwáis in Behar.

Deohar, a title of inoculators for small-pox, now applied to vaccinators in Behar.

Deorahir, a *pur* or section of Sákadwipi Brahmans in Behar.

Deori, a title of Sunris in Bengal.

Deradár, a title of Kewats in Behar.

Derhgáon, a *mul* or section of the Ayodhiá sub-caste of Hajjáms in Behar.

Desá-Asram, a sub-caste of Gandhabaniks in Bengal.

Desauri, a title of Kandhs in Orissa.

Deseriet, a *mul* or section of the Sátmuliá or Kishnaut sub-caste of Goálás in Behar.

Desi, a sub-caste of Kumhárs, Telis, and of Kaibarttas in Behar; a group of the Rájbansi sub-caste of Kochhs in Northern Bengal; of Goálás in the North-Western Provinces; a sub-caste of Bhandáris in Orissa, and of Bhumijs in Chota Nagpur.

Desjá, a *thar* or section of Nepáli Brahmans.

Deslá, a sub-caste of Telis in Bengal.

Desoar, a section of Ghásis in Chota Nagpur.

Deswál, a section of Goálás in the North-Western Provinces and Behar.

Deswáli, a sub-tribe of Santáls in the south of Manbhum who employ Brahmans and have adopted portions of the Hindu ritual.

Deswáli, *Deswari*, a title of natives of Upper India who settle in Bengal.

Deswár, a sub-caste of Kalwárs in Behar and of Máls in the Santál Parganas; a section of the Sakhiná and Turi Doms in Behar who perform their domestic worship outside of the *angan* or courtyard of their houses.

Deswári-Kharwár, a sub-tribe of Kharwárs in Chota Nagpur.

Deuli, a *gain* of the Bátsya *gotra* of Bárendra Brahmans in Bengal.

Deuri, a title of Kumhárs in Behar.

Devakotya, a *thar* or section of Nepáli Brahmans.

Devápáthi, a section of Kámis and a *thar* or sept of Mangars in Darjiling.

Deva-Sarmá, a synonym for Brahman.

Dewán, a section of the Yakha caste; originally a title conferred by the Nepal Raj.

Dewán ke asámi, a section of the Banodhiá and Jaiswár Kalwárs in Behar.

Dewárk, a *pur* or section of Sákadwipi Brahmans in Behar.

Dhabal, a title of Telis in Bengal.

Dhabalrishi, a section of Chásádhobás in Bengal.

Dhabhinchhwár, *Dabhauchwar*, a section of Bábhans.

Dhái, *Dái*, a nurse, wet-nurse, or midwife. See Dái.

Dhaiá, a section of Goálás in the North-Western Provinces.

Dháin, a *gáin* or sub-section of Saptasati Brahmans in Bengal.

Dhákáes, a *mul* or section of the Tinmuliá and Chhamuliá Madhesiá and Bhojpuria sub-castes of Halwáis in Behar.

Dhákái, a sub-caste of Kámárs in Eastern Bengal.

Dhákáich, a section of the Biyáhut and Kharidáhá Kalwárs in Behar.

Dhakaichhá, a section of Sonárs in Behar.

Dhákáis, a *mul* or section of the Naomuliá or Goriá sub-caste of Goálás in Behar.

Dhakait, a section of Bábhans and of Madhesiá Halwáis in Behar.

Dhákal, a *thar* of the Upamanya *gotra* of Nepáli Brahmans.

Dhakania, a section of Kanaujiá Lohárs in Behar.

Dhakaren, a *thar* or sept of Gurungs in Darjiling.

Dhákáwál, a sub-caste of Kámárs in Murshedabad.

Dháki, a beater of the *dhâk* or large drum; a title of the Báiti and Muchi, the only castes which use this kind of drum.

Dháli, an honorary title of Káyasths and Goálás in Bengal; of Kawális in Eastern Bengal.

Dhaliá, a sub-caste of Máls in Bankura.

Dhalo, a sub-caste of Korás in Western Bengal.

Dhaluá, a sub-caste of Karangás.

Dhamala, a *thar* or sept of Mangars in Darjiling.

Dháman, a *mul* or section of the Naomuliá or Majraut sub-caste of Goálás in Behar.

Dhamaniá, a class of professional beggars in Chota Nagpur who eat dead animals and snakes.

Dhamdi, a section of Kaibarttas in Orissa.

Dhami, a section of the Goria sub-caste of Goálás in Behar whose title is Mandar.

Dhámin, *Dhámi*, a low, probably non-Aryan, caste in Darbhanga, who make fans or brushes (*morchhal*) of peacock's feathers. In Gya the Dhámins officiate as priests to pilgrims in the ceremonies performed for the benefit of ancestors on the Rámsila and Pretsila hills, immediately above the town. They pretend to be a sort of Brahmans, but their social position is low, and orthodox Hindus will not take water from their hands.

Dhámna Sáp, a section of Ghásis in Chota Nagpur.

Dhán, paddy or rice soup, a totemistic sept of Chiks, Korwas, Lohárs, and Oraons; a sept of Mundas who are forbidden to take rice and rice soup, and eat only *gondli;* a section of Khariás; a sept of Rajputs in Behar.

Dhanái Mandal, a family name of the Grihasth group of Jugis in Bengal.

Dhánautá, a *mul* or section of the Tinmuliá Madhesiá sub-caste of Halwáis in Behar.

Dhandh, plum bushes, a totemistic sept of Chiks in Chota Nagpur.

Dhandhábe, a section of the Bahánnajáti sub-caste of Khatris in Bengal.

Dhánej, a *mul* or section of the Chhamuliá Madhesiá sub-caste of Halwáis in Behar.

Dhánesri, a section of Pods in Bengal.

Dhaneswar, a *mul* or section of the Tinmuliá Madhesiá sub-caste of Halwáis in Behar.

Dhángar, in Chota Nagpur Proper an agricultural labourer, usually non-Aryan, engaged by the year, who receives, if hired by a native, a lump sum varying from Rs. 4 to Rs. 6, at the time of hiring, besides monthly wages in grain and a cloth at the end of the year. Labourers of this class are also largely employed by European tea-planters on the Lohardagá plateau. In this case they get Rs. 9 on engagement, and Rs. 9 more in three instalments, besides a blanket and an umbrella. On the origin of the term there has been some discussion. "It is," writes Colonel Dalton, "a word that from its apparent derivation (*dáng* or *dháng*, 'a hill') may mean any hillman; but amongst several tribes of the Southern Tributary Mahâls the terms *Dhángar* and *Dhángarin* mean the youth of the two sexes both in highland and lowland villages, and it cannot be considered as the national designation of any particular tribe." So Mr. Oldham says in a note on *Some Historical and Ethical Aspects of the Burdwan district* that the Male Paharias call their men of fighting age Dhángar or Dhángaria. The Malé are cognates of the Oraons, the typical Dhangar labourers of Chota Nagpur, so that on this showing the word may well be nothing more than the Oraon for an adult. According to another interpretation, the name has reference to the fact that persons working as *dhángars* receive the bulk of their wages in *dhán*, or unhusked rice. *Rabi* or cold weather crops are not largely grown in Chota Nagpur Proper; and during the slack season, from December to the end of March, large numbers of Dhángars leave their own country in search of agricultural work in the central and eastern districts of Bengal, where the harvesting of the winter rice creates a great demand for labour. The *dhángar* system of payment is so general in Chota Nagpur that the term is virtually synonymous with labourer, and these nomadic labourers describe themselves, and are known throughout Bengal, as 'Dhángars.' When they settle, as they frequently do, they acquire the name of *Buna*, which is sometimes prefixed to their tribal name, thus Buna-Oraon, Buna-Munda.

Dhanichhwár, a section of Bábhans in Behar.

Dhánjaya, a *gotra* or section of Nepáli Brahmans.

Dhankai, Dhankoi, a *mul* or section of the Naiyá caste in Behar.

Dhanka-Oraon, a sub-tribe of Oraons in Chota Nagpur.

Dhankháriá, a section of the Biyáhut and Kharidahá Kalwárs in Behar.

Dhanki, a sept of Nágeswars in Chota Nagpur.

Dhanroár, a sub-caste of Goálás in Behar.

Dhanu, a title of Dakshin-Rárhi and Bangaja Káyasths; a section of Kishnaut Goálás in Behar.

Dhanuár, a section of Khariás in Chota Nagpur.

Dhánuk, one of the seven subdivisions of the Kurmis, who are supposed to have been archers, but are now employed in personal service and agriculture.

Dhánuk, a cultivating caste of Behar, many of whom are employed as personal servants in the households of members of the higher castes. Their origin is obscure. Buchanan considered them a "pure agricultural tribe, who, from their name, implying archers, were probably in former times the militia of the country, and are perhaps not essentially different from the Kurmis; for any Yasawár (Jaiswár) Kurmi who from poverty sells himself or his children is admitted among the Dhánuks. All the Dhánuks at one time were probably slaves, and many have been purchased to fill up the military ranks—a method of recruiting that has been long prevalent in Asia, the armies of the Parthians having been composed almost entirely of slaves; and the custom is still, I believe, pretty general among the Turks. A great many of the Dhánuks are still slaves, but some annually procure their liberty by the inability of their masters to maintain them, and by their unwillingness to sell their fellow-creatures." According to the Padma Purána quoted by Sir Henry Elliot, Dhánuks are descended from a Chamár and a female Chandál. Another equally mythical pedigree makes the mother a Chamár and the father an outcast Ahir. Such statements, however slight their historical value, serve to indicate in a general way the social rank held by the Dhánuks at the time when it was first thought necessary to enrol them among the mixed castes. In this point of view the degraded parentage assigned to the caste lends some support to the conjecture that they may be an offshoot from one of the non-Aryan tribes.

Traditions of origin.

Dhánuks are divided into the following sub-castes:—**Chhilatiá** or **Silhotiá, Magahyá, Tirhutiá** or **Chiraut, Jaiswar, Kanaujiá, Khapariyá, Dudhwár** or **Dojwár, Sunri-Dhánuk,** and **Kathautiá.** Sir Henry Elliot, writing of the Dhánuks of the North-West Provinces, gives a slightly different list, which will be found in Appendix I. Buchanan mentions Jaiswár, Magahyá, Dojwár, and Chhilatiyá. Little is known regarding the origin of any of the sub-castes. Magahyá, Tirhutiá, Kanaujiá, are common territorial names used by many castes to denote sub-castes who reside in, or are supposed to have emigrated from, particular tracts of country. The Dudhwár or Dojwár sub-caste pride themselves upon not castrating bull-calves.

Internal structure.

The **Sunri-Dhánuk** are said to have been separated from the rest of the caste by reason of their taking service with members of the despised Sunri and Teli castes. According to some authorities the Chhilatia sub-caste is also known by the name of Jaiswár-Kurmi, a fact which to some extent bears out Buchanan's suggestion that there may be some connexion between the Dhánuk and Kurmi—castes. Speculations based upon resemblances of names are, however, apt to be misleading, and I can find no independent evidence to show that the Dhánuks are a branch of the Kurmis, or, which is equally possible, that the Jaiswár sub-caste of the Kurmis derive their origin from the Dhánuks. It is curious that the distinction between personal service and cultivation, which has led to the formation of sub-castes among the Gangotá, Amát, and Kewat, should not have produced the same effect in the case of the Dhánuks. Throughout Behar, indeed, full expression is given to these differences of occupation in the titles borne by those who follow the one or the other mode of life; but it is only in Purniah that they form an impassable barrier to intermarriage between the **Khawásiá** sub-caste, who are employed as domestic servants, and the **Gharbait** and **Mandal**, who confine themselves to agriculture.

The sections of the caste are shown in Appendix I. They are comparatively few in number, and their influence on marriage seems to be gradually dying out, its place being taken by the more modern system of counting prohibited degrees. For this purpose the standard formula *mamerá*, *chacherá*, etc., is in use, the prohibition extending to seven generations in the descending line.

Marriage.

Both infant and adult-marriage are recognised by the Dhánuk caste, but the former practice is deemed the more respectable, and all who can afford to do so endeavour to get their daughters married before they attain the age of puberty. The marriage ceremony differs little from that in vogue among other Behar castes of similar social standing. In the matter of polygamy their custom seems to vary in different parts of the country. In Behar it is usually held that a man may not take a second wife unless the first is barren or suffers from an incurable disease; but in Purniah no such restrictions seem to exist, and a man may have as many wives as he can afford to maintain. A widow may marry again by the *sagai* or *chumauná* form, in which Brahmans take no part; and the union of the couple is completed by the bridegroom smearing red lead with his left hand on the forehead of the bride. In Purniah the deceased husband's younger brother or cousin, should such a relative exist, is considered to have a preferential claim to marry the widow; but elsewhere less stress is laid on this condition, and a widow is free to marry whom she pleases, provided that she does not infringe the prohibited degrees. Divorce is not recognised in Behar, but the Dhánuks of the Santál Parganas, following apparently the example of the aboriginal races, permit a husband to divorce an unchaste wife by making a formal declaration before the pancháyat of his intention to cast her off, and tearing a leaf in two to symbolise and record the separation. The proceedings conclude with a feast to all the relations, the idea of which appears to be that by thus entertaining his family the husband frees himself from the stain of having lived with a disreputable woman. Women so divorced may marry again, provided that their favours have been bestowed solely on members of the caste. Indiscretions outside that circle are punished by immediate expulsion, and cannot be atoned for by any form of penance except in the unusual case of a Dhánuk woman living with a man of notably higher caste.

Religion.

The religion of the Dhánuks presents no features of special interest. They worship the regular Hindu gods, and employ as their priests Maithil Brahmans, who are received on equal terms by other members of the sacred order. Among their minor gods we find Bandi, Goraiyá, Mahábir, Rám Thákur, Gahil, Dharm Ráj, and Sokha Sindabás. The last appears to be the spirit of some departed sorcerer. Dhánuks are also much given to the worship of the sun, to whom flowers, rice, betel-leaves, cloves, cardamoms, molasses, together with money and even clothes, are offered on Sundays during the months of Baisákh and Aghan. The offerings are taken by the caste Brahman or the Máli. The dead are burned, and the *sráddh* ceremony is performed on the thirteenth day after death. In the case of persons who die from snake-bite, their relatives offer milk and fried rice (*láwá*) to snakes on the Nágpanchami day in the month of Sráwan.

Social status and occupation.

Notwithstanding the degraded parentage assigned to them by tradition, and the probability that they are really of non-Aryan descent, the social position of Dhánuks at the present day is quite respectable. They rank with Kurmis and Koiris, and Brahmans will take water from their hands. They themselves will eat cooked food, drink and smoke with the Kurmi, Amát, and Kewat; and Bahiot Dhánuks will eat the leavings of Brahmans, Rajputs, and Káyasths in whose houses they are employed. Personal service, including palanquin-bearing and agriculture, are their chief occupations, and in some parts of the country they are engaged in the cultivation of hemp and the manufacture of string, whence they derive the title Sankatwár. Most of them are occupancy or non-occupancy raiyats, and the poorer members of the caste earn their living as agricultural day-labourers.

The following statement shows the number and distribution of Dhánuks in 1872 and 1881 :—

District.	1872.	1881.	District.	1872.	1881.
Bardwan	150	2	Maimansinh	172	16
Bankura	17	181	Chittagong	......	1
Birbhum	772	43	Patna	25,038	36,530
Midnapur	26	......	Gya	5,847	4,179
Hughli	162 (Hughli and Howrah, bracketed)	......	Shahabad	1,781	1,699
Howrah		18	Tirhut: Darbhanga ...	182,175 (Darbhanga and Mozufferpur, bracketed)	190,216
24-Parganas	181	63	Tirhut: Mozufferpur		52,773
Nadiya	308	......	Saran	15,516	17,868
Murshedabad	4,4[illegible]7	4,802	Champaran	9,906	15,235
Dinajpur	184	111	Monghyr	113,524	119,559
Rajshahye	54	......	Bhagalpur	98,597	161,606
Rangpur	2	7	Purniah	39,762	26,192
Bogra	3	......	Maldah	7,805	5,044
Pabna	199	2	Santal Parganas ...	12,429	12,388
Darjiling	19	11	Hazaribagh	620	1,326
Jalpigori	13	......	Lohardaga	2,107	1,872
Kuch Behar	......	11	Manbhum	124	24
Faridpur	191	13	Tributary States ...	......	1,566
Bakarganj	213	......			

Dhanuki, a sub-caste of Doms in Eastern Bengal who use bows and arrows to kill game; a *thar* or sept of Mangars in Darjiling.

Dhanutá, a section of Madhesiá Kándus in Behar.

Dhanwantari, a *gotra* or section of the Baidya caste in Bengal.

Dhaona, a sept of Chakmás in the Hill Tracts of Chittagong.

Dhaprá, a sub-caste of sweeper Doms in Behar who reverence one Syám Singh, an ancestral hero in process of conversion into a god.

Dhar, a family title of Sádhya Baidyas; of the Kut sub-caste of Gandhabaniks; of Sánkháris; of Dakshin-Rárhi and Bárendra Káyasths; and of Subarnabaniks in Bengal. Intermarriage is prohibited within the title.

Dhár, a sub-caste of Koiris in Behar.

Dhár or *Dhári*, a sub-caste of Dosádhs in Behar.

Dhárá, a title of Bágdis in Bengal.

Dharádhari, a *mel* or hypergamous sub-group of Rárhi Brahmans in Bengal.

Dharamdási, a sub-caste of Khatiks in Behar.

Dharampuriá, a *mul* or section of the Naomuliá or Majraut sub-caste of Goálás in Behar.

Dharan, a section of Bábhans in Behar.

Dharani, a title of Dakshin-Rárhi and Bangaja Káyasths.

Dháráni, a section of Bábhans in Western Bengal.

Dhardhar, a *gáin* or sub-section of Saptasati Brahmans in Bengal.

Dháren, a *thar* or sept of Gurungs in Darjiling.

Dhárh, a sub-caste of Chamárs in Behar.

Dhári, *Dári*, a class of Mahomedan musicians, generally women, who play, sing, and dance, and are regarded by connoisseurs in such matters as superior to the Mirasan. The men do no work, and live on their wives' earnings. This, however, is perhaps a recent development resulting from their conversion to Islam, for when Buchanan wrote he found the Dhári in Behar employed in digging tanks and ditches, and collecting firewood. They ate pork and worshipped Bandi and Rám Thákur.

Dháriwár, a section of Oswáls in Behar.

Dharkár, a sub-caste of Doms in Behar who make cane baskets, winnowing-fans, etc., and keep and sell pigs.

Dhárkia, a section of Bhojpuriá Halwáis in Behar.

Dharkiliár, a section of the Amashta Káyasths in Behar.

Dharmaghare, a religious group of Jugis in Bengal.

Dharmáhu, a section of Awadhiá Hajáms in Behar.

Dharmapandit, a title of Telis, Jugis, and Doms in Bengal, who officiate as priests in the religious ceremonies of their caste and of the rural god Dharma, who is said, in a Bengali Purána dedicated to him, to be an avatar of Vishnu, Dharma, represented by a square stone with human features roughly carved upon it, is particularly worshipped by women, and is believed to cause and cure skin diseases. Brahmans will not worship him.

Dharm-ásram or *Dharm-Sut*, a sub-caste of Mayarás in Central Bengal.

Dhároá, *Dhárua*, a sub-caste of Gonds, usually employed in washing gold from the sands of the rivers in Chota Nagpur.

Dhartá-Kausik, a *gotra* or section of Nepáli Brahmans.

Dharwár, a *kul* or section of Bábhans in Behar.

Dhaul, a sept of Rajputs in Behar.

Dhaundriá, a section of Sonárs in Behar.

Dhauráni, a section of Bábhans in Behar.

Dhausáni, a section of Bábhans in Behar.

Dhawá, a class of Mahomedan palanquin-bearers and fishmongers in Bengal.

Dhawan, a section of the Chhajáti sub-caste of Khatris in Bengal.

Dháyat, a title of Kanaujiá Brahmans.

Dhechuá, a black bird, a totemistic sept of Bedias, Oraons and Mundas in Chota Nagpur.

Dhek, a section of the Banwár sub-caste of Baniyás in Behar.

Dhekhá, a sept of Rajputs in Behar.

Dhelakata, a tree, at totemistic sept of Mundas in Chota Nagpur.

Dhelki, a section of Khariás in Chota Nagpur.

Dhelphor, 'clod-breaker,' a title of Koiris in Behar which is supposed to have reference to their skill and thoroughness in cultivation.

Dhemá, a *mul* or section of the Chhamuliá Madhesiá sub-caste of Halwáis in Behar.

Dhemál, a synonym for Dhimál.

Dhengar, a sub-caste of Gareris in Behar.

Dhenu, a section of Goriá Goálás in Behar.

Dhenuár, a small Dravidian caste of Chota Nagpur, whose totemistic sections seem to indicate a possible kinship with the Mundas. Very little is known of their customs, and their numbers are scanty.

Dhesiá Dháṛál or *Tapaspuriá*, a sub-caste of Doms in Bengal who remove dead bodies, etc.

Dhibar, a sub-caste of Kewats in Western Bengal, and a synonym for Kaibartha.

Dhilki, a section of Mahilis in Chota Nagpur.

Dhilki-Khariá, a sub-caste of Khariás in Chota Nagpur.

Dhimál, *Dhemál, Maulik*, a non-Aryan tribe of the Darjiling and Nepal Terai, classed by Fr. Müller as Lohitic. They belong to the same main stock as the Kochh, whom they resemble closely in features and complexion; and, like them, are rapidly losing their tribal identity by absorption into the large and heterogeneous Rájbansi caste. Rájbansis, who pretend to be Kshatriyas, strenuously deny that any such process is going on, but a shrewd observer[1] of social changes assures me that "any Dhimál can become a Rájbansi at any time if he is only prosperous enough," and instances are known in which a fee of Rs. 600 has been paid for this privilege. Formal promotions of this sort are, however, exceptional, and the average Dhimál who aspires to social elevation transforms himself into a Rájbansi by simply assuming that title. To this movement rather than to any lack of vitality in the race we may attribute the fact that, while in 1847 Hodgson[2] estimated the number of the Dhimáls at 15,000, no recent census[3] shows any approach to this figure, and they seem likely to disappear altogether as a separate tribe within the next generation. Already, indeed, they affect a dislike for the tribal name Dhimál, which is now used only by outsiders, and prefer to call themselves by the modern title of Maulik. They have no traditions of their own, and look upon themselves as the original inhabitants of the tract of country where they are now settled. The scanty legends current among other races regarding their origin are noticed in the article on the Mech tribe, with whom the Dhimál are associated by the Nepalese dwellers in the Terai.

Origin.

The Dhimál are divided into three classes—**Agniá, Láter,** and **Dungiá**—the members of which are not absolutely debarred from intermarriage, though the Agniá Dhimáls deem themselves superior to the other two classes, and as a rule marry within their own group. Marriages also occasionally take place between Dhimáls and Rájbansis of either sex, but in such cases the Rájbansis usually have to abandon their own caste and enrol themselves in the Dhimál community, giving a feast to the *panchâyat* by way of entrance-fee. There are four exogamous septs—**Chongá, Dauwá, Kauwá,** and **Rángá**. Prohibited degrees are reckoned by the standard formula down to seven generations on the male and three on the female side.

Internal structure.

Infant-marriage is almost unknown among the Dhimáls, and is practised only by the few well-to-do families, who strive to imitate the customs of high-caste Hindus. Among the main body of the tribe youths between the ages of sixteen and twenty marry girls from twelve to sixteen. Courtship is unrestricted, and the young people usually settle their own love affairs without the intervention of parents or guardians. It occasionally happens that a match affecting the proprietary interests of two families is arranged by the fathers of the

Marriage.

[1] Mr. W. B. Oldham, Bengal Civil Service, late Deputy Commissioner of Darjiling.
[2] *Essays*, i, 115.
[3] They numbered 873 in 1872 and 662 in 1881.

couple concerned, but as a rule the first step taken in the direction of marriage is for the girl to go off one evening with the man of her choice and quietly establish herself in his house. At this stage her parents come forward and demand a settlement of the bride-price (*chumna*), which formerly stood at Rs. 11, but now ranges from Rs. 20 to Rs. 80, according to the attractions of the girl and the value which her parents set upon her lover. The amount, however, is not paid, or even finally settled at once; the bride must first pass through a period of probation, extending often to a year or more, during which time her capabilities as a housewife are supposed to be tested. If she gives satisfaction, the bride-price is determined and paid, and the marriage formally celebrated. If she is rejected, the man with whom she eloped is bound to maintain her and her children; but instances of this very rarely occur. The procedure, however, is by no means uniform in all cases. Very commonly the marriage takes place a month or so after the elopement, while the question of bride-price stands over until the young woman's true value has been ascertained by the working test of domestic life. Dhimáls seem, however, to regard marriage as a form of minor importance. I know of a young Dhimál who took a girl to his house some three years ago. The two live happily together, and she has borne him a child, but the marriage ceremony has not yet been performed, owing probably to the parents being unable to agree about the bride-price. No social stigma attaches to the girl's position, and the women of the village receive her on equal terms; but she is not entitled to serve boiled rice to guests invited on any ceremonial occasion. From this curious laxity in ordering the relations of the sexes it follows of course that intercourse previous to elopement or marriage is tacitly recognised. But if a girl becomes pregnant while still in her parent's house, she is expected to disclose the name of her lover, and to prevail upon him to marry her or at least to take her to live with him.

The marriage ceremony has evidently been borrowed from the Hindus. Its essential portions are the standard rites of *sátpák* or carrying the bride seven times round the bridegroom and smearing vermilion on her head (*sindurdán*). The village barber attends to shave the front half of the bridegroom's head; the caste *guru*, usually a Rájbansi, mutters gibberish which passes muster as sacred texts, and the proceedings are completed by the assembled guests showering paddy, *dub* grass, sandal powder, and water on the heads of the married couple.

Polygamy is permitted up to a supposed maximum limit of three wives, but the tribe is a poor one, and very few Dhimáls can afford themelves the luxury of more than one wife. A widow may marry again, and is in no way restricted in her choice, except that the second marriage must take place from her parent's house and the prohibited degrees binding on her before her marriage may not be infringed. *Sindurdán* and the resumption of the massive shell bracelet, usually three or four inches wide, which distinguishes a married woman, are the essential portions of the ceremony in use. Traces of Hindu influence may be discerned in the tendency to think less highly of a remarried widow than of a woman, whether married or not, who is cohabiting with a man for the first time, and is therefore eligible for marriage by the full form. Divorce is permitted on the ground of unchastity with the sanction of the caste panchâyat, and divorced wives may marry again under the conditions applicable to widows. A man who seduces a married woman is supposed to be liable to repay to the injured husband the bride-price given for her when a virgin, and the panchâyat may be called upon to enforce this obligation by the various forms of social punishment which they have at their command. The tribe knows nothing of the Hindu systems of law, and the devolution of property is regulated by a tribal custom of their own, administered by the village council or panchâyat. Sons inherit by equal shares; failing sons the uterine brethren divide the property; next in order comes the wife, then the daughters; and next to them the cousins of the deceased.

Religion.

In the forty years which have passed since Hodgson published his *Essay on the Kochh, Bodo, and Dhimál Tribes*, the Dhimáls have made a marked advance in the direction of Hinduism. They now insist upon describing themselves as orthodox Hindus, and among their favourite objects of worship are Chháwál Thákur or Gopál Thákur (a form of Krishna), Chaitan, and Nitai (Chaitanya and Nityánanda, the great teachers of Vaishnavism), the Sálagrám or fossil ammonite, and the tulsi-plant (*Ocymum sanctum*). In the Darjiling Terai Dhimál temples may be seen in which Krishna is the central figure, having Chaitanya on his right hand and Nityánanda on his left; while the sacred tulsi is planted in front of the bamboo hut which contains these images. No better illustration could be given of the distance which separates the Dhimál religion of to-day from the simple Nature-worship described by Hodgson, to which temples and images were alike unknown. The river-deities of forty years ago seem entirely to have lost their hold on the people, who no longer mention them among the regular gods, though it is possible that they may still drag on an obscure existence as patrons of the village or the household. From the precincts of the recognised tribal pantheon they have been expelled beyond hope of recall by Káli, Bisahari, Manasá, Bura Thákur, Mahámái, and other celestial personages borrowed from the Hindu system. These adopted gods, however, are worshipped on just the same principle as the spirits of flood and field, whom they have displaced. None of the esoteric doctrines of Hinduism have accompanied the new divinities, who are propitiated for the avoidance of physical ills by much the same offerings as were presented to their predecessors. Thus, to Chháwál Thákur and Chaitanya plantains, milk, and parched rice are offered; to Káli, buffaloes, goats, and pigeons; to Bisahari, goats, pigeons, and ducks. In this *mélange* of Vaishnavism and Saivism the functions of priest are usually discharged by selected members of the Rájbansi caste, called Bámans, to distinguish them from the degraded Brahmans who are occasionally called in to assist in a specially important act of worship. These men, though belonging to the class of Barna Brahmans and serving the lowest castes of Hindus, would not deign to attach themselves regularly to the Dhimál tribe, and it seems likely enough that the whole of the Dhimáls may be absorbed in the Rájbansi caste without ever reaching the dignity of having Brahmans of their own.

Funeral.

Among the Dhimáls of the present day the Hindu practice of cremation, unknown at the time when Hodgson wrote, is fast displacing the more primitive usage of burial. The Agniá Dhimáls, indeed, who rank above the other sub-castes, are said to owe their name to their adoption of the custom of burning the dead. When burial is resorted to, the corpse is laid in the grave face upwards with the head pointing towards the north. A meagre imitation of the Hindu ceremony of *sráddh* is performed, usually on the tenth day after death; but the practice in this matter is by no means uniform, and some prefer the third day, some the seventh, and others again the thirteenth. A feast is always given to the relatives and friends of the deceased. Offerings for the benefit of ancestors in general are made in the month of Kártik (October–November).

Social status and occupation.

Standing as the Dhimáls do outside the regular caste system, their social status cannot be very precisely defined. They abstain from beef, snakes, rats, and similar vermin and the leavings of other people, but eat fowls, pork, lizards, and all kinds of fish. Rájbansis will take water from them and smoke in the same hookah, but all other castes regard them as unclean. Dhimáls in their turn profess not to take water from the Mech tribe, from Mahomedans, and from the large group of semi-Nepalese castes, vaguely termed Pahárias. Cooked food they will take from a Rájbansi or from a member of any higher caste. Agriculture, fishing, and pasturing cattle are their chief occupations, and a few work as coolies in the tea gardens of the Terai or carry on a petty trade in the commoner sorts of food-grain. In former years they were greatly addicted to the *jhúm* system of cultivation, but the limits within which this is possible have been greatly curtailed by the development of forest conservancy, and Dhimáls residing in British territory have for the most part taken to regular plough cultivation. In the Darjiling Terai a few of them are *jotdárs* under a ten years' settlement, the bulk of the tribe being ordinary raiyats or landless day-labourers. They still retain the nomadic habits noticed by Hodgson, and large numbers of them will at times desert their villages in order to settle in some locality better suited to their peculiar mode of life.

Dhimar, a sub-caste of Kahárs in Behar who say that they immigrated from the west. They carry palanquins and work as domestic servants, while some of them parch grain and keep petty shops. Socially they rank somewhat below the Rawani Kahars, and Brahmans will not take water from their hands. They practise widow-marriage, and have a remarkable ceremony for divorce on the ground of adultery, the concluding act of which is to pour a *gharráh* of water over the wife's head and turn her adrift.

Dhimire, a *thar* of the Kásyap *gotra* of Nepáli Brahmans.

Dhoár, a sub-caste of Gonrhis in Behar.

Dhobá, the washerman caste of Bengal and Orissa, who claim descent from Neta Muni or Netu Dhopáni, who washed the clothes of Brahmá. According to another story, Neta was the son of a devotee called Dhobá Muni, who washed his loin cloth (*kopin*) in a river, and thereby so fatigued himself that he could not fetch flowers for the daily worship. For this neglect his fellow-devotees cursed him, and he and his posterity were condemned to follow the profession of washing dirty clothes. The Skanda Purána quoted in the Játi Kaumudi makes the Dhobás the offspring of a Dhibar father and a Tibar mother—a statement quite unsupported by evidence, which is only mentioned here in illustration of the common tendency to insist on referring every caste now existing to some mode of mixed parentage.

Origin.

Owing to the universal custom which forbids a Hindu to wash his own clothes, the Dhobá caste is very widely distributed, and has in Bengal Proper been broken up into an unusually large number of sub-castes. Eighteen of these are shown in Appendix I, but I am by no means certain that the enumeration is exhaustive. In Eastern Bengal two great divisions are recognised—**Rámer Dhobá** and **Sitár Dhobá**; the former claiming descent from the washermen of Ráma, and the latter from those of Sita. Members of these two groups eat and drink together, but never intermarry. The story is that originally Rama's washermen worked only for men and Sita's only for women. The latter received a special payment of nine *pans* (720) of golden cowries for washing Sita's menstrual cloths, and this made Ráma's washermen covetous, so that one day they stole those garments and washed them themselves. From that time it is said each branch of the caste took to washing indifferently for either sex.

Internal structure.

In Central Bengal we find four sub-castes—**Sátisá**, **Athisá**, **Hájará Samáj**, and **Nitisiná**. The first two are said to have reference to the number of families originally comprised in each group; the third is supposed to consist of a thousand persons degraded for some breach of social rules; the fourth are day-labourers as well as washermen. The distinctions between the first three are said to be less strictly maintained of late years. The Hughli Dhobás have four sub-castes—**Bará Samáj**, **Chhota Samáj**, **Dhobá Samáj**, and **Rárhiya Samáj**, the members of which do not intermarry and cannot eat cooked rice together. In Noakháli we find three endogamous groups bearing the names of parganas **Bhuluá**, **Jugidiá**, and **Sundip**. In Orissa there appear to be no sub-castes. The Manbhum series, **Bangáli**, **Goriá**, **Maghayá**, and **Khottá**, seems at first sight akin to the Behar set of sub-castes, in that it recognises Bangáli and Maghayá as distinct geographical groups. I have, however, placed the Manbhum Dhobás in the Bengal division of the caste, because they speak Bengali themselves and are on the whole more subject to Bengal than to Behar influences.

The sections of the Bengal Dhobás present no points of special interest. All of them have been borrowed from the Brahmanical system, and are not taken into account in arranging marriages. There is, indeed, usually only one *gotra* current in each local community, and that seems to be retained mainly from the force of custom and as a badge of social distinction. The prohibited degrees are the same as in other castes of about the same position in society.

Marriage in Bengal.

Bengal Dhobás, including the Manbhum members of the caste, marry their daughters as infants, at the age of from seven to nine years. Boys are usually married between eleven and fifteen, but the sons of poor men, who cannot afford to pay the bride-price (*pan*), often remain unmarried till five-and-twenty, by which time a man has probably earned enough to secure a wife for himself. The marriage ceremony is the same as is observed by most of the lower castes. The carrying of the bride seven times round the bridegroom is regarded as its binding portion. Polygamy is fully recognised in the case of well-to-do men whose first wives are barren; for others it is allowed, but is not considered quite respectable. Widows may not marry a second time. Divorce is not allowed, but when a husband casts off his wife for adultery a reference is usually made to the pancháyat and a purificatory ceremony (*práyaschitta*), such as is described in the article on Chásádhobá, is gone through by the husband. Women thus cast off cannot marry again.

Among the Dhobás of Eastern Bengal some curious usages prevail in respect of marriage. Every *samáj* or local assemblage of the **Rámer-Dhobá** sub-caste is headed by three officials, known in order of rank as the **Náik**, the **Parámánik**, and the **Bárik**. The rest of the assemblage or community are known by the general name **Samájik**. For marriages between equals, that is between persons both of whom belong to the same class, whether official or Samájik, the bride-price is fixed at Rs. 50. But where the parties do not belong to the same class, the bride-price varies above or below this sum in relation to the rank of the bride and bridegroom. Thus a Samájik marrying the daughter of a Bárik, Parámánik, or Náik will pay Rs. 51, Rs. 52, or Rs. 53, as the case may be; while a Náik marrying in the classes below him pays Rs. 49, Rs. 48, or Rs. 47, according to the rank of the bride. A somewhat less elaborate system exists in the Sitar-Dhobá sub-caste. There the headman of the Samáj is called **Pradhán**, and the second **Parámánik**, but there is no third official. The amount of *pan* varies with the rank of the bride, but neither the normal amount nor the scale of variation is fixed by custom. In Murshedabad and other districts of Central Bengal the Samáj of the Dhobá caste is presided over by three officials—**Parámánik**, **Bárik**, and **Mandal**, who are consulted when a marriage is under consideration, and who decide any questions regarding affinity which may arise.

Marriage and structure in Orissa.

The Dhobás of Orissa differ in several important particulars from the Dhobás of Bengal. In the first place they have among their *gotras* the distinctly totemistic group Nágasa, the members of which revere the snake as their common progenitor, and observe the primitive rule of exogamy, which forbids a man to marry a woman who bears the same totem as himself. Prohibited degrees of course are recognised, but the form in which they are stated shows them to be later amplifications of a more archaic method of preventing marriages between persons of near kin.

Again, adult as well as infant-marriages are sanctioned, and there are no limits to polygamy. A man may take as many wives as he likes or can afford to maintain. Widows may marry again under much the same conditions as are recognised by the non-Aryan races of Chota Nagpur. The ritual observed is *sanga*. When such a marriage is under consideration, the widow appears before a caste council and solemnly cuts an areca nut (*supári*) into two pieces. This is supposed to symbolize her complete severance from the family of her late husband. The actual ceremony gone through on the day of the *sangá* is of the simplest character. The bridegroom decks the bride with new ornaments, denoting that she has put off the unadorned state of widowhood, and a feast is given to the members of the caste, their presence at which is deemed to ratify the marriage. While permitting widows to remarry, the Orissa Dhobás do not extend this privilege to divorced women. In dealing with women taken in adultery, the main point is whether the paramour is a member of the caste or not. If he is, I gather that the moral sense of the community is satisfied by the imposition of some slight penance, and that the husband by no means invariably insists on getting rid of his wife. A *liaison* with an outsider, however, admits of no atonement, and the offending woman is simply turned out of the caste.

Religion.

The religion of the Dhobá caste, whether in Bengal or in Orissa, exhibits no points of special interest. Most Dhobás belong to the Vaishnava sect, and a few only are Saktas. Like many other serving castes, they pay especial reverence to Viswakarmá. They employ Bráhmans for religious and ceremonial purposes, but the Dhobá-Bráhman, as he is usually called, ranks very low, and is looked down upon by those members of the priestly order who serve the higher castes. In the disposal of the dead and the subsequent propitiatory ceremonies they follow the standard customs of lower class Hindus. It deserves notice that the Dhobás of Orissa bury children up to five years of age face downwards—a practice which in Upper India is confined to members of the sweeper caste.

Occupation.

The necessities of Hindu society give rise to a very steady demand for the services of the Dhobá, and for this reason a comparatively small proportion of the caste have abandoned their distinctive occupation in favour of agriculture. The village Dhobá, however, besides receiving customary presents at all village festivals, often holds *chákarán* land in recognition of the services rendered by him to the community. In Eastern Bengal, according to Dr. Wise, the presence of the Dhobá is deemed indispensable at the marriages of the higher classes, as on the bridal morn he sprinkles the bride and bridegroom with water collected in the palms of his hands from the grooves of his washing-board (*pát*), and after the bride has been daubed with turmeric the Dhobá must touch her to signify that she is purified.

In Dacca, says the same accurate observer, the washerman is hard-working, regular in his hours of labour, and generally one of the first workmen seen in the early morning, making use of a small native bullock, as the donkey does not thrive in Bengal, for carrying his bundles of clothes to the outskirts of the town. He cannot, however, be said to be a careful washerman, as he treats fine and coarse garments with equal roughness; but for generations the Dacca Dhobás have been famous for their skill, when they choose to exert it, and early in this century it was no uncommon thing for native gentlemen to forward valued articles of apparel from Calcutta to be washed and restored by them. At the present day Dhobás from Kochh Behár and other distant places are sometimes sent while young to learn the trade at Dacca.

Mode of washing.

For washing muslins and other cotton garments, well or spring water is alone used; but if the articles are the property of a poor man, or are commonplace, the water of the nearest tank or river is accounted sufficiently good. The following is their mode of washing. The cloth is first cleansed with soap or fuller's earth, then steamed, steeped in earthen vessels filled with soap suds, beaten on a board, and finally rinsed in cold water. Indigo is in as general use as in England for removing the yellowish tinge and whitening the material. The water of the wells and springs bordering on the red laterite formation met with on the north of the city has been for centuries celebrated, and the old bleaching fields of the European factories were all situated in this neighbourhood. Dhobás use rice starch before ironing and folding clothes, for which reason no Brahman can perform his devotions or enter a temple without first of all rinsing in water the garment he has got back from the washerman.

Various plants are used by Dhobás to clarify water, such as the nir-malí (*Strychnos potatorum*), pui (*Basella*), nágphaní (*Cactus Indicus*), and several plants of the mallow family. Alum, though not much valued, is sometimes used.

The Dhobá often gives up his caste trade and follows the profession of a writer, messenger, or collector of rent (*tahsíldár*), and it is an old native tradition that a Bengali Dhobá was the first interpreter the English factory of Calcutta had, while it is further stated that our early commercial transactions were solely carried on through the agency of low-caste natives. The Dhobá, however, will never engage himself as an indoor servant in the house of a European.

Among the natives of Bengal the washerman, like the barber, is proverbially considered untrustworthy, and when the former says the clothes are almost ready he is not to be believed. The Bengali Dhobá is not so dissipated as his Hindustani namesake, whose drinking propensities are notorious, but he is said to indulge frequently in *gánja*-smoking.

Social status.

The Dhobá is reckoned as unclean because he washes the puerperal garments—an occupation which, according to Hindu ideas, is reserved for outcaste and abandoned races. His social rank therefore is low, and we find him classed with Chandáls, Jugis, Máls, and the like. Notwithstanding this he assumes many airs, and lays down a fanciful standard of rank to suit his pleasure. Thus in Bikrampur, in Dacca, he declines to wash for the Pátuni, Rishi, Bhuinmáli, and Chandál, but works for the Sunri, because the Nápit does so, and for all classes of fishermen. He also refuses to attend at the marriages of any Hindus but those belonging to the Nava-Sákha, and under no circumstances will he wash the clothes worn at funeral ceremonies.

The following statement shows the number and distribution of Dhobás in Bengal, Orissa, and Manbhum in 1872 and 1881 :—

District.	1872.	1881.	District.	1872.	1881.
Bardwan	7,152	4,904	Darjiling	85	330
Bankura	2,343	4,405	Jalpigori	166	979
Birbhum	2,131	3,209	Kuch Behar	......	310
Midnapur	34,896	41,607	Dacca	9,615	11,028
Hughli	12,152	7,988	Faridpur	4,132	9,815
Howrah		9,312	Bakarganj	27,395	21,628
24-Parganas	39,591	13,968	Maimansinh	12,587	17,419
Nadiya	4,815	6,834	Chittagong	11,136	11,446
Khulna	......	2,276	Noakhali	13,243	15,151
Jessore	7,624	9,866	Tipperah	16,197	16,592
Murshedabad	5,295	6,900	Hill Tracts	7	38
Dinajpur	2,177	2,071	Cuttack	27,560	36,139
Rajshahye	1,743	1,696	Puri	12,247	14,529
Rangpur	805	898	Balasore	16,475	21,350
Bogra	327	651	Tributary States ...	16,975	15,645
Pabna	1,376	2,225	Manbhum	7,816	9,404

Dhobi, the washerman caste of Behar, entirely distinct from the Dhobás of Bengal and Orissa. Except the vague story that they are descended from Gári Bhuiyá, one of the minor gods of Behar, Dhobis have no tradition respecting their origin, and the internal structure of the caste throws no light upon the sources from which it has been formed.

Origin.

Mr. Nesfield holds that the "washerman represents an impure caste, but are many degrees higher than that of the Bhangi, from whom he has sprung. Both are descended from the Dom, 'whose sole wealth,' according to Manu, 'must be dogs and asses.'[1] The Indian washerman has always been associated with the indigenous ass, which carries the soiled clothes down to the bank of the river or tank and takes them back clean to the house. No Hindu of any caste, even the lowest, will wash his own clothes, and so the Dhobi has been formed into a caste which shall bear the impurities of all." It seems to me open to question whether this ingenious hypothesis is borne out by the very scanty evidence that is available. Dhobis and Doms, as I understand the argument, are alleged to be cognate races, because both are associated with the donkey. Now in the first place the use of donkeys by the Dhobi caste is so far from being

[1] Manu, x, 52, speaks thus of the Chandáls, not of the Doms. There is nothing *primâ facie* improbable in the view that both are derived from a common stock, but I doubt whether the evidence justifies the assumption of their identity.

universal that it has given rise to the formation of a slightly inferior sub-caste called Gadhayá. Secondly, beyond the highly conjectural identification of the Doms with the Chandáls spoken of by Manu, there is nothing to show that Doms have the faintest partiality for the donkey. On the contrary, the Magahyá Doms of Behar, as is explained in the article on that caste, will not touch a donkey, and regard the Dhobi with very special aversion, in explanation of which they tell a curious story. So far as my knowledge extends, neither the physical characteristics nor the exogamous divisions of the Dhobi caste suggest any conclusion at all regarding the origin of the group; and for the present at any rate all that can be said is that it is probably a functional group evolved under the pressure of social requirements from whatever elements happened to be at hand in any particular locality. The tendency, no doubt, would be to relegate the ceremonially objectionable work of a washerman to the non-Aryan races; and in Orissa, as has been pointed out in the article on Dhobá, some evidence has survived to show that this has actually taken place. But it would be hopeless to attempt by any mode of analysis to trace the various elements which may have been combined in a large functional caste.

Internal structure.

The Dhobis of Behar are divided into the following sub-castes:—Kanaujiá, Maghayá, Belwár, Awadhiyá, Bathám, Gorsár, Gadhayá (keep donkeys), and Banglá (immigrants from Bengal). There is also a class of Mahomedan Dhobis known as Turkiá.

Magahya Dhobis have exogamous sections (*muls*) of the territorial type. The other sub-castes appear to have no sections, and to regulate their marriages solely by the standard Behar formula regarding prohibited degrees.

Marriage.

The usual practice among Dhobis is to marry their daughters as infants at ages ranging from five to twelve years; but cases sometimes occur in which a girl is married after puberty owing to her parents being too poor to arrange for her marriage before. The preliminary negotiations are conducted by a match-maker (*aguá*), who may or may not be a relative of the bride. A small customary price (*tilak*) is usually paid to the parents of the bridegroom. The ceremony is of the ordinary type. Polygamy is supposed to be prohibited, but a man may have two wives without incurring censure; and as a rule no one is rich enough to be able to keep more. A widow may marry again by the *sagai* form, in which the ritual consists of smearing vermilion on the parting of the bride's hair with the bridegroom's left hand, and presenting to her a lac armlet. If her late husband has left a younger brother or younger cousin, it is considered the right thing for the widow to marry him some four or five months after her husband's death. A divorce may be obtained with the assent of the caste panchâyat when a woman is taken in adultery with a member of the caste or for incompatibility of temper. Sexual intercourse with an outsider belonging to a lower caste would involve expulsion; but I infer from the case cited below that a woman would incur no social penalty by becoming the mistress of a man of high caste. A divorced woman may marry again by *sagai*. The man whom she marries is expected to give a feast to the members of the caste.

It is a singular fact that the Dhobis of Behar, like the Bauris and Bagdis of Bengal, admit into their community men of higher castes who have been expelled from their own group. In such cases the head of the new member is shaved, and he is bathed in any sacred stream that may be available. He must also worship Sat Náráyan, and give money and a feast to the Brahmans of the caste. A case of this kind occurred recently in Champáran. A Bhuinhár (Bábhan) of Khartari, thana Dháka, having been expelled from his own caste for eating and drinking with a Dhobi woman who was his mistress, was formally received into the Dhobi caste by the ceremony described above.

Religion.

In all that concerns the worship of the greater gods the religion of the Dhobis differs little from that of other castes of about the same social position. Siva, Vishnu, Kártikeya, or the Saktis are selected for worship, very much as the personal tastes of the worshipper may dictate. Maithil and Sákadwipi Brahmans are employed as priests, but these suffer in social estimation by serving so low a caste, and are distinguished by the opprobrious name of Dhobi Brahman. Besides these professional *purohits*, a Dhobi who turns Bairági may find employment as *guru* or spiritual adviser among the members of his caste. In addition to the minor gods common to them and other low castes of Behar, Dhobis pay especial respect to Gári, Bhuiá, whom they worship on the 5th of Srávan with offerings of he-goats, betel-leaves, flowers of the *urhál* tree, cakes of flour, rice boiled in milk, *ganjá* with a *chilam* ready for smoking, a *dhoti*, and a few coins. These offerings, with the exception of the *ganjá*, are afterwards consumed by the members of the family. The *dhoti* and the money are given to Brahmans. In the Monghyr district Barham Ghási appears to occupy much the same position as Gári Bhuiá does further north. On the last day of Asarh, Ghosi Pacháin is propitiated in very similar fashion. Some Dhobis are said to worship their flat iron (*istiri*), but I have been unable to find out the precise form of ritual appointed for such occasions. Jhunki Gosain and Rám Thákur are also reckoned among their gods.

Social status and occupation.

In point of social standing Dhobis hold but a low place among the castes of Behar, being classed with Beldars, Musahars, Chamárs, and the like. Brahmans of course cannot take water from their hands. They are not very particular about their food, and in some districts they are known to eat field-rats—a fact which suggests non-Aryan affinities. Most of them adhere to their traditional occupation of washing clothes, and only a few have taken to agriculture as non-occupancy raiyats. Some, however, work as cartmen, and others have taken to selling milk. In North-West Shahabad, says Mr. Grierson,[1] the village Dhobi receives as his perquisite ten *sers*

[1] *Behar Peasant Life*, s.v. Dhobi.

of grain for every plough in the village. This is called *jaurá*. In the same part of the country he also receives an armful of crop, known as *kharwan* or *kerá*, according as it is large or small. In the North-Western Provinces, and probably also in Behar, the Dhobi gets a special fee in cash or kind at child-birth and on the day when the mother first leaves her room. According to the same high authority[1] :—

"The honesty of the washerman and his tenderness for the clothes committed to his care are not considered of much account in Behár, and there are numerous proverbs coined at his expense, *e.g.*, *dhobi par dhobi base, tab kapra par sábun pare,*—no soap ever touches clothes unless many washermen live together (when owing to competition they wash well). Again, *dhobik báp ker kichhu nahiñ phát,*—nothing belonging to a washerman's father is ever torn by him (*i.e.*, those are the only clothes about which he is careful). It is also a wise precaution, which according to Behár ideas should universally be adopted, to disbelieve a washerman when he says the clothes are 'nearly' ready. A washerman's donkey is a bye-word, as in the proverb *gadha ken na dosar gosainyán, dhobiya ken na dosar parohan,*—an ass has only one master (a washerman). and the washerman has only one steed (a donkey). Again, *dhobi, náü, darji i tinu algarji,*—there are three careless people, the washerman, the barber, and the tailor."

The following statement shows the number and distribution of the Dhobi caste in Behar and Chota Nagpur during 1872 and 1881 :—

District.	1872.	1881.	District.	1872.	1881.
Patna	12,459	13,534	Bhagalpur	16,414	23,491
Gya	17,954	16,733	Purniah	10,775	13,616
Shahabad	14,564	18,750	Maldah	3,507	3,893
Tirhut { Darbhanga ...	46,197	21,075	Santál Parganas ...	10,497	7,905
Tirhut { Mozufferpur ...		28,433	Hazaribagh	7,530	11,872
Saran	15,122	20,804	Lohardagá	8,612	11,397
Champaran	16,911	17,969	Singbhum	2,096	2,695
Monghyr	15,772	20,061	Tributary States ...	2,592	3,863

Dhobáhá, a section of the Biyáhut and Kharidáhá Kalwárs in Behar.

Dhobá-Samáj, a sub-caste of Dhobás in Hughli.

Dhobdhar, a sept of Bairágis in Chota Nagpur who cannot wash their clothes when performing ceremonies for the birth of a child.

Dhobi, a sept of Kharwars in Chota Nagpur who cannot touch a washerman.

Dhokar-Gond or **Mángan-Gond**, a sub-tribe of Gonds in Chota Nagpur.

Dhokasan, a section of Goálás in Behar.

Dhokra, a sub-caste of Kámars or blacksmiths in Western Bengal who make brass idols.

Dhol, *Dhole*, a title of Barendra Brahmans and Bangaja Káyasths in Bengal.

Dholá, a sub-caste of Doms in Bengal who are supposed to come from Dhalbhum.

Dholi, *Dhuli*, *Dholiá*, *Dhuliá*, a beater of the *dhol* or small drum; a title of the Báiti, Hári, Kora, Muchi, and other low castes; a section of the Dhaprá

[1] *Behar Peasant Life*, s.v. Dhobi.

sub-caste of Doms in Behar; a title of Goálás.

Dholo, a sub-caste of Sunris in Western Bengal.

Dhondh, a water-snake, a sept of Páns in Chota Nagpur.

Dhongán, a *thar* or section of Nepáli Brahmans.

Dhor, a sept of Rajputs in Behar.

Dhorá, a sub-tribe of Bhuiyás in Chota Nagpur.

Dhorán, a section of Goálás in the North-Western Provinces and Behar.

Dhosáli, a *gáin* of the Bátsya *gotra* of Bárendra Brahmans in Bengal.

Dhrámar, a title of Maithil Brahmans in Behar.

Dhruba, a *gotra* or section of the Baidya caste in Bengal.

Dhukankorá, a sub-caste of Sunris in Behar.

Dhukursáni, a sub-caste of Kotáls in Bengal.

Dhuli, a *thar* or sept of Dámis in Darjiling, the members of which are drummers by profession.

Dhuliá or *Dhulo*, a sub-caste of Bauris in Western Bengal.

Dhum, a title of Bangaja Káyasths in Bengal.

Dhunakátá, a sub-caste of Máls in Midnápur and Manbhum.

Dhundhiá, a section of Goálás in the North-Western Provinces.

Dhundhlá, a section of Goálás in the North-Western Provinces.

Dhundhuri, a *gáin* of the Sábarna *gotra* of Bárendra Brahmans in Bengal.

Dhungiál, a *thar* of the Agasti *gotra* of Nepáli Brahmans.

Dhuniá, a cotton-carder, an occupation followed by Mahomedans.

Dhunkor, a section of Páns in Chota Nagpur.

Dhurári, a *thar* or section of Nepáli Brahmans.

Dhurfandá, a section of the Biyáhut and Kharidáhá Kalwárs in Behar.

Dhuriá, a sub-caste of Kándus and Kahárs in Behar.

Dhurjhár, a *mul* or section of the Ghosin sub-caste of Goálás in Behar.

Dhurjya, a sept of Chakmás in the Hill Tracts of Chittagong.

Dhurungia, a section of Ghásia in Chota Nagpur.

Dhusiá, Dhusiyá, a totemistic sept of Chamárs and Doms in Chota Nagpur; a sub-caste of Chamárs in Behar.

Diá, a section of Goálás in the North-Western Provinces.

Diáli, a section of Kámis in Darjiling.

Dian, a kind of fish, a totemistic sept of Bedias in Chota Nagpur.

Dichhit or **Dikshit**, a title of Kanaujiá Brahmans, Bábhans, and Rajputs in Behar.

Dighá, a title of Bauris in Western Bengal.

Dighal, a *gáin* of the Bátsya *gotra* of Rárhi Brahmans in Bengal.

Dighbáit, Dighwait, a *kul* or section of Bábhans in Behar.

Dighwará, a *mul* or section of the Tinmuliá Madhesiá sub-caste of Halwáis in Behar.

Dighwe-Tipri, a *mul* of the Sándil section of Maithil Brahmans and of Bábhans in Behar.

Dighwe-Nagar, a *mul* of the Sándil section of Maithil Brahmans in Behar.

Dighwe-Kankaurá, a *mul* of the Sándil section of Maithil Brahmans in Behar.

Dighwe-Sannahpur, a *mul* of the Sándil section of Maithil Brahmans in Behar.

Dighwe-Sakarpurá, a *mul* of the Sándil section of Maithil Brahmans in Behar.

Dihbans, a sept of Chiks in Chota Nagpur.

Dih-korwa, a sub-tribe of Korwas in Chota Nagpur.

Dihparsár, a local section of the Maghayá sub-caste of Koiris in Behar.

Dihwár, a *pur* or section of Sákadwipi Brahmans in Behar.

Diller, a sept of Goálás in Chota Nagpur.

Dilpáli, a *thar* or sept of Khambus in Darjiling.

Dingsáin, a *gáin* of the Bharadwája *gotra* of Rárhi Brahmans in Bengal.

Dip, a sept of Chiks in Chota Nagpur who may not eat after twilight.

Dipar, a section of Bábhans in Behar.

Dirgháti, a *gáin* of the Sándilya *gotra* of Rárhi Brahmans in Bengal.

Dirra, a kind of eel, a totemistic sept of Oraons in Chota Nagpur.

Dirwar, a jungle fruit, a totemistic sept of Mundas in Chota Nagpur.

Doai, *Doi*, *Chalanta*, *Baidya*, *Lakhiputra*, *Pátia Dás*, a low cultivating caste of Eastern Bengal, especially numerous along the banks of the Lakhya river in Dacca. The Doai are probably allied to the Hajang, a Mongrel Garo tribe of Maimansinh and Silhet, bordering on the Garo Hills, who under Brahmanical influence have broken off from the hillmen. A division of the Kochh Mandai, however, bears the name Doi, and the Danyi are described by Buchanan as the most depraved of the Kochh tribe, and the most impure of the Rájbansi.

The Doaís of Rungpúr, according to Mr. Damant, have no Brahmans, but employ members of their own caste as Purohits, and any stray Bairágí as Guru, the sráddha being held on the eleventh day after decease. They eat pork and drink spirits, while their principal occupation is carrying palankins and fishing.

The Doaí of Dacca are described by Dr. Wise as short, squat men, with an Indo-Chinese type of features; others are tall and muscular with large black eyes, acquiline noses, and a profusion of hair on the face, while their complexion is of a light brown. At the present day the Doaís have become so thoroughly Hinduised, and have so completely lost their original language and customs, that very little information can be got from them. They have Patit Brahmans of their own, who confess to having been their priests for three generations only. The weddings and funerals are the same as those of other low-caste Hindus, the sráddha being likewise celebrated on the thirtieth day. The Doaí will drink from the vessels of the lowest Súdras, but even the Bhúinmálí is disgraced if he drinks from theirs. They disavow the use of pork and spirits, although their neighbours affirm that indulgence in both is universal. They all belong to one gotra, the Aliman, and their sole title is Dás. Disputes are settled by a headman, Pradhán, whose office is not hereditary.

Their religious festivals are Hindu, the majority being Vaishnavas, while a Gosáin or Bairágí is the Guru. Before felling a Gujálí or Sál-tree, offerings are made to Chandí, or Durga, the Bráhman officiating; while according to their own account no religious rite is ever celebrated without the guidance of the family priest.

Living as they always do on the edge of the forest, they cut firewood for the market, and make matting (pat), whence the name Patia Dás, but do not catch fish for sale or engage themselves as boatmen. They have lost their ancestral language, and some of them occasionally learn to read and write Bengali, being employed as Tahsíldárs, or rent-collectors by landlords; while the illiterate become watchmen and messengers.

Doálak, a *mul* or section of the Naomuliá or Majraut sub-caste of Goálás in Behar.

Doálband, he who bears a sword, a soldier; one of the two main divisions of Kharwárs, the other being Pátband.

Doasli, *Dofasli*, a designation of the illegitimate offspring of parents of different castes.

Dobar, a section of Sunris in Behar.

Dobe, see **Dube**.

Dobháit, a *mul* or section of the Maghaya sub-caste of Barhis in Behar.

Dobhásia, Dubash, 'a man of two languages,' an interpreter; a title of the Rájbansi sub-caste of Kochhs in Northern Bengal.

Dobongwar, a sept of Mundas in Chota Nagpur.

Dodral, a kind of bird, a totemistic sept of Mundas in Chota Nagpur.

Doen, a *mul* or section of the Chhamuliá Madhesiá sub-caste of Halwáis in Behar.

Doeri, *Dwári*, *Darwán*, a door-keeper. The term is reserved for the door-keepers of the houses of considerable landholders in the mofussil.

Dogla, a mixed caste in Behar descended from fathers of the higher classes by women of the low castes. They are chiefly employed as writers.

Dohál, a *thar* of the Bachh *gotra* of Nepáli Brahmans.

Dohán, a section of Goálás in the North-Western Provinces.

Dohar, a sub-caste of Chamárs in Behar.

Doh-rahb-pá, one dwelling under the feet, a *rui* or sept of Dejong Lhoris, the members of which form the lowest class of Bhotias.

Doh-zepá, living in rough and craggy rocks, a *rui* or sept of Dejong Lhoris, the members of which form the lowest class of Bhotias.

Doi, a synonym for Doai; a section of the Kochh-Mandai in Dacca.

Doingnak, a sub-tribe of Chakmás in the Hill Tracts of Chittagong.

Dojwár, see **Dudhwár**.

Dokáne-Máli, a sub-caste of Mális in Bengal.

Dokhangpá, a *rui* or sept of the Bed tshan-gye sub-tribe of Dejong Lhoris or Bhotias of the south.

Dolbandhi, a sept of Kharwars in Chota Nagpur.

Dom, a sub-caste of Turis in Chota Nagpur.

Dom, *Domrá*, sometimes called Chandál by outsiders, a Dravidian menial caste of Bengal, Behar, and the North-Western Provinces, regarding whose origin much has been said. Dr. Caldwell[1] considers the "Doms and other Chandálas of Northern India and the Pareiyas and other low tribes of the Peninsula" to be the surviving representatives of an older, ruder, and blacker race, who preceded the Dravidians in India. Some of these were driven by the Dravidian invasion to take refuge in mountain fastnesses and pestilential jungles, while others were reduced to perpetual servitude like the Doms of Kumáon, whom Mr. Atkinson[2] describes as for ages the slaves of the Khasiyás—thought less of than the cattle, and, like them, changing hands from master to master. Sir Henry Elliot[3] says they "seem to be one of the aboriginal tribes of India. Tradition fixes their residence to the north of the Gogra, touching the Bhars on the east, in the vicinity of Rohini. Several old forts testify to their former importance, and still retain the names of their founders; as, for instance, Domdiha and Domangarh.[4] Rámgarh and Sahankot on the Rohini are also Dom forts." Mr. Carnegy[5] observes that the fort of Domangarh was the stronghold of the Domar, a degenerate clan of Rájputs, and suggests in a note that these Domar or Donwár may themselves have been a family of Doms who had risen to power locally and got themselves enrolled in "the conveniently elastic fraternity of Rajputs." In support of this theory he refers to the case of Ali Baksh Dom, who became Governor of Ramlabad, one of the districts of Oudh, and mentions that it was not uncommon for men of this class to rise to high office under kings by whom they were employed as musicians.

Traditions of origin.

[1] *Grammar of the Dravidian Languages*, p. 546.

[2] *North-Western Provinces Gazetteer*, vol. xi, p. 370.

[3] *Races of the North-Western Provinces*, i, 84.

[4] Buchanan, *Eastern India*, ii, p. 353, calls this the "Domingar or the castle of the Dom lady." It should be noted that Sir Henry Elliot misunderstands Buchanan, who nowhere gives it as his own opinion that the Doms are the same as the Domkatár section of the Bábhan caste, though he mentions (ii, 471) without comment a popular tradition to that effect.

[5] *Notes on the Races of Avadh (Oudh)*, p. 24.

Out of this somewhat profitless discussion there seems to emerge a general consensus of opinion that the Doms belong to one of the races whom, for convenience of expression, we may call the aborigines of India. Their personal appearance bears out this opinion. Mr. Beames describes the Magahiyá Doms of Champáran as "small and dark, with long tresses of unkempt hair, and the peculiar *glassy* eye of the non-Aryan autochthon;"[1] and Mr. Sherring remarks that "dark-complexioned, low of stature, and somewhat repulsive in appearance, they are readily distinguishable from all the better castes of Hindus."[2] The type, however, as is the case with most widely-diffused castes, seems to display appreciable variations. In Eastern Bengal, according to Dr. Wise, the Dom's hair is long, black, and coarse, while his complexion is oftener of a brown rather than a black hue; and among the Magahiyá Doms whom I have seen in Behar only a small proportion struck me as showing any marked resemblances to the aborigines of Chota Nagpur, who are, I suppose, among the purest specimens of the non-Aryan races of India. On the whole, however, the prevalent type of physique and complexion seems to mark the caste as not of Aryan descent, although evidence is wanting to connect it with any compact aboriginal tribe of the present day. The fact that for centuries past they have been condemned to the most menial duties, and have served as the helots of the entire Hindu community, would of itself be sufficient to break down whatever tribal spirit they may once have possessed, and to obliterate all structural traces of their true origin.

Internal structure: endogamy.

The Dom community is a large one, and the intricacy of its internal organization is doubtless due for the most part to the large area over which the caste is distributed. The sub-castes and sections are given in a tabular form in Appendix I. About most of these there is very little to be said. Enquiry into the origin of sub-castes is usually a difficult and unfruitful process, and it is attended with peculiar difficulties in the case of a caste regarded by all Hindus with extreme repulsion, and destitute of the social pride which delights to recall the reasons for minute internal divisions. The Magahiyá Doms of Behar have a legend that once upon a time Mahadeva and Párvati invited all the castes to a feast. Supat Bhakat, the ancestor of the Doms, came late, and being very hungry, mixed up and ate the food which the others had left. His behaviour was deemed so scandalous that he and his descendants were straightway degraded and condemned to eat the leavings of all other castes. Even at the present day if a Dom who comes to beg is asked to what caste he belongs, the answer will invariably be "*Jhutá-khái,*" or eater of leavings. This myth is unknown to the Doms of Central and Western Bengal, who trace their origin to a common ancestor called Kálubir, the son of a Chandál woman by her Let[3] husband. From his four sons, Pránbir, Manbir, Bhánbir, and Shánbir, the sub-castes Ankuriá, Bisdeliá, Bájuniá, and Magahiyá are said to

[1] *Races of the North-Western Provinces*, p. 85.
[2] *Hindu Tribes and Castes*, i, 401.
[3] Let is a sub-caste of the Bágdis in Murshedabad.

be descended. The two elder sons, Pránbir and Manbir, were, it is said, sent out to gather flowers for a sacrifice. Pránbir, who was lazily inclined, tore the flowers from the trees with a bamboo hook (*ánkuli*) and picked them up as they fell on the ground; while Manbir climbed the trees and gathered flowers carefully from branch to branch. The flowers brought in by Manbir were accepted, and he received the title of Bisdeliá (*bis*, 'twenty,' and *dál*, 'a branch'), because he had climbed twenty branches in the service of the gods. The elder brother's offering was rejected as unclean, and he and his descendants were named Ánkuriá in reference to the hook. On hearing this decision the third brother was greatly pleased, and drummed on his stomach in token of satisfaction. He and his offspring therefore were entitled Bajunia, or musician Doms. The Dhákál Dhesiá or Tapaspuriá Doms, who remove dead bodies and dig the cross trench which forms the base of the funeral pyre, also claim descent from Kalubir. One of his sons, they say, was sent by Mahadeva to fetch water from the Ganges. At the river bank he found a dead body waiting to be burned, and was tempted by offers of money from the friends of the deceased to dig the necessary trench. On his return to Mahádeva the god cursed him and his descendants to minister to the dead for all time. No special legend is given to account for the name Magahiyá, which doubtless originally denoted the Doms of South Behar. The Dái sub-caste owe their name to the circumstance that their women act as midwives in parts of the country where Chamains are not numerous enough to perform this function. The men are day-labourers. The Bánsphor or 'bamboo-splitter' sub-caste derive their name from the material out of which they make baskets; while the Chapariyá seem to be so called from building the bamboo frame-work by which a roof (*chapar*) is supported. The Uttariya Doms of South Behar work in *sirki*, and regard this as an important distinction between themselves and the Magahiyá, who in that part of the country till the soil and make mats and baskets of bamboo.

Internal structure: exogamy.

The exogamous sections of the caste are very numerous. In Behar they seem to be *territorial* or *titular;* while in Bankura the names are *totemistic*, and the members of particular sections refrain from injuring the animals after which they are called. In Central Bengal traces of totemism may perhaps be found, but the tendency is to borrow the Brahmanical *gotras*, while in the eastern districts all exogamous groups seem to have disappeared, and marriages are regulated by the more modern system of counting prohibited degrees down to and including the fifth generation in descent from a common ancestor. The Magahiyá Doms of Behar affect to observe a very elaborate method of working the rule of exogamy. They lay down that a man may not marry a woman belonging to the same section as his own (1) father, (2) paternal grandmother, (3) paternal great-grandmothers, (4) paternal great-great-grandmothers, (5) mother, (6) maternal grandmother, (7) maternal great-grandmothers. In applying the rule to a particular case, all the sections on both sides are taken into account in the manner described in the article on Bais, so that a marriage would be barred if one of the great-grandmothers of the proposed bride happened to have belonged to the same section as one of the great-great-grandmothers of the proposed bridegroom, even though the parties themselves belonged to different *muls*. This mode of calculation appears to be confined to Behar; and in Bengal wherever sections exist, the only rule observed is that a man may not marry a woman of the same section as himself. The standard formula for reckoning prohibited degrees is in general use. In Bankura it is ordinarily calculated to three generations in the descending line; but where *bhaiádi*, or mutual recognition of relationship, has been kept up between two families, the prohibition extends to five generations. The Doms of the 24-Parganas affect to prohibit marriage between *sapindas*, but this is a palpable imitation of the customs of the higher castes. Members of other castes may be received into the Dom community by paying a fee to the panchâyat and giving a feast to the Doms of the neighbourhood. At this feast the proselyte is required to wait upon his new associates and to eat with them. He must also have his head shaved and undergo a sort of baptism with water at the hands of the caste panchâyat in token of his adoption of the Dom religion. Instances of men of other castes thus joining themselves to the Doms are very rare, and occur only when a man has been ejected from his own caste for living with a Dom woman. Some say, however, that in these cases the proselyte, though ordinarily spoken of as a Dom, is not admitted to complete equality with the original members of the caste. His children, however, will be Doms of the same sub-caste as their mother.

Marriage.

In Central and Eastern Bengal Doms, following the example of the higher castes, nearly always marry their daughters as infants, and regard it as wrong for a girl over ten years of age to remain unmarried in her father's house. A small bride-price (*pan*), varying from Rs. 5 to Rs. 10, is paid to the parents of the girl. In Behar and Western Bengal adult-marriage still holds its ground for those who cannot afford the more fashionable practice, and sexual intercourse before marriage is said to be tolerated. Among the Doms of the Dacca district the marriage service is peculiar. The guests being assembled on a propitious day fixed by a Bráhman, the bridegroom's father takes his son on his knee, and, sitting down in the centre of the "Marocha" opposite the bride's father, who is holding his daughter in a similar posture, repeats the names of his ancestors for seven generations, while the bride's father runs over his for three. They then call God to witness the ceremony, and the bridegroom's father addressing the other asks him, "Have you lost your daughter?" The answer being in the affirmative, a similar interrogation and reply from the opposite party terminates the service. The boy-bridegroom then advances, smears the bride's forehead with *sindur* or red lead—the symbol of married life—takes her upon his knee, and finally carries her within doors. Like all aboriginal races, Doms are very fond of gaudy colours; the bridal dress consisting of yellow or red garments for the female, and a yellow cloth with a red turban for the male.

In the 24-Parganas a more Hinduised ritual is in vogue. The marriage takes place on a raised earthen platform (*bedi*), to which a branch of a banian-tree is fixed. An earthen vessel full of Ganges water is placed in the centre. On this vessel the bride and bridegroom lay their hands, one above the other, and the ceremony is completed by exchanging garlands of flowers. The Dom priest, Dharma-Pandit, presides and mutters words which purport to be sacred texts, and the actual marriage service is preceded by offerings to ancestors and the worship of Surya, Ganesa, Durga, Mahadeva, and Anti Kuldevatá. Further west again, in the districts of Bankura and Manbhum, the ritual appears to differ little from that already described in the article on the Bágdi caste. There is, however, no marriage with a tree and no symbolic capture of the bride, as in the case of the Bágdis; while in the joining of the hands which precedes *sindurdán*, the bride presents her right hand if she is given away by a male, and her left if by a female relative. On the night before the wedding the ceremony of *adhibás* is performed in the houses of both parties by anointing the body with turmeric and oil and tying a thread soaked in this mixture and knotted with a few blades of *durvá* grass on the right wrist of the bridegroom and the left wrist of the bride. The ritual followed in Behar is of the simplest character, consisting mainly of *sindurdán*, which is often performed in the open air under a tree. The wealthier Doms, however, erect a wedding canopy (*marwa*), and generally copy the Hindu ceremony with more or less accuracy of detail.

Polygamy is everywhere permitted, and poverty forms the only restriction on the number of wives a man may have. The standard of living however is low, and it is unusual to find a Dom with more than two wives, and most men content themselves with one. A widow may marry again, and in Behar it is deemed right for her to marry her late husband's younger brother; but in Bengal this idea does not seem to prevail, and a widow may marry any one she pleases provided that she does not infringe the prohibited degrees binding on her before her first marriage. The ritual (*sánga* or *sagái*) observed at the marriage of a widow consists mainly of *sindurdán* and the present of a new cloth. A *pan* is rarely paid, and never exceeds a rupee or two. In Murshedabad there is no *sindurdán*, and a formal declaration of consent before representatives of the caste is all that is required. Considerable license of divorce is admitted, and in some districts at any rate the right can be exercised by either husband or wife; so that a woman, by divesting herself of the iron bracelet given to her at marriage, can rid herself of a husband who ill-treats her or is too poor to maintain her properly. Dom women have a reputation for being rather masterful, and many of them are conspicuous for their powerful physique. It may be by virtue of their characteristics that they have established a right very rarely conceded to women in Bengal. A husband, on the other hand, can divorce his wife for infidelity or persistent ill-temper. In either case the action of the individual requires the confirmation of the panchâyat, which however is usually given as a matter of course, and is expressed in Bhágalpur by solemnly pronouncing the pithy monosyllable *jáo*. In North Bhagalpur the husband takes in his hand a bundle of rice straw and cuts it in half before the assemblage as a symbol of separation. Divorced wives may marry again by the same ritual as widows. Their children remain in the charge of their first husband. In Monghyr the second husband must give the panchâyat a pig to form the basis of a feast, and if convicted of having seduced the woman away from her first husband must pay the latter Rs. 9 as compensation. A husband, again, who divorces his wife has to pay a fee of 10 annas to the panchâyat for their trouble in deciding the case.

Most of the sub-castes seem to have a fairly complete organization for deciding social questions. The system of panchâyats is everywhere in full force, and in Behar these are presided over by hereditary headmen, variously called *sardár*, *pradhán*, *manjhan*, *marar*, *gorait*, or *kabiráj*, each of whom bears rule in a definite local jurisdiction, and has under him a *chharidar* or rod-bearer to call together the panchâyat and to see that its orders are carried out.

Religion.

The religion of the Doms varies greatly in different parts of the country, and may be described generally as a chaotic mixture of survivals from the elemental or animistic cults characteristic of the aboriginal races, and of observances borrowed in a haphazard fashion from whatever Hindu sect happens to be dominant in a particular locality. The composite and chaotic nature of their belief is due partly to the great ignorance of the caste, but mainly to the fact that as a rule they have no Brahmans, and thus are without any central authority or standard which would tend to mould their religious usages into conformity with a uniform standard. In Behar, for instance, the son of a deceased man's sister or of his female cousin officiates as priest at his funeral and recites appropriate *mantras*, receiving a fee for his services when the inheritance comes to be divided. Some Doms, indeed, assured me that the sister's son used formerly to get a share of the property, and that this rule had only recently fallen into disuse; but their statements did not seem to be definite enough to carry entire conviction, and I have met with no corroborative evidence bearing on the point. So also in marriage the sister's son, or occasionally the sister (*sawásin*), repeats *mantras*, and acts generally as priest. Failing either of these, the head of the household officiates. The possible significance of these facts in relation to the early history of the caste need not be elaborated here. No other indications of an extinct custom of female kinship are now traceable, and the fact that in Western Bengal the eldest son gets an extra share (*jeth-angs*) on the division of an inheritance seems to show that kinship by males must have been in force for a very long time past. In Bengal the sister's son exercises no priestly functions, these being usually discharged by a special class of Dom, known in Bankura as Degharíá, and in other districts as Dharma-Pandit. Their office is hereditary, and they wear copper rings on their fingers as a mark of distinction. In Murshedabad, on the other hand, most Doms, with the exception of the Bánukiá sub-caste and some of the Ánkuriás, have the services of low Brahmans, who may perhaps be ranked as

Barna-Brahmans. The same state of things appears to prevail in the north of Manbhum. In the Santál Parganas barbers minister to the spiritual wants of the caste.

In Bengal.

With such a motley array of amateur and professional priests, it is clearly out of the question to look for any unity of religious organization among the Doms. In Bankura and Western Bengal generally they seem on he whole to lean towards Vaishnavism, but in addition to Rádhá and Krishna they worship Dharam or Dharma-ráj in form of a man with a fish's tail on the last day of Jaishtha with offerings of rice, molasses, plantain, and sugar, the object of which is said to be to obtain the blessing of the sun on the crops of the season. Every year in the month of Baisákh the members of the caste go into the jungle to offer sacrifices of goats, fruits, and sweetmeats to their ancestral deity Kálubir; and at the appointed season they join in the worship of the goddess Bhádu, described in the article on the Bágdi caste. At the time of the Durga Puja, Bájuniá Doms worship the drum, which they regard as the symbol of their craft. This usage has clearly been borrowed from the artisan castes among the Hindus. In Central Bengal Káli appears to be their favourite goddess; and in Eastern Bengal many Doms follow the *Panth*, or path of Supat, Súpan, or Sobhana Bhagat, who is there regarded as a guru rather than as the progenitor of the caste. Others, again, call themselves Haris Chandís, from Rájá Haris Chandra, who was so generous that he gave away all his wealth in charity, and was reduced to such straits that he took service with a Dom, who treated him kindly. In return the Rájá converted the whole tribe to his religion, which they have faithfully followed ever since.[1]

The principal festival of the Doms in Eastern Bengal is the Srávannia Puja, observed in the month of that name, corresponding to July and August, when a pig is sacrificed and its blood caught in a cup. This cup of blood, along with one of milk and three of spirits, are offered to Náráyan. Again, on a dark night of Bhádra (August) they offer a pot of milk, four of spirits, a fresh cocoanut, a pipe of tobacco, and a little Indian hemp to Harí Rám, after which swine are slaughtered and a feast celebrated. A curious custom followed by all castes throughout Bengal is associated with

[1] This is the form of the legend current among the Doms of Dacca. It will be observed that the Chandála of the Márkandeya Purána has been turned into a Dom, and the pious king into a religious reformer. According to Dr. Wise, Haris Chandra is a well-known figure in the popular mythology of Bengal, and it is of him that natives tell the following story, strangely like that narrated in the xviiith chapter of the Koran regarding Moses and Joshua. He and his Ráni, wandering in the forest, almost starved, caught a fish and boiled it on a wood fire. She took it to the river to wash off the ashes, but on touching the water the fish revived and swam away. At the present day a fish called kálbosa (*Labeo calbasu*), of black colour and yellow flesh, is identified with the historical one, and no low-caste Hindu will touch it. In Hindustan the following couplet is quoted concerning a similar disaster which befell the gambler Nala, the moral being the same as that of the English proverb—"Misfortunes never come singly":—

"Rája Nal par bihat pare,
Bhúne machhle jal men tire.

the Dom, and may perhaps be a survival from times when that caste were the recognised priests of the elemental deities worshipped by the non-Aryan races. Whenever an eclipse of the sun or moon occurs, every Hindu householder places at his door a few copper coins, which, though now claimed by the Áchárji Brahman, were until recently regarded as the exclusive perquisite of the Dom.

In Behar.

Similar confusion prevails in Behar under the *régime* of the sister's son, only with this difference, that the advance in the direction of Hinduism seems to be on the whole less conspicuous than in Bengal. Mahadeva, Káli, and the river Ganges receive, it is true, sparing and infrequent homage, but the working deities of the caste are Syám Singh, whom some hold to be the deified ancestor of all Doms, Rakat Málá, Ghihal or Gohil, Goraiyá, Bandi, Lakeswar, Dihwár, Dák, and other ill-defined and primitive shapes, which have not yet gained admission into the orthodox pantheon. At Deodha, in Darbhanga, Syám Singh has been honoured with a special temple; but usually both he and the other gods mentioned above are represented by lumps of dried clay, set up in a round space smeared with cow-dung inside the house, under a tree or at the village boundary. Before these lumps, formless as the creed of the worshipper who has moulded them, pigs are sacrificed and strong drink offered up at festivals, marriages, and when disease threatens the family or its live-stock. The circle of these *godlings*, as Mr. Ibbetson has excellently called them, is by no means an exclusive one, and a common custom shows how simply and readily their number may be added to. If a man dies of snake-bite, say the Magahiyá Doms of the Gya district, we worship his spirit as a *Sámperiyá*, lest he should come back and give us bad dreams; we also worship the snake who bit him, lest the snake-god should serve us in like fashion. Any man therefore conspicuous enough by his doings in life or for the manner of his death to stand a chance of being dreamed of among a tolerably large circle is likely in course of time to take rank as a god. Judging, indeed, from the antecedents of the caste, Syám Singh himself may well have been nothing more than a successful dacoit, whose career on earth ended in some sudden or tragic fashion, and who lived in the dreams of his brethren long enough to gain a place in their rather disreputable pantheon. Systematic robbery is so far a recognised mode of life among the Magahiyá Doms that it has impressed itself on their religion, and a distinct ritual is ordained for observance by those who go forth to commit a burglary. The object of veneration on these occasions is Sansári Mái, whom some hold to be a form of Káli, but who seems rather to be the earth-mother known to most primitive religions. No image, not even the usual lump of clay, is set up to represent the goddess: a circle one span and four fingers in diameter is drawn on the ground and smeared smooth with cowdung. Squatting in front of this the worshipper gashes his left arm with the curved Dom knife (*katári*), and daubs five streaks of blood with his finger in the centre of the circle, praying in a low voice that a dark night may aid his designs; that his booty may be ample; and that he and his gang may escape detection.[1]

> "Labra movet metuens audiri: pulchra Laverna,
> Da mihi fallere, da justo sanctoque videri,
> Noctem peccatis et fraudibus objice nubem."[2]

Funeral ceremonies.

According to Dr. Wise it is universally believed in Bengal that Doms do not bury or burn their dead, but dismember the corpse at night, like the inhabitants of Tibet, placing the pieces in a pot and sinking them in the nearest river or reservoir. This horrid idea probably originated from the old Hindu law which compelled the Doms to bury their dead at night. The Doms of Dacca say that the dead are cast into a river, while the bodies of the rich or influential are buried. When the funeral is ended each man bathes, and successively touches a piece of iron, a stone, and a lump of dry cowdung, afterwards making offerings of rice and spirits to the manes of the deceased, while the relatives abstain from flesh and fish for nine days. On the tenth day a swine is slaughtered, and its flesh cooked and eaten, after which quantities of raw spirits are drunk until everybody is intoxicated. In Western Bengal and Behar the usual practice is to burn the dead and present offerings to the spirit of the deceased on the eleventh day, or, as some say, on the thirteenth. Before going to the place of cremation the Behar Doms worship Masán, a demon who is supposed to torment the dead if not duly propitiated. Burial is occasionally resorted to, but is not common, except in the case of persons who die of cholera or small-pox and children under three years of age. In these cases the body is laid in the grave face downward with the head pointing to the north.

Habits and customs.

"By all classes of Hindus," says Dr. Wise, "the Dom is regarded with both disgust and fear, not only on account of his habits being abhorrent and abominable, but also because he is believed to have no humane or kindly feelings. To those, however, who view him as a human being, the Dom appears as an improvident and dissolute man, addicted to sensuality and intemperance, but often an affectionate husband and indulgent father. As no Hindu can approach a Dom, his peculiar customs are unknown, and are therefore said to be wicked and accursed. A tradition survives among the Dacca Doms, that in the days of the Nawábs their ancestors were brought from Patna for employment as executioners (jallád) and disposers of the dead—hateful duties, which they perform at the present day. On the paid establishment of each magistracy a Dom hangman is borne, who officiates whenever sentence of death is carried out. On these occasions he is assisted by his relatives, and as the bolt is drawn shouts of 'Dohái

[1] The whole of this business was acted before me in the Buxar Central Jail by a number of Magahiyá Doms undergoing sentence there. Several of them had their left arms scarred from the shoulder to the wrist by assiduous worship of the tribal Laverna.

[2] Horace, *Epist.* i. 16, 60.

Mahárani!' or 'Doháí Judge Sáhib' are raised to exonerate them from all blame."

Attend Hindu funerals.

The peculiar functions which the caste performs at all Hindu funerals may be observed by all visitors to Benares, and are described by Mr. Sherring as follows:—"On the arrival of the dead body at the place of cremation, which in Benares is at the base of one of the steep stairs or *gháts*, called the Burning Ghát, leading down from the streets above to the bed of the river Ganges, the Dom supplies five logs of wood, which he lays in order upon the ground, the rest of the wood being given by the family of the deceased. When the pile is ready for burning, a handful of lighted straw is brought by the Dom, and is taken from him and applied by one of the chief members of the family to the wood. The Dom is the only person who can furnish the light for the purpose; and if from any circumstance the services of one cannot be obtained, great delay and inconvenience are apt to arise. The Dom exacts his fee for three things, namely, first, for the five logs; secondly, for the bunch of straw; and thirdly, for the light." It should be added that the amount of the fee is not fixed, but depends upon the rank and circumstances of the deceased. In Eastern Bengal, according to Dr. Wise, the services of the Dom at the funeral pyre are not now absolutely essential. Of late years, at any rate in Dacca, household servants carry the corpse to the burning ghát, where the pyre constructed by them is lighted by the nearest relative.

Social status.

The degraded position forced upon all Doms by reason of the functions which some of them perform is on the whole acquiesced in by the entire caste, most of whom, however, follow the comparatively cleanly occupation of making baskets and mats. Taking food as the test of social status, it will be seen that Doms eat beef,[1] pork, horse-flesh, fowls, ducks, field-rats, and the flesh of animals which have died a natural death. All of them, moreover, except the Bansphor and Chapariyá sub-castes, will eat the leavings of men of other castes. To this last point one exception must be noted. No Dom will touch the leavings of a Dhobi,[2] nor will he take water, sweetmeats, or any sort of food or drink from a man of that caste. The aversion with which the Dhobi is regarded is so pronounced that Doms of Behar have assured me that they would not take food from a Muhammadan who had his water fetched for him by a washerman of his own religion. The reason is obscure. Some people say the Dhobi is deemed impure because he washes women's clothes after childbirth; but this fact, though conclusive enough for the average Hindu, would not, I imagine, count for much with a Dom. Moreover, the Doms themselves say nothing of the kind, but tell a very singular story to account for their hatred of the Dhobis. Once upon a time,

[1] In Murshedabad and Eastern Bengal they profess to abstain from beef and hold themselves superior to Muchis and Bauris for so doing. In Assam buffalo meat is also forbidden.

[2] Some Doms say they will not eat the leavings of Dosadhs and Chamárs, but this refinement is not general.

they say, Supat Bhakat, the ancestor of the Doms, was returning tired and hungry from a long journey. On his way he met a Dhobi going along with a donkey carrying a bundle of clothes, and asked him for food and drink. The Dhobi would give him nothing and abused him into the bargain, whereupon Supat Bhakat fell upon the Dhobi, drove him away with blows, killed his donkey, and cooked and ate it on the spot. After he had eaten he repented of what he had done, and seeing that it was all the Dhobi's fault declared him and his caste to be accursed for the Doms for ever, so that a Dom should never take food from a Dhobi or eat in his house. The legend may perhaps be a distorted version of the breach of some primitive taboo in which Dhobis and donkeys somehow played a part. Doms will not touch a donkey, but the animal is not regarded by the caste in the light of a totem. In this connexion I may mention the curious fact that the Ankuriá and Bisdeliá Doms of Birbhum will not hold a horse or kill a dog, nor will they use a *dáo* with a wooden handle, explaining that their ancestors always worked with handleless *dáos*, and that they are bound to adhere to the ancient custom. The prejudice against killing a dog seems at first sight to suggest some connexion with the Bauris; but it may equally arise from the fact that one of the duties of scavenging Doms in towns is to kill ownerless dogs.

Occupation.

Doms believe their original profession to be the making of baskets and mats, and even the menial and scavenging sub-castes follow these occupations to some extent. About half of the caste are believed to have taken to agriculture, but none of these have risen above the rank of occupancy raiyats, and a large proportion are nomadic cultivators and landless day-labourers. In the south of Manbhum a small number of rent-free tenures, bearing the name *sibottar*, and supposed to be set apart for the worship of the god Siva, are now in the possession of Doms—a fact of which I can suggest no explanation. The Bajuniá sub-caste are employed to make highly discordant music at marriages and festivals. His women-folk, however, only perform as musicians at the wedding of their own people, it being considered highly derogatory for them to do so for outsiders. At home the Domni manufactures baskets and rattles for children. A single wandering branch of the Magahiyá sub-caste has earned for itself a reputation which has extended to the whole of that group. "The Magahiyá Doms of Champaran," says Mr. Beames, "are a race of professional thieves. They extend their operations into the contiguous districts of Nepal. They are rather dainty in their operations, and object to commit burglary by digging through the walls of houses: they always enter a house by the door; and if it is dark, they carry a light. Of course all this is merely done by way of bravado. Magahiyás never live long in one place. They move about constantly, pitching their ragged little reed tents or *sirkis* outside a village or on a grassy patch by the roadside, like our gipsies, till they have done all the plundering that offers itself in the neighbourhood, when they move off again." The popular belief that all Magahiyá Doms are habitual criminals is, however, a mistake.

Burglary is followed as a profession only by the wandering members of that sub-caste. The Magahiyás of Gya are peaceable basket-makers and cultivators, who regard thieving with as much horror as their neighbours, and know nothing of the Laverna cult of Sansári Mái, whom they identify with Jagadambá, the small-pox goddess, one of a group of seven sisters presiding over various diseases. There seems, indeed, reason to believe that the predatory habits of the gipsy Magahiyás of Champaran are due rather to force of circumstances than to an inborn criminal instinct; and the success of the measures introduced for their reclamation by Mr. E. R. Henry while Magistrate of Champaran affords grounds for the hope that they may in course of time settle down as peaceable cultivators.

The following statement shows the number and distribution of Doms in 1872 and 1881:—

District.	1872.	1881.	District.	1872.	1881.
Bardwan	52,327	38,856	Chittagong	15,491	9,117
Bankura	7,193	17,601	Noakhali	793	380
Birbhum	34,897	35,238	Tipperah	1,905	804
Midnapur	18,610	16,235	Patna	6,116	5,594
Hughli	10,715 (Hughli and Howrah)	10,729	Gya	7,627	6,773
Howrah		2,950	Shahabad	4,675	5,812
24-Parganas	6,478	3,159	Tirhut { Darbhanga ...	11,557 (Darbhanga and Mosufferpur)	10,618
Nadiya	2,937	2,247	Tirhut { Mosufferpur ...		10,042
Khulna	......	49	Saran	7,466	9,965
Jessore	1,078	2,054	Champaran	4,211	8,612
Murshedabad	10,490	7,577	Monghyr	10,769	12,910
Dinajpur	1,242	3,494	Bhagalpur	14,961	17,279
Rajshahye	582	405	Purniah	3,267	6,852
Rangpur	3,095	1,736	Maldah	1,227	1,377
Bogra	171	327	Santál Parganas	29,465	35,634
Pabna	1,566	1,231	Cuttack	2,252	1,785
Darjiling	88	166	Puri	2,113	2,232
Jalpigori	73	953	Balasore	1,397	1,582
Kuch Behar	......	281	Tributary States	4,853	3,929
Dacca	641	270	Hazaribagh	7,566	7,962
Faridpur	589	292	Lohardagá	5,395	5,673
Bakarganj	1,088	853	Singbhum	2,034	2,214
Maimansinh	3,717	1,112	Manbhum	17,342	18,610
			Tributary States	836	2,211

Domkatár, a section of Bábhans in Western Bengal and Behar to whom the members of other sections will not give their daughters in marriage, though they will marry Domkatár women. It perhaps deserves notice that *katár* or *katári* is the name of the peculiar curved knife used by the basket-making Doms.

Dom Khakha, a raven, a totemistic sept of Oraons in Chota Nagpur.

Dom-Pátni, Machhwá or **Naqárchi**, a sub-caste of Pátnis in Bengal.

Domrá, a sub-caste of Turis in Chota Nagpur; a synonym for Dom.

Domtakarái, a *mul* of the Bharadwáj section of Maithil Brahmans in Behar.

Domtáshi, a title of those Doms whose only profession is to sell bamboo articles, originally immigrants from Upper India.

Domtikár, a *kul* or section of Bábhans in Behar.

Don, a *mul* or section of the Chhamuliá Madhesiá sub-caste of Halwáis in Behar.

Dondchatra, a section of Páns in Chota Nagpur.

Dong-ba, a *rui* or sept of Sherpa Bhotias of Nepal.

Dongwár, a title of those who use canoes, generally Gond, Malla, or Oraon.

Donwár, a *kul* or section of Bábhans and a sept of Rajputs in Behar; a sept of the Rautár sub-tribe of Thárus.

Dopátiá, a sub-caste of Mayaás in Eastern Bengal.

Dorihar-jogi, a section of Rajwárs in Chota Nágpur.

Doroá-Gond or **Náik,** a sub-tribe of Gonds in Chota Nagpur.

Dorompá, a *rui* or sept of the Ruichhung sub-tribe of Dejong Lhoris or Bhotias of the south.

Dorowár, a sept of Rajputs in Behar.

Dorrá, a sub-tribe of Bhuiyás in Western Bengal.

Traditions of origin.

Dosádh, a degraded Aryan or refined Dravidian cultivating caste of Behar and Chota Nagpur, the members of which are largely employed as village watchmen and messengers, and bear a very evil reputation as habitual criminals. Dosádhs claim to be descended from the soldiers of the Pándava prince Bhima or Bhim Sen, and to be allied to the Cheros, who are supposed at one time to have ruled in Behar. Buchanan thought there was "some reason to suspect" that the Dosádhs might be the same tribe as the Chandáls of Bengal, basing this conjecture on the statement that "the two castes follow nearly the same professions and bear the same rank, while the Chandáls pretend to be descended of Ráhu, and, I am told, worship that monster." In fact, however, the Chandáls do not worship Ráhu or trace their origin to him, and the Dosádhs revere a host of deified heroes, a form of worship entirely unknown to the Chandál. The young men of the caste are often rather good-looking, and many of them have a yellowish brown complexion with wide, expanded nostrils and the tip of the nose slightly turned up. The complexion, however, and the shape of the nose show a range of variations which seems to indicate considerable mixture of blood.

Professor Mantegazza, following Dalton, describes them as "Aryans of a very low type;" and it seems about equally likely that the original stock may have been a branch of the Aryans degraded and coarsened by crossing with lower races, or a non-Aryan tribe refined in feature and raised in stature by intermixture with semi-Aryan castes. In Northern Behar there has probably been some infusion of Mongolian blood; and in all parts of the country some allowance must be made for the fact that members of any Hindu caste except the Dom, Dhobi, and Chamar may gain admission into the Dosádh community by giving a feast to the heads of the caste and eating pork and drinking liquor in token of their adoption of Dosádh usage. This privilege, no doubt, is not eagerly sought for, and most of those who join themselves to the Dosádhs after this fashion have probably got into trouble with their own people for keeping a Dosádh mistress or doing something disreputable. Still the existence of a regular procedure for enrolling recruits from other castes shows that such cases are not unknown, and they must tend in some measure to modify the physical type of the caste.

Internal structure.

The caste is divided into eight sub-castes:—**Kanaujiá, Magahiyá, Bhojpuriá, Pailwár, Kámar** or **Kánwar, Kuri** or **Kurin, Dhárhi** or **Dhár, Silhotia** or **Sirotiá, Báhaliá.** The members of nearly all these groups will eat cooked food together, but do not intermarry. The Dhárhi, however, who pretend to be descended from a Goálá who accidentally killed a cow, and disclaim all connexion with the Dosádhs, are excluded from this privilege; and the Kámar have only recently cleared themselves from the suspicion of eating beef and been admitted to social intercourse with the other sub-castes. Concerning the Báhaliá there is some question whether they are Dosádhs at all, and it has been maintained that they are a distinct caste of gypsy-like habits, and possibly akin to the Bediyás. Most Báhaliás, however, insist on their title to be considered Dosádhs, and in Bengal at any rate the Báhaliá and Dosádh eat and smoke together, and, though they do not intermarry, behave generally as if they were branches of the same stock. The sections (*dih, mul, párich,* or *pangat*), which are very numerous, are shown in Appendix I. In applying the rule of exogamy to a particular case the caste profess to exclude the sections of (1) the father, (2) the paternal grandmother, (3) the paternal great-grand-mothers, (4) the paternal great-great-grandmothers, (5) the mother, (6) the maternal grandmother, (7) the maternal great-grandmothers, and to follow the double method of reckoning explained in the article on Bais. So that if the proposed bridegroom's maternal grandmother should happen to have belonged to the same section as one of the proposed bride's paternal great-great-grandmothers, the marriage would be disallowed notwithstanding that the parties themselves belong to different sections. It is obvious, however, that entire conformity with so complicated and far-reaching a scheme of prohibitions requires that genealogies shall be carefully kept up and infringements of the rules jealously watched for by the headmen and panchâyats, who in the first instance determine the question whether a particular couple may marry or not. There are indeed officials called *panjiárs* or genealogists, who are supposed to act as referees in such matters, but the caste as a whole is on a very low educational level, and it is very doubtful whether the strict letter of these rules is invariably complied with. It will be seen that nearly all the sections of the Magahiyá and Páilwár sub-castes are *titular,* while most of the other sub-castes have *local* or *territorial* sections. The Báhaliá have no sections, and regulate their marriages by the standard formula for reckoning prohibited degrees calculated to seven generations in the descending line. This formula is also used by the other sub-castes as supplementary to their system of exogamy.

Marriage.

Dosádhs marry their daughters whenever they can afford to do so, but they do not hold the strict view of the spiritual necessity of infant-marriage which is current among the higher castes, and the fact of a girl's marriage being deferred until she has passed the age of puberty is not deemed to put any special slur on the family to which she belongs. Some Dosádhs, however, hold that an adult bride is not entitled to the full marriage service (*biyáh*), but must be married by the *sagai* form used at the remarriage of a widow. The marriage ceremony is a somewhat meagre copy of the ritual in vogue among middle-class Hindus. Well-to-do Dosádhs employ Brahmans to officiate as priests; but this practice is not general, and most members of the caste content themselves with getting a Brahman to fix an auspicious day for the event, and to mutter certain formulæ (*mantras*) over the vermilion, the smearing of which on the bride's forehead constitutes the binding portion of the rite. An infant bride is kept in her parent's house until she reaches puberty, at the age of twelve or fourteen, when the *gauná* ceremony is performed, her nails are cut and stained red, and her husband takes her to his own house. Consummation does not take place until after the *gauná* ceremony. Polygamy is permitted to a limited extent. A man may in no case have more than two wives, and he is not supposed to take a second wife at all unless the first is childless or suffers from an incurable disease. In the Santál Parganas, however, three wives are allowed, and the tendency is to follow the aboriginal usage of unlimited polygamy. A widow may marry again by the *sagai* form, and it is deemed right, on grounds of domestic convenience, for her to marry her late husband's younger brother if such a relative survives him. In the event of her marrying an outsider she takes no share in her late husband's property, and any children she may have had by him remain in the charge of his family. Divorce is permitted by all sub-castes except the Kámar, with the sanction of the pancháyat, for adultery and persistent disobedience or ill-temper on the part of the wife. In the Santál Parganas and Palámau a *sál* leaf is torn in two or a stick broken to symbolise the separation of the couple. Divorced women may marry again by the *sagai* rite, but they must first give a feast to the members of the caste by way of atonement for their previous misconduct.

Religion.

Most Dosádhs, if questioned about their religion, will persistently aver that they are orthodox Hindus, and in proof of this allegation will refer to the fact that they employ Brahmans and worship the regular gods. In most districts, indeed, degraded Kanaujiá or Maithil Brahmans serve the caste as priests in a somewhat irregular and intermittent fashion, being paid in cash for specific acts of worship and for attendance at marriages. Many Dosádhs, again, belong to the Sri Narayani sect, and some follow the *panth*, or doctrine of Kabir, Tulsi Dás, Gorakhnath, or Nának. This enthusiasm for religion, however, like the Satnámi movement among the Chamárs of the Central Provinces, appears to be a comparatively recent development, induced in the main by the desire of social advancement and existing side by side with peculiar religious observances, survivals from an earlier animistic form of belief, traces of which may perhaps be discerned in current Hindu mythology.

The god Ráhu.

Their tribal deity Ráhu has been transformed

by the Brahmans into a Daitya or Titan, who is supposed to cause eclipses by swallowing the sun and moon. Though placed in the orthodox pantheon as the son of the Danava Viprachitti and Sinhiká, Ráhu has held his ground as the chief deity of the Dosádhs. To avert diseases, and in fulfilment of vows, sacrifices of animals and the fruits of the earth are offered to him, at which a Dosádh Bhakat or Chatiyá usually presides. On special occasions a stranger form of worship is resorted to, parallels to which may be found in the rustic cult of the Roman villagers and the votaries of the Phœnician deities. A ladder, made with sides of green bamboos and rungs of sword-blades, is raised in the midst of a pile of burning mango wood, through which the Bhakat walks barefooted and ascends the ladder without injury. Swine of all ages, a ram, wheaten flour, and rice-milk (*khir*), are offered up: after which the worshippers partake of a feast and drink enormous quantities of ardent spirits.

His worship.

Another form of this worship has been described to me by Dosádhs of Darbhanga and North Bhágalpur. On the fourth, the ninth, or the day before the full-moon of the months Aghan, Mágh, Phálgun, or Baisákh, the Dosádh who has bound himself by a vow to offer the fire sacrifice to Ráhu must build within the day a thatched hut (*gahbar*) measuring five cubits by four and having the doorway facing east. Here the priest or Bhakat, himself a Dosádh, who is to officiate at the next day's ordeal must spend that night, sleeping on the *kusa* grass with which the floor is strewn. In front of the door of the hut is a bamboo platform about three feet from the ground, and beyond that again is dug a trench six cubits long, a span and a quarter wide, and of the same depth, running east and west. Fire-places are built to the north of the trench, at the point marked *d* in the plan below. On the next day, being the fifth, the tenth, or the full-moon day of the months mentioned above, the trench is filled with mango wood soaked in ghee, and two earthen vessels of boiling milk are placed close to the platform. The Bhakat bathes himself on the north side of the trench and puts on a new cloth dyed for the occasion with turmeric. He mutters a number of mystic formulæ and worships Ráhu on both sides of the trench. The fire is then kindled, and the Bhakat solemnly walks three times round the trench, keeping his right hand always towards it. The end of the third round brings him to the east end of the trench, where he takes by the hand a Brahman retained for this purpose with a fee of two new wrappers (*dhotis*), and calls upon him to lead the way through the fire. The Brahman then walks along the trench from east to west, followed by the Bhakat. Both are supposed to tread with bare feet on the fire, but I imagine this is for the most part an optical illusion. By the time they start the actual flames have subsided, and the trench is so narrow that very little dexterity would enable a man to walk with his feet on either edge, so as not to touch the smouldering ashes at the bottom. On reaching the west end of the trench the Brahman stirs the milk with his hand to see that it has been properly boiled. Here his part in the ceremony comes to an end. By passing through the fire the Bhakat is believed to have been inspired with the spirit of Ráhu, who has become incarnated in him. Filled with the divine or demoniac *afflatus*, and also, it may be surmised, excited by drink and gánjá, he mounts the bamboo platform, chants mystic hymns, and distributes to the crowd *tulsi* leaves, which heal diseases otherwise incurable, and flowers which have the virtue of causing barren women to conceive. The proceedings end with a feast, and religious excitement soon passes into drunken revelry lasting long into the night.

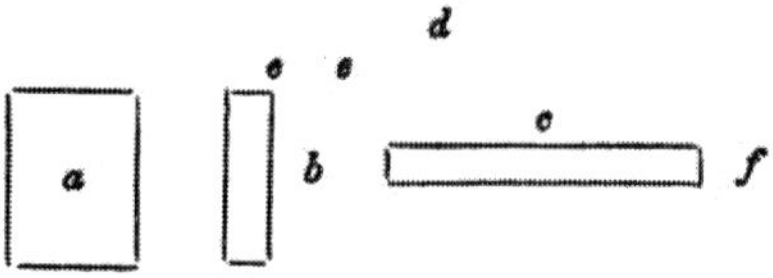

a. Bhakat's hut (*gahbar*).
b. Platform (*machán*),
c. Trench full of fire.
d. Fire-places.
e. Vessels of milk.
f. Point from which Brahman and Bhakat pass through the fire.

Next in importance to the worship of Ráhu is that of various deified heroes, in honour of whom huts are erected in different parts of the country. At Sherpúr, near Patna, is the shrine of Gauraiá or Goraiyá, a Dosádh bandit chief, to which members of all castes resort; the clean making offerings of meal, the unclean sacrificing a swine or several young pigs and pouring out libations of spirit on the ground. Throughout Behar, Salesh or Sáláis, said to have been the porter of Bhím Sen, but afterwards a formidable robber in the Morang or Nepal Terai, is invoked; a pig being killed, and rice, ghi, sweatmeats, and spirits offered. In other districts Choár Mal is held in reverence, and a ram sacrificed. In Mirzápúr the favoured deity is Bindháchal, the spirit of the Vindhya mountains. In Patna it is either Bandí, Moti Rám, Kárú or Karwá Bír, Miran, the Pánch Pir, Bhairav, Jagdá Má, Kálí, Deví, Patanesvarí, or Ketú, the descending node in Hindu astronomy, sometimes represented as the tail of the eclipse-dragon, and credited with causing lunar eclipses; while Ráhu, the ascending node, represented by the head of the dragon, produces a similar phenomenon in the sun. In none of these shrines are there any idols, and the officiating priests are always Dosádhs, who minister to the Súdra castes frequenting them. The offerings usually go to the priest or the head of the Dosádh household performing the worship; but fowls sacrified to Mirán and the Panch Pir are given to local Muhammadans.

In Eastern Bengal, says Dr. Wise, Sákadvípi Brahmans act as the hereditary purohits of the Dosádhs, and fix a favourable day for weddings and the naming of children. To the great indignation of other tribes, these Brahmans assume the aristocratic title of Misra, which properly belongs to the Kanaujiá order. The guru, called Gosáin, Faqír, Vaishnava, or simply Sádhu, abstains from all manual labour and from intoxicating drugs. His text-book is the Gyán-ságar, or Sea of Knowledge, believed to have been written by Vishnu himself in his form of Chatur-bhuja, or the four-armed. It inculcates the immaterial nature of god (Nirákára), which is regarded by the Brahmans as a most pernicious heresy. In the Santál Parganas Dhobis and barbers serve the Dosádhs as priests.

Dosádhs usually burn, but occasionally bury, their dead and perform a *sráddh*, more or less of the orthodox pattern, on the eleventh day after death. The female Dosádh is unclean for six days after child-birth. On the seventh day she bathes, but is not permitted to touch the household utensils till the twelfth day, when a feast (*bárahi*) is given and she becomes ceremonially clean.

Social status and occupation.

The social rank of Dosádhs is very low. No respectable caste will eat with them, while they themselves, besides eating pork, tortoises, fowls, and field-rats, and indulging freely in strong drink, will take food from any class of Hindus except the Dhobi and the specially unclean castes of Dom and Chamar. Some of them even keep pigs and cure pork. Their characteristic occupation is to serve as watchmen (*chaukidárs*), and in this capacity they afford an excellent illustration of the Platonic doctrine *ὅτου τις ἄρα δεινὸς φύλαξ, τούτου καὶ φὼρ δεινός*,[1] for they rank among the most persistent criminals known to the Indian police. We find them also as village messengers (*gorait*), grooms, elephant-drivers, grass and wood-cutters, pankhá coolies, and porters. They bear a high character as carriers, and are popularly believed to repress their criminal instincts when formally entrusted with goods in that capacity. In South Bhagalpur the occupation of a groom is considered degrading, and a Dosádh who takes service in that capacity is expelled from the caste. This seems to be a purely local practice. In Western Bengal and Behar Dosádhs occasionally work as cooks and grooms for Europeans. Some of the *chaukidárs* and *goraits* hold small allotments of land rent-free in lieu of the services rendered by them to the village,[2] but generally speaking Dosádhs hold a low place in the agricultural system. Their improvidence and their dissolute habits hinder them from rising above the grade of occupancy raiyat, and a very large proportion of them are merely tenants-at-will or landless day-labourers. During the Muhammadan rule in Bengal, says Dr. Wise, Dosádhs and Báhalias served in the army, and when Ali Vardi Khán was Nawáb Názim the native historian stigmatises their licentious conduct as a disgrace to the Government. From the days of William Hamilton it has been generally believed that in the early period of our military history "Bengali sepoys almost exclusively filled several of our battalions, and distinguished themselves as brave and active soldiers;" but, as is pointed out by Mr. Shore, for years before the battle of Plassey the troops in Bengal were chiefly composed of recruits enlisted in Hindustan. According to Mr. Reade, most of the sepoys who served under Lord Clive were Dosádhs, who of course cannot be regarded as Bengalis in the ordinary sense of the word. It must be remembered, however, that a few generations ago the

---

[1] *Plato. Rep.* i, 334.

[2] Buchanan, ii, 235, says that in Bhagalpur the Dosádh receives from two to ten bighas of land rent-free, with $\frac{1}{160}$ part, or a quarter of a seer per maund, of the rent in grain, all these charges being paid by the landlord.

word Bengal was used in a more extended and less accurate sense than is now the case, and it is quite likely that when Hamilton wrote of *Bengali* sepoys he merely meant to distinguish Natives of Hindustan from the Madras sepoys (see article **Telinga**), who were largely employed in our early campaigns in Bengal.

The following statement shows the number and distribution of Dosádhs in 1872 and 1881:—

District.	1872.	1881.	District.	1872.	1881.
Bardwan	596	400	Bakarganj	14	......
Bankura	19	24	Maimansinh	36	159
Birbhum	144	1,414	Tipperah	9	......
Midnapur	96	134	Chittagong	3	8
Hughli	479	254	Patna	85,084	100,631
Howrah		1,172	Gya	95,641	108,284
24-Parganas	5,606	1,304	Shahabad	77,974	90,845
Nadiya	1,357	309	Tirhut { Darbhanga ...	296,186	189,061
Khulna	......	15	Tirhut { Mozufferpur ...		179,758
Jessore	23	29	Saran	73,098	79,600
Murshedabad	2,436	1,886	Champaran	70,609	82,507
Dinajpur	1,100	6,692	Monghyr	99,892	111,331
Rajshahye	196	626	Bhagalpur	67,127	72,412
Rangpur	201	258	Purniah	27,374	31,084
Bogra	44	80	Maldah	2,393	2,848
Pabna	25	314	Santál Parganas	8,307	11,033
Darjiling	68	1,230	Hazaribagh	16,553	26,779
Jalpigori	142	6	Lohardagá	25,233	34,998
Kuch Behar	......	100	Singbhum	244	240
Dacca	50	137	Manbhum	903	1,674
Faridpur	4	394	Tributary States	4,030	2,786

Dosi, a title of Oswál Baniyas.

Doside, a sub-group of the Hele Kaibarttas in Central Bengal.

Dotiyál, a *thar* or section of Nepáli Brahmans.

Dowalbandhi, a section of Ghásis in Chota Nagpur.

Drábirí, Dráviri, a territorial division of the Pancha Drávira Brahmans who live in the south of the Vindhya range, a country of the Dravidian or Tamil language.

Duarbandha, a sub-caste of Sunris in Maldah.

Duárseni, a sub-caste of Ghásis in Chota Nagpur.

Dubaithiá, a section of Sonárs in Behar.

Dube or Dobe, a title of Gaura, Sáraswat, and Kanaujiá Brahmans, and of Bábhans in Behar; a title of the Brahmans who officiate as priests for lower castes in Bengal.

Dubhiár, Dobihár, a *mul* or section of the Kanaujiá sub-caste of Sonárs in Behar.

Dub Ság, a grass, a totemistic sept of Mundas in Chota Nagpur.

Dudhailá or *Maghayá*, a sub-caste of Dhánuks in Behar.

Dudhiá, a section of Mauliks in Western Bengal.

Dudhkatorá, a *mul* or section of the Ajodhiabasi sub-caste of Sonárs in Behar.

Dudh-Kaur, a sub-tribe of Kaurs in Chota Nagpur.

Dudhliá, a section of Goálás in the North-Western Provinces.

Dudhnáit, a *kul* or section of Bábhans in Behar.

Dudhpuriet, a *mul* or section of the Naomuliá or Majraut sub-caste of Goálás in Behar.

Dudhráj, a section of Kámis in Darjiling.

Dudhwár or **Dojwár**, a sub-caste of Dhánuks in Behar who are said never to castrate calves.

Dud-Khariá, a sub-caste of Khariás in Chota Nagpur.

Dudul, a kind of bird, a totemistic sept of Kharwars in Chota Nagpur.

Dugar, a sect of Dasnámi Sannyásis.

Dugra, a variant for Doglá or Dogra, *q.v.*

Dugriár, a section of Kurmis in Chota Nagpur and Orissa.

Dukhcháki, a *thar* or sept of Mangars in Darjiling.

Dulál, a *thar* or section of Nepáli Brahmans.

Duliá, a sub-caste of Bágdis in Bengal, who are fishermen, palki-bearers, and general labourers.

Dumala Goárá, a sub-caste of Goálás in Orissa.

Duman, a sub-caste of Sutradhars in Noakháli.

Dumániá, a section of Goálás in the North-Western Provinces and Behar.

Dumar, a section of Goálás in Behar.

Dumariár, a *pur* or section of Sákadwipi Brahmans in Behar.

Dumdoliá, a section of Goálás in the North-Western Provinces and Behar.

Dumján, a section of Murmis in Darjiling.

Dumrahar, a section of Báis Sonárs in Behar.

Dumráit, a section of Bábhans in Behar.

Dumri, a *mul* or section of the Tinmuliá Madhesiá sub-caste of Halwáis in Behar.

Dumriá, *Dumuriá*, *Dungriár*, *Dungri*, a totemistic section or sept of Kurmis, Lohars, Mundas, and Mahilis in Chota Nagpur, the members of which will not eat the wild fig (*dumur*).

Dumriába, a totemistic sept of Juángs in the Tributary States of Orissa, probably a variant of Dumriá, and having reference to the wild fig.

Dundoar, an owl, a totemistic sept of Chiks in Chota Nagpur.

Dundu, a kind of eel, a sept of Mundas in Chota Nagpur.

Dundwár, a section of Bábhans in Behar.

Dungdung, a river-fish, a sept of Mundas and Khariás in Chota Nagpur.

Dungiá, a sub-tribe of Dhimáls in the Darjiling Terai.

Dungmáli, a sept of Khambus in Darjiling.

Duntakarieh, a *mul* of the Bharadwája section of Maithil Brahmans in Behar.

Dunyá, a sept of the Tungjainya sub-tribe of Chakmás in the Hill Tracts of Chittagong.

Dura, a fruit, a totemistic sept of Mundas in Chota Nagpur.

Durál, a section of Kámis in Darjiling.

Durang, a section of Khariás in Chota Nagpur.

Durbichá, a *thar* or sept of Sunuwars in Darjiling.

Durgbansi, a sept of Rajputs in Behar.

Durgu, a section of the Koohh-Mandai in Dacca.

Durihar, a string-maker in Hazaribagh. Some of them bear the title of Gosáin.

Durihár, a religious group of Jugis.

Durjea, see **Darjea**.

Duryodhan, a title of Sunris in Bengal.

Dusád, a section of Goálás in the North-Western Provinces and Behar.

Dusre, a group of the Sribástab sub-caste of Káyasths in Behar.

Dut, a title of Bangaja Káyasths.

Dwádas, a sub-caste of Telis in Bengal.

Dwija, a synonym for Brahman.

Dwijáti, *Dijáti*, "twice-born," a title of Brahmans, Kshatriyas, and Vaisyas in the scheme of castes attributed to the mythical Manu. In the Census papers the term seems to have been used pedantically by Brahmans or Rajputs who wished to glorify themselves.

E

Echaghatu, a sept of Hos in Singbhum.

Eh-A'r, a sept of the Chandrabansi Rajputs in Behar.

Ekádas, a sub-caste of Telis in Bengal and Orissa; a section of the Rauniyár sub-caste of Baniyás in Behar.

Ekádasi, a functional group of Jugis in Bengal.

Ekauná, a section of the Biyáhut and Kharidáhá Kalwárs and of Awadhiá Hajáms in Behar.

Ekáhre-Orá, a *mul* of the Bharadwáj section of Maithil Brahmans in Behar.

Ekahre-Ruchaul, a *mul* of the Bharadwáj section of Maithil Brahmans in Behar.

Ekahre-Kanhauli, a *mul* of the Bharadwáj section of Maithil Brahmans in Behar.

Ekahre-Sagrám, a *mul* of the Bharadwáj section of Maithil Brahmans in Behar.

Ekahre-Torne, a *mul* of the Bharadwáj section of Maithil Brahmans in Behar.

Ekka, tortoise, a totemistic sept of Oraons in Chota Nagpur.

Ekpatiá, a sub-caste of Mayarás in Eastern Bengal.

Eksariá, a *kul* or section of Bábhans in Behar.

Ekside, a sub-group of the Hele Kaibarttas in Central Bengal.

Emboro, a sept of Hos in Singbhum.

Erengá-Khariá, a sub-caste of Khariás in Chota Nagpur.

Ergat, a kind of mouse, supposed to live in plum bushes, a totemistic sept of Mundas in Chota Nagpur.

Ergo, rat, a totemistic sept of Oraons in Chota Nagpur.

F

Fadung, a sept of Tipperahs in the Hill Tracts of Chittagong.

Fakir, a title of the Hárita section of Utkal Brahmans in Orissa.

Fakir, an Arabic word, properly denoting a Mahomedan religious mendicant, but vaguely used to denote beggars of all kinds. Of fakirs in the strict sense of the word, the following classes are enumerated by Wilson: "1. The Kádariá or Báuawá, who profess to be the spiritual descendants of Saiad Abdul-Kádir Jiláni, of Bagdad. 2. The Chishtiá, followers of Banda-nawáz, whose shrine is at Kalbarga; they are usually Shias. 3. Shutáriá, descendants of Abdul-shutar-i-nák. 4. Tabkátiá, or Madáriá, followers of Sháh Madár; many of these are jugglers, and bear or monkey-leaders. 5. Malang, descended from Jaman Jati, one of Shah Madár's disciples. 6. Rafái, or Gurz-már, descended from Saiad Ahmed Kabir Rafái, who appear to beat, cut, and wound themselves without suffering inconvenience, and who, in the belief of the faithful, can cut off their own heads and put them on again. 7. Jaláliá, followers of Saiad Jalál-ud-din Bokhári. 8. Sohágia, from Músa Soház, who dress like women, wear female ornaments, play upon musical instruments, and sing and dance. 9. Naksh-bandia, followers of Bahá-ud-din, of Nakshband, distinguished by begging at night and carrying a lighted lamp. 10. Báwá piári ka fakírán, who dress in white. There are other distinctions; and at the Muharram a number of the lower classes assume the character and garb of fakírs, of different ridiculous personations, for the amusement of the populace and the collection of contributions."

Fáluda-wálá, a maker of sherbets and syrups. In Behar the Faluda-wálá often opens a tea shop during the cold weather.

Fanigá, grasshopper, a totemistic sept of Parhaiyas in Chota Nagpur.

Farakhábádi, a sub-caste of Gareris in Behar.

Fariansa, a sept of the Tungjainya sub-tribe of Chakmás in the Hill Tracts of Chittagong.

Farrásh, *Farásh*, a servant whose business it is to spread and sweep mats, carpets, etc.

Fatehpuri, a section of Sonárs in Behar.

Fatehsing, a sub-caste of Telis in Murshedabad.

Faujdár, a title conferred by the local Rájás of Western Bengal on certain families who were engaged in police duties. The word also denotes the proselytizing officials of the Vaishava sects.

Fenga, a section of Máls in Bankura.

Feringi, a title of the Hárita section of Utkal Brahmans in Orissa.

G

Gábag, a section of Murmis in Darjiling.

Gácha, a *thar* or sept of Mangars in Darjiling.

Gachai, a sept of Parhaiyas in Chota Nagpur.

Gáchhuá or **Ghaná**, a sub-caste of Telis in Bengal from Gáchhu, a designation of persons who own *gáchh* or oil mills and sugarcane mills.

Gáchkátá, a wood-cutter, a title of Seulis who cut down date-trees for their juice.

Gadahiá, a sub-caste of Doms in Behar who are breeders of donkeys; a section of the Banodhiá and Jaiswár Kalwárs in Behar.

Gadahpurná, a *pur* or section of Sákadwipi Brahmans in Behar.

Gadáili, Gadál, a section of Kámis; a *thar* or sept of Mangars in Darjiling.

Gadaiyá, a section of Saraogis in Behar.

Gadariyá, a synonym for Gareri.

Gádásari, a sub-caste of Kurmis in Orissa.

Gáddi, a class of Mahomedan herdsmen in Behar.

Gáddi, Ghosi, or **Ghosin**, a sub-caste of Goálás in Behar.

Gadháriá, a section of Goálás in the North-Western Provinces and Behar.

Gadhayá, a sub-caste of Dhobis in Behar who keep donkeys; a title of Beldárs.

Gadheyiá, a section of the Biyáhut and Kharidáhá Kalwárs in Behar.

Gadhojiá, a section of Goálás in the North-Western Provinces and Behar.

Gadhuwal, a section of the Ját sub-caste of Goálás in Behar whose titles are Chaudhri, Singh, and Marár.

Gadibhárat, a section of Bágdis in Western Bengal.

Gadrahá, a *pur* or section of Sákadwipi Brahmans in Behar.

Gaegoal, a sept of Goálás in Chota Nagpur, who are forbidden to eat *pákar* fruit.

Gaek, a sept of Gonds in Chota Nagpur.

Gáger, a section of the Sátmuliá Maghayá sub-caste of Kándus in Behar.

Gághraba, paddy, a totemistic sept of Juángs in the Tributary States of Orissa.

Gagriá, a sept of Hos in Singbhum.

Gágrish, a section of Sunris in the Santál Parganas.

Gahalá, a section of Goálás in the North-Western Provinces and Behar.

Gahálaot, a sept of the Suryabans sub-tribe of Rajputs in Behar.

Gaharbári, a sept of the Rautár sub-tribe of Thárus in Behar.

Gaharwár, a sept of Suraj-bansi Rajputs and of the Rautár sub-tribe of Thárus in Behar.

Gahatráj, a section of Kámis in Darjiling.

Gahlaut, a sept of the Chandrabansi division of Rajputs in Behar.

Gah-oh, a *rui* or sept of Dejong Lhoris, whose ancestor had emigrated from Bhotan and the members of which now work as blacksmiths.

Gahui, a small caste of Hindu traders found in Hazaribagh.

Gahunágáoná, a *mul* or section of the Chhamuliá Madhesiá sub-caste of Halwáis in Behar.

Gái, cow, a totemistic sept of Kharwars in Chota Nagpur.

Gaibing, a sept of Tipperahs in the Hill Tracts of Chittagong.

Gaiduhá, a sub-caste of Pásis in Behar.

Gaighatiá, a section of Bháts in Behar.

Gáigwár, a sept of Rajputs in Behar.

Gaim, a section of Maghaiyá Kumhárs in Behar.

Gáim, a group of Maghaiyá Telis in Behar.

Gáin, a sept of Rajputs and a *pangat* or section of Bánsphor Doms and of Sunris in Behar; a class of Mahomedan singers; a low Nepali caste of musicians.

Gáin or **Grámin**, literally 'belonging to a village,' a term signifying a title of Rárhi and Bárendra Brahmans in Bengal, whose ancestors were given villages by Rájá Adisura when they were brought from Kanauj to perform ceremonies at his request.

Gaintwar, a sept of Lohárs in Chota Nagpur

Gairaha Pipli, a *thar* or section of Nepáli Brahmans.

Gaitháhá, a section of Bhojpuriá Halwáis in Behar.

Gaithaula, a *thar* or section of Nepáli Brahmans.

Gajamer, a *thar* or sept of Mangars in Darjiling.

Gajbania, a section of Páns in Chota Nagpur.

Gajkesar, a sept of Rajputs in Behar.

Gajmer, a section of Kámis in Darjiling.

Gajniyál, a *thar* or section of Nepáli Brahmans.

Galan, a section of Murmis in Darjiling.

Gálá-Tánti, a sub-caste of Tántis in Orissa.

Gamaiyá, *Parganá Kharakpur*, a *dih* or local section of the Maghaiyá sub-caste of Koiris in Bhágalpur.

Gambhariá, a *kul* or section of Bábhans in Behar.

Gámel, a section of the Biyáhut and Kharidáhá Kalwárs in Behar.

Gan, a title of Dakshin-Rárhi and Bangaja Káyasths in Bengal.

Gana, a hypergamous division of Tiyars in Behar.

Ganda, a sub-caste of Páns in Chota Nagpur.

Ganda, Gandak, a title of Dakshin-Rárhi and Bangaja Káyasths in Bengal.

Gandár, Gandá, a title of Goálás in Behar.

Gandark, a *pur* or section of Sákadwipi Brahmans in Behar.

Gandha, flying bug, a totemistic sept of Chiks in Chota Nagpur.

Gandhabanik, *Gandhabaniá*, *Putuli*, the spice-selling, druggist, and grocer caste of Bengal Proper. They claim to be a branch of the Aryan Vaisyas, and trace their descent from Chandra Bhava, commonly called Chánd Saudágar, "an accomplished man, the son of Kotís-Vara, the lord of crores," and Sáha Rájá of Ujjain, mentioned in the Padma Purána. Although this ancient lineage is assumed, the caste no longer wear the Bráhmanical thread; their marriage ritual does not include *Kusandiká*; and, instead of mourning like the Agarwálá Baniyás for thirteen days, they mourn, like pure Súdras, for thirty. A modern compiler of caste genealogies gives them a Baidya father and a Rájput mother, a *pratilomaj* pedigree wholly fatal to their claim to be Vaisyas. Another story of their origin is current. Kubja, the hunch-backed slave girl of Rájá Kansa, was carrying home spices and sandal wood when Krishna first met her. The son born of their subsequent *liaison* was naturally the first spice-seller and the father of all Gandhabaniks. A third tradition tells how Siva, being in need of spices for his marriage with Durgá, created the first of the Desá Gandhabanik from his forehead, the Sankha from his arm-pit, the Aut from his navel, and the Chhatris from his foot, and sent them out to the four quarters of the globe to fetch what he required. The Chhatris, who went to the east, got back first. All four were then appointed to sell spices to men.

Traditions of origin.

The Gandhabaniks are divided into four sub-castes—**Aut-Asram, Chhatris-Asram, Desá-Asram, Sankha-Asram.** In Dacca, according to Dr. Wise, the three last intermarry and eat together, but this appears not to be the case in Central Bengal. The sections shown in Appendix I are Brahmanical, with the single exception of the one called Rásrishi, which I am unable to trace or account for. The prohibited degrees are the same as among the Káyasths.

Internal structure.

Gandhabaniks marry their daughters as infants, and receive a bride-price (*pan*) varying according to the social status of the two families concerned. Thus the Gandhabaniks of Bikrampur in Dacca receive a higher price for their daughters and pay a lower price for their wives than members of families whose reputation stands less high for purity of lineage and propriety of ceremonial observances. The marriage ceremony is of the orthodox type. In Dacca city, says Dr. Wise, the Gandhabanik caste has six powerful *dals*, or unions; the *Dalpatis*, or headmen, being persons of great respectability. In one of the *dals* a curious marriage custom, said to have been observed by their forefathers when they first entered Bengal, is still preserved. The bridegroom climbs a champá-tree (*Michelia champaca*) and sits there while the bride is

Marriage.

carried round on a stool seven times. Should no tree be available, a champá log, placed beneath a canopy or a platform made of champá wood planks, is substituted and ornamented with gilt flowers resembling the real champá blossoms. The other *dals*, who follow the usual Sudra ritual, associate with this one in private, but not in public. In all cases the bridal dress is made of yellow silk (*cheli*) with a red striped border, and the bride wears hers for ten days after marriage.

Polygamy is permitted to the extent that a man may take a second wife if he has no children by the first. Widows are not allowed to marry again, nor is divorce recognised. A woman convicted of unchastity is simply turned out of the caste and ceases to be a member of respectable Hindu society. Her husband burns her in effigy, and performs for her a mimic *sráddh* as if she were actually dead.

Religion.

In matters of religion the Gandhabaniks conform entirely to the orthodox forms of Hinduism prevalent in Bengal Proper. The large majority of them are Vaishnavas, a few Sáktas, and still fewer Saivas. Their patron goddess is Gandheswari, 'our lady of perfume,' a form of Durgá, in whose honour they hold a special service on the full moon of Baisakh (April-May), arranging in a pyramidal form their weights, scales, drugs, and account-books, and placing in front a goblet daubed over with red lead. Flowers, fruit, rice, sweetmeats, and perfumery, are offered, and the caste Brahman repeats several invocations soliciting the favour of the goddess during the ensuing year. These Brahmans, it may be mentioned, are treated on terms of equality by other members of the sacred order, except those who decline to officiate as priests for even the most respectable Sudras.

Social status.

According to Dr. Wise, the Gandhabanik is a spice-seller, or "épicier," as well as a druggist. He will not sell rice, vegetables, salt, oil, or spirits, but he keeps almost every other grocery in stock. He is often called by the Hindi term Pansárí, which signifies a dealer in groceries, spices, and herbs. The comparatively high position of Gandhabaniks among Súdra castes is owing to the circumstance that the sandal-wood and spices, essential for Hindu religious rites, can only be procured at their shops. It may be surmised, however, that their admission into the ranks of the Nava-Sákha is of comparatively recent date, as their name does not appear in the passage of Parásara usually quoted as the standard authority for the composition of that group.

Occupation.

The Gandhabanik, says Dr. Wise, obtains his drugs and spices direct from Calcutta, or from the place where they are produced, and buys quinine, iodide of potassium, and sarsaparilla from English druggists. He also sells tin, lead, pewter, copper, and iron, and retails, if licensed, saltpetre, sulphur, and gunpowder, as well as chemicals used by pyrotechnists, and dispenses medicines ordered by Kabírájs. Although Gandhabaniks possess no pharmacopœia, and are ignorant of chemistry, they display wonderful sharpness in distinguishing salts and minerals. Every Gandhabanik has the reputation of being a doctor, and, like the druggists of Europe, he is often consulted and prescribes for trifling ailments. Drugs at the present day are sold by apothecary's weight, other articles by the bazar weight of eighty sicca rupees to a *ser*. Kabírájs, however, still use the old Hindu weights—*pala*, *ratí*, *máshá*, and *jau*. Boys able to read and write Bengali are apprenticed to a Gandhabanik, who make them familiar with the appearance, names, and prices of drugs, of which, it is said, a genuine Pansárí's shop may contain three hundred and sixty kinds. Most of these go to form the different kinds of *pát*, or alterative medicine, greatly relied on in Hindu therapeutics. The Gandhabanik is expected to know the proper ingredients in each *pát*, as well as the proper quantity of each. In the preparation of pills goat's milk, or lime-juice and water, are used, but by some druggists the juice of the Ghí-Kuwar (*Aloe perfoliata*) is preferred.

The Gandhabanik retails charas, bhang, opium, and ganja, but some have scruples about selling the last, and employ a Mahomedan servant to do so. Many shops for the sale of ganja, however, are leased by members of this caste, who pay a Sunri, or a Mahomedan, to manage them.

The following statement shows the number and distribution of Gandhabaniks in Bengal in 1872 and 1881:—

District.	1872.	1881.	District.	1872.	1881.
Bardwan	32,105	24,160	Dacca	6,634	4,365
Bankura	6,626	18,730	Faridpur	3,018	5,468
Birbhum	10,165	13,587	Bakarganj	3,290	2,865
Midnapur	10,140	10,596	Maimansinh...	2,238	5,458
Hughli	6,985	7,897	Chittagong	1,364	3,163
Howrah		3,642	Noakhali	1,316	1,676
24-Parganas	5,053	3,400	Tipperah	4,176	4,609
Nadiya	8,010	10,931	Hill Tracts	......	1
Khulna	......	2,199	Maldah	649	2,817
Jessore	4,511	7,211	Santál Parganas	......	1,434
Murshedabad	11,016	9,874	Cuttack	506	5,406
Dinajpur	1,331	1,797	Puri	......	8,690
Rajshahye	893	1,421	Balasore	......	4,822
Rangpur	758	1,178	Tributary States	948	6,404
Bogra	519	908	Hazaribagh	3,906	......
Pabna	2,315	2,531	Lohardagá	5,036	
Darjiling	17	73	Singbhum	695	1,196
Jalpigori	390	299	Manbhum	7,140	9,328
Kuch Behar	......	161			

Gandhabaniyá, a synonym for Gandhabanik.

Gandhár, a small caste said by some to be connected with Mallás, who sing and play on musical instruments.

Gandharma, a *thar* or sept of Mangars in Darjiling.

Gandharp, *Gandharb*, the caste which supplies Hindu dancing-girls, singers, and prostitutes. Mr. Nesfield classes them with the Kanchan.

Gandhauriá, a sept of Rajputs in Behar.

Gandhi, a sept of Chiks in Chota Nagpur.

Gandhi, *Gandhari*, a perfumer or dealer in scent, an occupation followed by both Hindus and Mahomedans.

Gandura, a big bird, a totemistic sept of Mundas in Chota Nagpur.

Ganesh, a subdivision of the Jugi caste, chiefly employed in agriculture, a title of potters in Nepal.

Ganesiá, a section of Ayodhiabási Sonárs in Behar.

Ganesrishi, a section of Mayarás in Bengal.

Ganet, a section of Sonárs in Behar.

Gangá, a sept of Gonds in Chota Nagpur.

Gangábandhu, a kind of religious mendicant, occasionally met with in Behar and the North-Western Provinces.

Gangábási, 'dwellers on the Ganges,' a title of those Doms who take clothes and ornaments from dead bodies and usually live close to the funeral places. They are also called Murdáfarásh.

Gangábisaiyi, a sub-caste of Telis in Bengal.

Gangágrámi, a *gáin* of the Kásyapa *gotra* of Bárendra Brahmans in Bengal.

Gangájali, a sub-caste of Gareris in Behar.

Gangájhi, a section of Gangotás in Behar.

Gangápáli, a *mul* or section of the Chhamuliá Madhesiá subcaste of Halwáis in Behar.

Gangáputra, "son of the Ganges," a sub-caste of Doms who prepare the funeral pile for cremation; also a class of Brahmans who attend pilgrims at bathing *gháts* on the Ganges; a title of Pátnis.

Gángar, a section of Maghayá Kándus in Behar.

Gángaulih, a *mul* or section of the Tinmuliá Madhesiá subcaste of Halwáis in Behar.

Gangaure, a *mul* of the Sándil section of Maithil Brahmans in Behar.

Gangautá, a synonym for Gangota.

Gángdahiá, a section of the Biyáhut and Kharidáhá Kalwárs in Behar.

Gángoli, a title of Brahmans in Bengal.

Gangotá, *Gangautá*, a cultivating, landholding, and labouring caste of Behar. Many of them live on the banks of the Ganges, and this is said to be the origin of the name. Their customs give no clue to their descent, unless we may infer non-Aryan affinities from the fact that in some parts of the country they are known to eat pork and field-rats. Gangotas are divided into two sub-castes—**Jethkar** and **Maghaya**—and have two sections—**Gangájhi** and **Jáhnavi**. A man may not marry a woman of his own section, nor a woman who comes within the formula *chachera*, *mamera*, etc., calculated to four generations in the descending line. He may not marry two sisters at the same time, but may marry his deceased wife's younger sister.

Origin and internal structure.

Gangotás profess to marry their daughters as infants, but adult-marriage is by no means unknown among the poorer classes. The ceremony is a meagre version of the standard ritual, *sindurdán* being deemed the essential and binding portion. Polygamy is permitted in the sense that a man may take a second wife with the consent of his first wife if

Marriage.

the latter is barren or suffers from an incurable disease. A widow may marry again, but she is expected to marry her deceased husband's younger brother if there is one. Divorce is not recognised.

Religion.

The religion of the caste presents no features of special interest. The small-pox goddess, Jagadambá, is worshipped twice or three times a month with offerings of husked rice and incense. At weddings and on occasions of sickness Bhagavati is propitiated with kids, rice, ghee, tulsi leaves, and vermilion. The eatable portions of the sacrifice are consumed by the members of the household. Brahmans who serve the Gangotás are said to incur no degradation by doing so.

Social status and occupation.

Gangotás rank with Kurmis and Koiris, and Brahmans will take water from their hands. In Bhagalpur they eat pork, but at the same time profess to abstain from fermented and spirituous liquors. In Monghyr, on the other hand, their practice in the matter of diet is reported to be the same as that of respectable Hindus of similar social position. Agriculture is their sole occupation. A few have risen to be small zamindars, but the bulk of the caste are occupancy or non-occupancy raiyats and landless day-labourers paid in cash or kind.

The following statement shows the number and distribution of Gangotás in 1872 and 1881:—

DISTRICT.	1872.	1881.	DISTRICT.	1872.	1881.
Kuch Behar	......	1	Bhagalpur	29,910	49,226
Gya	46	......	Purneah	36,762	12,702
Shahabad	272	......	Maldah	......	440
Tirhut	6	......	Santál Parganas	4	21
Saran	74	......	Hazaribagh	......	369
Champaran	55	5	Lohardagá	......	336
Monghyr	8,757	8,118	Tributary States	......	20

Gangotri, a sub-caste of Brahmans in Behar.

Gángthaiyá, a *mul* or section of the Naomulia or Majraut sub-caste of Goálás in Behar.

Gangtiáit, a *kul* or section of Bábhans in Behar.

Gánguli, a *gáin* of the Sábarna *gotra* of Rárhi Brahmans in Bengal.

Gángulwár-Sakuri, a *mul* of the Sándil section of Maithil Brahmans in Behar.

Gangulwár-Dumra, a *mul* of the Sándil section of Maithil Brahmans in Behar.

Gangye-pá, dwelling behind a hill, a *rui* or sept of Dejong Lhoris, the members of which form the lowest class of Bhotias.

Ganhwariá, a sept of Rajputs in Behar.

Ganjhu, Gaunjhu or *Gonjhu*, a sub-caste of Sunris in Behar; a title of Binjhiás, Gonds, Khandáits Kharwárs, Musahars, Rájwars, Rautiás, and Parhaiyas in Chota Nagpur.

Ganjhu Baiswár, members of the Kharwár caste who are worshippers of Vishnu.

Ganjwár, a sub-caste of Sunris in Behar who deal in liquor.

Gánr, fort-builder, a sub-sept of the Murmu sept of Santáls.

Ganrár, a boating, fishing and trading caste of Eastern Bengal, identified by M. Vivien de St. Martin with the Gangaridæ of Pliny and Ptolemy. They claim to be descended from Madhesia Kándús, whose ancestors were brought to Dacca five generations ago by the Muhammadan Government from Súrya-garhí in Bhagalpur to act as rowers on board the imperial dispatch boats. The caste is most numerous in Dacca, but they are also met with in Silhet, Tipperah, and Maimansinh, working as cultivators. Buchanan mentions that the Ganrár of Rangpur originally came from Dacca, two hundred families being in his time domiciled along the banks of the Brahmaputra.

In former times the Ganrár had the reputation of being the bravest of all boatmen, and the river dákáits never dared to attack boats manned by them. Now-a-days they are great traders, carrying in their large cargo-boats, called *Palwár*, rice, cotton, and linseed to Calcutta, Bhagwángolah, and other centres of trade. They generally do business on their own account, and being honest and straightforward, obtain advances of money on favourable terms from the bankers.

Ganrárs use the three-pronged harpoon (*tenta*) with great dexterity to kill alligators and Gangetic porpoises, a float being attached to the weapon with a rope. Porpoise oil is in great repute for burning, and as an embrocation for rheumatism. It usually sells for three to five rupees a *man*. Turtles are frequently harpooned for food, and turtle eggs are deemed a great delicacy. Ganrárs work at almost any trade, but in Dacca they will not take to cultivating the soil. The women are principally employed in parching grain and selling it in bázárs.

They all belong to one *gotra*, the Aliman, and the purohit is a Patit Bráhman. By religion the caste is mainly Vaishnava, but deities unknown to the Bráhmanical Pantheon are also worshipped. Like most of the low castes, the Ganrár set afloat the *Berá* in honour of Khwájah Khizr, and pay special adoration to Sat Náráyana. On the last day of Srávan they sacrifice a turtle to Manasá Deví, the goddess of snakes, and make offerings in the month of Paus to Bura-Burí. The Ganrárs of Dacca, through Bráhmanical influence, have relinquished the worship of Khala-Kumari, who is regarded by the Ganrárs of Rangpur as the Naiad of the river. This worship, probably like that of Bura-Burí, a survival of an earlier animistic faith, is only found in outlying districts, where Hinduism has imperfectly established its sway.

Ganrárs rarely eat flesh, but they freely indulge in spirits, and often in ganja. At the present day they marry their daughters as infants, and, unlike the Kándus, from whom they profess to be descended, forbid widows to marry again. Divorce is not recognised.

Gánrol, a section of the Sát-muliá Maghayá sub-caste of Kándus in Behar.

Gánthen, a section of Murmis in Darjiling.

Ganwár (abbreviation of *gáonwar*), a villager, as opposed to an inhabitant of a town: hence, an illiterate and stupid person.

Gáontiá, headman of a *gaon* or village; a title of Bhuiya feudatories in Gangpur and Bonai.

Gaprai, a section of the Amashta Káyasths in Behar.

Gárá, a section of Sunris in Behar.

Garabing, a big river-snake, a totemistic sept of Mundas in Chota Nagpur.

Garáet, a section of the Játhot division of the Parbatti-Kurin sub-caste of Gonrhis in Behar.

Garahiá, a section of Sonárs in Behar.

Garai, a section of Binjhiás in Chota Nagpur.

Garai or **Gorai**, a title of Kalus or Telis in Western Bengal, generally adopted by wealthy Kulin members of the caste.

Garain, a section of Kurmis and Sunris in Behar.

Gárál, a low sub-caste of Chandáls who prepare *chirá* or parched rice.

Garaur, a sept of Goálás in Chota Nagpur.

Garbariá, a section of Lohárs in Behar.

Garbetá, a sub-caste of Kaibarttas in Behar.

Garbháit, *Gorwáit*, or *Sághár*, a sub-caste of Kewats in Behar.

Gáre, a sub-caste of Sunris in Behar.

Gareri, *Gadariya*, *Bhenrihar*, the shepherd, goatherd, and blanket-weaver caste of Behar. Gareris appear to have no traditions, and cannot give any account of their origin beyond the vague statement that they came 'from the west.' It is possible that they may be an offshoot from the Goálás, differentiated by keeping sheep and taking to the comparatively degraded occupation of weaving, but I can offer no evidence in support of this conjecture, except the rather remarkable fact that Gareris will take both boiled rice (*kachi*) and sweetmeats, etc. (*pakki*), from members of the Goálá caste.

Origin.

The Gareris of Behar are divided into four sub-castes—**Dhengar**, **Farakhábádi**, **Gangájali**, and **Nikhar**—of whom the Dhengar have the exogamous sections shown in the Appendix. The other sub-castes appear to regulate their marriages by the standard formula *mamerá*, *chacherá*, etc., calculated to six generations in the descending line.

Internal structure.

The practice of infant-marriage is firmly established among the Gareris. *Tilak*, consisting of a loin-cloth (*dhoti*), some *chupattis*, and two or three rupees,

Marriage.

is paid to the bridegroom on an auspicious day by the parents of the bride. The marriage ceremony is of the standard type. Polygamy is permitted to the extent that a man may marry a second wife if his first wife is barren. A widow may marry again by the *sagai* form. It is considered right for her to marry her late husband's younger brother if there is one, but she is not positively obliged to do so. Some say that divorce is not recognised. If a woman has an intrigue with a man of another caste, she is excommunicated and turned adrift, but indiscretions within the brotherhood admit of being atoned for by various modes of penalty awarded by the headman (*manjan*) and panchâyat, and chiefly by a feast to the members of the caste. Others hold that divorce may be had on the oath of the husband, and that a divorced woman may marry again by *sagai*.

Religion.

In respect of religious and ceremonial observances the Gareris generally conform to the usages of the Vaishnava sect, and comparatively few Saivas are found among them. Many are followers of Daryá Dás, a Gareri, who founded a corrupt Vaishnava sect distinguished by abstinence from fish, flesh, and spirits. His disciples do not worship him as a deity, but simply regard him as their *guru* or spiritual guide. The *purohits* of the caste are Kanaujiá, or sometimes Jyoshi Brahmans; while Bairági or Dasnámi ascetics serve them as *gurus*. Their household worship, in which priests take no part, is addressed to Bandi, Goraiya, Dharam Ráj, Narsingh, the Pánch Pir, and Káli, to whom the males of the family offer cakes, rice boiled in milk, sweetmeats, and plantains on the 30th Sráwan. The offerings are eaten afterwards by the members of the family and the *deori* relations who can claim to participate in domestic worship. When a flock of sheep is sold, the Gareri keeps back a ram; and having assembled his brethren, sacrifices it to Banjári, after which its flesh is eaten by those who follow the Saiva ritual.

Occupation.

The large majority of the caste find employment as shepherds, goatherds, or blanket-weavers, and comparatively few have taken to cultivation. Mr. Hoey[1] gives the following account of the manner in which their characteristic occupation is carried on in the neighbourhood of Lucknow:—

"One Gareri will attend a flock of 100 sheep and goats, and is at no expense for fodder. He drives them out to graze on wild pasture. Goats and sheep drop young twice a year, and as many as four kids or lambs at a birth are not unusual. In a flock of one hundred sheep and goats let there be 60 sheep. It is the custom to cut the wool three times in the year,—after the cold weather, the

[1] *Monograph on Trade and Manufactures in Northern India*, by W. Hoey, Bengal Civil Service, p. 106. This valuable work is based on notes collected by Mr. Hoey while engaged in revising the assessments of license-tax in Lucknow city during 1879 and 1880—a fact which accounts for the minute attention paid to the profits of particular trades.

hot weather, and the rains. The idiom for shearing is *pairi karna*. The average is a quarter of a seer of wool at each *pairi*. Thus 60 sheep will yield 1 maund 5 seers of wool in a year. If the wool is sold, it will fetch about one rupee per 3 seers. But Gareris frequently weave their wool into small blankets (*kamli*) of 1½ seers each, which sell for one rupee each. But in this case they are at a cost of ½ anna per *kamli* paid to a *behna* for carding the wool. Thus from 60 sheep the Gareri may have either 45 seers of wool, value Rs. 15, or 30 *kamlis*, to sell at Rs. 30. In the latter case he pays the *behna* Re. 1-6-6 and clears Rs. 28-9-6. The latter method of disposing of the wool is chosen by Gareris who have grown sons and daughters, or wives without children, who weave.

"The lowest estimate which any Gareri has given me of the lambs dropped by 60 sheep in one year is 90. These sell as lambs for 8 annas each, as one-year olds for from Re. 1 to Re. 1-8, and as two-year olds for Rs. 2. This is an average computation.

"Gareris milk ewes, but draw never more than ¼ seer per diem, for they have regard to the value of the lambs. Sheep's milk is sold to Halwáis at 1 anna per seer to make *khoá*. There will always be 12 sheep in 60 in milk, and they thus bring 3 annas per diem by milk.

"Sheep's manure is sold to Dhobis for washing, and Muraos purchase it as a high-class manure for *dofasli* fields. It sells at Re. 1 per 5 maunds. The pen where 60 sheep are kept at night will, when swept in the morning, give 10 seers.

"Now take the 40 goats in the mixed flock of 100 sheep and goats. The estimate of kids from these is set at 90 in the year, and their milk 12 seers per diem. Goat's milk sells at 1 anna per seer. Kids are sold in the first year at from 12 annas to Re. 1 each, and in the second year from Rs. 2 to Rs. 3 (if females) and Rs. 4 (if males). Goats when in milk are given *bhusá*, but 4 annas at most per diem is spent on 40.

"Thus a flock of 100 sheep and goats in the proportion taken above is worth Rs. 405 per annum at the lowest computation—the sheep Rs. 157-8, the goats Rs. 247-8—after paying all expenses."

Social status.

According to Dr. Wise, the Gareri is reckoned higher in rank than the Ahir, and equal to the Majroti and Krishnaut Goalás, with whom, as has been mentioned above, Gareris will eat both *kachi* and *pakki* food and will smoke in the same *hookah*. It is not clear, however, that this intercourse is reciprocal, and that the Goálás will accept food on the same terms from a Gareri, while the fact that Gareris make wethers themselves must necessarily involve some measure of social degradation. In Behar and Bengal this caste is generally reckoned a clean one, from whose members a Brahman can take water; but in Puraniyá, says Buchanan, it is impure. The Gareri is often found working as a domestic servant, refusing, however, to carry bathing-water for his master or to rinse his body-clothes after bathing. He cannot, without incurring expulsion, serve as a shepherd with any but Gareri masters. He may, however, take household service with any class, even with Christians.

The following statement shows the number and distribution of Gareris in 1872 and 1881 :—

DISTRICT.	1872.	1881.	DISTRICT.	1872.	1881.
Bardwan	6	116	Patna	10,144	9,718
Bankura	......	60	Gya	14,381	15,633
Birbhum	1	33	Shahabad	18,259	24,055
Midnapur	236	1	Tirhut { Mozufferpur ...	} 16,855	10,530
Hughli	} 3	{ 44	Tirhut { Darbhanga ...		10,491
Howrah		......	Saran	7,070	9,881
24-Parganas	50	......	Champaran	8,759	6,805
Nadiya	1	217	Monghyr	4,471	6,009
Murshedabad	234	652	Bhagalpur	4,116	7,846
Dinajpur	......	16	Purniah	2,850	4,872
Rangpur	1	10	Maldah	65	310
Bogra	1	......	Santál Parganas	118	630
Pabna	13	......	Cuttack	354	103
Darjiling	......	37	Puri	......	29
Jalpigori	......	11	Balasore	123	......
Kuch Behar	......	23	Hazaribagh	......	935
Dacca	......	9	Lohardaga	3,124	4,788
Faridpur	1	......	Singbhum	67	287
Maimansinh	3	23	Manbhum	......	5
			Tributary States	109	352

Gareyiá, a section of Biyáhut and Kharidáhá Kalwárs in Behar.

Garg, an eponymous section of Agarwáls and Bábhans in Behar.

Garga, Gárgya, a section of Brahmans and of Sánkháris in Bengal.

Gargari, a *gáin* of the Sándilya *gotra* of Rárhi Brahmans in Bengal.

Gargarishi, an eponymous sept of Savars; a section of Nápits and Tántis in Bengal.

Gargbansi, a sept of Rajputs in Behar.

Garhatiá, a sept of Kumhars in Chota Nagpur.

Garhbiyar, a section of the Karan sub-caste of Káyasths in Behar.

Garhi, synonym for Gareri, *q.v.*

Garhiá, a section of Bábhans in Behar.

Garh-Náik or *Singha*, leader or lion of the fort, a title of Khandáits in Orissa.

Garhuk or *Garauwá*, a sub-caste of Kahárs in Behar.

Garhwár, a sept of Rajputs in Behar.

Gari, monkey, a totemistic sept of Mundas and Oraons in Chota Nagpur.

Gariá, a sub-caste of Dhobis in Western Bengal.

Garjang, a sept of Tipperahs in the Hill Tracts of Chittagong.

Garowá, a sub-caste of Kahars in Behar.

Garral, *Garial*, a title of Telis.

Garria, a kind of bird, a totemistic sept of Mundas in Chota Nagpur.

Garur, vulture, a totemistic section of Rautiás in Chota Nagpur, and of Máls in Bankura.

Garwál, a section of Goálás in the North-Western Provinces and Behar.

Garwe, a stork, a totemistic sept of Oraons in Chota Nagpur.

Garyá, a sub-caste of Goálás in Behar.

Gatáni, a section of Mahesris in Behar.

Gatpará, *Gatpáchha*, 'pock-puncturer,' a term applied to those who practise inoculation.

Gatsorá, a sept of Hos in Singbhum.

Gáudá, a sub-caste of Telis in Orissa.

Gaudanhá, a section of the Banodhiá and Jaiswár Kalwárs in Behar.

Gaudhal, a *mul* or section of the Naomuliá or Goria sub-caste of Goálás in Behar.

Gaudhaniá, a sept of Rajputs in Behar.

Gauláni, a sept of Rajputs in Behar.

Gauli, a section of Bhojpuriá Halwáis in Behar.

Gaunágahunár, a *mul* or section of the Tinmuliá Madhesiá sub-caste of Halwáis in Behar.

Gauna-Kulin, a hypergamous division of Rárhi Brahmans in Bengal made by Rájá Ballál Sen.

Gaura, a sub-caste of Káyasths and Sonárs, a section of Bábhans and a sept of Rajputs in Behar.

Gaura or **Gauriya**, a territorial division of the Pancha Gaura Brahmans, who live in the country of the Lower Ganges, deriving its name from Gaura, the ancient capital of the Hindu dynasty of the Pál Rájás.

Gaura, Gorho, a sub-caste of Goálás in Bengal and Orissa.

Gaurâli, a *samáj* or local group of the Basishtha *gotra* of Páschátya Baidik Brahmans in Bengal.

Gaurangi, a class of Vaishnava, followers of Gauránga.

Gaurihár, a sub-tribe of Thárus in Behar.

Gauripur, a *dih* or local section of the Maghayá sub-caste of Koiris in Bhagalpur.

Gauro, a sept of Thárus in Behar.

Gautama, a section of Bábhans in Behar. The name denotes the Vedic sage Saradwat, the husband of Ahalyá, who was seduced by Indra. It has probably been borrowed from the Brahmanical system in comparatively recent times. Most of the Bábhan section-names are territorial. The name also does duty as a sept of the Suryabansi Rajputs in Behar; a section of Brahmans; a *thar* of the Atri *gotra* of Nepáli Brahmans; a section of Káyasths, Mayarás, Tántis, Baidyas, Goálás, Subarnabaniks, Sunris, and Sankháris in Bengal.

Gauthâhá, a section of Bhojpuriá Halwáis in Behar.

Gáwá, a group of the Bárendra Goálás in Bengal.

Gáwál, a *gotra* or section of Agarwáls.

Gaya, a section of Awadhiá Hajáms in Behar.

Gayalpure, a section of the Bahánnajáti sub-caste of Khatris in Bengal.

Gáyán (a singer), a class of Muhammadans believed to have been originally Shándárs. They have learned from their teachers the myth that they are descended from Jihád Gáyán, who accompanied Sháh Jalál in his conquest of Silhet, and state that they emigrated from that country in covered canoes, differing in build from those used by other Bediyás.

The Gáyán is usually a cultivator, and when he is absent from home his wife watches the crops and tends the cattle. Any relationship with other Bediyás is warmly repudiated, for which reason the Farazi sect sometimes concedes to the Gáyán the rights and privileges of other Mussulmáns. This concession has transformed these vagrants into rigid Puritans. The Gáyán women are secluded, and the other Bediyas are reproached for indelicacy in allowing their women to wander about unveiled and unprotected.

The Gáyán sing Bengali songs in public, to the music of the violins, known as *sárangi* and *behlá*.

Gayáwál, *Gayál*, *Gayáli*, a degraded sub-caste of Debal Brahmans, who act as priests in the Vishnupada temple at Gya. They are remunerated by fees from pilgrims who offer *pindas* to the names of their ancestors. The name is also incorrectly applied to the touts or recruiters who are sent out from Gya by the Gyawals to collect pilgrims.

Gáysari, a sub-caste of Kurmis in Orissa.

Gede, duck, a totemistic sept of Oraons in Chota Nagpur.

Gehani, a section of Kamárkalla Sonárs in Behar.

Gehuaná, a sept of Rajputs in Behar.

Geláng, a *thar* or sept of Mangars in Darjiling.

Gelra, a section of Oswáls in Behar.

Ghager, field-bird, a totemistic sept of Mundas in Chota Nagpur.

Ghai, a section of the Bárajáti sub-caste of Khatris in Bengal.

Ghajári, a class of birdcatchers occasionally met with in Behar. I have been unable to ascertain whether the name has any definite and uniform relation to caste.

Ghale, a section of Gurungs and Murmis in Darjiling.

Ghaleh, a *thar* or sept of the Das-Gurung sub-tribe of Gurungs, so named after a village. The Gurung chief of Ghaleh in former times ruled at a place called Dong-ti in Nepal, and all the Gurungs were under his sway.

Ghali, a *thar* or sept of Mangars in Darjiling.

Ghamela, a sub-caste of Kurmis in Behar.

Ghámghotle, a section of Kámis in Darjiling.

Ghaná or **Gáchhuá**, a sub-caste of Telis in Bengal.

Ghani, a section of Kaibarttas in Orissa.

Ghaniá, a title of Bangaja Káyasths in Bengal.

Ghansi, fish, a totemistic sept of Kharwars in Chota Nagpur.

Ghanteswari, a *gáin* of the Sábarna *gotra* of Rárhi Brahmans in Bengal.

Ghar, Ghár, a title of Dakshin-Rárhi and Bangaja Káyasths.

Gharámi, a thatcher, an occupation followed by members of several different castes.

Gharbait or *Raut*, an endogamous sub-caste of Amats in Behar.

Gharbári, a householder, a title of religious sectarians who live a secular life.

Gharbári Atit, a class of Atit in Behar which, whatever may have been its original mode of formation, does not now differ materially in manner of life from any ordinary occupational caste.

Gharbeta or **Gharbait**, a sub-caste of Dhánuks in Behar.

Gharikárak, a section of the Biyáhut and Kharidáhá Kalwárs in Chota Nagpur.

Ghar Ráut, a division (not exogamous) of the Ráut Mehtar sub-caste of Doms in Behar.

Gharruk, a sub-caste of Kahárs in Behar.

Gharti, (i) a caste formed by those members of the Kamára or slave caste in Nepal who have been freed by their masters on payment of their manumission fee. The formation of the Kamára caste and its precise relations to the Gharti are rather obscure, but I understand that persons, who infringe the law of exogamy by marrying or having intercourse with a woman of their own *thars* are in Nepal liable to be sold as slaves or Kamáras. (ii) A section of Kamáras. (iii) A sub-tribe of Mangars.

Gharti, a *thar* or sept of Gurungs in Darjiling.

Gharti-ghaure, a section of Kámis in Darjiling.

Ghartmel, a *thar* or section of Nepáli Brahmans.

Ghartyál, a *thar* or section of Nepáli Brahmans.

Gharu, a *mul* or section of the Kanaujiá sub-caste of Sonárs in Behar.

Gharui, a title of Kaibarttas and of Goálás in Western Bengal.

Gharwár, a sept of Rajputs in Behar.

Gháscharái, a title of Goálás who graze cattle.

Ghaserá, a sub-caste of Doms in Bengal who cut grass for sale.

Ghási, a sub-section of the Kantsasa section of Utkal Brahmans in Orissa.

Ghási, a Dravidian fishing and cultivating caste of Chota Nagpur and Central India, who attend as musicians at weddings and festivals and also perform menial offices of all kinds. Ghási women act as midwives and nurses, and I have come across a case of a Brahman girl being nicknamed Ghásimani in her infancy and made over to a Ghási woman to bring up in order to avert the malevolent influences supposed to have caused the early death of previous children of the same mother.

Origin.

The Ghásis of Chota Nagpur are divided into three sub-castes—Sonaáti, Simarloká, and Hári. They have only one section (Kasiár), probably a corruption of Kásyapa. Ghásis marry their daughters in infancy when they can afford to do so, but adult-marriage is by no means uncommon. Their marriage ceremony is a debased form of that in ordinary use among orthodox Hindus. Polygamy is permitted without any limit being imposed on the number of wives. Widow-marriage and divorce are freely practised, and the women of the caste are credited with living a very loose life.

Internal structure.

The caste ranks socially with Doms and Musahars. They eat beef and pork, and are greatly addicted to drink. Their origin is obscure. Colonel Dalton regards them as Aryan helots, and says:—

Social status.

"But far viler than the weavers are the extraordinary tribe called Ghásis, foul parasites of the Central Indian hill tribes, and submitting to be degraded even by them. If the Chandáls of the Puráns, though descended from the union of a Brahmani and a Sudra, are the 'lowest of the low,' the Ghásis are Chandáls, and the people who further south are called Pariahs are no doubt of the same distinguished lineage. If, as I surmise, they were Aryan helots, their offices in the household or communities must have been of the lowest and most degrading kinds. It is to be observed that the institution of caste necessitated the organization of a class to whom such offices could be assigned, and when formed, stringent measures would be requisite to keep the servitors in their position. We might thence expect that they would avail themselves of every opportunity to escape, and no safer asylums could be found than the retreats of the forest tribes. Wherever there are Kols there are Ghásis, and though evidently of an entirely different origin, they have been so long associated that they are a recognised class in the Kol tradition of creation, which appropriately assigns to them a thriftless career, and describes them as living on the leavings or charity of the more industrious members of society. There are not fewer than 50,000 Ghásis in the Kol countries. Their favourite employment is no doubt that of musicians. No ceremony can take place or great man move without the accompaniment of their discordant instruments—drums, kettle-drums, and huge horns—to proclaim the event in a manner most horrifying to civilised ears."

The Simarloká sub-caste have a curious aversion for Káyasths, which they account for by the story that once upon a time some Ghási musicians, who were escorting the marriage procession of a Káyasth bridegroom to the house of his betrothed, were tempted by the valuable ornaments which he wore to murder him and cast his body into a well. The youth besought them to let him write a letter to his relatives informing them that he was dying and bidding them perform his funeral obsequies. This the Ghásis agreed to, after making him swear that he would not disclose the manner of his death. The Káyasth, however, did not think the oath binding, and on the letter being delivered the Ghásis were straightway given up to justice. For this reason, say the Simarlokás, trust not a Káyasth, for he is faithless even in the hour of death.

The following statement shows the number and distribution of Ghásis in 1872 and 1881:—

District.	1872.	1881.	District.	1872.	1881.
Bardwan	......	2	Champaran	......	5
Bankura	......	8	Monghyr	......	360
24-Parganas	......	894	Bhagalpur	......	813
Nadiya	......	47	Purniah	......	127
Khulna	......	160	Santál Parganas	......	236
Jessore	......	41	Cuttack	......	206
Murshedabad	......	14	Balasore	......	48
Bogra	......	67	Tributary States	2,014	2,769
Pabna	......	12	Hazaribagh	3,119	4,290
Darjiling	......	90	Lohardagá	15,700	16,394
Patna	......	40	Singbhum	3,976	2,667
Darbhanga	......	27	Manbhum	4,105	2,100
			Tributary States	5,358	9,863

Ghasuria, grass-cutters. The same as Ghási.

Ghatait, a section of Bábhans in Behar.

Ghatak, a title of Brahmans who by profession are match-makers and genealogists. Each sub-caste of Bráhmans in Bengal, as well as the Baidya and Káyasth castes, has its recognised staff of Ghataks, who are responsible for arranging suitable marriages and preserving the social and ceremonial purity of each family belonging to it. The organization of the society of Ghataks, the Herald's College of Bengal, is referred to Ballál Sen, who settled the Rárhi Ghataks in Jessore, Bakarganj, and Bikrampúr, where, with the exception of a few who have emigrated to Calcutta, they are domiciled at the present day. The Ghatak registers of the Rárhi Bráhmans, like those of the Kulin Káyasths, are said to go back twenty-three generations, or five hundred years, and although any Brahman may become a Ghatak, the highest estimation, and the title Pradhán, or chief, is only bestowed on the individual who can show a long and unbroken pedigree of Ghatak ancestors.

There are three grades of Ghataks. The first can repeat offhand the names of all the members of the main as well as collateral branches of any family in his particular part of the country; of the families with which they have married, and of the issue of such marriages. The second grade embraces those Ghataks who can only give the name of the *Kul* or family into which a Bráhman or his relatives have married; while the third comprises such as can only name the *Bans* or lineage to which the Bráhman belongs. It is not uncommon for one Ghatak to challenge another to display his powers of memory, and public contests are held somewhat after the manner of the logical disputations of the Middle Ages.

Ghataks seldom officiate at religious ceremonies, and always employ purohits for their own requirements. According to Dr. Wise, every Kulin Bráhman in Eastern Bengal is compelled to employ a Ghatak in negotiating the marriages of his family, otherwise the whole race of Ghataks revolt and ostracise him. The rich Bráhman zemindárs, who are willing and able to pay a large sum for an unexceptionable Kulin bride, often try to convince the Ghataks that their families are of purer and more honourable descent than they actually are. Bribes are often offered to establish the claim, but are rarely accepted. Disputes, however, are common, and the Ghataks who favour a claim that is fallacious, and who attend at an unauthorised marriage, fall in the estimation of those who have questioned its soundness and declined to be present. The scruples of a single Pradhán Ghatak often mar the otherwise perfect satisfaction of a parent on the marriage of his son to a family of higher rank than his own; and should all the leaders unite in forbidding the marriage, it is impossible for him to win any permanent promotion beyond that laid down in their registers.

Ghatakár, a synonym for Kumhár.

Ghatakarpar, "potsherds," the *nom-de-plume* of a poet at the Court of Vikramáditya who is said to have been a potter: hence, a title of Kumhárs.

Ghatáni, a section of Kámis; a *thar* or sept of Mangars in Darjiling.

Ghátiyá, a sub-caste of Utkal Brahmans in Orissa.

Ghát-mánjhi, a title of Pátnis in Bengal.

Ghatoar, a sept of Chiks in Chota Nagpur.

Ghát-Pátni, Balami, or **Ghátwál**, a sub-caste of Pátnis in Bengal.

Ghatráj, a *thar* or sept of Mangars in Darjiling.

Ghatra-Kámár, a sub-caste of Kámárs in Western Bengal.

Ghátu, a section of Máls in Bankura.

Ghátwál, (i) in Behar, a title of Mallahs who have charge of ferries and landing-places; (ii) in Western Bengal and Chota Nagpur a title of the holders of service tenures who act as rural police and are attached in that capacity to certain tracts of country or hill passes (*ghâts*). Most of them belong to Dravidian tribes or castes, such as Bhumij, Kharwár, Bauri, etc.

Gházipuriá, a division (not exogamous) of the Ráut Mehtar sub-caste of Doms in Behar.

Ghi, butter clarified, a totemistic sept of Mundas in Chota Nagpur.

Ghibihár, the *ghi*-eater, a title of the Bahiot sub-caste of Amats and Dhánuks in Behar who are personal servants in the houses of the higher castes. The term also denotes a sub-caste of Kewats in Bhagalpur, who are said to have been outcasted for eating the *jhuthá* or leavings of their masters.

Ghimirya, a *thar* or section of Nepáli Brahmans.

Ghingpá, a *rui* or sept of the Bed tshan-gye sub-tribe of Dejong Lhoris or Bhotias of the south.

Ghiohaddá, a section of Sonárs in Behar.

Ghising, a section of Murmis in Darjiling.

Ghiuádhár, a *mul* or section of the Naomuliá or Majraut sub-caste of Goálás in Behar.

Ghogro, a section of Páns in Chota Nagpur.

Ghoneh, a *thar* or sept of the Das-Gurung sub-tribe of Gurungs in Darjiling.

Ghorá, horse, a totemistic sept of Gonds in Chota Nagpur.

Ghorábach, a section of Páns in Chota Nagpur.

Ghoraila, a title of the Ghosin sub-caste of Goálás in Behar.

Ghorasaine, a *thar* or section of Nepáli Brahmans.

Ghorcharhá, a sub-caste of Kurmis in Behar; a section of the Banodhiá and Jaiswár Kalwárs in Behar.

Ghosh, a group of the Purbba Kuliyá Sadgops and a title of Káyasths and Goálás in Bengal.

Ghoshál, a *gáin* of the Bátsya *gotra* of Rárhi Brahmans in Bengal.

Ghoshli, a *gáin* of the Sándilya *gotra* of Rárhi Brahmans in Bengal.

Ghosi Bangsi, *Ghosi*, *Ghosin*, *Gonsia*, a sub-caste of Goálás, *q.v.*

Ghosin, a class of Mahomedan herdsmen in Behar.

Ghosináik, Náik, a sub-caste of Telis or oil-pressers in Hazaribagh.

Ghritakausika, a section of Brahmans, Baidyas, and Káyasths in Bengal.

Ghulám-Káyasth, a synonym for Sudra.

Ghumlá, a section of Goálás in the North-Western Provinces and Behar.

Ghundáne, a *thar* or sept of Gurungs in Darjiling.

Ghuni, a title of Bágdis, so-called from *ghuni*, a fish-trap.

Ghuniá, a sub-caste of Kewats in Western Bengal and of Mallas or fishermen in Behar.

Ghunri, a kind of fruit, a totemistic sept of Mundas in Chota Nagpur.

Ghurcholi, a *thar* or section of Nepáli Brahmans.

Ghusaute-Nagwár, a *mul* of the Bátsya section of Maithil Brahmans in Behar.

Ghybrim, a *thar* or sept of the Bárah-Gurung sub-tribe of Gurungs in Darjiling.

Gidad, a section of Goálás in the North-Western Provinces and Behar.

Gidh or *Gidhi*, vulture, a totemistic sept of Mundas, Oraons, and Parhaiyas in Chota Nagpur.

Gigániá, a section of Goálás in the North-Western Provinces and Behar.

Gilal, a *thar* or section of Nepáli Brahmans.

Ginmuar, a sept of Korwas in Chota Nagpur.

Ginuar, eel, a totemistic sept of Korwas in Chota Nagpur.

Giri, a sect of Dasnámi Sannyásis; a title adopted by Mahantas, trustees of religious endowments. There is also a low caste of the name somewhat akin to Jugis, etc., who string gold and silver ornaments and sometimes beg; their females make mats of date leaves. A title of Kaibarttas in Bengal.

Giriak, a *mul* or section of the Maghayá sub-caste of Kándus in Behar.

Giridhari, a class of Vaishnavas.

Giritar, a *mul* or section of the Maghayá sub-caste of Barhis in Behar.

Girnám, a class of Sannyási or hermit.

Gislihi, bird, a totemistic sept of Oraons in Chota Nagpur.

Gnyambipá, a *rui* or sept of the Bed tahan-gye sub-tribe of Dejong Lhoris or Bhotias of the south.

Goá, a section of the Biyáhut and Kharidáhá Kálwárs in Behar.

Goáit, a *kul* or section of Bábhans and Gonrhis in Behar.

Goál, a synonym for Goálá.

Goal, cow, a totemistic sept of Páns in Chota Nagpur.

Goálá, *Goár*, *Ahir* (Sanskr. A'bhira), the great pastoral caste of India. According to Manu, an A'bhira is the offspring of a Brahman by an Ambastha girl. Lassen[1] describes the A'bhira as a non-Aryan pastoral race, dwelling near the mouth of the Indus, and remarks that the modern word Ahir means cowherd. At the present day the designation Ahir seems to be confined to Behar and parts of Upper India, Goálá being more commonly used in Bengal. The traditions of the caste bear a highly imaginative character, and profess to trace their descent from the god Krishna, whose relations with the milkmaids of Brindában play a prominent part in Hindu mythology. Krishna himself is supposed to have belonged to the tribe of Yádavas, or descendants of Yadu, a nomadic race, who graze cattle and make butter, and are believed to have effected an early settlement in the neighbourhood of Mathurá. In memory of this tradition, one of the sub-castes of Goálás in the North-Western Provinces is called Yadu or Jadu-bansi at the present time. Another story quoted by Buchanan makes out the Goálás to be Vaisyas, who were degraded in consequence of having introduced castration among their herds, and members of the caste who are disposed to claim this distinguished ancestor may lay stress upon the fact that the tending of flocks and herds is mentioned by the authorities among the duties of the Vaisya order.

Traditions of origin.

Taken as a whole, the Goálá traditions can hardly be said to do more than render it probable that one of their earliest settlements was in the neighbourhood of Mathurá, and that this part of the country was the centre of distribution of the caste. The large functional group known by the name Goálá seems to have been recruited not merely by the diffusion along the Ganges Valley of the semi-Aryan Goálás of the North-Western Provinces, but also by the inclusion in the caste of pastoral tribes who were not Aryans at all. These of course would form distinct sub-castes, and would not be admitted to the *jus connubii* with the original nucleus of the caste. The great differences of make and feature which may be observed among Goálás seem to bear out this view, and to show that whatever may

[1] *Ind. Alt.* I², 947 and 652, note 4.

have been the original constituents of the caste, it now comprises several heterogeneous elements. Thus even in a district so far from the original home of the caste as Singbhum, we find Colonel Dalton remarking that the features of the Mathurábási Goálás are high, sharp, and delicate, and they are of light-brown complexion. Those of the Magadha sub-caste, on the other hand, are undefined and coarse. They are dark-complexioned, and have large hands and feet. "Seeing the latter standing in a group with some Singbhum Kols, there is no distinguishing one from the other. There has doubtless been much mixture of blood." These remarks illustrate both the processes to which the growth of the caste is due. They show how representatives of the original type have spread to districts very remote from their original centre, and how at the same time people of alien race, who followed pastoral occupations, have become attached to the caste and are recognised by a sort of fiction as having belonged to it all along.

Internal structure.

Owing to the wide range of the caste, and to the double process by which its members have been recruited, the internal structure is extremely complicated, and the number of sub-castes and sections unusually large. Taking the Goálás of the North-Western Provinces as the type, we find the following seven divisions recognised:—DESI, NANDBANSI, JADUBANSI, SURAJBANSI, GOALBANSI, AHIR, and KATHA. These again are subdivided into a very large number of sections, the names of which appear for the most part to have reference to locality rather than to descent. According to Sir Henry Elliot traces of hypergamy may be found among these groups, but his information on this point seems to be incomplete.

Among the Goálás of Behar a different series of sub-castes has been developed, and none of the names current in the North-Western Provinces are met with. As a rule, too, the names of the groups are in Behar of a different type, and instead of being based, as in the North-West, upon descent from a particular stock or from some mythical progenitor, have reference either to the number of *muls* or sections with which intermarriage is prohibited, or to some departure from traditional usage on the part of its members. Náomulia and Sátmulia are instances of the former type, the peculiarities of which are explained more fully in the paragraphs on marriage below. Sátmuliá has the alternative title Kishnaut, and seems to arrogate descent from the god Krishna. Náomulia is also called Majraut, a name which I am unable to interpret. In Bhagalpur members of the Kishnaut and Majraut groups will not make butter—an occupation which they consider degrading—and confine themselves to dealing in milk. The Goriá or Dahiárá sub-caste is said to have been degraded because its members make butter without first scalding the milk—a practice enjoined by the Hindu scriptures and recognised as a crucial test of purity by all Goálás. Dr. Wise spells the name Daira, and says it is generally believed to be merely a corruption of the Bengali *dári*, a beard, adding as a reason that many Dahiárá Goálás have become Mahomedans and wear beards. This seems to be a little far-fetched: a more probable etymology is from *dahi*, curds. The **Kantitáhá** derive their name from their custom of branding cows with a *kánti*, or hook, a practice confined to Ahirs and never resorted to by the higher grades of Goálás, except at *sráddhs*, when the Dharm-Sánr is branded and let go. The **Kanaujia** and **Bargowár** sub-castes believe their ancestors to have migrated to Behar from the North-Western Provinces, and on this ground claim to be superior to, and hold themselves aloof from, the other sub-castes. The **Sepári** are a writer sub-caste, largely employed as patwaris in some parts of Behar. They are looked down upon by the other sub-castes, because they do not call in the Chamai, the barber, or the Dhobi at the birth of a child, but cut the navel string and perform all necessary offices themselves.

Turning now to Bengal, we find the **Pallab** or **Ballabh** sub-caste tracing their descent from one Ghám Ghosh, who is said to have sprung from the sweat of Krishna; the **Bágre** or **Ujainia** sub-caste affect to have come from Ujain; while the **Gaura Ghosh** or **Gop-Goálá**, also known as Lathiáls, pretend to be pure Sudras, and resent the suggestion that they should intermarry with any other sort of Goálá. The **Rárhi** or **Bhoga Goálás**, like the Kántitáhá in Behar, are cut off from intermarriage with the rest and generally looked down upon, because they brand their cows with red-hot iron and castrate bull calves. Two curious groups are found in Dacca—the **Sádá** or white Goálás and the **Lál** or red Goálás, the names being derived from the colour of the clothes worn by the bride and the members of the bridal procession. With the Sádá Goálás all of these are dressed in white, while the Lál Goálás wear red. The Sádá are reckoned the higher of the two, and a *pan* or bride-price is given when a girl of this group marries a Lál Goálá. In all cases of intermarriage between Sádá and Lál Goálás the colour of the clothes to be worn by the bridal party follows that of the group to which the bridegroom belongs.

Goálás are very strong in Orissa, and a large proportion of the Uriyas employed as personal servants by Europeans belong to that caste. It is a question whether the **Gaura** or **Gopopuria** sub-caste or the **Mathurábási** rank higher. Both are very particular in all matters touching their ceremonial purity, and the Mathurábási lay stress on the duty of making occasional pilgrimages to the original home of the caste at Brindában. The **Dumalá** or **Jadupuria** Goárá seem to be a group of local formation. They cherish the tradition that their ancestors came to Orissa from Jadupur, but this appears to be nothing more than the name of the Jádavas, the mythical progenitors of the Goálá caste transformed into the name of an imaginary town.

In Chota Nagpur the distribution of sub-castes is very much what might be expected. In parts of Singbhum and the adjoining Tributary States a large Goálá population exists, holding rather a subordinate position in relation to the dominant Hos and Bhuiyas, but on the whole the most flourishing of the peasantry in that part of the country. These people belong to the sub-castes known in Orissa, and appear to have entered Chota Nagpur from the south. According to Colonel Dalton, the **Magadha** Goálás are suspiciously like Hos, and in most Ho villages a few of them will be found receiving pay for looking after the Hos' cattle. The Mathurábási Goálás, who are of a much more Aryan type and claim to be pure Gopas, will not condescend to take service with Dravidians. Without forsaking their hereditary calling, they frequently manage to gain possession of substantial farms, where they keep large herds of cows and buffaloes, and deal in milk and ghi. In the north and west of the division numerous representatives of the Behar sub-castes are met with, who come in from the crowded and over-cultivated districts of Behar to feed their cattle on the forest-clad table lands of Hazaribagh, Lohardagá, and Sarguja. Here they lead a nomadic life during the dry season, living in tents of bamboo matting and moving from place to place as the supply of forage requires.

Marriage.

The character of the exogamous subdivisions of the Goálás and of the rules by which intermarriage is regulated differs markedly in different parts of the country. In Bengal the caste recognises six *gotras*, borrowed from the Brahmanical system, and forbids a man to marry a girl who belongs to the same *gotra* as himself. The *gotra* of the mother, or, to speak precisely, of the maternal grandfather, is not excluded. The intermarriage of *sapindas* is also prohibited, though the rules on this point observed by the Goálás are hardly so elaborate as those followed by the higher castes. In Behar the Brahmanical *gotras* are unknown, and marriage among the Goálás is regulated by a very large number of *muls* or exogamous groups of the territorial type, the names of which are given in the appendix. In some places where the existing *muls* have been found inconveniently large, and marriage has been rendered unduly difficult, certain *muls* have broken up into *purukhs* or sub-sections. Where this has taken place, a man may marry within the *mul*, but not within the *purukh*, the smaller and more convenient group taking the place of the larger one. Some difference of opinion prevails concerning the precise manner in which the rule of exogamy is worked, and the subject is one of such extreme intricacy that it would be unreasonable to look for uniformity of practice everywhere. The Satmulia or Kishnaut Goálás in Bhagalpur forbid a man to marry a woman belonging to the following sections or *muls* :—

(*a*) His own *mul*.
(*b*) His mother's *mul*.
(*c*) His maternal grandmother's *mul*.
(*d*) His maternal great-grandmother's *mul*.
(*e*) His paternal grandmother's *mul*.
(*f*) His paternal great-grandmother's *mul*.
(*g*) His paternal great-great-grandmother's *mul*.

To these the Naomulia add—

(*h*) The *mul* of his paternal grandmother's mother.
(*i*) The *mul* of his paternal great-grandmother's mother.

In some cases a further complication is introduced by taking into account not only the bride's *mul*, but also that of some of her female ancestors, so that if, for example, the *mul* of the proposed bride's maternal grandmother should happen to have been the same as that of the proposed bridegroom's paternal grandmother, no marriage could take place between the parties, although the *mul* of the bride herself might not correspond with any of those prohibited to the bridegroom.

Elaborate as the system is, an examination of the annexed table will show that the prohibitions of intermarriage based on the *mul* or section require to be supplemented by the standard formula: *Chacherá, mamera, phuphera, maserá, ye chár nátá bacháke shádi hotá hai* ("The line of paternal uncle, maternal uncle, paternal aunt, maternal aunt,—these four relationships are to be avoided in marriage"). To a certain extent this rule overlaps the rule of exogamy reckoned from the *mul*. Thus in the first generation the whole of the paternal uncle's descendants, both male and female, would be excluded by the rule prohibiting marriage within the section. In the second and subsequent generations agnates would be barred, but descendants through females would not, for the paternal uncle's daughters having necessarily married out of the section, their children would belong to some other section, and their second cousins would be able to marry. On the other hand, the rule of exogamy, if it stood alone, would permit the marriage of first cousins in three out of four possible cases. A reference to the table will show how this conclusion is arrived at; for Propositus belonging himself to section *A* might, so far as the rule of exogamy is concerned, marry the daughters of his paternal and maternal aunts, who would not belong to any of the *muls* barred for him. The rule defining the prohibited degrees is usually calculated to four generations in the descending line.

Table illustrating exogamy as practised by Sátmulia and Naomulia Goálás.

[The small letters *a* to *n* show the *muls*. The Sátmulia exclude the 'Seven *muls*' *a* to *g* inclusive; the Naomulia further prohibit marriage within *h* and *i*.]

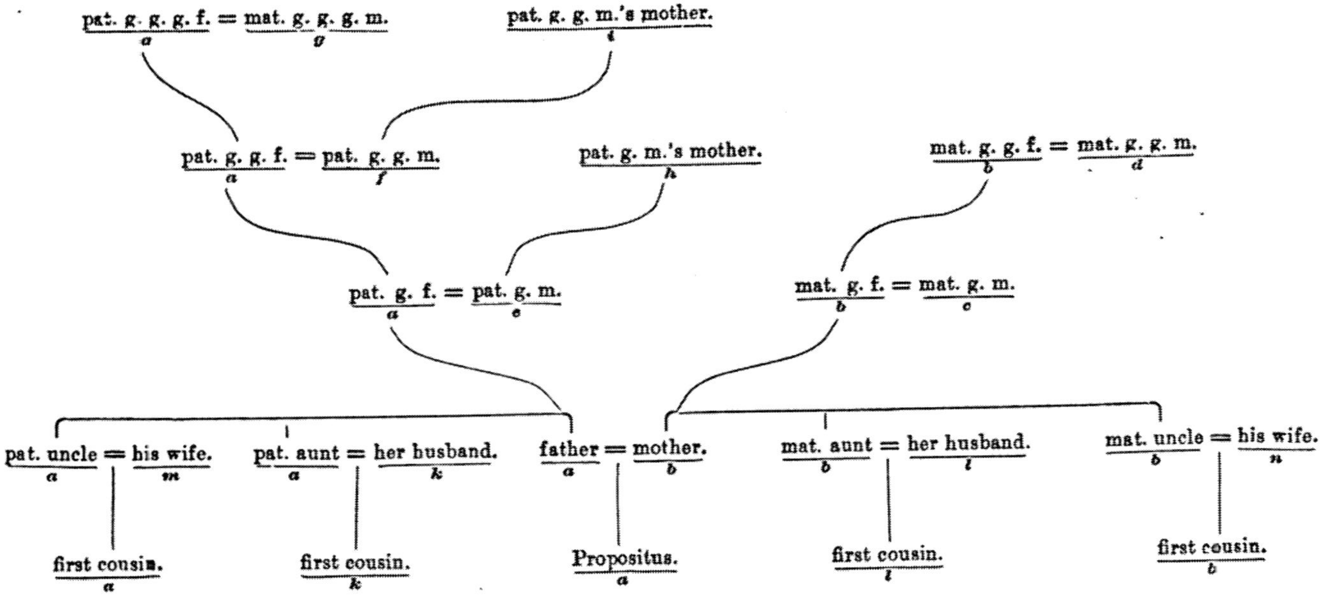

These elaborate precautions against consanguineous marriages appear to be unknown in Orissa and Chota Nagpur. In Chota Nagpur the Goálás have totemistic sections of the type common in that part of the country. A man may not marry a woman who belongs to his own totem, and is also bound to observe the standard rule concerning prohibited degrees. Regarding Orissa the information available on this point is defective, and I have been unable to ascertain the names of the exogamous subdivisions of the caste and the rules governing intermarriage.

Among the Goálás of Bengal and the higher Goálás of Orissa, the orthodox view of Hindu marriage is on the whole accepted. Girls are married as infants; widow-marriage is strictly prohibited, and divorce is unknown. If a woman commits adultery with another Goálá or with a man of higher caste, the matter is hushed up: an intrigue with a low-caste man is punished with instant exclusion from caste.

In Behar infant-marriage has established itself as a usage essential to the maintenance of social respectability; but a widow is allowed to marry again, and is generally expected to marry her late husband's younger brother. Under no circumstances may she marry the elder brother.

With the Goálás of Chota Nagpur both adult and infant-marriage are recognised, the latter being regarded as a counsel of perfection, which well-to-do persons may be expected to act up to. The rule that the *rukhsati* or final ceremony celebrating the departure of the bride to the house of the bridegroom and the commencement of regular connubial relations shall ordinarily take place four months after the wedding shows pretty clearly that infant-marriage cannot have been introduced in the strict sense in which it is understood in Bengal. A bride-price is paid, varying from Rs. 5 to Rs. 25, according to the status of the families concerned, and out of this sum the bride's father is expected to provide his daughter with ornaments. Brahmans officiate at the wedding. The smearing of vermilion on the bride's forehead is believed to be the most important part of the ceremony. Widows may marry again by the meagre ritual known as *sagai*. At this no Brahman attends; new *sáris* and some sweetmeats are presented to the bride and to her mother, and either the bridegroom himself or some widow of the company puts vermilion on the bride's forehead. This completes the marriage; no *rukhsati* is required, and the parties begin to live together at once. Among the Goálás of Singbhum a widow is required to marry one of her late husband's younger brothers; and failing these, she must select a husband from among the exogamous group to which her husband belonged. This deserves notice, as being in all probability a survival of earlier custom which has elsewhere fallen into disuse.

The usages current in Orissa do not differ very materially from those which prevail in Behar. In both infant-marriage is the standard to which every one seeks to conform, but it may be conjectured that this has not been so in Orissa for very long. The Goálás there say that if by chance a girl should remain unmarried in her father's house after she has attained puberty, the breach of ceremonial requirements may be got over by giving her in marriage to an old man or a man otherwise unfit for marriage. After the marriage she is at once divorced by her husband, and is then competent to marry again by the ritual appointed for widows. I have mentioned above that the higher Goálás of Orissa affect a high standard of orthodoxy, and look down upon the Behar and Bengal divisions of the caste. Among them widow-marriage is said to be forbidden. Most Uriya Goálás, however, allow a widow to remarry by the usual form.

Birth.

Some curious particulars concerning the birth customs of the Orissa Goálás may be given here. During labour and after delivery the mother is kept in a separate house, from which fresh air is excluded as much as possible, and which is kept artificially heated for a period of twenty-one days. Branches of *kendu* (Embryopteris Glutinifera) and *ligu* (Ligneolaria) are hung near the front door of the house; iron nails are driven into the door-posts, and *chimuai* (Hemidesmus Indicus), and *bholia* (Semecarpus Anacardium) are laid in the infant's bed. After the navel string has been cut the child is bathed in hot water in which leaves of *basanga* (Justicia Adhatode), *arka* (Asclepios Gigantea), *bigunia* (Viter Negnanda), *daukari*, and *dhatura* (Datura nutal) have been boiled. On the fifth day after the birth *harada* (Cytisus Cajan), *mung* pulse, *biri* (Phaseolus Mungo), rice, and wheat are fried together and distributed to friends. The worship of the goddess Shashthi is performed on the sixth day, when Vidhátá, or Brahmá, is believed to enter the house and write its destiny on the child's forehead. On this occasion two lumps of cowdung are placed at each side of the door, and for fifteen days red lead is smeared on them, and *dúb* grass well moistened laid on the top. On the eighth day a feast is given to relatives and members of the caste. Finally, on the 21st day new cooking pots are brought into use, an elaborate entertainment is prepared, and the child is named. During this period of three weeks not only the mother, but also the father, is deemed to be impure, and is required to abstain from all his ordinary occupations.

Religion.

There is little to be said about the religion of the caste. In Bengal most of them are Vaishnavas, and celebrate the Janmáshtami or festival of the birthday of Krishna with great circumstance. They employ Brahmans for religious and ceremonial purposes, but these are looked upon as degraded, and are not received upon equal terms by the higher orders of the priestly caste. In Behar the tendency to Vaishnavism does not seem to be so strong, and a considerable proportion of the caste are said to belong to the Saiva and Sákta sects. There Goálá Brahmans occupy a higher position than in Bengal, and are deemed as respectable as the Brahmans who serve other castes of the same status. It is, however, only for marriage, *sráddh*, and the worship of Sat Narain and the greater gods that the services of Brahmans are required. When it is only a question of propitiating the host of minor gods, who play so important a part in the domestic religion of the people, the householder himself officiates as priest. By Goálás special reverence is paid to Bisahari, Ganpat

Gohil, Gosawan, the god of cattle disease, Kalumánjhi, and a number of *gaián* or ghosts. To these vague shapes flowers, sweetmeats, milk, rice, and occasionally sacrifices of goats are offered and partaken of by the worshippers. Monday and Friday are considered the most auspicious days, Saturday being reckoned peculiarly unlucky. At the time of the Sankránti on the last day of Kártik, October-November, a pig is turned loose among a herd of buffaloes, who are encouraged to gore it to death. The carcase is then given to Dosádhs to eat. The Goálás or Ahirs, who practise this strange rite, aver that it has no religious significance, and is merely a sort of popular amusement. They do not themselves partake of any portion of the pig.

Social status

In point of social standing the Goálás of Behar rank with Kurmis, Amáts, and the other castes from whose hands a Brahman can take water. In Bengal they occupy a lower position, and are counted as inferior, not only to the Naba-Sákh, but also to the cultivating division of the Kaibartta caste. The Orissa Goálás, on the other hand, affect a high standard of ceremonial purity, and look down upon the Behar and Bengal divisions of the caste. Most Goálás combine cultivation with their hereditary pursuits, and in Orissa and Singbhum some members of the caste hold landed tenures of substantial value.

The following statement shows the number and distribution of Goálás in 1872 and 1881 :—

District.	1872.	1881.	District.	1872.	1881.
Bardwan	99,825	78,263	Noakhali	1,520	2,306
Bankura	38,572	59,662	Tipperah	9,023	11,089
Birbhum	17,448	16,125	Chittagong Hill Tracts ...	...	29
Midnapur	44,163	53,994	Patna	179,848	217,845
Huzhli	65,366	46,134	Gya	278,665	309,871
Howrah		17,317	Shahabad	214,605	242,721
24-Parganas	88,551	77,956	Mozufferpur	526,683	299,127
Nadiya	91,260	93,382	Darbhanga		349,112
Jessore	20,992	17,270	Saran	238,749	256,513
Khulná	...	14,021	Champaran	131,413	169,274
Murshedabad	39,953	36,411	Monghyr	197,669	217,616
Dinajpur	4,280	5,123	Bhagalpur	335,137	343,830
Rajshahye	9,594	9,273	Purniah	128,606	131,629
Rangpur	3,049	6,331	Maldah	14,389	16,875
Bogra	3,594	2,925	Santál Parganas	74,529	88,544
Pabna	11,646	11,788	Cuttack	105,840	140,870
Darjiling	420	1,494	Puri	43,227	66,662
Jalpigori	960	2,152	Balasore	56,649	69,581
Kuch Behar	...	1,710	Tributary States	94,386	136,420
Dacca	22,788	25,337	Hazaribagh	92,890	129,445
Faridpur	2,912	6,316	Lohardaga	60,433	78,677
Bakarganj	6,738	4,240	Singbhum	36,320	38,675
Maimansinh	17,613	22,593	Manbhum	35,176	29,081
Chittagong	327	664	Tributary States	29,002	45,742

Goalabhuiyá, a sub-caste of Sutradhars in Western Bengal.

Goálbansi, a sub-caste of Goálás in the North-Western Provinces and Behar.

Goár, a synonym for Goálá.

Gobans, cow-born, a sept of Bairágis in Chota Nagpur.

Gobansi, a title of the family of the Rájás of Pachet, in the district of Manbhum, referring to the legend that the founder of the house was deserted in the woods as an infant and was suckled by a cow.

Gobargárhá, a *mul* or section of the Naomuliá or Majraut sub-caste of Goálás in Behar.

Gobariá, a synonym for Sikhariá Bhuiyá, *q.v.*

Gobasi, "beef-eaters," an opprobrious designation of Bauris, Háris, and other low castes.

Gobhil, a *gotra* or section of Agarwáls.

Gobindpuriá, see **Govindpuriá**.

Gobolachan, a totemistic sept of Mundas in Chota Nagpur who cannot eat beef.

Gobra, *Gobrea*, a sub-caste of Bauris, so designated from their purifying the ground with cow-dung where they eat, while the other Bauris (Jhántias) simply sweep the ground; a sub-caste of Máls and Lohárs in Bankura.

Gochalya, a sept of the Tungjainya sub-tribe of Chakmás in the Hill Tracts of Chittagong.

Gochchhási, a *gáin* of the Bharadwája *gotra* of Bárendra Brahmans in Bengal.

Gochhpuriá, a *pur* or section of Sákadwipi Brahmans in Behar.

Godáhia, *Godágá*, a sub-caste of Goálás in Behar who brand cattle with a red-hot iron, see **Gujiár**.

Godahiyá, a sub-caste of Kumhárs in Behar.

Godhanpuriá, a *mul* or section of the Kamarkalla sub-caste of Sonárs and of Lohárs in Behar.

Godná-wálí, a female tattooer. In Eastern Bengal, according to Dr. Wise, Bediya women travel about the country with a bag, containing a variety of drugs, a cupping horn (*Singá*), and a scarificator (*Náran*). They attract attention by bawling "To tattoo, to cup, and to extract worms from decayed teeth!" They also prescribe for female disorders. It is said that small grubs are kept in a bamboo tube, and while the patient's attention is occupied by the talk of the operator, a maggot is presented as if it had been extracted from the hollow tooth. For this trick the Godná-wáli receives a suitable fee.

In tattooing the juice of the Bhangra plant (*Indigofera linifolia*) and woman's milk are the materials used, and the punctures are made with needles or the thorns of the Karaundá (*Carissa Carandas*). While the operation is being performed a very equivocal mantra is recited to alleviate pain and prevent any subsequent inflammation.

In respectable Hindu families an old nurse usually tattoos the girls. Now-a-days the ordinary tattoo design, either circular or stellate, is made at the top of the nose in the centre of the forehead; formerly the fashionable stain (*Ullikhi*) was at the same spot, but a line extended along the bridge of the nose, branching out into two curves over each ala. Tattoo marks were originally distinctive of Hindu females, but Muhammadan women copied them, and it is only since the Farazí revival that they have discontinued the habit.

Chandál women are often employed to cure goitre by tattooing. A circular spot on the most prominent part of the swelling is punctured with a bamboo spike, and common ink mixed with the sap of the Kálí Koshijia rubbed in.

Godo, crocodile, a totemistic sept of Oraons in Chota Nagpur.

Gográmi, a *gáin* of the Bharadwája *gotra* of Bárendra Brahmans in Bengal.

Goh, a sept of Gonds in Chota Nagpur.

Goherwar, a sept of Chiks in Chota Nagpur.

Gohori, a *thar* or sept of Gurungs in Darjiling.

Goil, a section of Agarwáls.

Goin, a half-*gotra* or section of Agarwáls.

Goit, a *mul* or section of the Ghosin sub-caste of Goálás in Behar; a totemistic sept of Bhuiyás in Chota Nagpur.

Goita, a sub-caste of Koiris in Behar.

Gojiá, a sub-caste of Kámárs in Hazaribagh.

Gola, a sub-caste of Bhandáris in Orissa.

Golaja, a sept of Oraons in Chota Nagpur.

Golángya, a *thar* or sept of Gurungs in Darjiling.

Golchiá, a section of the Oswál Baniyás.

Goldár, a title of Kalwárs in Behar.

Gole, a section of Murmis in Darjiling.

Goleg-pá, *go*, a head, and *leg*, good—the peaceful, a sub-sept of the Nah-pá sept of Sherpa Bhotias.

Golmetah, a section of Maghayá Dhobis in Behar.

Goloar, sweet potato, a totemistic sept of Lohárs in Chota Nagpur.

Golrám, a *mul* or section of the Naomuliá or Majraut sub-caste of Goálás in Behar.

Golsáz, see **Hawáigar.**

Golvar, a section of Ghásis in Chota Nagpur.

Gomdan, a section of Murmis in Darjiling.

Gond, a non-Aryan tribe, classed on linguistic grounds as Dravidian, properly belonging to the Central Provinces,[1] but found also in the Tributary States of Chota Nagpur, in the south of Lohardagá and in Singbhum. In the States of Sargujá, Koreá, and Udaipur most of the feudal tenures held on terms of military service directly under the Chief are in the hands of Gonds—a fact which suggests that the tribe must have been among the earliest permanent settlers in that part of the country. The Gonds of Bengal are divided into four sub-tribes:—**Gond, Ráj-Gond, Dhokar-Gond,** and

Origin.

[1] The present article deals only with the Gonds of Bengal, and does not attempt to give an exhaustive account of the entire tribe.

Doroá-Gond or Náik. The Gond represent the bulk of the tribe, while the Ráj-Gond are supposed to be descended from families who attained to the dignity of Chief. The Dhokar-Gond are a wandering race, who make a living by begging and thieving. The Doroá-Gond or Náik are found only in Singbhum. According to Colonel Dalton, they were the military retainers of the Mahápátra of Bámanghâti, a feudatory of the Rájá of Moharbhanj, who were driven out of Bámanghâti with their leader and permitted to settle in Singbhum in consequence of his having rebelled against his lord paramount. Their sections, shown in Appendix I, are totemistic. One of them, *Besrá* (hawk), occurs also among the Santáls.

Internal structure.

Marriage.

Gonds practise both infant and adult-marriage, but under Hindu influence the former practice tends continually to become more popular and to be looked upon as a badge of social distinction. The ceremony is modelled on that in use among the lower castes of Hindus. *Sindurdán* and marriage to a mango-tree form prominent parts of the ritual, while according to some the binding portion of the rite consists in the village barber pouring a vessel of water over both bride and bridegroom. Widows are allowed to marry again, the usual practice being for the widow to marry her late husband's younger brother. No religious ceremony is in use on such occasions, nor is it customary to send for the Brahman and Hajjám, who officiate at the marriage of a virgin. All that is necessary is to assemble a sort of committee of relations, before whom the bridegroom gives the bride a new cloth and a lac bracelet and promises to maintain her in a suitable fashion. The proceedings end, as is the manner of the non-Aryan tribes, with a feast, at which every one gets very drunk.

Religion.

The Bengal members of the tribe affect to be orthodox Hindus, and worship the standard gods with the assistance of a degraded class of Brahmans, who also officiate at their marriages. Although to this extent they have embraced the popular religion, they still worship the characteristic deities of the non-Hinduised Gonds—Bar Deo and Dulhá Deo. They burn their dead, but the relatives mourn for three days only, after which period they purify themselves by bathing and shaving, and make offerings of bread and milk to the spirit of the departed. Their social rank is very low, as in spite of their professed conformity to Hinduism they eat fowls and other unclean food. Concerning their appearance and characteristics, Colonel Dalton has the following remarks:—

Social status.

"Socially, I consider the Hinduised or semi-Hinduised Gonds to be the least interesting of the great families of the aborigines of India. They have none of the lively disposition of the Oraons or of the free, dignified demeanour which characterises many of the Singbhum Kols. They are in character reserved, sullen, and suspicious. They are indifferent cultivators and careless about the appearance of their homesteads, and they are withal singularly ill-favoured; and though some of the wealthier families have formed a series of alliances with other races, which have improved their looks, I can point to many who have tried this in vain, and who show to this day features more closely resembling the lower Negro type than any I have met with amongst the tribes of Bengal. They often have short crisp curly hair, and though it is said, and no doubt truly, that this is far removed from the regular woolly covering of a Negro's head, I have generally found such hair in conjunction with features very noticeably Negro in type, and accompanying a very dark skin. They are larger and heavier in build than the Oraons and Kols, and with none of the graceful physique to be found in both these tribes."

The following statement shows the number and distribution of Gonds in 1872 and 1881 :—

District.	1872.	1881.	District.	1872.	1881.
Bardwan	47	......	Bhagalpur	......	167
Bankura	3,860	9,636	Purniah	......	1,002
Birbhum	8	......	Santál Parganas	......	580
Midnapur	7,860	7,161	Cuttack	12	16
Hughli	......	3	Puri	3	......
Howrah	......	21	Balasore	6	......
24-Parganas	2	35	Tributary States	22,275	17,550
Gya	......	126	Hazaribagh	7	3
Shahabad	......	7,089	Lohardagá	1,338	3,842
Mozufferpur	......	25	Singbhum	4,838	2,168
Saran	......	11,653	Manbhum	......	30
Champaran	......	11,055	Tributary States	68,614	72,274

Gonda, a *thar* or sept of Mangars in Darjiling.

Gondh, a sub-caste of Binds in Behar.

Gondli, a kind of grain, a totemistic sept of Mundas in Chota Nagpur.

Gondrari, a tree, a totemistic sept of Oraons in Chota Nagpur.

Gonduk, a *thar* or sept of Gurungs in Darjiling.

Gongbá, a section of Murmis in Darjiling.

Gonr, a sub-caste of Kándus in Behar; a section of the Biyáhut and Kharidáhá Kalwárs in Behar; a stone-cutter and maker of stone plates and household utensils.

Gonrhi, a title of Malláhs in Behar.

Gonrhi, *Gunrhi, Malláh, Machhuá*, a fishing and cultivating caste of Behar, who claim descent from Nikhád or Nishád, a mythical boatman, who is said to have ferried Ram Chandra across the Ganges at Allahabad. The fact that the word Nishád, which is used in the Rig Veda as a general name for the non-Aryan races, should appear in the traditions of the Gonrhi as a personal eponym, suggests the conjecture that the caste may be descended from one of the aboriginal tribes whom the Aryans found in possession of the Ganges Valley. This view

Origin.

derives some support from the physical appearance of the caste, which approaches to the non-Aryan type. The internal structure of the group throws no light on its origin, unless we may attach weight to the fact that one of the sub-castes bears the name of Kolh. The other sub-castes are Banpar, Cháb or Chábi, Dhoár, Kurin, Parbatti-Kurin, Khunaut or Khulaut, and Semári. All of these are strictly endogamous, except the Kolh and Kurin sub-castes, which admit of intermarriage with each other, though not with members of other sub-castes. Some members of the Cháb sub-caste deny that they have any connection with the Gonrhi. The section-namse, which are shown in the Appendix, are in common use as titles among many other castes in Behar. Their precise bearing on marriage is not easy to ascertain. Gonrhis are not as a class intelligent enough to be able to explain their own customs very clearly, nor have they a sufficiently strong organization to secure uniformity of practice in different parts of the country. Thus according to some accounts the Cháb, Dhoár, and Kolh regulate their marriages solely by the standard formula for reckoning prohibited degrees, and the Khunaut sub-caste have no exogamous sections, while within the Parbatti-Kurin sub-caste only a special group, known as Játhot, observes the rule of exogamy in respect of its section-names. The rest of the sub-castes regard these names as titles having no special significance. The Kurin have no section-names, and affect to know nothing about the regular custom of exogamy, but they do not allow a man to marry a woman who lives in the same village as himself. The Banpar and Semári sub-castes, on the other hand, appear to have distinct sections, and also count prohibited degrees down to six, or as some say seven, generations in the descending line. In determining whom a man may marry regard is paid not merely to his own section, but to the section to which his mother and his paternal and maternal grandmothers belonged.

Internal structure.

Gonrhis marry their daughters as infants or as adults according to their means. Infant-marriage is deemed the more respectable, but no special disgrace attaches to a family because one of the daughters attains the age of puberty before being married. The marriage ceremony is of the standard type. Polygamy is permitted only to the extent that a man may take a second wife if his first wife is barren or suffers from an incurable disease. A widow may marry again by the *sagai* form, of which *sindurdán* constitutes the binding portion. She may marry her late husband's younger brother, but is not compelled to do so. Divorce is permitted with the consent of the pancháyat, on the ground of misconduct or incompatibility of temper. Divorced wives can marry again. Some hold, however, that a woman taken in adultery is debarred from this privilege, and I gather that divorce is generally regarded with disfavour by the respectable members of the caste.

Marriage.

Most Gonrhis are Vaishnava Hindus, but a few members of the Saurapatya sect of sun-worshippers are found among them. They employ Maithil Brahmans for the worship of the greater gods, but these priests are not usually

Religion.

recognised as equals by other members of the sacred order. They have a large number of minor gods, and many of them belong to the Pánch Píriya creed—an obscure but widely-spread cult, which appears to have arisen from the contact of Islam with the animistic beliefs of its aboriginal converts. Some, again, worship a water-god, called Koila-Bábá, described as an old grey-bearded person who, as *Gangáji ká Beldár*, 'the navvy of our lady the Ganges,' saps and swallows up whatever opposes the sacred stream. Before casting a new net or starting on a commercial venture, offerings of molasses and seven kinds of grain, kneaded into balls, are offered to him, and at the end of the ceremony one of the balls is placed on the edge of the water, another on the bow of the boat. Another rite common to many, if not to all, fisher castes is the Bárwaria or Bárahí Púja, when a subscription is made, and in the absence of a Bráhman a pig is sacrificed in a garden or on a patch of waste land outside the village. Jai Singh, Amar Singh, Chand Singh, Diyál Singh, Kewal, Marang, Bandi, Goraiyá, and a river named Kamaláji, are also regularly worshipped. Jai Singh, who is also a favourite deity of the Tiyar caste, is said to have been a Gonrhi of Ujjain, who had a large timber trade in the Sunderbuns. On one occasion the Rájá of the Sunderbuns imprisoned 700 Gonrhis in consequence of a dispute about the price of wood. Jai Singh slew the Rájá and released the prisoners, and has ever since been honoured with daily worship. Goats, sweetmeats, wheaten cakes, *pán supári*, and flowers are offered to him at regular intervals, and no Gonrhi will light a pipe or embark on a fishing excursion without first invoking the name of Jai Singh. Once a year, in the month of Sráwan, a flag is set up in honour of Hanumán on a bamboo pole in the courtyard, and offerings of sweetmeats and fruits are presented to the god. These offerings are received by the Brahmans who officiate as priests, while the articles of food given to the minor gods are eaten by the members of the caste. The dead are burned, usually on the brink of a river, and the ashes thrown into the stream. In Supul the practice is to burn in a mango grove. *Sráddh* is performed on the thirteenth day after death.

Social status.

The social status of the Gonrhi caste appears to vary in different parts of the country, and does not admit of very precise definition. All that can be said is that they rank below Barhis, Kumhárs, and Laheris, and that although Brahmans do not ordinarily take water from their hands, this rule is not observed everywhere. Their own practice in the matter of diet inclines towards laxity, as they eat scaleless as well as scaly fish, pork, water tortoises, and field-rats, and indulge freely in strong drink. There are, however, many Bhakats among them who abstain from liquor and from all kinds of animal food, and are held in respect by reason of their abstinence. The caste will take water and sweetmeats from Kewats, Dhánuks, and Gangotás, but will not eat cooked food prepared by members of those castes.

Occupation.

They believe boating and fishing to be their original and characteristic occupation, but many of them are engaged in agriculture as tenure-holders, occupancy or non-occupancy raiyats, and landless day-labourers.

The following statement shows the number and distribution of Gonrhis in 1872 and 1881:—

District.	1872.	1881.	District.	1872.	1881.
Bardwan	1,663	454	Chittagong	524	81
Bankura	1,333	2,463	Noakhali	106	......
Birbhum	466	3,157	Tipperah	2,510	1,720
Midnapur	1,896	15,244	Patna	17,724	21,335
Hughli	} 1,424	{ 647	Gya	11,933	12,458
Howrah		637	Shahabad	19,269	17,928
24-Parganas	2,304	991	Tirhut { Darbhanga ...	} 163,355	{ 116,228
Nadiya	13,237	10,679	Tirhut { Mosufferpur ...		89,339
Khulna	......	3,397	Saran	36,306	22,935
Jessore	12,129	10,766	Champaran	69,152	68,209
Murshedabad	7,322	8,302	Monghyr	27,437	36,674
Dinajpur	675	1,969	Bhagalpur	43,060	42,996
Rajshahye	1,768	1,714	Purniah	59,141	46,633
Rangpur	388	1,166	Maldah	1,656	1,955
Bogra	2,741	1,397	Santál Parganas	2,760	66,597
Pabna	7,530	5,844	Cuttack	8,417	10,983
Darjiling	26	549	Puri	262	334
Jalpigori	24	3	Balasore	17,213	21,331
Kuch Behar	......	361	Tributary States	1,522	1,317
Dacca	5,567	2,015	Hazaribagh	1,466	3,709
Faridpur	5,466	2,026	Lohardagá	7,250	12,318
Bakarganj	1,705	978	Singbhum	......	3,567
Maimansinh	10,061	22,361	Manbhum	1,671	53

Gonria, a sub-caste of Goálás in Behar.

Gop or **Ghosh**, a sub-caste of Goálás in Bengal.

Gopa, a synonym for Goálá; a title and a section of the Kanaujiá and Goriá sub-castes of Goálás in Behar.

Gopál, a synonym for Goálá.

Gopálghataki, a *mel* or hypergamous sub-group of Rárhi Brahmans in Bengal.

Gopál-Kárikar, a sub-caste of Sutradhars in Murshedabad.

Gop-Goálá, a synonym for Goálá.

Gopijan, a sect of Vaishnavas; a synonym for Sadgop.

Gopurbba, a *gáin* of the Bharadwája *gotra* of Uttar-Bárendra Brahmans in Bengal.

Gorahat, a small class of Bhuiyás in the south of Chota Nagpur who make a living by washing for gold in the sands of the rivers.

Goraheri, a synonym for Gareri in Behar.

Gorai, a title of Kaibarttas.

Gorâit, a title of the headmen of the Dom caste in Bhagalpur, who have under them servants, called Chharidárs, to execute or communicate their orders to villages; a watchman and messenger in Behar, usually of the Dosadh caste.

Gorait, *Korait*, *Baikar*, a non-Aryan caste of musicians, comb-makers, and cotton-carders found in the south-west of the Lohardagá district, and perhaps in Hazaribagh. It may be inferred from the totemistic character

Origin.

of their sections, a list of which is given in Appendix I, that they are an offshoot from one of the aboriginal races, while the variant Korait rather suggests that they may be connected with the Kora caste. Resemblances between names, however, are but blind guides in questions of tribal affinity, and I doubt whether we can safely do more than surmise that Korait may probably have been the original name of the caste, which was corrupted into Gorait from its similarity in sound to the familiar title of the village messenger and watchman. Their specialised and comparatively degraded avocations, and the fact that they are not employed as village messengers, exclude the supposition that the converse process can have been at work, and that the bond of a common occupation may have formed a number of Goraits properly so called into an endogamous group bearing that name. Indeed, although nearly every village in Behar and Chota Nagpur has its Gorait, the profession, owing perhaps to its members being so scattered, shows no tendency towards hardening into a caste.

Marriage.

Goraits marry their daughters both as infants and as adults, but the former practice is deemed the more respectable, and is followed by all who can afford it. After the bride has been selected, the parents of the bridegroom go to her parents' house to see her. On this occasion a feast is given by the bride's people, at which the liquor—an essential element in all non-Aryan rejoicings—is provided by the father of the bridegroom, and four annas, eight annas, or one rupee is presented to the bride as *muh-dekhi*, or fee for the privilege of seeing her face. On the next day the girl's parents visit the boy, and are entertained wholly at his father's expense. Lastly, if both parties are satisfied with this mutual inspection, the boy's people go to the bride's house and present to her a new *sári*, a he-goat, and Rs. 3 to buy ornaments with. These constitute the bride-price (*dali*).

On the day before the wedding the bridegroom's party march in procession to the bride's house and stop there for the night. Next morning the fathers of the bride and bridegroom shake hands and embrace one another (*samdhi milán*). Then, in the presence of some elders of the caste, the headman of the village and the priest of the rural gods (*páhn*), who are received with great ceremony, the marriage is completed by the bride and bridegroom smearing vermilion on each other's foreheads (*sindurdán*), while the elders solemnly exhort them to work hard, eat, drink, and prosper and not get divorced. This meagre ceremony takes place in a bamboo marriage shed (*marhwa*) erected in the courtyard. Brahmans are not called in, and the village barber takes no part in the ceremony. On the evening of the same day the bridegroom's party take the bride and bridegroom, both seated in the same palanquin, to the latter's house, where *sindurdán* is again performed. On that night the bridegroom, if he has attained puberty, sleeps with the bride. After three days the couple go to the bride's house and stay there nine days, returning finally to their own home on the tenth day.

Polygamy is permitted, and there is no rule limiting the number of wives. A widow may marry again, and her choice is not fettered by the obligation to marry her late husband's younger brother. The ritual used at the marriage differs from that in use at the marriage of a virgin in that no *marhwa* is constructed and the money portion of the bride-price is only Re. 1. *Sindurdán* is performed in the presence of the widow's relatives, but there is no marriage procession, and the bride is taken home without any display. According to some authorities if the widow elects to live on with her brother-in-law, it is sufficient to announce this intention to the relatives, and no ceremony of any kind is required.

A divorce (*chhorá-chhuri*) may be granted by the caste council (pancháyat) if the wife is proved to be unchaste, or if she frequently runs away to her father's house without the permission of her husband. Proceedings may also be initiated by the wife on the ground that her husband is too old for her or is an habitual drunkard. Divorced women may marry again by *sagai*.

Religion.

Goraits profess to be Hindus, but they have not yet attained to the dignity of employing Brahmans. They worship **Devi Mái** and a tribal spirit called **Purubia,** to whom a goat is sacrificed once a year. In cases of illness an exorcist (*mati baigá*) is called in to detect the demon or witch who is giving trouble. If this personage ascribes the visitation to the wrath of the tribal god, the *páhn* is sent for, and a goat, pig, sheep, or fowl sacrificed. Those who can afford to do so burn the dead, but the bodies of the poor are buried with the head to the north. No regular *sráddh* is performed. On the tenth day after death the nearest relative of the deceased gets himself shaved and gives a feast to the friends of the family.

Social status.

In point of social status Goraits rank with Lohrás and Ghásis, and no respectable people will take water from their hands. They eat beef, pork, and field-rats, and indulge freely in spirituous and fermented liquors. As has been already stated, they find employment as hired musicians at weddings and various kinds of festivities, as makers of bamboo combs and carders of cotton. Some are employed in agriculture as non-occupancy raiyats or agricultural labourers (*Dhángars*) engaged by the year for a lump sum of Rs. 5 paid down at the time of hiring, one *kát* and a half (about 38 seers) of paddy per month, and four yards of cloth at the end of the year.

In 1881 there were 61 Goráits in Hazaribagh, 3,856 in Lohardagá, and 43 in Singbhum. There was no separate entry for Goráits in 1872.

Goraksa, a section of Jugis.

Gorangi, a title of mendicant Vaishnavas, apparently a variant of Gaurangi.

Gorea, a sub-section of the Bharadwája section of Utkal Brahmans in Orissa.

Gorhárk, a *pur* or section of Sákadwipi Brahmans in Behar.

Goria, red earth, a totemistic sept of Mundas in Chota Nagpur.

Goria or *Dahiara*, a sub-caste of Goálas in Behar who hold the title of Mandar and belong to the

Prem Ghuno *gotra*. They make butter and sell milk and curds. Also a sub-caste of Dhobás in Manbhum, and of Chamárs in Behar who will not make shoes and disown the title Muchi.

Goriár, a section of Kurmis in Chota Nagpur and Orissa.

Goro, a sub-caste of Khatwes in Behar; a sub-caste of Goálás in Chota Nagpur.

Gorsár, a sub-caste of Dhobis in Behar.

Goru, cow, a totemistic section of Jagannáthi Kumhárs in Orissa.

Gosáin, *Goswámi*, *Gonsái*, *Gonsiá*, a master of his passions, a religious mendicant; a title of a class of Brahmans, the original disciples of Chaitanya, who are spiritual guides of the worshippers of Vishnu. In Bengal the term is usually applied to Jugis and the Grihi or Grihastha Vaishnavas, who are allowed to marry and follow secular pursuits. It is also used as a common title, just as Banarji, Bhattácharji, etc. Socially it denotes a class of people who manufacture and sell threads, corresponding to Jugis. A synonym for Bairági.

Gosáinji, a synonym for Brahman.

Gosáinpanthi, a sect of religious mendicants.

Gosti, a *thar* or sept of Gurungs in Darjiling.

Goswálambi, a *gáin* of the Bharadwája *gotra* of Bárendra Brahmans in Bengal.

Gotama, Gautama, a section of Brahmans.

Gotanya, a *thar* or section of Nepáli Brahmans.

Gothar, a section of Murmis in Darjiling.

Gothi, a *thar* or sept of Gurungs in Darjiling.

Gothwál, a section of Goálás in the North-Western Provinces and Behar.

Gotramási, a section of Báruis in Bengal.

Gotsobhni, a *mul* or section of the Naomuliá or Majraut subcaste of Goálás in Behar.

Govariyá, a hypergamous group of Tiyars found in Bhagalpur.

Govindpuriá, a sub-caste of Telis in Bengal and of Lohárs in the Santál Parganas.

Gowe, a section of Bábhans in Behar.

Gozar, a title of Dhobis in Behar.

Grahabipra, "Planet-Brahman," a title of Achárji Brahmans.

Graháchárji, *Griháchárjya*, "Teacher of the Planets," a title of Achárji Brahmans.

Grandan, a section of Murmis in Darjiling.

Gránjá, a *thar* or sept of Mangars in Darjiling.

Grihasodhani, a *gáin* of the Bátsya *gotra* of Uttar-Bárendra Brahmans in Bengal.

Grihasth, a synonym for Bábhan; a functional group of Jugis in Bengal composed of four families—Dhanái Mandal, Jnánbar, Bhagan Bhájan, and Paban.

Grihi, householders, a sept of Mál Paháriás in the Santál Parganas.

Guá, areca-nut, a sub-sept of the Hemrom sept of Santáls; a totemistic sept of Mundas in Chota Nagpur.

Guábári, a *mul* or section of the Naomuliá or Majraut sub-caste of Goálás in Behar.

Guáburi, the highest *thar* or sept of Gurungs in Darjiling, whose members, in the absence of a Brahman, are called in to perform the ceremony of *nuarmi*, that is, the purification of a woman after birth of a child. They are also employed for the ceremonies of marriage and funerals.

Gudar, a group of the Aoghar sect of Saiva ascetics founded in Guzerat by a Dasnámi mendicant named Brahmagiri. See **Aoghar**.

Guha, a title of Káyasths in Bengal.

Guhai, Gonhhi, a sub-caste of Baniyas.

Gui, a title of Dakshin-Rárhi Káyasths; of Mayarás, Tántis, and of Kaibarttas in Bengal.

Gujiár or **Godágá**, a sub-caste of Ahirs or Goálás in Behar who are cow-doctors.

Gujráti or **Gurjjara**, a territorial division of the Pancha Dravira Brahmans who live in the south of the Vindhya range in Gurjarashtra, the country of the Gujráti language. Persons bearing this title are found in Behar, they claim to have originally come from Gujrat, and are usually engaged in trade. In Patna they are said to make pickles.

Gulgo, a sept of the Bhumij tribe in Manbhum.

Gulguliá, a wandering non-Aryan tribe, who live by hunting, teaching monkeys to dance, selling indigenous drugs, begging, and petty thieving. Their origin is obscure, but it seems likely that they are a branch of the Bediyás. I have been unable to obtain any trustworthy information regarding the internal structure of the caste. Some Gulguliás in Gya assured me that they had three sub-castes—**Bantari, Pachpaniá**, and **Sukwár**—and I mention this statement in case it may be of use to other inquirers. My informants seemed to be stupid and ignorant men, and I doubt whether their evidence was worth much. They have a legend that Rukmini, the reputed ancestress of the Pási caste, had a son, called Mohabábá, who in his turn had seven sons, Gaiduha, Byádhá, Tirsuliá, Magháyá, Turk (the Mahomedan Pási), Gilehri, and Gulguliá. These seven sons challenged each other to jump off the top of a palmyra tree (*tár*). Gilehri (the squirrel) jumped first and landed unhurt. Tirsuliá, who went second, was killed on the spot, whereupon Mohabábá, seeing that Gilehri had led the others into trouble, smote him with his hand and cursed him to be reckoned among the inferior animals and to be fortunate only in this, that he should jump from great heights and come to no harm. This is the reason why the squirrel is a good jumper and bears the marks of five fingers on his back. The

Origin and internal structure.

story goes on, in a somewhat inconsequent fashion, to say that the next to leave the family was Gulguliá, who observed that his brothers, after serving their customers with *tári*, always washed the cup, however low the caste of the man who had drunk from it. This struck the youngest brother—in folklore it is usually the *youngest* brother who takes a line for himself—as showing a great want of self-respect, and he at once decided to throw over his family and adopt a wandering life. His descendants are true to the traditions of their mythical eponym, and during the dry season at least have no fixed habitations. In the rains they build themselves a sort of *tente d'abri* about eight feet long by six feet wide, of two bamboo uprights and a ridge pole covered in with a tilt of *sirki* matting (*Saccharum sara*, Roxb.), which reaches to the ground on either side. The whole thing can be struck and carried off at a moment's notice if the owner and his family want to change their quarters in a hurry—a common chance with a tribe of predatory instincts, whom the police are ever ready to credit with every petty theft that baffles their slender detective ability. Such huts or rather tents are usually found on the outskirts of large villages, and the Gulguliás, though they will never admit that they have a fixed residence anywhere, do in fact usually return, if not to the same village, at least to the same neighbourhood, for the rainy season, when frequent shifting even of the most portable habitation is apt to cause much discomfort, especially to people who keep no beasts of burden and carry their house themselves.

Marriage.

Gulguliás affect to practise infant-marriage, but admit that poverty often leads to a girl's marriage being deferred until she has passed the age of puberty. As is the case with gypsies in other parts of the world, their women have a certain reputation for chastity, and sexual indiscretions are said to be rare. When anything of the kind occurs, the woman in fault is turned out of the caste, and the man with whom she has gone wrong is fined Rs. 10 or so by the chief of the pancháyat. This official is elected by an assembly of the local representatives of the caste, and holds office until displaced by the same authority. The marriage ceremony is a meagre copy of the ritual followed by low-caste Hindus. The functions of priest are usually performed by two men selected at the time from the family of the bride and bridegroom, but sometimes the village barber is called in to officiate. A bride-price of from four to six maunds of rice and Rs. 3 in cash is usually paid. Polygamy is allowed, but is rarely resorted to owing to the extreme poverty of the caste. A widow may marry again, and it often happens that she marries her deceased husband's younger brother. To him in any case belongs the custody of her children by her late husband, but in some cases it would appear that the pancháyat of the caste exercises the right of allotting the children to the widow in the event of her marrying an outsider.

Religion.

The religion of the Gulguliás appears to be a form of the animism which characterises the aboriginal races. They worship a host of spiritual powers, whose attributes are ill-defined, and who are not conceived as wearing any bodily form. This at least may be inferred from the fact that they make no images, and that Baktáwar, the tutelary deity of the Patna Gulguliás, is represented by a small mound of hardened clay set up in an earthen plate. Among their objects of worship we find also Jagdamái or Devi, Rám Thákur, Baren, Setti, Goraiya, Bandi, Parameswari, and Dák. In Hazaribagh they worship Dánu in the form of a stone daubed with five streaks of red lead and set up outside the house. The offerings made to these deities consist usually of rice, milk, fruit, and sweetmeats, which are afterwards eaten by the worshippers.

Funerals.

In disposing of the dead they have the curious practice of pouring some country spirit into the dead man's mouth and killing a fowl, so that the spirit may be satisfied and may not come back to trouble his relatives with bad dreams. The corpse is then burned and the ashes thrown into a tank.

Although the squirrel is the reputed ancestor of the caste, Gulguliás are so far from regarding the animal as sacred that its flesh forms their favourite food. Spearing squirrels with a series of seven reeds (*narsar*), which fit one into the other like the joints of a fishing rod, is a pursuit at which they are specially expert, and some say that the name Gulguliá is derived from a peculiar noise, sounding like *gul gul*, which they make in order to attract the squirrel's attention while they are gradually bringing the *narsar* within stabbing distance. Another theory is that they are called Gulguliás, 'the chatterers,' because they use a peculiar *patois* or thieves' slang understood only among themselves. The *narsar* is also used for spearing birds. Gulguliás never cultivate themselves, but they are in the habit of gleaning what is left on the ground after the crops are cut.

Occupation.

Begging, pilfering, and exhibiting goats and monkeys are their chief means of livelihood. They buy monkeys from the Birhors, whom they affect to look down upon for their promiscuous habits in the matter of food. Gulguliás themselves profess to abstain from beef, but they eat pork, field-rats, a variety of small birds and animals, and the leavings of all Hindu castes except the Dhobi, Dom, Musáhar, Hári, and Chamár. Their women sell drugs and profess to cure a variety of small ailments, such as earache, toothache, rheumatism, and the like. It is rumoured that they also know remedies for barrenness, and will supply medicines which facilitate parturition and bring about abortion.

The following statement shows the number and distribution of the Gulguliás in 1881. There is no separate entry of them in 1872:—

District			Number	District			Number
Patna	...	...	254	Purniah	...	...	125
Gya	...	...	99	Hazaribagh	...	...	436
Darbhanga	...	...	113	Singbhum	...	...	12
Monghyr	...	...	77	Manbhum	...	...	92

Guli, a sub-caste of Bágdis in Western Bengal, among whom the men cultivate, while the women catch and sell fish.

Gumi, a section of Goálás in the North-Western Provinces and Behar.

Gumiá, a sub-caste of Goálás in Behar.

Gun, Guna, a title of Káyasths in Bengal.

Gundi, a section of Kaibarttas in Orissa.

Gundki, a kind of wood, a totemistic sept of Mundas in Chota Nagpur.

Gundli, a section of Mahilis in Chota Nagpur.

Gundri, a bird, a totemistic sept of Mundas in Chota Nagpur.

Gungambhir, a section of Kanaujiá Lohárs in Behar.

Gunj, a kind of fruit, a totemistic sept of Lohárs in Chota Nagpur.

Gunsaiyá, a *pur* or section of Sákadwipi Brahmans in Behar.

Gunwariá, a section of Rajputs in Bhagalpur, to which the Rájá of Sonbarsá belongs.

Gupta, a title of Dakshin-Rárhi and Bangaja Káyasths, and of Siddha Baidyas in Bengal.

Gupta Rai or *Rai Gupta*, a title of Baidyas in Bengal.

Gur, a *gáin* of the Kasyapa *gotra* of Rárhi Brahmans in Bengal; a title of Támbulis.

Gura Gáin, a *thar* of the Dhánjaya *gotra* of Nepáli Brahmans.

Guráh, a section of Goálás in the North-Western Provinces and Behar.

Gureni, a *mul* or section of the Tinmuliá Madhesiá sub-caste of Halwáis in Behar.

Guriá, the confectioner caste in Orissa. Also a sub-caste of Malláhs in Behar.

Guri-Báwá, a sub-caste of Korás in Chota Nagpur.

Gurjar Gaura, a sub-caste of Gaura Brahmans.

Gurmáchhan, a *thar* or sept of Mangars in Darjiling.

Gurni, a vegetable, a totemistic sept of Mundas in Chota Nagpur.

Guro, a sept of Thárus in Behar.

Guromani, a section of Mangars in Darjiling.

Guru, a totemistic sept of Mundas in Chota Nagpur who cannot eat beef.

Gurum, a synonym for Gurung in Darjiling.

Gurumbo, Gyu-rumbo, a *rui* or sept of Dejong Lhoris whose ancestor had emigrated from Bhotan.

Gurung, *Gurungá*, *Gurungáh*, one of the best of the fighting tribes of Nepal, divided into two endogamous sub-castes and a number of septs shown in Appendix I. Gurungs marry their daughters as adults, and like most Nepalese castes allow great license in the matter of divorce on repayment of the bride-price to the woman's father. Divorced women may marry again by the full ceremony, a privilege denied to the widow who may live with a man, especially with her late husband's younger brother (but not the elder) as his concubine, but cannot go through any ceremony. The caste was once Buddhist, and is now Hindu, Bhim Sen, the second of the Pandava brethren, being their favourite deity. They still retain pronounced traces of the primitive animism which they professed before their conversion to Buddhism, and worship the mountains and rivers, offering flowers and grass to the former and food to the latter. This worship seems to be of a propitiatory kind, and is celebrated more particularly for recovery from illness or relief from domestic calamity. Brahmans serve them as priests, but if no Brahman is available, a member of the Guaburi *thar* may take his place and may perform the ceremonies of marriage and disposal of the dead and *nuarmi* or purification after childbirth. All Gurungs bury their dead, except members of the Urunta *thar*, who burn their dead on a hill top and throw the ashes in the air. At funerals a man of the Leh-lama *thar* casts earth on the grave and recites mystical formulæ (*mantras*) supposed to put the soul of the dead man to rest. In other respects the ceremony is the same as that used by the Sunuwár tribe. Gurungs abstain from beef, pork, or vermin, but eat the flesh of the buffalo and wild pigs and the domestic fowl. The four castes—Chattri or Khas, Gurung, Mangar, and Sunuwár—are classed together as *mukhya* or chief. With members of the other castes included in this group a Gurung will not formally intermarry, but if one of them runs away with his daughter, he will accept the bride-price of Rs. 140 or some definite fraction of that amount. A woman thus married cannot cook rice or dal for her husband, but may make bread or cook meat. If a Gurung steals a wife from one of the other castes in this manner, her children will be admitted into the Gurung caste, but once admitted they may not eat rice cooked by their mother. If he marries a girl of the Kiranti group, her children are not reckoned as Gurungs.

Guru Táshi, the blessed *rui* or sept of the Tongdu sub-tribe of Dejong Lhoris, of which Guru Pema was guide.

Guta, a title of Dakshin-Rárhi Káyasths in Bengal.

Gyángmi, a *thar* or sept of Mangars in Darjiling.

Gyásáin, a section of the Amashta Káyasths in Behar.

Gyon-sah-pá, he of the new monastery, a *rui* or sept of the Bed tshan-gye sub-tribe of Dejong Lhoris or Bhotias of the south.

H

Habibpur Phupidih, a *mul* or section of the Naomuliá or Majraut sub-caste of Goálás in Behar.

Habin, a tree, a totemistic sept of Mundas in Chota Nagpur.

Hádá, a section of Goálás in the North-Western Provinces and Behar.

Hadauriár, a *pur* or section of Sákadwipi Brahmans in Behar.

Hadkwál, a section of Goálás in the North-Western Provinces and Behar.

Hadung, black tree-ant, a totemistic sept of Mundas in Chota Nagpur.

Háfiz, a reciter of the Koran.

Hah-po, a *rui* or sept of Dejong Lhoris whose ancestor had emigrated from North Bhotan.

Haiboru Lángi, a sept of Hos in Singbhum.

Haidibuthá, a *thar* or sept of Khambus in Darjiling.

Haio, a *thar* or sept of Mangars in Darjiling.

Hajam, a synonym for Bhandári.

Hajám,[1] *Nái*, *Náu*, *Nauá*, the barber caste of Behar, popularly supposed to have been specially created by Viswakarmá for the convenience of Mahádeva.

Origin.

There are seven sub-castes—**Awadhiá**, **Kanaujiá** or **Biáhut**, **Tirhutiá**, **Sribástab** or **Bástar**, **Magahiyá**, **Bangáli**, and **Turk-Nauwá**. Of these, the Awadhiá claim to have come from Oudh; the Kanaujiá from Kanauj; the Tirhutiá are located on the north, and the Magahiyá on the south of the Ganges; the Bangáli are immigrants from Bengal into the border districts of Behar; and the Turk-Nauwá are Muhammadans. The sections of the Awadhiá and Kanaujiá sub-castes are shown in Appendix I. Most of them are of the territorial type. The former observe a highly complex system of exogamy, which forbids marriage into the sections to which the following relatives belong:—(1) Father, (2) paternal grand-mother, (3) paternal great-grand-mothers, (4) paternal great-great-grand-mothers; (5) mother, (6) maternal grand-mother, (7) maternal great-grand-mothers. In applying these rules to a particular case, the double method of reckoning explained in the article on Báis is resorted to; so that if one of the bridegroom's paternal great-great-grand-mothers should have belonged to the same section as one of the bride's great-grand-mothers, the marriage will be disallowed, although the bride and bridegroom themselves belong to different sections. The other sub-castes appear either to have no sections or to have borrowed a few

Internal structure.

[1] Mr. Nesfield calls the Hindu barber Nápit, and says that the name Hajám is confined to the Muhammadan barber. This, however, is not the case in Behar.

of the Brahmanical *gotras*. All observe the standard formula for determining prohibited degrees, calculated to seven, or, in the case of the Awadhiá, to four generations in the descending line.

Marriage.

With rare exceptions, Hajáms marry their daughters as infants, and ordinarily pay a small bridegroom-price (*tilak*), varying with the means and relative status of the families. The ceremony is of the standard type, *sindurdán* being considered the essential and binding portion. Polygamy is permitted if the first wife be barren, but even in this case a man may not have more than two wives. He may marry his wife's younger sister during the former's life-time, but not an elder sister. In all the sub-castes, except the Biáhut and Sribástab, widows may marry again, and are restricted by no positive conditions in their selection of a second husband, though it is considered right and proper for a widow to marry her deceased husband's younger brother if there is one. Divorce is not generally recognised by the Hajáms of Behar: a faithless wife is turned adrift and ceases to be a member of the caste. In Palámau, the Santál Parganas, and parts of Darbhanga adultery by the wife and incompatibility of temper are admitted as grounds of divorce. A pancháyat is summoned to decide the question, and if cause is shown for a divorce a stick is solemnly snapped in two, a leaf torn, or an earthen vessel broken in pieces to symbolise the rupture of the marriage bond. Divorced wives may marry again by the *sagai* form.

Religion.

The religion of the caste does not differ materially from the average Hinduism of the middle classes in Behar. Kanaujiá or Srotri Brahmans serve them as priests, and are received on equal terms by other members of the sacred order. In addition to the minor gods recognised throughout Behar, the head of a Hajám household worships Banirám or Gaiyán with offerings of castrated goats, molasses, sweetmeats, betel leaves, and gánja. Dharm Dás, said to have been a Hajám himself, is also worshipped in similar fashion. The dead are burned, and the ceremony of *sráddh* is performed on the thirteenth day after death. Periodical libations (*tarpan*) are offered in the month of Asin for the benefit of deceased ancestors.

Social status.

The social standing of the caste is respectable, and Brahmans will take water from their hands. They themselves will eat *kachchi* food prepared by Brahmans, Rajputs, Bábhans, and high-caste Banias, and will take *pakki* articles from members of those castes from whom Brahmans will receive water. Their own rules regarding diet are the same as are followed by most orthodox Hindus, but they are believed not to be very particular as to the use of spirituous liquors.

Occupation.

The importance of the place taken by the barber in the constitution of the Hindu village community and the religious sanctions on which many of his functions depend are well brought out by Mr. Nesfield in the following remarks:—

"Every child after the age of six months or a year undergoes the ceremony of having its head for the first time touched with the razor. This is a ceremony of no little importance in the eyes of a Hindu, and is called *chura karan.* It is performed in the presence of some deity, or rather in that of his image, who is believed henceforth to take the child under his special patronage. The cutting off of the birth-hair is believed to remove the last trace of the congenital taint inherited from the maternal womb, and hence the ceremony has the same significance as that of a baptismal or lustral rite. The custom of cutting off the birth-hair has been widely practised among backward races elsewhere, and is not at all confined to the natives of India. The germs of the barber caste may therefore have existed in times before the Aryan had appeared.

"In funeral ceremonies the Nápit plays an important part. He shaves the head and pares the nails of the dead preparatory to cremation. He shaves the head of the man who puts the first light to the pyre. Ten days afterwards he shaves the head of every member of the household. By this time, after taking a final bath, they are purified of the contagion of death.

"In the celebration of marriage ceremonies he acts as the Brahman's assistant, and to the lowest castes or tribes, who cannot employ a Brahman, he is himself the matrimonial priest. The important part he plays in marriage ceremonies has led to his becoming the match-maker among all the respectable castes. It is he who hunts out the boy, finds out whether his clan or caste is marriageable with that of the girl, settles the price to be paid on both sides, takes the horoscopes to the Brahman to be compared, so as to see if the stars are favourable, carries the presents from one house to the other, and so forth. His function as match-maker is not an unimportant one in a state of society in which the rules of caste have imposed endless restrictions on the freedom of marriage.

"Shaving is not the only service that he is expected to render to his constituents. He is the ear-cleaner, nail-cutter, cupper, and bleeder, etc. In short, he performs any kind of operation on the body of man that requires a sharp knife, from shaving a beard to lancing a boil. He might therefore be fitly styled a barber-surgeon. In this double capacity he is the exact counterpart of the barber-surgeons of mediæval Europe, out of whom the modern medical profession has sprung. His wife acts as nurse to the mother and child for the last six days of the confinement. During the first six days they are in charge of the midwife—some woman of the less respected castes of Chamár, Dhánuk, or others. She also pares the nails of the new-born child, and receives a fee for doing so." In Behar the Hajám is sent round with invitations to weddings and funerals, and announces the birth of a child to the relations in the neighbourhood. For this he gets a small fee, which is higher in the case of a first-born child, especially if it be a son. The ordinary charge for shaving is one pice, but the regular village barber gets a variety of periodical perquisites, and does not charge by the job. Among these perquisites Mr. Grierson mentions[1] *kharwan*, an armful of the crop given at harvest-time; *kera*, a smaller bundle; and *púri*, three handfuls. Many Hajáms, besides practising their

[1] *Behar Peasant Life* p. 319.

hereditary functions, are also cultivators themselves, but none of them appear to have risen above the status of occupancy raiyats. In some parts of the country they hold tenures granted to them rent-free or at a quit-rent by the local zamindars as remuneration for their professional services. In the Chota Nagpur estate such tenures go by the name of *bhittáná*, a term which includes the holdings bestowed upon table-servants, gold and silversmiths, grooms, *chobdárs* or mace-bearers, palanquin-bearers, *khákis* or mendicants, and prostitutes. While actually in attendance on the Rájá, all these people usually received a small daily allowance in addition to the proceeds of their tenures. These lands are not alienable by the holders, and are believed to be liable to resumption when service is no longer required. In the Pachet estate in Manbhum, these petty *chákaran* are usually rent-free, but in a few they are subject to a very small quit-rent or *mughuli jamá*.

Social status of Turk-nauwas.

The Turk-nauwá or Muhammadan barber is not so intimately associated with religious offices as his Hindu namesake, and holds a far lower social position. His services are not indispensable, and he is therefore less independent and wayward than the Hindu barber is popularly supposed to be. Musicians (**Bajuniá**) used formerly to be selected from among Muhammadan barbers, but of late the two classes have been gradually separating. Like barbers in other countries, they dabble in medicine and surgery; consequently they are often styled **Bhedi**, from their skill in extracting worms from decayed teeth, and **Más-Káta**, from circumcising boys. In many parts of the country they are also the Abdál, who geld bulls; but any Mussulman peasant will castrate kids. When not otherwise employed, they cultivate the soil. Their women sell *mantras*, or magical formulæ, against toothache, earache, and neuralgic pains; and prepare liniments to cure colic and other internal disorders.

The following statement shows the number and distribution of Hajáms in 1872 and 1881:—

District.	1872.	1881.	District.	1872.	1881.
Birbhum	......	3	Saran	29,023	31,844
24-Parganas	......	3	Champaran	20,867	21,109
Dinajpur	......	63	Monghyr	27,020	39,106
Rangpur	......	39	Bhagalpur	27,181	34,927
Darjiling	......	138	Púrniah	18,350	18,704
Faridpur	......	1	Santál Parganas	12,338	7,628
Patna	35,570	39,165	Hazaribagh	16,230	23,659
Gya	37,190	37,859	Lohardagá	11,739	14,080
Shahabad	25,806	29,153	Singbhum	1,875	275
Tirhut { Mozufferpur ...	} 59,536	{ 38,643	Manbhum	13,604	25
Tirhut { Darbhanga ...		{ 31,961	Tributary States	1,413	3,946

Hajeri, a kind of tree or bush, a totemistic sept of Mundas in Chota Nagpur.

Hajjam Thákur, a title of barbers in Behar.

Hajrá, Házrá, (i) in Bengal a title of Kaibarttas; (ii) in Behar a title of Dosádhs, used in practice as a synonym for the caste.

Hakím, a Mahomedan physician.

Hakkák, a maker of glass beads, a lapidary; an occupation usually followed by Mahomedans.

Haladhar, a title of Chásádhobás and Kaibarttas in Bengal.

Halálkhor (*halál*, 'lawful,' and *khordan*, 'to eat,') one to whom all food is lawful: hence, a sweeper. A class of Mahomedan mehtars; also a class of musicians; a synonym for Mehtar, Khakrob, and Bhangi.

Háldár, a title of Srotriya Brahmans, Káyasths, Baniás, and Telis; a title of honour amongst the lower castes, such as Kaibarttas, Kapális, Chandáls, Chásádhobás, Máls, and some Mahomedans in Bengal.

Háldar-Parámánik, a sub-caste of Nápits in the 24-Parganas.

Haldiá, a sub-caste of Telis in Orissa and Chota Nagpur, characterised by their practice of yoking a pair of bullocks in their oil-presses.

Háliá Bálai, a hypergamous group of Kaibarttas in Bakarganj.

Háliá-Dás, a synonym for and a sub-caste of Kaibarttas.

Háliá, Mahasthán or **Mastán**, a sub-caste of Utkal Brahmans in Orissa.

Hálik, a sub-caste of Kaibarttas in Maldah.

Halkhori, a class of musicians who sing and play on pipes.

Haludboná, a group of the Ekádas Telis in Bengal.

Hálui, a *gáin* or sub-section of Saptasati Brahmans in Bengal.

Haluikar, a variant for Halwai.

Hálwa, a functional group of Jugis in Bengal.

Halwái, *Mithiyá*, the confectioner caste of Behar, often confounded with the Kándu, who is properly a grain-parcher, though he also deals in sweetmeats. The two castes, however, are entirely distinct, and do not intermarry with one another. The name Halwái is derived from *halwá*, a sweetmeat made of flour, clarified butter, and sugar, coloured with saffron and flavoured with almonds, raisins, and pistachio nuts.

Origin.

The sub-castes and sections of Halwáis are shown in Appendix I. They give no clue to the origin of the caste, which is clearly a functional group composed of members of respectable middle-class castes who adopted the profession of sweetmeat-making. The sections, which are very numerous, seem to be of the territorial type, and bear no traces of either totemism or eponymy. The rule of exogamy is carefully observed. A man may not marry a woman of his own section, or of the sections to which his mother and his paternal grand-mother belong. These sections, moreover, are taken into account on both sides; so that if the proposed bride's mother belonged to the same section as the bridegroom's paternal grand-mother, no marriage can take place, although the parties themselves belong to different sections. Prohibited degrees are reckoned by the standard formula calculated to seven generations in the descending line.

Internal structure.

Marriage.

As a general rule Halwáis marry their daughters as infants, but they do not take an extreme view of the necessity of doing so, and no slur attaches to a man who from poverty or any other reason is unable to get his daughter married before she attains the age of puberty. In fact some Halwáis of the Kanaujiá sub-caste have assured me that they do not think it right to get their daughters married under eleven or twelve years of age. The marriage ceremony in vogue does not differ materially from that used by other Behar castes of about the same social standing. *Sindurdán*, or the smearing of vermilion on the bride's forehead and the parting of her hair, is deemed to be the binding portion of the ritual. Polygamy is permitted when the first wife is barren, but in no case may a man have more than two wives. A widow may marry again by the *sagai* form. She is free to choose any one she will for her second husband, provided that the prohibited degrees are observed; and she is not required to marry her late husband's younger brother or cousin, as is the custom in some castes. In practice, however, it often happens that she does marry the next brother, as he in any case can claim the custody of the children she may have had by her first husband. A very singular custom is observed when a bachelor marries a widow. The ceremony takes place, as is the usual practice, in the widow's house, but before going there the bridegroom is formally married in his own house to a sword or a piece of iron, which he bedaubs with vermilion as if it were his bride. With this may be compared the usage common among the Kándu caste of marrying to a sword a daughter who by reason of some physical defect is not considered likely to find a husband. The theory seems to be that the full marriage ceremony is a sort of sacrament, which must be partaken of by every one at least once in life. On the question of divorce there is some difference of practice among the sub-castes. The Kanaujiá and Pachimi-Madhesia do not recognise the authority of the pancháyat as between husband and wife, and if a woman proves faithless turn her out of the house without further ceremony. In the Magahiya and Purbiya-Madhesia sub-castes a charge of unchastity on the part of the wife or of persistent ill-treatment on the part of the husband is laid before the pancháyat or caste council, who, after taking evidence and hearing what both parties have to say, may dissolve the marriage, either party being at liberty to marry again.

Religion.

The majority of the caste are Vaishnavas, and comparatively few adherents of other sects are found among them. For religious and ceremonial purposes they employ Maithil Brahmans, who are received on equal terms by all other members of the sacred order, except by those who regard it as unworthy of a Brahman to serve any man as priests. The minor god Ghanináth is worshipped on Saturdays with offerings of rice, fruit, and sweetmeats, which are afterwards eaten by the members of the household. At marriages a fee of one anna is paid by the bride, and two annas by the bridegroom for the worship of this deity. The members of the caste also hold in honour Bandi, Goraiyá, and other minor gods of Behar, and many of them are adherents of the Panch

Piriya sect. Halwáis burn their dead and perform the ceremony of *sráddh* on the thirty-first day after death.

Social status. The social standing of the Halwái is respectable, and Brahmans will take water from his hands. "His art," says Mr. Nesfield, "implies rather an advanced stage of culture, and hence his rank in the social scale is a high one. There is no caste in India which is too pure to eat what a confectioner has made. In marriage banquets it is he who supplies a large part of the feast, and at all times and seasons the sweetmeat is a favourite viand to a Hindu requiring temporary refreshment. There is a kind of bread called *puri*, which contains no sugary element, but yet it is specially prepared by men of the confectioner caste. It consists of wheaten dough fried in melted butter, and is taken as a substitute for the *chapáti* or wheaten pancake by travellers and others who happen to be unable to have their bread cooked at their own fire. With the exception of Brahmans, there is no class of men in India which declines to eat a buttered pancake prepared by the Halwái; and considering the immense amount of fuss (involving even forfeiture of caste) which is attached to the domestic fire-place, this says much for the respect in which the Halwái is held. As in the case of the Bári, the caste which makes leaf-plates for all classes of the community, considerations of general convenience have no doubt contributed something to the social respectability of the confectioner caste." The rules of the caste regarding their own diet are much the same as those followed by other Hindus of about the same standing. None of them will eat the leavings of the higher castes, even of the Brahmans who serve them as priests; and members of the Madhesia sub-caste profess to abstain from wine. Only a small proportion of the caste have taken to

Occupation. agriculture, and those are mostly occupancy raiyats. Men of the Magahia and Bantiriá sub-castes are often servants or petty shop-keepers, and many Magahia Halwáis combine grain-parching with the characteristic business of their caste. The Mahomedan Halwáis found in most districts of Bengal are an entirely distinct class, and there is no reason to suppose that they are recruited by conversion from among the ranks of the Hindu confectioners. According to Dr. Wise, the art of preserving fruits in sugar or vinegar is unknown to the Hindus, and all the preserves procurable in the bazars of the East are made by the Musalmán Halwái, who, however, destroys by too many spices and by excess of sugar the natural flavour of the fruit. The Halwái prepares jams of mango, cocoanut, ginger, and *bél*, and candies oranges, citrons, and *bél* fruit. The pickles (*áchár*), consumed in large quantities by all Muhammadans, are of three kinds, prepared with vinegar, mustard oil, or salt. The Halwái likewise makes his own vinegar with sugar, molasses, and water, and with it preserves vegetables and fruits of all kinds. Mangoes and limes are, however, often preserved in mustard oil to which pounded mustard seed has been added. Járaka, or fruit in brine, is highly recommended as an aid to digestion when eaten as dessert. Arab pedlars bring the best to Bengal, but in Dacca the aromatic lime, known as *kághazi*, from the fineness of its rind, is usually preserved in this way.

The following statement shows the number and distribution of Halwáis in 1872 and 1881:—

District.	1872.	1881.	District.	1872.	1881.
Bardwan	The figures are included in the table on Mayarás.	96	Patna	9,716	10,148
Bankura		1	Gya	11,126	13,064
Birbhum		598	Shahabad	4,552	4,835
Midnapur		129	Tirhut { Mozufferpur ...	45,567	10,722
Hughli		230	Tirhut { Darbhanga ...		38,313
Howrah		1	Saran	1,106	1,567
24-Parganas		351	Champaran	3,289	4,735
Nadiya		1,694	Monghyr	14,918	15,895
Jessore		105	Bhagalpur	21,096	22,287
Murshedabad		614	Purniah	7,889	9,905
Dinajpur		1,107	Maldah	......	69
Rajshahye		85	Santál Parganas	8,524	4,178
Rangpur		196	Cuttack	11	65
Bogra		58	Puri	1	13
Pabna		208	Balasore	1,040	1,044
Darjiling		180	Tributary States	7	109
Jalpigori		159	Hazaribagh	2,079	2,213
Kuch Behar		282	Lohardagá	2,995	3,051
Dacca		778	Singbhum	680	104
Bakarganj		13	Manbhum	9,640	2,765
Maimansinh		41	Tributary States	253	667
Chittagong		2			

Hamdábádi, a section of Sonárs in Behar.

Han, nest of ants, a totemistic sept of Mundas in Chota Nagpur.

Handi, a section of the Bahánnajáti sub-caste of Khatris in Bengal.

Hándi, earthen vessel, a subsept of the Murmu sept of Santáls.

Hangam, the king's officer, a sept of the Miákhola sub-tribe of Limbus in Darjiling.

Hanjait, *kutuna* fruit, a totemistic sept of Mundas in Chota Nagpur.

Hanre, a bird, a totemistic sept of Mundas in Chota Nagpur.

Hánriáo, a *mul* or section of the Tinmuliá Madhesiá sub-caste of Halwáis in Behar.

Hans, swan, a totemistic sept of Kharwars in Chota Nagpur.

Hansa, wild goose or swan, a totemistic sept of Mundas and Gonds in Chota Nagpur; a section of Kumhárs in Jessore.

Hánsá, a section of the Magahiyá, Pachainyá, and Tirhutiyá sub-castes of Doms in Behar.

Hansadaha-Parámánik, a sub-caste of Nápits in the 24-Parganas.

Hansarishi, a Brahmanical section of Khatris in Bengal.

Hansarwar, duck, a sept of Kharwars in Chota Nagpur.

Háṅsdá, Hasdak or **Hasdagiár**, a totemistic sept of the Bhumij, Turis, Kharwárs, Korás, Hos, Kurmis, Korwás, Santáls and Máhilis in Chota Nagpur, the members of which will not touch, kill, or eat a wild goose.

Hansi, a title of Tántis in Bengal and a section of Majraut Goálás in Behar.

Hansi-Tánti, a sub-caste of Tántis in Orissa.

Hansnemba, a sept of the Pánthar sub-tribe of Limbus in Darjiling.

Hánsotá, a section of the Pachainyá sub-caste of Doms in Behar.

Hánthi, elephant, a sept of Mundas in Chota Nagpur.

Hanuman, monkey, a totemistic sept of Mundas and Chiks in Chota Nagpur; a section of Sonárs in Behar.

Har, a *gáin* of the Kásyapa *gotra* of Rárhi Brahmans in Bengal.

Hár, plough, a totemistic sept of Korwas in Chota Nagpur; a section of the Tirhutiyá sub-caste of Doms in Behar.

Hárá, a sept of Rajputs in Behar.

Harabans, a sept of the Suryabansi sub-tribe of Rajputs in Behar.

Harariá, a section of Bábhans in Behar.

Harbang, a sept of Tipperahs in the Hill Tracts of Chittagong.

Harbans, a sept of Chamárs and Doms in Chota Nagpur, the members of which cannot wear bones in any shape.

Harchanpuriá, a section of the Banodhiá and Jaiswár Kalwárs in Behar.

Hardá, a section of Goálás in the North-Western Provinces and Behar.

Hardi, turmeric, a totemistic sept of Lohárs in Chota Nagpur.

Hardiál, a section of Báis Sonárs in Behar.

Hardwar, a sept of Mundas in Chota Nagpur.

Hardwár, a section of the Biyáhut and Kharidáhá Kalwárs; a *mul* or section of the Ayodhiábási sub-caste of Sonárs in Behar.

Hargambai, a section of the Amashta sub-caste of Káyasths in Behar.

Hargamiá, a section of Awadhiá Hajáms in Behar.

Hargurra, bone, a totemistic sept of Mundas in Chota Nagpur.

Hári, a synonym for Korá, used inaccurately by outsiders only; a synonym for Bhuinmáli; a sub-caste of Ghásis in Chota Nagpur; a totemistic sept of Mundas in Chota Nagpur whose ancestors are said not to have washed their mouths after eating; a section of the Dhaprá sub-caste of Doms in Behar.

Hári, *Mihtar*, *Har-Santán*, a menial and scavenger caste of Bengal Proper, which Dr. Wise identifies with the Bhuinmáli and regards as "the remnant of a Hinduised aboriginal tribe which was driven into Bengal by the Aryans or the persecuting Muhammadans." This conjecture is borne out by the physical features of the caste, and by the fact that

Origin.

wherever we can trace the affinities of the menial castes we find them to have been largely recruited, if not entirely drawn, from the ranks of the aboriginal races. The internal structure of the Hári caste throws no light upon its origin, as at the present day there are no sections, and marriage is regulated solely by counting prohibited degrees. The sub-castes are the following:—Bará-bhágiyá or Káorá-páik, Madhya-bhágiyá or Madhaukul, Khore or Khoriyá, Siuli, Mihtar, Bangáli, Maghayá, Karaiyá, Purandwár. Of these, the Mihtar sub-caste alone are employed in removing night-soil; the Bara-bhágiyá serve as chaukidárs, musicians, and palki-bearers; the Khore keep pigs; the Siuli tap date-palms for their juice; and the rest cultivate. Some authorities include Ghási among the sub-castes of Hári, but I have preferred to treat them as a separate caste.

Internal structure.

Háris admit both infant and adult-marriage, but the former practice is deemed the more respectable, and all parents endeavour to get their daughters married before the age of puberty. Adult-marriage, however, still holds its ground, and sexual intercourse before marriage is said to be more or less tolerated. Their marriage ceremony presents some curious features, which seem to be survivals of non-Aryan usage. After the bride-price has been settled and a lucky day fixed for the marriage, the parties meet in the bride's house. The bride and bridegroom are seated opposite to each other, each on the thigh of the father or nearest male relative of a full age. They then change places, the bride sitting on the lap of the bridegroom's father and the bridegroom on that of the bride's father. This is repeated five times. After that the right hand little finger of the bridegroom's sister's husband is pricked, and a drop or two of blood allowed to fall on a few threads of jute, which are rolled up into a tiny pellet. This the bridegroom holds in his hand, while the bride attempts to snatch it from him. Her success in the attempt is deemed to be of good omen for the happiness of the marriage. Last of all, the bridegroom smears vermilion on the forehead of the bride. Polygamy is permitted, but is rarely resorted to in practice, as few Háris can afford to maintain more than one wife. There seems to be no definite rule on the subject, and the caste inclines rather to the practice of the aboriginal races than to the more civilised restriction which allows a second wife to be taken only in the event of the first being barren. Some, however, favour this latter view, and hold that even if offspring fail, a man may in no case have more than three wives. A widow may marry again by the ceremony called *chumauná* or *nikáh*, of which the binding portion is the exchange of garlands of flowers, but she is not permitted to marry her husband's younger brother. No reason is assigned for thus prohibiting an alliance which is usually regarded with special favour by the castes which permit widow-marriage. But it may represent an advance towards the entire abolition of widow-marriage—a step which has already been taken by the Bhuinmáli-Háris of Eastern Bengal. Divorce is permitted with the sanction of the punchâyat of the caste. In some districts a leaf is torn in two

Marriage.

to symbolise separation. Divorced wives may marry again by the *nikáh* form.

Religion.

Although Háris profess to be Hindus and worship Káli and other of the standard gods in a more or less meagre fashion, it seems probable that they have embraced Hinduism at a comparatively recent date. In Hughli, indeed, they employ Brahmans for religious and ceremonial purposes, but these Brahmans are looked down upon by other members of the sacred order, and are generally regarded as only a little less degraded than Háris themselves. In other districts they have priests of their own caste, who bear the pretentious title of Pandit. The dead are usually burnt, and the ashes thrown into the nearest river. A pig is sacrificed on the tenth day after death to appease the spirit of the departed, the flesh being eaten by the relatives. On this occasion the nephew (sister's son) of the deceased person officiates as priest.

Social status and occupation.

Their social rank is of the lowest. No one will eat with a Hári or take water from his hands, and members of the caste are not permitted to enter the court-yard of the great temples. Some of them hold land as occupancy or non-occupancy raiyats, and many find employment as agricultural day-labourers. Tapping date-trees, making bamboo combs, playing musical instruments at weddings and festivals, carrying palanquins, serving as sycee, and scavenging, are among their characteristic occupations; but the removal of night-soil is confined to the Mihtar sub-caste. Their women often act as midwives. They are troubled by few scruples regarding diet. Fowls, pork, field-rats, scaly or scaleless fish, and the leavings of other castes, are freely eaten; while in districts where the aboriginal races are numerous, Háris will even indulge in beef. Their partiality for strong drink is notorious.

The following statement shows the number and distribution of the Hári caste in 1872 and 1881:—

DISTRICT.	1872.	1881.	DISTRICT.	1872.	1881.
Bardwan	31,418	23,996	Chittagong	6,589	5,520
Bankura	2,636	6,770	Noakhali	571	499
Birbhum	22,262	24,097	Hill Tracts	......	29
Midnapur	29,915	32,954	Patna	1,934	1,549
Hughli	44,700 (Hughli and Howrah)	22,610	Gya	1,246	1,436
Howrah		16,763	Shahabad	3,303	2,967
24-Parganas	70,637	52,283	Tirhut { Mozufferpur ...	8,063 (Tirhut)	6,034
Nadiya	6,859	6,535	Tirhut { Darbhanga ...		4,833
Khulna	......	3,020	Saran	3,335	3,993
Jessore	2,981	4,380	Champaran	3,065	3,401
Murshedabad	18,954	9,176	Monghyr	2,325	3,010
Dinajpur	36,661	32,383	Bhagalpur	3,197	5,822
Rajshahye	3,998	4,723	Purniah	38,339	29,950
Rangpur	8,511	7,872	Maldah	14,679	12,464
Bogra	6,839	7,618	Santál Parganas	6,853	10,734
Pabna	3,141	2,339	Cuttack	3,914	4,206
Darjiling	988	1,664	Puri	6,749	7,784
Jalpigori	4,866	8,410	Balasore	3,360	4,465
Kuch Behar	......	2,009	Tributary States	15,075	12,097
Dacca	4,554	2,789	Hazaribagh	1,871	5,169
Faridpur	1,828	2,886	Lohardagá	2,502	1,149
Bakarganj	6,406	574	Singbhum	1,269	1,357
Maimansinh	5,021	6,396	Manbhum	11,140	13,314
Tipperah	760	1,051	Tributary States	15	27

Hári or *Bangáli*, a sub-caste of Doms in Behar who are probably immigrants from Bengal.

Hariambá, a section of Bábhans in Behar.

Hariáme Rakhwári, a *mul* of the Bátsya section of Maithil Brahmans in Behar.

Hariáme-Sibá, a *mul* of the Bátsa section of Maithil Brahmans in Behar.

Hariáme-Balirájpur, a *mul* of the Bátsa section of Maithil Brahmans in Behar.

Hariáme-Katmá, a *mul* of the Bátsa section of Maithil Brahmans in Behar.

Hariáme-Ahil, a *mul* of the Bátsa section of Maithil Brahmans in Behar.

Harichandan Khandait, a sub-caste of Khandáits in Puri.

Harihobans, a sept of the Suryabansi Rajputs in Behar.

Hari Majumdári, a *mel* or hypergamous sub-group of Rárhi Brahmans in Bengal.

Harin, deer, a totemistic sept of Chiks and Mundas in Chota Nagpur.

Hárita, an eponymous section of Bábhans in Behar; a section of the Srotriya sub-caste of Utkal Brahmans.

Hariyán or **Jehariyá**, a sub-caste of Mauliks in Chota Nagpur.

Hariyana, a sub-caste of Gaura Brahmans.

Harkár, a sub-caste of Doms in South Behar who are scavengers.

Harkar, *Harkal*, a sub-caste of Háris in Bengal.

Harnátar, a section of the Biyáhut and Kharidáhá Kalwárs in Behar.

Haroha, a *thar* or sept of Sarkis in Darjiling.

Harpatti, 'plough-owner,' a group of Maghaiya Telis in Behar.

Harrá, myrabolam, a totemistic sept of Korwas in Chota Nagpur.

Har-Santán, a synonym for Hári.

Harsariá, a section of Lohárs in Behar.

Hartakiá, a section of Bábhans in Behar.

Hasa, earth, a sept of Goálás in Chota Nagpur.

Hasada, a sept of Mundas in Chota Nagpur, *see* **Hánsdá**.

Hasanpuriá, a section of Lohárs in Behar.

Hasará, a sept of Mundas in Chota Nagpur.

Hasdajiá, a synonym for Hansda, *q.v.*

Hassa ara, a kind of vegetable, a totemistic sept of Mundas in Chota Nagpur.

Hastaddá, a totemistic section of Turis in Chota Nagpur, signifying an eel.

Hastgáme, a *kul* or section of Bábhans in Behar.

Hastuar, a sept of Lohárs in Chota Nagpur.

Hastwár, a totemistic section of Kurmis in Chota Nagpur

and Orissa who will not touch a tortoise.

Hát, a section of Goáláa in Behar; a sub-sept of the Saren sept of Santáls.

Háth, a *pangat* or section of Bánsphor Doms and of Dosádhs in Behar.

Háthi, elephant, a totemistic sept of Khariás and Kharwars and a section of Kumhárs in Chota Nagpur; a title of Bangaja Káyasths; a section of Sunris in Behar.

Háthi or *Hátti*, elephant, a totemistic sept of Lohárs in Chota Nagpur.

Háthiákán, a section of the Sátmuliá Maghayá sub-caste of Kándus in Behar.

Háthiá Kándhá, a section of Koránch Kándus in Behar.

Háthián, a territorial section of Barhis in Behar.

Háthsukhá, a section of Madhesiá Kándus in Behar.

Háti, elephant, a title of Khandáits in Orissa.

Hátiá, a sub-caste of Bhuinmális found in Noakháli.

Hátisalaba, elephant, a totemistic sept of Juángs in Orissa.

Hátser, a *mul* or section of the Chhamuliá Madhesiá sub-caste of Halwáis in Behar.

Hátuá, a sub-caste of Bhandáris in Orissa.

Háturi, a *gáin* or sub-section of Saptasati Brahmans in Bengal.

Háturiá Baidya, a doctor who attends markets, or, according to Dr. Wise, a quack, a meddlesome fellow.

Hatuwáli, a *thar* or sept of Khambus in Darjiling.

Hátwál, a title of Bagdis and Háris in Bengal.

Hausakar, a sept of Mundas in Chota Nagpur.

Hawáigar, a maker of fire-works, always a Mahomedan, often called Golsáz, and in Behar Atash-baz. In Bengal the Hindu málákár makes a few simple fire-works for weddings, but this is never his exclusive business.

Házará, a title of Káyasth, Kaibartta, Sadgop, Chásádhoba, Kapáli, and Hari castes in Bengál; of Dosadhs in Behar; a section of Kewats.

Házárá-Samáj, a sub-caste of Dhobás in Central Bengal.

Hazári, a *pangat* or section of Dosadhs and Kádars in Behar.

Hazári pánre, a section of the Biyáhut and Kharidáhá Kalwárs in Behar.

Heding, a bird, a totemistic sept of Mundas in Chota Nagpur.

Hej, a hypergamous group of the Bárendra Káyasths in Bengal.

Hekoriá, tomato, a totemistic sept of Páns in Chota Nagpur.

Hele-Kaibartta, or **Helo**, a sub-caste of Kaibarttas in Bengal.

Hem, a title of Dakshin-Rárhi and Bangaja Káyasths.

Hembaran, a sept of Hos in Singbhum.

Hembowar, ancester, a totemistic sept of Mundas in Chota Nagpur.

Hemphá, a sept of Limbus in Darjiling.

Hemram, a kind of fish, a totemistic sept of Mundas in Chota Nagpur.

Hemramiá, betel palm, a totemistic section of Kurmis in Chota Nagpur and Orissa.

Hemremina, a sept of Kharwars in Chota Nagpur.

Hemriárk, a *pur* or section of Sákadwipi Brahmans in Behar.

Hemrom, a kind of fish, a totemistic sept of Birhors and Lohárs in Chota Nagpur.

Hemrom, Hembaram, betel palm, a sept of Santáls.

Hemromi, ashes, a totemistic sept of Mundas in Chota Nagpur.

Hemron, a totemistic sept of Bhumij, and Mahili, the members of which may not eat the horse.

Henduár, a section of Kurmis in Chota Nagpur and Orissa, the members of which do not observe the *Jita parab*, and celebrate marriage in the open and not in a house.

Heride, a bird, a totemistic sept of Mundas in Chota Nagpur.

Hermaniá, a sub-caste of Telis in Behar.

Hersiriá, a *mul* or section of the Kamar Kalla sub-caste of Sonárs in Behar.

Herung, a bird, a totemistic sept of Mundas in Chota Nagpur.

Hes, a title of Dakshin-Rárhi and Bangaja Káyasths.

Hesá, a sept of Hos in Singbhum.

Hiapela, a sub-caste of Telis in Chota Nagpur.

Hijrá, eunuch, a person of equivocal malformation, supposed to be a hermaphrodite and usually wearing female attire and bearing the name of a man.

Hinduá, a section of Tántis in Behar.

Hinga, a section of the Oswál Baniyás in Bengal.

Hingu, an exogamous section of Baidyas in Bengal.

Hirni, a *mul* or section of the Kanaujiá sub-caste of Sonárs in Behar.

Ho, *Larka Kolh*, a non-Aryan tribe of the district of Singbhum, classed for linguistic purposes as Kolarian. The name Ho seems to be merely a contracted form of the word *horo*, 'man,' which is used by the cognate tribes of Munda and Santál as their national designation.[1] The two latter tribes, it should be noted, are not called *horo* by outsiders, and a Santál will as often as not describe himself by the title of Mánjhi. In the case of the Hos, the tribal name of the original stock whence Hos, Mundas, and Santáls are sprung has obtained popular recognition, in a slightly altered form, as the distinctive name of the branch which inhabits Singbhum, and which may now be regarded as a separate tribe. For intermarriage between Hos and Mundas or Santáls, though not absolutely forbidden

[1] Nottrott, *Grammatik der Kolh-Sprache*, Gütersloh, 1882, Jellinghaus Sagen, *Sitten und Gebräuche der Munda-Kolhs in Chota Nagpur. Zeitschrift für Ethnologie*, iii, 328.

by custom, is certainly uncommon, and may be expected soon to fall into disuse. The internal structure of the tribe is shown in Appendix I. They have no sub-tribes, but the septs are very numerous, and many of them appear to be totemistic. Six of the sept names are common to them and to the Santáls. The rule of exogamy is strictly observed, and a man may on no account marry a woman of his sept. With this exception their views on the subject of prohibited degrees appear to be lax, and I understand that marriages with near relatives on the mother's side are tolerated provided that a man does not marry his aunt, his first cousin, or his niece. For the rest I have nothing to add to the passages quoted below from Colonel Dalton's classical account of the Ho tribe, which, so far as I can ascertain, is substantially correct at the present day. Owing to the use in the Census returns of the general name Kol to denote Mundas, Hos, and Oraons, it has been found impossible to draw up any statistical table showing the number of Hos in 1872 and 1881. In the former year 150,925 Kols were registered in Singbhum, while in 1881 the number of Kols in that district is given as 187,721, to which may be added 539 returned under various sept names. If, then, we might assume that all persons registered in Singbhum as Kols were really Hos, the figures would stand thus: 1872, 150,925; 1881, 188,260. But Oraons and Mundas are also found in Singbhum, and it is impossible to separate them from the total set down for Kols. I have therefore thought it best not to attempt to construct any statistical table showing the distribution of the tribe. It is the less necessary to do so as there are probably not many Hos outside of Singbhum. The tribe are fairly fortunate in their relations to the land, and presumably for this reason are not accustomed, like the Mundas and Oraons, to leave their homes during the cold weather to assist in gathering in the rice harvest of Bengal Proper.

Internal structure.

"The Hos appear to have no traditions of origin or migrations that throw much light on their history. They generally admit that they are of the same family as the Mundas, and that they came from Chota Nagpur. The Oraons sometimes say that the exodus of the Hos was caused by *their* invasion, but I cannot believe that the Hos could ever have given way to so inferior a race; and the tradition usually received is that the Oraons made friends with the Mundas and were allowed to occupy peaceably the north-western corner of the plateau, where the latter apparently have never taken root. The Hos are the only branch of the Kols that have preserved a national appellation. The Mundas of Chutiá Nágpur are sometimes called Kokpát or Konkpát Mundas, and that may be a national word; but Ho, Hore, or Horo means in their own language 'man,' and they are not the only people that apply to themselves exclusively the word used in their language to distinguish human beings from brutes. They probably left Chutiá Nágpur before their brethren there had assumed the Sanskrit word 'Munda' as their distinctive name, taking with them their old constitution of confederate village communities under hereditary headmen, which system they have

Tradition of origin.

retained to the present day. But they did not find in Singbhum an unoccupied country. It is admitted on all sides that one part of it was in possession of the Bhuiyás, and another held by the people who have left many monuments of their ingenuity and piety in the adjoining district of Manbhum, and who were certainly the earliest Aryan settlers in this part of India,—the Saráwaks or Jains. The former were driven from their possessions in what is now the Kolhán, and fell back into Paráhát. What became of the Jains we know not. They have left their marks in Dhalbhum and the eastern and north-eastern quarters of the district; and it is not improbable that the Súdras, Goálás, and Kurmís, now settled in Paráhát, Kharsáwán, Sáraikalá, and Dhalbhum, may be remnants of the colonies they founded. But it is also probable that many were absorbed into the family that conquered them; and this may account for the greater beauty of the Hos as compared with other Kols, and for their having in use a number of common vocables of Sanskrit origin, though they insulated themselves as much as possible, despised the Hindus, and for a long time had little or no intercourse with them.

"I propose to select the Hos as the branch of the people who, from their jealous isolation for so many years, their independence, their long occupation of one territory, and their contempt for all other classes that came in contact with them, especially the Hindus, probably furnish the best illustration, not of the Mundárís in their wildest state, but of what, if left to themselves and permanently located, they were likely to become. Even at the present day the exclusiveness of the old Hos is remarkable. They will not allow aliens to hold lands near their villages; and indeed if it were left to them no strangers would be permitted to settle in the Kolhán. Now there are settlements of Goálás, Kurmís, and others; but though such settlements are under the authority of the Kol *mánkí* of the *pír*, the Kols hold little communication with them, and jealously watch and circumscribe the spread of their cultivation. They argue that they are themselves rapidly increasing, and the waste lands should all be reserved for their progeny. The only persons of alien race they tolerate, and, so far as suits their own convenience, associate with, are the few Tántís (weavers), Goálás (herdsmen), potters, and blacksmiths who ply their respective trades for the benefit of the community; but these people, who are in all probability remnants of the Aryan colonies that the Hos subjugated, must learn their language and generally conform to their customs. The old Hos will not conform to theirs. It is only the rising generation that takes kindly to the acquisition of another language. The Hos have a tradition concerning the creation of the world and the origin of the human race, which is given in Colonel Tickell's account of the tribe, published in volume ix of the *Journal of the Asiatic Society of Bengal*, p. 797. Ote Borám and Sing Bonga were self-created; they made the earth with rocks and water, and they clothed it with grass and trees, and then created animals,—first, those that man domesticates, and afterwards wild beasts. When all was thus prepared for the abode of man, a boy and girl were created, and Sing Bonga placed them in a cave at the bottom of a great ravine;

and finding them to be too innocent to give hope of progeny, he instructed them in the art of making *illi*, rice-beer, which excites the passions, and thus the world became peopled. When the first parents had produced twelve boys and twelve girls, Sing Bonga prepared a feast of the flesh of buffaloes, bullocks, goats, sheep, pigs, fowls, and vegetables; and making the brothers and sisters pair off, told each pair to take what they most relished and depart. Then the first and second pair took bullocks and buffaloes' flesh, and they originated the Kols (Hos) and the Bhumij (Matkum); the next took of the vegetables only, and are the progenitors of the Bráhmans and Kshatriyas; others took goats and fish, and from them are the Súdras. One pair took the shell-fish, and became Bhuiyás; two pairs took pigs, and became Santáls. One pair got nothing; seeing which the first pairs gave them of their superfluity, and from the pair thus provided sprung the Gháais, who toil not, but live by preying on others. The Hos have now assigned to the English the honour of descent from one of the first two pairs—the elder. The only incident in the above tradition that reminds one of the more highly elaborated Santál account is the divine authority for the use of strong drinks.

Physical type.

"The Hos of Singbhum and the Mundáris of the southern *parganás* of the Lohardagá district are physically a much finer people than the Bhúmij, the Santáls, or any other of the Kolarians. The males average five feet five or six inches in height; the women five feet two. The average height of a number of the Juáng tribe I found to be—for males, less than five feet; and for women, four feet eight. In features the Hos exhibit much variety, and I think in a great many families there is considerable admixture of Aryan blood. Many have high noses and oval faces, and young girls are sometimes met with who have delicate and regular features, finely chiselled straight noses, and perfectly-formed mouths and chins. The eyes, however, are seldom so large, so bright, and gazelle-like as those of pure Hindu maidens; but I have met strongly-marked Mongolian features, and some are dark and coarse like the Santáls. In colour they vary greatly,—28, 29, and 30 of Brossac's table; the copper tints are the commonest ones. Eyes dark brown (about 2 of Brossac); hair black, straight, or wavy, and rather fine; worn long by males and females, but the former shave the forehead. Both men and women are noticeable for their fine erect carriage and long free stride. The hands and feet are large, but well formed. The men care little about their personal appearance. It

Dress and ornaments.

requires a great deal of education to reconcile them to the encumbrance of clothing; and even those who are wealthy move about all but naked, as proudly as if they were clad in purple and fine linen. The women in an unsophisticated state are equally averse to superfluity of clothing. In remote villages they may still be seen with only a rag between the legs, fastened before and behind to a string round the waist. This is called a *botoi*. The national dress is, however, a long strip of cloth worn as a girdle round the loins, knotted behind, and the ends brought between the legs and fastened to the girdle in front; but in the principal group of villages about Cháibásá the young women dress themselves decently and gracefully. The style of wearing the hair is peculiar, collected in a knot artificially enlarged, not in the centre of the back of the head, but touching the back of the right ear. Flowers are much used in the *coiffure.* The neck ornaments most in vogue a year or two ago were very small black beads; but in this one small item of their simple toilette fashion changes, and the beads most prized one year are looked on with repugnance the next. As with the Santáls, very massive bracelets and armlets are worn, and anklets of bell-metal. It is a singular sight to see the young women at the markets subjecting themselves to the torture of being fitted with a pair of these anklets. They are made so that they can just, with great violence, be forced on. The operation is performed by the manufacturers, who put moistened leather on the heel and instep to prevent excoriation. The girl, clinging to and resting on one of her companions, cries bitterly at the violence inflicted on her, and the operation is a long one; but when it is over, she admires her decorated foot and instep, and smiles through her tears. The Ho women have adopted as their distinctive mark or *godna* an arrow, which they regard as their national emblem. A Ho unable to write, if asked to attach his mark or sign manual to a document, does so by making a rude representation of an arrow. The Munda women use the same *godna* marks as the Juángs and the Kharriás. The Larkas are lightly assessed, and, cultivating their own lands, never join any of the numerous bands of labourers emigrating to the tea districts. They care not to work for hire, and never, if they can avoid it, carry loads. The use of the block-wheeled dray is universal among them, and all the carrying necessary in their agricultural operations is done by it.

Child-birth.

After the birth of a child both mother and father are considered unclean, *bisi*, for eight days, during which period the other members of the family are sent out of the house, and the husband has to cook for his wife. If it be a difficult case of parturition, the malignancy of some spirit of evil is supposed to be at work, and after divination to ascertain his name a sacrifice is made to appease him. At the expiration of the eight days the banished members of the family return, friends are invited to a feast, and the child is ceremoniously named. The name of the grandfather is usually given to the first-born son, but not without an ordeal to ascertain if it will prove fortunate. As the name is mentioned, a grain of *urid* (pulse) is thrown into a vessel with water; the name is adopted if it floats, rejected if it sinks.

Marriage.

"Owing to the high price placed on daughters by their fathers, the large number of adult unmarried girls seen in every considerable village in the Kolhán is a very peculiar feature in the social state of the community. In no other country in India are spinsters found so advanced in years. In many of the best families grey-headed old maids may be seen, whose charms were insufficient to warrant the large addition to the usual price, called *pan*, imposed in consideration of the high connection that the union would confer. The *pan* is calculated, and for the most part paid, in cattle, indicating that the custom dates from a time when there was no current coin; and fathers of *mánki* dignity demand from forty to fifty head of cattle for each of their girls. Dr. Hayes, finding that in consequence of this practice the number of marriages was annually diminishing and immoral intimacy between the sexes increasing, convened in 1868 a meeting of representative men for the express purpose of discussing this question; and after a long debate it was unanimously agreed that a reduction should be made. It was resolved that in future a *pan* was not to exceed ten head of cattle; and that if one pair of oxen, one cow, and seven rupees were given, it should be received as an equivalent for the ten head. For the poorer classes it was fixed at seven rupees. Even thus modified the *pan* in Singbhum is higher than it is in Chutiá Nágpur for the multitude. The *mánkis* and headmen of the latter country, conforming to the Hindu customs, have given up exacting it. In olden times young men counteracted the machinations of avaricious parents against the course of true love by forcibly carrying off the girl, and still at times evade extortion by running away with her. Then the parents have to submit to such terms as arbitrators think fair. This abduction it was necessary to put a stop to, and elopements are not considered respectable; so, until the conference, prices had a tendency to rise rather than fall. The old generation of *mánkis* vehemently opposed any reduction. The second generation, since the accession of the British, are now in the ascendant, and they entertained more enlightened views; but, notwithstanding the compact, I have not yet heard of a marriage in high life in which the reduced *pan* has been accepted. It is certainly not from any yearning for celibacy that the marriage of Singbhum maidens is so long postponed. The girls will tell you frankly that they do all they can to please the young men, and I have often heard them pathetically bewailing their want of success. They make themselves as attractive as they can, flirt in the most demonstrative manner, and are not too coy to receive in public attentions from those they admire. They may be often seen in well-assorted pairs returning from market with arms interlaced, and looking at each other as lovingly as if they were so many groups of Cupids and Psyches; but with all this the '*men will not propose.*' Tell a maiden you think her nice looking, she is sure to reply, 'Oh yes, I am; but what is the use of it? the young men of my acquaintance don't see it.' Even when a youth has fully made up his mind to marry, it may happen that fate is against the happiness of the young couple: bad omens are seen that cause the match to be postponed or broken off; or papa cannot, or will not, pay the price demanded. When a young man has made his choice, he communicates the fact to his parents; and a deputation of the friends of the family is sent to the girl's house to ascertain all that should be known regarding her family, age, appearance, and means. If the information obtained and the result of the inspection be satisfactory, and the omens observed on the road have been propitious, an offering is made on the part of the young man; and if it be received, the deputation are invited to stay, and are feasted. The report of the deputation being favourable, a day is fixed for a meeting between the parents, and the terrible question of the *pan* discussed. At this point many matches are broken off, in consequence of greed on one side or stinginess on the other. The amount agreed on has to be paid before the day can be fixed for the marriage; and when delivery of the cattle is made, a pot of beer has to be given from the bride's side for each animal. At last if all this is got over, the appointed day arrives, and the bride is escorted to the village for her intended by all her young female friends, with music and dancing. The young men and girls of the village, and those invited from neighbouring villages, form a cortege for the bridegroom. They go out and meet the bride's party, and, after a dance in the grove, in which the bride and bridegroom take part, mounted on the hips of two of their female friends, they enter the village together, where there is a great feast, a great consumption of the rice-beer, and much more dancing and singing. Ceremony there is none; but the turning point in the rite is when the bride and groom pledge each other. A cup of beer is given to each; the groom pours some of the contents of his cup into the bride's cup, and she returns the compliment. Drinking the liquor thus blended they become of one *kili*, that is, the bride is admitted into her husband's tribe, and they become one. This has, I believe, succeeded an older custom of drinking from the same cup. After remaining with her husband for three days only, it is the correct thing for the wife to run away from him and tell all her friends that she loves him not, and will see him no more. This is perhaps reparation to the dignity of the sex, injured by the bride's going to the bridegroom's house to be married, instead of being sought for and taken as a wife from her own. So it is correct for the husband to show great anxiety for the loss of his wife and diligently seek her; and when he finds her, he carries her off by main force. I have seen a young wife thus found and claimed and borne away, screeching and struggling, in the arms of her husband from the midst of a crowded *básár*. No one interferes on these occasions, and no one assists. If the husband cannot manage the business himself, he must leave her alone. After this little escapade the wife at once settles down, assumes her place as the well-contented mistress of the household, and, as a rule, in no country in the world are wives better treated. Dr. Hayes says:—' A Kol or Ho makes a regular companion of his wife. She is consulted in all difficulties, and receives the fullest consideration due to her sex.' Indeed, it is not uncommon in the Kolhán to see husbands so subject to the influence of their wives that they may be regarded as henpecked. Instances of infidelity in wives are very rare. I never heard of one, but I suppose such things occur, as there is a regulated penalty. The unfaithful wife is discarded, and the seducer must pay to the husband the entire value of the *pan*.

Occupation.

"The Hos are fair marksmen with the bow and arrow, and great sportsmen. From childhood they practise archery; every lad herding cattle or watching crops makes this his whole pastime, and skill is attained even in knocking over small birds with blunt arrows. They also keep hawks, and the country in the vicinity of their villages is generally destitute of game. In the months intervening between the harvest-home and the rains they frequently go in large parties to distant jungles; and with them, as with the Santáls, there is every year in May a great meet for sport, in which people of all classes of the neighbourhood and surrounding villages take part. From the setting in of the rains to the harvest the time of the people is fairly employed in cultivation, to which they pay great attention. The women have their full share of labour in the fields; indeed, the only agricultural work they are exempted from is ploughing. They work from early morn till noon; then comes the mid-day meal, after which their time is pretty much at their own disposal. The young people then make themselves tidy, stroll about the village, or visit neighbouring villages; and the old people, sitting on the gravestones, indulge in deep potations of rice-beer, and smoke, or gossip, or sleep. Amongst the amusements of the Hos I must not omit to mention *pegtops*. They are roughly made of blocks of hard wood, but their mode of spinning and playing them, one on another, is the same as with us. Pegtopping has been noticed as an amusement of the Khásias of Assam. Their agricultural implements consist of the ordinary wooden plough tipped with iron; a harrow; the *kodáli* or large hoe; a sickle; the *tángi* or battle-axe, which is used for all purposes; the block-wheeled dray; and an implement with which to remove earth in altering the levels of land to prepare it for irrigation and rice cultivation. The latter consists of a broad piece of board firmly attached to a pole and yoke, so that its edge touches the ground at an angle as it is drawn by oxen or buffaloes attached to it. The Hos make these agricultural implements themselves; every man is to some extent a carpenter, handy with his adze and clever in simple contrivances. The Kols plough with cows as well as oxen; but it is to be recollected that they make no other use of the animal, as they never touch milk. Buffaloes are preferred to bullocks as plough cattle. They have a rude kind of oil-press in every village. The Mundárís and Larkas raise three crops of rice,—the early or *gorá*, the autumnal or *bád*, and the late or *berá* crop. Indian corn and the millets, *maruá* and *gondli*, are also cultivated as early crops. Wheat, gram, mustard seed, and sesamum they have also taken to as cold weather and spring crops. Tobacco and cotton they have long cultivated, but not in sufficient quantities even for their own consumption. They have no notion of weaving, and if left to their own resources for clothing would probably resume their leaves; but every village has one or two families of Tántis, or weavers, who are now almost undistinguishable from the Hos. The villagers make over their cotton to the weavers, and pay for the loom labour in cotton or grain.

Festivals.

"The Hos are a purely agricultural people, and their festivals are all connected with that pursuit. In describing these festivals I avail myself of information on the subject kindly collated for me by W. Ritchie, Esq., District

Superintendent of Police, Singbhum. The chief requisite for festivities of all kinds is the preparation of an ample quantity of the home-made beer called *illi*. It is made from rice, which is boiled and allowed to ferment till it is sufficiently intoxicating; its proper preparation is considered one of the most useful accomplishments that a young damsel can possess. The Hos keep seven festivals in the year. The first or principal is called the *Mágh parab* or *Desauli Bonga*. This is held in the month of Mágh, or January, when the granaries are full of grain, and the people, to use their own expression, full of devilry. They have a strange notion that at this period men and women are so overcharged with vicious propensities that it is absolutely necessary to let off steam by allowing for a time full vent to the passions. The festival, therefore, becomes a Saturnale, during which servants forget their duty to their masters, children their reverence for parents, men their respect for women, and women all notions of modesty, delicacy, and gentleness,—they become raging Bacchantes. It opens with a sacrifice to Desauli of three fowls,—a cock and two hens, one of which must be black,—offered with some flowers of the *palás* tree (*Butea frondosa*), bread made from rice-flour, and sesamum seeds. The sacrifice and offerings are made by the village priest, if there be one; or if not, by any elder of the village who possesses the necessary legendary lore. He prays that during the year they are about to enter on they and their children may be preserved from all misfortune and sickness, and that they may have seasonable rain and good crops. Prayer is also made in some places for the souls of the departed. At this period an evil spirit is supposed to infest the locality, and to get rid of it the men, women, and children go in procession round and through every part of the village, with sticks in their hands as if beating for game, singing a wild chant and vociferating violently till they feel assured that the bad spirit must have fled,—and they make noise enough to frighten a legion. These religious ceremonies over, the people give themselves up to feasting, drinking immoderately of rice-beer till they are in the state of wild ebriety most suitable for the process of letting off steam. The Ho population of the villages forming the environs of Cháibásá are at other seasons quiet and reserved in manner, and in their demeanour towards women gentle and decorous. Even in the flirtations I have spoken of they never transcend the bounds of decency. The girls, though full of spirits and somewhat saucy, have innate notions of propriety that make them modest in demeanour, though devoid of all prudery; and of the obscene abuse so frequently heard from the lips of common women in Bengal, they appear to have no knowledge. They are delicately sensitive under harsh language of any kind, and never use it to others; and since their adoption of clothing, they are careful to drape themselves decently as well as gracefully. But they throw all this aside during the Mágh feast. Their natures appear to undergo a temporary change. Sons and daughters revile their parents in gross language, and parents their children; men and women become almost like animals in the indulgence of their amorous propensities. They enact all that was ever portrayed by prurient artists in a Bacchanalian festival or Pandean orgy; and as the light of the sun they adore, and the presence of numerous spectators seem to be no restraint on their indulgence, it cannot be expected that chastity is preserved when the shades of night fall on such a scene of licentiousness and debauchery. This festival is not kept at one period in all the villages. The time during which it is held in different villages of a circle extends over a period of a month or six weeks; and, under a preconcerted arrangement, the festival commences at each village on a different date, and lasts three or four days, so the inhabitants of each may take part in a long succession of these orgies. As the utmost liberty is given to girls, the parents never attempting to exercise any restraint, the girls of one village sometimes pair off with the young men of another, and absent themselves for days. *Liaisons* thus prolonged generally end in marriages. The ordinary Ho dance is similar to the *rasa* dance of the Santáls,—an amorous, but not a very rapid or lively movement; but the Mágh dance is like a *grande galope*,—a very joyous, frisky, harum-scarum scamper of boys and girls through the village and from one village to another. The Mundárís keep this festival in much the same manner as the Hos, but one day is fixed for its commencement everywhere,—the full of the moon in Mágh,—and there is less commingling of the boys and girls from different villages. The resemblance to a Saturnale is very complete, as at this festival the farm-labourers are feasted by their masters and allowed the utmost freedom of speech in addressing them. It is the festival of the harvest-home,—the termination of one year's toil and a slight respite from it before they commence again. At this feast the Mundárís dance the *jádúra*, remarkable for the very pretty and peculiar manner in which the lines of performers interlace their arms behind their backs. The next in the order of festivals is what is called *Bah Bonga* by the Hos, corresponding to the *Sarhúl* of the Mundárís. *Bah* means flower; and the festival takes place when the *sál* tree is in full bloom in March or April,—a favourite season with many tribes, for it is then that the death of Gautáma is commemorated. With the Hos and Mundárís it is held in honour of the founders of the village and the tutelary deity or spirit, called Darhá by the Oraons. The boys and girls collect basketsful of the flowers, make garlands of them, weave them in their hair, and decorate their houses with them. Each house makes an offering of these flowers, and sacrifices a cook. The people dance for a couple of days and nights incessantly, and refresh themselves meanwhile with beer; but in the Kolhán it is the quiet style of dance, and there are no open breaches of decorum. The dance on this occasion of the Mundárís is called the *bahni*. The boys and girls poussette to each other, clapping their hands and pirouetting, so as to cause *dos-á-dos* concussions, which are the source of much mirth. The selection of the *sál* flowers as the offering to the founders of the village is appropriate, as there are few villages that do not occupy ground once covered by *sál* forest; and at this period new ground, if there be any, is cleared for cultivation. The third festival is the *Damurai*, which is celebrated in May, or at the time of the sowing of the first rice crop.

It is held in honour of the ancestral shades and other spirits, who, if unpropitiated, would prevent the seed from germinating. A he-goat and a cock are sacrificed. The fourth festival is the *Hírá Bonga*, in June; the Mundárís call it *Harihur*. It is to propitiate Desauli and Jáhir Búrhi for a blessing on the crops. In the Mundárí villages every householder plants a branch of the *bhelwa* in his field and contributes to the general offering, which is made by the priest in the sacred grove, a fowl, a pitcher of beer, and a handful of rice. In Singbhum a he-goat is offered. This is followed by the *Bahtauli Bonga*, which takes place in July. Each cultivator sacrifices a fowl, and after some mysterious rites a wing is stripped off and inserted in the cleft of a bamboo and stuck up in the rice-field and dungheap. If this is omitted, it is supposed that the rice will not come to maturity. It appears more like a charm than a sacrifice. This corresponds with the *karam* in the Kol villages of Chutiá Nágpur, where the *hoja* is danced. The women in this dance follow the men, and change their positions and attitudes in obedience to signals from them. When the movement called *hoja* is asked for, the women all kneel and pat the ground with their hands in time to the music, as if coaxing the earth to be fruitful. On the day appointed a branch of the *karam* tree is cut and planted in the *ákhrá* or dancing place. This festival is kept by Hindus in Chutiá Nágpur as well as by Kols. The sixth festival is the offering of the first fruits of the harvest to Sing Bonga; it is solemnized in August, when the *gorá* rice ripens, and till the sacrifice is complete the new rice must not be eaten. The offering, in addition to the rice, is a white cock. This is a thanks-offering to the Creator and Preserver. It is called *Jum-nama*, and considered of great importance. To eat new rice without thus thanking God is regarded as impious. The seventh festival is the *Kalam Bonga*, when an offering of a fowl is made to Desauli on the removal of the rice straw from the threshing-floor, *kalam*, to be stacked. The *páhns* or priests of the Kol villages in Chutiá Nágpur have another festival, for the performance of which they are in possession of some rent-free land, called *dálikatári*. The sacrifices are, every second year a fowl, every third year a ram, every fourth year a buffalo, to Marang Búru; and the main object is to induce him to send seasonable rain. The above are all general festivals; but the Hos, on their individual account, make many sacrifices to the gods. In cases of sickness and calamity they commence by sacrificing what is small and of little value; but if the desired change is retarded, they go on until the patient dies or their live-stock is entirely exhausted.

Sorcery and witchcraft.

"All disease in men or animals is attributed to one of two causes,—the wrath of some evil spirit, who has to be appeased, or to the spell of some witch or sorcerer, who should be destroyed or driven out of the land. In the latter case a *sokha*, or witch-finder, is employed to divine who has cast the spell, and various modes of divination are resorted to. One of the most common is the test by the stone and *pailá*. The latter is a large wooden cup, shaped like a half cocoanut, used as a measure for grain. It is placed under a flat stone as a pivot for the stone to turn on. A boy is then seated on the stone, supporting himself by his hands; and the names of all the people in the neighbourhood are slowly pronounced, and as each name is uttered a few grains of rice are thrown at the boy. When they come to the name of the witch or wizard, the stone turns and the boy rolls off. This, no doubt, is the effect of the boy's falling into a state of coma and losing the power of supporting himself with his hands. In former times the person denounced and all his family were put to death, in the belief that witches breed witches and sorcerers. The taint is in the blood. When, during the Mutiny, Singbhum district was left for a short time without officers, a terrible raid was made against all who for years had been suspected of dealings with the evil one, and the most atrocious murders were committed. Young men were told off for the duty by the elders; neither sex nor age were spared. When order was restored, these crimes were brought to light, and the actual perpetrators condignly punished; and since then we have not only had no recurrence of witch murders, but the superstition itself is dying out in the Kolhán. In other districts accusations of witchcraft are still frequently made, and the persons denounced are subjected to much ill-usage if they escape with their lives. Some of the *sokhas*, instead of divining the name of the person who has cast the evil eye on the suffering patient, profess to summon their own familiar spirits, who impart to them the needed information. The *sokha* throws some rice on a winnowing sieve, and places a light in front of it. He then mutters incantations and rubs the rice, watching the flame, and when this flickers it is owing to the presence of the familiar; and the *sokha*, to whom alone the spirit is visible, pretends to receive from it the revelation, which he communicates to the inquirer, to the effect that the sufferer is afflicted by the familiar of some rival *sokha*, or sorcerer, or witch, whom he names. The villagers then cause the attendance of the person denounced, who is brought into the presence of the sufferer and ordered to haul out his evil spirit. It is useless for him to plead that he has no such spirit: this only leads to his being unmercifully beaten. His best line of defence is to admit what is laid to his charge, and to act as if he really were master of the situation. Some change for the better in the patient may take place, which is ascribed to his delivery from the familiar, andt he sorcerer is allowed to depart. But if there is no amelioration in the condition of the sick person, the chastisement of the sorcerer is continued till he can bear no more, and not unfrequently he dies under the ill-treatment he is subjected to, or from its effects. A milder method is when the person denounced is required to offer sacrifices of animals to appease or drive away the possessing devil; this he dare not refuse to do. And if the sickness thereupon ceases, it is of course concluded that the devil has departed; but if it continue, the sorcerer is turned out of his home and driven from the village, if nothing worse is done to him. It must not be supposed that these superstitions are confined to the Kols; they are common to all classes of the population of this province. I have elsewhere noticed their prevalence in the Southern Tributary Mahals, and the alleged existence of secret witch-schools, where damsels of true Aryan blood are instructed in the black art and perfected in it by practice on forest trees. Even Brahmans are sometimes accused. I find in a report by Major Roughsedge, written in 1818, an account of a Brahman lady who was denounced as a witch and tried; and having escaped in the ordeal by water, she was found to be a witch and deprived of her nose. The *sokha* does not always denounce a fellow-being; he sometimes gives out that the family *bhút* is displeased and has caused the sickness. And in such cases a most extensive propitiatory offering is demanded, which the master of the house provides, and of which the *sokha* gets the lion's share. I find an instance of the oracle giving out that Desauli, the village *bhút*, had caused the trouble; but on further inquiry it was averred that a spiteful old woman had on this occasion demoralised the honourable and respectable guardian of the village. And though he was propitiated, the hag was made to suffer very severely for her malignancy. It will be seen that it is not only women that are accused of having dealings with the imps of darkness. Persons of the opposite sex are as frequently denounced; nor are the female victims invariably of the orthodox old hag type. In a recent case eight women were denounced by a *sokha* as witches who had introduced epidemic cholera into the village and caused a terrible mortality, and among these were some very young girls. They were ill-treated until they admitted all that was imputed to them and agreed to point out and remove the spell they had prepared. They pretended to search for dead birds, which, it was said, they had deposited as charms, but nothing was produced; and one of the poor creatures, fearing further ill-usage, destroyed herself by jumping into a well. In Singbhum the wild Kharriás are looked upon as the most expert sorcerers; and the people, though they not unfrequently seek their aid, hold them in great awe.

Disposal of the dead.

"The funeral ceremonies of the Hos are deserving of special notice, as they show great reverence for the dead; and the variety and singularity of the rites performed may materially aid us in tracing the connection of the people we are describing. In my account of the Khásias I have already drawn attention to the similarity between their funeral ceremonies and those of the Hos. The funeral rites of the Hos and Gáros have also many points of resemblance. On the death of a respectable Ho a very substantial coffin is constructed and placed on faggots of firewood. The body, carefully washed and anointed with oil and turmeric, is reverently laid in the coffin; all the clothes, ornaments, and agricultural implements that the deceased was in the habit of using are placed with it and also any money that he had about him when he died. Then the lid of the coffin is put on, and faggots placed around and above it, and the whole is burned. The cremation takes place in front of the house of the deceased. Next morning water is thrown on the ashes, search made for bones, and a few of the larger fragments are carefully preserved, whilst the remainder, with the ashes, are buried. The selected bones are placed in a vessel of earthenware,—we may call it an urn,—and hung up in the apartment of the chief mourner, generally the mother or widow, that she may have them continually in view, and occasionally weep over them. Thus they remain till the very extensive arrangements necessary for their final disposal are effected. A large tombstone has to be procured, and it is sometimes so ponderous that the men of several villages are employed to move it. Some wealthy men, knowing that their successors may not have the same influence that they possess, select during their lifetime a suitable monument to commemorate their worth, and have it moved to a handy position to be used when they die. When required for use it is brought to the family burial place, which with the Hos is close to the houses, and near it a deep round hole is dug for the reception of the cinerary urn. When all is ready a funeral party collect in front of the deceased's house—three or four men with very deep-toned drums, and a group of about eight young girls. The chief mourner comes forth, carrying the bones exposed on a decorated tray, and a procession is formed. The chief mourner, with the tray, leads; the girls form in two rows, those in front carrying empty and partly broken pitchers and battered brass vessels; and the men, with drums, bring up the rear. The procession advances with a very ghostly dancing movement, slow and solemn as a minuet, in time to the beat of the deep-toned drums, not straightforward, but mysteriously gliding,—now right, now left, now marking time, all in the same mournful cadence—a sad dead march. The chief mourner carries the tray, generally on her head; but at regular intervals she slowly lowers it, and as she does so the girls also gently lower and mournfully reverse the pitchers and brass vessels, and, looking up for the moment with eyes full of tears, seem to say, 'Ah! see! they are empty.' In this manner the remains are taken to the house of every friend and relative of the deceased within a circle of a few miles, and to every house in the village. As the procession approaches each habitation, in the weird-like manner described, the inmates all come out, and the tray having been placed on the ground at their door, they kneel over it and mourn, shedding tears on the remains as their last tribute of affection to their deceased friend. The bones are also thus conveyed to all his favourite haunts,—to the fields he cultivated, to the grove he planted, to the tank he excavated, to the threshing-floor where he worked with his people, to the *ákhrá* or dancing arena where he made merry with them,—and each spot which is hallowed with reminiscences of the deceased draws forth fresh tears from the mourners. In truth, there is a reality in their sadness that would put to shame the efforts of our undertakers and the purchased gravity of the best mutes; and it is far less noisy and more sincere than the Irish 'keening.' When this part of the ceremony is completed the procession returns to the village, and, slowly gyrating round the great slab, gradually approaches its goal. At last it stops; a quantity of rice, cooked and uncooked, and other food is now cast into the grave, and the charred fragments of bone transferred from the tray to a new earthen vessel placed over it. The hole is then filled up and covered with the large slab, which effectually closes it against desecration. The slab, however, does not rest on the ground, but on smaller stones, which raise it a little. With the

Mundas, as among the Khásias, these slabs may cover the graves of several members of a family; but the ghost of a Ho likes to have his grave all to himself. A collection of these massive gravestones indelibly marks the site of every Ho or Mundárí village; and they may now be found so marking sites in parts of the country where there have been no Kols for ages. But in addition to the slab on the tomb, a megalithic monument is set up to the memory of the deceased in some conspicuous spot outside the village. The pillars vary in height from five or six to fifteen feet, and apparently fragments of rock of the most fantastic shape are most favoured. Close to the station of Cháibásá, on the road to Keunjhar, may be seen a group of cenotaphs of unusual size,—one eleven feet two inches, another thirteen feet, and a third fourteen feet above the earth; and many others of smaller dimensions. The groups of such stones that have come under my observation in the Munda and Ho country are always in line. The circular arrangement, so common elsewhere, I have not seen.

Religion.

"I do not find that the present generation of Kols have any conception of a heaven or a hell that may not be traced to Brahmanical or Christian teaching. They have some vague idea that the ghosts of the dead hover about, and they make offerings to them; and some have, like the Chinese, an altar in the house, on which a portion of the 'daily bread' is offered to them. But unless under a system of prompting, often inadvertently adopted, they will not tell you that this after-existence is one of reward or punishment. When a Ho swears, the oath has no reference whatever to a future state. He prays that if he speak not the truth, he may be afflicted with as many calamities as befell Job,—that he may suffer the loss of all his worldly wealth, his health, his wife, his children; that he may sow without reaping, or reap without gathering; and finally, that he may be devoured by a tiger. It is a tremendous oath, and it is a shame to impose the obligation of making it on so generally truthful a people; but they swear not by any hope of happiness beyond the grave, and the miserable wandering life they assign to the shades can only be looked forward to with dread. They fear the ghosts and propitiate them as spirits of a somewhat malignant nature, but can have no possible desire to pass into such a state of existence themselves. The funeral ceremonies I have described are what I myself witnessed. Colonel Tickell tells us that on the evening of the burning of the corpse certain preparations are made in the house in anticipation of a visit from the ghost. A portion of the boiled rice is set apart for it,—the commencement, we may presume, of the daily act of family devotion above noticed,—and ashes are sprinkled on the floor, in order that, should it come, its footprints may be detected. The inmates then leave the house, and, circumambulating the pyre, invoke the spirit. Returning, they carefully scrutinise the ashes and rice, and if there is the faintest indication of these having been disturbed, it is at once attributed to the return of the spirit; and they sit down apart, shivering with horror, and crying bitterly, as if they were by no means pleased with the visit, though made at their earnest solicitation. I have often asked the Kols if their custom of casting money, food, and raiment on the funeral pyre is at all connected with the idea of the resurrection of the body, or if they thought the dead would benefit by the gifts bestowed. They have always answered in the negative, and gave me the same explanation of the origin and object of the custom that I received from the Chulikata Mishmis of Upper Assam, namely, that they are unwilling to derive any immediate benefit from the death of a member of their family; they wish for no such consolation in their grief. So they commit to the flames all his personal effects, the clothes and vessels he had used, the weapons he carried, and the money he had about him. But new things that have not been used are not treated as things that he appropriated, and they are not destroyed; and it often happens that respectable old Hos abstain from wearing new garments that they become possessed of to save them from being wasted at the funeral. When the interment of the bones is accomplished, the event is made known far and wide by explosions that sound like discharges from heavy guns. This is sometimes done through the agency of gunpowder, but more frequently by the application of heat and cold to fragments of schistose rock, causing them to split with loud noises.

Social status.

"In summing up the character of the people I have been describing it is necessary to separate the Hos from their cognates. The circumstances under which the character of the former has been developed are different, and they are in my opinion physically and morally superior to the Mundas, Bhumij, and Santáls. They appear to me to possess a susceptibility of improvement not found in the other tribes. They have been directly under our government for about thirty-seven years; and, coming to us as unsophisticated savages, we have endeavoured to civilise them without allowing them to be contaminated. Whilst they still retain those traits which favourably distinguish the aborigines of India from Asiatics of higher civilisation,—a manner free from servility, but never rude; a love, or at least the practice, of truth; a feeling of self-respect, rendering them keenly sensitive under rebuke,—they have become less suspicious, less revengeful, less bloodthirsty, less contumacious, and in all respects more amenable to the laws and the advice of their officers. They are still very impulsive, easily excited to rash, headstrong action, and apt to resent imposition or oppression without reflection; but the retaliation, which often extends to a death-blow, is done on the spur of the moment and openly, secret assassination being a crime almost unthought of by them. As a fair illustration of their mode of action when violently incensed, I give the following:—A Bengali trader, accustomed to carry matters with a very high hand among his compatriots in the Jungle Mahals, demanded payment of a sum of money due to him by a Ho, and not receiving it, proceeded to sequestrate and drive off a pair of bullocks, the property of his debtor. The Ho on this took to his arms, let fly an arrow which brought down the money-lender, whose head he then cut off, went with it in his hand straight to the Deputy Commissioner, and explaining to that officer exactly what had occurred, requested that he might be condemned for the crime without more ado! Murders are not now more frequent in the Kolhán than in other districts, latterly less so; but when one does take place, the perpetrator is seldom at any trouble to conceal himself or his crime. The pluck of the Hos, displayed in their first encounter with our troops in former wars, I have often seen exemplified on minor occasions. In competitive games they go to work with a will and a strenuous exertion of their full force, unusual in natives of India. Once at the Ránchí Fair there was a race of carriages, often used by travellers in Chutiá Nágpur, drawn and propelled by men. One of these came from Singbhum and had a team of Hos; a collision took place early in the race, and the arm of one of the Ho team was badly fractured. It fell broken by his side, but he still held on to the shaft of the carriage, and, cheering and yelling like the rest, went round the course. The extreme sensitiveness of both men and women is sometimes very painfully exhibited in the analysis of the numerous cases of suicide that every year occur. A harsh word to a woman never provokes a retort, but it causes in the person offensively addressed a sudden depression of spirits or vehement outbreak of grief, which few persons would a second time care to provoke. If a girl appears mortified by anything that has been said, it is not safe to let her go away till she is soothed. A reflection on a man's honesty or veracity may be sufficient to send him to self-destruction. In a recent case a young woman attempted to poison herself because her uncle would not partake of the food she had cooked for him. The police returns of Singbhum show that in nine years, from 1860 to 1869, both inclusive, 186 men and women committed suicide in that district. I have already spoken of them as good husbands and wives, but in all the relations of life their manner to each other is gentle and kind. I never saw girls quarrelling, and never heard them abuse or say unkind things of each other; and they never coarsely abuse, and seldom speak harshly to women. The only exception I know is when they believe a woman to be a witch. For such a one they have no consideration. They have no terms in their own language to express the higher emotions, but they feel them all the same."

Hoduar, a bird, a totemistic sept of Mundas in Chota Nagpur.

Holongwár, a sub-caste of Sunris in Manbhum.

Hom, a title of Bangaja Káyasths.

Homjah, a sept of Mundas in Chota Nagpur.

Homodimchhá, a *thar* or sept of Khambus in Darjiling.

Homwár, a section of Kurmis in Chota Nagpur and Orissa.

Homyagain, a *thar* of the Dhánjaya *gotra* of Nepáli Brahmans.

Hondagiá, a section of the Dhusiá sub-caste of Chamárs in Behar.

Hone-hogá, a sept of Hos in Singbhum.

Hong, a bird with long tail, a totemistic sept of Mundas in Chota Nagpur.

Honti, a sept of Gonds in Chota Nagpur.

Hopthen, a section of Murmis in Darjiling.

Hor, a title of Dakshin-Rárhi and Bangaja Káyastha.

Horia, a bush, a totemistic sept of Mundas in Chota Nagpur.

Horo, red tree-ant, a totemistic sept of Mundas in Chota Nagpur.

Horo-hon, a synonym for Munda in Chota Nagpur.

Horongpáchhá, a *thar* or sept of Khambus in Darjiling.

Hosainpuriá, a section of the Banodhiá and Jaiswár Kalwárs in Behar.

Hotá, a section of Utkal or Orissa Brahmans.

Hrisi or *Rishi*, a synonym for Muchi in Bengal.

Hroimajusa, a sept of Maghs in the Hill Tracts of Chittagong.

Huddá, a sept of Rajputs in Behar.

Hudinwál, a section of Goálás in the North-Western Provinces and Behar.

Hui, a title of Dakshin-Rárhi and Bangaja Káyastha.

Hukpáh, a sept of Limbus in Darjiling.

Hularbaha, a flower, a totemistic sept of Mundas in Chota Nagpur.

Hundar, wolf, a totemistic sept of Mundas in Chota Nagpur.

Huni, mouse, a totemistic sept of Mundas in Chota Nagpur.

Hunjar, a section of Tántis and Páns in Chota Nagpur.

Hunri, a synonym for Sunri.

Hupachongbang, he who was blessed and prospered, a sept of the Phedab sub-tribe of Limbus in Darjiling.

Huru, paddy-bird, a totemistic sept of Binjhiás in Chota Nagpur.

Huruj, a sept of Korwas in Chota Nagpur.

Husoi, a sept of Tipperahs in the Hill Tracts of Chittagong.

Hutar, a flower, a totemistic sept of Mundas in Chota Nagpur.

I

Ichá, a sept of the Tungjainya sub-tribe of Chakmás in the Hill Tracts of Chittagong.

Ichapocha, a sept of Chakmás in the Hill Tracts of Chittagong.

Ichbariá, a section of the Sátmuliá Maghayá sub-caste of Kándus in Behar.

Ichommah, a sept of Limbus in Darjiling.

Idri, a jungle fruit, a sept of Bairágis in Chota Nagpur.

Ikahan, a section of the Karan Káyasths in Behar.

Ikteh, a sept of Limbus in Darjiling.

Ilámháng, a sept of Limbus in Darjiling.

Imli, tamarind, a totemistic sept of Mundas in Chota Nagpur.

Imsong, a sept of Limbus in Darjiling.

Indi, a title of Khatris and Mayarás in Bengal.

Indra, a title of Dakshin-Rárhi and Bangaja Káyasths.

Indrabárá, a *dih* or local section of the Maghayá sub-caste of Telis in Behar. The system of exogamy among this sub-caste of Telis seems, however, either to be dying out or to be of recent introduction, for some of the Maghayás say they have no *dihs*, but merely prohibit marriage within nine *pirhis* or degrees of relationship.

Indrapati, a sub-caste of Rástogis in Behar.

Indrawár, a section of Bábhans in Behar.

Indri, a *mul* or section of the Chhamuliá Madhesiá sub-caste of Halwáis in Behar.

Induar, a kind of eel, a totemistic sept of Nágeswars; a section of Goráits, Mahilis, Turis, and a sept of Chiks, Lohárs, and Oraons in Chota Nagpur.

Indur-katea, house rat, a totemistic sept of Mundas in Chota Nagpur.

Ingaria, moonlight, a sept of Mundas in Chota Nagpur.

Inglamphe, the liar, a sept of the Ahtharai sub-tribe of Limbus in Darjiling.

Ingmaba, he who kept fowls, a sept of the Pánthar sub-tribe of Limbus in Darjiling.

Ingyaromba, a sept of the Yangorup sub-tribe of Limbus in Darjiling.

Isar, a *pangat* or section of Bánsphor Doms and Dosádhs in Behar.

Isáre, a sept of the Agniá sub-tribe of Meches in the Darjiling Terai.

Isbo, name of a village, a sept of the Phedáb sub-tribe of Limbus in Darjiling.

Iswájitauni, a sub-tribe of Thárus in Nepal.

Itawá, a *mul* or section of the Kanaujiá sub-caste of Sonárs in Behar.

Itbár or *Itbál*, a title and a section of Tiyars in Behar.

Ithinku, a sept of Limbus in Darjiling.

Itwár, a section of Kewats in Behar.

J

Jabagrámi, a *gáin* or sub-section of Saptasati Brahmans in Bengal.

Jábáli, a section of Brahmans.

Jábáliá, a section of Bhojpuriá Halwáis in Behar.

Jáchandár, appraiser, a title of Jugis and Tántis in Bengal, dating back to the time when the East India Company traded in Indian woven goods.

Jádab-Mádhab, a section of the Mahmudábáz sub-caste of Nápits in Bengal.

Jádab-Ráy, a hypergamous group of Kaibarttas in Bakarganj.

Jádan, a sept of Rajputs in Behar.

Jádu, a section of the Magahiyá sub-caste of Doms in Behar; of Goálás in the North-Western Provinces and Behar.

Jáduá, *Jaduah* (*jádu*, 'magic'), a sub-caste of Kraunchdwipi Brahmans in Behar who practise fortune-telling.

Jadubansi, a sub-tribe of Rajputs (*Sher.* i. p. 123). The Ahir Paiks of Chota Nagpur also call themselves Jadubansi Rajputs. A sub-caste of Goálás in Behar and the North-Western Provinces.

Jadwál, a section of Goálás in the North-Western Provinces and Behar.

Jádwar, a sept of Rajputs in Behar.

Jagaha, a sept of Gonds in Chota Nagpur.

Jagái, a *gáin* or sub-section of Saptasati Brahmans in Bengal.

Jagannáthi or **Uriya-Kumhár**, a sub-caste of Kumhárs in Orissa.

Jagat, a sept of Gonds in Chota Nagpur.

Jagatpur, a *mul* or section of the Naomuliá or Majraut sub-caste of Goálás in Behar.

Jagdá, **Jagdar**, a sept of Mundas.

Jagmanrá, a section of the Biyáhut and Kharidáhá Kalwárs in Behar.

Jago, tamarind, a totemistic sept of Mundas in Chota Nagpur.

Jagsariá, a sept of Birhors in Chota Nagpur.

Jahari, a title of Lohárs, derived from their sharpening weapons, the gloss of which is called *jahar*.

Jáhnavi, a section of the Gangotá caste in Behar.

Jahur, a sub-sept of the Hemrom sept of Santáls.

Jaiá, **Pubiá**, a sub-caste of Utkal Brahmans in Orissa.

Jaibele, a sub-caste of Sunris in Western Bengal.

Jailak, a *mul* or section of the Naomuliá or Majraut sub-caste of Goálás in Behar.

Jaimini, a section of Brahmans.

Jainagariá, a section of Awadhiá Hajjáms in Behar.

Jaintimási, a section of the Bárui caste in Bengal.

Jaintpur, a section of the Biyáhut and Kharidáhá Kalwárs in Behar.

Jaipur, a *mul* or section of the Ayodhiá sub-caste of Hajjáms in Behar.

Jaipuriá, a section of Amashta Káyasths and a *mul* or section of the Banodhiá sub-caste of Kalwárs in Behar; a sept of Gonds in Chota Nagpur.

Jaisi, (i) in Behar a synonym for Jyotisi, *q.v.*; (ii) in Darjiling and Nepal a sub-caste of Brahmans, some of whom are probably Jaisi Brahmans who have immigrated from the plains, while others are the illegitimate children of Upádhya Brahmans by women of their own caste, or of Upadhya or Jaisi Brahmans by slave women.

Jaisi, Jotkhi, or **Jotsi**, a sub-caste of the Kraunchdwipi Brahmans in Behar.

Jai Singh, a section of Tiyars in Behar.

Jáiswár, *Jaiswára, Jessowára, Jashar, Jaswara, Jeswar*, a name of a sub-caste or sept of Rajputs; of Telis, Baniyas, Barais, Kurmis, Tántis, Dhánuks, Kalwárs, Chamárs, etc. Sir H. Elliot thinks the name may imply that the people bearing it "came originally from Jáis, a large manufacturing town in Oudh." The name is very widely diffused, and it is impossible to say for certain to what main caste we should refer persons who described themselves in the Census schedule as Jaiswárs by caste. Chamárs are particularly fond of assuming this designation, which appears to associate or identify them with the more respectable Kurmi.

Jaitar, a sept of the Suryabansi sub-tribe of Rajputs in Behar.

Jaithariá, a section of Bábhans in Behar.

Jaiwár, a hypergamous group of Maithil Brahmans in Behar.

Jájaki, a class of up-country Brahmans who come to Bengal in search of employment as priests.

Jáji, a section of Bábhans in Behar.

Jajim, a section of Bábhans in Behar.

Jájnabalkya, a section of Brahmans.

Jajpuriá, a sub-caste of Utkal Brahmans in Orissa.

Jajuwáre-Bharám, a *mul* of the Sándil section of Maithil Brahmans in Behar.

Jajuwáre-Udánpur, a *mul* of the Sándil section of Maithil Brahmans in Behar.

Jajuwáre-Jamuni, a *mul* of the Sándil section of Maithil Brahmans in Behar.

Jajuwáre-Pachahi, a *mul* of the Sándil section of Maithil Brahmans in Behar.

Jakhalpuriá, a section of Lohárs and Sonárs in Behar.

Jalaiwár-Jále, a *mul* of the Bátsya section of Maithil Brahmans in Behar.

Jalaiwár-Maránchi, a *mul* of the Bátsa section of Maithil Brahmans in Behar.

Jalaiwár-Ganraul, a *mul* of the Bátsa section of Maithil Brahmans in Behar.

Jalaiwár-Máll, a *mul* of the Bátsa section of Maithil Brahmans in Behar.

Jalálpur, a *dih* or local section of the Maghayá sub-caste of Koiris in Behar.

Jálbanuár, net, a totemistic section of the Kurmi caste in Chota Nagpur and Orissa, the members of which will not make or touch a net.

Jal Chhatri, a title of Surahiyás.

Jalewár (holder of fishing nets), a *kul* or section of Bábhans in Behar.

Jaliásinghi, a section of Goria Gowár or Dahiár Goálás in Behar.

Jálik, a sub-caste of Kaibarttas in Máldah.

Jáliyá, a title of Málos in Eastern Bengal.

Jáliyá, *Jaliyá*, *Jele*, *Jálo*, *Jalwá*, *Jeliyá*, a general name in use throughout Bengal Proper as the popular designation of all classes of people who are engaged in boating or fishing. The etymology of the word is uncertain: some derive it from *jál*, 'a net,' others from *jal*, 'water.' Strictly speaking it is not a caste name, but is applied indifferently to Málos, Tiyars, Kaibarttas, Bauris, Bágdis, Rájbansis, and Mahomedans. In Noakháli, however, the term seems to have developed into the designation of a caste divided into four endogamous groups—**Chátgáon Jáliyá**, **Bhuluá Jáliyá**, **Jhálo Jáliyá**, and **Kaibartta Jáliyá**. The last-named group consists doubtless of fishing Kaibarttas as distinguished from the cultivating members of that caste; while Jhálo may perhaps be a synonym for Málo. The other groups seem to be peculiar to Noákháli.

Origin.

Dr. Wise, who had special opportunities of observing the fishing castes, describes them as "remarkable for strength, nerve, and independent bearing. The finest examples of Bengali manhood are found among them, and their muscular figures astonish those accustomed to the feeble and effeminate inhabitants of towns. The physique of the Dacca fisherman is more robust than that of the same class on the Hughli, a fact noticed by Bishop Heber fifty years ago."

Physical type.

No one belonging to a fisher caste will fish with a rod and line, or use a harpoon, as the Shikárìs do. Bengal fishermen use the seine, drift, trawl, bag, and cast nets. The Kaibarttas, however, will not employ an Uthár or Ber net, which are favourites with the Tiyar and Málo.

Fishing apparatus.

Nets are made of hemp, never of cotton, and they are steeped in gáb (*Diospyrus glutinosa*) pounded and allowed to ferment, by which means the net is dyed of a dark brown colour, becoming after immersion in water almost black. Floats are either made of sholá or pieces of bamboo, but dried gourds are occasionally preferred. Sinkers are made of baked clay or iron.

The following are the common nets in use among Bengali fishermen:—

1. *Jhakí* or *kshepla* is the circular cast net[1] met with in all Eastern countries. It is usually six or seven cubits in diameter,

[1] Il giacchio of Italian fishermen.

and is either thrown from the bank of a stream or from a boat. The circumference is drawn up into loops, or rather puckered, and weighted with iron. It is folded on the left forearm, while the edge and the central string are held by the right hand. By a sudden and forcible swing of the body the net is cast, and if properly thrown alights on the surface of the water, forming a complete circle. On its touching the bottom the fisher slowly draws it towards him by the string just mentioned, and as he does so the heavily-weighted edge comes together, and no fish can escape. The outcast Bágdì in Central Bengal swings the net round his head before casting it, but no respectable fisherman would dishonour his calling by so doing.

2. The *uthár* and *gulti* are magnified cast nets, differing only in size and in the dimensions of the meshes. They are shot from a boat placed broadside to a stream, with the net folded on the edge. One man holds the centre rope, while two others gradually unfold and drop it overboard. As the boat drifts the net falls in a circle, and is then slowly drawn up. One of these nets is often forty feet in diameter, and a long boat like the jalká is required to shoot it from.

3. The *sángla* is a small trawl net, used for catching *hilsá*. The lower edge of the bag is weighted, and after being shot the boat drifts with the stream. When a fish passing over the lower lip of the net, to which a rope held by the fisherman is attached, is felt to strike the back of the net, it is suddenly raised and the fish secured.

4. The *baoti* is a fixed bag net, worked on the same principle.

5. *Chándi* is a large drift net, supported by gourds or bamboo floats, and in the water it hangs as a curtain, like the herring net, the fish being caught by the gills.

6. *Ber* is a large seine or sweep net, often thirty feet in depth and seven hundred and fifty in length. Several nets are usually joined together to form this "train fleet" or "drift of nets." The upper edge, or back, is buoyed by bamboos, while the lower, or foot, is weighted with iron. This is the favourite net with the Málos on the Meghna, but owing to its great length it has to be shot from two boats fastened together, and when drawn the two "wings," or ends, are slowly brought ashore.

7. *Besál* or *khára* is a fixed net, used either from the side of a boat, balanced by an outrigger, or fixed to posts on the banks of rivers. The net is attached to two bamboos, which meet at an acute angle in the boat, but branching off until separate about fifteen to twenty feet. One man stands at the angle and lowers the net into the water, while another sits at the stern working a paddle with his leg until a certain distance has been passed over, when the net, which is somewhat bagged, is leisurely raised. This net is fancied by Tiyars and Málos, who at the first dawn of day may be seen fishing with it off bathing ghâts and around steamers and vessels anchored in mid stream. Small fry are usually caught with it, but when fixed on the margin of a river, where there is a backwater or an eddy, large and weighty fish are often netted.

8. *Kona* is a large bag net used at the outlets of rivers and streams. The sides are fixed, and the mouth faces the current. The lower lip rests on the bottom, while the upper remains open, and at intervals the former is raised and the fish taken out.

Bengali fishermen are familiar with the habits of fish, and much might be learned from them on a branch of natural history strangely neglected in India. Night is the favourite time for fishing, quiet being necessary for success; and a full moon, or sunset and sunrise, are favourable times for shooting nets. The first of a spring tide is also a period when fish move.

It is a curious coincidence that the English fisherman, when looking for a place to shoot his large drift, or herring net, raps with a piece of wood the planks of his boat, close to the water line. The Málo is equally aware of the fact that brisk undulation of water frightens fish, causing them to move; and as the net is being drawn, a man beats the side of the boat with an oar, by which means the draught is increased.

During the month of mourning for a parent, no fisherman can ply his trade, or have any dealings in fish, unless he gets a special dispensation from the purohit.

All fishermen object to sell the skate (ságus), and will not retail in any way but whole the pangas (*Pimelodus pngasius*), garua (*Silurus garua*), and gagar (*Pimelodus gagora*). Neither will they catch or sell crabs, nor touch the "putká" or bladder fish.[1] Many of the fisher castes of India have the Muhammadan aversion to fish without scales, and few will eat, or even handle, the "singi" (*Silurus singeo*). Eels, however, they sometimes cook, but owing to the rich and heating properties of the flesh it is not a favourite article of food. Muhammadans of the Hanífí school never eat amphibious animals as the crab, consequently the only Bengali-Muhammadans who use them as food are the indigent residents of Chittagong.

The following statement shows the number and distribution of Jáliyás in 1872 and 1881:—

DISTRICT.	1872.	1881.	DISTRICT.	1872.	1881.
Bardwan	10,533	5,374	Darjiling	44	13
Bankura	1,261	3,310	Jalpigori	1,270	3,870
Birbhum	765	4,059	Kuch Behar	......	2,640
Midnapur	29,430	20,063	Dacca	32,269	40,733
Hughli	} 15,829	{ 10,369	Faridpur	20,460	23,607
Howrah		6,467	Bakarganj	12,603	13,183
24-Parganas	23,979	11,424	Maimansinh	36,399	34,587
Nadiya	20,398	14,998	Tipperah	7,106	12,616
Khulna	......	20,925	Chittagong	9,284	15,312
Jessore	43,642	36,836	Noakhali	9,313	8,602
Murshedabad	3,014	2,848	Hill Tracts	......	11
Dinajpur	10,296	13,398	Balasore	......	123
Rajshahye	16,692	13,774	Hazaribagh	34	......
Rangpur	16,301	8,387	Lohardaga	99	......
Bogra	5,163	5,218	Manbhum	2,648	1,206
Pabna	26,945	39,260			

[1] The *Tetrodon patoca*. It emits a sound when lifted out of the water and fills itself with air. Like the *T. Fahaca* of the Nile, it serves as a plaything for fisher children.

Jallád, an executioner, a hangman, a term which appears as a caste designation in the schedules of the Census of 1881. The persons who so described themselves were probably Doms.

Jálo, a title of Málos in Eastern Bengal.

Jáluá, a group of the Rájbansi sub-caste of Kochhs in Northern Bengal.

Jalwá, a title of Málos in Eastern Bengal.

Jalwar, net, a sept of Lohárs in Chota Nagpur.

Jámadagni pátra, a section of Utkal or Orissa Brahmans.

Jámadagnya, a section of Brahmans and Káyasths in Bengal.

Jamadár, a section of the Chaubhán sub-caste of Nuniás in Behar.

Jamádár, sergeant in a native regiment, a police officer, a cashier, and sometimes a sweeper, who is so called by his fellow-servants in derision, he being the lowest servant in the household.

Jamálpuri, a section of Sonárs in Behar.

Jamar Katyál, a *thar* of the Bharadwája *gotra* of Nepáli Brahmans.

Jamátya, a sept of the Tipperah tribe in the Hill Tracts of Chittagong.

Jambar, a section of the Oswál Baniyás.

Jamgot, a totemistic section of Nuniás in Behar.

Jamraián, a section of Bábhans in Behar.

Jámrukhi, a *gáin* of the Bátsya *gotra* of Bárendra Brahmans in Bengal.

Jamtuti, a kind of grain or vegetable, a totemistic sept of Mundas in Chota Nagpur.

Jamuáon, a section of the Biyáhut and Kharidáhá Kalwárs in Behar.

Jamuár, a *pur* or section of Sákadwipi Brahmans and of the Amashta sub-caste of Káyasths in Behar.

Jámulu, a sept of Hos in Singbhum.

Jáná, *Jená*, a sub-caste of Aguris in Bengal; a title of Chásás and Khandáits in Orissa, and of Goálás and Kaibarttas in Bengal.

Janágadhiá, a section of Awadhiá Hajáms in Behar.

Janakpuri, a sub-caste of Telis and Chamárs in Behar; a section of Sonárs in Behar.

Janam iar, a sept of Chiks in Chota Nagpur.

Janaráshi, a section of Tántis in Bengal.

Jándár, a title of Kewats in Behar.

Janeri (*Janeo-ri*), wearer of the *janeo* or sacred thread; a title of Brahmans and Rajputs.

Jangatras, cowbone, a totemistic sept of Mundas in Chota Nagpur.

Jangli, *Jangla*, a native of the jungles. The word is used in a special sense in connexion with inland emigration to denote non-Aryan coolies from Chota Nagpur, whose immunity from fever renders them the most valuable class of labourers for Assam.

Jánjdiá, a section of Goálás in the North-Western Provinces and Behar.

Janku Samrai, a sept of Hos in Singbhum.

Janwár, a section of Bábhans and Mahesris in Behar.

Jarangait, a section of Lohárs in Behar.

Járdár, a title of Hajáms.

Jarhuáit, a territorial section of Binds in Behar.

Jariár, a totemistic section of Turis in Chota Nagpur signifying a lizard.

Jarigámba, *jari* tree, a totemistic sept of Juángs in Orissa.

Jár-Kámi, a section of Kámis in Darjiling.

Jaru, a section of Awadhiá Hajjáms in Behar.

Járu, a totemistic sept of the Bhumij tribe in Manbhum.

Jaruhár, a sub-caste of Koiris in Behar who do permit widows to remarry.

Jas, a title of Dakshin-Rárhi and Bangaja Káyasths.

Jasatbár, a sept of Surajbansi Rajputs in Behar.

Jasiám, a section of Lohárs in Behar.

Jasográmi, a *gáin* of the Sábarna *gotra* of Bárendra Brahmans in Bengal.

Jaswár, a sub-caste of Dhánuks, Kándus, Kahárs, Kurmis, and Telis in Behar, see **Jáiswár**.

Ját, a sub-caste of Goálás in Behar whose sections are Gadhuwal, Chitosia, etc. They hold the title of Chaudhri, Singh, and Marár.

Játh, a class of Mahomedan herdsmen in Behar; a religious group of Jugis in Bengal.

Játham, a sub-caste of Dhobis in Behar.

Jathot, a division of the Párbatti-Kurin sub-caste of Gonrhis in Behar who are distinguished from the rest of the sub-castes by treating as exogamous groups the divisions which the others regard merely as titles having no bearing on marriage.

Játhot, a sub-caste of Kewats in Behar.

Játi-Karmakár, a sub-caste of Kámárs in Noakháli.

Játi-Madak, a sub-caste of Madhunápits in Bengal.

Játi-Mech, a sub-tribe of Meches in the Darjiling Terai.

Ját-Pátni, a sub-caste of Pátnis in Bengal.

Jatrama, a sept of Mundas in Chota Nagpur.

Jatria, a sept of Mundas in Chota Nagpur.

Jattia, *Jetti*, a class of wandering mendicants from the North-Western Provinces.

Játukarna, a section of the Dákshinátya Baidik Brahmans in Bengal, and of Utkal Brahmans in Orissa.

Jaum, a section of Awadhiá Hajjáms in Behar.

Jaunpuri, a sub-caste of Telis in Behar who sell oil, but do not manufacture it; also of Chamárs.

Jaunpuri Kamlapati, a sub-caste of Baniás in Behar.

Jawáliá, a *mul* or section of the Tinmuliá Madhesiá sub-caste of Halwáis in Behar.

Jayi, a sub-section of the Bharadwája section of Utkal Brahmans in Orissa.

Jebel, a *mul* or section of the Chhamuliá Madhesiá sub-caste of Halwáis in Behar.

Jedhriá, a *kul* or section of Bábhans in Behar.

Jeruhet, a section of Maghayá Kumhárs in Behar.

Jeseriet, a *mul* or section of the Sátmuliá or Kishnaut sub-caste of Goálás in Behar.

Jeshkuchá, a *thar* or sept of Sunuwars in Darjiling.

Jesiwár, a section of Bábhans in Behar.

Jespuchá, a *thar* or sept of Sunuwars in Darjiling.

Jeswár, a sub-caste of Baniyas; of Chamárs in Behar who are said to have come from the North-West Provinces and work as servants, syces, and labourers. See **Jáiswár**.

Jethaut, a sub-caste of Kaibarttas and Nágars in Behar.

Jethautiá, a *mul* or section of the Naomuliá or Goriá sub-caste of Goálás in Behar.

Jethkar, a sub-caste of Gangotás in Behar.

Jethman, a title of the Sangtarásh sub-caste of Gonrhis in Behar.

Jethuliar, a section of Bábhans in Behar.

Jethuriá, a section of Bábhans in Behar.

Jewal, a section of Madhesiá Halwáis in Behar.

Jewni, a section of Chandáls who catch and sell fish.

Jhá, Ujhá, or **Ojhá**, a title of Maithil Brahmans in Behar.

Jhádadiá, a section of Goálás in the North-Western Provinces and Behar.

Jhagdoliá, a section of Goálás in the North-Western Provinces and Behar.

Jhagreb, a *thar* or sept of the Bárah-Gurung sub-tribe of Gurungs in Darjiling.

Jháj, a *mul* or section of the Naomuliá or Majraut sub-caste of Goálás in Behar.

Jhámál, Jhampati, a *gáin* of the Bharadwája *gotra* of Bárendra Brahmans in Bengal.

Jhandáhá, a *mul* or section of the Banodhiá sub-caste of Kalwárs in Behar.

Jhángar, a variant for Dhángar, *q.v.*

Jhángdi, a *thar* or sept of Mangars in Darjiling.

Jhankai or **Jani**, a title of Kandhs in Orissa.

Jhankri, a quack doctor in Nepal.

Jhápábasriár, a section of Kurmis in Chota Nagpur and Orissa.

Jhári, a *thar* or sept of Mangars in Darjiling.

Jhárowá, a synonym for Mehtar or sweeper.

Jharuá, a sub-tribe of Savars in Orissa.

Jháruá, a sub-caste of Utkal Brahmans in Orissa.

Jhárukar, a broom-maker; a title applied roughly to several of the low castes.

Jhátiá or *Jhetiá*, a sub-caste of Bauris, Korás and Lohárs in Western Bengal.

Jhátideká, a section of Kurmis in Chota Nagpur and Orissa.

Jhauáit, a territorial section of Binds in Behar.

Jhiniá, a section of Pátnis.

Jhorá, *Khaki*, a small caste of Chota Nagpur, believed by Colonel Dalton to be a sub-tribe of Gonds. Babu Rakhal Das Haldar thought they were Kaibarttas, who had made their way up the valley of the Brahmani and settled in Chota Nagpur. He mentions in support of this hypothesis the fact that the Jhora Málik of parganas Biru and Kesalpur in Lohardagá bears the title Behara, which is used by the Kaibarttas in Bengal. But the title Behara is common among the Dravidian tribes of Orissa, and there is no need to go so far as the Kaibarttas to explain it. The Málik in question calls himself a Gangabans Rajput, and all landholding Jhoras claim similar rank. The Beharas of Biru were bound to supply diamonds to the Maharaja of Chota Nagpur, and several villages are said to have been granted to them on these terms. In the south of Lohardagá and in the Tributary States Jhoras earn a miserable and uncertain livelihood by washing gold in the beds of the streams. Their appliances are primitive to a degree—a scraper in the form of a flattened iron hook set in a wooden handle, and a shallow wooden dish about two feet long and eighteen inches wide. The scraper is used to collect what an Australian would call 'pay-dirt' from the chinks and corners of the rocks in the bed of the stream, and this dirt is then manipulated with water by dexterously rocking the dish this way and that, until the smallest particles of foreign matter have been separated and there remains only a fine deposit of black sand in which tiny specks of gold are seen to sparkle. The use of mercury being unknown, the very small and invisible gold is of course lost. As regards the earnings of the Jhorás, the evidence is necessarily somewhat uncertain. Colonel Haughton was told in 1854 that a vigorous man often earned as much as twelve annas in a day, a sum enormously exceeding the daily wages of unskilled labour, which cannot then have been more than an anna. Mr. Robinson found that men whom he paid at the latter rate got for him from three to four annas' worth of gold; and it may be taken for granted that men working for themselves would earn more than this. Colonel Dalton, on the other hand, speaks of gold washing as a very poor business, at which a man could not expect to earn more than a bellyful (*pet-bhar*) as the Jhorás simply put it. Doubtless the amount varies considerably in different localities, and the Jhoras themselves would be disposed to underrate it for fear the local Rájá might begin to take an interest in the subject. They are, moreover, a depressed and indolent class of people, and are believed to be not entirely free from a superstitious prejudice against trusting too much to their own exertions.

The Jhorás of Lohardagá have three sections—Kásyapa, Krishnátreya and Nag, and they observe the rule that a man may not marry a woman of his own section. In the matter of prohibited degrees supplementing the rule of exogamy, their practice is unusually lax, for they allow a man to marry the daughter of his maternal uncle or his paternal aunt, a departure from the ordinary rules which strikes one as curious. By religion they are Hindus, employing Brahmans as priests and burning their dead in the usual way except in the case of lepers, women who die in childbed, persons who die of small-pox or leprosy, and infants who die before the ceremony of Karnabedh or boring the ear has been performed. The landholding Jhorás profess to marry their daughters as infants in accordance with orthodox Hindu usage; the gold-washing class adhere to the adult marriage characteristic of the Dravidian tribes while untouched by Hindu influence.

Jhorá, a title of Kewats or fishermen in Behar.

Jhumurwála, a class of Mahomedan musicians.

Jhuri, dried bushes, a sept of Mundas in Chota Nagpur.

Jiá, a river fish, a sept of Mundas and Páns in Chota Nagpur.

Jiárwár, a section of the Sátmuliá Maghayá sub-caste of Kándus in Behar.

Jihu, a bird, a sub-sept of the Hansda sept of Santáls.

Jijicha, a *thar* or sept of Sunuwárs in Darjiling.

Jildgar, a book-binder, an occupation followed almost exclusively by Mahomedans.

Jimbá, a section of Murmis in Darjiling.

Jimdar, a title and synonym for Khambu in Darjiling.

Jimel, a *thar* or sept of Gurungs in Darjiling.

Jing-ba, a *rui* or sept of Sherpa Bhotias of Nepal.

Jirábasti, a *mul* or section of the Chhamuliá Madhesiá sub-caste of Halwáis in Behar.

Jirel, a *thar* or sept of Sunuwárs in Darjiling.

Jirhul, a kind of wild flower, a totemistic sept of Mundas in Chota Nagpur.

Jitiapipar, a fruit, a totemistic sept of Mundas in Chota Nagpur.

Jnánbar, a name of a family of Grihasth Jugis in Bengal.

Jog, a hypergamous group of Maithil Brahmans in Behar.

Jogi, a section of Rautiás; a sub-sept of the Saren sept of Santáls; a synonym for Bairági.

Jogidási, a sub-caste of Sunris in Maldah.

Joláhá, a synonym for Jolha.

Jolhá, *Joláhá*, *Juláhá*, *Momin*, the Mahomedan weaver caste of Bengal and Behar. Dr. Wise thinks that they "belonged to a despised Hindu caste who in a body became converts to Muhammadanism." It would seem, however, that the formation of a weaving caste within the ranks of the Mahomedans may be accounted for without supposing that any compact group was converted *en masse*. The structure of the large and heterogeneous aggregate known as the Tánti caste (see article Tánti) suggests, not that all Tántis derive their origin from a distinct tribe devoted to the weaving trade, but that separate weaving castes were formed in different parts of the country out of the materials which were at hand in each case. The same thing may well have happened among the Mahomedans; while the low esteem in which the profession of weaving is held would suffice to cut off those adopting it from intermarriage with their co-religionists.

Origin.

The customs of the Joláhás, says Dr. Wise, are essentially Shíah, and are observed with the punctiliousness which often characterises converts of dubious social position. During the month of Muharram they do not comb their hair, chew betel, or eat from vessels in which fish has been dressed. Besides, on the fifth, sixth, and seventh days of that month they wear the *baddhi* and *kafni* badges of the martyred Imams. In former days the Joláhás were peculiar among Mahomedans in never having the *Kábin*, or marriage settlement, drawn up in presence of the Qázi; but of late years the practice has been introduced, and in addition a *Mahr-Námah*, or deed of settlement, is executed. The titles of Joláhás are Kárigar, Málik, Mandal, and Shikdár. Their headman is called Muátabar.

Manners and customs.

In Behar during the Muharram Joláhá women abstain from chewing betel, combing their hair, using oil or vermilion, and putting spangles (*tikli*) on the forehead. They assume, in short, the garb of widowhood and mourn for Hassan and Hossein as the Greeks mourned for Adonis, sleeping on the bare ground and avoiding intercourse with their husbands. They wear *baddhi* and *kafni* on the 8th of the month, and on the night of the 9th they break their bangles, attire themselves in green *sáris*, and go forth with dishevelled hair, chanting dirges for the murdered Imams.

The following extract from *Behar Peasant Life* shows how low a place the Joláhá occupies in popular estimation. The sayings quoted by Mr. Grierson have very wide currency, and are by no means confined to Behar :—

Social status.

"The Musalman weaver or Jolhá is the proverbial fool of Hindu stories and proverbs. He swims in the moonlight across fields of flowering linseed, thinking the blue colour to be caused by water. He hears his family priest reading the Qurán, and bursts into tears to the gratification of the reader. When pressed to tell what part affected him most, he says it was not that, but the wagging beard of the old gentleman so much reminded him of a pet goat which had died. When forming one of a company of twelve he tries to count them, and finding himself missing wants to perform his own funeral obsequies. He finds the rear peg of a plough, and wants to set up farming on the strength of it. He gets into a boat at night, and forgets to pull up the anchor. After rowing till dawn he finds himself where he started, and concludes that the only explanation is that his native village could not bear to lose him, and had followed him. If there are eight weavers and nine *hukkas*, they fight for the odd one. Once on a time a crow carried off to the roof of the house some bread which a weaver had given his child. Before giving the child any more he took the precaution of removing the ladder. Like the English fool, he always gets unmerited blows. For instance, he once went to see a ram fight and got butted himself, as the saying runs :—

Karigah chhár tamása jáy,
Náhak chot Joláha kháy.

—'He left his loom to see the fun, and for no reason got a brushing.'

"Another story (told by Fallon) is, that being told by a soothsayer that it was written in his fate that his nose would be cut off with an axe, the weaver was incredulous, and taking up an axe kept flourishing it, saying, *yon karba ta gor kátbon, yon karba ta háth kátbon, aur yon karba tah ná–*,—if I do *so* I cut my leg, and if I do *so* I cut my hand; but unless I do *so* my no—, and his nose was off. A proverb—*Jolhá jánathi jau kátai?*—does a weaver know how to cut barley?—refers to a story (in Fallon) that a weaver, unable to pay his debt, was sent to cut barley by his creditor, who thought to repay himself in this way. But instead of reaping, the stupid fellow kept trying to untwist the tangled barley stems. Other proverbs at his expense are—*kaua chalal bás ken, Jolhá chalal ghás ken*,—the weaver went out to cut grass (at sunset), when even the crows were going home; *Jolhá bhutiailáh tisi khet*,—the weaver lost his way in the linseed field, an allusion to the swimming exploit already recorded. His wife bears an equally bad character, as in the proverb—*bahsali Jolhini bápak dánrhi noche*,—a wilful weaver's wife will pull her own father's beard."

The following statement shows the number and distribution of Jolhás in 1872 and 1881. It appears that some Jolhás are considered to be Hindus who are insignificant in number, and as such returned in the Census of the latter year as well as in certain districts of the former year.

District.	1872.	1881.
Bardwan	48	47
Bankura	......	192
Birbhum	205	180
Midnapur	899	......
Hughli }	53	19
Howrah }		......
24-Parganas	478	6
Nadiya	2,327	396
Khulna	......	267
Jessore	9,432	925
Murshedabad	766	199
Dinajpur	74	1,159
Rajshahye	6,023	163
Rangpur	280	40
Bogra	533	2
Pabna	7,793	709
Jalpiguri	17	......
Dacca	10,464	......

District.	1872.	1831.
Faridpur	6,036	319
Bakarganj	3,748	4
Maimansinh	1,138	7
Chittagong	......	56
Gya	144	49
Tirhut { Mozufferpur }	51	......
Tirhut { Darbhanga }		381
Champaran	......	851
Monghyr	77	3,184
Bhagalpur	23,085	21,716
Purniah	......	6,275
Maldah	800	189
Santál Parganas	698	2,356
Hazaribagh	38,144	......
Lohardagá	25,697	13
Singbhum	......	10
Manbhum	4,690	112
Tributary States	250	......

Jonáli, a *pathi* or hypergamous sub-group of Bárendra Brahmans in Bengal.

Jonári, an endogamous division of Páschátya Baidik Brahmans in Bengal.

Jongan, a section of Murmis in Darjiling.

Jonk Haper, leech, a totemistic sept of Mundas in Chota Nagpur.

Joriahá, a section of the Dhusiá sub-caste of Chamárs in Behar.

Joshi, a group of the Adi-Gaura sub-caste of Gaura Brahmans in Behar.

Josiám, a section of Kamárkalla Sonárs in Behar.

Juáng, *Patuá*, a non-Aryan tribe of Keunjhar and Dhenkanal in Orissa, classed by Colonel Dalton on linguistic grounds as Kolarian. Their language is said to approach more closely to the Khariá than to the other Kol dialects; but it has borrowed largely from Uriya, and also contains a number of words of uncertain origin.

Origin.

They are, says Colonel Dalton, a small race like the Oraons, the males averaging less than five feet in height, and the women not more than four feet eight inches. Their predominating physical characteristics appear to be great lateral projection of the zygomatic arches and general flatness of feature; upright, but narrow and low, foreheads projecting over a very depressed nasal bone; pug-noses with spreading nostrils; large mouths, thick lips, receding lower jaw and chin. The hair is coarse and frizzly, the prevailing colour being a reddish brown.

Physical type.

The opinion that the Juángs are closely related to the Mundas and the Khariás derives some support from the fact that the women tattoo their faces with the same marks as are used by these tribes—three strokes on the forehead just above the nose, and three on each temple. They swear on earth taken from an ant-hill and on a tiger skin. The Khariás hold the ant-hill sacred, and the oath on the tiger's skin is in common use among Hos and Santáls.

Head-quarters of the tribe.

The Keunjhar Juángs claim to be the autochthones of the country, and trace their descent on the male side to a race of celestial beings who danced in the Guptaganga hills with the leaf-clad daughters of men and took some of them to wife. The village of Gonasika, which is considered the head-quarters of the tribe, was visited by Colonel Dalton about twenty years ago. He found there twenty-five families of Juángs living in tiny huts measuring about six feet by eight, very low, and with very small doors. These were divided into two compartments—one used for stores, and the other being the living-room of the head of the house and his wife and daughters. The boys of each family slept in a large dormitory near the entrance of the village, which also served as a lodging for guests. All the habits of the tribe were then of the most primitive character. Ironsmiths and smelters of iron were unknown, and there was no word for iron in their language. The arts of spinning and weaving were equally strange to them, and, like the Australian aborigines, they had never attained to the simplest knowledge of pottery.

Manners and customs.

"The females," says Colonel Dalton, "had not amongst them a particle of clothing. Their sole covering for purposes of decency consisted in a girdle composed of several strings of beads, from which depended before and behind small curtains of leaves. Adam and Eve sewed fig leaves together and made themselves aprons. The Juángs are not so far advanced; they take young shoots of the Asan (*Terminalia tomentosa*) or any tree with long soft leaves, and arranging them so as to form a flat and scale-like surface of the required size, the sprigs are simply stuck in the girdle fore and aft and the toilet is complete. The girls were well-developed and finely-formed specimens of the race, and as the light leafy costume left the outlines of the figure entirely nude, they would have made good studies for a sculptor.

The beads that form the girdle are small tubes of burnt earthenware made by the wearers. They also wore a profusion of necklaces of glass beads, and brass ornaments in their ears and on their wrists, and it was not till they saw that I had a considerable stock of such articles to dispose of that they got over their shyness and ventured to approach us."

The men of the Juáng tribe, though still preserving a tradition that they used to wear *kopins* or loin-cloths made from the bark of the *tumba* tree, use instead of leaves a small strip of cotton cloth. Up to a few years ago the women were deterred from following their example by the tradition that the goddess of the Baitarani river "emerging for the first time from the Gonasika rock came suddenly on a rollicking party of Juángs dancing naked, and ordering them to adopt leaves on the moment as a covering, laid on them the curse that they must adhere to that costume for ever or die." In 1870 the curse was removed by Captain F. J. Johnstone, Superintendent of the Keunjhar State, who had acquired great influence with the people, and induced the women to dress themselves in cotton clothes.

The internal structure of the Juáng tribe is shown in Appendix I.

Internal structure.

There are no sub-tribes, and the entire community forms a single endogamous group. The septs are totemistic, the totems comprising the names of animals, trees, and plants. A man may not marry a woman of his own section, and must also observe certain rules regarding prohibited degrees which do not seem to be very precisely defined. I gather, however, that marriage with the descendants of the paternal uncle is prohibited for a certain number of generations, but that the rule is less strict concerning the descendants of a maternal uncle.

Marriage.

As a general rule Juángs give their daughters in marriage only after they are grown up; and sexual license before marriage, though not expressly recognised, is nevertheless tolerated as a necessary incident of a system of free courtship. Of late years instances of infant-marriage have occurred in the tribe; but these were exceptional cases, due to the desire of particular families to imitate Hindu usage. The marriage ceremony is simple. The bridegroom sends a party of his friends to propose for the girl, and if his offer is accepted the wedding day is fixed and a cart-load of unhusked rice delivered by way of bride-price. The bride is then brought to the bridegroom's house by his friends and hers, is dressed in new clothes, and has a set of brass ornaments put on. Consummation follows at once, and the night is spent in feasting. In the morning the bridegroom dismisses the bride's friends with a present of three measures of husked and three of unhusked rice. The presence of a priest is not ordinarily deemed essential, but in some cases the village *dehari* is called in to add a religious sanction by sprinkling rice and turmeric on the heads of the wedded pair.

Polygamy is permitted, and there appears to be no rule limiting the number of wives a man may have. No Juáng, however, says Colonel Dalton, has ventured on more than two at a time; and even this indulgence is only resorted to when the first wife proves barren or faithless. A widow may marry again, and is expected, though not compelled, to marry her deceased husband's younger brother. In the event of her choice falling upon an outsider, she is not allowed to marry until a year after her husband's death. No special ritual appears to be ordained for the marriage of a widow: the bridegroom merely gives her a new cloth and some bracelets, and provides a feast for the elders of the caste. Divorce is permitted, with the sanction of the *panchdyat*, for adultery, disobedience, scolding, and barrenness. The woman is simply taken back to her father's house and left there. In cases of special hardship, where the wife is held not to have been in fault, the husband is required to give a heifer or three or four rupees to the wife's family as compensation for his action in divorcing her. Divorced wives may marry again by the same form as widows.

"The Juángs appear to be free from the belief in witchcraft, which is the bane of the Kols, and perniciously influences nearly all other classes in the Jungle and Tributary Maháls. They have not, like the Khariás, the reputation of being deeply skilled in sorcery. They have in their own language no terms for 'god,' for 'heaven' or 'hell,' and, so far as I can learn, no idea of a future state. They offer fowls to the sun when in distress, and to the earth to give them its fruits in due season. On these occasions an old man officiates as priest: he is called Nágam. The even tenor of their lives is unbroken by any obligatory religious ceremonies."

Religious belief.

My own enquiries lead me to doubt the accuracy of this account. The Juángs of Keunjhar worship a forest deity called Barám, who stands at the head of their system and is regarded with great veneration. Next to him come Thánpati, the patron of the village, also known to the Savars, Másimuli, Kálápát, Básuli, and Basumati or mother earth. Buffaloes, goats, fowls, milk, and sugar are offered to all of these, and are afterwards partaken of by the worshippers. No regular days seem to be set apart for sacrifice, but offerings are made at seed time and harvest, and the forest gods are carefully propitiated when a plot of land is cleared from jungle and prepared for the plough. In addition to these elemental or animistic deities, the Hindu gods Siva, Durgá, and Balabhadra are beginning to be recognised, in a scanty and infrequent fashion, by the tribe. Brahmans as yet have not been introduced, and all religious functions are discharged by the *dehari* or village priest.

Juángs burn their dead, laying the corpse on the pyre with the head to the south. The ashes are left at the place of cremation or are cast into a running stream. A few days after death a meagre propitiatory ceremony is performed, at which the maternal uncle of the deceased officiates as priest. Offerings to departed ancestors are also made in October, when the autumn rice crop is harvested.

Disposal of the dead.

Agriculture is believed to be the original occupation of the tribe. "They cultivate," says Colonel Dalton, "in the rudest way, destroying the forest trees by the deadly process of girdling them, burning all they can of the timber when it dries and sowing in the ashes. They thus raise a little early rice, Indian corn, pulses, pumpkins, sweet potatoes, ginger, and red pepper,—seed all thrown into the ground at once to come up as it can. They declare they subsist every year more on wild roots and fruits than on what they rear, but I doubt if they are so badly off as they pretend to be. The area of their cultivation appeared proportionate to their numbers. They pay no rent, being under obligation to serve the Rájá, repair his house, and carry his burdens when required to do so in lieu of money payment, and they spend no money in clothes; it is difficult to understand, therefore, their not having a sufficiency of wholesome food, unless it be that they spend all their substance in drink.

Occupation.

They are no doubt addicted to ardent spirits, and they are obliged to buy what they consume, as they have not acquired the art of distilling or even of brewing rice-beer, which every Kol understands."

Food.

In regard to food they are not in the least particular, eating all kinds of flesh, including mice, rats, monkeys, tigers, bears, snakes, frogs, and even offal, and for them the jungles abound in spontaneously-produced vegetables. In the quest of such food they possess all the instinct of the animal, discerning at a glance what is nutritive, and never mistaking a noxious for an edible fungus or root.

The Juángs do not look a warlike people, but when urged to it by the Bhúiyas, whose lead they invariably follow, they are sometimes troublesome. They use the bow and arrow, but their favourite weapon is the primitive sling, made entirely of cord. They take "pebbles from the brook," or stones as they find them. They have no idea of fashioning them to produce more efficient projectiles."

Tribal dance.

The tribal dances of the Juángs, which seem to be totemistic in character, are thus described by Colonel Dalton:—

"In one figure the girls moved round in single file, keeping the right hand on the right shoulder of the girl in front; in another, with bodies inclined they wreathed their arms and advanced and retreated in line. In this movement the performance bore a strong resemblance to one of the Kol dances. Then we had the bear dance. The girls, acting independently, advance with bodies so much inclined that their hands touch the ground; thus they move not unlike bears, and by a motion from the knees the bodies wriggle violently, and the broad tails of green leaves flap up and down in a most ludicrous manner.

"The pigeon dance followed: the action of a love-making pigeon when he struts, pouts, sticks out his breast, and scrapes the ground with his wings was well imitated, the hands of the girls doing duty as wings. Then came a pig and tortoise dance, in which the motions of those animals were less felicitously rendered, and the quail dance, in which they squatted and pecked at the ground after the fashion of those birds. They concluded with the vulture dance, a highly dramatic finale. One of the men was made to lie on the ground and represent a dead body. The girls in approaching it imitated the hopping, sidling advance of the bird of prey, and, using their hands as beaks, nipped and pinched the pseudo-corpse in a manner that made him occasionally forget his character and yell with pain. This caused great amusement to his tormentors.

"I had heard of a 'ballet' called 'the Cocks and Hens,' but this they could not be induced to exhibit. It was admitted that it was impossible to keep the leaves in proper position whilst they danced it. It was too much of a romp, especially for a day performance."

Social status.

The social status of the tribe cannot be precisely defined. They are beyond the pale of Hinduism, and no member of any recognised caste will eat or drink with them. Juángs themselves will take cooked food, water and sweetmeats from the Bhuiyás, but a Bhuiyá will not take even water from a Juáng. In course of time no doubt they will attain a higher social position, and the first step in this direction has already been taken by their partial adoption of some of the Hindu gods.

In 1872 the Juángs numbered 9,398 in the Tributary States, while in 1881 only 3 were returned in Cuttack and 606 in the Tributary States.

Jubhingeh, a *thar* or sept of Khambus in Darjiling.

Jugi, a sub-caste of Tántis in Bengal.

Jugi, *Jogi*, a weaving caste of Eastern Bengal, many of whose members have of recent years been driven by the competition of English piece-goods to betake themselves to agriculture, lime-burning, goldsmith's work, and the subordinate grades of Government service. The origin of the caste is extremely obscure. Buchanan thought it probable that they were either the priesthood of the country during the reign of the dynasty to which Gopí Chandra belonged, or Ṣúdras dedicated to a religious life, but degraded by the great Ṣaiva reformer Ṣankara Áchárya, and that they came with the Pál Rájás from Western India. In Rangpur he found the Jogís living by singing an interminable cyclic song in honour of Gopí Chandra. This is all the information collected by that shrewd and trustworthy observer, and since the beginning of the century no fresh facts have been added. The Másya sub-caste of Jugís give the following account of their origin. In the Vrihad Yogini Tantra, their chief religious work, it is written that to Mahádeo were born eight passionless beings (Siddhas), who practised asceticism and passed their lives in religious meditation. Their arrogance and pride, however, offended Mahádeo, who, exercising his power of Máyá or illusion, created eight female energies, or Yoginís, and sent them to tempt the Siddhas. It was soon apparent that the virtue of the perfect ones was not so impregnable as they boasted, and the issue of their amours were the ancestors of the modern Másya Jugís. Another account is that a Sannyásí Avadhúta, or scholar, of Benares, who was an incarnation of Ṣiva, had two sons: the elder, by a Bráhman woman, becoming the progenitor of the Ekádaṣí Jugís—the younger, by a Vaiṣya woman, of the Másya; but it is probable that this legend has been invented to account for the fact that these two sub-castes perform the obsequial rites at different periods.

Traditions of origin.

The Ekadasi Jugís, when questioned about their descent, refer to a Sanskrit work called Vriddha Ṣátátapíya, in which the Muní Ṣátátapa relates how the divine Rishí Nárada was informed by Bráhma that near Benares resided many Bráhman and Vaiṣya widows, living by the manufacture of thread, who had given birth to sons and daughters the offspring of Avadhútas, or pupils of Náthas, or ascetics. The Rishí was further directed to proceed to Káṣí, and in consultation with the Avadhútas, to decide what the caste of these children should be. After much deliberation it was determined that the offspring of the Avadhútas and Bráhman widows should belong to the Ṣiva gotra, while the issue of the

Vaiṣya widows should form a class called Nath; the former, like the Bráhmans, being impure for eleven days, the latter like the Vaiṣya for thirty days. Both classes were required to read four Vedas, to worship their Mátris or female ancestors at weddings, to perform each household for itself the Nándí Ṣráddha in the name of their forefathers, and to wear the sacred cord. It was further enacted that the dead should be buried, the lips of the corpse being touched with fire by the son or grandson. It is from these Brahman widows that the modern Ekádaṣí Jugís claim to be descended, and being of that lineage, mourn for only eleven days, although they have never assumed the Brahmanical cord.

Modern history.

Turning from these mythical events to the history of the caste in more modern times, we find that most Jugís in Eastern Bengal regard the family of Dalál Bazár, in the Noakhali district, as the head of their race, and recall with some pride the fact that in the middle of last century Braja Ballabh Ráí, a Jugí, of this family was Dalál, or broker, his brother Radhá Ballabh Raí being Jachandár, or appraiser, of the English factory of Char Páta, on the Meghna. The son of the former developed the trade in Báftah cloth to so great an extent that the Company in 1765 bestowed on him the title and rank of a Rájá, presenting him at the same time with a *lákhiraj* or rent-free estate, which is still held by one of his descendants.

In the Presidency districts the Jugis are assuming the sacred thread *en masse*, and this pretension has given rise to numerous quarrels with the Brahmans, some of which have ended in protracted and vexatious litigation in the Criminal Courts.

On the evidence now available it is difficult to arrive at any definite conclusion regarding the manner in which the caste arose. There is nothing beyond the fact that they are generally looked down upon by Hindus, and follow a despised occupation to indicate a difference of race. Independent evidence of non-Aryan descent is wholly wanting. There remain the alternatives of degradation or mixed descent, both of which play a prominent part in the standard Indian theory of the formation of castes. But here, again, we have no data to form a basis for serious discussion. For the present, therefore, the problem must be abandoned as insoluble.

Internal structure.

The internal structure of the caste is stated in Appendix I, and may be briefly described here. In Eastern Bengal we find two main sub-castes—the **Másya**, who perform the *sráddha* thirty days (mása) after death, and the **Ekadasí**, who celebrate it after eleven (ekádaṣa) days. The former abound in the southern parts of Bikrampúr, Tipperah, and Noakhali; the latter in the north of Bikrampúr and throughout the Dacca district generally. No intermarriages take place between them, and each refuses to taste food cooked by the other, although they drink from each other's water-vessels. Besides these divisions arising from the observance of different funeral ceremonies, there are others based upon differences of habitat and occupation. The cultivating members of the caste form a distinct group called **Hálwa Jugi**, and it is alleged that they were outcasted for abandoning the traditional pursuit of weaving. The lime-burning Jugis of Tipperah are said to have incurred a similar condemnation. In Murshedabad, on the other hand, the Jugis who lived by weaving cotton cloth are said to have taken to agriculture without qualifying their original designation or forfeiting their position as the recognised main body of the caste; while sub-castes have been formed corresponding to the special pursuits which particular groups have adopted. Among these are the **Rangrej-Jugi**, who dye cotton thread, the **Kambule-Jugi**, who make blankets, and the **Manihári-Jugi**, who work in lac and weave ribands. Others again prefer a division into the three groups **Rárhi**, **Baidik**, and **Barendra**, which seem to have been borrowed from the higher castes in the struggle for social precedence. In Bardwan a fourth division—**Khelinda**—is added to these. In Noakhali this larger territorial grouping appears to be unknown, and the endogamous divisions are given as **Sundip-Náth**, comprising Jugis who live on the island of Sundip, and **Bhuluá-Náth**, or residents on the mainland. Even smaller local divisions occur in some districts. I am informed that in Murshedabad the Jugis of thâná Kandi will not intermarry with the Jugis of thana Barawá, while in Tipperah the Jugis of *pargana* Sarail marry only among themselves.

The **Dharmaghare Jugis**, who are found in Western Bengal, are looked down upon by the Jugis of other parts of the country. They worship Dharma, Sitalá, Manasá, and other aboriginal deities, and their only *sanskár* is the wearing copper in some form, such as that of a ring or bracelet. They beg from door to door, carrying the effigies of those deities in their hands, and singing songs in their honour.

They say that their original progenitor, an ascetic, after obtaining *siddhi*, success in *yog*, married the daughter of Kasyap Rishi and had a son by her. When he died his son went to his grand-father Siva (who is reckoned the father of all those that become ascetics) and asked his advice as regards the disposal of his father's dead body. Siva thought it should be buried after the manner of ascetics, but the widow wished it to be burned, because the deceased had been a *grihastha* or householder. So the son, wishing to please both, compromised matters by putting fire on the mouth of the corpse and then burying it. The more advanced among them affect to follow the Hindu system of the 10 *sanskárs* or *dasakarmas* and to use the same books as the Brahmans, such as the work of Bhabadeb Bhatta, used by all Sámvedi Brahmans. Some of them even attend *tols* or indigenous Sanskrit Colleges, but they have to sit in the courtyard, and are regarded more or less as intruders.

They say that they have only one *gotra*, the Siva, and four *pravaras*—Siva, Sambhu, Sankara, and Ápnabat; but as marriage in the same *gotra* is prohibited, they have devised a fiction by which the bride at the time of marriage becomes a member of the Kasyapa gotra.

The sections of the caste are of a mixed character. Some have clearly been borrowed from the standard Brahmanical series, while others, such as **Matsyendra**, **Goraksha**, and **Birbhairab**, seem to lend support to the conjecture hazarded above that the caste is an offshoot from some sect of ascetics. In some districts the three hypergamous groups of **Kulin**, **Madhyalá**, and **Bángál** appear to be recognised; while elsewhere there are only two Brahman-Jugi and Dandi-Jugi. In both cases the rule is said to be observed that a man of a higher group may marry a woman of a lower group, but a certain loss of social position is entailed by doing so.

Marriage.

Jugis marry their daughters as infants and follow the standard Hindu ritual, a member of their own caste officiating as priest. Their practice as to exogamy and the reckoning of prohibited degrees is the same as that in vogue among the higher castes. A second wife may be taken if the first is barren or suffers from an incurable disease. Divorce is not formally recognized: a woman found guilty of unchastity is cast off by her husband and turned out of the community. Widows are not allowed to marry again.

Religion.

The great majority of the caste worship Mahadeo or Siva, but a few Vaishnavas are also found among them. The Másya Jugís have no Brahmans who minister to them, but a spiritual leader, Adhikárí, elected by the Purohits referred to below, is invested with a cord and styled Brahman. In Tipperah and Noakhali the cord is still worn, but in Dacca of late years it has been discarded. The Adhikárí of the Másya Jugís in Dacca is Mathurá Ramana, of Bídgaon, in Bikrampúr, a very illiterate man, who can with difficulty read and write Bengali. The post has been hereditary in his family for eight generations, and now-a-days it is only in default of heirs that an election is held. It is a curious circumstance that the Adhikárí bestows the *mantra* on the Bráhmans of the Ekádasí, and occasionally on Sannyasi Jugís, although neither acknowledge any subjection to him. The Adhikárí has no religious duties to perform, as each household employs a Purohit to minister at its religious ceremonies. The Purohit is always a Jugí, inducted by the Adhikárí and subordinate to him. He is often a relative, or marries a daughter of his master. The Adhikárí, again, has his Purohit, without whose ministration neither he nor any member of his family can marry or be buried. The great festival of the Másya Jugís is the Sivarátrí, held on the fourteenth of the waning moon in Mágh (January-February); but they observe many of the other Hindu festivals, such as the Janmáshtamí, and offer sacrifices beneath the *bat* tree to the village goddess Siddhesvarí. In all religious services they use a twig of the Udumbara, or Jagyá dúmúr (*Ficus glomerata*), and regard with special reverence the tulasi, bat, pípal, and tamála (*Diospyrus cordifolia*). They have *sthâns*, or residencies, at Brindában, Mathurá, and Gokula, but their chief places of pilgrimage are Benares, Gayá, and Sítakund in Chittagong. The Ekádasí have Brahmans of their own, called "Varna-Sarman," and addressed as Mahátama, who trace their origin from the issue of a Srotriyá Bráhman and a Jugí woman. In Bikrampúr alone it is estimated there are at least a hundred of these Jugí Bráhmans. The majority of this division of Jugís are worshippers of Krishna, but a few who follow the Sákta ritual are to be met with. The Gosáins, who are followers of Nityánanda, admit Jugis into their communion, but those of Adwaita decline to have anything to do with them.

The Jugí Bráhmans are, with few exceptions, illiterate, but a few gain a livelihood as Páthaks, or readers of the epic poems. Jugís are the Mahants of the Kapila Muni shrine in the Sunderbuns, and officiate at the Váruni festival in Phálgun.

Disposal of the dead.

In the burial of their dead all Jugís observe the same ceremonies. The grave (*samádhi* or *ahsan*) is circular, about eight feet deep, and at the bottom a niche is cut for the reception of the corpse. The body, after being washed with water from seven earthen jars, is wrapped in new cloth, the lips being touched with fire to distinguish the funeral from that of a *sannyási* or ascetic and a Mahomedan. A necklace made of the Tulasi plant is placed around the neck, and in the right hand a rosary (*japa málá*). The right forearm, with the thumb inverted, is placed across the chest, while the left, with the thumb in a similar position, rests on the lap, the legs being crossed as in statues of Budha. Over the left shoulder is hung a cloth bag with four strings, in which four cowries are put. The body being lowered into the grave, and placed in the niche with the face towards the north-east, the grave is filled in, and the relatives deposit on the top an earthen platter with balls of rice (*pinda*), plantains, sugar, ghi, and areca-nuts, as well as a *huqqa* with its *chillam* (bowl), a small quantity of tobacco, and a charcoal ball. Finally, from three to seven cowries are scattered on the ground as compensation to Vasumati or mother earth for the piece of earth occupied by the corpse. Women are interred in the same way as men.

The bag with its four cowries, and the position of the body, are noteworthy. With the cowries the spirit pays the Cháran, who ferries it across the Vaitarani river, the Hindu Styx; while the body is made to face the north-east, because in that corner of the world lies Kailása, the Paradise of Siva.

The mourning dress of the Jugís is a cotton garment, called "Jala Kacha," literally netted end, manufactured by them, and identical with that worn by other Hindus between the death of a relative and the *sraddha*. In a corner of this raiment the Jugi ties a piece of iron, suspending it over his shoulder. On the eleventh day, when the funeral obsequies are about to be performed, the barber cutting off the iron, gives it to the wearer, who throws it into the water, then bathes, offers the *pinda* to the manes of the deceased and returns home.

All Jugís believe that the spirits of good men are at death absorbed into the Deity, while the bad reappear on earth in the form of some unclean animal; but women, however exemplary their conduct may have been in this world, are not cheered by any assurance of a future state, and in their case death involves annihilation.

Social status.

The social status of the caste is very low, and they are everywhere reviled by the Hindus without any intelligible reason being given for the treatment to which they are subjected. If questioned on the subject of the low position accorded to the Jugís, some Hindus will reply that it is because they bury their dead, while all orthodox people practise cremation. Others, again, will explain that the starch of size they use in weaving is made of boiled rice (*már*), while the Tántis use parched rice (*khai*) for this purpose. Whatever may be the reason, there can be no doubt as to the existence of a very strong prejudice against the caste, although the Jugís themselves, whom Dr. Wise describes as "a contented people," affect to laugh at it. The belief in their impurity is carried to such a length that the Jugí has peculiar difficulties in having his children educated, as no other boy will live with his son, who is consequently obliged to hire lodgings for himself and engage servants of his own. If men of this caste enter the house of any of the clean castes, all cooked food, and any drinking-water in the room, are regarded as polluted and are thrown away. In spite of this the barber and washerman who serve the Súdras work also for them. Jugís themselves, moreover, are not free from intolerance, but they can hardly be blamed for this in a society where a nice sense of ceremonial impurity in other people is a faculty essential to social advancement. They will, for example, eat food cooked by a Srotriyá Bráhman, but not that prepared by any Barna Bráhman, or by a Ṣúdra, however pure. The Sannyásí Jugí eats with the weaving Jugí, but a Bairágí will only touch food given by the Adhikárí. Furthermore, the Ekádaṣí Jugí will eat with the Sannyásí if he is a Bráhman observing the sráddha on the eleventh day.

Occupation.

Until the last few years the Bengali Jugís were all weavers, but now the cloth (*dhotí* and *gamcha*) manufactured by them is gradually being displaced by English piece-goods, and the Jugí finds it difficult to earn a livelihood by weaving. The Jugí uses a much more cumbrous loom than either the Tántí or Juláha, but employs the same comb, or *shánah*, while his shuttle (*nali*) is peculiar to himself. The women are as expert weavers as the men, the preparation of the warp being exclusively done by them.

The following table shows the number and distribution of Jugis in 1872 and 1881:—

DISTRICT.	1872.	1881.	DISTRICT.	1872.	1881.
Bardwan	7,451	5,364	Chittagong	32,314	27,351
Bankura	439	795	Noakhali	33,038	37,879
Birbhum	2,982	2,272	Hill Tracts	......	11
Midnapur	4,576	5,889	Patna	5,016	1,449
Hughli	} 8,060	{ 2,803	Gya	5,481	2,059
Howrah		4,234	Shahabad	2,914	2,167
24-Parganas	20,903	12,966	Tirhut { Mozufferpur ...	} 7,543	{ 616
Nadiya	15,368	12,374	Tirhut { Darbhanga ...		1,115
Khulna	......	11,085	Saran	3,143	1,047
Jessore	18,931	13,211	Champaran	2,441	494
Murshedabad	5,855	5,240	Monghyr	726	363
Dinajpur	7,741	5,844	Bhagalpur	1,491	1,623
Rajshahye	3,331	2,527	Purniah	5,507	2,098
Rangpur	6,819	4,707	Maldah	......	779
Bogra	4,589	3,650	Santál Parganas	3,493	1,889
Pabna	11,738	1,251	Cuttack	14,514	5,861
Darjiling	100	209	Puri	4,723	1,157
Jalpigori	813	2,111	Balasore	5,422	1,403
Kuch Behar	......	4,431	Tributary States	5,463	1,506
Dacca	16,410	17,080	Hazaribagh	2,067	1,553
Faridpur	1,698	5,312	Lohardagá	3,718	999
Bakarganj	28,198	21,515	Singbhum	1,015	285
Maimansinh	39,644	44,501	Manbhum	2,567	2,069
Tipperah	66,812	55,848	Tributary States	393	315

Jugidiá, a sub-caste of Dhobás in Noákháli.

Jugi Muchi or *Korá*, a sub-caste of Muchis in Bengal.

Juláhá, a synonym for Jolha.

Jungi, a synonym for Jugi.

Jurhá, a *pur* or section of Sákadwipi Brahmans in Behar.

Juruár, a section of Kurmis in Chota Nagpur and Orissa.

Jurvaunt, a section of Awadhiá Hajjáms in Behar.

Jutaut-Bind, a sub-caste of Binds in Eastern Bengal.

Juthasankhwár, a section of Kurmis in Chota Nagpur and Orissa.

Juthibariár, a *pur* or section of Sákadwipi Brahmans in Behar.

Jutiwálá, a dealer in boots and shoes. These articles are made by the Chamár and Rishi, and sold by all Sudras, and even by degraded Brahmans. The bulk of the trade, however, is in the hands of Mahomedans. The business is reckoned highly respectable, and in Eastern Bengal the Mahomedan jutiwalas are strict Farázis, never opening their shops or selling a pair of shoes on a Friday.

Jyotishi, Josi, an astronomer or astrologer. In Bengal the term usually denotes the Ácharji Brahman who prepares horoscopes.

K

Kabái, a section of Majraut Goálás in Behar.

Kabar, a section of Rautiás in Chota Nagpur.

Kabári, a synonym for Kunjrá in Behar.

Kabar Tantwa, a sub-caste of Tantwas or weavers in Behar.

Kabi-ballabh, a title or popular designation of Baidyas practising medicine, used by themselves.

Kabi-bhusan, a title or popular designation of Baidyas practising medicine, used by themselves.

Kabi-Indra, a title or popular designation of Baidyas practising medicine, used by themselves.

Kabiji, a title of Bháts.

Kabiráj, *Kabi*, a physician, a synonym for Baidya.

Kabiráj, a medical practitioner according to the Hindu system. The most respected among them, says Dr. Wise, are generally Baidyas. Kabírájs usually assume bombastic titles, such as Kabí-ratna, Kabí-ranjan, Kabí-chandra, Kabí-Indra, Kabí-bhúshana, Kabí-ballabha, and Baidya-nidhí; but the popular nickname for all doctors is Nárí-tepá, or pulse-feeler. Uneducated practitioners and quacks are known as Háthuria,[1] or meddlesome fellows, from *háth*, the hand; while a still more objectionable and dangerous character is the Ta'líqa Kabíráj, who goes about with a list (ta'líq) of prescriptions, selling them at random, and vaunting their virtues in curing all diseases. He is often a plucked student of the Calcutta College, or a young man too poor to prosecute his studies until qualified for graduation.

Formerly medicine was taught in páthsálas, or schools, the most famous being those of Bikrampur and Kánchrapárá, on the Hughli; but at the present day each practitioner of any reputation has a *tol*, or class, of pupils to whom he translates and expounds the Sástras, if the youths understand Sanskrit, but if they do not he merely lectures on the principles and practice of Hindu medicine. A class generally consists of from ten to twelve young men of various Súdra castes, and it is computed that about 12 per cent. of the Dacca Kabírájs are sufficiently versed in Sanskrit to interpret it.

The two principal text-books of the Bengal physicians are the Mádhava Nidána, or commentary on the Áyur-veda, and the Chakra-vání. The former, written by a celebrated doctor, Mádhava-Kara, chiefly treats of the diagnosis of diseases, while the latter, named after the writer, who was physician and steward of the court of Gaur, is a later and less valued work. Each Kabíraj has a particular master and system, but the greatest teacher, Dhanvantarí, the physician of the gods, is obeyed by all. In the Brahma-

[1] Buchanan, iii, 142, derives this sobriquet from *hát*, a market.

Vaivartta Purána the names of fifteen great physicians are preserved, but only the following are invoked by the modern doctor, namely :—

Dhanwantari.	Kási Rája.
Divodasa.	Nakula.

Sahadeva.

The first three are often identified with one person; the fourth and fifth are the twin sons of Súrya, the physicians of Svarga, or heaven. On all occasions of anxiety Mahádeva, or Vaidyanátha, "lord of physicians," is also addressed in prayer.

The chief causes of the stagnation of Hindu medicine, which has lasted from prehistoric times, appear to be the discontinuance of the study of anatomy; the belief that the medical Sástras, being of divine origin, are infallible; and the selfishness of successive generations of physicians in concealing the results of their experience and observation. Kabírájs of the present day often blindly follow the teaching of the Áyur-veda, notwithstanding the opinion that the habits and constitution of the human race and the prevailing type of diseases, have altered since the archaic days of their teachers.

The candid physician confesses that his brethren have not the magnanimity to divulge the merits of a drug which chance or experience has taught them to value; and although it is revealed to a son or favourite pupil, the secret is kept from the profession at large, and consequently is often lost at the death of the discoverer.

The real Baidya always dispenses his own prescriptions; but as this consumes much time and necessitates his limiting the number of his patients, apprentices are employed in pounding and triturating drugs, while the minute subdivision into powders is done by himself in a private recess of the house. Before beginning his work, the Baidya observes a custom, peculiar to physicians of his caste, namely, the worship of Vaidya-nátha, after which the medicine is divided into four parts, one being offered to the Elements, a second to a Bráhman, a third being retained by the physician, and a fourth sent to the patient. As a rule drugs are procured from the shop of the Gandha-banik, or Pansárí, but in olden days the physician had to go himself to the forest and collect whatever herb he wanted.

Consultations are usually held in difficult cases, but the physician who can quote the Sástras most fluently and interminably is too often deemed the most learned and skilful doctor. Although the Sástras declare that physic given by the hands of a Baidyá has an intrinsic virtue not possessed when it is administered by any other caste, the populace have no such conviction, and as soon as the treatment of a Baidya fails the patient has no hesitation in placing himself under any other doctor, whatever his caste or colour, who has acquired the reputation of curing his particular ailment.

The present state of Hindu medicine in Bengal is sketched in the following particulars, obtained from the Kabírájs themselves.

Kabírájs believe that the human race has degenerated, and that the constitutions of the present generation have changed, and they cite as an instance the type of fever now prevalent, which is more acute and less tractable than the fevers described in the Sástras. In these works it is enjoined that for seven days no medicines are to be given to a patient, and that he is to fast, or only take liquid food; but now, as soon as a diagnosis is formed, and a propitious hour found, the first dose is given. The examination of the pulse is regarded of primary importance, and many doctors are credited with being able to distinguish a disease by its character. The inspection of the urine is not considered, as it is by the Hakím, of much value, for should a drop touch the physician he becomes unclean, and must at once bathe. When it is inspected the sample is always mixed with mustard oil, and the density of the water estimated by the buoyancy of the oil.

Venesection is never performed at the present day, as the type of the ordinary diseases contra-indicates its use; but cupping or leeches are occasionally ordered. In apoplexy and some forms of hysteria the actual cautery is still employed, and the potential cautery (kshára) is used for destroying piles, and, in a fine state of division, is made into an embrocation and applied over the enlarged spleen and liver.

In the Sástras enemata are recommended, but, whether owing to the clumsy syringes employed, or to the strange aversion of all Eastern nations to their use, Hindu physicians ceased to order them. Kabírájs, however, are beginning to follow the example of English doctors, but much latent opposition is encountered.

Hindu physicians have arrived at the following conclusions regarding the most valued European drugs. Quinine, in extensive use throughout Bengal, is popularly regarded as a heating remedy, and as causing, when injudiciously used, the fever to take a permanent hold, or to return after a short interval. The masses further believe that it drives the fever into the bones, and that if once taken it prevents all other febrifuges from being of the slightest benefit. As a tonic, however, during convalescence from fever, it is admitted by all to be invaluable and unequalled. In extreme cases of fever, after violent delirium has set in, a pill containing a small quantity of cobra poison (*bish bari*), mixed with other ingredients, is administered by the Kabiráj. When a man is at the point of death and all other medicines have been tried, bits of all the other pills are pounded together and mixed with honey or juice of the betel leaf and given as the last resource.

With educated practitioners the use of mercury has quite gone out of fashion, and iodide of potassium taken its place; but the victims of its abuse are still lamentably common, and scarcely a hospital in Bengal is ever without several poor creatures permanently maimed or disfigured by it.

English or American sarsaparilla is not much esteemed, as a *pát* or *páchan* of from nine to sixty ingredients is considered a better alterative. The patient being given twenty-one powders, made of a jumble of herbs, takes one daily and boils it in a seer of water until only a quarter remains; then straining and putting aside the sediment, he drinks the decoction. After the twenty-one days have expired, all the sediments are taken, reboiled, and the decoction drunk for eleven days longer. Finally, the sediment is put into boiling water, and with it the patient takes a vapour bath (bhápra).

Cod-liver oil is considered inferior as a nutrient tonic to divers pills and powders prepared by Kabírájs, and in consumption an oil, called *sárchandanadi*, made of til oil and numerous herbs, is pronounced more beneficial.

Chicken broth, prohibited in health, is often prescribed in lingering diseases, while the good effects of port wine and brandy in the treatment of low types of fever are acknowledged.

Pills prepared at English druggists are objected to, as the magnesia sprinkled over them interferes, it is thought, with the action of the medicine: consequently the Hindu pills, rolled with the fingers and mixed with honey or the juice of the *bela*, or *pán* leaf, are preferred.

Such are the condition and opinions of the better class of native physicians, but the description would be incomplete if it omitted all allusion to the uneducated practitioner met with in every village of Bengal, who secures an extensive, and by no means unprofitable, practice among classes unable to pay for better medical advice. He is often a superannuated barber, or fisherman, who has obtained from some strolling "bairágí" or "faqír" a recipé to cure all diseases. There is perhaps no single complaint which so often awakens the inventive faculty of such men as enlargement of the spleen, and he who acquires notoriety as the possessor of a remedy is courted by all classes. A very nutritious diet of milk, fish, and vegetables is always ordered by these shrewd observers, and is generally assigned by sceptics as the explanation of cures which they undoubtedly sometimes effect.

An amateur doctor, residing in the outskrits of Dacca, earned a lasting reputation by using a vesicatory made with the root of the "Kálá-chítra," and applied over the spleen. He, however, assigned much of its efficacy to a secret invocation, addressed, in the act of applying the paste, to Lakshí Náráyana. The Hindu, moreover, relies as much on the virtues of a cup of water over which a mantra has been mumbled as any Muhammadan peasant, and the water of the Ganges, water taken from a tidal river at the turn of the tide, or water in which the Gosáin has bathed, have each their crowd of admirers.

In Bengal, as in ancient Egypt and Greece, certain shrines are still celebrated for the cure of intractable diseases. The most famous are those of Tárakesvara, in Hughli, sacred to Mahádeva; of Vaidyanátha, in the Santál Parganas; and of Gondalpárá, in Hughli, famous in cases of hydrophobia. The device followed at the last place is for the bitten person, after fasting, to defray the expense of a special service, and to receive a piece of red broadcloth (Sultání banát), impregnated with the snuff of a lamp wick and secreted in the heart of a plantain called *kathali kalá*. As long as this charm is preserved, and the patient abstains from eating this variety of plantain, the effects of the bite are warded off. Another plan is for the patient to take a secret medicine, probably cantharides, pounded with 21 pepper-corns, before the 21st day. The effect of this is to make the patient pass urine and mucus—the latter, believed to be *kukur ka bachá*, 'the dog's whelp,' leading to cure.

Kabiráj, a title of the headmen of the Dom caste in Behar, who have under them servants called Chharidárs to execute or communicate their orders.

Kabiranjan, a title or popular designation of Baidyas practising medicine, used by themselves.

Kabi-ratna, a title or popular designation of Baidyas practising medicine, used by themselves.

Kabirdás, *Kabirpanthi*, *Kabri*, a follower of the religious reformer Kabir (1488–1512), who taught a monotheistic and tolerant form of Vaishnavism.

Kableár, a section of Káyasths in Behar.

Kábra, a section of Mahesris.

Kach, tortoise, a totemistic sept of Bhuiyás in Chota Nagpur.

Kách, crab, a totemistic section cf the Paripál sub-caste of Sunris in Manbhum.

Kacháisá, a sub-caste of Kurmis in Behar.

Kácharu, a small caste of Eastern Bengal, who claim to be an offshoot of the Káyasths, and tell the following story to explain the separation :—A rich and aspiring Káyasth determined on celebrating the worship of Kálí in his own house, contrary to the wishes of his brethren, and performed the ceremony, but was punished by being excommunicated. This is a most improbable story, as the Kácharu caste is dispersed throughout Eastern Bengal, being very numerous at Madáripúr in Faridpur, and it has a Purohit of its own. The Súdra barber and washerman work for them, although their water-vessels are unclean. It is far more probable that, if they ever were Káyasths, which is unlikely, they were expelled, like the Chhotá-bhágiya Tantis, for adopting a new trade.

The caste has three gotras—Aliman, Kasyapa, and Parásara. Their patronymics are Datta, Dás, and Dé. The principal festival kept is in honour of Viswa-Karmá in Bhádra (August-September).

In Dacca the Kácharu are gradually relinquishing their caste trade, the manufacture of lac bracelets (*kácha*), in which Muhammadans also engage, and are acting as traders, grocers, and shopkeepers.

Kachá Simar, a *mul* or section of the Satmuliá or Kishnaut sub-caste of Goálás in Behar.

Kachchhap (the tortoise), a totemistic section of Bágdis, Bhars and Máls in Western Bengal.

Kachchhuá, a section of Cheros in Chota Nagpur.

Kachera, a *mul* or section of the Kanaujia sub-caste of Sonars in Behar.

Kachgawai, a section of the Amashta sub-caste of Káyasths in Behar.

Kach Gotra, a section of the Banwár sub-caste of Baniyás in Behar.

Káchhati, a *gáin* of the Bharadwája *gotra* of Bárendra Brahmans in Bengal.

Káchhgot, a totemistic section of Nuniás in Behar.

Kachhrá, a section of the Karan sub-caste of Káyasths in Behar.

Kachhriyá, a sept of the Rautár sub-tribe of Thárus in Behar.

Káchiári, a section of Kurmis in Chota Nagpur and Orissa.

Káchim, tortoise, a totemistic section of Kumhárs in the Santál Parganas; a section of Telis in Bengal.

Káchimár, a section of Kurmis in Chota Nagpur and Orissa.

Kachnariá, a sept of Rajputs in Behar.

Kachoár, a *mul* or section of the Tinmuliá Madhesiá sub-caste of Halwáis in Behar.

Kachrá-Mech, a sub-tribe of Meches in the Darjiling Terai.

Kachu, a title of Bangaja Káyasths in Bengal.

Kachuá, Kachhuá, or Kachchh, tortoise, a section of Kanaujiá Halwáis in Behar. The use of the word to distinguish an exogamous group may perhaps be regarded as a survival of totemism; a *gotra* or section of Hindu Jolahas and Goálás in Behar. A sept or section of Chiks, Lohárs, Goráits, Gonds, Ghásis, Oraons, Mundas, Turis, Tántis, Telis, and of Doms in Chota Nagpur; a sub-sept of the Kisku sept of Santáls, Asuras, Binjhiás, Goálás, Bedias, Bhuiyas, Chamárs, and Kharwars in Chota Nagpur; also of Khandaits in Orissa, and of Kámárs in Singbhum and the Santál Parganas.

Kachui, a sept of the Tungjainya sub-tribe of Chakmás in the Hill Tracts of Chittagong.

Kachwá, a tortoise; the totem of a section of Oraon-Dhángars settled for several generations in Behar; a sept of Rajputs in Behar.

Kachwáha, a sept of the Suryabansi sub-tribe of Rajputs in Behar.

Kádá, a *mul* or section of the Chhamuliá Madhesiá sub-caste of Halwáis in Behar.

Kádáchási, a title of Kaibarttas in Bengal.

Kadál, a *gáin* of the Sándilya *gotra* of Rárhi Brahmans in Bengal.

Kadam, *nauclea grandifolia*, a totemistic section of Khandaits in Orissa.

Kádar, a sub-caste of Kádars.

Kádar, *Bhuiyá*, a non-Aryan caste of cultivators, fishermen, and day-labourers in Bhagalpur and the Santál Parganas, probably a degraded offshoot from the Bhuiyá tribe. They are divided into two sub-castes—**Kádar** and **Naiyá**—the latter of which may possibly have been developed from among the priests of the forest gods, who are usually called Láyá or Náyá in Western Bengal. There is also a separate caste bearing the name Naiyá, the members of which disown all connexion with the Kádar. The sections of the Kádar are shown in Appendix I. Among them we find Rikhiásan, the characteristic eponym of the Musahars and the Northern Bhuiyás. Most of the others have names familiar as titles

Origin.

Internal structure.

of the lower castes in Behar. These have become exogamous groups among the Kádars, while at the same time the system has been greatly complicated by the fact that owing to supposed differences of descent and social standing some of the groups only intermarry with certain other groups. In all cases the rule of exogamy is one-sided, and alliances with near relatives not excluded by that rule are barred by the standard formula *mamerá*, *chacherá*, etc., calculated in the descending line to seven generations on the father's side and three on that of the mother. The conclusion suggested by a careful examination of the list is that the Kádar caste was originally a branch of the Bhuiyás, but has since been recruited from other sources. The vagueness of the word Bhuiyá would obviously rather lend itself to this process. Whatever may be the origin of the Kádars, they are certainly a group of considerable antiquity, for they are referred to in the account of the origin of the human race communicated to Lieutenant Shaw by the Mál Pahariás in 1798.

Marriage.

Kádars marry their daughters as infants or as adults, according to their means, the former practice being deemed the more respectable. Their marriage ceremony is of the type common among low-caste Hindus, *sindurdán* being the binding portion. The village barber officiates as priest. Polygamy is allowed in the sense that a man may take a second wife if he has no children by his first wife. Widows may marry again by the *sagai* form, and are subject to no restrictions in their choice of a second husband except those arising from the prohibited degrees. The ceremony consists simply of the application of vermilion to the woman's forehead in the presence of her relatives. It deserves notice that the Kádar custom requires a *sagai* marriage to be performed in the open air, and will not permit it to take place within the house, thus reversing the ordinary practice under which the marriage of a virgin is celebrated in the courtyard, while the less reputable *sagai* ritual is relegated to the women's apartments at the back of the house. Divorce is freely permitted, and divorced women may marry again.

Religion.

Special interest attaches to the religion of the Kádar as representing a comparatively early stage in the process of conversion to Brahmanism, which the aboriginal races of Bengal are now undergoing. The real working religion of the caste is in fact pure animism of the type which still survives, comparatively untouched by Hindu influences, among the Santáls, Mundás, and Oraons of Chota Nagpur. Like these, the Kádars believe themselves to be compassed about by a host of invisible powers, some of whom are thought to be the spirits of departed ancestors, while others seem to embody nothing more definite than the vague sense of the mysterious and uncanny with which hills, streams, and lonely forests inspire the savage imagination. Of these shadowy forms no images are made, nor are they conceived of as wearing any bodily shape. A roughly-moulded lump of clay set up in an open shed, a queer-shaped stone bedaubed with vermilion,—this is all the visible presentment that does duty for a god. Their names are legion, and their attributes barely known. No one can say precisely what functions are allotted to Káru Dáno, Hardiyá Dáno, Simrá Dano, Pahár Dáno, Mohanduá, Lilu, Pardona, and the rest. But so much is certain that to neglect their worship brings disasters upon the offender, death or disease in his household, murrain among his cattle, and blight on his crops. In order to avert these ills, but, so far as I can gather, without the hope of gaining any positive benefit from gods who are active only to do evil, the Kádar sacrifices pigs, fowls, goats, pigeons, and offers ghi, molasses, and heads of Indian corn in the *sarna* or sacred grove where his deities are believed to dwell. The priest is a man of the caste who combines these sacred functions with those of barber to the Kádars of the village and neighbourhood. The offerings are eaten by the worshippers. For all this the Kádars, if questioned about their religion, will reply that they are Hindus, and will talk vaguely about Parameswar, Mahádeo, and Vishnu, as if they lived in the very odour of orthodoxy instead of being, as in fact they are, wholly outside of the Brahmanical system. To talk about the Hindu gods is usually the first step towards that insensible adoption of the externals of Hinduism which takes the place of the formal and open conversion which sterner and less adaptive creeds demand. The next thing is to set up Brahmans whose influence, furthered by a variety of social forces, gradually deposes the tribal gods, transforms them into orthodox shapes, and gives them places in the regular Pantheon as local manifestations of this or that well-known principle, or relegates them to a decent and inoffensive obscurity as household or village deities. Last of all, if the tribe is an influential one, and its leading men hold land, they give themselves brevet rank as Rajputs.

Disposal of the dead.

Kádars burn their dead and bury the ashes at the place of cremation on the second day after death. On the thirteenth day a sort of propitiatory sacrifice is performed, which is repeated after an interval of six months. No periodical offerings are made for the benefit of ancestors in general.

Social status.

The social rank of the caste is very low if judged by the current standard of food. Doms and Háris are the only people who will take either food or water from the hands of a Kádar, and though he himself will eat with Kahárs and Bhuiyás, neither of these will return the compliment. Kádars eat beef, pork, fowls, and field-rats, and indulge freely in strong drink. Concerning beef the Kádars, on whose statements this article is mainly based, were careful to explain that they only ate the flesh of cattle that had died a natural death. This they said with reference to the popular belief that Kádars kill and eat cattle while grazing in the jungle. Most of the caste are agricultural day-labourers, and comparatively few have got land of their own or acquired occupancy rights. Fishing and wood-cutting are their other occupations. On certain occasions they worship the axe and sickle as symbols of their craft.

Occupation.

In 1872 there were 7,120 Kádars in Bhagalpur, while in 1881 they numbered in Gya 13, Darbhanga 4, Saran 5, Bhagalpur 11,470, and Santál Parganas 6,952.

Kádaral, Kádare, a section of Bábhans in Behar.

Kadayán, Kadián, a section of Goálás in the North-Western Provinces and Behar.

Káet, a synonym for Káyasth.

Kaethoar, curry vegetable, a totemistic sept of Lohárs.

Kághazi, a paper-maker, an occupation carried on exclusively by Mahomedans.

Kahál, a synonym for Kahar.

Kahár, a sub-caste of Tántis in Behar.

Kahár, a large cultivating and palanquin-bearing caste of Behar, many of whose members are employed as domestic servants by Natives and Europeans. The Brahmanical genealogists represent the Kahar as a mixed caste descended from a Brahman father and a Nisháda or Chandál mother; but it seems more likely that they are a remnant of one of the primitive races who occupied the valley of the Ganges before the incursion of the Aryans. In one sense, indeed, the Kahars may perhaps be regarded as a mixed caste, since their ranks have probably been recruited by members of other castes who adopted the same profession, while their employment as domestic servants in high-caste families may well have led to some infusion of Aryan blood. Like the Bauris and Bágdis of Bengal, they admit into their community Brahmans, Rajputs, Káyasths, and Kurmis and children of Kahar women by men of those castes on condition of performing certain religious ceremonies and giving a feast to the heads of the caste. Instances of men born in a higher caste applying for enrolment as Kahars are probably rare, and occur only when the applicant has been turned out of his own caste for an intrigue with a Kahar woman. Still the mere existence of the rule seems to show that such things do happen sometimes; and in any case the admission of the children of Kahár women by men of the higher castes must have had some effect on the type. The physical appearance of the caste rather bears out the view that they are of mixed descent. Their features often approach the Aryan type, but they generally have darker complexions than are met with among the higher castes. Mr. Nesfield renders the name Kahár as 'water-carrier,'[1] and considers the caste to be sprung from fishing tribes, such as the Gondh, the Turaha or Dhuria, and the Dhimar. He adds that Kahár is ambiguous as a caste designation, and is given specifically "to that caste which has entirely, and for many generations continuously, withdrawn from the occupation of fishing, boating, etc., and which now exclusively devotes itself to domestic service." Another, and I think more plausible, explanation is given by Sir Graves Haughton (Bengali-Sanskrit Dictionary, s.v. Kahár), who suggests that the word may be a corruption of *kandh* + *bhar*, meaning a man who bears burdens on the shoulder.

Traditions of origin.

Kahárs themselves claim descent from Jarásandha, king of Magadha, and tell an absurd story to account for their name.

[1] Lassen says (see his remarks quoted in article **Kewat**) that *Ka* is seldom used in this sense.

Bhagawán, it is said, had a beautiful garden on the Giriyak hill near Rájgir, in Gya, which in a year of unusual drought was nearly destroyed. He therefore promised the hand of his daughter and half his kingdom to any one who should water the garden plentifully with Ganges water in a single night. Chandrawat, the chief of the Kahárs, undertook the task. He built the long embankment called the Asurabándh to bring the waters of the Báwan Gangá to the foot of the hill, and from the reservoir thus formed his tribesmen watered the garden with a series of swing lifts (*chánr*). When Bhagawán saw the work was done, he repented of his promise to give his daughter to a man of low degree, and caused the cock to crow before dawn, at the same time taunting the Kahárs with having failed in their undertaking. Deceived by this ruse, and fearing that Bhagawán would slay them for attempting to win his daughter for their chief, the Kahárs fled in haste, and when morning broke not a man was there to claim fulfilment of the promise. Their flight was so hurried that they carried with them the implements used for watering the garden. Those who took the bamboos were called Kahárs, those who took the ropes were called Magahiyá Brahmans, while two other classes got the names of Dhánuk and Rajwár, for some reason which the story does not disclose. It is added that Bhagawán afterwards took pity on the Kahárs to the extent of paying them three and a half seers of food-grain (*anáj*) per man, and this or its money value is the proper wage of a Kahár to this day.

The following sub-castes of Kahárs are found in Behar:—

Internal structure.

Rawáni or Ramáni, Dhuria, Dhimar, Kharwárá, Turhá, Jaswar, Garhuk or Garauwá, Bisariá, and Magahiyá. The origin of these groups is obscure, and the distinctions between them seem to be very imperfectly understood. Some say that in former days there were no sub-castes at all, and that the entire caste had its head-quarters at Ramanpur, near Gya. The chief, however, married two wives, who quarrelled so violently that he was compelled to remove one of them to Jaspur. Her descendants formed the Jaswar sub-caste, while the members of the family who remained at Ramanpur were known as Ramánis or Rawánis. The Dhuriá are boatmen and fishermen, and also collect the *singhárá* or water chestnut (*Trapa Bispinosa*, Roxb.) The Dhimar carry palanquins, catch fish, make nets, and are employed as field-labourers and coolies. The Kharwárá say they came from Khairágarh, and may possibly be Kharwárs who have taken to carrying palanquins. The Turhá believe dealing in fish and vegetables to be their original occupation, but they cultivate and carry palanquins like the other sub-castes.

Among the Rawáni Kahárs of the Santál Parganas we find the

Marriage.

totemistic sections Nág and Kásyapa, while the same sub-caste in Behar have a local section, called Rawanpur. For the most part, however, the caste appears to have lost its sections, and marriage is regulated by the standard formula for reckoning prohibited degrees calculated to seven generations in the descending line. Some, however, say that the prohibition extends as far as any relationship can be traced. Girls are usually married in infancy, but this is not absolutely indispensable, and no disgrace attaches to a family which is unable on account of poverty to get its daughters married before the age of puberty. The marriage ceremony is of the standard type, and appears not to differ materially from that described by Mr. Grierson in *Behar Peasant Life*. Polygamy is allowed, but the number of wives a man may have is limited to three. A widow may marry again by the *sagai* form, and is not compelled to marry her deceased husband's younger brother, though it is considered very proper for her to do so. When a widow marries an outsider, he is expected to pay a bride-price of Rs. 2 to her relatives and a fee of Re. 1 to the headman of the caste. Divorce is permitted on the ground of adultery with the sanction of the pancháyat, and divorced wives may marry again. If a woman is convicted of an intrigue with a man of a lower caste, who would not be eligible for admission into the Kahár community, she is at once excommunicated. But if her paramour is a Brahman, Rajput, Kayásth, or Kurmi, the offence may be condoned by giving a feast to the pancháyat. This is a strong and well organised body, on which every head of a family is bound to serve when summoned. It is presided over by a *sardár*, whose office is hereditary. Under him, again, is a *chharidár* or staff-bearer, charged with the duty of calling the pancháyat together and seeing its orders carried out.

Religion.

So far as the worship of the greater gods is concerned, the religion of the Kahárs is much the same as that of other castes of similar social standing. Most of them are worshippers of Siva or the Saktis, and the proportion of Vaishnavas among them is very small. Members of the Rawáni sub-caste observe a peculiar worship in honour of Ganesa on the seventh day of the waxing moon of Kártik (October-November), when, accompanied by Brahmans, they proceed to a wood and make offerings of vegetables, fruits, and sweetmeats under an *ámlá* tree (*Phyllanthus emblica*), but never sacrifice any animal. A feast is then given to the Brahmans, after which the Kahárs dine and drink spirits to excess. The entertainment of Brahmans on this day is accounted as meritorious as the gift of five cows on any other occasion. In addition to Dák, Kartá, Bandi, Goraiya, Dharam Ráj, Sokhá, Sambhunáth, and Rám Thákur, whose worship is common throughout Behar, the caste pay special reverence to a deified Kahár called Dámubir, before whose effigy, rudely daubed in red and black paint, goats are sacrificed and betel leaves, sweetmeats, and various kinds of cakes offered at marriages, during harvest time and when illness or disaster threatens the household. As a rule these rites are performed only by the members of the family, who share the offerings among themselves. In Bhagalpur, however, the Maithil or Kanaujiá Brahmans, who serve the caste as priests of the greater gods, are called in to sacrifice to Dámubir, and receive half of the offerings as their perquisite. Mondays, Wednesdays, and Fridays are the days set apart for the worship of Dámubir. Throughout Behar the status of the Brahmans who work for Kahárs as priests appears to be a comparatively degraded one, and they are not received on equal terms by other members of the sacred order. The *guru* of the caste is often a Bairágí or Nanak-shahi ascetic. Kahárs burn their dead and perform the ceremony of *sraddh* on the thirty-first day after death. The ashes are buried near the burning place under a small platform of mud, on the top of which a *tulsi* tree is planted.

Occupation.

Agriculture, palanquin-bearing, and service in the houses of the higher castes, are the chief occupations of Kahárs at the present day. Mr. Nesfield, who regards the Kahár as an offshoot from one of the fishing castes, lays stress on the fact that "his primary function is that of drawing and bringing water for the bath or the table, and this has led to his being employed for various other uses, such as taking care of clothes, dusting the rooms, kneading the *chapati* preparatory to cooking it, carrying the palanquin, etc." It is, however, equally probable that the functions of the caste were developed in an order the reverse of that laid down by Mr. Nesfield. People who were qualified to perform the respectable duty of bringing drinking-water to men of the higher castes would hardly take to the comparatively menial occupation of carrying palanquins. Moreover, the fishing castes have always been regarded as specially unclean, and on the face of things would be the last people chosen for a duty so closely bound up with the caste system as that of giving water to their betters. On the other hand, when the members of a particular caste had once been established as palanquin-bearers, their employers would always be tempted on the ground of mere convenience to promote them to the higher duties of personal service. The fact of a man being on a journey has always been recognised as a ground for relaxing the strict letter of the rules regarding food and drink, and it would often happen that while travelling a man would have no one but his Kahárs to look after his personal wants. I have even heard it alleged against some of the landholders in Chota Nagpur, where proper Kahárs are scarce, that they had manufactured (*banáyá*) Kahárs out of Bhuiyás, Rajwárs, and the like in consequence of the trouble they were put to by having to travel with men from whose hands they could not take water without losing caste.

Social status.

Kahárs engaged in personal service consider themselves superior to those who merely carry palanquins or till the soil, and demand a higher bride-price when they give their daughters to them in marriage. Cultivating Kahárs are rarely found occupying any higher position than that of occupancy raiyats, while many of them are landless day-labourers paid in cash or kind.

Socially the caste ranks with Kurmis and Goalas, and Brahmans will take water and certain kinds of sweetmeats from their hands. Traces of their lowly origin may perhaps be discerned in the fact that many of them will eat fowls and even field-rats, and all except the Bhakat or ascetic members of the caste indulge freely in strong drink. Mr. Sherring says that some of them eat pork, but this does not appear to be the case in Behar or Chota Nagpur. In spite of this comparative laxity of diet, they observe some curious prohibitions of their own. Thus a Kahár engaged in personal service with a Brahman, Rajput, Babhan, Káyasth, or Agarwál, will only eat his master's leavings so long as he is himself unmarried. They are also particular to explain that their women may not wear nose-rings or have their foreheads tattooed.

Members of the caste domiciled in Bengal proper.

It was stated in the first paragraph of this article that the Kahárs are properly a Behar caste. A certain number of them, however, regularly seek employment outside beyond that province, and some of them become regularly domiciled. The following particulars regarding these outlying branches of the caste are taken from Dr. Wise's notes:—

The Kahár, being the most docile and industrious of workmen, is in much request throughout Bengal, and of late years he has been in great demand as a coolie for the tea gardens of Assam, Kachar, and Chittagong. A few also come yearly from Chaprah, being employed in the city of Dacca as coolies, porters, and domestic servants; but they always return home as soon as a little money has been saved.

Kahárs domiciled in Bengal, and known as Dolíya, are proscribed by their Hindustáni brethren, because, having ceased to observe the peculiar customs of the caste, they have adopted those of the despised Bengali Súdras. The Dolíya are met with along the old post road between Dacca and Calcutta, and at Mansúrábád, on the Padma river, twenty-five houses are occupied by them, while in Farídpur still larger settlements occur. Palanquin travelling being no longer the custom in the country, the Dolíyas have become cultivators, domestic servants, and palanquin-bearers in cities. The Rawání Kahár is an eager and indefatigable sportsman, but the Dolíya is content to catch fish in traps, and has given up hunting and snaring game. In one respect the Dolíya is unchanged. Spirit-drinking is to him, as to the Rawání Kahár, the *summum bonum* of life, but he rejects pork, which is still a favourite article of food with his Híndustání kinsmen. The Dolíyas, rejected by the Kahárs and by the Bengalí Súdras, have a Bráhman of their own, and all belong to a gotra called Aliman. The majority are Saiva worshippers, but a few are Vaishnavas.

In Bengal the Hindi name, Mahará, is applied to any palanquin-bearers not Kahárs, and in Dacca bearers either belong to the Mitra Sení subdivision of the Bhúinmálí caste or to the Kándho branch of the Chandál. A few Muhammadan palanquin-bearers, called Doli-wálas or Sawári-wálas, may occasionally be picked up, but their numbers are yearly diminishing.

Last century the title Kahár was at Patna the distinctive appellation of a Hindu slave, as Mauläzádah was of a Muhammadan; and the tradition in 1774 was that the Kahár slavery took its rise when the Muhammadans first invaded Northern India.[1] So Buchanan observes that the Rawánis have been entirely reduced to slavery; nor does any one of them pretend to a free birth, but many procure

[1] *Slavery in India*, by James Peggs, p. 6.

their liberty by the inability of their masters to maintain them, and many more are allowed to do as they please for a subsistence.

The following statement shows the number and distribution of the Kahárs in 1872 and 1881:—

DISTRICT.	1872.	1881.	DISTRICT.	1872.	1881.
Bardwan	1,156	1,744	Chittagong	7	2,063
Bankura	124	571	Noakhali	1,148	1,776
Birbhum	938	2,873	Hill Tracts	50	......
Midnapur	1,193	3,156	Patna	74,721	86,863
Hughli	947	1,409	Gya	106,788	118,644
Howrah		2,065	Shahabad	52,064	71,946
24-Parganas	10,491	2,921	Tirhut { Mozufferpur ...	33,320	39,544
Nadiya	2,583	1,526	Tirhut { Darbhanga ...		18,010
Khulna	......	1,352	Saran	31,566	56,536
Jessore	3,466	4,707	Champaran	12,629	46,628
Murshedabad	3,416	4,769	Monghyr	40,703	49,202
Dinajpur	758	3,661	Bhagalpur	22,127	31,348
Rajshahye	520	1,209	Purniah	9,758	18,117
Rangpur	707	3,986	Maldah	2,741	3,147
Bogra	211	864	Santál Parganas	12,918	16,385
Pabna	376	2,656	Cuttack	......	476
Darjiling	49	964	Puri	......	8
Jalpigori	178	1,577	Balasore	......	196
Kuch Behar	......	187	Tributary States	......	10
Dacca	1,456	1,898	Hazaribagh	24,674	36,849
Faridpur	1,910	3,842	Lohardaga	22,720	33,183
Bakarganj	557	361	Singbhum	175	329
Maimansinh	199	4,273	Manbhum	5,829	6,880
Tipperah	217	125	Tributary States	660	1,346

Kahhál, an oculist, a profession followed by both Hindus and Mahomedans. In Darbhanga there are schools of ophthalmic surgery, and Hindu oculists from that district travel about Behar in the cold season when operations can be most safely undertaken. Many oculists belong to the Khatri caste. In Eastern Bengal similar schools exist, but they are in the hands of Mahomedans.

Káhinoár, a *mul* or section of the Tinmuliá Madhesiá sub-caste of Halwáis in Behar.

Kahráur, a sept of the Chandrabansi division of Rajputs in Behar.

Kah-tsho-bo, a *rui* or sept of Dejong Lhoris in Darjiling, the members of which are of a low mixed origin.

Kahu, crow, a sub-sept of the Besrá sept of Santáls.

Kaiáre, a *mul* of the Bátsya section of Maithil Brahmans in Behar.

Kaibartta, a sub-caste of Kewats in Bengal.

Kaibartta, *Kaibartta-Dás, Chási-Dás, Háliá-Dás, Parásar-Dás, Dhivara, Khyán*, a large fishing and cultivating caste of Bengal Proper, taking rank below the Nava-sakha, or group of nine castes, from whose hands a Brahman may take water.

Traditions of origin.

No serious attempt can be made to trace the origin of the Kaibartta. The physical characters of the caste are not marked enough to throw any certain light on their descent, while their exogamous divisions, having been obviously borrowed from the Brahmans, contribute in no way to the solution of the question. All that can be said is that they are one of the characteristic castes of the deltaic districts of Bengal, that the nucleus of the group was probably Dravidian, but that their original cast of feature may have been to some extent refined by a slight infusion of Aryan blood. The type as it stands at present is distinctly an intermediate one, equally removed from the extreme types of Aryan and Dravidian races found in Bengal.

There seem to be good grounds for the belief that the Kaibarttas were among the earliest inhabitants of Bengal and occupied a commanding position. Many centuries ago five separate princedoms—Tamralipta or Tamluk, Bálisita, Turka, Sujamuta, and Kutabpur—are said to have been founded by them in the Midnapur district, and it is perhaps not unreasonable to infer from this tradition that that part of the country must have been one of the earliest seats of the tribe. The fact that none of them are now found occupying the position of large landholders is readily accounted for by the extinction of some families and the transformation of others into pseudo-Rajputs.

Concerning the etymology of the name Kaibartta there has been considerable difference of opinion. Some derive it from *ka*, water, and *vartta*, livelihood; but Lassen says* that the use of *ka* in this sense is extremely unusual in early Sanskrit, and that the true derivation is *Kivarta*, a corruption of *Kimvarta*, meaning a person following a low or degrading occupation. This, he adds, would be in keeping with the pedigree assigned to the caste in Manu, where the Kaibarta, also known as Márgava or Dása, is said to have been begotten by a Nisháda father and an Ayogavi mother, and to subsist by his labour in boats. On the other hand, the Brahma-Vaívartta Purána gives the Kaibartta a Kshatriya father and a Vaisya mother, a far more distinguished parentage; for the Ayogavi, being born from a Sudra father and a Vaisya mother, is classed as *pratiloma*, begotten against the hair, or in the inverse order of the precedence of the castes.

In another place† Lassen mentions a story told by an obscure Greek writer, Orthagoras, in his book *On Things Indian*, how the people of the village Koythos fed their goats upon fish, and goes on to say "seeing that in popular speech the name of the mixed caste *Kaibarta*, to whom the business of boating and fishing has been allotted, must become *Kevatta*, and the *v* would drop out in Greek, this village, doubtless situated on the sea or on a river, must have derived its name from the fact that it was inhabited by Kaibartas." Whatever may be thought of this as a specimen of a kind of conjecture of which Indian antiquarian research furnishes too many examples, the passage seems to deserve quotation partly for the curious and characteristic story which it contains, and partly for the opinion which it expresses that Kewat and Kaibartta are merely two names for the same tribe, or at any rate for the same occupation. Kaibartta, the Sanskrit or Prakrit form, has been preserved in Bengali, and is still in general use as the name of the caste in question, while the shorter form Kewat has become current in Behar.

* *Ind. Alt.* i, 770.

† *Ind. Alt.* iii, 342.

The simplest explanation of the relation between the Kaibartta and the Kewat appears then to be that both belonged to one and the same tribe, but that the branch which settled in Behar gradually became endogamous and adopted a Hindi name, so that the two groups are now virtually distinct castes and have been so treated in this book. Numerous instances could be cited in which endogamous groups originally formed within the body of an existing caste have in course of time severed their connexion with the parent group and come to be accepted as distinct castes. As is usual in such cases, the two groups stand, or affect to stand, on a different social level, and the group bearing a Sanskritised name arrogates to itself some sort of undefined superiority. In Orissa, on the other hand, the two names are current side by side; but Kaibartta is used by members of the caste, while only outsiders have the bad taste to talk of Kewats.

In the case of the Kewat and Kaibartta several legends have arisen to account for the separation of the two branches, which deserve notice for the light they throw upon the growth of this sort of folklore. One of these tells how in Bengal there was a powerful tribe called Kewat, whom Ballál Sen raised to the grade of pure Sudras, conferring on them the title of Kaibartta in return for their undertaking to abandon their original profession of fishing. The Kanaujia Brahmans, however, refused to officiate for them on their promotion, and the Vyásokta Brahmans were appointed to be their priests. Now these Brahmans are either the descendants of, or, as another story has it, were appointed by Vyása, himself the son of a fisher girl, Matsyagandhá, by Parásara Muni. The Kaibarttas of Bengal claim the same parentage, and allege that at the great assemblage of the castes before Ballál Sen they urged their right, as the descendants of the Muni Vyása, to be included among the Nabasákha. But Ballál Sen refused to listen to their plea, and allotted them one of the most degraded priests. At the present day the Brahmans who serve the Kaibartta are so generally despised that no clean Sudra will touch anything cooked by them, and in reality they rank beneath the Sudra.

A variety of legends are current in the Midnapur district concerning the origin of the Vyásokta Brahmans, who serve the Kaibarttas as priests. They are said to be descended from Barhu, a sage who composed heterodox Puránas and was cursed by Brahmá with the curse that he and his descendants should be priests to men of the Sudra caste. In consequence of this curse the Vyásoktas were told off to serve the Kaibarttas, the children of Bidur, on the banks of the Sarjyu river.

Another story tells how the Kaibarttas rendered a great service to Ballál Sen and were told to name their reward. They asked the King to compel the local Brahmans to serve them as priests; but the Brahmans refused to obey, and the King, in order to keep his promise, vowed that the first man he saw in the morning should be made the Kaibarttas' priest. Next morning early when the King looked out the first man he saw was his own sweeper sweeping out the courtyard. This was not quite what the Kaibarttas meant, but the

King's vow had to be kept, so the sweeper was invested with the sacred thread and sent to minister to the Kaibarttas.

A third legend says that after the Kaibarttas had settled in Midnapur a certain Kaibartta merchant dug a big tank in Parganá Kásijora. To consecrate this tank a Brahman had to be got who could kindle the sacred fire by the breath of his mouth. The Vyásokta were unequal to this feat, but a Drávida Brahman performed it. His caste brethren expelled him for having served a low caste, and he therefore settled in Midnapur.

Like the Kaibarttas themselves, the Kaibartta Brahmans of Midnapur are divided into two sub-castes, **Uttar Rárhi** and **Dakhin Rárhi**, the names of which enable them to pose before the ignorant as Rárhi Brahmans. Members of the higher castes, however, who will take water from the hands of the Kaibarttas will not take it from Kaibartta Brahmans, and the Kaibarttas themselves will not eat food cooked by their own Brahmans.

Internal structure.

The internal divisions of the caste differ in different districts. They are shown in tabular form in Appendix I. The exogamous divisions have been borrowed from the Brahmans and, as has been observed above, give no clue to the origin of the caste. The endogamous divisions are based either upon occupation or upon habitat, but these distinctions are not everywhere recognised to the same extent: thus in Central Bengal and Maldah we find the cultivating and fishing groups, variously called **Hálik** and **Jálik** or **Chásá** and **Jálwah** or **Jáliyá**, clearly differentiated, while in Dacca there is no **Chásá** or **Halwaha** division, and the **Dás Kaibarttas** have not yet separated into a distinct caste. In the latter district the Jalwah or fisher Kaibarttas are all members of one gotra, the Aliman, and have the common title of Dás, but a few individuals who practise medicine have assumed the title of Baidya. In Hughli there are four sub-castes, two territorial—**Uttar-rárhi** and **Dakhin-rárhi**—and two occupational, **Jeliyá** or **Málá**, who live by fishing, and **Tutiyá**, who rear silkworms. The name of the last group is derived from *tut*, the mulberry tree, on the leaves of which silkworms are fed.

The divisions of the caste in Bakarganj are curious and interesting, and deserve somewhat fuller examination by reason of the light they throw upon the process by which endogamous classes are formed, and even upon the growth of the caste system itself. There the Kaibarttas are divided into two groups—a cultivating group, known as **Háliá Dás, Parásara Das** or **Chási Kaibartta**, and a fishing group, known simply as **Kaibartta**. Clearly the latter group represents the main body of the caste, while the former comprises those Kaibarttas who have abandoned their original occupation and betaken themselves to the more respectable profession of agriculture. But the separation has not been long enough in force, or has not gained sufficient acceptance to render the two groups completely endogamous. Intermarriage is permitted between them, but is restricted by certain conditions. Girls of the Háliá-Dás class can be given in marriage to Kaibarttas, but if a man of the former class marries a Kaibartta girl, his family is deemed to have been guilty of a *mésalliance*, and descends a step in social estimation. Such marriages frequently take place, but a substantial price is paid by the Kaibartta family for the privilege of getting a bridegroom from the higher class. Similar relations exist in Jessore between the HELO, ploughing, and MECHO or fishing Kaibarttas. Among the Háliá Dás themselves the following families have the titular rank of Kulin:—Kálá Ráy, Háliá Bálái, Jádab Ráy, Bhuban Kuri, Mánji, Samaddár, Charmanái Ráy, and Majumdár. All the rest are classed as Bángáls. Kulins and Bángáls may intermarry, but the latter must pay to the former a bride or bridegroom-price for the honour which an alliance with them confers. The Kaibartta in their turn are divided into Chandradwipi and Bára hazári, the former being the superior group and demanding a premium in case of intermarriage. The following titles denote Kulin families:—Káwár, Mandal, Mánji, Páthar and Sikdár, the rest are Bángáls.

The subdivisions of the Dakhin-Rárhi group—Lalchatái, Eksidé, Dosidé, and Mákunda—found in Midnapur are of an uncommon type, and seem to have been originally hypergamous as regards the Lalchatái, the highest of the series. It is explained that they used to have a 'red mat' to sit on, as a mark of social distinction, at the meetings of the Kaibartta caste. The next two names are based on a marriage custom. The Eksidé, when they go with a wedding procession to fetch the bride, will not eat in her father's house on the wedding night. He therefore sends them a present (*side*) of food, which they cook and eat in a neighbour's house. The Dosidé extend this to the night after the wedding, and therefore are described as two-present men. Mákunda is said to be an eponymous group. They carry their own wedding presents to the bride's house, and they eat cooked food with any Kaibartta, whether he belongs to their class or not.

The Háliá Dás have the following sections:—Álamyán, Kásyap, Bharadwáj, Parásar, and Ghrita-Kausik, of which only the first two are recognised by Kaibarttas. But in both groups the rule prohibiting marriage within the section, though admitted to have been binding in former times, has fallen into disuse of late years. In Orissa, on the other hand, traces of totemism still survive among the caste, and the rule of exogamy is invariably enforced. I may remark here that in regard to the observance of this rule Eastern Bengal presents a remarkable contrast to Western Bengal and Behar. Not only is the number of sections recognised in any particular caste peculiarly small, but the law of sectional exogamy is often disregarded altogether. It may be conjectured that this is due in some measure to the example of the Mahomedans of the eastern districts. Islam knows nothing of exogamy, and enjoins the marriage of first cousins as a peculiarly suitable alliance. The large Mahomedan population of Eastern Bengal, coming of the same race as the Hindus and maintaining close social relations with them, could hardly fail to exercise considerable influence on their matrimonial arrangements.

Marriage.

Like most orthodox Hindus, the Kaibarttas of Bengal perform the ceremonial marriage of their daughters before they attain puberty, and sometimes when they are only three years old. The girls, however, do not go to live with their husbands until they are fully grown up. Complaints, indeed, are not uncommon of a girl being kept at home by her people to assist in household work long after the time when she was physically capable of entering upon married life. In the case of males marriage is often delayed by inability to pay the *pan* or bride-price for a suitable maiden, which runs rather high among respectable Kaibarttas, and may amount to as much as Rs. 200 or Rs. 300. Polygamy is permitted in this sense and to the extent in which it is permitted to orthodox Hindus; but in practice it is very rarely resorted to. Widows may not marry a second husband. Divorce is permitted on the ground of adultery, but divorced wives are not allowed to marry again.

The Kaibarttas of Orissa depart in certain material points from the orthodox standard in matters concerning marriage. Infant-marriage is allowed to be the more excellent way, and most parents endeavour to follow it; but no disgrace attaches to the marriage of a girl after puberty. The widow is allowed to marry again, and is expected to marry her late husband's younger brother. The ceremony is a simple one. A feast is given to the members of the caste, and a bracelet is put on the right wrist of the bride. Divorce may be effected by a *chhadapatra* or letter of divorce, written in the presence of the headman and a few of the leading members of the caste. Divorced wives are allowed to marry again.

Widows.

In connection with the recognition of widow-marriage in Orissa, I may mention the tradition current in the Contai subdivision of Midnapur that in the Amli year 1223 a famine occurred in those parts and some widows took to themselves second husbands. The chief Kaibartta Rájá is said to have put a stop to the practice. Can we argue from this that widow-marriage, still current among the Kaibarttas of Orissa, survived among the Kaibarttas of Bengal down to 1223?

Religion.

In religion the Kaibarttas conform to the ceremonial observances of Hindus in general. With very few exceptions, the entire caste belongs to the Vaishnava sect, their guru being a Gossain and their purohits *patit* or *barna* Brahmans. The period of mourning in Bengal Proper is thirty days, as is appointed for Sudras; but in Midnapur this is reduced to fifteen, and in Orissa to ten.

The characteristic festival of the caste is the *Jálpálani*, or laying by of the net, which begins on the 1st of Mágh (January–February). From this date commences a close period, lasting from two and a half to seven days, during which no fishing operations are carried on. On the last day the river Ganges is worshipped, the net being spread on the bank and smeared with red lead. Offerings are made to the river goddesses, prayers recited by the caste Brahman, and a live kid thrown into the water, which in Eastern Bengal becomes the perquisite of the Bhuinmáli or Pátni.

So far as I can ascertain, there are no minor gods peculiar to the caste. It is said, however, that Sitalá, the departmental goddess of small-pox, and Chandi, a form of Káli, are worshipped with especial devotion in Kaibartta villages. The offerings made to these two goddesses on ordinary occasions consist of rice, sweetmeats, fruits, and small coins. Goats are sacrificed and clothes and ornaments presented in fulfilment of vows made by persons suffering from illness or in recognition of some special stroke of good luck. Neither Sitalá nor Chandi have as yet attained to the dignity of having regular temples and images or special priests set apart for their service. In Bengal the caste Brahman of the worshipper, in Behar a Chatiyá or Bhakat, performs the simple ritual which custom prescribes. A rough block or slab of stone set up under a *pipal*, *banyan*, or *seorhá*[1] tree, smeared with red lead and bathed in clarified butter or milk, represents to the mind of the villagers an ill-defined, but formidable power, which must be propitiated at regular intervals on pain of sickness or death.

Another *grám devatá* or village deity of the same type commonly worshipped by Kaibarttas is Bura-Buri, literally old man and old woman, a well-known androgynous divinity of Eastern Bengal, which is believed to have been adopted by Hinduism from some more primitive system of belief. The annual festival of Bura-Buri falls on the Paush-Sankránti, or last day of the month of Paush, corresponding to December and January.

Occupation.

In the occupation of the cultivating Kaibarttas there is as a rule nothing to distinguish them from other Hindu castes who are engaged in agricultural pursuits. It is said, however, that in former days all Kaibarttas used to allow their bull calves to be castrated. In course of time it came home to them that this practice was abhorrent to all good Hindus, and a few families bound themselves to give it up. Their descendants now call themselves Lakhi-Náráyan, to denote their zeal in the cause of religion, and Tera-ghariá, to keep in remembrance the fact that thirteen families took part in the original resolution. All cultivating Kaibarttas now abstain from the practice in question. Regarding the fishing Kaibarttas of Eastern Bengal, Dr. Wise has collected some interesting information. When a man of this class has saved some money his first idea is to give up fishing and become a fishmonger (*nikári*), using in his leisure hours a cast net, but no other. Kaibarttas generally cultivate a field of hemp for their own use, or, if they hold no land, give an advance to a neighbour and get a patch planted out. They themselves prepare the fibre; their wives spin it; and in this way nets, ropes, and twine are manufactured.

Kaibarttas are the chief curers of fish in Eastern Bengal. They work during November and December, when fish are most abundant and the weather is cool. Early in November a piece of land is leased by the water side, and the fishermen of the neighbourhood are

---

[1] *Trophis aspera.* The Sanskrit name is sákhota. It is also known as Pisácha-dru, Pisácha-briksha or Bhuta-briksha, the tree of ghosts or goblins.

engaged to bring in large quantities of the small *poti* or *ponti* fish. The fish is placed between mats and trodden under foot and then slowly dried in the sun. No salt is used. The product is exported to districts where fish cannot be got in the cold weather. In Maimansinh larger fish are gutted, dried in the sun, and buried in pits. When dug up at the beginning of the rains, it is known as *sukhti*, and is exported to Sylhet and Kachar, where it is esteemed a great delicacy.

Social status.

The social status of the Kaibartta is not altogether easy to determine, as the fisher sub-castes would necessarily occupy a lower position than purely agricultural groups. The Háliá Kaibarttas are usually allowed to smoke in the same hooka with members of the Nava-sákha, and this fairly marks their position as standing first below that group. The same privilege is not accorded to Jáliyá Kaibarttas. At present Brahmans will not take water from the hands even of the Háliá sub-caste, but it seems likely, as time goes on, that this sub-caste will rise in social estimation, and will altogether sink the Kaibartta, so that eventually it is possible that they may succeed in securing a place with the Nava-sákha, an elastic group, which has already been expanded beyond its original limits.

The following statement shows the number and distribution of Kaibarttas in 1872 and 1881:—

District.	1872.	1881.	District.	1872.	1881.
Bardwan	56,702	31,592	Faridpur	13,649	24,010
Bankura	12,644	25,250	Bakarganj	29,341	18,080
Birbhum	11,081	9,129	Maimansinh	77,798	94,217
Midnapur	692,140	753,435	Chittagong	3,692	4,544
Hughli	} 288,620	142,526	Noakhali	20,263	16,151
Howrah		155,653	Tipperah	53,866	50,290
24-Parganas	182,486	179,758	Chittagong Hill Tracts ...	......	7
Nadiya	114,857	126,063	Darbhanga	484	379
Jessore	44,001	32,505	Saran	6	......
Khulna	......	25,895	Champaran	471	......
Murshedabad	102,517	100,355	Monghyr	55	......
Dinajpur	38,301	37,785	Bhagalpur	311	207
Rajshahye	60,440	63,154	Purniah	56,321	44,221
Rangpur	35,396	30,612	Maldah	27,566	23,556
Bogra	14,833	15,566	Santal Parganas	2,994	10,749
Pabna	19,255	23,306	Cuttack	......	5,129
Darjiling	24	219	Balasore	......	861
Jalpigori	2,970	5,838	Tributary States	......	319
Kuch Behar	......	2,678	Singbhum	......	800
Dacca	32,317	40,422	Manbhum	......	5,140

Kaibartta-Dás, a synonym for Kaibartta.

Káibtár, a section of the Dharkár sub-caste of Doms in Behar.

Kaikyal, a *thar* or section of Nepáli Brahmans.

Kailiá, a section of Bháts.

Kailwár, a sept of the Chandrabansi division of Rajputs in Behar; a section of Majraut Goálás.

Káin, Káinya, Kaiyá, a synonym for Sonár. In Darjiling and the Nepal Terai the word Káinya denotes a native of the plains who carries on business as a trader and money-lender, and is more especially used as a title of Marwaris, and generally of traders and money-lenders from Upper India.

Kainrála, a *thar* of the Mautkaha *gotra* of Nepáli Brahmans.

Kaiobanuár, a section of Kurmis in Chota Nagpur and Orissa.

Kairálá, a section of Kámis; a *thar* or sept of Mangars in Darjiling.

Kairawár, illegitimate issue, a section of Kurmis in Chota Nagpur and Orissa.

Kaisab, corruption of *Kásyapa*, a section of the Ayodhiá sub-caste of Hajjáms and of the Bhojpuriá sub-caste of Nuniás in Behar.

Kaisale, a sept of Lohárs in Chota Nagpur.

Kaisár, a section of Ghásis in Chota Nagpur.

Káit, a synonym for Káyasth.

Kaita, Kaith, curry vegetable, a totemistic sept of Chiks, Oraons, and Ahirs or Goálás in Chota Nagpur.

Kaithar, a section of the Biyáhut and Kharidáhá Kalwárs in Behar.

Kaitháwar, *Kaithá*, a sept of Asuras in Chota Nagpur.

Káiwar, a *mul* or section of the Ghosin sub-caste of Goálás in Behar.

Káji, a sept of Thárus in Behar.

Kajol, a sub-caste of Goálás in Bengal.

Kákan, a sept of the Surajbansi division of Rajputs in Behar.

Kákas, a section of Goálás in the North-Western Provinces and Behar.

Kákin, aunt, a totemistic sept of Mundas in Chota Nagpur.

Kakir, a sept of Rajputs in Behar.

Kakkar, a section of the Bárajáti sub-caste of Khatris in Bengal.

Kák ká Rakmal, a section of Kalwárs in Behar.

Kakra, hyena, a totemistic sept of Oraons in Chota Nagpur.

Kakroliá, a section of Goálás in the North-Western Provinces and Behar.

Kaksa, a section of Majraut Goálás in Behar.

Kákulu, a sept of Tipperahs in the Hill Tracts of Chittagong.

Kákusthi, a *mel* or hypergamous sub-group of Rárhi Brahmans in Bengal.

Kál, a section of Bágdis in Bengal.

Kalá, a sept of Chakmás in the Hill Tracts of Chittagong.

Kalaen, a section of Awadhiá Hajjáms in Behar.

Kalágáchi, a section of Pátnis in Bengal.

Káláí, a *gáin* of the Bátsya *gotra* of the Uttar-Bárendra Brahmans in Bengal.

Kalaigar, a tinman, a profession followed mostly by Mahomedans. *Occ.*

Kalait, a section of Lohárs in Behar.

Kalá Kháti, a *thar* or sept of Dámis in Darjiling, the members of which are drummers by profession.

Kalál, *Kalwár*, (i) in Bengal Mahomedan distillers and liquor-sellers, who are regarded as outcastes by reason of their profession, so that other Mahomedans will not eat, drink, or intermarry with them. Synonyms: *kárigar*, *mistri*, used by themselves; *sharábwálá*, looked upon as derogatory: (ii) in Behar the term *kalál* denotes a Mahomedan and *kalwár* a Hindu liquor-seller. A distiller is called *bhatthidár* or *ábkár*, and in Sáran *ránki*.

Kaláliá, a section of Goálás in the North-Western Provinces and Behar.

Kalalohár, a *thar* or sept of Mángars in Darjiling.

Kalálsunri, a sub-caste of Sunris in Behar.

Kálánuá, a section of the Biyáhut and Kharidáhá Kalwárs in Behar.

Kálá Ráy, a hypergamous group of Kaibarttas in Bakarganj.

Kálásan, a *mul* or section of the Naomuliá or Goriá sub-caste of Goálás in Behar.

Kalasdih, a *mul* or section of the Chhamuliá Madhesiá sub-caste of Halwáis in Behar.

Kaláwat, a sub-caste of Brahmans in Behar.

Kalemniá, a section of Bábhans in Behar.

Kalganiá, a section of Goálás in the North-Western Provinces and Behar.

Kálhans, a sept of Rajputs in Behar.

Kalhia, a section of Ghásis in Chota Nagpur.

Kali, a sept of Tipperahs in the Hill Tracts of Chittagong.

Kaliá, a title of Chási Kaibarttas and Sadgops in Bengal.

Káligrámi, a *gáin* of the Bátsya *gotra* of Bárendra Brahmans in Bengal.

Kálihái, a *gáin* of the Bátsya *gotra* of Bárendra Brahmans in Bengal.

Kálimba, tobacco flower, a totemistic sept of Juángs in Orissa.

Kálindi, a sub-caste of Doms in Bengal who are cultivators and basket-makers. Their chief occupation is basket-making, but they are employed to kill dogs, remove dead bodies, and sometimes as executioners. The name is said to refer to their being worshippers of the goddess Káli. A *gáin* of the Bátsya *gotra* of Bárendra Brahmans in Bengal; a title of Jáliyas.

Kalinwál, a section of Goálás in the North-Western Provinces and Behar.

Kalipa, a religious group of Jugis.

Kalit, a *mul* or section of the Kamarkalla sub-caste of Sonars in Behar.

Kallani, a section of Mahesris.

Kalmi, a section of Telis in Bengal.

Kalmut, a section of Brahmans in Behar.

Kalot, a section of Goálás in the North-Western Provinces and Behar.

Kalsarea, a man who works at a *kalsar*, the place where the juice of sugarcane is expressed.

Kalu, a sub-caste of Telis in Bengal and Orissa; also a synonym for Teli, and a title of Mahomedan oil-pressers and sellers in Northern Bengal.

Kálui, a *gáin* or sub-section of Saptasati Brahmans in Bengal.

Kalundiá, a sept of Hos in Singbhum.

Kalupitá, a term used in Western Bengal to denote a

hardworking man of the aboriginal castes, such as Báuris, Bágdis, and the like.

Kalvisha, a section of Brahmans and Káyasths in Bengal.

Kalwadiá, a section of Goálás in the North-Western Provinces and Behar.

Kalwár, a sub-caste of Baniyás and Sunris in Behar.

Kalwár, a liquor-selling, distilling, and trading caste of Behar, probably a degraded offshoot of one of the numerous branches of the Baniyás. Mr. Nesfield regards the name as "a variant of *Khairwár* or catechu-maker, a process which is very similar to that of drawing juice from the palm-tree and fermenting it into a spirit;" and adds that this etymology "implies that the caste has sprung out of such tribes as Chain, Khairwár, Musahar, etc., all of whom are skilled in making the intoxicating juice called catechu." It seems, however, more likely that *Kalwár* is a corruption of *Kalwálá*, a man who works a *kal* or machine; while there is no evidence whatever to connect the Kalwár with the jungle races who collect catechu, an astringent extract from the wood of several species of acacia, which, so far as I am aware, has no intoxicating properties.

Origin.

The caste is divided into six sub-castes—**Banodhiá**, **Biyáhut** or **Bhojpuri**, **Deswár**, **Jaiswar** or **Ajodhiábási**, **Khálsá**, and **Kharidáhá**. Mahomedan liquor-sellers are called **Ránki** or **Kalál**. Of these the Banodhiá say they came from the north-west of the Roy Bareilly district about a hundred years ago. The Biyáhut pretend that in former years they did not permit widows to marry again, though they admittedly to do so now. Another story is that they are descended from the *biyáhi* wife of the common ancestor of the caste, while the other sub-castes were the offspring of a *sagai* wife. They will not drink or sell alcoholic liquor, and will not milk cows with their own hands or allow bullocks to be castrated. The Kharidáhá, who are said to derive their name from a village in Gházipur, observe the two latter restrictions, but do not object to selling drink. The Jaiswár sub-caste are alleged to be the illegitimate descendants of a Kalwár by a mistress called Jaisiá. They themselves derive their name from a village called Jaispur, the precise locality of which they are unable to state. Most of the sub-castes appear to have sections of the territorial type, and to observe the standard formula stating prohibited degrees. The Biyáhut and Kharidáhá forbid a man to marry a woman of his own section, or of the sections to which his mother, his paternal grandmother, and his paternal great-grandmother belonged. One of the sections of the Jaiswár group is denoted by the curious formula *Báwan gali, tirpan bázár, chhatis lahr, battis parkár;* for a further notice of which see article **Báwan**. Jaiswárs follow the same rule regarding excluded sections as the Biyáhut and Kharidáhá sub-castes, except that they substitute the maternal grandmother for the paternal great-grandmother.

Internal structure.

Members of the Biyáhut and Kharidáhá sub-castes marry their daughters between the ages of five and twelve years; Jaiswárs from five to ten; while

Marriage.

Banodhiás regard from seven to fourteen as the marriageable age for a girl. Boys are married between eight and fourteen, but all sub-castes agree in holding it proper for the bridegroom to be a few years older than the bride. The marriage ceremony is of the standard type, *sindurdán* being the binding portion. Banodhiá Kalwárs omit the preliminary forms known as *ghardekhi*, *bardekhi*, and *panbáti*. The *tilak* paid to the parents of the bridegroom never exceeds a maximum amount of Rs. 21. Polygamy is permitted up to a limit of three or, as some say, four wives. It is not very clear, however, whether the permission to take more than one wife is not in any case conditional on the first being barren, and the practice of the caste on this point seems to vary in different districts. Widows are allowed to marry again by all sub-castes, and no restrictions are placed on their freedom of choice. Biyáhut Kalwárs, as has been stated above, say that they derived their name Biyáhut, 'the married,' from their prohibiting widow-marriage. But there is no independent evidence in support of their statement, and it is *primâ facie* unlikely that they should have retraced their steps after having travelled so far in the path of orthodoxy. Divorce is not generally recognised, a woman taken in adultery being simply turned out of the caste. In Champaran, however, the rule seems to be more lax, and divorced wives are allowed to marry again by the *sagái* form.

Religion.

Vaishnavism is the favourite religion of the caste, but in addition to the regular Hindu gods the Biyáhut and Kharidáhá offer rice and milk to Sokhá on Mondays during the light half of Sawan; goats and sweetmeats to Káli and Bandi on Wednesdays and Thursdays; and sucking pigs and wine to Goraiyá on Tuesdays. On Saturdays within the same period the Jaiswár sub-caste present cakes and sweetmeats to the Pánch Pir, while the Banodhiá make similar offerings to Barham Deo on the eleventh or thirteenth day of the dark half of Bhádra and the light half of Mágh. All these offerings are eaten by the members of the household except the sucking pigs, which are buried. In some families the articles of food presented to the Pánch Pir are made over to the Mahomedans of the village.

Kalwárs employ Brahmans for religious and ceremonial purposes, but they are deemed to be of inferior rank. Only the Kanaujiá Brahmans, who serve the Banodhiá sub-caste, are received on equal terms by other members of the sacred order. The dead are burned, and the ceremony of *sráddh* performed in accordance with orthodox usage on the thirteenth day after death. Banodhiá Kalwárs bury the bodies of children under seven years.

Social status.

The social rank of Kalwárs is low. Brahmans and members of the higher castes will on no account take water from their hands, and they are ordinarily classed with Telis, Tatwás, and Cháins. On this point Mr. Nesfield remarks:—"The Kalwár ranks a little higher than the Teli, because there is more skill and less dirt in the practice of his art. His trade as a private occupation has been destroyed by the British Government, which has taken the distilling and sale of liquors entirely into its own hands. The Kalwár still finds some opportunity, however, of following his old pursuit by working in the Government distilleries and taking out licenses for the sale of spirits. But the majority have taken to other kinds of trade or to agriculture, the common goal to which all the decayed industries of India are tending. The art of the Kalwár, like that of the Teli, has been known to almost all the backward races of the world, and cannot by any means be counted among the higher types of industry. Hence the status of the Kalwár has always been low." Distilling and selling liquor is believed to have been the original occupation of the entire caste; but most of its members, with the exception of the Banodhiá, Deswár, and Khálsá sub-castes, make their living by shop-keeping, money-lending, and various forms of trade. A few are engaged in the manufacture of sugar, and some have taken to agriculture in the capacity of tenure-holders and occupancy raiyats. The trading and money-lending Kalwárs have a reputation for squalid penury in the ordering of their household affairs, and for grasping extortion in their dealings with their poorer neighbours. Many of the Bhakats who infest Chota Nagpur and the Santál Parganas belong to this caste. They certainly have a remarkable talent for amassing money, while their standard of living is frequently no higher than that of an ordinary day-labourer. Their meanness in dress is almost proverbial, and I have heard them charged as a class with grudging the *dhobi* the trifle he gets for washing their clothes.

Occupation.

The following statement shows the number and distribution of the caste in 1881, the figures for 1872 having been included with the table on Sunris:—

District.	1881.	District.	1881.
Bardwan	15	Patna	8,747
Bankura	5	Gya	2,359
Birbhum	21	Shahabad	20,126
Howrah	47	Mozufferpur	29,039
24-Parganas	100	Darbhanga	11,949
Nadiya	1	Saran	23,979
Murshedabad	108	Champaran	30,357
Dinajpur	27	Monghyr	12,002
Rajshahye	60	Bhagalpur	26,576
Rangpur	6	Purniah	9,822
Bogra	5	Maldah	229
Pabna	6	Santál Parganas ...	4,577
Darjiling	104	Cuttack	25
Kuch Behar	19	Balasore	4
Dacca	7	Hazaribagh	1,116
Faridpur	2	Lohardagá	5,660
Maimansinh	13	Manbhum	1,617
		Tributary States ...	2,406

Kalwat Mallâh, a synonym for Surahiyá.

Kamal, lotus, a sept of Lohárs, Mundas, and Ahirs or Goálás in Chota Nagpur.

Kamalsar, a section of the Biyáhut and Kharidáhá Kalwárs in Behar.

Kamáni, a synonym for Pási, *q.v.*

Kámáni, a sub-caste of Pásis in Behar.

Kamár, a synonym for Kámár in Bengal and for Lohár in Behar; a sub-caste of Dosádhs peculiar to Behar.

Kámar, a sept of Rajputs in Behar.

Kámár, *Kamár*, the metal-working caste of Bengal and Behar distinguished from the Lohar by not confining themselves to the fabrication of iron implements, and by having no scruples about working with any kind of metal. The Kámárs or Karmakárs of Bengal are popularly believed to be descended from an intrigue between a woman of the Sudra caste and the celestial artificer Viswa-karmá. In the Midnapur district they have a legend curiously like the myth of the destruction of the Asuras quoted in the article on the Mundá tribe. Once upon a time, they say, there was a demon called Lohásura (*Lohá + asura*), who obtained by his austerities the gift of immortality, and warred successfully with the gods. Wearied with constant defeat, Indra at last appealed to Siva for help. As the demon was proof against all the weapons of the gods, a man was created to be their champion and armed by Siva with a set of blacksmith's tools. His hammer was formed from Siva's drum (*damaru*), a skull was converted into an anvil, pincers were made out of the snake girdle worn by the god, while the sacred bull parted with a piece of his skin to furnish the bellows. Thus equipped the first Kámár went forth to meet Lohásur, who laughed and declined to fight any one so small. On this the Kámár asked the Asura to give a proof that he was really immortal by getting into his furnace and letting him blow the bellows. With stupidity worthy of a giant in a fairy tale, the Asura complied; but the Kámár worked the bellows so hard that before the demon could turn he had become red hot and had run out of the furnace as molten iron. From this were forged eight different kinds of iron, corresponding, it is said, to the eight classes of Kámár known in Midnapur, viz. (1) **Lohár-Kámárs**, who work in iron; (2) **Pitule-Kámárs**, who make brass utensils; (3) **Kánsáris**, who work in bell-metal; (4) **Sarna-Kámárs**, or working goldsmiths; (5) **Ghatra, Kámárs**, who make imitation fruits, iron figures of owls and other birds used in the worship of Lakshmi, and *kajlautis* or iron snuffer-shaped vessels for collecting lampblack; (6) **Chánd-Kámárs**, whose specialty is the manufacture of brass mirrors; (7) **Dhokrás**, and (8) **Támrás**, two lower classes of Kámárs found in the Jungle Mahâls in the west of the district, who eat fowls, are reckoned unclean, and are served by a degraded class of Brahman. Of these groups the first two intermarry, while all the rest are endogamous. It is impossible at the present

Traditions of origin.

Internal structure.

day to determine whether all of them are really derived from the Kámár caste; and it seems probable that some of them may be separate castes, which have been classed as Kámárs on account of some real or supposed resemblance in their occupations. It is, however, undoubtedly the case that in other districts besides Midnapur the internal divisions of the Kámár caste are unusually intricate and multifarious. Thus in the 24-Parganas three sub-castes are recognised—**Uttar-Rárhi**, **Dakhin-Rárhi**, and **Ánarpuri**, the members of which do not intermarry; while the first two are further subdivided into the hypergamous groups Kulin and Maulik. In Eastern Bengal we find **Bhusnápati**, **Dhákái**, and **Paschimá**, the first being again broken up into **Naldipáti**, **Chaudda-Samáj**, **Pánch-Samáj**, between which intermarriage is permitted. The Kámárs of Murshedabad again reckon four groups—**Rárhi**, **Bárendra**, **Dhákáwál**, and **Khottá**. The last two are composed respectively of emigrants from Dacca and Hindustan, who have settled in Central Bengal. The **Rárhi** and **Bárendra** sub-castes are found also in Pabna under the names **Das-Samáj** and **Panch-Samáj**, while in Noakhali the caste is divided into **Játi-Karmakár** and **Sikhu-Karmakár**, who do not intermarry. **Belási**, **Máhmudpuriá**, and **Kámlá-Kámár** are met with in Bardwan. In Manbhum there are four sub-castes—**Magahiyá**, **Dhokrá**, **Lohsá**, and **Basuná**, and the same number in the Santál Parganas—**Ashtalal**, **Churálai**, **Belálai**, and **Sankhalai**. In Singbhum and throughout Behar no sub-castes seem to exist.

An equal degree of diversity prevails among the exogamous divisions of the caste. The Kámárs of Bengal have adopted the standard Brahmanical *gotras*; in Singbhum and the Santál Parganas totemistic sections are in vogue; while in Behar the corresponding groups are of the local or territorial type. In Bengal the *gotra* is looked upon as a sort of ornamental appendage testifying the respectability of the caste, but persons of the same *gotra* are allowed to marry provided that they are not of kin within the fifth degree on the mother's and the seventh on the father's side. In Behar and Chota Nagpur the usual rule that a man may not marry a woman belonging to his own section is still observed. These facts, taken in connexion with the prevalence of several different types of section-names seem to point to the conclusion that many distinct castes of metal-workers have sprung up in different parts of the country to meet local wants; that each caste has been formed out of recruits from the surrounding population; and that the name Kámár, so far from indicating a common origin, is merely the functional designation of an extremely heterogeneous group. In other words, the profession of metal-worker in its various branches has been adopted from time to time by Aryans, non-Aryans, and people of mixed race; but the fact of their following the same occupation, though it has led to their being called by a common name, has not welded them into a uniform group, and the component elements of the caste still remain entirely distinct. The caste, in fact, is a caste only in the loose popular sense of the word, and its multifarious internal divisions afford an excellent illustration of the general rule that while diversity of occupation undoubtedly leads to differentiation, community of occupation does not necessarily or generally bring about integration.

Marriage.

The Kámárs of Bengal marry their daughters as infants, between the ages of five and ten years. The usual maximum limit of age in Behar is twelve for a girl and fifteen for a boy; but it is essential that the bridegroom should be taller than the bride, and this point is ascertained by actual measurement. In Bengal, however, the marriage of a son is sometimes delayed till he is twenty-five or so by reason of the necessity of paying a *pan* or bride-price in order to obtain a wife. Among the Kámárs of Chota Nagpur adult-marriage still holds its ground even for girls, though it is considered more proper for them to be married before attaining puberty. The Kámárs of Midnapur, though regarding infant-marriage as essential, do not permit consummation to take place immediately after the ceremony, but keep their girls at home until they have reached puberty and may fairly be deemed *aptæ viro*. Another custom prevalent in that district is *káparparána*, or presenting a piece of cloth and certain spices to the bride elect before the marriage. The acceptance of this cloth is held finally to bind the bride's family to keep faith with the bridegroom, so that if the girl were afterwards given to another man her father would run the risk of being turned out of the caste. In Bengal the marriage ceremony is of the standard type, while in Behar it closely resembles that described in the article on the Kewat caste. One curious practice, known as *gháskáti*, or cutting grass, is peculiar to Kámárs. On the day after the marriage the wedded pair, followed by a number of women singing, are taken outside the house, and the bridegroom is given a sickle, with which he cuts a handful of grass. After this a maid-servant or one of the female members of the bride's household plants a stick in the ground at some distance off, and the bridegroom and his brother-in-law race for the stick, which the winner pulls up. In this contest it is an understood thing that the bridegroom must be allowed to win, and if the bride's brother seems to be getting the best of it he is headed back by the bridegroom's friends, so as to let the latter come in first. Polygamy is permitted in Bengal and Chota Nagpur, but is strongly disapproved of in Behar, where the rule is that a man may only take a second wife in the event of the first being barren or suffering from an incurable disease. Widow-marriage is forbidden in Bengal and Behar, but is still practised in Chota Nagpur by the Magahiyá Kámárs, who probably left Behar before the Kámárs of that province had taken to orthodox ways. Divorce is recognised only in Singbhum and the Santál Parganas, where a *sál* leaf is torn in two before the panchâyat as a symbol of separation, and divorced wives are allowed to marry again. In other districts a faithless wife is turned out of the caste, and either becomes a regular prostitute or joins some religious sect of dubious morality. Such measures, however, are only resorted to in extreme cases, and intrigues within the caste are usually condoned by the husband.

Religion.

The majority of the Kámárs in Bengal are Vaishnavas, but a few follow the Sákta ritual. Their favourite deity is Viswakarmá, who is worshipped on the last day of Bhádra with offerings of sweetmeats, parched rice, fruits, molasses, flowers, sandal-wood paste, Ganges water, cloth, silver ornaments, etc. At the same time they worship the hammer, anvil, and other tools used in their handicraft. In Behar they reverence as minor gods Hanumán, Bandi, Goraiyá, Káli, Jawálá Mukhi, Jalpá, Bhairab, and two Mahomedan saints—Miran or Shaikh Sadu and Saiyad. Cocks, *khir*, and *puri* are offered to the latter, and afterwards given away to poor Mahomedans. In Bengal the women perform the Ananta, Savitri, Sasthi, and Panchami *bratas*, and Nistárini, and Mangal Chandi are worshipped by the women and children with offerings of sweetmeats, milk, fruit, etc. For the service of the greater gods and in the performance of *bratas* the caste employ Brahmans, who are received on equal terms by other members of the sacred order. The dead are burned, and a regular *sráddh* performed on the thirty-first day after death.

Occupation.

Among the Kámárs of Dacca, says Dr. Wise, there exists a tradition that they were brought from Upper India by the Muhammadan Government. In the 'Aín-i-Akbari it is stated that there was an iron mine in Sarkár Buzúha, which included Dacca, and in later times jágirs called *áhangar* were granted to the skilled workmen employed in smelting iron from the red laterite soil of the Dacca district. At the present day, however, the Kámárs are unacquainted with the art of smelting iron, and they procure pig-iron from Calcutta when a local supply is not to be had. Iron-smelting, indeed, seems to be practised only by the aboriginal Lohárs and Asuras of Chota Nagpur and Western Bengal. Kámárs work in all metals, including gold and silver, and being themselves members of the Nava-Sákha group affect to despise the professional goldsmith or Sonarbanik, who is considered unclean. Most Sekrás or working goldsmiths are Kámárs, and more than half of the caste are employed as blacksmiths. The regular village blacksmith, whether Kámár or Lohár, is usually paid in kind, receiving four *árhis* (about a maund) of paddy per plough. Some Kámárs, again, are employed to slaughter the animals offered in sacrifice to Sakti. In Dacca, where the Kánsári or brazier caste is no longer met with, the manufacture of the brass utensils solely used in Hindu households devolves on the Kámárs, their only competitors being the Ghulám Káyasths, many of whom engage in this trade. They make an alloy (*bharn*) with three parts of copper and four of zinc, and with it manufacture cups, *lotás*, and other vessels. The Panní-wála, or tin-foil maker, is always a Kámár. The tin is obtained in bars from Calcutta, and being run into moulds, is, while still soft, beaten out until thin enough to be cut into strips, which are then stained with lac and turmeric so as to counterfeit the colour of gold. The foil so produced is then sold to the Muhammadan Chúrí-wála to ornament his glass bracelets, and to the Málákár to embellish chaplets, tiaras, images of gods and goddesses, and the platforms paraded on gala days. A small number of Kámárs have taken to agriculture and trade, and among these a few hold the position of zemindars or tenure-holders, while the majority are occupancy raiyats. The caste has always been an illiterate one, and very few of its members have made their way into Government service, or the learned professions. It is, in fact, a common allegation that they only learn enough reading and writing to enable them to keep accounts.

Social status.

The social standing of Kámárs is respectable. In Bengal they rank among the Navasákha, and in Behar they belong to the group of castes from whose hands a Brahman can take water. Except in Singbhum and the Santál Parganas, where fowls are deemed lawful food, they observe the same rules regarding diet as the higher castes, but do not consider themselves bound to abstain from spirituous liquors. Like the Ekádas Telis, Kámárs pride themselves upon not allowing their women to wear nose-rings. This prohibition is said to have been introduced by a Parámánik or headman of the caste because a Kámár woman dropped her nose-ring on his plate while serving him at a feast. In Midnapur the Parámániks hold a very high position, and marriages with their families are eagerly sought after. All questions bearing on the usages of the caste are laid before them for decision, and disregard of their orders may in the last resort be punished by excommunication. Ordinarily, however, a fine is inflicted, of which the Parámánik himself gets the largest share, while the rest is spent in giving a feast to the Kámárs who live within his jurisdiction.

The following statement shows the number and distribution of Kámárs in 1872 and 1881. The figures of the former year include those of Lohárs.

DISTRICT.	1872.	1881.	DISTRICT.	1872.	1881.
Bardwan	32,851	20,399	Chittagong	2,749	2,916
Bankura	22,750	32,328	Noakhali	1,350	2,118
Birbhum	10,365	9,709	Hill Tracts	......	53
Midnapur	32,348	38,474	Patna	The figures are shown in the table on the Lohárs.	77
Hughli	11,949 (Hughli and Howrah)	11,318	Gya		4,890
Howrah		4,373	Shahabad		2,295
24-Parganas	21,439	12,890	Mozufferpur		612
Nadiya	16,005	15,515	Darbhanga		4,491
Khulna	......	7,213	Saran		15
Jessore	14,384	18,759	Champaran		2,790
Murshedabad	7,450	8,952	Monghyr		2,940
Dinajpur	3,659	5,624	Bhagalpur		5,495
Rajshahye	4,508	5,109	Purniah		3,524
Rangpur	4,237	5,714	Santál Parganas ...		21,395
Bogra	1,475	1,768	Maldah	4,312	5,895
Pabna	6,740	8,109	Cuttack	11,071	14,627
Darjiling	456	319	Puri	5,785	6,454
Jalpigori	511	1,619	Balasore	9,704	12,789
Kuch Behar	......	619	Tributary States ...	17,162	8,993
Dacca	12,072	16,747	Hazaribagh	10,505	2,295
Faridpur	4,758	9,548	Lohardaga	31,996	654
Bakarganj	11,418	9,475	Singbhum	7,959	7,428
Maimansinh	9,019	14,859	Manbhum	22,615	25,523
Tipperah	5,403	7,482	Tributary States ...	6,243	2,765

Kamarhet, a *mul* or section of the Kamarkalla sub-caste of Sonars in Behar.

Kamarkalla, a sub-caste of Barhis, Lohárs, and of Sonárs in Behar who do not permit the marriage of widows.

Kámat, a title of Kewats in Behar.

Kámati, Kamtá, Kamti, a title of cultivating Dhánuks in Behar.

Kámbáháng, a sept of Limbus in Darjiling.

Kambaliá, a title of Gareris in Behar.

Kámbáng, a sept of Limbus in Darjiling.

Kambule, a functional group of Jugis in Bengal.

Kámendra, a *gáin* of the Sándilya *gotra* of Bárendra Brahmans in Bengal.

Kámi, *Kámiá,* the blacksmith caste of Nepal, some of whom also work in the precious metals. They claim descent from the mythical artificer Viswámitra, and profess to have entered Nepal from the plains of India. This indeed is probable enough, for their section-names, a list of which is given in the Appendix, are not of the type common among the Indo-Tibetan races, and seem to be of Indian origin. Their physical characteristics also appear to suggest the conclusion that they are immigrants from India, who have intermarried freely with some of the indigenous races of Nepal.

Traditions of origin.

A man may not marry a woman of his own *thar* or section, nor of the section to which his mother belonged before her marriage. Girls marry after they are grown up, and courtship is more or less recognised. Sexual intercourse before marriage is said not to be tolerated; but in fact the morals of the Kámi girls are not stricter than those of the young women of other castes in the hills. The marriage ceremony appears to have been borrowed from the Hindu system. It takes place at night. The bride and bridegroom stand facing each other on either side of an earthen vessel containing what is supposed to be a sacred fire. Round this they walk seven times, keeping the fire always on the right hand. The bride then takes her stand by the bridegroom and places her hands on his, while her parents, who conduct the ceremony, lay on the joined hands of the couple some *kusá* grass, some leaves of the *bel* and *tulsi,* and a piece of copper, muttering at the same time some gibberish which purports to be Sanskrit sacred texts. The rite is completed by the bridegroom smearing some red lead on the bride's forehead and the parting of her hair and putting a necklace (*poti*) of white beads round her neck.

Marriage.

Polygamy is permitted, and in theory at least a man may have as many wives as he can afford to maintain. Poverty, however, and the great liberty which is accorded to women in the hills, tend in practice to limit the number to two. Polyandry is unknown. A widow may marry again, and is restricted by no rules in her choice of a second husband, except that she may not marry her late husband's elder brother or elder cousin, and must observe the prohibited degrees which were binding on her before she married. The ceremony is of a simpler character than at the marriage of a virgin. No fire is kindled, nor are texts recited: the bridegroom merely puts vermiion on the bride's forehead and gives her a necklace, the proceedings being completed by a feast, at which the relations of both parties are present.

The utmost license of divorce prevails. A husband can get rid of his wife whenever he pleases by going through the symbolic form of cutting in two a kind of fruit (*pang-ro*) with a bit of wood called *sinko*. In reference to this ceremony, which prevails among several other castes, divorce is commonly spoken of in the hills as *sinko-pangro*. Wives are supposed to have somewhat less extensive powers of divorce, and the theory is that they can only divorce their husbands on the ground of positive ill-treatment. In fact, however, a woman who is tired of her husband goes off with any man who will take her, and by the custom of the caste the husband has only the right to demand from his rival the bride-price originally paid for the woman. Divorced wives marry again by the same ceremony that is used at the marriage of a widow.

Kámis admit into their caste members of any caste higher in rank than their own. No ceremony is performed on such occasions, and the consent of the panchâyat of the caste is all that is required to confer the privilege of membership. Instances of such changes of caste taking place do not, however, very frequently occur. The usual cause is that a man of a higher caste has taken a Kámi girl as a mistress, and has got into trouble with his own people for eating with a woman of lower rank.

The caste know nothing of Hindu law, and profess to be guided in matters of inheritance and succession by a tribal custom of their own. This, however, presents no features of special interest. Sons take equal shares in the property. Failing sons, brothers and brothers' sons inherit. If no male relatives survive, daughters and daughters' sons succeed.

Religion.

Kámis pose as orthodox Hindus, worshipping Káli and regarding Viswakarmá as their tutelary deity. The bonds of Hinduism, however, lie very lightly upon them, and their real worship is directed to certain animistic powers, known as Kuláin, Anardhá, Khodái, and Dáramastá, among whom the sections of the caste are parcelled out in a curious and uneven fashion. Of these ill-defined shapes, Kuláin is the most popular. To him all the thirty-eight sections sacrifice goats, sheep, and fowls twice in the year, besides burning incense at every full moon. The Gadáili, Sásankhar, and Darnál sections slay pigs in honour of Khodái; while Anardhá and Dáramastá are worshipped by the Gajmér and Kharká-Báyu sections, respectively, with the offering of a white cock. The offerings in each case are eaten by the worshippers. Kámis have no Brahmans, and any member of the caste who chances to have a turn for religion officiates as priest.

Disposal of the dead.

The dead are burned, thrown into a river, or buried, as may be found convenient at the time. The two former methods are considered the most respectable. Persons who affect special orthodoxy take the ashes of their dead to the Ganges, but such cases are comparatively rare. The funeral ceremony is a curious one. After the corpse has been disposed of, the mourners have their heads and faces entirely shaved, including the eyebrows. They put off their ordinary clothes and dress themselves in a waistcloth and a blanket, a bit of white linen being tied over the forehead. In this dress they stay at home for ten days, during which time they take only one meal a day, abstain from meat, salt, and oil, do not receive or pay visits, and, as far as may be, avoid conversing with their fellows. On the eleventh day a feast is prepared for the relatives of the deceased; but before they can partake of it a small portion of every dish must be put on a leaf-plate and taken out into the jungle for the spirit of the dead man, and carefully watched until a fly or other insect settles on it. The watcher then covers up the plate with a slab of stone, eats his own food, which he brings with him to the place, and returns to tell the relatives that the dead man's spirit has received the offering set for him. The feast can then begin. The watcher is a member of the caste, who is paid for his services as if he were a Brahman. No ceremonies are performed for the benefit of ancestors in general, childless ancestors, or men who have died a violent death.

Social status.

Notwithstanding that they abstain from eating beef and have adopted several Hindu usages, the social standing of Kámis among the hill castes is decidedly low, and Tibetans, Murmis, Mangars, and members of the Kiranti group will not eat, drink, or smoke with them. Their position is clearly marked by the fact that they eat with the Sarki caste. They regard pork and fowls as lawful food, and indulge freely in strong drink.

In 1881 the Kámis numbered 3,723 in Darjiling, 107 in Champaran, 9 in Bhagalpur, and 580 in the Tributary States of Chota Nagpur, while none were separately returned for 1872.

Kámiá, a synonym for Kámi.

Kamiá, a sub-caste of Lohárs in Chota Nagpur.

Kamila, a title of Sonárs in Singbhum.

Kamiya, an endogamous division of Nepáli Brahmans.

Kámkáli, a *gáin* of the Bátsya *gotra* of Bárendra Brahmans in Bengal.

Kamkar, a title of Kahárs in Chota Nagpur.

Kamláit, a section of the Kamár sub-caste of Dosádhs in Behar.

Kámlá-Kámár, a sub-caste of Kámárs in Bardwan.

Kampti, a section of the Kádar caste in Behar which intermarries with the Bárik, Kápari, Marik, Darbe, Mánjhi, and Báre sections, but not with the rest.

Kámrám, a *mul* or section of the Naomuliá or Majraut subcaste of Goálás in Behar.

Kamrupi, a sub-caste of Brahmans from Assam who serve as cooks or priests in Northern Bengal.

Kámsarke Máhto, a section of the Biyáhut and Kharidáhá Kalwárs in Behar.

Kamtariá, a section of Kanaujiá Lohárs in Behar.

Kámti, a section of the Kulsunri sub-caste of Sunris in Behar.

Kán, a very low caste of musicians akin to the Doms; Musalman workers in steel, who repair umbrellas, make fish-hooks, etc.

Kánái-Madan, a section of the Mahmudábás sub-caste of Nápits.

Kanaka, a section of Kumhárs in Jessore.

Kanakrishi, a section of Sutradhars in Bengal.

Kanakwár, a sept of Rajputs in Behar.

Káná-Machhri, a sept of Gonds in Chota Nagpur.

Kánáp, a section of the Sátmuliá Maghayá sub-caste of Kándus in Behar.

Kanaujia, a designation of numerous and widely-distributed sub-castes and sections of castes of very different social standing. In the case of the higher castes the name doubtless implies a notion of their having come originally from Kanauj or Kanya-Kubja, the famous old capital of Ajodhyá or Oudh, on the Kalindi, a tributary of the Ganges in the North-West Provinces. Its occurrence among the lower castes is accounted for by Mr. Beames in his edition of Sir Henry Elliot's Supplemental Glossary, by the remark that "whenever the lower castes begin to talk about their subdivisions, they always give them the grandest possible names, such as Chauhán, Kanaujiá, and so on." This is true so far as it goes, but it hardly goes far enough. One would like to know why the grand names are selected. The clue is probably to be found in the fact that many of the lower castes are attached in various sorts of servile capacities to the landholding families of the higher castes. In such cases it is in accordance with the passion for imitation which runs through the caste system that the servants should adopt the tribal designations of the masters, just as the Rajputs themselves have borrowed the *gotras* of the Brahmans. A sub-caste of Barhis in Behar who are said to have come from Gorakhpur. They make boxes, desks, etc., and do joiner's work of all kinds, but consider themselves debarred by custom from making panels, doors, windows, and the larger class of woodwork used in houses; a sub-caste of Ahirs or Goálás in Behar who bear the title Gop and belong to the Kasyap *gotra*. They make curds and serve the higher castes. A sub-caste of Halwáis in Behar, who are confectioners by occupation. A sub-caste of Hindu Joláhas (Tantwa or Tánti) in Behar; a sub-caste of Brahman, Dhanuk, Dhobi, Dosádh, Hajjam (barber), Kándu, Kumhar, Koiri, Lohár, Sonár, Támbuli, Tánti, Teli, and Thathera castes in Behar.

Kanauli, a section of the Pachainyá sub-caste of Doms in Behar.

Kánbindhá, pierced ears, a section of Kurmis in Chota Nagpur and Orissa.

Kánchaba, dog, a totemistic sept of Juángs in Orissa.

Kánchan, a section of Brahmans.

Kanchanbhár, a section of Bábhans in Behar.

Kánchanpur, a section of the Karan Káyasths in Behar.

Kand, a synonym for Kandh.

Kanda, a kind of sweet potato, a totemistic sept of Mundas, Lohárs, and Oraons in Chota Nagpur; a section of Kahárs in Behar.

Kándar, a *mul* or section of the Chhamuliá Madhesiá sub-caste of Halwáis in Behar.

Kándare, a *gáin* or sub-section of Saptasati Brahmans in Bengal.

Kandaria, a *thar* or section of Nepáli Brahmans.

Kandarpa, a sub-section of the Bharadwája section of Utkal Brahmans.

Kándeil, a *mul* or section of the Tinmuliá Madhesiá sub-caste of Halwáis in Behar.

Kandh, *Kondh*, *Khond*, *Kui-loka*, *Kui-enju*, a Dravidian tribe, inhabiting that part of the territory of the Rájá of Boad, one of the tributary states of Orissa, known as the Kandhmals, a hilly tract of country 40 miles in length, and in extreme breadth 24 miles, with an area of about 800 square miles. These Kandhs call themselves *Maliah* Kandhs as distinguished from the *Beniah* Kandhs, who inhabit Gumsur in Madras. The general character of the country is wild and mountainous; it consists of a confused succession of ranges covered with dense sál forests. The Kandhs live in scattered villages surrounded with patches of cultivation. There are 677 villages with a population of 58,959 souls. It is calculated that two-thirds of the country is covered with jungle. The people are shy and timid, hating contact with the inhabitants of the plains. They love the wild mountain gorges, and prefer the stillness of jungle life, and fly to the most inaccessible parts on the least alarm. They live by hunting and rude agriculture. Like many other wild tribes, they are in the habit of clearing patches of land in the forest during the cold weather, and firing it in the hot weather. Seed is sown among the ashes after the commencement of the rains. After the second year the land is abandoned, and a fresh clearing made. The people produce barely sufficient food for half the year, and supply their wants for the remainder by bartering turmeric, of which they raise large quantities. The Kandhs regard themselves as proprietors of the land, and insist upon their rights with that curious pertinacity which distinguishes the cognate tribes of Santál, Munda and Ho.

Origin.

The Kandhs call themselves Kui-loka or Kui-enju. The derivation of the name Kandh is obscure, nor has the critical study of the Kandh dialects gone far enough to throw any light on the subject. Some seek to identify it with the Uriya word *Khanda*, denoting a measure of land reckoned by the quantity of seed sown, and support this view by reference to the Kandh tradition that once upon a time they were a race of quiet cultivators dwelling in the plains of Orissa. But why should the fact of men having 'acres' to till lead them to call themselves by so obviously inappropriate a name, and that too in a language with which *ex hypothesi* they could have no acquaintance? Another theory refers to the mention in the Ramayana of a tribe of Asuras, called Skandh-Asuras, ruling over the forest of Dandaka, the hilly tract extending from the Vindhya hills to the river Krishna, and suggests that the Kandhs may be a remnant of these, the initial S having been dropped by phonetic corruption. A third and in some respects more plausible hypothesis derives the name from *Khanda*, the Uriya for a sword which is said to be the totem or distinguishing mark of the tribe. Where the data are so vague and uncertain, no opinion can be usefully put forward. I may, however, point out, arguing from analogous cases, that tribal names usually belong to one of two types. Either they consist simply of the word for 'man' in the tribal language, or they are epithets bestowed by Hindu neighbours usually casting some aspersion on the usages of the tribe in the matter of food. Horo or Ho is an instance of the former type; Musahar and, according to some authorities, Kol or Kolh of the latter. These lines of inquiry, if followed up by persons adequately acquainted with the various dialects concerned, ought, one would think, to lead in course of time to a satisfactory solution of the question.

Internal structure.

The Kandhs of the Orissa Kandhmals, with whom alone we are now concerned, are supposed to have entered the Kandhmals from the south about 250 years ago, driving out the feeble and unwarlike Kurums or Kurmis who appear to have been the original occupants of these tracts. They are divided into two classes—(1) Uriya Kandh, (2) Malua or Arria Kandh. The former are Kandhs who from social intercourse with the Uriyas have abandoned many Kandh usages and adopted Hindu customs in their place; while the Malua or hill Kandhs still adhere strictly to the original observances of the tribe. Within the limits of the Kandhmals these two groups have not yet become strictly endogamous, and owing perhaps to the sparseness of the population of these tracts, intermarriages still take place between them. But the Malua Kandhs already refuse to intermarry with the Uriya Kandhs of Bod Proper and Gumsur, whom they regard as having lowered themselves by taking to Hindu practices; and it seems probable that in course of time an equally complete separation will be brought about between the Uriya and Malua Kandhs of the Kandhmals.

The fine physique of the Kandhs—a point on which all observers agree—may perhaps be due in some measure to their custom of admitting into the tribe members of other stocks, always excepting the weaver Páns or Domnas and the sweeper Háris. The price paid for the privilege of admission into the Kandh community varies in different parts of the Kandhmals, but is invariably reckoned in buffaloes and strong drink. A great feast is made and the new member is formally inducted into the tribe.

In close contact with the Kandhs and dwelling in the same villages with them, we find three castes bearing names which seem to indicate some sort of connexion with the tribe. These are the Kui-Kumhárenju or Kandh-Kumhárs, the Kui-Lohárenju or Kandh-Lohárs, and the Kui-Gonrenju or Kandh-Gonds. Although these castes have adopted the religion, customs and dress of the Kandhs, they are still not recognised as members of the Kandh community, and Kandhs will not intermarry or eat with them. It is possible therefore that there may be no tie of blood between them and the Kandhs, and that their imitation of Kandh observances is due merely to their having been long settled in the Kandh country and having forgotten their own rites. On the other hand, if we compare these names with the similar combinations found among the Mundas, Oraons, and other tribes of Chota Nagpur, it is difficult to avoid the conclusion that the castes in question must have arisen from intermarriages between women of the Kandh tribe and Hindu artisans who had settled in Kandh villages.

Exogamy.

Ethnologists have long been aware that the custom of exogamy is rigorously observed among the Kandhs. In his *Essay on Primitive Marriage*, first published in 1865, the late Mr. J. F. McLennan refers to Major Macpherson's *Account of the Religion of the Khonds in Orissa* for "the distinct statement that among the Khonds inter-marriage between persons of the same tribe, however large or scattered, is considered incestuous and punishable by death." Notwithstanding the stringency of the rule, and although owing to the prevalence among them of human sacrifices and infanticide, the Kandhs have been under the close observation of British officers ever since 1837, I have had the greatest difficulty in ascertaining the precise form of exogamy practised by them, and indeed in getting any information at all on the subject. In reply to repeated inquiries addressed to several different correspondents well acquainted with the tribe and engaged in official work among them, I have been assured that the Kandhs have no exogamous subdivisions at all, and that their matrimonial arrangements are regulated, so far as the avoidance of consanguineous marriages is concerned, by the comparatively modern system of calculating prohibited degrees from a common ancestor. The facts now recorded, which I regret to say are still incomplete, reached me only a few days before the completion of these volumes. They were ascertained for me in a special inquiry conducted at my request by Mr. James Taylor, Tahsildar of the Kandhmals, whose intelligence in carrying out my instructions I am glad to have this opportunity of acknowledging. That the facts should have been ascertained with difficulty, and that they should have escaped the notice of so many observers, is quite in keeping with my experience in other parts of Bengal. The rules which govern the custom of exogamy, and the caste or tribal divisions by means of which that custom is worked, concern the inner life of the people, and leave no trace on their relations with the outside world. They are a sort of shibboleth, understood only by members of the tribe itself. Even among them this knowledge is often confined to heads of families or villages, priests, genealogists, match-makers, and such-like persons whose business it is to look after the matrimonial arrangements of the tribe. For this reason they form not only the most archaic, but also the most durable portion of the body of custom which a given tribe or caste observes, and are the least liable to be modified or destroyed by the operation of fiction and of the inveterate tendency to imitate the institutions of groups supposed to be socially superior, which has done and is constantly doing so much to force all tribal observances into conformity with the standard Brahmanical pattern.

The Kandhs of the Orissa Kandhmals are divided into fifty *gochis* or exogamous septs, each of which bears the name of a *muta* or village, believes all its members to be descended from a common ancestor, and as a rule dwells as a body of blood relations in the commune *muta* or group of villages after which it is called. The Kandh *gochi* appears therefore to represent the nearest approach that has yet been discovered to the "local exogamous tribe," supposed by Mr. McLennan to be the primary unit of human society. A list of the *gochis* is given in Appendix I. Each *gochi* is further split up into sub-septs called *klambus*. Each dwelling in one of the villages making up the *muta* or commune. Of these I have not yet been able to obtain a complete list.

The sub-sept, like the sept, traces its origin to a single ancestor, but he is a personage of more recent date than the progenitor of the sept. The relations included in the former are comparatively near, while the connexion between members of the *gochi* is much more remote, and in the modern sense of the word they can hardly be called relations at all. The sub-sept seems in fact to be a sort of joint-family expanded to form a village community, the members of which are invited to marriages, festivals and similar domestic ceremonies to which it would be impossible to bring together the larger group. On occasions of special importance, when, for example, a *casus belli* is thought to have arisen between a sept and its neighbours, the whole *gochi* is summoned to meet in council and consider the question laid before it.

Marriage.

A Kandh may not marry a woman of his own *gochi*, even though she belong to a different *klambu* from himself. Both *gochi* and *klambu* go by the father's side, and I can find no traces of female kinship having ever been recognised by the Kandhs. The use of the division into *klambus* can best be illustrated by an actual example. Let us suppose that a man of the Besringia *gochi* and Besera *klambu* marries a woman of the Kutrengia *gochi* and Bisunga *klambu*. Their son would belong to the same *gochi* and *klambu* as his father, and would be precluded from marrying a woman of the *klambu* to which his mother belonged, but might marry into any of the other four *klambus* of the Kutrengia *gochi*. This prohibition holds good for three generations in the descending line, and many Kandhs prefer to extend it to the fourth. They take, in fact, as Mr. Taylor pertinently remarks, much the same view of it as many Europeans take of intermarriage between first cousins. It will be seen from this that the rule forbidding marriage within the mother's *klambu* serves for the Kandhs much the same purpose as is ordinarily effected by the standard formula for reckoning prohibited degrees. This formula is unknown to the Kandhs of the Kandhmals, and their arrangements for guarding against consanguineous marriages cousist solely of the simple rules regarding the *gochi* and the *klambu* which have been explained above. A similar system exists among the Santáls, but the septs and sub-septs are not *localised* as they are among the Kandhs, and the prohibition of marriage within the mother's sub-sept is not so stringently enforced.

Kandh girls are usually married when of full age in most cases to men of their own choice, and after a regular process of courtship considerable license is allowed to the young men and maidens of the tribe, and sexual intercourse before marriage is tacitly recognised. Infidelity after marriage is said to be rare; the adulterer if found out atones for his fault by paying an indemnity to the husband. Until this has been done, the woman is excluded from social intercourse with her neighbours. Widows and divorced wives may marry again. A bride-price is paid to the father. The widow's choice of a second husband is in theory unfettered; but it is considered the right thing for her to marry her late husband's younger brother. In the event of her marrying an outsider, she retains the charge of her children until the girls attain puberty and the boys are old enough to hold the plough. In any case she has no rights over her late husband's property, which goes to his children, or failing them to his brother.

When a Kandh youth is of an age to marry, his parents find out who he has fallen in love with, and send a go-between, usually a man of the Pán caste, to ascertain the views of the girl's parents, and to approach the delicate question of the price to be paid for the bride. If these preliminary negotiations are successful, a deputation of the boy's relations go soon afterwards to the girl's house, and a general drinking bout is held, at which the amount of the bride-price is definitely fixed. The price is reckoned in *pots* or lives, a term of somewhat vague connotation, which includes buffaloes, cows, goats, brass plates and cooking vessels, ornaments and things in general. Its amount varies with the wealth of the bride's father, to whom it is paid. It may extend to as many as forty *pots*, and the payment may be spread over two or three years. Soon after the relations have reported the result of their negotiations, the bridegroom pays a visit to his future father-in-law's house, bringing with him the first instalment of the bride-price. The formal betrothal is then effected by the bridegroom putting a necklace round the girl's neck, while she pours oil over his head.

On the day before the wedding the bridegroom and his male relations go in procession to the bride's house, where they spend that evening and the next morning in feasting. The essential and binding portion of the marriage ceremony, in which the bride's father officiates as priest, is said to consist of his taking the right hands of the couple and spitting on the palm of each. The effect of this in the case of the bride is to remove her from her original sept, and to preclude her from re-entering her father's house. The married couple are carried off on the backs of the bridegroom's friends to his house, where the marriage is consummated. On the next day a feast is made, and the girl sits on a couch surrounded by the women of the village and pretends to weep. After this has gone on for some time she and her husband are seized by his friends and carried about in triumph. A short dance follows, and both are replaced on the couch. Then the bride's male relations take hold of the bride and run away with her, hotly pursued by the girls of the village who pummel the men soundly, recapture the bride, and bring her back to her husband. After this the bride's relations return to their own village. On the day after the marriage the bride and bridegroom, taking with them an old man to officiate as priest, go a little way outside the village and worship Dharma Pennu with offerings of fowls, eggs, rice and strong drink in order to secure a happy life and male offspring. A high standard of conjugal fidelity is observed among the Kandhs, and husbands usually treat their wives kindly. Polygamy as a practice is unknown. If a woman proves barren, the husband may take a second wife; but in such cases the two wives have separate houses and enjoy equal privileges.

Birth.

About a month before her confinement is expected, the woman and her husband pay a visit to her parent's house and get from them some toys for the child, consisting usually of a small bow and arrow, a winnowing fan, and a small basket. These are hung up in the house till they are wanted. A few days before the confinement both husband and wife leave their house and take up their abode in an outside room set apart for this purpose. There the husband cooks and eats with the wife, and in the case of a first confinement he or his father sacrifices a pig with offering of cooked and uncooked rice and libations of strong drink to the spirits of their ancestors, in order that nothing may go wrong. No one can enter the room while labour is going on on pain of becoming ceremonially unclean, and the husband has to give whatever assistance is necessary. After the placenta has passed, the cooking pots hitherto in use are broken and visitors are admitted; but they may not eat with the parents of the child until a further period of twelve days has elapsed, when a further breaking of pots takes place, and a feast is given to the neighbours. When the child is two or three years old, its head is shaved and a small ceremony is performed calling upon the dead ancestors to protect it from scald, itch, and similar diseases of the skin. From the age of ten or twelve the hair is allowed to grow again. No ceremonies are performed after birth or when a boy or girl attains puberty.

Succession.

As regards succession to property, the general rule is that the sons get equal shares, but the portion of the eldest is sometimes larger than that of the others. The widow gets a share equal to that of a son. If a man dies without male issue, leaving a widow and a daughter, the widow takes his moveable property in full ownership, but has only a life-interest in his land, which goes to his nearest male relatives on her death. Daughters never share in the inheritance, but are entitled to maintenance out of the estate until they are married. Adoption is unknown. A step-son has no rights in the estate of his step-father.

Religion.

Much has been written about the religion of the Kandhs, but the subject can hardly be regarded as having yet been fully cleared up. Major Macpherson's account of the matter ascribes to the Kandhs religious conceptions of a very advanced character, quite out of keeping with their primitive social organization, and one is inclined to suspect that the persons from whom he derived his information must have described to him rather their ideal view of what the religion of the tribe ought to be than what it actually was. For this reason instead of entering upon a lengthy discussion of the subject as treated by him, and endeavouring by analysis and comparison with the beliefs of cognate tribes to get at the actual facts underlying his account, I prefer to state very briefly what is known about the Kandhs of the Kandhmals, trusting to future research to work out the problem in fuller detail.

The Kandhs of the Kandhmals recognise three principal gods—Dharma Pennu, Sáru Pennu, and Táru Pennu. The functions of Dharma Pennu appear to be of a somewhat more general character than those assigned to the other two. No regular times or seasons are fixed for his worship, and he is appealed to only in cases of illness or at the birth of a first child. His worship is performed by a *guru* who may be of any caste, but is usually either a Kandh or a Pán. The *gurus* usually have the power of throwing themselves or feigning to throw themselves into a state of hypnotic trance, and are supposed to be able to cure diseases by touching people, tying them up with bits of thread, and similar mummery. On the whole Dharma Pennu may best be described as the god of the family and of the tribe itself. Sáru Pennu is the god of the hills, a divinity apparently of much the same type as the Marang Buru of the Santáls and Mundas. He is a jealous god, and does not like people to trespass on his domain, and the chief object of the worship which is performed in his honour in April and May is to induce him to protect from the attacks of wild animals people whose business takes them among the forest-clad hills of the Kandhmals, and also to secure a full yield of the jungle products which the Kandhs, like most similar tribes, use so largely for food. The priests of Sáru Pennu are called dehuri, and the appropriate offerings are a goat and a fowl with rice and strong drink. The offerings are partaken of by the worshippers. Táru Pennu, the earth god, takes the place among these Kandhs of Tári Pennu, the earth *goddess*, familiar to students of the voluminous official literature which treats of the suppression of human sacrifice among the Kandhs. He is believed to be very vindictive, and to wreak his anger upon those who neglect his worship, afflicting them with various diseases, destroying their crops, and causing them to be devoured by tigers and leopards. In order to avoid these evils the Kandhs offer buffaloes and goats to the god at irregular intervals, apparently whenever they think that he stands in need of being appeased. His priests are called *jhankar*, and the person who actually sacrifices the animals is known as *jani*. The functions of the *dehuri*, the *jhankar* and the *jani* are hereditary.

Human sacrifice.

Although human sacrifice has now been abandoned by the Kandhs, and the memory of it is believed to have almost died out in the Kandhmals of Orissa, an account of the tribe would be incomplete without some mention of the terrible practices which formerly prevailed. As I am not in a position to add any fresh facts to those already on record in the reports on the subject, I venture to quote the admirable description of this phase of Kandh superstition which is given by my friend, Mr. J. G. Frazer, of Trinity College, Cambridge, in volume I, pages 384–90 of *The Golden Bough*[1] :—"The best known case of human sacrifices systematically offered to ensure good crops is supplied by the Khonds or Kandhs, another Dravidian race in Bengal. Our knowledge of them is derived from the accounts written by British officers, who forty or fifty years ago were engaged in putting them down.[2] The sacrifices were offered to the earth goddess, Tari Pennu or Bera Pennu, and were believed to ensure good crops and immunity from all disease and accidents. In particular, they were considered necessary in the cultivation of turmeric, the Khonds arguing that the turmeric could not have a deep red colour without the shedding of blood.[3] The victim or Meriah was acceptable to the goddess only if he had been purchased, or had been born a victim, that is, the son of a victim father, or had been devoted as a child by his father or guardian. Khonds in distress often sold their children for victims, 'considering the beatification of their souls certain, and their death, for the benefit of mankind, the most honourable possible.' A man of the Panua (Pán) tribe was once seen to load a Khond with curses, and finally to spit in his face, because the Khond had sold for a victim his own child, whom the Panua had wished to marry. A party of Khonds, who saw this, immediately pressed forward to comfort the seller of his child, saying—'your child has died that all the world may live, and the earth goddess herself will wipe that spittle from your face.'[4] The victims were often kept for years before they were sacrificed. Being regarded as consecrated beings, they were treated with extreme affection, mingled with deference, and were welcomed wherever they went. A Meriah youth, on attaining maturity, was generally given a wife, who was herself usually a Meriah or victim, and with her he received a portion of land and farm-stock. Their offspring were also victims. Human sacrifices were offered to the earth goddess by tribes, branches of tribes, or villages, both at periodical festivals and on extraordinary occasions. The periodical sacrifices were generally so arranged by tribes and divisions of tribes that each head of a family was enabled, at least once a year, to procure a shred of flesh for his fields, generally about the time when his chief crop was laid down.[5]

"The mode of performing these tribal sacrifices was as follows. Ten or twelve days before the sacrifice, the victim was devoted by

---

[1] *The Golden Bough: a study in comparative Religion*, London, 1890.

[2] Major S. C. Macpherson, *Memorials of Service in India*, p. 113 *sq.*; Major-General John Campbell, *Wild Tribes of Khondistan*, pp. 52–58, etc.

[3] J. Campbell, *op. cit.*, p. 56.

[4] S. C. Macpherson, *op. cit.*, p. 115 *sq.*

[5] *Ib.*, p. 113.

cutting off his hair, which until then was kept unshorn. Crowds of men and women assembled to witness the sacrifice, none might be excluded, since the sacrifice was declared to be 'for all mankind.' It was preceded by several days of wild revelry and gross debauchery.[1] On the day before the sacrifice the victim, dressed in a new garment, was led forth from the village in solemn procession, with music and dancing, to the Meriah grove, which was a clump of high forest trees standing a little way from the village and untouched by the axe. In this grove the victim was tied to a post, which was sometimes placed between two plants of the sankissar shrub. He was then anointed with oil, ghee, and turmeric, and adorned with flowers; and 'a species of reverence, which it is not easy to distinguish from adoration,' was paid to him throughout the day.[2] A great struggle now arose to obtain the smallest relic from his person; a particle of the turmeric paste with which he was smeared, or a drop of his spittle, was esteemed of sovereign virtue, especially by the women. The crowd danced round the post to music, and addressing the earth, said, 'O God, we offer this sacrifice to you; give us good crops, seasons, and health.'[3]

"On the last morning the orgies, which had been scarcely interrupted during the night, were resumed, and continued till noon, when they ceased, and the assembly proceeded to consummate the sacrifice. The victim was again anointed with oil, and each person touched the anointed part, and wiped the oil on his own head. In some places the victim was then taken in procession round the village from door to door, where some plucked hair from his head, and others begged for a drop of his spittle, with which they anointed their heads.[4] As the victim might not be bound nor make any show of resistance, the bones of his arms and, if necessary, his legs were broken; but often this precaution was rendered unnecessary by stupefying him with opium.[5] The mode of putting him to death varied in different places. One of the commonest modes seems to have been strangulation, or squeezing to death. The branch of a green tree was cleft several feet down the middle; the victim's neck (in other places, his chest) was inserted in the cleft, which the priest, aided by his assistants, strove with all his force to close.[6] Then he wounded the victim slightly with his axe, whereupon the crowd rushed at the victim and cut the flesh from the bones, leaving the head and bowels untouched. Sometimes he was cut up alive.[7] In Chinna Kimedy he was dragged along the fields, surrounded by the crowd, who, avoiding his head and intestines, hacked the flesh from his body with their knives till he died.[8] Another very common

[1] S. C. Macpherson, *op. cit.*, p. 117 *sq.*; J. Campbell, p. 112.

[2] S. C. Macpherson, p. 118.

[3] J. Campbell, p. 54.

[4] J. Campbell, pp. 55, 112.

[5] S. C. Macpherson, p. 119; J. Campbell. p. 113.

[6] S. C. Macpherson, p. 127. "Instead of the branch of a green tree, Campbell mentions two strong planks or bamboos (p. 57) or a slit bamboo (p. 182)."

[7] J. Campbell, pp. 56, 58, 120.

[8] Dalton, *Ethnology of Bengal*, p. 288, quoting Colonel Campbell's Report.

mode of sacrifice in the same district was to fasten the victim to the proboscis of a wooden elephant, which revolved on a stout post, and, as it whirled round, the crowd cut the flesh from the victim while life remained. In some villages Major Campbell found as many as fourteen of these wooden elephants, which had been used at sacrifices.[1] In one district the victim was put to death slowly by fire. A low stage was formed, sloping on either side like a roof; upon it the victim was placed, his limbs wound round with cords to confine his struggles. Fires were then lighted and hot brands applied, to make him roll up and down the slopes of the stage as long as possible; for the more tears he shed the more abundant would be the supply of rain. Next day the body was cut to pieces.[2]

"The flesh cut from the victim was instantly taken home by the persons who had been deputed by each village to bring it. To secure its rapid arrival, it was sometimes forwarded by relays of men, and conveyed with postal fleetness fifty or sixty miles.[3] In each village all who stayed at home fasted rigidly until the flesh arrived. The bearer deposited it in the place of public assembly, where it was received by the priest and the heads of families. The priest divided it into two portions, one of which he offered to the earth goddess by burying it in a whole in the ground with his back turned, and without looking. Then each man added a little earth to bury it, and the priest poured water on the spot from a hill gourd. The other portion of flesh he divided into as many shares as there were heads of houses present. Each head of a house rolled his shred of flesh in leaves, and buried it in his favourite field, placing it in the earth behind his back without looking.[4] In some places each man carried his portion of flesh to the stream which watered his fields, and there hung it on a pole.[5] For three days thereafter no house was swept; and in one district strict silence was observed, no fire might be given out, no wood cut, and no strangers received. The remains of the human victim (namely, the head, bowels, and bones) were watched by strong parties the night after the sacrifice; and next morning they were burned, along with a whole sheep, on a funeral pile. The ashes were scattered over the fields, laid as paste over the houses and granaries, or mixed with the new corn to preserve it from insects.[6] Sometimes, however, the head and bones were buried, not burnt.[7] After the suppression of the human sacrifices, inferior victims were substituted in some places; for instance,

---

[1] J. Campbell, p. 126. The elephant represented the earth goddess herself, who was here conceived in elephant-form; Campbell, pp. 51, 126. In the hill tracts of Goomsur she was represented in peacock-form, and the post to which the victim was bound bore the effigy of a peacock, Campbell, p. 54.

[2] S. C. Macpherson, p. 130.

[3] Dalton, *Ethnology of Bengal*, p. 288, referring to Colonel Campbell's Report.

[4] S. C. Macpherson, p. 129, cp., J. Campbell, pp. 55, 58, 113, 121, 187.

[5] J. Campbell, p. 182.

[6] S. C. Macpherson, p. 128; Dalton, *l. c.*

[7] J. Campbell, pp. 55, 182.

in the capital of Chinna Kimedy, a goat took the place of a human victim.[1]

"In these Khond sacrifices the Meriahs are represented by our authorities as victims offered to propitiate the earth goddess. But from the treatment of the victims, both before and after death, it appears that the custom cannot be explained as merely a propitiatory sacrifice. A part of the flesh certainly was offered to the earth goddess, but the rest of the flesh was buried by each householder in his fields, and the ashes of the other parts of the body were scattered over the fields, laid as paste on the granaries, or mixed with the new corn. These latter customs imply that to the body of the Meriah there were ascribed a direct or intrinsic power of making the crops to grow, quite independent of the indirect efficacy which it might have as an offering to secure the goodwill of the deity. In other words, the flesh and ashes of the victim were believed to be endowed with a magical or physical power of fertilising the land. The same intrinsic power was ascribed to the blood and tears of the Meriah, his blood causing the redness of the turmeric and his tears producing rain; for it can hardly be doubted that, originally at least, the tears were supposed to produce rain, not merely to prognosticate it. Similarly, the custom of pouring water on the buried flesh of the Meriah was no doubt a rain-charm. Again, intrinsic supernatural power as an attribute of the Meriah appears in the sovereign virtue believed to reside in anything that came from his person, as his hair or spittle. The ascription of such power to the Meriah indicates that he was much more than a mere man sacrificed to propitiate a deity. Once more, the extreme reverence paid him points to the same conclusion. Major Campbell speaks of the Meriah as 'being regarded as something more than mortal,'[2] and Major Macpherson says—'A species of reverence, which it is not easy to distinguish from adoration, is paid to him.'[3] In short, the Meriah appears to have been regarded as divine. As such, he may originally have represented the earth deity, or perhaps a deity of vegetation; though in later times he came to be regarded rather as a victim offered to a deity than as himself an incarnate deity. This later view of the Meriah as a victim rather than a god may perhaps have received undue emphasis from the European writers who have described the Khond religion. Habituated to the later idea of sacrifice as an offering made to a god for the purpose of conciliating his favour, European observers are apt to interpret all religious slaughter in this sense, and to suppose that wherever such slaughter take place, there must necessarily be a deity to whom the slaughter is believed by the slayers to be acceptable. Thus their preconceived ideas unconsciously colour and warp their descriptions of savage rites."

Disposal of the dead.

The dead are burned and the ashes left at the burning ground until the next day. The relatives then go to the spot and burn over the ashes a cloth

[1] J. Campbell, p. 187.
[2] J. Campbell, p. 112.
[3] S. C. Macpherson, p. 118.

and some rice, at the same time calling upon the dead man to keep quiet and employ his spare time in ploughing or in gathering the leaves used for plates, and not to transform himself into a tiger and become a nuisance to his friends. A fowl is also killed and a portion of the flesh laid close to the ashes. Having thus done their best to provide for the comfort of the deceased in the next world, and to induce him to refrain from giving trouble to the living, the mourners return home and solace themselves with a drinking-bout. Relations who live in other villages are expected to pay visits of condolence to the dead man's house, and to bring with them a sufficient quantity of liquor.

Witchcraft.

The Kandhs have a strong belief in witchcraft, particularly in that exercise of the art which enables witches to transform themselves into tigers, leopards, wolves, and so forth, and in this shape to attack human beings or their cattle. For the detection of such persons the following ordeals are appointed:—In the ordeal by iron a bar of iron is put into the blacksmith's furnace and the guru works the bellows. If no one in particular is suspected, the names of the villagers are called out one after the other, and the person at whose name the iron melts is held to be the guilty one. If suspicion has fallen on some one, and it is desired simply to test his guilt, a fowl is taken, its legs are plunged into boiling water and rapidly withdrawn. If the skin peels off, the suspected person is held to be guilty, and he is turned out of the village unless he chooses to undergo the ordeal by fire. For this purpose a trench is cut seven cubits long and one cubit broad, and filled with burning embers. The legs of the accused are then smeared with *ghi*, and he is made to walk twice through the trench lengthwise. If the *ghi* catches fire and he is burned, it is a proof of his guilt.

Dress.

The dress of the Kandhs is simple. The only garment of the men is a long cloth, a few inches wide, which is passed round the waist and twice through between the legs, the ends usually brightly coloured, hang down behind like a tail. The hair is worn in a tight chignon on the right side of the head, into which metal pins, a fine tooth-comb and flamingo feathers are usually stuck as ornaments. The women's dress consists of a short petticoat reaching from the waist to the knee; on the upper part of the body they wear nothing but strings of beads. The face is tattooed on the cheeks and forehead with fine lines starting from the nose as a centre. Sometimes the legs are also decorated in this fashion. All observers agree in describing the men as a fine-looking, well-formed race of middle height, and great activity and fleetness of foot. The women, on the other hand, are ugly of feature, short and square of build, and exceedingly sturdy and robust. Similar differences of form and feature between the two sexes may be observed among the Rájbansi, the Tibetans, the Mundas and Oraons of Chota Nagpur, and among many other primitive races. It is, in fact, a general opinion among ethnologists that the tribal type is more sharply defined and more persistent among the women than among the men of a tribe.

Like the Santáls and Hos, the Kandhs are keen sportsmen and show remarkable skill in the use of very primitive weapons. Armed only with axes and bows and arrows, they run down the bison, the nilgao and the wild boar, and their accuracy of aim in the case of smaller animals is described as surprising. Agriculture is their sole pursuit, and none of them have taken to any sort of trade. They claim full rights of property in the soil in virtue of having cleared the jungle and prepared the land for cultivation. In some villages individual ownership is unknown, and the land is cultivated on a system of temporary occupation subject to periodical redistribution under the orders of the headman or *málik*. Every village has its headman or *málik*, and the office is hereditary in the male line. These officials have considerable influence, and act as arbitrators in petty disputes between the villagers. A group of villages supposed to be inhabited by the descendants of a single ancestor forms a *muta* or commune under a chief called the *muta-málik*, whose authority is invoked chiefly to settle social disputes. In addition to the *muta-málik*, each *muta* has a Hindu Superintendent, called *bisai* or *muta-sardár*. These men are believed to have been appointed and endowed with grants of land by the Kandhs themselves in order to act as intermediaries between them and the Hindu Rájás of the neighbourhood. Their authority is said to be rapidly declining.

Occupation.

The tables on the following pages show the names of relationships in use among the Kandhs.

A.—Relations through the father, whether of man or woman.

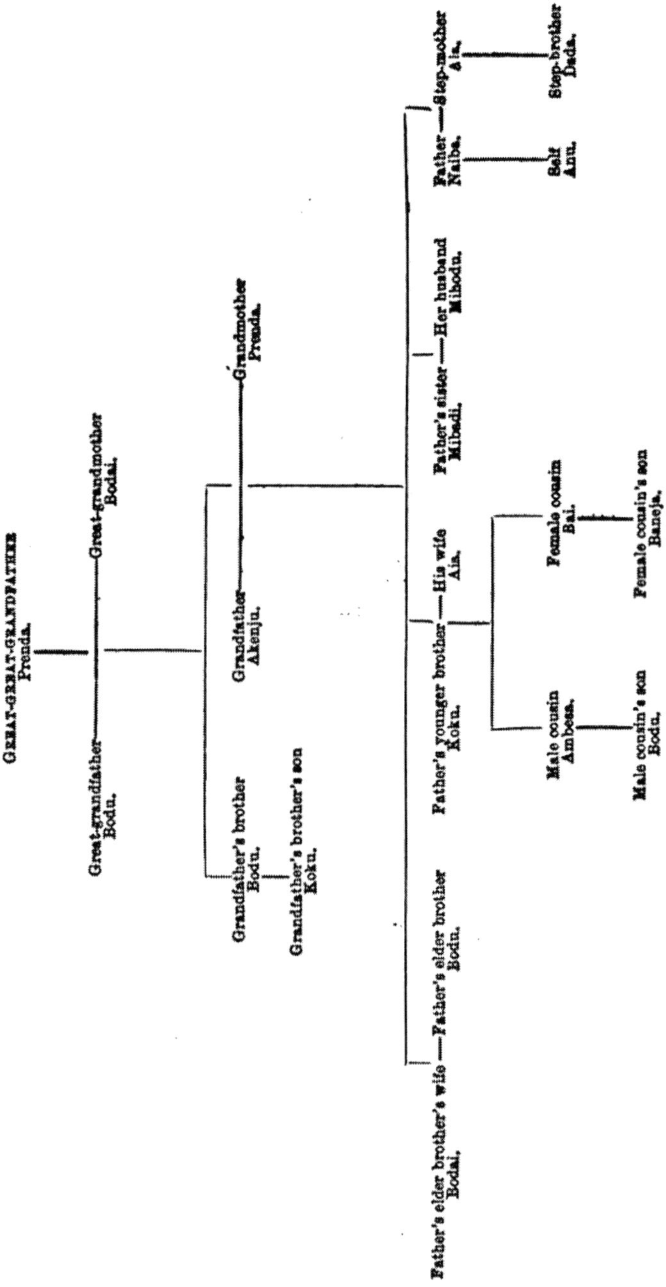

B.—Relations through the mother, whether of man or woman.

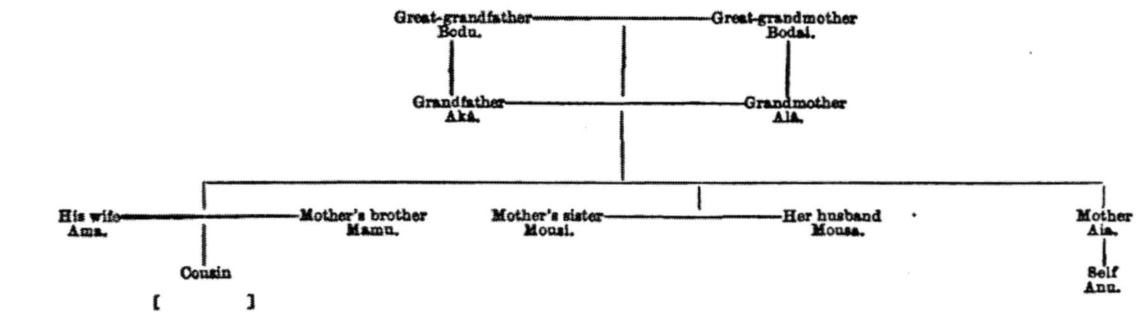

C.—Relations through the brother and sister, whether of man or woman.

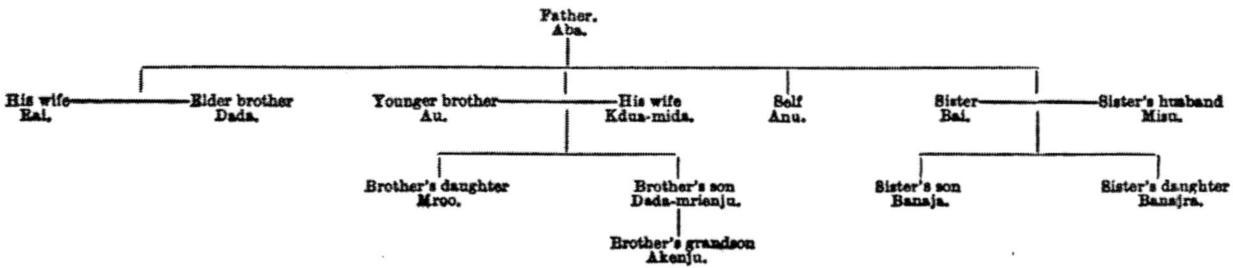

D (1).—*Relations through the wife, of a man.*

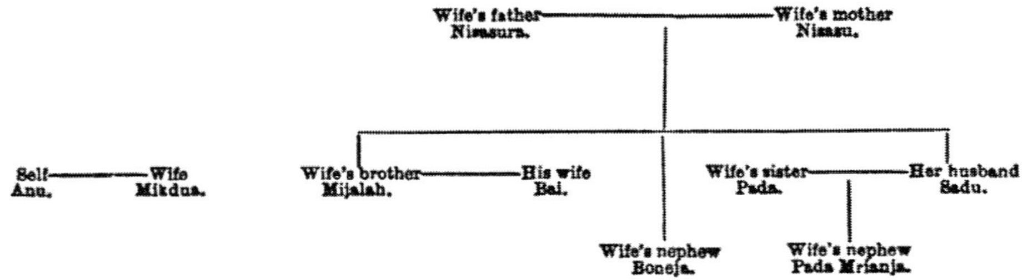

D (2).—*Relations through the husband, of a woman.*

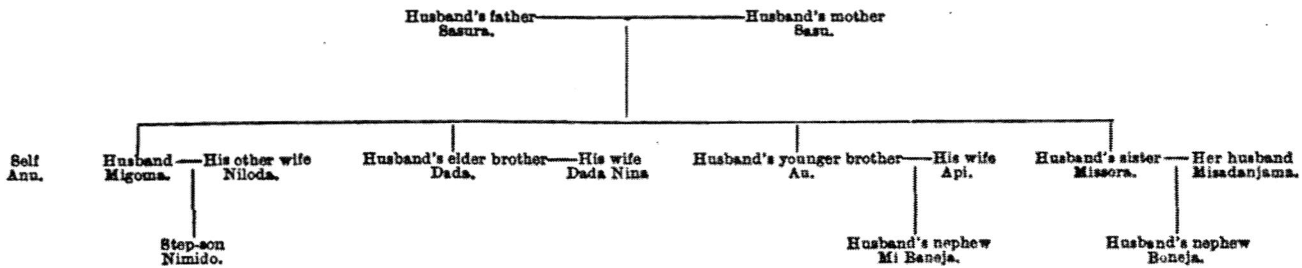

E (1).—*Relations through the son, whether of man or woman.*

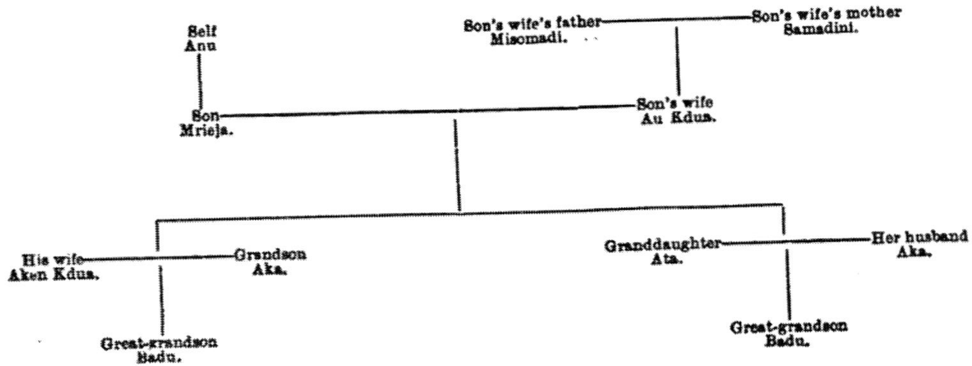

E (2).—*Relations through the daughter, whether of man or woman.*

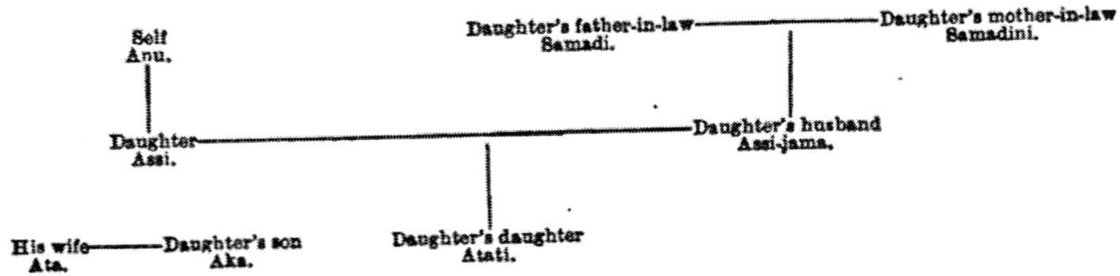

Kándh pákar, a section of the Biyáhut and Kharidáhá Kalwárs in Behar.

Kandir, a bird, a totemistic sept of Mundas in Chota Nagpur.

Kandru, fish, a totemistic sept of Mundas in Chota Nagpur.

Kándu, *Kánu*, *Bharbhunjá*, *Bhujári*, *Gonr*, the grain-parching caste of Behar and Bengal, supposed to be descended from a Kahár father and a Sudra mother, and ranking among the mixed castes. According to Buchanan,[1] indeed, the Kándus of Gorakhpur were reckoned as Vaisyas, but in this connexion the term Vaisya seems to have been used merely to mean merchant, and had no reference to the Vaisyas of early Indian tradition. The fact that the Kándus keep shops and often manufacture and sell sweetmeats has led to their being confounded with the Halwái or confectioners, who make sweetmeats, but do not usually parch grain themselves. This confusion has perhaps been more difficult to avoid owing to both castes being distributed over much the same area and having among their sub-castes groups bearing the same territorial names. The Kándus are divided into the following sub-castes:—

Origin.

Madhesiá, Magahiyá, Bantariá or **Bharbhunjá, Kanaujiá, Gonr, Koránch, Dhuriá, Rawáni, Ballamtiriá, Thather** or **Thatherá**. Among these the Madhesiá and Bantariá adhere strictly to their hereditary profession of parching grain and selling sweetmeats; the Kanaujiá sub-caste are said to make saltpetre, while the Madhesiá Guriya are cultivators, personal servants, and thatchers of houses; the Gonr cut and dress stones, sell sweetmeats, or act as personal servants in the houses of zemindars. Grain-parching, building mud walls, brick-laying, and thatching are the characteristic occupations of the Koránch, while the Dhuriá and Rawáni carry palanquins and make sweetmeats. All the sub-castes, or at any rate their women, practise grain-parching more or less; and the separation of each group from the main body seems to have been due either to geographical position or to the circumstance of the males of the group adopting other occupations in addition to their hereditary profession. The Dhuriá and Rawáni rank lowest of all, owing either to their having taken up the comparatively menial profession of palanquin-bearing or to their being branches of the Kahar caste, who went in for grain-parching and thus came to be associated with the Kándus. These two intermarry with each other. All the other sub-castes are strictly endogamous.

Internal structure.

The majority of the Dacca Kándus, says Dr. Wise, belong to the Madhesiá and Koranch sub-castes, and are usually called Bharbhunjás, from their parching and grinding grain and preparing *sattú* or flour. Another equally common designation is Pánch Píriya Kándus, from the religious sect to which they all belong. They originally came from Damdáhá, in Purniah, but having resided for several generations in Bengal are known as Khontá, or degraded, and

[1] *Eastern India*, ii, 465.

Deswálí, or alien, Kándus by their Hindustání brethren, who decline all communication with them.

The sections of the Magahiyá sub-caste, which are very numerous, are shown in Appendix I. Authorities differ as to the precise form of exogamy which is practised. Some say that a man may not marry a woman who belongs to the same section as (*a*) himself, (*b*) his mother, (*c*) his paternal grandmother, (*d*) his maternal grandmother, (*e*) his paternal and maternal grandmothers. According to others the four sections of father, mother, and both grandmothers are excluded on the side of the bridegroom, and the three sections of father, mother, and maternal grandmother on the side of the bride, and in reckoning consanguinity both sets are taken into account; so that if the bride's maternal grandmother should have belonged to the same section as the bridegroom's paternal grandmother, the marriage will be barred, even though the bride and bridegroom themselves belong to different sections. Probably both systems are in force in some part of the large area covered by the caste. As regards the other sub-castes, the information available is rather meagre. The Gonr, Kanaujiá, and Madhesiá have *muls* or sections, and exclude in marriage a man's own section and those to which his mother's and both his grandmother's belong. I have not been able to ascertain the names of the sections. Two of the Bantariá and five of the Koránch sections are given in Appendix I. The Dhuriá and Rawáni sub-castes regulate their marriages by the standard formula for calculating prohibited degrees.

Marriage.

As a general rule Kándus marry their daughters as infants, but cases of adult-marriage are by no means uncommon. The marriage ceremony is of the common type, and *sindurdán* is regarded as the binding portion. A *tilak* of cloth and ornaments is usually exchanged, the first gift being presented by the parents of the bride. But where the bride's people are very poor, a bride-price of from Rs. 10 to Rs. 20 is sometimes paid, and in such cases the marriage is celebrated in the bridegroom's house. Among the Gonr sub-caste I have come across a very singular practice, which appears to have been introduced with the object of avoiding the stigma incurred by a family which has a daughter unmarried at the age of puberty. Where a girl is sickly or deformed, or where, owing to the poverty of the family, it is thought doubtful whether she will get married, all the relatives are assembled, and in their presence she is formally married to a drawn sword. The full marriage ceremony is performed, the caste Brahman officiates as priest, and red lead is smeared on the girl's forehead with the point of the sword. A girl so married wears ornaments, bedaubs the parting of her hair with red lead, and in every respect demeans herself as a married woman, though living in her father's house. In the event of her afterwards procuring a husband, the entire ceremony is performed afresh. In the case of adults sexual intercourse before marriage may be atoned for by pay ment of a fine to the panchâyat; and if the fine is duly paid, the social position of the couple after marriage is not affected by their previous indiscretion.

Polygamy is permitted up to the customary limit of two wives; but in some districts it seems to be held that before taking a second wife a man must obtain the permission either of his first wife or of the headman and pancháyat of the caste. A man may marry his wife's younger sister, whether virgin or widowed, but may in no case marry an elder sister after being married to the younger. A widow may marry again by the *sagai* ritual, which is less meagre than is usual among other widow-marrying castes. A Brahman is employed to recite *mantras*, and *sindur* is besmeared seven times on the forehead of the widow. She is not obliged to marry her late husband's younger brother, should such a relative exist, but in practice it is usual for her to do so. If she prefers to marry an outsider, the members of her late husband's family may claim the custody of her male children by him. Female children, however, follow the mother. Most Kándus appear to allow of divorce for adultery with a member of the caste, and permit divorced wives to marry again. Among the Gonr sub-caste, however, divorce in the European sense of the word is unknown. If a woman goes wrong with a member of the caste, the matter is brought before the pancháyat, and is usually condoned. A second indiscretion is visited with expulsion from the caste, and this penalty is invariably inflicted when a woman has a *liaison* with an outsider.

Religion.

In matters of religion the caste seems to be pretty evenly divided between Vaishnavism and Sáktism. Maithil or Tirhutiá Brahmans serve them as priests, and are received on equal terms by other members of the sacred order. Their minor gods are numerous and deserve special notice. In Behar the entire caste worship Goraiyá in a fashion which seems hardly in keeping with their high social position, and which seems to be a survival of some non-Aryan rite. A lump of clay is set up outside the house to represent the deity, a Dosádh officiates as priest, and the victim is a pig which is bought for a price from the Dosádh, slain by him at the instance of the Kándu worshippers, and then eaten by the family of the priest. The Dosádh, in fact, performs exactly the same functions as the Páhan of Chota Nagpur, and is paid for them in exactly the same manner. The Bantariá or Bharbhunjá sub-caste worship Govinda as a household god on the Krishnáshtami (8th dark half of Bhádra) with offerings of parched paddy, plantain, curds, and sweetmeats, which are eaten by the members of the family and the *deádi* relations. The Gonr sub-caste perform *pujá* once a month to a small silver image of Bandi Mái; and on the tenth day of the Dasahará festival they wash the chisel, hammer, and T-square which they use for stone-cutting, and worship these tools with libations of ghi. The Koranch also worship Bandi, but make her image of cloth, like a doll. The Magahiyá Kándus of Bhagalpur and Monghyr worship a deified member of the caste, one Kangáli Sahu,[1] to whom goats, sweetmeats, boiled rice, parched grain, and ganja are offered in the months of Srávan and Bhádra.

---

[1] Otherwise known as Kangáli Maháráj, or Kangáli Bábá.

In the month of Mágh all grain-parching Kándus, instead of worshipping Sarasvatí, as most Hindus do, pay adoration to Sokha Sív Náth. At this festival a pot filled with ghi, flour, barley, and other articles of their trade, together with a large quantity of rosin (*dhúná*), is set fire to, and the dense smoke is regarded as the symbol or manifestation of their patron deity. Rám Thákur, Rangá Dhári, and Náyá Gosáin, are also mentioned among the minor gods of Behar, to whom goats are offered on Fridays in the month of Ashár.

The Dacca Kándus, although employing a Brahman as purohit, follow the singular creed called Pánch Píriyá. Many observe the fast of Ramazán, wear the *baddhi* or sash, and the *kafni* or mendicant's garb, offer sweetmeats (*shirni*) at Dargahs and at the Shíah Husainí Dalán, and put their trust in amulets (*tawiz*) given by the Khwánd-Kár. Like the Pánch Píriyá Binds and Kumhárs, their Guru is the Mahant of the Nának Sháhí Akhárá.

Their funeral ceremonies present no features of special interest. The dead are burned, and *sráddh* is performed on the thirty-first day after death.

Occupation.

Most Kándus believe the parching of grain to be their original and characteristic occupation, and the caste is spoken of by early English travellers under the quaint name of "the frymen." In Upper India they are often cultivators, but they also parch grain and use pack-bullocks, as the Banjárás do, for transporting merchandise and cereals. The Gonr sub-caste cut and dress stone for building, carve images of the gods, and prepare curry-stones and grain-mills for household use. They also work as masons, and many of them are employed as domestic servants in the houses of wealthy landholders. In this capacity they fetch water and do all kinds of culinary work. No money wages are paid them, but they get their homestead lands (*bári*) rent-free, and are also entitled to claim certain perquisites (*mángan*) when the crops are reaped. Their women parch grain, and sometimes make sweetmeats.

Throughout the caste, indeed, the actual work of parching grain is usually left to the women. The process is a simple one. A clay oven is built, somewhat in the shape of a beehive, with ten or twelve round holes in the top. A fire is lighted inside and broken earthen pots containing sand are put on the holes. The grain to be parched is thrown in with the sand and stirred with a flat piece of wood (*dabilá*) or a broom (*jháru*) until it is ready. The wages (*bhág*) of the parcher are a proportion of the grain, varying from one-eighth to one-fourth. In Dacca the Kándus are confectioners as well as watchmen, domestic servants, and coolies. Their lowly traditional origin does not prevent their providing the only food that strict Hindus can eat with unwashed hands. It should be explained that vegetable products, such as *gur* or molasses, and sweetmeats cooked without the addition of any other substance than sugar, are called *jálá* or *kánchá*, and may be eaten even by Brahmans without dishonour; but if water or milk be added, it is *pakka* or dressed, and becomes impure.

This rule is observed everywhere, but in Upper India the terms in which it is expressed are exactly the reverse of those used in Bengal. A native of Behar, for instance, speaks of sweetmeats, parched grain, etc., as *pakki* food, while by *kachchi* he means boiled rice, chupatties, etc., and anything in the preparation of which water has been used. The convenience of the distinction is obvious. It lightens the burden of taboo, and enables a traveller or a man who is in a hurry to stay his hunger without either risking his caste or being obliged to inquire minutely into the ceremonial status of the person who supplies him with food.

Social status.

In point of social standing Kándus may be classed with Koiris, Goálás, Gangautás, and the entire group of castes from whose hands a Brahman will take water. On this point Buchanan, writing of Gorakhpur, observes :—" The Kándus are considered as on a par with the lower Baniyas. One-half of them have Brahman gurus, the others are of all the sects which the Baniyás follow. Their purohits are pure Brahmans. Their widows become concubines, but they abstain from drinking liquor in public, and Rajputs do not scruple to drink their water, although they eat the wild hog." Kándus themselves will eat cooked food only with members of their own sub-caste. Gonr Kándus, indeed, are said to be so particular as not to allow even a Brahman to cook for them; but I am inclined to think that this statement may have been a piece of personal affectation on the part of my informant, for in Champáran, where all Kándus permit themselves to eat fowls, the Gonr sub-caste add to this the further iniquity of indulging in strong drink. As agriculturists the caste does not hold a very high position. A few members of the Kóránch sub-caste have risen to be zemindars and tenure-holders, but most Kándus are occupancy raiyats, while in Bhagalpur some have sunk to be *Kamiás* or landless day-labourers.

The following statement shows the number and distribution of Kándus in 1872 and 1881 :—

District.	1872.	1881.	District.	1872.	1881.
Bardwan	817	747	Tipperah	407	269
Bankura	193	721	Patna	30,430	31,513
Birbhum	70	492	Gya	22,753	25,072
Midnapur	328	2,111	Shahabad	60,145	65,751
Hughli	574 (Hughli and Howrah)	183	Tirhut { Mosufferpur ...	99,298 (Tirhut)	80,078
Howrah		1,106	Tirhut { Darbhanga ...		83,288
24-Parganas	1,847	632	Saran	111,921	88,723
Nadiya	2,268	840	Champaran	60,721	67,393
Khulna	......	66	Monghyr	52,259	59,207
Jessore	437	978	Bhagalpur	23,781	24,191
Murshedabad	2,384	1,112	Purniah	4,833	5,913
Dinajpur	1,083	389	Maldah	1,048	1,214
Rajshahye	22	31	Santál Parganas	2,121	9,084
Rangpur	16	517	Cuttack	59,598	58,644
Bogra	9	8	Puri	22,403	24,920
Pabna	144	184	Balasore	10,008	12,153
Darjiling	81	422	Tributary States	22,698	23,407
Jalpigori	640	181	Hazaribagh	5,087	6,969
Kuch Behar	......	73	Lohardaga	8,669	7,159
Dacca	1,611	330	Singbhum	42	156
Bakarganj	2	22	Manbhum	1,058	678
Maimansinh	314	267	Tributary States	120	1,700
Chittagong	7	......			

Kandwár, a sept of Rajputs in Behar.

Káneil, a section of the Biyáhut and Kharidáhá Kalwárs, and of Magahiyá Kándus in Behar.

Kangál, Kangáli, a beggar. Usually denotes the class of lepers, cripples, etc., who are maintained in ordinary years by the charity of their fellow-villagers. The obligation is held to cease when relief measures are undertaken by Government.

Kangali, a title of Goálás.

Kánhaiwar, a *mul* or section of the Naomuliá or Majraut sub-caste of Goálás in Behar.

Kanigáme-Kanigám, a *mul* of the Bharadwája section of Maithil Brahmans in Behar.

Kanjar, *Khangor*, a Dravidian gipsy caste of the North-West Provinces, who hunt jackals, catch and eat snakes, and make strings of hemp and cotton. In Behar they are chiefly rope-twisters.

Kanji, a title of Joláhas.

Kánjiári, a *gáin* of the Bátsya *gotra* of Rárhi Brahmans in Bengal.

Kánjilál, a *gáin* of the Bátsya *gotra* of Rárhi Brahmans in Bengal.

Kánkhojia, an ear-picker, generally a member of the barber caste.

Kánkol, a *mul* or section of the Chhamuliá Madhesiá sub-caste of Halwáis in Behar.

Kánkuli, a sept of Rajputs in Behar.

Kanniá, a *gotra* or section of Nepáli Brahmans.

Káno, a section of the Banapár sub-caste of Koiris in Behar.

Kanp, a *mul* or section of the Kanaujiá sub-caste of Sonárs in Behar.

Kánpákar, a *mul* or section of the Tinmuliá Madhesiá sub-caste of Halwáis in Behar.

Kánphát or **Sannyási**, a religious group of Jugis.

Kanphatá, a sept of the Rautár sub-tribe of Thárus in Behar.

Kánri, a Hindu caste of Purniah allied to the Doms and intermarrying with them. Their profession is hunting, and they are supposed to be experts in killing tigers and other wild beasts with poisoned arrows.

Kans, grass, a sept of Kharwars in Chota Nagpur.

Kansabanik, a synonym for Kánsári.

Kánsári, *Kansabanik*, the brazier caste of Bengal, popularly supposed to be an offshoot of the Subarnabanik, degraded because its members took to working in Kánsá or bell-metal. Another view is that they are merely a sub-caste of Kámárs who have severed their connexion with the parent caste and set up as an independent group. Kánsáris marry their daughters as infants by the orthodox Brahmanical ritual, prohibit the remarriage of widows, and do not recognise divorce. Their social rank is respectable. They employ the same Brahman, barber and waterman as the members of the Nabasakh group, and Brahmans take water from their hands In Eastern Bengal almost all Kánsáris belong to the Saiva sect, but in Central and Western Bengal Saivas are found among their number. Like other artisan castes, they are very particular about observing the festival of Viswakarmá, the mythical architect of the universe.

Kánsáris buy their material in the form of brass sheeting, which they hammer into the shapes required. In Eastern Bengal Chandáls often take service with them, and become very skilful workmen. The utensils made are sold to dealers (*paikár*) who retail them in villages inland.

Kánsari, a sub-caste of Kámárs in Midnapur.

Kansaunghiá, a section of Bábhans in Behar.

Kansi, field grass, a totemistic sept of Chiks, Kumhars, Páns, Telis, Goálás, and Bairágis in Chota Nagpur; a section of Kahárs in Behar.

Kant, a section of Awadhiá Hajjáms in Behar.

Kantáha, Mahábráhman, or **Mahápátra**, a division of Brahmans in Behar, who officiate as priests at the cremation of the dead.

Kántái, a group of the Rájbansi sub-caste of the Koch caste, by profession palki-bearers.

Kantaru, a sub-section of the Bharadwája section of Utkal Brahmans.

Kante ke rakmal, a section of the Biyáhut and Kharidáhá Kalwárs in Behar.

Kante ke ras, a section of the Biyáhut and Kharidáhá Kalwárs in Behar.

Kánthará, a *gáin* or sub-section of Saptasati Brahmans in Bengal.

Kanthwár, a territorial section of Rautiás in Chota Nagpur.

Kánti, Kantuár, a totemistic section of Máhilis in Manbhum, the members of which will not eat the ear of any animal.

Kantitáhá, a sub-caste of Goálás in Behar.

Kantithiá, a section of Kanaujiá Lohárs in Behar.

Kánu, a synonym for Kándu.

Kánungo, an honorary title of Káyasths in Bengal.

Kanwa or **Kánna**, a section of Brahmans.

Kanwad, a jungle fruit, a sept of Kharwárs in Chota Nagpur.

Kanwár, a sept of the Surajbansi division of Rajputs in Behar; a title of Cheros in Palámau.

Kánwar, a sub-caste of Dosádhs in Behar.

Kánwáyan, a kshatra-peta *gotra* or section of Brahmans.

Kanyá, a *gáin* or sub-section of Saptasati Brahmans in Bengal.

Kánwakubja or **Kanaujiá**, a territorial division of the Pancha Gaura Brahmans, deriving its name from the Kanauj country.

Káorá, a sub-caste of Háris in Bengal. They rear pigs and prepare *gur* or molasses from the juice of date-trees. Many of them also act as cooks for Europeans.

Kaorá, a synonym for Korá.

Kápa, Chhaghariá, a hypergamous group of Bárendra Brahmans in Bengal.

Kapáli, a *gáin* of the Sábarna *gotra* of Bárendra Brahmans in Bengal.

Kapáli, a cultivating and weaving caste of Eastern Bengal, who claim to be the offspring of a Kámár father and a Teli mother; others say that the father of the caste was a Tiyar and the mother a Brahman. Both pedigrees are wholly imaginary, and only deserve mention here as illustrating the persistence and vitality of the theory that all castes except the four supposed to have been originally created have arisen by marriage between the members of these four and members of the so-called mixed castes thus produced. Like many Bengal castes, the Kapáli have a vague tradition that their original home was in Upper India; but this tradition has never assumed a legendary form. Another theory is that up to the time of Adisura they were classed as the Sudras of Eastern Bengal, and that when he imported the ancestors of the Bengal Brahmans and Káyasths from Kanauj, he called upon the Kapális to supply the newcomers with water. This they declined to do, and in punishment for their refusal were reduced to the comparatively low position which they now hold. The internal structure of the caste throws no light upon its origin. They have only two sections—Sib (Siva) and Kásyapa—but these are not exogamous, and marriage is regulated by counting prohibited degrees down to three, or, as some say, seven generations in the descending line. We may perhaps hazard the conjecture that the section-name Sib, by no means a common one, may indicate remote kinship with the Sib-bansi Kochh, a very numerous tribe, from which in all probability many of the castes of Eastern Bengal have been derived. Kapális have no regular sub-castes, but a distinction seems to be drawn between those who make gunny-bags and those who only sell them. The latter consider themselves socially superior to the former and avoid intermarriage with them, though they have not yet reached the complete endogamy which is essential to the formation of a sub-caste properly so-called.

Origin.

Internal structure.

Kapális marry their daughters as infants by the standard Hindu ritual, the essential portion of which is *sampradán*, or the presentation of the bride to the bridegroom and his acceptance of the gift. The bride's parents receive a bride-price (*van*), the amount of which is slightly higher when the bride comes from a family bearing the title of Mandal, Mánjhi, or Shikdár. Polygamy is permitted when the first wife is barren, but is said to be rare in practice. Widows may not marry again. Divorce is not recognised. A woman taken in adultery is simply cast off by her husband and ceases to be a member of respectable society. She cannot marry her paramour, for *sángá* is not in force among Kapális, but she may live with him as his mistress, though in that case both run some risk of being expelled from the caste.

Marriage.

Religion.

The religion of the Kapáli presents no features of special interest. Most of them are Vaishnavas, comparatively few being Sáktas. Among the minor gods Kártikeya is held in special veneration. For religious and ceremonial purposes they employ degraded Barna-Brahmans, who are looked down upon by all members of the sacred order, except those who serve castes of still lower social status than the Kapálí. The dead are burned, and the *sráddh* ceremony is performed on the thirty-first day after death. In the case of persons who die a violent death, the *sráddh* takes place on the fourth day.

Occupation.

In Rangpur Buchanan found the Kapáli engaged in making umbrellas, but in Eastern Bengal at the present day they are weavers and cultivators. According to Dr. Wise, they chiefly cultivate jute (*koshtá*), preparing the fibre themselves and manufacturing from it coarse canvas (*tát*) for bags. Both men and women weave, their loom being the ordinary native one, but clumsier than that used by the Tántí. Their shuttle is called *váya*, and they dispense with the reed (*shána*). They are careful to explain that the shuttle is shot with the hands, as among the Tántís, and not driven by pedals, as with the outcaste Jogis.

The Kapáli manufactures three kinds of canvas: the first (*chhálá*) being used for the carriage of rape seed; the second (*chat*) for packing goods; while the third (*tát*) is in universal demand for floor-matting, for boat sails, rice bags, and bags for country produce generally. In Bikrampúr a finer kind of canvas, known as *bára-bastra*, is woven for the carriage of areca nut. The trade of the Kapáli has of late years suffered greatly by the importation of gunny-bags from Europe, but they always find a ready market for the sake of matting. Bamboo mats for floors are seldom used in Bengal, but canvas is laid down in every shop, and beneath bedding whenever people sleep on the ground. On the Vijayá Dasamí day of the Durgá Pújá all Bengali shopkeepers, often including the Muhammadan, regard it as a duty to throw away the old matting of their shops and to replace it by new.

The Kapális generally reside in villages, where they can cultivate jute, never in large towns, and would lose caste if they worked with hemp or cotton. Their occupation being different from that of the Tántí, the two castes live in amity with one another.

Social status.

They are usually poor, but in former days several of them are said to have risen to be táluqdárs. Some hold tenures, but the bulk of the caste are occupancy and non-occupancy raiyats. A few have relinquished their characteristic trade and become boatmen and shop-keepers. Socially they rank between Jeliyás and Dhobás. They claim to be of higher rank than the Bhuinmáli, Chandál, or Sunri, and the washerman and barber admit them to be clean Sudras, and have no objection to working for them. Their practice in the matter of food is the same as that of other orthodox Hindus of Eastern Bengal. They assert that they never taste spirits, but it is generally believed they do. Ganjá-smoking, however, is common among them.

The following statement shows the number and distribution of Kapális in 1872 and 1881:—

District.	1872.	1881.	District.	1872.	1881.
Bardwan	730	729	Pabna	5,811	6,378
Bankura	......	1	Darjiling	......	89
Birbhum	230	......	Jalpigori	838	690
Midnapur	130	71	Kuch Behar	......	12
Hughli	} 1,724	{ 337	Dacca	17,017	18,589
Howrah		1,698	Faridpur	9,359	12,189
24-Parganas	28,061	9,534	Bakarganj	8,378	7,009
Nadiya	12,961	5,728	Maimansinh	11,393	11,568
Khulna	......	14,719	Tipperah	8,197	6,443
Jessore	22,794	27,679	Chittagong	......	46
Murshedabad	1,536	100	Noakhali	417	582
Dinajpur	86	248	Purniah	......	55
Rajshahye	12	213	Maldah	17	......
Rangpur	316	265	Santál Parganas	......	10
Bogra	761	810			

Kápar, a section and a title of Kewats; a title of the Dhusiá sub-caste of Chamárs and of Maghayá Kumhárs in Behar.

Kapardár, the son of a wet-nurse; a title given by the Rájás of Rámgarh to some of their servants.

Kápari, a section of the Kádar caste in Behar.

Kaphalya, a *thar* or section of Nepáli and Utkal Brahmans.

Kapinjala, a section of Utkal Brahmans.

Kápri, a section of the Maghayá sub-caste of Barhis; a title of Aráyiyá Telis; a section of the Banapár sub-caste of Koiris in Behar; a title of Chamárs and a section of Sunris in Behar.

Kapur, a section of Awadhiá Hajjáms in Behar.

Kápur, a sept of the Chandrabansi division of Rajputs and a section of the Chárjáti sub-caste of Khatris in Behar.

Kar, a section of Utkal or Orissa Brahmans; a family name of Baidyas and Kayasths in Bengal; a title of the Áut sub-caste of Gandhabaniks, of Sánkháris, Tántis, and Sutradhars in Bengal.

Kará, buffalo, a sub-sept of the Besrá sept of Santáls and a sept of Chiks in Chota Nagpur.

Kárá, a group of the Srotriya sub-caste of Utkal Brahmans; a *mul* or section of the Tinmuliá and Chhamuliá Madhesiá and Bhojpuria sub-castes of Halwáis in Behar; a title of Kaibarttas.

Kárádhánautá, a *mul* or section of the Tinmuliá Madhesiá sub-caste of Halwáis in Behar.

Karaf, a section of Awadhiá Hajjáms in Behar.

Karaiáchor, a section of the Banodhiá and Jaiswár Kalwárs in Behar.

Karaiárk, a *pur* or section of Sákadwipi Brahmans in Behar.

Karaiyá, a sub-caste of Háris.

Karáiyá, a title of Bangaja Káyasths.

Kárak, a section of Sunris and Telis in Behar and Chota Nagpur.

Kárákátá Karwár, buffalo, a totemistic section of Kurmis in Chota Nagpur and Orissa.

Karál, *Kurál*, a sub-caste of Chandáls who sell fish caught by others. Their women prepare and sell *chirá*.

Karalái, a sub-caste of Kaibarttas in Noakhali.

Karam, a tree, a sept of Goálás in Chota Nagpur.

Karámati, a *thar* or sept of Gurungs in Darjiling.

Karamwár, a sept of Rajputs in Behar.

Karan, the indigenous writer-caste of Orissa. Karans recognise only two endogamous sub-castes—**Karan** proper and **Sristi-Karan** or **Uriya Sristi-Karan**. The former, like the Madhyasreni Brahmans and the Kásthas or Madhyasreni Káyasths, claim to have been originally Káyasths of Bengal who were driven to take refuge in Orissa, because they refused to accept the institution of Kulinism from Ballál Sen. The latter are supposed to be sprung from *liaisons* between Karans and members of the Nabasákhá group. They are generally employed as menial servants by the Karans, and I am informed that even now they do not object to admit the illegitimate children of Karans into their caste. Karans and Sristi-Karans, however, do not intermarry, and a Karan cannot eat food that has been cooked by a Sristi-Karan. As with the Káyasths of Bengal, cases occur among the Karans of outsiders being admitted into the caste, and it is said that several families of well-to-do Khandaits have thus been transformed into Karans. The children borne by maid-servants kept in the family are called Bhatuntara. They are recognised as Karans, but do not inherit the property of the head of the family.

Origin and internal structure.

Another group, which is not strictly endogamous, deserves special notice here. This is the class known as Nauli Karan or Karan with the sacred thread. Concerning these a curious story is told. Once upon a time the King of Orissa while out walking found two male infants, apparently twins, lying at the roadside. He had them carried home, and gave one to a washerwoman and the other to a sweeper (Hári) woman to nurse. When they were grown up, the boys were brought to the king, and he was asked to determine their caste. Seeing that no low-caste woman would be at the trouble of exposing her infants, the king concluded that they must be either Brahmans or Karans. As it was impossible to say which, he decided, as it were, to split the difference by investing them with the sacred thread as if they were Brahmans, and then enrolling them in the Karan caste. Their descendants still go through the form of investing their sons with the thread, though they only wear it for two or three months. At the time of their assuming the thread they perform a curious ceremony in memory of the vicissitudes of their ancestors. A post made of *bel* wood, and adorned with various kinds of devices in *sola* is set up at the place where the ceremony of investiture is performed, and shell bracelets, a piece of cloth, and other odds and ends are placed at the foot of it. On one side of the post stands a washerwoman, on the other a woman of the Hári caste, and when the initiate is taken inside the house, he is made to bow ostensibly to the *bel* post, but really, so it is explained, to the two women who represent the wet-nurses of the twin forefathers of the caste. The Nauli Karans intermarry with the Karans proper, but not with the Sristi-Karans.

The exogamous divisions of the Karan caste are shown in Appendix I. Most of them are of the standard Brahmanical type, though it is possible that Nágésa and Sankha may be totemistic. Prohibited degrees are reckoned by the method in vogue among the higher Hindu castes, with the curious exception that a man is permitted to marry his maternal uncle's daughter, an alliance distinctly forbidden by the ordinary rules.

Marriage.

Girls are usually married as infants, but instances not unfrequently occur where, owing to difficulties in procuring a suitable husband, a man will keep his daughters unmarried until they come to be eighteen or nineteen years old. In any case the Karans, like the Kásthas of Midnapur, are careful to guard against the physical objections to infant-marriage by forbidding the couple to cohabit until the bride attains sexual maturity. Contrary to the usual practice of Hindus, marriages in the Karan caste generally take place in the day-time. On the question what should be deemed the more binding portion of the ritual, there seems to be some difference of opinion. Some attach special importance to the offering of funeral cakes to the deceased ancestors of the bridegroom, which takes place on the fourth day after the initial ceremony of giving away the bride. Others again hold that the essential rite is the laying of the bride's right hand in that of the bridegroom, and binding their two hands together with a piece of thread spun in a special way. The wedding usually takes place at the bride's house. On the next day the bride is taken to the bridegroom's house, where she spends eight days, called the *ashta-mangalá*, or eight auspicious days. On the day and night immediately following the marriage, known as the *bisá rátri* or 'poison-night,' the bride and bridegroom are not allowed to see one another at all, nor in any case are they allowed to sleep together during the *ashta-mangalá* unless the bride has attained puberty.

Religion.

Most Karans are Vaishnavas, and their favourite divinity is Krishna. They employ Utkal Brahmans for religious and ceremonial purposes, and these are the only Brahmans from whose hands they will take food. The dead are burned; a period of mourning is observed for ten days, and the *sráddh* is performed in the orthodox fashion on the eleventh day. In the matter of personal law they are governed by the Mitákshará, as interpreted by the commentary of Sambhukar Bájpayi.

Social status.

Karans rank next to Brahmans in the scale of social precedence commonly recognised in Orissa. Most of them have a sound knowledge of their own vernacular and are ready scribes, and within the last few years many of them have taken to English education. Zemindars, patnidárs, holders of lákhiráj tenures, and occupancy and non-occupancy ryots are found among the caste, and many are employed as clerks and gomashtas by the various grades of landholders. They are strict as to diet, abstaining entirely from wine and strong drink, taking cooked or uncooked food from no other caste, water only from members of the Nabasákhá group, and never smoking in the same hookah with men of another caste.

Karan, a sub-caste of Káyasths and Támbulis in Behar.

Karan, Nauli-Karan, a sub-caste of Karans in Orissa.

Karangá, *Karga*, *Koranga*, a small Dravidian caste of Western Bengal, who make baskets, dig tanks, and work as carpenters. Their special business is the making of cart wheels and wooden articles, such as *pailás* or seers of standard measure. In Singbhum they are also stone-cutters. They have two exogamous subdivisions, Sálmách and Kachchap, and four endogamous sub-castes —Dhaluá, Maluá, Sikhariá and Tunga. The word also denotes persons who castrate goats and bullocks.

Karangá-Munda, a sub-tribe of Mundas in Chota Nagpur.

Karangarhyá, a sept of Rajputs in Behar.

Karania, kussum tree, a totemistic sept of Mundas in Chota Nagpur.

Karanja, a *gáin* of the Kásyapa *gotra* of Bárendra Brahmans in Bengal.

Karanjá, a sub-caste of Goálás in Bengal.

Karanjea, an oil-seed, a sept of Bairágis in Chota Nagpur.

Karar, a *mul* or section of the Chhamuliá Madhesiá sub-caste of Halwáis in Behar.

Karár, a section of the Kurmi caste in Manbhum, the members of which will not kill or eat a buffalo.

Kárárihá, a *mul* or section of the Tinmuliá Madhesiá sub-caste of Halwáis in Behar.

Karáti, a title of Chandáls who are employed as sawyers of wood.

Karauche, a section of Bábhans in Behar.

Karaunti, a section of Awadhiá Hajjáms in Behar.

Karbháia, a section of Kanaujiá Sonárs in Behar.

Karcholiá, a sept of Rajputs in Behar.

Kargáhá, a section of the Maghayá sub-caste of Koiris in Behar.

Karhar, a jungle fruit like *bel*, a totemistic sept of Kharwars, Chiks, and Lohárs in Chota Nagpur; a section of Rajwárs in Western Bengal.

Karian, a section of the Satmuliá Maghayá sub-caste of Kándus in Behar.

Kariar, a sept of Kaurs in Chota Nagpur.

Kárikar, *Kárigar*, iron-smiths and artificers generally.

Kariont, a section of the Kamár sub-caste of Dosádhs in Behar.

Karirá, a section of Goálás in the North-Western Provinces and Behar.

Karjáhá, a section of the Biyáhut and Kharidáhá Kalwárs in Behar.

Karjhuliá, a sept of Rajputs in Behar.

Kárji, a title of Binjhiás in Chota Nagpur.

Kárkádá, a *mul* or section of the Chhamuliá Madhesiá sub-caste of Halwáis in Behar.

Karkosa, cow, a totemistic sept of Lohárs in Chota Nagpur.

Karkusá, a bird, a totemistic section of Lohárs and Mahilis in Chota Nagpur.

Karma, a tree, a totemistic sept of Mundas and Gonds in Chota Nagpur.

Karmahe-Majhaurá, a *mul* of the Bátsya section of Maithil Brahmans in Behar.

Karmáhe Áhpur, a *mul* of the Sándil section of Maithil Brahmans in Behar.

Karmahe-Tarauni, a *mul* of the Bátsa section of Maithil Brahmans in Behar.

Karmahe-Naruár, a *mul* of the Bátsa section of Maithil Brahmans in Behar.

Karmahe-Behat, a *mul* of the Bátsa section of Maithil Brahmans in Behar.

Karmahe-Majhiám, a *mul* of the Bátsa section of Maithil Brahmans in Behar.

Karmahe-Alanpur, a *mul* of the Bátsa section of Maithil Brahmans in Behar.

Karmahe-Urái, a *mul* of the Bátsa section of Maithil Brahmans in Behar.

Karmakár, in Bengal a synonym for Kámár; in Hazaribagh a title of Kahárs.

Karmáli, a title of blacksmiths in Chota Nagpur.

Karminia, a sept of the Suryabansi sub-tribe of Rajputs in Behar.

Karmot, a sub-caste of Nuniás in Behar.

Karmuá, a section of Bábhans in Behar.

Karnamási, a section of Báruis in Bengal.

Karnáti, a territorial division of the Pancha Drávira Brahmans, who live in the south of the Vindhya range, in Karnátika, the country of the Canarese language.

Karnautiá, a *kul* or section of Bábhans in Behar.

Karnávati, a section of Bábhans in Behar.

Karni, a small and degraded caste of weavers in Eastern Bengal, whose claim to kinship with the Tántis is repudiated by the latter. Karnis are met with in the western thánas of the Dacca district, along the left bank of the Padma river, but are more numerous in Faridpur and Pabna. They have three *gotras*—Bharadwája, Aliman, and Kasyapa—which appear to have been borrowed from the Brahmanical system. Vaishnavism is the religion of the majority; Saivism of the minority. Their priests are Barna Brahmans, who serve them alone.

The Karni are exclusively engaged in weaving, agriculture and fishing being strictly forbidden. They manufacture the *dhoti* or waist-cloth, the *gámchá*, napkin or towel, as well as chequered bed-curtains (*chárkhán*). In some eastern districts they sell betel-leaf. Napits, Dhobas, and other servants of the Nava-sakha work for the Karní, which would hardly be the case if their origin were wholly impure.

Kárni, a *mul* or section of the Chhamuliá Madhesiá sub-caste of Halwáis in Behar.

Karnwár, a sept of the Surajbansi division of Rajputs in Behar.

Karo, a section of Madhesiá Halwáis in Behar.

Karpatne, a section of the Amashta Káyasths in Behar.

Karpur, a sub-section of the Bharadwája section of Utkal Brahmans.

Karrál, a sub-caste of Chandáls, which has become degraded from carrying on the business of fishmongers. Their kinsmen neither intermarry nor hold any social intercourse with them, but the same Brahman and servants work for both. The Karrál is to the Hindu population what the Mahífarosh or Panjárí is to the Muhammadan, and men and women, though they never fish themselves, retail fish in the markets, and often make advances to fishermen. This sub-caste is more numerous in Faridpur than in Dacca, but all along the left, or Dacca, bank of the Padma small colonies are established, while inland individuals are employed as constables and messengers.

The Karráls are all Vaíshnavas in creed, and united in one *gotra*, the Kasyapa. They confess to a partiality for spirits, but allege that they abstain from flesh, including pork, unless when the animal has been sacrificed.

Karsá, a sept of Rajputs in Behar.

Karsal, a sept of Goálás in Chota Nagpur.

Karsul, a section of Rautiás in Chota Nagpur.

Karthiá, a kind of *dál* or grain, a section of Goálás in Chota Nagpur.

Kártik-rási, a section of Málos in Eastern Bengal.

Karuá, a sept of the Tungjainya sub-tribe of Chakmás in the Hill Tracts of Chittagong.

Karuah, a title of the Ghási caste in Singbhum.

Karuná, a title of Kámárs in Behar.

Karunjua, a big black bird, a totemistic section of Páns in Chota Nagpur.

Karwá, a section of Chamárs in Behar.

Karwár, a section of Dhenuárs in Chota Nagpur.

Karwat, a sub-caste of Nuniás in Behar.

Kasa, a *mul* a section of the Ayodhiá sub-caste of Hajjáms in Behar.

Kasái, a butcher. Most butchers are Mahomedans, but in Bengal low Brahmans, Káorás, and Bágdis slaughter goats and sheep, and are known as Hindu *kasáis*. In Eastern Bengal Mahomedan butchers are classed as Bakri-kasái or goat-killers and Goru-kasái or cow-killers. The latter were formerly looked upon as degraded, but of late years the two groups have united and intermarry freely. All are followers of Moulavi Karamat Ali, and are very bigotted, eating with the Kuti, but declining to have anything to do with sweepers and Bediyas.

Kasái Kuliá, a sub-caste of Bágdis in Western Bengal, living on the banks of the Kasái river, who are boatmen and fishermen and are reckoned the highest in rank of the 14 sub-castes in which the Bágdis are divided.

Kasail, deer, a totemistic sept of Goálás in Chota Nagpur.

Kasarbáni, *Kasarwáni*, a section of the Biyáhut and Kharidáhá Kalwárs in Behar.

Kasarwáni, a sub-caste of Baniyas in Behar, who profess to have no less than ninety-six sections, of which the following are specimens:—**Sagelá Bagelá, Chanankát-Kathautiá, Laungjharájhari, Sonechanrupekedándi, Abkahilá, Chálániá, Chausowár, Málhátiá, Sonaul, Társi, Tirusiá.** A man may not marry a woman belonging to his own section, and must also observe the standard formula of prohibited degrees reckoned to the fifth generation in the descending line. The Kasarwáni marry their daughters as infants, and do not recognise divorce. Polygamy, however, is permitted, without any restriction on the number of wives a man may have. A widow is allowed to marry again, and is not compelled to marry her late husband's younger brother, though it is considered a very proper thing for her to do so. By religion most of them are Vaishnavas, and they also worship Banni and Sokhá-Sambhunáth as minor or household gods. Shop-keeping is their regular occupation, and only a few have taken to agriculture. Kasarwánis will not allow calves to be castrated, nor will they sell cattle to Muhammadans or to men of the Teli caste.

Kasaudhan, *Kasondhan*, or *Kasaunan*, a sub-caste of Baniyás in Behar, some of whom claim to be Bais Baniyás. The claim, however, is not generally admitted.

Kásbak, the heron, a totemistic section of Bágdis.

Kaserá, *Kanserá, Tamherá*, the brass-founding caste of Behar, probably an offshoot from one of the higher mercantile castes, which was separated from the parent group by adopting this special profession. The fact that the Kaserá have a well-defined set of exogamous sections and pride themselves on their purity of descent seems to indicate that the caste is a homogeneous one, and is not, like many of the functional castes, a collection of men from several different groups held together merely by the bond of a common occupation. On the distinction between the Kaserá and the cognate, but distinct, caste of Thatherá, Mr. Nesfield remarks[1] :—"The Kaserá's

Tradition of origin.

[1] *Brief View of the Caste System*, p. 29.

speciality lies in mixing the softer metals (zinc, copper, and tin) and moulding the alloy into various shapes, such as cups, bowls, plates, etc. The Thatherá's art consists in polishing and engraving the utensils which the Kaserá supplies."

Marriage.

The sections of the Kaserás are shown in Appendix I. A man may not marry a woman belonging to his own section, and must also observe the rules regarding prohibited degrees which are held binding by the Káyasths of Behar. All Kaserás who can afford to do so marry their daughters as infants, but they do not appear to regard this as an absolute necessity, and in poor families it often happens that girls do not find husbands until after they have attained the age of puberty. The marriage ceremony is of the standard type. Polygamy is permitted to the extent that a man may take a second wife if his first wife is barren. A widow is allowed to marry again by the *sagai* ritual, which consists of smearing vermilion on the bride's forehead. This must be done at night in a dark room. Only widows attend at the ceremony, married women deeming it unlucky to be present. No religious forms are gone through, nor is any entertainment given to the members of the caste. Divorce is not recognised.

Religion.

The religion of the Kaserás differs in no respect from that of other members of the middle class in Behar. For religious and ceremonial purposes they employ Brahmans, who are received on terms of equality by other members of the sacred order. They burn their dead and perform *sráddh* in the orthodox fashion. Their social rank is respectable,[1] and Brahmans will take water from their hands. The bulk of the caste are engaged in their characteristic occupation, and only a few have taken to agriculture.

The following statement shows the number and distribution of Kaserás in 1872 and 1881. The figures for Thátherá are included in the former year:—

DISTRICT.	1872.	1881.	DISTRICT.	1872.	1881.
Patna	4,344	2,358	Santál Parganas	402	91
Gya	4,768	2,558	Cuttack	7,559	4,106
Shahabad	2,258	694	Puri	4,774	2,796
Tirbut { Mozufferpur ...	6,805	362	Balasore	1,980	903
Tirbut { Darbhanga ...		485	Tributary States	5,139	3,404
Saran	817	361	Hazaribagh	763	719
Champaran	1,314	968	Lohardagá	2,016	1,139
Monghyr	3,421	532	Singhbhum	692	124
Bhagalpur	4,692	945	Manbhum	593	199
Purniah	5,959	648	Tributary States	490	525

[1] In describing the Kaserás of the North-Western Provinces, Mr. Sherring says:—"As artisans and traders, the Kaserá caste occupies a high position. They are said to be above the Vaisya, or commercial caste, and to hold a place between this and the Kshatriya caste. The reasons assigned for this opinion are that the tribe in all its subdivisions is more punctilious on many matters considered to be of importance by Hindus than the Vaisya or Sudra castes usually are, and that they all wear the sacred thread." These remarks do not appear to be applicable to the Kaserás of Behar.

Káshib, tortoise, a totemistic section of Rautiás in Chota Nagpur.

Káshmiri, a sub-caste of Brahmans.

Kashta-Srotriya, a hypergamous group of Rarhi Brahmans in Bengal.

Kási, kind of grass, a totemistic section of Rautiás, Binjhiás, Khariás, and Lohárs in Chota Nagpur; a section of Goálás and Sonárs in Behar; a *thar* or sept of Khambus in Darjiling.

Kásiám, a section of the Sátmuliá Maghayá sub-caste of Kándus in Behar.

Kásiáno, a *mul* or section of the Chhamuliá Madhesiá sub-caste of Halwáis in Behar.

Káslar, a section of Ghásis in Chota Nagpur.

Kásibak, heron, a totemistic sept of Savars; a section of Korás in Chota Nagpur and Western Bengal.

Kásil, a *gotra* or section of Agarwáls.

Kásipuriyá, a sub-caste of Aguris in Western Bengal.

Kasmal, a section of the Biyáhut and Kharidáhá Kalwárs in Behar.

Kasojan, a sub-caste of Baniyás in Behar.

Kaspai, a section of Bábhans in Behar.

Kastá, a title of Tantis or weavers.

Kástha, a cultivating and landholding caste peculiar to the districts of Midnapur and Balasore. It is divided into two sub-castes—**Madhyasreni-Káyasth** and **Kástha**. The former, who are as a rule wealthier and more highly esteemed than the latter, claim to be the descendants of certain legendary Káyasths who settled in Midnapur before the time of Ballál Sen, and so completely lost touch with their brethren in Bengal that even the growth of Kulinism passed them by unnoticed, and there are no Kulins among them to this day. The same tradition represents the Kásthas as the offspring of these Madhyasreni-Káyasths by women of lower castes. The theory derives some support from the analogous case of Rajput families who have settled in outlying parts of the country, lost connexion with their own people, and intermarried with the women of the land.

Origin.

It is, however, equally possible, and in my opinion rather more probable, that both Madhyasreni-Káyatths and Kásthas may be the descendants of an indigenous writer-tribe like the Karans of Orissa, the wealthier members of which disowned their humbler tribesmen and sought kinship with the well-known Káyasth caste of Bengal. The fact that both Kásthas and Madhyasreni-Káyasths are in possession of very old estates seems to tell in favour of this view.

Marriage.

Kásthas marry their daughters as infants, condemn the remarriage of widows, and do not recognise divorce. In one point, however, both divisions of the caste, and even the despised Karans of Orissa, are greatly in advance of the Káyasths of Bengal. While they accept and act up to the sacerdotal view that untold spiritual evils will befall the man who does not get his daughters married before the age of puberty, they carefully guard against the physical dangers of the practice by forbidding the married couple to cohabit until the bride has arrived at sexual maturity. In matters of religious and ceremonial observance they are at all points orthodox Hindus. Most of them belong to the Vaishnava sect. Madhyasreni-Brahmans officiate as their priests.

Social status and occupation.

Madhyasreni-Káyasths occupy much the same position in Midnapur as the Káyasths in Bengal Proper and the Karans in Orissa. Their social rank is high, and Brahmans take water from their hands. Some of them hold zemindaris and substantial tenures, while the majority are engaged in clerical pursuits. Of late years, however, they have had to compete with true Káyasths who have immigrated from Bengal and become domiciled in Midnapur. The Kásthas are for the most part cultivators, tilling their own lands, but in Balasore and the west of Midnapur a few of them are found holding estates.

Kástha, a sub-caste of Kásthas in Midnapur.

Kástogiri, a title of Baidyas in Bengal.

Kastuár, a section of Sonárs in Behar.

Kástu Rishi, a section of Kaibarttas in Central Bengal.

Kastwár, a section of Bábhans in Behar.

Kaswár, a sub-caste of Bais Baniyás in Behar.

Kasya, a *gotra* or section of Nepáli Brahmans.

Kásyab, Kásyap, a totemistic section of Bhars and of the Rajwar, Kumhar and Koiri castes in Chota Nagpur, the members of which will not touch, kill, or eat a tortoise; a section of Korás denoting a tortoise; a sept of Bhumij; a section of Sonárs and Tántis in Behar.

Kásyapa, a *gotra* or eponymous section of Brahmans denoting descent from the Vedic sage Kasyapa. It has been adopted by the following castes:—Kumhár, Tánti, Teli, Baidya, the Kasaudhan sub-caste of Baniyás and the Kanaujiá sub-caste of Lohárs in Behar, the Subarnabanik, Sunri, Khatri, Káyasth, Karan, Rajput, Goálá, Kaibartta, Kochh, Kámár, Dhanuk, Barhi, Beldar, Cháin, Nuniá, Bauri, Bágdi, Barui, Chásádhobá, Bind, Dhobi, Gandhabanik, Jugi, Kapáli, Khatwé, Khatik, Pod, Madhunápit, Máli, Mayará, Muchi, Nápit, Bábhan, Bhát, Kurmi, Sonár, Tánti, Chásá, Kewat, Sánkhári, Sukli, Támbuli, Pachim Kuliyá Sadgop, Surahiyá, Sutradhar, Tiyar, Nágar, Pási, Chero, and Kahár. The Kumhárs and Kurmis of Behar appear to have borrowed this section from the Brahmans in comparatively recent times, but as it is used indiscriminately by all Kumhárs and Kurmis of that province, it does not operate as a bar to intermarriage. In the case of Maghayá Kurmis, indeed, it has been superadded to an existing series of exogamous groups (*muls*) based on actual descent. Some of the Maghayá Kumhárs, however, have no *muls*, and reckon prohibited degrees by the formula referred to in the article on Kayasth. The same remark holds good of the Behar Kurmis, with the possible exception of the Ghámela sub-caste.

Kátádi, a *gáin* or sub-section of Saptasati Brahmans in Bengal.

Katáit, a *kul* or section of Bábhans in Behar.

Kátáiwár-Andhrá, a *mul* of the Kásyapa section of Maithil Brahmans in Behar.

Kataiwár-Phet, a *mul* of the Kásyap section of Maithil Brahmans in Behar.

Kataiwár-Malangiyá, a *mul* of the Kásyap section of Maithil Brahmans in Behar.

Kataiwár-Loám, a *mul* of the Kásyap section of Maithil Brahmans in Behar.

Kataiwár-Maráchi, a *mul* of the Kásyap section of Maithil Brahmans in Behar.

Kátáiyá, a *mul* or section of the Naomuliá or Majraut sub-caste of Goálás in Behar.

Kataki or *Ashtagrámi*, a sub-caste of Támbulis in Bengal.

Katalpuri, a section of Sonárs in Behar.

Kátáni, a *gáin* or sub-section of Saptasati Brahmans in Bengal.

Kátar, *katár*, a title of basket-making Doms in Behar.

Katari, a title of Telis in Behar.

Kátári, a *mul* or section of the Chhamuliá Madhesiá sub-caste of Halwáis in Behar.

Katariyár, a section of Káyasths in Behar.

Kataunia, a section of Bábhans in Behar.

Katea, field-mouse, a totemistic sept of Mundas in Chota Nagpur.

Káteár, a section of the Sátmuliá Maghayá sub-caste of Kándus in Behar.

Kátekâ Rakmal, a *mul* or section of the Biyáhut sub-caste of Kalwárs in Behar.

Kates, a section of the Biyáhut and Kharidáhá Kalwárs in Behar.

Kateswar, a section of the Biyáhut and Kharidáhá Kalwárs in Behar.

Katewár, a *kul* or section of Bábhans in Behar.

Kátha, a sub-caste of Goálás in the North-Western Provinces and Behar.

Káthádulárpur, a *mul* or section of the Naomuliá or Majraut sub-caste of Goálás in Behar.

Kathak, a sub-caste of Brahmans in Behar who rank very low, the male members of which sing and dance on ceremonial occasions in the houses of respectable people. The name Kathak, properly denoting a reciter of the Hindu sacred books, is also applied to musicians of any creed or caste who play on the violin. Dr. Wise mentions an instance of a Chhatri Kathak who went about in Dacca with a troop of Mahomedan dancing boys (Bhagtiya), and adds that none of his class would condescend to accompany Mahomedan *báis* or dancing girls.

Kathalmalet, a section of Maghaiyá Kumhárs in Behar.

Kathár, a section of Kanaujiá Lohárs in Behar.

Kathargách, a section of Mahilis in Western Bengal.

Kathariá, a sept of the Rautár sub-tribe of Thárus; a section of the Biyáhut and Kharidáhá Kalwárs in Behar.

Kathautia, a sub-caste of Dhánuks and Nágars in Behar.

Kathautiá, a section of Bábhans and of Kanaujiá Lohárs in Behar.

Kathautiá, *Katháwá*, a sub-caste of Beldárs in Western Bengal.

Kathautiar, a section of Káyasths in Behar.

Kathbaniyá, a sub-caste of Baniyás in Behar, who have no sections and regulate their marriages by the standard formula for reckoning prohibited degrees calculated to seven generations in the descending line. They practise infant-marriage and allow a man to take a second wife during the lifetime of the first. A widow may marry again, but is not compelled to marry her late husband's younger brother or younger cousin. In certain exceptional cases husbands are permitted to divorce their wives with the concurrence of the *pancháyat*, but women so divorced may not marry again.

Most Kathbaniyás belong to the Vaishnava sect. Maithil Brahmans serve them as priests, and are received on equal terms by other members of the sacred order. Sokhá Sambhunáth and Satnaráyan are among the minor gods to whom their domestic worship is directed. They burn their dead and perform *sráddh* on the thirty-first day. Shop-keeping and money-lending on a small scale are believed to be their characteristic occupations, but many of them have taken to agriculture and hold land as non-occupancy raiyats or work as landless day-labourers. Instances, however, are known of Kathbaniyás having risen to be zamindárs.

Káthej, a *mul* or section of the Chhamuliá Madhesiá sub-caste of Halwáis in Behar.

Katherá, a section of the Biyáhut and Kharidáhá Kalwárs in Behar.

Káthuriá, a sub-caste of Bauris in Western Bengal.

Kathwáit, a *kul* or section of Bábhans in Behar.

Katiá, a class of Hindu weavers in Western Bengal.

Katiáin, a section of Bábhans in Behar.

Kátiár, a totemistic section of Kurmis in Chota Nagpur and Orissa, the members of which pierce the ears of their boys at the Dharma pujá. They have the further peculiarity that they will not use cloth made of *tasar* silk.

Kátichá, a *thar* or sept of Sunuwárs in Darjiling.

Kati-chiore, a section of Kámis in Darjiling.

Katigrámi, a *gáin* of the Kásyapa *gotra* of Bárendra Brahmans in Bengal.

Katki-káet, a synonym for Karan in Orissa.

Kátki Phulbaria, a *mul* or section of the Sátmuliá or Kishnaut sub-caste of Goálás in Behar.

Kátniá, a section of Goálás in the North-Western Provinces and Behar.

Katosiá, a section of Lohárs in Behar.

Kátrás, a sub-tribe of Bhuiyás in Manbhum.

Katri, subject to fits, a sept of Chiks in Chota Nagpur.

Katriár, a sub-caste of Kurmis in Behar.

Katsaiá, a *mul* or section of the Kamarkalla sub-caste of Sonárs in Behar.

Katsarwá, a section of the Biyáhut and Kharidáhá Kalwárs in Behar.

Kattahwa, a section of Bábhans in Behar.

Katun, a sept of Pators in Chota Nagpur.

Katur, a section of Awadhiá Hajjáms in Behar.

Káture, a sub-caste of Tántis in Bengal.

Káturi, a *gáin* or sub-section of Saptasati Brahmans in Bengal.

Káturiá, a wood-cutter, a sub-caste of Sutradhars in Dacca. The name usually denotes an occupation, not a caste. In Bengal Káturiás are mostly Kaibarttas or Bágdis, and in Chota Nagpur they are generally Dhángars or members of one of the Dravidian races.

Katwál, an honorific title of Kotáls, who are *chaukidárs* or *simándárs*.

Katwár, a section of Rajwárs in Western Bengal.

Kátyáyan, a section of Brahmans.

Kauá, crow, a totemistic sept of Lohárs, Mundas, Oraons, Parhaiyas, and Páns in Chota Nagpur.

Kaiyá, an up-country trader. See **Káin**.

Kaukdaintsa, a sept of Maghs in the Hill Tracts of Chittagong.

Kaulika, a synonym for Sákta, *q.v.*

Kaundil or **Kaundin**, a *gotra* or section of Bábhans in Behar, borrowed from the Brahmanical system and superadded to the original exogamous groups (*kuls*) characteristic of the caste. A section of Nepáli Brahmans.

Kaundilya, a section of Brahmans; an eponymous section of Khandáits in Orissa.

Kaundilya-Kausik, a section of the Uttar-Bárendra Brahmans in Bengal.

Kaundinya, tiger, a totemistic section of Jagannáthi Kumhárs in Orissa.

Kaur, a caste of Jashpur, Udaipur, Sarguja, and other Tributary States of Chota Nagpur, who claim to be descended from the Kauravas or sons of Kuru, whose war with the Pándavas is described in the Mahábhárata. Colonel Dalton speaks of them as a dark, coarse-featured, broad-nosed, wide-mouthed and thick-lipped race, and the fact that some of their sections are totemistic seems to lend support to the view that they are of Dravidian origin. Kaurs are divided into five sub-castes—**Cháuti**, **Charwa**, **Dudh-Kaur**, **Paikará** and **Rathiyá**. The Dudh-Kaur follow Hindu doctrine and have Brahman priests The Paikará are also orthodox, but rank slightly below the Dudh

Origin and internal structure.

Kaur. The Rathiyá rear and eat fowls, have no Brahmans, and employ the village barber as their priest, while some of them also keep a Baiga to propitiate the forest gods.

Marriage.

Kaurs forbid marriage within the section, and observe much the same prohibited degrees as the Hindus, except that they allow a man to marry his maternal uncle's daughter. Infant-marriage is in vogue, *sindurdan* is reckoned the essential portion of the marriage ceremony, and those sub-castes who have Brahmans as priests employ them at marriages. A widow may marry again, and is expected to marry her late husband's younger brother if one survives. Failing a brother, she may marry an outsider. In the case of a widow no priest is employed: the husband applies vermilion to her forehead with his own hand and the marriage is complete. Divorce is allowed with the sanction of the *panchâyat* or caste council, and divorced women may marry again. Colonel Dalton mentions that the Kaurs of Sarguja at one time encouraged widows to become Satis, and describes the shrine of a Kaur Sati who was at the time of his visit the principal object of worship near Jilmilli in Sarguja. Every year a fowl was sacrificed to her, and very third year a black goat; whereas Hindu offerings at Sati shrines are strictly confined to fruit and flowers. Probably the family of the Sati in question were land-holding Kaurs who affected to be orthodox Hindus, and aspired in course of time to transform themselves into Rajputs.

Religion.

Generally speaking, Kaurs regard themselves as Hindus and look upon Káli·Mái as the goddess whom they are more especially bound to worship. But, except for marriages, they do not employ Brahmans as priests. They bury the dead. On the third day the chief mourner gets himself shaved, and on the tenth and eleventh days funeral cakes are offered and a feast given to the relatives.

Occupation.

Most Kaurs are common cultivators, a few hold farms of villages, and some are in possession of the clearing tenures known as *Korkar* and *Khunt-Katti*.

Kaur, a title of Karangás.

Kaurá, a sub-caste of Doms in Bengal who breed pigs and act as scavengers.

Kausalya, a Brahmanical section of Khatris.

Kausár, a *mul* or section of the Tinmuliá Madhesiá sub-caste of Halwáis in Behar.

Kausika, a *gotra* or eponymous section of Brahmans, Baidyas, and Káyasths in Bengal, and of Bábhans, and the Chandrabansi and Surajbansi divisions of Rajputs in Behar.

Kausikárk, a *pur* or section of Sákadwipi Brahmans in Behar.

Kausonjhiá, a section of Bábhans in Behar.

Kaustav, a section of Brahmans.

Kautsasa, a section of the Bhatta Misra sub-caste of Utkal Brahmans and of Karans in Orissa.

Kauwá, a sept of Dhimáls in the Darjiling Terai.

Kavirâj, a title of Baidyas and some other Hindu families.

Kawâl, a title of Kaibarttas.

Kawáli, *Kalwah*, *Kálwáli*, a caste of musicians, who were originally Kapális, but having adopted a different occupation were compelled to enrol themselves in a new caste. In Dacca they preserve a tradition that they are the offspring of a Káyasth father and a Dhobín, or washerwoman, and the Súdra servants work for them, as they also do for the Kapális. The Kawális all belong to one *gotra*, the Aliman. They have no surnames, but several honorary titles, such as Dhálí, Mála, Háldár, and Mánjhí, and the most respectful term by which to address them is Vidyádhara, a name given to the dancers in Indra's heaven.

The Kawálí plays on any instrument taught him by his *ustád*, *sardár*, or teacher. When young he is apprenticed to a master, whose credit depends on the proficiency of his pupil. Youths are also taught to dance, and it is said that the purohit does not disdain to join in a dance or to take a part in a theatrical play. The Kawálí will not play in the house of any caste who has not the services of the Sudra Nápit and Dhobá, and refuses to attend at the homes of the Muhammadan Dáí or Hajjám. They have no objections, however, to play in concert with the Nar, Rishí, or Hajjám. The dancing girls to whom they usually play are either Muhammadans (báí), or Chandálnís; but widows belonging to any caste, even to the Bráhman, are often found with them.

The great annual festival of the Kawális is the Srí Panchamí, in honour of Sarasvatí; but its observance is not allowed to interfere with their professional engagements, and they as readily accept employment on that day as on any other. The Kawális are all Vaishnavas, and are hired by Hindu villagers to sing the religious hymns called Hari San-kirtan.

They observe the *sraddhá* and *sashthi* ceremony on the same days as the Kapálí and Súdras generally.

Kawáni, a class of Banias.

Káwar, a title of Chhatris in Nepal; a hypergamous group of Kaibarttas in Bakarganj.

Kawnriá, a sort of newt, a totemistic sept of Mundas.

Káwot, the Behar equivalent of Kewat, *q.v.*

Kawwá dardáha, janawwir piprá, a formula or shibboleth denoting a *dih* or local section of the Hazári *pangat* of the Maghayá sub-caste of Dosádhs in Behar. Properly speaking, the Hazári *pangat* is itself an exogamous section, but it would appear to have expanded; so that a *dih* or local section distinguished by the shibboleth quoted above has formed itself within the original *pangat*. Any considerable increase of these *dihs* would probably convert the *pangat* into an endogamous group.

Kawwál, a class of Mahomedan singers and dancers.

Kayál, a title of Pods in Bengal.

Kayál, *Keál*, *Koyál*, a weighman, a petty broker, a negociator of the prices of grain between sellers and buyers. In Patna and South-East Behar the word denotes the person who weighs the grain when produce rent is collected on the system of *batai kharihâni* or division on the threshing-floor. In Bengal rents are rarely paid in kind, and the *Kayáls* enumerated in the Census were probably weighmen in municipal markets and small village *hâts*.

Káyastha, *Kaet, Kait, Káyath, Káya*, the writer-caste of Bengal Proper, a numerous and influential body, whose traditional origin has been the subject of much controversy. No mention of the caste occurs in Manu, and the Káyasths themselves reject the theory which gives them for an ancestor the Karan, the son of a Vaisya father by a Sudra mother. The earliest reference to the Káyasths as a distinct caste occurs in Yájnavalkya, who describes them as writers and village accountants, very exacting in their demands from the cultivators. In the Padma and Bhabishya Puránas the Káyasths are made out to be the children of Chitragupta, the supreme recorder of men's virtues and vices, who sprang from the body (*káyá*) of Brahma, and this was the first Káyastha. The Skanda Purána gives them a more distinguished ancestry. It tells how Parasu Rama's efforts to exterminate the Kshatriya race were time after time defeated by the birth of sons to the Kshatriya women whom he spared when their husbands were killed. Determined to clear the earth of the obnoxious tribe, he resolved to show mercy no longer, even to women in their pregnancy. In fulfilment of this vow he pursued the widow of the Kshatriya Rájá Chandra Sen into the hermitage of Dalabhya Rishi, where she had taken refuge, and demanded that she should be given up to him. But Dalabhya begged the life of the child in the Rani's womb, and his request was granted by Parasu Rama on the condition that the child should be called Káyastha and should be brought up to follow the ritual of the Sudras, and not that of the twice-born castes. On this showing the Káyasthas are by birth Kshatriyas of full blood, but by reason of their following the ceremonies of the Sudras they are called Vrátya or incomplete Kshatriyas. The faint suggestion of inferiority which this term implies seems on the whole to be borne out by the position assigned in the Mrichhakatiká to the Káyastha who sits with the Judge as assessor in the trial described in the ninth act of the play. He is charged with the ministerial duty of recording evidence under the orders of the Judge, and he, like the other assessor, Sreshthi, speaks Prakrit, while the Judge and the principal defendant use the more dignified Sanskrit. From the Mrichhakatiká we pass on to the more recent and more popular opinion that the forefathers of the Bengal Káyasths came from Kanauj with the five Brahmans whom King Adisura summoned to perform for him certain Vedic ceremonies. Around this tradition a bitter controversy has raged between the Káyasths, who sought to exalt their social status, and members of other castes who refused to admit their claims. One party alleged that the five Káyasths—Makaranda Ghosh, Dasaratha Vasu, Kalidása Mitra, Dasaratha Guha, and Purushottama Datta—came to Bengal as the menial servants of the five Brahmans. Their social standing therefore could have been no higher than that of the Kahárs, who in Upper India at the present

Traditions of origin.

day discharge personal services for members of the higher castes The Káyasths for their part repudiated this view as derogatory to their dignity, and some of them went so far as to argue that the five Káyasths of tho tradition were political officers in charge as Kshatriyas. of a mission from Kanauj to the King of Bengal, and that the five Brahmans played quite a subordinate part in the transaction, if indeed they were anything more than the cooks of the five Káyasths. An ingenious grammatical argument, based on the names of the two sets of immigrants, is brought forward in support of this view.

Putting tradition aside, and looking on the one hand to the physical type of the Káyasths and on the other to their remarkable intellectual attainments, it would seem that their claim to Aryan descent cannot be wholly rejected, though all attempts to lay down their genealogy precisely must necessarily be futile. It appears to be at least a plausible conjecture that they were a functional group, developed within the Aryan community, in response to the demand for an official and literary class, which must in course of time have arisen. This class would naturally have been recruited more largely from the peaceful Vaisyas and Sudras than from the warlike Kshatriyas, while the Brahmans would probably have held aloof from it altogether. It is possible, though I put forward the suggestion with much diffidence, that the tradition describing the Káyasths as the offspring of a Vaisya and a Sudráni may be merely an archaic method of saying that the writer-caste was composed of elements drawn from the two lower grades of Aryan society. This view of the origin of the Káyasths is entitled to whatever support it may derive from the statement of some of my correspondents, that even in recent times instances have occurred of members of other castes gaining admission into the Káyasth community. Some of these statements are curiously precise and specific. It is said, for example, that a few years ago many Magh families of Chittagong settled in the western districts of Bengal assumed the designation of Káyasth, and were allowed to intermarry with true Káyasth families. An extreme case is cited in which the descendants of a Tibetan missionary have somehow found their way into the caste, and are now recognised as high class Káyasthas. Another story tells how a certain Uriya Goálá, bearing the name Datta, which is one of the distinctive hypergamous titles of the Káyasthas, took service with a Káyasth family in Calcutta, where his principal duty was to boil the milk to be offered to certain idols. This man's sons grew up and were educated with the sons of the house, and were recently admitted as Káyasthas of the Datta group and of the Kasyapa gotra. Alongside of these instances, derived from inquiries in Western Bengal, we may set the statement of Dr. Wise that in the eastern districts of Bengal there exist a very numerous body called Ghulám, or slave, Káyasths, and also known as Shikdár, or Bhándárí. The Ghulám Káyasths are descended from individuals belonging to clean Súdra castes who sold themselves, or were sold, as slaves to Káyasth masters. It is stoutly denied that any one belonging to an unclean tribe was ever purchased as a slave, yet it is hard to believe that this never occurred. The physique of the low and impure races has always been better than that of the pure; and on account of their poverty and low standing a slave could at any time be more easily purchased from amongst them. However this may be, it is an undoubted fact that any Ghulám Káyasth could, and can even at the present day, if rich and provident, raise himself by intermarriage as high as the Madhalya grade, and obtain admission among the Bhadra-lok, or gentry of his countrymen. Datta being a Madhalya title, it will be observed that this is precisely the position to which in the instance quoted above the descendants of an Uriya Goálá are said to have attained.

Internal structure.

The Bengal Káyasths are divided into four sub-castes: (1) UTTAR-RARHÍ, (2) DAKHIN-RARHÍ, (3) BARENDRA, (4) BANGAJA. These groups are in theory endogamous, but within the last few years marriages have occasionally taken place between members of the Dakhin-Rárhí and Bangaja sub-castes. The Uttar Rárhí are met with in the districts of Birbhum, Bardwan, Murshedabad, parts of Rangpur, Dinajpur, Hughli, and Jessore. The Dakhin-Rárhí are massed in Bardwan, Hughli, Midnapur, 24-Parganas, Jessore, Kishnagar, and parts of Bakarganj, while in Dacca only two families reside. The Bangaja are established in Bakarganj, Jessore, 24-Parganas, Dacca, Faridpur, western part of Maimansinh, eastern part of Pabna, and in several villages of the Bogra district. The Barendra are settled in Rajshahye, Pabna, Maldah, Bogra, Dinajpur, as well as here and there throughout Faridpur, Jessore, and Kishnagar.

Within each of the sub-castes we find a series of three hypergamous groups, each comprising so many family names. These are given in tabular form in the Appendix. The rules governing the intermarriage of these groups differ in several material points from those in force among the Brahmans.

Marriage and Kulinism.

Ballál Sen is said to have divided the Káyasths into four sub-castes according to locality, thus:—Uttar-Rárhi, Dakshin-Rárhi, Bangaja and Bárendra. He selected eight members from each *kul* of the Dakshin-Rárhis in order to create *samajs* or hypergamous groups, *e.g.*, eight from each of the three families of Ghosh, Basu and Mitra, out of which two were made *Kulin* and six were made Bansaj. Prabhákar of the Akná group and Nisápati of the Báli group represented the *mukhya* of the Ghosh family; Sukti of the Bágánda group and Mukti of the Máhinagar group represented the Basu family; while Dhuin of the Barisá group and Guin of the Tek group represented the Mitra family. Thus according to the rules of Ballál Sen only these six men were made *Kulin*; the rest were made *Bansaj*, *i.e.*, born of the *Kulin* family. The following are the names of the *Bansaj* groups:—Amreswar, Dirghánga, Karáti, Seákhálá, Khaniá, and Sánkráli of the Ghosh family; Nimárká, Sáthuli, Chitrapur, Dirghánga, Gohari and Panchamuli of the Basu family; Dábarákupi, Chándará, Dántiá Chákłái, Kumárhatta and Báliá groups form the Mitra family.

The members of the Guha family lived in Eastern Bengal, where their ancestor, Dasaratha Guha, was ranked as a Kulin, but those who had been incorporated after Ballál's grouping into the Dakshin-Rárhi sub-caste were reckoned as *Mauliks*.

Those Káyasths who had been living at that time in Eastern Bengal, including Datta and Guha, were classed as *Mauliks*, out of which eight families—De, Datta, Kar, Pálit, Sen, Sinha, Dás, and Guha were Siddha Mauliks, and the remaining seventy-two families beginning with Hora were classed as Sádhya Mauliks. Formerly ten out of seventy-two families of Sádhya Mauliks used to intermarry with the Kulins, but afterwards 16 families became connected with the Kulins by intermarriage. The names of the sixteen families are—Pál, Nág, Arnab, Som, Rudra, Aditya, Aich, Ráhá, Bhauja, Hora, Teja, Brahma, Bishnu, Nandi, Rakshit and Chandra.

The kuls of Káyasths are of nine sorts, out of which five are known as *mul* or original and four as *sákhá* or branch. Following the order of social estimation, the *mul Kuls* are Mukhya, Kanishtha, Sharabhrátá or Chhabháyá, Madhyánsa and Turjyak or Teyaj. The *sákhás* or branches are—Dwitiya-Po (the second son of Kanishtha), Chhabháyá's Dwitiya-Po (second son of Chhabháyá) Dwitiya-Po (second son of Madhyánsa), and Dojo-Po (second son of Teyaj). Kulins belong to one or other of these nine varieties. They are further sub-divided into different grades, and they rise or fall in social estimation according to the marriage made by the eldest son and eldest daughter. If they marry into Kulin families, the reputation of their own family is secured, and the younger members may marry as they please.

Mukhya Kulins are of three kinds—Prakrita, Sahaj and Komal. Only the eldest son of each has the right to hold that title. Their other sons will descend a step or rise in social estimation in accordance with their observance of the marriage law.

It is a great distinction for a Mukhya to observe the "Navaranga" or nine-grade kul, the rules regarding which are—The *ágchhei*, or eldest daughter of a Mukhya, should be given in marriage to a Mukhya; the *dochhei*, or second, to a Kanishtha; the *techhei* or third, to a Chhabháyá; the *chauchhei*, or fourth, to a Madhyánsa; and the *panchami*, or fifth, to a Teyaj Kulin. Conversely, the eldest son of a Mukhya should be given in marriage to a Mukhya girl, the second to a Kanishtha girl, the third to a Madhyánsa girl, and the fourth to a Teyaj girl. The Mukhya who observes these rules of marrying and giving in marriage earns the title of Navarangi.

"Pancharanga" kul is observed in the following manner:—The first son of a Kanishtha Kulin ought to marry the *dochhei* or second daughter of a Mukhya; the second son that of a Madhyánsa girl; the third son that of a Teyaj girl. The Kanishtha Kulin who observes these rules is held in honour by his fellows and is called Pancharangi.

The following general rules are to be observed by all *Kulin* Káyasths, though some of them apply to other castes as well:—

A *Kulin* loses his *kul* by marrying or giving in marriage outside the *parjyá* or generation to which he himself belongs, counting from the first advent of Káyasths in Bengal. Whoever does so becomes a *Maulik*. A *Kulin* loses his *kul* by marrying a *randa* or daughter of a man having no male issue, or if he should by accident marry a *swagotra* or *swapinda*. An adopted son of a *Kulin* is not a *Kulin*. Though he has the privileges of a son in other respects, he has no such privilege as regards *kul*. He will simply remain a *Bansaj*. A *Kulin* by marrying the daughter of a *Kulin* of a lower degree descends to the level of the latter. For instance, if a *Mukhya* man marries a *Madhyánsa* girl, he becomes a *Madhyánsa*. Again, if a *Teyaj* man marries a girl of Madhyánsá's Dwitiya-Po, he becomes Dwitiya-Po of Madhyánsa. A man should not give in marriage his daughters one after another to *Kulins* of the same degree. For instance, if the first daughter is given to a *Mukhya*, it is not proper that the *dochhei* or second daughter be given to another *Mukhya*. In that case both the giver and taker become degraded.

Religion.

Subject to the exceptions noted above, the religious practice of the Káyasths does not differ materially from that of the highest Hindu castes in Bengal. It is a singular fact that while the teaching of Chaitanya has united almost all the artisan and agricultural castes in a common faith, the three highest and most intelligent castes in Bengal adhere as a rule to the Sákta ritual. In Eastern Bengal all Kulin Káyasths, and something like three-fourths of the other divisions, are believed to practise Śáktism, and it is said that a large proportion of these celebrate the Bamachári Kohár or Chakra ceremonies. For the fulfilment of domestic religious duties every Kulin family has a private temple, or sacred nook, where a Śiva-linga is erected and daily worship performed by the head of the household. All Káyasths observe the Srí Panchamí, or "Dawát Púja," on the fifth of the waxing moon in Mágh (January–February). This festival is held in honour of Saraswati, the goddess of learning, who is regarded by the Káyasths as their patron deity. On this day the courts and all offices are closed, as no Hindu penman will use pen and ink, or any writing instrument, except a pencil, on that day. When work is resumed a new inkstand and pen must be used, and the penman must write nothing until he has several times transcribed the name of the goddess Durgá, with which all letters should begin. Káyasths are expected to spend the holiday in meditating on the goddess Saraswatí after they have observed certain religious rites; but the extent to which this obligation is observed depends largely upon the inclinations of the individual. On this day, says Dr. Wise, the Káyasth must taste of a hilsá fish, whatever its price, while from the Srí Panchamí festival in January to the Vijaya Dasamí in September or October fish must be eaten daily; but from the last to the first month it must not be touched. This curious custom, probably founded on some hygienic superstition, is often reversed by Bengali Káyasths.

The following statement shows the number and distribution of Káyasths in 1872 and 1881:—

DISTRICT.	1872.	1881.	DISTRICT.	1872.	1881.
Bardwan	53,398	33,069	Noakhali	20,878	37,565
Bankura	11,676	20,575	Tipperah	72,804	69,373
Birbhum	8,319	8,902	Chittagong Hill Tracts ...	93	588
Midnapur	101,663	92,178	Patna	28,289	29,864
Hughli	38,722	25,484	Gya	40,222	43,965
Howrah		15,849	Shahabad	42,407	46,994
24-Parganas	82,803	82,364	Mozufferpur	70,992	42,552
Nadiya	39,719	40,780	Darbhanga		45,124
Jessore	90,040	62,611	Saran	47,686	51,065
Khulna	......	36,985	Champaran	24,547	28,411
Murshedabad	17,077	15,656	Monghyr	20,462	23,044
Dinajpur	4,523	6,024	Bhagalpur	17,170	21,810
Rajshahye	8,727	8,373	Purniah	11,833	12,761
Rangpur	10,387	11,449	Maldah	4,601	4,656
Bogra	5,483	3,759	Santál Parganas	5,940	7,820
Pabna	35,359	34,602	Cuttack	5,329	4,441
Darjiling	44	406	Puri	1,194	2,335
Jalpigori	587	3,782	Balasore	2,371	1,757
Kuch Behar	......	2,522	Tributary States	386	1,517
Dacca	102,084	92,909	Hazaribagh	6,300	9,232
Faridpur	57,026	84,193	Lohardagá	4,061	6,690
Bakarganj	125,164	87,834	Singbhum	611	993
Maimansinh	105,537	108,409	Manbhum	7,991	6,546
Chittagong	68,916	72,370	Tributary States	210	689

The statement includes the Káyasths of Behar and the Karans of Orissa which form the subject of separate articles. It would be impossible to distinguish the statistics relating to these three groups.

Káyasth, *Kaeth*, *Lala*, the writer-caste of Behar, who trace their mythical parentage to Chitragupta, the scribe or recorder of Yama, the regent of the dead, and pique themselves on being wholly distinct from the Káyasths of Bengal. The physical characters of the Behar Káyasths afford some ground for the belief that they may be of tolerably pure Aryan descent, though the group is doubtless a functional one recruited from all grades of the Aryan community. Káyasths themselves hand down a tradition that their progenitor Chitragupta was produced from the inner consciousness of Brahma for the purpose of managing the business affairs and keeping the accounts of the other castes, and each of the twelve sub-castes traces its pedigree back to some member of his family. Chitragupta himself and all his sons and grandsons are said to have been invested with the sacred thread marking the twice-born castes, and Káyasths claim to have, and occasionally to exercise, the right to wear this sacred symbol. The sub-castes are the following:—(1) **Aithání**, (2) **Amashta**, (3) **Bálmik**, (4) **Bhatnágar**, (5) **Gaur**, (6) **Karan**, (7) **Kulsrashta**, (8) **Mathur**, (9) **Nigam**, (10) **Saksena**, (11) **Sribástab**, (12) **Surajdwaj**. Of these the Aithání are supposed to come from Jaunpur in the North-Western Provinces. The Amashta may possibly, as Mr. Crooke suggests[1], be the modern representatives of the Ambastha tribe said

Origin and internal structure.

[1] *Ethnographical Handbook*, p. 105.

to be descended from a Brahman father and Vaisya mother. They, like the Karans, also in theory a mixed group, born of a Sudra woman by a Vaisya father, are found in large numbers in Gya, Patna and Tirhut. The Bálmik or Válmiki sub-caste are supposed to have come from Guzerat. Mr. Crooke thinks they may perhaps have taken their name from the author of the Rámáyana. Karans, Amashtas and Sribástabs will smoke in the same hooka, but will not eat *kachchi* food together. The two former, however, will eat *kachchi* that has been cooked by a Bábhan. Nigam (derived by the same authority from the Sanskrit *nigama*, meaning the veda, a town, road, traffic) are not met with in Behar. The Surajdwaj group—the word means having the sun for emblem—are said to be descended from the Brahman Mádhava Nal and Kám Kándla, a dancing girl of Vikramáditya's Court. The Máthur, Saksena, Bhatnágar and Sribástab sub-castes claim descent from the first wife of Chitragupta, said to have been a daughter of the Suraj-bansi race of Kshatriyas. The names appear to have reference to localities—the first to Mathura, Saksena to the ruined town of Sankisa in Farukhabad, Bhatnágar to Bhatner, and Sribástab either to Srinagar, the traditional place of origin of the sub-caste or to Srivatsa, an epithet of Vishnu, who is their favourite object of worship.[1] The Khare and Dusre subdivisions of the Sribastab sub-caste trace their origin to the grandsons of Chitragupta. According to Buchanan,[2] the Khare Sribástabs claim to be higher than the ordinary Sribástábs, and call themselves Páure. The two subdivisions do not intermarry or eat and drink together. Similar subdivisions are found in the Saksena sub-caste. Contrary to the common usage of Hindus, Káyasths of the Máthur, Bhatnágar and Saksena groups eat even *kachchi* meals fully dressed. The Gaur Káyasths believe that they derive their name from Gaur, the ancient capital of Bengal, and allege that the Sen kings of Bengal were really Gaur Káyasths. A curious story is told about the Gaur and Bhatnágar sub-castes which is worth quoting as an illustration of the growth of mythical traditions of that type. The Bhatnágar Káyasths, it is said, came to Bengal at the time of the Mahomedan conquest, and finding the Gaur Káyasths settled there, asked to be admitted to eat and drink with them. The Gaur Káyasths agreed to invite the Bhatnágars to their houses for food, but declined to accept their hospitality in return. After a time the Bhatnágars, who had friends at court, began to put pressure on the Gaurs in order to compel them to accept their invitations, and the latter fled to Delhi to lay their case before the Emperor Balban. Meanwhile Balban died, and the Bhatnágars prevailed upon his successor to order some of the Gaur Káyasths to be arrested and compelled to eat with their rivals. To avoid this dishonour the rest of the sub-caste took refuge with the Brahmans of Badaon, who passed them off as members of their own caste, and went so far as to eat with them in support of their allegation. For doing this the Brahmans were turned out of their caste, and became the family priests of the Gaur

---

[1] Crooke *op. cit.* p. 105.
[2] *Eastern India*, ii, 466.

Káyasths. After a time the Gaur Káyasths who had been forced to eat with the Bhatnágar were admitted on the intercession of the Badaon Brahmans to communion of food with their brethren. For the purpose of marriage, however, they were formed into a separate group under the name of Shamali or Northern Gaur. Traditions of this sort are not uncommon, and it is to be regretted that no means exist of testing their historical value. Their most singular feature is the conspicuous part alleged to have been played by the ruling power, whether Hindu or Mahomedan, in determining purely social questions. A caste is now regarded as an autocratic body, whose decisions on questions concerning its own members no one would dream of questioning. This does not seem to have been the view taken by the earlier rulers of Bengal, and the further back we go, the more frequent and pronounced do such instances of interference become.

Besides the regular Lála-Káyasths included in the twelve sub-castes enumerated above, people calling themselves Káyasths are found working as tailors in the Sewán subdivision of Saran, and some of the vermilion-selling Sindurias, who formerly acted as inoculators and now have turned vaccinators, claim to belong to this caste. The Lála-Káyasths disown all connexion with these groups. There is, however, nothing *primâ facie* improbable in the hypothesis that a certain number of Káyasths may have adopted the profession of tailors or vaccinators, and may thus have become separated from the main body of the caste. Nothing is more common than to find even a slight departure from the traditional occupation of a caste becoming the occasion for the formation of a new endogamous group. Signs of a tendency in this direction may be traced in the fact that many Káyasths object to marry their daughters in the family of those who have served as hereditary *patwáris* or village accountants. "Patwáris," says one of my correspondents, "however rich, are regarded as socially lower than other Káyasths, *e.g.*, Kánungo, Akhauri, Pánde, or Bakshi."

The system of exogamy practised by the Káyasths of Behar is shown in detail in Appendix I, and needs only brief explanation here. An examination of the names of the sections will show that intermarriage is really regulated by a number of *kuls* or exogamous sections, mostly of the territorial or titular type, and that the Brahmanical *gotras*, though recognised in theory, are really ineffective. Thus the Sribástab Káyasths reckon among their sections the Brahmanical *gotra* Kasyapa; but this is the only section of the Brahmanical type that they possess. All Sribástabs belong to the Kasyapa *gotra* and thus of necessity violate the primary rule of exogamy upon which the *gotra* system depends. Although the Brahmanical *gotra* is disregarded, the rule of exogamy is carefully observed in relation to the *kul*. Thus members of the Akhauri *kul* believe themselves to be descended from an ancestor holding the title of Akhauri, conferred many generations ago. Their original habitat was Churámanpur in Shahabad, and the full designation of the *kul* is *Churámanpur ke Akhauri*. The meaning of the term Akhauri is uncertain. Some say it is a corruption of Lakhauri, owner of a lakh of rupees. In further illustration of this system of using titles as the designations of exogamous groups and expanding or eking them out by prefixing the name of a village, the following *kuls* of the Sribástabs may be mentioned:—Amaundha ke Pánre; Dibia Koth ke Pánre; Mithabel ke Tewári; Morar ke Bakshi, Rái or Thakur; Batáha ke Misir; Hargáon ke Singh; Patar ke Tewári; Parsarma ke Thákur; Sahuli ke Sahuliár. The last appears to be of the local or territorial type. All *kuls* are strictly exogamous. Only the father's *kul* is excluded in marriage. The system is supplemented by a table of prohibited degrees calculated in the manner described in the article on Brahman.

Marriage.

All Káyasths who can afford to do so marry their daughters as infants, but the scarcity of husbands is greatly complained of, and daughters of poor Káyasth families frequently remain unmarried up to the age of eighteen or nineteen. When a girl is married before puberty, she lives with her own people apart from her husband until she has attained sexual maturity. Connubial relations cannot commence until the ceremony of *duragaman*, or bringing the bride home, has been performed. This may take place one, three, five or seven years (*numero Deus impare gaudet*) after the marriage according to the age of the bride. When a girl is married after puberty, this ceremony is added to the regular ritual, and the girl goes to live with her husband at once or at latest after a year. Widows may not marry again; nor is divorce recognised.

Among the Káyasths, as among the other high castes of Behar, the balance of the sexes seems to be uneven, and the number of girls marriageable at a given time is usually in excess of the number of possible husbands available for them. The first step therefore towards initiating proposals for marriage is taken by the parents or guardians of the bride who depute a Brahman (generally the purohit, or priest of the family) and the family barber to find out a suitable bridegroom. These emissaries select several suitable boys and report accordingly. Among Káyasths no marriage can take place unless the horoscopes of both the bride and bridegroom 'agree,' as the phrase goes, that is to say, unless from the dates of the births of both the girl and the boy it can be calculated by astrological methods that the bride will not become a widow, and that the marriage will prove fruitful and happy in every respect. If the two horoscopes do not 'agree,' the negotiations are broken off. In order to comply with these conditions, the Brahman who acts as go-between carries with him a copy of the bride's horoscope, takes copies of those of all the eligible boys, and reports to his employer on the prospects of each possible combination. Here it is that difficulties begin. Highly educated as the Káyasths are, they have not yet shaken off the trammels of astrology, and the custom of insisting on the 'agreement' of the horoscopes has such a strong hold upon their minds that it often proves the chief obstacle to a marriage desirable in other respects. Owing to this cause the marriage of the girls is delayed in many cases till long after they attain puberty, and the consequence is that the bride is often older than the bridegroom. In order to get their daughters married, parents are obliged to give them to bridegrooms of unequal age, doubtful education and character, and of unequal position and wealth. This practice, though often preventing the marriage of the girl in her infancy, turns out undesirable in many respects. Other difficulties arise from the exorbitant demand of *tilak* and *jahes* (dowry) by the parents of the bridegroom, which leads to unequal marriages and brings about the ruin of families unfortunate enough to have a number of girls to be married.

After the *gananá* has been made out to the satisfaction of both parties, and it has been ascertained that there are no objections to the marriage on the ground of consanguinity, etc., the question of bridegroom price and dowry (*tilak*, *jahes* or *dán pan*) is settled. This is too often exorbitant. If the terms are agreeable to the bride's parents, the marriage is at once agreed upon. In many cases the bride's parents depend wholly on the discretion of the Brahman and Hajjám in the selection of the bridegroom, and these either to save themselves trouble or in collusion with the parents of undesirable bridegrooms are said to make selections which the bride's family would not approve if they knew all the facts. The bridegroom's relations on the other hand are equally in the dark regarding the qualifications of the bride, and it thus happens that girls suffering from actual physical defects are enabled to obtain husbands by the collusion of the match-makers.

The following observances make up the marriage ceremony as celebrated by orthodox Káyasths of Behar:—

(1) When the marriage is agreed upon, a day is fixed for the betrothal or the taking of *sagun*. On that day the Brahman and Hajjám go to the bridegroom's house, where the latter's friends assemble at an auspicious time. His parents put rupees, rice, *haldi* and *supari* in a *tháli* before them, and the Brahman takes from this his fee at the rate of five per cent. on the amount of *tilak* and *jahes* agreed upon. If therefore the dowry be settled at Rs. 500, he will take out Rs. 25. Sometimes the bride's party pay cash as earnest-money instead of taking the *sagun*. This is called *bardekhi*, literally meaning the seeing of the bridegroom. It is also called *barchheka*, as a retaining fee is paid in advance in order to secure the bridegroom.

(2) After this the date for the *tilak* or the payment of the first instalment of the dowry is fixed. On that day a party, consisting of Brahmans and others and often a relative of the bride, about seven in all, proceed to the house of the bridegroom. He is adorned and made to sit in the *angan* or inner courtyard, where the gods are worshipped, after which the bride's party put a *tilak* or patch of curd on his forehead, and make a present to him of money, plates and clothes, amounting in all to the sum agreed upon to be paid at this time. This ceremony is called *tilak*. The bride's parents make a profit over the plates and cloth, which they estimate sometimes at double their value, thus reducing the actual cash payment agreed upon. It is for this reason that some astute guardians insist upon the payment of a certain amount in cash before giving the *sagun*, and if the money is not paid at the time of *tilak*, disagreements between the parties continue till after the celebration of the marriage. After the ceremony the bride's party, together with the friends of the bridegroom's family, receive *pakki* food. Before the *tilak* neither

the Brahman nor the Hajjám would even drink water at the bridegroom's house.

(3) On the following day the *tilak* party returns, being presented with dresses and money by the bridegroom's father according to his means. The latter at the same time addresses a letter to the bride's father, fixing an auspicious date for the marriage. This is called *lagnapatri*. If convenient to him, he agrees to it, otherwise some other date agreeable to both parties is fixed. After the *tilak* the betrothal becomes complete, and an engagement thus ratified is rarely broken off.

(4) On the eighth, fifth, and in some families on the third day before the marriage the ceremony variously known according to its date as *áthmangrá*, *panchmangrá* or *tinmangrá*, is performed. On that day the women troop out singing to fetch earth from some field outside the village, and put it in the courtyard where all the family gods and dead ancestors are invited to attend. This ceremony is performed at the houses of both parties. On an auspicious day the *mandap*, a sort of thatched canopy supported on nine new bamboos, is erected at the house of the bride's father. In the centre is placed an earthen vessel (*kalsa*) supposed to contain water from all Hindu places of pilgrimage. Under this *mandap* and near the *kalsa*, where all the family gods and ancestors are invited by *mantras* to be present and witness the marriage, the marriage ceremonies are subsequently performed. No *mandap* is erected at the bridegroom's house, but only a *haris* or plough shaft is set up in the *angan*, courtyard, and a *kalsa* similar to the bride's is placed beside it.

(5) Then the ceremony of *hardikahandan* takes place. Turmeric with oil is applied to the persons of the bride and bridegroom at their respective houses at stated times daily up to the day of marriage. This ceremony is not performed at the bridegroom's house when he is married a second time.

(6) *Matrik Pujah*—Is the ceremony of worshipping the wives of all the gods, *i.e.*, Sakti in all her forms. The gods are also invited to be present and worshipped. The women of the family invoke the spirits of departed ancestors, and *pindas* are offered to them.

(7) Ceremonies in propitiation of dead ancestors (*abhyudáik sráddh*) are also performed by the parents of the bride and the bridegroom at their respective houses on the day of the marriage.

(8) *Dwar Pujah.*—After performing the *matrik pujah* the women bathe the bridegroom and smear him with turmeric, and he eats with some unmarried boys his last meal as a bachelor. He is then dressed and made to sit on the lap of his mother, who drinks water which he has tasted. His brother also assists in this ceremony. After some other observances the bridegroom's party go in procession to the bride's house with as much show and noise as the means of the family permit, timing their journey so as to arrive after dark.

On arrival, and after their formal reception, the bridegroom is presented with money. This is called *dwár pujah*, the homage done to the bridegroom at the door of his father-in-law's house. After it the bridegroom's party proceed to the place (*janwása*) prepared for their temporary reception.

(9). *Ashuch parichhalan.*—After the procession has gone to the *janwása*, the ceremony of cutting the nails of the bride takes place. At the same time a drop of blood is drawn from her little finger, and preserved in *mahawar* (cotton soaked in red dye). Her feet are also marked with *mahawar*.

(10) *Bar Newatran* or *Dhurchhak*.—A party of the bride's relatives, Brahmans and others taking some *sherbet*, eatables, tobacco. etc., go to the *janwása* and present them to the bridegroom's party, The bridegroom is formally invited to dinner with a present of money, which his father accepts. But owing to the exorbitant demands of money and grain generally made by the bridegroom's father, which the bride's father cannot always meet, this dinner seldom comes off before noon on the following day. Thus the food prepared is wasted, and the bridegroom's party remain unfed. Sometimes the bride's father in order to make up for the high *tilak* he had to pay in order to secure the bridegroom tries to cut down the amount of *jahez* agreed upon, and also doles out the *rassad* or supplies to the bridegroom's party very sparingly. The bridegroom's father, on the other hand, tries to get as much as he can out of the arrangement.

(11) *Kanya Nirechhan*, seeing the bride.—After the invitation to dinner has been accepted, the elder brother or some other elder relative of the bridegroom proceeds to the house of the bride's father; the bride is made to sit under the *mandap*, and the bridegroom's brother going there presents to her jewels and clothes, after which she returns to the inner apartments and is dressed in those clothes and ornaments. By this time the bridegroom is also brought to the place.

(12) The bridegroom's feet are washed by the bride's father, and (13) he is given a wooden seat (*Pidha*) and a *Kusásan* or pad of *Kusa* grass to sit on. All these ceremonies are performed according to Vedic prescription.

(14) His feet are again washed after taking his seat (*Padanjali* and *Hast Argha*).

(15) Then *dahi*, honey and *ghi* and sugar (*madhuparkà*) are given him to eat by the bride's father. The bride also is brought and made to sit on his right side on a similar wooden seat.

(16) *Agnisthápan*, or the placing of the fire before them, is duly performed.

(17) *Gotranchara*, or the ceremony of transferring the bride into the family of bridegroom by reciting the names of the father and grandfather of each with vedic *mantras*, is performed, and the bride and bridegroom's clothes are knotted together. By this ceremony the bride gives up all claims on her father's family and is transferred to that of the bridegroom.

(18) *Kanyádan* or *pánigrahan*, by which the bride's father puts her hand into that of the bridegroom and entrusts her to his care, while he in his turn accepts the offer.

(19) Then the bridegroom changes his dress (*bastra bandhan*), and puts on a *dhoti* given by the bride's father.

(20) Next in order *hom* is performed by throwing *ghi* and sugar on the sacred fire in homage to all the Hindu gods.

(21) *Lájdhuti* or *Láwá Merdwan.*—Unhusked and parched paddy brought by both parties is mixed together. The bride and bridegroom go seven times round the sacred fire, which stands in the centre of the *mandap*, taking care to keep it always on their right hand. The bride puts her hands into those of the bridegroom, holding at the same time a small *supli* or basket for cleaning grain. Into this *supli* the bride's brother pours out the *láwá*, which the bride and the bridegroom jointly pour on to the fire. This offering is said to be made to a toothless god, named Pukha.

(22) *Silarohan* (*Sapta Bedi*).—The bride puts her foot on a *sil*, the stone used for grinding spices, and the bridegroom removes it. Both parties call the gods to witness that they have accepted each other as husband and wife.

(23) *Sumangli Karan* or *Sendur bandhan.*—The bridegroom smears vermilion on the bride's forehead. This form is now regarded merely as a token and memorial of the married state. Clearly, however, as has been pointed out in the article on Kurmi and elsewhere in these volumes, it is a survival of mixing the blood of the parties or drinking each other's blood which is found among the marriage customs of more primitive races.

(24) *Dachhina shankalp.*—The bride's father promises in a form authorised by the scriptures to pay a price for the bridegroom. The *tilak* and *jahes*, it appears, are not sanctioned by the Shastras.

(25) *Kudát mantra pathan.*—The bridegroom formally confers his blessing on the bride's father for the presents he has made to him.

(26) *Ashuch Karan.*—It has been mentioned above (No. 9, *ashuch parichhalan*) that a piece of coloured cotton containing a little of the bride's blood is kept. With this the bridegroom's neck is touched, and the bride's neck is also touched with a piece of simple coloured cotton brought by the bridegroom. The pieces of cotton are tied on their wrists (*kangan bandhan*). It is believed that this practice generates mutual affection. Clearly it is a survival of the earlier rite already referred to.

(27) *Pith Paritechan.* The couple exchange seats, and the bridegroom swears to protect and love his wife, and the bride swears to obey, respect and love her husband.

(28) After this the priest tells them that they have become *girhasta* and should live like married people, and explains to them their duties.

(29) *Ashirbád.*—The Brahmans and all present bless the bride and the bridegroom, and throw rice (*achhat*) over them. This ends the Vedic rites necessary to make a marriage binding. Neither the bridegroom nor the bride understand what is said, and in most cases the Brahmans recite even those parts which the parties to the marriage ought to pronounce themselves.

After the final blessing all the men present retire, leaving the bride and bridegroom under the *mandap*. Then the women come and do *chumawan*, *i.e.*, touch the feet, knee, and shoulders of the bridegroom with their fingers, at the same time holding rice in their hands. They are then taken into the *kohbar*, or the room prepared for their reception. There the women perform their own peculiar ceremonies, playing at the same time various tricks on the bridegroom till daybreak when he returns to the *janwása*. Then the marriage party is invited to dinner, or rather breakfast, which, as stated above, seldom comes before noon. At this time a present of plates, etc., is made to the bridegroom, and his relatives, all of which counts towards the amount of *jahez* agreed upon. At night, or rather next morning, comes a repast of *kachchi* food, after which the bridegroom's party prepare for return. Before leaving, each of the relatives of the bridegroom makes presents of money and ornaments to the bride. This is called *madwa* or *muhdekhai*, and at the same time all the relatives of the bride meet those of the bridegroom, and each of the former makes a present of money when embracing the latter. *Attar*, *pán*, etc., are distributed. The party returns to the *janwása* followed by the bride's people, who supply them with provisions for return journey. Thus ends the marriage. On the fourth day the ceremony of *chauthari* is performed. In some districts, especially in Patna, the bride accompanies the bridegroom to his house, where they jointly perform this ceremony. The bridegroom visits all the places of family worship. The family gods and all Hindu gods are worshipped, who having been invited to be present during the marriage are supposed then to take their departure to their respective abodes. After this the bride returns to her father's house. In such cases the ceremony of *duragawan* is performed just after the performance of the marriage rites. To complete the ceremony of *duragawan*, which means the going of the bride to the house of the bridegroom, only the nails of the bride are cut. Conjugal life cannot begin until this rite has been performed. In Shahabad and other places the bride does not accompany the bridegroom to his house after the marriage, and *chowthari* is performed by each at their respective fathers' houses. In these cases the ceremony of *durgaawan* is performed after one, three or five years according to the age of the bride and the convenience of the parties. The ritual observed is simple. The bridegroom goes with his friends to the bride's house. No *mandap* is constructed: only a *kalsa* is placed as in marriage. The bride and bridegroom are seated together, the gods and ancestors are worshipped, and the bride's nails are cut. *Chumawan*, etc., as in marriage, is performed by the women, and the bride sent to the bridegroom's house. On this occasion the bride's father gives her dresses, jewels, bed, bed-clothes, and presents to the bridegroom. Henceforth she lives with her husband and visits her parents whenever she likes.

Religion.

Votaries may be found among the Káyasths of nearly all the main Hindu sects—Vaishnava, Saiva, Sákta, Kabirpanthi, Nának-sháhi, and the like. The worship of Durga and the Saktis is believed, however, to be their favourite cult. Chitragupta, the mythical ancestor of the caste, is honoured once a year on the 17th Kartik, the festival of the *dawát pujá*, with offerings of sweetmeats and money, and the symbolical worship of pen and ink, the tools of the Káyasth's trade. For the worship of the greater gods an generally for religious and ceremonial purposes, the Káyasths employ Brahmans, who are received on equal terms by other members of the priestly caste. As regards the ceremony of *sráddh*, the practice of the caste appears to vary. Some Káyasths observe it on the 13th, some on the 16th, and some on the 29th day after death. The final funeral ceremony, known as *barki sráddh*, is performed at the end of a year in the case of a father, mother, or other ascendant, but after three months for the death of a wife.

Occupation.

Clerical work is believed to be the original and characteristic occupation of the caste, and an illiterate Káyasth is looked upon as a creature with no proper reason for existing. Káyasth tradition, however, puts a very liberal construction on the expression clerical work, and includes in it not merely clerkly pursuits of a subordinate character, but the entire business of managing the affairs of the country in the capacity of *dewan*, *sarbarahkar*, etc., to the ruling power. It is doubtless owing in some measure to this connexion with former governors that Káyasths are now in possession of considerable zemindaris and tenures of substantial value, while comparatively few of them are to be found among the lower grades of cultivators. In the course of the cadastral survey undertaken in 1886–87 of 235 villages in chakla Nai, pargana Bissarrah, Mozufferpur, a statement was drawn up at my suggestion showing the caste of the various grades of landholders. The following table shows the number of Káyasths in these villages possessing rights in connexion with the land and the proportion that number bears in each case to the total of the class of landholders concerned :—

	Number of Káyasths.	Percentage on total of class.
Proprietors	672	13·3
Lákherájdárs	3	4·8
Thikádárs	2	2·9
Tenants at fixed rents ...	58	3·9
Settled ryots	372	2·2
Occupancy but not settled ryots	8	6·2
Non-occupancy ryots ...	48	3·0

These figures cannot of course be taken to represent precisely the relations of Káyasths to the land in all districts of Behar, but they are of interest as showing the strong position that a caste, having in theory no connection whatever with agriculture and affecting to despise those of its own members who serve as village accountants, has managed to win for itself in the land system of the country. There could be no better comment on the numerous proverbial sayings current in Behar which have for their subject the cunning and the acquisitiveness of the Kayasth caste.

Notwithstanding the jealousy with which their less astute neighbours regard them, the social position of the Behar Káyasths is unquestionably a high one. Popular opinion ranks them next in order to the Bábhans and Rajputs, and like these, when they hold land as ryots, they get their homestead free of rent. All Káyasths will eat *kachchi* food that has been cooked by a 'good' Brahman, that is, by a Brahman who belongs to a respectable sub-caste, and whose ceremonial purity has not been affected by serving low people. The Amasht and Karan sub-castes will eat *kachchi* cooked by a Bábhan. None of the Káyasth sub-castes will eat *kachchi* food prepared by a member of another sub-caste. Sribástabs, Amashtas, and Karans will sometimes eat *pakki* off the same plate and smoke out of the same hookah. Ordinarily speaking, Káyasths take *pakki* food from any caste from whose hands water can be taken. The Vaishnava members of the caste abstain from flesh and wine; but Káyasths usually eat mutton and goat's flesh, hare, game birds, and are notorious for their indulgence in strong drink.

Social status.

The following statement shows the number and distribution of Káyasths in 1872 and 1881:—

DISTRICT.	1872.	1881.	DISTRICT.	1872.	1881.
Patna	28,289	29,864	Purniah	11,833	12,76
Gya	40,222	43,965	Maldah	4,601	4,656
Shahabad	42,407	46,994	Santál Parganas	5,940	7,830
Mozufferpur	70,992	48,551	Hazaribagh	6,300	9,232
Durbhanga		45,124	Lohardagá	4,061	6,690
Saran	47,686	51,065	Singbhum	611	996
Champáran	24,547	28,411	Manbhum	7,991	6,506
Monghyr	20,452	23,044	Tributary States	210	689
Bhagalpur	17,170	21,810			

Kayát, a synonym for Darzi, *q.v.*

Káyat, *Káyath*, a synonym for Kayastha.

Kechengia, a sept of Chiks in Chota Nagpur.

Kekrá, crab, a sub-sept of the Márndi sept of Santáls.

Kelatoni, a *thar* or section of Nepáli Brahmans.

Keli, a *thar* or sept of Mangars in Darjiling.

Kelobo, bee, a totemistic sept of Juángs in Orissa.

Kendi, a tree, a totemistic sept of Oraons in Chota Nagpur.

Kendwár, a sept of Rajputs in Behar.

Kenu, fish, a totemistic sept of Oraons in Chota Nagpur.

Keoli, a section of the Bahánnajáti sub-caste of Khatris in Bengal.

Keond, fruit, a totemistic sept of Oraons in Chota Nagpur.

Keophasa, a sept of Maghs in the Hill Tracts of Chittagong.

Keora, a flower, a totemistic sept of Chiks in Chota Nagpur.

Keoya, a sept of Tipperahs in the Hill Tracts of Chittagong.

Kephuk, a sept of Limbus in Darjiling.

Kerá, plantain, a totemistic sept of Mundas in Chota Nagpur.

Kerálaba, pumpkin, a totemistic sept of Juángs in Orissa.

Kerketa, a bird which makes a noise like 'ket ket,' a totemistic sept or section of Oraons, Lohárs, Korwas, Mundas, Doms, Asuras, Chamárs, Goráits, Khariás, Mahilis, Turis, and Kharwars in Chota Nagpur.

Kerungma, a sept of the Pánthar sub-tribe of Limbus in Darjiling.

Kerwar, a sub-sept of the Hansda sept of Santáls.

Kerwári, a sept of Pators in Chota Nagpur.

Kesarari, a section of Páns in Chota Nagpur.

Kesargia, a sept of Kharwárs in Chota Nagpur.

Kesariá, a totemistic section of Kurmis in Chota Nagpur and Orissa, the members of which will not cut or touch *kesar* grass.

Kesarkuni, a *gáin* of the Sándilya *gotra* of Rárhi Brahmans in Bengal, to which the Rájá of Nadiya belongs.

Kesaur, a *mul* or section of the Chhamuliá Madhesiá sub-caste of Halwáis in Behar.

Kesrá, a totemistic sept of Páns in Chota Nagpur, who are forbidden to eat *rahar dál*.

Keswál, a section of Goálás in the North-Western Provinces and Behar.

Ket-Chhutár, a sub-caste of Sutradhars in the Santál Parganas.

Ketugrámi, a *gáin* of the Sábarna *gotra* of Bárendra Brahmans in Bengal.

Kevala Gaura, a group of Gaura Brahmans.

Kewat, a sub-caste of Malláhs in Behar, mostly boatmen and fishermen; a section of Ghásis in Chota Nagpur.

Kewat, *Kiot*, a fishing and cultivating caste of Behar, also largely engaged in personal service among the higher classes of natives. Its origin is uncertain. Buchanan[1] thought it not improbable that the Kewats of Behar and the Kaibarttas of Bengal belonged in the earliest times to one aboriginal tribe bearing the name Kewat, and that the Sanskrit name Kaibartta might "have been adopted when Ballál Sen raised the tribe to the rank of purity." Lassen's remarks on these two names have been quoted in the article on *Kaibartta*, at p. 376 above. It will be seen that he differs from the Indian grammarians in holding that *Kaivarta* has nothing to do with fishing, but denotes a person who follows a low occupation, and from Buchanan in thinking that *Kewat* or *Kevat*, so far from being the 'barbarous' name of an aboriginal tribe, is merely a popular corruption of *Kaivarta*.

Origin.

[1] *Eastern India*, iii, 530.

At the present day the Kewats of Behar are divided into five sub-castes—**Ajudhiabási**; **Bahiáwak, Bahiot** or **Ghibihár**; **Garbháit, Gorwáit,** or **Sághár**; **Játhot**; and **Machhuá**. The Ájudhiábási are believed to have immigrated in comparatively recent times from Oudh, and are engaged solely in cultivation. The Bahiáwak sub-caste, called Ghibihár or ghi-eater, from a story that one of them once ate the leavings of his master, also believe that they came from Upper India, where they followed the occupation of boatmen and fishermen. In those days it is said the personal servants of the Darbhanga Ráj were Kurmis; but one of them, named Biru Khawás, who had risen to be a *tahsildár*, dealt dishonestly with the Rájá, and owing to his treachery all the Kurmis were turned out and Kewats from the North-West Provinces established in their places. Various titles were conferred upon the Kewats, according to the offices which they held. Thus the Khawás was the Rájá's personal servant; the Bhandári had charge of the *bhandár* or granary, where rent paid in kind was stored; the Derádár worked in the kitchen; the Kápar looked after the Rájá's clothes; and the Kámat saw to the cultivation of his *sirát* or private lands. In course of time the distinction between agriculture and personal service became accentuated: the cultivators drew together into the Garbháit sub-caste, and the serving class formed the Bahiáwak group. The names Ghibihár, 'ghi-eater,' and Sághár, 'vegetable-eater,' appear to indicate that supposed divergences of practice in the matter of food gave rise to the separation. The Bahiáwak Kewats living in and about their employers' houses would necessarily fall under the suspicion of eating forbidden food, and this would of itself be sufficient to cut them off from their cultivating brethren. Those Kewats, on the other hand, who adhered to their original profession of boating and fishing, formed the nucleus of the Machhuá sub-caste.

Internal structure.

Infant-marriage is in full force among the Kewats, the marriageable age for boys being ordinarily from five to ten, and for girls from three to ten years of age. Curiously, it is deemed less material that the bridegroom should be older than the bride than that he should be *taller*. This point is of the first importance, and is ascertained by actual measurement. If the boy is shorter than the girl, or if his height is exactly the same as hers, it is believed that the union of the two would bring ill luck, and the match is at once broken off. The marriage ceremony corresponds in its main features with that described by Mr. Grierson at page 362 of *Behar Peasant Life*. Some points, however, seem to deserve special notice. After the first proposal has been made, the bridegroom's people pay a visit to the bride's house (*ghardekhi*) for the purpose of seeing the bride. This is followed by a return visit on the part of the bride's people, known as *bardekhi*, seeing the bridegroom. Then comes *tilak*, which consists in the bride's father or guardian going to the bridegroom's house with a present of money, clothes, etc., proportionate to the respective rank of the two families. If, for example, a Bahiáwak Kewat employed in the family of the Maháraja of

Marriage.

Darbhanga marries the daughter of a Kewat who serves a man of inferior rank, or marries into a family of Kewats who allow their women to do menial offices in the houses of their employers, the family of higher rank claims and receives a proportionately large *tilak*. *Tilak* having been paid, a Tirhutiá Brahman is called in to fix a lucky day for the marriage. On the day before the wedding, not five or eight days before, as in the case described by Mr. Grierson, the ceremony called *kumram* or *matkorwá* is performed by the relatives of both bride and bridegroom. The women of each family with their female friends go forth singing to a tank outside the village. There, after bathing the bride or bridegroom as the case may be, the mother or female guardian digs up and brings home a clod of earth. From this clod a rude fireplace is made, on which ghi is burned and paddy parched in honour of the household god on the threshold of the kitchen, where he is supposed to dwell. A goat is sacrified at the same time. Some of the parched paddy is kept to be used in the ceremony of the following day.

On the wedding day *parchhan* is performed in the manner described by Mr. Grierson. For the *bukuá urái* or *dhurchhak* ceremony, noticed in paragraph 1320 of *Behar Peasant Life*, the Kewats substitute *sirhar*. The females of the bride's household, one of them bearing on her head a *ghará* of water, go in a body to the *ianwánsá*, where the bridegroom's party are lodged, and assail them with abusive songs and personal ridicule. This is kept up until one of the bridegroom's friends comes out and drops some prepared betel and some money. Then the women retire; but one of them, usually the wife of one of the brothers of the bride, returns armed with a scarf, which she throws round the neck of the bridegroom and drags him away to the courtyard of the bride's house. On his arrival there he is made to walk round the *marhwa*, scattering on the ground the paddy parched in the *matkorwa* ceremony of the preceding day. Both parties are then seated under the *marhwa*. The family Brahman makes his appearance, and the religious portion of the ceremony begins, which need not be described in detail. *Sindurdán* is believed to be its essential and binding portion. Before, however, *sindurdán* is performed the *purohit* writes the names of the bride and bridegroom and their ancestors up to the third degree on two mango leaves, and binds one of these on the wrist of each. After *sindurdán* again there follows a curious rite, called *sonch*, which looks as if it were a survival of the primitive form of *sindurdán* described in the article on Kurmi. The bridal pair are taken into one of the rooms, where two dishes of boiled rice and milk are standing ready. A tiny scratch is then made on the little finger of the bridegroom's right hand and of the bride's left, and the drops of blood drawn from these are mixed with the food. Each then eats the food with which the other's blood has been mingled.

Polygamy is permitted only in the event of the first wife being barren, and in no case can a man have more than two wives. A widow may marry again by the *sagai* form. She is not obliged to marry her late husband's younger brother, but she may do so if she pleases, and this arrangement is usually favoured by the other members of the family. Divorce is not permitted. Adultery within the caste is atoned for by a penalty fixed by the *manjan*, while an intrigue with an outsider involves instant expulsion.

Religion.

In religion the Kewats are orthodox Hindus, who regard Bhagavati as their special goddess. They also worship the snake god Bisahari, and some members of the caste abstain altogether from killing snakes. Maithil Brahmans officiate as their priests, and their gurus are Sannyasi ascetics. Among the minor gods, so numerous in Behar, they worship Bandi Goraiyá, Nar Singh, and Káli with offerings of goats, rice, milk, sweetmeats, and various kinds of cakes. Cocks are sacrificed to Bandi alone, but these may not be slain within the house, nor may they, like the other articles mentioned, be eaten by the worshippers. Sanái Maháraj and Baba Dayál Singh, both supposed to be deified Kewáts, are also reckoned among their gods.

Social status.

In point of social standing Kewats occupy much the same position as Kurmis, Koiris, Dhánuks, and other members of the group of castes from whom Brahmans can take water and certain kinds of sweetmeats. Their own rules as to diet differ little from those of other orthodox Hindus, except that Bahiáwak Kewats will eat the leavings of the Brahmans, Rajputs, Bábhans, and Káyasths whom they serve, while Machhuá Kewats eat fowls and indulge freely in strong drink. They will take water and sweetmeats, etc., from Goalas, Koiris, and Dhánuks, but will eat *kachchi* food with no other caste except Amáts of good family. Most cultivating Kewats hold the position of raiyats with or without occupancy rights in the land which they till. Some few have risen to hold small zemindaris, while the poorest members of the cultivating sub-caste work as agricultural labourers.

Members of the caste domiciled in Eastern Bengal.

It deserves mention that the Kewats, though properly a Behar caste, are very widely distributed in Bengal and Orissa. A colony of them, says Dr. Wise, has for centuries been settled in the city of Dacca, but no traces of them are to be found in the interior of the district. A tradition still survives that they were brought from Behar by the Mahomedan rulers of Eastern Bengal and employed as messengers and watchmen. They repudiate the idea of relationship with the Kaibarttas, although they do not object to eat or smoke with them. The Dacca Kewats have three subdivisions—Seo Rámi, Gauri or Gonrhi, and Dhun Kewat. These names, however, must be regarded rather as titles than as the designations of true sub-castes, for their members not only eat together, but intermarry just as Kewats who happen to bear different titles do in Behar. These Kewats are all included in one gotra, Kásyapa; and though domiciled in Bengal, are not excluded from caste privileges when on a visit to Behar. Owing to association with more orthodox or more bigoted people, widow-marriage has been discontinued. In Dacca the caste have relinquished fishing, and have generally adopted the occupation of fishmongers, although a few are poddárs or bankers.

The Kewat fishmonger usually makes advances to the fishermen, and finds it more profitable to buy small fish by the basket and large ones by weight than to haggle for each day's catch. The Kewat generally brings the supply from the fishing ground himself if it is near, but a servant is sent if it is distant.

Their religion.

Dr. Wise remarks on the strange fact that the Dacca Kewats have become followers of the Nának Sháhi faith. Their guru is the Mahant of the Akhárá of that sect in the suburb of Shuj'áatpur; their purohit a Maithil Brahman. The Kantha Brahman performs their funeral service, and attends at the *sráddha* observed fifteen days after death; but he is charged with being extortionate, and with demanding more than poor Kewat families can afford.

Festival.

The great annual festival of the Kewats of Dacca is the Nauámí, or ninth lunar day of Paush (December-January), when every one visits the Akhárá, and after prayers receives *Mohan Bhog*, a sweetmeat specially prepared for the occasion. The Chhath, on the sixth of Kártic, is a great bathing rite observed by Kewats and all Hindustání castes; while the Ganga Pújah, as well as the principal Hindu festivals, are kept. Sacrifices, too, are offered at the proper seasons to Bura-Buri, the androgynous village deity of Eastern Bengal, whose worship has been described at length in the article on the Chandáls.

The following statement shows the number and distribution of Kewats in 1872 and 1881:—

District.	1872.	1881.	District.	1872.	1881.
Bardwan	......	631	Shahabad	706	......
Bankura	......	1,747	Tirbut { Mozufferpur ...	} 52,977	{ 3,447
Birbhum	......	1,162	Tirbut { Darbhanga ...		42,064
Midnapur	......	2,678	Saran	46	......
Hughli	......	1	Champaran	2,279	5,166
Howrah	......	1	Monghyr	3,101	2,319
Khulna	......	39	Bhagalpur	64,594	35,516
Jessore	......	53	Purniah	20,067	39,641
Murshedabad	......	341	Maldah	......	1,119
Rajshahye	......	2	Santál Parganas	1,212	538
Bogra	......	12	Cuttack	57,373	10,989
Pabna	......	288	Puri	27,188	4,668
Julpigori	......	1	Balasore	34,442	21,311
Dacca	......	26	Tributary States	31,384	3,744
Tipperah	......	7	Hazaribagh	632	636
Chittagong	......	1	Lohardagá	678	1,073
Patna	427	584	Singbhum	1,529	1,471
Gya	293	22	Manbhum	692	1,042
			Tributary States	2,660	9,271

Khádhnu, a section of the Sátmuliá Maghayá sub-caste of Kándus in Behar.

Khadohar, tattooers; also employed as vaccinators.

Khadoliá, Khadotiá, a section of Goálás in the North-Western Provinces and Behar.

Khadumiá, a section of Goálás in the North-Western Provinces and Behar.

Khagaur, a *mul* or section of the Kanaujiá sub-caste of Sonárs in Behar.

Khairá, a small caste in Hazaribagh who grow vegetables

and other crops. They are believed to be akin to Kharwárs.

Khairá, a cultivating sub-caste of Bágdis in Bengal; also a synonym for Korá.

Khairi, a sub-tribe of Kharwárs in Palámau.

Khairwál, a section of Goálás in the North-Western Provinces and Behar.

Khajkaliá, a sub-caste of Sunris in Behar.

Khajurárk, a *pur* or section of Sákadwipi Brahmans in Behar.

Khajuri, a *mul* or section of the Naomuliá or Majraut sub-caste of Goálás in Behar.

Khalang, a section of Khambus in Darjiling.

Khalhad, a section of Goálás in the North-Western Provinces and Behar.

Kháling, a *thar* or sept of Khambus in Darjiling.

Khalkho, a section of Goráits in Chota Nagpur.

Khalkhoa, a totemistic sept of Oraons who may not eat fish that have been caught by baling water out of a tank or pool.

Khalrihá, a section of the Banodhiá and Jaiswár Kalwárs in Behar.

Khálsa, a sub-caste of Kalwárs in Behar.

Kham, a synonym for Sherpa Bhotia of Nepal.

Khamapong, the dweller under the *bar* (*Ficus religiosa*) tree, a sept of the Phedáb sub-tribe of Limbus in Darjiling.

Khámáru, a synonym for Bhuinmáli, *q.v.*

Khamba, a sub-tribe of Lepchas in Darjiling.

Khambe, a sept of Chakmás in the Hill Tracts of Chittagong.

Khambha, fork of a tree, a totemistic sept of Chiks in Chota Nagpur.

Khambu, *Jimdár*, *Rái*, one of the fighting tribes of Nepal, forming with the Limbu and Yákhá the Kiranti group who have their original home in the Kirant Des or mountainous country lying between the Dud-Kosi and Karki rivers. Like several other Nepalese tribes, the Khambu cherish a tradition that they came to Nepal from Kási or Benares. A mythical ancestor, Parubang, is still worshipped as a household deity. Khambus marry their daughters as adults, and tolerate sexual license before marriage on the understanding, rarely set at defiance, that a man shall honourably marry a girl who is pregnant by him. Men usually marry between the ages of 15 and 20, and girls between 12 and 15, but marriage is often deferred in the case of the former to 25, and of the latter to 20. The preliminary negotiations are entered upon by the bridegroom's family, who send an emissary with two *chungas* or bamboo

Marriage.

vessels of *marwa* beer and a piece of ham to the bride's house to ask for her hand. If her parents agree, the bridegroom follows on an auspicious day about a fortnight later, and pays the standard bride-price of Rs. 80. The wedding takes place at night. Its essential and binding portion is the payment of one rupee by the bridegroom as *saimundi* or earnest-money to the bride's father, the smearing of vermilion on the bride's forehead and putting a scarf round her neck. The bride-price may be paid in instalments if the bridegroom's family cannot afford to pay in a lump. A widow is allowed to marry again, but her value is held to have declined by use, and only half the usual bride-price is paid for her if she is young, and only a quarter if she has passed her first youth. Divorce is permitted for adultery ; the adulterer must pay to the husband the full amount that the woman originally cost, and he can then marry her. In actual practice the marriage bond is very readily broken among the Khambus and among many other of the Nepalese tribes. Women are faithful to the men they live with while they live with them, and secret adultery is believed to be rare, but they think very little of running away with any man of their own or a cognate tribe who takes their fancy; and the state of things which prevails approaches closely to the ideal *regimé* of temporary unions advocated by would-be marriage reformers in Europe.

Religion.

By religion Khambus are Hindus, but they have no Brahmans, and men of their own tribe, called Homé, corresponding closely to the Bijuás employed by the Tibetans, serve them as priests. Their special god is the ancestral deity Párubang, who is worshipped in the months of March and November with the sacrifice of a pig and offerings of incense and *marwa* beer. Him they regard as a *ghardevatá* or household deity, and he is held in greater honour than the unmistakeably Hindu divinity Devi to whom buffaloes, goats, fowls and pigeons are occasionally sacrificed. Another of their minor gods, Sidha, is honoured with offerings of *dhuba* grass and milk. His origin is uncertain; but it seems to me possible that the name may be a survival of the stage of Buddhism through which the Khambus, like many other Nepalese castes, have probably passed.

Funerals.

The practice of the Khambus in respect to disposing of the dead varies greatly, and appears to depend mainly on the discretion of the Homé called in to supervise the operation. Both burial and cremation are resorted to on occasion, and the mourners sometimes content themselves with simply throwing the body into the nearest river. A *sráddh* ceremony of a somewhat simple character is performed once for the benefit of the deceased in the next world, and to prevent him from coming back to trouble the living. Land-owning and cultivation are believed by the Khambus to be their original and characteristic occupation, but a certain number of them adopt military service and enter Gurkha regiments under the title of Rai. A Khambu if asked to what caste he belongs will usually reply Jimdár (a corruption of zamindár) or

Occupation.

Rai-Jimdár. A few Khambus have also taken to weaving. Their social status, so far as Nepal is concerned, is best marked by the statement that they belong to the Kiranti group, and are recognised as equals by the Limbus and Yakhas. In the matter of food they are less particular than the Hindus of the plains, for they eat pork and the domestic fowl, and indulge freely in strong drink.

Khámid, a title of Máls.

Khámtá, a section of Goálás in the North-Western Provinces and Behar.

Khámthák, a sept of Limbus in Darjiling.

Khán, a title of Rajputs and a section of Sunris in Behar; a title of the Desá sub-caste of Gandhabaniks; of Nápits and of Bágdis in Bengal; a section of the Biyáhut and Kharidáhá Kalwárs; a title of Thárus and Karangás.

Khána, a title of Maithil Brahmans in Behar.

Khanál, a *thar* or section of Nepáli Brahmans.

Khandabati, a *gáin* of the Sábarna *gotra* of Bárendra Brahmans in Bengal.

Traditions of origin.

Khandáit, *Khandáyat*, a swordsman, from Uriyá *khandá*, 'a sword,' the generic title of the feudal militia of Orissa, the leading members of which claim to be descended from a band of pure Kshatriyas who came in as conquerors from Northern India. A good observer writes of them as follows:—"Although a numerous and well-defined body, the Khandáits do not appear to be really a distinct caste. The ancient Rájás of Orissa kept up large armies, and partitioned the lands on strictly military tenures. These armies consisted of various castes and races, the upper ranks being officered by men of good Aryan descent, while the lower ones were recruited from the low castes alike of the hills and the plains. On the establishment of a well-defined caste system such troops took their caste from their occupation, and correspond to the military class in the fourfold division in Northern India; but with this difference, that in Northern India the military class consists of an ethnical entity, whereas in Orissa the Khandáits exhibit every variety of type, from the high Aryan of good social position to the semi-aboriginal mongrel taken from the dregs of the people." In this passage, taken from the *Statistical Account of Balasore District*, Mr. Beames appears to regard the Khandáits as a heterogeneous group, made up at the one end of Aryan immigrants from Upper India and at the other of recruits from a number of indigenous non-Aryan tribes.

The data now available enable us to carry the analysis a step further, and to show that the Khandáit caste is for the most part, if not entirely, composed of Bhuiyás of the southern tribe, whose true affinities have been disguised under a functional name, while their customs, their religion, and in some cases even their complexion and features, have been modified by long contact with Hindus of relatively pure Aryan descent. The evidence for this view consists of the following facts:—*first*, that the Khandáits of the Chota Nagpur Division, who say that they immigrated from Orissa some twenty generations ago, and many of whom still speak Uriya, regulate their marriages by the totemistic sections characteristic of the Southern Bhuiyás, and call themselves Bhuiyá-Páiks; *secondly*, that among the numerous titles of the Khandáits in Orissa we find the very singular names **Uttar, Dakhin,** and **Paschim-Kapát,** which are assumed by the Bhuiyás of Singbhum; *thirdly*, that as late as 1825[1] the term Bhuiyá was current as a synonym for Khandáit even in Orissa, where it now seems to have fallen into disuse.

Internal structure.

The sub-castes and sections of both Orissa and Chota Nagpur Khandáits, so far as I have been able to ascertain them, are shown in Appendix I. The relations of the subdivisions of the **Bar-gohri** sub-caste are rather intricate. Members of all four groups may intermarry, but the women of the **Pánchsaughariá** and **Pandrasaughariá** subdivisions, if married to men of the **Dasghariá** or **Pánchghariá** classes, are supposed to be to a certain extent degraded, and members of their own groups will not take food from their hands. So also the **Das** and **Pánch-ghariá** will eat food cooked by the **Pánchsau** and **Pandrasau-ghariá,** but the latter will not return the compliment. The **Panchsau,** again, will take boiled rice, etc., from the **Pandrasau-ghariá,** but only the unmarried men of the former class are deemed pure enough to prepare food of this kind for members of the latter class. The whole of the **Bar-gohri** sub-caste profess to maintain a high standard of ceremonial propriety, and will on no account intermarry with the **Chhot-ghori,** who eat fowls and indulge in strong drink like their non-Aryan neighbours. The Orissa sub-castes seem to be based on the social difference between the **Mahanáik** or **Sresta Khandáits** holding large *jagir* tenures, who represent the officers of the ancient feudal militia, and the rank and file of that body who now bear the name of **Chásá-Khandáit, Orh-Khandáit,** or **Khandáit-Páik,** and occupy the lower position of village *chaukidárs* and ordinary cultivators. Intermarriage between the two groups, though not absolutely forbidden, occurs very rarely, and they may properly be regarded sub-castes. The latter class still retain totemistic sections of the same type as are found among the Khandáits of Chota Nagpur, while the former have borrowed the Brahmanical *gotras*. In all cases the rule of exogamy extends only to a man's own section, and is supplemented by a table of prohibited degrees closely corresponding to that given in the article on the Rautias. The Chásá or Orh-Khandáit sub-caste admit into their own ranks members of the Chásá caste, but this appears to be effected simply by intermarriage, and not to form the occasion of any special ceremony.

Marriage.

The main body of Khandaits marry their daughters after they are grown up, and the practice of infant-marriage is confined to those landholding families who pretend to be Rajputs and affect strict conformity with orthodox usage. Even among these, however, special care is

[1] Stirling, *Account of Orissa*, p. 60.

taken to guard against premature consummation, and the husband is not allowed to take his wife home until she has attained the age of puberty. The ceremony is supposed to be in the Prájápatya form, referred to by Manu. The essential portions of the ritual are *hátgaultri*, or binding the hands of bride and bridegroom together with *kusa* grass, and *ganthiyán*, or knotting their clothes. Polygamy is permitted, and in theory at least there is no restriction on the number of wives a man may have. This luxury, however, is sparingly indulged in even by the wealthier members of the caste, and in practice few Khandáits take a second wife unless the first is barren or suffers from an incurable disease. In Chota Nagpur widows may marry again, and are bound by no conditions in their choice of a second husband, except that they must avoid the prohibited degrees binding upon them before marriage, and that they cannot marry elder brothers or elder cousins of their first husband. Marriage with the first husband's younger brother or younger cousin is allowed, and is deemed a very proper arrangement on the ground of family convenience. In Orissa the Sresta Khandaits forbid widow-marriage: in other sub-castes it is allowed on the same terms as in Chota Nagpur. Divorce may be decreed by the pancháyat on the application of the husband if a woman is convicted of unchastity, persistent disobedience, or serious misconduct. In such cases the divorced wife generally gets alimony for a year; but the more orthodox hold that she is only entitled to the jewels and property which she brought with her at marriage. All sub-castes except the Sresta Khandáits of Orissa allow a divorced wife to marry again by the *sagai* ritual.

Religion.

The majority of Khandaits follow the tenets of the Vaishnava sect, and comparatively few Sáktas or Saivas are met with among them. Their religious observances present no features of special interest. In Orissa the Sásani Brahmans, who serve them as priests, are received on equal terms by other members of the sacred order, and are deemed socially superior to the Sebak or Panda Brahmans, who minister to the spiritual necessities of the Chásá caste. Among minor gods Gramdevati in Orissa, and in Chota Nagpur the unmistakeably aboriginal deity Bar Pahár, corresponding to the Marang-Buru or great mountain of the Mundas and Santáls, are worshipped by the head of each household with offerings of goats, sweetmeats, and fruit, which are afterwards divided among the members of the family. The Orissa Khandáits profess great reverence for the sword as the symbol of their rank, and at the Dasahara festival the family weapons are solemnly cleaned and worshipped by laying flowers and fruit before them. This practice, however, seems to be merely a reflex of the common Hindu usage which leads every artificer to worship the tools of his craft, and cannot be regarded as of itself giving any clue to the tribal affinities of the caste. As a rule Khandáits burn their dead and perform a *sráddh* ceremony of the orthodox pattern on the eleventh day after death.

Social status.

In the social system of Orissa the Sresta Khandáits rank next to the Rajputs, who are comparatively few in number and have not the intimate connexion with the land which has helped to raise the Khandáits to their present position. A Sresta Khandáit assumes the sacred thread at the time of his marriage, a practice not uncommon among castes of dubious origin, who are pressing to be counted among the number of the twice-born. The Chásá Khandáits do not wear the thread, but Brahmans will take water from their hands, and they occasionally intermarry with the Karan caste. Khandáits themselves will take cooked food only from their own Brahmans, whose leavings also they will eat. Sweetmeats and water may be given to them by Chásás, Gor-Goálás, and Karans. In Chota Nagpur Kanaujiá Brahmans take water from Bar-Gohri Khándaits, but not from the Chhot-Gohri, who eat fowls, indulge freely in spirituous liquors, and generally order their lives in a fashion entirely inconsistent with the Hindu standard of ceremonial purity. Their traditions aver that shortly after their immigration from Orissa they were in possession of eight forts (*áth garh*) at Biru, Básia, Belsián, Dimba, Gorra, Lachrá, Lodhma, and Sonpur, and it is certain that at one time entire parganas in Chota Nagpur were held by Khandáits on terms of military service. These, however, passed out of their hands as the country settled down under British rule, and at the present day very few families retain tenures of any substantial value. The Orissa Khandáits seem to have held their ground more firmly; and it may be that our settlement of the land revenue, by recording the rights of all persons connected with the land, has enabled them to resist the modern tendency towards the resumption of ancient service grants. However this may be, the leading families of the caste still hold estates and rent-free tenures directly under Government, while the rank and file are occupancy raiyats or have small tenures in payment for their services as headmen (*sarbarahkárs*) or watchmen (*chaukidárs*) of villages; others, again, are occupancy or non-occupancy raiyats and landless day-labourers. Khandáits who wear a sword and do not cultivate with their own hands consider themselves superior to those who are working agriculturists; but this distinction does not seem to coincide exactly with the existing division into sub-castes.

Occupation.

The following statement shows the number and distribution of the Khandáits in 1872 and 1881. In Bengal Proper the figures for Ghatwáls are included in the former year:—

District.	1872.	1881.	District.	1872.	1881.
Bardwan	331	23	Bogra	336	......
Bankura	3	9	Pabna	1,910	......
Birbhum	184	......	Dacca	11	......
Midnapur	797	1,239	Maimansinh	383	......
Hughli ... ... }	8	{ 53	Chittagong	3	......
Howrah		132	Maldah	328	......
24-Parganas	1,340	1,107	Cuttack	263,308	343,596
Nadiya	......	14	Puri	7,847	34,292
Khulna	......	5	Balasore	135,955	184,773
Jessore	8	......	Tributary States ...	54,374	80,341
Murshedabad	1,545	1	Lohardagá	322	3,714
Dinajpur	35	......	Singbhum	2,255	505
Rajshahye	209	......	Tributary States ...	84	809

Khandáit-Paik, a sub-caste of, and a synonym for, Khandáits in the Orissa Tributary States.

Khandania, a sept of Mundas in Chota Nagpur.

Khandáyat, a synonym for Khandáit.

Khandelvála, a group of the Sanádhya sub-caste of Gaura Brahmans in Behar.

Khandiwár, a sub-caste of Bais Baniyás in Behar.

Khandsap, a *pur* or section of Sákadwipi Brahmans in Behar.

Khanduar, a section of Goálás in Behar.

Khandwal, a sub-caste of Goálás in Singbhum.

Khangar, a section of Mahilis in Western Bengal.

Khangar-Munda, a sub-tribe of Mundas in Chota Nagpur.

Khangbha, a *thar* or sept of Gurungs in Darjiling.

Khangor, a synonym for Khanjar.

Kháni Khor, a section of Murmis in Darjiling.

Khanjar, a small caste in Behar whose women practise prostitution.

Khánná, a sept of Rajputs and a section of the Chárjáti sub-caste of Khatris in Behar.

Khánrsimriá, a *mul* or section of the Naomuliá or Majraut sub-caste of Goálás in Behar.

Khantwár, a *pur* or section of Sákadwipi Brahmans in Behar.

Khápangi, a *thar* or sept of Mangars in Darjiling.

Khapariyá, a sub-caste of Dhánuks in Behar.

Khapráhá, a section of the Biyáhut and Kharidáhá Kalwárs in Behar.

Khaptari, a *thar* or sept of Gurungs and Mangars in Darjiling.

Khapu, a bird, a totemistic sept of Kharwárs in Chota Nagpur.

Khará, a hypergamous group of Karans in Orissa.

Kharádi (*Kharád*, a lathe), the caste of turners in Behar chiefly employed in making and painting legs of bedsteads and toys.

Kharait, a title of Sadgops in Bengal.

Kharáit, a *mul* or section of the Magháya sub-caste of Barhis in Behar.

Kharak, sword, a totemistic section of Rautiás in Chota Nagpur.

Kharakwár, a territorial section of Rajwárs and Rautiás in Chota Nagpur.

Kharáont, a sub-caste of Nuniás in Behar.

Kharaunre-Bhaur, a *mul* of the Sándil section of Maithil Brahmans in Behar.

Kharaunre-Khutti, a *mul* of the Sándil section of Maithil Brahmans in Behar.

Kharaunre-Gurdi, a *mul* of the Sándil section of Maithil Brahmans in Behar.

Kharaunre-Ekmá, a *mul* of the Sándil section of Maithil Brahmans in Behar.

Kharbahiá, a sept of Rajputs in Behar.

Kharchwár, a sub-caste of Kurmis in Behar.

Khardaha, a *mel* or hypergamous sub-group of Rárhi Brahmans in Bengal.

Khare, an endogamous division of the Sribástab sub-caste of Káyasths in Behar.

Khárgá, a section of Sunris in Behar.

Khargpur, a group of Maghaiya Telis in Behar.

Khariá, blade of grass, a totemistic section of Rautiás in Chota Nagpur. A sub-caste of Bhandáris in Orissa.

Khariá, a Dravidian cultivating tribe of Chota Nagpur, classed on linguistic grounds as Kolarian. In physique the settled members of the tribe resemble the Mundas, but have rather coarser features and a figure not so well proportioned. One of their traditions alleges that they succeeded the Oraons as settlers in the country between Rohtasgarh and Patna, while another says that their original home was in Moharbhanj, of which State they and the Puráns were the first inhabitants, being born there from a pea-fowl's egg,—the Puráns from the white, the Khariás from the shell, and the family of the chief (Bhanj) from the yolk. Thence they made their way up the valley of the Koel into the south-western corner of the Lohardagá district, where we now find them massed in tolerably large communities. Colonel Dalton endeavours to reconcile these conflicting accounts, but with no great success. In truth, legends of this kind are for the most part a highly unprofitable study. As often as not they refer to some recent migration of a comparatively small section of the tribe, and it is hopeless to expect that they should contain the clue to any really ancient history. Barbarous people like the Khariás have no means of handing down a statement of fact for any length of time. Writing is unknown to them, their language is rapidly dying out, and they have no form of poetry or modulated prose suited to the preservation of the early traditions of their race.

Traditions of origin.

The Khariás of Lohardagá are divided into four sub-tribes:—**Dhilki-Khariá, Dud-Khariá, Erengá-Khariá**, and **Munda-Khariá**. The Dud-Khariá affect a leaning towards Hinduism, and do not eat beef. The Munda-Khariá are supposed to be the offspring of an intrigue with a Munda woman. This statement is in accordance with the hypergamous relations which subsist between the two tribes. Khariás speak of the Mundas as their elder brethren, and Khariá women are sometimes taken as wives by the Mundas, who, however, will on no account give their girls in marriage to the Khariás. The septs of the tribe are shown in Appendix I. All of them are totemistic, but I am informed that the usual rule making the totem taboo is not now very generally observed. It must, however, at one time have been in force, for a sept of wild Khariás whom Mr. Ball observed on the Dalma range in Manbhum had the sheep for their totem, and were not allowed to eat mutton, or even to use a woollen rug. Exogamy is regularly practised, and a man may not marry a woman of his own sept. Beyond the circle defined by the sept name, the ideas of the Khariás on the subject of consanguineous marriages are said to be lax, and on the maternal side they appear to content themselves with forbidding a man to marry his aunts, his nieces, and his first cousins. Girls are usually married after they have attained puberty, and sexual intercourse before marriage is tacitly tolerated. Of late

Internal structure.

Marriage.

years the richer members of the tribe have adopted the Hindu fashion of infant-marriage. The preliminary negotiations for a marriage are carried on by the parents, and a bride-price (*sukmur*) of from one to ten head of cattle must be paid before the day can be fixed. This must be some time in Mágh (January-February), as Khariás can only marry during that month. On the day before the wedding the bride's family escort her to the bridegroom's house, great care being taken that she does not put her foot into a running stream on the way. The bridal party establish themselves under a tree, where a place has been prepared for them. There they are met by the bridegroom's party, each side being provided with an earthen jar of water wreathed round with ears of rice and crowned with a lighted lamp. The rest of the day is spent in feasting and in songs and dances, all bearing[1] "more directly than delicately on what is evidently considered the main object of the festivities—the public recognition of the consummation of the marriage." Early next morning the bride and bridegroom are anointed with oil and taken to bathe. Five bundles of straw are then spread on the ground, and the yoke (*juár*) of a plough laid upon them. The bride and bridegroom stand facing each other on the yoke, and the bridegroom smears vermilion on the bride's forehead and the parting of her hair, while she makes a small round spot of the same colour on his forehead. This completes the marriage, and the whole party sit down under a tree to feast at the expense of the bridegroom. While the feast is going on the bride is brought before the company and is made to wash a cloth in hot water, in token, apparently, of her willingness to do any form of household work. After this she is finally handed over to the bridegroom. If the full bride-price has been paid, the bride's father is expected to provide his daughter with a trousseau of seven pieces of cloth, and to give one ox to his son-in-law within a month after marriage.

A widow may marry again by the *sagai* form, which consists of the bridegroom presenting her with a new cloth. If her husband leaves a brother younger than himself, the widow is expected to marry him, but is not compelled to do so. It may indeed be inferred, from the fact that one head of cattle is the customary bride-price for a widow, that she frequently does marry outside of her late husband's family. Divorce is permitted on the ground of adultery, in which case the wife's family are required to give back the cattle which they received as the bride-price. A divorced woman may marry again, and her customary market value is stated to be two head of cattle.

Inheritance.

The Dud-Khariás profess to be guided in matters of inheritance and succession by the principles of the Mitákshará. This, however, is mere pretence, for they, like the rest of the tribe, follow a customary law of their own, administered by a pancháyat or council of elders, at which the tribal priest usually presides. The chief features of Khariá custom, so far as I have been able to ascertain them, may be summarised

[1] Dalton, *Ethnology of Bengal*, p. 160.

as follows. Sons inherit to the exclusion of all other heirs; but the eldest son gets two shares more than any of his brothers, and on him is supposed to rest the obligation of providing for the maintenance of the daughters. In dividing property a distinction is drawn between sons by a *biháí* wife, married by the full ceremony, and sons by a *sagai* wife, who may have been a widow or a divorced woman. Thus, supposing a man dies leaving two sons by a *biháí* and two by a *sagai* wife, and the property to be divided consists of sixteen *kanwas* of rice land, the land would be divided into two lots, one containing twelve *kanwas* and the other four. The elder of the two *biháí* sons would get seven *kanwas*, and the younger five *kanwas*; while the *sagai* sons would get two *kanwas* apiece. Brothers and uncles exclude widows and daughters.

Religion.

The religion of the Khariás may be defined as a mixture of animism and nature-worship, in which the former element on the whole predominates. As the nominal head of their system we find **Bar Pahār**, to whom buffaloes, rams, and cocks are offered at uncertain intervals. He seems to be a *fainéant* sort of deity, who brings neither good nor ill-fortune to men, and is not in charge of any special department of human affairs. He has no Khariá name, and it is possible that the practice of worshipping him may have been borrowed from the Mundas and Oraons. The working deities of the Khariá pantheon are the following:—(1) **Dorho Dubo**, who delights in muddy places and takes care of the *dárhis* or springs of water, which are a notable feature in the Lohardagá district. Pigs, goats, and red fowls are the offerings set apart for him. (2) **Nasán Dubo**, the god of destruction, who scatters death and disease abroad, and must be propitiated with sacrifices of five chickens. (3) **Giring Dubo**, the sun, whom Colonel Dalton mentions under the name of Bero, adding that "every head of a family should during his lifetime make not less than five sacrifices to this divinity; the first of fowls, the second of a pig, third of a white goat, fourth of a ram, and fifth of a buffalo. He is then considered sufficiently propitiated for this generation, and regarded as an ungrateful god if he does not behave handsomely to his votary. In praying to Bero they address him as 'Parameswar,' the Hindi word for God. The Ho term 'Sing bonga' they do not know. The sacrifices are always made in front of an ant hill, which is used as an altar. This peculiar mode of sacrificing has fallen into desuetude among the Hos and Mundas; but on my making some enquiries on the subject from old men of those tribes, I was informed that it was orthodox, though not now generally practised."[1] (4) **Jyolo Dubo**, the moon—offering, a black cock. (5) **Pát Dubo**, a god who loves rocky places—offering, a grey goat or reddish-brown fowls. (6) **Donga Dárhá**, a hill god—offering, a white goat. (7) **Mahádán**, another hill god, to whom rams are sacrificed. (8) **Gumi**, the god who lives in the *Sarná* or sacred grove, which serves as temple for most of the aboriginal deities—offering, a sow. (9) **Agin Darhá**, the protector of the rice crop—offering, a

[1] *Ethnology of Bengal*, p. 159.

white goat. (10) **Kárá Sarná**, the god of cattle-disease, to whom buffaloes are sacrificed on the occasion of an outbreak.

Khariás have not yet attained to the dignity of employing Brahmans for religious and ceremonial purposes, but have priests of their own, called Kálo, whose office is usually hereditary. They also avail themselves of the services of the village Páhan, who is usually a Munda or an Oraon. In their funeral rites they observe a curious distinction: the bodies of married people are burned, while persons who die unmarried are buried. When cremation is resorted to, the bones and ashes of the dead are put into a new earthen vessel with some parched rice and thrown into the deepest pool of a river, or, should there be no river near, into a rocky chasm or a tank in the *bhuinhári* village of the deceased, that is to say, the village in which he ranks among the descendants of the original clearers. If this village cannot be traced, the ashes may be thrown into any tank that is near, only in that case a feast must be given to the *bhuinhárs* of the village, and a *sidhá* of rice presented to the landlord. The relations and friends of the deceased are entertained at a feast, and a tall slab of unhewn stone is set up near his house, before which daily oblations are supposed to be offered in order to appease his spirit and avert the danger of his returning to trouble the living.

Funerals.

The settled Khariás are fair cultivators, and in the south-west of Lohardagá, where they are fairly numerous, many of them claim to be *bhuinhárs*, holders of *korkar* tenures, and occupancy raiyats. In other parts of the district they are mostly tenants-at-will and farm-labourers. The wild Khariás who frequent the Dalmá range in Manbhum and the forest-clad hills of Gángpur and other Tributary States know no other mode of agriculture than the barbarous *jhúm* or *dáhá* system, which consists in burning down a patch of jungle and sowing *bajrá*, *biri*, or *kodo* in the ashes between the stumps of the trees. They are said to be not over-fastidious feeders, eating monkeys and various kinds of small animals and cattle which have been killed by wild beasts or have died from disease. The settled Khariás have much the same notions as the Mundas on the subject, but the Dud-Khariá sub-tribe, as has been mentioned above, profess to abstain from beef, and eat *kachchi* only with men of their own tribe. "Some Khariás," says Colonel Dalton, "profess to be intensely exclusive in regard to cooking and eating. This characteristic I found most developed in villages of Chota Nagpur, where Khariás were associated with Oraons under Brahman proprietors; and it is a common saying in that part of the country that every Khariá must have his *hariah*, *i.e.*, cooking pot. He may not allow even his wife to cook for him, and if a stranger enters a house in which he keeps his earthen drinking and cooking vessels and water pots, every vessel is polluted, and the whole are destroyed or thrown away. This class of Khariás are specially filthy in their habits, and it is not improbable that Hindus may have been more than ordinarily harsh in excluding them from their kitchens and inner apartments, and that the Khariás retaliate by outcasting everybody."

Occupation.

The foregoing paragraphs treat for the most part only of the settled agricultural Khariás of the Lohardagá district, a people who are respectably dressed, comfortably housed, and well supplied with wholesome food. Some of them hold landed tenures of appreciable value, and there are signs of a tendency among them towards the adoption of Hinduism—a step which, whenever taken, will speedily obliterate all traces of primitive usage. Even now there is little left to show that they come of the same stock as the wild Khariás who inhabit the crests of the highest ranges in Manbhum, Singbhum, and the Tributary States of Chota Nagpur and Orissa, and are shunned even by the Hos and Bhumij on account of their reputation as wizards. These wandering savages, like the Birhors of Hazaribagh and Palamau, who Colonel Dalton supposes may belong to the same tribe, are now believed to be rapidly dying out, and very few Europeans have had the opportunity of seeing them in their homes. No apology therefore is needed for quoting Mr. V. Ball's description of the Khariás whom he met with on the Dalmá range in Manbhum during the cold weather of 1866–67[1] :—

Social status.

"The Khariás show a marked dislike for civilization, constantly leaving places where they have any reason for supposing that they are overlooked. Their houses, generally not more than two or three together, are situated on the sides or tops of the highest hills; they stand in small clearances, a wretched crop of *bajrá* being sown between the fallen and charred trunks of trees.

Khariás of Manbhum.

"Close to the south boundary of Manbhum there are a succession of hill ranges, of which Dalmá (3,407 feet), the rival of Párasnáth, is the highest point. On this hill I saw three or four neat little Khariá cottages, made of wattled bamboo, which, together with the small standing crop, had for no apparent reason been deserted. Further west, just outside the boundary of Manbhum, on a plateau formed of trap, where there was a good water-supply, the small Khariá villages had assumed a somewhat permanent appearance. Occasionally Khariá cottages are to be seen on the outskirts of villages, but this is a departure from what is one of the most characteristic customs of the race.

"The first Khariás I met with were encamped in the jungle at the foot of some hills. The hut was rudely made of a few *sál* branches, its occupants being one man, an old and two young women, besides three or four children. At the time of my visit they were taking their morning meal; and as they regarded my presence with the utmost indifference, without even turning round or ceasing from their occupations, I remained for some time watching them. They had evidently recently captured some small animal, but what it was, as they had already eaten the skin, I could not ascertain. As I looked on, the old woman distributed to the others, on plates of *sál* leaves, what appeared to be the entrails of the animal, and, wrapping

---

[1] *Jungle Life in India*, p. 89 ff.

up her own portion between a couple of leaves, threw it on the fire in order to give it a very primitive cooking. With regard to their ordinary food, the Khariás chiefly depend upon the jungle for a supply of fruits, leaves, and roots. I got them to collect for me specimens of the principal species they used." The list of edible plants will be found in full in the *Statistical Account of Hazaribágh* (vol. xvi). "Besides these, however, the Khariás eat rice, which they obtain in the villages in exchange for several jungle products, such as honey, lac, *dhuná*, *tasar* cocoons, *sál* leaves, and bundles of bamboo slips, called *khurki*, wherewith the leaves are stitched into plates. That the rice which they thus obtain, though small in quantity, is an important element in their daily food, seems apparent from the fact that a large number of them are said to have died in the famine. I can only explain this by supposing that they lost heart on being deprived of what had been a regular source of supply, and failed to exert themselves in the collection of an extra quantity of roots. An explanation somewhat similar to this was given to me by a Santál, who said, speaking of his own race, that those who underwent the labour of searching the jungles escaped, while those who sat in their houses wishing for better times died. The roots are dug up with considerable labour from the rocky ground, by means of an instrument called *khunti*—an iron spike firmly fixed in a wooden handle. The point of this, as it is natural it should be, frequently becomes blunted. To avoid the necessity of taking it to be sharpened, perhaps half a dozen miles to the nearest Kámár, the Khariás have invented for themselves a forge, the blast of which is produced by a pair of bellows of the most primitive construction. They consist of a pair of conical caps about eighteen inches high, which are made of leaves stitched together with grass. These are firmly fixed down upon the hollows in the ground, whence a pair of bamboo nozzles conveys the blast produced by alternate and sudden elevations and depressions of the caps to a heap of ignited charcoal. In this the iron spikes are heated until they become sufficiently soft to be hammered to a point by a stone used as a hammer on a stone anvil.

"The Khariás never make iron themselves, but are altogether dependent on the neighbouring bázárs for their supplies. Had they at any period possessed a knowledge of the art of making iron, conservative of their customs as such races are, it is scarcely likely that they would have forgotten it. It is therefore not unreasonable to suppose that there was a period anterior to the advent of the Hindus when iron was quite unknown to them,—when, owing to the absence of cultivation in the plains, they were even more dependent on the supply of jungle food than they are at present. In those times their axes and their implements for grubbing up roots were in all probability made of stone, and their arrows had tips made of the same material.

"In their persons the Khariás are very dirty, seldom, if ever, washing themselves. Their features are decidedly of a low character, not unlike the Bhumij, but there seemed to me to be an absence of any strongly-marked type in their faces or build, such as enables one to know a Santál, and even a Kurmi, at a glance."

The following statement shows the number and distribution of Khariás in 1872 and 1881 :—

District.	1872.	1881.	District.	1872.	1881.
Bardwan	1,926	......	Rangpur	......	721
Bankura	17,936	311	Darjiling	......	25
Birbhum	231	......	Tributary States, Orissa	3,948	8,404
Midnapur	2,399	3,343	Hazaribagh	......	73
Hughli	} 120	{ 1	Lohardagá	21,019	4,616
Howrah		1,274	Singbhum	1,463	884
24-Parganas	7	3	Manbhum	2,298	2 431
Nadiya	1	......	Tributary States ...	1,618	28,074
Murshedabad	......	4			

Khariá-Munda, a sub-tribe of Mundas in Chota Nagpur.

Khariá-Oraon, a sub-tribe of Oraons in Chota Nagpur.

Khariár, a section of Mahilis in Western Bengal.

Khariát, a sub-caste of Binds in Behar.

Kharidáhá, a sub-caste of Kalwárs in Behar.

Kharihi, a title of Goálás in Behar.

Kharipárá, a sub-caste of Sutradhars in Western Bengal.

Kharkábáyu, a section of Kámis in Darjiling.

Kharnáke ke ráut, a section of the Biyáhut and Kharidáhá Kalwárs in Behar.

Kharniá, a section of Goálás in the North-Western Provinces and Behar.

Khárpáik, a *mul* or section of the Kanaujiá sub-caste of Hajjáms in Behar.

Kharsán, a section of Goálás in the North-Western Provinces and Behar.

Kharuá, a section of Kumhárs in Singbhum.

Kharura, makers of brass ornaments in Western Bengal.

Kharwal, *Kherwal*, a sub-caste of Bhuiyas in Singbhum.

Kharwár, *Kherwár*, a Dravidian cultivating and landholding tribe of Chota Nagpur and Southern Behar, regarding whose origin there has been much discussion. Speaking of the Kharwárs of Shahábád, Buchanan says that great confusion prevails concerning them, because in different places they have adopted the precepts of Hinduism in different degrees. The social position of the tribe also varies greatly. Some are found amongst the labouring classes bearing burdens and carrying palanquins, some have attained positions as land-owners, lording it over Brahmans and Rajputs, their raiyats, whilst others occupy the table-land unmixed with any other tribe, and there is little reason, no doubt, that they are its original inhabitants. These, he observes, have retained the features by which the aboriginal tribes of the Vindhyan mountains are distinguished, but no one has met with any of the tribe who retain a trace of their original language. Some Kharwárs declare their original seat to have been the fort of Rohtás, so called as having been the chosen abode of Rohitaswa, son of Harischandra, of the family of the sun. From this ancient house they also claim descent, call themselves Surjabansis, and wear the *janeo* or caste thread distinguishing the Rajputs. A less flattering

Traditions of origin.

tradition makes them out to be the offspring of a marriage between a Kshatriya man and a Bhar woman contracted in the days of King Ben, when distinctions of caste were set aside and men might marry whom they would.

The difficulty experienced by Buchanan in arriving at any conclusions regarding the true affinities of the tribe in Shahábád is well illustrated by Colonel Dalton's account of their status in Chota Nagpur :—

"The Rajas of Rámgarh and Jashpúr are members of this family, who have nearly succeeded in obliterating their Turanian traits by successive intermarriages with Aryan families. The Jashpúr Raja is wedded to a lady of pure Rájpút blood, and, by liberal dowries, has succeeded in obtaining a similar union for three of his daughters. It is a costly ambition, but there is nc doubt that the infusion of fresh blood greatly improves the Kharwár physique. The late Maharaja Sambhunáth Sing, of Rámgarh, was a remarkably handsome man, sufficiently so to support his pretensions to be a true child of the sun; but according to the traditions and annals of his own family his ancestors must have been very low in the social scale when they first came to Rámgarh. They are descended from the younger of two brothers who, generations ago, came as adventurers and took service under the Maharaja of Chútiá Nágpúr. The elder obtained Rámgarh as a fief on his doing homage to the Maharaja and receiving the 'tilak,' or mark of investiture, from that potentate's great toe. Almost all the men of ancient standing with proprietary rights in the Rámgarh estate are Kharwárs. The Thákurs of Húsir Sáram and Babu Dalgovind of Khoyra, of Rajput lineage, have become Kharwárs by marrying into the Raja's family."

In another place Colonel Dalton notices the traditional connexion between the Kharwárs and the Cheros, who are said to have invaded Palámau frcm Rohtas and driven the Rajput Chief of the country to retire and found a new kingdom in Sargújá.

"It is said that the Pálámau population then consisted of Kharwárs, Gonds, Márs, Korwás, Parheya, and Kisáns. Of these the Kharwárs were the people of most consideration. The Cheros conciliated them, and allowed them to remain in peaceful possession of the hill tracts bordering on Sargújá; all the Cheros of note who assisted in the expedition obtained military service grants of land, which they still retain. It is popularly asserted that at the commencement of the Chero rule in Palámau, they numbered twelve thousand families, and the Kharwárs eighteen thousand, and if an individual of one or the other is asked to what tribe he belongs, he will say, not that he is a Chero or a Kharwár, but that he belongs to the twelve thousand or to the eighteen thousand, as the case may be. * * * * Intermarriages between Chero and Kharwár families have taken place. A relative of the Palámau Raja married a sister of Maninath Sing, Raja of Rámgarh, and this is amongst themselves an admission of identity of origin; as both claiming to be Rájpúts they could not intermarry till it was proved to the satisfaction of the family priests that the parties belonged to the same class."

Others, again, regard the Cheros as a sub-tribe of Kharwárs, but this opinion appears to have been based on observations in Southern Lohardagá, where the Cheros have gone down in the world and ceased to be of any social importance.

Colonel Dalton describes the low Kharwárs as strongly resembling the Santáls in feature. "They are," he says, "very dark, with pyramidal-shaped low noses, thick protuberant lips, and cheek-bones or zygomata that project so as to make the temples hollow." The landholding classes, on the other hand, have refined the type by intermarriages with higher castes, and are quite as high bred in appearance as most of the pseudo-Rajput families of Chota Nagpur and Western Bengal.

Internal structure.

An examination of the internal structure of the tribe, which is given in Appendix I, leaves little doubt as to their Dravidian descent. Many of their septs are certainly totemistic; although the animals associated by other tribes with septs bearing the same names appear not to be deemed sacred by the Kharwárs. Further research among more primitive members of the tribe may, however, show that the older ideas have not altogether died out. Special interest attaches to the fact that the Kharwárs of South Lohardagá regard the *khar* grass as the totem of their tribe, and will not cut or injure it while growing. The adoption of the *khar* as a totem may of course be due merely to the consonance of names—a factor which plays an important part in the speculations of savages regarding their own descent. If, on the other hand, the case is one of genuine survival, it goes far to suggest the inference that the Kharwár tribe of the present day may be merely an enlarged totem-sept which broke off from some larger group and in course of time developed a separate organization. Instances of septs splitting up into sub-septs are by no means uncommon, and it is obvious that circumstances favouring separation might easily lead to the transformation of the original sept into a distinct tribe.

Among the endogamous divisions of the tribe the Bhogtás are the most important. They are found, says Colonel Dalton, "in the hills of Palámau skirting Sargújá, in Tori and Bhanwar Pahár of Chútiá Nágpúr and other places. They have always had an indifferent reputation. The head of the clan in Palámau was a notorious freebooter, who, after having been outlawed and successfully evading every attempt to capture him, obtained a jágir on his surrendering and promising to keep the peace. He kept to his engagement and died in fair repute, but his two sons could not resist the opportunity afforded by the disturbances of 1857-58. After giving much trouble they were captured: one was hanged, the other transported for life, and the estate was confiscated." Bhogtás do not intermarry with ordinary or Deswári Kharwárs, and although living side by side with them, affect to repudiate the idea of tribal relationship between the two groups. There is, however, no reason to question the accuracy of the general opinion that the Bhogtás are a branch of Khárwárs who have formed themselves into an independent group.

Marriage.

Throughout the tribe the form of exogamy practised is the simple one that a man may not marry a woman of his own sept. Outside that circle of relationship, prohibited degrees are reckoned by the standard formula. All who can afford to do so arrange for the marriages of their children while they are still too young to choose for themselves, and adult-marriage is looked upon as a sign of poverty and social insignificance. Deswári Kharwárs profess to disapprove of the practice of taking money for a daughter, but among Bhogtás and Manjhias a bride-price, ranging from Rs. 5 to Rs. 12, is regularly paid. Remnants of non-Aryan usage may be discerned in the marriage ceremony itself. Both parties must first go through the form of marriage to a mango tree, or at least to a branch of the tree; and must exchange blood mixed with *sindur*, although in the final and binding act *sindur* alone is smeared by the bridegroom upon the bride's forehead and the parting of her hair. Polygamy is permitted, but not generally practised, except in the event of failure of offspring by the first wife. The Bhogtá and Manjhia sub-castes sanction the marriage of a widow, and deem it right for her to marry her late husband's younger brother. Deswári Kharwárs, however, require widows to remain unmarried. Divorce is permitted if the wife is convicted of unchastity or if the couple cannot agree. Divorced women may marry again by the *sagai* form, which is the same as that in use among the Rautias.

Inheritance.

In matters of inheritance Kharwárs follow tribal customs of their own, and cannot be described as formal adherents of any of the recognised schools of Hindu law. The eldest son of the senior wife, even if younger than one of the sons of a second wife, inherits the entire property subject to the obligation of providing all other legitimate children. If the inheritance consists of land, the heir is expected to create separate maintenance grants in favour of his younger brothers. Daughters can never inherit, but are entitled to live in the ancestral house until they are married.

Religion.

"The Kharwárs," says Colonel Dalton, "observe, like the Kols, triennial sacrifices. Every three years a buffalo and other animals are offered in the sacred grove, 'sarna,' or on a rock near the village. They also have, like some of the Kols, a priest for each village, called páhn. He is always one of the impure tribes—a Bhúiya, or Kharwár, or a Parheya, and is also called baiga, and he only can offer this great sacrifice. No Brahmanical priests are allowed on these occasions to interfere. The deity honored is the tutelary god of the village, sometimes called Duár Pahár, sometimes Dharti, sometimes Purgahaili or Daknai, a female, or Dura, a sylvan god, the same perhaps as the Darhá of the Kols." In Sargújá a village of Kharwárs was found employing a baiga of the wild Korwa tribe to offer sacrifices in the name of the village every second year to Chindol, a male spirit, Chanda, a female spirit, and to Parvin. Buffaloes, sheep, and goats were offered to all of these. These people made no prayers to any of the Hindu gods, but when in great trouble they appealed to the sun. The apparent anomaly of their having a Korwa for their priest was explained by the belief that "the hill people, being the oldest inhabitants, are best acquainted with the habits and peculiarities of the local spirits, and are in least peril from them;

besides, they are wholly pagan, whilst the people in whose behalf they make offerings, having Hindu and Brahmanical tendencies, could only offer a divided allegiance to the sylvan gods, which it might not be safe to tender."

The main body of the tribe, and particularly those who belong to the landholding class, profess the Hindu religion, and employ Sákadwipi Brahmans as priests. Mahadeo and Sitaram are the popular deities; Gauri and Ganesh being worshipped during marriages. In addition to these, the miscellaneous host of spirits feared by the Mundas and Oraons are still held in more or less reverence by the Kharwárs, and in Palámau members of the tribe sometimes perform the duties of páhan or village priest. *Sráddh* is performed ten days after death, and once a year in the month of Aswin regular oblations are made for the benefit of deceased ancestors in general.

Social status.

The social standing of the tribe varies greatly in different places, and seems to depend chiefly upon the hold they have on the land. This appears to be strongest among the Deswári Kharwárs. A landed proprietor of this sub-tribe will wear a *janeo* and pose as a kind of Rajput; while Bhogtás, Manjhias, and the like aspire to no such distinction. Similar differences may be observed in matters of diet. Beef is forbidden to all members of the tribe; but Bhogtás, Manjhias, and Rauts eat pigs and fowls, which the Deswári regard as unclean. Kharwárs profess to take water and sweetmeats only from Brahmans, Rajputs, the higher classes of Banias, Jhoras, and Rautias. In Chota Nagpur they regard

Occupation.

landholding as their traditional occupation; some are zamindars, many hold substantial *khuntkátti* and *korkar* tenures, and the rest of the tribe are raiyats with occupancy rights. Very few have sunk to the position of landless day-labourers; but many of the Bhogtás have taken up the comparatively degraded occupation of making baskets and working in bamboos.

The following statement shows the number and distribution of Kharwárs in 1872 and 1881:—

District.	1872.	1881.	District.	1872.	1881.
Bardwan	266	82	Shahabad	5,883	5,969
Bankura	......	455	Tirhut { Mozufferpur ...	135	457
Birbhum	14	37	Tirhut { Darbhanga ...		817
Midnapur	80	693	Saran	26	1,315
24-Parganas	......	94	Champaran	47	801
Nadiya	14	......	Monghyr	21	8
Murshedabad	141	188	Bhagalpur	6,019	9,043
Dinajpur	......	269	Purniah	4,068	3,776
Rajshahye	11	10	Maldah	6,005	4,095
Rangpur	......	247	Santál Parganas	431	3,866
Bogra	......	16	Hazaribagh	28,569	38,010
Darjiling	......	213	Lohardagá	67,495	74,832
Dacca	......	56	Singbhum	3,872	2,233
Maimansinh	......	63	Manbhum	25,978	13,152
Chittagong	......	84	Tributary States	11,591	17,959
Gya	3,538	1,243			

Kharwara, a sub-caste of Kahárs in Behar.

Khát, a sept of Rajputs in Behar.

Khátádiá, a section of Goálás in the North-Western Provinces and Behar.

Khataiá, a section of the Biyáhut and Kharidáhá Kalwárs in Behar.

Khatait, a sept of Thárus in Behar.

Khatauri, a small cultivating and landholding caste of the Santál Parganas who claim to be Rajputs, but are believed by Mr. Oldham to be Mals, who, by virtue of being owners of landed estates, were enabled to claim a higher social position.

Kháti, a sept of the Suryabansi sub-tribe of Rajputs in Behar; a section of Kámis; a *thar* or sept of Gurungs and Mangars in Darjiling.

Khatik, a sub-caste of Khatiks in Behar.

Khatik, a cultivating and vegetable-selling caste of Behar, divided into two sub-castes—**Khatik** and **Dharamdási**. They have only one section (Kásyapa), and regulate their marriages by the standard formula, calculated to five generations in the descending line. Khatiks marry their daughters as infants, between the ages of five and twelve years. When a marriage is under consideration, the headman and *pancháyat* are consulted regarding the prohibited degrees. If their opinion is favourable, mutual visits of inspection (*ghar-dekhi*) follow, at which presents of betel-leaves, areca nut, and sweetmeats are exchanged. After this a *tilák*, consisting of new clothes, brass feeding utensils, and one rupee in cash, is given to the parents of the bridegroom, and a Tirhutiá Brahman is called in to fix an auspicious date for the wedding. This is celebrated in the form usually followed by the lower castes, the place of the Brahman being taken by a Bairági ascetic belonging to the Khatik caste. Polygamy is not expressly recognised, but a man may take a second wife if the first is barren. Divorce is effected by the pancháyat in the manner described in the article on the Khatwe caste.

Khatiks follow the Hindu law and profess the Hindu religion as usually understood in Behar. Their minor gods are Bandi and Mirá, to whom sacrifices of kids, cakes, and sweetmeats are offered on Wednesdays and afterwards eaten by the worshippers. The latter, it should be observed, is common to them and to the Khatwes, and appears to be worshipped by no other castes. Khatiks do not employ Brahmans, and Bairági members of their own caste serve them as priests.

In point of social standing Khatiks rank little higher than Musahars. Their rules as to food differ little from those of respectable middle-class Hindus, but they make no secret of their partiality for spirituous liquors.

The following statement shows the number and distribution of Khatiks in 1872 and 1881. The figures of 1872 include other vegetable-selling castes, hence the discrepancy:—

District.	1872.	1881.	District.	1872.	1881.
Murshedabad	......	3	Champaran	22,657	942
Rajshahye	......	1	Monghyr	2,548	535
Patna	1,746	623	Bhagalpur	1,391	1,191
Gya	2,124	284	Purniah	806	275
Shahabad	3,472	238	Santál Parganas	330	69
Tirhut { Mozufferpur ...	} 19,694	2,394	Hazaribagh	......	61
Tirhut { Darbhanga ...		1,827	Lohardaga	......	150
Saran	17,102	1,289			

Khátimahará, or pure *Mahara*, a sub-caste of Chamárs in Behar.

Khatiwára, a *thar* of the Atri *gotra* of Nepáli Brahmans.

Khatkalá, a sub-tribe of Thárus in Behar.

Khatri, a sub-caste of Baniyás in Behar.

Khatri, a mercantile caste of the Panjáb, described by Mr. Ibbetson as superior in physique, in manliness, and in energy to the rest of the trading community of that province. Many of them have settled in Bengal and Behar, and the Mahárájá of Bardwan is considered the head of the caste. The *locus classicus* for the Khatris is Sir George Campbell's paper on 'The Ethnology of India,' published in the *Journal of the Asiatic Society of Bengal* for 1866, from which I quote the following passages:—

Sir George Campbell's account.

"Trade is their main occupation, but in fact they have broader and more distinguishing features. Besides monopolising the trade of the Panjab and the greater part of Afghanistan and doing a good deal beyond those limits, they are in the Panjab the chief civil administrators, and have almost all literate work in their hands. So far as the Sikhs have a priesthood, they are, moreover, the priests or gurus of the Sikhs. Both Nának and Govind were, and the Sodhis and Bedis of the present day are, Khatris. Thus, then, they are in fact in the Panjab, so far as a more energetic race will permit them, all that Mahratta Brahmans are in the Mahratta country, besides engrossing the trade, which the Mahratta Brahmans have not. They are not usually military in their character, but are quite capable of using the sword when necessary. Diwan Sáwan Mal, governor of Multan, and his notorious successor, Mulraj, and very many of Ranjit Singh's chief functionaries, were Khatris. Even under Mahomedan rulers in the west they have risen to high administrative posts. There is a record of a Khatri diwan of Badakshan or Kunduz, and, I believe, of a Khatri governor of Peshawar under the Afghans. The Emperor Akbar's famous minister, Todur Mal, was a Khatri, and a relative of that man of undoubted energy, the great commissariat contractor of Agra, Joti Parshad, lately informed me that he also is a Khatri. Altogether there can be no doubt that these Khatris are one of the most acute, energetic, and remarkable races in India, though in fact, except locally in the Panjab, they are not much known to Europeans. The Khatris are staunch Hindus, and it is somewhat singular that while giving a religion and priests to the Sikhs, they themselves are comparatively seldom Sikhs. The Khatris are a very fine, fair, handsome race, and, as may be gathered from what I have already said, they are very generally educated.

"There is a large subordinate class of Khatris, somewhat lower, but of equal mercantile energy, called Rors or Roras. The proper Khatris of higher grade will often deny all connexion with them, or at least only admit that they have some sort of bastard kindred with Khatris; but I think there can be no doubt that they are ethnologically the same, and they are certainly mixed up with Khatris in their avocations. I shall treat the whole kindred as generically Khatris.

"Speaking of the Khatris then thus broadly, they have, as I have said, the whole trade of the Panjab and of most of Afghanistan. No village can get on without the Khatri, who keeps the accounts, does the banking business, and buys and sells the grain. They seem, too, to get on with the people better than most traders and usurers of this kind. In Afghanistan, among a rough and alien people, the Khatris are as a rule confined to the position of humble dealers, shopkeepers, and money-lenders; but in that capacity the Pathans seem to look at them as a kind of valuable animal, and a Pathan will steal another man's Khatri, not only for the sake of ransom, as is frequently done on the Peshawar and Hazara frontier, but also as he might steal a milch-cow, or as Jews might, I dare say, be carried off in the middle ages with a view to render them profitable.

"I do not know the exact limits of Khatri occupation to the west, but certainly in all Eastern Afghanistan they seem to be just as much a part of the established community as they are in the Panjab. They find their way far into Central Asia, but the further they get the more depressed and humiliating is their position. In Turkistan Vambery speaks of them with great contempt, as yellow-faced Hindus of a cowardly and sneaking character. Under Turcoman rule they could hardly be otherwise. They are the only Hindus known in Central Asia. In the Panjab they are so numerous that they cannot all be rich and mercantile, and many of them hold land, cultivate, take service, and follow various avocations.

"The Khatris are altogether excluded from Brahman Kashmir. In the hills, however, the 'Kakkas,' on the east bank of the Jahlam, are said to have been originally Khatris (they are a curiously handsome race), and in the interior of the Kangra hills there is an interesting race of fine patriarchal-looking shepherds called Gaddis, most of whom are Khatris. Khatri traders are numerous in Dehli; are found in Agra, Lucknow, and Patna; and are well known in the Bara Bazar of Calcutta, though there they are principally connected with Panjab firms.

"The Khatris do not seem, as a rule, to reach the western coast: in the Bombay market I cannot find that they have any considerable place. In Sindh, however, I find in Captain Burton's book an account of a race of pretended Kshatriyas, who are really Banias of the Nanak-Sahi (Sikh) faith, and who trade and have a large share of public offices. These are evidently Khatris. Ludhiana is a large and thriving town of mercantile Khatris, with a numerous colony of Kashmiri shawl-weavers."

Traditions of origin.

Khatris allege themselves to be the direct descendants of the Kshatriyas of early Indian tradition, and in support of this claim refer to the fact that they assume the sacred cord and commence the study of the Vedas at the age of eight years, as is enjoined in the sacred books, and that Sáraswat Brahmans will eat *kachchi* food prepared by them. Mr. Nesfield thinks the claim a good one, adding that "the cause which detached the Khatri from the Chattri or Kshatriya and shut out all possibility of a return to the ancestral caste was the establishment of a marriage union between fragments or clans drawn from several different sub-castes of Kshatriyas between whom no connubial rights had hitherto existed, or from sub-castes of Kshatriyas mixed with those of Brahmans. There is much reason to believe that Brahmans as well as Kshatriyas have contributed to form the new caste of Khatri; for Brahmans of the Sáraswat sub-caste will to this day eat food cooked by Khatris, but no Brahman of any sub-caste will eat food cooked by a Kshatriya." Mr. Ibbetson puts the question by with the remark that "the validity of the claim is as doubtful as are most other matters connected with the fourfold caste system." It seems to me that the internal organization of the caste furnishes almost conclusive proof that they are descended from neither Brahmans nor Kshatriyas, and that the theory connecting them with the latter tribe rests upon no firmer foundation than a resemblance of name, which for all we know may be wholly accidental. Their features and complexion, indeed, entitle them to be ranked as Aryans of comparatively pure lineage, but among their numerous sections we find none of those territorial names which are characteristic of the Rajput septs. The section-names of the Khatris belong to quite a different type, and rather resemble those in vogue among the Oswals and Agarwáls. Were they descended from the same stock as the Rajputs, they must have had the same set of section-names, and it is difficult to see why they should have abandoned these for less distinguished patronymics. In addition to their own sections, they have also the standard Brahmanical *gotras*; but these have no influence upon marriage, and have clearly been borrowed, *honoris causâ*, from the Sáraswat Brahmans who serve them as priests. If, then, it is at all necessary to connect the Khatris with the ancient fourfold system of castes, the only group to which we can affiliate them is the Vaisyas. This conjecture is at least in keeping with the present occupations of the caste, and gets us out of the difficulty which led Sir George Campbell to propound the doubtful theory that in the ordinary course of history the warlike conquerors of one age become the astute money-dealers of another. In truth, however, all speculations which profess to connect existing castes with the four traditional castes are on the face of things futile and misleading. We do not know enough about these primitive groups to be able to apply to their internal structure that minute analysis which alone can determine their precise tribal affinities.

The exogamous sections of the Khatris are shown in Appendix I.

Internal structure.

As I have stated above, there is a double series,—one original and the other borrowed from the Brahmans. Only the original or tribal series is taken into account for the purposes of marriage. The rule is absolute that a man may not marry a woman of the same tribal section as himself; but the fact that two persons belong to the same Brahmanical *gotra* does not operate as a bar to intermarriage, provided that their tribal sections are different. Thus the three sections Kapur, Khanná, and Mehará all belong to the Kausalya *gotra*, but members of these groups intermarry freely. Apart from the section rule, prohibited degrees are reckoned on the system in vogue among the Brahmans; marriage with *sapindas*, *samánodakas*, *pitribandhus*, and *mátribandhus* being forbidden.

The endogamous divisions of the Khatris are exceedingly obscure and complicated. "Within recent times," says Mr. Ibbetson, "there has sprung up a system of social graduation, in accordance with which certain Khatri tribes refuse to intermarry with any save a certain specified number of their fellow tribes, and the distinctions thus created have been formulated in a set of names, such as *Árháighar*, 'he who only marries into two and a half houses;' *Chárzáti*, 'he who marries into four tribes;' *Chhezáti*, 'he who marries into six tribes;' and so on. This purely artificial and social classification has obscured the original tribal divisions of the caste; for Khatris of the same tribe may be in one part of the province Chárzátis, and in another Bárázátis, and so forth."

In describing the Khatris of the Panjab, Mr. Ibbetson gives the following abstract:—

Bunjáhi ... Sarin ... Báhri ... Khokhrán ...	Tribal groups.
Árháighar ... Chárzáti ... Panjzáti ... Chhezáti ...	Artificial divisions.
Sodhi ... Bedi ... Kapur ... Khanna ... Marhotra ... Seth ...	Exogamous sections.

"The origin of the division into the four sections called Bunjáhi, Sarin, Báhri, and Khokhrán is said to be that Ala-ul-din Khilji attempted to impose widow-marriage upon the Khatris. The Western Khatris resolved to resist the innovation, and sent a deputation of 52 *báwan* of their members to represent their case at court; but the Eastern Khatris were afraid to sign the memorial. They were therefore called followers of *Shara Ayin* or the Mahomedan customs —hence Sarin; while the memorialists were called *Báwanjai*, from the number of the deputation or of the clans respectively represented by the members of the deputation—hence Bunjáhi. The Khokhrán section is said to consist of the descendants of certain Khatris who joined the Khokhars in rebellion, and with whom the other Khatri families were afraid to intermarry; and the Báhri section, of the lineage of Mahr Chand, Khan Chand, and Kapur Chand, three Khatris who went to Dehli in attendance upon one of Akbar's Rajput wives, and who, thus separated from the rest of the caste, married only within each other's families. But these are fables, for the same division into Báhri and Bunjáhi appears among the Brahmans of the Western plains. The number of clans is enormous. The most important in point of social rank are the Marhotra or Mahra, the Khanna, the Kapur, and the Seth, the first three of which are said to be called after the names of the three men just mentioned, while Seth is a term now used for any rich banker. These four clans belong to the Báhri section of the caste, and constitute the Dháighar and Chárzáti divisions, which stand highest of all in the social scale. The origin of the term Dháighar lies in the fact that the families of that division exclude not only the father's clan, but also such families of the mother's clan as are closely connected with her, and thus reduce the clans available for intermarriage to two and a half. I should say that each division will take wives from the one below it, though it will not give its daughters to it in marriage. The Bedi and Sodhi clans belong to the Bunjáhi tribe, and owe most of their influence and importance to the fact that Bába Nának belonged to the former, and Guru Rám Dás and Guru Hargovind to the latter. They are commonly said to be the descendants of these men, but this appears to be a mistake, the two clans dating from long before Bába Nának. The Sodhis played an important part during the Sikh rule. They claim descent from Sodhi Rái, son of Kál Rai, King of Lahore, and the Bedis from Kálpat Rai, brother of Kál Rai and King of Kasur, who being deprived of his kingdom by his nephew, studied the Vedas at Benares and was known as Vedi. The modern head-quarters of the Bedis is at Dera Nának, in Gurdáspur, where Bába Nának settled and died, and of the Sodhis at Anandpur, in Hushyárpur, which is also the great centre of the Nihang devotees." The divisions recognised in Bengal are shown in Appendix I, where I have attempted by brief explanatory notes to clear up the confusion in which the subject is involved.

The Khatris of Bengal trace their origin to the Panjab, and the main body of them is said to have emigrated from Lahore in the reign of Aurangzib. These eastern or Purbiyá Khatris are spoken of in a somewhat slighting fashion by the Pachhainya Khatris of Upper India, and are charged with having departed from the high standard of ceremonial purity supposed to be characteristic of the caste. I do not understand that any specific allegation is made against the Bengal Khatris, and the latter appear to pique themselves on keeping the usages of their original home. But in most cases where a branch of a caste domiciled in Upper India has settled in Bengal Proper, we find that the settlers fall under the suspicion of infringing the customs of the caste and indulging in acts forbidden by the sacred texts. The Khatris are no exception to this general rule. Rightly or wrongly, the Bengal members of the caste are to a certain extent looked down upon by their brethren in Upper India, and intermarriage between the Purbiyá and Pachhainya groups is comparatively rare.

The relative positions of the Khatris of Bengal and the Panjab are, I believe, stated in the last paragraph as precisely as the nature of the subject permits. So far as my knowledge extends, the bulk of the Bengal Khatris endeavour to conform on the whole to the traditional usages of the Panjab branch of the caste. They look on the Panjab as the original home of their race, and in theory at least Panjab custom is the standard by which their social and domestic affairs are regulated. On the other hand, at Paikpárá, in the Dacca district, and in villages around Barmi Hát on the Lakhya, Dr. Wise came across a class of Hindus calling themselves Rándá or Randak Khatri, who gave a confused account of themselves, repeating the names of Ballál Sen and Rájá Mán Singh, as if connected in some mysterious way with their settlements in Bengal and their degraded position among Hindus. Kanaujiá Brahmans officiate as their purohit, and they have a Bengali Brahman for their guru. Being naturalised Bengalis, they have relinquished the names of the characteristic Khatri sections and adopted the common Sudra *gotra* Alyamán along with Bengali titles such as Chakravarti, Prasád, and the like. Sudras eat with them in private, but in public refuse to take water from their hands. They are employed as shopkeepers and cultivators, and some of them are talukdárs.

Marriage.

Khatris marry their daughters as infants and make use of the standard marriage ceremony, the binding element in which is the giving away of the bride by her father or guardian and the acceptance of the gift by the bridegroom. Polygamy is permitted, nor is there any definite limit to the number of wives a man may have. Fashion, however, is on the whole adverse to his taking more than one. On the other hand, many Khatris keep concubines of their own and other castes. The children of these women form a separate class, bearing the name *Piruwál*, and as a rule marry among themselves. Widows may not marry a second time, and divorce is not recognised.

Religion.

Most Khatris belong to the Vaishnava sect, and comparatively few worshippers of Siva are found among them. Sáraswat or Sarsut Brahmans serve them as priests. In Eastern Bengal, says Dr. Wise, Chandiká, a form of Durgá, is the patron deity of the caste; but each *gotra* has its own peculiar idol. An interesting tradition connects the modern Khatris with the foundation of the Muhammadan city of Dacca. When the Khatri Rájá Mán Singh occupied Dacca in 1595 with the Mughal army, he encamped on a tract clear of jungle, ever since called Urdu. Here was found an image of Durgá, believed to have been the property of Vedabati, the divorced wife of Adisura. The image was deposited in a shrine, and under the name of Dhakeswari is still regarded as the palladium of the city. At the present day the revenue of this sanctuary is divided between several old Khatri families and the Brahmachári Mahant of the Ramná Ákhárá.

Occupation and social status.

The majority of the Bengal Khatris are engaged in some form of trade. A few of them are zemindars and tenure-holders, and a certain number are occupancy raiyats. They never touch the plough themselves, and employ hired labourers to cultivate their lands. The Maharaja of Bardwan is the head of the caste in Bengal. Their social rank is high. All Brahmans take water from their hands, and Sáraswat Brahmans will eat *kachchi* food prepared by them.

The following statement shows the number and distribution of the Khatris in 1872 and 1881:—

District.	1872.	1881.	District.	1872.	1881.
Bardwan	13,630	5,237	Tipperah	......	623
Bankura	497	4,132	Chittagong	143	228
Birbhum	528	614	Noakhali	68	96
Midnapur	1,268	3,807	Patna	1,938	1,538
Hughli	701	3,937	Gya	850	1,863
Howrah		906	Shahabad	353	319
24-Parganas	863	930	Tirhut { Mozufferpur ...	4,675	8,099
Nadiya	1,314	597	Tirhut { Darbhanga ...		7,519
Khulna	......	196	Saran	450	468
Jessore	378	274	Champaran	676	638
Murshidabad	9	670	Monghyr	356	343
Dinajpur	1,258	18,934	Bhagalpur	634	2,203
Rajshahye	224	238	Purniah	767	1,256
Rangpur	118	1,950	Maldah	388	251
Bogra	717	6,401	Santál Parganas	......	9,643
Pabna	737	898	Cuttack	......	5,235
Darjiling	146	249	Puri	......	506
Jalpigori	1	1,766	Balasore	......	849
Kuch Behar	......	1,481	Tributary States	......	3,895
Dacca	621	2,769	Hazaribagh	......	860
Faridpur	36	260	Lohardagá	......	195
Bakarganj	112	266	Singbhum	......	375
Maimansinh	941	2,068	Manbhum	......	964
			Tributary States	......	69

Khatsopárk, a *pur* or section of Sákadwipi Brahmans in Behar.

Khatwah, *Khatwe*, a sub-caste of Kahárs in Behar who live by weaving and cultivation. They rank below both Rawáni and Dhimar Kahárs, and the higher castes will not take water from their hands.

Khatwe, a sub-caste of Joláhas in Behar.

Khatwé, a small palanquin-bearing and cultivating caste of Behar, divided into two sub-castes,—**Bahio** and **Goro**, names which appear to have reference to the original avocations of the members, though at the present day the Goro are not exclusively engaged in cultivation, nor the Bahio in carrying palanquins. They have only one section, **Kásyapa**, and regulate their marriage by the standard formula defining prohibited degrees, calculated to seven generations, in the descending line. Khatwés marry their daughters as infants, between the ages of five and twelve years. The marriage ceremony is of the standard Behar type. The headman of the caste (*manjan*) is consulted on the question of prohibited degrees, and *tilak* is paid to the bridegroom's parents in the form of a present of clothes. Tirhutiá Brahmans are called in to fix an auspicious date for the wedding, but they take no part in it themselves. Polygamy is permitted to the extent that a man may take a second wife if the first is barren. Widows may marry again, and are bound by no conditions in their choice of a second husband, except that they must not infringe the rules regarding prohibited degrees. Divorce is supposed not to be recognised, but in actual practice I understand that when a woman has gone wrong

Origin.

Marriage.

with a member of the caste her husband may get rid of her by solemnly abjuring her society before the headman and the *panchâyat*, while the woman may marry again by the *sagai* form, provided that her previous indiscretions are duly atoned for by a fine in the form of a feast to the caste brethren. Intrigues outside the caste admit of no atonement.

Religion.

In matters of religion Khatwés affect to be orthodox, and regard Bhagawati with especial reverence. They have, however, not attained to the dignity of having Brahmans of their own, and Bairági members of their own caste serve them as priests. Their minor gods are Sasiá, Káli, Dharam-ráj, Nar-Singh, and Mirá. Sheep, goats, pigeons, cakes, milk, rice, and sweetmeats are offered to these on Mondays, Wednesdays, Fridays, and Saturdays, and are afterwards eaten by the worshippers. The priests take no part in this worship, which is confined to the members of the household. The dead are burned, and the ashes buried near the burning place on the third day. Libations of water (*tarpan*) are poured forth for the propitiation of ancestors in the month of Asin.

Occupation and social status.

Palanquin-bearing and cultivation are believed by the Khatwés to be their original occupations. With the decline in the demand for bearers caused by the railway extensions of recent years, the caste tends more and more to fall back upon cultivation as a means of livelihood. In some districts they have taken to weaving and assumed the title Joláhá. Their social rank is low, being much the same as that of Tatwás and Musahars. Nevertheless they are cleaner feeders, according to Hindu ideas, than the latter, for they will eat neither fowls nor field-rats, both of which the Musahars freely indulge in. All of them, except those who call themselves Bhakats and profess to abstain from flesh and strong drink, make free use of fermented and spirituous liquors.

The following statement shows the number and distribution of Khatwés in 1872 and 1881:—

DISTRICT.	1872.	1881.	DISTRICT.	1872.	1881.
Gya	34	......	Bhagalpur	16,875	8,909
Tirhut { Mozufferpur ...	} 40,047	{ 2,010	Purniah	41	328
Tirhut { Darbhanga ...		{ 44,356	Santál Parganas	......	140
Sarun	1	......	Hazaribagh	......	4
Champaran	478	......			

Khatya, a sub-caste of Kumhárs in Dacca and Orissa who are supposed to have immigrated from Upper India.

Khauniá, a section of Kaibarttas in Orissa.

Khavur, a section of Awadhiá Hajjáms in Behar.

Khawás, "servant," a title of those members of the Amát, Dhanuk, and Kewat castes in Behar who are employed as personal servants by the higher castes. A sub-caste of Ghartis in Darjiling.

Khawásiyá, a sub-tribe of Thárus in Behar.

Khebangba, the native of Khebang, a sept of the Yangorup sub-tribe of Limbus in Darjiling.

Khechá Kesria, a section of Kurmis in Chota Nagpur and Orissa.

Khechar, a sept of Rajputs in Behar.

Khechinjiá, a section of Páns in Chota Nagpur.

Kheksa, curry vegetable, a totemistic sept of Oraons in Chota Nagpur.

Kheláut, a *mul* or section of the Sátmuliá or Kishnaut sub-caste of Goálás in Behar.

Kheldá, a class of hereditary prostitutes in Behar.

Khelenda, a sub-caste of Jugis in Eastern Bengal.

Khelri, a woman retained for purposes of dancing and amusement, a prostitute.

Khema, a pheasant, apparently a totemistic sept of the Chhothar sub-tribe of Limbus in Darjiling. This *thar* will not eat a pheasant or fowl or any bird of that class. The story is that the founder went out to shoot pheasants in a fir copse, but found none, and vowed never to eat a pheasant again.

Khendro-Oraon, a sub-tribe of Oraons in Chota Nagpur.

Kherá, a sub-caste of Máls in Bankura.

Kheresanchhá, a *thar* or sept of Khambus in Darjiling.

Khereswar ke pánre, a section of the Biyáhut and Kharidáhá Kalwárs in Behar.

Kherho, a *mul* or section of the Naomuliá or Majraut sub-caste of Goálás in Behar.

Kheri, a section of Maghaiyá Kumhárs in Behar.

Kheroar, a sept of Mundas; a title of Parhaiyas in Chota Nagpur.

Kherwár, a synonym for Kharwár.

Kherwár or **Safá-Hor**, a sub-tribe of Santáls in the Santál Parganas who affect a high degree of ceremonial purity.

Khes, a totemistic sept of Oraons in Chota Nagpur who cannot eat corn that grows in ponds.

Kheswá, a section of Goálás in the North-Western Provinces and Behar.

Khetta, cobra, a totemistic sept of Oraons in Chota Nagpur.

Khichengia, a totemistic sept of Kharwars in Chota Nagpur who cannot eat *jengia*, a fruit.

Khil, a title of Dakshin-Rárhi and Bangaja Káyasths in Bengal.

Khili-wálá, a title of Támbulis in Behar.

Khingba, a sept of the Yangorup sub-tribe of Limbus in Darjiling.

Khiongje, a sept of Chakmás in the Hill Tracts of Chittagong.

Khiráha, a section of the Kanaujiá sub-caste of Goálás in Behar.

Khirheri, a title of Goálás in Behar.

Khirkatorá, a *mul* or section of the Tinmuliá Madhesiá sub-caste of Halwáis in Behar.

Khobaipong, a sept of Limbus in Darjiling.

Khodál or **Khandyal**, a *thar* of the Dhartá-Kausik *gotra* of Nepáli Brahmans.

Khodlá, a section of Goálás in the North-Western Provinces and Behar.

Khoepa, wild dog, a totemistic sept of Oraons in Chota Nagpur.

Khojom, he who ate his earnings, a sept of the Chhothar sub-tribe of Limbus in Darjiling.

Khojwár, a sept of Thárus in Behar.

Khol, a *rui* or sept of the Ruichhung sub-tribe of Dejong Lhoris or Bhotias of the south of Tibet.

Khon, a sept of the Rautár sub-tribe of Thárus in Behar.

Khond, a synonym for Kandh, *q.v.*

Khondua, a sept of Mundas in Chota Nagpur.

Khonrá-rási, a section of Málos in Eastern Bengal.

Khontá, a *mul* or section of the Chhamuliá Madhesiá sub-caste of Halwáis in Behar.

Khopariá, a sub-caste of Dhánuks in Behar.

Khopchá, an owl, a sept of Bediás in Chota Nagpur.

Khopriha, a *mul* or section of the Tinmuliá Madhesiá sub-caste of Halwáis in Behar.

Khor, a title of Báruis in Bengal.

Khore or **Khoriyá**, a sub-caste of Háris in Bengal.

Khorlá, a sub-caste of Kurmis in Chota Nagpur.

Khorjár, a *gáin* of the Bharadwája *gotra* of Bárendra Brahmans in Bengal.

Khosá, a section of Goálás in the North-Western Provinces and Behar.

Khosbediá, a synonym for Bediyá, *q.v.*

Khosle, a section of the Bahánnajáti sub-caste of Khatris in Bengal.

Khotawá, a class of Beldárs in Western Bengal.

Khoti, a sept of the Surajbansi division of Rajputs in Behar.

Khottá, (i) a generic name in Bengali for natives of the North-Western Provinces and Upper India. I cannot ascertain the derivation of the word, but the fact that the dialect of broken Hindi spoken in the north of Manbhum is known locally as *Khattá bháshá* may perhaps warrant the conjecture that it has reference to the linguistic peculiarities of up-country men. (ii) A designation of up-country barbers who have settled in Bengal. Such persons practically form a separate sub-caste, as Bengali barbers will not intermarry with them, and they are regarded as impure by the barbers of Upper India and Behar by reason of their having taken up their residence in Bengal. (iii) A sub-caste of Kámárs in Murshedabad and of Dhobás in Western Bengal.

Khottá or **Mauná**, a sub-caste of Pods.

Khowáre-Nahás, a *mul* of the Kásyap section of Maithil Brahmans in Behar.

Khowáre-Mahuá, a *mul* of the Kásyap section of Maithil Brahmans in Behar.

Khowáre-Mahnaurá, a *mul* of the Kásyap section of Maithil Brahmans in Behar.

Khowáre-Kokrahi, a *mul* of the Kásyap section of Maithil Brahmans in Behar.

Khowáre-Khari, a *mul* of the Kásyap section of Maithil Brahmans in Behar.

Khowáre-Murajpur, a *mul* of the Kásyap section of Maithil Brahmans in Behar.

Khoyea, a wild dog, a totemistic sept of Mundas in Chota Nagpur.

Khoyra, a title of Bagdis in Bengal.

Khuadang, a sept of Limbus in Darjiling.

Khujiriá, a section of Kámárs in Singbhum and the Santál Parganas.

Khukri, a kind of mushroom, a totemistic sept of Chiks and Mundas in Chota Nagpur.

Khulál, a *thar* or sept of Gurungs and Mangars in Darjiling.

Khunaut or **Khulaut**, a sub-caste of Gonrhis in Behar.

Khungbá, a section of Murmis in Darjiling.

Khur, a title of Támbulis in Bengal.

Khurdá, a sub-caste of Bhandáris in Orissa.

Khuskhelia, a sub-caste of Telis in Behar.

Khuthá Bhagwánpur, a *mul* or section of the Naomuliá or Majraut sub-caste of Goálás in Behar.

Khutibaran, a section of Páns in Chota Nagpur.

Khuturiá, a sub-caste of Máls in Birbhum.

Khwánd-Kár, a teacher or reader in Persian, who in Eastern Bengal performs for the lower classes several singular functions arising from the corrupt and Hinduised character of Muhammadanism in India. He is often styled the Murshíd, or religious guide, and Akhúnd or tutor. As a rule he is very illiterate and only able to read Arabic with difficulty, but he makes much of this smattering of knowledge Thirty years ago the Khwánd-Kárs were important persons, their services being in great demand, but the reformed teaching of modern times has been gradually undermining this influence, and they are now little respected and seldom consulted. During the early years of this century, when Islám in Bengal was still paralyzed by the revolution that had occurred, the Khwánd-Kárs educated boys, instructing them in the rudiments of their religion. At the present day, however, Munshís generally teach children, although a Khwánd-Kár is often preferred by strict Muhammadans to instruct their children in the doctrines of the faith, and teach them the Kalma, or confession of faith.

The Khwánd-Kár, moreover, makes Murı́ds or disciples, exorcises persons possessed of devils, and cures diseases by preparing charms (ta'wíz) ; while many families consult him on all occasions of sickness; and his ability to relieve suffering is never for a moment questioned by women. Should a child be attacked by fever or convulsions, the father goes to the Khwánd-Kár and obtains a charm, usually consisting of a sentence of the Korán scribbled on a piece of paper, which is fastened to the child's hair or arm; or the Khwánd-Kár mumbling a few sentences from the same book, blows into a cup of water and gives it to the father as a medicinal draught. Parents put implicit faith in the efficacy of these charms, and every Muhammadan can relate wonderful cures effected by them. It is said that if an adult disabled by a neuralgic or rheumatic pain, drinks water in which the written charm of a Khwánd-Kár has been dipped, immediate relief is procured, and no native will deny the possibility of this occurring.

Khyán, *Kolita*, a trading and cultivating caste of Northern Bengal and Assam, who claim to be descended from a Kayasth who was employed at the Court of the Rájá of Kuch Behar to determine auspicious times and seasons for doing particular things. Colonel Dalton describes them as a good-looking race with "oval faces, well-shaped heads, high noses, large eyes, well-developed eye-lids and eye-lashes, and the light supple frame of the pure Hindu." In Assam they are called Kolita, in Northern Bengal they are known by the name of Khyán.

The sections of the caste are shown in Appendix I. They are of the ordinary Brahmanical type, with slight modifications such as might easily arise from maladroit borrowing. A Khyán may not marry a girl belonging to his own section, nor may he marry within the usual formula of prohibited degrees reckoned to the seventh generation in the descending line. Girls are married as infants at ages varying from five to thirteen. The marriage ceremony is of the standard Brahmanical type, the gift of the bride to the bridegroom and his acceptance of her being reckoned the essential and binding portion. Widows are not allowed to marry again, nor is divorce permitted.

As to their religion, Khyáns are orthodox Hindus. Most of them belong to the Sákta sect, but Vaishnavas are also found among them. They employ Brahmans as priests, who are received on terms of equality by other members of the sacred order. Their social rank is respectable, and Brahmans, Káyasths and Baidyas take water, fruit and sweetmeats from their hands.

Khyán, a synonym for Kaibartta.

Khyaurakár, a title of Nápits in Bengal.

Khyungpo, a *rui* or sept of Dejong Lhoris, whose ancestor is said to have emigrated from North Bhotan.

Khyung-toipá, a *rui* or sept of the Bedtshan-gye sub-tribe of Dejong Lhoris or Bhotias of the south.

Kidat, a section of Goálás in the North-Western Provinces and Behar.

Kilkhágaur, a *mul* or section of Sonárs in Behar.

Kinda, date palm, a totemistic sept of Oraons in Chota Nagpur.

Kintichá, a *thar* or sept of Sunuwárs in Darjiling.

Kinwar, a sept of the Suryabansi Rajputs and a section of Bábhans in Behar.

Kiot, a synonym for Kewat.

Kiral, a *gáin* of the Kásyapa *gotra* of Bárendra Brahmans in Bengal.

Kiránti, Kiráti, a native of the Kiránt-des or mountainous country lying between the Dud-Kosi and the Karki rivers in Nepal. The term includes the Khambu, Limbu, and Yákhá tribes; and the Danuár, Hayu, and Thámi also claim to be Kiránti. Their title, however, to be included in this category is not admitted by the three tribes first mentioned, who claim to be, and are generally recognised as being, of superior social status.

Kiri, weevils in rice, a totemistic sept of Mundas in Chota Nagpur.

Kiro or **Bágh**, a section of Khariás in Chota Nagpur.

Kirtoliá, a *mul* or section of the Naomulia or Majraut sub-caste of Goálás in Behar.

Kirttan, a title of Sunris in Bengal.

Kirtti, a title of Dakshin-Rárhi and Bangaja Káyasths in Bengal.

Kisán, a *mul* or section of the Biáhut sub-caste of Kalwárs in Behar; a title of Khariás in Chota Nagpur.

Kisangir, a sect of religious mendicants who worship Krishna.

Kisánsinduriá, a class of cultivators in Chota Nagpur said to have come from Gángpur.

Kisán Turi, a sub-caste of Turis in Chota Nagpur.

Kisauriá, a section of Kanaujiá Lohárs in Behar.

Kishanpakshi, one born in the dark half (*Krishna paksha*) of the month; a title of the illegitimate offspring of members of two different castes in Behar.

Kishnaut, a sub-caste of Ahirs or Goálás in Behar and Chota Nagpur whose title is Mandar. Their *gotra* is Prem Ghuno. They churn milk.

Kisku, a sept of the Ho and Santál tribes.

Kisnot, a sept of Lohárs in Chota Nagpur.

Kispotta, pig's entrails, a totemistic sept of Oraons in Chota Nagpur.

Kissan, a totemistic sept of Mundas in Chota Nagpur; also a synonym for the Nágeswar tribe.

Kissauriá, a section of Kanaujiá Lohárs in Behar.

Kissi, a sept of Mundas in Chota Nagpur.

Kistobagal, a sub-caste of Goálás, who eat fowls, drink wine, etc.

Koá, cocoon, a totemistic sept of Mundas in Chota Nagpur.

Koáljibhá Thákur, a title of Bábhans in Behar.

Koári, a *gáin* of the Kásyapa *gotra* of Rárhi Brahmans in Bengal.

Kochh, *Kochh-Mandai*, *Rájbansi*, *Paliyá*, *Desi*, a large Dravidian tribe of North-Eastern and Eastern Bengal, among whom there are grounds for suspecting some admixture of Mongolian blood. At the present day the name Kochh, without doubt the original designation of the tribe, is so carefully tabooed in the districts where they are most numerous, and where there is every reason to believe them to represent the earliest permanent settlers, that in Kuch Behar itself at the Census of 1881 not a single Kochh was to be found. The transformation of the Kochh into the Rájbansi, the name by which they are now known in Rangpur, Jalpaiguri, and Kuch or Kochh Behar, is a singular illustration of the influence exercised by fiction in the making of caste. As described by Buchanan at the beginning of the century and by Hodgson some fifty years ago, the Kochh tribe was unquestionably non-Aryan and non-Hindu. Now the great majority of the Kochh inhabitants of Northern Bengal invariably describe themselves as Rájbansis or Bhanga-Kshatriyas—a designation which enables them to pose as an outlying branch of the Kshatriyas who fled to these remote districts in order to escape from the wrath of Parasu-Ráma. They claim descent from Rájá Dasarath, father of Ráma; they keep Brahmans, imitate the Brahmanical ritual in their marriage ceremony, and have begun to adopt the Brahmanical system of *gotras*. In respect of this last point they are now in a curious state of transition, as they have all hit upon the same *gotra* (Kasyapa), and thus habitually transgress the primary rule of the Brahmanical system which absolutely prohibits marriage within the *gotra*. But for this defect in their connubial arrangements—a defect which will probably be corrected in a generation or two as they and their purohits rise in intelligence—there would be nothing in their customs to distinguish them from Aryan Hindus, although there has been no mixture of blood and they remain thoroughly Kochh under the name of Rájbansi. Although there is no historical foundation for the claim of the Rájbansis to be a provincial variety of the Kshatriyas, it is a singular fact that the title Rájbansi serves much the same purpose for the lower strata of the Hindu population of Northern Bengal as the title Rajput does for the landholding classes of dubious origin all over India. The one term, like the other, serves as the sonorous designation of a large and heterogeneous group bound together by the common desire of social distinction. The original nucleus of the Rajput group may have been Aryan, as that of the Rájbansi was certainly Dravidian. Both, however, have been, and continue to be, recruited by very similar methods. Only the recruits of the one are drawn from the landholders; of the other from the cultivating classes.

Traditions of origin.

A good observer[1] describes the Rájbansi as "the most conspicuously Dravidian race in Bengal. Their men are tall and robust, and neither in feature nor dress strikingly Tamulian; but at a market or village gathering thronged by their women one could imagine oneself transported to Kanara or Tamil land. The Rájbansi women, whose cast of feature is singularly homely

[1] Mr. W. B. Oldham, then Deputy Commissioner of Darjiling.

and rough-hewn, leave the head uncovered and wear a dress in which blue or purple invariably predominates, reaching only to the knee and bound over the bosom, leaving both shoulders bare in a fashion not seen among other people in Bengal; while the ornaments of the head and limbs recall those worn in Southern India. Their language, however, is only Bengali, and they have no separate dialect or *patois*. That their adhesion to Hinduism is comparatively recent is shown by their own customs as regards burial, food and marriage, as well as by the existence of the Dhimal, who might be defined as a non-Hinduised Kochh or Rájbansi among them and beside them."

A medical officer, resident in Kochh Behar, whose opinion is quoted by Colonel Dalton, describes the Kochh of that country as having flat square faces; eyes black and oblique; hair black and straight, in some curling; nose flat and short; cheek bones prominent; beard and whiskers rather deficient; colour of skin in most instances black. Colonel Dalton himself says that the Rájbansi are all very dark, and that the Kochh display the thick protuberant lips and maxillaries of the negro.

A comparison of these opinions with my own observations and with the average cephalic, nasal and naso-malar indices of the caste ascertained by a large number of actual measurements seems to me to warrant the conclusion that the Kochh, Rájbansi, Paliyá, Desi and other varieties by whatever names they are called are descended from a Dravidian stock which may probably have occupied the valley of the Ganges at the time of the Aryan advance into Bengal. Driven forward by this incursion into the swamps and forests of Northern and North-Eastern Bengal, the tribe were here and there brought into contact with the Mongoloid races of the Lower Himalayas and of the Assam border, and their type may have been affected to a varying degree by intermixture with these people. But on the whole Dravidian characteristics predominate among them over Mongolian.

Internal structure.

The endogamous divisions of the caste differ slightly in different districts, but are based everywhere upon the degree of ceremonial purity which the members of particular groups are believed to have attained. In Northern Bengal the principal sub-caste is the **Rájbansi**, who also call themselves **Sivbansi** with reference to the legend which traces their origin to a *liaison* between the God Siva and Hira, the daughter of Háju, chief of the Kochh tribe, about the middle of the sixteenth century. Other synonyms—Bhanga-Kshatriya, Patita-Kshatriya, Kshatri-Sankoch, and Suraj-bansi—rest on the tradition which makes them out to be a remnant of the Kshatriyas scattered by Parasu Ráma, who cast off their sacrificial threads, hid themselves in the swampy jungles of Northern Bengal, and thus for the time being abdicated the proud position which the Rájbansi are now anxiously striving to reclaim. Alongside of the Rájbansi, but usually[1]

---

[1] I have come across Rájbansis who said that members of the two groups intermarried, and that Rájbansi and Paliyá were practically convertible terms.

distinct in respect of intermarriage and the eating of cooked food, we find the large sub-caste of **Paliyá**. The name Paliyá is said by some to refer to the flight (*paláyan*) of the supposed Kshatriya ancestors of the tribe; but it is equally possible that it may be merely a variant of the first half of the name Pani-Kochh by which the people now calling themselves Paliyá were known at the beginning of this century, when Dr. Buchanan made his survey of Dinájpur and Rangpur. They are further subdivided into two subordinate groups, known as **Sádhu** or pure and **Bábu Paliyá**. The latter name is regarded by the members of the sub-caste themselves as a title of distinction, or at least of respectability, connecting them with the Maharaja of Kuch Behar and the Ráikat of Jalpaiguri, whom they regard as the heads of the large heterogeneous body known as Rájbansi or Paliyá. By the Sádhu Paliyás, on the other hand, it is explained as a corruption of Byábahári from *Byábahár* usage, implying that the observances of the Bábu group are not up to their own standard of ceremonial purity. It is by no means easy to say how far these imputations are justified in regard to the entire Bábu sub-caste. Custom varies from district to district, and the tendency to imitate the usages of the higher castes is continually raising the ideal to which people endeavour to conform. Subject to this limitation, I think it is true as a general rule that the main distinction between the Sádhu and Bábu Paliyá consists in the fact that the latter eat pork, fowls, crocodiles, lizards and the leavings of men of their own caste, and indulge freely in strong drink, while all these things are forbidden to the Sádhu Paliyá. Another sub-caste known in Dinajpur is **Desi**, who regard themselves as somewhat superior to the Paliyás. A Desi can take rice, water, sweetmeats, etc., from a Paliyá man, but not from a Paliyá woman; nor is there any intermarriage between the two groups. One is tempted to conjecture that this group, which is not a particularly large one, may be the modern representatives of the Deosi, a sort of rudimentary priests among the Pani-Kochh, who, according to Buchanan, were "supposed to know more than their neighbours of the manner in which the gods are to be pleased." The Desi claim to be better than the Paliyás, in that they do not plough with cows or use them to turn oil-mills.

In Jalpaiguri the general name is Rájbansi, and three sub-castes are found—the **Dobhásir**, who eat pork and fowls and drink spirits; the **Modási**, who eat pork and drink spirits, but abstain from fowls; and the **Jáluá** or **Jháluá**, who catch and sell fish. It is curious to learn that within comparatively recent times the Rájbansis of the Darjiling Terai were divided into three endogamous sub-castes, bearing names having reference to the character of their dwellings. The **Tongia** lived in houses raised from the ground on piles, such as the Mongoloid races of the north-eastern border usually build; the **Khopria** contented themselves with low huts on the level of the ground; while the **Gobria** kept their cattle in the houses which they lived in themselves. These distinctions have now died out, and have been replaced by the divisions **Paliyá** and **Bábu** Kochh, and they are only mentioned here as showing how tribes which adopt Hinduism tend continually to get rid of their pre-Hindu methods of grouping and to remodel their internal structure on lines which indicate the degree in which particular groups approach the orthodox standard of food and usage.

The **Kántái** Rájbansi are a smaller group found scattered in several districts of Northern Bengal, who cultivate the soil, hold various kinds of tenures, serve as gomashtas, and sometimes practise medicine. The **Tiár** or **Dalai** are a fishing group mentioned by Buchanan, whose characteristic pursuit is fishing in the shallow drains or ditches connected with swamps and rice-fields. "In these they lay a long trap, called *dhanggi*, made of split bamboos. The mouth may be six or eight feet in length and one and a half to two feet wide. It slopes to an edge behind, being about two and a half or three feet broad. The fish that enter are prevented from returning by a row of bamboo splits placed as in a mouse trap, and they are shaken out by a hole at one corner which is plugged when the trap is set. Where there is any stream, the fish enter of their own accord; but they are often collected from a whole marsh and driven to the trap by dragging through the water a rope made of twisted ribs of the plantain tree leaves, the sides of which hang down like a fringe and alarm the fish as the rope approaches."

The **Kochh-Mandai** of the Bhowal forest tract in the north of Dacca appear to be a branch of the Kochh who have long been separated from the main body of the tribe and have to some extent intermingled with the Garos. The latter half of the name Kochh-Mandai is said to be the Garo word for man, and the entire name may be taken to be analogous to those double names which occur among several Dravidian tribes and denote groups owing their origin to crossing.

Mention has been made above of the singular fact that in seeking to copy the Brahmanical method of exogamy, the Rájbansi have been content to borrow one *gotra* only. All Rájbansis in fact belong to the same *gotra* Kasyapa, and thus habitually disregard the leading principle of the system which they proudly profess to follow. In theory intermarriage is regulated by the standard formula calculated to seven generations in the descending line from the paternal and maternal uncles, and to three generations from the aunts. But great laxity is said to prevail on this point throughout the caste, and in one district I am informed that marriage with a uterine half-sister is not prohibited. Another circumstance which tends rather to encourage consanguineous marriages is the prejudice entertained against marrying any one who comes from a distance. The result of this is that for matrimonial purposes the Rájbansi are broken up into a number of small territorial groups which bear no distinctive names and the limits of which do not admit of being precisely defined.

Marriage.

The Rájbansis profess to marry their daughters as infants, between the ages of four and ten years; but this custom has only recently been adopted, and it is difficult to ascertain to what extent it is really followed even among those sub-castes which profess to be pure Hindus. In the more primitive groups adult-marriage still prevails, and a breach of chastity before marriage is readily condoned, though the tendency is continually towards the adoption of what is believed to be the more orthodox usage. The same remark applies to the remarriage of widows. The Rájbansis in Rangpur if questioned on this point aver most positively that nothing of the sort is permitted; while their brethren in the Darjiling Terai make no secret at all of allowing a widow to remarry outside the degrees prohibited to her before her marriage, and subject to the further condition that she may not marry any of the elder relations of her late husband. Where a widow happens to be the head of the family, she enjoys the further privilege of choosing any man not within the prohibited degrees to live with her as her husband without going through any ceremony whatever. This looks like a survival, and may possibly furnish an explanation of the statement made by Buchanan[1] about the Páni-Kochh that "women who happen to be unmarried after they have grown up select a husband according to their own discretion," which by itself seems rather unlikely. If, however, we suppose the privilege to have been limited to women who had control of the property of their family, it bears a different aspect, and falls into line with several points of primitive practice in matters affecting property. Curiously enough, the Rájbansis, who prohibit widow-marriage, nevertheless recognise divorce,—a fact sufficient in itself to show, if further proof were wanting, that the former prohibition cannot have been long in force among them. Such divorces are effected before a *pancháyat*, at which the *purohit* and the barber of the caste,—the former a Rájbansi-Brahman or Barna-Brahman,—are present. The husband states his case, the wife has or is supposed to have the right of reply, and the judgment of the *pancháyat* is given by acclamation. If, as usually happens, it is adverse to the wife, her hair is shaved close to her head by the barber and the husband turns her out of the Rájbansi community.

Hypergamy.

Among the Rájbansi of Rangpur the feeling against widow-marriage has given rise to a curious form of hypergamy. Not content with adopting from the higher castes an artificial and inconvenient restriction which causes special hardship in a country where girls are married as children, they have proceeded to manufacture for themselves an imitation of Kulinism based upon the extent to which particular families have kept themselves free from the sin of allowing their widows to marry. Just as Ballál Sen appraised the virtues of the Brahmans of his day and allotted them graded rank accordingly, so Rájbansi opinion has seized upon the one tangible quality of having refrained from countenancing widow-marriage, and has made this the test of social respectability. Families of whom it can be said that none of their widows have been allowed to take second husbands rank in Rájbansi circles as Kulins; their members are spoken of as *mahat* or "great;" and people who wish to marry their daughters have to pay a substantial bride-price for the privilege. In point of stringency and completeness the copy falls far short of the model it professes to reproduce. Kulin women are not restricted in marriage to their own grade, and the alliances contracted by them have not, as among the Brahmans, the property of tainting the entire family to which they belong.

---

[1] *Eastern India*, iii, 540.

Match-making.

Professional match-makers (*ghataks*) are employed to arrange marriages. The initiative is taken by the father of the bridegroom, who sends the *ghatak* with two hundred leaves of the betel and eighty areca nuts to the bride's house. The *ghatak* stays there three days, which are spent in discussing the *pros* and *cons* of the match and haggling about the amount of the bride-price. If this time is disturbed by any unlucky event, such as the house catching fire, or a cloth being accidentally burned, or a cooking pot or water pot broken, the negotiations are abandoned and cannot be afterwards renewed, it being believed that grave misfortunes would follow if the omens were disregarded. Supposing all goes well, the *ghatak* returns to the bridegroom's house and reports the result of his mission, laying stress upon the attractions of the bride, and stating the bride-price that is asked for her. This of course depends mainly upon the circumstances of the families. When the bride's father is rich he may decline to accept money. Again, the amount sometimes varies in proportion to the age of the bridegroom. An elderly man may have to pay Rs. 80 or Rs. 90 for a wife, while in the case of a boy of fourteen to eighteen the sum would ordinarily range in tolerably well-to-do families from Rs. 20 to Rs. 25. After the *ghatak's* report has been duly considered, for nothing may be done in a hurry, a party of the boy's relatives go to the girl's house with the *ghatak*, bearing an offering of curds, which they distribute to the members of the bride's family. This is the right time to pay the bride-price, or at least half of it, should the bridegroom's father not be able to pay the whole at once.

Marriage ceremony.

The offer made through the *ghatak* having thus been ratified by the bridegroom's family, the wedding day is fixed with due regard to the auspicious days determined by the priests of the caste. On the appointed day the bridegroom is taken in procession to the bride's house, where four women (*baráti*) of the bride's family lift him out of his palanquin, place him on a seat, and offer him *pán* and tobacco after his journey. In the courtyard of the house a *marua* or wedding canopy has been erected, consisting of five plantain stems, about three feet high, arranged in the form of a quincunx, with an earthen pot (*ghará*) of water placed at the foot of each. The distance between the plantain stems is the distance from the bridegroom's foot to his ear. Outside the figure are a sieve and a winnowing fan with two extra pots of water. The following plan illustrates the arrangement:—

Bride

•O O•

•O

•O O•

Bridegroom

§O O¶

• Plantain stems.	¶ Winnow.
O Water pots.	§ Sieve.

The four *baráti* or processional women already referred to lead in first the bridegroom and then the bride, and put them in their places on either side of the *marua*, which they walk round five times, conducted by the *baráti*. As they reach their places after each complete turn, the bridal pair stand still and pelt each other with *átab*, rice and imitation cowries made of pith (*solá*). While this goes on a cloth is held up across the centre of the *marua* and suddenly raised when the bride throws, so that only a few of her missiles reach the bridegroom while it is dropped for the latter so as to give him a clear shot at the bride. Throughout the ceremony the couple wear high crowns or helmets made of *solá* pith.

After the *marua* has been duly circled, a cloth is spread in front of the winnow and sieve, and the couple sit down on it, cross-legged, the bride being on the right. Her left hand is then tied with *kusa* grass on the top of the right hand of the bridegroom; the father of the bride puts a rupee or half a rupee into her hand, and she gives the coin to the bridegroom, while a priest sitting at one side recites *mantras* or mystical formulæ supposed to be in Sanskrit. This completes the giving of the maiden (*kanyádán*) which the more orthodox Rájbansi affect to regard as the binding and essential portion of the ceremony. The father of the bride then gives her a new cloth, a *lotá*, a cow, jewellery, etc., according to his means, and presents are also made to the bridegroom.

A basketful of cowries is now brought for the couple to foretell the fortunes of their wedded life. The girl takes a handful and passes them to the boy, who in his turn picks them up and lays them down by the girl. The *baráti* women then count the shells and observe how many of them are lying with the hollow side upwards. If the greater number are in this position, the girl is said to have won the game, and this is an omen of her triumph in connubial disputes hereafter. If, however, most of the shells lie the other way, it is believed that the husband will get the best of it. After this the bride and bridegroom give one another curds and molasses to eat and afterwards betel, and the *baráti* women conduct the bride inside the house, while the bridegroom returns to his own party. The night is spent in feasting, and early next morning the bridegroom takes the bride to his own house. Here a sort of duplicate ceremony is gone through, under the name of *bási bibáha*, the four *baráti* women accompanying the procession in order to lift the bride out of her palanquin and to attend upon her during the celebration.

It is curious to observe that *sindurdán*, the smearing of vermilion between the bride's eyebrows and on the parting of her hair, which ordinarily forms the binding portion of the marriage ceremony of the lower castes, is relegated by the Rájbansi to a position of comparative obscurity. It is performed by two of the *baráti* women before the bridegroom arrives, at the time when the bride is washed with turmeric. The bridegroom merely puts a small black spot (*kájol*) of oil and lamp-black between the bride's eyebrows. In Darjiling, on the other hand, *sindurdán* holds its ground as the binding portion of the marriage ceremony, and as soon as it has been completed grass, water and rice, symbolising happiness and fertility, are showered upon the couple from the sieve and winnowing fan which lie ready.

The Rajbansis of Jalpaiguri vary in some particulars the ritual described above. They use four plantains instead of five, and wind cotton thread seven times round each. The place of the fifth plantain stem in the centre of the quincunx is taken by some glowing embers supposed to represent the sacred fire of orthodox tradition, across which the bride and bridegroom pelt each other with flowers. The fire is circled seven times, not five, and in marching round the couple keep the fire on their *left* hand, thus going counter to the path of the sun—a remarkable deviation from orthodox usage sufficient of itself to indicate that the Rájbansis have borrowed a ritual which they understand very imperfectly. In giving the bride to the bridegroom, the father of the bride must touch the bridegroom's knee with the second and third fingers of his left hand, repeating at the same time certain *mantras* dictated by the priest.

Religion.

The precise form of Hinduism followed by the Rájbansis seems to vary in different parts of the country according to the influences to which they are subjected. In Rangpur they profess to be Vaishnavas, while in Darjiling, where Tantric ideas are perhaps more prevalent, their favourite goddess is alleged to be Káli. Bisahari or Manasá, Grámi, Tistu Buri, Hanuman, Bindur Tulsi, Rishi Kishtho, Petháni, Jogini, Hudum Deo, Bahastho or Bahustho, Balibhadra Thákur, and Kora-Kuri are mentioned as among their minor gods. Some curious particulars of their worship deserve mention here. When a drought has lasted long, the Rájbansi women make two images of Hudum Deo from mud or cowdung, and carry them away into the fields at night. There they strip themselves naked and dance round the images, singing obscene songs, in the belief that this will cause rain to fall. The household god, Bahastho or Bahustho, is worshipped in Baisakh (April-May) twice daily and at other times whenever the family enters a new house. A round lump of clay made smooth by smearing it with cowdung is set up at the foot of a bamboo to represent the god, and to this offerings of rice are made which are eaten by the worshippers. If this duty is neglected, disease or some similar calamity is believed to come upon the family. To Satya-Narain, whom the Mahomedans revere under the name of Satya-Pir, fresh milk, wheat flour, plantains and sugar are offered by the Brahmans who serve the caste on an auspicious day in Jaishtha (May-June). For this god wheat flour is said to be essential, and no substitute is admitted. Balibhadra Thákur is propitiated at sowing time under the form of a yoked plough, before which the worshippers prostrate themselves and do homage as at the shrine of a regular divinity. The germination of the seed is deemed to depend on the due performance of this ceremony. Seven months after child-birth, when the child is given rice to eat for the first time, Sháti (probably a variant of Shashthi) is worshipped with offerings of *kántlá* plantain, *atab* rice, and the leaves of the *bel* and the *tulsi*. Rude image of the goddess are made by the Máli caste in the form of cylinders of *solá* about seven inches high, roughly moulded into human form and mounted on the backs of *solá* ducks. The cult of *Kora Kuri* is confined to women and children. During the month of Paush (December-January) a small earthen pot *(ghat)* is set up in the yard, offerings of *duba* grass, plantain and turmeric are laid on it, and it is smeared with vermilion and oil. Petháni and Jogini are worshipped only by women, Sannyási only by boys.

In Rangpur, Kamakhya or Kámrup Brahmans superintend the religious observances of the Rájbansi caste. These rank as Barna-Brahmans, and are not received on equal terms by other members of the sacred order. In Darjiling and Jalpaiguri the caste seem hardly to have attained to the dignity of having Brahmans of their own, and any one among them who has acquired a reputation for sanctity may be called in to officiate as priest.

Funeral.

Orthodox Rájbansis burn their dead: the less Hinduised members of the caste resort to either burial or cremation as happens to be convenient. Children, lepers and persons who die of snake-bite are buried. Some set up over the grave a small white flag or canopy, usually of muslin, two or three feet square; others put a pot of water and a *tulsi* tree there. The period of mourning seems to vary in different districts. Thus the Rájbansis of Darjiling perform *sráddh* on the thirteenth day after death, those of Jalpaiguri on the eleventh, and the Rájbansis of Rangpur on the thirty-first. During the thirty days following the funeral, these latter take their meals in wet clothes, changing afterwards to dry ones, sleep on jute, eat *átap* rice, and abstain from fish, flesh, *pán*, *masur dál*, condiments and salt. Every year on the eighth or ninth day of the new moon in the month of Bhádra (August-September) *sráddh* is performed for three generations of deceased ancestors by throwing into a river milk, wheat, *átap* rice, sesamum, barley, plantains, *bel* leaves and sprays of the *tulsi* plant, and uttering at the same time the names of the three ancestors who are to be held in honour.

Social status and occupation.

In spite of their pretentions to be Kshatriyas, the social status of the Rájbansi is still extremely low, and no well-known caste will take cooked food from their hands or smoke in their hookahs. In the Darjiling Terai, where the caste is numerous, Hindus take water from them, but this is one of those concessions to circumstances of which caste custom offers many examples. The caste as a whole may be described as agricultural, though many, as has been mentioned above, make their living as fishermen, and carpenters, blacksmiths, jewellers, and money-lenders are also found among them. Most Rájbansis, however, are cultivating ryots with or without occupancy rights, some are landless day-labourers paid in cash or kind, and others hold their fields as *ádhiárs* or *métayers*, paying half the produce to their immediate landlord. There are said to be no *zamindars* among them, the fact probably being all the *zamindars* who were originally Rájbansis have long ago got themselves transformed into Rajputs. Many of them in Darjiling and Jalpaiguri hold the tenures known as *jotdári*, the incidents of which closely resemble those of a *táluk*.

The following statement shows the number and distribution of the Kochh tribe in 1872 and 1881:—

District.	1872.	1881.	District.	1872.	1881.
Bardwan	......	1,006	Kuch Behar	......	299,458
Bankura	3	224	Dacca	15,600	13,498
Birbhum	1	4,861	Faridpur	3,862	1,886
Midnapur	17	2,523	Bakarganj	572	924
Hughli	23	5	Maimansinh	32,351	31,997
Howrah		96	Chittagong	10,866	180
24-Parganas	170	1,757	Noakhali	43	210
Nadiya	1,532	15,335	Tipperah	1,296	2,495
Jessore	2,317	4,768	Chittagong Hill Tracts ...	......	41
Khulna	......	2,012	Gya	......	4
Murshedabad	17,646	17,582	Bhagalpur	164	38
Dinajpur	446,641	407,923	Purniah	61,724	71,833
Rajshahye	11,850	10,459	Maldah	63,217	60,700
Rangpur	427,671	432,498	Santál Parganas	352	61
Bogra	15,649	19,055	Orissa Tributary States ...	......	27
Pabna	3,078	4,875	Hazaribagh	......	3
Darjiling	23,124	30,801	Manbhum	......	862
Julpigori	139,647	206,322	Tributary States	......	116

Kochhi Bediá, a sub-caste of Bediás whose original home was in Kuch Behar; also called Kochh Bediá.

Kochila, a sub-tribe of Thárus in Nepal; a sept of the Rautár sub-tribe of Thárus in Behar.

Kochohina, a sept of the Suryabansi sub-tribe of Rajputs in Behar.

Kodaria, worker with the spade, a section of Bábhans in Behar.

Kodbariá, a *mul* or section of the Maghayá sub-caste of Kándus in Behar.

Kodo Ság, a kind of water vegetable, a totemistic sept of Mundas in Chota Nagpur.

Kodriá, a synonym for Kadar or Kadarwa, who dig earth like Beldárs and work as labourers.

Kodriwe or **Kodarye**, a *mul* of the Sándil section of Maithil Brahmans in Behar.

Koeá, a wild beast, a totemistic sept of Lohárs in Chota Nagpur.

Koftgar, a craftsman who practises the art of inlaying gold and silver on iron, usually, though not invariably, a Mahomedan.

Kogdengsa, a sept of Maghs in the Hill Tracts of Chittagong.

Kohli, a *thar* or sept of the Das-Gurung sub-tribe of Gurungs in Darjiling.

Koiri, *Muráo*, a very numerous cultivating caste of Behar and Chota Nagpur, whom Dr. Wise believed to be "closely allied to the Kurmi, with whom they drink, but do not eat, while the Kurmi attend their marriages and partake of the feast." Mr. Nesfield again identifies the Koiri with the Káchhi, and adds that the name Koiri "shows that the wandering and semi-savage Kol, who is still to be found in the districts south of

Origin.

the Ganges," was the remote ancestor of the caste, "though every tradition of such descent appears now to have been forgotten." Both theories appear to me to go much farther than the evidence justifies. There is nothing specially improbable in the suggestion that both Koiris and Kurmis may be descended from the same stock, nor even in the conjecture that the parent tribe was of non-Aryan origin; but we can point to no definite facts tending to affiliate the Koiris to the group of tribes included in the general name Kolh, nor are the cases of social intercourse noticed by Dr. Wise sufficient to prove tribal affinity between the two castes. All that can be said is that the Koiri have too long been a distinct caste, and have been too much affected by Hindu influences for it to be possible to frame any plausible hypothesis regarding the elements of which they are made up. Their own tradition, that they were created by Siva to tend the radish (*murái*) and to look after the sacred gardens of Benares, is of the common mythological type and gives no clue to their descent.

Internal structure.

We find among Koiris in different parts of the country the following thirteen sub-castes:—Barki-Dángi,[1] Chhotki-Dángi, Banapár, Jaruhár, Kanaujiá, Magahiyá, Tirhutiá, Chirmáit, Kumárh, Goitá, Dhár, Reutiá, Pauriá, Barákar, and Palmohá. The common story regarding the origin of these groups is that the first Koiri, the son of Mahádeva and Párvati, was placed by them in charge of a garden, and that the sub-castes are descended from girls of various castes who came to pick flowers in the garden and conferred their favours on the gardener. The sections are shown in Appendix I. In Behar they are territorial or titular; while in Chota Nagpur and the Santál Parganas survivals of totemism may be traced in the Kásyap and Nág *gotras*, the members of which will not kill or molest tortoises and snakes. The Kásyap Koiris, indeed, carry their reverence for the tortoise to such a length that if one is caught they smear its shell with oil and vermilion and put it back into the water. Some of the Behar section-names, again, are a kind of shibboleth, referring to the occupation of the caste or reciting at length the supposed habitat of the section. The usual rule is that a man may not marry a woman of his own section, but in Bhagalpur as many as nine sections are said to be excluded. The standard formula calculated to seven generations in the descending line is used for reckoning prohibited degrees not covered by the rule forbidding marriage within the section.

Marriage.

Koiris usually marry their daughters as infants between the ages of seven and ten, but rich men sometimes have the ceremony performed when the girl is only three or four years old: "after she has got her teeth," as the saying goes; while both in Behar and Chota Nagpur a girl's marriage may be deferred for special reasons until she has passed the

[1] The Barki-Dángi, who forbid widow-remarriage, are supposed to be the highest in rank; then come the Chhotki-Dángi and the Jaruhár, followed by the territorial divisions Kanaujiá, Magahiyá, and Tirhutiá. The Goitá and Dhár groups, found in Champaran, keep fowls, and are believed to be the illegitimate descendants of a Koiri woman by a Kunjrá or vegetable-seller.

age of puberty without the family incurring serious reproach thereby. Colonel Dalton gives the following account of a Koiri marriage in Chota Nagpur, which does not appear to differ materially from the usage current in Behar:—

"The preliminaries are first arranged by mutual friends, who meet at the house of the bride. If they come to an agreement, small sums of money are interchanged. The boy's friends give four annas and a half, and the girl's friends one and a half, and this is an engagement.

"But as a betrothal it is incomplete till the ceremony called *sugan bándhná* is performed. Ten or more of the boy's friends with music and a Brahman go to the girl's house; her friends are also invited, and the ceremony commences by the father of the girl and the father of the boy each spreading a new cloth on the ground. The Brahman then takes some *dhán* from the store of the bride's father and places it in the hands of the maiden, who throws it on the cloth spread by her father-in-law that is to be. The Brahman next takes some grain that has been brought from the bridegroom's house, and this is thrown on the cloth spread by the father of the maiden. The cloths are then rolled up with the grain in them: the bride retains that which was brought from her betrothed's house. The friends of the latter take away the cloth produced by the bride's father.

"Eight days after the above ceremony the marriage takes place. A Brahman priest presides, and the service is strictly Brahmanical. At the conclusion of the orthodox ritual the bride and *var*, their scarfs tied together, are made to perform seven times a circuit round a collection of vessels containing water, grain, oil, and a light. This is called the *bhanwar*. The girl goes first: she carries one of the cloths with grain, and the boy the other, and, allowing the grain to drop, they thus mark the circuits they make.

"When all is over, the boy is taken into the women's apartments and invited to eat, but he will not touch food till a present is made to him. In the same manner, when the bride first appears amongst the females of her husband's house she obstinately declines all refreshments till bribed to eat. The *jahás* is used by the Koiris as well as by the Kurmis."

Polygamy is permitted, and there does not appear to be any positive rule limiting the number of wives a man may have. The caste, however, is not a wealthy one, and it is unusual to find a man with more than two wives, while a second wife is commonly taken only in the event of the first being barren.

All the sub-castes except the Barki-Dángi allow a widow to marry again by the *sagai* or *sangá* form, and impose no restrictions on her choice of a second husband. It is, however, deemed the right thing for her to marry her late husband's younger brother (*dewar*) if such a relative exists; and the fact that a woman who marries an outsider must give up her male children to her late husband's family tends on the whole to make marriage with the *dewar* a very common arrangement. The *sangá* ritual as performed by the Koiris of Manbhum is a very simple one. Late in the evening the bridegroom accompanied by a few of his friends goes without any special display to the bride's house, where he is received by her relations and given a seat in the courtyard. There he is joined by the bride, who is brought in by two widows, and takes her seat on a *sál* leaf in front of the bridegroom. The bridegroom presents to her a new *sári*, and touches with the little finger of his left hand some powdered vermilion, which is brought to him in a *sál* leaf. A widow then smears some of this powder on the bride's forehead and the parting of her hair; this act, which completes the ceremony, being greeted with a cry of "Haribol" by the lookers-on. The proceedings end with a feast provided by the bridegroom, who takes his wife home quietly the same night. In the north of Manbhum (thánás Jhariá and Topchánchi) a different custom prevails, which may perhaps represent a state of transition towards the abandonment of widow-marriage. There no ceremony of any kind is performed; but if a man wishes to keep a widow as his mistress, he announces his intention to the headmen. If they agree, he simply takes the woman to live with him.

The practice of the caste in the matter of divorce appears to vary with the surroundings of the caste, and to depend on the extent to which they have been influenced by the example of the higher castes. In Chota Nagpur and parts of Behar considerable license of divorce is allowed. Reference is made to the caste *pancháyat;* and if it is found that the husband has just cause of complaint, he is permitted to put away his wife. Divorced wives may marry again. The Koiris of Bhagalpur and Patna, on the other hand, profess not to recognise divorce, and a woman who goes wrong is simply turned out of the caste. In Champaran the rule is said to be that a man may obtain from the *pancháyat* authority to divorce his wife for adultery or for serious faults of temper. A woman so divorced may marry a man of a different (presumably lower) section, but may not marry within her own section without the express permission of the leading members of the group—the caste Brahmans and the local zamindar. For this permission certain fees have to be paid. This seems to imply the opinion that a woman having by marriage become a member of her husband's section does not revert to her own section when divorced, and thus is not precluded from marrying a man who before her marriage would have been deemed a blood relation.

Religion.

Koiris profess to be orthodox Hindus belonging to the Saiva or Sákta sects, and Vaishnavism has hitherto made little progress among them. The quality of their orthodoxy, however, seems to vary with locality, and may perhaps be gauged by the degree of consideration accorded to their Brahmans and by the character of their minor gods. Thus in Chota Nagpur the Brahmans who serve the Koiris as priests are not received on equal terms by other members of the sacred order; while among their minor gods we find the aboriginal Marang-Buru or Barpahári alongside of Sokhá, Parameswari, Mahávira, and Hanumán. Mounds of dried clay representing these are found in every house, and there is often a larger mound with a *tulsi* tree in the courtyard, which, according to Colonel Dalton, is sacred to the entire group of deities. In addition to the Hindu festivals of

Janmáshtami and *Sivarát* they observe the aboriginal feasts of *Karma* and *Jittá parab*, and invoke Marang-Buru at certain intervals, specially when rain does not fall in due season. In Behar, on the other hand, the Kanaujiá, Srotri, or Tirhutiá Brahman, who is employed by the Koiri for religious and ceremonial purposes, seems to hold a fairly high position and not to be looked down upon by his brethren. Their village gods are Bandi, Goraiyá, Sokhá, Hanumán, Rám Thákur, Kurlál, and Dharm-Ráj, who are worshipped by the head of the household with the usual offerings of sheep, goats, and sweetmeats of various kinds. In Arrah the Koiris, like the Kándus, worship the Pánch Pir and hold a festival in their honour on the ninth and tenth days of the Dasahará in Aswin (September–October). A few are found following the tenets of Kabir, Nának, and Daryá Das.

Koiri women are unclean for twelve days after child-birth, at the end of which time the mother bathes twice, and after each bath plasters the house floor with cowdung. She then marks with red lead five spots on the rim of the well, draws a jar of water, and her purification is complete. The dead are burned, the body being laid on the pyre with the head pointing to the north, and the ashes thrown into the Ganges or into any river that may happen to be handy. The ceremony of *sráddh* is performed in the regular method on the thirteenth day after death. Cakes and libations of water are offered every Aswin for the propitiation of ancestors in general. In Chota Nagpur a curious custom prevails, under which on the day of death the friends and relatives of the deceased, and even the members of other castes, give the family a few handfuls of rice and receive in return a small quantity of milk.

Social status.

The social position of Koiris is respectable. They rank with Kurmis and Goálás, and Brahmans will take water from their hands. In the matter of food the practice of the caste, in some districts at any rate, seems to fall below the ordinary Hindu standard of purity. Thus the Koiris of Champaran eat fowls, and in North Bhagalpur field-rats are mentioned as a legitimate article of diet. On the other hand, they will not touch the leavings of even the highest castes, nor will they take personal service—a point wherein they consider themselves to be raised above the Dhánuks, Kewats, and Amáts. They will, however, eat *pakki* with, and take water from, men of these castes, and will smoke in the same hookah when on a journey. Their pursuits are purely agricultural, but they are distinguished from the Kurmis and other purely cultivating castes by their skill in rearing tobacco, opium, and other special produce requiring more careful cultivation than the staple crops. In the neighbourhood of large towns they work as market-gardeners, growing and selling all kinds of vegetables. Many Koiris are tenure-holders, and here and there members of the caste have risen to be petty zemindars. Most of them are prosperous cultivators holding occupancy rights, and comparatively few have sunk to the position of landless day-labourers. In fact, their skill and industry are so notorious that a Koiri, even if he has no land of his

Occupation.

own, is usually rather in demand as a partner on the *bhág-jot* system of cultivation.

The following statement shows the number and distribution of Koiris in 1872 and 1881:—

District.	1872.	1881.	District.	1872.	1881.
Bardwan	709	344	Tipperah	529	232
Bankura	2,397	624	Chittagong	17	18
Birbhum	468	87	Noakhali	402	......
Midnapur	2,140	380	Patna	81,561	86,738
Hughli	} 143	{ 153	Gya	131,030	142,068
Howrah		343	Shahabad	130,394	152,846
24-Parganas	1,539	1,633	Tirhut { Mozufferpur ...	} 227,046	{ 141,551
Nadiya	8,702	65	Tirhut { Darbhanga ...		129,027
Khulna	......	3	Saran	141,209	150,354
Jessore	359	47	Champaran	82,074	103,893
Murshedabad	7,171	930	Monghyr	77,741	92,650
Dinajpur	211	233	Bhagalpur	81,117	82,368
Rajshahye	580	55	Purniah	24,025	26,138
Rangpur	21,626	295	Maldah	462	226
Bogra	1,607	211	Santál Parganas	9,341	11,304
Pabna	741	8	Cuttack	......	31
Darjiling	61	409	Puri	......	4
Jalpigori	62	181	Balasore	......	997
Kuch Behar	......	41	Hazaribagh	27,321	41,495
Dacca	838	282	Lohardagá	24,232	23,538
Faridpur	1,516	......	Singbhum	42	52
Bakarganj	436	62	Manbhum	4,528	2,404
Maimansinh	3	46	Tributary States	1,320	3,661

Kokarsá, a section of Sonárs in Behar.

Kokás, a sub-caste of Barhis in Behar who are said to have come from Gorakhpur, and work only in wood; a sub-caste of Lohárs.

Kokenamba, he who rises with the sun, a sept of the Pánthar sub-tribe of Limbus in Darjiling.

Koki, a *thar* or sept of Gurungs in Darjiling.

Kokras, a section of the Sátmuliá Maghayá sub-caste of Kándus in Behar.

Kol, a sub-caste of Gonrhis in Behar which, though endogamous as regards the other sub-castes of Gonrhis, allows of intermarriage with the Parbatti Kurin sub-caste. The Kols say they are not Gonrhis, and distinguish themselves as Gonrh.

Kol or **Kolh**, a generic name applied by Hindus to the Munda and Oraon tribes, and sometimes also to the Bhumij and Kharias. Herr Jellinghaus[1] thinks that it means pig-killer; but the question is a very obscure one, and it is at least equally likely that the word may be a variant of *hor* or *horo*, the Mundári for 'man,' which is used by both Mundas and Santáls in speaking of themselves.

Kolandh, a section of the Pachainyá sub-caste of Doms in Behar.

Kola-Parámánik, a sub-caste of Nápits in the 24-Parganas.

Kolasa, a sept of Maghs in the Hill Tracts of Chittagong.

Koleman or **Kalu**, a hypergamous group of Telis in Bengal.

Kolh-Ásur, a sub-tribe of Asuras in Chota Nagpur.

[1] *Zeitschrift für Ethnologie*, iii, 326.

Kolita, *Kolita Tása Orh Tása*, an agricultural caste of the Southern Tributary Mahals of Chota Nagpur, whose traditions say that they came originally from Mithila in the days of Rama. Colonel Dalton describes them as of fair complexion with good features and well-proportioned limbs, and pronounces them to be mainly Aryan in blood with "a slight deterioration arising from intermixture with the less comely aborigines." They generally allow their daughters to grow to maturity before giving them in marriage, and Colonel Dalton saw many full-grown girls in the villages that he visited. Nothing is known about the internal structure or the religion of the caste. They usually call themselves Tása, a corruption of Chása, and I think it is an open question whether they are not merely Orh-Chasas who have settled in the Tributary Mahals and acquired the name Kolita.

Kolita, an endogamous sub-division of Káyasths in Assam.

Kolkatári, a sept of Kaurs in Chota Nagpur.

Kol-Munda, a sub-tribe of Mundas in Chota Nagpur.

Konári, an endogamous division of Páschátya Baidik Brahmans in Bengal.

Konárk, a *pur* or section of Sákadwipi Brahmans in Behar.

Kondongwa, the vagabond, a sept of the Ahtharai sub-tribe of Limbus in Darjiling.

Kongaddi, crow, a totemistic sept of Mundas in Chota Nagpur.

Konhar, a sept of the Rautár sub-tribe of Thárus in Behar.

Konkpát, a title of Mundas in Chota Nagpur.

Konkpát-Munda, a sub-tribe of Mundas in Chota Nagpur.

Konr-Gop, a hypergamous division of the Purbba Kuliyá Sadgops in Murshedabad who take their wives from other Sadgops, but give their daughters only in their own group.

Kons, grass, a totemistic sept of Lohárs in Chota Nagpur.

Kopetah, a section of Maghayá Dhobis in Behar.

Kopinyar, a section of Awadhiá Hajjáms in Behar.

Koput, a sept of Gonds in Chota Nagpur.

Korá, a sub-caste of Tántis in Bengal; a *mul* or section of the Kanaujiá sub-caste of Sonárs in Behar; a sept of Hos in Singbhum.

Korá, *Káorá*, *Khairá*, *Khayrá*, a Dravidian caste of earth-workers and cultivators in Chota Nagpur, Western and Central Bengal, probably an offshoot from the Mundá tribe. The Korás or Khayrás of Manbhum and Bankura have well-marked totemistic sections[1] of the same type as the Mundas, and the latter admit that some sort of affinity may at one time have been recognised. The Korás of the Santál Parganas on the other hand claim to have come from Nagpur. The Bárdá section of the Korás have a curious legend concerning their totem. They say that one of their ancestors went out hunting

Tradition of origin.

[1] See Appendix I, *s.v.* Korá.

with his two brothers in the jungle, but found no game. While they were wandering about, they noticed a bundle wrapped in *sál* leaves hanging from the branch of a *bárdá* or *pitháli* tree. The bundle contained meat, which, being very hungry, they cooked and ate without further inquiry. Afterwards they found out that what they had eaten was a human placenta, and expressed their horror by making the fruit of the *bárdá* tree taboo for themselves and their descendants. The Álu section, on the other hand, believe that their first ancestor was born under a Phal-álu tree, and for this reason they will not eat the bulb-like fruit of this tree, or any bulbs, such as potatoes, which bear a resemblance to it. Both stories seem to be attempts to find a rational explanation for a prohibition which seemed unreasonable to men who had got beyond the stage of believing in their actual descent from trees. Further east these characteristic section-names have been dropped, but the caste is divided into four sub-castes, bearing the names Dhalo, Molo, Sikhariá, and Bádámia, of which the first three still preserve the memory of their original settlements. Thus the Dhalo sub-caste say that they came from Dhalbhum, the eastern pargana of Singbhum; the Molo from Manbhum; and the Sikhariá from the tract of country between the Dámodar and Barákar rivers bounded on the east by Samet Sikhar or Párasnáth Hill. In Bankura, again, besides the Sikhariá we find three other groups—Sonárekhá, Jhetiá, and Guri-Báwá, of which the first is associated with the Sonárekhá or Subarnarekhá river, which rises in the Mundári country, while the second bears the same name as one of the sub-castes of the Bágdis. In Bankura all four sub-castes are strictly endogamous; in the districts further east Molos and Sikhariás intermarry. In Manbhum no sub-castes appear to have been formed, and the caste is still more or less in the tribal stage.

Internal structure.

The Hinduised Khairás of Central Bengal have developed a legend of the common mythological type, to the effect that they were generated by the bellowing of the miraculous cow Kámadhenu when Viswámitra came to take her away from the sage Vasishtha, and that they with other soldiers born from the cow drove off the intruding Kshatriya. Another tradition current in the Santál Parganas says that the Khairás came from the west, and that their special function is to prepare catechu (*khair*) for use in conjunction with betel. There is nothing to show that the Korás ever followed this particular occupation, and the statement is referred to here merely as an instance of the striving after a meaning which meets us so frequently in the popular derivations of caste names.

Where the exogamous groups have been preserved, the rule is that a man may not marry a woman of the same totem as himself; but on the mother's side the totem is not taken into account, and the rule of exogamy is supplemented by the standard formula *mamerá*, *chacherá*, etc., calculated to three generations in the descending line.

Marriage.

The Korás of Western Bengal marry their daughters both as infants and as adults, and in Chota Nagpur sexual intercourse before marriage is regarded as a venial offence. This measure of toleration, so characteristic of the aboriginal races, is no longer recognised in Bankura, where sexual indiscretions are visited with severe social penalties, although adult-marriage still maintains its ground. In Bengal Proper the caste has fully adopted the more fashionable custom of infant-marriage.

The marriage ceremony of the Bankura Korás corresponds precisely with that described at length in the article on the Bágdis, with the curious difference that vermilion is applied to the bride's forehead with the handle of the cutter (*chimta*) used for slicing areca nut. In Manbhum the bride and bridegroom are made to stand one behind the other on a bundle of straw laid on the top of a bullock-yoke (*jorán*), and the bridegroom, whose place is in the rear, treading on the heels of the bride, reaches forward and smears vermilion three times on the bride's forehead. This, which is deemed to be the binding portion of the ritual, has clearly survived or been borrowed from the marriage ceremony of the Mundás. The Eastern Korás follow the regular Hindu ritual.

Polygamy is everywhere permitted, and in theory there is no limit to the number of wives a man may have. Custom, however, and the standard of living imposed by the comparative poverty of the caste, combine in actual life to bring about the result that hardly any one has more than two wives, and most men content themselves with one.

Among the Korás of Manbhum and the Santál Parganas a widow is allowed to marry again, and her choice of a second husband is unfettered, save that she must observe the prohibited degrees, and that she may not marry her deceased husband's elder brother. She may marry his younger brother, but she is under no special obligation to do so, though such marriages are deemed both respectable and convenient, and very commonly take place. The ceremony (*sangá*) is much the same as that described in the article on the Koiris. In the Korá ritual, however, the bridegroom does not himself apply the vermilion to the bride's forehead. He merely touches the powder, which is then smeared on the parting of the bride's hair by the widows who are present. In Bankura and the districts further east the example of the rest of the population has induced the Korás to abandon widow-marriage. The working of the same influence may be observed in the matter of divorce, which is prohibited in the eastern districts, while in Chota Nagpur and the Santál Parganas aboriginal usage still holds its ground and divorce is granted by the caste council on the application of either husband or wife. Persons so divorced, whether men or women, are allowed to marry again.

Like the Bauris and Bágdis, Korás admit into their community members of any caste ranking above their own in social standing. The occasions on which this privilege is sought are doubtless rare, and usually occur only when the outsider has been turned out of his own caste for carrying on an intrigue with a Korá woman and eating food which she has prepared. A case of this kind, which has been reported to me from one of the districts of Central Bengal, throws a curious light upon the working of the caste system at the present day. A man of the highly respectable Águri caste fell in love with a Korá girl, and after keeping the intrigue secret for some time was ejected from his caste and turned out of his household. He then went to live with his mistress, and at first thought of turning Vaishnava. Finally, however, at the girl's suggestion he decided to join the Korá community, and his case was laid before a meeting of the headmen (*mandals*) of the caste. These worthies the convert propitiated with a liberal feast, and was thereupon formally admitted to be a member of the Korá caste.

Like most of the lower castes, the Korás settle the bulk of their civil disputes through the agency of their own *panchâyats*, and very seldom resort to the regular courts. In fact the value of the property in question is usually too small to bear the costs of a regular suit. In matters of inheritance and succession they affect to be governed by the standard codes recognised in the locality, by the Dáyabhága in Bengal districts and by the Mitákshará in Chota Nagpur. Their customs, however, imperfectly as it has been possible to ascertain them, show some curious deviations from the ordinary Hindu rules of law. In Bankura the custom of giving the eldest son an extra share (*jeth-angs*) is in full force, and even in the eastern districts traces of this practice still survive. The Korás of Manbhum, on the other hand, divide a man's property equally among his sons, but where he leaves sons by more than one wife, they follow the custom known in the Panjab as *chundávand*, under which the sons, however many, of one wife get no more than the sons, however few, of another wife.

Religion.

In matters of religion Korás affect to be orthodox Hindus, worshipping the regular gods and calling themselves Śáktas or Vaishnavas, according as they incline to the cult of Káli, Durgá, and Manasá, or to that of Rádhá and Krishna. Manasa, the heavenly patroness of snakes, and Bhádu, the virgin daughter of the Pachete house, whose worship has been described in the article on the Bágdis, are their favourite deities. Their village and household deities are Bhairab Thákur, Grám-Deoti, and Kudra, to whom goats, fowls, pigeons, rice, sugar, and plantain are offered on no fixed dates, and are divided between the worshippers and the Deoghariá Brahmans, who serve them as priests and keep in order the shrines (*Kudrasthán* and *Bhairabsthán*) of the village gods. In Manbhum the Korás do not employ Brahmans, but a member of the caste, styled the Láyá or Náyá acts as priest, and is sometimes remunerated by a grant of rent-free land held on the tenure known as *láyáli*. Further east they are served by Barna Brahmans, who are looked down upon by other members of the sacred order, and occupy about the same position as the Brahmans who look after the spiritual welfare of the Bauris and Bágdis.

Like the Bauris, the Korás of Chota Nagpur admit both burial and cremation as modes of disposing of the dead; and when burial is resorted to, the corpse is laid in the grave face downwards and with the head pointing north. In Bankura and further east the rule is to burn, burial being confined to the case of those who have died of cholera, small-pox, or any disease supposed to be infectious. Here also the fashion of placing the body face downwards is observed, the idea being apparently that this affords some security against the spirit of the dead man 'walking' and giving trouble to the living—a danger which is always supposed to be greater in the case of those who have died by a comparatively sudden or violent death. A meagre imitation of the orthodox *sráddh* is performed on the eleventh day after death, and annual offerings of rice, ghi, and *gur* are made to deceased ancestors in the months of Kártik and Chait.

Social status.

The social position of Korás is very low, and they are usually classed with Bágdis, Bauris, Bunas, and other dwellers on the confines of Hinduism. Their own practice in the matter of diet varies in different parts of the country. In Chota Nagpur they eat beef, pork, and fowls, and all manner of fish, whether scaly or scaleless, but refrain from eating field-rats, snakes, lizards, and animals which have died a natural death. Further east they are more particular. No Korá will touch beef, and some members of the caste abstain from fowls and from strong drink, in the belief that by doing so they acquire some sort of social distinction. These comparatively ascetic Korás have not as yet formed themselves into a sub-caste, but there is no reason why this should not hereafter take place. In Bankura Korás will eat sweetmeats, etc., with members of the Bágdi caste, but will not take water from their hands or smoke in the same *hookah*. Boiled rice they will take only from members of the Nabasákha group.

Occupation.

The caste believe tank-digging, road-making, and earthwork generally to be their characteristic profession, and it may be surmised that their adoption of a comparatively degraded occupation, necessarily involving a more or less wandering manner of life, may have been the cause which led to their separation from the Mundás, who are above all things settled agriculturists, conspicuous for their attachment to their original villages. As earth-workers they rank next to the Beldárs, but, unlike these, they carry earth in a pair of triangular baskets slung on a shoulder-yoke (*bahangi*), and will on no account carry it on their head. Beldárs, on the other hand, always use single baskets, borne on the head, and refuse to touch a *bahangi*, deeming it an indignity to carry anything on their shoulders. Within the last generation many Korás have taken to cultivation, holding land as occupancy or non-occupancy raiyats, and working as agricultural labourers. In Bankura, however, and in other districts of Western Bengal, their connexion with the land must be of very ancient date, for we find a certain number of them at the present day in possession of substantial *ghatwáli* tenures—a fact which indicates that they were among the earliest settlers in that part of the country.

The following statement shows the number and distribution of Korás in 1872 and 1881:—

District.	1872.	1881.	District.	1872.	1881.
Bardwan	726	3,211	Chittagong	......	4
Bankura	1,216	5,054	Patna	1	......
Birbhum	3,776	5,079	Monghyr	3,301	2,927
Midnapur	6,181	3,608	Bhagalpur	74	13
Hughli	......	3,117	Maldah	......	238
24-Parganas	11	330	Santál Parganas ...	2,211	3,760
Nadiya	3	......	Cuttack } ...	The figures are included with other "labouring castes."	......
Khulna	......	15	Puri } ...		
Jessore	312	217	Balasore } ...		554
Murshedabad	606	967			
Dinajpur	......	28	Hazaribagh	315	334
Rajshahye	......	143	Lohardagá	828	......
Rangpur	......	183	Singhbhum	156	474
Bogra	......	219	Manbhum	103	11,121
Pabna	564	701	Tributary States ...	......	391

Korabania, a synonym for Korá in Western Bengal.

Korait, a synonym for Goráit.

Koránch, a title of Koiris and Kándus in Hazaribagh, said to refer to the mythical island Kraunchdwip; a section of Bábhans and of Awadhiá Hajjáms in Behar; also a sub-caste of Halwais and Kándus.

Korángi, a *thar* or sept of the Das-Gurung sub-tribe of Gurungs, having derived its name from Koren, a place in Tibet.

Korankárk, a *pur* or section of Sákadwipi Brahmans in Behar.

Korár, a sub-caste of Chamárs in Behar.

Koriár, a section of Koránch Kándus in Behar.

Korisá, a *mul* or section of the Chhamuliá Madhesiá sub-caste of Halwáis in Behar.

Korla, fig, a totemistic sept of Chiks in Chota Nagpur.

Korwá, a Dravidian tribe of Sarguja, Jashpur and Palamau, who claim to be the original inhabitants of the country they occupy, and whose claim is in some measure borne out by the fact that the priests who propitiate the local spirits are always selected from this tribe. The hill Korwás of Sarguja have the singular legend that they are descended from the scare-crows set up to frighten wild animals by the first men who raised crops in Sarguja, which were animated by the great spirit to save his votaries the trouble of continually making new ones. The male Korwás are described by Colonel Dalton as short of stature, dark-brown in complexion, strongly built and active with good muscular development. Their foreheads are narrow, and the lateral projection of the zygomatic arches very marked. Some of the wilder specimens have black skins, flat faces and projecting lower jaws, while their matted hair has acquired a tawny shade from constant neglect. "The women," says Colonel Dalton, "appear ground down by the hard work imposed on them, stunted in growth, black, ugly, and wretchedly clad, some having only a few dirty rags tied round their persons, and in other respects untidy and unclean. On them falls the double task of labour in the fields and of providing the daily bread for the miserable household.

Origin and appearance.

They have all the burdens, but none of the privileges, of women. The man may follow his instincts as a hunting animal, and bow and arrow in hand search the hills for the meat that his soul loveth; but he, day after day, returns unsuccessful, and in the meantime the woman has been hunting for and digging up wild esculent roots, or cutting wild vegetables, hewing wood, and drawing water, and woe betide her if she has not been more successful than her lord."

Internal structure.

The Korwás appear to be divided into four sub-tribes, the **Agaria-Korwa**, probably a cross with the Agarias, the **Dand-Korwa**, the **Dih-Korwa**, who are settled in regular villages, and the **Paharia-Korwa**, who live in the hills, and are the wildest branch of the tribe. Colonel Dalton mentions that he failed to find among them any tribal distinctions by which restrictions on intermarriage were imposed such as are observed by cognate stocks. I am indebted to Mr. W. H. P. Driver, of Ranchi, for the interesting list of septs given in Appendix I. Most of these, it will be seen, are totemistic. Among the totems we find the tiger, the snake, the parrot, the wild goose, two kinds of eel, a fish, the *kerketa* bird, the mango, myrabolam, unhusked rice, ploughs and pestles used for pounding grain, also a curious group called Muri, alleged to derive its name from the fact of its ancestors having made a *chulha*, out of four skulls, and cooked their dinner on this uncanny sort of fireplace. This is clearly a sept of the nickname type such as are common among the Tibetans, Limbus and the people of the Chittagong Hill Tracts. To what extent the totems mentioned above are taboo to the septs which bear their names is a point on which no certain information is as yet forthcoming. The general tendency is for such prohibitions to fall into disuse, and the only rule about the sept-name that really holds its ground is the rule forbidding marriage within the circle which it defines.

Korwas, says Colonel Dalton, are considered formidable as bowmen, but he was not struck with the accuracy of their aim. Their bows are surprisingly strong, and they use arrows with barbed heads, nine inches long by an inch and a half wide. The feathers are arranged in a spiral, which is supposed to give great steadiness to the flight of the shaft. They make battle-axes from iron of their own smelting, and are very expert in the use of this weapon.

Agriculture.

Their system of agriculture is primitive. They cultivate only virgin soil, resorting freely to fire for the purpose of clearing away the jungle, and changing their homesteads every two or three years as the land becomes exhausted. Rice, vetches, millets, pumpkins, yams, chillies and arrowroot are their standard crops, and they eke out the scanty yield of their fields with a variety of jungle products. Grain they store under ground done up in small packets of leaves, and thus packed they say it will keep for years. They also trade in honey, bees-wax, arrowroot, resins, gum, stick lac and iron.

Religion.

Of their religion little is known. According to Colonel Dalton the Korwas of Sarguja sacrifice only to the spirits of their ancestors, and as this must be done by the head of each family, they have no priests. In Jashpur, on the other hand, Baigas serve them as priests, and the Khuria Rani, a bloodthirsty goddess, dwelling in a cave overhanging a stream, is worshipped with offerings of slain buffaloes and goats. The families of the Dewan of Jashpur and the Thakur of the Kallia estate—the only Korwás who now hold any considerable landed property—affect to have adopted Hinduism and "spurning alliances with the ordinary Korwás have continued inter-breeding for several generations," although "they dare not altogether disown the spirits of the hills and forests that their ancestors adored, and they have each at their head-quarters a Korwa Baiga or pagan priest to propitiate the gods of the race."

Korwár, a sept of Rajputs in Behar.

Koshta, *Máhárá*, a weaving and cultivating caste of Chota Nagpur, who believe their ancestors to have immigrated from Sambalpur, Raijah and Chattisgarh in the Central Provinces. The caste call themselves Máhárá, and the name Koshtá is used only by outsiders. The exogamous sections of the Koshtás are shown in Appendix I. With three exceptions, they appear to be totemistic; but there is nothing to show whether the members of the sections pay any reverence to the totems whose names they bear. As a rule Koshtás marry their daughters after they have attained maturity, and infant marriage is also resorted to occasionally by comparatively wealthy men, who believe that they perform an act of social merit by giving a daughter in marriage before puberty. The marriage ceremony differs little from that in force among the lower classes of Hindus. *Sindurdán* or the smearing of vermilion on the bride's forehead and the parting of her hair is deemed the essential and binding portion. A widow may marry again by the *sagai* ritual, and is expected to marry her late husband's younger brother if one survives him. Divorce is permitted on various grounds. No special formalities are prescribed. A simple declaration before the *panchäyat* that the parties propose to dissolve their marriage is all that is necessary. As a rule the husband is the person who moves, and it is a doubtful point whether a woman is entitled to take steps to obtain a divorce from her husband.

The principal god of the Koshtás is the Gond divinity Dulha Deo, a boy-bridegroom raised to divine honours by reason of his tragic death in the midst of his own bridal procession. There are also many Kavirpanthis, owing, it is said, to the activity of the missionaries of this sect among them of recent years. Koshtás have no Brahmans; the village barber (*náwá*) presides at marriages, and on all other occasions the heads of families are priests unto themselves. Both burial and cremation are in vogue. Members of the Kavirpanthi sect are always buried.

In respect of diet, Koshtás observe most of the rules held binding by middle class Hindus, but they do not consider themselves bound to abstain from strong drink. They eat *pakki* and drink with Brahmans, Rajputs, Khandaits, Kharwas, Jhorás, Ahirs, Kumhars. *Kachchi* they can take only from Gonds and Rantias, a fact which, taken in connexion with their traditions of origin and their worship of Dulha Deo, seems to imply some affinity with the former tribe. It is curious to find that the children of Koshtá men by women of any of the *Jáláoharaniya* castes from whom a Brahman may take water are readily admitted into the Koshtá community.

Kosliá, a section of Goálás in the North-Western Provinces and Behar.

Kosuar, fish, a totemistic sept of Oraons in Chota Nagpur.

Kotá, a sub-caste of Báruis in Bengal; a section of Madhesiá Kándus in Behar.

Kotábándab, a totemistic sept of Juángs in Orissa.

Kotah Kaisi, a small vulture, a totemistic sept of Mundas in Chota Nagpur.

Kotál, *Kotwál*, a small Dravidian cultivating caste of Central Bengal, frequently employed as village watchmen. They believe themselves to be descendants of Guhak Muni, the traditional ancestor of the Chandáls, and it is possible that they may be a branch of that caste separated from the main group by their adopting the profession of *Kotwál* or village policeman. In Murshedabád they are divided into four sub-castes—**Atpárá**, **Dhukursáni**, **Kutabpur**, and **Manoharsáhi**. They have no sections, and regulate their marriages by counting prohibited degrees down to the seventh generation in the descending line. Kotáls marry their daughters by the regular ceremony followed by the lower castes of about their own standing. The binding portion of the rite is *sátpák*, the carrying of the bride seven times round the bridegroom. Polygamy is permitted when a man's first wife is barren, but is rarely resorted to. Neither widow-marriage nor divorce is recognised.

Origin.

Marriage.

By religion the Kotáls are Saiva Hindus, worshipping Káli in the month of Kártik and Dharmaráj in Jaishta. Sasthi and Lakshmi are held in special reverence by their women. Their priests are a low class of Brahmans, who are looked down upon by other members of the sacred order.

Religion.

Their original occupation they believe to be to perform the duties of village watchman, an office for which they sometimes hold small allotments of land rent free. Of late years, however, and especially since the introduction of the Chaukidari Act, they have rather tended to abandon these functions, their place being taken by members of other low castes. As cultivators, they usually hold land as non-occupancy raiyats, or work as agricultural labourers. Their social rank is much the same as that of the Chandáls. Some of them drink spirits, but this practice is by no means universal. For the rest their practice in the matter of diet is very much that of orthodox Hindus in general, and they look down upon the Bágdis and Háris as unclean feeders.

Occupation.

The following statement shows the number and distribution of Kotáls in 1881. The figures for 1872 are included with those of Chandáls.

District.	1881.	District.	1881.
Bardwan	10,324	Rajshahye	4
Bankura	225	Dacca	93
Birbhum	673	Chittagong	3
Midnapur	16	Purniah	113
Hughli	51	Maldah	19
24-Parganas	69	Santál Parganas	580
Nadiya	260	Manbhum	57
Jessore	11	Tributary States	1,463
Murshedabad	1,768		

Kotálipárá, a *samaj* or local group of the Bharadwája *gotra* of Páschátya Baidik Brahmans in Bengal.

Kothádomar, a section of Sonárs in Behar.

Kothipál, a section of the Karan sub-caste of Káyasths in Behar.

Kotoliá, probably a corruption of *Kotwál*, a title of a class of rural policemen who hold allotments of land for keeping watch and ward in the town of Darbhanga, in Behar.

Kotri, a small deer, a totemistic sept of Chiks in Chota Nagpur.

Kotsá or *Korsá*, a *mul* or section of the Chhamuliá Madhesiá and Bhojpuria sub-castes of Halwáis in Behar.

Kotsobhni, a *mul* or section of the Naomuliá or Majraut sub-caste of Goálás in Behar.

Kotwal, *Kotál*, a *pangat* or section of Bánsphor Doms and Dosadhs in Behar; a title of the Bágdi, Chandál, Hári, and other castes in Bengal employed as chaukidars.

Kotwál, a synonym for Dámi.

Kotwár, a title of Khandáits and Rautiás and a sept of Kharwárs in Chota Nagpur.

Kowriar, a sept of Chiks and Kharwars in Chota Nagpur.

Koyá, the wild dog, a totemistic section of Rautiás in Chota Nagpur.

Kraunchdwipi, a division of Brahmans in Behar including Jaisi, Jotkhi or Jotsi, Dákutiá, Bhadariá or Bhareri, Jadwá, Saguniá, Sanicherá.

Krishak, *Krishan*, *Krishi*, a title of those who work in the fields, whether as day-labourers or as cultivators of their own land.

Krishnakándári, a title of Pátnis, *q.v.*

Krishnátreya, a *gotra* or section of the Brahman, Baidya, Káyasth, and Gandhabanik castes in Bengal, and the Jhoras in Chota Nagpur.

Kritanya, a group of Gaura Brahmans in Behar.

Krong Khyungtsa, a sept of Maghs in the Hill Tracts of Chittagong.

Krubchhági, a *thar* or sept of Mangars in Darjiling.

Kshám, a title of Dakshin-Rárhi and Bangaja Káyasths in Bengal.

Kshatri-Sankoch, a synonym for Kochh.

Kshatriya, the warrior caste in the traditional Hindu system. The word is now used mainly as a synonym for Rajput.

Kshem, a title of Dakshin-Rárhi and Bangaja Káyasths.

Kshetragrámi, a *gáin* of the Bharadwája *gotra* of Bárendra Brahmans in Bengal.

Kshir, a sub-caste of Tántis in Bengal.

Kshom, a title of Dakshin-Rarhi and Bangaja Káyasths in Bengal.

Kshuri, razor, a title of Bhandáris in Orissa.

Kuar, a hypergamous division of the Maghaya sub-caste of Barhis in Behar.

Kuardar, a sept of Kharwars in Chota Nagpur.

Kuásanchhá, a *thar* or sept of Khambus in Darjiling.

Kuchal, a section of the Bahánnajáti sub-caste of Khatris in Bengal.

Kuchhainá, a sept of Rajputs in Behar.

Kujhariá, a section of Awadhiá Hajjáms in Behar.

Kujri, a fruit, from which oil is made; a sept of Mundas; a section of Goráits in Chota Nagpur.

Kujur, a fruit, the oil of which is used in anointing horns of cattle at the Sohorai festival; a totemistic sept of Oraons; a section of Goráits.

Kuká, a sept of Rajputs in Behar.

Kukar, a group of the Aoghar sect of Saiva ascetics founded in Guzerat by a Dasnami mendicant named Brahmagiri. See **Aoghar**.

Kukkuti, a *gáin* of the Bátsya *gotra* of Bárendra Brahmans in Bengal.

Kukrar, a *mul* or section of the Kanaujiá sub-caste of Sonárs in Behar.

Kuktáiáre, a sept of the Agniá sub-tribe of Meches in the Darjiling Terai.

Kukur, **Kukura**, dog, a totemistic sept of Mundas in Chota Nagpur.

Kukurbandhá, a *pur* or section of Sákadwipi Brahmans in Behar.

Kukurbans, a sept of Rajputs in Behar.

Kukuriá, a sept of Páns in Chota Nagpur.

Kukurjhampar, a section of Kanaujiá Lohárs in Behar.

Kul, a group of the Bárendra sub-caste of Sunris in Eastern Bengal.

Kulabhi, a *gáin* of the Sándilya *gotra* of Rárhi Brahmans in Bengal.

Kulál, a synonym for Kumhár.

Kulchuliá, a sept of the Suryabansi sub-tribe of Rajputs in Behar.

Kulden, a section of Murmis in Darjiling.

Kulhá, a section of Bábhans in Behar.

Kulhai, a tiger, a totemistic sept of Chiks in Chota Nagpur.

Kulhariá, a sept of the Suryabansi sub-tribe of Rajputs in Behar.

Kulhasia, a sept of Páns in Chota Nagpur.

Kulin, (i) a hypergamous division of Rárhi Brahmans in Bengal attributed to Rájá Ballál Sen, who is said to have instituted similar divisions among the Baidyas and Káyasths. Other Hindu castes below the latter in rank have adopted the same system as they have done in the case of *gotras* or sections; (ii) a hypergamous division of the Paschim Kuliyá Sadgops, including Bhálki, Kánkse, Praharáj, and Siur, and of the Purbba Kuliyá Sadgops in Midnapur, including Biswás, Neogi, and Sur; (iii) a hypergamous group of Chásá-dhobás and Subarnabaniks in Bengal; of Karans in Orissa; (iv) a hypergamous group of Jugis comprising four families—Raghu, Mádhab, Nimái, and Págmal. For a fuller treatment of the subject, see the article on Brahman.

Kulin-rási, a section of Málos in Eastern Bengal.

Kulisá or **Kulkuli**, a *gáin* of the Sándilya *gotra* of Rárhi Brahmans in Bengal.

Kulkhwár, a *mul* or section of the Naiyá caste in Behar.

Kulsreshta, a sub-caste of Káyasths in Behar.

Kulsunri, a sub-caste of Sunris in Behar.

Kulthari Mallik, a section of Kanaujiá Lohárs in Behar.

Kulu or *Kachchhuá*, a section of Khariás in Chota Nagpur.

Kulung, a *thar* or sept of Khambus in Darjiling.

Kulusurhi, a section of Goriá Gowár or Dahiár Goálás in Behar.

Kulwant or **Kulwat**, a sub-caste of Malláhs in Behar.

Kulyá Rishi, a section of Tántis in Bengal.

Kum, a section of Rautiás in Chota Nagpur.

Kumair, a section of Awadhiá Hajjáms in Behar.

Kumár, a section of the Pargah caste in Behar, and of Rautiás in Chota Nagpur; a sub-sept of the Hemrom sept of Santáls.

Kumár or *Komar-Bhág*, a sub-tribe of Mal Páháriyás.

Kumára, a sub-caste of Koiris and a title of Maithil Brahmans in Behar.

Kumbhakár, *Kumár*, a synonym for Kumhár in Bengal.

Kumedwár, a section of Babhans in Behar.

Kumhar, a sept of Mundas in Chota Nagpur.

Kumhár, *Kumár*, *Kumbhakár*, the potter caste of Bengal, Behar, and Orissa. Concerning their traditional parentage there seems to be a wide difference of opinion among the recognised authorities on that subject. Thus the Brahmavaivartta Purána says that the Kumbhakár, or maker of water jars (*kumbha*), is born of a Vaisya

Traditions of origin.

woman by a Brahman father; the Parásara Sanhitá makes the father a Málákar (gardener) and the mother a Chamár; while the Parásara Padhati holds that the ancestor of the caste was begotten of a Tili woman by a Pattikár, or weaver of silk cloth. Sir Monier Williams, again, in his *Sanskrit Dictionary*, describes them as the offspring of a Kshatriya woman by a Brahman. Conjectures of this kind do not pretend to have any historical basis, and their only object is to reconcile the fact that there are many castes with the Brahmanical theory that there are only four. All beyond the canonical number are therefore supposed to have arisen from a complicated series of courses between the original four and their descendants; and if a new caste is formed, it is some one's business to find a mythical pedigree for it. Such pedigrees, however, are not taken very seriously, even by the people most concerned, and stories ascribing the origin of a caste to an act of special creation seem to be quite as popular as traditions of mixed descent. The Kumhárs, for example, say that at the marriage of Siva a water jar (*ghat*) was wanted, but no one knew how to make one. The god therefore took a bead from his necklace and with it created a potter; while with a second he made a woman, who became the potter's wife. This man was the father of all those who work in pottery, and in memory of their creator all potters bear the title Rudra Pál.

Internal structure.

The endogamous subdivisions of the caste are very numerous, and vary a good deal from district to district. In Dacca, for instance, we find the five subdivisions **Bará Bhágiyá, Chhotá Bhágiyá, Rájmahálíá, Khatya,** and **Magi.** The Bará Bhágiyá Kumhárs have separated into two divisions. The first, descended from Tílak Pál, only make black utensils; the second, sprung from Mádhava Pál, like the Chhotá Bhágiyá, only manufacture red. In both sub-castes, again, there is a further grouping into **Lál** and **Sádá,** so called from the custom of wearing red or white clothes at the marriage ceremony.

The Rájmahálíá potters are quite distinct from the **Khatya** Kumhárs on the one hand and the Bengali Kumhár on the other. They originally came from Rájmahál with a member of the Banga Adhikárí family, and having tarried in Dacca for several generations lost caste, while those who subsequently arrived from Hindustán were in their turn likewise degraded. There are about two hundred houses belonging to these potters in Ja'farganj, Sultánganj, Rái Bázár, and Kárwán, suburbs of Dacca, and the caste still speaks a language made up of Hindi and Bengali. Having been settled in Bengal for many years, the clean Ṣúdra castes drink from their water-vessels, while the Ṣúdra Brahman and other servants work for them. The *sráddha,* moreover, is celebrated after thirty days, as with the Nava-ṣákha.

The Khatya, or debased Kumhárs of Dacca, claim to belong to the Maghaiyá potter family of Patna. They drink water from the vessels of the other Kumhárs, and may give water to them, but hold no communication with the Rájmahálíá Kumhárs. None of the other Bengali Ṣúdras, however, admit their equality. In Dacca they are all Nának Sháhís in creed, the Mahant of the Shujá'atpúr

Ákhára being the Guru. Unlike the other sub-castes, they work throughout the month of Baisákh, and on the Dashará make oblations of rice, wheat-flour, clay, and red lead to Mahádeo, their patron deity.

Khatya Kumhárs only work with *chikni-matti*, or potter's earth, manufacturing with the *chák*, or horizontal wheel, long-necked flasks (*suráhí*), lotahs, pipes, water-spouts, balusters (*garádiá*), and toys, but never idols. On the tenth day after death the Kantahá Brahman performs a religious service, at which he tastes the oblation rice. On the following day the *sráddha* is celebrated as among Chaṇḍáls and Ekádaṣí Jogís.

The Magi subdivision is outcasted, having a purohit of its own. Their debasement is referred to the days when the Maghs harried Eastern Bengal, and, entering houses, defiled the inmates. There seems no reason, however, for concluding that these degraded potters are the offspring of Maghs by Kumhár women, as they resemble in every feature the genuine stock of potters.

One of my correspondents in Dacca describes an entirely different arrangement of sub-castes, thus:—**Chhota Bhágiyá, Bikrampuriyá, Jahángirnagariá, Faitábájiá, Bhágaldáspuriá.** The last four names have a purely local significance. Jahángirnagar is the old name of Dacca, and its derivative is applied to the potters of the city; Faitábáj is the name of a *pargana*, and Bhágaldáspur is a village in Bhowál. It appears, however, that these groups are not invariably endogamous, and that intermarriages between them are not absolutely prohibited. At present, then, they cannot certainly be ranked as sub-castes; and it is possible that they are merely organizations for trade purposes. Dr. Wise mentions that in the city of Dacca the Kumhárs have two *dals*, or trade unions—one known as Islámpúr, the other as Bhágalpúr, after two quarters of the city where the potters chiefly reside; while outside the city every four or five villages have a *dal* to promote the interests of the trade. The headman is styled Parámánik, who, on account of the increase in the size of the caste, is obliged to employ assistants, Náiks or Gumáshtas. They are treated with little deference, and merely execute the orders of their master.

The four sub-castes found in Noakhali—**Bhuláiya, Sarállá, Chátgáinyá**, and **Sandwipá**—appear to be based on differences of original habitat. In Pabna five sub-castes have been formed—**Sirasthán, Májhásthán, Chandansára, Chaurási**, and **Daspárá**. The first are believed to have come from the North-Western Provinces, and are said to be descended from Premánanda, third son of the original potter, Rudra Pál. Their habits are supposed to be unclean, and Brahmans will not take water from their hands. The Daspárá are said to be descended from Kulávanda, the eldest of Rudra Pál's sons. The Chaurási, according to local tradition, were originally a branch of the Chandansára sub-caste, who settled among the Daspárá, but were not admitted by them to equal social rights. The immigrants waited their time, and took the first opportunity which offered of righting themselves. When the Nawáb of Murshedabad chanced to be travelling in that part of the country, they presented to him a number of artificial flowers and fruits made of pottery. The imitation was so exact that in reward for their skill the Nawáb gave the settlers eighty-four villages, and permitted them to call themselves by the title Chaurási. From that time their social supremacy was secured, and they were able to impose upon the Daspárá sub-caste the condition that only those who admitted the superiority of the Chaurási should hold the title **Parámanik**; that those who served them with *pán* at marriage and social ceremonies should be called **Pánpátra**; and that those who still insisted on holding aloof should be degraded to the lowest rank under the designation **Mujgarni**.

In Murshedabad and Hughli the sub-castes **Bárendra** and **Rárhi** are met with, the theory being that the original settlements of each group were in the large tracts of country whose name it bears. Some, however, say that the Bárendra Kumhárs are descended from one of the sons of Rudra Pál, who had forcible intercourse with his own sister. The Daspárá sub-caste is also known in Murshedabad, where it is believed to be the offspring of one of Rudra Pál's sons by a maid-servant. Its special function is supposed to be the manufacture of the shell bracelets which are worn by married women. The Jessore sub-castes appear to be only local.

In Behar, Chota Nagpur, and the Santál Parganas a wholly different set of sub-castes is met with. The **Maghaiya**, **Kanaujiá**, and **Tirhutiá** are named after large tracts of country; the **Ayodhiábási** claim to be immigrants from Oudh; the **Bangáli** or **Rárhi** are Bengal Kumhárs who have settled in Behar; and the **Turk-Kumhár** are Mahomedans. Of the rest, the **Biahut** forbid widows to marry again, and the **Chápuá** take their name from a particular kind of earthen vessel which they make.

The Kumhárs of Orissa are divided into two endogamous sub-castes—**Jagannáthi** or **Uriya Kumhárs**, who work standing and make lagre earthen pots, and **Khatya Kumhárs**, who turn the wheel sitting and make small earthen pots, cups, toys, etc. The latter are immigrants from Upper India, whose number is comparatively insignificant.

Exogamy.

In the matter of exogamy the practice of Kumhárs differs widely in different parts of the country. In Eastern Bengal, where the influence of Mahomedan usage is strong, only one or two sections are known to the caste, and marriage within the section is permitted. The Maghaiyá Kumhárs, on the other hand, and probably most of the Behar sub-castes, have a long array of sections, mainly of the titular type, but referring in some instances to local and territorial areas. A man may not marry a woman of his own section or of the sections to which his mother, paternal grandmother, or maternal grandmother belonged. The Jagannáthi Kumhárs of Orissa, who hold a tolerably high social position in that province, are subdivided for matrimonial purposes into the following exogamous sections:—**Kaundinya**, tiger; **Sarpa**, snake; **Neul**, weazel; **Goru**, cow; **Mudir**, frog; **Bhad-bhadriá**, sparrow; **Kurma**, tortoise. The members of each section express their respect for the animal whose name the section bears by refraining from killing or injuring it, and by bowing when they meet it. The entire caste also abstain from eating, and even go so far as to worship, the *sál* fish, because the rings on its scales resemble the wheel, which is the symbol of their craft. The Khatya Kumhárs in Orissa have only one section (Kásyapa), and thus, like the Rájbansis of Rangpur, are really endogamous in spite of themselves. The reason probably is that there are too few of them in Orissa to fit up a proper exogamous system, and they content themselves with the pretence of one. Both sub-castes appear to be conscious that the names of their sections are open to misconception, and explain that they are really the names of certain saints, who being present at Daksha's horse sacrifice transformed themselves into animals to escape the wrath of Siva, whom Daksha, like Peleus in the Greek myth, had neglected to invite. It may well be that we owe the preservation of these interesting totemistic groups to the ingenuity of the person who devised this respectable means of accounting for a series of names so likely to compromise the reputation of the caste. In the case of the Khatya Kumhárs, the fact that their single section bears the name of Kásyapa, while they venerate the tortoise (*kachhap*), and tell an odd story by way of apology for the practice, may perhaps lend weight to the conjecture, in itself a fairly plausible one, that many of the lower castes in Bengal who are beginning to set up as pure Hindus have taken advantage of the resemblance in sound between *kachhap* and *kasyap* (*chh* and *s* both become *sh* in colloquial Bengali) to convert a totemistic title into an eponymous one, and have gone on to borrow such other Brahmanical *gotras* as seemed to them desirable. If, for example, we analyse the matrimonial arrangements of the Bhars of Manbhum, many of whom are the hereditary personal servants of the pseudo-Rajput Rájá of Pachete, we find the foregoing conjecture borne out by the fact that two out of the seven sections which they recognise are called after the peacock and the *bel* fruit, while the rest are eponymous. But this is an exceptionally clear case of survival, and I fear it is hardly possible to simplify the diagnosis of non-Aryan castes by laying down a general rule that all castes with a section bearing the name Kásyapa, who have not demonstrably borrowed that appellation from the Brahmans, are probably offshoots from some non-Aryan tribe.

Marriage.

In Behar, Orissa, and Chota Nagpur Kumhárs still permit girls to be married as adults, though they hold infant-marriage to be more respectable. In Singbhum and the Tributary States of Orissa adult-marriage is the rule. The Kumhárs of Bengal, on the other hand, have long conformed to the usage of the higher castes, and marry their daughters before the age of puberty.

Everywhere a bride-price (*pan*) is paid to the father of the bride, and in determining the amount of this the comparative social position of the parties is not usually taken into consideration. "It is considered," says Dr. Wise, "a dishonouring act for a Kumhár to accept a wife without paying money to the father. Of late years the price has risen so much that the poorer young men find it difficult to procure wives at all." One of my correspondents says, indeed, that it ranges from Rs. 300 to Rs. 1,000, but I am inclined to suspect some exaggeration here. There are, however, signs of the development of a system of hypergamy, modelled on the Kulinism of the higher castes, which may lead in time to the conversion of the bride-price into a bridegroom-price. The Parámánik, Pánpátra, and Mujgarni groups mentioned above seem on the way to become hypergamous; and I am informed that a Kumhár of Bikrampur in Dacca would, within that district at any rate, be able to obtain a higher price for his daughter than would be paid to a member of another group. The marriage ceremony is of the orthodox type; the essential and binding portion of the ritual is usually *sindurdán*, or smearing vermilion on the bride's forehead and the parting of her hair. The Jagannáthi Kumhárs of Orissa regard the knotting together of the clothes of the married couple as the most important feature in the ceremony. This is done by a Brahman after the offering of *hom* has been made. The Khatya Kumhárs follow much the same ceremony, but substitute for *hom* the worship of the goddess Bindubásini.

Polygamy is permitted to the limited extent that a man may take a second wife if his first wife has not borne him a son. Some say that he can only do so if the wife gives permission. It is certain, however, that polygamy is not much in vogue. Widow-marriage and divorce are not recognised by the Kumhárs of Bengal, who adhere strictly to the customs of the higher castes on these points. In Behar, Chota Nagpur, and Orissa a widow of any but the Biáhut sub-caste may marry again by the *sagai* or *chumauná* form, and is not ordinarily[1] restricted in her choice by any positive obligation to marry her deceased husband's younger brother should such a relative exist. Divorce is permitted on the ground of unchastity, with the sanction of the *panchâyat* of the caste. In Orissa the finding of the *panchâyat* is usually recorded on a palm-leaf, and the woman is allowed maintenance for six months. Divorced women are looked upon as degraded, but are permitted to marry again by the same ritual as widows.

Religion.

Notwithstanding their alleged descent from the god Siva, Vaishnavism seems to be the favourite religion of the caste. In Eastern Bengal, Dr. Wise states that Kumhárs still worship the ancient Vedic deities Agní, Brahma, Indra, and Pavana, and on the first of Jaishtha (May-June), at the termination of the idle month, special services are held in their honour, at the same time as the festival of Viswa-Karmá is celebrated. With this exception, their religious observances in Bengal and Behar do not appear to differ materially from those of other Hindu castes of similar social standing. In Orissa Rádhá, Krishna, and Jagannáth are the deities most revered by the Uria Kumhárs. The Khatya Kumhárs, on the other hand, in Cuttack, as in Dacca, profess to follow the precepts of Guru Nának, while at the same time they worship Durgá under the name

---

[1] In Singbhum she is expected to marry her deceased husband's younger brother.

of Bindubásini. Among the Uria Kumhárs, Rudra Pál, the mythical ancestor of the caste, is worshipped as a sort of patron saint. His image is placed between the images of Rádhá and Krishna in the Bhagwat gadi, or room set apart for the reading of the sacred books of the Vaishnava sect, and on the *Sukla Sasti*, the sixth day of the new moon of the month of Aghrán, fried paddy, plantains, cocoanuts, and similar offerings are presented to him. A Brahman recites *mantras*, or mystic invocations, and receives as his perquisite the articles offered to Rudra Pál. This festival is called Ohran Sasti. The Khatya Kumhárs pay a similar tribute to **Kunwár**, whom they regard as their ancestor, in the month of Srában. **Sitalá**, the goddess of small-pox, is worshipped in the same month, and Chaitra is regarded as sacred to the tutelary goddess Bindubásini. **Kunwár** is revered in Behar as the chief of the **Gáián**, or spirits of departed Kumhárs, who exercise some vague sort of influence over human affairs, and have to be appeased by periodical sacrifices of goats and sweetmeats, which are afterwards divided among the members of the caste who attend at the ceremony. The snake goddess **Bisohari**, **Sokhá**, **Sambhunáth**, Bandi, Goraiyá, and the Pánch Pir, also rank among the minor deities of the caste, and are worshipped four times a year, in the months of Mágh, Phálgun, Baisákh, and Sráwan. In Chota Nagpur the religion of the caste seems to be of a more primitive type. Although professing Hinduism and worshipping in a general way all the gods of the regular pantheon, they also offer goats, molasses, ghi, and milk to the mountain gods **Káná Buru**, **Máthá Buru**, and **Kánki Buru**, who are reverenced by the non-Aryan tribes. On the occasions of this worship Brahmans officiate as priests and take the offerings. It might perhaps be argued that the cult is a genuine survival, indicating that the Kumhárs of that part of the country are merely an offshoot from a non-Aryan tribe; but I think it equally possible that we have to deal with mere imitation, encouraged by the desire to appease the local gods.

On the first of Baisákh the Bengal Kumhárs put an image of the god Siva on their wheel (*chák*), and leave the wheel unturned during the whole month. On the thirtieth day Siva is formally worshipped, and his effigy is thrown into a river or tank. The wheel is then again brought into use. Viswakarmá, the artificer of the gods, is worshipped on the last day of Paus. All the implements of the potter's craft are laid before him, and offerings of fruits, sweetmeats, and the like are presented.

For the service of the greater gods Kumhárs, like other members of the Nava-Sákha group, employ Brahmans, who are for the most part received on equal terms by other members of the sacred order, although less esteemed than those Brahmans who themselves serve Brahmans only.

Disposal of the dead.

The dead are burned by all except the very poor, who cannot afford the wood for the funeral pyre. The Kumhárs of Bengal and Orissa perform the ceremony of *sráddh* on the thirtieth day after death, in much the same fashion as the higher castes. Among the Kumhárs of Behar and Chota Nagpur and the Khatya Kumhárs of Bengal and Orissa, the Kanthá Brahman celebrates a religious service and tastes the oblation rice on the tenth day after death, and the regular *sráddh* is performed on the eleventh day. Some, however, say the thirteenth, and it is possible that the practice may differ in different parts of the country. Libations (*tarpan*) for the benefit of ancestors in general are poured forth in the month of Aswin every year.

Social status.

The social standing of the caste is respectable. In Bengal they are recognised as members of the Navasákha group, and in Behar and Orissa Brahmans take water from their hands. The Jagannáthi Kumhárs of Orissa, though professing Vaishnavism and deeming it praiseworthy to abstain from the flesh of any living creature, nevertheless eat goats which have been sacrificed to the gods, deer, wild boars, and all fish except the *sál*. They also partake of the leavings of Brahmans, and at the *mahotsab*, or sacred feast of the Vaishnava sect, they will eat cooked food with Khandáyats. Orh-Chásás, Guriás, Chhutárs, Kámárs, Goálás, Telís, Nápits, and Tántis. On no other occasion will they eat with, or take water from, a man of a caste lower than Teli. Smoking from a hookah is governed by the rule about water, but cigars may be taken from any one. Khatya Kumhárs eat goats and all kinds of scaly fish, and also the leavings of Nának Sháhi priests. Neither sub-caste permits the use of strong drink. In Bengal the Kumhárs eat sacrificial animals—deer, ducks, geese, and pigeons. Boiled rice they take only from Brahmans; water and sweetmeats from members of the Nava-Sákha group. The Kumhárs of Behar eat cooked food and smoke only with their own caste, but take sweetmeats and water from Koiris, Gangotas, and the large group of castes from whom a Brahman may take water. Goat flesh and mutton, and all kinds of fish except the *bagár*, are lawful food. Strong drink is also indulged in, but it is thought more respectable to abstain.

Occupation.

In Dacca, says Dr. Wise, the manufacture of pottery is still in its infancy, and no improvement can be looked for so long as the obligation of breaking all cooking utensils after a death, or any sort of ceremonial polution, limits Hindus to the use of the cheapest kinds of pottery. The wheel in use is the Roman rota, a circular table of baked clay weighted along the rim, revolving rapidly on a pivot cut from the heart of a tamarind tree. The neck and shoulders of all globular vessels are made with the wheel (*chák*), but the body is fashioned by hand, often by women. A round ball of hardened clay (*boilá*) is held inside, while with a wooden mallet (*pitná*) the material is beaten from the outside into the requisite shape and thinness. Two kinds of earth are used by the Dacca Kumhárs: one called *báli*, the other *kála mattí;* and one part of the former mixed with two of the latter are employed in the production of the strongest pottery. For making the common red earthenware vessels red laterite earth from Bhowál is used, the colour of the rim being deepened by coating it with a mixture of catechu (*kath*) and fuller's earth. The cheap red and black earthenware are both prepared with the same clay, the latter being blackened by covering up the kiln at a certain stage and adding oil-cake to the fire. Bengali potters cannot glaze or fix the colours on the ware, but are content to paint the vessel after it has been baked. Their colours are always mixed with mucilage, obtained from *bela* or tamarind seeds. Red paints are prepared with red lead; yellow with arsenic (*hartál*); green by mixing yellow arsenic and indigo; and black with lamp-black, charred rice, or *nal* reeds. A gloss is often imparted with the white of duck's eggs, but as this washes off before long, *garjan* oil is more generally used. Idols, toys, and tobacco-bowls are also painted with these colours, and the images of deities are further embellished by having powdered mica sprinkled over them while the paint is still wet. The Dacca Kumhárs manufacture bricks, tiles, earthenware of all shapes and sizes, idols, and toys; the two last being moulded if of small size.

The manufactory of the Kumhár well repays a visit. Beneath the same thatched roof are the kiln, storehouse, and dwelling-house, while at the door the clay is prepared. The kiln is called the *pan*, from the Sanskrit Pavana, that which purifies, and the hut the *panghar*. The kiln is divided into compartments, in which the newly-made vessels are arranged, earth being heaped over all. Wood is never used to heat it, but grass, reeds, or bamboo stems are the ordinary combustibles.

Although Kumhárs are prohibited from using the *chák* during the month of Baisákh, because Viswakarmá, the great artificer, rested from his labours during that month, they are permitted to dig and store clay. A potter never cultivates the soil or serves as a domestic servant, but he has no objections to become a trader, a cloth merchant, a writer, or a servant to a shopkeeper. The village potter occasionally holds chákarán land, on the condition that he supplies the vessels required at all festivals observed by the zamindár or the village community. Hindu households generally contract for their annual supply of earthenware, while a few pay the market rate for what is wanted. The pottery made at Rái Bazár, in Dacca, bears a great name throughout Eastern Bengal, and in the cold season boats laden with cocoanuts arrive from Sondíp, Noakhali, and Bárganj, returning full of pots and pans from this mart. Vijayapur, in Tipperah, is another bazár famous for the excellence of its pottery.

Rájmahāliá Kumhárs have a curious custom, which is a source of much wit among Bengalis. They thatch the drying houses with green grass, merely fastening it down with weights, but never tying it, and when dry the thatch is used for lighting the kiln fire. They manufacture cooking pots for vegetables, milk-pans (*ras-dohana*), and salvers on which sweetmeats and other delicacies are handed round at weddings, but will not make idols or platters used in offerings to deities.

Like the Bengali Kumhárs, they do no work during the month of Baisákh, and on the first Saturday of that month celebrate the worship of Viswakarmá. They work double during the previous month Chaitra, and it is lawful to bake the pottery in Baisákh. At the time of worship their trade implements and manufactures are arranged on the top of the kiln and ornamented with *bel* leaves, while the usual oblations are presented. The purohit, meanwhile, mutters a few incantations, soliciting the favour of the divine workman. Once a year, when the kiln is filled, the caste Brahman officiates at the Agni Pujá. Offerings are made of rice, plantains, cocoanut, sweetmeats, and a piece of cloth.

The wives of these Kumhárs assist their husbands, fashioning the globular part of the vessels, while the men make the necks and rims. Kumhárs are singular in placing over their wells an earthenware rim or *chák*, admirably suited for preventing the ingress of filth. It is made by themselves, but has not been adopted by any other class.

The foregoing description of the occupation of the potter caste is substantially correct at the present day. Kumhárs, however, are not so exclusively devoted to their characteristic profession as Dr. Wise makes them out to be. In Orissa some of them follow the trade of carpenters and bricklayers, and everywhere a certain proportion of the caste is engaged in agriculture. This, however, is a comparatively recent departure, and few of them have risen above the status of tenure-holders or occupancy raiyats. Cultivating Kumhárs still regard the *chák* as the symbol of their caste, and brand their cattle with a rude representation of it. In Chota Nagpur the Maghaiya Kumhárs are looked down upon by the Kanaujia sub-caste because they castrate bullocks.

The following statement shows the number and distribution of Kumhárs in 1872 and 1881 :—

District.	1872.	1881.	District.	1872.	1881.
Bardwan	19,947	13,020	Tipperah	10,945	9,705
Bankura	4,518	7,992	Chittagong	3,826	6,423
Birbhum	7,583	8,892	Noakhali	3,518	4,640
Midnapur	29,122	30,650	Patna	20,581	24,069
Hughli	14,872	9,688	Gya	25,868	22,282
Howrah		5,712	Shahabad	18,931	23,814
24-Parganas	16,474	12,036	Tirhut { Mozufferpur ...	48,030	33,408
Nadiya	20,420	15,855	Tirhut { Darbhanga ...		25,241
Khulna	......	9,332	Saran	21,911	24,594
Jessore	22,022	19,335	Champaran	17,151	18,807
Murshedabad	11,278	10,487	Monghyr	20,361	31,007
Dinajpur	6,408	5,319	Bhagalpur	25,669	35,939
Rajshahye	7,856	6,999	Purniah	11,912	18,732
Rangpur	6,769	6,063	Maldah	3,804	5,908
Bogra	3,748	3,710	Santál Parganas	14,765	21,419
Pabna	10,202	9,841	Cuttack	16,812	22,268
Darjiling	342	687	Puri	9,666	13,135
Jalpigori	3,215	1,892	Balasore	10,589	12,681
Kuch Behar	......	1,101	Tributary States	16,559	26,553
Dacca	14,835	17,378	Hazaribagh	14,058	21,966
Faridpur	8,196	10,783	Lohardaga	15,589	19,579
Bakarganj	13,748	9,540	Singbhum	7,145	6,882
Maimansinh	19,323	18,618	Manbhum	24,391	32,844
			Tributary States	4,508	9,099

Kumhariá, a section of the Banodhiá and Jaiswár Kalwárs in Behar; a sept of Chiks in Chota Nagpur.

Kuna, a stone quarry, a title of the Karangá caste in Singbhum.

Kunbáhong, a sept of Limbus in Darjiling.

Kunbi, a synonym for Kurmi.

Kunchbandhwá, a maker of the *kas-kas* brushes (*kunch*), used by weavers to smooth the threads of the warp before it is put into the loom. The occupation is usually followed by Nats and by Mahomedans, who combine with it the castration of cattle.

Kundail, a sept of Rajputs in Behar.

Kundalál, a *gáin* of the Sábarna *gotra* of Rárhi Brahmans in Bengal.

Kundárk, a *pur* or section of Sákadwipi Brahmans in Behar.

Kundi, a section of Awadhiá Hajjáms in Behar.

Kundiar, a section of Kurmis in Chota Nagpur and Orissa; a section of Mahilis in Western Bengal.

Kundil, a section of Rautiás in Chota Nagpur.

Kundkar, a turner, denoting more particularly workers in horn, who are always Mahomedans. The Kundkar makes combs, pegs for shoes, small boxes (*dibiya*) for keeping medicines and various odds and ends. They despise the Kasai and the Kuti and decline to intermarry with them.

Kundri, a vegetable used in making curry, a totemistic sept of Oraons in Chota Nagpur.

Kundu, *Kunda*, a title of Aguris, Gandhabaniks, Kaibarttas, Káyasths, Tántis, Telis, Sánkháris, Sutradhars, and certain other castes in Bengal.

Kundula, a sept of Mundas in Chota Nagpur.

Kunjakuli, a section of Páns in Chota Nagpur.

Kunjalwár, a section of Bábhans in Behar.

Kunjasiri, a section of Páns in Chota Nagpur.

Kunjilwár-Malangiá, a *mul* of the Kátyáyan section of Maithil Brahmans in Bengal.

Kunjilwár-Sater, a *mul* of the Kátyáyan section of Maithil Brahmans in Behar.

Kunjilwár-Ullu, a *mul* of the Kátyáyan section of Maithil Brahmans in Behar.

Kunjilwár-Bhakrain, a *mul* of the Kátyáyan section of Maithil Brahmans in Behar.

Kunjilwár-Digaun, a *mul* of the Kátyáyan section of Maithil Brahmans in Behar.

Kunjilwár-Bhakhrauli, a *mul* of the Kátyáyan section of Maithil Brahmans in Behar.

Kunjrá, a greengrocer who sells *tarkári* and *sabji*—an occupation usually, but not exclusively, followed by Mahomedans in Behar. In Dacca, according to Dr. Wise, Kunjra is used as a term of abuse, and the fruit sellers call themselves Mewa-farosh, Sabzi-farosh or Bepári.

Kunkál, a title of Kumhárs.

Kunot, a sub-caste of Gonrhis in Behar.

Kuns, a section of Binjhiás in Chota Nagpur.

Kuntiá, a sept of Hos in Singbhum.

Kunwar, a section of Bháts.

Kunwardár, a section of Cheros in Chota Nagpur.

Kurá, a sept of Chakmás in the Hill Tracts of Chittagong.

Kurái, a *pur* or section of Sákadwipi Brahmans in Behar; a sept of Páns in Chota Nagpur.

Kurál, a title of Kaibarttas in Bengal.

Kurambi, a synonym for Kurmi.

Kurga, a sub-caste of Karangas in Western Bengal who are employed in making bamboo baskets.

Kuri, a sub-caste of Dosádhs who make their living as bird-catchers, and occasionally as pedlars. A synonym for Mayará, Madhukuri, or Madhunápit, *q.v.*

Kurin, a sub-caste of Dosádhs and Gonrhis in Behar; of Malláhs in Behar, usually employed as boatmen.

Kurisarjan, a subdivision of the Meches, also called Mechkuri, who sell oil.

Kurji, a section of Goálás in Behar.

Kurjya, a sept of Chakmás in the Hill Tracts of Chittagong.

Kurkuti, red ant, a totemistic sept of Mundas in Chota Nagpur.

Kurki Dholiar, a *thar* or sept of Dámis in Darjiling, the members of which are drummers by profession.

Kurma, tortoise, a totemistic section of Jagannáthi Kumhárs in Orissa.

Kurmi, *Kunbi, Kurambi*, a very large cultivating caste of Upper India, Behar, Chota Nagpur, and Orissa. Their origin is obscure, and their meagre traditions throw no light upon the subject, being for the most part mythological tales of a trivial character, or legends relating to recent migrations of comparatively small sections of the caste. Writing of the Kurmis of Behar, Buchanan classes them among the "aboriginal Hindu nations that were not of sufficient consequence to be admitted into the order of Kshatris, but too powerful to be thrust into the dregs of impurity."[1] In another place he mentions as not wholly untenable the opinion that the Kurmis of Gorakhpur are the same as the Thárus, adding, however, that the Kurmis strenuously deny the connexion, they being nearly as pure as the Ahirs.[2] The only evidence in support of this view seems to be the fact that the title Dhelphor, or 'clod-breaker,' given by Buchanan as the name of a Kurmi 'tribe,' is found also among the Thárus. This, however, proves nothing, as the term might obviously be applied to any class of regular cultivators. On the other hand, it is perfectly possible that a branch of the Thárus on taking to settled cultivation may have sought to connect themselves, under the name of Dhelphor Kurmis, with the leading agricultural caste of the Ganges Valley. Sir Henry Elliot,[3] Mr. Sherring,[4] and Mr. Nesfield[5] treat the caste as an accomplished fact, and venture on no conjecture regarding its probable origin. Sir George Campbell, speaking of the Kurmis of Hindustan, says they are on an average darker and less good-looking

Traditions of origin.

[1] *Eastern India*, i, 166.
[2] *Ibid*, ii, 469.
[3] *Races of the North-Western Provinces*, p. 155.
[4] *Hindu Tribes and Castes*, i, 323.
[5] *Brief View of the Caste System*, p. 14.

than Brahmans and Rajputs, but still quite Aryan in their features, institutions, and manners.[1] Colonel Dalton regards them as the descendants of some of the earliest of the Aryan colonists of Bengal—"a brown, tawny-coloured people, of average height, well-proportioned, rather lightly framed, and with a fair amount of good looks. They show well-shaped heads and high features, less refined than Brahmans, less martial than Rajputs, of humbler mien even than the Goálás; but, except when they have obviously intermixed with aborigines, they are unquestionably Aryan in looks. Grey eyes and brownish hair are sometimes met with amongst them. The women have usually small and well-formed hands and feet."[2]

The foregoing description clearly refers only to the Kurmis of Behar, who are on the whole a fine-looking race, though perhaps hardly so Aryan in appearance as Colonel Dalton seeks to make out. The caste bearing the same name in Chota Nagpur and Orissa belongs to an entirely different type. Short, sturdy, and of very dark complexion, these Kurmis closely resemble in feature the Dravidian tribes around them. In Manbhum and the north of Orissa it is difficult to distinguish a Kurmi from a Bhumij or a Santál, and the latter tribe, who are more particular about food than is commonly supposed, will eat boiled rice prepared by Kurmis; and according to one tradition regard them as half-brethren of their own, sprung from the same father, who begot the Kurmis on the elder and the Santáls on the younger of two sisters. The distinct and well-preserved totemism of the caste is noticed at length below.

The question then arises—Are these Kurmis a degraded branch of the Kurmis of Behar and Upper India, or should they be treated as a separate caste formed out of Dravidian elements and owing their name to the accident of their having devoted themselves exclusively to cultivation? Colonel Dalton does not distinctly commit himself to either view; but it is clear from his account of the caste that he was conscious of the difficulty, and was inclined on the whole to dispose of it by the hypothesis of degradation. This theory, however, fails entirely to account either for the remarkably uniform type of the Chota Nagpur Kurmis or for their totemistic usages. The latter point, however, appears to have been unknown to Colonel Dalton, and might possibly have induced him to change his opinion. Three hypotheses seem to be more or less tenable:— (1) that the class Kurmi is made up of two distinct stocks, the one Aryan and the other Dravidian; (2) that the entire group comes of an Aryan stock, the type of which has been modified to a varying extent by mixture of blood and vicissitudes of occupation; (3) that the entire group was originally Dravidian, but that those portions of it which lay in the track of the Aryan invasion were refined by intercourse with the immigrants, while those who settled in remote parts of the country preserved their primitive type.

---

[1] *Ethnology of India*, p. 92, in *J. A. S. B.*, vol. xxxv, part II.
[2] *Ethnology of Bengal*, p. 320.

Internal structure.

The internal structure of the Kurmi caste is shown in a tabular form in Appendix I. In Behar the chief sub-castes are the following:—**Ayodhiyá** or **Awadhiyá, Chanaur, Ghamelá, Jaiswár, Kachaisá, Ramaiyá, Sanswár.** The Ayodhiya claim to be of the highest dignity and purest blood, coming, as their name indicates, from Oudh, where they are usually cultivators, while in Bengal they often enlist in the native army or serve as constables. The Jaiswár, less punctilious than the Ayodhiyá, are husbandmen, proverbial for industry and skill, who, from indulging in spirits and permitting their widows to marry, are held to be degraded. In Manbhum we find four endogamous groups,—**Kurum, Ádh-Kurmi** or **Madhyam-Kurmi, Sikhariá** or **Chhota-Kurmi,** and **Nich-Kurmi.** The Kurum aver that they are the original nucleus of the entire caste, and explain that the other groups were degraded for eating fowls and drinking spirituous liquor. To these ceremonial offences the Nich-Kurmi add great sexual laxity, and pay little regard to the chastity of young girls before marriage. In the north of Chota Nagpur two sub-castes appear to exist, **Magahiá,** who are supposed to be immigrants from Behar and conform on the whole to Hindu practices, and **Bagsariá** or **Bágsariá,** whose usages are more of an aboriginal type. The latter group is popularly supposed to derive its name from Buxar, in Shahabad; but the traditional reverence with which its members regard the tiger, and the occurrence of the same name as a section among wilder cognate castes, incline me to look upon it as totemistic. There is no evidence whatever in favour of the opinion that this sub-caste came from Buxar, and this notion is merely another instance of the common striving to find a rational explanation of terms the meaning of which has been forgotten. In Orissa we have **Gáysari, Maisásari, Bagsari,** and **Gádásari.**[1] The first two are more Hinduised than the others, and are said to have given up eating pork, fowls, etc. The two lower divisions have no objection to marry into the upper divisions, but such marriages are extremely rare, and entail degradation of the members of the higher groups. The sections in use among the Kurmis of Chota Nagpur and Orissa are purely totemistic, and it will be seen from Appendix I that a large proportion of the totems are capable of being identified. In Behar, on the other hand, the section-names are titular, and the tendency is to discard the primitive rule of exogamy in favour of the more modern system of reckoning prohibited degrees by the formula quoted in the article on Bais. Where the section rule is in force, it is usually held that a man may not marry a woman of his own section, or of the sections to which his mother and his paternal and maternal grandmothers belonged. These facts tell in favour of the theory that all Kurmis are derived from a Dravidian stock: for, if the Behar Kurmis had been originally Aryans, they could have had no motive for discarding their original section-names; whereas a Dravidian tribe intimately associated with Aryans and

[1] Some interpret these names as having reference to the cow, the buffalo, the crane, and a pit or hollow in the ground (*gádá*). I mention the explanation for what it may be worth.

subjected to Aryan influences would certainly be anxious to cast off totemistic designations which would serve only as a badge of social inferiority. It should be observed, moreover, that even in Behar the Kurmis have not risen high enough to establish a claim to use the Brahmanical *gotras*, and have had to content themselves with a titular series of names; while in Bengal they are excluded, on the ground of their Dravidian descent, from the group of castes from whose hands a Brahman can take water.

Marriage.

Among Behar Kurmis the general practice is that girls are married as infants, adult-marriage being resorted to only in those cases where the girl's parents are too poor to conform to the fashion which requires that she should have been provided with a husband before reaching the age of puberty. The ceremony is of the orthodox type, and was formerly followed by an elaborate entertainment given by the bridegroom. In course of time, however, the rivalry of neighbouring families made this a source of such heavy expense that the Kurmis determined to abolish the custom, and now refuse to ask for or to give money on such occasions. In Chota Nagpur and Orissa, though the tendency is on the whole towards infant-marriage, adult-marriage is still in full force, and sexual intercourse between unmarried people is tacitly recognised, it being understood that if the girl becomes pregnant her lover will come forward to marry her before her child is born. In such intrigues the law of exogamy must be strictly observed, and intercourse between members of the same totem is reckoned as incest and punished by expulsion from the caste. The marriage ceremony is of a highly primitive character, and comprises several usages of special interest. After the preliminary negotiations have been completed and a bride-price (*pan*), varying from Rs. 3 to Rs. 9, has been paid to the parents of a girl, an auspicious day for the marriage is fixed on the basis of certain astrological data, which are usually arrived at by consulting a Brahman skilled in such matters. Early on the wedding morning the betrothed pair, each in their own homes, are separately married to trees—the bride to a *mahuá* (*Bassia latifolia*), and the bridegroom to a mango (*mangifera Indica*). This curious rite merits full description. Wearing on the right wrist a bracelet of the leaves of the *mahuá*, the bride walks round the tree seven times, and then sits in her mother's lap on an earthen platform built close to the trunk. While sitting in this position her right hand and right ear are tied to the tree with thread by her elder sister's husband or by some male member of the household, and she is made to chew *mahuá* leaves, which are afterwards eaten by her mother. Last of all, lights are lit round the tree, and it is solemnly worshipped by all present. The same ritual is separately performed by the bridegroom, with the difference that in his case the tree is a mango, and is circled nine times instead of seven. The people who practise this singular ceremony believe that by it all misfortunes of the bride and bridegroom are somehow forestalled and transferred to the tree, which thus acts as a sort of scapegoat. Instances of similar superstitions are given by Tylor and Peschel.[1] It occurs to me,

[1] *Primitive Culture*, ii, 149: *Völkerkunde*, 263.

however, as possible that we may have here a survival of a still more ancient idea—the notion that a virgin, before being married, must be dedicated to some god, who exercises the right to her person, which, int he first beginnings of communal life, is supposed to have been claimed by the tribe.

On the completion of the rite by the bridegroom (the bride, as I have stated, goes through it separately in her own home), his friends form a procession and escort him to the bride's house, the time of starting being arranged so that the party shall arrive in the evening. On reaching the house the bride's people come out to meet the bridegroom, and daub sandal wood paste on his forehead, using the point of an areca nut for this purpose. He is then taken to a wedding canopy made of *sál* branches, where the bride joins him, and both march seven times round a sacred fire represented by an earthen vessel with a lamp burning inside it. Meanwhile the maternal uncles of the bride and bridegroom exchange plates of rice in token of friendship and social intercourse. After circling the fire the wedded pair sit down together on a platform of dried clay built under the canopy, and the bridegroom touches the bride between the breasts with a drop of his own blood, drawn by cutting through the nail of his little finger and mixed with lac-dye. This symbolical transfusion of blood marks the transfer of the bride from her own to her husband's section, and is evidently the original form of the widespread custom of *sindurdán*.

Oddly enough, the next stage of the ritual is *sindurdán*, performed in the ordinary way by smearing vermilion on the bride's forehead and the parting of her hair. At the same time an iron bracelet (*kháru*) is put on the bride's left wrist. This double observance of *sindurdán*, in its original and its derivative form, may probably be accounted for by supposing the latter to have been adopted from the Hindus after its connexion with the former and less civilised practice had been lost sight of. It gives an excellent illustration of the facility with which customs, like myths, pass from tribe to tribe and are adopted by men as the fancy strikes them, without any one taking the trouble to inquire into their original meaning.

The Kurmis of Behar usually employ Brahmans to preside at their marriages and to recite sacred texts (*mantras*) at certain stages of the ceremony. In Chota Nagpur and Orissa Brahmans are not called in: the eldest male of the household, the Láyá of the village, or in some cases the brothers-in-law of the bride and bridegroom, take the leading part in the ritual. In the matter of polygamy the Behar Kurmis profess to hold that a man may only take a second wife in the event of the first being barren; but this rule is frequently transgressed in practice by those who can afford to maintain several wives. In Orissa, again, polygamy appears to be regarded with disfavour, and it is deemed more respectable for a man to have but one wife. The Kurmis of Chota Nagpur, on the other hand, recognise no restrictions at all except those imposed by the standard of living common in the caste.

All Kurmis except the Ayodhiá sub-caste in Behar allow a widow to marry again, and require her to marry her husband's younger brother or younger cousin, even though he be already married, on pain of forfeiting not merely all claims to a share in her husband's property, but also the custody of all children whom she may have had by him. The idea seems to be that she has been bought at a price, and belongs to the family that bought her. If she is perverse enough to fall in love with an outsider, no active measures are taken to prevent her from marrying him, but she may take nothing with her—not even the children begotten on her by her late husband. In some cases she is allowed to retain temporary charge of female children or of infants at the breast; but she is bound to make them over before they attain a marriageable age, in order that her late husband's family may not be deprived of the bride-price payable for the girls. The ceremony in use at the marriage of a widow is comparatively simple, consisting merely of putting on bracelets and applying vermilion, which is touched by the bridegroom and then smeared on the bride's forehead by some of the married women of her own or the bridegroom's family. Others, again, say that this must be done by widows; and in parts of Manbhum the widow has to undergo the indignity of receiving *sindur* from the bridegroom's great toe.

Divorce is permitted, with the sanction of the *panchâyat*, on the ground of the wife's adultery or barrenness, or if the couple cannot get on together. The husband pours some water on the ground or tears a leaf in two to symbolise separation, while the wife must give up the iron ring (*khâru*) which was placed on her wrist at her marriage. Three months' alimony is usually given to the wife. Divorced women may marry again by the same ceremony as widows. The Midnapur Kurmis profess not to allow divorce, and there are symptoms among them of a tendency to abandon widow-marriage.

Inheritance.

In the matter of inheritance Behar Kurmis follow the standard Hindu law; while in Chota Nagpur and Orissa traces of an earlier tribal custom may still be discerned, under which the eldest son gets twice the share of his brothers, and a son by a *bihâi* wife, married as a virgin by the full ceremony, has a similar advantage over sons by *sagai* wives. An actual instance will illustrate the working of the rule. A Kurmi dies leaving three sons and three *khâris* of land; the eldest gets a *khâri* and a half, the two younger three-fourths of a *khâri* apiece. If there were two sons—one by a *bihâi* and the other by a *sagai* wife, the former would get two *khâris* and the latter one. Daughters and daughters' sons are excluded by male agnates, such as cousins; but in Orissa an only daughter may claim something on account of her marriage expenses.

Religion.

The religion of the Behar Kurmis differs little from that of other Hindu castes of similar social standing. Maithil or Tirhutiá Brahmans usually serve them as priests, and are received on terms of equality by other members of the sacred order. By preference they appear to incline rather to Vaishnavism, but votaries of Siva and the Saktis are also found among them. Besides the minor gods ordinarily worshipped in Behar, the members of the Sanswár sub-caste have a special deity of their own, called Mokini Mahato, who is said to have been a Kurmi. I have been unable to ascertain on what grounds he was deified. He-kids are sacrificed to him occasionally, and various kinds of sweetmeats offered, but there appear to be no fixed days for his worship. In Eastern Bengal members of the Ayodhyá sub-caste employ Sakadwipí Brahmans for religious and ceremonial purposes, and have Atit or Vaishnava mendicants for their Gurus. The majority are followers of Kabír, Daryá Dás, or Rámánand. In the same parts of the country the Jaiswár Kurmis favour the Pánch Píriyá creed, eating any animal offered in sacrifice to a Hindu deity, and at the same time keeping the Muharam and fasting during the Ramazan, while a few are followers of Nának Sháh and Kabír.

In Chota Nagpur and Orissa the Kurmis are in a still earlier stage of religious development. The animistic beliefs characteristic of the Dravidian races are overlaid by the thinnest veneer of conventional Hinduism, and the vague shapes of ghosts or demons who haunt the jungle and the rock are the real powers to whom the average Kurmi looks for the ordering of his moral and physical welfare. Chief among these is **Bar-Pahár**, the mountain deity of the Santáls; **Gosain Rái**, perhaps a variant of **Gosain Erá**; **Ghát**, any striking hill pass, such as the Dhangárá Pass, near Chatra, which figures in the early traditions of the caste; **Gároár**, who watches over cows; **Grámeswari**, the patron goddess of the village; **Kinchekeswari**; **Boram-devi**; **Sát-bahani**; **Dakum Buri**, and **Mahámái**. The functions and attributes of these deities are not susceptible of close definition, and the worshippers seem to be conscious of little more than a vague notion that by sacrificing goats, sheep, fowls, etc., and offering libations of rice-beer, certain material calamities, such as disease and bad harvests, may be warded off. In this worship Brahmans usually take no part, and either the head of the household officiates or a professional hedge-priest (*dehari* or *láyá*) is called in; but to this rule there is a curious exception in the Bámanghâti pargana of Moharbhanj, where Brahman priests offer fowls to the goddess Kinchekeswari on behalf of her Kurmi votaries. Jitibáhan, again, a deity whose attributes I cannot ascertain, is said to be worshipped only by women, assisted by degraded Brahmans. In respect of the employment of Brahmans, the practice of the Kurmis of Chota Nagpur and Orissa is by no means uniform. In Midnapur they call in the assistance of Brahmans on all religious and ceremonial occasions, but these priests are held to be degraded by rendering this service, and are not received on equal terms by other members of their own order. In Manbhum, Lohardagá, and Moharbhanj Brahmans assist only in the funeral ceremonies of the caste, and all other religious functions, including marriage, are discharged by the eldest Kurmi who is present at the time. The Moharbhanj Kurmis affect to get their Brahmans from Sikharbhum, and some of these claim to be of the Rárhi sub-caste, though such pretensions would of course not be recognised by the Brahmans of Bengal.

Besides the Bándhná Parab, which is common to them and the Santáls, the Akhan Játrá, or cake festival, deserves notice as being peculiar to the Kurmis.

Festivals.

"On the last day of the month of Pús (in the middle of January), when the granaries are full, the people make cakes in the shape of a double cone, called *gargaria pithá*, put on their best attire, and assemble on a green outside their village, and the young men and women form circles and dance and sing. This is followed by a joust of archery: a cock is thrown up in the air, and this is continued till one of the young men manages to shoot the bird with an arrow. The successful archer is then treated as the hero of the day."[1]

Disposal of the dead.

As a general rule all Kurmis, except the very poor, burn their adult dead, and perform obsequies resembling the regular *sráddh* more or less closely according to the standard of ceremonial purity recognised in the caste. Thus the Jaiswár Kurmis celebrate the *sráddh* on the thirty-first day after death, following herein the traditional period of mourning ordained for the Sudras; the Ayodhiá, claiming higher rank and greater purity of blood, mourn for twelve days only, and perform the *sráddh* on the thirteenth; while the Kurmis of Chota Nagpur and Orissa, like most Dravidians working up to Hinduism, observe the term of mourning laid down for Brahmans, and hold obsequies on the eleventh day. In Gyá unmarried persons of either sex are buried, but this appears to be merely an extension of the common practice of burying children, which is probably traceable to the desire to avoid the expense of cremation. Burial is also resorted to in Chota Nagpur and Orissa in cases where death has been caused by cholera or small-pox, and the body is laid in the grave face downwards, the idea being that the spirits of those who die by a rapid and fatal disease, arising from the malice of a special demon, can be prevented by this device from returning after death and spreading infection among the living.

A Kurmi woman is unclean until three ceremonies have been performed. On the sixth day after birth the *Gulhatti Chhathi* is observed, at which the mother is obliged to drink rice-gruel. On the twelfth day the *Bárahi* is kept, and a feast provided for ten or twelve children. Lastly, on the *Bisái*, or twentieth day, the mother paints the well with red lead, draws water, and is deemed clean.

Social status.

In Behar the social rank of the caste is respectable, and Brahmans will take water from their hands; while they themselves profess to follow the rules of diet which are binding on all respectable Hindus. The Jaiswár sub-caste, however, are supposed in some districts to eat fowls and field-rats. In Chota Nagpur and Orissa their practice is far more lax. By abstaining from beef and pork[2] they have raised themselves a step higher than the Santáls, Oraons, and other non-Hinduised tribes; but the fact that they eat fowls and field-rats, both abominable in the eyes of the orthodox, and indulge freely in spirituous liquors, excludes them from the circle of castes

[1] Dalton's *Ethnology of Bengal*, p. 320.
[2] In Orissa this reform has been adopted quite recently.

from whose hands a Brahman can take water. Their standing in these districts, though not very clearly defined, is sufficiently indicated by the circumstance that in the north of Orissa Magahiyá Kumhárs, Bhuiyás, and Rajwárs are the highest castes who will admit that they can take water and sweetmeats from Kurmis. On the other hand, the Kurmis themselves have some curious prejudices in the matter of food, in which perhaps we may discern traces of the traditional antipathy to Brahmans which distinguishes the Santál. A Kurmi, for example, will not touch food cooked by any Brahman except his own *guru;* while a Kurmi woman will not eat food prepared by her husband's *guru*. Santáls will eat food cooked by a Kurmi, but the Kurmis will not return the compliment, though they will smoke from the same hookah as a Santál, and will take water from his hands. In Eastern Bengal, according to Dr. Wise, Káyasths, but not Brahmans, will drink from a Kurmi's water-vessel and smoke from his hookah.

Occupation.

Agriculture is regarded by the Kurmis as their original and characteristic profession, and no marked tendency to engage in other occupations seems to be traceable among them, although of late years a few have taken to trading in grain. In Behar Kurmis are sometimes employed as personal servants in the households of the higher castes; and this practice, which seems to have been more widely prevalent in Buchanan's time,[1] must have played an important part in the refinement of their physical type. The great majority of the caste are occupancy or non-occupancy raiyats; some have acquired substantial tenures. In Orissa many are *pradháns*, or village headmen, holding service lands; a small proportion make a livelihood as landless day-labourers; while, at the other end of the scale, the few who have risen to be considerable zamindars have managed to transform themselves into Rajputs, and cannot now be recognised as Kurmis. Two instances of this have come to notice. The zamindar of Khelar, in Nayábásán pargana of the Midnapur district, is said to have been a Kurmi, who attempted to reform his brethren by urging them to abandon the custom of widow-marriage, and to give up yoking cows to the plough. His efforts, however, were unsuccessful, and the Khelár family now call themselves Kshatriyas, and strenuously disown all connexion with the Kurmis. Another case is that of the well-known house of Pachet in Eastern Manbhum. The Pachet Rájá claims to be a Go-bansi Rajput, and traces back his ancestry fifty-two generations to a child discovered in the woods by the Kurmis being suckled by a cow. The Kurmis of those parts say they have been there just the same number of generations, and Colonel Dalton seems to have thought that the Pachet people were probably of Kurmi extraction, basing his opinion partly on the coincidence in the number of generations, and partly on the fact that the family cannot rationally trace back their origin out of the district, while there is no particular reason for supposing them to be Bhumij or Munda. Any attempt, however, to account for

[1] *Eastern India*, i, 166.

the fact that hardly any Kurmi zamindars are to be found at the present day must, from the nature of the case, be purely conjectural. The settlement of the caste on the land must have taken place in very early times, and in Manbhum many Kurmis claim even now to hold their lands at a moiety of the current rates of rent, on the ground that they were the original clearers of the soil. Some of these pioneers of cultivation must in the nature of things have developed into zamindars or local Rájás; but on attaining this position they would undoubtedly set up as Rajputs, and in the course of a generation or two would be accepted locally as members of that very heterogeneous group.

Kurmis are excellent cultivators, and a large proportion of the raiyats who grow opium in Behar are drawn from their ranks. They are said, however, to be less painstaking and less skilful in the management of special crops than the Koiris, who show a remarkable talent for spade husbandry and all forms of gardening. Kurmis, on the other hand, are noted for their industry in the management of the staple food-crops, and are particularly successful wheat-growers. To render thanks for the harvest already reaped and garnered, as well as to ensure an abundant crop next season, the Ayodhyá sub-caste annually celebrate a harvest home in the following manner. In the centre of a piece of ground, levelled and plastered for the purpose, a lofty pole is erected, to which the cattle are tethered and made to tread out a portion of the new wheat crop. This being finished, the pole is removed and the hole filled with water, and sweetmeats (*laddu*) consecrated to Mahádeva and Paramesvara, after which a feast of parched barley and various kinds of confectionery is given to the Brahmans of the village. All Kurmis worship the plough at the time of the Dasahará festival.

The following statement shows the number and distribution of the Kurmis in 1872 and 1881:—

District.	1872.	1881.	District.	1872.	1881.
Bardwan	890	2,561	Chittagong	47	105
Bankura	672	11,810	Noakhali	13	3
Birbhum	364	1,591	Hill Tracts	1	27
Midnapur	40,410	45,290	Patna	165,463	194,272
Hughli	} 696	{ 634	Gya	40,826	43,838
Howrah		702	Shahabad	58,540	66,284
24-Parganas	4,275	3,469	Tirhut { Mozufferpur ...	} 142,303	{ 115,117
Nadiya	1,654	2,961	Tirhut { Darbhanga ...		61,060
Khulna	......	493	Saran	101,015	112,570
Jessore	383	544	Champaran	77,641	87,736
Murshedabad	3,222	4,515	Monghyr	33,029	38,610
Dinajpur	400	2,245	Bhagalpur	16,827	30,423
Rajshahye	1,480	2,798	Purniah	5,418	14,578
Rangpur	1,360	4,283	Maldah	1,592	3,995
Bogra	262	56	Santál Parganas	9,777	13,240
Pabna	449	2,338	Cuttack	191	365
Darjiling	260	689	Puri	45	69
Jalpigori	142	368	Balasore	222	5,912
Kuch Behar	......	3,583	Tributary States	11,051	19,810
Dacca	508	2,831	Hazaribagh	45,528	62,144
Faridpur	328	784	Lohardagá	35,688	45,539
Bakarganj	20	137	Singbhum	19,667	9,708
Maimansinh	659	1.723	Manbhum	137,934	168,380
Tipperah	221	372	Tributary States	1,547	14,472

Kurminiá, Karminiá, a sept of Rajputs in Behar.

Kurmuri, a *gáin* of the Bátsya *gotra* of Bárendra Brahmans in Bengal.

Kurnat, a section of Awadhiá Hajjáms in Behar.

Kurno Beheri, a *thar* or sept of Dámis in Darjiling, the members of which are musicians by profession.

Kurram, a sub-caste of Támbulis in Behar.

Kursi, fruit, a totemistic sept of Mundas in Chota Nagpur.

Kuru, the local and popular name of af ragment of the Pardhiá, a hunting sub-tribe of Savars, who are found in the south of pargana Biru in Lohardagá. The Kuru speak a dialect of Mundari, but do not eat or intermarry with Mundas, Kharias or Oraons; marriage is both infant and adult, and the practice of marrying one or both of the parties to a mango tree is in vogue. The *Sarhul* and *Kuram* festivals are observed in spring and autumn.

Kurus eat beef and pork, and it is doubtful whether they can be classed as Hindus at all, though the fact that they will take water, sweetmeats, etc., only from the hands of Brahmans, Rajputs, Rautias, Kharwárs, Jhoras and Khandaits, seems to indicate a desire on their part to rise in the scale of social distinction. For the most part they earn a miserable livelihood by collecting jungle products and watching the crops of their more civilised neighbours. Some, however, have taken to cultivation, and a few are recognised as having acquired *Korkar* rights.

Kurum, a sub-caste of, and a synonym for, Kurmi in Western India, occasionally used in Behar.

Kurumánik, a synonym for Kurmi.

Kurumbár, a sept of the Suryabansi sub-tribe of Rajputs in Behar.

Kurumbhong, the divider of the village, a sept of the Chhothar sub-tribe of Limbus. The founder of this *thar* is said, for reasons not stated, to have divided his village into two parts by drawing a line down the middle.

Kurunkh, a synonym for Oraon.

Kurur, a sub-caste of Muchis in Bengal.

Kusadái or *Saptagrámi,* a sub-caste of Támbulis in Bengal.

Kusal, a *thar* or sept of Newars; a section of Brahmans.

Kusalá, a *gáin* or sub-section of Saptasati Brahmans in Bengal.

Kusári, a *gáin* of the Sándilya *gotra* of Rárhi Brahmans in Bengal.

Kusarpákri, a *mul* or section of the Chhamuliá Madhesiá sub-caste of Halwáis in Behar.

Kusbhabáni, a sept of Rajputs in Behar.

Kusbhansi, a sept of the Chandrabansi division of Rajputs in Behar; a title of Bágdis in Bengal.

Kushihár, a synonym for Arkasiya, *q.v.*

Kusiet, a *mul* or section of the Ghosin sub-caste of Goálás in Behar.

Kusik, a section of Káyasths in Bengal.

Kusmáre-Sabás, a *mul* of the Kásyapa section of Maithil Brahmans in Behar.

Kusmáre-Dhanauli, a *mul* of the Kásyap section of Maithil Brahmans in Behar.

Kusmetiá, *Kusmátiá*, or *Kusputra*, a sub-caste of Bágdis in Western Bengal, said to be named after the *kusa* grass, and apparently totemistic.

Kusro, a sept of Gonds in Chota Nagpur.

Kussum, a fruit, a totemistic sept of Bhuiyás and Kharwars in Chota Nagpur.

Kusuar, fish, a totemistic sept of Lohárs in Chota Nagpur.

Kusum, a sept of Páns in Chota Nagpur.

Kusumbaha, *kussum* flower, a sept of Mundas in Chota Nagpur.

Kusumkali, a *gáin* of the Sándilya *gotra* of Rárhi Brahmans in Bengal.

Kusumni, a tree or its fruit; a sept of Chiks in Chota Nagpur.

Kusuwa, fish, a totemistic sept of Oraons in Chota Nagpur.

Kutabkháni, a *pathi* or hypergamous sub-group of Bárendra Brahmans in Bengal.

Kutabpur, a sub-caste of Kotáls in Chota Nagpur.

Kutabpuri, a sub-caste of Telis in Bengal.

Kutár, a section of Goálás in Behar.

Kutári, *Káthurá* (*Kuthar*, an axe), a degraded sub-caste of Sutradhars who work as carpenters and also deal in lime.

Kutba, a *mul* or section of the Ayodhiá sub-caste of Sonárs in Behar.

Kútí, a subdivision of Mahomedans in Eastern Bengal, deriving their name from the Hindustani *Kútna*, to pound or beat. They are regarded as a most degraded class, it being the popular belief that they joined the ranks of Islám only a few generations ago, while, like all new converts, they are most intolerant, affecting to be more orthodox than their neighbours and regarding foreigners with extreme suspicion. They are either followers of Dúdhú Míyán, or of Maulaví Karámat Alí; and, although punctilious in their religious duties out of doors, cling to many Hindu superstitions. In October they worship the Dhenkí used for husking grain, at the same time making offerings to Lakshmí, the goddess of plenty, and every morning bowing thrice before it; while nothing, according to them, is more ominous of evil than for a stranger to sit down or to rest his foot on it. When small-pox attacks their families the Sítala pújah is observed, the same offerings being made to the goddess as among Hindus.

Kútís are divided into the three following classes, who intermarry and hold social intercourse with each other—Páon Kútí, Háth Kútí, Chutkí Kútí. The Páon Kútí, by far the most numerous, are masons, thatchers, goldsmiths, boatmen, water-carriers, but their principal occupation is husking rice. Bepárí is their ordinary title, while those who are expert at weighing grain are called Kayyál, the equivalent of Dándi-dár, or weighman.

The wives of the Kútí alone among Mussulman women appear unveiled in public, making purchases in the bazár, fetching water from the river, and boiling and husking rice in the open air. Among the richer families the women are expert workers of Kashída cloth, and often take service as wet-nurses. The Páon Kútí have a pancháyat of their own, like any Hindu caste, and a headman called Sardár. The Háth Kútí pound bricks for road metal with an iron pestle or mallet, and makes surkhí for mortar. This subdivision is a small one, and is being gradually absorbed by the first.

According to Buchanan, the Chutkí probably take their name from carrying about samples or a pinch (*chutkí*) of rice to show the quality of the whole, and as all Kútís deal in rice, the designation was applied to them collectively. At the present day the usual occupation of the Chutkí is extracting the kernel of the cocoanut for the manufacture of oil, and polishing the shells to make hookahs.

No respectable Mahomedan will marry, eat, or associate with the Kútí, although they are admitted into the public mosques and buried in the public graveyard. It is a plausible conjecture that the entire Kútí class may be made up of Chandáls converted to Islam, and this view gains some support from the fact that in Eastern Bengal Kútís and Chandáls annually compete in boat races on the popular Shashthí Pújah—a circumstance which would account for their low rank among Mahomedans.

Kutua, a sept of Chakmás in the Hill Tracts of Chittagong.

Kutunjiá, a section of Páns in Chota Nagpur.

Kwinjusa, a sept of Maghs in the Hill Tracts of Chittagong.

Kyabohchá, a *thar* or sept of Sunuwárs in Darjiling.

Kyágchhági, a *thar* or sept of Mangars in Darjiling.

Kyaukmatsa, a sept of Maghs in the Hill Tracts of Chittagong.

Kyaukpiatsa, a sept of Maghs in the Hill Tracts of Chittagong.

W. J.—Reg. No. 4044J—120—3-12-91.

The
Tribes *and* Castes *of* Bengal

by

Herbert Hope Risley

INDIAN CIVIL SERVICE, COMPANION OF THE INDIAN EMPIRE,
OFFICER D'ACADÉMIE FRANÇAISE

ETHNOGRAPHIC GLOSSARY

Vol. 2

(In Two Volumes)

τίς πόθεν εἷς ἀνδρῶν ; πόθι τοι πόλις ἠδὲ τοκῆες ;

ODYSSEY i, 170.

Low Price Publications
2017

First Published 1892
Reprinted in **LPP** 2017

ISBN 10: 81-7536-560-9 (Set)
ISBN 13: 978-81-7536-560-5 (Set)

ISBN 10: 81-7536-562-5 (Vol. 2)
ISBN 13: 978-81-7536-562-9 (Vol. 2)

Published by
Low Price Publications
A-6, 2nd Floor, Nimri Commercial Centre,
Ashok Vihar Phase 4, Delhi 110052 (INDIA)
tel.: +91-11-27302453 fax.: +91-11-47061936
url: www.LPPindia.com e-mail: info@LPPindia.com

Printed at
D.K. Fine Art Press Pvt. Ltd.
Delhi

PRINTED IN INDIA

Official edition, circulated for criticism.

THE

TRIBES AND CASTES OF BENGAL.

By H. H. RISLEY,

INDIAN CIVIL SERVICE, COMPANION OF THE INDIAN EMPIRE,
OFFICIER D'ACADÉMIE FRANÇAISE.

ETHNOGRAPHIC GLOSSARY.

Vol. II.

τίς πόθεν εἰς ἀνδρῶν; πόθι τοι πόλις ἠδὲ τοκῆες;

ODYSSEY i, 170.

CALCUTTA:

Printed at the Bengal Secretariat Press.

1892.

TO THE MEMORY OF

Dr. James Wise,

SOME TIME CIVIL SURGEON OF DACCA,

THIS VOLUME,

EMBODYING IN PART THE RESULTS OF HIS RESEARCHES DURING THIRTEEN

YEARS' RESIDENCE IN EASTERN BENGAL,

IS DEDICATED.

L

Láb, a title of Baniyás, of the Khandiwár sub-caste of Bais Baniyás and of the Oswal Baniyás in Behar.

Lábar, a *gáin* of the Sándilya *gotra* of the Uttar-Bárendra Brahmans in Bengal.

Labnagar Kumet, a section of the Majraut sub-caste of Goálás in Behar.

Lachh, a section of Rautiás in Chota Nagpur.

Ladilá, a section of Bábhans in Behar.

Ladu, a sub-section of the Kautsasa section of Utkal Brahmans in Orissa.

Láek, a section of Utkal or Orissa Brahmans.

Lagdingpá, a *rui* or sept of the Bedtshan-gye sub-tribe of Dejong Lhoris or Bhotias of the south.

Lagmetá, a *mul* or section of the Naomuliá or Majraut sub-caste of Goálás in Behar.

Lagori, a sept of Hos in Singbhum.

Láhá, a title of the Desá sub-caste of Gandhabaniks; of Mayarás, Kaibarttas, and of Subarnabaniks in Bengal.

Láhágot, a *mul* or section of the Naomuliá or Goriá sub-caste of Goálás in Behar.

Lahakpá, a *thar* or sept of Mangars in Darjiling.

Lahaniá, a section of Goálás in the North-Western Provinces and Behar.

Lahati, a section of Newars in Darjiling.

Laher, a sub-sept of the Hemrom and Márndi septs of Santáls.

Laherá, a synonym for Láheri.

Láheri, a group of the Bárendra Goálás in Bengal.

Láheri, a *gáin* of the Sándilya *gotra* and a title of Bárendra Brahmans in Bengal.

Laheri, *Laherá*, a Behar caste engaged in the manufacture and sale of lac bangles (*láh ká churi*). The group is probably a functional one, consisting of members of several different castes who happened to adopt that particular profession. In Behar it is divided into two sub-castes—**Dakhinhá** and **Tirhutiá**—residing respectively north and south of the Ganges. There are two sections,—**Kási** and **Mahuriá**. Prohibited degrees are reckoned by the standard formula calculated to seven generations in the descending line.

Origin and internal structure.

Laheris admit both infant and adult-marriage, but regard the former practice as the more respectable. The ceremony is of the standard type, but no *tilak* is paid to the parents of the bridegroom. Polygamy is resorted to only in the event of the first wife proving barren. Widows are allowed to marry again by the *sagai* form. In such cases it is deemed right and proper for a woman to marry her late husband's younger brother if one has survived him, but she is under no positive obligation to do so. A faithless wife can be divorced by establishing her guilt before a panchâyat. If, however, the offence

Marriage.

has been committed with a member of the caste, it is usually condoned on payment of a fine in the form of a feast given to the heads of the caste. Adultery with an outsider involves instant expulsion from the community.

Inheritance. In deciding questions of inheritance and succession the caste profess to be guided by the Mitákshará, which is the personal law of most Hindus in Behar. Disputes, however, rarely go beyond the pancháyat, a highly primitive tribunal, which cannot be credited with very precise knowledge of the written law. To this circumstance, no doubt, we owe the preservation among their scanty customs of the usage known in the Panjáb as *chundávand*, by which the sons, however few, of one wife take a share equal to that of the sons, however many, of another. In applying this rule no distinction is drawn between the status of the wives, and the sons of a wife married by the *sagai* form get the same share as the sons of a woman who was married as a virgin by the regular ceremony.

Religion. Laheris consider themselves to be orthodox Hindus, and regard Bhagavati as the deity whom they are more especially bound to worship. Tirhutiá Brahmans serve them as priests, and do not suffer in social esteem by so doing. Their functions, however, extend only to attendance at marriages and watching over the observances due to the greater gods of the Hindu Pantheon. The minor deities, Bandi and Goraiyá, are worshipped by the heads of families themselves without the assistance of Brahmans. Goats, wheaten cakes, milk, and sweetmeats form the usual offerings, which are afterwards eaten by the members of the household.

Social status and occupation. In point of social standing the Laheris rank with Koiris and Kurmis, and Brahmans will take water from their hands. Besides their original occupation of making lac bracelets, many of them are engaged in cultivation as occupancy raiyats. As a rule, however, they will not guide the plough with their own hands, and none of them are found in the lower grades of the agricultural system.

The following statement shows the number and distribution of the Laheri caste in 1872 and 1881:—

District.	1872.	1881.	District.	1872.	1881.
Bardwan	333	158	Tirhut { Mozufferpur...	6,643	2,212
Bankura	28	8	Tirhut { Darbhanga ...		2,673
Birbhum	98	149	Saran	617	324
Midnapur	206	15	Champaran	1,273	995
Hughli	246	24	Monghyr	1,995	2,209
24-Parganas	282	......	Bhagalpur	1,306	1,046
Nadiya	30	205	Purniah	501	708
Khulna	......	103	Maldah	163	......
Murshedabad	274	81	Santál Parganas ...	11	393
Dinajpur	98	74	Cuttack	4,656	3
Pabna	5	......	Puri	1,879	......
Dacca	2	79	Balasore	1,018	39
Faridpur	353	153	Tributary States ...	914	......
Tipperah	6	826	Hazaribagh	......	884
Noakhali	18	2	Lohardagá	......	1,430
Patna	1,424	1,081	Singbhum	......	9
Gya	2,651	714	Manbhum	......	99
Shahabad	243	24	Tributary States ...	......	65

Lah-ogpá, dwelling below *la* or mountain-top or pass; a *rui* or sept of the Ruichhung sub-tribe of Dejong Lhoris or Bhotias of the south.

Lahoni, a *thar* or section of Nepáli Brahmans.

Lahtaur, a sept of Rájputs in Behar.

Láhuliá, a sept of Rájputs in Behar.

Láik, a title of Telis and Mayarás in Bengal.

Laiyál, a *thar* or section of Nepáli Brahmans.

Lakándri, a *thar* or sept of Mangars in Darjiling.

Lakargarhá, a sub-caste of Sunris in Manbhum.

Lákat, a sept of Rájputs in Behar.

Lakhansariá, a section of Madhesiá Halwáis in Behar.

Lakhauriá, a division of Brahmans in Behar.

Lakhauriár, a section of Káyasths in Behar.

Lakhiputra, a synonym for Dosi.

Lakhnauá, a section of the Banodhiá and Jaiswár Kalwárs in Behar.

Lakhotia, a section of Maheswris in Behar.

Lakhsariá, a section of Bháts.

Lakrihár, a section of Bansphor Doms in Western Behar.

Laksha, a *gáin* of the Bátsya *gotra* of Bárendra Brahmans in Bengal.

Laksham Seriá, a section of the Biyáhut and Kharidáhá Kalwárs in Behar.

Lakshan or *Saranbanda*, a class of Sannyásis or Fakirs.

Lakshanpuriá, a *mul* or section of the Naomuliá or Majraut sub-caste of Goálás in Behar.

Laktomáháng, a sept of Limbus in Darjiling.

Lakwár, a section of the Maghayá sub-caste of Barhis in Behar.

Lál, **Lála**, a title of Káyasths, Khatris, of the Banodhiá sub-caste of Kalwárs and Sunris in Behar.

Lálá, a synonym for Káyasth in Behar.

Lálbegi, a class of Mahomedan sweepers supposed to have come from Upper India, some with sepoy regiments, others as wanderers in search of work. Though styled Mahomedans, they neither practise circumcision nor abstain from pork. The Lalbegí are employed as sweepers in European households, and are always addressed as jama'dár by the other servants.

They eat the leavings of Europeans, and drink any sort of wine or spirits. They will not, however, eat with the Raut, who in their turn pride themselves on abstaining from food thathas come from a European table. Nor will they touch a dead body.

The religious rites of the Lalbegi are partly Hindu, partly Muhammadan. As with Mussulmáns generally, marriages are arranged by an old woman who acts as match-maker. No *kabin* or marriage settlement is drawn up, but an *ikrár* or bond is executed, in which both promise to love one another, and the bridegroom undertakes not to bring a second wife into his house. Previous to the wedding day the Khandúrí ceremony is observed, as well as other Muhammadan customs, but the services of the Acharjí Brahman are not required. Should the marriage be celebrated in the bridegroom's house, a fee of twenty annas is paid to the pancháyat; if in the bride's, only five annas.

A few of the Lalbegi keep the fast of Ramazán, although they dare not enter a public mosque.

Their funeral ceremonies are peculiar. The dead may not be buried in a Mussulmán cemetery, but are consigned to the ground in some waste and jungly spot. The corpse is wrapped in five shrouds, a handkerchief is placed under each arm and in each hand, a *kasáwá* or napkin is bound round the head, and a *khirqá* or blouse is put on the body. After the grave has been filled in, a cloth cover (*phúl ka chadar*) is laid over it, while four pieces of "Agar" wood are inserted at the corners and set fire to. The rest of the funeral ceremonies are strictly Mahomedan. For four days after a death a fire is not allowed to be lighted in the dwelling-house of the deceased, the family in the meantime receiving food from their neighbours; but on the fifth day a tray laden with betel-nuts and adorned with flowers is placed in front of the hut, and a feast is given to the whole tribe.

The Lalbegis follow many Hindu customs, observing the Díwálí and the Holí as the greatest festivals of the year. On these occasions a mud image of a mosque with five domes is made, supposed to be a model of one still existing at Ghazní, in Kábul, which belonged to Lál Beg, the eponymous ancestor of the tribe. In front of the image a cock is sacrificed, and offerings of *pilao*, *sherbet*, and sweetmeats are made in his name. Lál Beg is identified by Sir H. Elliot[1] with Lál Guru, the same as the Rákshasa Aronákarat; but in Benares[2] he is confounded with Pír Zahr, perhaps the famous Chishtíya saint Sayyíd Sháh Zuhúr. In the Panjáb, again, Mihtars adore Lál Pír, or Bábá Faqír, as the dyers do Pír 'Alí Rangrez, and the blacksmiths Hazrat Dáúd. It seems not improbable, therefore, that the Lalbegí, like many other tribes converted to Mahomedanism, have adopted a Mahomedan saint as their common ancestor.

Lál-Chátái, a sub-group of Hele Kaibarttas in Central Bengal.

Lál-Gámia, a group of the Mihtar sub-caste of Telis in Behar.

Lál-Goálá, a hypergamous group of Goálás in Eastern Bengal.

Lalihar, a bird, a totemistic sept of Lohárs in Chota Nagpur.

Láma, a *thar* or sept of Gurungs in Darjiling.

Lámá Khor, a section of Murmis in Darjiling.

Lamamaka, a sept of Hos in Singbhum.

Lámbá, a section of Goálás in the North-Western Provinces and Behar.

Lambacha, a sept of the Tungjainya sub-tribe of Chakmás in the Hill Tracts of Chittagong.

Lámgáde, Lamgadeh, a section of Kámis and a *thar* or sept of Mangars in Darjiling.

Lamgoriá, a section of Bábhans in Behar.

[1] *Supplemental Glossary*, i, 32.
[2] Sherring, *Hindu Tribes of Benares*, p. 397.

Lámi Chhanya, a *thar* or sept of Gurungs and Mangars in Darjiling.

Lamjál, a *thar* or sept of Mangars in Darjiling.

Lampochhá, a sept of the Rautár sub-tribe of Thárus in Behar.

Lamsani Tongi, a *thar* or sept of the Das-Gurung sub-tribe of Gurungs in Darjiling. It was separated from its parent *thar*, the Lehbo Lamsani.

Lang, a kind of bird, a totemistic sept of Mundas in Chota Nagpur.

Láng Chenre, a section of the Mahili-Munda sub-caste of Mahilis in Chota Nagpur.

Langjharájhari, a *mul* or section of Kesarwáni Baniyás in Behar.

Langsál or **Lamsál**, a *thar* of the Bachh *gotra* of Nepáli Brahmans.

Laoti, he who was obeyed, a sept of the Pánthar sub-tribe of Limbus in Darjiling.

Láphaunchhá, a *thar* or sept of Khambus in Darjiling.

Lápung, a small bird, a totemistic sept of Mundas in Chota Nagpur.

Larapá, monkey-eater, a sept of Mundas in Chota Nagpur.

Larauni, a *mul* or section of the Chhamuliá Madhesiá sub-caste of Halwáis in Behar.

Larhora or *Purbál Mehter*, a sub-caste of Doms in Behar who reverence Supat Bhagat, a devotee whom they believe to be the *purka* or founder of their sub-caste. They make baskets and remove filth.

Lari, a sub-caste of Goálás in Chota Nagpur.

Larka, the fighters, a title of the Ho tribe in Singbhum.

Larkor, a title of Jaunpuri Chamárs in Behar whose women act as midwives.

Larma, a sept of Chakmás in the Hill Tracts of Chittagong.

Larsunar, a sept of Mundas in Chota Nagpur.

Lartangar, a *mul* or section of the Kanaujiá sub-caste of Sonárs in Behar.

Láruli, a *gáin* of the Bharadwája *gotra* of Bárendra Brahmans in Bengal.

Larwár, a *dih* or exogamous section of the Gharbait sub-caste of Amáts in Behar.

Larwariá, a section of Bábhans in Behar.

Laskar, a title of Pods in Bengal.

Lát, a sub-sept of the Kisku, Saren, and Tudu septs of Santáls, whose ancestor baked meat in a leaf platter.

Latá-baidya, a synonym for Bárui.

Latá Punra, a section of Pundarik or Pundas, so called from their selling vegetables grown from *latá* or creeper.

Láter, a sub-tribe of Dhimáls in the Darjiling Terai.

Lathaur, a sub-caste of Telis in Behar, a section of Rajwárs and Rautiás in Chota Nagpur.

Latihar, a variant for **Láheri** or **Churihár**, who manufacture lac bracelets or *churis*.

Lau, a sub-section of the Hárita section of Utkal Brahmans in Orissa.

Laugi, a title of Nágars in Behar.

Lauki, a title of Hindu Joláhas in Behar.

Laungijarhuá, a *mul* or section of the Sátmuliá or Kishnaut sub-caste of Goálás in Behar.

Lauriá, a section of Goálás in Behar.

Lautni, a sept of Rájputs in Behar.

Láwápur, a section of Majraut Goálás in Behar.

Láyá, a synonym for Maulik.

Leba, a sept of Chakmás in the Hill Tracts of Chittagong.

Lechenche, the dissolute one, a sept of the Yangorup sub-tribe of Limbus in Darjiling.

Legbahang, a sept of the Tambrkhola sub-tribe of Limbus in Darjiling.

Legma, the worker in mud, a sept of the Chhothar sub-tribe of Limbus in Darjiling.

Leh Láma, a *thar* or sept of Gurungs in Darjiling the members of which are called in to officiate at the obsequies of the dead by throwing earth on the grave, and to read the funeral prayers.

Lekhogma, he of the swollen testes, a sept of the Yangorup sub-tribe of Limbus in Darjiling.

Lenda, earthworm, a totemistic sept of Mundas in Chota Nagpur.

Leng, a totemistic sept of the Bhumij tribe in Manbhum, the members of which will not touch or eat a mushroom.

Lenká, a title of Chásás in Orissa.

Lepcha, *Rong*, *Khamba*, *Mon*, a Mongolian tribe of Sikkim, Western Bhutan, Eastern Nepal, and Darjiling. They are divided into two branches—**Rong** and **Khamba**. The former claim to be the original inhabitants of Sikkim, while the Khamba are believed to have immigrated some 250 years ago from the Kham province of China, whither a deputation of Lamas had been sent to choose a ruler for Sikkim. The Raja selected by them brought with him a number of his own tribe, who retained the name of their original home as associating them with the ruling family. The distinction, however, has not operated as a bar to intermarriage, and the two branches are now thoroughly amalgamated. Both, in fact, probably come of the same original stock, and represent two successive migrations of Mongols into Sikkim.

Origin.

"In person," says Dr. Campbell,[1] "the Lepchas are short, averaging about five feet in height: five feet six inches is tall, and four feet eight inches is a common stature among the men. The women are shorter in the usual proportion. The men are bulky for their height, but rather fleshy than sinewy. The muscular development of their limbs is inferior to that of the Mágárs, Gurungs, Murmis, and other

Physical type.

[1] *Journal of Ethnological Society of London*, vol. I, No. 2.

Parbattiahs. They are very fair of skin, and boys and girls in health have generally a ruddy tinge of complexion. This is lost, however, in adolescence, although the fairness continues. The features are markedly Mongolian, but there is a fulness and roundness of feature accompanied by a cheerful expression and laughing eye which renders the face a most pleasing one. The total absence of beard and the fashion of parting the hair along the crown of the head adds to a somewhat womanly expression of countenance in the men, and the loose bedgown sort of jacket, with wide sleeves, which they wear, contributes still more to render it rather difficult for strangers to distinguish the sexes, especially in middle age. The men very often look like women, and the women sometimes like men. The hair is worn long by both sexes; the younger men allowing it to hang loose over the shoulders, the elders plaiting it into a tail, which sometimes reaches to the knees. The women of rank wear their hair in two, and sometimes in three tails, tying it with braids and silken cords and tassels. The Lepchas, both male and female, are dirty in person, rarely having recourse to ablution. In the cold and dry season this renders them unpleasant inmates of a close dwelling, but in the rains, when they move about and are frequently wet, they are clean and sweet. The temperament of the Lepcha is eminently cheerful, and his disposition really amiable. In ordinary intercourse they are a very fascinating people, and possess an amount of intelligence and rational curiosity not to be met with among their Bhotia, Limbu, Murmi, or Gurung neighbours, and indeed rarely, if ever, to be seen among people so completely secluded from foreign intercourse as they always have been. The marked contrast in these respects between the Lepchas and the listless, uninquiring natives of the plains renders association with them a source of much pleasure to Europeans. They are wonderfully honest, theft being scarcely known among them; they rarely quarrel among themselves. I have never known them to draw their knives on one another, although they always wear them. For ordinary social purposes of talking, eating, and drinking, they have great unanimity, but for any more important purposes of resistance to oppression, the pursuit of industry or trade, their confidence in one another is at a low pitch; they fly bad government rather than resist it, and used to prefer digging for yams in the jungle and eating wretchedly innutritious vegetables to enduring any injustice or harsh treatment. They are singularly forgiving of injuries, when time is given them, after hasty loss of temper. Although they were ready enough to lodge complaints before the Magistrate against one another in cases of assault and other offences, they rarely prosecuted to a decision, generally preferring to submit to arbitration or making mutual amends and concessions."

Internal structure.

The internal structure of the tribe, so far as I have been able to ascertain it, is shown in Appendix I. The subject is most obscure, and Lepchas themselves seem unable to throw much light upon it. Besides the main divisions of Rong and Khamba, which, as has been stated above, have no special bearing on marriage, the Lepchas recognize ten groups, which they call *thars*. These appear to have been at one time exogamous, and the Adinpuso *thar* is said to be so still. The rest, however, have lost their exogamous character, and their members may marry women of their own or of other groups. Two *thars*, Barphungpuso and Adinpuso, rank higher than the other eight, and do not permit intermarriage with them. The distinction is said to arise from the fact that the officials of the Sikkim State are invariably chosen from these two *thars*, and they probably are the descendants of the Khamba clansmen who followed the chief from Tibet. Village headmen (*mandals*) are drawn from among the eight lower *thars*, and these groups represent the main body of cultivators in Sikkim. Members of these *thars* again may intermarry with Limbus, which is forbidden for Barphungpuso and Adinpuso.

The primitive rule of exogamy having thus fallen into disuse, the Lepchas supply its place by a table of prohibited degrees which does not differ materially from that expressed by the common formula *mamera*, *chachera*, etc., already often referred to. Intermarriage is barred only for three generations in the descending line, except when a *mith* or adoptive relationship has been entered into, in which case the prohibition is said to extend to nine generations. The ceremony observed in *mith* is of the same general character as among the Murmis, but Lamas, not Brahmans, officiate as priests, and Tibetan scarves are exchanged as pledges of amity instead of the rupees used by the Murmis. The wives of the two friends take part in the ceremony, and are not troubled by the strict etiquette which among the Nepalese regulates the conduct of a wife towards her husband's *dost*.

Marriage.

Lepcha girls usually marry between the ages of sixteen and eighteen. Men marry later owing to the difficulty of getting together the bride-price, which ranges from Rs. 40 to Rs. 100 according to the rank of the parties. The freest courtship is permitted, and sexual license before marriage is tolerated. If a girl becomes pregnant, the man is expected either to marry her or to pay some compensation to her parents for the reduction in value which she has undergone. Formal proposals of marriage are usually made to the bride's parents by *pibus* or go-betweens acting on behalf of the lover. If the proposal is accepted, the *pibus* go to the bride's house with Rs. 5 as earnest-money, and ten seers of *maruá* beer and a Tibetan scarf. An auspicious day for the marriage is then fixed by the Lamas. The ceremony, performed first at the bride's and then at the bridegroom's house, is of a very simple character. Bride and bridegroom sit side by side on a carpet, and the Lama ties a silk scarf round the neck of each and then changes the scarves, so that the bride wears the bridegroom's and *vice versâ*. Rice is sprinkled over their heads, they eat together, and drink *maruá* beer out of the same cup. The proceedings end with a feast. The married couple spend three days in the husband's house, and then usually go on a month's visit to the bride's parents.

When a man is too poor to pay the bride-price, he is often allowed to marry, as it were, on credit; but the bride does not leave her father's house, and the husband goes to live with her and work for his father-in-law until the full amount has been made up.

Polyandry, though comparatively rare, is not entirely unknown among the Lepchas. As might be expected, the Tibetan form of the custom is followed, and the younger brothers share the favours of the eldest brother's wife. Polygamy is permitted, but is not practised on a large scale.

A widow may marry again, and is subject to no express restrictions in her choice of a second husband. It is considered, however, proper for her to marry her late husband's younger brother, and if she marries an outsider, this brother-in-law usually keeps the children, and in any case may claim repayment of the bride-price. The full ceremony may be employed at the marriage of a widow, but the parties usually content themselves with the mere announcement by a Lama that they have become man and wife.

If a married couple cannot agree, arbitrators (*pibus*) are appointed to attempt to adjust their differences. If they fail after two or three attempts, a formal divorce is effected with the concurrence of the Lama who married the pair. The wife returns to her father's house, and her husband pays some compensation to her parents. When a woman is taken in adultery, a panchâyat considers the case and determines the amount of fine (*gysh*) to be paid to her husband by the paramour. The amount of the fine is not fixed by custom, nor does it bear any stated proportion to the bride-price. Where adultery is proved, the husband has a right to divorce his wife without paying compensation to her parents, and to take away her ornaments. Physical chastisement is never inflicted, nor is the right of divorce invariably exercised. Divorced wives may marry again by the same ceremony as is in use at the marriage of a virgin.

Inheritance.

In matters of inheritance and succession the Lepchas follow a tribal custom of their own, which is administered by the panchâyats of the tribe, and rarely comes before the regular courts. At a man's death his property is supposed to be divided equally among his sons, but the rule of equal division is liable in practice to be modified by other considerations. Thus the widow and daughters of the deceased usually live with the eldest son, and where this is the case he gets an extra share of the property. In Sikkim, again, it is held that the rule of equal division only applies where the sons render equal service to the Raja of the country, so that if one son does service and the others do not, that one gets an extra share of the property. A similar principle is recognized by the Lepchas of Darjiling. In dividing an inheritance account is taken by the panchâyat of the extent to which the different heirs have contributed to the improvement of the property, and their shares are adjusted accordingly. Brothers have no claim by right of descent, but shares may be awarded to them by the panchâyat in proportion to the work they have done during the lifetime of the deceased. Wills are unknown; but a father may make a verbal declaration in favour of a particular son, and the panchâyat will give effect to this declaration of his wishes. If sons survive, the unmarried daughters are maintained by them, and neither they nor married daughters take any share in the property. If, however, there are no sons, a married daughter may succeed, provided that she and her husband have lived in her father's house. The whole system, however, is extremely fluid and indefinite, and the rules stated above are in practice constantly modified by the panchâyat with the object of doing substantial justice to the various claimants.

Religion.

Most Lepchas at the present day profess to be Buddhists, and follow in a more or less intelligent fashion the observances of the northern sect of that religion. It is clear, however, that at no very distant time their sole belief was a form of Shamanistic Animism of the same general character as that described in the article on the Limbus. Conspicuous traces of this faith still survive among them, imperfectly hidden by the thin veil of Buddhistic usage. In the belief of the average Lepcha, mountain and forest, rock and stream represent ill-defined but formidable powers who threaten mankind with a variety of physical ills, and require to be constantly appeased through the agency of Bijuás or exorcists. Not all of these powers are evil, and some are even credited with taking a kindly interest in human affairs. But savage theology, expressing doubtless the experience of primitive man as to the distribution of good and evil in the world, teaches that the good gods abide in their own place and take no heed of mankind, while the malevolent deities are in a constant state of jealous and mischievous activity. The former therefore gradually drop out of notice and fade from the memories of men, while the latter, strong in the fears they inspire, may even outlive an entire change of religion on the part of their votaries. The snow-clad giant Kinchinjanga, chief among the elemental deities of the Lepchas, who vexes men with storm and hail and sends down avalanches and torrents to wreck their fields and sweep away their homes, has been translated to the milder system of Buddhism, where he figures as the tutor of Sakya Muni himself. Eshegenpu, Palden Lhamo, Lapen-Rimbuchi, Genpu-Maling-Nagpu, and Wasungma are less easy to identify; but the fact that they receive offerings of meat and *maruá* beer in addition to the flowers, fruit, rice, and incense sanctioned by Buddhist usage, lends some weight to the conjecture that they belong to an earlier and more barbarous system. Chirenzi or Lachen-Om-Chhup-Chhimu is said by the Lepchas to be the same as Mahadeva. His wife is Umadeva. Both are believed to have been worshipped by the Lepchas before the introduction of Buddhism.

Tibetan Lamas serve the tribe as priests, and preside at all Buddhist ceremonies. Lepchas themselves rarely become Lamas, but many of them are exorcists (Bijuás or Ojhas), and exercise considerable influence by their power of averting the ill-will of the gods and appeasing the spirits of the dead.

Disposal of the dead.

The dead are usually buried, fully clothed and in a sitting position, facing towards the east. Before burial the corpse is kept sitting in the house for two or three days with food before it. The grave is lined with stones and a round cairn built on the top surmounted by a flag. Among the Rong Lepchas an Ojha is called in about a month after death to perform a simple propitiatory rite, at which a cow or a goat is killed and much *maruá* beer is drunk. This is sometimes repeated on the first anniversary of the death. The object is to put the dead man's spirit to rest, and to prevent him from plaguing the living with bad dreams. At harvest time offerings of rice, *maruá* beer, and various kinds of food are presented by the head of the household for the benefit of ancestors in general.

The higher classes of Khamba Lepchas burn their dead, pound the fragments of the bones which remain, and throw them into a river, not into a *jhorá* or hill stream. The subsequent propitiatory ceremony is sometimes very elaborate, as in the case of the obsequies of the sister of the Sikkim Raja, described by Mr. J. Ware Edgar, C.S.I., in the following passage[1]:—

"Before the figure [meant to represent the dead person, in this case the Sikkim Rajah's sister, who was a nun] was a table on which were different kinds of food; on another table at the side were various things which had belonged to the woman when alive; while on a third, 108 little brass lamps were arranged in rows. Long lines of monks in dark red robes and with very tall caps of bright crimson on their heads sat on carpets placed in the middle of the chapel and chanted litanies throughout each day of my stay at Toomlong.

"It chanced that I saw the conclusion, and learned the meaning of this ceremony at Pemiongchi, where the lay-figure of the nun was taken some days after I left Toomlong. There for three days the figure was seated before the altar, and the monks chanted the litanies for the departure of the soul of the dead nun * * *. On the third day the relations, friends, and dependents of the deceased brought or sent gifts of food or clothing or money, which were all laid before the figure of the dead woman; while the head Lama, standing in front of his chair and turning towards the figure, stated the nature of each gift and the name of the donor. Towards evening the tea-cup of the nun was freshly filled with tea and her murwa jug with murwa, and all the monks solemnly drank tea with her. Then many people who had known and loved the nun when alive went up, and, prostrating themselves before the figure, kissed the hem of the robe as a last farewell, while the monks chanted the litanies more zealously than ever, and the head Lama, who had left his chair and gone to one of the tables, went through some elaborate ceremonies the meaning of which I could not make out. At about nine o'clock the chanting ceased, and the Lama again standing in front of his chair made a long speech to the soul of the nun, in which he told her that all that could be done to make her journey to another world easy had been done, and that now she would have to go forth alone and unassisted to appear before the king and judge of the dead * * * * * * *
When the Lama had finished his address, some of the monks took

[1] *Report of a Visit to Sikkim*, pp. 57-58.

down the lay-figure and undressed it; while others formed a procession and conducted the soul of the nun into the darkness outside the monastery, with a discordant noise of conch-shells, thigh-bone trumpets, Tibetan flutes, gongs, cymbals, tambourines, drums, and other most disagreeable but nameless instruments."

"The Lepchas," says Dr. Campbell,[1] "have no caste distinctions. Those who live under the Nepal Government are obliged to conform to the Hindu laws of that State, which prohibit the killing of the cow. This they do, however, with a very bad grace, and rarely forego an opportunity of visiting Darjiling to indulge their beef-eating propensities. They are gross feeders, eating all kinds of animal food, including the elephant, rhinoceros, and monkey, and all grains and vegetables known to us, with the addition of many roots and plants altogether excluded from our culinary list. Pork is their most favourite flesh; next to that beef, goat, and mutton. The yak is considered the best beef, the next to that the flesh of the Sikkim cow, a fine animal, and last the Bengali and common cow. All birds are included in their list of eatable game. Of the carrion of wild animals, that of the elephant is most prized. The favourite vegetable food is rice; next to it wheat, barley, maize, millet. murwa, and a fine species of yam called "bookh," which grows all over these mountains, at elevations of from 1,500 to 3,000 feet. During the rains, when grain is scarce, they contentedly put up with ferns, bamboo roots, several sorts of fungi, and innumerable succulent plants found wild on the mountains. A large-rooted arum is much used at this season, after being soaked in water for six days to remove its acrid juice; still it often produces colic, and is poisonous. Fond of fermented and spirituous liquors, the Lepchas are nevertheless not given to drunkenness; their common beverage is a kind of beer made from the fermented infusion of Indian corn and murwa, which is weak, but agreeably acid and very refreshing. They drink this at all times when procurable, and when making a journey it is carried in a large bamboo "chunga," and diligently applied to throughout the day. They have no distilled liquor of their own, but they greatly admire and prize all our strong waters—our port and sherry, cherry brandy, and maraschino. Tea is a favourite beverage, the black sort brought from China in large cakes being that preferred. It is prepared by boiling, after which the decoction is churned up in a "chunga," with butter and salt. Milk is never taken with tea. Their cooking is careless, coarse, and not cleanly. Rice is generally boiled when travelling in pieces of the large bamboo; at home, in coarse iron pots. Vegetables are always boiled in oil, when the latter is procurable, and spiced with capsicum and ginger, of which these hills possess very fine kinds. Salt is not a commonly used condiment, the chief source of its supply till lately being Tibet, whence rock-salt is brought on men's backs: the easier communication with the plains of Bengal by the new Darjiling road admits of the importation of this article at a cheaper rate, and sea-salt is rapidly taking the place of the other.

Food.

---

[1] *Journal of the Ethnological Society of London*, vol. I, No. 2, pp. 147-49.

"The Lepcha dress is simple and graceful. It consists of a robe of striped red and white cotton cloth crossed over the breast and shoulders, and descending to the calf of the legs, leaving the arms bare; a loose jacket of red cotton cloth is worn over the robe by those who can afford it, and both are bound round the waist by a red gridle; some strings of coloured beads round the neck, silver and coral earrings, a bamboo bow and quiver of iron-pointed arrows, and a long knife complete the dress of the men. The knife, called "ban" by the Lepchas, and "chipsa" by the Bhotias, is constantly worn by the males of all ages and ranks; it hangs on the right side, suspended from the left shoulder, and is used for all purposes. With the "ban" the Lepcha clears a space in the forest for his house and cultivation; it is the only tool used by him in building; with it he skins the animals that fall a prey to his snares and arrows; it is his sword in battle, his table knife, his hoe, spade, and nail-parer. Without the "ban" he is helpless to move in the jungle; with it he is a man of all work: the expertness with which it is used by the boys of a few years old even is the astonishment of strangers.[1] The women are less neatly dressed than the men: a piece of plain unbleached cotton cloth, or the cloth of the castor oil insect—the indi—rolled round to form a sort of petticoat, with a loose red gown of the same, and a profusion of mock coral and coloured bead necklaces, form their entire wardrobe. They are the domestic and farm drudges of the men, performing all out and in-door work along with their husbands, and much besides. It is not unusual to meet a stout and active man, bow in hand, sauntering along the road followed by his wife and sisters heavily loaded with grain or merchandise. It is the delight of a Lepcha to be idle; he abhors the labour of practising any craft, but he expects that while he is amused and unemployed the female part of the household shall be busily engaged in the field, or in looking after the pigs and poultry. In recent times they have taken to work in tea plantations and as chair-bearers: and the necessity for money, since we introduced it into their country, has made them more steady workers."

Dress.

[2] "The Lepchas are poor agriculturists, their labours in this art being confined to the careless growing of rice, Indian corn, murwa (*Sessasum Orientalis*), and a few vegetables, of which the brinjal, cucumber, and capsicum are the chief. Their habits are incurably erratic: they do not form permanent villages, and rarely remain longer than three years in one place, at the expiration of which they move into a new part of the forest, sometimes near, often distant, and there go through the labour of clearing a space for a house, building a new one, and preparing the ground for a crop. The latter operations consist in cutting down the smaller trees, lopping off the branches of the large ones, which are burnt, and scratching the soil with the "ban," after

Occupation.

[1] The "ban" is a straight sword with a wooden scabbard open along one side.

[2] *Journal of the Ethnological Society of London*, vol. I, No. 2, p. 151.

which, on the falling of a shower of rain, the seed is thrown into the ground. Their houses are built entirely of bamboo, raised about five feet from the ground, and thatched with the same material, but a smaller species, split up."

The Lepchas numbered 3,952 in 1872 and 202 in 1881 in the district of Darjiling.

Lepuriet, a *mul* or section of the Naomuliá or Majraut sub-caste of Goálás in Behar.

Let, a sub-caste of Bágdis found in Murshedabad and Birbhum.

Lethrani, the designation of the women of the Limbu caste in Darjiling.

Levátiá, a section of Majraut Goálás in Behar.

Lhasung, a sub-sept of the Pon-po sept of Dejong Lhoris or Bhotias of the south, the members of which officiate as priests of all the septs.

Lha-yo, a *thar* or sept of Mangars in Darjiling.

Lhebo Lamsani, a *thar* or sept of the Das-Gurung sub-tribe of Gurungs. There is a tradition that in ancient times two Gurungs —father and son—quarrelled and separated from each other. The father's party remained at Lehbo and the son's party emigrated to a distant place. The latter were called Lamsani Tangi (*tangi* in Gurung means 'separated').

Lhopa, a native of Bhotan.

Lhopa Bhotia, a synonym for Dejong Lhori.

Lhoringten, the chief of Morang, a sept of the Chaibisa sub-tribe of Limbus. This *thar* was formerly under the Morang Raja.

Lhorong, a sub-tribe of Yakhas in Darjiling.

Libang, the archer, a sept of the Miákhola sub-tribe of Limbus in Darjiling.

Lihimba, dove, a totemistic sept of Juángs in Orissa.

Lila, fish, a totemistic sept of Oraons in Chota Nagpur.

Lilla, wild cow, a totemistic sept of Mundas in Chota Nagpur.

Liluai, a sept of Birhors in Chota Nagpur.

Limbu, a large tribe, probably of Mongolian descent, ranking next to the Khambu and above the Yakha among the three upper divisions of the Kiránti group. The precedence given to the Khambus is supposed to be due to their having a larger proportion of Khas and Newar blood, while the Limbus have interbred freely with the Lepchas. The Yakha are a minor tribe, concerning which little is known. Unlike the other two, they have no generally recognized honorific title, though they claim to be addressed as *dewan* and call themselves Yak Thomba or yakherds, with reference to the tradition that this was their characteristic occupation before the tribe crossed the Himalaya into Eastern Nepal. The name Limbu, or Das Limbu, from the ten sub-tribes (really thirteen) into which they are supposed to be divided, is used only by outsiders. Tibetans have no special name

Traditions of origin.

for the Limbus; they call all the tribes of the Indian side of the Himalaya by the general name Monpa or dwellers in the ravines. The Lepchas and Bhotias or Tibetans settled in Bhotan, Sikkim, and Nepal speak of the Limbus as Tsong, because the five *thums* or sub-tribes included in the class known as Lhása-gotra emigrated to Eastern Nepal from the district of Tsang in Tibet. Lepchas call them Chang, which may be a corruption of Tsong. By other members of the Kiránti group they are addressed by the honorific title of Subah or Suffah, a chief.

The Limbus, according to Dr. Campbell, "form a large portion of the inhabitants in the mountainous country lying between the Dud-Kosi and the Kanki rivers in Nepal, and are found in smaller numbers eastwards to the Mechi river, which forms the boundary of Nepal and Sikkim. In still fewer numbers they exist within the Sikkim territory, as far east as the Tista river, beyond which they rarely settle. In Bhutan they are unknown except as strangers." Hodgson locates them between the Arun Kosi and the Mechi, the Singilela ridge being their boundary on the east. The Limbus themselves claim to have held from time immemorial the Támba Khola valley on the upper waters of the Támba Kosi river; and the fact that one of their sub-tribes bears the name Támbakhola suggests that this valley may have been one of their early settlements. They have also a tradition that five out of their thirteen sub-tribes came from Lhása, while five others came from Benares. The former group is called the Lhása-gotra, and the latter the Kási-gotra; but the term *gotra* has in this case no bearing on marriage. All that can safely be said is that the Limbus are the oldest recorded population of the country between the Támra Kosi and the Mechi, and their flat features, slightly oblique eyes, yellow complexion, and beardlessness may perhaps afford grounds for believing them to be the descendants of early Tibetan settlers in Nepal. They appear to have mixed little with the Hindus, but much with the Lepchas, who of late years have migrated in large numbers from Sikkim to the west. Dr. Campbell compares the two tribes in the following words:—"The Limbu is a very little taller in stature than the Lepcha, somewhat less fleshy, and more wiry in the limbs, as fair in complexion, and as completely beardless. He is scarcely ever as ruddy as the Lepchas sometimes are; his eyes are, if anything, smaller, and placed more to the front than the Lepcha's, and his nose, although somewhat smaller, is rather higher in the bridge than that of the Lepcha. He wears his hair long, but does not plait it into a tail; has no fancy for bead necklaces; wears a *kukri* instead of the *bán*,[1] and wide trousers and a jacket or *chapkan* in preference to the robe and long jacket of the Lepchas."

At the time of the Gurkha conquest of Nepal the country east of the Arun Kosi was held by petty Limbu chiefs on quasi-feudal terms from the Hindu Rajas of Bijapur and Makwánpur, at whose courts representative Limbus discharged the duties of *Chauntra* or prime minister. Taking refuge in the hill forts with which each

[1] The long, straight knife used by the Lepchas.

chiefship was provided, the Limbus offered a gallant resistance to the invading Gurkhas, and the latter underwent many repulses before their supremacy was fully established. Although used to bearing arms, and deeming themselves a military race, they do not rank among the regular fighting tribes of Nepal, and they are not admitted into the Gorkháli regiments of the Nepalese army. Their principal occupations at the present day are agriculture, grazing, and petty trade. They serve in the Kiranti regiments raised about 30 years ago by Jang Bahadur, and some of them have enlisted in our own Gurkha battalions. Some authorities believe them, with the rest of the Kiranti, to be inferior in soldierly qualities to the Khas, Mangar, and Gurung tribes, from whom our best recruits are drawn, but this opinion seems to be giving away, among the present generation of Gurkha officers, to a more favourable estimate of their military capacity, and their behaviour in the Sikkim compaign of 1888 is understood to have borne out the latter view.

Internal structure.

The internal structure of the tribe is extremely complicated, and can best be studied in the Appendix, where it is shown in a tabular form. The Limbus are divided into thirteen endogamous sub-tribes, each of which is again broken up into a number of exogamous septs. The names of the septs are extremely curious. Two or three at the most are totemistic, a few are local or territorial, and one only is eponymous. By far the greater number of them refer to some personal adventure or peculiarity of the original founder of the sept, and they suggest the existence of a considerable body of rather grotesque folklore. The rule of exogamy goes by the male side, and is supplemented by forbidding intermarriage between persons descended in a direct line from the same parents as long as any relationship can be traced. Intermarriage between cousins is barred for three generations, or, as some say, for seven. In practice, however, while the rule forbidding marriage within the *thar* is most strictly observed, there seems to be much uncertainty about prohibited degrees, and I believe near alliances with the mother's kindred are by no means uncommon. A further complication is introduced by the restrictions on intermarriage arising from *mith* (Limbu *saiba*) friendship or on fictitious brotherhood among most of the hill races. Two men contract friendship by a special ritual at which a Brahman, or, when the parties are Buddhists, a Lama, officiates, and reads *mantras* or mystic formulæ, while the two friends thrice exchange rupees, handkerchiefs, or scarves, and daub each other between the eyebrows with the paste made of rice and curds which is used in the marriage ceremony. The effect of the union is that the friends are reckoned as brothers, and intermarriage between the two families is prohibited for several (some say eighteen) generations. Any breach of the rule is punished in British territory by exclusion from caste. In Nepal, I am informed, more severe punishments, such as death or slavery, are inflicted.

Members of the Murmi, Lepcha, and Bhotia tribes may be admitted into the Limbu tribe after being approved by the tribal council, called by the Limbus *thum-thum*, and giving a feast to the local community. In some cases the new member is required to file a written statement to the effect that he has entered the tribe and will abide by its rules. Khambus and Yakhas, being Kirántis themselves, may be admitted into the tribe by the simpler and more direct process of adoption. In any case the children of a Limbu man by a Bhotia, Lepcha, Gurung, Sunawar, Mangar, or Murmi woman, or of a Limbu woman by a man of any of these groups, are admitted without question into the Limbu community.

Religion.

The phlegmatic and utilitarian habit of mind which a German ethnologist has noticed as characteristic of the Mongolian races comes out conspicuously in the nonchalant attitude of the Limbus towards religion. Where their surroundings are Hindu, they describe themselves as Saivas, and profess to worship, though with sparing and infrequent observance, Mahádeva and his consort Gauri, the deities most favoured by the lax Hinduism of Nepal. In a Buddhist neighbourhood the yoke of conformity is still more easy to bear: the Limbu has only to mutter the pious formula, *om mani padme om*, and to pay respect and moderate tribute to the Lamas, in order to be accepted as an average Buddhist. Beneath this veneer of conformity with whatever faith happens to have gained local acceptation, the vague shapes of their original Pantheon have survived in the form of household or forest gods, much in the same way as Dionysus and other of the Greek gods may be traced in the names and attributes of the saints who preside over the vintage, the harvest and rural festivals of various kinds in remote parts of Greece at the present day. Under such disguises, which serve to mask departures from the popular creeds, the Limbus worship a host of spiritual beings whose attributes are ill-defined, and whose very names are not easy to ascertain. Yumá, Kápobá, and Thebá rank as household gods, and are propitiated once in five years, or whenever disease or loss of property threaten the family, by the slaughter, outside the house, of buffaloes, pigs or fowls. The votaries eat the sacrifice, and thus, as they express it, "dedicate the life-breath to the gods, the flesh to ourselves." No special days are set apart for the ceremony; but it cannot be performed on Sunday, as that day is sacred to Himáriyá. Those who wholly neglect the duty are supposed to suffer in person or property, and the common hill disease of goitre is believed to be one of the special modes by which the gods manifest their displeasure. Temples and idols are alike unknown, nor, so far as I can ascertain, does the imagination of the Limbus trouble itself to clothe its vague spiritual conceptions with any bodily form.

Himáriyá, the god of the forest, is propitiated on Sundays by offerings of sheep, goats, fowls, pigeons and Indian-corn. A stone under a tree by the roadside is smeared with vermilion and bound with thread, and this place of sacrifice is marked by consecrated rags tied to a bamboo pole.

In addition to these more or less beneficent, or at least neutral, divinities, the Limbus are compassed about by a multitude of nameless evil spirits, "who require peculiar management in warding off their caprices." To appease and propitiate these is the special function of the Bijuás, a class of wandering mendicants peculiar to Sikkim and the eastern parts of Nepal. Bijuás are wholly illiterate, and travel about the country muttering prayers and incantations, dancing, singing, prescribing for the sick and casting out devils. They wear a purple robe and broad-brimmed hat, and are regarded with great awe by the people, into whom they have instilled the convenient belief that their curses and blessings will surely be fulfilled, and that ill-luck will attend any one who allows a Bijuá to leave his door dissatisfied.

While the Bijuá acts as exorcist and devil-worshipper for all the Himalayan races, the equally illiterate Phedangma is the tribal priest of the Limbus for the higher grades of spirits, and officiates at sacrifices, marriages, and funerals. He is also called in at births to foretell the destiny of the infant, and to invoke the blessings of the gods. The office frequently descends from father to son, but any one may become a Phedangbo who has a turn for propitiating the gods, and for this reason the occupation shows no signs of hardening into a caste.

Animism.

It will be apparent from the facts stated above that the leading principle of the Limbu religion is *animism*, "the belief in the existence of souls or spirits of which only the powerful—those on which man feels himself dependent, and before which he stands in awe—acquire the rank of divine beings and become objects of worship."[1] Among the Limbus, as among the aborigines of Chota Nagpur, who appear to have reached a very similar stage of development, this belief has given birth to a number of primitive miscellaneous divinities whose functions are very vaguely defined, and who do not owe allegiance to any centralised authority. This multiplicity of deities would of itself seem to favour the growth of Shamanism, a phenomenon which Sir John Lubbock regards as a widely distributed phase of thought forming a necessary stage in the progress of religious development. Others have gone so far as to use Shamanism as a sort of general name for all those animistic religions which make prominent use of the agency of the Shaman. Without disputing the convenience, or indeed the necessity, of introducing a class-name of some kind, I would urge that Shamanism is a term singularly ill-suited to serve as the designation of a large group of religions. For in the first place the practice which it denotes is common to religions of all varieties of culture, and is by no means confined to the religions specially called Shamanistic; and secondly, the word, while calling attention to the superficial, fails to connote the essential characteristics of the class of religions in question. It may, indeed, possibly be the case, as has been hinted above, that the complicated departmentalism of certain animistic religions, where the supreme power is cut up into fractions and distributed among an army of gods, ghosts and demons, has led to the development of Shamanism by leaving it uncertain to whom a man should apply for the alleviation of any particular evil. The Shaman, like the touts who

[1] Tiele, *Outlines of the History of the Ancient Religions*, p. 9.

hang about our public offices, professes to help people out of this difficulty, and to show them not only to what god their petitions should be addressed, but in what form they should be couched, and by what ceremonies introduced. But even on this showing the practice is the consequence, not the cause, of certain primitive ideas; and it is these ideas, not any of their more or less variable consequences, which a definition should aim at expressing. Taken by itself, then, the word Shamanism seems to fall short of completeness as a description of the Limbu religion. For all religions of that type the term animism should be retained as denoting the *entourage* of vague spiritual influences which is of their essence. In dealing with these surroundings different agencies are resorted to: sometimes the fetish predominates; sometimes the medicine man. According as one or the other of these predominates, the particular form of animism may conveniently be styled fetishistic or Shamanistic. Following this principle, the Limbu religion may be defined as a rather elementary form of Shamanistic animism, in which the Bijuá and Phedangma play the part of Shaman, the former operating on the demons, and the latter having for his department the gods. Finally, we may perhaps hazard the conjecture that the original religion of the Limbus is closely akin to the Pon or ancient religion of Tibet. In both we find the forces of nature and the spirits of departed men exalted into objects of worship. In both systems temples and images are unknown, while propitiatory offerings occupy a prominent place. To complete the parallel, neither recognize a definite priestly order, while both encourage resort to Shamans or medicine men to ward off the malign influences which surround the human race.

Disposal of the dead.

Both cremation and burial are in vogue among the Limbus, the latter being the more common, and probably the older, practice. The corpse is placed lying on its back with the head to the east. The grave is lined with stones, and a cairn, consisting of four tiers for a man and three for a woman, erected on the top. The Phedangma attends at the funeral and delivers a brief address to the departed spirit on the general lot of mankind and the doom of birth and death, concluding with the command to go whither his fathers have gone and not to come back to trouble the living with dreams. Neither food nor clothes are placed in the grave, but sometimes a brass plate with a rupee in it is laid under the head of the corpse. For nine days after the funeral the sons of the deceased live on plain rice without any salt; and for a month or two the relatives wear flowers in their hair and avoid merry-makings. The special and characteristic sign of mourning is a piece of white rag tied round the head. There is no periodical ceremony for the propitiation of ancestors.

Inheritance.

At a man's death his sons, natural or adopted, divide his property; but an adopted son or a natural son by a wife informally married (*kachchi sádi*) takes only one-half of a legitimate son's share. The division of the property is usually made by the tribal council (*thum-thum*), who set apart an extra share for the eldest son. The youngest son is allowed to choose his share first, and the other shares are then allotted by the *thum-thum*. Failing sons, the sons-in-law actually living in or willing to live in the family homestead are entitled to divide the property. Brothers are the next heirs, and married sisters, if they attend the funeral, usually get a small share in the inheritance, although it is said that they have no positive right to claim this concession. An exception to these rules of devolution occurs in the case of *daijo* or property given to a sister or daughter or acquired from a maternal uncle or father-in-law. This is equally distributed among the sons of the woman to whom or on whose behalf it was given, and in the event of her dying without children it reverts to her own family. This simple customary law is administered by the headmen of the tribe, and hardly any instances are known of Limbus having resorted to our courts for the settlement of disputes regarding property.

Social status.

The Limbus stand wholly outside of the Hindu caste system, and their social position can only be defined with reference to the other Himalayan races. They belong to the upper division of the Kiránti group, which inhabits the middle hills of the Himalayas, and rarely descends below an elevation of 2,000 feet. Within this division the Limbu take rank below the Khambu and above the Yákha, but this distinction is probably unknown beyond the limits of the Kiránti group, and in the eyes of society at large the three tribes occupy practically an equal position. They consider themselves, and are regarded by others, as superior to the Danuár, Hayu, and Thámi, who make up the lower division of the Kiránti. Their relations to the people of Nepal are less easy to define. They are certainly deemed inferior to the Khas, and probably also to the Mangars and Gurungs, both of whom are classed as military tribes. Newars hold a place second only to the Khas; Gurungs are inferior to the Newars. Mangar and Sunwar have their place next to the Gurungs; Limbus, Khambus, and Yakhas are inferior to the Mangar and Sunwar.

In the matter of food, they have very few prejudices. They eat beef, pork, and the flesh of all clean-feeding animals, and drink wine. In fact, the only restrictions on their diet appear to be those imposed on certain *thars* by the obligation not to eat the totem or beast-eponym of the group. They will eat with all the castes of the hills except the Kami, Damai, Sarki, and Gain.

The Census Report of 1881 returned 2,429 Limbus in the district of Darjiling.

Linda, eel, a totemistic sept of Oraons in Chota Nagpur.

Lin-dseh-bo, a *rui* or sept of the Bedtshan-gye sub-tribe of Dejong Lhoris or Bhotias of the south.

Lingdam, a sept of the Char-khola sub-tribe of Limbus, said to be admitted from the Lepchas.

Lingden, a sept of the Yan-gorup sub-tribe of Limbus, said to be admitted from the Lepchas.

Lingdenbeh, a sept of Limbus in Darjiling.

Lingkhim, a sept of the Tam-brkola sub-tribe of Limbus in Darjiling.

Linglámphen, a sept of Limbus in Darjiling.

Ling-tamba, a *rui* or sept of Dejong Lhoris, whose ancestor had emigrated from Bhotan.

Liokichá, a *thar* or sept of Sunuwárs in Darjiling.

Lipo, a tree, a totemistic sept of Mundas in Chota Nagpur.

Litiya, a bird, a totemistic sept of Mundas in Chota Nagpur.

Lo, a section of Murmis in Darjiling.

**Lodyat*, a synonym for Kuri or Mayará in Tipperah.

Lodah, a sub-tribe of Bhumijs in Chota Nagpur.

Lodarwa, a *mul* or section of the Kanaujia sub-caste of Sonárs in Behar.

Lodh, a title of Dakshin-Rárhi and Bangaja Káyasths in Bengal.

Lodhiyá, a sub-caste of Binds in Behar.

Logáin, a *mul* or section of the Kanaujia sub-caste of Sonárs in Behar.

Logna Kotra, small deer, a totemistic sept of Mundas in Chota Nagpur.

Logo, a sept of Mundas in Chota Nagpur believed to be totemistic.

Lohá, iron, a totemistic sept of Tántis, Oraons, and Gonds in Chota Nagpur.

Lohágun, a section of Kámis; a *thar* or sept of Mangars in Darjiling.

Lohâit-Kuri, a small caste found along the banks of the Meghna, who represent themselves as the descendants of a Kaibartta fisherboy, bought during a season of famine by a Kuri, or parcher of grains, who took this means of securing a husband for his daughter. The caste has separated into two subdivisions, those following the father's profession of fisherman having repudiated connection with the maternal branch, who parch grain.

The Lohâit-Kuri at present associates neither with the Kaibarttas nor with the Kuri or Mayará. The majority are fishermen, who will not cast a net or fish from the shore, but angle with a rod from boats drifting with the stream. The name Lohait-Kuri is said to come from their using large rectangular iron hooks, with a shank nearly two inches long. Iron sinkers are preferred to leaden ones, and the only bait used is a small fish.

A Patit Brahman ministers to them, and the *sráddha* is kept at the expiry of a lunar month. Like other fishermen, they observe the Jál-pálani for seven days. A heavy fee is paid for a wife, as the caste is a small one, and one hundred rupees is not an unusual bride-price, while a widower may have to pay as much as two hundred. The Lohâit-Kuris carry on a considerable trade with their own boats, but will not accept service with any other caste.

Lohar, a sub-caste of Barhis in Behar who work only in iron. They are, however, distinct from, and do not intermarry with, the Lohár caste. The latter are probably of Dravidian descent, while the former appear to be an occupational group.

Lohár, a synonym for Kámár in Behar; a *mul* or section of the Naomuliá or Majraut sub-caste of Goálás in Behar; a section of Kámis in Darjiling.

Lohár, the blacksmith caste of Behar, Chota Nagpur, and Western Bengal. The Lohárs are a large and heterogeneous aggregate, comprising members of several different tribes and castes, who in different parts of the country took up the profession of working in iron. Of the various sub-castes shown in Appendix I, the **Kanaujiá** claim to be the highest in rank, and they alone have a well-marked set of exogamous sections. They regard Viswámitra as their legendary ancestor, and worship him as the tutelary deity of their craft. The **Kokás** Lohárs seem to be a branch of the Barhis, who have taken to working in iron and separated from the parent group for that reason. The **Maghaiya** seems to be the indigenous Lohárs of Behar, or opposed to the Kanaujiá and **Mathuriyá**, who profess to have come in from the North-West Provinces. **Kamár-Kalla** Lohárs may perhaps be a degraded offshoot from the Sonar caste. The **Mahur** or **Mahulia** say they came from the North-Western Provinces, and the fact that all Hindus can take water from their hands renders it likely that they may have broken off from some comparatively respectable caste. Their traditions, however, are not definite enough to enable this conjecture to be verified. The **Kamiá** Lohárs found in Champáran have immigrated from Nepal, and are regarded as ceremonially unclean. Many of them have become Mahomedans. In the Santál Parganás, a sort of ethnic border land between Bengal and Behar, we find three sub-castes of Lohárs,—**Birbhumiá**, from the neighbouring district of Birbhum; **Govindpuriá**, from the subdivision of Govindpur, in Northern Manbhum; and **Shergarhiá**, from the *parganá* of that name in Bardwan. The names give no clue to the tribal affinities of these three groups, but the fact that they have the totemistic section **Sal-máchh** shows them to be of non-Aryan descent, probably Bauris or Bágdis, who took to iron-working and called themselves Lohárs. Of the four sub-castes into which the Lohárs of Bankura are divided, two bear the names **Gobrá** and **Jhetiá**, which occur among the sub-castes of the Bauris. Two others—**Angariá** and **Pánsili**—I am unable to trace. The Manbhum Lohárs acknowledge three sub-castes,—**Lohár-Mánjhi**, **Danda-Mánjhi**, and **Bágdi-Lohár**, names which suggest a connexion with the Bágdi caste. Lastly, in Lohardagá we have the **Sad-Lohárs**, claiming to be immigrant Hindus; the **Manjhal-Turiyás**, who may well be a branch of the Turi caste; and the **Mundá-Lohárs**, who are certainly Mundás. The great number of the sub castes, coupled with the fact that in some cases we can determine with approximate certainty the tribes of which they once formed part, seem to point to the conclusion, not merely that the aggregate termed the Lohár caste is made up of drafts locally levied from whatever groups were available for employment in a comparatively menial occupation, but that all castes whose functions are concerned with the primary needs of social life are the result of a similar process.

Further indications of the different elements from which the caste has been formed may be traced in its social customs. The Lohárs of Chota Nagpur and Western Bengal practise adult as well as infant-marriage, a price is paid for the bride, and the marriage ceremony is substantially identical with that in use among the Bágdis. Polygamy they allow without imposing any limit on the number of wives a man may have, and they recognize the extreme license of divorce characteristic of the aboriginal races. In Behar, on the other hand, infant-marriage is the rule and adult-marriage the rare exception. The ceremony is modelled on the orthodox type. A bridegroom-price is paid, and polygamy is lawful only on failure of issue by the first wife. As to divorce, some diversity of practice seems to prevail. Kanaujiás profess to prohibit it altogether, while other sub-castes admit it only with the permission of the panchâyat, and regard the remarriage of divorced wives with disfavour. Widow-marriage is recognized both in Behar and elsewhere; but this is by no means a distinctively Dravidian usage, but rather a survival of early Aryan custom, which has fallen into disuse among the higher castes under the influence of Brahmanical prejudice.

Marriage.

Equally characteristic differences may be observed in the religious usages of the main branches of the caste. Kanaujiá Lohárs and all the Behar sub-castes, except the Nepalese Kamiás, pose as orthodox Hindus, employ Maithil Brahmans, and worship the standard gods. In Chota Nagpur and Western Bengal, though some profession of Hinduism is made, this is little more than a superficial veneer laid on at a very recent date, and the real worship of the caste is addressed to Manasá, Rám Thákur, Baranda Thákur, Phulai Gosáin, Dalli Gorai, Bhádu, and Mohan Giri. In the latter we may perhaps recognize the mountain god (Marang Buru) of the Mundas and Santáls. To him goats are sacrificed on Mondays or Tuesdays in the months of Mágh, Ashár, and Agraháyan, the flesh being afterwards eaten by the worshippers. The Lohárs of Bankura and the Santál Parganás have taken to employing low Brahmans, but in Lohardagá the aboriginal priest (*páhan*) and the local sorcerer (*mati*, *ojhá*, or *sokhá*) minister to their spiritual wants. The Sad-Lohárs alone show an advance in the direction of orthodoxy, in that they employ the village barber to act as priest in the marriage ceremony.

Religion.

In Behar the caste work as blacksmiths and carpenters, while many have taken to cultivation. They buy their material in the form of pigs or bars of iron. Iron-smelting is confined to the Lohárs of Chota Nagpur, and is supposed to be a much less respectable form of industry than working up iron which other people have smelted. In the Santál Parganás Lohárs often cultivate themselves, while the women of the household labour at the forge. None of the Western Bengal Lohárs combine carpentry with working in iron.

Occupation.

In Behar Lohárs rank with Koiris and Kurmis, and Brahmans take water from their hands. The status of the caste in Western Bengal is far lower, and they are associated in matters of food and drink with Bauris, Bágdis, and Máls.

Social status.

The following statement shows the number and distribution of Lohárs in 1872 and 1881:—

District.	1872.	1881.	District.	1872.	1881.
Bardwan	The figures are included in the table on Kámárs.	202	Gya	17,216	16,659
Bankura		5,507	Shahabad	27,959	30,268
Birbhum		1,007	Tirhut { Mozufferpur ...	57,341	38,245
Midnapur		312	Tirhut { Darbhanga ...		11,831
Hughli		87	Saran	38,449	42,025
24-Parganas		57	Champaran	26,953	24,015
Nadiya		1	Monghyr	7,179	4,232
Jessore		238	Bhagalpur	23,405	9,789
Dinajpur		101	Purniah	16,063	7,952
Rajshahye		10	Maldah	......	307
Bogra		19	Santál Parganás	14,870	2,913
Pabna		10	Cuttack	The figures are included in the table on Kámárs.	300
Darjiling		577	Balasore		33
Kuch Behar		3	Tributary States		1,387
Faridpur		2	Hazaribagh		8,422
Maimansinh		6	Lohardagá		34,106
Chittagong		19	Singbhum		1,826
Patna	7,304	8,064	Manbhum		1,531
			Tributary States		10,302

Lohará, a sept of Mundas in Chota Nagpur.

Lohar-Agariá, a sub-tribe of Agariás in Chota Nagpur.

Lohartengi, a section of Rajwárs in Western Bengal.

Loharbans, iron, a totemistic sept of Chiks; a section of Ghásis in Chota Nagpur.

Lohár-Kámár, a sub-caste of Kámárs in Midnapur.

Lohárkoriyá, a section of Bháts.

Lohár Mánjhi, a sub-caste of Lohárs in Manbhum.

Lohatiá, a section of Sonárs in Behar.

Lohchab, a section of Goálás in the North-Western Provinces and Behar.

Lohrá, a synonym for Asura and Lohár.

Lohra Asur, a sub-tribe of Asuras in Chota Nagpur.

Lohrakhukhri, a kind of wild mushroom, a totemistic sept of Mundas in Chota Nagpur.

Lohriá, an iron-smelter.

Lohsá, a sub-caste of Kámárs in Manbhum.

Lohtamiá, a sept of Rájputs in Behar.

Lohutiá, a *mul* or section of the Ghosin sub-caste of Goálás in Behar.

Loityal, a *thar* or section of Nepáli Brahmans.

Lokándri, a section of Kámis in Darjiling.

Lokárk, a *pur* or section of Sákadwipi Brahmans in Behar.

Lokmahung, a sept of the Phedáb sub-tribe of Limbus in Darjiling.

Loksohm, a sept of the Yongorup sub-tribe of Limbus, said to be admitted from the Lepchas.

Lolutra, a *mul* or section of the Chhamuliá Madhesiá sub-caste of Halwáis in Behar.

Lomasá, a Brahmanical section of Khatris in Bengal.

Longa, a bird with long tail, a totemistic sept of Mundas in Chota Nagpur.

Lopáte, a *thar* or sept of Gurungs in Darjiling.

Lopchan, a section of Murmis in Darjiling.

Lori, a *dugu* or section of the Kochh-Mándái in Dacca.

Loskra, a sept of Chakmás in the Hill Tracts of Chittagong.

Lotháng, a *thar* or sept of Gurungs in Darjiling.

Lowa, a sept of Páns in Chota Nagpur.

Loyá, a section of Mahesris in Behar.

Loyna, a sept of Chiks in Chota Nagpur.

Lu, a title of Tántis in Bengal.

Ludhi, a sub-caste of Baniyás who deal in *lodh* or catechu.

Ludhna, a sub-caste of Bhuiyas in Singbhum.

Lugniár, hare, a totemistic sept of Mundas in Chota Nagpur.

Lugum, a tree, a totemistic sept of Mundas in Chota Nagpur.

Lugumah, a sept of Limbus in Darjiling.

Lugunki, a sept of Mundas in Chota Nagpur.

Luhá, a sept of the Pánthar sub-tribe of Limbus in Darjiling.

Lukhasan, a section of Goálás in Behar.

Luksom, a sept of Lepchas in Darjiling.

Lukum, a sept of Rájputs in Behar.

Lulang, a sept of the Tungjainya sub-tribe of Chakmás in the Hill Tracts of Chittagong.

Lumphongma, those who shared the land, a sept of the Phedáb sub-tribe of Limbus in Darjiling.

Lumria, fox, a totemistic sept of Lohárs in Chota Nagpur.

Lungyeli, a *thar* or sept of Mangars in Darjiling.

Luniá, a synonym for Nuniá.

Luniwál, a section of Goálás in the North-Western Provinces and Behar.

Lupu, paddy husks, a totemistic sept of Mundas in Chota Nagpur.

Luti, small black fly, a totemistic sept of Mundas in Chota Nagpur.

M

Machhilhá, a section of Sonárs in Behar.

Machhuá, a sub-caste of Bagdis and Kewats; a synonym for Gonrhi, Kewat, and Tiyar; a title of Máls and of low class Mahomedans who sell fish retail. The latter do not catch fish themselves, but obtain their supplies on a system of advances from the regular fishing castes. Hindus who follow the same avocation are called Nikári, *q.v.*

Machi, a section of Sonárs in Behar.

Machiwár, fish, a totemistic sept of Páns in Chota Nagpur.

Machli, fish, a totemistic sept of Mundas; a section of Sáráks in Chota Nagpur.

Madak, a synonym for Madhunápit and Mayará.

Mádalwár, a section of Turis in Chota Nagpur.

Madán, a *thar* or sept of Gurungs in Darjiling.

Madári, a sub-caste of Máls, who are often employed as snake-charmers.

Maden, the son of his mother, a sept of the Chhothar and Phedáb sub-tribes of Limbus in Darjiling. The name may possibly have reference to a system of female kinship which has now fallen into disuse.

Maderwár, a sept of Kharwars in Chota Nagpur.

Mádhab, a family of the Kulin group of Jugis in Bengal.

Mádhabáchárjya, a sect of Vaishnavs in Bengal.

Madha Gaurá, a sub-caste of Gaura Brahmans in Behar.

Mádhái, a *mel* or hypergamous sub-group of Rárhi Brahmans in Bengal.

Madhepuriet, a *mul* or section of the Naomuliá or Majraut sub-caste of Goálás in Behar.

Madhesia, a sub-caste of Goálás, Halwáis, and Kándus in Behar.

Madhubaniá, a *pur* or section of Sákadwipi Brahmans in Behar.

Madhu Goálá, a sub-caste of Goálás in Bengal.

Madhugrámi, a *gáin* of the Bátsya *gotra* of Uttar-Bárendra Brahmans in Bengal.

Madhukari, a sub-caste of Tántis in Bengal.

Madhukuliya, Madhukulya, an exogamous section of Baidyas; of Baruis and Nápits in Bengal, a section of Sánkháris, Tántis, Telis, and Subarnabaniks in Bengal; of Kaibarttas in Central Bengal; of Sutradhars and Bauris in Western Bengal; of Khyáns in Northern Bengal.

Madhu-Madak, a sub-caste of Madhunápits in Bengal.

Madhunapit, *Madak*, a confectioner caste of Bengal Proper who regard themselves as distinct from the Mayará. In explanation of their origin the story is told that the religious reformer Chaitanya being one day in

Origin.

a hurry ordered two of his servants to shave him. They carried out the command, but pointed out to their master that expulsion from caste privileges was the penalty which their obedience had brought upon them. Chaitanya accordingly bade them become confectioners and make sweetmeats for him. Since that time their descendants have followed the same trade, and their purity, according to Hindu ideas, is such that even goddesses partake of the dainties they prepare. Another more romantic version is that a barber named Madhu, who was called in to shave the head of Chaitanya on the occasion of his becoming a Sannyási, was so impressed with the importance of the function he had performed that he asked to be released from his hereditary profession; for, he said, having touched the head of Chaitanya, how could he cut the toe-nails of ordinary men? As Chaitanya flourished about the beginning of the sixteenth century, this legend would make the Madhunápit caste a comparatively recent offshoot from the Nápit. Such an origin, however, is not in great favour among the members of the caste, who prefer to assume a special act of creation.

Marriage.

The sub-castes and sections of the Madhunápit are shown in Appendix I. Neither series throws any light upon the origin of the caste. A man may not marry a woman belonging to his own section, nor one who stands towards him in the religious relation of *sapinda* or *samánodaka*. Madhunápits marry their daughters as infants, forbid widows to remarry, and do not recognize divorce. Although not mentioned by name in the various couplets defining the Nava-Sákha, the Madhunápit are generally admitted to belong to that group, and Brahmans will take water from their hands. Considering that the Napit and Madak are unquestionably members of the Nava-Sákha group, and the Madhunápit certainly derive their origin from one or other of these castes, their title to be Nava-Sákha seems to be beyond dispute. Most of them are Vaishnavas by creed.

Occupation.

The Madhunápit, says Dr. Wise, is the most respected confectioner in Eastern Bengal, for the caste Mayará or Madak is rarely met with, and the Halwai is usually a Ghulám Káyasth, a Khontta Brahman, or a Kándu. They assume great airs, neither intermarrying with other castes—not even with barbers—nor shaving themselves. In former days they would not fry sweetmeats in ghi or butter, but now they are less fastidious. The common sweetmeats prepared by the Madhunápit are *jalebi*, *amriti*, *khájá*, *chhená-perá*, *laddu*, *gajá*, and *sar-bhájá*. The delicacies offered to idols are *perá*, *barfi*, *iláchi dáná*, *batásá*, and *sandes*.

The Madhunápit do not cultivate the soil, but are found employed as writers, goldsmiths, grocers, cloth merchants, and policemen.

Madhurá, a sub-caste of Bábhans in Behar.

Madhuras, a totemistic sept of Mundas in Chota Nagpur who cannot eat honey.

Madhurasiárk, a *pur* or section of Sákadwipi Brahmans in Behar.

Madhurishi, a section of Mayarás in Bengal.

Madhust, a section of Maghaiyá Kumhárs in Behar.

Madhwál, a sept of Rájputs in Behar.

Madhyabhág, a *samáj* or local group of the Sándilya *gotra* of the Páschátya Baidik Brahmans in Bengal.

Madhya-bhág or **Madhyamkul**, a sub-caste of Háris in Bengal.

Madhyagrámi, a *gáin* of the Kásyapa *gotra* of Bárendra Brahmans in Bengal.

Madhyakul, a group of the Aswini Tántis in Bengal.

Madhyalá, a hypergamous group of Jugis in Bengal.

Madhyalya, a hypergamous group of the Bangaja Káyasths.

Madhyam Kurmi, a sub-caste of Kurmis in Manbhum.

Madhya-sreni, a sub-caste of Brahmans and Káyasths in Western Bengal.

Madhyasreni Káyastha, a sub-caste of Káyasthas in Midnapur.

Mádowán, a *mul* or section of the Ghosin sub-caste of Goálás in Behar.

Madrishi, honey-bee, a totemistic section of Sunris in the Santál Parganás and Manbhum.

Madrisi or **Madhukulya**, a section of Goálás in Bengal.

Mádura, *Mádar*, a contraction of Mahádanda, a sub-caste of Kewats in Behar who sell *sál* leaves and wood.

Mag, a synonym for Magh.

Mágadha, a territorial division of Brahmans in Behar.

Magadha Goárá, a sub-caste of Goálás in Orissa.

Magahgoriah, a variant for Maghaya Goálá or Maghaya Gonrh.

Magahiyá, a sub-caste of Doms in North Behar, who are cultivators and thieves, in Gya basket-makers, and in Bengal musicians and basket-makers; a sub-caste of Dhánuks, Dosádhs, Hajjáms in Behar, and of Kámárs in Manbhum; of Kándus, Támbulis, Kahárs, and Chamárs in Behar; and of Máls in the Santál Parganás.

Magai or *Mágadhi*, a sub-caste of Goálás in Bengal.

Magar, a synonym for Mangar.

Maggah, a section of the Tirhutiya sub-caste of Doms in Behar.

Magh, *Mag*, the popular designation of a group of Indo-Chinese tribes, who describe themselves by the various titles of **Maraṁagri**, **Bhuiyá Magh**, **Baruá Magh**, **Rájbansi Magh**, **Marmá** or **Myam-ma**, **Roáng Magh**, **Thongtha** or **Jumiá Magh**. Concerning the use and derivation of the name Magh there has been much discussion, and the question cannot be considered as having been finally settled.

Origin.

Wilson,[1] followed by Ritter,[2] Fr. Muller,[3] and Colonel Yule,[4] defines it as "a name commonly applied to the natives of Arakan, particularly those bordering on Bengal or residing near the sea,—the people of Chittagong." Sir Arthur Phayre, quoted by Colonel Yule, derives the name from "*Maga*, the name of the ruling race for many centuries in *Magadha* (modern Behar). The kings of Arakan were no doubt originally of this race; for though this is not distinctly expressed in the histories of Arakan, there are several legends of kings from Benares reigning in that country, and one, regarding a Brahman, who marries a native princess and whose descendants reign for a long period." Dalton[5] appears to take much the same view regarding the Arakanese as an outlying branch of the Burmese, and adding that the name Magh is exclusively a foreign epithet, unknown to the Arakanese themselves. Mantegazza[6] follows Dalton on the whole, but seems to look upon the term Magh as rather a tribal name than the general designation of the people who inhabit a particular tract of country.

Internal structure.

In its actual use at the present day the term Magh includes three endogamous groups:[7] the Thongtha, Thongcha, or Jumiá Magh;[8] the Marma, Myamma, Roáng or Rakhaing Magh;[9] and the Máramagri, otherwise known as Rájbansi, Baruá, or Bhuiyá Magh. The first and second have been described by Lewin under the name Khyoungtha or 'children of the river,' a designation based upon locality and not corresponding to any real tribal distinction. Both the Jumiá and the Roang Maghs probably belong to the same original stock, but the former have so long been settled in the Chittagong country that they regard themselves as the aborigines of the Hill Tracts, while the latter belong to a more recent stream of immigrants from Arakan.[9] The physical characteristics of both tribes are unmistakeably Mongolian. Their stature is low, the face broad and flat, cheekbones high and wide, nose flat and bridgeless,

---

[1] *Glossary, s.v.* Magh.

[2] *Erd-Kunde*, v, 324.

[3] *Allgemeine Ethnographie*, 405.

[4] *Anglo-Indian Glossary, s.v.* Mugg.

[5] *Ethnology of Bengal*, 112.

[6] *Studii sull' Etnologia dell' India*, p. 331.

[7] *Hill Tracts of Chittagong*, p. 36.

[8] Some remarks on the defects of Captain Lewin's classification of the hill tribes into Khyoungtha and Toungtha will be found in the article on Chakma above. To those objections it should be added that the classes Khyoungtha and Toungtha do not appear to be mutually exclusive. Captain Lewin himself states (p. 37) that "Khyoungtha means those who inhabit the banks of mountain streams and support themselves by hill cultivation;" and if this definition be accepted, it is difficult to see how the line between the two classes should be drawn.

[9] Roáng seems to be a corruption of Rakhaing, the indigenous name for the Arakan country or its inhabitants. Arakan, again, is the European form of Rakhaing or Rakhang. Colonel Yule (*Anglo-Indian Glossary*, art. Arakan) thinks that we may have got Arakan through the Malay, but the early connexion of the Arabs with Chittagong seems to justify the conjecture that the word may be simply Al-Rakhang.

and eyes small with eyelids obliquely set;[1] while according to Lewin the men have neither beard nor moustache. The Maramagri or Rájbansi Magh are of an entirely different type. They are supposed by Colonel Phayre to be "the offspring of Bengali women by Burmans when the latter possessed Chittagong;" and this theory of their origin is borne out by the fact that their exogamous septs are similar to those of the Thongtha and Marmá. All external indications of their Mongolian descent have, however, been obliterated by generations of intermarriage with the non-Aryan Bengalis of Chittagong and Noakhali; and the Rájbansi Maghs, who are largely employed as cooks in Calcutta, have the glossy black complexion, wavy hair, and abundant beard and moustache which characterise the lower castes of Eastern Bengal. It may be added that their somewhat insolent bearing and excitable manner of speech complete the contrast with the stolid, but amiable Mongolians, from whom they are remotely descended.

The septs of the three sub-tribes are shown in Appendix I. Most of them, as Lewin has pointed out, appear to be the names of the rivers on which the original settlements of the sept were situated. They observe the simple rule that a man may not marry a woman of his own sept, supplemented by a table of prohibited degrees, which does not differ materially from that arrived at by the standard formula already often referred to. In applying these prohibitions, however, there seems to be some laxity where descent is traced through females, for I am informed that a man may marry the daughters of his father's sister and of his mother's brother—a connexion which would not ordinarily be allowed.

Marriage.

The Maramagri marry their daughters either as infants or as adults, and there is some tendency among them to regard the former usage as more respectable from the social point of view. Marmás and Thongchas adhere to the more primitive custom of adult-marriage, and more or less expressly tolerate sexual intercourse as one of the necessary incidents of pre-matrimonial courtship. Their marriage ceremony, says Lewin,[2] "is distinctive and uncommon. On a young man attaining a marriageable age, that is, about 17 to 18, his parents look about for some young girl who would be a good wife to him, unless, as is more often the case, he has fixed upon a partner for himself. Having determined upon a suitable match, a male relative of the family is sent off to the girl's parents to arrange matters. On arriving at their village he proceeds to the house, and before going up the house ladder he gives the usual salutation, with both hands joined and raised to the forehead. '*Ogatsa*,' he says, 'a boat has come to your landing place; will you bind it or loose it?' A favourable response is given, and he then goes up into the house. On seating himself he asks, 'Are the supports of the house firm?' If the

---

[1] The apparent obliquity of the Mongolian eye is due to a peculiar conformation of the eyelids, and does not extend to the orbit itself. See Topinard, *Eléments d'Anthropologie Générale*, p. 998.

[2] *Hill Tracts of Chittagong*, p. 49.

answer is, 'They are firm,' it is favourable, and matters may then be more fully entered into. The affair is taken into consideration, and he returns to his own village to report good progress to the bridegroom's parents, and to request them to fix a day for taking the omens. On the appointed day the parents meet, the young people being supposed to know nothing of all this. A fowl is killed by the fathers, its tongue taken out, and, according to certain marks thereon, the matter is pronounced good or bad. The bridegroom's parents sleep for the night at the house of the intended bride, and all parties look anxiously for dreams by which to foretell the happiness or the reverse of the union. On going away, should everything be propitious, their intended daughter kneels at their feet for a blessing, and they present her with a new petticoat and a silver ring. Learned persons are then called in, who, by consulting the stars and casting the nativity of the parties, determine a favourable day and hour when the ceremony shall be undertaken. Meantime the parents on both sides prepare pigs and spirits, rice and spices, unlimited, for the marriage feast. They also send round to all their kith and kin a fowl and a letter giving notice of the intended marriage; in some places a pice or copper coin is substituted for the fowl. On the auspicious day, and at the hour appointed, the bridegroom and all his relatives set out for the bride's house, dressed in the gayest colours, both men and women, with drums beating before them. On arriving at the entrance of the village the female relatives of the bride bar the approach with a bamboo. Across this barrier the bridegroom has to drink a loving cup of fraternity, generally spirits. Should the females on the bride's side muster strong, the road will probably be barred five or six times before the entry into the village is fairly made. The bridegroom, however, does not drink all that is given him, but after taking the liquor in his mouth he is allowed to eject it again upon the ground.

"In the village, on some open turfy spot, a number of bamboo booths have been erected, adorned with flowers and green boughs, and filled with materials for feasting. Here also sit an opposition party of drummers, and mighty is the row as the bridegroom's party defiles on to this spot. A separate and specially beautified booth has been erected for the young lover and his parents, and here they sit in state and receive visits from all the village. The bride in like manner, surrounded by her near relatives, sits in her father's house. The boys of the village, irrepressible as is the wont of that species, make raids upon both parties, for the purpose of chaffing and getting alternate feasts of comestibles. They also organize an amateur band of music, and serenade the bride towards evening with fiddles and flutes. Of course, all the girls of the village are congregated at the bride's father's house, and, as license and riot are the order of the day, the fun here grows fast and furious. Towards nightfall the bridegroom ascends to his bride's house amid a tempest of cheers and a hailstorm of drums. After this outburst a temporary lull ensues, to permit of the ceremony being performed. The bride is brought forth from an inner chamber in the arms of the women. On the floor of the house are placed water in jars, rice, and mango leaves. Round these a new-spun cotton-thread is wound and carried again round the two contracting parties as they stand opposite to each other. The 'poong-yee,' or priest, now comes forward; he recites some prayers in a language that is not understood even by himself (probably Pali), and then taking cooked rice, a handful in each hand, he crosses and recrosses his arms, giving seven alternate mouthfuls to the bride and bridegroom; after this he takes their hands and crooks the little finger of the bridegroom's right hand into the little finger of the bride's left. The ceremony is then concluded by more unintelligible mutterings. The bridegroom now takes the bride by the hand, and together they make the circuit of the room, saluting lowly the elder relatives of both families. They then sit down—the bride to the left of her husband, and their clothes are tied together. The wedding guests then come forward and place at their feet, each according to his or her means, some presents of clothes or household furniture. After this a saturnalia ensues, of dancing, drinking, fighting, and love-making. The bride and bridegroom are expected to sit up all night. I should add that the happy man does not consummate his marriage until he and his wife (sleeping apart) have for seven days eaten together seven times a day."

The bride-price among Thongchas and Marmas is said to be about Rs. 30. With the Maramagris, who as a class are wealthier, the average amount paid for a wife is Rs. 60, which may rise to Rs. 80 if the bridegroom is of inferior status, as, for example, in the event of a Bhuiyá Magh marrying the daughter of a Rájbansi Magh. The ceremony in use among the Máramagris is of the same general character as that described above, the essential portion being the crooking together of the little fingers of the bridegroom's left hand and the bride's right, while the priest pours water over the hands thus joined. This is followed by *sindurdán* or smearing vermilion on the bride's forehead—a form which appears to have been borrowed from the Hindus. The Marmá ritual is still more like that of the Thongchas, and does not include *sindurdán*. In the course of the wedding the bride and bridegroom eat some curry and rice from the same dish, and what they leave is kept in a covered earthen vessel for seven days, during which time the married couple may not leave the village or cross running water. On the eighth the vessel is opened, and if maggots are found in the food it is deemed an excellent omen, showing that the marriage will be a fruitful one.

Polygamy is recognized: a man may have as many wives as he can afford to maintain. The first wife, however, is regarded as the highest in rank, and takes precedence of all subsequent wives, who are expected to treat her with special consideration.

In all the sub-tribes widows are allowed to marry again, and are fettered by no restrictions in their choice of a second husband. No special ritual is ordained for this purpose, and as a rule the parties simply go and live together as man and wife. Divorce is permitted, with the sanction of the tribal pancháyat, on the ground of adultery or inability to live happily together. A written agreement is usually drawn up, and sometimes, when the authority of the pancháyat is deemed insufficient, this "writing of divorcement" is laid before the Magistrate of the district. Among the Thongchas the parties give one another flowers, and after bathing go off in different directions, exchanging all kinds of abusive epithets. Divorced wives may marry again by the ritual in use for the remarriage of widows.

Religion.

All Maghs are Buddhists of the Southern school, and regard the northern Buddhists of Tibet as wholly unorthodox. The wilder sections of the Thongchas, however, retain some vestiges of an earlier animistic faith, which bids them sacrifice cattle, goats, and swine, and make offerings of rice, fruits, and flowers to the spirits of hill and river. Among the Maramagris, on the other hand, the tendency is to follow after modern Hinduism, particularly in its Tantric developments, and to add the gross worship of Siva and Durga to the simple observances prescribed by their own communion. It thus comes to pass that while the Buddhist *Phungyis* or *Ráolis* are the recognized priests of all the tribes, considerable respect is shown to Brahmans, who are frequently employed to determine auspicious days for particular actions, and to assist in the worship of the Hindu gods. Among the Thongchas old women often devote themselves to the service of religion, and although not charged with special ceremonial functions, are regarded as in some sense priestesses, and are called by the distinctive name *lerdama*.

Disposal of the dead.

The funeral ceremonies of the Maghs are thus described by Lewin :—" When a person has died, his relatives assemble. Some one of them sits down and commences to beat the funeral roll on the drum; the women weep and cry, and the men busy themselves, some in performing the last offices to the corpse, of washing, dressing, etc., while others go off to the woods and bring wood for the funeral pile, and bamboos with which to construct the bier. About 24 hours generally elapse from the time of death to that of cremation. In bearing the corpse from the house to the burning ground, if the deceased were a man of wealth or influence, the body may be borne on a wheeled car; all women also have this privilege; the plebs, however, are simply carried to the funeral pile on the shoulders of their relatives. The procession is after this fashion :—First come the priests, if there are any in the vicinity to attend; they march gravely at the head of the party, bearing on their shoulders their curved palm-leaf fans, clad in their ordinary saffron-coloured robes, and attended by their disciples. Next come relatives of the deceased, two and two, bearing food, clothes, etc., which have been offered as alms to the priests on behalf of the departed. Next is borne the bier, carried on bamboos by six men, and accompanied by as many drums as can be procured. Behind the coffin come the male relatives; and lastly, the procession is closed by the women of the village, clad in their best. The funeral pile is composed of four layers of wood for a woman, three for a man. The body is placed on the pile; the leading priest takes an end of the dead man's turban, and, holding it, repeats some passages of the law, four of the deceased's male relatives standing meanwhile at the four corners of the pile and sprinkling a few drops of water thereon. The nearest blood relative, male or female, of the dead man then fires the pile. When the fire is extinguished the ashes are scrupulously collected together and buried over the spot; a small conical mound of earth is heaped up, and a very long bamboo pole, with an equally lengthy flag, is erected over the grave. On returning from the place all parties bathe themselves. If it is the master of the house who has died, the ladder leading up to the house is thrown down, and they must effect an entrance by cutting a hole in the back wall and so creeping up. The relatives eat and drink, and each contributes according to his means to defray the expenses incurred. After seven days the priests reassemble at the house to read prayers for the dead."

In the case of priests and persons of high social position the corpse is dried or embalmed and kept for a year in a special coffin, while arrangements are being made for an elaborate funeral, which usually takes place on the 1st of Baisakh. A temporary pagoda is built of bamboo decorated with coloured paper and flags, and is set up in some open place faced by a row of bamboo cannon mounted on wheels, crammed to the muzzle with tightly-rammed powder and fitted with a long fuse. These cannon are presented by persons desirous of doing honour to the deceased, and it is deemed an act of great merit to send a cannon to the funeral of a Phungyi. On the arrival of the coffin a mimic conflict—a 'tug of war'—takes place over it, the women pulling it one way and the men the other. According to another account the contest is not between the men and the women, but between the unmarried and married persons of either sex. The coffin is then placed in the pagoda, and the bamboo cannon are discharged in order of the precedence of those who presented them. Last of all the pagoda and coffin are burned, and a long bamboo, carrying a triangular flag forty-five feet long, is set up on the place. A funeral offering (*kongmu*) of various kinds of food is placed on the ground on the eighth day, and this ceremony is repeated every year.

Social status.

The social status of the Maghs does not admit of very precise definition, as the entire community is outside of the regular caste system, and orthodox Hindus will take neither food nor water from their hands. In the matter of diet they are highly promiscuous, eating beef, pork, fowls, fish of all kinds, snakes, field-rats, lizards, and certain kinds of worms. Both sexes indulge freely in spirituous liquors. For all this they are not wholly free from prejudice as to the caste of the persons with whom they will take food; and no Maghs, except those who are fishermen themselves, will eat, drink, or smoke in the same hookah with members of the fishing castes, such as Kaibarttas and Málos, or with the Jugi caste of weavers. Tántis and Nápits, on the other hand, are considered ceremonially pure, and Maghs will take water from their hands.

Occupation.

The Thongcha sub-tribe live almost entirely by the peculiar method of cultivation known in Chittagong, Assam, and Northern Bengal by the name *jhúm;* in Burmah and Arakan as *tungyá;* and in Chota Nagpur and the Central Provinces called *dáhá* or *paráo.* Captain Lewin describes the system as follows:—

Jhum cultivation.

"In the month of April a convenient piece of forest land is fixed upon, generally on a hillside, the luxuriant under-growth of shrubs and creepers has to be cleared away, and the smaller trees felled: the trees of larger growth are usually denuded of their lower branches, and left standing. If possible, however, the jhumiá fixes upon a slope thickly covered with a bamboo jungle of the species called 'dolloo.' This compared with a dense tree jungle is easy to cut, and its ashes, after burning, are of greater fertilising power. Although the clearing of a patch of dense jungle is no doubt very severe labour, yet the surroundings of the labourer render his work pleasurable in comparison with the toilsome and dirty task of the cultivators of the plains. * * * * * *

By his comparatively pleasurable toil the hill-man can gain two rupees for one which the wretched ryot of the plains can painfully earn, and it is not to be wondered at that the hill people have a passion for their mode of life, and regard with absolute contempt any proposal to settle down to the tame and monotonous cultivation of the dwellers in the low-lands.

"The jhum land once cleared, the fallen jungle is left to dry in the sun, and in the month of May it is fired: this completes the clearing. The firing of the jhums is sometimes a source of danger, as at that season of the year the whole of the surrounding jungle is as dry as tinder and easily catches fire. In this way sometimes whole villages are destroyed, and people have lost their lives. I have myself seen a whole mountain-side on fire for four days and four nights, having been ignited by jhum-firing. It was a magnificent sight, but such a fire must cause incalculable injury to the forest: young trees especially would be utterly destroyed. Generally, however, by choosing a calm day, and keeping down the fire at the edges of the jhum, by beating with boughs, the hill people manage to keep the firing within certain prescribed limits. A general conflagration, such as I have mentioned, is of quite exceptional occurrence. If the felled jungle has been thoroughly dried, and no rain has fallen since the jhum was cut, this firing will reduce all, save the larger forest trees, to ashes, and burn the soil to the depth of an inch or two. The charred trees and logs previously cut down remain lying about the ground: these have to be dragged off the jhum and piled up all round, and with the addition of some brushwood form a species of fence to keep out wild animals.

"Work is now at a standstill, till the gathering of the heavy clouds and the grumbling of thunder denote the approach of the rains. These signs at once bring a village into a state of activity; men and women, boys and girls, each bind on the left hip a small basket filled with the mixed seeds of cotton, rice, melons, pumpkins, yams, and a little Indian corn; each takes a 'daô'[1] in hand, and in a short time every hillside will echo to the 'hoiya,' or hillcall (a cry like the Swiss jodel), as party answers party from the paths winding up each hillside to their respective patches of cultivation. Arrived at the jhum, the family will form a line, and steadily work their way across the field. A dig with the blunt square end of the daô makes a narrow hole about three inches deep: into this is put a small handful of the mixed seeds, and the sowing is completed. If shortly afterwards the rain falls, they are fortunate and have judged the time well; or (unparalleled luck) if they get wet through with the rain as they are sowing, great will be the jollification on the return home, this being an omen that a bumper season may be expected.

"The village now is abandoned by every one, and the men set to work to build a house, each in his own jhum, for the crop must be carefully watched to preserve it from the wild pig and deer, which would otherwise play havoc among the young shoots of the rice. The jhums of the whole village are generally situated in propinquity: a solitary jhum is very rare. During the rains mutual help and assistance in weeding the crop is given; each one takes his turn to help in his neighbour's jhum; no hoeing is done; the crop has merely to be kept clear from weeds by hand labour, and an ample return is obtained. If the rain be excessive, however, the cotton crop is liable to be spoilt, as the young plants die from too much water.

"The first thing to ripen is Indian corn; this is about the end of July. Next come the melons, of which there are two or three sorts grown in the jhums: afterwards vegetables of all sorts become fit for gathering; and finally, in September, the rice and other grain ripens. At this time the monkeys and jungle fowl are the chief enemies of the crop. In the month of October the cotton crop is gathered last of all, and this concludes the harvest. The rice having been cut, is beaten from the ear in the jhum: it is afterwards rolled up in rough, straw-covered bales and carried to the granary in the village.

* * * * *

---

[1] "The 'daô' is the hill knife, used universally throughout the country. It is a blade about 18 inches long, narrow at the haft, and square and broad at the tip; pointless, and sharpened on one side only. The blade is set in a handle of wood; a bamboo root is considered the best. The fighting 'daô' is differently shaped. This is a long pointless sword, set in a wooden or ebony handle; it is very heavy, and a blow of almost incredible power can be given by one of these weapons. With both the fighting and the ordinary daô one can make but two cuts; one from the right shoulder downwards to the left, one from the left foot upwards to the right. The reason of this is that in sharpening the blade one side only gives the edge, slanting to the other straight face of the blade. Any attempt to cut in a way contrary to those mentioned causes the daô to turn in the hand on the striker, and I have seen some bad wounds inflicted in this manner. The weapon is identical with the "parang latok" of the Malays. The ordinary hill daô is generally stuck naked into the waist-band on the right hip, but the fighting daô is provided with a scabbard and worn at the waist. The daô to a hillman is a possession of great price. It is literally the bread-winner. With this he cuts his jhum and builds his houses; without its aid the most ordinary operations of hill life could not be performed. It is with the daô that he fashions the women's weaving tools; with the daô he fines off his boat; with the daô he notches a stair in the steep hillside leading to his jhum; and to the daô he frequently owes his life, in defending himself from the attacks of wild animals."

Besides grain and cotton, the hill tribes grow tobacco. This is planted principally in small valleys on the banks of the hill streams." In order to scare birds, deer, and wild pigs from the growing crop, a cleft bamboo is planted in the middle and connected by a long cane with the hut built for watching the crop in such a manner that by pulling the cane the two halves of the bamboo can be clashed together and a harsh rattling noise produced.

The Marmás and Maramagris have for the most part adopted a settled mode of life and taken to plough cultivation. They also catch and sell fish, hew wood, dug-out canoes, and weave baskets and mats. The Rájbansi Maghs are accomplished cooks, and are largely employed by Europeans in that capacity. As a rule they take a keen interest in their profession, and it may be that their skill is in some measure due to their freedom from the social and religious prejudices which debar other classes of native cooks from tasting the dishes which they prepare.

Maghá Chewár, a *mul* or section of the Sâtmuliá or Kish-naut sub-caste of Goálás in Behar.

Maghad Khandi, a sub-caste of Telis in Bengal.

Maghaiá, a sept of Lohárs in Chota Nagpur.

Maghaiyá, a sub-caste of Kumhárs and Telis in Behar and Chota Nagpur.

Maghayá, a native of Mag-há (Magadha) or South Behar; a designation of numerous sub-castes, such as Barai, Beldar, barber, Dhanuk, Dhobi, Gangotá, Goálá, Kándu, Nunia, Sunri, and Teli castes in Behar; a sub-caste of Barhis in Behar who work in both wood and iron and do the rougher woodwork required for houses, as distinguished from the Kanaujiás, who are joiners and cabinet-makers. Representatives of this sub-caste are found both in the town of Bhágalpur and in the north of the district, but intermarriage between the two groups is believed to be rare. The headman of the former is styled *Sátun*, while the headman of the latter bears the usual title of *Manjhan*; a sub-caste of Bhars in Manbhum, comprising the five sections of Mayur, Bel, Básrisi, Kásyab, and Bráhmarshi, of which the first four are totemistic and the last appears to have been borrowed from the Brahmans; a sub-caste of Doms in Behar who play the *dhol* and *turi*; a sub-caste of Halwáis or confectioners in Behar, who have to some extent abandoned their distinctive occupation and find employment as servants and petty shopkeepers dealing in miscellaneous articles. Many of them fry rice, *chura*, etc., and are called *bhuja bhura*; a sub-caste of Koiris in Behar, which, though endogamous as regards the rest of the caste, intermarries with the Chirme or Chirmáit sub-caste; a sub-caste of Kumhárs in Behar and Western Bengal, which used formerly to be endogamous, but now intermarries with the Tirhutiá sub-caste; a sub-caste of Thatherá or brass-chaser in Behar.

Maghayá Bráhman, a synonym for Bábhan.

Maghi, a sept of Chiks in Chota Nagpur.

Maghniá, a sept of Lohárs in Chota Nagpur.

Magi, a sub-caste of Kumhárs in Dacca and Tántis in Bengal; a sub-caste of Báitis in Faridpur.

Magrathi, a *thar* or sept of Mangars in Darjiling.

Maguri, a title of Bangaja Káyasths in Bengal.

Mahabara, a totemistic sept of Chiks in Chota Nagpur who never kill or chase the wild boar.

Mahabhát, a section of the Kamár sub-caste of Dosádhs in Behar.

Mahábrahman, Mahápátra or **Kantáha**, a division of Brahmans in Behar who officiate as priests on cremation.

Mahádanda, a sub-caste of Kewats in Behar.

Mahádanta, a title of Brahmans.

Mahájan, money-lender, a title of the Ariár sub-caste of Bais Baniyás.

Máhakariá, a section of Goálás in the North-Western Provinces and Behar.

Mahalá, a section of Goálás in the North-Western Provinces and Behar.

Mahaldár, a title of men who measure grain for Mahajáns, also called Kayáls; a title of Jaunpuri Chamárs and Muchis in Behar whose women act as midwives; a title of certain Musalmans, also called Pajrá, who sell fish and are boatmen.

Mahali, a synonym for Mahili; a sept of Lohárs in Chota Nagpur.

Mahali-Munda, a sub-tribe of Mundas in Chota Nagpur; a sept of Lohárs in Chota Nagpur.

Mahallá-navis, an honorary title of Káyasths in Bengal.

Mahámandá, a section of the Mahmudábáz sub-caste of Nápits in Central Bengal.

Mahánadi, a river, a sept of Bediyas and Chiks in Chota Nagpur.

Mahánadiá, a sept of Gonds in Chota Nagpur.

Mahánáik or *Sreshta-Khandáit*, a sub-caste of Khandáits in Balasore and Cuttack.

Mahánandiá, a sept of Páns in Chota Nagpur.

Maháni, a title of Támbulis, Telis, and other trading castes.

Mahant, S.; the head of a religious establishment of the mendicant orders of the Hindus.

Mahanta, a priest of the Jugi caste in Tipperah; a spiritual guide in the Vaishnava sect; a title of Kurmis in Western Bengal.

Mahanti, *Máhinti*, a titular section of Utkal or Orissa Brahmans; a title of Chásás and Karans in Orissa.

Mahápátra, a hypergamous group of the Bangaja sub-caste of Káyasths in Bengal; a title of Brahmans and Karans in Orissa; a title of Khandáits in Chota Nagpur.

Mahar, a section of Goálás in Behar.

Mahará, a title of the Dhusiá sub-caste of Chamars; a title of Kahars in Behar who carry palanquins and work as boatmen.

Mahárái, a title of Kurmis in Behar.

Mahráj, a title affected by certain mendicants and Brahmans; a title of respect applied to Behar Brahmans who are employed as cooks.

Mahárání, a title of Nágars in Behar.

Mahárano, a *mul* or section of the Naomuliá or Majraut sub-caste of Goálás in Behar.

Maháráshtra, a *thar* or section of Nepáli Brahmans.

Maháráshtriya, a territorial division of the Pancha Drávira Brahmans who live in the south of the Vindyá range, a country of the Marathi language.

Mahárath or *Mahárathi*, great charioteer, a title of Khandáits in Orissa.

Maháraus, a sept of the Suryabansi sub-tribe of Rájputs in Behar.

Maharná, a section of Kewats in Behar.

Maháset, a group of Maghaiyá Telis and Sunris in Behar.

Mahásib, literally 'an accountant,' a section of the Maghayá sub-caste of Telis; a title of Sunris in Behar.

Mahasthán, Mastán or **Háliá**, a sub-caste of Utkal Brahmans in Orissa.

Mahat, a sub-caste of Goálás in Chota Nagpur; a title of up-country Brahmans and of some trading castes; a title of the Kochh tribe in Northern Bengal.

Máhátá, a title of Khatris in Bengal.

Maháthá, a section of Maghaiyá Kumhárs in Behar.

Mahathwár, a section of the Chamár and Bhuiyá castes.

Mahátmá, a *mul* or section of the Ghosin sub-caste of Goálás; a section of the Chaubhán sub-caste of Nuniás and a section of the Banodhiá and Jaiswár Kalwárs in Behar.

Mahátman, a section of the Maghayá sub-caste of Kumhárs in Behar.

Mahato, a title of Goálás, Kurmis, Koiris, Kahárs, Kumhárs, Rajwárs, Dhánuks, Mundas, Chiks or Páns and Pásis; a sept of Oraons in Chota Nagpur.

Mahatoar, a sept of Páns and Agariás in Chota Nagpur.

Mahauliá, a section of Kaserás in Behar.

Mahaut, a sept of Thárus in Behar.

Máhbariá, a *kul* or section of Bábhans in Behar.

Mahbho, a sept of the Yangorup sub-tribe of Limbus in Darjiling; branch of the same sept may not intermarry.

Mahbu, the physician, literally a shaker—one who, being ridden by ghosts or devils, shakes himself free: hence a physician; a sept of the Charkola sub-tribe of Limbus in Darjiling.

Mahdauriár, a *pur* or section of Sákadwipi Brahmans in Behar.

Mahendra Khyáni, a group of the Bárendra Sunris in Eastern Bengal.

Máhepurá, a *mul* or section of the Chhamulia Madhesiá sub-caste of Halwáis in Behar.

Maher, a section of Kumhárs in Singbhum.

Mahesbaráit, a section of the Kamár sub-caste of Dosádhs in Behar.

Maheśri, a trading caste of Northern India and Marwar, closely allied to the Agarwáls and Oswáls with whom they eat and drink. Like the Agarwáls, they have a sub-caste called Dasá, said to be illegitimate and perhaps coming of slave mothers. The Maheśri are almost invariably Hindus, while the Agarwál and Oswál castes contain a large proportion of Jains. They have 72 exogamous subdivisions (*gots*), a few of which are shown in Appendix I. Like the Agarwáls, they observe a complex rule of exogamy. A man may not marry into (*a*) his own section, (*b*) his mother's, (*c*) his maternal grandmother's, (*d*) his father's maternal grandmother's, (*e*) his mother's maternal grandmother's.

Maheswar, a *pur* or section of Sákadwipi Brahmans, and of Maghaiyá Kumhárs in Behar.

Mahili, *Mahali*, a Dravidian caste of labourers, palanquin-bearers, and workers in bamboo found in Chota Nagpur and Western Bengal. They are divided into five sub-castes—**Bansphor-Mahili**, who make baskets and do all kinds of bamboo work; **Pátar-Mahili**, basket-makers and cultivators; **Sulunkhi-Mahili**, who are cultivators and labourers; **Tánti-Mahili**, who carry palanquins; and **Mahili-Munda**, a small outlying sub-caste confined to Lohardagá. A comparison of the totemistic sections of the Mahilis shown in Appendix I with those of the Santáls seems to warrant the conjecture that the main body of the caste, that is to say the group comprising the Bansphor, Sulunkhi, and Tanti Mahilis, is merely a branch of the Santáls, separated at a comparatively recent date from the parent tribe. The exact causes of the separation are, of course, lost in the obscurity which enshrouds the early history of all tribal movements. But the fact that the Mahilis make baskets and carry palanquins, occupations which every Santál would deem degrading, suggests that the adoption of these pursuits may have given the first impulse to the formation of the new group. The Mahili-Munda possibly parted from the Mundá tribe for similar reasons. Besides the sections shown in the Appendix the entire sub-caste regard the pig as their totem, and consider it wrong to eat pork. It is rumoured, indeed, that appetite often gets the better of tradition, but that in such cases the carcase alone is eaten, and the consequences of breaking the taboo averted by throwing away the head. The Pátar-Mahili are a Hinduised sub-caste of South-East Manbhum, who employ Brahmans as priests and abstain from eating beef.

Origin and internal structure.

A man may not marry a woman of his own section or of the section to which his mother belonged before her marriage. Beyond these limits marriage is regulated with reference to the standard formula for prohibited degrees.

Marriage.

Mahilis marry their daughters both as infants and as adults, but the former practice is deemed the more respectable, and there can, I think, be little doubt that in this, as in other castes on the borders of Hinduism, the tendency at the present day is towards the entire abolition of adult-marriage. The customary bride-price paid for a Mahili girl is supposed to be Rs. 5, but the amount is liable to vary according to the means of the bridegroom's parents. On the wedding morning, before the usual procession starts to escort the bridegroom to the bride's house, he is formally married to a mango tree, while the bride goes through the same ceremony with a mahuá. At the entrance to the bride's house the bridegroom, riding on the shoulders of some male relation and bearing on his head a vessel of water, is received by the bride's brother, equipped in similar fashion, and the two cavaliers sprinkle one another with water. The bride and bridegroom are then seated side by side on a plank under a canopy of sál leaves erected in the courtyard of the house, and the bridegroom touches the bride's forehead five times with vermilion, and presents her with an iron armlet. This is the binding portion of the ritual.

So far as positive rules are concerned, the Mahilis appear to impose no limit on the number of wives a man may have. It is unusual to find a man with more than two; and practically, I understand, polygamy is rarely resorted to unless the first wife should happen to be barren. Widows may remarry, and are under no restrictions in their choice of a second husband, though it is deemed right and proper for a widow to marry her deceased husband's younger brother if such a relative exists. Divorce is permitted on the ground of adultery or inability to agree. When a husband divorces his wife he gives her a rupee and takes away the iron armlet (*lohár kháru*) which was given her at her wedding. He must also entertain his caste brethren at a feast by way of obtaining their sanction to the proceedings. Divorced wives may marry again.

Like the Bauris and Bágdis, the Mahilis admit into their caste men of any caste ranking higher than their own. The conditions of membership are simple. The person seeking admission into the Mahili community has merely to pay a small sum to the headman (*parganáit*) of the caste and to give a feast to the Mahilis of the neighbourhood. This feast he must attend himself, and signify his entrance into the brotherhood by tasting a portion of the food left by each of the guests on the leaf which on these occasions serves as a plate.

Inheritance.

In matters of inheritance and succession the Mahilis profess to follow whatever law applies to the Hindus of the locality—the Dáyabhága in Manbhum and the Mitákshará in Lohardagá. Statements of this kind, however, import little more than a vague assumption of conformity with what is supposed to be the custom of all respectable men; and there is no reason to believe that the headman (*parganáit*) and caste-council (*pancháyat*), who settle the civil disputes of the caste, have any knowledge of, or pay the smallest regard to, the rules of the regular Hindu law. The questions which come before this primitive tribunal are usually very simple. Its decisions are accepted without question, and I know of no instance where an attempt has been made to correct them by appealing to the regular courts. It does not follow, however, that Mahilis and castes of similar standing have escaped the influence of the Codes and have preserved a distinct customary law of their own. On the contrary, the written law certainly filters down to these lower grades of society, not through the regular channels of text-books and courts, but in virtue of their tendency to imitate the usages of the groups immediately above themselves. If men of these lower castes are asked what law they follow, a common answer is that they have the same law as their landlords; and the landlords, to whatever caste they may belong, almost invariably get their law from the text-books and the courts. To this influence it is probably due that the practice of giving an extra share (*jeth-angs*) to the eldest son in dividing an inheritance is gradually dying out among the Mahilis, and the tendency is towards an equal division of property.

Religion.

The religion of the Mahilis is at present a mixture of half-forgotten animism and Hinduism imperfectly understood. They affect indeed to worship all the Hindu gods, but they have not yet risen to the distinction of employing Brahmans, and their working deities seem to be Bar-pahári and Manasá. The former is merely another name for the well-known mountain god of the Mundas and Santáls, while the latter is the snake goddess, probably also of non-Aryan origin, whose cult has been described in the article on the Bágdis. To these are offered goats, fowls, rice, and ghi, the offerings being afterwards eaten by the worshippers themselves.

Disposal of the dead.

The Mahilis of Northern Manbhum bury their dead face downwards; but this practice is not universal, for the Pátar Mahilis and the Mahilis of the Santál Parganas burn their dead and bury the ashes near at hand. On the eleventh day after death offerings of milk, ghi, and rice are made at the place of burial. Similar offerings are presented in the months of Kártik and Chait for the propitiation of departed ancestors in general. The anniversary of the death of an individual ancestor is not observed.

Social status and occupation.

Mahilis rank socially with Bauris and Dosadhs. They eat beef, pork, and fowls, and are very partial to strong drink. Field-rats, which are reckoned a special delicacy by the Oraons, they will not touch. They will eat cooked food with the Kurmi, the Bhumij, and the Deswali Santáls. They believe their original occupation to be basket-making and bamboo work generally. Many of them are now engaged in agriculture as non-occupancy raiyats and landless day-labourers.

The following statement shows the number and distribution of Mahilis in 1872 and 1881:—

DISTRICT.	1872.	1881.	DISTRICT.	1872.	1881.
Bardwan	64	57	Maldah	1,365	218
Bankura	......	77	Santál Parganás	9,521	1,252
Birbhum	......	85	Cuttack	......	53
Midnapur	3,497	966	Balasore	......	7
Nadiya	18	31	Tributary States	......	604
Khulna	......	10	Hazaribagh	1,979	2,256
Dinajpur	3	302	Lohardaga	8,999	7,510
Rajshahye	28	196	Singbhum	1,301	1,196
Pabna	60	......	Manbhum	7,895	4,772
Monghyr	375	......	Tributary States	111	13
Bhagalpur	548	......			

Mahili-Mundá, a sub-caste of Mahilis in Western Bengal.

Mahintá, a *gáin* of the Bátsya *gotra* of Rárhi Brahmans in Bengal.

Mahisirupján, a *mul* or section of the Naomulia or Majraut sub-caste of Goálás in Behar.

Máhkur, Mákur, a sub-caste of Goálás in Chota Nagpur.

Mahlaingtsa, a sept of Maghs in the Hill Tracts of Chittagong.

Mahli, a sept of Birhors in Chota Nagpur.

Mahmudábáz, a sub-caste of Nápits in Eastern Bengal.

Máhmudpuriá, a sub-caste of Kámárs in Western Bengal.

Mahrá, a *mul* or section of the Biahut sub-caste of Kalwárs in Behar.

Máhrá, a title of Chamárs and men employed to herd cattle.

Mahrághási, a sub-caste of Ghásis in Chota Nagpur who serve as bearers.

Mahrajiá, a section of Bháts.

Mahrána, a *pangat* or section of Bánsphor Doms, and of Dosadhs in Behar.

Mahrano, a title of Hindu Joláhás in Behar.

Mahrasiá, a *pur* or section of Sákadwipi Brahmans in Behar.

Mahrat, a *mul* or section of the Ayodhiá sub-caste of Hajjáms in Behar.

Mahraul, a *mul* or section of the Goria sub-caste of Goálás in Behar.

Mahraur, a sept of the Chandrabansi Rájputs in Behar. They cannot intermarry with persons of the Besáin and Chaubhán septs, being supposed to have had their common origin in the same saint.

Mahtá, a section of Goálás in the North-Western Provinces and Behar.

Mahtha, a section of the Amashta sub-caste of Káyasths in Behar.

Máhto, (i) a village headman; (ii) a title applied in Behar to Kurmis who by age or by personal influence have attained a leading position in their villages. In some parts of the country the title is used as almost synonymous with Kurmi; and a Kurmi, when asked to what caste he belongs, will reply "Máhto;" (iii) a title of the following castes:—Dhánuks, Dosádhs, Goria Goálás, Koiris, Sunris; the Bhojpuriá and Ayodhiá sub-castes of Nuniás in Behar; also Thárus; the Bediyas, Mahilis, Nágeswars, and Kharwars in Chota Nagpur; Cheros and the Malwe Rájputs in Chota Nagpur; Tántis, Kewats, Binds and Dhobis in Behar.

Mahtoar, a totemistic sept of Chiks in Chota Nagpur.

Mahtwar, a section of Goálás in Behar.

Mahuá, a tree, a totemistic sept of Páns, Doms, Bedyas, and Chamárs in Chota Nagpur.

Mahuár, a sept of Rájputs in Behar.

Mahuári, a section of Bábhans and of the Biyáhut and Kharidáhá Kalwárs in Behar.

Mahukal, a bird, a totemistic sept of Mundas, Bediyas, and Kharwars; a section of Mahilis in Chota Nagpur.

Mahuli, a section of the Sátmuliá Maghayá sub-caste of Kándus in Behar.

Mahur or *Mahuliyá*, a sub-caste of Lohárs in Behar.

Máhuri, a sub-caste of Baniyás in Behar, who occupy nearly as high a rank as the Agarwáls in social estimation. Like the Sikhs, the Máhuris strictly prohibit the use of tobacco, and a man detected smoking would be expelled from the community. Another peculiar usage is that marriages are always celebrated at the bridegroom's house, and not at the bride's. Trade and money-lending are the proper occupations of the Máhuri. Some of them have acquired substantial tenures and set up as landholders and zamindars.

Mahuriá, a section of Láheris in Behar.

Mahwá, a section of the Tirhutia sub-caste of Doms in Behar.

Maiduchhá, a *thar* or sept of Khambus in Darjiling.

Maikam, a *thar* or sept of Khambus in Darjiling.

Mai ketári begunâ bágh, "harrow, sugarcane, egg-plant, garden," a formula or shibboleth distinguishing a section of the Maghayá sub-caste of Koiris in Behar.

Maikhola, a sub-tribe of Limbus in Darjiling.

Máil, a *mul* or section of the Chhamuliá Madhesiá sub-caste of Halwáis in Behar.

Máilidhurlak, a *mul* or section of the Naomuliá or Majraut sub-caste of Goálás in Behar.

Mailwár, a section of Cheros, Khariás, Kharwars, and Lohárs in Chota Nagpur.

Máilwar, a *mul* or section of the Naomuliá or Majraut sub-caste of Goálás in Behar.

Mainá, a bird, a totemistic sept of Goálás, Parhaiyas, Mundas, and Bediyas in Chota Nagpur.

Mainkiswar, a section of the Kamár sub-caste of Dosádhs in Behar.

Mainpuri, a class of Baniyás in Behar.

Máir, a sub-caste of Sonárs in Behar who do not permit the remarriage of their widows.

Mairiá, a section of Bábhans in Behar.

Maisásari, a sub-caste of Kurmis in Orissa.

Máitál, a title of Kánsáris or braziers in Western Bengal.

Maitbukru, a place where he buries his bones, being his ancestral birthplace, a section of Mahilis in Chota Nagpur.

Maithil or **Tirhutiá**, a territorial division of the Pancha Gaura Brahmans in Behar, deriving its name from Mithilá or Tirhut.

Máiti, *Máti*, a title of Utkal Brahmans and of Kaibarttas in Orissa and Bengal.

Maitra, a *gáin* of the Kásyapa *gotra* of Bárendra Brahmans in Bengal.

Majar or **Minjur**, peacock, a totemistic sept of Mundas and Páns in Chota Nagpur.

Májháliár, a *mul* or section of the Sátmuliá or Kishnaut sub-caste of Goálás in Behar.

Majhal-Turiyá, a sub-caste of Rajwárs in Lohardagá.

Májhasthán, a sub-caste of Kumhárs in Pabna.

Májhaurá, a section of the Biyáhut and Kharidáhá Kalwárs in Behar.

Majhiaur, a sept of the Rautár sub tribe of Thárus in Behar.

Majhiya, a section of Rajwárs in Western Bengal.

Majhrot, a title of Maithil Brahmans in Behar.

Majhwat, a sub-caste of Goálás in Chota Nagpur.

Máji, a title of Kandhs in Orissa.

Majilpur, a *samáj* or local group of the Dákshinátya Baidik Brahmans in the 24-Parganás.

Majlishi, a sub-caste of Sunris in Eastern Bengal.

Majlisi (Maudgalya), a section of Kaibarttas in Murshedabad.

Majraut or **Naomuliá**, a sub-caste of Goálás in Behar.

Majumdár, an honorary title of Brahmans, Káyasths, Báruis, Jugis, and Sunris in Bengal; a hypergamous group of Kaibarttas in Bakarganj.

Majurrishi, a section of Mayarás in Bengal.

Makadá, a section of Goálás in the North-Western Provinces and Behar.

Makhaiwár, a *pur* or section of Sákadwipi Brahmans in Behar.

Mákhpawár, a *pur* or section of Sákadwipi Brahmans in Behar.

Maki, *Muki*, a synonym for Ghási.

Mákunda, a sub-group of the Háliyá or Hele Kaibarttas in Central Bengal.

Makundpuri, a section of Sonárs in Behar.

Mál, a Dravidian cultivating caste of Western and Central Bengal, many of whom are employed as *chaukidárs* or village watchmen and have gained an evil reputation for their thieving propensities. Beyond the vague statements current among the Máls of Eastern Bengal, that they were wrestlers (*Malla*, *Mála*) at the court of the Dacca Nawábs and gained their name from this profession, the caste appear to have no

Traditions of origin.

traditions, and their origin has formed the subject of much discussion, the general drift of which is stated by Mr. Beverley[1] as follows:—

"In his late work on the Ancient Geography of India, General Cunningham quotes a passage from Pliny, in which the *Malli* are mentioned as this:—'*Gentes: Calingæ proximi mari, et supra Mandei Malli, quorum mons Mallus finisque ejus tractus est Ganges.*' In another passage we have, '*Ab iis (Palibothris) in interiore situ Monedes et Suari, quorum mons Mallus*'; and putting the two passages together, General Cunningham 'thinks it highly probable that both names may be intended for the celebrated Mount Mandar, to the south of Bhagalpur, which is fabled to have been used by the gods and demons at the churning of the ocean.' The *Mandei* General Cunningham identifies 'with the inhabitants of the Mahanadi river, which is the *Manada* of Ptolemy.' 'The *Malli* or *Malei* would therefore be the same people as Ptolemy's *Mandalæ*, who occupied the right bank of the Ganges to the south of Palibothra,' the *Mandalæ* or *Mandali* having been already identified with the *Monedes* and the modern Munda Kols. 'Or,' adds General Cunningham, 'they may be the people of the Rajmahal hills who are called Maler, which would appear to be derived from the Canarese *Male* and the Tamil *Malei*, a 'hill.' It would therefore be equivalent to the Hindu *pahári* or *párbatiya*, a 'hillman.'" Putting this last suggestion aside for the present, it seems to me that there is some little confusion in the attempt to identify both the *Monedes* and the *Malli* with the Mundas. If the *Mandei* and the *Malli* are distinct nations—and it will be observed that both are mentioned in the same passage—the former rather than the latter would seem to correspond with the *Monedes* or Mundas. The *Malli* would then correspond rather to the *Suari, quorum mons Mallus*—the hills bounded by the Ganges at Rajmahal. They may therefore be the same as the Mals. In other words, the Mals—the words Maler and Malhar seem to be merely a plural form—may possibly be a branch of the great Sauriyan family to which the Rajmahal Pahárias, the Oraons, and the Sabars all belong, and which Colonel Dalton would describe as Dravidian. Fifteen hundred or two thousand years ago this people may have occupied the whole of Western Bengal. Pressed by other tribes, they have long since been driven into corners, but not without, as it were, leaving traces of their individuality behind. In Mal-bhumi (Manbhum) instead of 'the Country of the Wrestlers,' as Dr. Hunter puts it, we seem to have the land of '*Mons Mallus*' and the Mals. The Maldah district may also possibly owe its name to their having been settled there. As to the name, indeed it is quite possible that it means nothing more than highlanders; the word *Mallus* being simply the Indian vernacular for the Latin *mons*. If a native were asked the name of a hill in the present day, he would reply, as Pliny's informant probably replied years ago, that it was a 'hill;' and if asked the name of the people who lived there, he would probably say they were 'hillmen.'

"These Mals appear to have been driven eastwards and to have spread over the whole of Bengal, where they have become merged

[1] *Report of the Census of Bengal*, 1872, by H. Beverley, p. 184.

in the mass of low-caste Hindus. This will account to some extent for what Colonel Dalton calls the Dravidian element in the composition of the Bengali race. Under the Hindu system the Mals, like other aboriginal tribes who came within the pale of Hinduising influences, appear to have formed one of the forty-five tribes of Chandals, the lowest or sweeper class among Hindus. Chandals are found in every district of Bengal, their aggregate number in the present day being over a million and a half. In Mymensingh, where we find 20,000 Mals, we have 123,000 Chandals. In the south-eastern districts they seem to have lost their name in the generic term of Chandals, but in the eastern districts they still retain it. In Birbhum and Bankura, in each of which districts there are about 9,000 Mals, there are not as many hundred Chandals. In Murshedabad there are 29,000 Mals against 22,000 who described themselves as Chandals. Most officers say the Mals are identically the same as the Chandals. Some say they are wrestlers, others attribute to them the same occupation as that of the Madaris or Sampheriyas, viz., that of snake-charmers. Others, again, say they are Musalmans, and identify them with Bediyas or Babajiyas; but in this explanation there seems to be some confusion, the two last tribes not being generally considered identical. The Babajiyas, though an itinerant tribe like the Bediyas, are employed, like the stationary Pasaris, in selling drugs. The returns, however, show that some of the Mals are Musalmans."

Internal structure.

The most primitive specimens of the caste are met with in Bankura, where they have distinctly totemistic sections, and are divided into the following sub-castes:—**Dhaiiá**, **Gobrá** or **Gurá**, **Khera**, **Rájbansi**, and **Sánágánthá**. In Midnapur and Manbhum we find **Dhunakátá**, **Rájbansi**, **Sápuryá** or **Bedya Mál**, and **Tungá**; in Birbhum **Khaturía**, **Mallik**, and **Rájbansi**; in the Santál Parganás **Deswar**, **Magahiyá**, **Rajbansi** or **Rájá Mál**, **Rárhi Mál**, and **Sindurá**; while in Murshedabad the sub-castes are the same as in Bankuar, except that Dhaliá is not known. The origin of these groups is extremely obscure, and I doubt whether any amount of inquiry would throw much light on the subject. Rájbansi, for example, is the name adopted by a very large proportion of the Kochh tribe; but there is no reason to suppose that the Máls are Kochh, and they might easily have acquired the name Rájbansi in the same manner as the Kochh have done by identifying themselves with the lineage of a local Rájá, who may or may not have belonged to the same race. The simplest solution of the difficulty appears to be to assume that Mál is nothing more than a variant of Málé, 'man,' the name by which the Málé Pahāriás describe themselves. It is possible, again, that the Rájbansi Máls may be the same as Rája Máls whom Buchanan noticed among the Mál Pahāriás at the beginning of the century. The monkey-catching Gobras bear the same name as one of the sub-castes of Bágdis; and Khera is not far removed from Khairá, whom some regard as a branch of the Doms. The Sánágánthá take their name from making *sánás*, the uprights through which weavers pass their thread. The **Dhunákátá Máls** collect resin (*dhuna*) by tapping *sál* trees; the **Tungá** sub-caste are cultivators; while the **Sapuriá** or **Bedya Máls** live by charming snakes, catching monkeys, hunting or conjuring, and roam about the country carrying with them small tents of coarse gunny-cloth. Although they catch snakes, Sápuriá Máls hold the animal in the highest reverence, and will not kill it, or even pronounce its name, for which they use the synonym *latá*, 'a creeper.'

Kinship with the Bediyás.

The names of the last-mentioned group raise the probably insoluble question of the connexion of the Máls with the Bediyás. Dr. Wise treats both Mál and Samperiá or Sápuriá as subdivisions of the Bediyá tribe; but it is equally possible that the Mál may be the parent group, and that the Bediyás may have separated from it by reason of their adhering to a wandering mode of life when the rest of the tribe had taken to comparatively settled pursuits. There certainly seem to be reasons for suspecting some tolerably close affinity between the two groups. The Máls of Dacca, for instance, are called **Ponkwah**, from their dexterity in extracting worms from the teeth, a characteristic accomplishment of the Bediyás. They repudiate the suggestion of kinship with the latter tribe, but it is said that many can recollect the time when relationship was readily admitted. At present, however, in spite of some survival of roving habits, peculiar physiognomy, and distinctive figures, Máls are with difficulty recognized. Many of them are small bankers (*mahájans*), never dealing in pedlar's wares, but advancing small sums, rarely exceeding eight rupees, on good security. The rate of interest charged is usually about fifty per cent. per annum; but this demand, however exorbitant, is less than that exacted by many money-lenders in the towns. The Dacca Máls never keep snakes, and know nothing about the treatment of their bites. The women, however, pretend to a secret knowledge of simples and of wild plants. They are also employed for cupping, for relieving obscure abdominal pains by friction, and for treating uterine diseases, but never for tattooing. The Máls of Eastern Bengal do not intermarry with Bediyás, and even within the limits of their own group a sharp distinction used to be observed between settled Máls and gipsy Máls; so that if one of the former sought to marry a girl of the latter class, he was required to leave his home, give up his cultivation, and adopt a wandering life. This custom has gradually given way to a keener sense of the advantages of settled life, but its general disuse is said to be still resented by the elders of the caste.

Plausible as the conjecture may be which would trace some bond of kinship between the Bediyás and the Máls, the evidence bearing on the point is not precise enough to enable us to identify the Sápuriá Máls of Midnapur with the Sámperiya Bediyás of Eastern Bengal. Snake-charming is an occupation likely enough to be adopted by any caste of gipsy-like propensities, and there is no reason why both Máls and Bediyás should not have taken to it independently. Further particulars will be found in the article Bediyá.

The Máls of Western and Central Bengal seem on the whole to be the most typical representatives of the original Mál tribe. Among them the primitive rule of exogamy is in full force, and a man may not marry a woman who belongs to the same totem group as himself. Prohibited degrees are reckoned by the standard formula calculated in the descending line to five generations on the father's and three on the mother's side. Outsiders belonging to higher castes may be admitted into the Mál community by giving a feast to the Máls of the neighbourhood and drinking water in which the headman of the village (*mánjhi*) has dipped his toes. No instance of any one undergoing this disagreeable ordeal has been quoted to me, and such cases must be very rare.

Exogamy.

Girls may be married either as infants or after they have attained puberty, the tendency being towards the adoption of the former custom. The ceremony takes place just before daybreak in a sort of arbour made of *mahuá* and *sidhá* branches in the courtyard of the bride's house. After the bride has been carried seven times round the bridegroom the couple are made to sit side by side facing the east, and a vessel of water which has been blessed by a Brahman is poured over their heads after the manner of the Mundas and Oraons.[1] Garlands of flowers are then exchanged, the clothes of the pair are knotted together, and if adult they retire into a separate room in order to consummate their union. On their reappearance they are greeted by the company as husband and wife. Polygamy is permitted, but most Máls are too poor to maintain more than one wife. A widow may marry again,[2] but no special ritual is in use, except among the Rájá Máls of Birbhum, who exchange necklaces of beads or seeds of the tulsi (*Ocynum sanctum*); and such marriages, which are called *sanga*, are effected by paying a small fee to the headman (*khámid* or *mánjhi*) and to the father of the widow. Divorce may be effected, with the sanction of the pancháyat, on the ground of adultery by the wife, and divorced women may marry again in the same manner as widows.

Marriage.

Máls profess to have completely adopted Hinduism, and no vestiges of any more primitive religion can now be traced among them. They seem to belong to whatever Hindu sect is popular in the locality where they are settled; and in different districts they describe themselves as Vaishnavas, Saivas, or Sáktas, as the case may be. The snake goddess Manasá is believed to be their special patroness, and is worshipped by them in much the same fashion as by the Bágdis. Sacrifices of rice, sweetmeats, and dried rice are also offered by the heads of families to the tutelary goddess of each village, who bears the name of the village itself with the termination *sini*

Religion.

---

[1] According to some accounts Jalmá, the goddess of water, must first be worshipped with gifts of flowers at a neighbouring tank, and water drawn from this tank must be used in the marriage in addition to water blessed by a Brahman.

[2] This is the general rule, but the Rájbansi Máls of Midnapur have recently abandoned widow-marriage.

added; so that the goddess of the village Páthará would be called Pátharásini. In most districts they have not yet attained to the dignity of employing Brahmans, but elders of the caste or headmen of villages serve them as priests (*khámid*). In the Santál Parganás, however, the Brahmans of the Let sub-caste of Bágdis officiate also for the Rájá Máls. The dead are burned, usually at the side of a stream, into which the ashes are thrown. A meagre imitation of the orthodox *sráddh* ceremony is performed on the eleventh day after death in ordinary cases, and on the third day for those who have died a violent death. On the night of the Káli Pujá in Kártik (October–November) dried jute stems are lighted in honour of departed ancestors, and some even say that this is done to show their spirits the road to heaven. Libations of water are offered on the last day of Chait. Female children are buried mouth downwards, and the bodies of very poor persons are often buried with the head to the north in the bed of a river.

Disposal of the dead.

Agriculture is supposed to be the original profession of the caste, and most Máls, except those of distinctly gipsy habits, are now engaged in cultivation as occupancy or non-occupancy raiyats and landless day-labourers. None appear to have risen to the higher rank of zamindar or tenure-holder, except in Bankura, where one *sardár ghatwál*, one *sadiál*, 56 *tábidárs*, and 35 *chákarán chaukidárs* are Máls. In Manbhum, on the other hand, which some believe to be the original home of the caste, no Máls are found in possession of these ancient tenures, though some are employed as ordinary village *chaukidárs*. The women of the caste and some of the men often make a livelihood by fishing—a fact which accounts for their bearing the title of Machhuá. Their social status is very low, and is clearly defined by the fact that Bágdis and Koras will not take water from their hands, while they will take water and sweetmeats not only from those castes, but also from Bauris. Máls pride themselves on abstaining from beef and pork, but eat fowls, all kinds of fish, field-rats, and the flesh of the *gosámp* (*Lacerta godica*). The Rájá Máls, however, do not touch fowls.

Occupation and social status.

The following statement shows the number and distribution of Máls in 1872 and 1881:—

DISTRICT.	1872.	1881.	DISTRICT.	1872.	1881.
Bardwan	3,078	734	Jalpigori	16	......
Bankura	8,436	12,348	Dacca	4,663	7,835
Birbhum	9,346	21,630	Faridpur	957	2,273
Midnapur	5,726	4,042	Bakarganj	2,945	877
Hughli	} 1,058	{ 607	Maimansinh	20,166	14,782
Howrah		16	Tipperah	3,970	4,755
24-Parganás	955	329	Chittagong	1	9
Nadiya	4,407	4,696	Noakhali	3	21
Khulna	......	70	Shahabad	907	7,016
Jessore	5,577	2,398	Bhagalpur	71	607
Murshedabad	29,281	8,368	Maldah	2,063	885
Dinajpur	1,446	1,026	Santál Parganás	8,820	469
Rajshahye	1,064	267	Tributary States, Orissa...	1,082	......
Rangpur	386	318	Lohardagá	950	......
Bogra	818	743	Singbhum	1,367	21
Pabna	1,682	1,310	Manbhum	4,031	1,675
Darjiling	2	......	Tributary States	1,042	......

Mál, a sub-caste of Bhuiyas in Singbhum; a title of Kaibarttas; a section of the Maghayá sub-caste of Koiris and a section of Turis; a sub-sept of the Saren sept of Santáls.

Mál or **Már**, a sub-caste of Mauliks in Chota Nagpur.

Málá, a title of Kapális and Kawális in Eastern Bengal.

Málabhumiá, a sub-caste of Muchis in Bengal.

Máládhárkháni, a *mel* or hypergamous sub-group of Bárhi Brahmans in Bengal.

Malár, a synonym for Kathak in Singbhum.

Malar, a sept of Mundas and Ghásis in Chota Nagpur.

Malauriár, a *pur* or section of Sákadwipi Brahmans in Behar.

Máldhiá, a section of the Sátmuliá Maghayá sub-caste of Kándus in Behar.

Málé, *Mál, Sámariá Malé, Savar Pahâriá, Sauriá, Sámil Pahâriá, Asal Pahâriá, Sangi*, a Dravidian tribe of the Rajmahál hills, closely akin to the Oraons, and probably an isolated branch of the large and widely diffused Savar tribe. The actual name of the tribe appears to be Mál, which is combined with the pronouns *en*, *em*, and *é* in order to form the present of the verb substantive. Thus Málen is the first person singular, I am a Mál; Málé, the third person singular; Malem, the first person plural; and Máler (used in the spelling Malair by Lieutenant Shaw as the name of the tribe), the third person plural. The selection of Málé as the tribal name for the purpose of this work is therefore both arbitrary and incorrect, and can only be justified by the necessity of having some distinctive designation to mark off these Máls from the Mál Pahâriás of the southern hills and from the Mál caste of Bengal. In respect of physical characteristics the Málé represent the extreme type of the Dravidian race as we find it in Bengal. The nasal index measured on 100 men of the tribe yields an average of 94·5, which closely approaches the proportions ascertained for the Negro. The average stature is low, the complexion dark, and the figure short and sturdy.

Origin.

Early history of the tribe.

Owing to the rocky and forest-bound character of their country, and their incessant internal struggles, the Málés of the Rájmahál hills maintained a virtual independence during the period of Musalmán ascendancy in Bengal. It appears that, although they never completely recognized the imperial authority, they had a rude indigenous system of government, which was worked in moderate accord with the *zamindárs* of the low country bordering on the hills. The hills included in each *tappá* or subordinate fiscal division were subject to one or more divisional headmen, called *sardárs*, to whom the village headmen (*mánjhis*) were in their turn subordinate. The *sardárs*, who were possibly more civilized than the rest of the tribe, received from the *zamindárs* allotments of land in the plains on *jágir* or service tenures, in consideration of which they made themselves responsible for the prevention and detection of crime among the hill people. Besides this, the passes leading from the hills into the plain country were guarded by outposts of Málés, whose duty it was to stop any bodies of men from making raids upon the plains, and to give warning of an impending inroad. For further security, the *zamindárs* themselves maintained at the foot of the hills a chain of *chaukís* or police outposts, which were independent of the Málé guardians of the passes within the hills. Once every year, at the Dasahará festival, the divisional headman (*sardár*) of each *ṭappá* came down to the plains with his subordinate *mánjhís*, and there partook of a feast and received a turban at the *zamindár's* expense, at the same time formally renewing his engagements to keep the peace within his jurisdiction. For a long time this system kept crime within bounds, and promoted good feeling between the Málés and the people of the low country; but about the middle of last century a show of independence on the part of the hill people was treacherously resented by the *zamindárs*, who took the opportunity of the annual public feast to murder several of the village headmen. On this the Málés within the hills gave up the guardianship of the passes, and commenced a series of depredations, which were held in some check up to 1770 by the line of *zamindárí* police posts without the hills. In that year, however, the famine which desolated the neighbouring districts pressed with peculiar severity upon the alluvial strip of country lying between the Rájmahál hills and the Ganges; the police outposts were abandoned, and the plains thus lay at the mercy of the Málés, who, owing to their aboriginal practice of living upon jungle foods, had escaped the extremity of distress. It was therefore in the years following the famine of 1770 that the raids of the hillmen upon the low country became most frequent and most systematic. Plunder no doubt was their main object, and the desire to revenge the treacherous murder of their headmen; but many of their inroads were in the first instance instigated by the landholders, who were in the habit of offering the Málés a free passage through their own lands on condition that they ravaged those of the neighbouring *zamindárs*. At any rate, the terror they occasioned was so widespread that the alluvial country was deserted by its cultivators; no boat dare moor after dusk on the southern bank of the Ganges; and even the Government mail-runners, who in those days passed along the skirts of the hills, by way of Rájmahál and the Teliá Garhí Pass, were frequently robbed and murdered at the foot of the hills. Up to 1778 the British Government, like the Muhammadans before them, made various attempts to suppress the Málés by military force. In 1772 a corps of light infantry, armed expressly for jungle fighting, was raised and placed under command of Captain Brooke. But the Málés never gave the troops a chance in the open country; while in the tangled undergrowth of the hills firearms had no decided advantage over the strong bamboo bows and heavy poisoned arrows of the hillmen. Besides this, the absence of roads, the difficulty of keeping up supplies, and the fatally malarious climate of the Rájmahál jungles, made the permanent subjection of the Málés a hopeless undertaking for native troops. In 1778 Captain Brown, then commanding the corps of light infantry, submitted to

Government a scheme for the pacification of the hillmen, the essential elements of which were the following:—*First*, the *sardárs* or divisional headmen of the Málés were to be restored to their original position as chiefs of the tribe, receiving formal *sanads* of appointment from Government, and in their turn entering into engagements, renewable annually, to perform certain specified duties. Similar engagements were to be taken from the *mánjhis* or village headmen, binding them to obey the *sardárs* in all matters laid down in the *sanads*. *Second*, those *sardárs* whose *tappás* bordered upon the public road were to receive a fixed pecuniary allowance, nominally for the purpose of maintaining police to protect the mail-runners, but in fact as a bribe to deter them from committing robberies themselves. *Third*, all transactions with the hill people were to be carried on through their *sardárs* and *mánjhis*, but intercourse with the inhabitants of the plains was to be encouraged by establishing markets on the outskirts of the hills. *Fourth*, the old *chauki bandi* or chain of police outposts, which had been abandoned in 1770, was to be completely re-established and maintained by Government until the service lands attached to them had been brought under cultivation. But the control of these outposts was to be taken from the *zamindárs* and made over to *thánádárs* or police officers appointed by Government, who were again to be subordinate to *sazáwals* or divisional superintendents. This police force was further to be strengthened by conferring grants of lands below the hills on invalid sepoys, on the condition that they settled on their allotments and gave assistance in the event of a Málé inroad. The total annual expense of the scheme was estimated at £100. Early in 1778 Captain Brown's scheme was approved by Government; and both the chain of police posts below the hills and the system of allowances to the *sardárs* on the public road were partially established before the end of the year. But in 1779 the hill country of Rájmahál was transferred from Captain Brown's jurisdiction, and it thus fell to Mr. Augustus Cleveland, who had been appointed Collector of Bhágalpur, to carry out the foregoing scheme. In the following year (1780) Mr. Cleveland reported that forty-seven hill chiefs had of their own will submitted to Government authority. With the view of retaining these men as loyal subjects he subsequently proposed that a corps of hill archers, four hundred strong, should be enrolled from among the Málés and officered by eight *sardárs* or divisional headmen, under the command of the Collector of Bhágalpur. The officers were to be paid Rs. 5, and the common soldiers Rs. 3, per mensem. Every village headman, he suggested, should be called upon to furnish recruits to the corps, and should receive for this service an allowance of Rs. 2 a month. The yearly expense of this arrangement, including the cost of the purple jackets and turbans which were to form the uniform of the corps, was estimated by Mr. Cleveland at £3,200. Warren Hastings, who was then Governor-General, at first objected to the enrolment of the corps of archers on the ground of this heavy expense, and sanctioned a scheme which Mr. Cleveland had proposed in the meantime, for granting pensions of Rs. 10 a month to all divisional headmen (*sardárs*) and of Rs. 5 a month to their *náibs* or deputies; *mánjhis* or village headmen were to receive no allowance at all. But towards the end of 1780 the enrolment of a corps of archers was sanctioned, mainly in consequence of the Commander-in-Chief having expressed his approval of the scheme when passing through Bhágalpur on his way to the Upper Provinces. At the same time the fiscal divisions of Ambár and Sultánábad were transferred to Mr. Cleveland's jurisdiction, it having been found that the chiefs of the southern portion of the Rájmahál hills would not give in their allegiance as long as they were exposed to continual inroads from the inhabitants of those *parganás*. Shortly afterwards, at the special request of the *sardárs* and *mánjhis* of Belpattá, that fiscal division was also placed under Mr. Cleveland, pensions being granted to the chiefs and recruits furnished for the hill archers.

Not long after the enrolment of the hill archers an outbreak that occurred in the hills was quelled by them so effectively that a proposal by Mr. Cleveland that the corps should be drilled and armed like regular sepoys was readily sanctioned, and Lieutenant Shaw was appointed adjutant; the name of the corps being at the same time changed to "The Bhágalpur Hill Rangers," by which name they were known until disbanded on the reorganization of the Native army after the Mutiny in 1857.

From the first enrolment of the hill archers petty offences committed by the members of the corps were punished by a rude court-martial of the officers. In 1782, however, one of the archers murdered a Málé woman, and in order to punish this, the first serious crime that had occurred, Mr. Cleveland proposed the formation of a distinct tribunal, the jurisdiction of which should be limited to members of the corps. This, which was at first styled court-martial, and afterwards hill assembly, was to consist of three or more officers of the corps, the power of appointing and dissolving the court resting with Mr. Cleveland. Mr. Cleveland was also to approve of all sentences passed by the court, except when capital punishment was awarded. In that case an assembly of five or more hill chiefs (*sardárs*) was to be convened, and a final decision to be passed in accordance with the opinion of the majority. Mr. Cleveland further proposed that offences committed by the inhabitants of the hills generally, with the exception of those who were enrolled in the corps of archers, should be withdrawn from the jurisdiction of the ordinary courts and placed under a tribunal of chiefs (*sardárs*) presided over by himself. The entire scheme, both as regards the court-martial for the archers and the assembly of *sardárs* for the hillmen generally, was approved by Government in April 1782. Shortly afterwards Mr. Cleveland reported that he had arranged for assemblies to be held twice a year, and gave the following account of the proceedings of the first trial:—"I have settled with the chiefs that they are regularly to assemble here twice a year for the purpose of trying all prisoners who may be brought before them; and as particular cases occur which may require immediate inquiry, they have agreed to attend whenever I find it necessary to summon them. One assembly has been already held, at which 1 principal chief (*sardár*), 74 *mánjhis*, and 120 common hill people were tried for plundering the *parganá* of Kharakpur of near nine hundred head of cattle. The trial lasted three days, and was conducted with as much ceremony and formality as the nature and disposition of the people would admit of. I have the pleasure to observe, however, that the chiefs appeared to conduct themselves throughout the trial with the greatest attention and impartiality, and the result of their proceedings, which I have confirmed, is as follows:—One principal chief, Bidji of Titoriá, and one common hill man, Chandra of Pupat, to be hanged immediately; and the sentence was accordingly carried into execution this morning, in the presence of the corps of hill archers and all the principal hill chiefs and *mánjhis*. One *mánjhi*, Jaruá of Tátakpárá, to be hanged twenty days hence, unless the whole cattle plundered are delivered up in that time, in which case he is to be pardoned. Seven *mánjhis* to be confined for their lives, unless the whole of the cattle plundered are delivered up in twenty days, in which case they are to be pardoned. Sixty-five *mánjhis* and 120 common hill people acquitted."

The rules of Mr. Cleveland's Hill Assembly were subsequently incorporated in Regulation I of 1796, which "provided that the Magistrate should commit all important cases to be tried before an assembly of hill chiefs. He was to attend the trial as superintending officer, and confirm or modify the sentence, if not exceeding fourteen years' imprisonment. Higher sentences were referred to the Nizámat Adalat, as the Supreme Criminal Court was then called. This unusual procedure was followed till 1827, when the law was repealed by Regulation I of that year; the mountaineers were then declared amenable to the ordinary courts, but some of the hill *mánjhis* were to sit with the Magistrate as assessors when he tried cases in which the hill men were concerned; and the *mánjhis* were also authorized to adjudicate summarily in disputes about land, succession, and claims to money when the value of the claim did not exceed one hundred rupees." It appears that the Hill Assembly, when no longer kept together by the personal influence of Mr. Cleveland, became almost unmanageable. Considerable difficulty was experienced in getting the chiefs to meet at all; and when present they would not attend to the proceedings of the court, while their sentences were hasty and capricious in the extreme. It was found, too, that even when the assemblies could be induced to do their work, the power they had been entrusted with was too uncontrolled, and that the total personal exemption of the Málés from the jurisdiction of the ordinary courts was a measure of doubtful policy, the more so as it seems to have been held that under Regulation I of 1796 the Magistrate had no power to try and punish Málés for petty offences on his own motion. Regulation I of 1827 has now been repealed by Act XXIX of 1871.

In 1783, the year before his death, Mr. Cleveland proposed that the Málés should be given extensive grants of waste land at the foot of the hills on the following terms:—(1) Every *sardár* was to have a rent-free *jágir* or service tenure, in perpetuity, of from 100 to 300 *bighás* of land. (2) Any Málé of lower rank than a chief might be allowed any quantity of land rent-free for ten years, it being liable to subsequent assessment at equitable rates. (3) In order to secure that the foregoing provisions should really come into operation, Mr. Cleveland suggested that all *sardárs* and *mánjhis* holding pensions from Government should forfeit their pensions unless they settled in the plains within twelve months. It was hoped that by thus forcing the hill men to settle in the plains they would become civilized by intercourse with the lowlanders; while as they learned more productive methods of agriculture it would be possible to make them contribute to the cost of administration. But the scheme was never carried out, and the immigration of Santáls from the west has now almost completely cut off the Málés from close intercourse with the plains. In any case, it may be doubted whether they would have left their hills; while from all that is known of the Oraons and other Dravidian races, Mr. Cleveland's expectation that the Málés would take to manufactures appears to have been utterly unfounded.

Traditions.

The traditions of the Málé are meagre. In Lieutenant Shaw's well-known monograph on the tribe[1] published in 1795, a story is told of seven brothers who were deputed by the gods to people the earth. A feast was made, and it was arranged that each brother was to take of such food as he liked and go to the land which he had chosen to dwell in. One took one thing and one another, and their choice determined the caste of their descendants. From the brother who took goat's flesh sprang the Hindus; another who took flesh of all kinds, but refused pork, became the father of the Mahomedans; another chose pork, and from him are the Kiratis; another is the ancestor of the 'Kawdir' (Kádar), and so on. Only the eldest brother, who was sick, got all sorts of food in an old dish. He was left in the hills as an outcast, and from him the Málé are descended. This myth is clearly only an echo of the similar story told by the Mundas and Hos. Both versions agree in their general tenor and in some of their details; both must have arisen after the tribes had been for some time in contact with Hindus, and both, it may be added, find it necessary to provide a place for the English in their account of the making of mankind.

Internal structure.

All my correspondents agree in assuring me that the Málés have no endogamous or exogamous subdivisions, and that their marriages are regulated solely by the standard formula for reckoning prohibited degrees which is explained in the introduction. If this is correct, a point upon which I am not yet fully convinced, the fact is remarkable. The Málés have been less exposed to Hindu influences than their kinsmen, the Oraons, yet the latter retain a long list of exogamous totems, while the former have no exogamous groups at all, and in this respect are more modern than most Hindu castes. The question seems to me to call for further inquiry. One would wish to know whether the Málé ever observed the characteristic Dravidian system of exogamy; and if so, how it came to fall into disuse.

---

[1] *Asiatic Researches*, vol. IV.

Marriage.

Free courtship is allowed, and girls are married, when of full age, to men of their own choice. Sexual intercourse before marriage is not recognized in theory, but if an unmarried girl becomes pregnant a sacrifice is offered to atone for the indiscretion, and arrangements are made to get her married without delay.

Marriage brokers (*sithu*) are employed to conduct the preliminary negotiations, and to settle the difficult question of the bride-price. When this has been satisfactorily arranged, an auspicious day is fixed, when the bridegroom goes with his friends to the bride's house, taking with him a goat to furnish forth the wedding feast, and the bride-price, a portion of which is sometimes paid beforehand through the *sithu*. The parties are made to sit opposite each other, the bridegroom facing east and the bride west, while her girl friends comb and oil her hair. Then the father takes the bride by the hand and gives her to the bridegroom, pointing out that she is not halt, maimed or blind, and enjoining him to treat her kindly. This done, the *sithu* takes the bridegroom's right hand, dips the little finger in *sindur*, and makes five dots with it on the girl's forehead, afterwards using her finger to perform the same office for the bridegroom. Guns are fired to mark the completion of this essential rite, and the married couple then eat together out of the same dish in symbol of their union. The proceedings are concluded by a feast.

Divorce.

Divorce is permitted with the sanction of the leading men of the village. If the husband demands a divorce on the ground that his wife is barren, that she has committed adultery, or that she is incurably lazy, he is entitled to claim a refund of the bride-price which he paid for her in the first instance. He forfeits this right if the reasons which he gives are deemed to be frivolous and insufficient. If the wife claims a divorce on whatever grounds, her family must refund the bride-price. The ritual observed consists in tearing a *sál* leaf or breaking a small branch or a piece of string in token of separation, and pouring a vessel of water over the woman's head. Divorced women may marry again.

Religion.

The religion of the Málés is animism of the type common among Dravidian tribes. At the head of their system stands the Sun called Dharmer Gosain, and represented by a roughly-hewn post set up in front of each house. He is worshipped with offerings of fowls, goats, sindur, and oil at the commencement of the harvest season, and at other times when any misfortune befalls the family. When people are gathered together for this purpose, the village headman, who acts as priest, goes round the congregation with an egg in his hand, and recites the names of certain spirits. He then throws away the egg, apparently as a propitiatory offering, and enjoins the spirits to hold aloof and abstain from troubling the sacrifice. Among the minor gods mentioned by Lieutenant Shaw, Raksi now appears as the tutelar deity of strong drink, who is worshipped by the headman of the village before beginning to distil liquor from the fresh *mahua* crop.

According to Lieutenant Shaw, Rakai is sought out when a man-eating tiger infests a village or a bad epidemic breaks out, and is worshipped in the form of a black stone set up under a tree and hedged round with *Euphorbia* plants. Chal or Chalnad is a god presiding over a group of ten villages, and represented by a black stone set up under a *mukmum* tree. Goats and pigs are the animals usually offered to him, and the sacrifice of a cow, said by Lieutenant Shaw to be performed every three years, seems to have fallen into disuse. Pau-Gosain, the god of highways, lives under a *bel*, *kurare*, or *mukmum* tree. He is invoked by persons going on a journey. When Lieutenant Shaw wrote the offering was a cock. Now it is a white goat, and the sacrifice is said to be a very expensive one, by reason of the large amount of rice-beer—ten or twelve maunds—that must be offered to the god and drunk by his assembled votaries. The tutelary deity of the village, spoken of by Lieutenant Shaw under the name of Dwára Gosain, is now called Bára-Dwári, because he is supposed to live in a temple with twelve doors. The whole village worship him in the month of Mágh. Colonel Dalton suggests that this god may perhaps be the same as the Oraon Dárá. Kul Gosain, 'the Geres of the mountaineers,' and Autga, the god of hunting, appear not to be known at the present day. Gumo Gosain, or the god of the pillar, is represented in every household by the wooden post (*gumo*) which supports the main rafters of the roof. On this the blood of a slain goat is sprinkled to propitiate the spirits of ancestors. The fact that this god is common to the Málés and Mál Paháriás (see page 70 below), and is worshipped by both in the same way, seems to tell strongly in favour of the common origin of the two tribes. As in Lieutenant Shaw's time, Chamda Gosain still ranks high among the tribe, and demands offerings on a larger scale than any other god. A sacrifice consisting of twelve pigs and twelve goats, with rice, oil and *sindur* in proportion, must put a severe strain on the resources of a Málé villager. In order to commemorate the event, three bamboos decorated with streamers of bark painted black and red at the ends, the natural colour being left in the centre, are set up to represent Chamda Gosain in front of the house of the person who organizes the sacrifice. One bamboo has ninety streamers, another sixty, and the third twenty, and the poles are also decorated with peacock's feathers. The night is spent in dancing, and in the morning sacrifices are offered in the house and in the fields for a blessing on the family and on the crops. The bamboos are then taken inside and suspended from the roof of the house to show that the owner has performed the full sacrifice.

The question whether the Málés have any functionaries who can properly be called priests is in some respects an obscure one. According to Buchanan, they formerly had priests called Naiyas or Laiyas, a designation common enough in Western Bengal, but these, it is said, have now disappeared, and their functions have devolved upon the Demános, who were originally only diviners selected for their supposed intimacy with the spirits, their capacity for going into trances, and so forth, these powers being in some mysterious way bound up with their long hair, which may on no account be cut. More recent observers, however, assure me that the Demáno merely directs religious and ceremonial observances, but does not himself officiate as priest. The duties of priest are discharged by the village headman or the chief member of the household, or by any influential person chosen for the occasion, and the Demáno is merely a spiritual director endowed with certain supernatural powers, such as that of discerning the causes of all diseases, so that when a man falls ill he can say which of the gods has afflicted him and what sort of sacrifice should be offered to bring about his recovery. On the occasions when Chamda Gosain and Gumu Gosain are worshipped, the Demáno is decorated with a necklace of cowrie shells. No Demáno may eat turmeric. Besides the Demáno there is another class of divines called Cherin, whose duty is to select persons to officiate as priests. This he does by balancing a bow on his two hands and watching its oscillations, while he calls out one by one the names of the persons present, the idea being that the god thus signifies from whose hands he wishes to receive the offering. The flesh of the animals offered in sacrifice is eaten by the male worshippers: women may not partake of it.

Disposal of the dead.

As a rule the Málé bury their dead, the corpse being laid on a layer of *bhelak* leaves with the head pointing towards the north. The bodies of those who died of snake-bite or have come to a violent end are exposed in the jungle. According to Colonel Dalton, the bodies of Demános are dealt with in this fashion, on the ground that if they are buried in the village, their ghosts walk and cause annoyance to the living. On the fifth day after death a feast is given, to which all members of the family are invited. Six months or a year later a special ceremony is held for the purpose of appeasing the spirit of the dead man. The chief part is played by the Demáno, who represents the deceased, and is dressed so as to personate him as closely as possible. In this character he demands clothes, ornaments, food and whatever the dead man was fond of in this life, the belief being that if they are given to the Demáno, the spirit will in some unexplained fashion have the use of them in the world of the dead. When the Demáno has got all that he asked for, he goes into a fit and remains insensible for some minutes, during which time he is supposed to be in communication with the spirit of the deceased. On his revival the company partake of a feast.

The property left by the dead man cannot be divided until this second feast has taken place. According to Colonel Dalton, the eldest son takes half, and the remainder is equally divided among the agnates. Some say, however, that division among the sons takes place on a sort of diminishing scale according to order of birth, the eldest getting the largest share, the second less, and so on.

Mode of living.

The Málé villages are usually built on the summits of the range of hills occupied by the tribe. Their houses are constructed of wattled bamboo, the interstices of which are filled with grass, no mud being used. They cultivate by burning the underwood and sowing seed in the ashes, a system usually known as *jhum* or *paráo*, but by them called *kale mandote*, or 'jungle-burning.' Although addicted to this destructive method of agriculture, the Málé are great lovers of trees, which they plant freely on their village sites. In matters of diet they acknowledge none of the restrictions recognized by Hindus. They eat beef, pork, domestic fowls, all kinds of fish, and the leavings of people of other castes, and indulge freely in strong drink.

Male Kumchhá, a *thar* or sept of Khambus in Darjiling.

Malhá, a title of Kaibarttas in Orissa.

Malhán, a section of the Baranwar sub-caste of Baniyás in Behar.

Málhátiá, a *mul* or section of Kesarwáni Baniyás in Behar.

Máli, *Málákár*, a caste employed in making garlands and providing flowers for the service of Hindu temples. In Bengal the caste is included among the Nava-Sákha, and its members profess to trace their descent from the garland maker attached to the household of Rája Kansa of Mathurá, who, when met by Krishna, was asked for a chaplet of flowers and at once gave it. On being told to fasten it with a string, he, for want of any other, took off his sacred thread and tied it, on which Krishna most ungenerously rebuked him for his simplicity in parting with his *paitá*, and announced that for the future his caste would be ranked among the Súdras. Like others of the higher castes, the Málákárs claim to have originally come from Mathurá in the reign of Jahangír. They are few in number, but in every Hindu village there is at least one representative, who provides daily offerings of flowers for the temples and marriage tiaras for the village maidens.

Tradition of origin.

They are divided into two main groups—the **Phulkátá-Máli**, who make ornaments, toys, etc., from the pith of the solá, and the **Dokáne-Máli**, who keep shops. The former group is again broken up into **Rárhi**, **Bárendra**, and **Áthghariá**, the last of whom are supposed to be descended from eight families outcasted for some cause now forgotten. Their sections, which are shown in Appendix I, belong to the ordinary Brahmanical series, and are supplemented by the regular rules regarding prohibited degrees. In Dacca, according to Dr. Wise, the caste has only one *gotra*, Alamyán, and two *dals*, or unions, between which there is no real difference. If, however, a member of one union marries into a family belonging to the other, the marriage feast will be more expensive than if he took a bride from his own, as he must invite the members of both *dals* to the ceremony. The bridal dresses must be made of red silk brought from Murshedabad, as cotton cloth is prohibited. The bride is always carried in a pálkí or palanquin, while the bridegroom rides on a pony or in a Sedan chair. Mális marry their daughters as infants, forbid widows to marry again, and do not recognize divorce. If a wife is proved to be unfaithful, she is turned out of the caste, and her husband performs a sort of penance to purify himself from the slur of having associated with her.

Internal structure.

The Málákárs are all Vaishnavas by creed, and it is said that none of them worship Siva. A Gosáin is their guru, while their Brahman is common to them and to the Nava-Sákha.

Religion.

"A Máli will not cultivate with his own hands, and never works as a kitchen-gardener, the gardeners of Bengal being generally Chandáls and Uriyas. Many Mális, however, hold land as occupancy raiyats, which they cultivate by means of hired labourers. In Dacca members of the caste keep shops for piece-goods, practise medicine, act as vaccinators, and take service in temples. Their principal occupations, however, are making wreaths, fabricating artifical chaplets and toys from the pith of the solá (*Hedysarum lagenarium*). The garlands placed every morning before idols are collected and arranged by Málákárs, who nevertheless refuse to paint figures, this being the profession of the Ganak and Rangrez. All the tinsel decorations put on the images and their carriages are designed by Málákárs. At marriages their services are indispensable, for they prepare the crowns (*Mukuta*) worn by the bridal pair. Morover, no bride would consider the attire complete unless her hair was adorned with a Khopajúrá, or ornament for the hair-knot, made with leaves of the jack-tree mixed with white Bela blossoms, while at one side of it they place a rose or some other bright flower. For the bouquet delivered on the bridal morning the Málákár expects to be paid a rupee.

Occupation.

"The profession of a Málákár requires a considerable knowledge of flowers, for some are forbidden to be used in religious services and others can only be exhibited before the shrines of the deities to whom they belong. Thus the 'Dhatúrá' is sacred to Siva; the 'Aparájitá' (*Clitoria ternatea*) to Káli; the 'Bákas' (*Justicia adhatoda*) to Saraswati; and the 'Asoka' (*Jonesia asoca*) to Sashthi. The 'Javá' (*Hibiscus rosa Sinensis*) or China rose is of most unlucky omen, and can only be presented to Káli, but not to other idols, nor employed at weddings.

"Strong scented blossoms are selected for religious offerings, and these in Bengal are the 'Champá' (*Michelia Champaca*), 'Chamelí' (*Jasminum grandiflorum*), 'Juí' (*Jasminum auriculatum*), 'Bela' (*Jasminum Zambac*), 'Gandhráj' (*Gardenia florida*), and the 'Hársingár' (*Nyctanthes arbor tristis*).

"Chaplets offered to idols must be tied with the dried fibres of the plantain stem, not with string, and if picked and arranged by one not a Málákár they are unclean. From sixteen to twenty-four annas a month are received by the garland-maker for providing a daily supply of flowers to a temple; but, as with everything else, the price of bouquets has greatly risen, and a rupee only procures about half the quantity it formerly did.

"One of the chief occupations of this caste is inoculating for small-pox and treating individuals attacked by any eruptive fever. Hindus believe that Sítalá, the goddess of small-pox, is one of seven sisters, who are designated Motiya, Matariyá, Pakauriya, Masúriká, Chamariya, Khudwá, and Pansá. The first four are varieties of small-pox, the names referring to the form, size, and colour of the pustules; the fifth is *Variola maligna*; the sixth is measles; and the seventh is water-pox. Every Málákár keeps images of one or more of these goddesses, and on the first of Chait (March 15th) a festival is held, and the Málákárs superintend the details. It is popularly called 'Málíbágh,' from the garden where the service is performed, and thither Hindus and Muhammadans repair with offerings of clotted milk, cocoanuts, and plantains in the hope of propitiating the dreaded sisters.

"When small-pox rages, the Málákárs are busiest. As soon as the nature of the disease is determined, the Kabíráj retires and a Málákár is summoned. His first act is to forbid the introduction of meat, fish, and all food requiring oil or spices for its preparation. He then ties a lock of hair, a cowrie-shell, a piece of turmeric, and an article of gold on the right wrist of the patient. The sick person is then laid on the 'Májh-pattá,' the young and unexpanded leaf of the plantain tree, and milk is prescribed as the sole article of food. He is fanned with a branch of the sacred *ním*, and any one entering the chamber is sprinkled with water. Should the fever become aggravated and delirium ensue, or if a child cries much and sleeps little, the Málí performs the Máta pujá. This consists in bathing the image of the goddess causing the disease and giving a draught of the water to drink. To relieve the irritation of the skin, pease-meal, turmeric, flour, or shell-sawdust is sprinkled over the body.

"If the eruption be copious, a piece of new cloth in the figure of eight is wrapped round the chest and shoulders. On the night between the seventh and eighth days of the eruption the Málí has much to do. He places a waterpot in the sick room, and puts on it alwá rice, a cocoanut, sugar, plantains, a yellow rag, flowers, and a few *ním* leaves. Having mumbled several *mantras*, he recites the *kissa*, or tale, of the particular goddess, which often occupies six hours.

"When the pustules are mature, the Máli dips a thorn of the karaundá (*Carissa*) in til oil, and punctures each one. The body is then anointed with oil, and cooling fruits given. When the scabs (dewli) have peeled off, another ceremonial, called 'Godám,' is gone through. All the offerings on the waterpot are rolled in a cloth and fastened round the waist of the patient. These offerings are the perquisite of the Máli, who also receives a fee.

"These minute, and to our ideas absurd, proceedings are practised by the Hindus and Muhammadans, including the bigoted Farazi, whenever small-pox or other eruptive fever attacks their families. Government vaccinators earn a considerable sum yearly by executing the Sítalá worship, and when a child is vaccinated a portion of the service is performed."

Social status.

The Mális of Behar hold a respectable position among the castes of that province. They rank with Kumhárs, Koiris, and Kahars, and Brahmans will take water from their hands. The main difference between them and the Bengal Mális is that they practice widow-marriage, and do not take an extreme view of the necessity of getting their daughters married as infants. With this exception, the account given above of the Bengal Mális applies for the most part to the Behar members of the caste.

The following statement shows the number and distribution of Mális in 1872 and 1881:—

DISTRICT.	1872.	1881.	DISTRICT.	1872.	1881.
Bardwan	3,376	2,171	Chittagong	856	106
Bankura	535	1,634	Noakhali	339	37
Birbhum	536	2,225	Patna	4,995	5,611
Midnapur	6,156	7,942	Gya	8,577	7,671
Hughli	} 2,652	{ 2,469	Shahabad	3,432	5,100
Howrah		1,163	Tirhut { Mozufferpur ...	} 16,222	{ 11,543
24-Parganás	2,586	2,390	Tirhut { Darbhanga ...		10,004
Nadiya	2,980	6,345	Saran	4,691	6,909
Khulna	......	2,176	Champaran	4,974	7,367
Jessore	1,811	4,323	Monghyr	5,360	5,249
Murshedabad	2,483	3,613	Bhagalpur	2,877	4,428
Dinajpur	2,184	3,133	Purniah	4,663	25
Rajshahye	452	890	Maldah	567	883
Rangpur	2,068	1,456	Santál Parganás	1,262	3,728
Bogra	1,075	864	Cuttack	3,346	4,493
Pabna	2,986	1,731	Puri	11,669	11,186
Darjiling	143	220	Balasore	1,305	1,690
Jalpigori	500	960	Tributary States	10,606	9,777
Kuch Behar	......	2,156	Hazaribagh	1,556	2,765
Dacca	2,757	2,769	Lohardagá	5,205	2,750
Faridpur	1,347	2,310	Singbhum	34	2,369
Bakarganj	2,204	1,401	Manbhum	4,105	3,601
Maimansinh	11,836	2,379	Tributary States	224	452
Tipperah	5,244	2,480			

Máli, a synonym for Bhuinmáli; a sept of the Malwe Rájputs in Chota Nagpur.

Malik, a title of Rájputs, Telis and Doms in Behar.

Málik, a title of Kandhs in Orissa.

Malikauliá, a section of Bábhans in Behar.

Malitwár, a section of Bábhans in Behar.

Maljáda, a bastard or son of a harlot.

Málkarnauti, a *mul* or section of the Sátmuliá or Kishnaut sub-caste of Goálás in Behar.

Málkas, a section of Oswáls.

Malkhájania, from *malkhájaná*, a payer of land revenue, a zemindar.

Málkiá, a *mul* or section of the Sátmuliá or Kishnaut sub-caste of Goálás in Behar.

Malla, wrestler, a title of Khandáits in Orissa and of the Aguri or Ugrakshatri caste in Western Bengal.

Mallabhumia, a sub-caste of Bauris in Western Bengal.

Malláh, *Ar.*, a sailor, a boatman, a generic term current in Behar and Bengal as the popular designation of various boating and fishing castes. Mr. Sherring notices this general use of the word, but adds that there is a special tribe of Malláhs divided into the following sub-castes:—(1) **Malláh**, (2) **Muria or Muriári**, (3) **Pandubi**, (4) **Bathawa or Badhariyá**, (5) **Chaini, Chain or Chai**, (6) **Suráyá**, (7) **Guriyá**, (8) **Tiar**, (9) **Kulwant or Kulwat**, (10) **Kewat**,

He also mentions the tradition that all these "are descended from a common father, by name Nikhád, but that the Kewats alone were born in lawful wedlock." Nikhád is merely a variant for Nishád or Nishada, a Dravidian tribe mentioned in the Rig-Veda, from which several of the fishing castes may possibly derive their origin. It is clear, however, that while the ten groups enumerated by Mr. Sherring may at one time have belonged to a single tribe, that tribe must have broken up some time before the Arabic word *Malláh* can have been current in India long enough to stand any chance of being adopted as a tribal name. If, then, Mr. Sherring's statement is correct, a point on which there is room for some difference of opinion, it merely shows that a certain number of distinct fishing castes believe themselves once to have formed part of a larger group, to which they give the modern name Malláh, a foreign word denoting an occupation, not a caste, and throwing no light on the affinities of the people who use it.

The castes to which the term Malláh is ordinarily applied in Bengal are the following:—Gonrhi, Chain, Bind, Kewat, Tiyar, Muriári, Surahiya, Málo, and Jáliyá Kaibartta.

Mallametiá, *Mátiá*, or *Mátiál*, a sub-caste of Bágdis in Bengal, by profession fishermen and earth-workers.

Mallik, a sub-caste of Máls in Birbhum; an honorary title of Brahmans, Doms, Káyasths, Kaibarttas, and Subarnabaniks in Bengal; a section of the Biyáhut and Kharidáhá Kalwárs and of Mális and Sonárs in Behar.

Malo, a sub-section of the Kautsasa section of Utkal Brahmans.

Málo, a title of the class of Rájputs to which the Raja of Bishenpur claims to belong. It is a plausible conjecture that this name, unheard of among admitted Rájputs, may have arisen from the connexion of the Raja with the Mál tribe, who are numerous in Bankura.

Málo, *Málo-Pátni*, a Dravidian boating and fishing caste, supposed by Buchanan to have come from Western India. This opinion, however, is unsupported by any evidence beyond a resemblance of names, which may be either wholly accidental or may have arisen from the tribal name Málo being confounded with the Arabic word Malláh, 'a boatman.' Dr. Wise considers the three fisher castes—the Kaibartta, Málo, and Tiyar—to be "undoubtedly representatives of the pre-historic dwellers in the Gangetic delta. As a rule they are short and squat, of a dark-brown colour, often verging upon black. Although Hindus by creed, they are fond of showy garments, of earrings, and of long hair, which is either allowed to hang down in glossy curls on their shoulders or fastened in a knot at the back of the head. The whiskers and moustaches are thin and scrubby, the lips often thick and prominent, the nose short with the nostrils expanded. The physiognomy indicates good temper, sensuality, and melancholy rather than intelligence and shrewdness." The sections of the Málos, shown in Appendix I, seem on the whole to bear out the view that

Internal structure.

they are the remnant of a distinct aboriginal tribe, and not merely an occupational group. These sections are peculiar to the Málos, and do not appear to have been borrowed from any other caste. I am unable to analyse them completely, but I venture the conjecture that some of them are totemistic, the totems being the rivers, which the Málos regularly worship. There are no sub-castes. The Rájbansi, which some authorities are disposed to regard as a sub-caste of the Málo, are clearly Kochh, who have taken to fishing, while the Kátar or Bepári Málo, who deal in, but do not catch, fish, and derive their name from their practice of cutting up their wares and selling them by weight, are Muhammadans in no way connected with the Málo caste.

Marriage.

The rule of exogamy is in full force among the Málo. A man may not marry a woman of his own section or of the section to which his mother belongs. For the rest, marriage is regulated by counting degrees down to seven generations in the descending line. Females are married as infants. A price is paid for the bride, which of late years has risen to the large sum of Rs. 100. The ceremony is of the orthodox type, the giving of the bride and the bridegroom's formal acceptance of the gift being the essential and binding portion of the rite. Polygamy is permitted in theory, and a man may marry two sisters, provided that he takes the eldest first. In practice, however, I understand it is unusual to marry a second wife unless the first proves barren. Widows may not marry again, nor is divorce permitted. A woman taken in adultery is abandoned by her husband and turned out of the caste.

Religion.

Málos as a rule belong to the Vaishnava sect. Their *purohit* is a Patit Brahman, and their *guru* a Gosain. Special reverence is paid by them to the great rivers on which they live, and these, together with their boats and nets, have their regular seasons of worship. Khala-Kumári is worshipped in Srávan (July–August), offerings are made to Bura-Buri in fulfilment of vows, and lights are launched on the water in honour of Khwája Khizr.

Disposal of the dead.

The dead are usually burned on the bank of a river, and the ashes cast into the water. *Sráddh* is performed on the thirty-first day after death, then once a month for a year, and again on the first anniversary of the death. Usually, however, the monthly *sráddhs* are lumped together towards the close of the year. In the case of persons who die a violent death, the first *sráddh* is performed on the fourth day, and a final *sráddh* on the thirty-first day.

Social status.

Although the social rank of the Málos is low, and Brahmans will not take water from their hands, the Nápit and Dhobá usually work for them. They are on good terms with the Tíyar and Kaibartta, and members of the three castes will even smoke together. The Málo, however, says Dr. Wise, "is the lowest in rank, while the Kaibartta and Tiyar still dispute about their relative positions. The Kaibartta, again, is more thoroughly Hinduised than either of the other two. A ridiculous distinction is always cited in proof of the inferior rank of the Málo. The Kaibartta and Tiyar in netting always pass the netting needle from above downwards, working from left to right; while the Málo passes it from below upwards, forming his meshes from right to left. It is remarkable that the same difference is adduced by the Behár fisherman as a proof of the degraded rank of the Banpar." The only titles met with among Málos are Mánjhi, Pátra, and Bepári, while among other fisher castes no honorary distinctions exist. Under the Muhamadan Government they served as boatmen, chaprásís, mace-bearers (asabardár), and staff-bearers (sonte-bardár) in processions. They were also employed in conveying treasure from Dacca to Murshedabad, while a tradition still survives that early in this century two of their number became great favourites with Nawáb Nasrat Jang, who presented them with golden spinning wheels for their wives' use. The Málos therefore extol the golden age that has passed, and inveigh against the equality and degeneracy of the present.

Occupation.

Málos generally use a shorter Jalká boat than the Tiyars, but when they fish with the long Uthár net they fasten two boats stem to stern. Like the Kaibartta, the Málo is often a cultivator, and in Bhowál he has been obliged by changes in the course and depth of the rivers to relinquish his caste trade. Málos manufacture twine, but not rope, and traffic in grain, while those who have saved a little money keep grocer's shops or become fishmongers. Málo women sell fish in the bazars, but in some places this practice is considered derogatory to their gentility and is prohibited.

The following statement shows the number and distribution of Málos in 1872 and 1881:—

District.	1872.	1881.	District.	1872.	1881.
Bardwan	9,333	454	Bakarganj	1,751	989
Bankura	6,933	22,079	Maimansinh	13,999	11,454
Birbhum	586	3,158	Tipperah	2,600	1,720
Midnapur	39,804	40,236	Chittagong	525	31
Hughli	} 1,820	{ 2,097	Noakhali	110	......
Howrah		657	Patna	17,559	19,099
24-Parganás	2,333	1,542	Gya	11,518	11,906
Nadiya	13,311	10,672	Shahabad	15,267	14,943
Khulna	......	3,390	Tirbut { Mozufferpur ...	} 159,730	{ 89,273
Jessore	12,600	10,765	Tirbut { Darbhanga ...		{ 115,217
Murshedabad...	7,386	7,598	Saran	21,849	22,599
Dinajpur	1,203	1,222	Champaran	45,531	55,222
Rajshahye	1,768	1,484	Monghyr	13,996	21,850
Rangpur	1,392	1,148	Bhagalpur	11,754	18,891
Bogra	3,637	1,120	Purniah	21,016	27,570
Pabna	16,490	6,566	Maldah	1,656	4,281
Darjiling	26	1,175	Santál Parganás	1,865	2,889
Jalpigori	251	3	Hazaribagh	1,466	3,475
Kuch Behar	......	133	Lohardagá	7,250	10,924
Dacca	6,437	1,949	Singbhum	......	443
Faridpur	6,033	2,389	Manbhum	1,671	1,918

Málo-Pátni, a synonym for Málo.

Mál Pahária, a Dravidian tribe inhabiting the Rámgarh Hills in the Santál Parganás, who until recently lived by hunting and *jhúm* or *karáo* cultivation Their tribal affinities are extremely obscure, and have formed

Origin.

the subject of some discussion. Buchanan[1] gives the following account of them:—"The northern tribe[2] consider their southern neighbours as brethren, and call them **Maler**,[3] the name which they give themselves; but the southern tribe, shocked at the impurity of the others, deny this consanguinity, and most usually call the northern tribe **Chet**, while they assume to themselves the denomination of **Mál** or **Már**, which, however, is probably a word of the same derivation with **Maler**. The Mál, however, divide themselves into three tribes—**Kumárpali**, **Dángrpali**, and **Márpali**; and they often call the northern mountaineers Sumarpali, thus, as it were, acknowledging a common origin, which I have little doubt is the fact. The manners and language of the three southern Pali are the same, and they speak a very impure dialect of the Bengalese. The three Pali were originally local distinctions, but now all live intermixed, have exactly the same customs and language, and intermarry but there are five real hereditary distinctions, which descend in the male line. The highest rank consists of the Rajas or chiefs and their descendants, all of whom are called Singhas or lions. Next to these are certain families that were at one time rich, and are called Grihi. They assisted their poorer brethren with loans, and seem to have been a kind of bankers, like the Vaisyas of the Hindus. They never seem to have held any office in the State. The third in rank were the Manjhis or chiefs of villages, and none but persons of this rank were ever permitted to hold this office. The persons of the Ahriti or fourth class were by birth hunters, and at first in all probability were the lower and labouring class, like the Sudras of the Hindus; for what is now considered as the lowest and fifth class is composed of the Naiyas, who are allowed to have originally been the priests, but have been totally discarded from that office." Against Dr. Buchanan's description of the Mál Pahárias as a Hinduised branch of the Maler, we have to set Colonel Dalton's opinions[4] that the former tribe "appear to be altogether unconnected with the Rájmahál hillmen," and Mr. Ball's statement,[5] based upon personal observation, that the Mál Pahárias "are altogether distinct in appearance, customs, and language from the Asal Pahárias, who occupy the Rájmahál hills proper." It should be observed, however, that even in Dr. Buchanan's time (1807–1814) a wide breach had been established between the two groups, and the southern Pahárias at least strenuously disowned all kinship with the northern. Sixty years later the breach must have been greatly widened by the Mál Pahárias continually adopting Hindu customs, while the Malés seem to have stubbornly resisted all impulses in that direction, and this movement may possibly account for the impression formed by Mr. Ball. On the question of language the evidence seems to be inconclusive. Colonel Dalton gives a very meagre list of words obtained by Dr. Coates from a Mál Pahária prisoner in the Hazáribágh Central Jail. On this he observes:—"I cannot say I have

[1] *Eastern India*, ii, 126.
[2] The Malés of Rajmahal.
[3] Malér is the plural of Malé.
[4] *Ethnology of Bengal*, p. 274.
[5] *Jungle Life in India*, p. 229.

found in it analogues sufficient to justify its association with the Dravidian dialects, but it is equally unlike Kol."[1] A comparison of the list with Mr. Droese's Malto Vocabulary shows, however, that some slight correspondence may be traced between the language of the Malé and the mongrel dialect spoken by the Mál Pahárиás. Thus, *chapta*, 'the foot'; Malto, sole of the foot: *ekore*, 'to go'; Malto, *eke*: *tindiáná*, 'to eat,' seems to be a causal formed in Hindi fashion from the Malto *tinde*, 'to feed:' *maler*, 'a man,' is the nominative plural of *male*: *bátker*, 'a woman,' and *batker*, 'a daughter,' are curiously like the Malto *batg*, 'virginal,' and *bátgni*, 'a maiden': *chichu* is the Malto word for fire: *ámma* is not far removed from *amu*, the Malto for water: *chiore*, 'to give,' appears to be from the same root as *chiye*: *malaga*, 'no,' merely adds a syllable to the Malto *mala*: and *kúkrá*, 'a cock,' may perhaps be connected with the Malto *kúkre*, 'to cry out.' These slight resemblances of course fall far short of establishing the identity of the two tribes, but they tend on the whole to show that Buchanan's opinion is not so clearly untenable as has been sometimes supposed to be the case. Mr. Droese, with whom I discussed the subject some years ago, considered the two tribes to be of common origin. This view is borne out by the fact that they understand one another's language readily, though they assert that the dialects are different; as well as by the identity of their ancestral worship, a point in which all races display a remarkably conservative spirit. As for the antagonism which at present prevails between the north and south Pahárиás, it is only another instance of what has been commonly observed in Chota Nagpur, that two sections of the same tribe which in any way happen to become separated are often far more strongly opposed to one another than if they had been originally distinct tribes.

Internal structure.

The Mál Pahárиás are divided into two sub-tribes—**Mál Pahárиá** proper and **Kumár** or **Komar-Bhág**. The latter group, which corresponds with Buchanan's Kumárpali, is the more Hinduised of the two. The septs are given in Appendix I. They appear to be identical with Buchanan's "hereditary distinctions." He would doubtless have discovered the fact that they are exogamous had the subject of exogamy attracted any attention at the time when he wrote. Their names are apparently titular, and throw no light upon the affinities of the tribe. The Mál Pahárиás also observe a table of prohibited degrees, which differs little from that defined by the standard formula referred to in the article on **Bais**. They have no traditions worth mentioning, except a vague legend that their first parents were born from a cow. The same story is told of the ancestor of the Pachete family in Manbhum, whose estate borders on the country where the Mál Pahárиás are now found. It is possible, indeed, that the Pachete Ráj may in early times have extended further to the east, and that the head of that house may have been the Raja of whom Buchanan speaks as having formerly appointed from among the Mál

[1] *Ethnology of Bengal*, p. 274.

Paháriás a dewan, a faujdár to command in predatory expeditions, and the mánjhis or headmen of villages. This, however, is the purest conjecture. The tendency to borrow a myth current in a landholding family may be frequently observed in Chota Nagpur.

Marriage. Marriage is either infant or adult. Girls are rarely married before the age of ten or eleven, and usually not until they are fully grown up. In the latter case sexual intercourse before marriage is tacitly recognized, it being understood that if an unmarried girl becomes pregnant her lover will come forward and marry her. A professional match-maker (*sithu*) is usually employed by the bride groom's people to search for a suitable wife. When his selection has been made, a visit of inspection is paid by the parents; and if the proposed bride is approved of, the price to be paid for her is settled by personal discussion. Custom ordains that the amount shall be an *odd* number of rupees, not less than five, nor more than twenty-five. It must be paid either in a lump sum or by instalments before the marriage can be celebrated. On the occasion of the final payment the bridegroom's parents send by the *sithu* some *bájrá* beer and a *sári* for the bride, which is made over to her maternal uncle to be kept till the day of the wedding. Particular inquiries were made regarding the reason for thus selecting the maternal uncle as a sort of trustee for the bride's *peculium*, but no definite result was arrived at; and this usage, undoubtedly one of great antiquity, seems only to be explicable as a survival of female kinship, a system of which no other traces are met with in the tribe. Shortly after the bride-price has been paid, the *sithu* is again sent to the bride's house, this time bearing an arrow wound round with yellow thread tied in as many knots as there are days to the date proposed for the wedding. The bride's people make their preparations accordingly, undoing a knot as each day passes. On the day before the bridegroom arrives and is lodged near the bride's house. Early next morning a big feast is given, after which the bridegroom takes his seat facing the east in a sort of arbour of *sál* branches built for the purpose. Here he is joined by the bride, dressed, like him, in a new cotton wrapper dyed yellow with turmeric, who sits besides him while the maidens of his company comb out her hair. A *sál* leaf cup is offered to the bridegroom, containing red lead, which he daubs on the bride's forehead and the parting of her hair. The girls who combed the bride's hair take her hand, dip a finger into the red lead, and make seven spots on the bridegroom's forehead. This final and binding rite is received with a shout of applause, which is the signal for the Dom musicians in attendance to beat the drums for a dance. Towards evening the wedded pair go off to the bridegroom's house, where the whole party spend the night in dancing and drinking. Polygamy is permitted, and, in theory at least, there are no restrictions on the number of wives a man may have. Practically, however, the poverty of the tribe and their hand-to-mouth fashion of living set strict limits to the exercise of this right, and few Paháriás indulge themselves with the luxury of a second wife, except when the first happens to be barren. A man may marry two sisters, but he must follow the order of age, and if already married to a younger sister, may not take an elder sister to wife.

A widow may marry again. She is expected to marry her late husband's younger brother if there is one; but if he does not wish to marry her, any member of the caste not barred by the prohibited degrees may have her on paying a bride-price of Rs. 2 to her late husband's relatives. No ceremony is required, nor is *sindur* used. The husband merely gives the woman a new cloth and takes her to his house. A wife may be divorced with the sanction of the caste council or pancháyat for adultery or persistent and incurable ill-temper. As a rule arrangements of this sort are effected by mutual consent, the parties tearing a *sál* leaf in two before the pancháyat as a symbol of separation. The seducer of a married woman is required to repay to her husband the sum which she cost him as a virgin. Divorced wives may marry again in the same manner as widows, and for the same bride-price, which is paid to their own, not to their late husband's relations.

Religion.

At the head of the Pahária religion stands the sun, to whom reverential obeisance is made morning and evening. On occasional Sundays a special worship is performed by the head of the family, who must prepare himself for the rite by eating no salt on the previous Friday and fasting all Saturday, with the exception of a light meal of molasses and milk, taken at sunset after bathing. Before sunrise on Sunday morning a new earthen vessel, a new basket, some rice, oil, areca nuts, and vermilion, and a brass *lota* of water with a mango branch stuck in it, are laid out on a clean space of ground in front of the house. The worshipper shows these offerings to the rising sun and prays, addressing the luminary as 'Gosain,' that he and his family may be saved from any specific danger or trouble that is supposed to threaten them. The rice is then given to a goat, which is decapitated while eating by a single blow from behind. The body of the animal is then cooked and served up at a feast, of which the neighbours partake; the head alone, which is deemed *prasád*, or sacred, being carefully reserved for the members of the family. Next in honour to the sun are Dharti Mái, mother earth; her servant, or as some say sister, Garámi; and Singhbáhini, who bears rule over tigers, snakes, scorpions, and all manner of noxious beasts. To the earth goats, pigs, fowls, etc., are offered in Ashar and Magh, and buffaloes or goats are sacrificed about the time of the Hindu Durga Pujá to the goddess Singhbáhini, who is represented for sacrificial purposes by a lump of clay daubed with vermilion and oil and set up in front of the worshipper's house. The village Mánjhi officiates as priest. The Mágh worship of Dharti Mái is clearly the festival described by Colonel Dalton under the name Bhuindeb, the earth god.[1]

"The Máls plant in their dancing place two branches of the *sál* tree, and for three days they dance round these branches, after which they are removed and thrown into a river, which reminds one of

---

[1] *Ethnology of Bengal*, p. 274.

the Karma festivals as solemnised by the Oraons and Kols in Chota Nagpur. On this occasion the men and women dance *vis-à-vis* to each other, the musicians keeping between. The men dance holding each other above their elbows, the left hand of one holding the right elbow of the other, whose right hand again holds the left elbow of the arm that has seized him. The fore-arms touching are held stiffly out and swayed up and down. They move sideways, advance, and retire, sometimes bending low, sometimes erect. The women hold each other by the palms, interlacing the fingers, left palm upon right palm, and left and right fore-arms touching. They move like the men."

Two curious points may be added. The man at whose instance or for whose benefit the ceremony is performed must sleep the night before on a bed of straw; and the dancing party, who are greatly excited with drink, shout continually *búr, búr* (*pudendum muliebre*), a mode of invocation believed to be especially acceptable to the goddess. In this somewhat indelicate cry we may perhaps see a barbarous and undraped reference to the *vis genetrix naturæ* so prominent in many early forms of belief.

Besides these greater elemental deities, the Mál Pahárías recognize and propitiate a number of vaguely-defined animistic powers, chief among whom is Chordánu, a malevolent spirit, needing to be appeased at certain intervals with sacrifices and the first fruits of whatever crop is on the ground. To the same class belongs Mahádáná, for whom eggs are the appropriate offering. Among the standard Hindu deities Kali and Lakhi Mai (Lakshmi) are honoured with sparing and infrequent worship, the offerings in this case being the perquisite of the village headmen.

Ancestor worship is in full force, and the *sacra privata* of a Mál Paháríá household correspond precisely with those observed by the Málé tribe. The Lares are known to both by the familiar term Gumo Gosain or Deota, the gods of the wooden pillar (*Gumo*),[1] which supports the main rafters of the house. Around this centre are grouped a number of balls of hardened clay, representing the ancestors of the family, to whom the first fruits of the earth are offered, and the blood of goats or fowls poured forth at the foot of the pillar that the souls may not hunger in the world of the dead. As every household is guarded by its ancestral gods, so every village has a tutelary deity of its own—*Larem agri custodem*, who lives in a *sál* tree within the village. This tree is daubed with red lead and worshipped on certain occasions, and may on no account be cut down. The tribe have no priests, and the head of the household or village, as the case may be, performs all religious and ceremonial observances. Brahmans, however, are to some extent held in honour, and presents are given to them on festal occasions.

Disposal of the dead.

The dead are usually burned, and a piece of bone is saved from the flames to be thrown into a river or a deep tank the waters of which do not run dry. The relatives are deemed impure, and may not eat salt for five days. At

[1] The word is Malto.

the end of that time they are shaved, and partake of a feast provided by the eldest son. The funeral expenses are a first charge on the estate, and after these have been paid the balance is equally divided among the sons, daughters getting no share. Very poor persons, who cannot afford to give a feast, bury their dead in a recumbent position with the head towards the south, and give nothing but a little salt and meal (*sattu*) to the friends who attend the funeral. In Buchanan's time it was the universal custom to bury the dead on the day of death. No *sráddh* is performed by the Mál Pahárías proper, but some of the wealthier members of the Kumár Bhág sub-tribe are beginning to adopt a meagre form of this ceremony in imitation of their Hindu neighbours.

Occupation.

The tribe believe *jhúm* tillage and hunting to be their original occupations, and a large proportion of the tribe still adhere to these primitive modes of livelihood. Their system of *jhúm* cultivation is thus described by Buchanan:—"On the hills the *bári* is neither ploughed nor hoed. The men cut the trees and burn them, and the women sow the seed. In the first year they scatter over the surface seed of the kinds of millet called *kheri* and *kangni*, and with a stick pointed with iron (*khantá*) form small holes, in which they drop seed of maize, *janirá*, and a pulse called *borá* or *kalai*. In the second year they plant only maize and *janirá*." By the third year the land is worked out, and the cultivator must seek a fresh patch of jungle for his operations. A large tract of hill land is therefore required to keep a Pahária village going. Buchanan observed that although their progress in agriculture was greater than that of their northern neighbours, their huts were much more wretched and dirty, their clothing more scanty, and their women less cleanly and worse provided with ornaments. In bad seasons they supplement their scanty food-supply with jungle roots and herbs, of which, like the Sikkim Lepchas, they have a minute empirical knowledge. Of late years many have taken to plough cultivation at the foot of the hills, where they hold land as occupancy raiyats at the rents fixed in the current settlement. Standing as they do wholly outside the regular caste system, they can hardly be said to have any social status in the ordinary sense of that phrase. From the Hindu point of view their diet is certainly unclean, for pork, fowls, and all kinds of fish are deemed lawful food; but the fact of their abstaining from beef, snakes, lizards, and field-rats would probably lead the average Hindu to regard them as a shade purer than the Málés and their congeners the Oraons.

Mál Pahária proper, a sub-tribe of Mál Pahárías in the Santál Parganás.

Málpáni, a section of Mahesris in Behar.

Malta, a sept of Chiks in Chota Nagpur.

Maluá, *Máluá*, a sub-caste of Bauris in Western Bengal whose original residence is said to have been Manbhum; a section of Chiks or Páns in Chota Nagpur; a sub-tribe of Kandhs in Orissa.

Máluá or Manuá, a sub-caste of Karangás in Western Bengal.

Malwar, a class of braziers who make *khâru* and other brass ornaments for the hand.

Malwe or **Már-Rájput**, a sub-tribe of Rájputs in Chota Nagpur.

Mán, a title of Bangaja Káyasths in Bengal.

Mana, a title of Dakshin-Rárhi and Bangaja Káyasths.

Mananmanáras, a *mul* or section of the Chhamuliá Madhesiá sub-caste of Halwáis in Behar.

Manár, a title of Cheros in Chota Nagpur.

Manariá, a section of Bábhans in Behar.

Manchhihá, Manchiá, a *kul* or section of Bábhans in Behar.

Mándái, a synonym for Kochh.

Mandal, (i) a headman of a village; (ii) a title of Kaibarttas, Chandals, Goálás, Sunris, Sadgops, Telis, Tantis, and Báuris; of Nápits, Kurmis, Kapális, Pods, Santáls, and Subarnabaniks; (iii) a sub-caste of Dhánuks in Purniah. Some Brahmans in Bankura bear the title; of Rájputs in Behar; a title of Khambus in Darjiling.

Mandap, a section of Kumhárs in Singbhum.

Mandar, probably a variant of Mandal, a title of cultivating Dhánuks; a *pangat* or section of Dosadhs and Kadars; a title of the Cháb and Kurin sub-castes of Gonrhis; a title of the Maghayá sub-caste of Koiris and Telis; a section of the Chaubhán sub-caste of Nuniyás and of Sunris and Khatwes in Behar; a section of the Kanaujiá sub-caste of Goálás and a title of Kishnaut Goálás in Behar; a title of Gangotás and Kowats and of Kharwárs in Lohardagá.

Mandaráná, a sub-caste of Sutradhars in Western Bengal.

Mandárane, a sub-caste of Sunris in Western Bengal.

Mandari, a title of Hindu Joláhas in Behar.

Mándároná, a group of the Aswini Tántis and of Dwádas Telis in Bengal; a sub-caste of Doms in Bengal.

Mándhayá, a section of Goálás in the North-Western Provinces and Behar.

Mándiár, a sept of Rájputs in Behar.

Mandilwár, a section of the Amashta sub-caste of Káyasths in Behar.

Manding, *man*, medicine, a practiser of medicine, a sub-sept of the Nah-pá sept of Sherpa Bhotias.

Mandrá, a section of Bábhans in Behar.

Mandri, a section of the Kádar caste in Behar.

Mandriár, a section of Mahilis in Chota Nagpur.

Mandus, a title of Ganjwár Sunris in Behar.

Manem-ma, a sept of the Phágu sub-tribe of Yakhas in Darjiling.

Maner, a section of the Sátmuliá Maghayá sub-caste of Kándus in Behar.

Manerar, a section of Awadhiá Hajjáms in Behar.

Maneriá, a section of the Biyáhut and Kharidáhá Kalwárs in Behar.

Mángaf, a section of the Biyáhut and Kharidáhá Kalwárs in Behar.

Mangal, a section of the Agarwála caste in Behar.

Mangar, crocodile. a totemistic section of Kurmis in Chota Nagpur and Orissa; a section of Binjhiás in Chota Nagpur.

Mangar, *Magar*, *Thapi*, one of the fighting tribes of Nepal, belonging, with the Gurung Khas and Sunuwar, to the Mukhya group, and highly esteemed for their military qualities. The Mangars believe their original *habitat* to have been the valley of Dhoreh on the banks of the Karnali-Bheri river in Western Nepal: thence they spread to Likhukhola, and thus gradually made their way into Eastern Nepal. The internal structure of the tribe, so far as I have been able to ascertain it, is shown in tabular form in Appendix I. The subject, however, is an extremely obscure one, and I am not yet in a position to throw much light upon it. There are four sub-tribes—**Athárah Panth, Burathoki, Gharti,** and **Sakhali.** The Gharti are probably descended from emancipated slaves (see article **Gharti**); the origin of the rest is uncertain. The exogamous septs are very numerous, and the list given in Appendix I contains many names of the territorial type common in India along with others which seem to be nicknames of the founders of septs, such as are found among the Tibetans and Limbus. Judged by their physical characteristics, the Mangars must be classed as Mongoloid, their naso-malar index being slightly lower than that of the Tibetans, while their complexion, eyelids, stature and the general cut of their features stamp them as a cross in which the Mongolian element on the whole predominates. The septs are exogamous, the rule being that a man may not marry a woman of his own sept. There seem to be no rules excluding more than one sept in marriage. Prohibited degrees are reckoned by the standard formula for three generations in the descending line.

Origin and internal structure.

Girls are married after they attain maturity, and sexual license before marriage is tolerated on the understanding that if a girl becomes pregnant, the father of her child shall at once be called upon to marry her. The marriage ceremony is of the Hindu type, *sindurdán*, or the smearing of vermilion on the bride's forehead, being its binding portion. Brahmans usually officiate, but this is not essential. A man may marry two or three wives, the only limit in practice being his ability to maintain them. A widow may not marry again by the standard ritual (*byáh*) appointed for the wedding of a spinster, but a man may take her to live with him, and she is counted as his wife. Her children by her second husband are considered legitimate; they rank as Mangars (instead of belonging to a special category like the offspring of Brahman widows in Nepal), and they share

Marriage.

in their father's property on equal terms with the children of a wife married in the regular form. Moreover, if any one runs away with a widow, he has to pay damages to the man she is living with just as if she were his regular wife. In Nepal husbands are entitled to wreak summary vengeance on the seducers of their wives. An adulterer taken in the act is killed offhand, and the faithless wife has her nose cut off. In such cases the question of divorce clearly does not arise. But in British territory, and I believe frequently in Nepal itself, disagreements of this sort are settled without resort to bloodshed. The wife goes off with her paramour, and the husband claims from the latter as damages the amount of the bride-price which he paid for the woman in the first instance. The pancháyat enforces his claim, and justice is held to have been satisfied.

Religion.

The religion of the Mangars may best be described as lax Hinduism tempered by survivals of an earlier animistic cult. Satya Narain is one of their favourite deities. Sansári and Aitábáreh are also worshipped with offerings of goats, fowls and pigeons. Upadhya Brahmins assist at the cult of Satya Narain and of the recognized Hindu gods; but Sansari and Aitábáreh are worshipped by the heads of households without the assistance of priests. Brahmans are not held to be degraded by serving as priests in Mangar families.

Disposal of the dead.

The funeral ceremonies of the Mangars, which are the same as those of the Gurung and Sunuwars, are curious and interesting. Immediately after death the corpse is tied with three pieces of rope to a stout pole and carried to the grave. There it is stripped, dressed in new clothes, and laid on its back in the grave with the head pointing to the north. The forehead is smeared with sandal wood paste. One of the maternal relatives of the deceased, usually the maternal uncle, is then chosen to act as priest for the occasion, and to conduct the ritual appointed for the propitiation of the dead. First of all he puts in the mouth of the corpse some silver coins and some coral, which is greatly prized by the Himalayan races. Then he lights a wick soaked in clarified butter, touches the lips with fire, scatters some parched rice about the mouth, and lastly covers the face with a cloth called *pujunri*. Two bits of wood, about three feet long, are set up on either side of the grave. In the one are cut nine steps or notches forming a ladder for the spirit of the dead to ascend to heaven ; on the other every one present at the funeral cuts a notch to show that he has been there. As the maternal uncle steps out of the grave, he bids a solemn farewell to the dead and calls upon him to ascend to heaven by the ladder that stands ready for him. When the earth has been filled in, the stick notched by the funeral party is taken away to a distance and broken in two pieces, lest by its means the dead man should do the survivors a mischief. The pole used to carry the corpse is also broken up, and the spades and ropes are left in the grave.

When the mourners return home, one of their party goes ahead and makes a barricade of thorn bushes across the road midway between the grave and the house of the deceased. On the top of the thorns he puts a big stone on which he takes his stand, holding a pot of burning incense in his left hand and some woollen thread in his right. One by one the mourners step on the stone and pass through the smoke of the incense to the other side of the thorny barrier. As they pass, each takes a piece of thread from the man who holds the incense and ties it round his neck. The object of this curious ceremony is to prevent the spirit of the dead from coming home with the mourners and establishing itself in its old haunts. Conceived of as a miniature man, it is believed to be unable to make its way on foot through the thorns, while the smell of the incense, to which all spirits are highly sensitive, prevents it from surmounting this obstacle on the shoulders of one of the mourners.

Occupation and social status.

Agriculture, trade and soldiering are the chief occupations of the Mangars, but no means of earning a livelihood comes amiss to them, provided that it does not involve doing things which are recognized as the proper business of the lower castes. They abstain from beef, but eat pork and domestic fowls, and indulge freely in strong drink. Before marriage a Mangar will eat any sort of food with a Gurung or Khas, but after he has been married, he can only take chupatties from these castes, and may not take rice or dál. Mangars smoke in the same hookah with Gurungs, Khas and Brahmans.

Mangaráj, a title of Khandáits in Orissa.

Mán-Gauránga, a sub-caste of Sutradhars in Murshedabad.

Mang-beh-pá, a *rui* or sept of Dejong Lhori Bhotias, the members of which are of a low mixed origin.

Manglagpa, a sept of the Pánthar sub-tribe of Limbus in Darjiling, whose ancestor was ridden by a god and danced.

Mangmu, a sept of the Yangorup sub-tribe of Limbus in Darjiling.

Mangoyak, a sept of Limbus in Darjiling.

Mangráti, a section of Kámis in Darjiling.

Mangrauni, a section of Bábhans in Behar.

Mangthong, a sept of the Phágu sub-tribe of Yakhas in Darjiling.

Mang-tshang-wa, a *rui* or sept of the Ruichhung sub-tribe of Dejong Lhoris or Bhotias of the south.

Mangyong, a sept of Limbus in Darjiling.

Manháriá, shopkeepers who deal in miscellaneous goods, chiefly fancy articles.

Mani, a sub-caste of Sunris in Maldah.

Manihári, a functional group of Jugis in Bengal.

Manikchakdudhpurá, a *mul* or section of the Naomuliá or Majraut sub-caste of Goálás in Behar.

Mánikmahanta, *Mánikmanta*, a title of Kurmis.

Manikshariá, a section of Bábhans in Behar.

Manimanáras, a section of Madhesiá Halwáis in Behar.

Manjar, cat, a totemistic section of Rautiás and a sept of Kharwars in Chota Nagpur.

Manjari, a section of Kámárs in Singbhum and the Santál Parganás.

Manjhal-Turiyá, a sub-caste of Lohárs in Chota Nagpur.

Manjhan, the title of the headman of the Tior and Dom castes in Behar who has under him a messenger bearing the title of *Chharidár*. The Maghaya Barhis and the Aráiyá Telis of North Bhágalpur also have headmen bearing this title. In the case of the latter the jurisdiction of each *manjhan* is said to extend to 22 villages.

Mánjhi, (i) the steersman of a boat, a ferryman: hence, a boatman generally. (ii) A village headman among the Santáls, and a title by which Santáls frequently describe themselves in answer to inquiries as to their caste. (iii) A title used by the Kaibartta, Kahár, Kumhár, Teor, Patni, Kochh, Bágdi, Málá, Jeliá, Goálá, the Máls of the Rájmahál hills, the Khetauris in the Santál Parganás; a section of Sunris in Behar; a title and a sept of Bauris and Kharwars; a title of Asuras, and Korwas in Chota Nagpur; a sept of Págesars in Chota Nagpur; a title of Binjhiá, Rautiá, Oraon, Turi; a title of Kapális and Kawális in Eastern Bengal; a section of Kádars; a title of Málos in Eastern Bengal; of Parhaiyas and Khandáits in Chota Nagpur; a section of Doms and Dosádhs in Behar; a title of Cheros and Mahilis; a title and a sept of Mál Pahárías; a title of Tántis in Behar.

Manjhiá, a sub-tribe of Kharwárs in Southern Lohardagá.

Mánjhi-Khil, a sub-sept of the Hansda, Marndi, and Tudu septs of Santáls.

Mánki, *Mánki Sáhib*, an honorific title bestowed in Bankura on the eldest son of a well-to-do cultivator of the Bhumij tribe. In Chotá Nagpur Proper the term denotes the headman of a group or circle of villages. It is also the designation of a sept and a sub-tribe of Mundas. See **Murá**.

Mánná, a title of Kaibarttas, Mayarás, and Nápits in Bengal.

Manoharshahi, a group of the Fatehsing Telis in Murshedabad; a sub-caste of Kotáls in Western Bengal.

Manrayá, a *kul* or section of Bábhans in Behar.

Mantiáni, a title of the Bárui caste in Bengal.

Mantrawár, a section of Kurmis in Chota Nagpur and Orissa.

Már, *Máhwé Rajput*, a small cultivating caste of Chota Nagpur, who say that they came from Malwa and were formerly Kshatriyas, but dropped the sacred thread and took to the plough. Colonel Dalton thought them 'more Aryan than anything else, with a dash of aboriginal blood.' But if this view be correct, it seems difficult to account for their abandoning the characteristic Rájput sept names and adopting the totems peculiar to Dravidian tribes. 'They have Brahmans for priests, worship the host of Hindu gods, and, like the Kandhs, especially adore those among their ancestresses who became Sátis, though in their present degraded state they allow of widow-marriage, and a man always takes to wife, by the custom called *sagai*, his elder brother's widow.'

Már, rice broth, a totemistic sept of Mundas in Chota Nagpur.

Marai, a wild animal, a totemistic sept of Páns and Gonds in Chota Nagpur.

Maraiá, a section of the Kádar caste in Behar.

Maraiya, a title of Barhis in Behar.

Maralbai, a sept of Rájputs in Behar.

Máramagri, *Rájbansi*, *Baruá* or *Bhuiyá Magh*, a sub-tribe of Maghs in the Hill Tracts of Chittagong.

Marandi, a sept of Santáls.

Marar, a title of Kumhárs and Tántis in Behar; a title of Surahiyás, Tiyars, Kewats, and of Gareris; a section of the Bánsphor sub-caste of Dóms in Behar.

Marár, a title of Amáts in Behar, indicating some degree of social importance and deemed superior to either Ráut or Khawas; a title of Sunris, Jolhas; a title of the headmen of the Dom caste in Behar who have under them servants called Chharidárs to execute or communicate their orders; a title of the Dhusiá sub-caste of Chamárs; a title of the Majraut sub-caste of Goálás; a section of the Játhot division of the Párbatti-Kurin sub-caste of Gonrhis; a title applied in Behar to Kurmis who by age or personal influence have attained a leading position in their villages; a title of Beldárs and Nuniás.

Marare-Sihaul, a *mul* of the Kásyap section of Maithil Brahmans in Behar.

Marare-Jagaul, a *mul* of the Kásyap section of Maithil Brahmans in Behar.

Marare-Ukki, a *mul* of the Kásyap section of Maithil Brahmans in Behar.

Marare-Barhampur, a *mul* of the Kásyap section of Maithil Brahmans in Behar.

Marare-Adauri, a *mul* of the Kásyap section of Maithil Brahmans in Behar.

Marare-Misrauli, a *mul* of the Kásyap section of Maithil Brahmans in Behar.

Marare-Rajaurá, a *mul* of the Kásyap section of Maithil Brahmans in Behar.

Marare-Jagatpur, a *mul* of the Kásyap section of Maithil Brahmans in Behar.

Mardahá, a *pangat* or section of Dosádhs in Behar.

Mardaniá, barbers, a sept of the Rautár sub-tribe of Thárus in Behar.

Márh, a title of Kaibarttas in Bengal.

Márhwár, a sept of Rájputs in Behar.

Maria, a sept of Chiks in Chota Nagpur.

Mariáli, a sub-caste of Tántis in Bengal.

Mariár, a sept of Rájputs in Behar.

Marich-bhuswal, a section of Sonárs in Behar.

Marichigrám, a *samáj* or local group of the Sábarna *gotra* of

Páschátya Baidik Brahmans in Bengal.

Marichwár, a sub-tribe of Thárus in Behar.

Marik, a title of Tántis and a section of the Bánsphor sub-caste of Doms in Behar.

Márik, a title of Báruis in Bengal; a section of the Kádar caste in Behar which intermarries with the Bárik, Kápari, Mánjhi, Mandar, and Naiyá sections, but not with the rest; a title of Hindu Jolhas, Doms, Dosádhs, Goálás, Koiris, Kumhárs, and other castes in Behar.

Marj-bhuswal, a section of Sonárs in Behar.

Markam, a sept of Goálás in Chota Nagpur.

Márkanda, Márkandárk, a *pur* or section of Sákadwipi Brahmans in Behar.

Márkande, a small cultivating caste found in Bhágalpur and the Santál Parganás. They have neither sub-castes nor sections, and I can find no evidence tending to affiliate them with any existing caste or tribe. Their own tradition is that they are descended from Márkandeya Muni, a sage who was outcasted for eating the leavings of certain Brahmans who had invited him to a feast.

Origin.

The Márkande practise infant-marriage and allow polygamy without setting any definite limit on the number of wives a man may have. Widows may marry again, and enjoy full freedom of choice in selecting a second husband. Divorce is not recognized. A faithless wife is simply turned out of the caste.

Marriage.

In matters of religious and ceremonial observances the Márkande exhibit little divergence from the standard of orthodox Hinduism. In the worship of the greater gods they employ Brahman *purohits*, who are not held to be degraded by serving the caste in this capacity. The minor god Karmani is worshipped by the members of the household without the assistance of priests.

Religion.

In point of social standing Márkandes rank with Goalas, Kurmis, and Koiris. Brahmans will take water and certain kinds of sweetmeats from their hands. Their sole occupation is agriculture. The bulk of the caste are occupancy raiyats, but some have risen to the position of tenure-holders.

Social status.

The following statement shows the number and distribution of the Márkande caste in 1872 and 1881:—

District.	1872.	1881.
Shahabad	6	......
Darbhanga	......	5
Monghyr	5,780	1,983
Bhagalpur	3,587	3,384
Purniah	6,561	3,598
Santál Parganás	3,044	4,390

Márkandeya, a *gotra* or section of the Baidya caste in Bengal.

Marli, a sept of Hos and Santáls.

Marmá, *Myammá* or *Roáng Magh*, a sub-tribe of Maghs in the Hill Tracts of Chittagong.

Marmu, a sept of Mundas in Chota Nagpur.

Márndi, grass, a totemistic sept of Santáls.

Marotsa, a sept of Maghs in the Hill Tracts of Chittagong.

Márre, a section of Bábhans in Behar.

Marri, a section of Máhilis in Manbhum, the members of which do not allow their daughters to enter their houses after marriage.

Marrik, a section of Rajwárs in Western Bengal.

Marsyángdi, a *thar* or sept of Mangars in Darjiling.

Marturiá, a section of Lohárs in Behar.

Maruá, a *mul* or section of the Chhamuliá Madhesiá sub-caste of Halwáis in Behar.

Maruá, *Maruábádi* (*maruá* = Indian corn (*Eleusine corocana*) and *ábádi* = cultivator), a contemptuous epithet applied to Hindustanis and especially to up-country boatmen who ply on the Bengal rivers on account of their stupidity in comparison with Bengalis.

Maruáhá, a *mul* or section of the Tinmuliá Madhesiá sub-caste of Halwáis in Behar.

Maruiporá, a sub-caste of Brahmans in Bengal, who have degraded themselves by officiating as priests at the funerals of Sudras.

Marwahe, a section of the Baháunajáti sub-caste of Khatris in Bengal.

Márwári, literally a native of Málwa or Márwár. Most of the Márwáris found in Bengal are bankers and traders, usually Jains. The name gives no definite indication of caste, but it will be found as a rule that a Márwári belongs to the Agarwal, Oswal, Maheswari, or Srimal castes. In fact all traders from Rajputana and the neighbouring districts are commonly called Márwáris.

Máryá, a small iron-working caste, possibly of Dravidian descent, found in the Santál Parganas. The information at my disposal does not warrant any conjecture regarding their origin. So far as I can ascertain, they have neither sub-castes nor sections, and their marriages are regulated by a very rough enumeration of prohibited degrees, which admits of intermarriage between persons descended from the same parents after the expiry of three generations on the father's side and one on the mother's. Daughters are married either as infants or as adults, and polygamy is allowed without any theoretical limitation on the number of wives a man may take. Widows may marry again, but are under no restriction in their choice of a second husband. Divorce is permitted for adultery or for inability to agree, and divorced women may marry again.

Marriage.

Máryás profess to be Hindus, but they do not employ Brahmans for religious and ceremonial purposes, and the functions of the priest are discharged by selected members of the caste. The dead are burned and the ashes

Religion.

buried, but no regular *sráddh* is performed, and the only funeral observance consists of a feast given to the caste brethren by a man's heir ten days after his death.

Social status. The caste ranks with Lohárs, Chamárs, and the lowest grades of Dravidian Hindus. They eat fowls and indulge freely in spirituous and fermented liquors. Iron-working is believed to be their original occupation, and most of them are blacksmiths at the present day. Some, however, have taken to cultivation, and a few are said to have risen to the comparatively high position of tenure-holders.

The Census Report of 1881 returned 857 Máryás in the Santál Parganás.

Masálchi, a title of Bágdis, probably arising from their employment as palanquin-bearers, one of the duties of a bearer being to carry a torch. It is also possible that the term may denote an office held by the Bagdi caste under one of the Rajas of Western Bengal.

Masanta, a title of Tilis in Bengal.

Masáre keraut, a section of the Biyáhut and Kharidáhá Kalwárs in Behar.

Másaur, a section of the Sátmulia Maghayá sub-caste of Kándus in Behar.

Masawár, a sub-caste of Kumhárs in Chota Nagpur and Behar.

Máschatak, a *gáin* of the Sándilya *gotra* of Rárhi Brahmans in Bengal.

Máski, a *thar* or sept of Mangars in Darjiling.

Másle, a sub-caste of Telis in Bengal.

Masnath, a sub-caste of Telis in Behar.

Masrakhiyá, a section of the Bánsphor sub-caste of Doms in Behar.

Mastán, Mahasthán or **Háliá**, a sub-caste of Utkal Brahmans.

Másya, a functional group of Jugis in Bengal.

Matasyási, a *gáin* of the Sándilya *gotra* of Bárendra Brahmans in Bengal.

Matha Ság, a vegetable, a totemistic sept of Mundas in Chota Nagpur.

Mathgrámi, a *gáin* of the Kásyapa *gotra* of Bárendra Brahmans in Bengal.

Mathia, brass bracelet, a totemistic sept of Mundas in Chota Nagpur.

Mathrwár, a section of Kurmis in Chota Nagpur and Orissa.

Máthur, a division of Brahmans and a sub-caste of Káyasths in Behar.

Mathurábási, a section of Goálás in Behar.

Mathurá or **Mathurábási**, a sub-caste of Goálás in Orissa.

Mathuriá, a sub-caste of Telis, Barhis and Lohars in Behar and Chota Nagpur.

Mátiá, a sub-caste of Bágdi in Bengal who are cultivators and earth-workers.

Mátial, a sub-caste of Kewats in Orissa.

Mátiál, a sub-caste of Bágdis in Bengal who sell fish and vegetables.

Mátiál, *Metel*, *Metiá*, "terræ filius," a title of Kaibarttas in Orissa and also of Bágdis, Bauris, Koras, and other earth-working castes in Bengal. As a rule the term is used only by outsiders.

Matibans-Tánti, a sub-caste of Tántis in Orissa.

Mat·um, a title of the Bhumij tribe in Manbhum.

Matsendra, king of fish, a section of Jugis.

Mattariá, a sub-caste of Halwáis in Behar.

Matti, a title of Goálás in Behar.

Matwárá, a section of Rajwárs in Western Bengal.

Maudgalya, a *gotra* or section of Brahmans, Baidyas, Káyasths, Subarnabaniks and Telis in Bengal; a section of Sudras in Eastern Bengal; of the Paschim Kuliyá Sadgops; an eponymous section of Kámárs, Mális, Madhunápits, and Nápits in Bengal; a section of Bárendra Sunris in Eastern Bengal.

Maudgalya or **Madhukulya**, a section of Pods in Central Bengal.

Maugh, fish, a totemistic sept of Mundas in Chota Nagpur.

Maughá, a group of the Bárendra Sunris in Eastern Bengal.

Mauhariá, a sub-caste of Rástogis in Behar.

Maulavi, a title of Bauris in Western Bengal.

Maulik, a synonym for Dhimál.

Maulik, a hypergamous group of Káyasths, of the Dákshinátya Baidik Brahmans, Baidyas, Sadgops, Chásádbohás, and Subarnabaniks in Bengal. The name appears to be connected with *mul*, root, stock, or origin.

Maulik, *Láyá*, *Náyá*, a Dravidian caste of Manbhum and Western Bengal, who claim affinity with the Mal Pahāriás of Rájmahál, and who may possibly be an offshoot from that tribe, to whom, as being the earliest settlers in the country, the duty of propitiating the forest gods may easily have come to be assigned.

Internal structure.

The Maulik of Northern Manbhum and the Santál Parganás are divided into six sub-castes—**Chandana**, **Hariyán** or **Jehariyá**, **Mál** or **Már**, **Sauriyá**, **Rájbansi**, and **Deobansi**. The last two groups call themselves Hindus, and allege that their ancestors were at one time in possession of the Pándra estate in Manbhum. The sections of all the sub-castes are totemistic. A man may not marry a woman belonging to his own section, nor one who falls within the usual formula for reckoning prohibited degrees.

Marriage.

Adult-marriage was formerly in vogue among the Mauliks, as it is still among the Mundas and Oraons. Of late years the example of the Hindus around them has led to the adoption of infant-marriage; and this practice, involving, as is ordinarily believed, an advance in social respectability, tends to become constantly more popular. The earlier custom, however, still survives, and sexual indiscretions before marriage are said to be not uncommon, and as a rule are leniently dealt with. After the bride has been selected and a small bride-price paid, the bridegroom is married to a mango-tree and the bride to a mahuá. This is followed by the ordinary ceremony performed under an open canopy made of sál leaves. The two Hinduised sub-castes employ a Brahman to recite *mantras* on this occasion; for the others a man of their own caste serves as priest. The binding portion is the marking of the bride's forehead with vermilion, which is done by the bridegroom with the *jánti* or cutter used for slicing areca nut.

Polygamy is not formally recognized, but a man is allowed to take a second wife if his first wife is barren. A widow may marry again by the *sangá* form, and is subject to no restrictions in her choice of a second husband. Great license of divorce is allowed, the tearing of a *sál* leaf in symbol of separation being the only form required to complete the act. Divorced wives may marry again.

Religion.

Although, as has been stated above, the Deobansi and Rajbansi sub-castes call in Brahmans of low rank, known locally as Pánres, to assist in their marriage ceremony, even they have not yet taken to worshipping Hindu deities or employing Brahmans as their family priests, and the caste as a whole still adheres to the rude animism characteristic of the aboriginal races of Western Bengal. Their offices as priests of the various spiritual powers who haunt the forests, rocks, and fields and bring disease upon man and beast are in great request. A Bhumij or a Kurmi who wishes to propitiate these dimly-conceived but potent influences will send for a Maulik to offer the necessary sacrifices in preference to a Láyá or priest of his own caste—a fact which speaks strongly for the antiquity of the settlement of the former in the country. Besides serving as priests, they also collect lac, catechu, and other jungle produce, and work as cultivators and day-labourers. Their social rank, according to orthodox ideas, is exceedingly low, and no Hindu will take water from their hands. Mauliks themselves will eat boiled rice with Bhuiyas, and sweetmeats, etc., with Santáls and Mundas. The more advanced Deobansi and Rájbansi sub-castes abstain from beef, and believe themselves to be thereby raised in ceremonial purity and social estimation above their fellows. It is curious to observe that while the non-Hinduised Mauliks will eat no one's leavings, the more orthodox sub-castes have no prejudices on this point so far as the members of the higher Hindu castes are concerned, and will eat the leavings of Brahmans, Rájputs, and Káyasths.

The following statement shows the number and distribution of Mauliks in 1872 and 1881:—

DISTRICT.	1872.	1881.	DISTRICT.	1872.	1881.
Monghyr	5,492	606	Lohardagá	371	......
Bhagalpur	......	95	Singbhum	578	......
Santál Parganás	9,179	3,524	Manbhum	687	5,446
Hazaribagh	628	18	Tributary States	......	179

Maulo, a title of Muchis in Western Bengal.

Maulwár, a sept of the Surajbansi division of Rájputs in Behar.

Maunachh, a sept of Rájputs in Behar.

Maunas, a section of Brahmans; a sept of Rájputs in Behar.

Maura, a *mul* or section of the Kanaujiá sub-caste of Hajjáms in Behar.

Maureswari, a sub-caste of Telis in Bengal.

Maurhiá, a section of the Banodhiá and Jaiswár Kalwárs in Behar.

Mauriyár, a *pur* or section of Sákadwipi Brahmans in Behar.

Mautkaha, a *gotra* or section of Nepáli Brahmans.

Mawáli, a title of Chandáls in Eastern Bengal.

Mawar, peacock, a totemistic sept of Chiks in Chota Nagpur.

Mawár, a title of Bábhans in Behar.

Mayáháng, a *thar* or sept of Khambus in Darjiling.

Mayará, *Modak*, *Mairá*, *Kuri*, the confectioner caste of Bengal Proper, a heterogeneous functional group, to be distinguished from the Madhunápit, on whom popular usage sometimes confers the titles Modak and Kuri. Some, indeed, regard the Madhunápit as merely a sub-caste of Mayará, but it will be seen from the article on Madhunápit that there are grounds for believing that group to be a distinct homogeneous caste owing its origin to a schism among the Nápits. In Central Bengal the Mayará caste is divided into four sub-castes—**Rárh-ásram**, **Máyur-ásram**, **Aja-ásram**, and **Dharm-ásram** or **Dharm-sut**. In Dacca, where there are comparatively few Mayarás and the occupation of sweetmeat-making is almost wholly in the hands of the Madhunápit, the former group has only two sub-castes—**Ekpátiá** and **Dopátiá**. The distinction between these is curious: the former in their marriage ceremony simply carry the bride seven times round the bridegroom, while the latter carry both round in concentric circles, the bridegroom following the inner and smaller circle of the two.

Origin and internal structure.

The sections of the Mayará caste which are given in the Appendix show a singular mixture of elements derived from the Brahmanical *gotras* and survivals from the earlier totemistic sections which we find among the non-Aryan castes. It is impossible now to determine what tribes may have contributed to form the Mayará caste as we now find it, but the fact that distinct traces of totemism may be discerned will perhaps be held to justify the conjecture that the group is not wholly of Aryan extraction. As a rule marriage within the section is strictly prohibited, but in some parts of the country the law of exogamy is disregarded, and marriage is regulated solely by calculation of prohibited degrees. Mayarás have not yet developed a full-blown system of hypergamy, but they appear to be on the road towards doing so, for the families who bear the titles **Ásh**, **Barát**, **Dás**, and **Nandi** are called

Kulins. At present, however, the distinction is meaningless so far as marriage is concerned. Men belonging to Maulik families may marry Kulin women, and the only privilege attached to Kulinism is the right to receive presents of cloth, etc., at marriages and other domestic festivals.

Marriage.

Mayarás profess to marry their daughters as infants, but they are not so particular in this matter as the higher castes, and instances of girls marrying after puberty, though rare, are said to occur occasionally without entailing any serious loss of reputation for the family concerned. The marriage ceremony is performed in accordance with orthodox usage; *sampradán*, or the giving and receiving of the bride, being the essential portion of the rite. A price, varying according to the social status of the parties, is paid for the bride. Polygamy is permitted, no limit being placed, in theory at least, on the number of wives a man may have. Widows may not marry again, and divorce is not recognized. A woman taken in adultery is turned out of the caste.

Religion.

The caste profess to be orthodox Hindus, belonging for the most part to the Vaishnava sect. They regard Ganes as their special deity, and make images in his honour. The special season for his worship is towards the end of the cold weather, before the sugarcane crop has been cut, and freshly-prepared molasses cannot be used in the manufacture of sweetmeats until the god has been duly propitiated. Brahmans officiate as their priests, and are not looked down upon by other members of the sacred order. In Manbhum, Mohan Giri, Sahib Miá, Sashthi, and Bhádu are among their minor gods, whom the members of each household worship with sacrifices of goats and offerings of rice, fruit, and sweetmeats. In this domestic worship Brahmans take no part. The dead are burned and the ashes thrown into the Ganges or any river that may be conveniently situated for the purposes. *Sráddh* is performed on the thirty-first day after death.

Occupation.

Mayarás believe the making of sweetmeats to be their original occupation, but many of them at the present day have entered Government service or taken to trade, while a few are engaged in agriculture as tenure-holders and occupancy raiyats. They will, however, on no account cultivate sugarcane themselves or take any part in the preparation of molasses. In a country where sweetmeats form a staple article of diet, and are often the only food that an orthodox Hindu can partake of on a journey, when he has no time to go through the elaborate process of preparing his own food, it is essential that there should be no doubt about the social status and ceremonial purity of the caste which supplies the community with sweetmeats. Mayarás therefore rank among the Navasákha, and Brahmans will take water from their hands. Their own rules regarding diet are those of most respectable Hindus. They will eat cooked food only with Brahmans, and will take water or sweetmeats from members of the Navasákha group.

The following statement shows the number and distribution of Mayarás in 1872 and 1881, the figures for Halwáis being included in the former year for the districts of Bengal Proper:—

District.	1872.	1881.	District.	1872.	1881.
Bardwan	17,040	12,240	Darjiling	90	65
Bankura	3,719	7,579	Jalpigori	270	1,104
Birbhum	10,066	8,165	Kuch Behar	......	336
Midnapur	6,010	7,066	Dacca	2,112	1,297
Hughli	} 8,278	{ 6,382	Faridpur	897	831
Howrah		{ 2,769	Bakarganj	1,450	270
24-Parganás	6,864	2,990	Maimansinh	5,017	4,780
Nadiya	9,337	17,076	Tipperah	5,901	666
Khulna	......	737	Chittagong	231	233
Jessore	1,942	3,322	Noakhali	616	428
Murshedabad	3,062	5,359	Maldah	279	1,219
Dinajpur	546	494	Santál Parganás	The figures are included in the table on Halwás.	9,045
Rajshahye	969	898	Lohardagá		26
Rangpur	5,798	18,150	Singbhum		572
Bogra	200	1,080	Manbhum		11,363
Pabna	1,522	1,894	Tributary States		71

Mayur, a totemistic section of the Bhar caste in Manbhum, the members of which will not touch or kill the peacock.

Mayur-ásram, a sub-caste of Mayarás in Central Bengal.

Mazumdár, a title of Nápits in Bengal.

Mech, *Mechi*, a Mongoloid tribe found in the Goalpárá district of Assam and in the Himalayan Terai from the Bhutan Duárs westward to the Konki river. In Northern Bengal they have given their name to the Mechi river, and in Goalpárá to the large tract of country called Mechpárá, the proprietor of which, however, calls himself a Rájbansi and repudiates all connexion with the Mech tribe.[1] Ritter[2] identifies them with the Dhimál, and remarks that in point of agricultural skill they are about on a level with the Gáros. Fr. Müller[3] classes them among the Lohitic races, and says they are of the same stock as the Káchári or Bodo. A good observer[4] writes thus of the Mech:—"They are probably the original inhabitants of the Darjiling Terai, and are a distinctly Mongolian race, with fair skins and large bones and limbs. Their physical appearance and characteristics are quite distinct from the Tháru of the Western Terai. They are disappearing, absolutely dying out, faster than any race of which I have known or read. The reason is, no doubt, that their distinctive cultivation is by *jhum*, which is barred by Government forest conservancy, and the spread of settled plough cultivation from the South." In another place Mr. Oldham speaks of the Dhimál and Rájbansi as "dark-skinned Dravidians, and lays stress on the contrast between them and the fair-complexioned Mech. The compiler of the *Assam Census Report*, on the other hand, includes the Mech and the Kochh under the generic term Bodo, and appears to regard both as belonging substantially to the same race.

Origin.

[1] Dalton, *Ethnology of Bengal*, p. 88.
[2] *Erdkunde*, iv, 109.
[3] *Allgemeine Ethnographie*, p. 406.
[4] Mr. W. B. Oldham, late Deputy Commissioner of Darjiling.

A singular reference to both Mech and Dhimál is met with in the Limbu legend that when the three brothers, their ancestors, were first dropped by the gods from Heaven they fell in Benares, whence they wandered northward, seeking the place appointed for them to dwell in. So they came to the *Khachar*, or *mule-country*, as the Nepalese call the tract at the foot of the hills between the Brahmaputra and Kosi rivers. There the youngest brother determined to settle, and became the father of the Kochh, Dhimál, and Mech; while the two others went further into the hills, and their descendants are the Limbus and Khambus of Nepal. A third story makes Assam the proper home of the Mech, and seeks to connect them with the Gáros. Others, again, say that the Mech and Dhimál are descended from Nepalese who, being driven out of Nepal for breaches of caste rules, settled in Khachar and married women of the locality. Without attaching any historical value to these traditions, we may perhaps infer from them that considerable intermixture of blood has taken place between the inhabitants of the hills and the plains, and that types originally distinct may in this way have been greatly modified and to some extent amalgamated. The process of fusion has, however, not yet gone so far as to render it impossible to discern in the Mech traces of a primary Mongolian stock, while the Dhimál tribe appears to be connected by features and complexion with the black races, who may be conveniently designated aboriginal.

Internal structure.

The Mech of the Darjiling and Jalpigori district are divided into two sub-tribes[1]—**Agniá-Mech** and **Játi-Mech**, which are practically endogamous, seeing that a member of the former group cannot marry into the latter without thereby forfeiting his position in his own group. The Agniá sub-tribe have twelve exogamous septs, which are shown in Appendix I, while the Játi-Mech regulate marriage by the standard formula calculated to three generations in the descending line. The same rule is observed on the mother's side by the Agniá-Mech, who, however, extend the prohibition in the male line to seven generations.

The Agniá-Mech admit only Rájbansis into their own group; while the Játi-Mech receive also Dhimáls, Dhekrás, and Agniá-Mech. In all cases the new member has to give a feast as a sort of entrance-fee and by way of proclaiming his membership. Such admissions are usually brought about by men of the higher groups taking mistresses from the women of the lower, and thus forfeiting their place in their own society.

Marriage.

Among the Agniá-Mech the usual age for marriage is twelve years for females and sixteen for males, though here, as elsewhere, the influence of Hinduism shows itself in the desire on the part of well-to-do people to get their daughters married at a still earlier age. For the most part, however, the earlier usage of free courtship still holds its ground, and the

[1] Further east, I understand, that four sub-tribes are known—Agniá-Mech, Assam-Mech, Káchrá-Mech, and Thampái-Mech. Káchrá-Mech are probably the same as the Kachári.

consent of the parents is sought only after the young people have arranged matters between themselves. Even then, if objections are raised, the girl often solves the difficulty by going off with her lover and thus compelling her parents to take steps to get her married. The same system prevails among the Játi-Mech, but with them the age for marriage ranges from sixteen to twenty for both males and females, and it is not uncommon to find a woman married to a man younger than herself. The bride-price, called *mothom theká* by Agniá and *chumná* or *sodhá* by the Játi-Mech, is supposed to be fixed with reference to the beauty and accomplishments, and may rise in the Agniá sub-tribe as high as Rs. 120 or even more. Among the Játi-Mech it is supposed to be fixed at Rs. 63, but this amount may be, and usually is, reduced by haggling.

In both sub-tribes the marriage ceremony is exceedingly simple. Among the Agniá-Mech the essential and binding portion of the rite is the formal washing of the bride's feet in the presence of the friends and relatives of both parties with water poured from a bamboo water-vessel (*chungá*). This being done, she enters a room where the bridegroom is awaiting her, and consummation is supposed to take place at once. When she comes out a cock and a hen are sacrificed and two betel leaves and areca nuts offered to Siva, the latter articles being afterwards eaten by the wedded pair. Feasting then commences by the bride serving first the bridegroom, and after him the other guests, with meat and boiled rice. The Játi-Mech do not wash the bride's feet, but make the pair exchange betel leaves and areca nuts. This is held to be the essential rite, and is followed by the sacrifice of a cock and hen to Siva.[1]

A widow may marry again, but if she has children it is deemed more respectable for her to live as a widow with her late husband's relatives, to whom in any case her children belong. If, however, she determines to contract a second marriage, she may not marry any relative, whether elder or younger, of her deceased husband, but must return to her parents' house and get married from there by an informal ceremony called *nika*, in which the bridegroom makes with his little finger a single spot of vermilion on the bride's forehead. Fowls are sacrificed as in the regular form, but the bride's feet are not washed, nor does she exchange betel leaves and areca nuts with the bridegroom. The bride-price for a woman marrying a second time is reduced to one-half of the original amount, and if she marries a third time to one-fourth. In the presumably rare case of a woman marrying for the fourth time, no bride-price at all is paid. A remarried widow is deemed to be socially the inferior of a woman

---

[1] Some of my correspondents distinguish three modes or forms of marriage: thus—(1) the ordinary marriage, in which the parents' consent is obtained before the girl goes to her husband; (2) the *dakud* marriage, in which the bride elopes or is carried off, and may be reclaimed by her parents if the bride-price is not paid; (3) the *ghar sundi* marriage, when a girl takes a fancy to a man, goes to his house of her own accord, and sits as a suppliant by the symbol of the *ghar-devi*, which stands in the corner of the chief room. In such cases, after refusing the girl as a matter of form, the man is bound ultimately to yield to her importunity. Clearly, however, these are not so much forms of marriage as modes of proposing marriage.

married as a virgin, and is not entitled to serve boiled rice to the guests assembled on any public or ceremonial occasion. Divorce may be effected, with the sanction of the panchâyat, at the wish of the parties or on the ground of the wife's adultery. In the latter case the seducer is liable to repay the bride-price to the injured husband, and cannot marry the woman until he has done so. Divorced wives can only be remarried by the curtailed ceremony in use at the remarriage of a widow, and they hold the same social status as the latter. Their children also belong to the father. It would seem at first sight that the unrestricted courtship permitted by the Mech can hardly promote a high standard of female chastity, and in fact sexual intercourse before marriage, though not expressly recognized, is virtually tolerated, it being understood that if a girl becomes pregnant her lover will at once come forward and marry her. Regarding married women, however, a different order of ideas prevails, and as soon as a girl has finally pitched upon a husband, she is required to be strictly faithful to him. A curious usage, to which parallels may be found in European folklore, deserves notice in this connexion. In the courtyard of every Mech house a sij plant (*Euphorbia Indica*) is carefully tended as the abode of the god Siva and as the emblem of conjugal fidelity. Should the leaves of the plant wither, this is supposed to show that something is wrong with one of the women of the household. Rice is deposited under the tree, and on the next day a panchâyat is called, before which all the women are summoned and a handful of rice is given to each to chew. She who fails to masticate her portion is held guilty of unchastity, and if married is at once turned out of the house. If it is an unmarried girl who breaks down in the chewing ordeal, she is called upon to disclose the name of her paramour, so that arrangements may be made to get her married at once.

Religion.

The religion of the Mech, like that of the Dhimál, is still in an early stage of transition from animism to Hinduism. They describe themselves as Hindus of the Saiva sect, and worship Siva under the name of Batho, and his consort Káli as Bali Khungri. To the former the Agniá-Mech sacrifice buffaloes, goats, and pigeons; while his wife has to put up with the less respectable offerings of pigs, fowls, and goats, which the Játi-Mech offer indifferently to either. The Játi-Mech also reverence as a household goddess (*ghar-devi*), a nameless personage, supposed to be the mother of Siva, who is represented by a lump of sun-dried clay set in the corner of the chief room. Pigs, fowls, plantains and parched rice are offered to her on any day in the week except Sunday, Tuesday, or Wednesday. Among their other deities may be mentioned Tsimising, Tista Burhi (Buchanan's 'old lady of the Tísta'), Mahesh Thákur, Sonnisi and Mahákál. They have no Brahmans, and priests (*dhámi* or *ojhá*) chosen from among the tribe to serve them for religious and ceremonial purposes.

Disposal of the dead.

Those who can afford a funeral pyre prefer to burn the dead, while the poorer members of the tribe bury, placing the corpse face upwards with the head pointing towards the south. In the latter case a small fire is kindled upon the grave, in which food and drink are burned for the benefit of the deceased. The Agniá-Mech perform a meagre propitiatory rite on the eighth day, and the Játi-Mech on the fourth day, after death. With both the important part of the proceedings is the feast which is given to the friends and relatives of the deceased. Some repeat the ceremony every year after the manner of the Hindus, but this is unusual.

Social status.

Judged by the Hindu standard, the social status of the Mech is extremely low. Both Rájbansis and Dhimáls look down upon them; and they themselves, while claiming higher rank than Garos, Lepchas, and Tibetans, admit the social superiority of the Rájbansis. Dhimáls they appear to look upon as standing on much the same level as themselves, though the former profess to be stricter in matters of food and drink, and strenuously disclaim kinship and social intercourse with the Mech. They eat pork, fowls, all kinds of fish, lizards, and the *imphu* silk-worm, but abstain from beef, the flesh of the long-tailed sheep, snakes, field-rats, and the leavings of other people. Buffalo flesh now ranks as beef, at any rate with the Agniá-Mech; but this seems to be a comparatively modern reform, for some Mech are said to eat buffalo flesh, and those who do not seem to pride themselves on their asceticism. Spirituous liquors are indulged in without stint.

A curious story is told in the Terai to account for the fact that the Nepalese will take water from the hands of the Mech. It is said that some twenty years ago Jang Bahadur, then Prime Minister of Nepal, while shooting in the Terai, fell in love with a Mech girl, the daughter of Ujir Singh Jamadar, of Dhulábári, and took her with him to Nepál as his mistress. As the price of her person, and in accordance with the wishes of the tribe, he issued an edict that in future no subject of Nepal should refuse to take water from a Mech, or, as my informant adds, from a Dhimál also. I am unable to say what amount of truth there may be in this tale, but if such an edict were ever actually published, it can hardly have done more than recognize and confirm a practice already existing. Even Jang Bahadur's despotic power must have yielded to popular prejudice if the Nepalese had really deemed the Mech unclean. The fact, however, seems to be that there is a considerable strain of Nepalese blood among the Mech, and other facts may be mentioned which go to confirm this view. Like the Nepalese, for example, the Mech have much greater liberty in matters of food before marriage than after, so that an unmarried man may take rice from people who are not deemed pure enough to give food to a married man. Both observe the Tihar festival; both call the bride-price *sodhá* or *theká*. These coincidences may of course be due merely to that transfusion of custom which is everywhere observable; but taking all the circumstances into consideration, I think it more likely that they have arisen from intermixture of the two races.

Occupation.

Husbandry by the *jhúm* method is regarded by the Mech as their original occupation, but of late years many have taken to settled cultivation as raiyats of *jots* in the Terai. The rearing of the *imphu* silkworm, which spins the silk used in the chequered cloths worn by the Mech, was at one time a regular industry, but has fallen off notably within the last generation.

The following statement shows the number and distribution of the Mech tribe in 1872 and 1881:—

DISTRICT.	1872.	1881.
Bogra	......	31
Rangpur	......	6,836
Darjiling	893	1,063
Jalpigori	40	8,760
Kuch Behar	......	224

Mechari, a sept of Tántis in Chota Nagpur.

Mechi, a synonym for Mech.

Mecho, a hypergamous group of Kaibarttas in Jessore.

Medari, a *gáin* of the Sábarna *gotra* of Bárendra Brahmans in Bengal.

Meghalbariárpur, a *mul* or section of the Naomuliá or Majraut sub-caste of Goálás in Behar.

Meghi, a *thar* or sept of Gurungs in Darjiling.

Mehalo, a title of Doms in Behar.

Meháus, a section of the Sátmuliá Maghayá sub-caste of Kándus in Behar.

Mehdipur Mohdia, a *mul* or section of the Naomuliá or Majraut sub-caste of Goálás in Behar.

Meheden, a section of the Bárajáti sub-caste of Khatris in Bengal.

Meherá, a section of the Chárjáti sub-caste of Khatris in Bengal.

Mehmánpur, a *mul* or section of the Naomuliá or Majraut sub-caste of Goálás in Behar.

Mehos, a *mul* or section of the Maghayá sub-caste of Kándus in Behar.

Mehrá, a sept of Rájputs in Behar.

Mehran, a section of Sunris in Behar.

Mehrána, a title of the Tirhutiá sub-caste of Kumhárs in Behar.

Mehri, a sept of Rájputs in Behar.

Mehtar, *Mihtar*, a sub-caste of Háris who remove night-soil.

Mehtar, a section of Maghayá Kumhárs; a title of Nuniás, of the Dhusia and Dohar sub-castes of Chamárs; a section of the Kulsunri sub-caste of Sunris and of the Dharkár sub-caste of Doms in Behar.

Mehtaria, a section of Maghayá Dhobis in Behar; also a title of Chamárs.

Mekchan, a section of Murmis in Darjiling.

Mekhun, a *dugu* or section of the Kochh-Mandai in Dacca. The name indicates the original habitat of the group, probably a hill or village in Assam, and at the present day has no bearing upon marriage.

Memophagpa, a sept of the Chaibisa sub-tribe of Limbus in Darjiling.

Mendru, a sept of Rájputs in Behar.

Meng, a *thar* or sept of Mangars in Darjiling.

Mengi, a *thar* or sept of Gurungs in Darjiling.

Menwár, a section of Bháts in Behar.

Menyangbo, the unsuccessful one, a sept of the Yangorup sub-tribe of Limbus in Darjiling.

Meongba, a sub-sept of the Thekim sept of Limbus in Darjiling.

Mephagpa, the butcher, literally pig-roaster, a sept of the Pánthar sub-tribe of Limbus in Darjiling.

Mert, a sept of Bhuiyás in Chota Nagpur.

Mesha, sheep, a title of Tántis in Bengal.

Mesh-rási, a section of Málos in Eastern Bengal.

Mete, a title of Kaibarttas in Bengal.

Methi, a section of Oswáls in Behar.

Methuá, a synonym for Dhángar in Chota Nagpur.

Mewakhola or **Terothar**, a sub-tribe of Limbus in Darjiling.

Mihtar, a sub-caste of Telis in Behar.

Millak, a section of Mahesris in Behar.

Millong, a sept of the Tungjainya sub-tribe of Chakmás in the Hill Tracts of Chittagong.

Min, *sál* fish, a totemistic section of the Kumhár caste in Manbhum; a section of Jugis in Bengal.

Minag-pá, a *rui* or sept of Sherpa Bhotias of Nepal.

Mind, a sept of Mundas in Chota Nagpur.

Minj, a snake, the totem of a section of Oraon-Dhángars settled for several generations in Behar.

Minji, eel, a totemistic sept of Oraons in Chota Nagpur.

Mir or *Mair*, a sub-caste of Sonárs in Behar.

Mirchaiá, a section of the Baranwar sub-caste of Baniyás in Behar.

Mirchwán, a section of Sonárs in Behar.

Mirdáha, a section of the Kádar caste in Behar which intermarries with the Darbe, Mánjhi, Kampti, and Báre sections, but not with the rest; a section and a title of Maghaya Doms; a title of men of the Turi and Dosadh castes who follow the profession of hawkers or falconers; a title of Binjhiás and Khandáits in Chota Nagpur.

Miriásin, a class of Mahomedan musicians in Behar who also deal in and apply leeches.

Mirich bhusait, a *mul* or section of the Ayodhiabási sub-caste of Sonárs in Behar.

Mirshikár, a chief huntsman; a low class of Mahomedans who live by snaring birds.

Mising, a sept of Tipperahs in the Hill Tracts of Chittagong.

Misir, a section of the Sribástab sub-caste of Káyasths in Behar.

Misr or **Misra**, a title of Gaura, Maithil, Kanaujiá, and Sáraswat

Brahmans and of Bábhans in Behar.

Misra, a title of the Dákshinátya Baidik Brahmans in Bengal; a *thar* of the Atri *gotra* of Nepáli Brahmans; a section of Gaura Brahmans in Behar; a section of Utkal or Orissa Brahmans.

Mistri, a synonym for Barai, Karangá, and Dhobi in Behar.

Mistri, a carpenter or mason, *Occ.* A title of Barhis, Kanaujiá Lohárs, and of Kámárs in Behar; a title of Sutradhars, Chásádhobás, Dhobás, and Pods in Bengal.

Mithan, a section of Agarwáls in Behar.

Mithoriá, a section of Majraut Goálás in Behar.

Mitra, a title of Káyasths and Báruis in Bengal.

Mitraseni Behará, a sub-caste of Bhuinmális in Bengal.

Mittal, a *gotra* or section of Agarwáls in Behar.

Moáli, a *gáin* of the Kásyapa *gotra* of Bárendra Brahmans in Bengal.

Mobrishya, a section of Sánkháris in Bengal.

Mochháre, a sept of the Agniá sub-tribe of Meches in the Darjiling Terai.

Mochi, a title of Jaunpuri Chamárs who make shoes; also a title of Dhusiá Chamars in Behar.

Mochián, a *mul* or section of the Kanaujiá sub-caste of Sonárs in Behar.

Modak, a synonym for Mayará.

Modási, a group of the Rájbansi sub-caste of Kochhs in Northern Bengal.

Modgalya, a section of Gandhabaniks in Bengal.

Modhágrámi, a *gáin* of the Kásyapa *gotra* of Bárendra Brahmans in Bengal.

Modi, a title of Baniyás, Halwáis, Kalwars, Koras, and Sunris in Behar.

Mogalkáchá, a *mul* or section of the Naomuliá or Majraut sub-caste of Goálás in Behar.

Mogha, a title of men who dress as females and earn their living by dancing and singing.

Moghaliá, a section of the Dhusiá sub-caste of Chamárs.

Mohali, a sub-caste of Doms in Behar. The similarity of name suggests a connection with the mat and basket-making caste of Mahili in Western Bengal.

Mohani, a title of Gonrhis in Behar.

Mohár, a *mul* or section of the Chhamuliá Madhesiá sub-caste of Halwáis in Behar.

Mohara, a *thar* or sept of Dámis in Darjiling whose chief profession is sewing.

Mohbaita, a section of the Pachainyá sub-caste of Doms in Behar.

Mohdiar, a section of Ghásis in Chota Nagpur.

Moirá, a synonym for Mayará.

Moktán, a section of Murmis in Darjiling.

Molá, a sub-caste of Báuris in Western Bengal.

Molá, a section of Doms in Western Bengal.

Molán, a section of Goálás in the North-Western Provinces and Behar.

Moldhiá, a section of Goálás in the North-Western Provinces and Behar.

Moldiar, a section of Bábhans in Behar.

Molima, **Molima-Sege**, a sept of Chakmás in the Hill Tracts of Chittagong.

Molo, a sub-caste of Korás in Western Bengal.

Momin, 'faithful'; a synonym for Musalmán; a designation of Mahomedan Jolahas which distinguishes them from the Hindu Jolahas.

Mon, a synonym for Lepcha.

Mongar, a section of Goálás in Behar.

Mongbai, a sept of Tipperahs in the Hill Tracts of Chittagong.

Monghyr, a *dih* or local section of the Maghayá sub-caste of Telis in Behar. The system of exogamy among this sub-caste of Telis seems, however, either to be dying out or to be of recent introduction, for some of the Maghayás say they have no *dihs*, but merely prohibit marriage within nine *pirhis* or degrees of relationship.

Monglá, a sept of the Tungjainya sub-tribe of Chakmás in the Hill Tracts of Chittagong.

Mongri, thorny fish, a totemistic sept of Páns in Chota Nagpur.

Mongtupo, a sept of the Yangorup sub-tribe of Limbus in Darjiling.

Monmatar, *Motia*, *Motari* (from *mot*, *B.*, 'a burthen') a porter, a carrier of burthens, and generally a day-labourer employed otherwise than in agriculture.

Mor, peacock, a totemistic section of Khandáits in Orissa and Chota Nagpur.

Mormu, deer, a totemistic sept of Lohárs in Chota Nagpur.

Morpachi, a sept of Goálás in in Chota Nagpur.

Moti, a sept of Gonds in Chota Nagpur.

Motiomán, a sept of Kaurs in Chota Nagpur.

Motliá, a section of Goálás in the North-Western Provinces and Behar.

Motrihá, a section of the Banodhiá and Jaiswár Kalwárs in Behar.

Mo-u, a sept of the Tungjainya sub-tribe of Chakmás in the Hill Tracts of Chittagong.

Mowar, a section of Bábhans in Behar.

Mowl, a sept of Mundas in Chota Nagpur.

Mradha, a title of Háris in Bengal.

Mridha, the head of the menial servants in a zamindár's establishment.

Mrung, a synonym for Tipperah.

Muchi, *Rishi*,[1] the leather-dressing and cobbler caste of Bengal, by origin doubtless a branch of the Chamárs, though its members now repudiate that name and claim to be a distinct caste of somewhat higher social position. Mr. Nesfield observes that "the industry of tanning is preparatory to, and lower than that of, cobblery: and hence * * * * the caste of Chamár ranks decidedly below that of Muchi. The ordinary Hindu does not consider the touch of a Muchi so impure as that of a Chamár, and there is a Hindu proverb to the effect that 'dried or prepared hide is the same thing as cloth,' whereas the touch of the raw hide before it has been tanned by the Chamár is considered a pollution. The Muchi does not eat carrion like the Chamár, nor does he eat swine's flesh; nor does his wife ever practise the much-loathed art of midwifery. He makes the shoes, leather aprons, leather buckets, harness, portmanteaux, etc., used by the people of India. As a rule he is much better off than the Chamár, and this circumstance has helped amongst others to raise him in the social scale." It may be gathered from this description that in the North-West Provinces the Muchi never dresses freshly-skinned hides, but confines himself to working up leather already tanned by the Chamár. This distinction does not appear to be so sharply drawn in Bengal, where Muchis tan hides like the Chamárs, but will only cure those of the cow, goat, buffalo, and deer.

Traditions of origin.

The origin of the Muchi caste is given in the following legend, related to Dr. Wise by one of their Brahmans, and afterwards reported to me substantially in the same form from an independent source:—One of the Prajá-pati, or mind-born sons of Brahmá, was in the habit of providing the flesh of cows and clarified butter as a burnt offering (Áhuti) to the gods. It was then the custom to eat a portion of the sacrifice, restore the victim to life, and drive it into the forest. On one occasion the Prajá-pati failed to resuscitate the sacrificial animal, owing to his wife, who was pregnant at the time, having clandestinely made away with a portion. Alarmed at this he summoned all the other Prajá-patis, and they sought by divination to discover the cause of the failure. At last they ascertained what had occurred, and as a punishment the wife was cursed and expelled from their society. The child which she bore was the first Muchí, or tanner, and from that time forth mankind being deprived of the power of reanimating cattle slaughtered for food, the pious abandoned the practice of killing kine altogether. Another story is that Muchirám, the ancestor of the caste, was born from the sweat of Brahmá while dancing. He chanced to offend the irritable sage Durvása, who sent a pretty

---

[1] Buchanan met with a tribe of fishermen in Puraniya called Rishi, and considered them to be an aboriginal tribe of Mithilá. Rishi, however, is often used as a pseudonym to hide the real paternity of a caste: thus the Músahar often calls himself "Rishi-bálaka," or son of a Rishi, and the Bengali Chamár tries to pass incognito as a Rishi. In the case of the Músahar it is possible that Rishi may be Rikhi or Rikh-Mun, the bear, one of the original totems of the Bhuiyá or Músahar tribe, and the same may hold good for the Chandál. This explanation, however, is mainly conjectural.

Brahman widow to allure him into a breach of chastity. Muchirám accosted the widow as mother, and refused to have anything to do with her; but Durvása used the miraculous powers he had acquired by penance to render the widow pregnant, so that the innocent Muchirám was made an outcaste on suspicion. From the widow's twin sons Bara Rám and Chhota Rám descended the **Bará-bhágiyá** and **Chhota-bhágiyá** sub-castes, which are the two main divisions of Muchis at the present day. The **Chhota-Bhágiyá** deal in hides, act as musicians, and do various kinds of leather work; while the **Bará-bhagiyá** profess to be only cultivators. The latter are again divided into **Uttar-Rárhi** and **Dakin-Rárhhi**, who do not intermarry or eat together. The other sub-castes, **Cnásá-Kurur** or **Chásá-Kolai**, are agriculturists; the **Betuá** make cane baskets and also cultivate; the **Jugi-Muchi** or **Korá** weave coarse cloth of cotton, often mixed with silk; the **Tikákar Konai**, who make the *tiká* or charcoal balls used for lighting pipes; and the **Baitál, Kurur, Mála bhumiá, Sabarkárá,** and **Sánki**, are shoemakers, cobblers, and curriers. Muchis have only two sections, Kásyapa and Sándilya, which have been borrowed from the Brahmanical system, and has no bearing upon the prevention of intermarriage between near relatives.

Marriage.

They follow the ordinary rules as to prohibited degrees, and permit the marriage of two sisters to the same man, provided that the younger is not married first. Both infant and adult-marriage are recognized for girls, but the former practice is deemed the more respectable, and is resorted to in the large majority of cases. In the Dacca district a father generally receives from fifty to sixty rupees for his daughter, from which it may be inferred that the custom of polygamy has tended on the whole towards the preponderance of males in the caste. In other districts, however, the bride-price is not so high, and in Pabna it is said to vary from Rs. 5 to Rs. 25-4, according to the means of the bridegroom. The marriage ceremony is a simplified form of that in use among the higher Hindu castes; *sindurdán*, or according to some the burning of *khai* or parched paddy before the bride and bridegroom, being the binding portion. The bride is dressed in red garments. In former years, says Dr. Wise, the marriage ceremonies of the Rishi were scenes of debauchery and intemperance, but of late intoxicating liquors have been prohibited until all the regular forms have been observed. Even Hindus, who rarely have anything favourable to say of the Rishi, confess that now-a-days, owing to some unknown cause, both the Chamárs and Rishis have become more temperate and more attentive to their religious duties than formerly. Polygamy is permitted with no restriction on the number of wives, except the man's ability to maintain them and their children. Divorce is permitted on the ground of adultery. Usually the pancháyat of the caste are called together by their president (*parámánik* or *moiáli*) to give their sanction to the proceedings; and if this is not done at the instance of the husband, the wife has a right to appeal to the pancháyat. With the permission of that body divorced wives may marry again by the *sanga* or *nika* form. Widows also may marry a second time by this ritual, the binding portion of which consists of exchanging garlands made of the flowers of the *tulsi* (*Ocymum sanctum*). Here also the sanction of the panchâyat is required, and a feast is given to the members. A small sum, varying from Re. 1 to Rs. 5, is paid as *pan*. Indications are not wanting that the opinion of the caste tends to condemn widow-marriage, and that the custom may be expected to die out within a generation or two unless some special influence is brought to bear in its favour. Already some Muchis hold that only virgin widows can properly marry again, and that the remarriage of a full-grown woman who has already lived with her husband is little better than concubinage. The children of *sanga* marriages are deemed to be in some sense degraded, and, if males, have to pay a heavy fine before they can obtain wives. Like Bauris and Bágdis, the Muchis admit into their community members of any caste higher than their own. The new member is required to give a feast to the caste panchâyat, and to eat with them in token of fellowship. Instances of men of other castes thus becoming Muchis are rare, and occur only when a man has been turned out of his own caste for having intercourse with a Muchi woman and taking food from her hands.

Religion.

The majority of the caste are believed to belong to the Saiva sect, but a large proportion of the Betuá sub-caste are Vaishnavas. They imitate the Sudras in most of their religious ceremonies, while others peculiar to themselves resemble those of the Chamárs. Though regarded as utterly vile, they are permitted to make offerings at the shrines of Káli, which a Jugi is not allowed to do. They keep many Hindu festivals, the chief being that in honour of Viswakarmá on the last day of Bhádra. When small-pox prevails they offer a pig to Sitalá, first of all smearing the animal's snout with red lead and repeating certain incantations, after which it is set free, and any one can seize it. Like the Chamár, Dhobá, Dosadh, and other low castes, the Muchis worship Jalka Devi whenever cholera or other epidemic disease breaks out. The Muchi women, however, only collect contributions in their own quarter, and wear the wreath of plantain, date-palm, or *bená* (*Andropogon muricatus*) for two and a half days instead of for six, as is the custom of the Chamárs. Muchirám Dás, the reputed ancestor of the caste, and Rui Dás, are also popular objects of worship.

Priests.

A Brahman was bestowed on the Bará-bhágiyá Muchis by Ballál Sen, and the story goes that in the palace of that monarch a certain Brahman, having made himself especially troublesome by insisting upon being appointed as priest to one of the newly-formed castes, had it intimated to him by the Raja that he would belong to the caste which should first appear to him in the morning. There was also a Muchi, a celebrated player on the *naqárah*, or kettledrum, whose duty it was to sound the *reveille*. It was easily arranged that the Brahman should first cast his eyes on him when he awoke, and his descendants have ever since ministered to this despised race. They rank among the lowest of the Barna-Brahmans, and neither members of the sacred order nor men belonging to the *A'charani* castes will take water from their hands. The Chhota-bhágiyá have priests of their own. Muchis burn their dead and perform *sráddh* on the thirtieth day after death. In the case of men who have died a violent death there is no *sráddh*, but a *práyaschitta*, or expiatory ceremony, is performed.

The Chhota-bhágiyá and Betuá sub-castes, like the Chandáls, observe ten days of impurity and celebrate the *sráddh* on the eleventh.

Social status.

The social position of Muchis is, as has been intimated above, perhaps a shade higher than that of Chamárs, but this is not saying much, and both castes may properly be placed in one class at the bottom of the scale of precedence recognized by the average Hindu. None of the regular village servants will defile himself by working for a Muchi, and thus the caste has been compelled to provide itself with barbers and washermen from among its own members. Illegitimate children are usually brought up to these professions, and wherever the community is a large one no inconvenience is felt. Their rules regarding diet are in keeping with their standing in society. The Chhota-bhágiyá sub-caste eat beef, as the Chamárs do; are very partial to chickens, and regard pork as a delicacy. The Bara-bhágiyá, Betuá, and Chásá-kolai abstain from beef and pork, but not from fowls; and they are far less particular than the higher castes as to the kinds of fish which they eat. Like the Chamárs, all Muchis are great spirit-drinkers, and notorious for their indulgence in the more dangerous vice of gánja-smoking. No other caste will eat food prepared by a Muchi, but Doms will take water from their hands and will smoke from the same hookah.

Occupation.

Muchis work as tanners, shoe-makers, saddlers, musicians, and basket-makers. Their mode of preparing skins is as follows:—The raw hide is rubbed, and then soaked for fifteen to twenty days in a strong solution of lime. It is then deprived of its hair and of any fat that remains, and steeped for six days in acid tamarind juice. Finally, it is put in a vat containing a solution of lac and pounded babúl (*Acacia*), garan (*Cerions Roxburghianus*), and sundarí (*Heritiera minor*) barks, the hide being after this immersion regarded as properly cured.

The town Muchis buy hides from their brethren resident in those parts of the country where cattle abound. The village Muchis of the Chhota-bhágiyá sub-caste, while they pride themselves on not skinning the carcasses of their own cattle, row up and down the rivers in their neighbourhood in search of carcasses, and when epidemic diseases attack the herds they find so much to do that the villagers attribute the spread of the disease to them. It is doubtless often the case that they puncture a healthy cow with an Acacia thorn impregnated with virus, but they are rarely, if ever, detected at this villainous trade. The people, however, firmly believe that they increase their profits in this way. In Western Bengal and Chota Nagpur, where the *sál* jungles form the chief pasturing grounds, Muchis destroy cattle with arsenic rolled up in a bundle of *mahuá* petals. These are a favourite food for cows, and can be strewn on the ground without rousing any suspicion.

The Muchi will not touch a corpse, but will skin the carcass of a dead animal. The skin of the buffalo sacrificed at the Durgá Púja is their perquisite, and the skinning of the animal often gives rise to bitter quarrels between rival families.

Most Muchis make shoes, but of inferior quality to those manufactured by the Chamárs. The Betuá sub-caste are famous for making baskets with rattan (*Calamus rotang*), which natives assert are so closely woven that they will hold water. They also collect the roots of the dub grass (*Panicum*), and manufacture the brush (*manjan*) used by weavers for starching the warp. In some parts the Muchi castrates bull calves, but this they stoutly deny. Others, again, work as sweepers and remove night-soil, but those who do so are excluded from intermarriage with the rest of the caste, and appear to be on the way to form a sub-caste of their own.

The tablá-wála, or drum-maker, is always a Muchi. Goats' skins are used for the covering, while cows' hides supply the strings for tightening the parchment. On every native drum, at one or both ends, black circles (*khiran*) are painted to improve the pitch. The Muchi prepares a paste of iron filings and rice, with which he stains the parchment. At all Hindu weddings they are employed as musicians, and engaged in bands, as among Muhamadans. Their favourite instruments are drums of various shapes and sizes, the violin, and the pipe.

The female Muchi differs from the Chamáín in never acting as a midwife, in wearing shell bracelets instead of huge ones of bell-metal, and in never appearing as a professional singer.

The following statement shows the number and distribution of Muchis in 1881, the figures for 1872 having been included with those of Chamárs :—

District.	1881.	District.	1881.
Bardwan	48,684	Darjiling	74
Bankura	9,094	Dacca	411
Birbhum	25,716	Faridpur	3,336
Midnapur	11,854	Bakarganj	1,547
Hughli	10,909	Maimansinh	6,902
Howrah	3,517	Tipperah	2,613
24-Parganás	24,814	Chittagong	584
Nadiya	34,068	Noakhali	221
Khulna	41,147	Maldah	2,883
Jessore	22,347	Santál Parganás ...	5,651
Murshedabad	10,076	Cuttack	862
Dinajpur	3,305	Puri	56
Rajshahye	2,795	Balaosre	249
Rangpur	2,834	Tributary States ...	571
Bogra	1,908	Singbhum	577
Pabna	4,899	Manbhum	7,307

Muchirám Dás, a title of Muchis in Bengal.

Muddapuriá, a section of the Kamár sub-caste of Dosádhs in Behar.

Mudgal, a section of Karans in Orissa.

Mudgul, a section of the Srotriya sub-caste of Utkal Brahmans.

Mudi, petty shop-keepers selling rice, *dál*, sugar, etc.; a title of Binds and Bágdis; a synonym for Korá, professional diggers and excavators; a title of bullock-drivers engaged in trade; a section of Oraons whose chief profession is earthwork. They also carry palanquins and cultivate land.

Mudir, frog, a totemistic section of Jagannáthi Kumhárs in Orissa.

Mudu, a sept of Tántis in Chota Nagpur.

Muduk, a sept of Mundas in Chota Nagpur.

Muduli, a title of Chásás in Orissa.

Mugrish, a section of Khyáns in Northern Bengal.

Muharrir, Mohari, a vernacular writer, a clerk who either does not know English or is employed in a post which requires no knowledge of English.

Muhkim, supervisor, a title of Tántis in Bengal.

Mujaimiya, a *kul* or section of Bábhans in Behar.

Mujaniar, a sept of Korwas in Chota Nagpur.

Mujganji-Parámánik, a sub-caste of Nápits in the 24-Parganás.

Mujgarni, a group of the Daspárá sub-caste of Kumhárs in Pabna.

Mujni, a section of Koiris in Behar.

Mujniá, a section of the Biyáhut and Kharidáhá Kalwárs in Behar.

Mukáranchhá, a *thar* or sept of Khambus in Darjiling.

Mukariá, a section of the Dhaprá sub-caste of Doms in Behar.

Mukeri, a person employed in grinding wheat-flour.

Mukh, a section of Maghaiyá Kumhárs in Behar.

Mukhaiti, a *gáin* of the Bharadwája *gotra* of Rárhi Brahmans in Bengal.

Mukhi, a section of Ghásis in Chota Nagpur: hence *Mukhiáin*, an opprobrious term applied to women of the Ghási and other low castes from their quarrelsome habits.

Mukhiá, a *mul* or section of the Ghosin sub-caste of Goálás in Behar; a section of Kewats; a title of Binds and Kurmis in Behar; a title of Khambus in Darjiling.

Mukhiár, a title of Tiors and of the Cháb sub-caste of Gonrhis in Behar.

Mukhiyá, a section of the Játhot division of the Párbatti-Kurin sub-caste of Gonrhis in Behar.

Mukhya-Kulin, a hypergamous group of Rárhi Brahmans in Bengal.

Mukmed, a section of the Maghayá sub-caste of Barhis in Behar.

Mukruár, spider, a sept of Asuras in Chota Nagpur.

Muktáng, a section of Murmis in Darjiling.

Mukta-sil, a title of barbers in Eastern Bengal.

Mukund, a section of Barhis in Behar.

Mul, a *gáin* of the Kásyapa *gotra* of Rárhi Brahmans in Bengal; a sept of Tántis in Chota Nagpur.

Mula, a group of the Bárendra Goálás in Bengal.

Mulhatiá, a section of the Kasarwáni sub-caste of Baniyás in Behar.

Mulki, a sub-tribe of Rájputs in Western Bengal.

Mulmaháli, a section of the Biyáhut and Kharidáhá Kalwárs in Behar.

Mulukjuri, a *gáin* or sub-section of Saptasati Brahmans in Bengal.

Mulukuas, a *thar* or sept of Khambus in Darjiling.

Munda, *Mura*, *Horo-hon*, a large Dravidian tribe of Chota Nagpur classed on linguistic grounds as Kolarian, and closely akin to the Hos and Santáls, and probably also to the Kandhs. The name Munda is of Sanskrit origin. It means headman of a village, and is a titular or functional designation used by the members of the tribe, as well as by outsiders, as a distinctive name much in the same way as the Santáls call themselves Mánjhi, the Bhumij Sardár, and the Khambu of the Darjiling hills Jimdár. The general name Kol, which is applied to both Mundas and Oraons, is interpreted by Herr Jellinghaus to mean pig-killer, but the better opinion seems to be that it is a variant of *horo*, the Mundári for man. The change of *r* to *l* is familiar and needs no illustration, while in explanation of the conversion of *h* into *k*, we may cite *hon*, the Mundári for 'child,' which in Korwa becomes *kon* and *koro*, the Muási form of *horo*, 'a man.' It may be added that the Khariss of Chota Nagpur call the Mundas Kora, a name closely approaching Kol.

Origin.

The Munda myth of the making of mankind tells how the self-existent primeval deities Ote Borám and Sing Bonga created a boy and a girl and put them together in a cave to people the world. At first they were too innocent to understand what was expected of them, but the gods showed them how to make rice-beer, which inflames the passions, and in course of time their family reached the respectable number of twelve of either sex. As is usual in myths of this class, the children were divided into pairs; and Sing Bonga set before them various kinds of food for them to choose from before starting in the world. The fate of their descendants depended on their choice. Thus "the first and second pair took bullocks' and buffaloes' flesh, and they originated the Kols (Hos) and the Bhumij (Matkum); the next took of the vegetables only, and are the progenitors of the Brahmans and Chhatries; others took goats and fish, and from them are the Sudras. One pair took shell-fish and became Bhuiyás; two pairs took pigs and became Santáls. One pair got nothing, seeing which the first pairs gave them of their superfluity, and from the pair thus

Tradition.

provided spring the Ghasis, who toil not, but live by preying on others."[1]

Internal structure.

The Mundas are divided into thirteen sub-tribes, several of which, such as Kharia-Munda, Mahili-Munda, Oraon-Munda, appear to be the result of crosses with neighbouring tribes, while others again, like Bhuinhár-Munda and Mánki-Munda, have reference to the land and communal system of the tribe. The Mahili-Munda sub-tribe has the pig for its totem, and for them pork is tabooed. But appetite has proved stronger than tradition, and the taboo is satisfied by throwing away the head of the animal, the rest of the carcase being deemed lawful food. The septs or *kilis*, which are very numerous, are mainly totemistic, and the totem is taboo to the members of the sept which bears its name. A list of the septs is given in Appendix I. If it were possible to identify them all, and to ascertain precisely to what extent and in what manner the taboo of the totem is observed by each, the information would probably throw much light upon the growth of early tribal societies.

Marriage.

A Munda may not marry a woman of his own sept. The sept-name goes by the father's side, and intermarriage with persons nearly related through the mother is guarded against by reckoning prohibited degrees in the manner common in Behar. Adult marriage is still in fashion, and sexual intercourse before marriage is tacitly recognized, but in all respectable families matches are made by the parents, and the parties themselves have very little to say in the matter. The bride-price varies from Rs. 4 to Rs. 20. *Sindurdán*, or the smearing of vermilion on the bride's forehead by the bridegroom and on the bridegroom's forehead by the bride, is the essential and binding portion. The practice described by Colonel Dalton of marrying the bride to a *mahuá* tree and the bridegroom to a mango seems now to have been abandoned. Traces still survive among the Mundas of a form of marriage, resembling the Santáli *nir bolok*. It is called *dhuko era*, meaning a bride who has entered the household of her own accord. The children of a woman thus married seem to have an inferior status in respect of their rights to inherit the landed property of their father. The late Babu Rákhál Dás Háldár, Manager of the estate of the Maharájá of Chota Nágpur, gave me an illustration of this fact. Some years ago the *mundá* or headman of one of the villages of the Government estate of Barkagarh died, leaving an only son by a *dhuko era* wife, and a question was raised as to the latter's right to succeed. Under Colonel Dalton's orders, a number of headmen of villages were called together, and their opinions were taken. No decided results, however, could be arrived at. Some thought the son should get the whole property. Others proposed to exclude him altogether, and a third party considered him entitled to maintenance. Eventually the question was compromised by admitting the son's right to one-fourth of the land and the whole of the personal property. The case is a curious comment on the

[1] Dalton, *Ethnology*, p. 185.

uncertainty of tribal custom. Widows may marry again by the ritual known as *sagai*, in which *sindurdán* is performed with the left hand. Divorce is allowed at the instance of either party, and divorced women are permitted to marry again. In cases of adultery the seducer is required to pay to the husband the full amount of the bride-price.

Religion.

At the head of the Munda religion stands Sing-Bonga, the sun, a beneficent but somewhat inactive deity, who concerns himself but little with human affairs, and leaves the details of the executive government of the world to the gods in charge of particular branches or departments of nature. Nevertheless, although Sing-Bonga himself does not send sickness or calamity to men, he may be invoked to avert such disasters, and in this view sacrifices of white goats or white cocks are offered to him by way of appeal from the unjust punishments believed to have been inflicted by his subordinates. Next in rank to Sing-Bonga comes Buru-Bonga or Marang-Buru, also known as Pát-Sarná, a mountain god, whose visible habitation is usually supposed to be the highest or most remarkable hill or rock in the neighbourhood. "In Chota Nágpur," says Colonel Dalton,[1] "a remarkable bluff, near the village of Lodhma, is the Marang-Buru or Maha-Buru for a wide expanse of country. Here people of all castes assemble and sacrifice—Hindus, even Mahomedans, as well as Kols. There is no visible object of worship; the sacrifices are offered on the top of the hill, a bare semi-globular mass of rock. If animals are killed, the heads are left there, and afterwards appropriated by the páhan or village priest." Marang-Buru is regarded as the god who presides over the rainfall, and is appealed to in times of drought, as well as when any epidemic sickness is abroad. The appropriate offering to him is a buffalo. Ikir Bonga rules over tanks, wells and large sheets of water; Garhá-era is the goddess of rivers, streams and the small springs which occur on many hill sides in Chota Nágpur; while Náge or Nága-era is a general name applied to the minor deities or spirits who haunt the swampy lower levels of the terraced rice-fields. All of these are believed to have a hand in spreading disease among men, and require constant propitiation to keep them out of mischief. White goats and black or brown cocks are offered to Ikir Bonga, and eggs and turmeric to the Náge. Deswáli or Kárá-Sarná is the god of the village who lives with his wife Jáhir Burhi or Sarhul-Sarná in the Sarná or sacred grove, a patch of the forest primeval left intact, to afford a refuge for the forest gods. Every village has its own Deswáli, who is held responsible for the crops, and receives periodical worship at the agricultural festivals. His appropriate offering is a *kárá* or he-buffalo; to his wife fowls are sacrificed. Gumi is another of the Sarná deities whose precise functions I have been unable to ascertain. Bullocks and pigs are sacrificed to him at irregular intervals. Chandor appears to be same as Chando Omol or Chanala, the moon worshipped by women, as the wife of

[1] *Ethnology of Bengal*, 188.

Sing Bonga and the mother of the stars. Colonel Dalton mentions the legend that she was faithless to her husband, and he cut her in two, 'but repenting of his anger he allows her at times to shine forth in full beauty.' Goats are offered to her in the Sarná. Háprom is properly the homestead, but it is used in a wider sense to denote the group of dead ancestors who are worshipped in the homestead by setting apart for them a small portion of every meal and with periodical offerings of fowls. They are supposed to be ever on the watch for chances of doing good or evil to their descendants, and the Munda fully realise the necessity for appeasing and keeping them in good humour.

Festivals.

The festivals of the tribe are the following:—(1) Sarhul or Sarjum-Bábá, the spring festival corresponding to the Baha or Bah-Bonga of the Santáls and Hos in Chait (March-April) when the *sál* tree is in bloom. Each household sacrifices a cock and makes offerings of *sál* flowers to the founders of the village in whose honour the festival is held. (2) Kadletá or Batauli in Asarh at the commencement of the rainy season. "Each cultivator," says Colonel Dalton, "sacrifices a fowl, and after some mysterious rites a wing is stripped off and inserted in the cleft of a bamboo and stuck up in the rice-field and dung-heap. If this is omitted, it is supposed that the rice will not come to maturity." (3) Naná or Jom-Naná, the festival of new rice in Asin when the highland rice is harvested. A white cock is sacrificed to Sing-Bonga, and the first fruits of the harvest are laid before him. Until this has been done, it would be an act of impiety to eat the new rice. (4) Khariá puja or Kolom Singh, called by the Hos Deswáli Bonga or Mágh Parab celebrating the harvesting of the winter rice, the main crop of the year. Five fowls and various vegetables are offered to Deswáli, the god of the village at the *khalihan* or threshing floor. Among the Hos of Singbhum the festival is kept as a sort of *saturnale*, during which the people give themselves up to drunkenness and all kinds of debauchery. This is less conspicuously the case with the Mundas of the plateau who live scattered among Hindu and Christian neighbours, and do not form a compact tribal community like the Hos of the Kolhan. The festival, moreover, is kept by the Mundas on one day only, and is not spread over a month or six weeks, during which time the people of different villages vie with each other in dissipation, as they do in the Kolhán.

The funeral ceremonies of Mundas do not differ materially from those of the Hos, of which Colonel Dalton's description has been quoted in the first volume of this Glossary.

Succession.

Succession among the Mundas is governed by their own customs, which appear to have been little affected by the influence of Hindu law. Property is equally divided among the sons, but no division is made until the youngest son is of age. With them, as with the Santáls, daughters get no share in the inheritance; they are allotted among the sons just like the live-stock. "Thus if a man dies, leaving three sons and three daughters and thirty head of cattle, on a division each son would get ten head of cattle and one sister; but should there be only one sister, they wait till she marries and divide the *pan*," or bride-price, which usually consists of about six head of cattle. Among the Hos of Singbhum the bride-price is higher than with the Mundas, and the question of its amount has there been found to affect seriously the number of marriages.

Village communes and officials.

According to ancient and universal tradition, the central table land of Chota Nagpur Proper was originally divided into *parhás* or rural communes, comprising from ten to twenty-five villages, and presided over by a divisional chief, called the *rájá* or *múnda* of the *parhá*. In 1839, titular *rájás* of the *parhá* were still existing in the Fiscal Division of Khukrá near Ránchí, who retained considerable authority in tribal disputes, and at times of festival and hunting. But this element in the Munda village system has now fallen into decay, and survives only in the *jhandás* or flags of the *parhá* villages, and in the peculiar titles bestowed on the cultivators themselves. The exclusive right to fly a particular flag at the great dancing festivals is jealously guarded by every Munda village, and serious fights not unfrequently result from the violation of this privilege. Besides this, individual villages in a *parhá* bear specific titles, such as *rájá*, *diwán*, *kunwár*, *thákur*, *chhotá lál*, etc., similar to those which prevail in the household of the reigning family, which obviously refer to some organization which no longer exists. I am informed that these officials still make the arrangements for the large hunting parties which take place at certain seasons of the year.

A Kol village community consists, when perfect, of the following officers:—*Múnda*, *máhato*, *páhn*, *bhandári*, *goráit*, *goálá*, and *lohár*. Washermen, barbers, and potters have been added since 1839, and even now are only found near much frequented halting places, and in villages where the larger Hindu tenure-holders live. The Kols invariably shave themselves, and their women wash the clothes.

(1) MUNDA.—The *múnda* is the chief of the *bhuinhárs*, or descendants of the original clearers of the village. He is a person of great consequence in the village; and all demands from the *bhuinhárs*, whether of money or labour, must be notified by the owner of the village through the *múnda*. He is remunerated for his trouble by the *bhuinhári* land, which he holds at a low rate of rent, and receives no other salary. In parganá Lodhmá, and in the south-eastern portion of Lohardagá he sometimes performs the *máhato's* duties as well as his own, and he then gets a small *jágir* of half a *páwá* of land rent-free.

(2) MAHATO.—The functions of a *máhato* have been compared to those of a *patwári* or village accountant, but he may be more aptly described as a rural settlement officer. He allots the land of the village among the cultivators, giving to each man a *goti* or clod of earth as a symbol of possession; he collects the rent, pays it to the owner, and settles any disputes as to the amount due from the *raiyats*; and, in short, manages all pecuniary matters connected with the land. He is appointed by the owner of the village, and receives one *páwá*

of *rájhas* land rent-free, as a *jágir* or service-tenure. But the office is neither hereditary nor permanent, and the *máhato* is liable to be dismissed at the landlord's discretion. Dismissal, however, is unusual, and the *máhato* is often succeeded by his son. Where the *máhato* collects the rents, he almost universally receives a fee, called *báttá*, of half an *ánná* from each cultivator, or of one *ánná* for every house in the village. In one village *báttá* amounts to four *ánnás* and a half on every *páwá* of land. Occasionally, where there is no *bhandári* or agent for the owner's rent-paying land, the *máhato* gets three bundles (*karais*) of grain in the straw, containing from ten to twenty *sers* apiece, at every harvest. Thus during the year he would receive three bundles of *gondli* from the cold weather crop, and the same amount from the *gorá* or early rice, and the *don* or late rice. In *khálsá* villages, which are under the direct management of the Mahárájá, the *máhato* often holds, in addition to his official *jágir*, a single *páwá* of land, called *kharcha* or *rozina kket*, from the proceeds of which he is expected to defray the occasional expenses incurred in calling upon cultivators to pay their rent, etc.

The functions of the *máhato* are shown in greater detail in the following extract from Dr. Davidson's Report of 1839 :—" On a day appointed, the *thikádár* or farmer proceeds to the *akhrá* or place of assembly of the village, where he is met by the *máhato*, *páhn*, *bhandári*, and as many of the *rayats* as choose to attend. He proceeds, agreeably to the dictation of the *máhato*, to write down the account of the cultivation of the different *rayats*, stating the number of *páwás* held and the rent paid by each. Having furnished this account, any new *rayats* who may wish to have lands in the village, after having the quantity and rent settled, have a *goti* given to them. If any of the old *rayats* require any new land, a *goti* is taken for that, but not for the old cultivation. The *máhato* collects the rent as the instalments become due, according to the above-mentioned account given to the farmer; and all differences as to the amount of rent payable by a *rayat*, if any ever arise, which very seldom happens, are settled by the opinion of the *máhato*. So well does this mode answer in practice, that in point of fact a dispute as to the amount of rent owed by a *rayat* is of rare occurrence. When a farmer wishes to cheat a *rayat*, he accuses him of having cultivated more land than he is entitled to, or of owing him *maswár* or grain-rent for land held in excess; and if such a thing as a dispute as to the amount of rent owed ever does arise, the *máhato's* evidence is generally considered conclusive by both parties."

(3) Pahn.—The importance of the *páhn*, or priest of the village gods, may be inferred from the current phrase in which his duties are contrasted with those of the *máhato*. The *páhn*, it is said, " makes the village" (*gáon banátá*), while the *máhato* only " manages it" (*gáon chalátá*). He must be a *bhuinhár*, as no one but a descendant of the earliest settlers in the village could know how to propitiate the local gods. He is always chosen from one family; but the actual *páhn* is changed at intervals of from three to five years by the ceremony of the *súp* or winnowing-fan, which is used as a divining rod, and taken from house to house by the boys of the

village. The *bhuinhár* at whose house the *súp* stops is elected *páhn*. On the death of a *páhn*, he is frequently, but not invariably, succeeded by his son. Rent-free lands are attached to the office of *páhn* under the following names:—(1) *Páhnt*, the personal *jágír* or service-tenure of the priest, generally containing one *páwá* of land. (2) *Dálikatári*, for which the *páhn* has to make offerings to Jáhir Búrhí, the goddess of the village. It is called *dálikatári*, as it is supposed to defray the expenses of the *Karm* festival, when a branch (*dáli*) of the *karma* tree is cut down and planted in the fields. (3) *Desauli*, a sort of *bhutkheta* or devil's acre, the produce of which is devoted to a great triennial festival in honour of Desauli, the divinity of the grove. This land is either cultivated by the *páhn* himself, or by *raiyats* who pay him rent. (4) *Pánbhárá* and *táhálu* are probably the same. Lands held under these names are cultivated by the *páhn* himself or his near relations; and whoever has them, is bound to supply water at the various festivals.

(4) BHANDARÍ.—The *bhandári* or bailiff is the landlord's agent in respect of the management of the village. He is usually a Hindu, and represents the landlord's point of view in village questions, just as the *páhn* is the spokesman of the *bhuinhárs* or original settlers. He generally holds one *páwá* of land rent free from the owner, receiving also from every *raiyat* three *karats* or sheaves of each crop as it is cut—one of *gondli*, one of early rice, and one of wet rice. Instead of the land, he sometimes gets Rs. 3 or Rs. 4 in cash, with 12 *káts* or 4½ cwt. of paddy.

(5) GORAIT.—The *goráit* is, in fact, the *chaukidár* or village watchman. He communicates the owner's orders to the *raiyats*, brings them to the *máhato* to pay their rents, and selects coolies when required for public purposes. As a rule he holds no service land, but receives the three usual *karats* or sheaves from every cultivator.

(6) ÁHIR or GOALA.—The *áhir's* duty is to look after the cattle of the village, and to account for any that are stolen. He is remunerated by a payment of one *kát* of paddy for each pair of plough-bullocks owned by the cultivators whose cattle are under his charge. He also gets the three *karats* or sheaves at harvest time, besides an occasional *súp* or winnowing fan full of paddy. If cows are under the *áhir's* charge, the milk of every alternate day is his perquisite. In the month of *Ághan* (December) he takes five *sers* of milk round to the cultivators, receiving in return *pakhirá* or 20 *sers* of paddy as a free gift. He always pays the *ábwáb* known as *dádani ghí*, and in some villages has to give the *baitháwán ghí* as well. In a very few cases the *áhir* holds half a *páwá* of land rent-free.

(7) LOHAR.—The *lohár* or blacksmith gets one *kát* of paddy and the three *karats* for every plough in the village, and is also paid two or three *ánnás* for every new *phár* or ploughshare. In a very few villages he holds half a *páwá* of land rent-free.

The *kotwál* or constable and the *chaukidár* or watchman do not belong to the genuine Munda village system, and need not be mentioned here.

In the Fiscal Division of Torí the bulk of the inhabitants belong to the Kharwár sub-tribe of Bhogtás, and the village system differs from that which prevails on the central plateau. Here the *páhn* is the only official who holds service land, and he gets half a *pátti*, or not quite two standard *bighás*. He performs the village *pujás*, and often does the work of a *máhato*, when the owner of the village is an absentee. But even then the landlord sometimes employs a bailiff, called *bárhil*, to collect the rents.

In the tract known as the Five Parganás, including Támár, Bundu, Sillí, Ráhe, and Barandá, as well as in the *Mánkipatti*, or that part of Sónpur *parganá* which borders on Singbhum district, we meet with *mánkis* and *múndas* who are undoubtedly the descendants of the original chiefs, and still hold the villages which their ancestors founded. Here the *parhá* divisions exist in their entirety, as groups of from twelve to twenty-four villages, each of which has its own *múnda* or village head; while the whole commune is subject to a divisional headman called *mánki*, who collects the fixed rents payable by the *múndas*. The chief village officer is the *páhn*, who holds from one to five *káts* of land rent-free as *dálikatári*. A *kát* in this sense is a measure of land analogous to, if not identical with, the *khandi* of the Kolhán in Singbhum, and denotes the quantity of land which can be sown with one *kát* of seed. In this part of the country the *múnda* sometimes has a deputy called *diwán* who assists him to collect his rents, and *bhandáris* are occasionally met with.

Mundabárik, a class of barbers in Chota Nagpur who only shave Mundas.

Munda-Khariá, a sub-caste of Khariás in Chota Nagpur.

Munda-Lohár, a sub-caste of Lohárs in Lohardagá.

Mundá-Mahili, a sub-caste of Mahilis in Chota Nagpur.

Munda-Mánjhi, a sub-tribe of Mundas in Chota Nagpur.

Munda-Oraon, a sub-tribe of Oraons in Chota Nagpur.

Mundiba, *mahuá* tree, a totemistic sept of Juángs in Orissa.

Mundoraj, a tree, a totemistic sept of Mundas in Chota Nagpur.

Mundra, a section of Mahesris in Behar.

Mundri, quail, a totemistic sept of Mundas in Chota Nagpur.

Mundu or **Badar**, a dense jungle, a sub-sept of the Saren sept of Santáls.

Munduáb, small mushroom, a totemistic sept of Juángs in Orissa.

Munduia, a sept of Hos in Singbhum.

Mundus, a section of the Kulsunri sub-caste of Sunris in Behar.

Munga, coral, a totemistic sept of Kharwars in Chota Nagpur; a section of the Karan sub-caste of Káyasths in Behar.

Munga Ság, a vegetable, a totemistic sept of Mundas in Chota Nagpur.

Muniar-Ganjhu, a sub-caste of Kharwárs in Hazaribagh.

Munis, an agricultural labourer.

Munjaniar, a fruit from which oil is made, a totemistic sept of Chiks in Chota Nagpur.

Munjniar, a wild creeper, a totemistic sept of Oraons in Chota Nagpur.

Munri, fried rice, a totemistic sept of Mundas in Chota Nagpur.

Munshi, an honorary title of Brahmans.

Munsif, an honorary title of Káyasths in Bengal.

Muntri, a section of Goálás in Behar.

Mura, a synonym for Munda, an honorific title bestowed in Bankura on the eldest son of a well-to-do cultivator of the Bhumij tribe. See **Mánki**.

Muráo, a synonym for Koiri.

Murári, *Muráli*, a corruption of Mundári, sometimes used outside of Chota Nagpur as a synonym for Munda.

Murba, a section of the Dhaprá and Pachainyá sub-caste of Doms in Behar.

Murchulia, a sept of Páns in Chota Nagpur.

Murdáfarash, a sub-caste of Doms in Bengal who attend to the cremation and disposal of dead bodies, or undertakers, each in charge of a burning *ghát*. They do the same work as Gangáputras, but the latter rank higher.

Murga, cock, a totemistic sept of Oraons in Chota Nagpur.

Murgear, a section of Khariás in Chota Nagpur.

Murgi, hen, a totemistic sept of Binjhiás and Kharwars in Chota Nagpur.

Murhia or **Sebaka**, a group of the Pandá sub-caste of Utkal Brahmans in Orissa.

Muri, a totemistic sept of Korwas in Chota Nagpur whose ancestors made a *chulá* of four soulls and cooked their dinner; a sept of Mundas whose totem is wild fowl.

Muria or **Muriári**, a sub-caste of Malláhs in Behar.

Muriari, *Mariyári*, a boating, fishing, and cultivating caste of Behar. The origin of the Muriari is uncertain. Buchanan,[1] who calls them Mariyári Málas, was of opinion that they belonged to an aboriginal race from the upper valley of the Ganges. Other authorities, however, connect them with the Kewat. Their only tradition is the somewhat vague one that their progenitor was a certain Kál Dás, who came from 'the south country.'

Origin.

The Muriyári marry their daughters as infants or as adults according to their means, the former practice being of course the more fashionable of the two. Polygamy is sanctioned in theory, but is found too expensive in actual life for many to indulge in it. A widow may marry again by *sagai*. She is expected to marry her husband's younger brother if he leaves one, but otherwise her choice is free. Divorce is not allowed.

Marriage.

Their religion, marriage ceremony, funeral observances, and so forth, are of the orthodox type. Maithil Brahmans act as their priests, and are said to

Religion.

[1] Martin's *Eastern India*, i, 172.

incur no social degradation by doing so. Bandi, Parameshwari, and the Panch Pir are their favourite minor gods, to whom they offer flowers, betel leaves, sweetmeats, etc., in a part of their own houses which is plastered with cow-dung for the occasion and called *gosainghar*.

Social status.

The social position of the Muriyári is much the same as that of Gangotás, Kurmis, and Koiris, and Brahmans will take water and certain kinds of sweetmeats from their hands. Their diet is that of most orthodox Hindus, except that, like most of the boating and fishing castes, they indulge freely in spirits. In Bhágalpur Muriyáris who have taken to cultivation call themselves **Maghaya'**, and profess to look down upon the boating and fishing members of the caste, whom they represent as having come from the North-Western Provinces. It is not clear that this divergence of occupation has as yet led to the formation of two distinct sub-castes. The cultivating section of the caste, indeed, appears not to be a very strong one, and few of its members have risen above the status of a non-occupancy raiyat, while many are landless day-labourers paid in cash or kind. In this connexion it deserves notice that in Arrah, where the Mariyári are very numerous, they are employed as ferrymen, boatmen, and fishermen, but refuse to carry palanquins or to settle down as cultivators. Many large boats manned by them arrive at the Váruni fair in November, laden with pulse and other vegetable products.

The following statement shows the number and distribution of the Muriári caste in 1881 :—

Monghyr	385
Bhágalpur	272
Purniah	1,764
Maldah	1,051
Santál Parganás	255

Murkia, a section of Mahesris in Behar.

Internal structure.

Murmi, *Tamang Bhotia*, *Isháng*, *Sain*, a Mongolian or semi-Mongolian caste, who claim to be among the earliest settlers in Nepal. About their origin little is known, nor do their own traditions throw much light upon the question ; but their physical characteristics, and the fact that their exogamous divisions (*thars*) bear Tibetan names, seem to lend support to the opinion that they are descended from a Tibetan stock, modified more or less by intermixture with Nepalese races. Like most Himalayan castes, the Murmis have a large number of *thars*, which are shown in Appendix I. The form of exogamy observed is the simple one that a man may not marry a woman of his own *thar*. For the rest marriage is regulated by the standard formula *mamera*, *chachera*, etc., calculated to seven generations in the descending line. In the case of descents through females these prohibitions are not so strictly observed, and public opinion does not disapprove of marriages with tolerably near relatives, provided that the primary rule of marrying outside the *thar* is not departed from. The question of prohibited degrees among the Murmis is greatly complicated by the rules regarding adoptive brotherhood (*mith*, *dosti*, *kanyaketi*)—a very obscure subject which I have been unable to work out thoroughly. When a man desires to adopt another man as his brother, he sends a message intimating his feelings, and if the reply is favourable presents are exchanged. A day is then fixed for the performance of the regular ceremony, at which a Brahman officiates as priest. The two friends stand facing one another, each with a rupee at his feet. The rupees are solemnly interchanged, and the pair bedaub one another between the eyebrows with the mixture of rice and curds used in the marriage ceremony. A fee of Re. 1 is paid to the Brahman, and the proceedings end with a feast.

Marriage.

The fictitious relationship thus established is regarded as equivalent to actual kinship. The adopted brothers may not address or speak of one another by name, nor may they talk to each other's wives, even though these may have taken part in the ceremony. Their descendants, again, are supposed not to intermarry till seven generations have passed. Some, indeed, say that this prohibition extends to the entire *thar*, and enumerate several *thars* which may not intermarry by reason of their founders having contracted *mith*. Others, again, say that *mith* can only be entered into by members of the same *thar*, whose descendants in the first generation would in any case be forbidden to intermarry. Great importance is attached to the observance of the rules connected with *mith*. In British territory a man who infringes them by marrying a woman within the forbidden degrees is punished by exclusion from the caste, and no Murmi will eat, drink, or smoke with him. In Nepal the penalties are said to be far more severe: the offender is denounced as *hár-phurá*, and is liable to be sold as a slave, or, according to some accounts, to be punished capitally. Murmis may contract *mith* with Bhotias, Lepchas, Limbus, Khambus, Yakhas, Mangars, Gurungs, and Sunwars; and members of the last six castes may even be admitted into the Murmi community.

With the Murmis, as with most of the Himalayan castes, adult-marriage prevails, and sexual intercourse before marriage is tolerated, it being understood that if a girl becomes pregnant she will disclose the name of her lover, and he will come forward to marry her. A bride-price (*sot*) of Rs. 50 to Rs. 60 in ornaments and cash is paid to the bride's parents. The marriage takes place at night in the house of the bride. A Lama officiates as priest and besmears the foreheads of the couple with a mixture of curds and rice. The bridegroom then puts vermilion on the bride's forehead and the parting of her hair and changes places with her, after which the Lama brings their heads together so that their foreheads touch (*lagan*). This is deemed the binding portion of the ceremony. Polygamy is permitted, but is not much resorted to in practice, and it is unusual to find a Murmi with more than one wife. Widows are not allowed to marry again by the regular ritual; but they may be kept as mistresses, and the children of women so kept are said to be considered not inferior to those born in regular wedlock. Divorce is permitted on the ground of adultery or unsuitability of temper. Divorced wives may not marry again, but become concubines on the same terms as widows.

In the matter of inheritance the Murmis follow a tribal custom of their own. Sons inherit in equal shares; failing sons, the father succeeds; then the daughters take equal shares. Failing daughters, the widow inherits, and in any case she must be maintained by the persons who succeed to the property.

Religion.

The religion of the caste is not easy to define. We may discern in it a substratum of primitive animism overlaid by elements borrowed from Hinduism, and, less freely, from Buddhism. Everything tends towards gradual adoption of the Nepalese form of Hinduism, and Buddhist usages are believed to be on the decline, though the Lama still serves as priest at a Murmi wedding, and flags stamped with the sacred *om* may be seen flying in Murmi villages. Notwithstanding this general tendency towards the triumph of Hinduism, some of the popular deities of the caste seem to belong to an earlier type. The stone fetish called Thangbaljho is honoured by winding cloth round it and sprinkling rice on its top; and every September goats and fowls are sacrificed and their blood poured forth on the stone. Similar offerings are made to Purbujá devatá, a forest god who lives in a tree and visits with fever and rheumatism those who neglect his worship. Bhim Singh, one of the Pándava brothers, is worshipped at the Durga Puja with sacrifices of buffaloes, goats, fowls, and ducks. Sherkijho is a fetish of ill-defined attributes; while Gyong and Changreshi appear to be deified Lamas. Behind these again are the village and household gods, a shifting and shadowy multitude, which no man can number or describe, clamouring, like the ghosts who crowded round Odysseus, for their share of sacrifice and libation.

Brahmans have not yet been called in to organize this chaotic Pantheon. Their functions are confined to presiding over the ceremony of *mith*, and occasionally assisting at the worship of some of the standard Hindu gods. The daily religion of the caste is looked after by Lamas or by any Murmi who has a turn for ceremonial ministration.

Disposal of the dead.

The rich burn their dead and preserve a piece of bone to be deposited in a private *gumpa*. The ordinary practice is to bury, the body being laid in the grave with the head to the north and fire applied to the mouth. A small enclosure roofed in with a big stone is built round the grave, a cairn is piled on the stone, and a flag is planted hard by. For seven days after death the relatives of the deceased observe formal mourning and do not eat salt with their food. On the eighth day a propitiatory offering of meat, rice, eggs, plantains, and sweetmeats is presented at the grave, and a feast is given by the chief mourner. For the next six months small daily offerings are made in the house to a piece of cloth torn from the shroud of the deceased: at the end of that time a Lama is called in and the final ceremony is performed.

Occupation and status.

The bulk of the Murmi caste are cultivators, and regard agriculture as their original and fitting occupation. Many of them serve in the police, and Lama Murmis are enlisted as recruits by the 1st Gurkhas. In Nepal they are not reckoned among the regular fighting castes, but they are admitted into the Kiránti regiments raised by Jang Bahadur some thirty years ago. A considerable number are employed as labourers on the tea gardens near Darjiling. In the matter of diet they have few scruples: they eat beef, pork, fowls, and frogs, and indulge freely in spirituous liquors. Notwithstanding this, their social status in the Himalayan region is respectable, and Nepalese Brahmans and Chattris will take water and sweetmeats from their hands. They themselves eat with Limbus, Khambus, Lepchas, and Bhotias.

In 1872 the Murmis numbered 6,557 in Darjiling and 23 in Jalpigori, while in 1881 they numbered 5,324 only in Darjiling.

Murmu, nilgao, a totemistic section of Kurmis in Chota Nagpur and Orissa; a sept of Hos and Santáls.

Murmuár, a totemistic section of Máhilis in Manbhum, the members of which will not touch, kill, or eat the murmu or nilgái.

Murmurwar, a sept of Kharwars in Chota Nagpur.

Muro, a sub-sept of the Murmu sept of Santáls.

Muromah, a sept of Mundas in Chota Nagpur.

Murtel, a *thar* of the Gargya *gotra* of Nepáli Brahmans.

Murti, a section of the Sátmuliá Maghayá sub-caste of Kándus in Behar.

Murum, stag, a totemistic sept of Mundas in Chota Nagpur.

Murwá, a section of the Tirhutiyá sub-caste of Doms in Behar.

Mus, rat, a totemistic sept of Goálás, Chamárs, and Kharwars in Chota Nagpur; a section of Kurmis in Chota Nagpur and Orissa; a totemistic sept of Chiks and Doms.

Musa or **Musu**, mouse, a totemistic sept of Mundas and Páns in Chota Nagpur.

Musahar, *Bhuiyá*, *Sádá Banráj*, *Banmánush*, a Dravidian cultivating and servile caste of Behar, who appear to be an offshoot from the Bhuiyá tribe of Chota Nagpur. The grounds for this opinion are stated at length in the article **Bhuiyá** and need not be repeated here. The question of the origin of the caste has been examined by Mr. J. C. Nesfield in an elaborate monograph on *The Musheras of Central and Upper India*, published in the *Calcutta Review* for January 1888.

Origin according to Mr. Nesfield.

Mr. Nesfield's inquiries into the traditions of the Musahars (as I prefer to spell the name) tend to connect them with the Cherus and Savars, who play a prominent part in the legendary history of the Ganges valley. From this it would follow, if the standard classification be accepted, that the Musahars belong to the Kolarian group of tribes, while my hypothesis would class them among the Dravidians. The distinction, however, between Kolarian and Dravidian appears to me, and, I believe, also to Mr. Nesfield, to rest solely upon peculiarities of language, which in this case at any rate do not correspond to real differences of race. If the test of language is rejected, and we look only to physical characteristics, the so-called Dravidians and Kolarians can only be regarded as local varieties of one and the same stock. This being so, there is really no material difference between Mr. Nesfield's view and my own. He connects the Musahars of the North-Western Provinces with the Dravidian Savars and Cherus; I trace the Musahars of Behar to the equally Dravidian Bhuiyás of Southern Chota Nagpur. Both hypotheses may conceivably be correct. We both agree in thinking the Musahars a fragment of some Dravidian tribe recently and imperfectly absorbed into the Hindu caste system; and if this main point be conceded, it is not very important to determine from which of the known Dravidian tribes the fragment was broken off.

The meaning and derivation of the name Musahar have often been discussed, and Mr. Nesfield has the following remarks on the subject:—

"The name given to the tribe in this essay has been spelt throughout as Mushéra, which is a slight departure from the spelling or spellings hitherto adopted in English books. The name has been supposed to be made up of two Hindi words signifying 'rat-taker.' Hence in Buchanan's *Eastern India* they are described as a people 'who have derived their name from eating rats.' But rat-catching or rat-eating is by no means the peculiar, or even a prominent, characteristic of the tribe; and the name in Upper India at least is pronounced by the natives of the country as Mŭshera, and not as Mūsahar (rat-taker) or Mūsarhá (rat-killer). In an old folk-tale which has recently come to my knowledge, the name is made to signify flesh-seeker or hunter, being derived from *mâsŭ*, 'flesh,' and *héra*, 'seeker,' and a legend is told as to the event which led to the tribe being driven to maintain itself by hunting wild animals. This is a more comprehensive title than rat-catcher, besides resting on better authority. Probably, however, both derivations are fanciful,—Hindi versions of a name which is not of Hindi origin. It is certain that the more isolated members of the tribe, who still speak a language of their own unconnected with Hindi, call themselves by a name which sounds like Mŭshéra; and it is not likely that men who have preserved their original speech continuously for so many centuries would have designated themselves by a name borrowed from a foreign language.

"There are one or two other names by which the tribe is known besides Mushéra. In all the districts of Oudh in which the tribe is found, they are commonly, and in some places exclusively, known by the title of Banmánush, or man of the forest. The name Banmánush is of purely Hindi origin; and though intended to be a term of reproach applied by Hindus to a people from whom they stand aloof as impure and savage, it has been accepted by Mushéras themselves, many of whom scarcely know themselves by any other title, and all of whom are entirely ignorant of its origin and meaning. Other names, less commonly known or used, are Deosiyá, derived from their great ancestor Deosi; Banráj, or king of the forest, a less contemptuous, or perhaps an ironical, form of the name Banmánush; and Maskhán, or eater of flesh, another form of the name Maséhra or Mushéra. Sometimes, if a Mushéra is asked to which of the great Indian castes he belongs, he will tell you that he is an Ahir, or rather a subdivision of Ahir, the caste of cowherd; and he appears to be rather anxious to have his title to this honour recognized. But in point of fact he has no claim to any such lineage. Mushéras are the hereditary enemies of Ahirs, as all their legends testify, and many are the petty raids that they have made against them for the possession of cattle and forest."

I am myself inclined to believe that the popular etymology "rat-catcher" or rat-eater is the true one, and that the word is an opprobrious epithet bestowed by the Hindus on the caste with reference to their fondness for eating field-rats. From Vedic times down to the present day we find the promiscuous habits of the non-Aryans in respect of food exciting the special aversion of the Aryan colonists and forming the basis of depreciatory names which tend to supplant the original tribal designation. It can hardly be expected that the givers of contemptuous names should be guided by a nice sense of scientific precision, and would stop to consider whether the practice of eating rats was really the peculiar or prominent characteristic of a particular tribe. The nickname would be bestowed at random, and it is conceivable that even in the same part of the country it might be conferred upon several different tribes.

Internal structure.

The internal structure of the caste is shown in Appendix I. So far as I can ascertain, the only sub-castes are Tirhutiá and Maghaiyá, and it is doubtful whether the distinction between these amounts to true endogamy or represents anything more than the fact that marriage between families living on opposite sides of the Ganges is comparatively uncommon. The divisions Rikhmun and Balakmun appear now to be purely titular groups, which bear no definite relation to marriage. It is a plausible conjecture that they were at one time exogamous sections, which broke up into smaller groups and thus lost their exogamous character. On the north of the Ganges the system of exogamy followed by the Tirhutiá Musahars is very elaborate, and a man may not marry a woman belonging to his own section, or the sections of which his mother and his paternal and maternal grandmothers were members. If, again, the excluded ascendants of a particular couple happened to be of the same section, the marriage is forbidden, although the boy and girl themselves belong to different sections. Among the more primitive Musahars further south the simpler rule prevails that a man may not marry a woman of his own section. This is the case also among the Bhuiyás; and there seem to be grounds for inspecting that the minute regulations which the Tirhutiá Musahars affect to observe have been borrowed by them from some of their Hindu neighbours.

On the north of the Ganges, Tirhutiá Musahars are said to practise infant-marriage; while in Shahabad girls are usually not married until they have passed the age of puberty, and sexual intercourse before marriage is said to be tolerated. A bride-price of Rs. 2 is paid for a virgin, but the tender is reduced to half if there are reasons to doubt her integrity. The marriage ceremony is based on the Hindu model, and does not differ materially from that in vogue among other low castes in Behar. The well-known formula—

Marriage.

> Gangá ká páni samundar ki sank
> Bar Kanyá jag jag anand
>
> (May Ganges water and sea-shell betide
> Enduring bliss to bridegroom and to bride)

is recited by one of the elders present, and water and rice are sprinkled on the bridegroom's head. The bride is then lifted by her mother, and the bridegroom marks her forehead five times with vermilion. Consummation follows at once, and the married couple usually leave for the bridegroom's house next day.

Polygamy is said to be unknown. The remarriage of widows by the *sagai* form is permitted, and is not fettered by the common condition requiring the widow to marry her late husband's younger brother. Divorce is allowed, with the sanction of the caste panchâyat, for infidelity on the part of the wife. The husband breaks in two a piece of dried grass (*khár*) in the presence of the panchâyat, and formally renounces his wife by saying that in future he will look upon her as his mother. Divorced women may marry again by the ritual appointed in the case of widows.

The religion of the Musahars illustrates with remarkable clearness the gradual transformation of the fetichistic animism characteristic of the more primitive Dravidian tribes into the debased Hinduism practised in the lower ranks of the caste system. Among the standard gods of the Hindu Pantheon, Káli alone is admitted to the honour of regular worship. To her the men of the caste sacrifice a castrated goat, and the women offer five wheaten cakes with prayers that her favour may be shown to them in the pains of childbirth. In parts of Gya and Hazaribagh an earlier stage of her worship may be observed. Her shrine stands at the outskirts of the village, and she is regarded as a sort of local goddess, to be appeased on occasion, like the Thakuráni Mai of the Hill Bhuiyas, by the sacrifice of a hog. It is curious to observe that the definite acceptance of Káli as a member of the Hindu system seems rather to have detracted from the respect in which she was held before she assumed this comparatively orthodox position. Her transformation into a Hindu goddess seems to have rendered her less malignant. Her worship, though ostensibly put forward as the leading feature of the Musahar religion, seems to be looked upon more as a tribute to social respectability than as a matter vitally affecting a man's personal welfare Káli, or Debi Mai, as she is commonly called, may be appeased by an occasional

Religion.

sacrifice, but the Birs require to be kept constantly in good humour, or they may do serious mischief. The six Birs or heroes known as Tulsi Bir, Rikmun, Ram Bir, Bhawár Bir, Asan Bir, and Charakh Bir are believed to be the spirits of departed Musahars who exercise a highly malignant activity from the world of the dead. Rikmun is often spoken of as the *purka* or ancestor of the caste, and when a separate sacrifice is offered to him the worshipper recites the names of his own immediate forefathers. On ordinary occasions the Birs are satisfied with offerings of sweetmeats prepared in ghi, but once in every two or three years they demand a collective sacrifice of a more costly and elaborate character. A pig is provided, and country liquor, with a mixture of rice, molasses, and milk is offered at each of a number of balls of clay which are supposed to represent the Birs.[1] Then a number of Bhakats or devotees are chosen, one for each Bir, with the advice and assistance of a Brahman, who curiously enough is supposed to know the mind of each Bir as to the fitness of his minister. The shaft of a plough and a stout stake being fixed in the ground, crossed swords are attached to them, and the Bhakats having worked themselves up into a sort of hypnotic condition, go through a variety of acrobatic exercises on the upturned sword-blades. If they pass through this uninjured, it is understood that the Birs accept the sacrifice. The pig is then speared to death with a sharp bamboo stake, and its blood collected in a pot and mixed with country liquor. Some of this compound is poured forth on the ground and on the balls of clay, while the rest is drunk by the Bhakats. The ceremony concludes with a feast in which the worshippers partake of the offerings.

Priesthood.

The Musahars have not yet attained to the dignity of keeping Brahmans of their own, though they call in Brahmans as experts to fix auspicious days for marriages and important religious ceremonies, to assist in naming children, and even to interpret the will of characteristic Musahar deities like the Birs. In the matter of funeral ceremonies the tendency is to imitate Hindu usage. A meagre version of the standard *sráddh* is performed about ten days after death, and once a year, usually in the month of October, regular oblations are made for the benefit of deceased ancestors. It deserves notice that with Musahars, as with Doms, the sister's son of the deceased officiates as priest at the *sráddh*.

Social status.

The social status of the caste is pretty closely defined by the fact that they will eat any kind of food with all Hindu castes except Chamars, Dosadhs, Dhobi, Dom, and Mihtar, but Doms alone will take food from them. In matters of diet they have few scruples, eating pork, fowls, frogs, tortoises, alligators, jackals, cats, wild and tame snakes, snails, and various sorts of lizards, particularly the gosámp or iguana, while field-rats are esteemed a special delicacy. Beef and the flesh of

[1] Some speak of the balls as the "houses" of the Birs, but this seems to be a modern refinement on the primitive idea, which recognizes no distinction between the god himself and the fetish which represents him.

horses and donkeys they hold to be forbidden. In the North-West Provinces, according to Mr. Nesfield, the Dolkárha or palanquin-bearing Musahars eat horse flesh and keep fowls, while the Paháhri and Deháti sub-tribes abstain from both, and regard the horse as a tabooed animal, whom it is sin for a Musahar to touch. The Paháris, however, eat beef when they can get it, and are only deterred from extensive cattle-lifting by their fear of the pugnacious grazier castes. Musahars are skilled, too, above other men in the knowledge of forest products, and use for food a number of roots, leaves, and fruits of which the ordinary Hindu knows nothing. They will not, however, cut or injure the *karhar* tree, which is also held sacred by the Chamárs.

Occupation.

In Behar the bulk of the caste are field-labourers and palanquin-bearers, and only a few have attained to the dignity of cultivating on their own account, or have become possessed of occupancy rights. Further west the hill Musahars, described by Mr. Nesfield, "do not even know the use of the plough," but burn patches of forest and raise small crops in the ashes. Wherever the caste is found they strive to eke out the scanty yield of their agricultural labours by a variety of semi-savage pursuits, their heritage from more primitive modes of life. The rearing of *tasar* silkworms, collecting stick-lac, resin and gum, making catechu, supplying Baidyas and Pansaris with indigenous drugs, stitching leaf plates and cutting wood for sale—all these may be reckoned among the characteristic occupations of the Musahar. We may add the watching of fields and crops by night, which Mr. Nesfield shrewdly connects with the notion that the Banmánush, or "man of the forest" (a common designation of Musahars), is best able to propitiate the primeval deities whose ancient domain has been invaded by the plough. An interesting parallel may be found in Colonel Dalton's statement that in Keonjhar, Bonai, and other Tributary States to the south the Bhuiyás, whom I hold to be the parent tribe from which the Musahars have sprung, "retain in their own hands the priestly duties of certain old shrines to the exclusion of Brahmans." The whole subject of the occupations of the Musahars is discussed with the utmost thoroughness in Mr. Nesfield's admirable monograph.

The following statement shows the number and distribution of Musahars in 1872 and 1881 :—

District.	1872.	1881.	District.	1872.	1881.
Bardwan	......	3	Gya	60,895	16,247
24-Parganás	......	5	Shahabad	10,117	13,213
Murshedabad...	......	1,091	Tirhut { Mozufferpur ...	} 83,668	{ 33,555
Dinajpur	......	45	Tirhut { Darbhanga ...		66,822
Rangpur	......	17	Saran	5,317	6,465
Bogra	......	18	Champaran	26,844	38,053
Darjiling	......	383	Monghyr	117,585	128,337
Faridpur	......	1	Bhagalpur	69,907	79,584
Maimansinh	......	159	Purniah	20,014	31,225
Chittagong	......	6	Santál Parganás	16,353	18,548
Maldah	......	139	Hazaribagh	4,297	8,753
Patna	27,208	36,884	Lohardagá	54	......

Musalmániá or *Turk-Naua*, a sub-caste of Hajjáms in Behar who are Mahomedans.

Musamiá, a section of Kamárkalla Sonárs in Behar.

Musawir, a painter.

Mushahar, a subdivision of Bhuiyas—low Bhuiyas as distinguished from the higher Ghatwal Bhuiyas. The former take service, while the latter do not.

Mushrif, an honorary title of Káyasths in Bengal.

Musipur, a group of Maghaiyá Telis in Bengal.

Mustaufi, an honorary title of Káyasths in Bengal.

Musuhang, the lowland chief, a sept of the Phedáb sub-tribe of Limbus in Darjiling.

Mutabar, a title of Kapális, signifying a headman of the panchâyat of the caste.

Mutai, a *thar* or sept of Dámis in Darjiling whose chief profession is sewing.

Muthá, a section of Koránch Kándus; a title of headman among the Kandh tribe in Orissa.

Muthbári, a *thar* or section of Nepáli Brahmans.

Mutri, a sept of Mundas in Chota Nagpur.

Mutriar, a sept of Lohárs in Chota Nagpur.

N

Nábik, a title of Kaibarttas.

Nád, a title of Bangaja Káyasths.

Nadhiá, a section of Goálás in the North-Western Provinces and Behar.

Nadi Samp, river snake, a totemistic sept of Mundas in Chota Nagpur.

Nág, "snake," a totemistic section of the Kumhár, Koiri, and Rajwár castes in Chota Nagpur, the members of which will not touch or kill a snake; a title of Káyasths; of the Kut sub-caste of Gandhabaniks; a totemistic section of Nuniás; a family title of Kashta Baidyas; a section of Binjhiás, Barais, Báruis, Rautiás; a totemistic sept of Ahirs, Bairágis, Bedias, Birhors, Chamárs, Bhuiyás, Kharwárs, and Nágesars in Chota Nagpur; a section of Goálás and a sept of Rájputs in Behar; a sept of Asuras, Gonds; a section of Kahárs, Khariás; a section of Chiks or Páns in Chota Nagpur; of Telis in Bengal; a totemistic section of Khandaits; of Kámárs in Singbhum and the Santál Parganás; of Dhanuks and Doms; a sub-sept of the Kisku sept of Santáls; a title of Sánkháris; a section of Máls in Bankura; a sept of Bhumij, Mundas, Santáls, Lohars, Parhaiyas, Pators; a title of Mayarás in Bengal.

Nágá, *Nάger*, *Nágabás*, *Nága-mahanta*, (i) corruption of *Nanga*, 'naked;' a small sect of religious mendicants, many or most of whom have now taken to cultivation, call themselves a caste, and are regarded by other people as low-caste Brahmans; they take alms at *sráddhs*: (ii) a title of Maháráshtriya Brahmans.

Nagar, a section of Goálás in Behar.

Nágar, a small cultivating caste of Bhágalpur and the Santál Parganás. The affinities of the Nágars are obscure. They have lost their original sections, and the whole caste now professes to belong to the *Kásyapa gotra*, a section-name borrowed from the Brahmanical system and inoperative for the purpose of controlling intermarriage. They are divided into five sub-castes—**Jethaut, Pulauns, Nágbansi, Káthautiá, Bhátnágar.** Of these all are endogamous except the first two, which have begun to intermarry within the last fifteen years. In all the sub-castes the degrees prohibited for marriage are defined by the formula *chacherá*, *mamerá*, etc., calculated to seven generations in the descending line.

Origin and internal structure.

Both infant and adult-marriage are in vogue, and polygamy is recognized in the event of the first wife being barren. The marriage ceremony is of the standard low-caste type, *sindurdán* being its essential portion.

Marriage.

Widows may marry again by the *sagai* form, and are subject to no restrictions in their choice of a husband. Divorce is not permitted.

Religion. In their religious and ceremonial observances Nágars do not appear to depart materially from the standard ordinances of popular Hinduism. They employ Brahmans as their priests, who are received on terms of equality by other members of the sacred order.

Social status. Their social status is low, and they rank just above the Dosádhs, with whom they will smoke, using the same hookah. Neither Brahmans nor members of the castes from whom Brahmans can take water will accept water from the hands of a Nágar. Some few have risen to the position of tenure-holders, but the large majority of the caste are occupancy or non-occupancy raiyats and landless day-labourers.

The following statement shows the number and distribution of Nágars in 1872 and 1881:—

District.	1872.	1881.	District.	1872.	1881.
Murshedabad	......	2,463	Monghyr	7,876	9,784
Dinajpur	......	4	Bhágalpur	3,998	2,284
Jalpigori	......	94	Purniah	2,853	1,030
Shahabad	2	......	Maldah	......	12,319
Darbhanga	696	473	Santál Parganás	211	247
Champaran	1,254	171			

Nágar, a hypergamous group of Maithil Brahmans; in Behar a synonym for Nat, *q.v.*

Nágarchi, a synonym for Dámi in Darjiling.

Nagare-Chhutár, a sub-caste of Sutradhars in the Santál Parganás.

Nagariá, a section of the Banodhiá and Jaiswár Kalwárs in Behar.

Nágasá, an eponymous section of Karans and Khandáits in Orissa.

Nágásan, a *mul* or section of the Naomuliá or Goriá sub-caste of Goálás in Behar.

Nágasya, a section of Telis in Chota Nagpur.

Nágbans, cobra, a totemistic sept of Oraons in Chota Nagpur.

Nágbansi, (i) in Behar a section of Bábhans and also of Dosádhs and Nágars; a sept of Rájputs; a title of Támbulis; (ii) in Chota Nagpur a sub-tribe of pseudo-Rájputs, probably of Dravidian descent, to which the Maharaja of Chota Nagpur belongs; a title of Mundas in Chota Nagpur.

Nágbansi Munda, a sub-tribe of Mundas in Chota Nagpur.

Nágbasriár, a section of Kurmis in Chota Nagpur and Orissa.

Nag-Chhang Shakzang, a synonym for Sherpa Bhotia of Nepal.

Nágduar, a water insect, a totemistic sept of Mundas in Chota Nagpur.

Nagen, a sept of Limbus in Darjiling.

Nager, a maker of stones for rings, an occupation followed by Mahomedans.

Nágesar, *Nágasia*, *Kisan*, a small Dravidian tribe of Chota Nagpur, described by Colonel Dalton as of dark complexion, short stature, and very ugly features. They have two sub-tribes, one of which uses vermilion (*sindur*) in their marriage ceremony, while the other substitutes oil. The names Sendará and Teliá have reference to this practice. Their sections bear totemistic names which occur among the Mundas and among many other Dravidian tribes. According to Colonel Dalton adult-marriage is in vogue, but matches are arranged by the parents. The standard bride-price is two baskets of rice and one rupee in cash.

In Sargujá the Nágesar worship the sun with offerings of white cocks, and sacrifice goats to Shikária deota, but their chief god is said to be the tiger. In Jashpur they swear by the tiger, but do not worship him, and their chief god is Moihidhúnia, to whom fowls are offered every year and a buffalo once in three years. They also recognize Darha, the village god of the Mundas, and keep the Sarhed festival like them.

Nágeswar, a *mul* or section of the Chhamuliá Madhesiá sub-caste of Halwáis in Behar.

Nágh, a *mul* or section of the Ghosin sub-caste of Goálás in Behar.

Nágneswar, a *mul* or section of the Chhamuliá Madhesiá sub-caste of Halwáis in Behar.

Nagpuriá, a sept of Birhors in Chota Nagpur.

Nágrá, a *mul* or section of the Sátmuliá or Kishnaut sub-caste of Goálás in Behar.

Nágraj, a *mul* or section of the Goriá sub-caste of Goálás in Behar.

Nágrishi, snake, a totemistic section of the Paripál sub-caste of Sunris in Manbhum; a section of Mayarás and Subarnabaniks in Bengal.

Nagrua, a kind of mud, a totemistic sept of Mundas in Chota Nagpur.

Naguriá, a sept of Hos and Santáls.

Náha, Náhá, a title of Báruis in Western Bengal; a title of Bangaja Káyasths in Bengal.

Nahadiá, a section of Goálás in the North-Western Provinces and Behar.

Nah-dik, a sub-sept of the Pon-po sept of Dejong Lhoris or Bhotias of the south.

Nah-pá, a *rui* or sept of Sherpa Bhotias of Nepal.

Naheri, a title of Hajjáms in Behar.

Nahlibo, he who chased his wife, a sept of the Miákhola sub-tribe of Limbus in Darjiling. The story is that the wife of the founder of the *thar* ran away from him, but he caught her and brought her back and afterwards had a large family by her.

Nahmah-pá, a *rui* or sept of the Ruichhug sub-tribe of Dejong Lhoris or Bhotias of the south.

Nái, a synonym for Nápit in Bengal and for Hajjám in Behar.

Naia, the village priest in the communal organization of a village (*Sans.* Náyaka), vulgarly called *laya*.

Náiár, a section of the Bahánnajáti sub-caste of Khatris in Bengal.

Naigrámi, a *gáin* of the Sábarna *gotra* of Bárendra Brahmans in Bengal.

Náik (*Sans.* Náyaka), leader, a title of Acharji or astrological Brahmans in Orissa; of Khandáits in Chota Nagpur and Orissa; of the Dhusiá sub-caste of Chamárs in Behar; of Kaibarttas in Bengal; of Chásás and Kewats in Orissa; of Mál Paháriás, Rájputs, and Telis in Behar; of Khariás, Binjhiás, Ghásis, Chiks, Paturias, and Telis in Chota Nagpur; also a section of Sunris in Behar.

Náiki-Khil, a sub-sept of the Hansda, Hemrom, Marndi, and Tudu septs of Santáls.

Naimba, a coolie class in Nepal.

Naini, a woman who performs the duties of a Naiá or village priest.

Naitam, a sept of Gonds in Chota Nagpur.

Naithung, a sept of Tipperahs in the Hill Tracts of Chittagong.

Naiyá, a small Dravidian caste found only in Bhágalpur. The sections of the Naiyás appear to be totemistic, and this fact, coupled with their bearing the title **Pujáhá**, leads me to regard them as a caste formed by the fortuitous aggregation of a number of Naiyás or Láyás, priests of the aboriginal forest deities, into an endogamous group. For an instance of this process having taken place under very similar conditions, see the article on **Maulik**. A sub-caste of the Kádar bears the same name, and it is perhaps owing to this that the Naiyás were not separately enumerated in the Census of 1881.

Naiyá, a sub-caste of Kádars; a section of the Kádar caste in Behar which intermarries with all the other sections except the Marik, Hazári, Naiyá, Kampti, and Báre.

Nakat, a section of Oswáls.

Nákhudá, a commander of a vessel, a title of Gonrhis in Behar.

Naknesá, a section of Madhesiá Halwáis in Behar.

Nakutwár, a *mul* of the Kausika section of Maithil Brahmans in Behar.

Nalakhiá, a section of the Biyáhut and Kharidáhá Kalwárs in Behar.

Nálsi, a *gáin* or sub-section of Saptasati Brahmans in Bengal.

Nal Tiyar, a sub-caste of Tiyars in Bengal.

Nalu, a title of Bangaja Káyasths in Bengal.

Nama, a synonym for Chandál.

Namadháni, a title of Chandáls in Eastern Bengal who live on agriculture.

Namah, short for Nama Sudra, a title of Chandáls in Bengal.

Namahatá, a title of Brahmans and Kayasths in Bengal.

Namang-po, a *rui* or sept of Dejong Lhoris, the members of which are of a low mixed origin.

Nama Sudra, a synonym for Chandál.

Námátá, a synonym for Lohárs in Manbhum who serve as servants to local zamindars.

Námbochhá, a *thar* or sept of Khambus in Darjiling.

Nambon, a sub-sept of the Pon-po sept of Dejong Lhoris or Bhotias of the south.

Námdung, a *thar* or sept of Khambus in Darjiling.

Namjali, a *thar* or sept of Mangars in Darjiling.

Nam-tsang-koba, a *rui* or sept of the Bedtshan-gye sub-tribe of Dejong Lhoris or Bhotias of the south.

Námzingmung, a sept of Lepchas in Darjiling.

Nánaksái, a *gáin* or sub-section of Saptasati Brahmans in Bengal.

Nánakshâhi, a worshipper of Guru Nának, a synonym for Sikh.

Nanda, a group of the Srotriya sub-caste of Utkal Brahmans.

Nandan, a title of Bangaja Káyasths.

Nandanábási, a *gáin* of the Sándilya *gotra* of Bárendra Brahmans in Bengal.

Nandark, a *pur* or section of Sákadwipi Brahmans in Behar.

Nandbansi, a sub-caste of Goálás in the North-Western Provinces and Behar.

Nandi, a *gáin* of the Sábarna *gotra* of Rárhi Brahmans in Bengal; a family title of Kashta Baidyas, Báruis, Káyasths, Mayarás, Nápits, Sánkháris, Subarnabaniks, Tántis, and Tilis in Bengal.

Nándi, a section of the Bahánnajáti sub-caste of Khatris in Bengal.

Nandigrámi, a *gáin* of the Bharadwája *gotra* of Bárendra Brahmans in Bengal.

Nandkiriár, a section of Káyasths in Behar.

Nangeswari, a class of mendicants who go about naked.

Nángtoyár, a section of Kurmis in Chota Nagpur and Orissa who give children their first rice naked.

Náníá, a section of Goálás in the North-Western Provinces and Behar.

Naniár, a section of Khariás in Chota Nagpur.

Nanjorá, a section of Bábhans in Behar.

Nánkár, a section of the Dhengar sub-caste of Gareris in Behar.

Naomuliá or **Majraut**, a sub-caste of Goálás in Behar.

Naorakhiá, a section of Bhojpuriá Halwáis in Behar.

Náphák, a *dugu* or section of the Kochh-Mandai in Dacca. The name indicates the original habitat of the group, probably a hill or village in Assam, and now-a-days has no bearing upon marriage.

Nápit, the barber caste of Bengal, descended, according to one opinion, from a Kshatriya father and Sudra mother, and according to Parásara from a Kuveri father and a Pattikár mother. Some, again, ascribe the origin of the caste to an act of special creation on the part of Siva, undertaken to provide for the cutting of his wife's nails. Several different versions of this myth are current, all of which are too childish to be worth quoting here. The caste is clearly a functional group, formed in all probability from the members of respectable castes who in different parts of the country adopted the profession of barbers.

Origin.

Nápits are divided into the following sixteen sub-castes:—**Anarpuriá, Bámanbane, Bárendra, Uttar-rárhi, Dakshin-rárhi, Paschim-rárhi, Mahmudábáz, Saptagrám, Sátghariá, Khottá.** There are two sub-castes

Internal structure.

in Noakháli—**Bhuluá-Nápit** and **Sundipá-Nápit**, while in the 24-Parganás there are four—**Háldár-Parámánik, Koliá-Parámánik, Hansadahá-Parámánik,** and **Mujganji-Parámánk.** No trustworthy tradition seems[1] to be extant regarding the origin of these groups, but their names appear to indicate that they are based upon territorial distinctions, and refer to the early settlements of certain main divisions of the caste. The Uttar-rárhi claim to be of higher rank than the Dakshin and Paschim-rárhi, and support their claim by the foolish tale that one of their ancestors was so skilful an operator that he used to shave the Raja of Nadiya without waking him. In recognition of his services he received a large grant of land, with the injunction that neither he nor his descendants should touch the feet of a woman or of a man of low caste. The three Rárhi sub-castes have Kulins and Mauliks among them; but these divisions are not strictly hypergamous, and a Maulik man may marry a Kulin woman, an arrangement wholly impossible among the castes which regularly practise Kulinism. Anarpuriá Nápits do not practise the profession of the caste, but make their living by trade, medicine, and all kinds of clerical work. Many of them are employed as *náibs* and *muharrirs* in the management of landed property. The sections, which are shown in Appendix I, have for the most part been borrowed from the Brahmans; and the exceptions to this rule observed among Mahmudábáz Nápits throw no light upon the origin of the caste as a whole. The theory is that a man may not marry a woman of his own *gotra*; but this prohibition appears not to be very strictly observed, and marriage is regulated for the most part by counting prohibited degrees.

Marriage.

Girls are married as infants between the ages of from six to ten years. A professional matchmaker (*ghatak*) belonging to the Nápit caste, or one of the friends of the bridegroom's family, finds out a suitable match and carries on the preliminary negotiations. A formal visit is then paid by the bridegroom's people for the purpose of seeing the bride and settling the important question of bride-price (*pan*), the amount of which is supposed never to be less than Rs. 100, while it may rise as high as Rs. 200 or Rs. 250. The guardians of the bride also visit and inspect the bridegroom. On these occasions small presents of betel-leaves, areca nuts, fresh fish, milk, etc., are exchanged. The amount of *pan* having been agreed to, the guardians of the bridegroom bestow their blessing (*ásirbad*) on the bride and present her with some article of jewellery. Her people do the same for the bridegroom and give him a few rupees. The date of the wedding is then fixed, and an instalment of the *pan* is paid.

Two days before the bridegroom himself, and the bride through her guardians, perform *nándimukh sráddh* for the propitiation of their ancestors. This is followed on the next day by *adhibás*, when the bridegroom, copiously anointed with turmeric and mustard oil, wearing new clothes, and having his right wrist bound round with cotton and blades of grass, sits on a wooden seat, while a basket containing

[1] Some authorities regard the Madhunápit as a sub-caste of barbers. This opinion, however, rests merely on an obscure tradition, and I have preferred to treat them as a separate caste.

five saucers (*pradip*) for burning oil, five lumps of coloured earth, a looking-glass, a small wooden box (*kotuá*), some vermilion, turmeric, paddy, and grass is carried seven times round him by a married woman whose husband is alive. The basket, with the things in it, is carefully kept that it may be taken next day to the bride's house.

On the wedding day the bridegroom is seven times rubbed with mustard oil and turmeric, and after bathing is dressed in a red silk wrapper. Towards evening he is taken in a palanquin with much discordant music to the bride's house, where the women of the family receive him and carry the basket already referred to round him seven times, touching him with it on the forehead at each turn, and crying *ulu ulu* for good luck.

The bride and bridegroom, both dressed in red silk, are then conducted to the *chháyá-mandap* or ceremonial canopy, which is set up in the courtyard. A sketch plan of this, showing approximately the relative positions of the chief parties to the ceremony, is given below:—

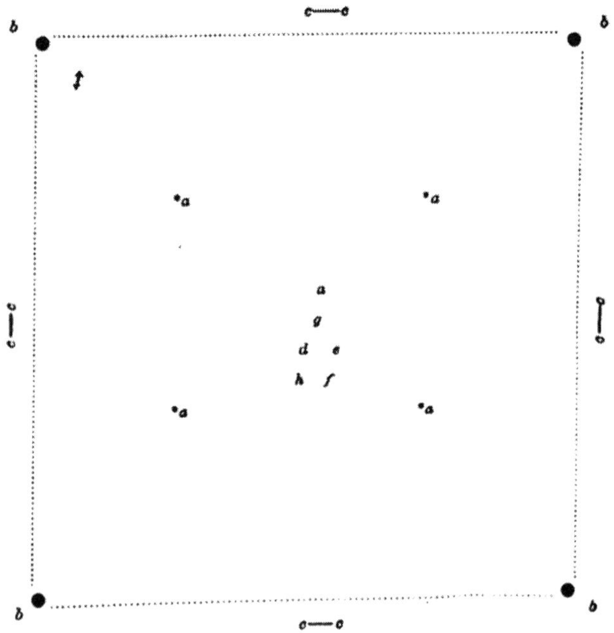

a Vessels of water covered with mango boughs.
b Tall shoots of bamboo drawn together at the top, so as to meet over the central water vessel.
c—c Lines of cotton thread joining the bamboos at about five feet from the ground.
•a Plantain stems fixed in the ground.
d The bridegroom, facing east.
e The bride, facing west.
f The bride's father, facing north.
g The priest.
h The barber, facing the bride and pronouncing the Gaur-vachana discourse.

The leading persons being placed as shown above, the priest dictates certain *mantras* or sacred texts, which are repeated by the bridegroom, the bride, and her father in turn, while the bride places her hands, palm downward, on the palms of the bridegroom, where a silver coin or some small fruit has been previously placed. This joining of the hands completes the ceremony, and it remains only for the barber to repeat to the wedded pair *Gaur-vachana*, an admonitory discourse about the marriage of Siva and Párvati, having for its moral the duty of submitting to one another and of bearing with each other's infirmities of temper. The bride and bridegroom are then taken to the *básarghar*,[1] a room in the house where they spend the night in the company of a number of young married women, friends of the family, who enjoy the privilege of tormenting the bridegroom with all manner of small witticisms and practical jokes. Early next morning the bride is taken in procession to the bridegroom's house, where she stays for a week and consummation usually takes place. At the end of that time she returns to her father's house and stays there until finally fetched by the bridegroom a year or so afterwards.

Polygamy is permitted, and there seems to be no theoretical limit to the number of wives a man may have. In practice, however, most people content themselves with one. Divorce is allowed on the ground of unchastity with the sanction of the panchâyat, a powerful and well-organized body, who summon both husband and wife before them and inquire into the facts. If the panchâyat decline to grant a divorce their orders are enforced, and the husband compelled to take his wife back by the penalty of excommunication.

Religion.

Most Nápits are Vaishnavas, and comparatively few Sáktas or Saivas are found among the caste. They employ Brahmans as priests, who are received on equal terms by other members of the sacred order. The dead are burned, and *sráddh* performed in the orthodox fashion on the thirty-first day after death.

Social status.

The social standing of the caste is high. They are included in the standard couplet of Parásara defining the Nabasákh group, and Brahmans will take water from their hands. Their own rules regarding diet are the same as are followed by most respectable Hindus. Vaishnava Nápits do not eat flesh, but as a rule allow themselves fish, except the *nánen*, *gháruá pángurá*, *bághár*, and *gajár*. Some, however, affect special purity by abstaining from all kinds of animal food. Sáktas, on the other hand, may take mutton and the flesh of goats which have been sacrificed. Indulgence in spirituous or fermented liquors is supposed to be prohibited, but in practice this question seems to depend more upon individual tastes than upon any general rule.

Occupation.

In Bengal, as elsewhere in India, the barber is an indispensable member of the village community, and the office often descends from father to son, carrying with it in some cases a small allotment of service land, held rent-free

---

[1] For a description of a typical scene in the Básarghar, see pp. 95 ff of *Bengal Peasant Life* by the Rev. Lál Behári Day.

or at a low quit-rent. In large towns they work independently, and there is no regulation against their following their occupation wherever they like. As a rule, the working classes only shave every eight days, but the higher ranks do so every four, sometimes every second day. For shaving every four days, eight annas a month is usually charged, and for a single shave one *paisá*, which also includes the charge for ear-cleaning, nailparing, shampooing, and cracking each joint of the body. In the houses of the rich the barbership is often a hereditary post, as is that of the purohit, dhobá, and dái, while he, like them, has free access to all parts of the house during the day. The barber pares the nails of Hindu females as well as males, and his presence is required at all domestic occurrences. The day a child is born he pares the mother's nails, and returns on the ninth and thirtieth days to repeat the operation. At the houses of Muhamadans he is only present on the sixth day, the *chhathi*. For these services he is given pulse, rice, oil, salt, turmeric, and two *paisá*, the rich generally adding a piece of cloth and a rupee. At marriages, as has been mentioned above, his presence is essential, and for some castes he performs the functions of a priest. His wife, unlike the Hajjámin of Behar and Upper India, has usually no occupation in Bengal, but the women of the Saptagrámi sub-caste are employed as female barbers.

In addition to all these vocations, the barber, like his European namesake of the seventeenth century, practises surgery, opening boils and abscesses, inoculating for small-pox, and prescribing in all forms of venereal disease. Often he is also an exorciser of devils, and is called in to cure convulsions in newly-born children by *jharna-phunkná*, or muttering spells and making passes with a *nim* branch. When a member of the Nápit caste wishes to study medicine, he is associated with a Kabíráj, who is then called Adhyápaka, or tutor. The pupil is not bound as an apprentice, but he must obey his master as implicitly as the disciple his guru. He compounds salves and simples, and daily receives instruction from his teacher. The Nápits who practise inoculation for small-pox are generally most reckless, spreading the disease without the slightest consideration for the unprotected. They possess a text-book, Vasanta-ṭiká, but few study it.

Nápits have the reputation of being thrifty and very acute, and many plying their trade in one of the large towns hold land in the country, which is sublet to others. Those who practise medicine often amass considerable wealth and attain great influence in rural society. Others, again, make a living by trade; some few have found their way in Government service and the legal profession; while many devote themselves to agriculture as tenure-holders or occupancy raiyats, rising in rare cases to the position of zamindars. A Nápit, however, will on no account till the soil with his own hands or earn his living by fishing, nor will he, like the Hajjám of Behar, accept domestic service in the houses of low-caste men. In Eastern Bengal he poses as a clean Súdra, condescending to shave Europeans and Muhamadans, but refusing to have anything to do with the Chandál, Bhúinmálí, and castes of similar standing. He will shave a Sunri, but will not pare his nails, and will not attend at the wedding of any but the clean Súdras.

Although the Bengal Nápits, unlike the barber-surgeon of the Middle Ages in Europe, does his work more or less in the open air, and has no shop where idlers lounge and the plethoric are bled, he enjoys much the same reputation for loquacity and spreading scandal. Constant observation of his neighbours gives him remarkable insight into the character of all ranks in Hindu society. His experience takes a wider range than that of the average villager, and renders him by comparison a man of the world, full of anecdote and repartee, and often gifted with a talent for debate which enables him to take a prominent part in the affairs of the community. The secrets of many households are known to him, and, if rumour is to be believed, he plays the go-between in many an intrigue. Nápits are very clannish, and an insult received by one is resented by the whole body; while melancholy indeed is the fate of a Hindu who offends his barber. The whole *dal* or union of the village will refuse to shave him, and at last, driven to desperation, he is glad, by the payment of an exorbitant fee, to be restored to their good graces.

The following statement shows the number and distribution of Nápits in 1872 and 1881:—

District.	1872.	1881.	District.	1872.	1881.
Bardwan	26,098	17,897	Darjiling	435	830
Bankura	7,428	12,222	Jalpigori	2,506	4,834
Birbhum	7,746	8,194	Kuch Behar	......	3,048
Midnapur	42,249	45,989	Dacca	18,208	21,715
Hughli	} 22,287	13,987	Faridpur	12,685	18,897
Howrah		11,454	Bakarganj	40,044	33,456
24-Parganás	36,660	21,803	Maimansinh	19,875	32,768
Nadiya	21,657	19,449	Tipperah	21,642	22,206
Khulna	......	16,289	Chittagong	15,697	15,400
Jessore	29,660	25,002	Noakhali	10,528	12,671
Murshedabad	15,057	13,459	Hill Tracts	4	104
Dinajpur	11,653	13,206	Purniah	......	11
Rajshahye	7,949	8,465	Maldah	6,357	7,864
Rangpur	13,726	12,940	Santál Parganás	......	14,673
Bogra	3,854	3,917	Singbhum	1,875	1,423
Pabna	10,623	11,686	Manbhum	13,504	15,174

Nápit, a synonym for Bhandári.

Nar, *Nat*, *Nartak*, *Nátak*, a dancing and musician caste of Eastern Bengal, whom Dr. Wise identifies with the Brahmanical Kathak of Hindustán, mainly on the strength of a tradition that they first came to Dacca in the days of the Nawabs. Another theory of their origin makes them out to be the same as the Nuri who manufacture lac bracelets. Ward mentions that in his day none of the caste were to be found in Bengal, and that the Brahmans trace their descent from a Málákár and a female Şúdra. The modern Naṭas, not satisfied with this pedigree, claim to be the offspring of Bharadwája Muní and a dancing girl, and assert that the Gaṇak Brahmans are sprung from a son of the same holy man, so the Naṛs of Bikrampur affect to trace their origin to a dancer banished from Indra's heaven and condemned to follow his profession on earth. In

Hindustán the Kathaks still wear the Brahmanical cord and confer the Ásír-bád, or benediction, on Ṣúdras; but in Bengal the Naṛs no longer do so, as the original settlers, being few in number, were obliged to take wives from mean castes, and became degraded. Although the Naṛ caste requires to support a Brahman of its own, the Ṣúdra Nápit and Dhobá work for it. The Naṛs have one *gotra*, the Bharadwája, and their patronymics are Nandí and Bhakta, by which latter title the caste is sometimes known, but whenever an individual excels in music, he is dignified by the title Ustád. Like other Ṣúdras, the Naṛs celebrate the *sráddha* on the thirtieth day, are generally Vaishnavas in creed, and have a Patit Bráhman to officiate to them. They decline to play in the houses of the Chaṇḍáls, Bhúinmális, and other low castes, and as their services are no longer required, have ceased to perform before Muhamadans. The Hindu Naṛ occupies a position corresponding to that of the Muhamadan Bájunia, but the former is more sought after, as no Hindu will have a Muhamadan musician in his house if he can possibly avoid it.

When young the Naṛ boys, then called Bhagtiyás, are taught dancing, but on reaching manhood they become musicians, or Sampardá, and attend on dancing girls (Báí), who are usually Muhamadans. If they have no ear for music, they become cultivators or shop-keepers. In former days no Hindu girls ever danced in public, although dancers among the Bází-gar and other vagrant tribes were common, but at present Baistabís and Hindu prostitutes are found among professional Nách girls. There has been a tendency within the last thirty years for the Naṛ caste to separate into two classes—one teaching boys to dance and playing to them, the other attending the Muhamadan Báí. The latter class are the better paid and more skilful musicians, and a band (Sampardáí) accompanying a popular dancing girl often earn as much as twenty rupees a night, while the former consider they are well paid if they get five rupees for one night's amusement. The musical instruments generally used by the Naṛs are the Sárungí, Behla and Kásí varieties of fiddles, the Tablá or drum, and the Manjírá or cymbals. Naṛs treat their instruments with great veneration, and always, on first rising in the morning, make obeisance before them. On the Ṣrí Panchamí in Mágh, sacred to Saraswatí, a Naṛ will not play a note until the worship of the goddess is finished. Like the Ṛishí women, the Naṛ women will not play, sing, or dance in public, although at marriages of their own people they still do so.

It is currently believed that many Naṛs have of late years become Muhamadans, but this accusation is denied by the caste. It is nevertheless true that when a Sampardá falls in love with a dancing girl, his only chance of marrying her is by becoming a Muhamadan.

Naradwár, a section of Bábhans in Behar.

Narangbali, a section of the Karan sub-caste of Káyasths in Behar.

Nara-Sundar, a title of Nápits in Bengal.

Naraune-Teghrá, a *mul* of the Parásara section of Maithil Brahmans in Behar.

Naraune-Saktárápur, a *mul* of the Parásar section of Maithil Brahmans in Behar.

Narauni, (i) a *mul* or section of the Tinmuliá, Madhesiá, and Bhojpuriá sub-castes of Halwáis in Behar; (ii) a sept of Chandrabansi Rájputs.

Nárbá, a section of Murmis in Darjiling.

Nardauchhá, a *thar* or sept of Khambus in Darjiling.

Narhan, a *dih* or exogamous section of the Gharbáit sub-caste of Amáts in Behar.

Narhatiár, a section of Káyasths in Behar.

Nári, a low class of people who make lac bracelets. *Occ.*

Nárikátá, cutters of the navel-string, a sub-caste of Háris. The men cultivate and the women act as nurses (*dhái*).

Nári-tepá, pulse-feeler, a title of Baidyas used by outsiders.

Nariyá, a *mel* or hypergamous sub-group of Rárhi Brahmans in Bengal.

Narjenáre, a sept of the Agniá sub-tribe of Meches in the Darjiling Terai.

Nartoroá, a sub-caste of Korwás in Chota Nagpur.

Narwáre-Rámpur, a *mul* of the Kásyapa section of Maithil Brahmans in Behar.

Naskar, a title of Brahmans, Kayasths, and Kaibarttas in Bengal.

Naskarpurá, a section of Pátnis in Bengal.

Natabaidya, a synonym for Nat.

Natanya, a section of Kumhárs in Singbhum.

Náth, (i) a lord; master; a title, perhaps ironical of, and a synonym for, the Jugi caste in Bengal. (ii) A title of Dakshin-Rárhi and Bangaja Káyasths and Subarnabaniks in Bengal. Intermarriage is prohibited within the title. (iii) A section of the Orissa Brahmans. (iv) A title of Binjhiás.

Náthán, a sub-caste of Báruis in Bengal.

Náthji, a title of Jugis in Bengal.

Nathur, a title of Rájputs in Singbhum.

Nau, Nauá, a synonym for Nápit in Bengal and for Hajjám in Behar.

Nauá, a sub-tribe of Thárus in Nepal.

Nauákuri, a section of Kurmis in Chota Nagpur and Orissa.

Nauhatta, a sub-caste of Beldars in Behar.

Naukandri, a Nepal caste who work as carpenters.

Nau-lákh Khambu, a synonym for Khambu.

Nauli-Karan, a sub-caste of Karans in Orissa.

Nauniyár, a synonym or variant for Rauniár, which is a sub-caste of Baniyás in Behar.

Nauriyá, a section of the Bansphor sub-caste of Doms in Behar.

Nautana, a sub-caste of Kumhárs in Jessore.

Nauthni, a sept of Chandrabansi Rájputs in Behar.

Navadwip, a *samáj* or local group of the Bharadwája *gotra* of Páschátya Baidik Brahmans in Nadiya.

Nawalpuriá, a sept of the Rautár sub-tribe of Thárus in Behar.

Naya, priests (worshippers of the titular deity) of Santáls, Bhuiyas, Mauliks, Rajwars, etc.

Náyá, a synonym for Maulik.

Náyári, a *gáin* of the Sábarna *gotra* of Rárhi Brahmans in Bengal.

Necháhli, a *thar* or sept of Khambus in Darjiling.

Nedhuri, a *gáin* of the Sábarna *gotra* of Bárendra Brahmans in Bengal.

Nekári, *Nikári*, a synonym for Machhuá, *q.v.*

Neki, a section of Murmis in Darjiling.

Nekutwár-Barahi, a *mul* of the Kausik section of Maithil Brahmans in Behar.

Nembang, the swollen one, a sept of the Charkhola sub-tribe of Limbus in Darjiling.

Nembong, a sub-sept of the Phejom sept of Limbus in Darjiling.

Nenijor, a section of the Sátmulia Maghayá sub-caste of Kándus in Behar.

Neogi, an honorary title of Brahmans, Kayasths, Sadgops, etc., in Bengal.

Neopáni, **Nivipánya**, a *thar* of the Kaundin *gotra* of Nepáli Brahmans.

Nepáli, a sub-caste of Brahmans in Nepal.

Nepáliyá, a *thar* of the Dharta-Kausik *gotra* of Nepáli Brahmans.

Neprá, a section of the Sátmuliá Maghayá sub-caste of Kándus in Behar.

Nermáh, a sept of Limbus in Darjiling.

Nesur, a section of Murmis in Darjiling.

Netriá, a section of Kámárs in Singbhum and the Santál Parganás.

Neul, weasel, a totemistic section of Jagannathi Kumhárs in Orissa.

Neurádarvesh, *Náradarvesh*, *Neurájáti*, *Nárajati*, a title of a sect of Vaishnavas who shave their heads.

Newra, mongoose, a totemistic sept of Chiks in Chota Nagpur.

Niáli, a section of Kaibarttas in Orissa.

Nich Kurmi, a sub-caste of Kurmis in Chota Nagpur who marry their daughters as adults and permit sexual license before marriage.

Nichondia, a sub-caste of Baniyás in Behar.

Nidráli, a *gáin* of the Bátsya *gotra* of Bárendra Brahmans in Bengal.

Nigam, a sub-caste of Káyasths in Behar.

Nigániá, a section of Goálás in the North-Western Provinces and Behar.

Nigham, a *mul* or section of the Kanaujiá sub-caste of Sonárs in Behar.

Nij, a sub-sept of all the septs of Santáls.

Nikari, a *gáin* of the Sábarna *gotra* of Bárendra Brahmans in Bengal.

Nikári, *Nikiri*, Hindu fishmongers, who do not catch fish themselves, but obtain their supplies on a system of advances from the regular fishing castes. Mahomedans who follow the same avocation are called Mechuá, *q.v.*

Nikhar, a sub-caste of Gareris in Behar.

Nikharbans, a sept of Chiks in Chota Nagpur.

Nikhati, a *gáin* of the Bharadwája *gotra* of Bárendra Brahmans in Bengal.

Nikitia-Kandh, a sub-tribe of Kandhs in Orissa.

Niktawár, Nikutwár, a section of Bábhans in Behar.

Nikthá, a section of the Banodhiá and Jaiswár Kalwárs in Behar.

Nikum, a section of Goálás in the North-Western Provinces and Behar.

Nikumbh, a sept of the Surajbansi division of Rájputs in Behar.

Niluá, a sub-caste of Jugis in Northern Bengal whose special business it is to dye in blue.

Nimáchandpurá, a *mul* or section of the Naomuliá or Majraut sub-caste of Goálás in Behar.

Nimái, a family of the Kulin group of Jugis in Bengal.

Nimak, salt, a totemistic sept of Mundas in Chota Nagpur.

Nimámbaunchhá, a *thar* or sept of Khambus in Darjiling.

Nimandih, a section of Káyasths in Behar.

Nimavat, a sect of Vaishnavas.

Nimri, a sept of Rájputs in Behar.

Nimuani, a sept of Chiks in Chota Nagpur.

Nimundih, a sept of the Suryabansi Rájputs in Behar.

Ninauchhá, a *thar* or sept of Khambus in Darjiling.

Ninglehku, one who cuts poisonous plants, a sept of the Phedáb sub-tribe of Limbus in Darjiling.

Ninhiám, a *mul* or section of the Chhamuliá Madhesiá sub-caste of Halwáis in Behar.

Niparia, a *mul* or section of the Kanaujiá sub-caste of Hajjáms in Behar.

Nir, a sub-caste of Tántis in Bengal.

Nirábil, a *pathi* or hypergamous sub-group of Bárendra Brahmans in Bengal.

Nirbán, a section of Goálás in the North-Western Provinces and Behar.

Nirbhaya, a title of Sunris in Bengal.

Nirola, a *thar* or section of Nepáli Brahmans.

Nisán, a sept of the Chandrabansi division of Rájputs in Behar.

Nisank, a group of the Srotriya sub-caste of Utkal Brahmans.

Nishi, a synonym for Muchi.

Niskalanka, a section of Telis in Bengal.

Niti Siná, a sub-caste of Dhobás in Central Bengal.

Niyárishi, a section of Telis.

Niyáriyá, *Neyári*, *Niyariyá*, *Niyárdhoá*, a low caste who sift and wash the ashes and refuse of goldsmiths' shops for the scraps of precious metal which may be recovered by this process.

Nobáiáre, a sept of the Agniá sub-tribe of Meches in the Darjiling Terai.

Nobonapuria, a section of the Kamár sub-caste of Dosádhs in Behar.

Nodá, a sub-caste of Bágdis found in the 24-Parganás and Hughli, said to have come from Bankura.

Nogo, a sept of Limbus in Darjiling.

Nohár, a variant of Lohár.

Noinjorá, a section of Sonárs in Behar.

Nois, a sept of Mundas in Chota Nagpur.

Nolka, a section of Oswáls in Behar.

Nomahang, a *thar* or sept of Khambus in Darjiling.

Nonaitwár, a *mul* of the Sándil section of Maithil Brahmans, and a *kul* or section of Bábhans in Behar.

Noniyán, a synonym for Nuniá.

Nonoár, a section of Goráits in Chota Nagpur.

Non-pá, a *rui* or sept of Sherpa Bhotias of Nepal.

Nowattiá, a sept of Tipperahs in the Hill Tracts of Chittagong.

Nrisingha, a section of Gandhabaniks in Bengal.

Nunáon, a section of the Biyáhut and Kharidáhá Kalwárs in Behar.

Nun-Bind, a sub-caste of Binds in Eastern Bengal.

Nuneswar, a section of the Biyáhut and Kharidáhá Kalwárs in Behar.

Nunetwár, a *mul* of the Sándil section of Maithil Brahmans in Behar.

Nungoliá, a synonym for Nuniá.

Nunhar, a section of the Biyáhut and Kharidáhá Kalwárs in Behar.

Nuniá, *Noniyán*, a Dravidian caste of Behar and Upper India engaged in cultivation, saltpetre-making, and various kinds of earthwork. The caste seem to have no traditions except of a silly story that the Awadhia are descended from an ascetic named Bidur Bhakat, who broke his fast on salt earth, and being thereby disqualified for the higher life of meditation, was condemned by Rám Chandra to betake himself to the manufacture of saltpetre. This throws small light on the origin of the Nuniás. It seems, however, to be generally believed that they are closely connected with the Binds and the Beldárs, and I venture the conjecture that the Binds may be the modern representatives of an aboriginal tribe from which the Nuniás have branched off as saltpetre-makers and the Beldárs as earth-workers. All three groups are now endogamous. The hunting and fishing proclivities of the Binds seem to suggest that they are the oldest of the three, while the totemistic sections of the Nuniás stamp them as Dravidian. The Beldars are probably a more recent offshoot, but the fact that the name Beldár (mattock-bearer) is assumed by members of any caste when employed on earthwork renders it difficult to determine their precise affinities.

Origin.

The Nuniás of Behar are divided into seven sub-castes:—Awadhiá or Ayodhiabási, Bhojpuriá, Kharáont, Maghayá, Orh, Pachainyá or Chauhán, and Semarwár. Their sections, which are given in Appendix I, appear to be for the most part totemistic. A man may not marry a woman belonging to his own section, but no other sections are barred to him; and the rule of simple exogamy is supplemented by the standard formula *mamerá*, *chacherá*, etc., already quoted. It deserves notice that intermarriage in the *chacherá* line is forbidden as long as any relationship can be traced, while in the other three lines the prohibition only extends to three or, as some say, to five generations. All Nuniás who can afford to do so marry their daughters as infants, adult-marriages being considered unfashionable, if not disreputable. Polygamy is permitted, but it is unusual to find a man with more than two wives; and I gather, although there is no distinct rule on the subject, that practice is held to be justified only by the necessity of procuring offspring. Widows are allowed to marry again by the *sagai* form, and are subject to no restrictions in their choice of a second husband except those arising from consanguinity. It is considered, however, right for a widow to marry her deceased husband's younger brother. Divorce is effected on grounds of adultery or incompatibility of temper by the order of the caste council (panchâyat). A divorced woman may marry again by the *sagai* form unless she has gone wrong with a man of another caste—an offence which entails summary expulsion.

Internal structure.

Tirhutiá Brahmans serve the Nuniás as priests, and officiate at their marriages. The marriage ceremony is of the standard type. The bridegroom-price (*tilak*) is fixed by custom at a sum varying from Re. 1 to Rs. 5

Marriage.

and a pair of *dhotis*. After the marriage the bride does not go with the *barát* to her husband's house, but stays with her parents until she attains puberty, when her husband goes to fetch her with a few of his friends and brings her home in procession (*dira gawau*). Consummation is not effected until after this ceremony. Kwadhiya Nuniás have a curious custom called *ásmáui shádi*, which requires that the bride and bridegroom shall be held off the ground during the marriage ceremony.

Religion.

In matters of religion the Nuniás follow the ordinary forms of Hinduism current in Behar. Most of them are Sáktas, and there are said to be comparatively few Vaishnavas in the caste. Bhagavatiji is their favourite goddess. Bandi, Goraiyá, and Sitalá are worshipped on Tuesdays, Wednesdays, and Saturdays. There are no deities specially worshipped by women and children, but women take part in the worship of Sitalá. Sannyási fakirs are the gurus of the caste. The dead are burned, and *sráddh* performed on the thirteenth day after death. The ashes are thrown into any river that may be handy. The bodies of children dying under five years of age are buried—a point wherein Nunias depart from the usual custom, which is to bury after eighteen months.

Occupation.

The caste believe the extraction of salt and saltpetre from saline earth to be their original occupation, and it is possible, as has been suggested above, that they may have broken off from the Binds by reason of their adopting this profession. At the present day we find them also employed in road-making, tank-digging, well-sinking, building and thatching houses, and all kinds of agricultural field labour. Many of them also hold lands of their own, and a few have gained a more secure position as occupancy raiyats. Nuniás who have no land often wander about during the dry season in search of work, and build small grass huts for temporary shelter. None of them are artisans. In Bengal, according to Dr. Wise, Nuniás readily obtain service with Goálás or other clean Sudras, but refuse to work as labourers or domestic servants with low-caste families. The social standing of Nuniás seems to vary in different parts, and does not admit of very precise definition. In Patna, Mozufferpur, and parts of Monghyr they rank with Kurmis, Koiris, Kumhárs, etc., and Brahmans will take water and certain kinds of sweetmeats from their hands. In Bhágalpur, Purniah, Champarun, Shahabad, and Gya they are placed on the same level as Tantis, and none of the higher castes will take water from them. In addition to the various kinds of food that are lawful for Hindus of the middle class, Nuniás eat field-rats and pork, and drink fermented and spirituous liquors. It is significant of the Nuniás' point of view in such matters that they think little of Bhakats, who practise small forms of asceticism by abstaining from certain kinds of food and drink; and I am informed that very few Bhakats are found among them.

Social status.

The following statement shows the number and distribution of Nuniás in 1872 and 1881:—

District.	1872.	1881.	District.	1872.	1881.
Bardwan	......	33	Patna	10,316	18,249
Bankura	......	1	Gya	14,916	16,608
Birbhum	......	28	Shahabad	13,183	18,606
Midnapur	......	4,667	Tirhut { Mozufferpur	} 69,343	{ 41,616
Hughli	......	39	Tirhut { Darbhanga		27,776
24-Parganás	......	451	Saran	65,654	68,368
Nadiya	......	25	Champaran	35,103	45,394
Murshedabad	......	80	Monghyr	9,218	9,369
Dinajpur	......	1,336	Bhágalpur	3,436	7,377
Rajshahye	......	23	Purniah	971	1,984
Rangpur	......	1,365	Santál Parganás	847	1,662
Bogra	......	287	Cuttack	} *	{ 736
Pabna	......	28	Puri		......
Darjiling	......	362	Balasore		1
Jalpigori	......	275	Tributary States		1
Kuch Behar	......	702	Hazaribagh	278	2,316
Maimansinh	......	2,218	Lohardagá	2,635	4,116
Maldah	......	344	Singbhum	4	32
			Manbhum	228	533

* The figures are included with "other labouring castes."

Nuniár, a subdivision of Baniyas who deal in saltpetre.

Nuniyár, a section of Káyasths in Behar.

Nunkhariá, a section of the Biyáhut and Kharidáhá Kalwárs in Behar.

Nuri, a title of Joláhas in Behar who make lac bracelets, dye for the lips, etc.; the same as Churihár and Laheri. A Bengal caste of jewellers and lac-workers said to have been brought from Orissa by one of the Rajas of Krishnagar.

O

Oari, a section of the Karan sub-caste of Káyasths in Behar.

Oaria, verandah, a totemistic sept of Mundas in Chota Nagpur.

Obarsári, a totemistic sept of the Bhumij tribe in Chota Nagpur.

Obung-gyakpa, the dweller above the fountain, a sept of the Phedáb sub-tribe of Limbus in Darjiling.

Odania, a territorial section of Binds in Behar.

Odhalaba, fox, a totemistic sept of Juángs in Orissa.

Oh-Ár, a sept of the Chandrabansi Rájputs in Behar.

Ohdár, a title of Khandáits and Kharwárs in Chota Nagpur.

Oinwár, a *mul* of the Kásyapa section of Maithil Brahmans in Behar.

Ojhá, a group of the Ádi-Gaura sub-caste of Gaura Brahmans; a title of Bábhans; a section of the Pargah caste in Behar.

Ojhá, Ujhá, or Jhá, a title of Maithil Brahmans in Behar.

Ojhaiyá, a sept of the Rautár sub-tribe of Thárus in Behar.

Okinwár, a *kul* or section of Bábhans in Behar.

Okrabo, a sept of the Phágu sub-tribe of Yakhas in Darjiling.

Olingthopa, a section of Mangars in Darjiling.

Om, a title of Dakshin-Rárhi Káyasths in Bengal.

On-chhombo, the horse-seller, a sept of the Tambrakhola sub-tribe of Limbus in Darjiling.

Ongdáhba, a *rui* or sept of Dejong Lhoris whose ancestor had emigrated from Bhotan.

Ongyo, a sept of the Tungjainya sub-tribe of Chakmás in the Hill Tracts of Chittagong.

Onwár, a section of Bábhans in Behar.

Ophia, a sept of Parhaiyas in Chota Nagpur.

Or, a sub-caste of Turis in Chota Nagpur.

Orá, a sept of Maghs in the Hill Tracts of Chittagong.

Oráon, *Uráon*, *Kunokh*, *Kunrukh*, a Dravidian cultivating tribe of Chota Nagpur, classed on linguistic grounds as Dravidian, and supposed to be closely akin to the Málés of the Rájmahál hills. Their traditions say that their

Tradition of origin.

original home was in the west of India, whence they came to the Kaimur hills and the plateau of Rohtás in Shahabad. Driven from Rohtás by the Muhamadans, the tribe split into two divisions. One of these, under the Chief, followed the course of the Ganges, and finally settled in the Rájmahál hills; while the other, led by his younger brother, went up the Son into Palamau, and turning eastward along the Koel took possession of the north-western portion of the Chota Nagpur plateau. Some say that they expelled the Mundas from this portion of the country, and forced them to retire to their present settlements in the south of Lohardagá; but this statement is not borne out by local tradition, nor can it be reconciled with the fact that the few Mundas found in the Oráon *parganás* on the plateau are acknowledged and looked up to as the descendants of the founders of the villages in which they live.

Physical characteristics.

The colour of most Oráons is the darkest brown, approaching to black; the hair being jet black, coarse, and rather inclined to be frizzy. Projecting jaws and teeth, thick lips, low narrow foreheads, broad flat noses, are the features which strike a careful observer as characteristic of the tribe. The eyes are often bright and full, and no obliquity is observable in the opening of the eyelids. No signs of Mongolian affinities can be detected in the relative positions of the nasal and malar bones, and the average naso-malar index for a hundred Oráons measured on the system recommended by Mr. Oldfield Thomas omes to 113·6.

Dress and ornaments.

"The dress of the men," says Colonel Dalton, "consists of a long narrow strip of cloth carefully adjusted as a middle garment, but in such a manner as to leave the wearer most perfect freedom of limb, and allow the full play of the muscles of the thigh and hip to be seen. They wear nothing in the form of a coat; the decorated neck and chest are undraped, displaying how the latter tapers to the waist, which the young dandies compress within the smallest compass. In addition to the cloth, there is always round the waist a girdle of cords made of *tasar* silk or of cane. This is now a superfluity, but it is no doubt the remnant of a more primitive costume, perhaps the support of the antique fig leaves. After the age of ornamentation is passed, nothing can be more untidy or unprepossessing than the appearance of the Oráon. The ornaments are nearly all discarded, hair utterly neglected, and for raiment any rags are used. This applies both to males and females of middle age. The ordinary dress of the women depends somewhat on the degree of civilization, and on the part of the country in which you make your observations. In the villages about Lohardagá, a cloth from the waist to a little below the knee is the common working dress; but where there is more association with other races, the persons of young females are decently clad in the coarse cotton cloth of the country, white with red border. Made-up garments are not worn except by the converts to Christianity. The one cloth, six yards long, is gracefully adjusted so as to form a shawl and a petticoat. The Oráons do not, as a rule, bring the upper end of the garment over the head, and so give it the functions also of a veil, as it is worn by the Bengali women; they simply throw the end of the dress over the left shoulder, and it falls with its fringe and ornamented border prettily over the back of the figure. Vast quantities of red beads and a large heavy brass ornament, shaped like a torque, are worn round the neck. On the left hand are rings of copper, as many as can be indued on each finger up to the first joint; on the right hand a smaller quantity. Rings on the second toe only, of brass or bell-metal, and anklets and bracelets of the same material are also worn. The hair is, as a rule, coarse and rather inclined to be frizzy, but by dint of lubrication they can make it tolerably smooth and amenable; and false hair or some other substance is used to give size to the mass (the chignon) into which it is gathered, not immediately behind, but more or less on one side, so that it lies on the neck just behind, and touching the right ear; and flowers are arranged in a receptacle made for them between the roll of hair and the head. The ears are, as usual with such people, terribly mutilated for decorative purposes; spikes and rings are inserted into holes made in the upper cartilage, and the lobe is widely distended. When in full dancing costume, they add to their head-dress plumes of heron feathers, and a gay bordered scarf is tightly bound round the upper part of the body."

Bachelor's dormitory.

In matters of domestic economy the Oráons are a slovenly race, and their badly-built mud huts afford no sufficient accommodation for the unmarried members of the family. In the older Oráon villages this difficulty is provided for by a house called the dhúmkúria, in which all the bachelors must sleep under penalty of a fine. Where the girls sleep is, says Colonel Dalton, "somewhat of a mystery." In some villages a separate building, under the charge of an elderly woman, is maintained for their use; and more commonly they are distributed among the widows of the village. "But however billeted, it is well known that they often find their way to the bachelors' hall, and in some villages actually sleep there."

This curious institution is not peculiar to the Oráons. We meet with it among the Juángs, the Hill Bhuiyás of Keonjhur and Bonai, and the Jhumiá Maghs of the Chittagong Hill Tracts. The Oráon system, though already looked upon as an ancient custom, and apparently tending to disuse in newly-formed villages, is still very elaborate. "The Dhúmkúria fraternity are under the severest penalties bound down to secrecy in regard to all that takes place in their dormitory; and even girls are punished if they dare to tell tales. They are not allowed to join in the dances till the offence is condoned. They have a regular system of fagging in this curious institution. The small boys serve those of larger growth, shampoo their limbs, and comb their hair, etc., and they are sometimes subjected to severe discipline to *make men* of them." It is difficult not to see in this a survival of more primitive modes of life, possibly even of the initiatory ceremonies to which many tribes of savages attach so much importance.

Internal structure.

The internal structure of the Oráon tribe is shown in a tabular form in Appendix I. The exogamous septs are extremely numerous, and all that can be identified are totemistic, the totem being taboo to the members of the sept. The rule of exogamy in force is the simple one that a man may not marry a woman of his own sept. The sept name descends in the male line, and there is no objection to a man marrying a woman belonging to the same sept as his mother. In addition to this some system of prohibited degrees seems to exist among them, though no one can state it clearly, nor is it expressed in a definite formula. Still every Oráon will admit that he cannot marry his maternal aunt or his first cousin on the mother's side, though he will probably not be able to say how far these prohibitions go in the descending line. So also no one can marry his younger brother's widow or the elder sister of his deceased wife, though marriage with an elder brother's widow or a deceased wife's younger sister is deemed permissible.

Marriage.

Seventeen years ago, when Colonel Dalton published his account of the Oráons, infant-marriage is said to have been entirely unknown among the tribe. A few of the wealthier men, who affect to imitate Hindu customs, have now taken to this practice, and marry their daughters before they have attained puberty. Among the mass of the people, however, girls marry after they are grown up, and the freest courtship prevails at dances, festivals, and social gatherings of various kinds. Young men woo their sweethearts with offerings of flowers for the hair and presents of grilled field-mice, "which the Oráons declare to be the most delicate of food." Sexual intercourse before marriage is tacitly recognized, and is so generally practised that in the opinon of the best observers on Oráon girl is a virgin at the time of her marriage. To call this state of things immoral is to apply a modern conception to primitive habits of life. Within the tribe indeed the idea of sexual morality seems hardly to exist, and the unmarried Oráons are not far removed from the condition of modified promiscuity which prevails among many of the Australian tribes. Provided that the exogamous circle defined by the totem is respected, an unmarried woman may bestow her favours on whom she will. If, however, she becomes pregnant, arrangements are made to get her married without delay, and she is then expected to lead a virtuous life. Prostitution is unknown. Intrigues beyond the limits of the tribe are uncommon, and are punished by summary expulsion.

Colonel Dalton gives the following account of the Oráon marriage system :—

"When a young man makes up his mind to marry, his parents or guardians go through a form of selection for him; but it is always a girl that he has already selected for himself, and between whom and him there is a perfect understanding. The parents, however, have to arrange all preliminaries, including the price of the damsel, which is sometimes as low as Rs. 4 (8s.) In the visits that are interchanged by the negotiators, omens are carefully observed by the Oráons, as by the Mundas, and there are, consequently, similar difficulties to overcome; but when all is settled, the bridegroom proceeds with a large party of his friends, male and female, to the bride's house. Most of the males have warlike weapons, real or sham, and as they approach the village of the bride's family the young men from thence emerge, also armed, as if to repel the invasion, and a mimic fight ensues, which, like a dissolving view, blends pleasantly into a dance. In this the bride and bridegroom join, each riding on the hips of one of their friends. A bower is constructed in front of the residence of the bride's father, into which the bride and bridegroom are carried by women, and made to stand on a curry-stone, under which is placed a sheaf of corn, resting on a plough yoke. Here the mystery of the *sindúrdán* is performed; but the operation is carefully screened from view, first by cloths thrown over the young couple, secondly by a circle of their male friends, some of whom hold up a screen cloth, while others keep guard with weapons upraised and look very fierce, as if they had been told off to cut down intruders, and were quite prepared to do so. In Oráon marriages the bridegroom stands on the curry-stone behind the bride, but in order that this may not be deemed a concession to the female, his toes are so placed as to tread on her heels. The old women under the cloth are very particular about this, as if they were specially interested in providing that the heel of the woman should be properly bruised. Thus poised the man stretches over the girl's head and daubs her forehead and crown with the red powder *sindúr;* and if the girl is allowed to return the compliment (it is a controverted point whether she should do so or not), she performs the ceremony without turning her head, reaching back over her own shoulder and just touching his brow. When this is accomplished, a gun is fired; and then, by some arrangement, vessels full of water, placed over the bower, are capsized, and the young couple and those who stand near them receive a drenching shower-bath. They now retire into an apartment prepared for them, ostensibly to change their clothes, but they do not emerge for some time, and when they appear they are saluted as man and wife. Dancing is kept up during their retirement, one of the performers executing a *pas seul* with a basket on her head, which is said to contain the trousseau. The Oráons have no prescribed wedding garments. They do not follow the Hindu custom of using saffron-coloured robes on such occasions. The bride is attired in ordinary habiliments, and no special pains are taken to make her lovely for the occasion. The bridegroom is better dressed than usual. He wears a long coat and a turban. Nor have the Oráons any special days or seasons for marriages. The ceremony may take place in any month of the year, but, with all natives, the hot, dry months are generally selected if possible. There is then not much work on hand; granaries are full, and they prefer those months for marching and camping out."

Polygamy is permitted, and in theory at least there is no limit to the number of wives a man may have. This luxury, however, is but little sought after. Oráons are usually too poor to maintain many wives, and the majority content themselves with one. Widows may marry again, and are subject to no restrictions in selecting their second husbands. In such marriages the full ceremony is not performed: it is deemed sufficient for the female relatives of the bridegroom to smear vermilion on the bride's forehead and the parting of her hair. Sometimes even this meagre form is omitted, and a valid marriage is constituted by the mere fact of the parties living together. Notwithstanding this laxity of formal observance, the children of a widow are recognized as holding equal rank with those of a woman married by the full ritual used in a first marriage. Divorce is readily effected at the will of either husband or wife. The consent of the panchâyat is not required, nor is the intention to separate attested by any particular form. A husband turns away his wife, or a wife runs off from her husband, and the fact in either case is accepted as constituting a valid divorce. If a woman has children, her husband may be compelled to contribute to their maintenance if he divorces the mother on any other ground than adultery. Similarly, when a wife deserts her husband, not on account of ill-treatment, but merely because she takes a fancy to another man, her parents may be called upon to repay the bride-price which they received at her marriage. Divorced wives may marry again on the same terms and by the same form as widows.

Religion.

"The religion of the Oráons," says Colonel Dalton, "is of a composite order. They have, no doubt, retained some portion of the belief that they brought with them to Chota Nagpur; but, coalescing with the Mundas and joining in their festivals and acts of public worship, they have to a certain extent adopted their ideas on religion and blended them with their own. There is, however, a material distinction between the religious systems of the two people. The Mundas have no symbols and make no representations of their gods; the Oráons, and all the cognates whom I have met with, have always some visible object of worship, though it may be but a stone or a wooden post, or a lump of earth. Like the Mundas, they acknowledge a Supreme God, adored as Dharmi or Dharmesh, the Holy One, who is manifest in the sun; and they regard Dharmesh as a perfectly pure, beneficent being, who created us, and would in his goodness and mercy preserve us, but that his benevolent designs are thwarted by malignant spirits whom mortals must propitiate, as Dharmesh cannot or does not interfere if the spirit of evil once fastens upon us. It is therefore of no use to pray to Dharmesh or to offer sacrifices to him; so though acknowledged, recognized, and reverenced, he is neglected, whilst the malignant spirits are adored.

"I do not think that the Oráons have an idea that their sins are visited on them, either in this world or in a world to come. It is not because they are wicked that their children or their cattle die, or their crops fail, or they suffer in body; it is only because some malignant demon has a spite against them, or is desirous of harming them. Their ideas of sin are limited. Thou shalt not commit adultery, thou shalt not steal, thou shalt not bear false witness against thy neighbour, is about as much of the Decalogue as they would subscribe to. It is doubtful if they see any moral guilt in murder, though hundreds of them have suffered the extreme penalty of the law for this crime. They are ready to take life on very slight provocation, and in the gratification of their revenge an innocent child is as likely to suffer as the actual offender. There is one canon of the Mosaical law that they in former years rigorously enforced—'Thou shalt not suffer a witch to live.' I have dwelt on this subject in treating of the Mundas. If left to themselves, the life of elderly females would be very insecure. As it is, a suspected old woman (and sometimes a young one, especially if she be the daughter of a suspected old one) is occasionally condemned, well drubbed and turned out of the village; and she does not always survive the treatment she is subjected to. If we analyse the views of most of the Oráon converts to Christianity, we shall, I think, be able to discern the influence of their pagan doctrines and superstitions in the motives that first led them to become catechumens. The Supreme Being who does not protect them from the spite of malevolent spirits has, they are assured, the Christians under His special care. They consider that, in consequence of this guardianship, the witches and *bhúts* have no power over Christians; and it is, therefore, good for them to join that body. They are taught that for the salvation of Christians one great sacrifice has been made, and they see that those who are baptized do not in fact reduce their live-stock to propitiate the evil spirits. They grasp at this notion; and long afterwards, when they understand it better, the atonement, the mystical washing away of sin by the blood of Christ, is the doctrine on which their simple minds most dwell. I have not found amongst the pagan Oráons a trace of the high moral code that their cousins of the Rájmahál hills are said to have accepted. I consider that they have no belief whatever in a future state, whilst to the Rájmahálís is attributed a profound system of metempsychosis. The Oráons carry that doctrine no further than to suppose that men who are killed by tigers become tigers, but for other people death means annihilation. As the sole object of their religious ceremonies is the propitiation of the demons, who are ever thwarting the benevolent intentions of Dharmesh, they have no notion of a service of thanksgiving; and so far we may regard the religion of the Mundas as of a higher order than theirs. When suffering or misfortune befall a man, he consults an augur, or *ojhá*, as to the cause of his affliction, and acts according to the advice given. The *ojhá* has it in his power to denounce a mortal or a particular devil. The method employed has been described in the account of the Mundas, and the result is the same. If a fellow-being is denounced, it is said that he has caused his familiar to possess and afflict the sufferer; and the person denounced is seized and tortured, or beaten, to force him to effect the expulsion of the evil spirit. But the family or village *bhút* may be accused. The *ojhá*, under inspiration, of course, decides what is to be sacrificed, and frequently ruins, if he does not cure, the patient consulting him. In the process of propitiation, the fetish nature of the Oráon belief is shown. The sorcerer produces a small image of mud, and on it sprinkles a few grains of rice. If fowls are to be the victims, they are placed in front of this image; and if they peck at the rice, it indicates that the particular devil is satisfied with the intention of his votaries, and the sacrifice proceeds. The flesh of the animals killed is appropriated by the sorcerer, so it is his interest to have a hecatomb if possible. In regard to the names and attributes of the devils, the Oráons who live with Mundas sacrifice to Marang Búrú and all the Munda Bongas. The Oráons on the western portion of the plateau, where there are few Mundas, ignore the Bongas and pay their devotion to Darhá, the Sarna Burhi (Lady of the Grove), and the village *bhúts*, who have various names. Chanda or Chandi is the god or goddess of the chase, and is always invoked preparatory to starting on great hunting expeditions. Any bit of rock, or stone, or excrescence on a rock, serves to represent this deity. The hill near Lodhma, known to the Mundas as Marang Búrú, is held in great reverence by the Oráons. To the spirit of the hill, whom they call Baranda, they give bullocks and buffaloes, especially propitiating him as the *bhút*, who, when malignantly inclined, frustrates God's designs of sending rain in due season to fertilise the earth. In some parts of the country Darhá is almost the only spirit they propitiate. If fowls are offered to him, they must be of divers colours, but once in three years he should have a sheep from his votaries; and once in the same period a buffalo, of which the *ojhá* or *páhn* gets a quarter. The Oráon must always have something material to worship, renewed every three years. Besides this superstitious dread of the spirits above named, the Oráon's imagination tremblingly wanders in a world of ghosts. Every rock, road, river, and grove is haunted. He believes that women who die in childbirth become ghosts, called *chorail;* and such ghosts are frequently met hovering about the tombstones, always clad in robes of white, their faces fair and lovely, but with backs black as charcoal, and inverted feet, that is, they walk with their heels in front. They lay hold of passers-by and wrestle with them, and tickle them; and he is lucky, indeed, who, thus caught, escapes without permanent injuries." Women who die within fifteen days of their confinement are believed to be likely to become *chorails;* but this danger may be averted by offering sacrifices for the repose of their spirits.

The Oráons do not employ Brahmans, and their religious and ceremonial observances are supervised by priests of their own tribe known as Naiyas.

Festivals.

"The Oráons and Mundas keep the same festivals; but, according to Mr. Luther, the *Karm* is, with the former, the most important. It is celebrated at the season for planting out the rice grown in seed-beds, and is observed by Hindus as well as by Kols and other tribes. On the first day of the feast the villagers must not break their fast till certain ceremonies have been performed. In the evening a party of young people of both sexes proceed to the forest, and cut a young *karma* tree (*Nauclea parvifolia*), or the branch of one, bearing which they return in triumph,—dancing, and singing, and beating drums,—and plant it in the middle of the *ákhra*. After the performance of a sacrifice to the Karma Deota by the *páhn*, the villagers feast, and the night is passed in dancing and revelry. Next morning all may be seen at an early hour in holiday array; the elders in groups, under the fine old tamarind trees that surround the *ákhra*, and the youth of both sexes, arm-linked in a huge circle, dancing round the *karma* tree, which, festooned with garlands, decorated with strips of coloured cloth, sham bracelets and necklets of plaited straw, and with the bright faces and merry laughter of the young people encircling it, reminds one of the gift-bearing tree so often introduced at our own Christmas festival, and suggests the probability of some remote connection between the two. Preparatory to the festival, the daughters of the headmen of the village cultivate blades of barley in a peculiar manner. The seed is sown in moist, sandy soil, mixed with a quantity of turmeric, and the blades sprout and unfold of a pale yellow or primrose colour. On the *karma* day, these blades are taken up by the roots, as if for transplanting, and carried in baskets by the fair cultivators to the *ákhra*. They approach the *karma* tree, and, prostrating themselves reverentially, place before it some of the plants. They then go round the company, and, like bridesmaids distributing wedding favours, present to each person a few of the yellow barley blades, and all soon appear, wearing, generally in their hair, this distinctive decoration of the festival. Then all join merrily in the *karma* dances, and malignant indeed must be the *bhút* who is not propitiated by so attractive a gathering. The morning revel closes with the removal of the *karma*. It is taken away by the merry throng and thrown into a stream or tank; but after another feast dancing and drinking are resumed. On the following morning the effects of the two nights' dissipation are often, I fear, very palpable." Colonel Dalton notices that the *karma* festival is celebrated by Hindus as well as by the aboriginal tribes, and quotes a passage from the Bhavishya Purána, the object of which appears to be to explain how a festival of an aboriginal people came to be adopted by the Hindus. He also points out that the necessity of the females of the family joining in the ceremony is an argument against its Hindu origin.

"The Oráons have some observances during the Sarhúl festival that differ a little from those of the Mundas. Their idea is that at this season the marriage of Dharti, the earth, is celebrated; and this cannot be done till the *sál* trees give the flowers for the ceremony. It takes place, then, towards the end of March or beginning of April; but any day whilst the *sál* trees are in blossom will answer. On the day fixed the villagers accompany their *páhn* to the *sarna*, the sacred grove, a remnant of the old *sál* forest, in which the Oráons locate a popular deity, called the Sarna Búrhi, or woman of the grove, corresponding with the Jáhir Era and Desauli of the Mundas. To this dryad, who is supposed to have great influence on the rain (a superstition not unlikely to have been founded on the importance of trees as cloud-compellers), the *páhn*, arriving with his party at the grove, offers five fowls. These are afterwards cooked with rice, and a small quantity of the food is given to each person present. They then collect a quantity of *sál* flowers and return laden with them to the village. Next day the *páhn*, with some of the males of the village, pays a visit to every house, carrying the flowers in a wide, open basket. The females of each house take out water to wash his feet as he approaches, and, kneeling before him, make a most respectful obeisance. He then dances with them, and places over the door of the house, and in the hair of the women, some of the *sál* flowers. The moment that this is accomplished, they throw the contents of their water-vessels over his venerable person, heartily dousing the man whom a moment before they were treating with such profound respect. But to prevent his catching cold they ply him with as much of the home-brew as he can drink, consequently his reverence is generally gloriously drunk before he completes his round. The feasting and beer-drinking now become general; and after the meal the youth of both sexes, decked with *sál* flowers (they make an exceedingly becoming head-dress), flock to the *ákhra*, and dance all night and best part of next day."

Disposal of the dead.

"Where a death occurs in an Oráon family, it is made known by the lamentations of the women, who loosen their hair (a demonstration of grief which appears to prevail in all countries) and cry vigorously. They lay out the body on the common cot, called *chárpái;* and, after washing it carefully, convey it to the appointed burning-place, covered with a new cloth, and escorted by all the villagers, male and female, who are able to attend. In some families the funeral procession proceeds with music, but others dislike this custom, and nothing is heard but the cries of the women. When they have arrived at the place where the funeral pile has been prepared, the body is again washed, and the nearest relations of the deceased make offerings of rice, and put rice into the mouth of the corpse, while others put pice or other coin. The body is then placed on the pile and anointed; further offerings of rice are made, and the pile is ignited by a father or mother, a wife or husband. When the body has been consumed, notice is given in the village, and there is another collection of friends and relatives to collect the charred bones which remain. These are placed in a new earthen vessel, and ceremoniously taken to the village; and as the procession returns, parched rice is dropped on the road to mark the route selected. The cinerary urn is suspended to a post erected in front of the residence of the deceased; the guests are feasted, and the party then breaks up. In the month of December or January next ensuing, the friends and relations are all again collected to witness the disposal of the bones in the place that, from the first establishment of the community, has been appropriated to the purpose. This is a point on which the Oráons are exceedingly tenacious; and even when one of them dies far from his home, his relations will, if possible, sooner or later, recover the fragments of his bones, and bear them back to the village, to be deposited with the ashes of his ancestors. The burial ground is always near a river, stream, or tank. As the procession proceeds with music to this place, offerings of rice are continually thrown over the cinerary urn till it is deposited in the grave prepared for it, and a large flat stone placed above. Then all must bathe, and after paying the musicians the party returns to the village. The money that was placed in the mouth of the corpse and afterwards saved from the ashes is the fee of the musicians. The person who carried the bones to the grave has to undergo purification by incense and the sprinkling of water. It is to be observed that this ceremony occurs in each village but once in the year; and on the appointed day the ashes of all who have died during the year are simultaneously relegated to their final resting place. No marriage can take place in a village whilst the bones of the dead are retained there. The most ardent lovers must patiently await the day of *hadbári* or sepulture. The marriage season commences shortly afterwards."

Social status.

In the eyes of the average Hindu the Oráons have no social status at all, and are deemed to be entirely outside the regular caste system. In the important matter of diet the main body of the tribe have as yet made no concessions to Hindu prejudice. Beef, pork, fowls, all kinds of fish, alligators, lizards, field-rats, the larvæ of bees and wasps, and even the flesh of animals which have died a natural death, are reckoned lawful food. Oráons, in fact, will eat almost anything, and are looked down upon as promiscuous feeders by the Bagdis, Bauris, and other dwellers upon the outskirts of Hinduism. A common charge is that they eat snakes and jackals, but this is only partially true, for the flesh of these animals is used solely for certain obscure medicinal purposes, and is not recognized as a regular article of diet. It is a singular fact that the Oráons hold the ass to be sacred, and will not kill it or eat its flesh, thus assigning to the animal much the same position and dignity as the Hindus give to the cow. No reason can be given by the members of the tribe for delighting to honour an animal which is in no way characteristic of heir present habitat; nor do I find any evidence to support the obvious conjecture that the ass may have been a tribal totem. The question of such totems and its bearing upon the problem of the origin of exogamy has been discussed at length in the Introduction to the first volume.

Occupation.

The Oraons claim to have introduced plough cultivation into Chota Nagpur, and thus to have displaced the barbarous *dáhá* method of tillage which is carried on by burning the jungle and sowing a crop of pulse or Indian-corn in the ashes. They were certainly among the earliest settlers on the plateau of Chota Nagpur, and many of them even now hold *bhuinhári* tenures in right of being the first clearers of the soil. These rights, however, are now fast passing out of their hands, and the modern competition for land tends rather to reduce them to the position of tenants-at-will or landless agricultural labourers. "Their lot," says Colonel Dalton, "is not a happy one. Not one of their own people now occupies a position which would give him the power to protect, or the influence to elevate, them from the state of degradation into which a majority of the tribe have long fallen. They submit to be told that they were especially created as a labouring class. They have had this so often dinned into their ears, that they believe and admit it; and I have known instances of their abstaining from claiming, as authorised by law, commutation for the forced labour exacted by their landlords, because they considered that they were born to it. There are indeed some amongst them, stern yeomen, who cling with tenacity to the freeholds they have inherited, and will spend all they possess in defending them; but the bulk of the people seldom rise, in their own country, above the position of cottiers and labourers. There the value of labour has not risen in proportion to the advance that has taken place in other parts of India; and Oráons are easily induced to migrate for a time to other climes, even to regions beyond the great 'black water,' where their work is better remunerated. But those who return with wealth thus accumulated regard it not. They spend in a month what would have made them comfortable for life, and relapse into their lot of labour and penury, as if they had never had experience of independence and plenty. I believe they relish work, if the task-master be not over-exacting. Oráons sentenced to imprisonment without labour, as sometimes happens, for offences against the excise laws, insist on joining the labouring gangs, and wherever employed, if kindly treated, they labour as if they felt an interest in the work. In cold weather or hot, rain or sun, they go cheerfully about it; and after some nine or ten hours of toil, they return blithely home, in flower-decked groups, holding each other by the hand or round the waist, and singing.

"The constitution of the Oráon village is the same as that of the Mundárí. In each the hereditary *múnda* or headman and the hereditary *páhn* or priest have their lands on privileged terms, as the descendants of the founders of the village. The hereditary estates of the two families are called *khúnts*, and there is sometimes a third *khúnt*, called the *máhato;* on all of these a very low rent is fixed, but there are conditions of service attached. These may now be commuted to cash payments at the instance of either party. There is also, under charge of the *páhn*, the land dedicated to the service of the village gods. The priestly office does not always descend from father to son. The latter may be ignorant and disqualified, or he may be a Christian; therefore, when vacated, it is filled by divination. The magic *súp*, or winnowing-sieve, properly spelled like a divining-rod, conducts the person holding it to the door of the man most fitted to hold the office. A priest there must be; an Oráon community cannot get on without one. The fate of the village is in his hands; in their own phraseology, it is said that 'he makes its affairs.' He is also master of the revels which are for the most part connected with religious rites. The doctrine of the Oráons is that man best pleases the gods when he makes merry himself; so that acts of worship and propitiatory sacrifices are always associated with feasting, drinking, dancing, and love-making. The *múnda* or *máhato* is the functionary to whom the proprietor of the village looks for its secular administration. In contradistinction to the *páhn* who makes (*bandtá*) the affairs, the *máhato* administers (*chalátá*) them; and he may be removed if he fail to give satisfaction."

The following statement shows the number and distribution of Oráons in 1872 and 1881 :—

District.	1872.	1881.	District.	1872.	1881.
Bardwan	991	2,413	Chittagong	1	43
Bankura	106	76	Noakhali	......	25
Birbhum	5,169	5,567	Patna	6	97
Midnapur	838	83	Gya	35	11
Hughli	626	240	Shahabad	712	104
Howrah		19	Darbhanga	886	1,224
24-Parganás	3,362	1,439	Saran	37	108
Nadiya	265	633	Champaran	2,288	1,492
Khulna	......	14	Monghyr	8	43
Jessore	2	133	Bhagalpur	5,612	3,182
Murshedabad	6,131	2,499	Purniah	8,066	7,864
Dinajpur	2,735	2,187	Maldah	3,165	2,623
Rajshahye	6,619	2,825	Santál Parganás	3,064	1,964
Rangpur	248	79	Cuttack	......	20
Bogra	167	423	Balasore	......	67
Pabna	200	185	Tributary States	......	50
Darjiling	1,648	603	Hazaribagh	1,775	1,493
Jalpiguri	433	210	Lohardagá	151,810	90,914
Kuch Behar	......	3	Singbhum	1,237	1,506
Dacca	2	......	Manbhum	19	670
Faridpur	11	......	Tributary States	53,342	48,975
Maimansinh	5	60			

Oráon, a section of Ghásis; a sept of Mundas in Chota Nagpur.

Oráon-Khariá, a sub-caste of Khariás in Chota Nagpur.

Oraon-Munda, a sub-tribe of Mundas in Chota Nagpur.

Orea, basket-maker, a sept of Mundas in Chota Nagpur.

Orgonra, hawk, a totemistic sept of Oraons in Chota Nagpur.

Orh, a sub-caste of Nuniás in Behar and of Kaibarttas in Orissa. It deserves notice that Od or Odh is a well-known vagrant caste of earth-workers in the Panjáb, Rájputána, and Western Hindustan. See Mr. Ibbetson's Report on the Census of the Panjáb, p. 308.

Orha, *Ourha*, synonyms for Uriya, a native of Orissa.

Orhchásá or *Mundi-chásá*, a sub-caste of Chásás in Orissa.

Orh-Pán or **Uriya-Pán**, a sub-caste of Páns in Orissa.

Oriá, a sub-caste of Sonárs in Behar.

Or-Máhali, a sub-caste of Máhilis who are basket-makers, the same as Doms.

Osái, a section of the Biyáhut and Kharidáhá Kalwárs in Behar.

Osiár, a *pur* or section of Sákadwipi Brahmans in Behar.

Ostá, **Ostad**, a title of Hajjáms in Behar.

Osti, a *thar* or section of Nepáli Brahmans.

Osui, a sept of Tipperahs in the Hill Tracts of Chittagong.

Origin. **Oswál**, a wealthy and respectable trading caste of Behar and Upper India, who say that their name is derived from Osiá or Osnagar, a town in Márwár. Colonel Tod places them among the mercantile clans of Rájputs, and they themselves, like many other trading castes, claim to be pure Vaisyas. However this may be, no one can fail to observe in them a refined type of features and a comparatively fair complexion—characteristics which can only be accounted for by supposing them to be of tolerably pure Aryan descent. A few of the sections of the caste are shown in Appendix I. They differ entirely from those of the Agarwáls. The Oswáls observe a complex rule of exogamy. A man may not marry into (*a*) his own section, (*b*) his mother's, (*c*) his maternal grandmother's, (*d*) his paternal grandmother's, (*e*) his paternal great-grandmother's. This, though reaching much further than the common rule which bars only a man's own section, does not enable the caste to dispense entirely with the usual system of counting prohibited degrees. There is only one sub-caste, the **Dasá**, which is debarred from intermarriage with Oswáls proper. According to Mr. Ibbetson[1] the word "means 'hybrid,' and is used for members of other castes who have departed from the custom of the caste or whose descent is not pure."

Marriage.

Oswáls marry their daughters as infants, prohibit widow-marriage, and do not recognize divorce. Like the Agarwáls, they also forbid polygamy. Many of the caste are Swetambari Jains, but in spite of this difference of religion they intermarry freely with Hindu Oswáls, most of whom belong to the Vaishnava sect, and thus do not offend Jain prejudice by partaking of animal food. Gaur Brahmans serve the Oswáls as priests, and do not forfeit their high position by doing so. The social rank of Oswáls is about the same as that of Agarwáls, and Brahmans will take water and certain kinds of sweetmeats from their hands.

The Oswáls were not returned separately in the Census Report of 1872. The following statement, however, will show the distribution of the caste in 1881:—

DISTRICT.	1881.	DISTRICT.	1881.
Bardwan	2	Maimansinh	11
Rangpur	106	Patna	2
Pabna	3	Shahabad	41
Bogra	4	Monghyr	23
Darjiling	164	Santál Parganás	3
Jalpigori	3	Lohardagá	7
Kuch Behar	20		

Otoniá, a section of the Biyáhut and Kharidáhá Kalwárs in Behar.

[1] *Panjáb Census Report*, para. 533.

P

Páb, a synonym for Pán.

Pábai ke kisán, a section of the Biyáhut and Kharidáhá Kalwárs in Behar.

Paban, a family name of the Grihasth group of Jugis in Bengal.

Pacháin, a *thar* or sept of Mangars in Darjiling.

Pacháinya, a sub-caste of Doms in Behar.

Pachainyá or *Chauhán*, a sub-caste of Nuniás in Behar.

Páchak, a maker of digestive pills and preserves; also a title applied to a Brahman cook.

Páchál, a title of Kaibarttas.

Pachás-ghariá, a group of the Bar-gohri sub-caste of Khandáits in Chota Nagpur.

Pachautá, a section of Madhesiá Halwáis in Behar.

Pachbhajuá, a section of Bábhans in Behar.

Pacheriá, a section of Goálás in the North-Western Provinces and Behar.

Pachgauti, a section of Rájputs in Behar.

Pachgotya, a section of Bábhans in Behar.

Pachhainya, a sub-caste of Agarwáls.

Pachhainyá Madesiá, a sub-caste of Halwáis in Behar.

Pachhaniá, a sept of Rájputs in Behar.

Pachhián, a sub-caste of Chamárs in Behar.

Pachhimá Bráhman, a synonym for Bábhan.

Pachhwár, a *pur* or section of Sákadwipi Brahmans in Behar.

Pachia, a sept of Gonds in Chota Nagpur.

Pachimá or *Kanaujiá*, a sub-caste of Kumhárs in Manbhum.

Pachi Pargana, a *mul* or section of the Naomuliá or Majraut sub-caste of Goálás in Behar.

Pach Kásyapa, a section of Sonárs in Behar, apparently adopted from the Brahmanical system.

Pachlor, a *mul* or section of the Kanaujiá sub-caste of Sonárs in Behar.

Pachmait, a section of Maghayá Kumhárs in Behar.

Páchnariá, a section of the Biyáhut and Kharidáhá Kalwárs in Behar.

Páchottar, a *mul* or section of the Tinmuliá and Chhamuliá Madhesiá and Bhojpuriá sub-castes of Halwáis in Behar.

Pachpákar, a section of Sonárs in Behar.

Pachpaniá, a sub-caste of Gulguliás in Hazaribagh and Gya.

Pachtar, a section of Madhesiá Kándus in Behar.

Pachtariá, a sept of Rájputs in Behar.

Padahári, a group of the Pandá sub-caste of Utkal Brahmans.

Paderáchhá, a *thar* or sept of Khambus in Darjiling.

Padhán, corruption of Pradhán, a title of Chásás in Orissa.

Padhániá, a section of Goálás in the North-Western Provinces and Behar.

Padmaráj, *Padaráj*, lotus-king; a title of Pods and Jaliyas in Bengal.

Padma-rási, a section of Málos in Eastern Bengal.

Padowar, a sept of Páns in Chota Nagpur.

Págmal, a family name of the Kulin group of Jugis in Bengal.

Págulwár-Barhiám, a *mul* of the Sándil section of Maithil Brahmans in Behar.

Pagulwár-Tarálohi, a *mul* of the Sándil section of Maithil Brahmans in Behar.

Pagulwár-Dhen, a *mul* of the Sándil section of Maithil Brahmans in Behar.

Páhari, a sub-caste of Ghásis in Chota Nagpur; a section of Saraogis in Behar.

Pahāriá-Agariá, a sub-tribe of Agariás in Chota Nagpur.

Paháriá-Asur, a sub-tribe of Asuras in Chota Nagpur.

Paháriá-Binjhiá, a sub-tribe of Binjhiás in Chota Nagpur, so called from living in the hills.

Paharia-Korwa, a sub-tribe of Korwas in Chota Nagpur.

Pahasrait, a section of the Pachainyá sub-caste of Doms in Behar.

Pahlampuri, a section of Kanaujiá Lohárs in Behar.

Pai, a title of Bangaja Káyasths.

Paiharwáre, a section of Madhesiá Halwáis in Behar.

Páik, a foot soldier, a title of Goálás, Khandáits, Chásádhobás, Pods, and Dhobis. In Midnapur and Cuttack the *Páiks* hold small landed tenures and serve as rural police and village watchmen. Ahir Paiks prepare *churá*.

Paikár, a dealer, a wholesale purchaser, a broker. In the silk industry of Bengal the term is applied to the agents who buy silk cocoons from the cultivators and deliver them to the factory.

Paikará, a sub-tribe of Kaurs in Chota Nagpur.

Pailáhá, a section of the Biyáhut and Kharidáhá Kalwárs in Behar.

Pailá-Sudhá, a sub-caste of Sudhás in Orissa.

Pailwár, a sub-caste of Dosádhs; a sept of Rájputs in Behar.

Paindi, a *thar* or sept of Gurungs in Darjiling.

Painju, a *thar* or sept of the Das-Gurung sub-tribe of Gurungs, so named after a place in the frontiers of Nepal and Tibet near the head waters of the Káligangá.

Paitál, a title of Tántis or weavers, who manufacture silk cloth and also mats.

Paithán, a section of Awadhiá Hajjáms in Behar.

Paitl, a title of Támbulis in Behar.

Pákar, a fruit, a totemistic sept of Konrs in Chota Nagpur.

Pakarye-Maheshi, a *mul* of the Kásyap section of Maithil Brahmans in Behar.

Pákari, a *gáin* of the Sábarna *gotra* of Bárendra Brahmans in Bengal.

Pákbasanta, bird, a totemistic section of Bágdis in Bengal.

Pákháli, a synonym for Dhobá.

Pakharpailo, a sub-section of the Bharadwája section of Utkal Brahmans.

Pakhichátá, a section of Telis in Chota Nagpur.

Pákhimárá, 'bird-killer,' a title of Bediyás.

Pakhora, a sept of Mundas in Chota Nagpur.

Pakhrin, a section of Murmis in Darjiling.

Pakhuá, a sept of Korwas in Chota Nagpur.

Pakli, a section of Karan Káyasths in Behar.

Pakonyal, a *thar* or section of Nepáli Brahmans.

Pakra, a section of Goriá or Dahiár Goálás in Behar.

Pákrási, a *gáin* of the Kásyapa *gotra* of Rárhi Brahmans in Bengal.

Pákuri, a title of Goálás in Behar.

Pál, a title of Dakshin-Rárhi and Bangaja Kayasths, Telis, Sadgops, Kumhars, Támbulis, Tántis, Subarnabaniks, and Sutradhars in Bengal. Intermarriage is usually prohibited within the title.

Páladhi, a *gáin* of the Kásyapa *gotra* of Rárhi Brahmans in Bengal.

Palainggritsa, a sept of Maghs in the Hill Tracts of Chittagong.

Palaingtsa, a sept of Maghs in the Hill Tracts of Chittagong.

Palak Pánre, a *mul* or section of the Biáhut sub-caste of Kalwárs in Behar.

Palámi, a *thar* or sept of Gurungs in Darjiling.

Palankhái, a title of Bágdis in Western Bengal.

Palása, a sept of Maghs in the Hill Tracts of Chittagong.

Palásram, a group of the Sundi sub-caste of Sunris in Bengal.

Palaur, a section of Mahesris in Behar.

Páli, a *mul* or section of the Sátmuliá or Kishnaut sub-caste of Goálás, and a section of the Sátmuliá Maghayá sub-caste of Kandus in Behar.

Pálit, a title of Káyasths in Bengal.

Páliwár-Mangrauni, a *mul* of the Bátsya section of Maithil Brahmans in Behar.

Paliwár-Mahesi, a *mul* of the Bátsa section of Maithil Brahmans in Behar.

Paliwár-Dibrá, a *mul* of the Bátsa section of Maithil Brahmans in Behar.

Paliwár-Sakuri, a *mul* of the Bátsa section of Maithil Brahmans in Behar.

Paliwár-Haripur, a *mul* of the Bátsa section of Maithil Brahmans in Behar.

Paliwár-Samaul, a *mul* of the Bátsa section of Maithil Brahmans in Behar.

Paliwár-Kachhrá, a *mul* of the Bátsa section of Maithil Brahmans in Behar.

Paliwár-Phuldáha, a *mul* of the Bátsa section of Maithil Brahmans in Behar.

Paliwár-Mahendra, a *mul* of the Bátsa section of Maithil Brahmans in Behar.

Paliwár-Jarhatyá, a *mul* of the Bátsa section of Maithil Brahmans in Behar.

Paliya, *Poliya*, *Pola*, a Dravidian cultivating caste of Northern Bengal, originally Kochh.

Paliyár-Parghá, a sub-caste of Parghás.

Pálki, a sept of Rájputs in Behar.

Pallab or Ballabh, a sub-caste of Goálás in Bengal.

Pallal, a group of Bárendra Goálás in Bengal.

Palli, a sub-tribe of Savars in Orissa.

Palmohá, a sub-caste of Koiris in Behar.

Palsái, a *gáin* of the Kásyapa *gotra* of Rárhi Brahmans in Bengal.

Pálu, a sept of Limbus in Darjiling.

Palwár, an up-country caste, by profession dealers in *ghi*, boatmen, cultivators, makers of brick-dust; some are also engaged as moharirs in the firms of tradesmen. Suryabansi is their title.

Pamár, a sept of the Suryabansi division of Rájputs in Behar.

Pamia, a tree, a totemistic sept of Mundas in Chota Nagpur.

Pán, *Pánwa*, *Pánr*, *Páb*, *Pánika*, *Chik*, *Chik-Baráik*, *Baráik*, *Ganda*, *Mahato*, *Sáwasi*, *Tánti*, a low weaving, basket-making, and servile caste scattered under various names throughout the north of Orissa and the southern and western parts of Chota Nagpur. "In feature," says Colonel Dalton, "these people are Aryan or Hindu rather "than Kolarian or Dravidian. Their habits are all much alike, "repudiating the Hindu restrictions upon food, but worshipping "Hindu gods and goddesses, and having no peculiar customs which "stamp them as of the other races.[1]" In Singbhum they are said by the same authority to be "domesticated as essential constituents of every Ho village community," and "now almost undistinguishable from the Hos.[2]" In another place they are described as "in all probability remnants of the Aryan colonies that the Hos subjugated.[3]"

Origin.

From these somewhat contradictory utterances it is not quite easy to gather what was Colonel Dalton's final opinion as to the origin of the Páns. In one place he credits them with features of an Aryan or Hindu type, in another he speaks of them as almost undistinguishable from the Hos—the most markedly Negrito-like

[1] Dalton, *Ethnology of Bengal*, p. 325.
[2] Dalton, *op. cit.*, 196, 325.
[3] Dalton, *op.cit.*, p. 185.

representatives of the Dravidian race. The distinction between Kolarian and Dravidian mentioned by him is of course purely linguistic, as has been explained in the introduction to these volumes.

The suggestion that the Páns may be the remnants of Aryan colonies subjugated by the Hos takes us back into prehistoric times, and raises the probably insoluble question: Were there ever Aryan colonies in the region where we find the Páns; and if so, is there anything to show that the Hos subjugated them? To the best of my knowledge the only evidence for the existence of such colonies consists of certain scanty architectural remains buried here and there in the jungles of Chota Nagpur, and of the shadowy tradition that the Singbhum copper mines were worked by the Jains. This seems a slender foundation for the conjecture that the Páns of the present day are the descendants of prehistoric Aryan colonists who were subdued by the Dravidian races of Chota Nagpur and settled down as helots in communities of alien blood, retaining their religion, but parting with that purism in matters of food which has always distinguished the Aryan in comparison with the Dasyu.

Traditions.

Fortunately there is no necessity to enter upon this speculative line of inquiry. Not only do their own traditions claiming descent from the snake throw doubt on the Aryan pedigree which has been made out for them, but the most cursory examination of the exogamous divisions of the Páns affords convincing evidence of their Dravidian origin. The caste has a very numerous set of totems, comprising the tiger,[1] the buffalo, the monkey, the tortoise, the cobra, the mongoose, the owl, the king-crow, the peacock, the centipede, various kinds of deer, the wild fig, the wild plum, and a host of others which I am unable to identify. They have in fact substantially the same set of totems as the other Dravidian tribes of that part of the country, and make use of these totems for regulating marriage in precisely the same way. The totem follows the line of male descent. A man may not marry a woman who has the same totem as himself, but the totems of the bride's ancestors are not taken into account, as is the case in the more advanced forms of exogamy. In addition to the prohibition of marrying among totem kin, we find a beginning of the supplementary system of reckoning prohibited degrees. The formula, however, is curiously incomplete. Instead of mentioning both sets of uncles and aunts and barring seven generations, as is usual, the Páns mention only the paternal uncle and exclude only one generation. They are therefore only a stage removed from the primitive state of things when matrimonial relations are regulated by the simple rule of exogamy, and kinship by both parents has not yet come to be recognized.

Like most castes which are spread over a large area of country, the Páns appear under several different names, the origin of

[1] It is a singular fact that the tiger gives its name to two separate groups. One of these is called *Kulhai*, a word which must have denoted tiger in the original language of the Pans (compare the Santali Kulh); while the other, *Bághail*, is obviously of Hindi origin.

which it is now difficult to trace. Thus in Manbhum they call themselves **Baráik**, 'the great ones,' a title used by the Jadubansi Rájputs, the Binjhias, Rautiás, and Khandáits; in Western Lohardagá and Sargujá we meet them under the name of **Chik** or **Chik Baráik**; in Singbhum they are **Sawási** or **Tánti**, and in the Western Tributary States they are called **Ganda**, a name which suggests the possibility of descent from the Gonds, a tribe which in former times appears to have extended further to the east, and to have occupied a more dominant position than is the case at the present day.

Internal structure.

In Orissa five sub-castes are known:—(1) **Orh-Pán** or **Uriya-Pán**, a semi-Hinduised group supposed to have sprung from a *liaison* between a Pán woman and a member of one of the lower Uriya castes, but now claiming a higher social status than the Páns of the original stock; (2) **Buna-Pán**, including those Páns who weave cloth only; (3) **Betra-Pán** or **Ráj-Pán**, basket-makers and workers in cane, also employed as musicians, syces, and chaukidárs. (4) **Pán-Baistab**, composed of Páns who have become Vaishnavas and who officiate as priests for their own caste. As a general rule it may be laid down that religious differences within the pale of Hinduism do not lead to the formation of endogamous groups. Among Agarwals and Oswals Jains and Hindus intermarry. It is only in Orissa that the Vaishnava members of several castes seem to cut themselves off from their own caste and from the general body of Vaishnavas, and form a new subcaste under a double name denoting the origin of the groups. (5) **Patradiá**, consisting of those Páns who live in the villages of the Kandh tribe, work as weavers and perform for the Kandhs a variety of servile functions. The group seems also to include the descendants of Páns, who sold themselves as slaves, or were sold as Merias or victims to the Kandhs. The precise history of the Patradiá sub-caste is of course obscure, but I see no reason to doubt the possibility of an endogamous group being formed in the manner alleged. There is no question whatever as to the Páns occupying a separate quarter,—a kind of Ghetto,—in the Kandh villages, where they weave the cloth that the tribe requires, and also work as farm-labourers, cultivating land belonging to the Kandhs, and making over to their landlords half the produce as rent. These Páns naturally come to be looked down upon by other Páns who serve Hindus or live in villages of their own and then come to be ranked as a separate sub-caste as regards the slave class alleged to be included in the group. We know that an extensive traffic in children destined for human sacrifice used to go on in the Kandh country, and that the Páns were the agents who "sometimes purchased, but more frequently kidnapped, the children, whom they sold to the Kandhs, and were so debased that they occasionally sold their own offspring, though they knew of course the fate that awaited them." Moreover, apart from the demand for sacrificial purposes, the practice of selling men as agricultural labourers was until a few years ago by no means uncommon in the wilder parts of the Chota Nagpur Division, where labour is scarce and cash payments are almost unknown. Numbers of formal bonds have come before me whereby men sold not only themselves, but their children for a lump sum to enable them to marry, and on several occasions attempts have been made to enforce such contracts in the courts, and to prevent the *Kamiá*, as a slave of this class is called, from emigrating to the tea districts of Assam, or from otherwise evading the obligations he had taken upon himself. There is nothing therefore antecedently improbable in the existence of a slave sub-caste among the Páns.

Marriage.

Pán girls are usually married after they are fully grown up, and the Hindu practice of infant-marriage is confined to a few well-to-do members of the Orh-Pán sub-caste, who have borrowed it from their orthodox neighbours as a token of social respectability. The standard bride-price is said to be Rs. 2 in cash, a maund and a half of husked rice, a goat and two *sáris*—one for the bride and one for her mother-in-law. In Orissa the simple marriage ceremony in vogue is performed by a member of the Pán-Vaishnava sub-caste, who, as has been mentioned above, serve the Páns as priests, and are often spoken of inaccurately as their "Brahmans." In Chota Nagpur, where the organization of the caste is less elaborate than in Orissa, men of the Nágeswar caste not unfrequently serve the Páns as priests; or again any member of the caste with a turn for ceremonial functions may officiate, and the post is usually filled by a Bhakat or devotee. The most essential portions of the ritual are believed to be *sindurdán*, the smearing of vermilion on the bride's forehead, and the parting of her hair and tying together the hands of the bride and bridegroom.

The widows may marry a second time, and it is deemed the proper thing for her to marry her deceased husband's younger brother. She may in no case marry the elder brother. Divorce is permitted, for almost any reason, with the sanction of the caste panchâyat. In Orissa the headman of the caste, styled Dalai or Behera, presides on such occasions, and a *chháda-patra* or bill of divorcement is drawn up. The husband is also required to provide her with food and clothing for six months. Divorced wives are allowed to marry again.

Religion.

The professed religion of the Páns is a sort of bastard Hinduism, varying with the locality in which they happen to be settled. In Orissa and Singbhum they incline to Vaishnavism, and tell a silly story about their descent from Duti, the handmaiden of Rádhá, while in Lohardagá the worship of Mahádeva and Devi Mái is more popular. This veneer of Hinduism, however, has only recently been laid on, and we may discern underneath it plentiful traces of the primitive animism common to all the Dravidian tribes. Man is surrounded by unseen powers—to call them spirits is to define too closely—which need constant service and propitiation, and visit a negligent votary with various kinds of diseases. The Páns seem now to be shuffling off this uncomfortable creed and deserting their ancient gods, while as yet they have not taken vigorously to Hinduism, and they are described by one observer as having very little religion of any kind. Among the minor gods in vogue among them mention may be made of Pauri Pahári or Bar-Pahár, a divinity of unquestionably Dravidian origin, who inhabits the highest hill in the neighbourhood and demands the sacrifice of a he-goat in the month of Phálgun, and occasional offerings of ghi all the year round. The snake is also worshipped as the ancestor of the caste. An attempt was made recently by the Páns of Moharbhanj to induce Brahmans to officiate for them as priests at marriages and funeral ceremonies, but no Brahmans could be persuaded to undertake these offices.

Disposal of the dead.

The southern Páns usually bury their dead in Orissa with the head pointing to the east, while in Singbhum it is turned towards the north. In Lohardagá both cremation and burial are in vogue. Rape seed and water are offered to the deceased and to his ancestors on the eleventh day after death.

Social status and occupation.

The social status of the caste according to Hindu ideas is exceedingly low. They eat beef, pork, and fowls, drink wine, and regard themselves as better than the Hári in virtue of their abstaining from horse flesh. In Lohardagá they eat *kachi*, drink and smoke with Mundas and Oraons. Their original occupation is admitted to be weaving, but many of them have now taken to cultivation. The Buná Páns of Orissa are noted thieves.

The following statement shows the number and distribution of Páns in 1872 and 1881 :—

District.	1872.	1881.	District.	1872.	1881.
Birbhum	......	36	Chittagong	2	......
Midnapur	9,709	......	Tipperah	......	5
24-Parganás	11	......	Cuttack	64,765	78,967
Khulna	......	2	Puri	5,242	6,124
Rangpur	......	57	Balasore	36,546	48,193
Bogra	......	15	Tributary States	112,638	106,567
Dacca	52	......	Lohardagá	12,387	217
Bakarganj	41	41	Mánbhum		536
Maimansinh	94	......	Tributary States	30,463	719

Pán, a sect of Dasnámi Sannyásis; a title of Telis and Aguris in Western Bengal.

Panarha, a title of Chamárs in Behar.

Panchabati, a *gáin* of the Sábarna *gotra* of Bárendra Brahmans in Bengal.

Pancha Drávira, one of the two main divisions of Brahmans dwelling in the south of the peninsula.

Pancha Gauriya, one of the two main divisions of Brahmans dwelling in the valleys of the Ganges and Jumna.

Panchakoti, a sub-caste of Brahmans, Baidyas, and Bauris in Western Bengal.

Panchapándava, "the five Pándus," a title of Kshatriyas.

Panchaparibár, a man with five families, a *pangat* or sect of Bairágis in Bengal.

Panchásiá, a sub-caste of Sunris in Tipperah.

Panchaubhe-Khajuli, a *mul* of the Sábarna section of Maithil Brahmans in Behar.

Panchaubhe-Jhauá, a *mul* of the Sábarna section of Maithil Brahmans in Behar.

Panchaubhe-Birpur, a *mul* of the Sábarna section of Maithil Brahmans in Behar.

Panchaubhe-Barhmaul, a *mul* of the Sábarna section of Maithil Brahmans in Behar.

Panchaubhe-Bhithi, a *mul* of the Sábarna section of Maithil Brahmans in Behar.

Panchaubhe-Dadri, a *mul* of the Sábarna section of Maithil Brahmans in Behar.

Panchaubhe-Kariaun, a *mul* of the Sábarna section of Maithil Brahmans in Behar.

Panchbatiár, a *pur* or section of Sákadwipi Brahmans in Behar.

Panchbhaiá, a functional section of Bábhans and Turis in Behar.

Panchbiha, a section of Tántis and Páns in Chota Nagpur.

Panchhai, a *pur* or section of Sákadwipi Brahmans in Behar.

Panchhiá, a sept of Páns in Chota Nagpur.

Panchjáti, a sub-caste of Khatris in Bengal.

Panchkanthi, a *pur* or section of Sákadwipi Brahmans in Behar.

Panchkuti, a *thar* or sept of Dámis in Darjiling whose chief profession is sewing.

Panchnámá mandar, a title of Nágars in Behar.

Panchobe, a *kul* or section of Bábhans in Behar.

Panchsamáj, a group of the Bárendra Sunris in Eastern Bengal.

Pánchsata Baháttarghar, a sub-caste of Kaibarttas in Central Bengal.

Pánchsau-ghariá, a group of the Bar-gohri sub-caste of Khandáits in Gángpur.

Pánchuriá, an endogamous division of Bárendra Brahmans in Bengal. They are held in the same estimation among Bárendras as Pirális among Rárhis.

Pandá, a sub-caste of Utkal Brahmans in Orissa, who serve in temples resorted to by pilgrims. The term is especially applied to temple priests in Orissa.

Pandar, a tree, a totemistic sept of Mundas in Chota Nagpur.

Pánde, a title of Bábhans; a section of the Sribástab sub-caste of Káyasths in Behar; also a designation of clerks of the Káyasth caste in Chota Nagpur.

Pánde or **Panre**, a title of Gaura, Kanaujiá, and Sáraswat Brahmans in Behar.

Pándiám, a section of Telis in Chota Nagpur.

Pandiár, a *pur* or section of Sákadwipi Brahmans in Behar.

Pandit, (i) a learned man: hence, ironically, a title of Bágdis, Doms, Jugis, and other low castes, who do not employ Brahmans. (ii) A section of the Banpár sub-caste of Gonrhis in Behar. (iii) A title of Kumhárs. (iv) A title of Sáraswat Brahmans in Behar; a *thar* or section of Nepáli Brahmans. (v) A title of priests of Barnasankar castes in Tipperah.

Panditratni, including Kesabi, Gurbhabáni, Máládhári, and Brahmachári, a *mel* or hypergamous sub-group of Rárhi Brahmans in Bengal.

Pandki, a section of Ghásis in Chota Nagpur.

Pándrá, a section of Saraogis in Behar.

Pandrasau-ghariá, a group of the Bar-gohri sub-caste of Khandáits in Gangpur and Bonai.

Pandubi, a sub-caste of Malláhs in Behar.

Panduchone, a sept of Mundas in Chota Nagpur.

Panduki or *Pandki*, dove, a totemistic sept of Mundas and Telis in Chota Nagpur.

Paner, *Paneri*, *Panhári*, a seller of *pán* or betel leaf, a title of Barais and Támbulis in Behar.

Paneru, a *thar* or section of Nepáli Brahmans.

Pang-Karmo, *pang*, 'pasture,' and *karmo*, 'white'—a dweller in high pastures, a sub-sept of the Nah-pá sept of Sherpa Bhotias.

Páni, a section of Utkal or Orissa Brahmans.

Pániá, a dealer in pán or betel-leaf, a title of Barais and Támbulis in Behar.

Pánihá chaur, a section of the Biyáhut and Kharidáhá Kalwárs in Behar.

Pánika, a synonym for Pán.

Paniyár, a section of the Maghayá sub-caste of Kumhárs in Behar.

Pánjá, heap of bricks, a title of Bárendra Brahmans and Kaibarttas in Bengal.

Panjiár, **Panjiárá**, a caste official who keeps up genealogies and registers of marriages in Behar; a section of Maghayá Kumhárs and a *pangat* or section of Dosádhs; a title of Nágars; a section of the Banapár sub-caste of Koiris and Sunris; a title of Goálás and Telis in Behar; a title of Kharwárs in Lohardagá.

Pánjibaddh, a hypergamous group of Maithil Brahmans in Behar.

Pánkharayá, a section of the Biyáhut and Kharidáhá Kalwárs in Behar.

Pankhi, a bird, a totemistic sept of Mundas in Chota Nagpur.

Pánkunda, a *samáj* or local group of the Sándilya *gotra* of Páschátya Baidik Brahmans in Bengal.

Pánpátra, a group of the Daspárá sub-caste of Kumhárs in Pabna.

Panr, a sept of Mundas in Chota Nagpur.

Pánr, a synonym for Pán.

Pánre, a section of Kanaujiá Lohárs and of the Banpár sub-caste of Gonrhis in Behar.

Pánre ke pánre, a section of the Biyáhut and Kharidáhá Kalwárs in Behar.

Pánru, snake, a totemistic sept of Lohárs in Chota Nagpur.

Pansain, a section of the Amashta Káyasths in Behar.

Pánsha, a sub-caste of Támbulis in Behar who deal in betel-leaves.

Pánsili, a sub-caste of Lohárs in Chota Nagpur.

Pán-Tanti, a class of Tántis or weavers in Chota Nagpur who allow widows to marry, eat fowls, drink wine, etc., while the other class, Aswini Tántis, do no such things.

Panthar, a sub-tribe of Limbus in Darjiling.

Pánthi, a *thar* or sept of Mangars in Darjiling. See **Pánti**.

Panthpákar, a section of the Biyáhut and Kharidáhá Kalwárs; a *mul* or section of the Tinmuliá Madhesiá sub-caste of Halwáis and of the Ayodhiábási sub-caste of Sonárs in Behar.

Pánti, *Pánthi*, a title of Telis and Támbulis in Bengal who sell *pán* (piper betel).

Pánwa, a synonym for Pán.

Panwár, a sept of the Surajbansi division of Rájputs in Behar.

Pápriwál, a section of Saraogis in Behar.

Papson, the adopted one, a sept of the Chaibisa sub-tribe of Limbus in Darjiling.

Parabwár, a *dih* or exogamous section of the Gharbáit sub-caste of Amáts in Behar.

Párájuli, a *thar* of the Kaundin *gotra* of Nepáli Brahmans.

Parak, a *dugu* or section of the Kochh-Mandai in Dacca. The name indicates the original habitat of the group, probably a hill or village in Assam, and now-a-days has no bearing upon marriage.

Paramánanda Misra, a *mel* or hypergamous sub-group of Rárhi Brahmans in Bengal.

Parámánik, a title of Tántis, Telis, Nápits, Bágdis, Doms, Bauris, and of Goálás in Bengal; of Kurmis in Behar; a section of Pátnis and of the Chapotá sub-caste of Hindu Joláhas in Behar; a hypergamous division of Telis and Tiyars in Bengal.

Paramánna, a title of Kaibarttas in Bengal.

Parásara, a *gotra* or section of Brahmans; of Tántis in Bengal; an eponymous sept of Rájputs in Behar; a section of Bábhans in Behar, borrowed from the Brahmanical system and superadded to the original exogamous groups (*kuls*) characteristic of the caste; a *gotra* or section of Joláhas in Behar. This designation has been borrowed from the Brahmans in comparatively recent times, and, being used indiscriminately by all Joláhas, does not operate as a bar to intermarriage. In fact, the Behar Joláhas have no working exogamous sections, and reckon prohibited degrees by the formula *mamera*, *chachera*, etc., explained in the article on Bais. A section of Karans in Orissa; of Káyasths, Madhunápits, Támbulis, Sánkhá-ris, and Subarnabaniks in Bengal; an eponymous section of Bhuinmális in Eastern Bengal.

Parásar Dás, a synonym for, and sub-caste of, Kaibarttas.

Páráswar, a *thar* of the Basishth *gotra* of Nepáli Brahmans.

Parayá, a sept of Hos in Singbhum.

Parbate, a section of Kámis in Darjiling.

Parbateh, a *thar* or sept of Mangars in Darjiling.

Parbatti-Kurin, a sub-caste of Gonrhis in Behar, which, though endogamous as regards the other sub-castes of Gonrhis, allows of intermarriage with the Kol sub-caste.

Parbatya, a *thar* or section of Nepáli Brahmans.

Párbbat, a sect of Dasnámi Sannyásis.

Parbe, a *pangat* or section of Dosádhs in Behar.

Pardhán (Pradhán), a title of Khandáit Páiks, Khariás, and Kharwars in Chota Nagpur; a section of Sunris in Behar.

Pardhiel Kokaw, a totemistic sept of Mundas in Chota Nagpur.

Parel, a title of Kaibarttas in Bengal.

Parel, Pondyál, a *thar* of the Atrái *gotra* of Nepáli Brahmans.

Parewá, pigeon, a totemistic sept of Bediás in Chota Nágpur.

Párgáchá, a *thar* or sept of Sunuwárs in Darjiling.

Parganábhusári, a *dih* or local section of the Maghayá sub-caste of Koiris in Behar.

Parghá, *Parighá*, a small cultivating and labouring caste, probably of Dravidian descent, found in Monghyr, Bhágalpur, and the Santál Parganás.

Origin.

The origin of the Parghá is obscure, and their traditions throw no light upon their tribal affinities. One legend of the common miraculous type says that the first Parghá was created from the sweat of one of the Hindu gods in order to be a warrior. Another describes them as Paliyá or 'fugitive' Rájputs, who fled from the north-west before the avenging Parasu Rám, and on the way tore off their Brahmanical threads and threw them into the river Son. The Paliyás of Dinájpur, themselves originally Kochh, have a similar tradition, and so have other Dravidian castes whom fortune has placed in a position to pass themselves off as Rájputs. There would indeed be nothing *primá facie* improbable in the hypothesis that the Parghá may be nothing more than an outlying branch of the Paliyá; but arguments based on similarity of names are apt to prove fallacious, and I know of no definite evidence either for or against such a conjecture. Mr. C. F. Magrath, in his memorandum on the castes of Behar included in the Report of the Census of Bengal for 1872, was disposed to infer from their location that they must be a Hinduised offshoot of the Bhuiyás; but this suggestion again seems to be unsupported by any tangible evidence.

Internal structure.

The Parghás of Bhágalpur are divided into two sub-castes—**Supá-Parghá** and **Paliyár-Parghá**, and into several sections, which are shown in Appendix I. The section-names are of no special interest. Most of them are terms, such as Marar, Raut, and the like, used by many other castes as titles. I am informed, however, on good authority that among the Parghá these groups are exogamous. Prohibited degrees are reckoned by the usual formula calculated to seven generations in the descending line.

Marriage.

Girls of the Parghá caste may be married either as infants or as adults, but the former practice is deemed the more respectable, and no father who could afford to get his daughter married as a child would allow her to reach the age of puberty unmarried. The standard low-caste ritual is followed, in which the smearing of vermilion on the bride's forehead is believed to constitute the valid and binding portion. Polygamy is permitted in the sense that a man may take a second wife if the first is barren. Widows may marry again, and are bound by no restrictions, except those arising from the prohibited degrees, in their choice of a second husband. Divorce is not formally recognized; and when a woman goes wrong, she is simply cast off by her husband. She is not, however, turned out of the caste, and she may marry again.

Religion.

The religion of the Parghás offers no points of special interest, and appears to differ little from that of other Hindus of about the same social standing. Maithil Brahmans serve them as priests, but their rank is low among those of the sacred order. The funeral ceremonies of the caste are for the most part framed on the orthodox model, and are performed on the thirteenth day after death; but in the case of persons who die by a violent death, some Parghás construct a small round heap of dried mud, which is called after the dead and worshipped with offerings of goats and sweetmeats as a minor god.

Occupation and social status.

The bulk of the caste are occupancy or non-occupancy raiyats and landless day-labourers; some are tenure-holders, and a few exceptionally fortunate individuals have risen to the status of zemindars holding petty estates. In point of social standing Parghás rank a little lower than Dhánuks. They observe the standard scruples regarding food, and profess to abstain from spirituous liquors.

The following statement shows the number and distribution of the Parghá caste during 1872 and 1881: –

District.	1872.	1881.
Champaran	4	...
Monghyr	979	444
Bhágalpur	6,466	6,145
Santál Parganás...	1,850	1,161

Parhaiyá, *Parhiá*, a small Dravidian tribe of Palamau, described briefly by Colonel Dalton and at greater length by Mr. L. R. Forbes in his report on the settlement of Palamau. Their sections are totemistic. Colonel Dalton speaks of them as 'the mere remnant of a tribe who, according to their own traditions in this district and the traditions of other races (Lohardagá), once formed an important section of the population.' They worship Dharti Mai, the earth goddess, and Gohet.

Parhápe, a section of Bábhans in Behar.

Parhar, a section of Goálás in the North-Western Provinces and Behar.

Parhatiá, a sub-section of the Bharadwája section of Utkal Brahmans.

Páriál, a *gáin* of the Sábarna *gotra* of Rárhi Brahmans in Bengal.

Parián, a section of Sonárs in Behar.

Pariár, a *pur* or section of Sákadwipi Brahmans in Behar.

Párich, a *mul* of the Kásyapa section of Maithil Brahmans in Behar.

Párichsardár, a head of the *párichs* or exogamous sections into which some castes are divided.

Paridá, a title of Chásás in Orissa.

Parighá, a synonym for Parghá.

Párihál, a *gáin* of the Sándilya *gotra* and a *mel* or hypergamous sub-group of Rárhi Brahmans in Bengal.

Parihar, a section of Kumhárs in Lohardagá.

Parihár, a sept of the Chandrabansi and Suryabansi sub-tribes of Rájputs; a section of the Banpár sub-caste of Gonrhis and of Sunris in Behar.

Pariharbári, a section of the Biyáhut and Kharidáhá Kalwárs in Behar.

Parihasta, a title of Maithil Brahmans in Behar.

Parijai Kavala, a *thar* or section of Nepáli Brahmans.

Paripál, a sub-caste of Sunris in the Santál Parganás and Manbhum.

Parirá, a sub-tribe of Savars in Orissa.

Parjá, a title of Agariás, Asuras, Binjhiás, Oraons, and Khariás in Chota Nagpur.

Párkhari, a sept of Limbus in Darjiling.

Parkhiá, a virtuoso, an examiner of jewels.

Párnágrahi, a group of the Srotriya sub-caste of Utkal Brahmans.

Párni, a title of several fishermen castes—Chandál, Málo, Kochh, etc., who act as ferrymen.

Parrarit, a section of Maghaiyá Kumhárs in Behar.

Parsaiá, a *mul* or section of the Ayodhiabási sub-caste of Sonárs in Behar.

Parsariá, a *kul* or section of Bábhans in Behar.

Parsautiá, a section of the Sátmuliá Maghayá sub-caste of Kándus in Behar.

Parselá, a *mul* or section of the Ghosin sub-caste of Goálás in Behar.

Parsi, Parsu, a bush, a totemistic sept of Mundas in Chota Nagpur.

Parubo, a *rui* or sept of Dejong Lhoris whose ancestor had emigrated from Bhotan.

Parue-Mahendra, a *mul* of the Kásyap section of Maithil Brahmans in Behar.

Párui, a sub-caste of Chandáls in Eastern Bengal; a title of Kaibarttas in Bengal.

Parurá, a section of Awadhiá Hajjáms in Behar.

Parus, a section of the Maghayá sub-caste of Barhis in Behar.

Parwariá, a section of the Dhaprá sub-caste of Doms in Behar.

Paryá, *Parkyá,* "a low Brahman who takes from Hindus alms, such as oil, old black blankets, etc.; all black things on every Saturday, which is accounted a black day." *Fallon, s.v.*

Pásbán, "watchman," a title of Dosádhs in Behar, where members of that caste are largely employed as *chaukidárs* or village watchmen.

Páschátya Baidik, a sub-caste of Baidik Brahmans in Bengal.

Paschimá, a sub-caste of Kámárs in Eastern Bengal.

Paschim-Kabát, west gate, a title of Khandáits in Orissa.

Paschim-Kuliyá, a sub-caste of Sadgops in Bengal.

Paschim-rárhi, a sub-caste of Nápits in Bengal.

Paserea, a class of people who hawk about goods for sale; pedlars.

Pási, a Dravidian caste of Behar, whose original occupation is believed to have been the tapping of the palmyra, date, and other palm trees for their sap. The name Pási is usually derived from *pása*, a noose or cord, which Mr. Nesfield interprets as disclosing that they have only recently emerged from the hunting state. It seems, however, more probable that the name refers, not to the snaring of wild animals, but to the sling or noose used by Pásis in climbing palm trees.

Origin.

Pásis are divided into four sub-castes—**Báydhá, Gaiduha, Kamáni,** and **Tirsuliá.** There are also Mahomedan Pásis, distinguished by the designation **Turk.** The Byádhá sub-caste say that their original occupation was to collect the water-chestnut or singhárá (*Trapa bispinosa*, Roxb.), but now they tap date trees like the other sub-castes. There is only one section, **Kásyapa,** which has been borrowed from the Brahmanical system in comparatively recent times, and has no bearing on the regulation of marriages. Prohibited degrees are reckoned by the standard formula *mamerá, chacherá,* etc., calculated to seven generations in the descending line. Pásis marry their daughters as infants or as adults according to their means, the former practice being deemed the more respectable. The marriage ceremony is of the ordinary low-caste type. It is preceded by *lagan*, when a Brahman stirs up in water two grains of rice, representing the bride and bridegroom, and sprinkles vermilion over them as soon as the grains float into contact with each other. This favourable omen having been observed and a trifling sum paid as bride-price, a date for the marriage is fixed. The binding portion of the ceremony is the smearing of vermilion on the bride's forehead with the bridegroom's left hand. Opinions differ as to the practice of the caste in the matter of polygamy. Some say that a man may have as many wives as he can afford to maintain; others that he can only take a second wife with the consent of his first wife, and for the purpose of obtaining offspring. A widow may marry again by the *sagai* form, but is expected to marry her deceased husband's younger brother if there is one. Failing him, she may marry any one not within the prohibited degrees. Divorce is effected, by the consent

Internal structure.

Marriage.

of the panchâyat, when a woman is convicted of adultery with another member of the caste. Women divorced on these grounds may marry again on paying a fine, which usually takes the form of a feast to the caste panchâyat. Adultery with an outsider admits of no such atonement, and a woman detected in this offence is turned out of the caste, and usually becomes a regular prostitute.

Succession.

In matters of inheritance the caste professes to be guided by the principles of the Mitaksharâ law, which are enforced in cases of dispute by the caste-council (panchâyat). Daughters, however, and daughters' sons, do not inherit so long as any *deádi* relative survives.

Religion.

Most Pásis belong to the Sákta sect of Hindus, and regard Bhagavati as the goddess whom they are chiefly bound to worship. In their religious and ceremonial observances the Kamáni sub-caste alone employ Tirhutiá Brahmans, who are said to incur no social degradation by serving them. The other sub-castes call in degraded (*patit*) Brahmans for marriges only. Such Brahmans rank very low in social reputation, and their employment by the Pásis seems to be a reform introduced at a very recent date, for in all funeral ceremonies and at sacrifices offered to the greater gods whenever the services of a Brahman are not available the worshipper's sister's son (*bhánjá*) performs the functions of the priest. Among the Pásis of Monghyr this ancient custom, which admits of being plausibly interpreted as a survival of female kinship, still prevails in such force that the caste has not yet been convinced of the necessity of engaging Brahmans at all. The guru of the Pásis is usually a Nának-Shahi ascetic.

The minor gods of the Pásis are very numerous. Bandi, Goraiyá, Sokhá, Sambhunáth, Mahámáyá, Rám Thakur, Mián Kabutrá, Naiká Gosáin, Masán, Ostád, and Kartar are the names mentioned in different parts of Behar. Goats, pigeons, cakes, milk, etc., are offered to them six times in the year, the offerings being afterwards eaten by the worshippers. In the month of Jeth the sickle (*hansuli*) used for cutting the palm tree is set up and solemnly worshipped with offerings of flowers and grain.

Social status and occupation.

Pásis rank socially below Tatwás, and on much the same level as Binds and Cháins, except that, unlike these, they nowhere attain to such consideration that Brahmans will take water from their hands. Most of them eat fowls and field-rats, and indulge freely in spirituous and fermented liquors. Many of them have taken to cultivation instead of, or in addition to, their traditional avocation, and hold land as occupancy or non-occupancy raiyats. Others are employed as day-labourers, porters, coolies, or servants to low-caste shop-keepers. In Bengal there is comparatively little demand for their services as palm-tappers, for the owners of toddy and date palms either extract the juice themselves or employ Bhuinmális to do so, and shops for the sale of spirituous liquors are usually owned by Sunris or outcaste Sudras. According to Dr. Wise, the extraction of the juice of the *tál*, or palmyra palm, as well as that of the *khajúr*, or date palm, is a most important operation in

Eastern Bengal, although it has not given rise to the formation of a special caste. The *tál* trees are tapped from March to May; the date palms in the cold season. The juice of the former, or toddy (*tári*), is used in the manufacture of bread, and as an intoxicating liquor by adding sugar and grains of rice. Hindustáni drunkards often add *dhatúrá* to increase its intoxicating properties. In Dacca a *tál* grove is usually rented, and on an average twelve annas a tree are obtained. The quantity of juice extracted varies from an average of five to ten pounds. When fresh this sells for two annas a seer, but if a day old for only one anna. Date palm *tári* is rarely drunk, being popularly believed to cause rheumatism, but is extensively used in preparing sugar. A date palm is generally leased for seven annas a year.

The following statement shows the number and distribution of Pásis in 1872 and 1881:—

District.	1872.	1881.	District.	1872.	1881.
Bardwan	318	254	Tipperah	21	......
Bankura	4	6	Patna	33,299	37,135
Birbhum	6	45	Gya	34,060	39,309
Midnapur	643	213	Shahabad	9,541	11,973
Hughli	813 (Hughli and Howrah)	75	Mosufferpur	19,339 (Mosufferpur and Darbhanga)	11,711
Howrah		446	Darbhanga		12,810
24-Parganás	1,226	648	Saran	4,767	5,562
Nadiya	1	1	Champaran	1,668	2,535
Khulna	......	1	Monghyr	12,362	13,996
Murshedabad	265	56	Bhagalpur	5,258	6,690
Dinajpur	90	47	Purniah	520	2,030
Rajshahye	1	924	Maldah	312	567
Rangpur	194	1	Santál Parganás	1,716	2,206
Bogra	......	2	Cuttack	1,062	631
Pabna	12	2	Puri	1,246	3,074
Darjiling	......	13	Balasore	1,266	63
Jalpigori	4	63	Tributary States	206	164
Kuch Behar	......	3	Hazaribagh	3,404	3,882
Dacca	19	43	Lohardagá	1,103	2,400
Faridpur	25	9	Singbhum	27	36
Bakarganj	66	......	Manbhum	97	57
Maimansinh	25	......	Tributary States	41	172

Pasupatiyá, a worshipper of Siva under the name of Pasupati, 'Lord of Animals.'

Pataiwár, a *dih* or exogamous section of the Gharbáit sub-caste of Amáts in Behar.

Patálang, a sept of Limbus in Darjiling.

Pátalkat, a class of stone-cutters in Gyá whose ancestors are said to have been brought from Jaipur to build the Vishnupad temple. They make stone cups, idols, and toys.

Pátar (*Sans.* Pátra), a title of Kaibarttas and various other castes; a section of the Pargha caste in Behar.

Pátár, a section of Bhojpuriá Halwáis in Behar.

Patá-Ratnauli, a sub-group of Maghaiya Telis in Behar.

Pátári, a *gáin* or sub-section of Saptasati Brahmans in Bengal.

Patariár, a section of Mahilis in Chota Nagpur.

Pátar Máhili, a sub-caste of Máhilis in the south of Manbhum.

Pata Sayá, a sept of Hos in Singbhum.

Patatri, a Sanskrit word for 'bird,' a title of the low class mountebanks called *Harbolás*, who imitate the tunes of birds and make their livelihood thereby.

Pátbandh, a sub-tribe of Kharwárs in Palámau.

Pate, a group of the Srotrya sub-caste of Utkal Brahmans.

Páthá, goat, a title of Bárendra Brahmans in Bengal.

Pathaiár, a *pur* or section of Sákadwipi Brahmans in Behar.

Páthak, a title of Kanaujiá and Sáraswat Brahmans in Behar; of Dákshinátya Baidik Brahmans in Bengal; a section of Utkal or Orissa Brahmans; a title of Bábhans in Behar.

Pathal, a section of Khariás in Chota Nagpur.

Páthar, a headman among tank-diggers in Tipperah; a hypergamous group of Kaibarttas in Bakarganj.

Pather, *Pattar*, *Patra*, a title of Bhuiyas in Western Bengal.

Patheri, a title borne by persons employed in stringing beads and trinkets with silk.

Páthu, a title of Maithil Brahmans in Behar.

Pathuri, a title of Kaibarttas.

Páthuri, dealers in articles of stone.

Pathuriá, a *mul* or section of the Ayodhiabási sub-caste of Sonárs in Behar. A prostitute.

Pati, a section of Utkal or Orissa Brahmans.

Pátia Dás, a synonym for Doai.

Pátial, a mat-making caste of Eastern Bengal who deny that they ever cultivate the soil with their own hands. Some say that they are a branch of the Káyasths, but no tangible evidence in support of this view seems to be available. The mats made by them, coarse, dark-coloured, and thick, are called Motápátí, to distinguish them from the finer kinds made at Silhet, known as Sítalpátí. The only plant cultivated for mat-making is the Mathara (*Maranta dichotoma*), which grows luxuriantly in low, marshy country. It flowers in June and July, and is cut, while still green, about the middle of September, the stems being divided into slips and hung from the rafters, and when required for use steeped in water.

Among the Silhet Pátials women make the mats; consequently the money value of a girl who is a skilful workman is considerable, and a father receives from three to five hundred rupees when his daughter marries. In Dacca, on the other hand, men are the sole workers. Although chiefly found in Dacca, the Pátials are scattered throughout Eastern Bengal, wherever the nature of the soil admits of the cultivation of the Maranta. The caste is eclusively Vaishnava. The headman has the title Pradhán, or Mu'tabar.

Pátikar, *Patuá*, *Sálubi*, an endogamous class of low Mahomedans, who paint pictures illustrating Hindu mythology and hawk them from door to door with songs. Although Pátikars are supposed to be Mahomedans, they, like the Nasyas of Rangpur, are very lax in their religious practices. They worship the rose as a *pir*, and have a great respect for the black kite, which they believe to be a bird of good omen.

Patila-Kshatri, a synonym for Kochh.

Patiyár, a *pur* or section of Sákadwipi Brahmans in Behar.

Pátkumiá, a sub-tribe of Bhumij in Manbhum.

Patmurmurara, a sept of Kharwars in Chota Nagpur.

Patnáik, a title of Kaibarttas in Bengal.

Pátni, *Pátuni*, *Pátauni*, *Dom-Pátni*, a low boating, fishing, basket-making, trading, and cultivating caste of Eastern Bengal, whose dark complexion, short and muscular frame, snub nose, and expanded nostrils stamp them as of Dravidian descent. They are, says Dr. Wise, very reserved and uncommunicative, but there can be little doubt they were originally Doms. In Rangpur, and throughout the valley of the Brahmaputra, they are still designated Dom-Pátni, and in Bengal this is applied to them as a term of abuse. Their other titles are Gangáputra, Ghát-mánjhí, or simply Mánjhí.

Origin.

According to some authorities they are descended from a Rajaka, or washerman, and a woman of the Vaisya caste. Pátnis, however, claim to be the offspring of Mádhava, who ferried Ráma across a river on his way from Ayodhyá to Mithila, and relate how Mádhava, having witnessed the resuscitation of Ahalyá, was afraid to transport the god to the other bank until he had extracted the promise that Ráma would sit on the gunwale with his feet in the water. The simplicity of this ferryman was remarkable. When Ráma landed, Mádhava complained that the colour of the boat had been changed to a hideous yellow, and that he was ruined. The reply was that the ferry-boat had been converted into pure gold, and as a punishment for the Pátni's stupidity Ráma announced that his descendants would always be ferrymen, and that he himself would after death become the ferryman of the Vaitarani, or Hindu Styx.

Another fiction in the history of the Pátnis pertains to the reign of Ballál Sen. The monarch became enamoured of a ferryman's daughter named Padmá-vatí, and married her. At the feast *Pákasparsa*, when the bride cooks and the bridegroom for the first time eats from her hands, the Pátnis, with inborn obtuseness, and to the great grief of the queen, presented themselves at the end of the festival. For this misconduct they were degraded and enrolled among the *Nicha* or low castes.

Internal structure.

The Pátnis are divided into five sub-castes—**Ját-Pátni**, who are agriculturists and small traders, usually keeping shop as *mudis* or grocers; **Ghát-Pátni**, **Balami** or **Ghátwál**, who work as boatmen and take charge of ferries; **Dom-Pátni**, **Machhwá**, or **Nagárchi**, who fish, keep pigs, and get casual employment as musicians at weddings and festivals of various kinds; **Bansphor** and **Dágará**, who hunt, manufacture sieves and baskets of cane, and tie the framework of *kánchá* houses. The last two, from the nature of their pursuits, are more or less nomadic, making only temporary settlements in neat round huts of *sirki*, which they build on the outskirts of villages near rivers. All the sub-castes are endogamous. The Dom-Pátnis are said to admit outsiders into their sub-caste on condition of undergoing a degrading ceremony, one feature of which is that the proselyte must drink water in which the others have washed their feet.

The exogamous sections of the Pátnis shown in Appendix I appear to be for the most part of the territorial type, and do throw no light upon the tribal affinities of the caste. It deserves notice that one of the sections bears the name Tentuliá, which also denotes one of the Bágdi sub-castes. The prohibited degrees are much the same as with other low-caste Hindus.

Marriage.

Pátnis marry their daughters as infants by the standard ceremony. A bride-price (*pan*) is paid by the parents of the bridegroom to those of the bride. Polygamy is recognized in theory, but rarely resorted to in practice. Widows are not allowed to marry again, and divorce is not permitted. Traces of widow-marriage still survive among the Pátnis of Noakháli, but even there the custom is looked upon as disreputable, and seems likely soon to die out.

Religion.

In religious and ceremonial observances Pátnis conform on the whole to the practice of orthodox low-caste Hindus. They employ Patita or Varna Brahmans, who generally assume pompous titles, such as Chakravartti and the like, by way of covering the degradation incurred by serving the Pátni as priests. The Gosains, on the other hand, who act as the gurus of the caste, are received on equal terms by other Brahmans. Most Pátnis belong to the Saiva sect, whose tenets involve little interference with their flesh-eating and spirit-drinking propensities. Only a few Vaishnavas are to be found among them, except in Noakháli, where Vaishnavism is the prevalent faith, and the Pátnis give to it a nominal adherence, which does not, however, prevent them from indulging their tastes in matters of food and drink.

Disposal of the dead.

The dead are burned, and *sráddh* is performed on the thirty-first day after death. Like most Hindu boatmen, they invoke the Pánch Pir on embarking or when overtaken by a storm. The chief religious festival is the Gangá Pujá, and Pátnis never enter upon the work of a ferry without first sacrificing a white kid to the river goddess. They also propitiate Pavan, the Hindu ruler of the winds, with offerings of salt, sugar, milk, and *gánjá*.

Social status.

In point of social status Pátnis rank with Jeliyás, Málos, and the fishing Kaibarttas. Brahmans will not take water from their hands, and they have barbers and washermen of their own caste, as the regular Nápit and Dhobá will not work for them. They consider, however, that they have raised themselves in the social scale by prohibiting the remarriage of widows, and in various small matters they ape the prejudices of the higher castes. For example, they will caulk a boat, but deem it derogatory to paint it, and though they indulge freely in intoxicating drinks, they will never own to doing so.

The following statement shows the number and distribution of the Pátnis in 1872 and 1881 :—

District.	1872.	1881.	District.	1872.	1881.
Bardwan	125	14	Bogra	1,407	1,134
Bankura	......	51	Pabna	3,551	4,782
Birbhum	104	33	Jalpigori	35	60
Midnapur	195	842	Kuch Behar...	......	93
Hughli	} 393	{ 174	Dacca	4,695	4,147
Howrah		115	Faridpur	1,369	3,363
24-Parganás	1,374	592	Bakarganj	4,518	3,836
Nadiya	3,564	3,696	Maimansinh	21,726	26,952
Khulna	......	3,670	Tipperah	6,305	5,814
Jessore	4,369	312	Chittagong	150	51
Murshedabad	2,529	2,066	Noakhali	2,419	2,104
Dinajpur	1,906	1,296	Purniah	......	6
Rajshahye	2,052	1,167	Maldah	1,126	1,066
Rangpur	2,178	1,770	Santál Parganás	......	8
			Maubhum	......	17

Pátni, a section of Saraogis in Behar.

Pátodi, a section of Saraogis in Behar.

Pátoli, a title of Jaliyás, fishermen.

Pátori, a section of Majraut Goálás in Behar.

Páthpariya, synonym for *páthak*, a Brahman who reads epic poems, Puranas, etc., in public.

Patra, *Pathara*, a title of Tántis, cocoon-weavers.

Pátra, *Pátor*, a synonym for Mahápátra, *q.v.*; a title of Kaibarttas, Pods, and Tántis in Bengal; a title of Málos in Eastern Bengal; a sept of Mál Pahářiás; a title of Mahilis, Khandáits, and Telis in Chota Nagpur.

Patradás, a title of the Kurar or Kural sub-caste of Muchis, who work as cobblers and beat drums at festivals.

Patraḍiá, a sub-caste of Páns in Orissa.

Pátrishi (the bean), a totemistic section of Bágdis; a section of Máls in Midnapur and Manbhum.

Pattadár, an honorary title of Káyasths in Bengal.

Páttar, a sub-caste of Tántis in Bengal; a class of fishermen in Eastern Bengal who enclose portions of newly-formed *char* lands at high tide by small weirs made of reed grass (*sirki*), and catch the fish when the water recedes. They do not use nets. Páttars also sell fish purchased from Jeliyás and other fishing castes.

Páttár, a class of Mahomedans who string silver and gold ornaments.

Pátuá, a group of the Karalái sub-caste of Kaibarttas in Noakháli.

Pátua, *Patu*, *Potá*, *Pote*, *Potuá*, *Patudár*, a class of people, both Hindu and Mahomedan, whose profession is painting Hindu deities.

Pátuli, a title of Kaibarttas.

Pátuni, a synonym for Dom in Northern Bengal.

Páturá-Chhutár, a sub-caste of Sutradhars in the Santál Parganás.

Paturiá, a Mahomedan dancing girl.

Páturiá, a sub-caste of Bauris in Western Bengal.

Patwa, *Pathera*, *Patheri*, a maker of fancy silk strings and fringes. Patwas also prepare and hawk about *tasar* silk. They are divided into three endogamous groups—**Gauria**, **Rewar**, and **Tánti**.

Patwár, a generic term in Central Bengal for persons employed in *zamindári* business, possibly a survival from times when there were *patwáris* in Bengal.

Patwári, a sept of Thárus in Behar.

Patwe, a *pangat* or section of Dosádhs in Behar.

Pátyakar, a synonym for Patiál, mat-makers and labourers.

Paulastya, a section of Brahmans.

Paundrakáli, a *gáin* of the Bátsya *gotra* of Bárendra Brahmans in Bengal.

Paunia, certain castes in Behar entitled to receive gifts from the village community, viz. Nauá, Dhobi, Lohár, Kumhár, Churihár, Teli, Chamár, Máli, Barhi, Laheri, Ghási, and Koiri.

Pauriá, a sub-caste of Koiris in Chota Nagpur.

Pauriá or **Pauliá**, a sept of Santáls.

Pauriár, a section of Awadhiá Hajjáms in Behar.

Pawaiyár, a *pur* or section of Sákadwipi Brahmans in Behar.

Páwariá, *Pauriá*, a class of Mahomedan women who dance and sing in male costume at the births of children in the houses of well-to-do people.

Pechá, a bird, a totemistic sept of Bediyas in Chota Nagpur.

Pechgotra, a section of the Ayodhiá sub-caste of Nuniás in Behar.

Pekhá, a sept of Limbus in Darjiling.

Pengi, a *thar* or sept of Gurungs in Darjiling.

Penkál-Máchh, a section of Máls in Midnapur and Manbhum.

Peo, a bird, a totemistic sept of Mundas in Chota Nagpur.

Peroan, pigeon, a totemistic sept of Mundas in Chota Nagpur.

Peshákar, *Peshákárin*, a prostitute.

Petehimba, a sub-sept of the Thekim sept of Limbus in Darjiling.

Pethokote, a sept of Mangars in Darjiling.

Petungbah, a sept of Limbus in Darjiling.

Phádám, a sept of the Agniá sub-tribe of Meches in the Darjiling Terai.

Phágu, a sub-tribe of Yakhas in Darjiling.

Phaguahi, a sept of Gonds in Chota Nagpur.

Phaksa, a sept of Chakmás in the Hill Tracts of Chittagong.

Phalechhuah, a sept of Limbus in Darjiling.

Phansia, a section of Ghásis in Chota Nagpur.

Pharia, a synonym for Kunjrá —vegetable-sellers.

Pharkiet, a section of the Maghayá sub-caste of Kumhárs in Behar.

Pharphar, a *gáin* or sub-section of Saptasati Brahmans in Bengal.

Pharsádhenti, a sept of Kaurs in Chota Nagpur.

Phawahong, the name of a village, a sept of the Yangorup sub-tribe of Limbus in Darjiling.

Phedáb or **Bhuiphuta**, a sub-tribe of Limbus in Darjiling.

Phe-dang-sirri, a sept of Chakmás in the Hill Tracts of Chittagong.

Phedungsa, a sept of Chakmás in the Hill Tracts of Chittagong.

Phehim, the singer, a sept of the Phedáb sub-tribe of Limbus in Darjiling.

Phejom, the *kukri*-bearer, including (*a*) Nembong, (*b*) Sardakpeapi, a sept of the Pánthar sub-tribe of Limbus in Darjiling.

Phekuram, a special ancestral deity of the Bahiot sub-caste of Amáts in Behar.

Phema, a sept of Chakmás in the Hill Tracts of Chittagong.

Phenduá, the hammerer of iron, a sept of the Tambrkhola sub-tribe of Limbus in Darjiling. This *thar* were formerly the blacksmiths of the tribe.

Phensa-pá, a *rui* or sept of Dejong Lhoris who are descendents of emigrants from Bhotan and Nepal.

Pheodan, the water-carrier, a sept of the Pánthar sub-tribe of Limbus in Darjiling.

Pherká, a title of Bágdis in Western Bengal.

Phetiá, a sept of Rájputs in Behar.

Pheyak, a sept of Limbus in Darjiling.

Phirti, a group of the Karalái sub-caste of Kaibarttas in Noakháli.

Phlumáchhá, a *thar* or sept of Khambus in Darjiling.

Pho-omphu, the hangman, a sept of the Phedáb sub-tribe of Limbus in Darjiling.

Photádár, a title of the Ariár sub-caste of Bais Baniyás and a *pangat* or section of Dosádhs in Behar.

Photro, a sept of the Charkhola sub-tribe of Limbus in Darjiling.

Phrangroatsa, a sept of Maghs in the Hill Tracts of Chittagong.

Phul, a group of the Bárendra sub-caste of Sunris in Eastern Bengal; flower, a sept of Chiks in Chota Nagpur.

Phulaus, a sub-caste of Nágars in Behar.

Phulehli, a *thar* or sept of Khambus in Darjiling.

Phulgot, a totemistic section of Nuniás in Behar.

Phulhári, a title of Háris in Eastern Bengal who are not sweepers, but are engaged as chaukidárs and gardeners.

Phuli, a *mul* or section of the Chhamuliá Madhesiá sub-caste of Halwáis in Behar.

Phuliá, a *mel* or hypergamous sub-group of Rárhi Brahmans in Bengal.

Phulkátá-Máli, a sub-caste of Mális in Bengal.

Phulmáli, a synonym for Máli.

Phulnápit, a sub-caste of Nápits in Western Bengal who have given up their profession of shaving and taken to cultivation.

Phulwar, a sept of Goálás in Chota Nagpur.

Phungthag, he who stole to order; a sept of the Phedáb sub-tribe of Limbus in Darjiling.

Phungun, a sept of Chiks in Chota Nagpur.

Phunknali, a sub-section of the Bharadwája section of Utkal Brahmans.

Phunvál, a *thar* or section of Nepáli Brahmans.

Phuowali, a mendicant caste of the Darjiling Terai regarding which little is known.

Phurkeli, a *thar* or sept of Khambus in Darjiling.

Phurti, a sept of Mundas in Chota Nagpur.

Phuti, rainbow, a totemistic sept of Mundas in Chota Nagpur.

Phutka, vegetable, a totemistic sept of Lohárs in Chota Nagpur.

Phyagpa, the knife-grinder, a sept of the Pánthar sub-tribe of Limbus in Darjiling.

Phyuyáli, a *thar* or sept of Mangars in Darjiling.

Pichagma, the son of the monkey, a sept of the Chaibisa sub-tribe of Limbus in Darjiling. This *thar* is said to have formerly worshipped the monkey.

Pikord, a bird, a totemistic sept of Mundas in Chota Nagpur.

Pil, a title of Dakshin Rárhi and Bangaja Káyasths.

Pilá, a totemistic sept of the Bhumij tribe in Chota Nagpur.

Pilchwár, a section of Bábhans in Behar.

Pilich, a section of the Sát-muliá Maghayá sub-caste of Kándus in Behar.

Piliksawár, a section of Báb-hans in Behar.

Pilkhait, a section of Báb-hans in Behar.

Pilua, a section of Mahilis in Chota Nagpur.

Pindwál, a section of Koránch Halwáis in Behar.

Pinguá, a sept of Hos in Singbhum.

Pipar, a fruit, a sept of Telis in Chota Nagpur.

Pipariá, a *mul* or section of the Kanaujiá sub-caste of Sonárs in Behar.

Pipi, a title of Bangaja Káyasths.

Pippalái, a *gáin* of the Bátsya *gotra* of Rárhi Brahmans in Bengal.

Pippali, a *gáin* of the Bharadwája *gotra* of Bárendra Brahmans in Bengal.

Pipret, a *mul* or section of the Naomuliá or Majraut sub-caste of Goálás in Behar.

Pipriáti, a section of Barhis in Behar.

Pirabhanga, a sept of Chakmás in the Hill Tracts of Chittagong.

Piráli, an endogamous division of the Rárhi Brahmans in Bengal. The popular story of the origin of this group is that their ancestor was degraded for having accidentally smelled food which had been prepared in the house of a Mahomedan. They are held in the same estimation among Rárhis as Pánchuriás among Bárendras.

Piruwal, a sub-caste of Khatris in Bengal.

Pishle, a sub-caste of Telis in Bengal.

Pitamundi, a *gáin* of the Kásyapa *gotra* of Rárhi Brahmans in Bengal.

Pithákoteh, a *thar* or sept of Mangars in Darjiling.

Pithári, a *gáin* or sub-section of Saptasati Brahmans in Bengal.

Pithoár, a section of Goráits in Chota Nagpur.

Pitraihá, a *mul* or section of the Banodhiá sub-caste of Kalwárs in Behar.

Pitule-Kámár, a sub-caste of Kámárs in Midnapur.

Plembochhá, a *thar* or sept of Khambus in Darjiling.

Poa, a sept of Chakmás in the Hill Tracts of Chittagong.

Pod, *Padmaráj*, *Chási*, a fishing, cultivating, landholding, and trading caste of Lower Bengal, found in large numbers in the 24-Parganás. Their origin is uncertain. Babu Bankim Chandra Chatterji, quoted at page 188 of the Census Report of 1872, notices their "marked approach to the Turanian and aboriginal type" of features, and seeks to identify them with the Pundra mentioned in the Mahábhárata as one of the five chief races of Eastern India between Magadha and the sea. The educated members of the caste claim for it a mixed descent from a Káyasth father and a Nápit mother. Others tell a highly indelicate story regarding the miraculous birth of the first Pod from Revati, the wife of Balarám.

Origin.

The Pods are divided into four sub-castes—**Bágande, Banglá, Khottá,** or **Mauná** and **Uraiya.** The first two are found chiefly in the 24-Parganás and Jessore, the third in Murshedabad and Maldah, and the fourth in Midnapur and Balasore. All these groups are endogamous. Each is subdivided into *gotras* or sections borrowed from the Brahmanical system. The prohibited degrees are the same as among the higher castes.

Internal structure.

Pods marry their daughters between the ages of five and nine years, forbid widow-marriage, and do not recognize divorce. The morality of Pod widows, however, is alleged to be singularly lax, and the caste is tolerant

Marriage.

towards sexual indiscretions, so that the illegitimate children of widows and of divorced women are received into the community. Their marriage is of the orthodox type, the ceremony of *Kusandika* alone being omitted. *Sampradán*, or the offering of the bride to the bridegroom and his acceptance of the gift, forms the binding portion of the ritual.

Religion.

In addition to the well-known sects of Saiva, Sákta, and Vaishnava, we find among the Pods a large number of Sauras and Gánapatyas, sects very sparingly represented among the higher classes of Hindus in Bengal. The caste employ as their priests Rárhi Brahmans, who are held to be so far degraded by serving them that high class Brahmans will not take food or water from their hands. The gurus of the Pods are Rárhi Gosáins, but these, I understand, have in no way forfeited their position among Brahmans, though in some cases they eat and drink in Pods' houses. An instance of this was brought to my notice recently as evidence of the growth of the spirit of religious toleration among the educated Hindus of Calcutta and its suburbs.

Social status.

The social status of Pods is decidedly low. They will eat sweetmeats, drink and smoke with the fishing sub-castes of Bágdis; and these are ordinarily deemed to be nearly their equals in rank. Brahmans and members of the Nava Sákha group will not take water from them; and the Sutradhar and Kapáli, while they will eat sweetmeats, drink and smoke in company with a Pod, will not use the same pipe or drink from the same *lotá*. In matters of diet their practice is orthodox on all points except the indulgence in strong drink. They will eat the leavings of Brahmans. Vaishnava Pods abstain from all kinds of flesh. The great majority of the caste are engaged in agriculture, as tenure-holders, and occupancy or non-occupancy raiyats. A few have risen to be zamindárs, and some at the other end of the scale work as nomadic cultivators on freshly-cleared land in the Sundarbans, changing their location every two or three years according to the fortune of their crops. Many Pods have taken to trade, and goldsmiths, blacksmiths, tinsmiths, carpenters, thatchers, etc., are found among them.

Occupation.

The following statement shows the number and distribution of Pods in Bengal in 1872 and 1881:—

District.	1872.	1881.	District.	1872.	1881.
Bardwan	216	43	Dinajpur	24	71
Bankura	3	196	Rajshahye	12	41
Birbhum	68	30	Rangpur	1	67
Midnapur	4	10,530	Bogra	4	50
Hughli	} 16,727	1,968	Pabna	......	9
Howrah		14,138	Dacca	101	......
24-Parganas	249,075	217,236	Faridpur	73	
Nadiya	4,250	2,220	Bakarganj	314	......
Khulna	...	66,790	Maimansinh	65	18
Jessore	21,562	7,047	Tipperah	35	53
Murshedabad	86	8,137	Maldah	66	8,216

Poddár, a title of the Ariár sub-caste of Bais Baniyás and of Sonárs in Behar; of Sunris and of Subarnabaniks in Bengal who are money-lenders and dealers in gold and silver ornaments.

Podoro, a sept of Hos in Singbhum.

Podret, a section of Maghayá Kumhárs in Behar.

Pohobait, a section of the Pachainyá sub-caste of Doms in Behar.

Poiá, a sept of Gonds in Chota Nagpur.

Poiti, a sept of Gonds in Chota Nagpur.

Pokharmiá, a section of Lohárs in Behar.

Pokhrel, a section of Kámis in Darjiling.

Poma, a sept of Chakmás in the Hill Tracts of Chittagong.

Pomo, the large family, a sept of the Ahtharai sub-tribe of Limbus in Darjiling.

Pondha, the wanderer, a sept of the Yangorup sub-tribe of Limbus in Darjiling.

Pongwar, a *thar* or sept of Mangars in Darjiling.

Pongyangu, he who carries his goods on his back, a sept of the Phedáb sub-tribe of Limbus in Darjiling.

Ponkrishi (jungle cock), a totemistic section of Bágdis in Western Bengal

Pon-po, a *rui* or sept of the Bedtshan-gye sub-tribe of Dejong Lhoris or Bhotias of the south. This sept is composed of the five ollowing sub-septs:—Chhungpá, Lhasung, Nah-dik, Nambon, and Yo-chang.

Ponthák, a sept of Limbus in Darjiling.

Porári, a *gáin* of the Kásyapa *gotra* of Rárhi Brahmans in Bengal.

Poriál, a title of Telis.

Porri, a sept of Gonds in Chota Nagpur.

Portel, a section of Kámis in Darjiling.

Porti, crocodile, a totemistic sept of Mundas in Chota Nagpur.

Potá, a section of Kámárs in Singbhum and the Santál Parganás.

Potadár, *Poddar* (properly Fotadár, from Persian *fotáh*, a bag or purse), a cash-keeper, a money-changer; an officer in Government treasuries who examines and weighs coins.

Prachanda, furious, a title of Bárendra Brahmans in Bengal.

Práchir, a section of Pátnis in Eastern Bengal.

Pradhán, (i) a title of Kaibarttas, Suklis, Sunris, and others in Bengal; a title of Kotáls and Binjhiás; of Khandáits in Chota Nagpur; Pátnis, Chamárs, and Santáls; (ii) a village headman in Singbhum; (iii) a section of Sunris in Behar; (iv) a hypergamous division of Tiyars.

Praharáj, a title of Khandáits in Orissa.

Prajápati, a synonym for Kumhár.

Prámánik, a group of the Daspárá sub-caste of Kumhárs in Pabna. See **Paramánik**.

Pramodni, a *mel* or hypergamous sub-group of Rárhi Brahmans in Bengal.

Prási, a section of the Biyáhut and Kharidáhá Kalwárs in Behar.

Prasidha, an eponymous sept of Rájputs in Behar.

Pratihár, including Bangrám and Gográm, a hypergamous group of the Paschim Kuliyá Sadgops in Western Bengal.

Pratilomaj, see **Anulomaj**.

Prayágwál, a priestly class of Brahmans in Prayág or Allahabad.

Prohá-kerauta, a section of Sonárs in Behar.

Puár, a sept of Rájputs in Behar.

Pubiá, Jaiá, a sub-caste of Utkal Brahmans in Orissa.

Puhániá, a section of Goálás in the North-Western Provinces and Behar.

Puhár, a title of Chásás in Orissa.

Puhoá, a sub-caste of Goálás in Behar.

Puilá, a title of Bágdis in Western Bengal.

Puin, a title of Bangaja Káyasths.

Pujáha, a title of the Naiyá caste in Behar, which appears to have reference to their original functions as priests of the aboriginal or forest deities.

Pujhor, priests, a sept of Mál Pahárias in the Santál Parganás.

Puktebu, a sept of the Yangorup sub-tribe of Limbus in Darjiling.

Pulámi, a *thar* or sept of Mangars in Darjiling.

Pulauns, a sub-caste of Nágars in Behar.

Pumá, a sept of the Tungjainya sub-tribe of Chakmás in the Hill Tracts of Chittagong.

Pun, a *thar* or sept of Mangars in Darjiling.

Pundárika, the white lotus (*Nelumbium speciosum*), a title of Pods, Kaibarttas, and occasionally of Jáliyas.

Pundarikáksha, *Pundari*, *Punra*, lotus-eyed; a name of Vishnu ; a title of Pods who rear cocoons and cultivate chillies, ginger, etc.

Pundárk, a *pur* or section of Sákadwipi Brahmans in Behar.

Pundul, a sept of Rájputs in Behar.

Pung, a *thar* or sept of Mangars in Darjiling.

Pungi, a *thar* or sept of the Das-Gurung sub-tribe of Gurungs in Darjiling, so called after the name of a place in Nepal.

Pungsika, a *gáin* of the Sábarna *gotra* of Rárhi Brahmans in Bengal.

Punrakhiá, a *pur* or section of Şákadwipi Brahmans in Behar.

Punrapaita, a title of Punras who rear silk-worms only.

Punriár, a section of Kurmis in Chota Nagpur and Orissa.

Pur, a section of Goálás in Behar.

Pura, a title of Maithil Brahmans in Behar.

Purá, a hypergamous group of Karans in Orissa.

Purabi, an endogamous division of Nepáli Brahmans.

Puráin, a section of Awadhiá Hajjáms in Behar.

Puraliá, a section of Kámárs in Singbhum and the Santál Parganás.

Puran, a section of Bháts who read out verses in *sabhás* or caste assemblies; a sept of Tipperahs in the Hill Tracts of Chittagong; a synonym for Bhuiyá in Moharbhanj.

Purandari, a sub-caste of Tántis in Bengal.

Purandwár, a sub-caste of Háris in Bengal.

Purásaini, a *thar* or section of Nepáli Brahmans.

Purbba, a *gáin* of the Bátsya *gotra* of Rárhi Brahmans in Bengal.

Purbba Banga, a *samáj* or endogamous group of the Páschátya Baidik Brahmans in Eastern Bengal.

Purbbakul, a sub-caste of Tántis in Bengal.

Purbba Kuliyá, a sub-caste of Sadgops in Bengal.

Purbbastháli, a *samáj* or endogamous group of the Páschátya Baidik Brahmans in Nuddia.

Purbe, a section of Sunris and of the Chapotá sub-caste of Hindu Joláhas in Behar.

Purbiá, a sub-caste of Sunris in Behar.

Purbiya, Purbiyá, a sub-caste of Agarwáls, a sub-tribe of Thárus in Nepal.

Purbiyá Khatri, the distinctive designation of the Bengal branch of the Khatri caste.

Purbiyá Madesiá, a sub-caste of Halwáis in Behar.

Puri, a sect of Dasnami Sannyásis.

Purthi, a sept of Hos in Singbhum.

Purti, a section of Khariás; a sept of Lohárs and Páns in Chota Nagpur.

Purubansi, a sept of Rájputs in Behar.

Purukhinu Naráin, a section of the Kamár sub-caste of Dosádhs in Behar.

Pusá, a section of the Pachainyá sub-caste of Doms in Behar.

Pusadih, a section of the Tirhutiya sub-caste of Doms in Behar.

Pusáitá, a section of the Dhaprá sub-caste of Doms in Behar.

Pusál, a *thar* or sept of Mangars in Darjiling.

Pusetá, a section of the Pachainyá sub-caste of Doms in Behar.

Pushali, Pushilál, a *gáin* of the Kásyapa *gotra* of Rárhi Brahmans in Bengal.

Pushána, a *gáin* of the Sándilya *gotra* of Bárendra Brahmans in Bengal.

Pusra, fruit of kusum tree, a totemistic sept of Oraons in Chota Nagpur.

Pusway, a section of Binjhiás in Chota Nagpur.

Putam, dove, a totemistic sept of Mundas in Chota Nagpur.

Puti, a *gáin* of the Bharadwája *gotra* of Bárendra Brahmans in Bengal.

Putitunda, a *gáin* of the Bátsya *gotra* of Rárhi Brahmans in Bengal.

Putri, a tree, a totemistic sept of Oraons in Chota Nagpur.

Pu-tsho-bo, a *rui* or sept of the Bedtshau-gye sub-tribe of Dejong Lhoris or Bhotias of the south, whose ancestor was a mixed progeny of Lepcha mother and Tibetan father.

Pu-tsibo, a *rui* or sept of Dejong Lohris, the members of which are the descendants of emigrants from Bhotan and Nepal.

Putuli, a synonym for Gandhabanik.

Puyi-rási, a section of Málos in Eastern Bengal.

Pyakarel or **Pokharyál**, a *thar* of the Gargya *gotra* of Nepáli Brahmans.

Pyo-chhembo, a *rui* or sept of Dejong Lohris, the members of which are the descendants of emigrants from Bhotan and Nepal.

R

Rábad, a section of Goálás in the North-Western Provinces and Behar.

Rabchháli, a *thar* or sept of Khambus in Darjiling.

Rabi-Dás, a synonym for Chamár.

Rachhuáni, a sept of Rájputs in Behar.

Rádháli, a worshipper of Rádhá, the favourite mistress of Krishna; a title of Vaishnavas.

Radhar, a sept of Kharwars in Chota Nagpur.

Rafugar, a professional shawl-mender; generally a Mahomedan.

Ràghab, a section of the Mahmudábáz sub-caste of Nápits in Eastern Bengal.

Rághab Ghosháli, a *mel* or hypergamous sub-group of Rárhi Brahmans in Bengal.

Rághopurdih, a *mul* or section of the Naomuliá or Majraut sub-caste of Goálás in Behar.

Raghu, a family of the Kulin group of Jugis in Bengal.

Raghubansi, a sub-tribe and a sept of Rájputs in Behar; a bastard caste in Chota Nagpur, like Rautia, who act as servants and are said to have originated since the time of Maharaja Raghunath Shahi.

Raghunáthiá, a sub-caste of Utkal Brahmans in Orissa.

Raghunáthpurdiár, a *mul* or section of the Naomuliá or Majraut sub-caste of Goálás in Behar.

Ráhá, a title of Dakshin-Rárhi and Bangaja Káyasths.

Rahapál, a section of Kámis; a *thar* or sept of Mangars in Darjiling.

Rahdauriár, a *pur* or section of Sákadwipi Brahmans in Behar.

Rahpáchá, a *thar* or sept of Sunuwárs in Darjiling.

Rahtaur, a sept of the Surajbansi division of Rájputs in Behar.

Ráhu, a title of Dosadhs in Behar who worship the demon Ráhu.

Ráhul, a *thar* or sept of the Das-Gurung sub-tribe of Gurungs in Darjiling. The name is said to have arisen in consequence of Rahul, the ancestor of the *thar*, showing courage worthy of the demon Ráhu in certain tribal feuds.

Ráhut, a title of Dakshin-Rárhi and Bangaja Káyasths.

Rái, a *gáin* of the Bharadwája *gotra* of Bárendra Brahmans in Bengal; a title of Brahmans; a section of the Sribástab sub-caste of Káyasths in Behar; an honorary title of Káyasths and Subarnabaniks in Bengal; a title of Rájputs, Bábhans, Dhánuks, and Goálás in Behar; of Jugis, Baitis, and Sunris in Bengal; a section of Khambus; a hypergamous division of the Maghaya sub-caste of Barhis; a title of Chásádhobás, Kapális, Korás; a title and a sept of Thárus; an honorific title common among many other castes.

Raibhuiya Ghatwal, a well-to-do class of Bhuiyas, Rai being their title; some also call themselves Singh.

Raikwár, a sept of Rájputs in Behar.

Raini, a *kul* or section of Bábhans in Behar.

Ráipur, a section of Pátnis in Bengal.

Ráj, a title of Mayarás in Bengal.

Ráj, *Rájmistri*, *Rájmajur*, a mason or bricklayer, an occupation mostly followed by Kaibarttas, Chásádhobas, Bágdis, Chandáls, and Mahomedans

Raja, a bird, a totemistic sept of Mundas in Chota Nagpur.

Rája, a family title of Kashta Baidyas and of Dakshin-Rárhi and Bangaja Káyasths.

Rájá, a section of the Magahiyá sub-caste of Doms in Behar.

Rajabin, a *thar* or sept of Khambus in Darjiling.

Rájáiswar, a section of the Kamár sub-caste of Dosádhs in Behar.

Rajak, a synonym for Dhobá in Bengal.

Rajandipur, a section of the Ariár sub-caste of Bais Baniyás in Behar.

Rájápáker, a *mul* or section of the Sátmuliá or Kishnaut sub-caste of Goálás and of the Kanaujiá sub-caste of Sonars in Behar.

Rájápákur, a section of Majraut Goálás in Behar.

Rajápati-Sobhni, a *mul* or section of the Naomuliá or Majraut sub-caste of Goálás in Behar.

Rajata-kausik, a section of the Uttar-Bárendra Brahmans in Bengal.

Rajbandh, a section of Ghásis in Chota Nagpur.

Rájbangsi, a Dravidian caste of Northern Bengal, originally Kochh, but now claiming to be an outlying branch of Kshatriyas.

Rájbansi, a synonym for Kochh, Rajwár, and for Tiyar; a sub-caste of Tiors in Behar who are said to wear the *janeo* or sacred thread; a sub-caste of Mauliks; a title of Bágdis in Western Bengal.

Rajbansi or *Rájá-Mál*, a sub-caste of Máls in Western Bengal.

Rájbansiá, a sept of Páns in Chota Nagpur.

Rájbhar, an up-country caste engaged in Bengal as gardeners and cowherds. They claim to be a distinct caste from the Bhars, with whom they do not eat or intermarry. In the North-Western Provinces they are engaged purely in agricultural pursuits, and rank socially with the Kurmis and Koiris.

Rajbhat, a sub-caste of Bháts, who are the hereditary bards and genealogists of the higher classes, and are said to wear the sacred thread.

Rájdom, a sub-caste of Doms who affect Brahmanical customs.

Rajgiri, Rájgrihi, a section of the Sátmuliá Maghaya sub-caste of Kándus and of the Kanaujiá sub-caste of Sonars in Behar

Raj Gond, a sub-tribe of Gonds in Chota Nagpur who affect Hindu customs.

Rájhans, wild goose, a totemistic sept of Goálás in Chota Nagpur.

Rájhasia, swan, a totemistic sept of Páns in Chota Nagpur.

Rájib, a section of the Mahmudábáz sub-caste of Nápits in Eastern Bengal.

Ráj-Kástha, see **Kástha.**

Rájkuar, a sept of Rájputs in Behar.

Rájkumát, a sept of Rájputs in Behar.

Rájkurin, a section of Maghayá Dhobis in Behar.

Rájmahaliá, a sub-caste of Kumhárs in Dacca.

Rájmor, a section of Kurmis in Chota Nagpur and Orissa.

Rájpur, a *samáj* or local group of the Dákshinátya Baidik Brahmans in the 24-Parganás.

Rajput, a section of Ghásis; a sept of Mundas in Chota Nagpur.

Rájput, *Kshatriya*, *Chhatri*, *Chhettri*, the fighting and landholding caste of Northern India, who claim to be the modern representatives of the Kshatriyas of classical tradition, and who are in many cases entitled to appeal to their markedly Aryan cast of feature in support of their claim. Besides these Aryan Rájputs, the large group designated indifferently by the name Rájput or Chhatri includes many families of doubtful or non-Aryan descent, whose pretensions to membership of the twice-born warrior caste rest solely upon the circumstances that they have, or are supposed to have, some sort of proprietary dominion over land. It would be out of place to attempt to give here an exhaustive account of the Rájput community as it exists in Ráj-putana and North-Western India. The peculiar characteristics of the pure-blooded Rájput have been described by several competent observers. Among the most conspicuous are a pride of blood, which delights in endless genealogies and ranks every one according to descent; a strong passion for field sports, combined with an equally pronounced distaste for peaceful and prosaic means of earning a livelihood; and an exaggerated idea of the saving virtues of ceremonial purity and precision in the matter of food and drink.

Origin.

The same characteristics are doubtless to some extent traceable among the Rájputs of the Lower Provinces; but the pressure of different conditions of life has tended to obliterate many distinctions, and the eastern Rájput is far less peculiar than the Western. It is commonly said that the Rájput can only be studied in his original surroundings, and that an account of the tribe as it exists in Bengal must necessarily be valueless and misleading. There is much truth in this view: at the same time it may be observed that outlying branches of a tribe which have wandered far away from the original habitat often preserve survivals of usages which have died out among the original stock or have been overlaid and obscured so as to be no longer traceable. Again, if there is reason to believe, as several good observers think there is, that the Rájput tribe itself has been recruited now and again by irregular methods from men of alien lineage, may there not be a better chance of observing the working of this process in distant districts than in Rájputáná itself, where all departures from the strict theory of descent are speedily condoned and hidden by the operation of fiction?

In Chota Nagpur, for example, the methods by which many of the chief landholding families have transformed themselves into Rájputs may be traced beyond question at the present day. The Maharajas of Chutia Nagpur Proper, that is of the elevated table land forming the southern portion of the Lohardagá district, call themselves Nágbansi, and claim descent from a mysterious child found in the jungle, concerning whose origin a singular story is told. The myth of the birth of the founder of the Chutia Nagpur house from a Brahman mother and a snake father, with the picturesque incidents which Colonel Dalton relates, seems to be nothing more than an ingenious invention contrived to mask the fact that a family of Munda chieftains had assumed the rank of Rájput. To this day ladies of Nágbansi families will not employ a Munda to carry their palkis, because they say he is their elder brother-in-law (*bhaisur*), and they veil their faces before him as they would before an elder brother-in-law. The Pachete family call themselves Gobansi Rájputs and tell a strange story, analogous to the Nágbansi myth, of the birth of their progenitor from a cow in the jungle near Pachete. The zamindars of Barabhum, Patkum, Nawagarh and Katiar in Manbhum all claim to be Rájputs, and boldly affiliate themselves to the Raksel and Chandel clans. Some minor landholders of the Bhumij tribe who hold ghatwali tenures in Barabhum have followed the example of the zamindar of that estate, and call themselves Rájputs, though in some cases it can be shown by documentary evidence that their ancestors in the last generation called themselves Bhumij.

Traditions.

The traditions of the tribe go back to the dateless antiquity in which so many royal pedigrees seek refuge. Accordnig to the usually accepted version there are two branches of Rájputs—the Surajbansi or Solar Race and the Chandrabansi or Lunar Race. To these must be added the four Agnikulas or Fire Tribes. Surajbansi Rájputs claim descent from Ikshwáku, son of the Manu Vaivaswat, who was the son of Vivaswat, the Sun. Ikshwáku, it is said, was born from the nostril of the Manu as he happened to sneeze. The elder branch of the Solar race sprang from Ikshwáku's eldest son Vikukshi, and reigned in Ayodhyá at the beginning of the second or Tretá Yuga. Another son named Nimi founded the dynasty of Mithilá. The Lunar race affect to be descended from the moon, to whom they trace through Ayus, Pururavas and Budha or Mercury, the son of Soma by Rohini or by Tárá, wife of Brihaspati. The Agnikulas or Fire Tribes are supposed to have been brought into existence by a special act of creation of comparatively recent mythological date. After the Kshatriya had been slain by Parasu Ráma, gods and men, and more particularly the Brahman, began to feel the consequences of the loss of their natural protectors. The earth was overrun by giants and demons (*Daityas* and *Asuras*), the sacred books were held in contempt, and there was none to whom the devout could call for help in their troubles. Viswámitra, once a Kshatriya, who had raised himself to be a Brahman by the might of penance determined to revive the race that had been exterminated, and moved the gods to assemble for this purpose on Mount Abu in Rájputáná. Four images of *Dhuba* grass were thrown into the fire fountain, and called into life by appropriate incantations. From these sprung the four fire-tribes, Pramar, Sulanki, Parihár and Chauhán.

Turning from mythology to fact, the first point to be noticed about the Rájput tribe is that, in theory at any rate, it has no endogamous subdivisions. All Rájputs are supposed to be of one blood, and no distinctions are formally recognized among them as forming a conclusive bar to intermarriage. The groupings **Surajbansi, Sombansi** and **Agnikula** refer only to traditions of origin, and there is nothing to prevent a man belonging to one of these divisions from marrying a woman who belongs to another subdivision. It is no doubt the case that some exogamous divisions are of higher rank than others, and that to give a daughter in marriage into one of these groups degrades her family in respect of future marriages for a period of seven years. But with a few doubtful exceptions in outlying districts the principle of hypergamy has not been pushed to the point of forming strictly endogamous groups.

Internal structure.

The original septs of the Rájput tribe appear to be for the most part of the territorial type, that is to say, their names seem to denote the tract of country in which the sept or its founder had their earliest habitat. **Sesodia** and **Bhadauria** may be taken as examples of this type. Other names again, such as **Jadubansi**, clearly refer to descent from particular families or stocks. In addition to their original septs, long lists of which are given in Appendix I, the Rájputs of Behar also recognize the Brahmanical *gotras*, and the tendency is for the latter series to supplant and take the place of the latter. Usually where the original sept names are still held to govern intermarriage, the rule is that a man may not marry a woman who belongs to the same sept as his father or his mother, and the prohibition is often extended to the septs, of the paternal and maternal grandmothers. Notwithstanding this rule a case has been brought to my notice in which the son of a Salanki Rájput of Behar married a woman of the Chandel sept, although his father had married into the same sept. At the time of the betrothal a question was raised as to the correctness of the procedure, and the Brahmans held that, as the son's betrothal, though of the same *tribal sept* as his mother, belonged to a different Brahmanical *gotra*, the rule of exogamy would not be infringed by the marriage. The standard formula for reckoning prohibited degrees is also recognized by the Behar Rájputs, who in theory considered it binding down to seven generations on the father's, and five on the mother's side. A man may marry two sisters, but he must take them in the order of age, and he cannot marry the elder sister if he is already married to the younger.

Isogamy and hypergamy.

In theory, as has been already stated, the whole body of Rájputs constitutes a single tribe divided into a very large number of septs or clans of descent, each of which is supposed to be descended from a common ancestor. Marriage within the sept is of course interdicted to its member, and in theory a Rájput belonging to any given sept has the whole community to choose from in seeking a bride for his son or a bridegroom for his daughter. In fact, however, the field of selection is greatly restricted by the operation of the laws of isogamy and hypergamy, the nature of which has been explained in the Introductory Essay. In a society so organized as to give the fullest play to the idea of purity of descent and the tradition of ceremonial orthodoxy, it must needs be that offences should come, and should be deemed to affect not only the offender himself and his family in the narrower sense, but the entire sept to which he belongs, which is conceived as an enlarged family. Thus in course of time is developed an infinite series of social distinctions giving rise to complicated and burdensome obligations in respect of marriage. In the case of the Rájputs these distinctions have not led to the formation of endogamous groups, as commonly happens among other castes, nor have they hardened into fixed hypergamous groupings, such as are exemplified by the Kulinism of Bengal. But running through the entire series of septs we find the usages of isogamy and hypergamy which have exercised and continue to exercise a profound influence on Rájput society. Isogamy or the law of equal marriage is defined by Mr. Ibbetson[1] as the rule which arranges the septs of a given locality in a scale of social standing, and forbids a father to give his daughter to a man of any sept which stands lower than his own. Hypergamy or the law of superior marriage is the rule which compels him to wed his daughter with a member of a sept which shall be actually superior in rank to his own. In both cases a man usually does not scruple to take his wife, or at any rate his second wife, from a sept of inferior standing. It will be readily seen how the working of these rules must have given rise to all sorts of reciprocal obligations as between septs, and must have restricted the number of available husbands in any particular locality. The men of a higher sept can take their wives from a lower sept, while a corresponding privilege is denied to the women of the higher sept. Hence results a surplus of women in the higher septs and competition for husbands sets in, leading to the payment of a high price for bridegrooms, and enormously increases the expense of getting a daughter married. Under these circumstances poor families are under a strong temptation to get rid of their female infants by poison or intentional neglect in order to be saved the expense of finding them suitable husbands or the disgrace of being compelled to marry them to men of lower degree.

Infanticide.

There is no reason to believe that infanticide has ever been practised by the Rajputs of Bengal on the scale on which it has been known to occur in North-Western India. The sentiment which would tend to the commission of the crime is probably not so strongly developed among the Eastern Rájputs, who are, as has been indicated above, probably of much more mixed descent than the Rájputs of Rájputáná.

[1] Report on the Census of the Panjab, p. 356.

Marriage.

The demand being for husbands, not for wives, it follows that the negotiations leading to marriage are opened by the father or guardian of the girl, who sends his family priest and family barber to the boy's house to make inquiries and to answer any questions that may be asked. Sometimes a professional match-maker, *aguá* or *ghatak*, is employed. In any case these preliminary negotiations are known as *aguái* or *bartuhari.* If these results are satisfactory, and the girl's family find that their offers are likely to be accepted, the same emissaries pay a second visit to the boy's house, accompanied by the girl's father, and bringing with them her horoscope, which is compared by the Brahmans of the two families with the horoscope of the boy in order to ascertain whether the match is likely to be auspicious. When this point has been satisfactorily settled, the question of the bridegroom-price (*tilak* and *dahej*) to be paid by the girl's family is discussed, and a certain proportion of it, usually half, is paid on the spot by way of clinching the bargain. This is called *bar chhenka* or *phaldán*, and by receiving it the boy's people are deemed to bind themselves to marry him to no other woman. Sometimes the father of the boy also pays a small sum (*sagun*) as earnest money to the family of the girl. This practice, however, is said to be unusual, and is only resorted to when it is thought that the girl's family may be disposed to evade fulfilment of their obligations. The first instalment of the *tilak* or bridegroom-price is paid by one of the girl's relations to the boy himself in the presence of the family Brahman. At the same time a cocoanut is presented to him and a mark (*tilak*) is made with curds on his forehead. Both the gift and the mark are supposed to bring good luck. The balance of the bridegroom-price is paid in two equal instalments later on—one before and one after the marriage. On the occasion of paying the first instalment of *tilak*, presents are made to the Bráhmans and barbers who have taken part in the proceedings, and a date is fixed for the celebration of the marriage, an interval of fifteen days being usually allowed.

A few days before the wedding *dhanbatti* takes place, a barber is sent from the girl's house to the boy's with a present of unhusked rice. The boy's guardian takes this, mixes with it some rice of his own, and has the mixture parched. Two days before the wedding the women of the family scatter this parched rice about in the court-yard, singing songs which are supposed to bring good luck. On the next day, that is the day before the wedding, the rite of *ghidhári* is performed in the houses of the bride and bridegroom separately. The parents and nearest relations of the latter put on yellow clothes, and in the presence of the family priests worship Ganesa, the deity, who presides over success in life. The bridegroom is then smeared with oil, turmeric and *ghi*, offerings are made to the family gods, and the hair of the bridegroom's mother or his nearest female relative is anointed with oil. The same ceremony is gone through in the house of the bride, the only difference being that her family clothe themselves in red for the occasion. On the day of the marriage, but before the wedding procession is arranged, the ceremony of *belonki mangna* is often, though not necessarily, performed. The parents of the betrothed couple distribute cakes to the neighbours, demanding in return small presents of money (*belonki*).

The marriage procession is formed at the house of the bridegroom, and makes a somewhat noisy progress to the house of the bride. There the entire party is entertained. The bride and bridegroom are seated under a *marwa* or wedding canopy, and after the recital of appropriate *mantras* or texts, the family priest of the bride's household fills the bridegroom's right hand with *sindur*, and makes a mark with it on the bride's forehead, the women of the family meanwhile singing songs to celebrate the event. Among the Rájputs of Tirhut this is deemed the binding portion of the ritual, and the practice of walking round the sacred fire, usually considered essential in the marriage of the higher castes, is said to be unknown. The married couple then leave the *marwa* and go to the *kohbar* or house, where the family deity has been placed for the occasion. They worship and make offerings to him, and this concludes the marriage. The bridegroom then returns to the *janwásá* or lodgings reserved for his party, while the bride remains in her own house. Early next morning they are brought out and each is made to chew betel with which has been mixed a tiny drop of blood drawn from the other's little finger. This usage in which we may trace an interesting survival of primitive ideas is called *sineh jorua*, the joining of love. When it is over the bride is taken to her husband's house where she remains. On the fourth day after her arrival she and her husband stand together on a yoke such as is used for oxen, and a washerwoman pours water over them. This symbolical washing is supposed to be the first occasion on which the couple see each other by daylight after marriage. Among the Rájputs of North-Western India, and in some parts of Behar, the bride and bridegroom do not live together until after a second ceremony (called *gauná*, or with reference to the bride's 'going' to her husband's house) has been performed, which may take place one, three, five or even seven years after the marriage, and is fixed with reference to the physical development of the bride. In Tirhut, however, the custom of premature consummation, mentioned by Buchanan as prevalent among the Rájputs of Behar, seems to have been introduced, and it is said to be unusual for a bride to be kept at home until she attains puberty. Another custom connected with marriage, which students of comparative ethnography will also recognize as a survival of more primitive ideas, may be referred to here. In Rájput families of Tirhut it is considered contrary to etiquette for a young married couple to see each other by day so long as the husband's parents are alive, and in particular they must avoid being seen together by the husband's parents, and must not speak to one another in their presence. It is of course extremely difficult to ascertain how far a rule of this sort is actually observed, but I am assured that young married couples are very careful to avoid infringing it, although as they grow older their solicitude on this point is apt to wear off.

The remarriage of widows is strictly forbidden among the Rájputs of Behar. Divorce is also prohibited, and when a woman is taken in adultery, she is summarily expelled from the caste, and either becomes a prostitute or joins herself to some religious sect of more or less dubious morality. In certain cases, however, where a married couple find themselves unable to live in harmony together, a separation is arrived at by mutual consent, each agreeing to look upon the other as a parent. In such cases the wife returns to her father's house, and the husband marries again. This is not, however, looked upon as a divorce.

Religion.

Rájputs are orthodox Hindus, and worship the Hindu divinities favoured by the sect to which they happen to belong. By the Surajbansi division, special honour is done to the sun, whom they regard as their eponymous ancestor. Among minor gods Bandi and Narsingh appear to be most in favour. Ancestors are worshipped with offerings of milk, flowers and rice. Mondays and Wednesdays are believed to be the most propitious days for this worship. On the 15th day of Asin married women offer cakes and oil to the souls of their mother-in-law, grandmother-in-law and great grandmother-in-law. This custom, known as the Jitia puja, has obviously been copied from the *sraddh* celebrated in honour of the three immediate descendants. The popular explanation of it is that it is intended to express the gratitude that every married women ought to feel for her good fortune in getting a husband. Mr. Grierson, in *Behar Peasant Life*,[1] speaks of the jitiya puja as "a fast and worship performed by women on the 8th of the dark half of Kártik (late in October) for the benefit of their children. Further inquiry on the subject would perhaps bring out points of interest and might clear up the discrepancy of date

Disposal of the dead.

For religious and ceremonial purposes Rájputs employ Brahmans, who are received on equal terms by other members of the sacred order. The dead are burned and the ashes thrown into the Ganges or ones of its tributaries. *Sraddh* is performed on the thirteenth day after death, and on the fourteenth a feast is given to the Brahmans of the neighbourhood. It is followed by the *barki sraddh* on the first anniversary of the death, when the members of the dead man's family shave their heads and faces, and present a *pinda* to the deceased, while the Brahmans recite mantras. Then the priests and the members of the family partake of a feast. It is said to be a tradition that the expenditure on this ceremony must not exceed half of that incurred on the original *sraddh*. After the *barkhi* the *tarpan* or *nit-tarpan*, a daily offering of water is presented regularly by all the sons of the deceased, and particularly by the eldest. This practice, however, is observed only by highly-educated Rájputs, who know their religious obligations in this matter. On the first fifteen days of Ásin the *pitri paksh* or ancestors' fortnight is observed with offerings of water to all deceased ancestors. If a man dies sonless, leaving a wife and daughter, the *sraddh* and the *barki* are performed by one of them, the other ceremonies being

---

[1] Page 402.

omitted. Failing these the nearest agnate *gotia* will take upon himself these pious duties. In the event of a man dying away from his people and being burned or buried without the proper rites, his body is burned in effigy by his relatives, and the other ceremonies are performed in the usual fashion. When a man has died a sudden or violent death, it is thought right for his son to make a pilgrimage to Gya and perform the *sraddh* ceremony there in order to secure the repose of his soul.

Occupation and social status.

The high-flown titles—Bhupál, Bhupati, Bhusur, Báhuja—in use among Rájputs, and the name Chhatri itself indicate the exalted pretensions of the tribe and their traditions concerning their original occupation. Many Rájputs still cling to the belief that Government and the trade of arms are their proper business in life; and these notions lead them to regard education, and more especially the higher education, in much the same light as a medieval warrior looked upon the clerkly studies of his time. For this reason the Rájputs as a body have rather dropped behind in the modern struggle for existence, where book-learning counts for more than strength of arm, and the more intelligent members of the tribe are quite conscious that their position is by no means what it was in the classical ages of Hindu tradition. Their relations to the land still help them to maintain a show of respectability and importance. Many of them are zamindars, and those who hold cultivating tenures claim in virtue of their caste a remission of rent of their homestead lands. The *jeth-raiyat* or headman of a Behar village is frequently a Rájput. He collects the rents and receives in return a yearly allowance, known as *pagri*, from the zamindar. Rájputs are never artisans, and it is unusual to find them engaging in any kind of trade. In theory their social status is second only to that of the Brahman, but in Bengal Proper, where great Rájput houses do not exist, popular usage would, I think, place them below the Baidya and the Káyasth. Even in Behar the Bábhans claim precedence over them on the ground that they will not touch the handle (*parihath* or *lagna*) of the plough, and that they use the full *upanayan* ritual when investing their children with the *janeo* or sacred thread, whereas the Rájputs plough and milk cows with their own hands, and shuffle on the *janeo* in a rough-and-ready fashion when a boy gets married.

In respect of diet the Rájputs conform generally to the practice of high-caste Hindus. The flesh of the goat, the deer and the hare, the pigeon, quail and ortolan may alone be eaten, and these animals, if not killed in hunting, must be slaughtered in a particular way (*jhataha*) by cutting the head off at a single stroke. Fish is lawful food. Wine is supposed to be forbidden. As regards the taking of food from members of other castes, the following rules are in force :—

A Rájput cannot take *kachchi* food, *i.e.*, rice or *dál* or anything that is cooked with water from anyone but a Brahman. *Pakki* food, such as parched grain, sweetmeats and the like, he may take from a man of any caste higher than his own or from a Dhánuk, Kurmi, Kahár, Lohar, Barhi, Kumhár, Goálá, Mallah, Hajjám, Máli, Sonár, Láheri, or Gareri, provided that no salt or turmeric has been used in the making. These condiments he will add himself. Water is governed by the rules applicable to *pakki* food. Rájputs may not use the hookahs of any other caste, but may smoke tobacco prepared by men of any caste except the Dosadh, Dom, Chamár, Musahar and Dhobi.

The following statement shows the number and distribution of Rájputs in 1872 and 1881:—

District.	1872.	1881.	District.	1872.	1881.
Bardwan	12,359	7,218	Noakhali	350	158
Bankura	9,180	13,967	Tipperah	2,161	1,168
Birbhum	7,028	8,344	Chittagong Hill Tracts ...	47	7
Midnapur	17,003	19,573	Patna	60,079	64,333
Hughli	} 6,993	{ 5,539	Gya	102,918	114,402
Howrah		1,039	Shahabad	183,896	207,195
24-Parganás	8,693	12,604	Mozufferpur	} 227,236	{ 167,594
Nadiya	5,017	6,047	Darbhanga		90,0[illegible]3
Jessore	1,114	903	Saran	213,348	243,972
Khulna	......	551	Champaran	69,614	80,764
Murshedabad	13,141	8,955	Monghyr	47,006	56,067
Dinajpur	1,813	2,887	Bhágalpur	52,579	60,491
Rajshahye	1,541	1,233	Purniah	23,663	48,465
Rangpur	2,404	2,325	Maldah	3,207	5,104
Bogra	3,426	372	Santál Parganás	33,337	28,124
Pabna	664	455	Cuttack	10,728	10,782
Darjiling	8,972	6,352	Puri	2,946	3,898
Jalpigori	523	1,269	Balasore	2,053	2,770
Kuch Behar	......	3,197	Tributary States	6,510	3,551
Dacca	1,665	5,362	Hazaribagh	31,387	37,404
Faridpur	901	533	Lohardagá	37,752	47,471
Bakarganj	952	468	Singbhum	1,718	1,919
Maimansinh	2,470	2,167	Manbhum	16,588	15,948
Chittagong	359	1,040	Tributary States	2,589	5,258

Rajwár, a Dravidian cultivating caste of Behar, Western Bengal, and Chota Nagpur, who are probably a branch of one of the aboriginal races. This opinion was held by Buchanan, who went so far as to identify them with the Rachewárs or Rajawárs whom he came across in Mysore. Colonel Dalton reckoned them among the mongrel tribes. "Traditionally," he says, "they appear to connect themselves with the Bhuiyás; but this is only in Behar. The Rajwárs in Serguja and the adjoining States are peaceably-disposed cultivators, who declare themselves to be fallen Kshatriyas: they do not, however, conform to Hindu customs, and they are skilled in a dance called Chailo, which I believe to be of Dravidian origin. The Rajwárs of Bengal admit that they are derived from the miscegenation of Kurmis and Kols. They are looked upon as very impure by Hindus, who will not take water from their hands." The Rajwárs of Behar told Buchanan "that their common ancestor was a certain Rishi, who had two sons From the eldest are descended the Rajwárs, who became soldiers and obtained their noble title; from the younger are descended the Musahars, who have obtained their name from eating rats, which the Rajwárs reject." The suggestion of affinity with the Musahars seems to support Colonel Dalton's statement that the Rajwárs connect themselves with the Bhuiyás, for Musahars and Bhuiyás are certainly closely related, if not one and the same. On the other hand, it should be observed that the Rajwárs of Gyá will not eat with Bhuiyás. The Rajwárs of Manbhum have

Origin.

a tradition that they came from Nagpur. They say that the king of that country had two daughters, the elder of whom was lawfully married to the elder of two brothers, while the younger daughter ran away with the younger brother. On the death of the king the brothers fought among themselves for the kingdom, but after a time it was settled that the one who came first to the capital on a certain morning should be king. On his way to the city the younger brother saw a golden crab and dismounted to get it, tying his horse to a tree. As he was reaching for the crab, a kite screamed over his head. He mistook the kite's scream for the neighing of his horse, assumed that it had broken loose and went off to look for it. This took him so long that he never got to Nagpur at all, but gave up his claims to the crown and went home. The Rajwár caste are his descendants. The legend may well have been suggested by the name Rajwár or the title Rájbansi. The internal structure of the caste is shown in Appendix I. Some of the sections are totemistic —a fact which may be taken as certainly indicating Dravidian descent. The sub-castes are the following—Angrok or Angwár, Chapwár, Sikhariá, Sukulkárá, Bar-Gohri, Majhal-Turiyá, and Berra-Rajwár. The last three are found only in Lohardagá. The third occurs among several castes of Western Bengal, and refers to the tract of country between the Dámodar and Barákar rivers, east of the Parasnáth range of hills. The Doms of Behar have a section called Angwár. All the sections are exogamous, but in Behar the Marrik, Majhiyá, and Matwárá profess not to intermarry with members of the Bhogtá group. For the rest they follow the standard formula for calculating prohibited degrees.

Internal structure.

Rajwárs marry their daughters either as infants or as adults. In the latter case sexual intercourse before marriage is condoned, as with the Mundas and Oraons, provided that the lover marries the girl. An intrigue with a man of another caste would of course be punished by summary excommunication. The marriage closely resembles that in use among the Kurmis, *sindurdán* being the binding portion. Polygamy is permitted. A man may have as many wives as he can afford to maintain. A widow may marry a second time by the *sangá* form. She is not bound to marry her late husband's younger brother. Some Rajwárs of Gya and Shahabad assured me that only childless widows might marry again, and that the privilege was under no circumstances extended to a widow with children. This looks like a first step towards the introduction of further restrictions, but I doubt whether my informants were correct in their statement; or, if they were, whether the modified usage extended beyond a small number of families. Divorce is allowed for adultery or incompatibility of temper, and divorced wives may marry again.

Marriage.

The members of the caste profess to be Hindus of the Vaishnava sect, and employ degraded Brahmans (Jyosi or Maithil) for religious and ceremonial observances. In Behar they also worship Goraiyá, Dihwár, Jagdambá, and the other standard minor gods. They burn their dead and perform a rather meagre *sráddh* ceremony on the eleventh day. A

Religion.

piece of bone is saved from the fire in order that it may be thrown into the Ganges or the Dámodar. The reverence thus shown for the latter river deserves notice, as it is always associated with the funeral rites of the aboriginal races.

Social status.

The social rank of the Rajwárs is low, and Brahmans will not ordinarily take water from their hands. Those Brahmans, however, who serve them as priests, and the Vaishnava ascetics, who act as their spiritual guides, will eat sweetmeats and similar *pakki* food in their houses. In virtue of their abstinence from beef and pork they believe themselves to be raised above the Bauris and Doms; while the fact that they eat fowls and the leavings of the higher castes, and indulge freely in strong drink, cuts them off from the respectable classes from whose hands Brahmans will take water. The Kurmis are the lowest caste from whom they will take cooked food. Agriculture is their sole occupation. Some of them are occupancy raiyats, but a large proportion have not risen above the condition of landless day-labourers.

The following statement shows the number and distribution of Rajwárs in 1872 and 1881:—

District.	1872.	1881.	District.	1872.	1881.
Bardwan	......	230	Patna	3,244	3,960
Bankura	......	61	Gya	39,454	43,773
Birbhum	......	135	Shahabad	4,451	6,302
Midnapur	......	10,265	Mozufferpur	72	531
Hughli	......	2	Saran	117	304
Howrah	......	133	Champaran	37	33
24-Parganás	......	469	Monghyr	114	......
Nadiya	......	113	Bhagalpur	289	334
Murshedabad	......	163	Purniah	218	62
Rajshahye	......	211	Maldah	......	23
Bogra	......	41	Santál Parganás	5,080	6,178
Pabna	......	4	Hazaribagh	1,265	9,291
Darjiling	......	20	Lohardagá	3,559	5,657
Faridpur	......	51	Singbhum	33	101
Chittagong	......	13	Manbhum	10,091	15,541
			Tributary States	11,510	14,475

Rajwár, a sept of Rájputs in Behar.

Rakhál, a *thar* or sept of Mangars in Darjiling.

Rakhali, a section of Khámbus in Darjiling.

Rakhi, a sub-caste of Kalwárs in Behar.

Raksa, a section of the Kanaujiá sub-caste of Goálás in Behar.

Raksáin, a sept of the Suryabansi sub-tribe of Rájputs in Behar.

Raksel, a sept of Rájputs in Behar.

Rakshit, *Rakhit*, a title of Baidyas, of Dakshin-Rárhi and Bangaja Káyasths; Báruis, Támolis, and Telis, of Mayarás and Sutradhars in Bengal.

Raksise, a *mul* or section of the Chhamuliá Madhesiá sub-caste of Halwáis in Behar.

Rakwár, a section of Rájputs in Behar.

Rám, (i) a title applied to Kurmis in Behar until by age or personal influence they attain a leading position in the village, when they are called Marár or Máhton; (ii) a title of Dosádhs; (iii) a section of the Mahmudábáz sub-caste of Nápits.

Rámáiyá, an endogamous branch of the Chauan sub-caste of Kurmis in Behar who are said to have been outcasted for eating by mistake for a goat the body of a dog which had been roasted in a fire which burned down a village. The Rámáiyás deny the truth of this story, but, while claiming to belong to the Chauan sub-caste of Kurmis, can assign no reason for their exclusion from rights of food and intermarriage.

Rámánuja, a sect of Vaishnavas.

Rámávat, a sect of Vaishnavas.

Ramayá, a section of Bábhans in Behar.

Rámdyat, *Rámáth*, a celibate sect of Vaishnavas who worship Rama and Krishna, wear the *paita*, and are usually treated as Brahmans.

Rámer-Dhobá, a sub-caste of Dhobás in Eastern Bengal.

Rámgarhiá, a sept of Bairágis and Mundas in Chota Nagpur.

Rámi dhámi ke asámi, a section of the Banodhiá and Jaiswár Kalwárs in Behar.

Ramjani, a caste of dancers, singers, and prostitutes, synonymous with Gandharvin.

Rámkisán, a section of the Biyáhut and Kharidáhá Kalwárs in Behar.

Rámpái, a section of Bábhans in the north of Manbhum to whom the members of other sections will not give their daughters in marriage, though they allow the men to marry Rámpai women.

Rámpuri, a section of Báis Sonárs in Behar.

Rámpurlá, a section of the Banodhiá and Jaiswár Kalwárs in Behar.

Rámudán, a section of Kámis in Darjiling.

Ráná, a title of the Bhar and Mayará castes; a *pangat* or section of Dosadhs; a section of the Surajbansi division of Rájputs in Behar; a title of Dakshin-Rárhi and Bangaja Káyasths; a title of Aguris and Sutradhars; of Kumhárs in Behar; of Mangars in Darjiling; a section of the Magahiyá sub-caste of Doms in Behar.

Ráná Lamsani, a *thar* or sept of the Das-gurung sub-tribe of Gurungs in Darjiling.

Ranasinha or *Samarsinha*, lion of the fight, a title of Khandáits in Orissa.

Ránauchhá, a *thar* or sept of Khambus in Darjiling.

Ranauni, a sept of the Suryabansi sub-tribe of Rájputs in Behar.

Ráncho, a section of Bágdis in Western Bengal.

Ráne, a section of Kanaujiá Lohárs in Behar.

Ranga, a title of Dakshin-Rárhi and Bangaja Káyasths.

Rángá, a sept of Dhimáls in the Darjiling Terai.

Rangataba, a yellow bird, a totemistic sept of Juángs in Orissa.

Rángdhári, *Rangdháriá*, a maker of tin (*rángá*) or pewter ornaments, an occupation followed by Mahomedans; also a synonym for Sonár.

Rangomung, a sept of Lepchas in Darjiling.

Rangpiár, a section of the Biyáhut and Kharidáhá Kalwárs in Behar.

Rangres, Rangráj, a dyer, an occupation usually followed by Mahomedans.

Rangroz, a functional group of Jugis.

Rani Poka, a red worm, a totemistic sept of Mundas in Chota Nagpur.

Ranka, a section of Oswáls in Behar.

Rankankar, a sept of Kaurs in Chota Nagpur.

Ránki or **Kalál**, a sub-caste (Mahomedan) of Kalwárs in Behar.

Rankwár, a sept of Rájputs in Behar.

Ransadiyá, a section of Bábhans in Behar.

Ranubád, a section of Kumhárs in Singbhum.

Ranyacelunya, a sept of Chakmás in the Hill Tracts of Chittagong.

Ranyin, a sept of Chakmás in the Hill Tracts of Chittagong.

Ráorh, a section of Maghayá Kumhárs in Behar.

Ráori, a title of Kándus in Behar.

Raot, a totemistic sept of Doms and Chamárs in Chota Nagpur.

Raotiá, crab, a totemistic sept of Páns in Chota Nagpur.

Rápungchhá, a *thar* or sept of Khambus in Darjiling.

Rárh-ásram, a sub-caste of Mayarás in Central Bengal.

Rárher Rárhi, a sub-caste of Sunris in Eastern Bengal.

Rárhi, a sub-caste of Brahmans in the Lower Provinces of Bengal who derive their name from the Rárh, or the high-lying alluvial tract on the west bank of the river Bhagirathi. They claim descent from five Kanaujiá Brahmans brought by Ádisur to perform certain ceremonies which the local Brahmans, who are now known as Saptasatis, were incompetent to undertake; a sub-caste of Kewats in Orissa; of Kumhárs, Tántis, Telis; of Baidyas, Baruis, Kayasths, Goálás, Kaibarttas, Jugis, Subarnabaniks, and Sunris in Bengal; of Kámárs in Murshedabad, and in Pabna also called Dás-Samáj; a group of Phulkátá Mális.

Rarhi-Mál, a sub-caste of Máls in the Santál Parganás.

Rárhiya-Samáj, a sub-caste of Dhobás in Hughli.

Ráriá, a section of Goálás in the North-Western Provinces and Behar.

Rasáili, a section of Kámis; a *thar* or sept of Mangars in Darjiling.

Rasákmáre, a *mul* or section of the Naomulia or Majraut sub-caste of Goálás in Behar.

Rásamba, mushrooms that grow on ant-hills, a totemistic sept of Juángs in Orissa.

Rasáunmare, a *mul* or section of the Naomulia or Majraut sub-caste of Goálás in Behar.

Rás-rishi, a section of Gandhabaniks in Bengal.

Rást, a title of Goálás in Behar.

Rástogi, a trading caste of Behar, usually engaged in selling cloth and money-lending, but sometimes also dealing in grain and native medicines. They practise two peculiar forms of petty money-lending by *bahi*, that is by entry in books of account without the security of a separate bond. These are known as *augáhi* or *ugáhi* and *rozáhi*. Mr. Hoey gives[1] the following account of them:—

"*Augáhi* is lending of money to be repaid with interest at 20 per cent. in monthly instalments. Thus, if a Rástogi lends on the 1st January ten rupees, he receives one rupee on the first of each month for twelve months, and thereby realises twelve rupees, of which two rupees are interest. A Rástogi's *augáhi bahi* is a curiosity. It is ruled like a chess-board, but has twelve columns. As each month's instalment is realised, it is entered in a square until the twelve squares are filled. He generally keeps also a separate *bahi*, in which the principal is noted when lent. It may, however, be noted in the margin of his check-pattern account. *Rozáhi* is money lent to be realised in daily instalments with interest at 25 per cent. Thus, if a rupee be lent, one-half anna (*táká roz*) will be realised daily. The account of this money is kept in a similar way, but the account-book will be ruled in lines of 40 squares. A Rástogi keeps his accounts by locality, that is, he has several *khets*, as he calls them; one, say, is Saadatganj, another Hasanganj, a third Deori Agha Mir, and so on. Debtors are called *asámis*, and the amount to be collected is called *lagán*. A separate set of account-books is kept for each *khet*, and a servant (generally a Brahman on Rs. 3 per mensem) is employed to collect each *khet*."

Mr. Sherring mentions three sub-castes—**Amethi**, **Indrapati**, and **Mauhariá**, which do not intermarry. Rástogis marry their daughters as infants, forbid widows to remarry, and do not recognize divorce. In matters of diet they affect to be extremely punctilious, and thus married women of the caste will not eat food that has been prepared, or even touched by their husbands.

The following statement shows the number and distribution of Rástogis in 1881. They were not returned separately in 1872:—

District.	1881.	District.	1881.
Patna	258	Champaran	24
Gya	8	Monghyr	296
Shahabad	186	Purniah	17
Mozufferpur	10	Hazaribagh	164
Darbhanga	36	Lohardagá	44
Saran	1,470		

Rat, a section of Awadhiá Hajjáms in Behar.

Rathiá, a sub-tribe of Kaurs in Chota Nagpur.

Rathitara, a section of the Páschátya Baidik Brahmans in Bengal; a Kshatrapeta *gotra* or section of Brahmans.

Ratnábali, a *gáin* of the Bharadwája *gotra* of Bárendra Brahmans in Bengal.

Ratwariá, a section of Lohárs in Behar.

Rauná, a synonym for Rawáni, *q.v.*

Ráuniá, a section of the Sátmuliá Maghayá sub-caste of Kándus in Behar.

[1] *Trade and Manufactures of Northern India*, p. 144.

Rauniár, *Raunia, Noniár*, a sub-caste of Baniyás[1] in Behar. Writing of the members of this group in the North-West Provinces, Mr. Nesfield says:—"Raunia, more fully written Ravaniyá, is from *ravan*, which means the crying or hawking of wares for sale." In another place he adds:—"The Rauniá (which means literally a crier) moves in a circle of some eight or ten villages surrounding his own; and if he cannot get cash for his grain, he barters it for spices, sugar, condensed treacle, etc. In these days he is seldom able to live by trade alone, and in the intervals of business he raises his own crops. But trade, and trade only, was his original function."

Internal structure.

The Rauniárs of Behar profess to have come from the North-West Provinces, and their allegation is likely enough to be correct. They are divided into exogamous sections (*muls* or *gotras*), but the only section-names I have been able to ascertain are **Ekadasi** and **Ekassi**, referring possibly to the number of families comprised, or supposed to be comprised, in each section. Their titles are **Sáhu** and **Modi**, which are common to them and to many other trading groups. In Champáran they have broken up into two endogamous groups—**Chhatri** and **Samri**, the former of whom claim to be Rájputs from the North-West Provinces who were degraded for intermarrying with women of the Baniyá caste.

Marriage.

Rauniárs profess to marry their daughters as infants, but I am informed that cases of girls being married after puberty are not uncommon where the parents are poor or for any special reason there has been difficulty in finding a husband. It is clear therefore that the caste does not take the extreme sacerdotal view of the necessity of infant-marriage which prevails among Hindus of the higher classes, especially in Bengal Proper. Their marriage ceremony is of the standard type, and a price (*tilak*) is paid to the parents of the bridegroom. Polygamy is allowed, but is rarely resorted to in practice, except when the first wife proves barren. Widows are allowed to remarry by the *sagai* form, of which *sindurdán* is the binding portion. The widow is under no obligation to marry her deceased husband's younger brother. Divorce is not generally recognized; but in Champáran it appears to be the practice to bring cases of unchastity before a panchâyat, which makes an order of divorce; and if the offence has been committed with a member of the caste, the woman is allowed to marry again by *sagai*.

Religion.

In their religious and ceremonial observances the Rauniárs are orthodox Hindus and employ Brahmans, whose social position is in no way affected by serving them. Rauniárs are not conspicuous for adhesion to any particular sect, but in some parts of the country they are said to regard

[1] I have treated the Rauniár as a sub-caste of Baniyá, instead of as a separate caste, in order to avoid doing violence to popular usage. Both Natives and Europeans speak of the Baniya caste, and ignore the fact that the expression denotes a group comprising several distinct castes, which cannot now be traced to any common stock. The subject is discussed at greater length in the article on Baniyá.

Mahádeva as their tutelary deity. Like the Agarwals, they pay special reverence to Lakhsmi, and celebrate the Diwáli festival with great pomp. They also worship Bandi, Goraiyá, Sokhá, and Máhábirji as household or village gods.

Occupation.

Trading in grain, cloth, etc., and lending money, are their special functions, but of late years some of them have taken to agriculture, and a few have risen, probably as a consequence of money-lending transactions, to be zemindars. In Champaran Rauniyárs are found as occupancy raiyats, but such cases are rare.

Rausan, a synonym for Teli.

Raut, a sub-tribe of Kharwárs in Southern Lohardagá.

Ráut, *Rahut*, a title of Amáts, Chamárs, Dhanuks, Dosádhs, Gonrhis, Goálás, Kadars, Kumhars, Nágars, Pargahs, Rájputs, and Sunris in Behar; in Bengal of the Bhát Brahmans. As a title of Mális in Behar, it seems to be in process of development into a sub-caste, for the Ráut Mális intermarry among themselves; a title of Beldars, Nuniás, Barais, Kahárs, Binds, and of Dhobis in Behar; a section and a title of Kurmis in Behar; a sept of Thárus; a title of Gareris; a title of Chásás and Khandáits in Chota Nagpur and Orissa; a section of Dharkár Doms in Behar; a title of Bhuiyás; a sept of Mundas in Chota Nagpur.

Rautar, a section of Sonárs in Behar.

Rautár, a sub-tribe of Thárus in Behar.

Rauti, a section of Mahesris in Behar.

Origin.

Rautiá, a landholding and cultivating caste of Chota Nagpur, probably Dravidian in its original affinities, but since refined in features and complexion by a large infusion of Aryan blood. The name Rautiá suggests some connexion with Rajpúts, and Mr. Beames has noticed that the cognate term Ráut is used in some districts to denote an inferior Rajpút, "the corruption of the name betokening the corruption of the caste."[1] Their traditions say that they formerly dwelled in Sinhal-dwip (Ceylon), whence they migrated to Barhar, in Mirzapur. In the time of the Emperor Jahángir some Rautias were serving as sentinels in the fort at Gwálior when Maharája Durjan Sáh of Chutiá Nagpur was imprisoned there for failure to pay his tribute to Dehli.[2] During his confinement the Rautiás treated the Raja kindly, and he repaid their good offices on his release by giving them lands in parganá Panári of Lohardagá. Further grants of villages, groups of villages, and entire parganás were afterwards made to them in *jágir*, and many of these are in existence at the present day. The titles of Baráik, Gaunjhu, and Kotwár were at the same time conferred upon them.

---

[1] *Supplemental Glossary*, vol. i, p. 24.

[2] See extracts from *Tuzuk-i-Jahángíri* and MS. history of Chutiá Nagpur in *J. A. S. B.* for 1871, and *Statistical Account of Bengal*, vol. xvi, p. 447 *et seq.*

Internal structure.

The Rautiás are divided into two endogamous sub-castes—**Bargohri** and **Chhot-gohri**. The origin of this division is obscure. The Rautiás themselves tell an absurd story to account for it. They say that the Bar-gohris were the first to arrive in their present habitat. When the Chhot-gohris came they were asked with what cooking pots and on what fire-places they had cooked their food after the Bar-gohris had started. On their replying that they had used the pots and fire-places left behind by the Bar-gohris, but had cleaned them, the latter straightway took offence, and from that time forth have refused to eat cooked food (*kachi*) with the Chhot-gohri. Following the analogy of similar schisms in castes formerly united, it seems more likely either that the Chhot-gohri were the first settlers and were outcasted for some such breach of caste rules as people are apt to commit, or to be taxed with committing, when they settle in outlandish parts of the country, or that the Chhot-gohri are the offspring of alliances between the Bar-gohri and women of inferior caste or purity of lineage. At the present day the Chhot-gohri eat fowls and wild pig and drink spirits, all of which things are forbidden for members of the higher group.

Within each sub-caste we find a group called **Berrá Rautiá**, who are admittedly descendants of Rautiás by concubines of other castes. Although not strictly endogamous, the Berrás observe certain special restrictions in the matter of marriage. Thus a Berrá whose mother was a Rájput will not marry a girl whose mother was a Ghási.

Both sub-castes have a long list of sections (*páris* or *got*), which will be found in the Appendix. The fact that the list contains totemistic, eponymous, and territorial names, tells on the whole in favour of the view that the Rautiás are people of mixed descent. The rule that the totem is taboo to its bearers seems only to apply to the animal-totems, which may be named, but not killed or eaten; for a Rautiá of the sword or axe groups is not forbidden to use those weapons, nor is a man of the Kási group forbidden to touch the grass from which his section is supposed to be descended.

The section name goes by the male side, and the prohibition attached to it affects only a man's own section and does not prevent him from marrying a woman belonging to the same section as his mother. This simple rule of exogamy is therefore supplemented by a table of prohibited degrees made up, like our own, by enumerating the individual relatives whom a man may not marry, and not, as is more usual, by prohibiting intermarriage with certain large classes of relations or with the descendants within certain degrees of particular relations.

Marriage.

Girls are married either as infants or adults, usually between the ages of eight and eighteen. Sexual license before marriage is not openly recognized, as it is among the aborigines of Chota Nagpur; but I am informed that grown-up girls enjoy considerable liberty in this respect, it being understood that in case of pregnancy a husband will be at once forthcoming. In theory polygamy is allowed without any restriction being laid on the number of wives or any antecedent condition being insisted on, such as that the first wife must be barren or be inflicted with an incurable disease in order to entitle her husband to take another wife. In actual life, however, it is unusual to find a man with more than three or four wives. One simple reason for this is that few men can afford to keep many wives or have house-room to accommodate them, as by universal custom each wife must have a separate room.

A widow is allowed to marry again by the *sagai* form, and it is considered right for her to marry her late husband's younger brother. Under no circumstances can she marry the elder brother. If she marries an outsider, her late husband's brother, father, or uncle have the right to the custody of all her children, both male and female. In any case she acquires no rights in her late husband's property, the whole of which passes to his eldest son, subject to certain obligations to provide, by way of maintenance, for younger brothers. If a widow marries her late husband's younger brother, her children by him are not deemed the children of her first husband, nor have they any rights in respect of his property.

The ritual used at the marriage of a widow is very simple. Five married women whose husbands are living take a *sári*, a pair of lac bracelets, and a little vermilion (*sindur*) to the bridegroom and get him to touch each article. They then return to the bride, attire her in the *sári* and bracelets, and daub the vermilion on her forehead. As in the case of a regular marriage, the proceedings conclude with a feast to the friends and relatives of the newly-married couple.

A woman may be divorced for adultery or for eating with a member of another caste. For lighter offences than these, separation is the only punishment awarded; and in that case the husband is bound to maintain his wife. A divorced woman may not marry again. If she lives with a man, she ranks as a concubine and her children are illegitimate.

The ceremony performed at the marriage of a virgin bride contains several features of a primitive and non-Aryan character. In the first instance, both parties go through the form of marriage to a mango tree (*ambá bihá*). The essential and binding portions of the ritual are the knotting together of the clothes of the bride and bridegroom and *sindurdán*, which is effected by smearing on the bride's forehead a drop of blood drawn from the little finger of the bridegroom, and *vice versâ*. Sákadwipi Brahmans officiate, and offerings are made to Gauri and Ganesa.

Marriages are arranged by the parents or guardians of the parties, who have no freedom of choice in the matter. Professional marriage-brokers are unknown. The first offer is made by the father of the bridegroom, and a bride-price (*dáli taká*), varying according to the means of the bridegroom's parents, is paid to the parents of the bride, by whom it is retained. No portion of the bride-price becomes the special property of the bride.

Succession. The Mitákshará commentary, which forms the personal law of most Hindus in Lohardagá, does not apply to Rautiás, who are governed by special customs of their own. The eldest son by a regularly-married (*bihái*) wife inherits the whole of his father's property, subject to the obligation of creating maintenance grants in favour of his younger brothers. These grants are not equal in value, but are supposed to decrease in the order of age of the grantees, so that each younger brother gets a smaller grant than his immediate elder, and so on. Instances, however, have occurred among the Bar-gohri Rautiás in which, with the consent of the eldest son, an entire property has been equally divided. Sons by a *sagai* wife are included in this arrangement, but get smaller grants than sons by a *bihái* wife. The rule that sons by a *bihái* wife take precedence of sons by a *sagai* wife is subject to the important exception that an elder brother's widow, though married by the *sagai* form, ranks in all respects as a *bihái* wife, and her sons have the full rights of succession to their father. This principle was affirmed by the Civil Courts in a case which occurred a few years ago. One of the Rautiá Baráiks of Basia died leaving a widow and infant son; the widow married in the *sogai* form her late husband's younger brother, who was already married to a *bihái* wife. Both of the wives bore sons, the *sagai* wife a few months earlier than the *bihái* wife. Meanwhile the infant son of the original proprietor died: the whole property passed to his brother, and on his death was disputed between his sons. It was held that the son of the *sagai* wife, being the eldest, was entitled to succeed under the custom of the caste, and that the son of the *bihái* wife had only a right to maintenance. It will be seen from this instance that a brother excludes a widow from succession. The latter is in fact entitled only to maintenance, and may forfeit even that by misconduct or infringement of caste rules. Brothers and uncles, or their descendants, exclude daughters and their descendants. Succession indeed is strictly agnatic throughout; the eldest male of the eldest line taking the entire inheritance subject to the obligation to provide maintenance for relatives within certain degrees on a scale progressively diminishing in relation to the age and propinquity in relationship of the claimants. The distinction between ancestral and self-acquired property, which has acquired such prominence in the standard Hindu law, does not seem to be very clearly recognized in the customary law of the Rautiás. I gather, however, that such property is not subject to the rule of primogeniture, but is ordinarily divided equally among the male descendants.

Step-sons are not entitled to maintenance from the estate of their step-father. Owing, however, to the fact that a widow may marry her late husband's younger brother and may *not* marry his eldest brother, it happens that a large proportion of the step-sons among the Rautiás are really the heirs to the estates of which their step-fathers happen for the time being to be in charge. A *ghár díjuá*, or son-in-law who lives with his wife in his father-in-law's household, retains his claims on his natural father's property, but acquires no right to a maintenance grant from his father-in-law's estate.

Adoption is unknown—a circumstance from which we may either infer that the Rautiás are free from the curse of childlessness, so common in the higher ranks of Hindus, or that one of the inducements to adopt sons has been removed by the rule regarding land referred to in the next paragraph.

In the event of a Rautiá dying without male heirs, his immovable property reverts to his superior landlord or the legal representative of the person by whom the land was originally granted. In such cases the landlord is expected to make some small provision for the maintenance of the females of the family. His movable property goes to the person who performs his funeral rites.

An elder brother can transfer to a younger brother all his rights in the family property, but the effect of such a transfer is limited to his own lifetime, and does not curtail the rights of his son, who will succeed, in preference to the uncle on attaining his majority.

Religion.

The religion of the Rautiás may best be described as a mixture of the primitive animism characteristic of the aboriginal races and the debased form of Hinduism which has been disseminated in Chota Nagpur by a class of Brahmans markedly inferior in point of learning and ceremonial purity to those who stand forth as the representatives of the caste in the great centres of Hindu civilization. Among the Bar-gohri Rautiás many have of late years become Kabirpanthis; the rest, with most of the Chhot-gohri and the Berrás of both sub-castes, are Rámáyat Vaishnavas. A few only have adopted the tenets of the Saiva sects. Rama, Ganesa, Mahadeva, and Gauri are the favourite deities, whose worship is conducted by Sakadwipi Brahmans more or less in the orthodox fashion. Behind the fairly definite personalities of these greater gods there loom in the background, through a fog of ignorance and superstition, the dim shapes of Bar-pahár (the Marang Buru or mountain of the Mundas); Bura-buri, the supposed ancestors of mankind; the seven sisters who scatter cholera, small-pox, and cattle-plague abroad; Goraiá, the village god—a sort of rural Terminus; and the myriad demons with which the imagination of the Kolhs peoples the trees, rocks, streams, and fields of its surroundings.

To Bar-pahár are offered he-buffaloes, rams, he-goats, fowls, milk, flowers, and sweetmeats; the animals in each case being given some rice to chew and decked with garlands of flowers before being sacrificed. When offered in pursuance of a special vow, the animal is called *charáol*, and is slain in the early morning in the *sarná* or sacred grove outside the village; rice, ghi, molasses, vermilion, flowers, and *bel* leaves being presented at the same time. No female may be present at the ceremony. The carcase of the victim is distributed among the worshippers, but no part of it may be taken into the village, and it is cooked and eaten on the spot, even the remnants being buried in the *sarná* at the end of the feast. The head is eaten by the man who made the vow and the members of his family, but no others share in it, owing to the belief that whoever partakes of the head would thereby render himself liable to perform a similar *pujá*.

When a buffalo is sacrificed, the Rautiás do not eat the flesh themselves, but leave the carcase to the Mundas, Kharias, and other beef-eating folk who may happen to be present.

To the seven sisters (*devis*) and their brother Bhairo a rude shrine (*devigarhi*) is erected in the centre of every village, consisting of a raised plinth five cubits square covered by a tiled or thatched roof resting on six posts of *gulaichi* trees (*Plumeria*). In the middle of the plinth, on a line running north and south, stand seven little mounds of dried mud, representing the seven goddesses, while a smaller mound on one side stands for Bhairo. In front of the *Devigarhi*, at some ten or fifteen cubits distance, is a larger mound representing Goraiyá, the village god, to whom pigs are sacrificed by the village priest (*páhan*) and by men of the Dosádh caste. Regarding the names and functions of the seven sisters there seems to be much uncertainty. Some Rautias enumerate the following :—

Burhiá Mái or Sitalá.
Kankárin Mái.
Káli Mái.
Kuleswari Mái.
Bágheswari Mái.
Mareswari Mái.
Dulhári Mái.

Others substitute Jwálá-mukhi, Vindhyabásini, Málat Mái, and Joginiá Mái for the last four. Jwálá-mukhi is a place of pilgrimage in the Lower Himalayas north of the Panjáb, where inflammable gas issues from the ground and is believed to be the fire created by Parbati when she desired to become a *sati*. Vindhyabásini is a common title of Sitalá Devi, who presides over small-pox throughout Northern India. I cannot find out which sisters are supposed to be responsible for cholera and cattle-plague. Kuleshwari (*kul* = 'tiger' in Mundári) and Bágheswari apparently have to do with the tiger. He-goats, flowers, fruit, and *bel* leaves are offered to the seven sisters in front of the *devi-gurhi*. Women and children are present at the worship. A Sakadwipi Brahman presides, but does not slay the victims.

Festivals.

The following are the festivals observed by the Rautiás :—

(1) **Nawa Khani**—eating new rice with milk, molasses, and ghi. On the 12th of the light half of Bhádon (middle of September) and the 15th of the light half of Aghan (middle of November). These periods correspond respectively to the harvesting of the low land and high land rice crops.

(2) **Jitia parab.**—On the 8th of the dark half of Ásin (end of September). The females of the village, after fasting a day, bring a twig from a *jitia pipal* tree (*Ficus religiosa*) and an ear of rice, and plant them in the courtyard of a house, usually that of the chief man of the village. Vermilion, *arwá* or rice husked without boiling, flowers, and sweetmeats, are offered to the twig. Dancing, singing, and processions of various kinds follow, and in

the morning, after watching the twigs all night, the women offer *mánr* or rice gruel to their deceased ancestors.

(3) **Dasahará**—corresponding to the Devi-pujá and Vijayá dasmi of the Hindus.—On the 10th of the light half of *Asin* (early in October).

(4) **Debathan**—a fast, followed by eating various kinds of boiled fruit and roots—observed only by bachelors and spinsters on the eleventh of the light half of Kartik (middle of November).

(5) **Ganesh Chauth.**—On the 4th of the dark half of Mágh (middle of January). An image of Ganesa is made out of cow-dung and is worshipped with *laddus* or cakes of *til*, legends being recited at the same time.

(6) **Phagua**—corresponding to the Holi of the Hindus.—On the 15th of the light half of Phágun (middle of March), when ancestors are propitiated.

(7) **Karma.**—On the 11th of the light half of Bhádon (beginning of September). This festival is similar to the Jitiá, except that a branch of a *karam* tree (*Nauclea cordifolia*) is planted in the courtyard and the fasting is not continuous as in the *Jitiya Parab.*

The foregoing festivals are observed by all Rautiás. The more Hinduised members of the caste add to them the Rath-jatrá, the Janmashtami, the Rámnabami, and the Ind Parab.

Disposal of the dead.

The dead are usually disposed of by burning, except in the case of Kabirpanthi Rautiás, who are buried standing upright and facing to the north. In the former case the corpse, covered with a new cloth, is taken to the place of cremation (*masán*) and there shaved, bathed, and clothed in a new waistcloth and sheet. If the body be that of a woman whose husband is alive, it is bathed, anointed with oil, and dressed in a new *sári*. In the case of a widow the oiling is omitted. The corpse is then placed on the funeral pile with the head to the north, and the chief mourner, lighting a torch made of five dry twigs of a *bel* tree tied to the end of a bit of wood and soaked in *ghi*, walks round the pile seven times, applies the torch to the mouth of the deceased, and then sets fire to the pile. Before doing so however, he takes a portion of the sheet in which the corpse is dressed and wraps up in it a knife or a piece of iron. This piece of cloth must be kept for ten days. After the body has been consumed, the ashes are collected in a new earthen vessel (*ghánti*). On returning home the mourners wash their feet with water previously placed for them outside the house. Inside the courtyard a shallow brass dish (*tháli*) is laid ready with leaves of the *tulsi* (*Ocymum sanctum*) and *kareli* (*Momordica charantia*), one pice, and a vessel of water. Some person, not a member of the family, pours a little water into the hand of each mourner, who drinks it off. For ten days after the cremation the ashes of the deceased (*santh*) are hung up in the vessel in which they were placed. During this time the chief mourner must make daily libations to the ashes, and must keep on his person the piece of sheet and the iron already referred to. He may not change his clothes, sleep on a bed, or eat salt, and he can only take one meal a day, which he must cook himself. At the end of this time the ashes are either buried at the *masna*, or, where the family are wealthy enough to undertake the journey, are kept for transport to Benares or Gya. On the tenth day he and the other relatives bathe, shave, anoint themselves with a mixture of oil and oil-cake, and put on clean clothes. The chief mourner also offers to the deceased ten cakes (*pinda*) made of rice, milk, linseed, barley, and honey. On the eleventh day the regular *sráddh* ceremony is performed with the assistance of a Kanaujiá, or, failing him, of a Sakadwipi Brahman who mutters unintelligble nonsense, supposed to be Vedic texts, and the Kantáha or Mahábráhman is fed and receives presents. On the twelfth day Sakadwipi Brahmans and friends of different castes are entertained, and one *pinda* is offered in order that the deceased may be united to the company of ancestors. On the thirteenth day relatives are fed and final purification is obtained. The anniversary of the death is celebrated only once (*barkhi sráddh*). While this is going on no marriage can take place in the family; and in order to avoid this inconvenience the *barkhi sráddh* is often performed some months before a year has elapsed from the time of death. Offerings to ancestors in general (*tarpan*) are made through the agency of Brahmans on the 15th of the dark half of Ásin (end of September), and by the people themselves at the Nawá Kháni, Jitiá, and Phaguá festivals. Childless relatives, lepers, persons who die a violent death, and women who die in child-birth, get only one *pinda*, and are not counted as ancestors. Lepers are usually buried.

Ceremonies.

The Rautiás do not perform any of the ceremonies usual among other castes during pregnancy. At child-birth assistance is rendered by the Kusrain or Dagrin, who cuts the umbilical cord. The ceremonies of *chhatthi*, *barhi*, and *ekaisi* are performed on the sixth, twelfth, and twenty-first days after birth. If the child is born under an unlucky star (*asubh lagan*), a fourth ceremony, called *Jataisi*, is added on the twenty-seventh day, at which Brahmans are fed, and Gauri, Ganesa, Mahadeo, and the *Kul devatas* or family gods worshipped. The father of the child does not lie up after its birth, or give up his ordinary occupations, but he is supposed to contract impurity (*chhutká*) by reason of the event, and must keep away from his neighbours until after the sixth day, when, if a poor man, he is purified by bathing and by giving a feast to his relatives and to Brahmans. The richer a man is, the longer is his term of impurity. Tolerably well-to-do Rautias remain impure till the twelfth day, while the wealthier of the castes cannot get purified till the twenty-first.

When a child is six months old, its first meal of rice is commemorated—the ceremony of *munghuti*, followed by *mundan* or tonsure. The effect of this latter rite is to remove from the mother the last traces of the pollution of child-birth, and to qualify to eat flesh and to worship the family gods. *Karnabedh*, the boring of a boy's ears by the village barber, is done between the ages of six and fourteen, and is deemed to admit a boy among the grown men of the caste. Kabirpanthi members of the Bargohri sub-caste assume the sacred thread (*janeo*) when initiated into the tenets of the sect. The thread so worn is a *Chhatri janeo*, which differs from a Brahman's in the form of the knot with which it is tied.

Superstitions. Spirits.

The Rautias, though less plagued by the terrors of the unseen world than are the Mundas and Oraons, have certain superstitions which are worth recording. Women who die in child-birth, persons killed by a tiger, and all *ojhas* or exorcists, are liable after death to reappear as *bhuts*, or malevolent ghosts, and give trouble to the living. In such cases an exorcist (*ojhá* or *mati*) is called in to identify the spirit at work, and to appease it by gifts of money, goats, fowls, or pigs. Usually the spirit is got rid of in a few months, but some are specially persistent and require annual worship to induce them to remain quiet. Spirits of this type, who were great exorcists or otherwise men of note during their life-time, often extend their influence over several families, and eventually attain the rank of a tribal god.

Babu Rakhal Das Haldar, Manager of the Chutia Nagpur estate, gives the following instance of exorcism from his personal experience. In December 1884, when the Manager was in camp at the foot of the Báragáin hills in Lohardagá, a Kurmi woman of Kukui was killed by a tiger, and the tiger-demon in her form was supposed to be haunting the village. An *ojhá* who was sent for to lay the ghost, took a young man to represent the tiger-demon, and after certain incantations put him into a kind of mesmeric condition, in which he romped about on all fours, and generally demeaned himself like a tiger. A rope was then tied round his loins and he was dragged to a cross-road, where the volent fit passed off and he became insensible. In this condition he remained until the *ojha* recited certain *mantras* and threw rice on him, when he regained his senses, and the demon was pronounced to have quitted the village.

Occupation.

Rautias believe military service to have been their original occupation, but this is little more than a distant memory of times long past, and at the present day most members of the caste in Lohardagá are settled agriculturists. The chief men of the caste hold *taluks*, *jágirs*, *báraik* grants, and similar tenures paying quit-rents direct to the Mahárája of Chutia Nagpur, while the rank and file are raiyats paying light rents and possessing occupancy rights. A few only are found in the comparatively reduced position of tenants of *raja's* lands at full rents. In many of the tenures and occupancy holdings *khuntkáti* rights, entitling the tenant to hold at a low quit-rent, are claimed; while others are *korkar*, paying only one-half of the standard rates of rent.

Social status.

Socially the caste ranks fairly high, and Brahmans will take water and sweetmeats from their hands. Bargohri Rautias will not eat cooked food, smoke, or drink with any but members of their own sub-caste; but they will take sweetmeats from Brahmans, Rajputs, and Srawaks. Chhot-gohris are equally particular about cooked food, but will take water and sweetmeats from, and will smoke with, Bhogtás, Ahirs, Jhorás, and Bhuyiás. They also drink spirits and fermented liquors, and eat wild pigs and fowls, all of which are forbidden for the Bar-gohri sub-caste.

Representative assembly.

The Chhot-gohri Rautias have a representative assembly (*mandli*) for groups of from five to fifteen villages, which decides questions of caste usage. Each village sends one member to the *mandli*, which is presided over by an official called *mahant*, whose office is hereditary. When the *mahant* is a minor, his duties are carried on by an adult member of his family or by any Rautiá unanimously chosen for this purpose by the *mandli*. The orders of the *mandli* are enforced by fines, by refusing to eat and drink with the offender, and by depriving him of the services of the barber and washerman of the caste. Certain acts entailing ceremonial impurity, such as accidentally killing a cow or having incestuous intercourse (*gotra-badh*) with a woman of the same *gotra*, admit of being atoned for by giving a feast to Brahmans and the caste brethren. But the wilful slaughter of a cow, the repetition of the offence of *gotra-badh*, and the cardinal sin of eating with a person of low caste, cannot be expiated, and in such extreme cases the offender is turned out of the caste. The Bar-gohri have no standing assembly, and pancháyats are summoned to deal with caste questions as occasion requires.

Sorcery.

The services of the *ojhá* are also called in to ascertain what spirit (*bhút*) or witch (*dáin* or *bisáhi*) has caused a particular illness, and to prescribe the cure. On such occasions he comes after sun-down and demands a winnowing fan, a small earthen lamp, rags for a wick, a handful of *arwa* rice, and some oil. Having twisted a wick into the rude semblance of a hooded snake, the *ojha* lights his lamp and proceeds, by shaking the rice in the winnowing fan, to divine the name of the *bhút* or *dáin* who is to blame. This point having been cleared up, he is presented with a fowl to be sacrified to his own *birwat* or *ishta deva*, and he then performs the ceremony of *kat bándh*, by which he binds the patient or his family to the spirit or witch. This is supposed to put matters in train towards recovery, and the *ojhá* departs, receiving from the patient's family a promise of presents of goats, etc., in the event of the treatment proving successful. Rautiás are in great terror of witches, and believe, like many people, that they can act upon their victims through objects belonging to or intimately associated with them, such as bits of cut hair or nails ; but no special care is taken to preserve or destroy such articles.

Dreams are believed to be caused by recently deceased relatives of the dreamer, who appear to him in sleep and complain of hunger and want of clothes, etc. Such importunate spirits are easily appeased by sending for a Brahman and giving him the things which have been demanded in the dream.

Among other curious superstitions may be noticed the notion that a woman in the early stages of pregnancy should not cross running water. The evil eye is believed in, but its influence is attributed to inordinate appetite on the part of the person who has overlooked any one. Its effects may be averted by mixing red mustard seeds and salt, waving the mixture round the head and then throwing it into the fire. To ward off the evil eye from the crops, a blackened earthen pot with rude devices scrawled on it in white paint is stuck up in the fields.

Oaths and ordeals are sometimes resorted to for the settlement of personal disputes and the decision of questions affecting caste. Ganges water, rice that has been offered to Jagannath, a mixture of rice and cow-dung or copper and tulsi leaves, are held in the hand and a solemn statement is made touching the matter in dispute. It is believed that some sort of misfortune will befall the person who under these circumstances speaks falsely, but the consequences of lying do not seem to be clearly defined. In former days a more severe test was in vogue: a ring was thrown into a deep pan of boiling ghi, and the person whose conduct was in question was required to take it out with his fingers.

Boys whose elder brothers have died in infancy are given opprobrious names, such as Akhaj, Bechan, Bechu (he who is for sale), Khudi, Chuni, Gandaur, Kinu, Lohar, Chamár, Dom or Doman, Mochi, Ghási, Mahili (names of low castes). Girls are called by the feminine forms of these names—Akhji, Chámin, etc. Rautias do not follow the custom, common among the higher castes, of giving two names—one for ceremonial purposes and the other for common use.

Lucky days for ploughing are the 12th of the light half of Kátik and the 5th of the light half of Aghán for low rice lands (*don*), and the 1st of the dark half of Chait for high lands. The 3rd of the light half of Baisakh is good for sowing; but if there is early rain, a Brahman may be got to fix a lucky day before this date. For transplanting the rice seedlings a lucky day may be arranged by a Brahman at any time between the 2nd of the dark half of Ásár and the 11th of the light half of Bhádo. It is specially unlucky to plough during the Mrigdáh or Nirbisrá period, called Ambubáchi in Bengal, when the sun is for three days in the Mrigasirá constellation; during the Karam festival (10th—12th of light half of Bhádo); and on the day of the Sarhúl. Rain during the Mrigdáh brings bad luck; but rainy weather, while the sun is in the Rohini or Swáti constellation, betokens good fortune. When rice is transplanted, the village *pahán* performs the *bangari puja* to the god of the village. When a well is sunk a Brahman is consulted as to the site and the proper time for commencing work, and a *pratishthá* or dedicatory sacrifice is performed before the water is used.

The following statement shows the number and distribution of Rautiás in 1872 and 1881:—

DISTRICT.	1872.	1881.	DISTRICT.	1872.	1881.
Santál Parganás	......	12	Singbhum	......	1
Hazaribagh	4	......	Manbhum	......	64
Lohardagá	16,387	18,533	Tributary States	5,242	8,264

Rautiá, a sub-caste of Koiris and a title of Cheros in Chota Nagpur.

Raut Mehter, a sweeper sub-caste of Doms in Behar.

Rawáni, a sub-caste of Kándus in Behar.

Rawáni or *Ramáni*, *Raoni*, *Rohání*, a sub-caste of Kahárs in Behar.

Rawanpur, a section of Kahárs in Behar.

Raworh, a section of Maghaiyá Kumhárs in Behar.

Ráya, a title of Bráhmans, Káyasths, and several other castes in Bengal and Behar; of Khairás in Chota Nagpur.

Ráyi, a *gáin* of the Bharadwája *gotra* and a *mel* or hypergamous sub-group of Rárhi Brahmans in Bengal.

Regálaunchhá, a *thar* or sept of Khambus in Darjiling.

Regmi, a *thar* of the Kausika *gotra* of Nepáli Brahmans.

Rekhaur, a sept of Rájputs in Behar.

Reláti-Madak, a sub-caste of Madhunápits in Bengal.

Renta, a sept of Páns in Chota Nagpur.

Reson, a synonym for Teli.

Retha, fruit, a totemistic sept of Lohárs in Chota Nagpur.

Riáng, a sept of Tipperahs in the Hill Tracts of Chittagong.

Richil, a *dugu* or section of the Kochh-Mandai in Dacca. The name indicates the original habitat of the group, probably a hill or village in Assam, and now-a-days has no bearing upon marriage.

Rigretsa, a sept of Maghs in the Hill Tracts of Chittagong.

Rijál, a *thar* of the Dhánjaya *gotra* of Nepáli Brahmans; a section of Kámis; a *thar* or sept of Mangars in Darjiling.

Rikhab, a section of Brahmans.

Rikhi, a section of Rajwárs and Rautiás in Chota Nagpur.

Rikhiásan, a sub-caste of Bhuiyas in Hazaribagh; a sept of Kharwars in Chota Nagpur; a section of Kádars and Musahars in Behar; a totemistic sept of Chiks in Chota Nagpur who may not eat beef or pork.

Rikhiásan or **Pátrise**, a section of Mauliks in Western Bengal.

Rikmun, a section of Musahars in Behar.

Rimál, a *thar* or section of Nepáli Brahmans.

Rimching, a *thar* or sept of Khambus in Darjiling.

Rimrimiá, a section of Kurmis in Chota Nagpur and Orissa.

Rishi, a title of the patit or degraded priests, who minister to the spiritual wants of the lower castes; a section of the Bhar caste in Manbhum. The term appears to have been borrowed from the Brahmanical system in comparatively recent times, as the caste has also a set of the totemistic sections characteristic of the Kolarian race.

Rishi, *Rishiputra*, a synonym for, and a title of, Muchis in Bengal.

Risyál, a *thar* or section of Nepáli Brahmans.

Riti, a title of Bangaja Káyasths.

Rochingáchhá, a *thar* or sept of Khambus in Darjiling.

Rohilá, a *pathi* or hypergamous sub-group of Barendra Brahmans in Bengal.

Rohini, a title of Káhárs in Behar.

Rohita, a section of Brahmans and Káyasths in Bengal.

Roh-Lutur, ear-pierced, a sub-sept of the Hansda, Hemrom, Kisku, and Tudu septs of Santáls.

Roht, *pánjaun* tree, a sub-sept of the Márndi sept of Santáls.

Rol, a title of Bangaja Káyasths.

Rojá, a title of Kaibarttas in Bengal.

Rondiar, a section of Mahilis in Chota Nagpur.

Rong, a sub-tribe of Lepchas in Darjiling.

Rorah, a sept of Rájputs in Behar.

Rori, a fruit, a totemistic sept of Oraons in Chota Nagpur.

Rosráit, a section of the Dhaprá sub-caste of Doms in Behar.

Rote, a sept of the Asuras in Chota Nagpur.

Rudra, a title of Baidyas and of Dakshin-Rárhi and Bangaja Káyasths in Bengal.

Rudrabagchhi, a *gáin* of the Sándilya *gotra* of Bárendra Brahmans in Bengal.

Rudrabanik, a title of Baniyás in Bengal.

Rudrabans, a synonym for Kumhár.

Rudrapal, a synonym for Kumhár in Bengal.

Rugri, a kind of mushroom, a totemistic sept of Mundas in Chota Nagpur.

Ruhidás, a title laid claim to by all Chamárs, as denoting their descent from a Bhagat ancestor of that name; also a title of Dosadhs in Behar.

Rui, a title of Khandáits in Orissa.

Ruichhung, a sub-tribe of Dejong Lhori or Bhotia of the south.

Ruidás, a title of Muchis in Bengal.

Rujál, a section of Kámis in Darjiling.

Rujichá, a *thar* or sept of Sunuwárs in Darjiling.

Rukái, a *thar* or section of Nepáli Brahmans.

Rukhar, a group of the Aoghar sect of Saiva ascetics founded in Guzerat by a Dasnámi mendicant named Brahmagiri. See **Aoghar**.

Rukhi, squirrel, a sept of Mundas in Chota Nagpur.

Rukhiár, a section of the Amashta sub-caste of Káyasths in Behar.

Rumbá, a section of Murmis in Darjiling.

Runda, fox, leopard (wild cat?), a totemistic sept of Mundas, Oraons and Lohárs in Chota Nagpur.

Rupakheti, a *thar* or section of Nepáli Brahmans.

Rutá, a tree, a totemistic sept of Mundas in Chota Nagpur.

S

Sabáláre, a sept of the Agáni sub-tribe of Meches in the Darjiling Terai.

Sabar, a synonym for Savar.

Sabarkárá, a sub-caste of Muchis in Bengal.

Sábarna, a *gotra* or section of Baidyas, Brahmans, Gandhabaniks, Káyasths, Tántis, and Subarnbaniks in Bengal; a Brahmanical section of Bábhans in Behar.

Sábarnia, a sept of the Chandrabansi division of Rájputs in Behar.

Sabarnika, a section of Utkal Brahmans.

Sabhaiyár, a *pur* or section of Sákadwipi Brahmans in Behar.

Sabhá-Sundar, a title of Dhobás in Bengal.

Sabkota, a *thar* or sept of Mangars in Darjiling.

Saboktsa, a sept of Maghs in the Hill Tracts of Chittagong.

Sabor, a sub-caste of Goálás in Chota Nagpur.

Sabri, a section of Kanaujiá Lohárs in Behar.

Sābu, a section of Mahesris in Behar.

Sadá, a section of Sunris in Behar.

Sádá, a sub-sept of all the septs of Santáls.

Sadábarti, a section of the Banodhiá and Jaiswár Kalwárs in Behar.

Sádá Goálá, a hypergamous group of Goálás in Eastern Bengal.

Sadásankar, a *thar* or sept of Mangars in Darjiling.

Sadgop, *Satgop*, *Chásá*, a cultivating caste of Bengal Proper, who are supposed to have separated themselves from the Goálás by abandoning pastoral pursuits and taking exclusively to agriculture. They are divided into two sub-castes—the **Paschim Kuliyá**, who live to the west of the Bhágirathi, and the **Purbba Kuliyá**, whose settlements are on the east of that river. The separation between the two is said to have taken place in the time of Ballál Sen, when the ancestors of the Paschim Kuliya group refused to accept the institution of Kulinism, which was introduced among them at a later date and in a somewhat different form. The Purbba Kuliyás, a much smaller body, adopted the new rules and parted on that account from the main body of the caste. Originally both sub-castes were strictly endogamous, but of late years the rule has been relaxed and marriages have taken place between members of the two groups. The Purbba Kuliyás. however, recognize a further division of their own sub-caste into the two endogamous groups of Ghosh and Sarbesia. The hypergamous divisions of both sub-castes and the sections of the Paschim Kuliyá are shown in the Appendix. One of the hypergamous groups, the **Konr Gop**, seems

Origin and internal structure.

to have developed in comparatively modern times among the Sadgops of Murshedabad, and deserves special notice for the light it throws upon the mode in which hypergamous groups are formed. The Konr Gop are in no sense of purer lineage than their brethren. They are merely Sadgops who have grown rich and have risen above the necessity of cultivating with their own hands. They affect some sort of ill-defined social pre-eminence, and while taking their wives from among ordinary Satgops will not give their daughters in marriage outside their own circle. The Purbba Kuliyá have no sections, and regulate their marriage by the standard rules defining prohibited degrees.

Marriage.

Infant-marriage is in full force among the Sadgops, and it would be deemed an indelible disgrace for a girl to be unprovided with a husband before she reaches the age of puberty. Men, on the other hand, marry comparatively later in life, and the operation of the law of hypergamy, popularly known as Kulinism, sometimes puts men of the lower groups to considerable difficulty in finding wives. The marriage ceremony is of the orthodox type, the binding portion being *sátpák*, the carrying of the bride seven times round the bridegroom. Although this is technically the essential rite, the marriage is held to be complete at an earlier stage, as soon as the *ásirbád*, or blessing on the married pair, has been pronounced. Polygamy is recognized so far that if a man's first wife is barren or proves faithless he may take a second; but such cases are said to be rare, and for all practical purposes the caste may be regarded as monogamous. Widows are not allowed to marry a second time. Divorce is not formally recognized; but if a woman commits adultery or otherwise disgraces herself, her husband may get rid of her by undergoing the ceremony of *práyaschitta* or expiation for impurity and by performing her *sráddh* as if she were actually dead. Women so divorced may not marry again.

Religion.

The religious and ceremonial observances of the caste exhibit no departure from the average Hinduism of the middle classes in Bengal. Almost all Sadgops are Vaishnavas, Hari and Satya Náráyan being their favourite deities. Lakshmi is also regarded with special reverence as watching over their welfare, while Sashti and Mangalchandi are worshipped by the women of the caste. The Brahmans who serve them as priests are received on equal terms by other members of the sacred order. The dead are burned, and the *sráddh* ceremony is performed according to the orthodox system.

Occupation and social status.

Agriculture is their characteristic pursuit, and they are commonly spoken of and addressed as Chásá. In Central Bengal large numbers of them are engaged in rearing silk-worms and selling raw silk. The bulk of the caste are occupancy or non-occupancy raiyats. Some hold tenures, and a few, particularly in Midnapur, have risen to be zamindars of fairly high position. Their social rank is sufficiently defined by stating that they belong to the Nabasákha group, and that Brahmans will take water and certain kinds of sweetmeats from their hands. Their rules as to diet are the same as are observed by all orthodox Hindus in Bengal Proper. One curious custom may be noticed here. Sadgops will not eat pumpkin (*láu*) and *dál* in the month of Ásár, and by way of accounting for this prohibition tell the absurd story that they are descended from one Kálu Ghosh, who, being appointed by one of the gods to look after his cattle, killed and ate the sacred animals. Oddly enough, instead of being punished for his sacrilege, the story goes on to say that his descendants, who thenceforth applied themselves to cultivation, were permitted to rank above the children of the other brother, Murári Ghosh, who faithfully discharged his trust. Valueless as the legend is, it deserves notice as a specimen of the folk-lore current among the people regarding the origin of particular castes.

The following statement shows the number and distribution of Sadgops in 1872 and 1881 :—

District.	1872.	1881.	District.	1872.	1881.
Bardwan	185,804	112,128	Faridpur	693	320
Bankura	17,971	45,201	Bakarganj	186	240
Birbhum	109,446	82,764	Maimansinh	581	698
Midnapur	187,996	196,360	Tipperah	158	456
Hughli	} 63,774	{ 61,025	Chittagong	85	167
Howrah		12,693	Noakhali	25	......
24-Parganás	38,066	20,570	Patna	......	21
Nadiya	17,506	16,177	Monghyr	37	......
Khulna	......	6,021	Bhagalpur	......	12
Jessore	7,539	9,316	Purniah	11,674	1,323
Murshedabad	29,321	26,008	Maldah	1,385	1,548
Dinajpur	2,316	3,923	Santál Parganás	1,109	2,581
Rajshahye	396	782	Cuttack	218	338
Rangpur	136	603	Puri	9	18
Bogra	565	942	Balasore	2,097	7,694
Pabna	449	893	Tributary States	51	125
Jalpigori	276	500	Lohardagá	69	9
Kuch Behar	......	133	Singbhum	1,413	1,239
Dacca	1,065	2,361	Manbhum	6,415	2,966

Sádhak, a *mul* or section of the Ghosin sub-caste of Goálás in Behar.

Sádhu, a title of the Desá sub-caste of Gandhabaniks and of Tántis in Bengal.

Sádhubagchhi, a *gáin* of the Sándilya *gotra* of Bárendra Brahmans in Bengal.

Sádhupaliyá, a sub-caste of Kochhs in Dinajpur.

Sádhya, a hypergamous group of the Bárendra Káyasths.

Sádhya-Maulik or **Bahátture**, a hypergamous group of the Dakshin-Rárhi Káyasths in Bengal.

Sádhya-Srotriya, a hypergamous group of Rárhi Bráhmans in Bengal.

Sad-Kámár, a sub-caste of Kámárs who are cultivators.

Sad-Lohár, a sub-caste of Lohárs or Hindu blacksmiths in Lohardagá.

Sad-Munda, a sub-tribe of Mundas affecting to follow the Hindu religion.

Sadom, horse, a totemistic sept of Mundas in Chota Nagpur.

Sadonga, a sept of Chakmás in the Hill Tracts of Chittagong.

Sadra, a section of Mahesris in Behar.

Sáfi, cleaner, a synonym for Dhobi in Behar, only used by persons who are not members of the caste.

Ság, vegetable, a totemistic sept of Chiks in Chota Nagpur.

Sagáhut, a sub-caste of Sunris in Behar who permit widows to marry again by the *sagái* form, often opposed to *Biáhut*, who do not tolerate such a practice. They are ordinarily grain-dealers and shopkeepers.

Ságáin, a *gáin* or sub-section of Saptasati Brahmans in Bengal.

Ságarbansi, a synonym for Ságarpeshá.

Ságarpeshá, in Orissa a designation of the illegitimate offspring of a Brahman woman by a Káyasth man.

Sagela Bagela, a *mul* or section of Kesarwáni Baniás in Behar.

Saghár, "vegetable-eater," a title of the Bahiot sub-caste of Amáts and of Dhanuks in Behar who are employed as personal servants to the higher castes.

Ságí, a section of Lohárs in Behar.

Sagin, the name of female attendants in shops for the sale of opium and its compounds, said to be kept for the purpose of attracting customers, and believed not to be above reproach in matters of morals.

Ságmá, a totemistic sept of the Bhumij tribe in Manbhum.

Saguniá, a sub-caste of the Kraunchdwipi Brahmans in Behar.

Sagun-ure, a title of the Kochh caste in Northern Bengal.

Sáh, a section of Saraogis in Behar.

Sáhá, *Sáhu*, a title of the Desá sub-caste of Gandhabaniks in Bengal; a title of Nápits, Sonárs, Telis, and Sunris. The latter invariably style themselves Sáhás or Sauloks. Tradition says that they were created from the sweat of the trunk (*sunda*) of the elephant-mouthed Ganesa to guard the celestial nectar for his mother Durgá; and hence they were called Sundis (corrupted into Sunris). Ballál assigned to them such a low rank on account of their tribal arrogance.

Sahadar, a section of the Biyáhut and Kharidáhá Kalwárs in Behar.

Sáhál, a section of the Biyáhut and Kharidáhá Kalwárs in Behar.

Sáhani, a title of Malláhs in Behar.

Sahar, a section of Bháts.

Sáhari, a *gáin* of the Bátsya *gotra* of Bárendra Brahmans in Bengal.

Sáharik, a *gáin* of the Bharadwája *gotra* of Rárhi Brahmans in Bengal.

Saharwár, a section of Kamárkalla Sonárs in Behar.

Sahasnangiá, a section of Bábhans in Behar.

Sahbar, a section of Goálás in Behar.

Sahdauliá, a *kul* or section of Bábhans in Behar.

Sáhjáwán, a section of Goálás in the North-Western Provinces and Behar.

Sahmbahang, a sept of the Tambrkhola sub-tribe of Limbus in Darjiling.

Sahni, a title of Gonrhis in Behar.

Sáho, a title of the Ariár and Khandiwár sub-castes of Bais Baniyás; of Halwáis, Kahárs, Kalwárs, Kandus, Sonárs, Sunris, and Telis in Behar.

Sahrwár, a *mul* or section of the Naomulia or Majraut sub-caste of Goálás in Behar.

Sahsradih, a *mul* or section of the Naomulia or Majraut sub-caste of Goálás in Behar.

Sáhu, a title of Khatris; of Baniyás, Kalwárs, and Kándus in Behar; a title of Kewats in Orissa; of Sonárs in Behar; a section of the Kulsunri sub-caste of Sunris in Behar; a title of Láheris in Chota Nagpur.

Sáhul, a section of Khariás in Chota Nagpur.

Sahuliar, a section of the Sribastab sub-caste of Káyasths in Behar.

Sahun, a *mul* or section of the Biahut sub-caste of Kalwárs in Behar.

Sahuri, a *mul* or section of the Chhamuliá Madhesiá sub-caste of Halwáis in Behar.

Sái, a title of Brahmans.

Saidábád, a section of Pátnis in Bengal.

Saigal, a section of the Panchjáti sub-caste of Khatris in Bengal.

Sailum, porcupine, a totemistic sept of Mundas in Chota Nagpur.

Sáin, a *gáin* or sub-section of Saptasati Brahmans in Bengal; a title of Dakshin-Rárhi and Bangaja Káyasths.

Sáini, a sub-caste of Sutradhars in Noakháli.

Sainthwár, a sub-caste of Kurmis in Behar.

Sair, a small agricultural caste of Western Bengal, believed to be closely related to Bágdis.

Sais, a *mul* or section of the Maghayá sub-caste of Koiris in Behar.

Saisarunduar, a sept of Mundas in Chota Nagpur.

Sai Sonarwar, a sept of Kharwars in Chota Nagpur.

Sáitghariá, a sub-caste of Sutradhars in Noakháli.

Saitiya, a section of the Oswál Baniyás.

Saiva, a worshipper of Siva.

Saival, a *thar* or section of Nepáli Brahmans.

Sakaddi, a section of Sonárs in Behar.

Sákadwipi or **Sakaldwipi**, a division of Brahmans in Behar.

Sákalya, a title of Dhobás in Bengal.

Sakar-Ghore, a *mul* of the Sándil section of Maithil Brahmans in Behar.

Sakarpuriet, a *mul* or section of the Naomuliá or Majraut sub-caste of Goálás in Behar.

Sakarwár, a *mul* or section of Bábhans; of the Bhojpuriá sub-caste of Halwáis; a sept of the Chandrabansi division of Rájputs in Behar.

Sákati, a *gáin* of the Bharadwája *gotra* of Bárendra Brahmans in Bengal.

Sakerbasá, a *mul* or section of the Kamárkalla sub-caste of Sonárs in Behar.

Sákhá, a title of Brahmans in Western Bengal.

Sakhali, a sub-tribe of Mangars in Darjiling.

Sakhwait, a *kul* or section of Bábhans in Behar.

Sakin, a section of the Purbiyá Madesia sub-caste of Halwáis in Behar.

Sakmait, a section of Bábhans in Behar.

Sákori, a *mul* or section of the Chhamuliá Madhesiá sub-caste of Halwáis in Behar.

Sakráit, a section of Bánsphor Doms in Western Behar.

Sakraiwár-Harari, a *mul* of the Kásyapa section of Maithil Brahmans in Behar.

Sakraiwár-Tatail, a *mul* of the Kásyap section of Maithil Brahmans in Behar.

Sakraiwár-Chhámu, a *mul* of the Kásyap section of Maithil Brahmans in Behar.

Sakraul, a *mul* or section of the Naomuliá or Goriá sub-caste of Goálás in Behar.

Sakri, a *mul* or section of the Kanaujiá sub-caste of Sonárs and of Gháṣis in Behar.

Sakrol, a *mul* or section of the Chhamuliá Madhesiá sub-caste of Halwáis in Behar.

Saksena, a sub-caste of Káyasths in Behar.

Sákta, a worshipper of the female principle in nature, of the female forms of the Hindu deities, and especially of Devi, the sakti or female energy of Siva. Sáktas are divided into two classes: Dakshináchári̇s, or Dakshinamárgis, "followers of the right-hand path," and Vámácháris or Vámamárgis, "followers of the left-hand path." The former base their religion on the Puránas and do not practise mystical or secret rites; the latter derive their ritual from the magical treatises known as Tantras, and are addicted to practices of a grossly licentious character. The Tantras are said to be founded on the Kaula Upanishad, and the left-handed Sáktas are therefore called Kaulikas.

Sakti, a title of Dakshin-Rárhi Káyasths in Bengal.

Saktri, a *gotra* or section of Brahmans and Baidyas in Bengal.

Sakuntalá, a sub-caste of Brahmans in Behar.

Sál, fish, a totemistic section of Khandáits; a sept of Mundas and Oraons; a title of Dakshin-Rárhi Káyasths.

Sál or **Saula**, a section of Korás, signifying a fish.

Sálákhá, a synonym for Sherpa Bhotia of Nepal.

Sálák-khá, a merchant carrying on trade, a sub-sept of the Nah-pá sept of Sherpa Bhotias.

Sálangiá, a section of Goálás in the North-Western Provinces and Behar.

Salankáyana, an exogamous section of Baidyas in Bengal.

Sálbanwár, *sál* jungle, a totemistic section of Kurmis in Chota Nagpur and Orissa.

Salhariá, a *kul* or section of Bábhans in Behar.

Salkar, a kind of potato, a totemistic sept of Mundas in Chota Nagpur.

Sálkhini, a *mul* or section of the Naomuliá or Majraut sub-caste of Goálás in Behar.

Sálmáchh, fish, a totemistic sept of Savars in Orissa; a section of Máls in Midnapur and Manbhum.

Sálodiá, a section of Goálás in the North-Western Provinces and Behar.

Sálrishi or *Sálmách* (the *sál* fish), a section of Bágdis in Bengal and of Chásás in Orissa; a totemistic sept of the Bhumij tribe in Manbhum, the members of which will not touch or eat the *sál* fish; a section of Lohárs in the Santál Parganás.

Sálu, a root in pond, a totemistic sept of Mundas in Chota Nagpur.

Sálubi, a synonym for Pátikár, *q.v.*

Sám, Syám, a title of Dakshin-Rárhi and Bangaja Káyasths.

Sámá, a section of Korás in Chota Nagpur.

Samaddar, a title of Chásá-dhobás in Bengal and a hypergamous group of Kaibarttas in Bakarganj.

Sámagáu, a singer of the Sáma Veda, a title of Brahmans.

Samaiár, a section of Káyasths in Behar.

Samal, a title of Khandaits in Orissa.

Sámal, a title of Chásás in Orissa.

Samal or **Samar**, deer, a totemistic sept of Mundas.

Sámanta, a chief, a group of the Srotriya sub-caste of Utkal Brahmans; a title of Aguris, Brahmans, Khandáits, Rájputs, Sadgops, Telis, and some other castes.

Sámantasár, a *samaj* or local group of the Saunaka *gotra* of Páschátya Baidik Brahmans in Bengal.

Sámánya-Maulik, a hypergamous group of the Uttar-Rárhi sub-caste of Káyasths.

Samári, a sub-caste of Malláhs in Behar.

Sámariá, a synonym for Málé.

Samastipur, a *mul* or section of the Naomuliá or Majraut sub-caste of Goálás in Behar.

Samat, pestle, a totemistic sept of Korwas in Chota Nagpur.

Samdiá, a section of Khariás in Chota Nagpur.

Samdoar, a sept of Mundas in Chota Nagpur.

Samduar, a sept of Agariás in Chota Nagpur.

Sámigrihi, a section of Utkal or Orissa Brahmans.

Sámil Thákur, a section of Kanaujiá Lohárs in Behar.

Samjhar, a sept of Chiks in Chota Nagpur.

Sámp, snake, a totemistic sept of Korwas; a section of Turis; a section of Goálás in the North-Western Provinces and Behar.

Sámperiyá, Sámp-wálá, a sub-caste of Bediyas who catch and charm snakes.

Samswár, a sub-caste of Kurmis in Behar.

Samudra, a *gáin* of the Sábarna *gotra* of Bárendra Brahmans in Bengal.

Samudwar, a sept of Kharwars in Chota Nagpur.

Samundar-Khorá, a section of Sonárs in Behar.

Samwah, a sept of Limbus in Darjiling.

San, heron, a totemistic sept of Lohárs in Chota Nagpur.

Sán, a title of Chásádhobás in Bengal.

Sáná, a title of Dakshin-Rárhi Káyasths in Bengal.

Sanádhya, a sub-caste of Gaura Brahmans.

Sánágánthá, a sub-caste of Máls in Bankura.

Sanahlá, a title of Hindu Joláhas in Behar.

Sánchi, a sub-caste of Doms in Bengal.

Sanda, a *pangat* or section of Dosádhs in Behar.

Sandaliá, a section of Bábhans in Behar.

Sándh, bullock, a totemistic sept of Lohárs; a section of Goráits; a totemistic sept of Chamárs and Doms in Chota Nagpur.

Sandhawár, a section of the Amashta sub-caste of Káyasths in Behar.

Sandhoá, a synonym for Niyáriya, *q.v.*

Sandi, plough, a totemistic sept of Mundas in Chota Nagpur.

Sandiguriá, black monkey, a totemistic sept of Mundas in Chota Nagpur.

Sandil, full moon, a totemistic sept of Mundas in Chota Nagpur.

Sándil, a *gotra* or section of Bábhans in Behar, borrowed from the Brahmanical system and superadded to the original exogamous groups (*kuls*) characteristic of the caste; a section of the Kumhár caste in Western Bengal, apparently borrowed from the Brahmanical system and added to the totemistic sections characteristic of the caste; a section of Utkal Brahmans; a section of Cháins.

Sándil or **Sanrishi,** a bull, a totemistic section of the Paripál sub-caste of Sunris in Manbhum, the members of which do not castrate their own cattle, but purchase bullocks and sell their own bulls.

Sandilai, a sept of Pators in Chota Nagpur.

Sándilya, a *gotra* or section of the Aguri, Baidya, Brahman, Kámár, and Subarnabanik castes in Bengal; a section of the Sárák caste in Manbhum; of Kumhárs, Tántis, Telis and Káyasths in Bengal; an eponymous sept of Rájputs and Savars; a section of Goálás, Kaibarttas, Madhunápits, Mális, Mayarás, Muchis, Nápits, and Sunris in Bengal; an eponymous section of Barhis, Baruis, Rautiás, Chásádhobás, Gandhabaniks; a sept of Bhumijs; a section of Sánkháris, Bháts; of Suklis in Midnapur; of the Paschim Kuliyá Sadgops; of Sutradhars and Támbulis in Bengal.

Sandipurti, cock, a totemistic sept of Mundas in Chota Nagpur.

Sandi Sarin, fowl, a totemistic sept of Mundas in Chota Nagpur.

Sandwipá, a sub-caste of Kumhárs in Noakháli.

Sanga, a title of Bangaja Káyasths.

Sangá, or *Sangoar*, sweet potato, a totemistic sept of Mundas in Chota Nagpur.

Sángá, a section of the Mahili-Munda sub-caste of Mahilis in Chota Nagpur.

Sangalwár, a sept of Lohárs in Chota Nagpur.

Sángbá, a section of Murmis in Darjiling.

Sángbah, a sept of Limbus in Darjiling.

Sang-behbo, a *rui* or sept of Dejong Lhoris, the members of which are the descendants of emigrants from Bhotan and Nepal.

Sang Chiria, a kind of bird, a totemistic sept of Mundas in Chota Nagpur.

Sangda, a sub-sept of the Murmu sept of Santáls.

Sángdan, a section of Murmis in Darjiling.

Sangi, a synonym for Málé.

Sángir, a sept of the Suryabansi sub-tribe of Rájputs in Behar.

Sangiri Thákur, a section of Kanaujiá Lohárs in Behar.

Sangma, a buffalo, apparently a totemistic sept of the Chhothar sub-tribe of Limbus in Darjiling. The buffalo is taboo to this *thar*: the legend is the same as that of the Khema *thar*.

Sangmi, a sept of Lepchas in Darjiling.

Sángpáng, a *thar* or sept of Khambus in Darjiling.

Sangskár, a performer of ceremonies, a title of Brahmans.

Sangtarás, stone-cutters of various castes.

Sangtarásh, a sub-caste of Gonrhis in Behar. They say they are not Gonrhis, and distinguish themselves as Gonrh. They work in stone.

Sangwe, a title of Aráiya Telis in Behar.

Sanhá, a section of the Biyáhut and Kharidáhá Kalwárs in Behar.

Sanhakiá, a section of Bháts.

Sanicherá, a sub-caste of the Kraunchdwipi Brahmans in Behar.

Sanichrá, a mul or section of Kalwárs in Behar.

Sanj·kmah, a sept of Limbus in Darjiling.

Sankar, a title of Sannyásis and Bairágis.

Sankarjáti, a generic term for the castes supposed to have been formed by marriages or illicit connexions between members of the four primary castes.

Sankarpur, a *mul* or section of the Naomuliá or Majraut sub-caste of Goálás in Behar.

Sankarshan, a section of the Páschátya Baidik Brahmans in Bengal.

Sankarwár, a sept of Rájputs in Behar.

Sankatwár, a title of Dhánuks in Behar.

Sánkh, conch shell, a sub-sept of the Saren sept of Santáls.

Sankha, a section of Karans in Orissa.

Sankha-Asram, a sub-caste of Gandhabaniks in Bengal.

Sankhabanik, a synonym for Sánkhári in Bengal.

Sankhakár, a synonym for Sánkhári in Bengal.

Sankhalai, a sub-caste of Kámárs in the Santál Parganás.

Sánkhári, *Sankhakár. Sankhabanik,* the shell-cutting caste of Bengal, some of whom have taken of late years to working in gold and silver. Tradition ascribes the origin of the caste, as of the goldsmiths, jewellers and Kánsáris, to one Dhanapati Saudagar of Karnáta, from whose third son, Srikánta, the Sánkhári believe themselves to be descended. They claim to be Vaisyas, and say that up to the time of Adisur they wore the Brahmanical thread, but were degraded by him at the same time as the Subarnabaniks, because the latter had cut to pieces a golden cow which the king had given to certain Brahmans at the celebration of a special sacrifice. Sánkháris have the Brahmanical *gotras* and observe the same table of prohibited degrees as the higher castes.

Tradition of origin.

Internal structure.

In Dacca they are divided into two sub-castes—**Bara-Bhágiya** or **Bikrampur Sánkhári** and **Chhota-Bhágiya** or **Sunargáon Sánkhári.** The latter are a comparatively small group, who work at polishing shells, which they purchase ready cut—a departure from traditional usage, which may account for their separation from the main body of the caste. In other districts, owing possibly to the smallness of the caste, no similar divisions seem to have been formed.

Character and habits.

The Sánkhári, says Dr. Wise, have the character of being very penurious and unusually industrious, young and old working to a late hour at night. Boys are taught the trade at a very early age, otherwise their limbs would not brook the awkward posture and confined space in which work is carried on. When sawing, the shell is held by the toes, the semi-circular saw, kept perpendicular, being moved sideways. The caste are notoriously filthy in their domestic arrangements. A narrow passage, hardly two feet wide, leads through the house to an open courtyard, where the sewage of the household collects and is never removed. Epidemic diseases are very prevalent among them, and owing doubtless to their unhealthy mode of life the men as a rule are pale and flabby and very subject to elephantiasis, hernia, and hydrocele.

Dr. Wise describes the women as "remarkable for their beauty, confinement within dark rooms giving them a light wheaten complexion. They are, however, squat, becoming corpulent in adult life, and their features, though still handsome, inanimate. They are very shy, but the fact that in former days their good looks exposed them to the insults and outrages of licentious Muhammadan officials is a sufficient excuse for their timidity. Even now-a-days the recollection of past indignities rouses the Sánkhári to fury, and the greatest abuse that can be cast at him is to call him a son of Abdúl

Razzáq or of Rája Rám Dás. The former was a zamindár of Dacca; the latter the second son of Rája Ráj Ballabh, Diwán of Bengal. It is stated that they frequently broke into houses and carried off the Sánkhári girls, being shielded by their rank and influence from any punishment."

Marriage.

Sánkháris marry their daughters as infants by the ceremony in use among the highest castes. It is the fashion for the bridegroom to ride in the marriage procession, while the bride, dressed in red, is carried in a palanquin. Polygamy is permitted subject to the same restrictions as are in force among the Brahmans and Káyasths. Widows are not allowed to marry again, nor is divorce recognized.

Religion.

Nearly all Sánkháris belong to the Vaishnava sect, and comparatively few Sáktas are found among them. Their principal festival is held on the last day of Bhádra (August-September), when they give up work for five days and worship Agastya Rishi, who, according to them, rid the world of a formidable demon called Sankha Asura by cutting him up with the semi-circular saw used by shell-cutters. Others say that they revere Agastya, because he was the *guru* or spiritual guide of their ancestor Dhanápati Saudágar. Rice, sweetmeats, and fruit are offered to him, and are afterwards partaken of by the Brahmans, who serve the caste as priests. These Brahmans act also as priests for the Káyasths, and are received on equal terms by other members of the sacred order. They also observe the *Jhulanjátrá* and *Janmáshtami* festivals in honour of Krishna, kept by all Bengali Vaishnavas. Sánkháris burn their dead, mourn for thirty days, and perform *sráddh* in the orthodox fashion.

Social status.

In point of social standing the Sánkháris rank with the Navasákha, and Brahmans will take water and certain kinds of sweetmeats from their hands. Their own rules regarding diet are the same as those of the highest ranks of Hindus. Many of them indeed are vegetarians, and abstain even from fish. Taken as a whole, the caste have been singularly constant to their hereditary occupation—a fact which is due partly to the smallness of their number, and partly to the steady demand for the articles which they produce. In Bengal Proper every married woman of the respectable castes wears shell-bracelets, which are as much a badge of wedded life as the streak of red lead down the parting of the hair. Of late years, however, a certain proportion of the Sánkháris have become traders, writers, timber and cloth merchants, and claim on that account to be superior in social rank to those who manufacture shell bracelets.

Occupation.

Dr. Wise collected from various sources the following interesting particulars regarding the traditional occupation of the Sánkháris:—

The shells used for manufacturing bracelets are imported from the Gulf of Manaar. Natives distinguish many varieties, differing in colour and size, but the ordinary conch shell is the Mazza or Turbinella napa. The trade in these shells has flourished from the earliest historical times. The "chank" is mentioned by Abù Zaid in the tenth century of our era. Tavernier includes shell bracelets among the exports of Dacca in 1666, and adds that in Patna and Bengal there were over two thousand persons employed in manufacturing them.[1]

Towards the end of the seventeenth century the shell trade became a monopoly in the hands of the Dutch. A French missionary in 1700 writes[2] :—"It is scarcely credible how jealous the Dutch are of this commerce. It was death to a native to sell them to any one but to the factory servants at Ceylon. The shells were bought for a trifle, but when despatched in their own vessels to Bengal, the Dutch acquired great profit."

The chank fishery[3] became a royalty of the English Government, yielding an annual revenue of 4,000*l.*, but it is now open to all the world. In former days six hundred divers were employed, and in a single season four and a half millions of shells were frequently taken, of the gross annual value of 8,000*l.* The shells are imported by English merchants into Calcutta, purchased by rich Sánkháris, and retailed to the cutters.

On the arrival of the shells the remains of the mollusc (*pitta*) are extracted and sold to native physicians as a medicine for spleen enlargement. The base (*gherá*), the lip, and point of the shell are then knocked off with a hammer, the chips being used as gravel for garden walks or sold to agents from Murshedabad, where beads are made of the larger pieces, and a paint, *Mattiya Sindúr*, of the smaller. From two to eight bracelets are made from one shell. The sawdust is used to prevent the pitting of small-pox, and as an ingredient of a valuable white paint.

In the ordinary shell the whorls turn from right to left, but when one is found with the whorls reversed, "Dakshiná-varta," its price is extravagant, as it is believed to ensure wealth and prosperity. One belonging to a Dacca zamindar is so highly prized that he refused an offer of 300 rupees.

The following statement shows the number and distribution of Sánkháris in 1872 and 1881 :—

District.	1872.	1881.	District.	1872.	1881.
Bardwan	1,146	1,001	Dacca	853	1,317
Bankura	479	687	Faridpur	......	335
Birbhum	574	159	Bakarganj	1,157	708
Midnapur	1,513	1,438	Maimansinh	192	460
Hughli	} 968	533	Tipperah	171	95
Howrah		823	Chittagong	89	68
24-Parganás	1,326	366	Noakhali	253	240
Nadiya	175	73	Maldah	34	71
Khulna	......	218	Hazaribagh	53	......
Jessore	1,450	555	Lohardagá	153	......
Murshedabad	423	871	Singbhum	410	......
Dinajpur	179	31	Manbhum	859	40
Rajshahye	88	87	Cuttack	1,135	1,061
Rangpur	35	3	Puri	270	289
Bogra	13	67	Balasore	408	313
Pabna	158	93	Tributary States	57	105
Kuch Behar	......	1			

[1] Tavernier, part ii, book ii, 183-84.

[2] *Lettres Edifiantes*, ii, 278.

[3] Accounts of this shell or "sea-horn" fishery are given by Jan Nieuhof in A. and J. Churchill's *Voyages and Travels*, vol. ii, 298, and, of a later date, in *Lettres Edifiantes* x, 121 (ed. 1781).

Sankhi, a sub-tribe of Rájputs in Chota Nagpur.

Sankhwár, a section of the Kurmi caste in Chota Nagpur the members of which may not wear *sankuá* or shell ornaments. Another peculiarity of the section is that its members wear a *pagri* in the marriage ceremony, and are prohibited from wearing the ornamental head-dress (*mukut*) made of *solá* pith, generally used on such occasions.

Sánki, a sub-caste of Muchis in Bengal.

Sánkoá, a totemistic section of the Rajwár caste in Manbhum.

Sánkriti, a section of Brahmans.

Sankura, king crow, a totemistic sept of Mundas in Chota Nagpur.

Sankwá, a section of Rajwárs in Western Bengal.

Sanmaulik, a hypergamous group of the Uttar-Rarhi Káyasths in Bengal.

Sánnyál, a *gáin* of the Bátsya *gotra* of Bárendra Brahmans in Bengal.

Sannyási Atit, a class of Atit in Behar who adopt a purely ascetic and celibate life, and transmit their property to their pupils (*chelás*) by a sort of spiritual succession.

Sannyási or **Kánphát**, a religious group of Jugis.

Sáno or **Kabátkoniá**, a sub-caste of Sudhás in Orissa.

Sánpu, a totemistic section of the Korá caste in Manbhum, the members of which will not touch or kill a bull.

Sanpuri, a sept of Mundas in Chota Nagpur.

Sánrári (Jaideb), a section of Majhraut Goálás in Behar.

Sansáit, a section of the Dhaprá sub-caste of Doms in Behar.

Sansári, an epithet applied by Christian Kolhs in Chota Nagpur to their heathen neighbours.

Sanswár, a sub-caste of Kurmis in Behar.

Santál, *Sonthál*, *Saontár*, a large Dravidian tribe, classed on linguistic grounds as Kolarian, which is found in Western Bengal, Northern Orissa, Bhágalpur and the Santál Parganás. According to Mr. Skrefsrud the name Santál is a corruption of Sáontár, and was adopted by the tribe after their sojourn for several generations in the country about Sáont in Midnapur. Before they went to Sáont they are said to have been called Kharwár, the root of which, *khar*, is a variant of *hor*, 'man,' the name which all Santáls use among themselves. As regards the derivation of the name of the tribe from Saont, an obscure village, somewhat off the main line of their recent migrations, it may be observed that Colonel Dalton suggested a doubt whether the name of the place may not have been taken from the tribe, and this view seems to derive some support from his discovery of a small tribe of Saonts in Sarguja and Keunjhar. The point, however, is not one of great importance. At the present day when a Santál is asked what caste he belongs to, he will almost invariably reply 'Mánjhi' (literally 'village

Origin and traditions.

headman,' one of the commonest titles of the tribe), adding 'Santál Mánjhi' if further explanation is demanded of him.

In point of physical characteristics the Santáls may be regarded as typical examples of the pure Dravidian stock. Their complexion varies from very dark brown to a peculiar, almost charcoal-like, black; the proportions of the nose approach those of the Negro, the bridge being more depressed in relation to the orbits than is the case with Hindus; the mouth is large, the lips thick and projecting; the hair coarse, black, and occasionally curly; the zygomatic arches prominent, while the proportions of the skull, approaching the dolichocephalic type, conclusively refute the hypothesis of their Mongolian descent.

Santál tradition traces back the origin of the tribe to a wild goose (*hâsdak*) which laid two eggs. From these sprang Pilchu Haram and Pilchu Burhi, the parents of the race, who begat the first seven sub-tribes. Their earliest abode was Hihiri or Ahiri Pipiri, a name which Mr. Skrefsrud derives from *hir* origin, and which others identify with parganá Ahuri in Hazaribagh. Thence they went westward to Khoj-Kaman, where all of them were destroyed for their wickedness by a deluge of fire-rain, except a single pair who were saved in a cleft of the mountain Hara. From Hara they went to Sasangbera, a plain on the banks of a great river, and after that to Jarpi, where is the great mountain Marang Buro, through which they could find no pass. Here they offered sacrifices to the mountain god, and prayed him to let them through. After a while they found a pass leading into a country called Ahiri, where they dwelled for a time, passing on to Kendi, Chai, and finally Champa. In Champa they sojourned many generations, and the present institutions of the tribe were formed. At last the Hindus drove them out of Champa, and they established themselves in Saont, and ruled there for two hundred years. Again pressed by the Hindus, they wandered on under a Raja called Hambir Singh to the eastern part of the Manbhum district near Pachet. Here after a while their Rajas adopted the Hindu religion and set up as Rajputs, so that at the present day they intermarry with the family of the Raja of Sarguja. But the people would not change their religion, so they left their chief to rule over Hindus, and wandered on to the Santál Parganás, where they are settled now.

Neither as a record of actual wanderings nor as an example of the workings of the myth-making faculty does this story of the wandering of the Santáls appear to deserve serious consideration. A people whose only means of recording facts consists of tying knots in strings, and who have no bards to hand down a national epic by oral tradition, can hardly be expected to preserve the memory of their past long enough or accurately enough for their accounts of it to possess any historical value. An attempt has indeed been made by Mr. Skrefsrud to prove from these legends that the Santáls must have entered into India from the north-west, just as Colonel Dalton uses the same data in support of his opinion that the tribe came originally from Assam. The one hypothesis is as tenable or as untenable as the other, and all that can be said is that there is not a fraction of substantial evidence in support of either. If, however, the legends of the Santáls are regarded as an account of recent migrations, their general purport will be found to be fairly in accord with actual facts. Without pressing the conjecture mentioned above, that Ahiri Pipri may be no other than pargana Ahuri in the north-west of Hazaribagh district, it is clear that a large and important Santál colony was once settled in parganás Chai and Champá in the same district. A tradition is noticed by Colonel Dalton of an old fort in Chai occupied by one Jaura, a Santál Raja, who destroyed himself and his family on hearing of the approach of a Muhamadan army under Sayyid Ibráhim Ali *alias* Malik Bayá, a general of Muhammad Tughlak's, who died in 1353. This tradition, so far as it refers to the existence of a Santál fort in Chai Champá, is to some extent corroborated by the following passage from the legends of the Southern Santáls collected by the Revd. J. Phillips and published in Appendix G to *Annals of Rural Bengal*, ed. 1868:—"Dwelling there (in Chai Champá) they greatly multiplied. There were two gates, the Ahin gate and the Báhini gate, to the fort of Chai Champá." If, moreover, the date of the taking of this fort by Ibráhim Ali were assumed to be about 1340 A.D., the subsequent migrations of which the tribal legends speak would fill up the time intervening between the departure of the Santáls from Chai Champá and their settlement in the present Santál Parganás. Speaking generally, these recent migrations have been to the east, which is the direction they might *primâ facie* have been expected to follow. The earliest settlements which Santál tradition speaks of, those in Ahiri Pipri and Chai Champá, lie on the north-western frontier of the table land of Hazaribagh and in the direct line of advance of the numerous Hindu immigrants from Behar. That the influx of Hindus has in fact driven the Santáls eastward is beyond doubt, and the line which they are known to have followed in their retreat corresponds on the whole with that attributed to them in their tribal legends.

Internal structure.

The internal structure of the Santál tribe is singularly complete and elaborate. There are twelve exogamous septs, (1) Hásdak, (2) Murmu, (3) Kisku, (4) Hembrom, (5) Marndi, (6) Saren, (7) Tudu, (8) Baske, (9) Besra, (10) Páuria, (11) Chore, (12) Bedea. The first seven are believed to be descended from the seven sons of Pilchu Haram and Pilchu Burhi or Ayo. The five others were added afterwards. All are exogamous. In order that members of the various septs may recognize each other when they meet, each sept, except Páuria, Chore and Bedea, has certain pass-words peculiar to itself, which are supposed to be the names of the original homes of the septs in Champá or in one of the earlier settlements of the tribe. The pass-words are as follows:—(1) Hásdak—Tatijhári, Gangijauni, Kárá Guja, Sohodoro; (2) Murmu—Champágarh, Bagsumbha, Naran Manjhi; (3) Kisku—Kundagarh; (4) Hembrom—Kunda, Khairigarh, Jalaghatia; (5) Marndi—Badoligarh, Jelen Sinjo, Dhano Mánjhi; (6) Saren—Anbali, Barha, Pero Pargana; (7)

Tudu—Simgarh, Sukrihutup, Baru Mánjhi; (8) Baske—Ranga, Chunuk-jhandu; (9) Besra—Dhokrapalania, Gulu, Phagu Mánjhi. These pass-words or shibboleths seem to serve among the Santáls the purpose for which Australian and North American savages tattoo the totem on the body. They preserve the memory of the tie of blood which connects the members of the sept, and thus furnish an additional security against unconscious incest. They further go to show that the sept in its earliest form must have been a group of purely local character analogous to the communal septs which have been mentioned in the article on Kandh. If due allowance is made for the causes which must tend in course of time to scatter the members of any particular sept over a number of different villages, it will be seen to be a remarkable circumstance not that so few local septs are now to be found, but that any traces of such an organization have survived to so late a period.

Concerning the origin of the five additional septs the following stories are told. The eighth tribe, Baske, at first belonged to the seven, but by reason of their offering their breakfast (*baske*) to the gods while the Santáls were still in Champá, they were formed into a separate sept under the name of Baske. The Besras (No. 9) were separated on account of the immoral behaviour of their eponym, who was called Besra, the licentious one. The tenth sept, Páuria, are called after the pigeon, and the eleventh, Chore, after the lizard; and the story is that on the occasion of a famous tribal hunting party the members of these two septs failed to kill anything but pigeons and lizards, so they were called after the names of these animals. The twelfth sept, the Bedea, was left behind and lost when the Santáls went up out of Champá. They had no father, so the story goes—at least the mother of their first ancestor could not say who his father was, and for this reason they were deemed of lower rank than the other septs. This sept is believed to have arisen during the time of Mando Singh in Champá when the Santáls had begun to come in contact with the Hindus. Some Santáls say the father was a Rájput and the mother a girl of the Kisku sept. There would be nothing antecedently improbable in the conjecture that the well-known gypsy tribe of Bedea may owe its origin to the *liaison* of a Rájput with a Santál girl; but the mere resemblance of the names is a slender foundation for any such hypothesis. Santáls are very particular about the honour of their women, so far at least as outsiders are concerned, and it is quite in keeping with their ideas that a sept formed by a *liaison* with a Hindu should have been looked down upon, and eventually banished from the community. Any way it seems to be clear that the legend need not be taken to indicate the prevalence of the custom of female kinship in the tribe.

Marriage.

No Santál may marry within his sept (*páris*), nor within any of the sub-septs (*khunt*) (shown in Appendix I) into which the sept is divided. He may marry into any other sept, including the sept to which his mother belonged. A Santál proverb says:—No one heeds a cow track or regards his mother's sept.

Although no regard is paid in marriage to the mother's sept, the Santáls have precisely the same rule as the Kandhs concerning the sub-sept or *khunt*. A man may not marry into the sub-sept or *khunt* to which his mother belonged, though it is doubtful whether the Santáls observe this rule for as many generations in the descending line as is customary among the Kandhs. Many of the sub-septs have curious traditional usages, some of which may be mentioned here. At the time of the harvest festival in January the members of the Sidup-Saren sub-sept set up a sheaf of rice on end in the doorway of their cattle sheds. This sheaf they may not touch themselves, but some one belonging to another sub-sept must be got to take it away. Men of the Sádá-Saren sub-sept do not use vermilion in their marriage ritual; they may not wear clothes with a red border on such occasions, nor may they be present at any ceremony in which the priest offers his own blood to propitiate the gods. The Jugi-Saren, on the other hand, smear their foreheads with *sindur* at the harvest festival, and go round asking alms of rice. With the rice they get they make little cakes which they offer to the gods. The Mánjhi-Khil-Saren, so called because their ancestor was a mánjhi or village headman, are forbidden, like the Sádá-Saren, to attend when the priest offers up his own blood. The Náiki-Khil-Saren, who claim descent from a náiki or village priest may not enter a house the inmates of which are ceremonially unclean. They have a *jáhirthán* or sacred grove of their own, distinct from the common *jáhirthán* of the village, and they dispense with the services of the priest who serves the rest of the village. The Ok-Saren sacrifice a goat or a pig inside their houses, and during the ceremony they shut the doors tight and allow no smoke to escape. The word *ok* means to suffocate or stifle with smoke. The Mundu or Badar-Saren offer their sacrifices in the jungle, and allow only males to eat the flesh of the animals that have been slain. The Mál-Saren may not utter the word *mal* when engaged in a religious ceremony or when sitting on a pancháyat to determine any tribal questions. The Jihu-Saren may not kill or eat the *jihu* or babbler bird, nor may they wear a particular sort of necklace known as *jihu málá* from the resemblance which it bears to the babbler's eggs. The *jihu* is said to have guided the ancestor of the sept to water when he was dying of thirst in the forest. The Sankh-Saren may not wear shell necklaces or ornaments. The Barchir Saren plant a spear in the ground when they are engaged in religious or ceremonial observances. The Bitol-Saren are so called because their founder was excommunicated on account of incest.

Girls are married as adults mostly to men of their own choice. Sexual intercourse before marriage is tacitly recognized, it being understood that if the girl becomes pregnant the young man is bound to marry her. Should he attempt to evade this obligation, he would be severely beaten by the Jag-mánjhi, and in addition to this his father would be required to pay a heavy fine. It is curious to hear that in the Santál Parganás, shortly after the rebellion of 1855, it became the fashion among the more wealthy Santáls to imitate the usages of high-caste Hindus and marry their daughters between the ages of eight and twelve. This fashion has, however, since been abandoned, and it is now very unusual for a girl to be married before she attains puberty. Polygamy is not favoured by the custom of the tribe. A man may take a second wife if his first wife is barren, or if his elder brother dies he may marry the widow. But in either case the consent of his original wife must be obtained to the arrangement. Instances no doubt occur in which this rule is evaded, but they are looked upon with disfavour.

There seem to be indications that fraternal polyandry may at some time have existed among the Santáls. Even now, says Mr. Skrefsrud, a man's younger brother may share his wife with impunity; only they must not go about it very openly. Similarly a wife will admit her younger sister to intimate relations with her husband, and if pregnancy occurs scandal is avoided by his marrying the girl as a second wife. It will of course be noticed that this form of polyandry need not be regarded as a survival of female kinship.

The following forms of marriage are recognized by the Santáls and distinguished by separate names:—(1) Regular marriage (*bapla* or *kiring behu*, literally bride-purchase); (2) *Ghardi jáwáe*; (3) *Itut*; (4) *Nir-bolok*; (5) *Sanga*; (6) *Kiring jawae* or husband-purchase. The negotiations antecedent to a regular marriage are opened by the father of the young man, who usually employs a professional match-maker to look for a suitable girl. If the match-maker's proposals are accepted by the girl's parents, a day is fixed on which the girl, attended by two of her friends, goes to the house of the jag-mánjhi or superintendent of morals, in order to give the bridegroom's parents an opportunity of looking at her quietly. A similar visit of inspection is paid by the bride's parents to the bridegroom's house, and if everything is found satisfactory the betrothal is concluded and an instalment of the bride-price is paid. The ordinary price of a girl is Rs. 3, and the bridegroom must also present a cloth (*sári*) to the girl's mother and to both her grandmothers if alive. If more than this is paid, the bridegroom is entitled to receive a present of a cow from his father-in-law. In the case known as a *golát* marriage, when two families, each having a daughter and a son of marriageable age, arrange a double wedding, one daughter is set off against the other, and no bride-price is paid by either party. For a widow or a woman who has been divorced the bride-price is only half the standard amount, the idea being, as the Santáls pointedly put it, that such women are only borrowed goods, and must be given back to their first husbands in the next world. As the second husband has the use of his wife only in this world, it is clearly fair that he should get her for half-price. In an early stage of the marriage ceremony both bride and bridegroom separately go through the form of marriage to a *mahuá* tree (*Bassia latifolia*). In the case of the bride a double thread is passed three or five times from the little toe of her left foot to her left ear, and is then bound round her arm with some blades of rice and stems of *dhuba* grass. The conjecture suggests itself that this may be a survival of some form of communal marriage, but from the nature of the case no positive evidence is available to bear out this hypothesis, or to throw any light upon the symbolism of the usage. The essential and binding portion of the ritual is *sindurdán*, the smearing of vermilion on the bride's forehead and on the parting of her hair. This rite, however, is supposed to have been borrowed from the Hindus. The original Santál ceremony is believed to have been very simple. The couple went away together into the woods, and on their return were shut up by themselves in a room. When they came out they were considered to be man and wife. A practice closely resembling this was found by Colonel Dalton to be in vogue among the Birhors, and it is quite in keeping with what is known of the doings of primitive man in the matter of marriage. The memory of it, however, only survives among the Santáls in the form of a vague and shadowy tradition upon which no stress can be laid. *Sindurdán*, on the other hand, is nothing but a refined and specialised form of the really primitive usage of mixing the blood of a married couple and making them drink or smear themselves with the mixture, and although it is possible that the Santáls may have borrowed *sindurdán* from the Hindus, there are certainly good grounds for believing that the Hindus themselves must have derived it from the Dravidian races.

The second mode of marriage, *ghardi jáwáe*, is resorted to when a girl is ugly or deformed and there is no prospect of her being asked in marriage in the ordinary way. An instance has been reported to me in which a girl who had on one foot more than the proper number of toes was married in this fashion. The husband is expected to live in his father-in-law's house and to serve him for five years. At the end of that time he gets a pair of bullocks, some rice and some agricultural implements, and is allowed to go about his business.

The third form, *itut*, is adopted by pushing young men who are not quite sure whether the girl they fancy will accept them, and take this means of compelling her to marry them. The man smears his fingers with vermilion or, failing that, with common earth, and, watching his opportunity at market or on any similar occasion, marks the girl he is in love with on the forehead and claims her as his wife. Having done this, he runs away at full speed to avoid the thrashing he may expect at the hands of her relations if he is caught on the spot. In any case the girl's people will go to his village and will obtain from the headman permission to kill and eat three of the offender's or his father's goats, and a double bride-price must be paid for the girl. The marriage, however, is legal, and if the girl still declines to live with the man, she must be divorced in full form and cannot again be married as a spinster. It is said that an *itut* marriage is often resorted to out of spite in order to subject the girl to the humiliation of being divorced.

The fourth form, *nirbolok* (*nir*, to run, and *bolok*, to enter) may be described as the female variety of *itut*. A girl who cannot get the man she wants in the regular way takes a pot of *hándiá* or rice-beer, enters his house and insists upon staying there. Etiquette forbids that she should be expelled by main force, but the man's mother, who naturally desires to have a voice in the selection of her daughter-in-law, may use any means short of personal violence to get her out of the house. It is quite fair, for example, and is usually found effective, to throw red pepper on the fire, so as to smoke the aspiring maiden out; but if she endures this ordeal without leaving the house, she is held to have won her husband and the family is bound to recognize her.

The fifth form, *sanga*, is used for the marriage of widows and divorced women. The bride is brought to the bridegroom's house attended by a small party of her own friends, and the binding portion of the ritual consists in the bridegroom taking a *dimbu* flower, marking it with *sindur* with his left hand, and with the same hand sticking it in the bride's back hair.

The sixth form, *kiring jáwáe*, is resorted to in the comparatively rare case when a girl has had a *liaison* with, and become pregnant by, a man of her sept whom she cannot marry. In order that scandal may be avoided, some one is procured to accept the post of husband, and in consideration of his services he gets two bullocks, a cow and a quantity of paddy from the family of the man by whom the girl is pregnant. The headman then calls the villagers together, and in their presence declares the couple to be man and wife, and enjoins the girl to live with, and be faithful to, the husband that has been provided for her.

A widow may marry again. It is thought the right thing for her to marry her late husband's younger brother, if one survives him, and under no circumstances may she marry his elder brother. Divorce is allowed at the wish of either husband or wife. If neither party is in fault, the one who wants a divorce is expected to bear the expenses. The husband, for example, in such a case would not be entitled to claim a refund of the bride-price originally paid, and would also have to pay a fine and give the woman certain customary dues. If, on the other hand, it is the wife who demands a divorce without just cause, her father has to make good the bride-price in addition to a fine for her levity of behaviour. The divorce is effected in the presence of the assembled villagers by the husband tearing asunder three *sál* leaves in token of separation, and upsetting a brass pot full of water.

Inheritance.

In the matter of inheritance Santáls follow their own customs, and know nothing of the so-called codes which govern the devolution of property among Hindus. Sons inherit in equal shares; a daughter has no claim to a portion as of right, but usually gets a cow given to her when the property is divided. Failing sons, the father takes; failing him, the brothers; after them, the male agnates. Failing agnates, the daughter inherits with succession to her children. If a man dies leaving young sons, his widow manages the property till all the sons are old enough to divide and start separate households. She then takes up her abode with the youngest. Should the widow marry outside the family, the male agnates take the property in trust till the sons are of age, and she gets nothing. If a man has male relatives, he cannot give away his property even to a son-in-law. Wills are unknown.

According to Mr. Skrefsrud traces may be discerned in the background of the Santál religion of a *fainéant* Supreme Deity called Thakur, whom the Santáls have long ceased to worship for the sufficient reason that he is too good to trouble himself about anybody and does neither good nor ill to mankind. Some identify him with the Sun, whom the Santáls regard as a good god and worship every fifth or tenth year with sacrifices of slain goats. But this point is uncertain, and I am myself inclined to doubt whether a god bearing the Hindu name Thakur, and exercising supreme powers which mark a comparatively late stage of theological development, can really have formed part of the original system of the Santáls. However this may be, the popular gods of the tribe at the present day are the following:—(1) **Marang Buru**, the great mountain or the very high one, who now stands at the head of the Santál Pantheon, and is credited with very far-reaching powers, in virtue of which he associates both with the gods and with the demons. (2) **Moreko**, fire, now a single god, but formerly known to the Santáls under the form of five brothers. (3) **Jáir Era**, a sister of Moreko, the goddess of the sacred grove set apart in every village for the august presence of the gods. (4) **Gosain Era**, a younger sister of Moreko. (5) **Parganá**, chief of the bongas or gods, and more especially master of all the witches, by reason of which latter functions he is held in especial reverence. (6) **Mánjhi**, a sort of second in command to Parganá, a personage who is supposed to be particularly active in restraining the gods from doing harm to men. The two latter are clearly deities constructed on the model of the communal and village officials whose names they bear. The idea is that the gods, like men, need supervising officials of this sort to look after them and keep them in order. All the foregoing gods have their allotted place in the sacred grove (*Jáhirthán*), and are worshipped only in public. Marang Buru alone is also worshipped privately in the family.

Religion.

Each family also has two special gods of its own—the Orak-bonga or household god, and the Abge-bonga or secret god. The names of the Orak-bongas are (1) Baspahar, (2) Deswáli, (3) Sás, (4) Goraya, (5) Barpahar, (6) Sarchawdi, (7) Thuntatursa. The Abge-bongas are the following:—(1) Dharasore or Dharasanda, (2) Ketkomkudra, (3) Champa-denagarh, (4) Garhsinka, (5) Lilachandi, (6) Dhanghara, (7) Kudrachandi, (8) Bahara, (9) Duárseri, (10) Kudraj, (11) Gosáin Erá, (12) Achali, (13) Deswáli. No Santál would divulge the name of his Orak-bonga and Abge-bonga to any one but his eldest son; and men are particularly careful to keep this sacred knowledge from their wives for fear lest they should acquire undue influence with the bongas, become witches, and eat up the family with impunity when the protection of its gods has been withdrawn. The names given above were disclosed to Mr. Skrefsrud by Christian Santáls. When sacrifices are offered to the Orak-bongas the whole family partake of the offerings; but only men may touch the food that has been laid before the Abge-bongas. These sacrifices take place once a year. No regular time is fixed, and each man performs them when it suits his convenience.

There still lingers among the Santáls a tradition of a 'mountain-god' (Buru-bonga) of unknown name, to whom human sacrifices used to be offered, and actual instances have been mentioned to me of people being kidnapped and sacrificed within quite recent times by influential headmen of communes or villages, who hoped in this way to gain great riches or to win some specially coveted private revenge. These are not the motives which prompted human sacrifice among the Kandhs of Orissa, a tribe whose internal structure curiously resembles that of the Santáls. The Kandh sacrifice was undertaken for the benefit of the entire tribe, not in the interest of individual ambition or malevolence. It is curious to hear that one of the men credited with this iniquity was himself murdered during the Santál rebellion of 1855, by being slowly hewn in pieces with axes, just as his own victims had been—a mode of execution which certainly recalls the well-known procedure of the Kandhs.

Human sacrifice.

The chief festival of the Santáls is the Sohrai or harvest festival, celebrated in Posh (November–December), after the chief rice crop of the year has been got in. Public sacrifices of fowls are offered by the priest in the sacred grove; pigs, goats and fowls are sacrified by private families, and a general saturnalia of drunkenness and sexual license prevails. Chastity is in abeyance for the time, and all unmarried persons may indulge in promiscuous intercourse. This license, however, does not extend to adultery, nor does it sanction intercourse between persons of the same sept, though even this offence, if committed during the Sohrai, is punished less severely than at other times. Next in importance is the *Baha puja*, kept in Phalgun (February-March) when the *sál* tree comes into flower. Tribal and family sacrifices are held, many victims are slain and eaten by the worshippers, every one entertains their friends, dancing goes on day and night, and the best songs and flute-music are performed. A peculiar feature of this festival is a sort of water-bottle in which men and women throw water at each other until they are completely drenched.

Festivals.

Mention may also be made of Erok-sim, the sowing festival kept in Asar (May–June); Hariar-sim, the feast of the sprouting of the rice in Bhadra (September–October); Trigundli nauai, the offering of the first fruits of the millets *iri* (Panicum millaceum) and *gundli* (Panicum frumentaceum) also in Bhadra; Janthar puja in Aghran (October–November), the first fruits of the winter rice crop; Sankránt puja on the last day of Posh, when bread and chira and molasses are offered to dead ancestors; Mágh-sim in the month of Mágh, when the jungle grass is cut. This is the end of the Santál year. Servants are paid their wages and fresh engagements are entered into. On this occasion all the village officials, the Manjhi, Parámánik, Jag Manjhi, Jag-parámánik, Gorait. Náiki and Kudam-naiki go through the form of resigning their appointments, and all the cultivators give notice of throwing up their lands. After ten days or so the manjhi or headman calls the village together and says he has changed his mind and will stay on as manjhi if the village will have him. His offer is accompanied with free drinks of rice-beer, and is carried by acclamation. One by one the other officials do the same; the ryots follow suit, and after a vast amount of beer has been consumed the affairs of the village go on as they did before. The Sima-bonga or boundary gods are propitiated twice a year with sacrifices of fowls offered at the boundary of the village where these gods are supposed to live. Jom-sim puja is an offering of two goats, or a goat and a sheep, to the sun. Every Santál ought to perform this sacrifice at least once in his life. After a year's interval it is, or ought to be, followed by Kutam dangra, when a cow is offered to the household god, and an ox to Marang buru and to the spirits of dead ancestors. Mak-more puja, literally 'the cut five,' is a sacrifice of three goats and many fowls offered to More-ko, the god of fire, supposed to have been originally five brothers, on occasions of public calamity, such as a failure of the crops, an outbreak of epidemic disease, and the like.

The following statement shows the number and distribution of Santáls in 1872 and 1881:—

District.	1872.	1881.	District.	1872.	1881.
Bardwan	4,487	5,806	Dacca	1	......
Bankura	25,378	20,034	Maimansinh	75	......
Birbhum	6,954	728	Chittagong	4	12
Midnapur	96,921	568	Patna	4	......
Hughli	46	36	Tirhut	6	......
Howrah		67	Monghyr	13,967	......
24-Parganás	514	31	Bhágalpur	16,468	48
Nadiya	6	29	Maldah	215	833
Jessore	23	55	Santál Parganás	4,55,513	9,148
Khulna	......	19	Cuttack	3	...
Murshedabad	3,002	1,663	Balasore	1,176	389
Dinajpur	1,039	6,813	Tributary States	76,548	922
Rajshahye	5	139	Hazaribagh	35,306	......
Rangpur	......	7	Lohardaga	1,204	7
Bogra	75	252	Sinhbhum	51,133	51,954
Pabna	......	130	Manbhum	132,445	86,403
Darjiling	......	19	Tributary States	9	17,216

Communal organization.

The communal organization of the Santáls is singularly complete. The whole number of villages comprising a local settlement of the tribe is divided into certain large groups, each under the superintendence of a *parganait* or circle headman. This official is the head of the social system of the inhabitants of his circle; his permission has to be obtained for every marriage, and he, in consultation with a *pancháyat* of village headmen, expels or fines persons who infringe the tribal standard of propriety. He is remunerated by a commission on the fines levied, and by a tribute in kind of one leg of the goat or animal cooked at the dinner which the culprits are obliged to give. Each village has, or is supposed to have, the following establishment of officials holding rent-free land:—

1. *Manjhi.*—Headman, usually also *ijardar* where the village is held on lease under a zamindar, collects rents, and allots land among the ryots, being paid for this by the proceeds of the *mân* land which he holds free of rent. He receives Re. 1 as *marocha* at each wedding, giving in return a full *handi* of rice-beer.

2. *Paramanik.*—Assistant headman, also holding some *mán* land.

3. *Jag Manjhi*
4. *Jag Paramanik*
— Executive officers, respectively, of the *manjhi* and the *paramanik* who, as the Santáls describe it, "sit and give orders," which the *Jag Manjhi* and *Jag Paramanik* carry out.

5. *Naiki.*—Village priest of the aboriginal deities.

6. *Kudam Naiki.*—Assistant priest, whose peculiar function it is to propitiate the spirits (*bhúts*) of the hills and jungles by scratching his arms till they bleed, mixing the blood with rice, and placing it in spots frequented by the *bhúts*.

7. *Gorait.*—Village messenger, who holds *mán* land and acts as peon to the headman. The gorait is also to some extent a servant of the zamindar. His chief duty within the village is to bring to the *manjhi* and *Paramanik* any ryot they want.

The communal circles of the Santáls seem to correspond closely to the *mutas* of the Kandhs and the *parhas* of the Mundas and Oraons. It is a plausible conjecture that among all these tribes this organization was once connected with marriage, as it is among the Kandhs at the present day.

Santari, a section of the Magahiyá sub-caste of Doms in Behar.

Sántaru, a *samáj* or local group of the Sábarna *gotra* of Páschátya Baidik Brahmans in Bengal.

Sántrá, *Sánt*, a title of Kaibarttas, Telis, and Bágdis in Bengal.

Santu Kusáet, a section of the Ghosin sub-caste of Goálás in Behar.

Sanuani, a sept of Dhenuárs in Chota Nagpur who cannot wear gold.

Sanuár, a section of Goálás in Behar.

Sanukra, a section of Ghásis in Chota Nagpur.

Sanwani, a sept of Kaurs and Rautiás in Chota Nagpur.

Sanwar, a goldsmith; a section of the Kámi caste in Darjiling.

Sanwasi, a section of Ghásis in Chota Nagpur.

Sánwát, a title of Cheros in Palamau.

Saoasi, a synonym for Pán and Tánti.

Sáolá, a sept of the Bhumij tribe in Manbhum.

Saonra, a title of Goálás in Behar; a sub-caste of Goálás in Chota Nagpur.

Saonsiá, a sept of Páns in Chota Nagpur.

Sáontár, a synonym for Santál.

Sapankotyá, a *thar* of the Kanniá *gotra* of Nepáli Brhamans.

Sapdohá, a section of Bábhans in Behar.

Saphárk, a *pur* or section of Sákadwipi Brahmans in Behar.

Sápkotá, a section of Kámis in Darjiling.

Saptagrámi, a sub-caste of Nápits and Telis in Bengal.

Saptagrámi or *Kusadái*, a sub-caste of Támbulis in Bengal.

Saptagrámi or **Nadiyá**, a sub-caste of Subarnabaniks in Bengal.

Saptasati or **Sátsati**, a sub-caste of Brahmans in Bengal who numbered seven hundred when Ádisur brought the five Brahmans from Kanauj in order to perform certain *jajna*, owing to their want of ceremonial purity. They have since become mixed with the later emigrant Brahmans, and consequently very few families of them are now recognized by the name of Saptasati.

Sápui, a title of Pods in Bengal.

Sápurya or *Bediyá-Mál*, a sub-caste of Máls in Midnapur and Manbhum.

Sar, a synonym for Savars.

Sár, a sub-caste of Ràjus in Midnapur.

Saráf, a title of the Ariár sub-caste of Bais Baniyás.

Sarai, a jungle fruit, a totemistic sept of Korwas and of Mundas in Chota Nagpur.

Saráihát, a section of the Sátmuliá Maghayá sub-caste of Kándus in Behar.

Saraiyár, a section of Káysths in Behar.

Sárák, *Sráwak*, a small caste of Chota Nagpur, who seem to be a Hinduised remnant of the early Jain people, to whom local legends ascribe the ruined temples, the defaced images, and even the abandoned copper mines of that part of Bengal. The temples and images indeed are proved by their well-marked and characteristic symbolism to be the handiwork of Jain artists, while there is nothing *primâ facie* improbable in the supposition that the mines also may be due to the energy of this comparatively civilised race, whose well-wrought stone pillars and lintels far surpass anything that the present inhabitants of the province can execute. Neither history nor tradition throws any clear light upon the causes which compelled these peaceful settlers to desert the picturesque valleys, where we find vestiges of their faith; but if we may suppose the majority of them to have been gradually driven out by the incursion of the non-Aryan races, nothing would be more likely than that the remnant who remained behind, surrounded as they were by barbarians of alien blood and religion, should have hardened into a caste such as the Sáráks form at the present day.

Origin.

The Sáráks have no sub-castes. Their sections are of the eponymous type, and this fact, coupled with their comparatively refined cast of features and light complexion, seems to confirm their claims to be deemed of Aryan descent. The prohibited degrees are the same as in the case of high-caste Hindus. They marry their

Internal structure and marriage.

daughters as infants, forbid widows to remarry, and do not recognize divorce. Polygamy is permitted in so far that a man may take a second wife if he has no hope of obtaining male issue by his first wife. The marriage ceremony is of the standard type.

Religion.

The Sáráks of Manbhum, while retaining the tradition that their ancestors were Jains, appear themselves to have completely adopted Hinduism. They worship the ordinary Hindu gods with the assistance of Brahmans; nor have they retained, as might perhaps have been expected, any of the characteristic *tirthankaras* or glorified saints of the Jains under the disguise of minor or household gods. In Lohardagá, on the other hand, Párswanáth, the twenty-third *tirthankara*, who is believed to have attained *nirvána* on Párasnáth Hill in Hazaribagh, is still recognized by the Sáráks as their chief deity, though they also worship Shyám Chánd, Rádhá Mohán, and Jagannáth. Brahmans officiate as their priests, and in no way forfeit their social reputation by doing so. In all Jain temples, indeed, the ministrant priests are Brahmans.

Occupation and social status.

Sáráks are skilful agriculturists, and are credited with having introduced sugarcane cultivation on the plateau of Chota Nagpur. Most of them are occupancy raiyats, and in pargana Sonpur of Lohardagá a few villages are held by Sáráks in permanency and at a fixed rent by the tenure known locally as *britt-bhandár*. In point of social standing they rank high, and Brahmans will take water and *pakki* articles of food from their hands. Sáráks themselves retain all the prejudices of the Jains in regard to eating the flesh of any kind of animal. Life may on no account be taken. Their diet therefore consists entirely of vegetables; and it is said that if in preparing their food any mention of the word 'cutting' is made, the omen is deemed so disastrous that every thing must be thrown away. Subject to these conditions, Sáráks will eat the leavings of Brahmans, and will take water or sweetmeats from Rájputs, Baidyas, and Kayásths.

The following statement shows the number and distribution of Sáráks in 1872 and 1881:—

District.	1872.	1881.	District.	1872.	1881.
Bardwan	......	38	Monghyr	......	37
Bankura	......	601	Santál Parganás	......	446
Rangpur	......	3	Hazaribagh	......	108
Patna	......	342	Lohardagá	1,659	1,518
Gya	......	123	Manbhum	8,327	8,218
Shahabad	......	5	Tributary States	......	56
Mozufferpur	......	8			

Sárálíá, a sub-caste of Kumhárs and Bhuinmális found in Noakháli.

Sáramba, a tigress, a totemistic sept of Juángs in Orissa.

Sarangi, a section of Utkal or Orissa Brahmans.

Sarángi, a *thar* or sept of Mangars in Darjiling.

Sárangihár, a religious group of Jugis.

Saraogi, a mercantile caste of Northern India closely allied to the Agarwals and Oswals. Like these, Saraogis are mostly adherents of the Jain faith. They profess to have 84 exogamous groups deriving their names from villages in Khandela and Shekhawati. In marriage they exclude both *gots*, like the Maheari, and reckon them on both sides.

Sarari, a title of Byádhs who kill birds by *sar* or arrows.

Sáras, a water-fowl, a totemistic sept of Bhuiyás and Kharwars in Chota Nagpur.

Sáraswat, *Sársath*, *Sársati*, a territorial division of the Pancha Gaura Brahmans found in Behar, said to derive its name from having originally dwelled in the country watered by the river Saraswati in the Panjáb.

Saraswati, a sect of Dasnámi Sannyásis.

Sarauli, a *mul* or section of the Chhamuliá Madhesiá sub-caste of Halwáis in Behar.

Sarbbánandi, a *mel* or hypergamous sub-group of Rárhi Brahmans in Bengal.

Sarbesia, a group of the Purbba Kuliyá Sadgops.

Sardak-peapi, a sub-sept of the Phejom sept of Limbus in Darjiling.

Sardár, a headman, a chief. (i) In Bengal Proper an ironical title of Tántis, Bágdis, Háris, Doms, Káhárs, and other low castes; (ii) in Manbhum a title of the Bhumij tribe, many of whom are headmen of *ghatwali* villages; (iii) in the Santál Parganás a title of Mal Pahariás and Santáls.

Saren, a sept of Santáls.

Sares Parganá Dadádih, a *mul* or section of the Naomuliá or Majraut sub-caste of Goálás in Behar.

Sárgátiá, a section of the Biyáhut and Kharidáhá Kalwárs in Behar.

Sargrámi, a *gáin* of the Kásyapa *gotra* or Bárendra Brahmans in Bengal.

Sarihin, a sept of the Patar-Mahili sub-caste of Máhilis in Chota Nagpur.

Sarin, a section of the Dharkár sub-caste of Doms in Behar.

Sariswe-Khángor, a *mul* of the Sándil section of Maithil Brahmans in Behar.

Sariswe-Sakuri, a *mul* of the Sándil section of Maithil Brahmans in Behar.

Sariyál, a *gáin* of the Bharadwája *gotra* of Bárendra Brahmans in Bengal.

Sarjál, a sept of Kaurs in Chota Nagpur.

Sarjupari, see **Sarwariá**.

Sarkár, a title of Brahmans; of Kurmis in Manbhum, used both by members of the caste and by outsiders; of Jugis, Kaibarttas, Kayasths, Nápits, Pods, Sadgops, and Tántis in Bengal.

Sarkatá, a *mul* or section of the Kanaujiá sub-caste of Sonárs in Behar.

Sarki, the cobbler caste of Nepal.

Sarmá, a synonym for Brahman; a title of Dakshin-Rárhi and Bangaja Káyasths.

Sarnabanik, a synonym for Subarnabanik.

Sarna-Kámár, a sub-caste of Kámárs in Midnapur.

Sarnakár, *Sekrá*, the working goldsmith and silversmith caste of Bengal, an artisan group, probably traceable to the Karmakar and wholly distinct from the Subarnabanik, who never work in metal themselves. Sarnakárs are divided into four sub-castes: **Brahman-desi, Dakhin-Rárhi, Khatangi** and **Uttar-Rárhi**. They have five exogamous groups, three Brahmanical and two Sabanta-Rishi and Sa-rishi, suggestive of less distinguished associations. Girls are usually married as infants, but this is said not to be obligatory—a view which is to some extent borne out by the fact that a bride-price is paid, and the bridegroom-price characteristic of the full development of infant-marriage has not yet been introduced. The marriage ceremony is of the orthodox type; its essential and binding portion being the gift of the bride to the bridegroom and his formal acceptance of the gift. Widows may not marry again, and divorce is permitted only on the ground of the wife's adultery.

The religion of the caste is that of the average middle class Hindu—Sákta or Vaishnava as the case may be. The divine artisan, Viswakarmá, is reverenced as the special patron of the caste. The women have a special ceremony called Kulai, which is performed during the rains without the assistance of any priest. Brahmans are employed for religious and ceremonial purposes, but these are not received on equal terms by those members of the sacred order who serve the higher castes. The dead are burned, and the *sráddh* ceremony performed one month after death. The caste believe the business of a goldsmith to be their original occupation, but some of them engage in agriculture. Their social status is low. None of the higher castes will take water from them, and they admit that they will take water and sweetmeats from any one except the very lowest castes, such as Hári, Muchi and Dom.

Sarnar, a curry vegetable, a totemistic sept of Mundas in Chota Nagpur.

Sarniá, a sept of the Surajbansi division of Rájputs in Behar.

Sarno, a sept of Oraons in Chota Nagpur.

Sarpa, snake, a totemistic section of Jagannáthi Kumhárs in Orissa.

Sáru, a *thar* or sept of Mangars in Darjiling.

Saruá, a group of the Pandá sub-caste of Utkal Brahmans.

Sarwál, a section of the Panchjáti sub-caste of Khatris in Bengal.

Sarwariá or **Saryupari**, a sub-caste of Kanaujiá Brahmans and Telis in Behar.

Sarwat, a section of Kanaujiá Lohárs in Behar.

Sarwe, a section of Bábhans in Behar.

Sásani or **Srotriya**, a sub-caste of Utkal Brahmans in Orissa.

Sásankhar, a section of Kámis in Darjiling.

Sásmal, a title of Suklis and Kaibarttas in Midnapur.

Satal, a *thar* or sept of the Bárah-Gurung sub-tribe of Gurungs in Darjiling.

Satánandkháni, a *mel* or hypergamous sub-group of Rárhi Brahmans in Bengal.

Satapasti, Satpati, a group of the Srotriya sub-caste of Utkal Brahmans.

Satarwár, a *mul* or section of the Kanaujiá sub-caste of Hajjáms in Behar.

Satchásá, a synonym for Sadgop in Bengal.

Sáteswari, a *gáin* of the Sábarna *gotra* of Rárhi Brahmans in Bengal.

Sátghariá, a sub-caste of Nápits in Bengal.

Satgop, a synonym for Sadgop in Bengal.

Sat Gosáin, a sub-sect of Vaishnavas recruited from the higher castes and distinguished for their proselytising zeal.

Sáthiet, a *mul* or section of the Naomuliá or Majraut subcaste of Goálás in Behar.

Sátisá, a sub-caste of Dhobás in Central Bengal.

Sátlakshe-Sataur, a *mul* of the Kásyapa section of Maithil Brahmans in Behar.

Sátlakshe-Sátlaksha, a *mul* of the Kásyap section of Maithil Brahmans in Behar.

Sátling, a sept of Limbus in Darjiling.

Satola, a *thar* or section of Nepáli Brahmans.

Sátoriá, a section of Goálás in the North-Western Provinces and Behar.

Satrá, a section of Sunris in Behar.

Sátsaikiyá, a sub-caste of Aguris in Western Bengal.

Satsudra, a group of castes from whose hands a Brahman can take water.

Sáttá, a section of Pátnis in Eastern Bengal.

Sattyal, a *thar* or section of Nepáli Brahmans

Sátun, a title of Barhis in Behar.

Satya, truth, a section of Jugis.

Sáu, a section of Goálás in Behar.

Sau or **Chalita-Sau**, a subcaste of Sunris in Western Bengal.

Sauar, a *mul* or section of the Maghayá sub-caste of Kándus in Behar.

Saubarniá, a section of Babháns in Behar.'

Sauchánd, a sub-caste of Kurmis in Behar.

Saudá Báek, a *mul* or section of the Satmuliá or Kishnaut subcaste of Goálás in Behar.

Saudarpurái Mahiá, a *mul* of the Sándil section of Maithil Brahmans in Behar.

Saudarpurái-Katká, a *mul* of the Sándil section of Maithil Brahmans in Behar.

Saudarpurái-Jagaur, a *mul* of the Sándil section of Maithil Brahmans in Behar.

Saudarpurái-Sarso, a *mul* of the Sándil section of Maithil Brahmans in Behar.

Saudarpurái-Suket, a *mul* of the Sándil section of Maithil Brahmans in Behar.

Saudarpurái-Hansauli, a *mul* of the Sándil section of Maithil Brahmans in Behar.

Saudarpurái-Khoir, a *mul* of the Sándil section of Maithil Brahmans in Behar.

Saudarpurái-Digaun, a *mul* of the Sándil section of Maithil Brahmans in Behar.

Saudarpurái-Kanhauli, a *mul* of the Sándil section of Maithil Brahmans in Behar.

Saudarpurái-Mánik, a *mul* of the Sándil section of Maithil Brahmans in Behar.

Saudarpurái-Rohár, a *mul* of the Sándil section of Maithil Brahmans in Behar.

Saudarpurái-Sundar, a *mul* of the Sándil section of Maithil Bráhmans in Behar.

Saudarpurái-Dhaul, a *mul* of the Sándil section of Maithil Brahmans in Behar

Saudarpurái-Baghát, a *mul* of the Sándil section of Maithil Brahmans in Behar.

Saudarpurái-Gaul, a mul of the Sándil section of Maithil Brahmans in Behar.

Sauiá, a sept of Hos in Singbhum.

Saukálin, a section of Brahmans and of Káyasths in Bengal.

Saul, fish, a sept of Páns in Chota Nagpur.

Sáulok, a general term for members of the Sáhá or Sunri caste.

Saunaka, a Kshatra-peta *gotra* or section of Brahmans.

Saundika, a synonym for Sunri.

Saunt, a section of the Bánsphor sub-caste of Doms in Behar.

Sauntia-Kandh, a sub-tribe of Kandhs in Orissa.

Saupáyan, a section of Brahmans and of Káyasths in Bengal.

Saur, a synonym for Savar; a *mul* or section of the Kanaujiá sub-caste of Sonárs and of Goálás in Behar; a totemistic section of Khariás and Turis signifying a fish; a totemistic sept of Doms and Chamárs in Chota Nagpur.

Saurástriya, a sub-caste of Brahmans found in Behar.

Sauriyá, a sub-caste of Maulíks in Chota Nagpur.

Saursambár, a section of the Sátmuliá Maghayá sub-caste of Kándus in Behar.

Traditions of origin.

Sabar,[1] *Subar, Saur, Sar, Sayar, Suir, Swiri,* a Dravidian cultivating and servile tribe of Orissa, Chota Nagpur, Western Bengal, Madras, and the Central Provinces. Colonel Dalton regards them as Dravidian,[2] while Friedrich Müller,[3] General Cunningham,[4] and Mr. R. Cust,[5]

[1] "The origin of the name of *Savara,*" says General Cunningham, "must be sought for outside the language of the Aryans. In Sanskrit *savara* simply means a 'corpse.' From Herodotus, however, we learn the Scythian word for an 'axe' was *sagaris;* and as *g* and *v* are interchangeable letters, *savar* is the same word as *sagar.* It seems therefore not unreasonable to infer that the tribes who were so called took their name from their habit of carrying axes. Now it is one of the striking peculiarities of the Savaras that they are rarely seen without an axe in their hands. This peculiarity has been frequently noticed by all who have seen them."—*Archæological Survey,* xvii, 113.

[2] *Ethnology of Bengal,* p. 149.

[3] *Allgem. Ethnog.,* 462.

[4] *Achæolog. Survey,* vol. xvii, p. 122.

[5] *Modern Languages of the East Indies,* p. 85.

place them on linguistic grounds in the Kolarian group of tribes. The evidence from language, however, is meagre and inconclusive; while on the other hand it is tolerably certain that the Savars, scattered and partially Hinduised as they are, represent the main body of an ancient race, an isolated fragment of which survives in the Málé or Saur of the Rajmahal hills. The Savars are usually identified with the Suari and Sabarai mentioned by Pliny[1] and Ptolemy.[2] General Cunningham shows in the paper referred to above that the tribe is very widely diffused at the present day; and local tradition ascribes to the Savars the conquest of the Cheros, and their expulsion from the plateau of Shahabad, in about the year 421 of the Sálivâhana era, or A.D. 500. A number of ancient monuments in the Shahabad district are still put down to the Savars or Suirs, who are supposed to have been driven south by the inroad of Rájputs under the Bhojpur chief, which made an end of their rule.

Physical characteristics.

A good observer[3] describes the Savaras near Mahendragiri in Ganjam as small but wiry, often very dark in colour and sometimes quite black, which agrees with Stirling's account.[4] "Their hair is generally tied in a top-knot, and sometimes it is cut short over the forehead, two long locks being permitted to hang over the ears. A few individuals have frizzled shocks, with which no such arrangement is attempted. Most of the men have small, square beards. The nose is in general broad, with wide nostrils. Of those races in Bengal with whose appearance I am familiar, they reminded me most strongly of the Bhumij, who belong to the Munda family; but I could also perceive in them some points of resemblance to the Dravidian Paharias of the Rajmahal hills. They have not, however, the manly bearing and good physique of the latter . . . . Their manner of dancing resembles that of the Rajmahal Paharias, as I have on one occasion witnessed it, rather than that of either the Santáls or Kols."

Internal structure.

The exogamous septs current among the Savars of Bankura are shown in Appendix I. The totems **Sálmachh** and **Kásibak** occur also among the Bágdis and several other Dravidian races of Western Bengal. The eponyms **Gargarishi** and **Sándilya** appear to have been borrowed from the Brahmanical system. The Savars of Orissa are said to have no septs, and it is possible that the Bankura branch of the tribe may have picked up their totemistic septs locally. The case of the Telingas (see article on that caste) rather bears out this view. Mention has been made in the article on the Málé tribe of the remarkable fact that they have no exogamous divisions, and regulate marriage by the more modern system of counting prohibited degrees. It follows from this that the section-names of the Savars throw no light upon their connexion with the Málé. Mr. W. B. Oldham,

---

[1] *Nat. Hist.*, vol. vi, 23. "Suari, quorum Mons Mallus."

[2] Ptolemy VII, 1, 80. Lassen states that Karkaradama, the most western of the cities of the Sabarai, was probably somewhere in Singbhum.

[3] V. Ball *Jungle Life in India*, p. 267.

[4] Stirling, *Orissa*, p. 42.

however, considers the two tribes to be one and the same, and this view may, I think, be accepted as correct.

The Savars of the Orissa Tributary States are divided into four sub-tribes—Bendkar, Parirá, Jharuá, and Palli—which are strictly endogamous. The origin of the names is obscure, but it seems possible that both Palli and Parirá may have some reference to the practice of using leaves as clothing. Varáha Mihira, quoted by General Cunningham, speaks of the Parna or leaf-clad Savaras[1]; and a Savara messenger mentioned in the Kathá Sarit Ságara is a described as carrying a bow in his hand "with his hair tied up in a knot behind with a creeper, black himself and wearing a loin cincture of vilwa leaves."

Marriage.

Girls may be married either as infants or after they have attained the age of puberty. Infant-marriage is deemed the more respectable usage, but no social stigma attaches to a family which is unable by reason of poverty or any other cause to comply with the demands of fashion on this point. Sexual license before marriage, though vehemently condemned, is said to be tolerated, and if an unmarried girl becomes pregnant her fault is condoned by marriage to the father of her child. The Savars of Bankura observe a Hinduised ceremony, the binding portions of which are *gotrántar*, or the transfer of the bride from her own sept to that of the bridegroom, and the smearing of vermilion on her forehead and the parting of her hair. In Orissa the ritual is more simple, and appears to have been less affected by the influence of Brahmanical usage. On the arrival of the bridegroom at the bride's house he is met by her female relatives, who greet him with cries of *lu lu*, and burn ghi, rice, areca nuts, turmeric, etc., in his honour. This is followed by a curious practice, called *seka*, believed to be peculiar to the Savars, in which the bridesmaids warm the tips of their fingers at a lamp and press them on both cheeks of the bridegroom. The couple then pass on towards the *bedi*, a raised platform of earth, in the courtyard of the house, stopping on the way to sprinkle each seven times with a mixture of mustard seed and salt. On reaching the *bedi* they make two and a half turns round a pot of water, in which are mango leaves, after which an elder of the tribe, nominated as priest for the occasion, makes them sit down side by side, and binds their hands together with *durba* grass and leaves of the *borkoli* plum tree. This is the closing and essential part of the ceremony. The bride-price varies with the means of the families. Among the Bendkar Savars, according to Colonel Dalton, it comprises two bullocks—one for the girl's father and another for her maternal uncle—and a cloth and one rupee presented to her mother.

Polygamy is permitted, and no theoretical limit is set to the number of wives a man may have Few Savars, however, indulge in more than two, and usually a second wife is only taken in the event of the first being barren. In Orissa (but not in Bankura), a widow may marry again, and is ordinarily expected to marry her

[1] Professor Kern identifies the Parna Savaras with the Phyllitæ of Ptolemy, but explains the name to mean "feeding upon leaves," which seems improbable.

first husband's younger brother or cousin. No compulsion, however, is exercised in the matter. and a widow may marry any one she pleases, provided that she returns to her father's house and remains unmarried for a year after her first husband's death. No regular ceremony is ordained for use on such occasions, and the union is celebrated by a feast given to the relations of both parties. Divorce is permitted for adultery or any other serious conjugal offence. The case is considered by the members of the husband's family, who, if they find it impossible or unadvisable to effect a reconciliation between the parties, formally escort the woman to the house of her father or guardian and leave her there. Divorced wives may marry again in the same manner as widows.

Religion.

The Savars of Bankura have become thoroughly Hinduised, and Brahmans serve them as priests in the worship of the standard gods. These Brahmans are received on equal terms by the *purohits* of Bagdis, Koras, Kewats, and other low castes. In Orissa the original faith of the tribe has been less modified by the influence of Hindu usage. The worship of the Brahmanical deities is indeed gaining ground among them, but the elder gods, Thánpati, who dwells in the *thán* or sacred grove of the village, and "Bansuri or Thákuráini, no doubt the same as the blood-thirsty she-devil revered by the Bhuiyás,"[1] still receive offerings of goats or fowls at the hands of the elders of the community, who have not yet been supplanted in their office by the professional Brahman.

Disposal of the dead.

The Orissa Savars recognize both burial and cremation as proper modes of disposing of the dead. The Bankura branch of the tribe only burn, and perform the ceremony of *sráddh* more or less in accordance with regular Hindu usage.

Occupation.

The Savars believe their original condition to have been that of a wandering tribe, roaming through the hills of Orissa and Chota Nagpur, living on the fruits of the forest and acknowledging the rule of no recognized chief. The memory of this primitive state is almost the only tradition which the tribe still preserve, and it can hardly be doubted that this primitive mode of life must have lasted, at any rate among some branches of the Savars, down to comparatively recent times.

The bulk of the tribe have taken to plough cultivation and massed themselves in regular villages; but the Bendkars of Keunjhar still adhere in the main to the nomadic habits which their traditions describe. An interesting account of this branch of the Savars was given in 1842 by Colonel Tickell, of the South-West Frontier Agency, who found them inhabiting a tangled tract of hill and forest bounded on the north and north-east by the cultivated land of the Ho communities or *pirs* of Kotgarh and Bar. They had lost their primitive dialect, and spoke either Ho or Uriyá. In physical appearance they resembled the Bhuiyás of that part of the country, and were fair,

[1] Dalton, *Ethnology*, p. 149. Thakuráini, it should be stated, is the name of a range of hills in the north of Keunjhar.

well-made, and intelligent. They worshipped Káli, with several minor tutelary deities. In matters of food they appear to have been rather exclusive. A Bendkar would take water from a Ho, but would not eat with him, nor would he touch any food that had been cooked by a Hindu. Their material condition was extremely poor. They possessed no cattle, and only a few fowls. The houses were mere hovels, not massed together in villages, but dotted about on the hillside in separate groups of two or three, like those of Birhors in Palámau. The crops usually cultivated were maize, high-land rice (*gora dhán*), and gram (*chaná*), which were grown in straggling fields formed by banking up the hillside water-courses. Edible jungle products were largely used for food, and frequently made up an entire day's subsistence. They paid no rent for their land, but were liable to be called upon for *begári* or gratuitous labour by the Rájá of Kalikáprasád in Keunjhar. Their funeral ceremony consisted in simply burning the dead body; they did not collect the ashes from the pyre, nor did they, like the Kols, destroy any of the deceased person's property with his corpse.

Dancing.

In writing of the same people Colonel Dalton[1] specially notices their style of dancing:—"The girls dance with their heads covered, bodies much inclined, and faces looking to the ground or to their feet, which have to perform a somewhat intricate step; the right hand holds down at arm's length the portion of the dress that is thrown over the head. The men, playing on tambourines or half drums, sing as they dance. The girls appear too intent on their steps to respond to them; but their peculiar attitude in the dance, the steps, and the melody, are the same for all Bhuiyás, and are unmistakeable characteristics of the race from the Ganges to the Mahánadi. The Kolarian dances are quite different." It seems to me that the argument from similarity of custom to tribal affinity has in this case been pressed too far. Subject races everywhere have not been slow to imitate the usages of the dominant people with whom they were brought into contact, and the Savars have been too long under the virtual control of the Bhuiyás for it to be at all surprising that they should have adopted the dances characteristic of the latter. The Kolarian races, on the other hand, have either maintained their isolation and independence or have been brought in contact only with Hindus, whose ideas on the subject of dancing would certainly not commend themselves to a sociable non-Aryan community.

Mode of agriculture.

Regarding the Bendkar methods of agriculture, Colonel Dalton[2] observes—"When first I saw the Bendkar hand-plough it was of wood,—only a branch cut with a large piece of the stem, from which it sprung attached, and that shaped so as to give it the appearance of a miniature Native plough; but they have improved on this, and now insert a piece of iron as a share, in further imitation of the Native plough. The implement answers well enough in preparing for seed the light

---

[1] *Ethnology of Bengal*, p. 150.
[2] *Ditto*, p. 152.

vegetable mould of the forest, to which they confine their cultivation; but in a stiff clay it would be inoperative. The hill Bendkars cultivate *kangni* (Panicum Italicum), *kheri*, *khodo* (Eleusine coracana) or *maruá*, *gangoi makai* (Zea mays) or maize, a species of coxcomb, the seeds of which they eat, a cereal called *siko*, and a large bean, which is intoxicating or acts as an emetic if eaten raw, but is pleasant and wholesome when well cooked; also *urid*. They have ordinarily no rice cultivation. They know well and use all the spontaneous edible productions of the forests, and showed me some wild yams, which they largely consume; they take an immensity of cooking." Here the suggestion seems to be that the Bendkar plough was consciously shaped in imitation of the implement commonly in use in India. It is, however, possible, and I think on the whole more probable, that it represents the earliest form of the Indian plough—a type which, though improved out of all recognition in the plains, may still be traced back to the clumsy wooden hoe which the Bendkar drags after him through the light ashes of his plot of *jhum* land.

Social status.

The social position of the Orissa Savars, like that of many non-Aryan tribes, does not admit of precise definition. Hindus alone are recognized members of the caste system, and the Savars have not yet come to be admitted as members of the Hindu community, though their promotion to that position cannot long be deferred. Their first step will doubtless be to provide themselves with Brahmans, as the Savars of Bankura have already done. The latter affect to maintain a high standard of ceremonial purity, and will not take cooked food from the hands of any one except a Brahman. Their pretensions, however, are not admitted by their neighbours, and at present their social rank is certainly not higher than that of Bágdis, Lohárs, Koras, and similar castes who hang on the outskirts of the Hindu social system.

The following table shows the number and distribution of the Savar tribe in 1872 and 1881:—

District.	1872.	1881.	District.	1872.	1881.
Midnapur	......	1,462	Tributary States, Orissa...	36,845	20,871
Cuttack	16,589	20,217	Singbhum	277	494
Puri	14,179	17,238	Manbhum	......	197
Balasore	446	692	Tributary States	106	190

Savar-Munda, a sub-tribe of Mundas in Chota Nagpur.

Sawani, a sept of Gonds in Chota Nagpur.

Sáwant, a section of the Magahiyá sub-caste of Doms in Behar.

Sawási, a synonym for Pán.

Sayar, a synonym for Savar.

Sebak, a title of the so-called pure Sudras who perform personal service for Brahmans.

Sebaka or **Murhia**, a group of the Pandá sub-caste of Utkal Brahmans.

Seduah, a sept of Limbus in Darjiling.

Sege, a sept of Chakmás in the Hill Tracts of Chittagong.

Segmang, a *thar* or sept of the Bárah-Gurung sub-tribe of Gurungs in Darjiling.

Segul, a sept of Rájputs in Behar.

Sejagá, a *gáin* of the Sándilya *gotra* of Rárhi Brahmans in Bengal.

Sekowa, a sept of Chakmás in the Hill Tracts of Chittagong.

Sekrá, a synonym for Sarnakár.

Sekri, a sweeper caste of Eastern Bengal, now converted to Islam and admitted to worship in the mosque and to the privilege of burial in the public graveyard. With their conversion the Sekris have abandoned their original occupation and now taken to cultivation and to the manufacture of lucifer matches, or rather spills of wood tipped with sulphur. All of them assume the title Shaikh, of which Sekri may perhaps be a derivative. Their personal names are generally taken from the day of the week, or from the month in which they were born. Thus Shaikh Ramazán and Shaikh Itwári are common appellations.

Sekwahdeng, a sept of Limbus in Darjiling.

Sem, a title of Kaibarttas in Bengal.

Semanohangiar, a sept of Lohars in Chota Nagpur.

Semárbár, a sub-caste of Beldárs in Behar.

Semári, a sub-caste of Kaibarttas and Gonrhis in Behar.

Semarkanda, root, a sept of Mundas in Chota Nagpur.

Semarwár, a sub-caste of Nuniás in Behar.

Semerya, a sub-caste of Barais in Behar.

Semraián, a section of Bábhans in Behar.

Sen, a family title of Siddha Baidyas, Báruis, and Mayarás; of Dakshin-Rárhi and Bangaja Káyasths and of Subarnabaniks; of Báitis, Sánkháris, and of Támbulis in Bengal.

Senápat, a section of Maghaiya Kumhárs in Behar.

Senápati, general, a group of the Srotriya sub-caste of Utkal Brahmans; a title of Khandáits in Orissa.

Senbhumiá, a sub-caste of Telis in Western Bengal.

Sendara-Nagasia, a sub-tribe of Nágesars who use *sindur* at marriage.

Senduriár, a *pur* or section of Sákadwipi Brahmans in Behar.

Sene, a sept of Limbus in Darjiling.

Senel, a *dugu* or section of the Kochh-Mandai in Dacca. The name indicates the original habitat of the group, probably a hill or village in Assam, and has no bearing upon marriage.

Sengár, a sept of the Chandrabansi division of Rájputs in Behar.

Sengra, horse, a totemistic sept of Mundas in Chota Nagpur.

Senihang, sons of the snow-chief, a sept of the Phedab sub-tribe of Limbus in Darjiling.

Senpuriá, a section of Banodhiá and Jaiswár Kalwárs in Behar.

Senthá, a sept of the Rautár sub-tribe of Thárus in Behar.

Seonáráyani, a religious sect found in Behar. See *Sivnáráini*.

Seorniá, a sept of Mundas in Chota Nagpur.

Sepári, a sub-caste of Goálás in Behar.

Serhar, a kind of bird, a totemistic sept of Mundas in Chota Nagpur.

Serling, the thief, a sept of the Yangorup sub-tribe of Limbus in Darjiling.

Serma, rent-collector, a sept of the Pánthar sub-tribe of Limbus in Darjiling.

Serwa, a section of Mangars in Darjiling.

Set, *Seth*, a chief merchant, from Sanskrit *sreshtha*, 'best' or 'chief,' (i) a title of Telis; (ii) a leading banker or trader among the Marwari Baniyás, usually Jains; (iii) a section of the Oswál Baniyás.

Set or **Set-tálwár**, a section of the Chárjáti sub-caste of Khatris in Bengal.

Setarapa, dog-eater, a totemistic sept of Mundas in Chota Nagpur.

Seth, a section of the Banodhiá and Jaiswár Kalwárs in Behar.

Setisurwál, a *thar* or sept of Mangars in Darjiling.

Setu, a *gáin* of the Sábarna *gotra* of Bárendra Brahmans in Bengal.

Setu-Suruál, a section of Kámis in Darjiling.

Seuli, people of different lower castes in Central Bengal who extract the juice of the date-palm and prepare molasses from it. See **Siuli**.

Sewar, moss, a totemistic sept of Mundas in Chota Nagpur.

Shahá, a sub-caste of Sunris in Eastern Bengal who have given up their original and taken to other professions, and thereby raised themselves above their caste brethren who sell wine, so that at present they consider the Sunris to be a caste different from, and considerably inferior to, them.

Sháha, a synonym for Sunri.

Sháhá, see **Sáhá**.

Sháhi Ugrakhatri, a sub-caste of Aguris in Western Bengal bearing the title Sháh.

Shaini, a *dugu* or section of the Kochh-Mándái in Dacca.

Shakya Láma, a *thar* or sept of Gurungs in Darjiling.

Shalankyana, a *gotra* or section of the Baidya caste in Bengal.

Shang-dah-bo, a *rui* or sept of the Tongdu sub-tribe of Dejong Lhoris, whose ancestor was born at his maternal uncle's when some tutelary deities were being propitiated.

Shári, a synonym for Bhát.

Shehedpuria, a section of Maghayá Dhobis in Behar.

Shelo, sub-tribe of the Bhumij tribe in Chota Nagpur who are iron-smelters.

Sheo, a *thar* or sept of Mangars in Darjiling.

Sheor, fish, a totemistic sept of Kharwars in Chota Nagpur.

Sherbá Khor, a section of Murmis in Darjiling.

Shergarhiá, a sub-caste of Lohárs in the Santál Parganás.

Shewa, a *thar* or sept of Dámis in Darjiling, whose chief profession is sewing.

Shikhu Karmakár, a sub-caste of Kámárs in Noakhali.

Sikkhdar, *Shikdar, Sikdar,* a title of Sudras in Eastern Bengal; an honorary title of Káyasths and Nápits in Bengal; an officer in charge of a *shikk* or fiscal division under the Mahomedan revenue system; a title of Brahmans, possibly of families descended from some one who held the office of shikdar; a title of Kapális and Sunris.

Shirasina, a sub-caste of Sunris in Maldah.

Shoályiá, a sept of Chakmás in the Hill Tracts of Chittagong.

Shushichá, a *thar* or sept of Sunuwárs in Darjiling.

Shyag-chom-bo, a *rui* or sept of Dejong Lhoris, the members of which are the descendants of emigrants from Bhotan and Nepal.

Shyag-ding-pá or **Shyag-tshang-pá,** a *rui* or sept of the Rui-chhung sub-tribe of Dejong Lhoris or Bhotias of the south.

Shyag-tsangpá, a *rui* or sept of Dejong Lhoris, the members of which form the lowest class of Bhotias.

Shyah-pá, a *rui* or sept of Dejong Lhoris whose ancestor had emigrated from North Bhotan.

Shyang-ba, a *rui* or sept of Sherpa Bhotias of Nepal.

Siár, jackal, a totemistic section of Kurmis in Chota Nagpur and Orissa; a sept of Asuras.

Siárahá, a section of the Banodhiá and Jaiswár Kalwárs in Behar.

Siárik, a *gáin* of the Sábarna *gotra* of Rárhi Brahmans in Bengal.

Siár Tuyio, jackal, a totemistic sept of Mundas in Chota Nagpur.

Sibala, a sub-sept of the Besrá sept of Santáls.

Sibingáre, a sept of the Agniá sub-tribe of Meches in the Darjiling Terai.

Sib-rási, a section of Málos in Eastern Bengal.

Siddh, a *thar* or sept of Gurungs in Darjiling.

Siddha, a hypergamous group of the Bárendra Káyasths in Bengal.

Siddhal, a *gáin* of the Sábarna *gotra* of Rárhi Brahmans in Bengal.

Siddha-Maulik, a hypergamous group of the Dakshin-Rárhi Káyasths in Bengal.

Siddha-Srotriya, a hypergamous group of Rárhi Brahmans in Bengal.

Siddhi-putra, a synonym for Bhuinmáli.

Sidhpur, a *mul* or section of the Chhamuliá Madhesiá sub-caste of Halwáis in Behar.

Sidhyál, a *thar* or section of Nepáli Brahmans.

Sidup or **Siduk**, a bundle of straw, a sub-sept of the Saren sept of Sántals.

Sigadiá, a section of Goálás in the North-Western Provinces and Behar.

Sihari, a *gáin* of the Sándilya *gotra* of Bárendra Brahmans in Bengal.

Sihásme-Khor, a *mul* of the Sándil section of Maithil Brahmans in Behar.

Sihásme-Sihásam, a *mul* of the Sándil section of Maithil Brahmans in Behar.

Sihogiá, a section of Bábhans and a sept of Rájputs in Behar.

Sihoriá, a section of Bábhans in Behar.

Sihujiá, a section of Bábhans in Behar.

Sijapati, a *thar* or sept of Mangars in Darjiling.

Sikalgar, a section of the Maghayá sub-caste of Barhis in Behar; a title of Lohárs or Kámárs.

Sikári, a section of Kumhárs in Singbhum.

Sikáuriár, a *pur* or section of Sákadwipi Brahmans in Behar.

Sikbandhera, a section of the Ariár sub-caste of Bais Baniyás in Behar.

Sikcharo, a bird, a totemistic sept of Mundas in Chota Nagpur.

Sikdár, a sept of Mál Paháriás; a hypergamous group of Kaibarttas in Bakarganj.

Sikhariá, a sub-caste of Bauris, Karangás, Korás, and Kurmis in Chota Nagpur, who derive their name from Sikharbhum, the tract of country north of the Dámudar river, corresponding roughly to the limits of the Pachet estate. In this connexion it deserves notice that Samet Sikhar is an old name for Párasnáth Hill, which is conspicuously visible from every part of Sikharbhum, and may almost be looked upon as forming the western boundary of the tract. See Statistical Account of Hazaribagh, p. 217. In the case of the Bauris, the Sikhariá sub-caste is also called Gobariá, which may perhaps have some reference to *gobar*, 'cow-dung,' as Bauri women earn money by making the cow-dung cakes used for fuel; a sub-caste of Rajwárs, and of Doms in South Manbhum.

Sikhariá or **Sindurtopá**, a sub-caste of Telis in Western Bengal.

Sikhariyá or *Meno*, a sub-tribe of Bhumijs in Chota Nagpur.

Sikhoriá, a sub-caste of Sunris in Behar who deal in liquor.

Sikhwád, a section of Goálás in the North-Western Provinces and Behar.

Sikiá, a *mul* or section of the Chhamuliá Madhesiá sub-caste of Halwáis in Behar.

Sikilgar, a cleaner of weapons.

Sikiyá, chain, a sub-sept of the Murmu sept of Santáls.

Sikrá, hawk, a totemistic sept of Mundas and Páns in Chota Nagpur.

Sikrar, a *pangat* or section of Bánsphor Doms in Behar.

Sil, a title of Subarnabaniks and Nápits; of Dakshin Rárhi and Bangaja Káyasths and of Tántis in Bengal; a section of Oswál Baniyás in Behar.

Silaichiá, a section of Sonárs in Behar.

Ṣilári (Sansk. *Silá*, a stone), a magician employed in Eastern Bengal to protect crops from hailstones. Formerly the Ṣilárí, like the Gárapagárí of the Central Provinces, was a paid village servant; and officiated as priest at an annual festival performed for the benefit of the crops. Now the festival has fallen into disuse, and a member of any caste may become a Ṣilárí, being remunerated in kind—it is unlucky to give him money—according to the success of his enchantments. Chaṇḍáls, Jogís, and Bairágís are the ordinary Ṣilárís, but a Muhamadan often acts as one, his co-religionists believing as implicitly in this occult science as their Hindu brethren.

"At the present day," says Dr. Wise, "this magical art is falling into disrepute, and it is no unusual thing for the peasantry to punish a Ṣilárí who fails to protect their fields. The Ṣilárís confess that their skill is inadequate to call down a storm on a neighbour's crop, as was formerly done; but they still profess ability to drive away a cloud threatening any tract of country.

"As hailstorms in Bengal occur usually in March and April, when the Boro-dhán, or spring rice, is in the ear, the services of the magician are called for in low lands, where this crop is cultivated. When a storm is impending the Ṣilárí, summoned by the peasantry, rushes, almost naked, from his hut, with a rattan wand in his right hand. Invoking Parameṣwara, the supreme god, he ascends a mound, where, spreading abroad his hands, and waving his rod to indicate the direction the storm-cloud is to take, he recites one or other of the following doggerel incantations in the vernacular:—

I.

O Narasiṉha! Narasiṉha! mighty Narasiṉha! whom the fourteen gods fear;
On hearing the name Narasiṉha the gods and spirits bend their heads;
My Guru's name is Híra. Wherever you go that quarter of the world is subdued,
Whether it consists of hills or mountains, trees or jungle.
Should this charm of mine fail, Mahádeva's hair will be uprooted and fall off.

II.

Diamonds cut stones.
Rivers retire before them.
A gold knife is keen as a diamond.
I have cut it this day into thirty-two.
Begone to the mountains of the north
Having paid you tribute to the south.
Having scattered you, I go home.
My name is Ṣiva Ṣankara.

"The above metrical rhapsody was obtained from Rái Chánd Bairágí, a celebrated Şilárí, residing at Shámgáon, in Tipperah."

Silewár, a sept of Rájputs in Behar.

Silhatia or *Sirotia*, a sub-caste of Dosádhs in Behar.

Silhotia or *Jeswar Kurmi*, a sub-caste of Dhánuks in Behar who call themselves *Kulin*.

Silli, a sept of the Patar sub-caste of Mahilis called after the ancestral burying place of the group; a kind of fish, a totemistic sept of Korwas and Páns in Chota Nagpur.

Silongchhá, a *thar* or sept of Khambus in Darjiling.

Silotháer, a section of Majraut Goálás in Behar.

Simalwál, a section of Goálás in the North-Western Provinces and Behar.

Simar, a section of Kamárkalla Sonárs in Behar.

Simarlásá, a tree, a totemistic section of Ghásis in Chota Nagpur.

Simarloká, a sub-caste of Ghásis in Chota Nagpur.

Simbi, a *gáin* of the Bharadwája *gotra* of Bárendra Brahmans in Bengal.

Simkhárá, a *thar* or section of Nepáli Brahmans.

Simlái, a *gáin* of the Kásyapa and Bátsya *gotras* of Rárhi Brahmans in Bengal.

Simli, a *gáin* of the Bátsya *gotra* of Bárendra Brahmans in Bengal.

Sinágar, a *mul* or section of the Chhamuliá Madhesiá sub-caste of Halwáis in Behar.

Sincheuli, a *thar* or sept of Mangars in Darjiling.

Sinchiori, a section of Kámis in Darjiling.

Sindhikuriá, a totemistic sept of Páns in Chota Nagpur who cannot touch the horns of a bull.

Sindhurishi, a section of Telis in Bengal.

Sindhwatiá, a section of Bhats.

Sindur, a totemistic sept of Mundas in Chota Nagpur who do not use vermilion in marriages.

Sinduriá, *Sindurhár*, a class of Bania who sell *sindur* or vermilion; also a class of Brahmans or Kayasths who formerly practised as inoculators, but are now employed as vaccinators; a sub-caste of Máls in the Santál Parganás.

Sinduriá, a red paint, a section of Binjhiás; a sept of Rájputs.

Sing, a title of Khambus and Mangars in Darjiling.

Singá-ore, a section of Kámis in Darjiling.

Singar, a section of Murmis in Darjiling; a sept of Kaurs in Chota Nagpur.

Singauri, a *thar* or sept of Mangars in Darjiling.

Singden, a section of Murmis in Darjiling.

Singdiár, a *gáin* of the Sábarna *gotra* of Bárendra Brahmans in Bengal.

Singdyang, a sept of Lepchas in Darjiling.

Singh, a title of Oswál Banyás, Bábhans, Goálás, Kshatriyas, Kurmis, and Rájputs in Behar; a title of Subarnabaniks in Manbhum. Intermarriage is prohibited within the title. A section and a title of Káyasths in Behar; a section of Rajwárs; a sept of Mundas and Páns in Chota Nagpur whose totem is horn; a title of Támbulis in Bengal.

Singhal, a *gotra* or section of the Agarwáls in Behar.

Singháras, a section of Madhesiá Halwáis in Behar.

Singhazári, a sub-caste of Sunris and Telis in Western Bengal.

Singhi, fish, a sept of Páns in Chota Nagpur; a section of Oswáls.

Singh-rási, a section of Málos in Eastern Bengal.

Singhror, a section of Goriá Goálás in Behar.

Singi, horn, a totemistic sept of Chiks in Chota Nagpur.

Singjangkuk, a sept of Limbus in Darjiling.

Singjuk, a sept of Limbus in Darjiling.

Singogpa, a sept of the Phedáb sub-tribe of Limbus in Darjiling.

Singpuriá, a sept of Birhors in Chota Nagpur.

Singyál, a *thar* or section of Nepáli Brahmans.

Sing-yangma, a sept of the Phágu sub-tribe of Yakhas in Darjiling.

Sinha, lion, a title of Khandáits in Orissa; of Káyasths and Subarnabaniks in Bengal; of Rájus in Midnapur.

Sinhi, a section of Kumhárs in Singbhum.

Sinhiniá, a sept of Rájputs in Behar.

Sinjali, a *thar* or sept of Mangars in Darjiling.

Sinjhikhariá, a sept of Páns in Chota Nagpur.

Sinjikuria, a sept of Chiks in Chota Nagpur.

Sinkoi, a sept of Hos in Singbhum.

Sipáhi, a title of Rájputs in Behar.

Sipahiyá, a section of Bánsphor Doms in Western Behar.

Sir, arrow, a totemistic sept of Goálás in Chota Nagpur.

Sirá, a section of Maghayá Kándus in Behar.

Sirasinthi, a *gáin* of the Bharadwája *gotra* of the Uttar-Bárendra Brahmans in Bengal.

Sirasthán, a sub-caste of Kumhárs in Pabna.

Siriár, a section of Bábhans in Behar.

Sirkar, a section of the Bánsphor sub-caste of Doms in Behar.

Sirkiá, 'the dweller in a *sirki* hut,' a designation of Nats, Bediyás, and other wandering castes of the gipsy type, derived from the materials of the temporary huts which they build.

Sirmaur, a sept of Rájputs in Behar.

Sirmauriár, a *pur* or section of Sákadwipi Brahmans in Behar.

Sirnáit, a sept of the Surajbansi division of Rájputs in Behar.

Sirnet, a sept of Rájputs in Behar.

Sirniá, a sept of the Surajbansi division of Rájputs in Behar.

Sirotá, a sub-caste of Dhanuks in Behar.

Sirpur, a section of the Tirhutiyá sub-caste of Doms in Behar.

Sirsait, a section of Bábhans in Behar.

Siruar, a sept of Birhors in Chota Nagpur.

Sirwár, a section of the Dhaprá and Pachainyá sub-castes of Doms in Behar.

Sisab, a section of Karan Káyasths in Behar.

Sisaundiá, a section of Sonárs in Behar.

Sisauriá, a *mul* or section of the Ayodhiábási sub-caste of Sonárs in Behar.

Sisingi, a river fish with two thorns on its head, a totemistic sept of Kumhars in Chota Nagpur.

Sisodhiá, a sept of Surajbansi Rájputs in Behar.

Sisodiá, a section of Goálás in the North-Western Provinces and Behar.

Sisoniá, a sept of Rájputs in Behar.

Sisotár, a *mul* or section of the Chhamuliá Madhesiá sub-caste of Halwáis in Behar.

Sisungi, fish, a sept of Mundas in Chota Nagpur.

Sisutbansi Loharia, a sub-caste of the Lohar caste (iron-smith); also called Lohondia.

Sit, a title of Telis in Bengal.

Sitali, a *gáin* of the Sábarna *gotra* of Bárendra Brahmans in Bengal.

Sitár-Dhobá, a sub-caste of Dhobás in Eastern Bengal.

Sithung, a *thar* or sept of Mangars in Darjiling.

Siuli or *Seuli*, a sub-caste of Háris in Bengal; a title of Chandáls, Doms, Haris and similar lower castes, as well as Mahomedans who extract juice from date-trees for the manufacture of *gur*, molasses, or toddy.

Siva, a section of the Mahmudábáz sub-caste of Nápits; of Jugis and Kapális; of Rautiás.

Siva-bansi, *Sivakul*, a synonym for, and a title of, Kochh or Rájbansi, probably a vague term for worshippers of Siva, in use among natives of Kuch Behar, many of whom claim to be Sivabansi, descended from Siva.

Sivnáráini, a worshipper of Siva and Náráyan, a class of religious sectarians who live a secular life.

Siwarwár, a sub-caste of Nuniás in Behar.

Siyár, a section of the Pargah caste in Behar.

Skandhasura, a synonym for Kandh.

Smár, Swar, a title of Dákshin-Rarhi and Bangaja Káyasths.

Smatti, a sept of Pators in Chota Nagpur.

Smritiratna, a literary title of Brahmans.

Soa, a kind of vegetable, a totemistic sept of Mundas in Chota Nagpur.

Soai, a bird, a totemistic sept of Mundas in Chota Nagpur.

Soási, a synonym for Pán.

Sobarnarekhá, a sept of Mundas in Chota Nagpur.

Soberi, a *thar* of the Kausika *gotra* of Nepáli Brahmans.

Sobhádih, a *mul* or section of the Naomuliá or Majraut sub-caste of Goálás in Behar.

Sobhni Tajpur, a *mul* or section of the Naomuliá or Majraut sub-caste of Goálás in Behar.

Sochari, a section of Báis Sonárs in Behar.

Sodemba, the spy, a sept of the Phedáb sub-tribe of Limbus in Darjiling.

Soeka, a bush, a totemistic sept of Mundas in Chota Nagpur.

Sogani, a section of Saraogis in Behar.

Sohagrámi, a *gáin* of the Kásyapa *gotra* of Bárendra Brahmans in Bengal.

Sohanpur, a section of the Biyáhut aud Kharidáhá Kalwárs in Behar

Sohek, a kind of fish, a totemistic sept of Mundas in Chota Nagpur.

Sohidamochi, a title of Chamárs or Muchis.

Soi, spring, a totemistic sept of Mundas in Chota Nagpur.

Sokhait, a sept of the Rautár sub-tribe of Thárus in Behar.

Sokhwá, a sub-caste of Barais in Behar.

Sokiriá, a sub-caste of Sunris in Behar.

Sokoe, a kind of fruit, a totemistic sept of Mundas.

Sokulkárá, a sub-caste of Rajwárs in Chota Nagpur.

Solai, fish, a totemistic sept of Mundas in Chota Nagpur.

Soma, a family title of Kashta Baidyas and Kayasths in Bengal.

Somáj, a hypergamous division of the Paschim Kuliyá Sadgops.

Somal, deer, a sub-sept of the Kisku sept of Santáls.

Sombansi, a sept of Rájputs in Behar.

Somnidih Sagun Máhta Purukh, a *mul* or section of the Naomuliá or Majraut sub-caste of Goálás in Behar.

Somrishi, a section of Mayarás in Bengal.

Somwár, a sept of the Surajbansi division of Rájputs in Behar.

Son, a title of Bangaja Káyasths; a sub-sept of the Beará sept of Santáls.

Soná, gold, a totemistic section of Kurmis in Chota Nagpur and Orissa; a totemistic sept of Goálás in Chota Nagpur who cannot wear gold.

Sonáchain, a section of the Chain sub-caste of Nuniás in Behar.

Sonaibar, a section of Bábhans in Behar.

Sonákánt, a section of the Biyáhut and Kharidáhá Kalwárs in Behar.

Sonaman, a section of Kanaujiá Lohárs in Behar.

Sonamati, a sept of Páns in Chota Nagpur.

Sonámdih, a *mul* or section of the Naomuliá or Majraut sub-caste of Goálás in Behar.

Sonaome, a sept of Lohárs in Chota Nagpur.

Sonápur Sakarwár, a *mul* or section of the Sátmuliá or Kishnaut sub-caste of Goálás in Behar.

Sonar, goldsmith, a sept of Bairágis and Kharwars in Chota Nagpur who do not wear gold.

Traditions of origin.

Sonár, *Káin, Kainyá, Zargar,* the goldsmith caste of Behar; also engaged to some extent in money-lending and general trade. Concerning the origin of the caste little is known, and it appears to be an occupational group consisting of the members of respectable middle-class castes who adopted the business of working in the precious metals. Sonárs are not rich in traditions, and the few they have are of the ordinary mythological type, and throw no light on the antecedents of the caste. A common story is that in the beginning of time, when the goddess Devi was busy with the construction of mankind, a giant called Sonwa-Dwaitya, whose body consisted entirely of gold, devoured her creations as fast as she made them. To baffle this monster the goddess created a goldsmith, furnished him with the tools of his art, and instructed him how to proceed. When the giant proposed to eat him, the goldsmith suggested to him that if his body were polished his appearance would be vastly improved, and asked to be allowed to undertake the job. With the characteristic stupidity of his tribe, the giant fell into the trap, and having had one finger polished was so pleased with the result that he agreed to be polished all over. For this purpose, like Œetes in the Greek legend of Medea, he had to be melted down, and the goldsmith, who was to get the body as his perquisite, giving the head only to Devi, took care not to put him together again. The goldsmith, however, over-reached himself. Not content with his legitimate earnings, he must needs steal a part of the head, and being detected in this by Devi, he and his descendants were condemned to be for ever poor.

Internal structure.

The internal structure of the caste is shown at length in Appendix I. Both sub-castes and sections belong to the local or territorial type, and their names do not help us to trace a connexion between the Sonárs and other similar groups. The system of exogamy followed is very complete. A man may not marry a woman belonging to the same section as (1) himself, (2) his mother, (3) his paternal grandmother, (4) his maternal grandmother, (5) his father's paternal grandmother, (6) his father's maternal grandmother. In applying this set of prohibitions to any particular case, the sections of both parties are taken into account; so that if the proposed bride's mother belonged to the same section as the proposed bridegroom's maternal grandmother, no marriage would be possible, although the parties themselves both belonged to different sections. The standard formula for calculating prohibited degrees is also taken into consideration down to the seventh generation in the descending line.

Marriage.

All Sonárs who can afford to do so marry their daughters as infants; and when a girl's marriage is delayed after the age of puberty, poverty is usually the sole cause. The marriage ceremony corresponds in all essential particulars to that observed by the higher castes in Behar. In rich families it is considered right for the bridegroom to go on horseback to fetch the bride. Polygamy is permitted, but is rarely resorted to except when the first wife is childless. In the Kanaujiá, Ajodhiapuri, Mair, and Kamarkalla sub-castes widow-marriage is prohibited. The other sub-castes allow a widow to marry again, and ordinarily deem it incumbent on her to marry her late husband's younger brother. Among the Sonárs of Chota Nagpur the custom of widow-marriage is recognized in the devolution of property, which proceeds *per stirpes*, the shares being so divided that the sons of a *sagai* wife get six-sixteenths and those of a *bihai* wife ten-sixteenths between them. In Behar the ordinary law of inheritance is followed by the caste, but a daughter's son is excluded from succession by the nearest male of the same *kul* or section. The sub-castes which permit widow-marriage also allow divorce, which is effected with the sanction of the panchâyat when a woman is suspected of unchastity.

Religion.

The religion of the Sonár caste differs little from that of other orthodox Hindus of about the same standing in society. Some Vaishnavas are found among them; but most Sonárs belong to the Sákta sect, and pay especial reverence to Devi. The popular minor gods of Behar are also worshipped. For the service of the *di majores* of the standard Hindu Pantheon, Maithil or Tirhutiá Brahmans serve them as priests, and are received on equal terms by other members of the sacred order. In the cult of the minor gods, on the other hand, traces of a more primitive state of things may perhaps be discerned. Thus the offerings made to Goraiá are the perquisite of the Dosádhs, which looks as if the priests of the deity were at one time chosen from that caste; while the *pakwáns* or cakes given to Bandi are eaten by the members of the family. Some Sonárs worship a Mahomedan *pir*, Sháh Sharf-ud-din; and all offer up silver images of Bandi at marriages.

Disposal of the dead.

The dead are burned, and the standard ceremony of *sráddh* is performed on the thirteenth day after death. Libations for the benefit of ancestors in general are also presented in the first fortnight of Ásin every year.

Social status and occupation.

The social standing of the caste is respectable, and their practice in the matter of diet does not differ materially from that of other orthodox Hindus in Behar. Brahmans take water and sweetmeats from the caste; while Sonárs themselves are on similar terms with Kewats, Dhánuks, and Goálás. In former days, it is said, they wore the sacred thread and abstained from spirituous drinks; but these marks of distinction have now fallen into disuse. Their chief occupations are working in metal, mostly in gold and silver, money-changing (*sardfi*), and *khichri-faroshi* or dealing in food-grains. In parts of the country where rent is paid in kind on the *bháoli* system, Kanaujiá Sonárs usually act as weighmen, and receive an allowance of a quarter or half a seer to every maund weighed. A few Sonárs are landholders or cultivators themselves, but as a rule the connexion of the caste with agriculture is only the indirect one of lending money to the raiyat.

It is fair to add that the Sonár does not bear a high reputation for honesty. As a goldsmith he is suspected of substituting base metal for the gold or silver supplied to him in order to be made up into ornaments; as a money-lender he is charged with numberless devices for extorting money from his clients. A fair idea of the opinion held of the caste by the agricultural classes may be derived from the following verses:—

Kainyá dub dubiyá
Suthan le gai Tágo bhái
Ek Suthan menminuá ke dehu
Sab Suthan mangá lehu.

"As he crossed the ford the Kainyá was drowned,
The Bábhan stole his gold mohars away:
Give one to the Judge, and if justice be found,
You will get all the others within the day."

The story is that once upon a time a Sonár and a Bábhan went forth from the same village to seek their fortunes. Both returned at the same time and met on the road—the Bábhan almost penniless and the Sonár with a bag full of gold mohars. As they were crossing a river, the Bábhan decided to drown the Sonár and steal his money. The latter gave himself up to his fate, only asking his murderer to repeat the foregoing verses as his last message to his kinsfolk. The stupid Bábhan did so, and thus himself furnished the clue which led to the detection of the crime. The story affords a curious illustration of the popular estimate of the comparative intellectual capacity of the castes concerned. A somewhat similar tale, in which a Káyasth plays the part here assigned to the Sonár, is quoted in the article on Ghási.

The following statement shows the number and distribution of Sonárs in 1872 and 1881. In certain cases the figures of Sekrás and Subarnabaniks seem to have been included in the Census Reports.

District.	1872.	1881.	District.	1872.	1881.
Birbhum	......	715	Monghyr	13,348	18,167
Nadiya	......	1	Bhágalpur	9,646	16,917
Dinajpur	......	186	Purniah	9,419	8,000
Rangpur	......	1	Maldah	......	14
Pabna	......	20	Santál Parganás	3,758	4,281
Darjiling	......	505	Cuttack	13,987	117
Kuch Behar	......	16	Puri	5,900	832
Chittagong Hill Tracts ...	......	7	Balasore	4,297	671
Patna	21,101	23,278	Tributary States	4,670	457
Gya	16,258	15,809	Hazaribagh	4,352	6,822
Shahabad	14,997	18,139	Lohardagá	3,302	4,495
Tirhut { Mozufferpur ...	} 34,720	{ 23,899	Singbhum	176	251
Tirhut { Darbhanga ...		16,988	Manbhum	1,812	2,553
Saran	20,157	21,472	Tributary States	1,290	1,304
Champaran	11,288	15,037			

Sonár, a synonyn for Sarnakár or goldsmiths.

Sonārbaniá, a synonym for Subarnabanik.

Sonárekhá, a sub-caste of Korás in Chota Nagpur.

Sonarwa, a bird, a totemistic sept of Mundas in Chota Nagpur.

Sonarwar, gold, a sept of Kharwars in Chota Nagpur.

Sonaul, a *mul* or section of Kasarwáni Baniyás in Behar.

Sonbesra, a bird, a totemistic sept of Lohárs in Chota Nagpur.

Sonbhadriá, a section of Bábhans in Behar, so named after the village Sonbhadra; or who live on the banks of the Son river.

Soncheri, a section of Kanaujiá Sonárs in Behar.

Sone, a totemistic sept of Mundas in Chota Nagpur who cannot wear gold.

Sonechaurupekedándi, a *mul* or section of Kasarwáni Baniyás in Behar.

Sonerupekhichri, a *mul* or section of Kasarwáni Baniyás in Behar.

Sonewár, a *kul* or section of Bábhans in Behar.

Songbangphe, the new settler, a sept of the Pánthar and Phedáb sub-tribes of Limbus in Darjiling.

Songden, a section of Murmis in Darjiling.

Songyokpa, a sept of the Phágu sub-tribe of Yakhas in Darjiling.

Sonhar, a *mul* or section of the Chhamuliá Madhesia subcaste of Halwáis and of Biyahut and Kharidáhá Kalwárs in Behar.

Soni, a section of the Bárajáti sub-caste of Khatris in Bengal; a section of Oswáls and Saraogis in Behar.

Soniyár, a *pur* or section of Sákadwipi Brahmans in Behar.

Sonkhare, a section of Káyasths in Behar.

Sonkharihan, a place of worship before cutting grain, a totemistic sept of Mundas in Chota Nagpur.

Sonkhariká, a sept of Páns in Chota Nagpur.

Sonkoka, a sept of Páns in Chota Nagpur.

Son Maghaia, a sept of Lohárs and Mundas in Chota Nagpur.

Sonmain, a section of Maghaiyá Kumhárs in Behar.

Sonmanik, a sept of Chiks in Chota Nagpur.

Sonoár, gold, a sept of Agariás in Chota Nagpur.

Sonoáti, a sub-caste of Ghásis in Chota Nagpur.

Sonpur, a section of the Tirhutiyá sub-caste of Doms in Behar.

Sonpuri, a sub-sect of Vaishnavas.

Sonpuriá, a section of Lohárs and Sonárs in Behar.

Sonpursa, a section of the Dhusiá sub-caste of Chamárs in Behar.

Sonpuryá, a section of the Pachainyá sub-caste of Doms in Behar.

Son Tirki, a sept of Lohárs and a section of Goráits in Chota Nagpur.

Sonwan, a section of Ghásis in Chota Nagpur.

Sonwani, a totemistic sept of Goálás, Nagesars, who cannot wear gold; a section of Cheros in Chota Nagpur.

Sonwár, a synonym for Sunuwár.

Sonwasi, a sept of Chiks in Chota Nagpur.

Sonyokpa, the guardian of the new fort, a sept of Chaibisa sub-tribe of Limbus in Darjiling.

So-onkobu, a resident of So-onko, a sept of the Phedáb sub-tribe of Limbus in Darjiling.

Sorahaiyá, a synonym for Surahiyá.

Soraiyá, a section of Kanaujiá Brahmans.

Soraniá, a section of Cheros in Palámau.

Sorawár, a section of Bábhans in Behar.

Soriyár, a *pur* or section of Sákadwipi Brahmans in Behar.

Soso bheloa, a fruit, a totemistic sept of Mundas in Chota Nagpur.

Sote, Srotriya, a hypergamous group of Maithil Brahmans in Behar.

Sothángeh, a *thar* or sept of Khambus in Darjiling.

Sothiwár, a section of Lohárs in Behar.

Sothung, name of a village, a sept of the Phedáb sub-tribe of Limbus in Darjiling.

Soti, a *thar* or section of Nepáli Brahmans.

Sotri, a title of Bábhans in Behar.

Sowáni, a section of Mahesris in Behar.

Sparshan, a title of Muchis in Bengal.

Spashta Dáya a, a sect of Vaishnavas, said to have been founded by one Rup Rám Kabiráj, a disciple of Krishna Chandra Chakravartti of Saidábád.

Srávak, literally, a hearer; (i) a lay member of the Jain religion; (ii) a Hinduised branch of Jains in Manbhum who appear to have lost their religion and become an ordinary caste.

Srávaka, a synonym for Sárák.

Srávak, a synonym for Sárák.

Sreshta-Khandait, a sub-caste of Khandáits in the Orissa Tributary States.

Srestikaran, (i) a title of traders generally; (ii) a title of the Madhyasreni Brahmans of Midnapur.

Sri, a sub-caste of Sutradhars in Noakháli.

Sriangabhatti, a *mel* or hypergamous sub-group of Rárhi Brahmans in Bengal.

Sribakariá, a section of Gonds in Chota Nagpur.

Sribarddhani, a *mel* or hypergamous sub-group of Rárhi Brahmans in Bengal.

Sribastab or *Bástar*, a sub-caste of Hajjams and Káyasths in Behar.

Sribitiá, a section of Madhesiá Kándus in Behar.

Sri-Gaura, a sub-caste of Gaura Brahmans.

Srikrishna, a sub-caste of Sutradhars in Noakháli.

Srimal, a section of Oswáls in Behar.

Srimaurhá, a section of the Banodhiá and Jaiswár Kalwárs in Behar.

Sringa, a *gáin* of the Bharadwája *gotra* of Bárendra Brahmans in Bengal.

Sringi, a *gáin* of the Sábarna *gotra* of Bárendra Brahmans in Bengal.

Sripáli, a *thar* or sept of Mangars in Darjiling.

Srisampad, a title of Brahmans.

Srishti-Karan, Bhatuntara, a sub-caste of Karans in Orissa.

Srisrimal, a section of Oswáls in Behar.

Srotriya, a hypergamous division of the Rárhi and Bárendra Brahmans in Bengal.

Srotriya or **Sásani**, a sub-caste of Utkal Brahmans in Orissa.

Srotriya, Sote, a hypergamous class of Maithil Brahmans in Behar.

Srutabati, a *gáin* of the Bátsya *gotra* of Bárendra Brahmans in Bengal.

Ssahoden, born in famine time, a sept of the Tambrkhola sub-tribe of Limbus in Darjiling.

Sser-Gomba, a *rui* or sept of Sherpa Bhotias of Nepal.

Sser-Lungchan, a *rui* or sept of Sherpa Bhotias of Nepal.

Sserpa, a *rui* or sept of Sherpa Bhotias of Nepal.

Sser-Phen-Zangná, a *rui* or sept of Sherpa Bhotias of Nepal.

Suá, a section of Goálás in Behar.

Suar, hog, a totemistic sept of Oraons; a section of Kahárs.

Suarait, a section of Bháts.

Suargane, a section of Bábhans in Behar.

Subansi, a sept of Chandrabansi Rájputs in Behar.

Subarna, a *gáin* of the Sándilya *gotra* of Bárendra Brahmans in Bengal.

Subarnabanik, *Baniá, Banik, Sarnabanik, Sonárbaniá*, a mercantile caste of Bengal Proper, who claim to be the modern representatives of the ancient Vaisya. In spite of the wealth and influence of the Subarnabanik, their high-bred appearance, and the notorious beauty of the women of the caste, their claim to this distinguished ancestry has failed to obtain general recognition. They are excluded from the ranks of the Nabasákha, or nine clean Sudra castes, and none but Vaidik Brahmans will take water from their hands. To account for the comparatively low status assigned to them the Subarnabaniks narrate a variety of traditions, some of which, however unsupported by historical evidence, deserve to be briefly mentioned here as illustrations of the kind of stories which would tend to grow up wherever the business talents and practical ability of a particular community advance it in the eyes of the world conspicuously beyond its rank in the theoretical order of castes. The Subarnabaniks say that their ancestors came to Bengal from Oudh during the reign of Adisura, who was struck by their financial ability and conferred on them the title of Subarnabanik, or trader in gold, as a mark of his favour. They then wore the Brahmanical

Traditions of origin.

thread, studied the Vedas, and were generally recognized as Vaisyas of high rank. The stories of their degradation all centre round the name of Ballál Sen, king of Bengal in 1070 (A.D.) His intrigue with a beautiful Pátni girl is said to have been ridiculed on the stage by some young men of the caste, while the Subarnabaniks in a body refused to be present at the penance whereby the king affected to purify himself from the sin of intercourse with a maiden of low caste. Another cause of offence is said to have been the refusal of a leading Subarnabanik to lend Ballál large sums of money to carry on a war with Manipur. Authorities differ concerning the method by which the king obtained his revenge. Some say that in the course of the penance already referred to a number of small golden calves had been distributed to the attendant Brahmans. One of these Brahmans was suborned by Ballál Sen to fill the hollow inside of a calf with lac-dye, and to take the figure to a Subarnabanik for sale. In testing the gold the Subarnabanik let out the lac-dye, which was at once pronounced to be blood. Having thus fastened upon the caste the inexpiable guilt of killing a cow, Ballál Sen publicly declared them and their Brahmans to be degraded, deprived them of the right to wear the sacred thread, and threatened with similar degradation any one who should eat or associate with them. Up to this time Subarnagram, near Dacca, had been the head-quarters of the caste in Bengal. Many had settled at Puri, in Orissa, beyond the jurisdiction of Ballál Sen, while others went to Gour in attendance on Lakhsman Sen.

In default of independent testimony to the accuracy of this tradition I do not see how it can be regarded as a narrative of historical events. It is no doubt conceivable that a despotic monarch might order the social degradation of a particular class of his subjects provided that it were not too numerous or too influential; and it is generally believed that Ballál Sen did effect some changes of this kind in the relative status of certain families of Brahmans. Notwithstanding this, the story of the depression of an entire caste from a very high to a comparatively low rank in the social system makes a very large demand on our belief, and inclines one to suspect that it may have been evolved in recent times to account for the position actually occupied by the caste being lower than that to which their riches and ability would entitle them to lay claim. From this point of view, Dr. Wise's conjecture that the Subarnabaniks are Hindustani Baniyás who lost rank by residing in Bengal seems to deserve some consideration.

Internal structure.

According to Dr. Wise the Subarnabaniks of Eastern Bengal recognize four sub-castes—**Banga**, **Dakhin-Rárhí**, **Uttar-Rárhí**, and **Saptagrámi** or **Nadiyá**. The Banga "claim to be descendants of Sonars resident in Bengal during the reign of Ballál Sen, and are undoubtedly the oldest branch of the family. Two Srenis are met with, Kulina and Varendra, or Maulika, inferior, which never intermarry. Every Maulika, however, asserts that he is a Kulina, and village Sonárs, by assuming similar claims, cause endless squabbles and feuds.

Ward distinguishes between the Sauvarna-kár and the Sauvarnabanik; the former being goldsmiths, the latter money-changers. It is remarkable that members of the Banga engaging in the caste profession of goldsmiths are styled Sankara, or mixed, baniks, and excommunicated from the society of their brethren. In the city of Dacca about forty families reside, twenty-five of whom belong to the pure town stock and fifteen to the Grámí, or rural. These two branches are still further sundered by having two distinct dals, or unions.

The Bangas have three gotras—Kásyapa, Gautama, and Vyáṣa. The "Padavi," or titles, are—

Sena.	Borál.	Pál.
Dhar.	Maulika.	Sinha.
Datta.	Laha.	Aḍḍi.
Dé.	Chanda.	

The marriage ceremonies are copied from those observed at the wedding of Ṣrí Rámachandra and Ṣíta, while in Western Bengal the marriage service is that of Mahádeva and Párvatí. At the former the bridal pair, seated on stools, are carried round the court; at the latter the bridegroom stands while the bride is borne round him. The bride wears a red dress, as well as a lofty diadem (*mukuta*) with a red turban, from which tinsel pendants hang. The bridal attire becomes the perquisite of the barber; the dress worn on the second day falls to the Ghaṭaka.

The "Pradhán," or president of the caste assembly, is always a Kulina. The Kulina sometimes marries a Maulika girl when her dowry is large, but this alliance does not exalt her family.

The Banga Sonárs are jewellers, but as a rule do not manufacture ornaments. They are often bankers, traders, and shop-keepers. The poorer class accept employment as writers, but would sooner starve than cultivate the soil. The large majority are Vaishnavas, but a few follow the Tantric ritual.

In the city of Dacca reside about seventy families of the Dakhin-Ráṛhí sub-caste, who originally sought shelter in Eastern Bengal, along with the Uttar-Ráṛhí and Nadiyá Sonárs, from the Marhatta invasion of 1741. Among them rage interminable disputes about precedence, and the confusion is increased by the Padavis being the same as those of the Banga.

The houses of Nílámbara Datta and Potiráj Dé are reckoned the first of Kulinas, and next, but at a great interval, are the children of two brothers, Chanda and Madhu, who are Síls, and reside at Balgonah, in Burdwan. Families with the titles of Borál, Laha, Chand, and Aḍḍi are deemed more aristocratic than the Maulika.

The gotras of this division are—

Madhu Kulyá.	Sáṇḍilya.
Káṣyapa.	Savarṇa.
Gautama.	Bharadwája.

As a general rule the Dakhin-Ráṛhí do not intermarry with the Uttar-Ráṛhí, but take *púri*, or cake, from them, and even cooked food, if on friendly terms. The daughter of a Kulina marrying a Maulika bridegroom sinks to his level, but the daughter of a Maulika marrying a Kulina is raised to his. Dakhin-Rárhí women dress like other Hindu females of Eastern Bengal; the Uttar-Rárhí as women of Bardwan and Hughli.

The Dakhin-Rárhí worship Lakshmí daily, when rice, sugar, and flowers are offered, and no woman will touch food until this duty is performed. The "goddess of wealth" is also worshipped with especial honour four times every year.

The members of this subdivision are usually employed as writers.

Many peculiarities of their earlier home in Western Bengal are retained by the Uttar-Rárhí subdivision. The women still speak the Burdwan "Bháshá," or dialect, and their dress is that of Central Bengal. The gotras are many, and the following are the most important:—

Madhu Kulyá.	Kaşyapa.
Şáṇdilya.	Bharadwája.
Paráşara.	Brahma Ṛishi.
Nága-Ṛishi.	Gautama.
Aliman.	Savarṇa.

The titles are the same as those of other Sonárs, but they have no Maulika. Their president is styled "Múrdhanya," a Sanskrit word for highest.

The Uttar-Rárhí still prepares the marriage space, called Marocha, which has been given up by the Dakhin-Rárhí, and the bride wears the lofty diadem and appendages of the Banga.

In Dacca there are about seventy families, the men being employed as clerks, accountants, and bankers. Only four annual festivals in honour of Lakshmí are kept, that on the Díwálí being omitted. Manasá Deví is propitiated with great ceremony, and on the Bhagíratha Dashará a branch of "Síj" (*Euphorbia ligularia*), sacred to the "goddess of snakes," is planted in the courtyard, and on every Panchamí, or fifth lunar day of each fortnight up to the Dashará of the Durgá Pújah, the Sonárs make offerings to it. On the great day of the feast, the Vijaya Daşamí, the plant is plucked up and thrown into the river.

The Saptagrámi or Nadiyá subdivision constitutes a small body, numbering some thirty-five households. Driven from their former homes by the Marhattas, they crossed the Ganges and settled in Dacca.

The principal gotras are—

Madhu Kuliyá.	Savarṇa.
Nága-Ṛishi.	Şúra-Şrí.
Şáṇdilya.	

The patronymics are Síl, Borál, Pál, Sena, Maulika, Dé, Harí, Priya Dás, and Karaṇa Varí Dás.

Being a small community, the Nadiyá Sonárs intermarry with the Dakhin and Uttar-Rárhí, and easily obtain wives by giving a large dowry.

While the Ták-sál, or Mint, was open at Dacca, the Nadiyá Sonárs worked as *Son-dhoas*, gold-washers, or Niyáriyás, infusing and purifying metals, but since its closure they have worked as Son-dhoas on their own account. The dust and refuse (*gád*) of goldsmiths' shops are bought for a sum varying from eight annas to five rupees a *ser*, according to the amount or nature of the business. The refuse being carefully washed, the metallic particles in the sediment are transferred to shallow earthen pans, and the larger separated by a skilled workman, or *Kárigar*. The smaller, mixed with cow-dung and a calx of lead, form a ball named *pindi* or *perá*. This ball being placed in a hole partially filled with charcoal, fire is applied, and as the lead melts it carries with it all gold and silver filings, forming a mass called *liná*. This *liná* is then dissolved in a crucible, and the gold and silver, being unmelted, are easily separated."

Dr. Wise's interesting information regarding the Subarnabaniks was collected by him nearly twenty years ago from members of the caste residing in the city of Dacca. Since that time a tendency towards the amalgamation of sub-castes seems to have set in. The Subarnabaniks of the present day do not seem to lay much stress on the distinction between the Uttar-Ráṛhí and Dakhin-Ráṛhí groups, and sometimes include both under the designation Ráṛhí. Members of the Ráṛhí sub-caste may, as is mentioned by Dr. Wise, marry into the Saptagrámi or Nadiyá sub-caste, subject only to the condition that the titles or family names of the parties shall not be the same.

Marriage.

Subarnabaniks marry their daughters as infants, and observe the standard marriage ceremony in vogue among the higher classes of Hindus. Betrothal, *nándi sráddha*—performed on the forenoon of the day of gift, and the formal gift of the bride on the same night, are the essential features of the ceremony.

The rules regarding the avoidance of marriage within the *gotra* or section, and the practice in the matter of prohibited degrees, are the same as are followed by the higher castes. Polygamy is permissible, but is rarely resorted to except in the event of failure of offspring by the first wife. Widow-marriage and divorce are under no circumstances allowed.

Religion.

The great majority of the caste belong to the Vaishnava sect of Hindus. Rádhá, Krishna, and Chaitanya, the modern incarnation of the latter, are their favourite objects of worship. Rádhá, the favourite mistress of Krishna, is in their view identical with Lakshmi, and a grain-measure (*kátá*, *kunki*, or *khunchi*) filled with paddy and shells, and daubed with vermilion, is worshipped daily as her emblem by the females of the family. In Central Bengal the goddess of learning, Bageswari, is also worshipped on the day following a marriage. For religious and ceremonial purposes the Subarnabaniks employ Brahmans of their own, who are not received on equal terms by other members of the sacred order. They claim nevertheless to be the descendants of certain Vaidik Brahmans of the highest learning and sanctity, who were opposed to the policy of Ballál Sen and elected to follow the fortunes of the Subarnabaniks even at the cost of sharing in their degradation.

Disposal of the dead.

The caste burn their dead and perform the ceremony of *sráddh* in the orthodox fashion on the thirty-first day. The obsequies of persons who die a violent death are performed on the fourth day.

Social status and occupation.

The social status of the caste, according to the recognized scale of precedence, is comparatively low. They rank below the Navasakha, and the Brahmans who serve the higher castes will not take water from their hands. There seems nevertheless to be a tolerably widespread feeling that the standing allotted to them by tradition is ludicrously incompatible with their wealth and abilities, and with the aptitude which they have shown of late years for taking advantage of English education. Trade has always been their chief function, and it was as successful merchants that the families of Síl, Mallik, and Laha first won for themselves a place among the leading citizens of Calcutta. In the present generation Subarnabaniks have come to the front as officials, and have attained some literary distinction. They number among their community a District Judge, an Inspector of Schools, four Subordinate Judges, five Deputy Magistrates, and fifteen Munsifs. The Revd. Lal Behari Dey is well known in Bengal as the author of the clever *genre* novel *Govinda Sámanta*, while Babu Bholanath Chandra's *Travels of a Hindu* has certain quaint merits of its own which seem likely to keep its memory alive.

The following statement shows the number and distribution of Subarnabaniks in 1872 and 1881. In certain districts the figures of Sekrás and Sonárs seem to have been included in the Census Report of 1872:—

DISTRICT.	1872.	1881.	DISTRICT.	1872.	1881.
Bardwan	13,318	4,754	Dacca	4,696	3,965
Bankura	5,259	6,683	Faridpur	2,280	2,843
Birbhum	5,268	3,467	Bakarganj	2,144	1,458
Midnapur	11,499	7,733	Maimansinh	3,106	3,522
Hughli ... ... }	8,887	5,511	Tipperah	1,841	2,046
Howrah ... ... }		2,464	Chittagong	5,165	4,446
24-Parganás	27,615	2,370	Noakhali	1,190	1,570
Nadiya	6,628	3,766	Chittagong Hill Tracts ...	......	4
Khulna	......	2,799	Maldah	440	196
Jessore	6,929	3,073	Santál Parganás	......	1,541
Murshedabad	5,342	3,286	Hazaribagh	1,778	73
Dinajpur	888	27	Lohardagá	2,736	2
Rajshahye	869	815	Manbhum	6,486	7,725
Rangpur	414	299	Singbhum	233	......
Bogra	400	150	Cuttack	13,987	10,397
Pabna	947	93	Puri	5,990	4,190
Darjiling	49	......	Balasore	4,297	5,209
Jalpigori	81	579	Tributary States	4,670	715
Kuch Behar	......	128			

Subarnabisayi, a sub-caste of Telis in Bengal.

Subarniá-panchbhá, a section of Bábhans in Chota Nagpur.

Suberi, a *thar* of the Bharadwája *gotra* of Nepáli Brahmans.

Subha or **Suffah** (chief), a title of Limbus in Darjiling.

Subharájkháni, a *mel* or hypergamous sub-group of Rárhi Brahmans in Bengal.

Suchait, a section of Oswál Baniyás.

Suchári, a *mul* or section of Sonárs in Behar.

Sudhá, a small caste of Orissa, who believe their original occupation to have been personal service, but are now for the most part engaged in cultivation. In the census of 1872 they appear to have been recorded under the name of Amáyat or Amát, which is one of their titles, and which, taken in connexion with their traditions of occupation, rather goes to suggest some affinity between them and the Amáts of Behar. Sudhás are divided into four sub-castes:—Bara-Sudhá, Sáno or Kabátkonia Sudhá, Pailá-Sudhá, and Butká-Sudhá. Concerning their exogamous groups my information is incomplete. The Bara-Sudhá profess to have gotras and to observe the rule that a man may not marry a woman of his own gotra. But I have not been able to ascertain the names of the *gotras*.

The most primitive of the three sub-castes regarding which tolerably full data are available appears to be the Butká-Sudhá. They are a nomadic race, who believe themselves to have immigrated into Orissa from Rerákhol in the Central Provinces. They wander about reclaiming waste lands and tapping date and palm-trees for their juice. Having found a suitable spot for their operations, they build small huts of mats, bamboos, and any light materials that are available and settle down for two or three years, deserting the place and seeking a fresh locality as soon as the soil shows signs of becoming exhausted. Marriage is adult, and courtship is a recognized preliminary; but after the parents have given their consent to an engagement it is not etiquette for the young people to meet until the marriage is celebrated. The marriage ceremony is simple. The parties sit side by side before a *bedi*, or elevated platform of earth, the bridegroom having the bride on his right. The headman (Beherá) of the caste ties their right hands together with a piece of string, which is afterwards untied or cut by the brother-in-law of the bridegroom, or the younger sister of the bride, who receives a piece of cloth from the bridegroom for doing him this service. Then some old women—not less than three or more than seven—sprinkle *atap* rice and turmeric powder over the couple and give them their blessing.

Widows may marry again. No regular ceremony is performed. The headman of the caste and the woman's relatives take her to her new husband's house and make her over to him. A feast is given to the caste if the bridegroom can afford it. Divorce is permitted with the sanction of the caste pancháyat, and divorced women are permitted to marry again in the same manner and by the same form as widows.

The regular Hindu deities seem to be unknown to the caste. They worship a goddess, called Pancha-Khanda (five swords), with offerings of he-goats, fowls and rice, which are partaken of by the worshippers. The full moon of the month of Aghran is the proper time for this sacrifice. The Beherá or headman of the caste officiates as priest at this and all other acts of public worship. The Butká-Sudhás have no Brahmans. The dead are burned and the ashes left on the spot. No sráddh ceremony is performed. The caste abstain from beef, but eat the wild buffalo, the wild boar, and domestic fowls.

The Bara and Sáno-Sudhá sub-castes have travelled further than the Butká on the road towards orthodox Hinduism. The first-mentioned group have entirely adopted infant marriage, while the Sáno, though still permitting adult marriage, regard infant marriage as the standard to which all respectable people should endeavour to conform. Widow remarriage, however, still holds its ground. A number of women headed by the barber's wife give the widow their blessing along with some *atap* rice and *duba* grass, and a priest mutters a few mantras. Divorced women may marry again.

For the service of the regular Hindu gods, the celebration of *sráddh*, and the like, Brahmans are employed, who are received on equal terms by other members of the sacred order The goddess Khambeswar, a divinity of a more primitive type, having her chief seat in the wild country of Bod, is worshipped every year in the month of Bhadra with sacrifices of goats. The goddess is represented by a wooden peg (*khamba*) fixed in the ground, and the Brahmans take no part in her worship, which is conducted by a Dehuri or tribal priest supposed to be specially acquainted with the way of the local gods.

Bara-Sudhás believe military or personal service to have been their original occupation. Some of them hold service-tenures under the Chiefs of the Orissa Tributary Mahals, and the fact that they bear the title Páik seems to show that they must have formed part of the rude militia which once existed in that part of the country. The Sáno-Sudhá believe that their original profession was the cultivation and management of date and palm-trees, and regard the *katári* or pruning knife as their characteristic implement. The social status of both groups is considerably higher than that of the Butká Sudhá, who can hardly be reckoned as coming within the pale of Hinduism at all. The higher caste of Orissa Brahmans, Chhatris, Karans and Goalas take water and sweetmeats from the hands of the Bara and Sáno-Sudhás, but the Bhandáris or barbers alone will receive boiled rice from them.

Sudra, the lowest and servile caste in the fourfold grouping adopted by early Indian writers, and, in theory at least, more or less recognized by the Natives of India at the present day. The opinion has been expressed by Lassen[1] and concurred in by Zimmer[2] that the name Sudra is not of Sanskrit origin, but was probably the tribal designation of one of the chief aboriginal races of Hindustan who adopted the Aryan faith and were admitted as servile members of the Aryan polity. Tribes who followed the example of the Sudras were naturally enrolled in the same class, and thus came to be called by the same

Origin.

[1] *Ind. Alt.*, i, 947.
[2] *Alt. Ind. Leben*, 216.

name. Weber, on the other hand, thinks that the Sudra caste "was composed of various mixed elements, partly, perhaps, of an Aryan race which had settled earlier in India, partly of the aborigines themselves, and partly, again, of those among the immigrants, or their Western kinsmen, who refused adherence to the new Brahmanical order." It would be foreign to the purpose of this book to enter upon a lengthy examination of the position of the Sudra in relation to the other three castes of the Manavic system, or to discuss the vexed question how far the precepts of the Mánava-dharma-sástra were at any time in correspondence with the facts of actual life. The following extract from Mr. E. W. Hopkins' work on the subject sums up the main features of the social status of the Sudra as represented by Manu :—

"The Sudra, once-born, is to be regarded in two lights—the one as general representative of his caste, irrespective of his master, where he is the abject slave of the twice-born, whose touch is unholy, in whose presence the Brahman may not remain, contact with whom is as polluting as with the lowest wretches and outcasts; on the other hand, as the settled servant of one master in whose house he is perhaps born, where his position is by no means so ignoble, though the fact of his slavery and lowness cannot be done away with. The personal contact with the Brahman is here greatly eased of the strict abhorrence with which the *dwija* is bound in general to regard the Sudra caste. As a servant his position is not in many respects different from the, indeed, not comfortable, because dependent and servile, yet still endurable and not very severe, position of an American house-slave prior to 1860. It is true that the Sudra has no mercy to expect on insulting his betters, and torture and death may be the consequence; but so long as he retains a respectful demeanour towards the upper castes, he is tolerably secure from danger. His master may give him advice, and bestow on him such old furniture and goods as are no longer fitted for the Brahman himself. He has his family, and his wife is as carefully guarded from freedom with other castes as the wives of the upper orders. His daughter or wife, if wronged by the upper castes, have the right of law, and a heavy fine is visited upon the offender. His master has, indeed, the right of punishing him, but only, as in the case of son and wife, for his own good. The striking is, moreover, limited in kind, and the fact that he may not be smitten upon the back shows that even he had an honourable part of the body.[1] He may not study, nor hear the Vedas recited, but he may be present at the small family sacrifices and religious ceremonies, and is indeed even praised for so doing. His legal privileges are few, but his rights are granted him with the other castes. He has the right of demanding redress for an injury of personal character even from the Brahman himself. He is held separate from the very lowest, the mixed castes, and should hold himself from their occupations till driven thereto by want. He represents his master in occasional business matters. As a matter

[1] In the last two particulars he stood, indeed, upon a higher level than the Negro!—E. W. H.

of principle he can have himself no property, as all belongs to his master, but practically he is a householder and receives a support suited to his need, and has property returned him if it is stolen. He is enjoined not to acquire very much, but evidently often managed to do so; and if his property in the eye of the law is dependent on the whim of the Brahman, it is at least in respect to other castes not regarded as a fiction. The rights of the Sudra are generally on a graded scale in respect to the other castes, and here no distinction is made between family-slave and general Sudra.[1] Distinct mention of Sudra as teacher when others fail, and the possibility of his being a king, show that he sometimes gained a position superior to the one he generally occupies."[2]

The modern use of the term Sudra is not easy to define. "In the present time," says Mr. Beames,[3] "there are no Sudras and no Vaisyas; no Kshatriyas except the Rájput: only the Brahman is recognizable. The lower castes fused more readily than the higher, and the Sudras probably were soon absorbed in the mixed classes, and ceased to have any distinct existence as Sudras." A Native writer[4] dealing with the same subject takes much the same view as Mr. Beames, admitting that the Kshatriyas are represented by the Rájputs, while in Bengal, at any rate, the Vaisyas have fallen to the rank of Sudras. The Sudras, again, he divides into the four following classes:—

i. Satsudra, including the Káyasths and the Nabasákh.
ii. Jalácharaniya Sudra, being those castes not technically belonging to the Nabasákh group from whom Brahmans and members of the higher castes can take water.
iii. Jalabyahahárya Sudra, castes from whose hands a Brahman cannot take water.
iv. Asprishya Sudra, castes whose touch is so impure as to pollute even Ganges water.

Here it seems to me that in the attempt to reconcile the existing state of things with the traditional system, and at any cost to unearth the survivors of the fourth caste, the author quoted has given to the term Sudra a wider significance than is warranted by popular usage. It may of course be argued that the scheme propounded by Manu treats all men who are not twice-born as Sudras, and that the same principle, if applied at the present day, requires us to include every caste below the Rájput in that category.

[1] How far the legal arrangements of fines in personal injuries, etc., contained in Manu were regarded as matters of fact and had a practical working, and how far they were held as legal fiction resulting from a desire to adjust and systematise the relations of all four castes before the law with arithmetical exactness, cannot be my purpose to determine. That Yajnavalkya, however, as a rule follows the arrangement of Manu, and settles such cases also according to higher or lower rank, so well by stated amounts as by general determination, shows the relative worth of these laws was as valid with him as with Manu.

[2] *The Mutual Relations of the Four Castes according to the Mánavadharma Cástram.* Leipzig, 1881.

[3] *The Races of the North-Western Provinces*, vol. i, p. 167.

[4] *Sambandhanirnaya.* By Lál Mohan Vidyánidhi, p. 89 ff.

Still I do not believe that the castes classed as Asprishya would be spoken of by any Hindu as Sudras at all, though the members of any particular group might possibly in a vague kind of way claim that title for themselves. At the other end of the scale the classification is equally open to criticism. No place is assigned to the Baidyas, Khatris, and Bháts; while the Káyasths, though not technically twice-born, invariably claim to rank above the Nabasákh, and by virtue of their wealth and intelligence occupy a position which fully bears out their claim.

Failing, then, any classical and authoritative definition, we have only to consider what is ordinarily understood by the term. Both in Bengal and Behar I think it is commonly used to denote the entire group of castes from whose hands a Brahman can take water. Káyasths, Baidyas, Bháts, and Khatris are not generally spoken of or regarded as Sudras, though persons of a pedantic turn of mind, who are bent on finding survivals of the original fourfold division, would probably set down both Káyasths and Baidyas as technically Sudras. In Orissa the definition by water offered above seems to hold good in the main, but the Karan, or writer caste, does not hold so high a status as the Káyasths of Bengal, and ranks as a Sudra in popular estimation.

Internal structure.

Although in most parts of the country the term Sudra is not strictly speaking a caste-name at all, but rather a general designation of a certain number of castes, there appears to exist in the eastern districts of Bengal a numerous body of people who call themselves **Sudras**, and are also known by the names of **Ghulám** (slave), **Káyasth**, **Shikdár**, and **Bhandári**. They form a distinct caste, and as a rule marry only among themselves, though in Maimansinh and Sylhet they marry women of the Sunri caste, and even bestow their own daughters on Sunri bridegrooms. In the latter case the girl forfeits her caste, but her family are not held to be degraded. The origin of the Sudras is obscure, and some say that they are descended from individuals belonging to the Sat-Sudra group, who sold themselves or were sold as slaves to Káyasth masters, and thus, by discharging the same functions as were assigned to the ancient Sudras, came to be called by the same name. The following deed of sale, given to Dr. Wise by Babu Brijo Sundar Mittra, a member of one of the oldest and most respected Káyasth families of Dacca, is quoted in illustration of this view :—

"I, Rám Kisto Pál, son of Túla Rám Pál, and grandson of Rám Deva Pál, do hereby execute this deed of sale :—

"Owing to the debts incurred at my marriage, and which I am unable to pay, I, in my proper mind, and of my own free will, sell myself to you on my receiving a sum of Púrojonodohomasi[1] rupees twenty-five, and I and my descendants will serve you as slaves as long as we are given subsistence allowance and clothing. You, your sons,

---

[1] Mr. J. D. Ward, C.S., suggests the following reading and interpretation :—Púra (full), jana, or gana, dáhá (ten), másha. Each rupee was to value ten full máshas. A "másha" equalled 17$\frac{3}{8}$ grains, and a rupee ten máshas.

and grandsons shall make us work as slaves, and have power to sell or make a gift of us to others. On these conditions I execute this bond.

"Dated 19th Kártik, 1201 B.S. (November 1794)."

Dr. Wise adds that, although slavery is illegal, and has been so for many years, the buying and selling of domestic slaves still goes on, and it may be safely said that there is hardly a family of any distinction which has not several Bhándárís on its establishment. The life of the Nafr, or Shahna, as the slave is called in other parts of the country, is most congenial to the Bengali. With rare exceptions he is kindly treated, and in return he regards the welfare and happiness of each member of the family as inseparable from his own. Owing to the deaths of their masters many thousands are scattered throughout Bengal, who are found working at all trades, and in Chittagong, Noakháli, and Tipperah do not consider themselves degraded by holding a plough or wielding a mattock. In Bikrampúr they are often boatmen, while in Dacca Sudras are employed as confectioners, coolies, braziers, shop-keepers, and vendors of *pán* and Indian hemp. Even at the present day, however, any Sudra who is rich and provident can raise his family by judicious marriages with pure Káyasths as high as the Madhalya grade of that caste. Such families drop the title Sudra, and after a generation or two become absorbed in the ranks of recognized Káyasths. This circumstance is the more remarkable as the Sudras are certainly to some extent recruited from among castes inferior in social standing to the Káyasths. So far as I am aware, no parallel instance can be quoted within the range of the modern caste system. Thus, according to Dr. Wise, Brahmans, Baidyás, Sunris, and Baniyas possess slaves, but none of these castes have ever permitted their servants to rise in rank or assume an equality with their masters. It is suggested by the Káyasths that the Sudras of the present day are the descendants of the tribe resident in Bengal before the advent of the Kanauj families; but this conjecture is erroneous, for not only are individuals being added even now to the servile branch, but admissions such as that of Rám Kisto Pál, the subject of the deed of sale, who was a Telí by caste, can be proved by existing documents.

Marriage.

In the case of a girl the Sudras deem infant-marriage indispensable, and it would disgrace a family to have a daughter unmarried at the age of puberty. Their sections are the same as those of the Brahmans, and they observe the same set of prohibited degrees. They have, however, no hypergamous groups, such as Kulin or Maulik. A bride-price (*pan*) is paid to the parents of the bride, and girls seem as a rule to be rather in demand. This is probably due to the fact that the lower grades of pure Káyasths take wives from among the Sudras, but do not give their daughters to men of that class. For this reason there is a slight surplus of males in the Sudra group, and Sudra men often marry comparatively late in life, and always have to purchase their wives.

Social status.

For the rest, Sudras conform on the whole to the customs of the Káyasth caste. Widows are not allowed to marry again, and divorce is not recognized.

The status of the caste is respectable, and they rank immediately below the Nabasákh group. Brahmans take water from their hands, and will as a rule permit them to eat in the same room with themselves. Káyasths, except the very orthodox, will eat cooked food prepared by a Sudra. In matters of diet Sudras themselves follow the same rules as Hindus of the higher castes. In former years they used to eat the leavings of influential Brahmans, Baidyas, and Káyasths in whose houses they were employed as servants. This custom, however, is now dying out.

The following statement shows the number and distribution of Sudras in 1872 and 1881 :—

District.	1872.	1881.	District.	1872.	1881.
Bankura	......	17	Dacca	......	17,892
Midnapur	23	12	Faridpur	86	15,109
Jessore	131	......	Bakarganj	8,969	9,573
Murshedabad	31	6	Maimansinh	3,617	13,892
Dinajpur	......	5	Tipperah	2,513	9,199
Rajshahye	......	16	Chittagong	30,638	28,112
Rangpur	6	......	Noakhali	4,292	2,213
Pabna	......	1	Chittagong Hill Tracts ...	......	13

Suga, parrot, a totemistic sept of Korwas and Mundas in Chota Nagpur.

Sugáin, a *gáin* or sub-section of Saptasati Brahmans in Bengal.

Sugardhar, a section of the Biyáhut and Kharidáhá Kalwárs in Behar.

Sugargane-Loám, a *mul* of the Parásara section of Maithil Brahmans in Behar.

Suia, a kind of little bird, a totemistic sept of Bediás, Kharwars and Lohárs in Chota Nagpur.

Suir, a synonym for Savar.

Sukalnaki, a sept of the Suryabansi sub-tribe of Rájputs in Behar.

Sukalvála, a group of the Ádi Gaura sub-caste of Gaura Brahmans.

Sukarbár, a sept of the Suryabansi sub-tribe of Rájputs in Behar.

Sukhar, a group of the Aoghar sect of Saiva ascetics founded in Guzerat by a Dasnámi mendicant named Brahmagiri. See **Aoghar**.

Sukhong, a sept of Limbus in Darjiling.

Sukhsárá, a *pur* or section of Sákadwipi Brahmans in Behar.

Sukli, a sub-caste of weavers in Western Bengal ranking below the Tantis. They use a wooden shuttle; the Tantis an iron one. Brahmans will eat sweetmeats, etc., in a Tanti's house, not in a Sukli's.

Sukli, a small cultivating caste peculiar to the district of Midnapur. Suklis claim to be the descendants
Origin. of a Sulanki Rájput named Bir Singh, who came to Midnapur about six hundred years ago and built himself

a fort at Birsinghpur in parganá Kedárkunda. The remains of the fort are still visible. It is flanked by two large mounds, called Mundamárui and Gardámárui, the former of which is said to cover the heads, and the latter the bodies, of seven hundred Bágdis who were slain by Bir Singh because they could not pronounce the word *hesh*, meaning a mat made of date-leaves. The legend goes on to say that after a time Bir Singh himself was defeated, and that his followers then discarded the sacred thread, changed the name Sulanki to Sukli, and settled down as cultivators. The internal structure of the caste throws no light on its origin. It is divided into three sub-castes—**Barabháiyá, Báhattarghari**, and **Dasásai**. The first, which is reckoned the highest in rank, is supposed to be descended from the twelve grandsons of Bir Singh. Their sections are of the ordinary Brahmanical type.

Internal structure.

Suklis marry their daughters as infants, forbid widows to marry again, and do not recognize divorce. For religious and ceremonial purposes they employ Brahmans, who however are not received on equal terms by other members of the sacred order. Most of them are Vaishnavas. They burn their dead and perform the ceremony of *sráddh* in the orthodox fashion on the thirty-first day after death.

Marriage.

Notwithstanding their conformity with all standard observances, the social position of Suklis is very low. They rank with Pods and Dhobás, and Brahmans will not take water from their hands. Agriculture is their sole occupation. A few hold tenures and small zamindáries, the bulk of the caste being occupancy raiyats.

Social status and occupation.

In the Census Report of 1872 the Suklis were included with the Tántis. The following statement, however, shows their number and distribution in 1881:—

Bardwan	...	20	Hughli	...	45
Birbhum	...	2	Howrah	...	1,326
Midnapur	...	19,886	24-Parganás	...	339

Sukru, potato, a totemistic sept of Mundas in Chota Nagpur.

Suksárini, probably a class of religious mendicants.

Sukul, a title of Kanaujiá, Sáraswata and Gaura Brahmans in Behar.

Sukulbans, a sept of Rájputs in Behar.

Sukuliyá, a sub-caste of Chásás in Orissa.

Sukwabah, a sept of Limbus in Darjiling.

Sukwár, a sub-caste of Gulguliás in Gya and Hazaribagh.

Sulankhi, a sub-tribe of Rájputs.—Tod's *Rajasthan*, i, p. 74; *Sher.*, i, p. 122; a sept of the Chandrabansi division of Rájputs in Behar; a bird, a totemistic sept of Bediás and Mundas in Chota Nagpur.

Sultánpuriá, a section of Sonárs in Behar.

Sulunkhi-Mahili, a sub-caste of Mahilis in Manbhum who are generally labourers and servants.

Sumai, a kind of fish, a totemistic sept of Dhenuárs in Chota Nagpur.

Suman, a title of Bangaja Káyasths.

Sumat, a totemistic section of Turis, signifying a deer.

Sumedhiar, a tree, a totemistic sept of Kharwars in Chota Nagpur.

Sunaka, a *gotra* or section of Brahmans in Bengal.

Sunam, a *thar* or sept of Dámis in Darjiling whose chief profession is sewing.

Sunári, a *thar* or sept of Mangars in Darjiling.

Sunáriá, a section of Goálás in the North-Western Provinces and Behar.

Sundar, a section of the Kishnaut sub-caste of Goálás in Behar.

Sundas, a *thar* or sept of Dámis in Darjiling whose chief profession is sewing.

Sundi, a synonym for, and a sub-caste of, Sunris in Bengal; a section of Goálás in Behar. In Chota Nagpur, a totemistic sept of Bediás, signifying *mahud* flower.

Sundi Baniyá, a sub-caste of Baniyás in Behar.

Sundi Deogam, a sept of Hos in Singbhum.

Sundip, a sub-caste of Dhobás in Noakháli.

Sundipá, a sub-caste of Jugis and Nápits in Noakhali.

Sundipe, a sub-caste of Kaibarttas in Noakhali.

Sundriába, red mushroom, a totemistic sept of Juángs in Orissa.

Sung, a sub-sept of the Beará and Tudu septs of Santáls.

Sungaru, a *thar* or sept of Dámis in Darjiling, the members of which are drummers by profession.

Sunga Sarbbánandi, a *mel* or hypergamous sub-group of Rárhi Brahmans in Bengal.

Sungdele, a *thar* or sept of Khambus in Darjiling.

Sungutmung, a sept of Lepchas in Darjiling.

Sunkewar, a sept of Ráj-puts in Behar.

Sunri, *Saundika*, *Sundaka*, *Sháhá*, a large and widely-diffused caste, found in most districts of Bengal and Behar, whose original profession is believed to be the manufacture and sale of spirituous liquors. Many of its members have now taken to mercantile pursuits, call themselves by the title Sháhá, and disown all connexion with those who still follow the characteristic occupation of the caste. Their striving for social advancement has as yet not been entirely successful, and in spite of their wealth and enterprise ancient associations still hold them down. The bond of tradition is hard to break. According to Hindu ideas distillers and sellers of strong drink rank among the most degraded castes, and a curious story in the Vaivarta Purana keeps alive the memory of their degradation. It is said that when Şani, the Hindu Saturn, failed to adapt an elephant's head to the mutilated trunk of Ganesa, who had been accidentally beheaded by Siva, Viswa-Karmá, the celestial artificer, was sent for, and by careful dissection and manipulation he fitted the incongruous parts together and made a man called Kedára Sena from the slices cut off in fashioning his

Traditions of origin.

work. This Kedára Sena was ordered to fetch a drink of water for Bhagavati, weary and athirst. Finding on the river's bank a shell full of water he presented it to her, without noticing that a few grains of rice left in it by a parrot had fermented and formed an intoxicating liquid. Bhagavati, as soon as she had drunk, became aware of the fact, and in her anger condemned the offender to the vile and servile occupation of making spirituous liquors for mankind. Another story traces their origin to a certain Bháskar or Bháskar Muni, who was created by Krishna's brother, Balarám, to minister to his desire for strong drink. A different version of the same legend gives them for ancestor Niranjan, a boy found by Bháskar floating down a river in a pot full of country liquor, and brought up by him as a distiller. Others, again, following the traditional method of accounting for the formation of castes, believe that Sunris are descended from a Vaisya man and a Tiyar woman.

Internal structure.

Putting these fables aside, we may, I think, find in the internal structure of the Sunri caste, and most of all in the number and diversity of its endogamous and exogamous divisions, some ground for believing that it probably comprises several independent groups, which have arisen in different parts of the country to supply the wants of the community in the matter of strong drink. In Manbhum, for example, eight sub-castes are said to be known: **Ariyár, Biáhut, Maghaiyá, Lakargarhá, Holongwár, Paripál, Sikhariyá, Chaturthán.** The first three admit intermarriage and have practically become amalgamated into a single endogamous group. These Sunris have totemistic sections, permit the adult-marriage of girls and the remarriage of widows, allow divorce by the tearing of a *sál* leaf, and generally show the characteristics of non-Aryan races who are beginning to come under the influence of Hinduism. In Behar, as a reference to Appendix I will show, the sub-castes and sections are very numerous; but the latter are mostly titular, and I cannot find that any totemistic usages are connected with the two (*Háthi* and *Bichhu*) which appear to bear animal names. In Bhagalpur the **Kul-Sunri** sub-caste is further subdivided into groups called *chatáis* (mats, hence those who sit together on the same piece of matting), the members of which may not intermarry. So far as I am aware, the *chatáis* have no distinctive names.

In Central and Western Bengal four sub-castes are found—**Rárhí, Bárendra, Bangá,** and **Magi.** In Eastern Bengal, according to Dr. Wise, the caste is subdivided into two sections, or Ṣreṇi Ráṛhí and Bárendra. The former are distillers, called Súnṛí; the latter traders, who have assumed the title of Sáhá or merchant, which is said to be a corruption of Sádhu, 'perfect, honest.' Sáhás usually object to being called Súnṛís, and affect to belong to a distinct caste from the latter. By some authorities, however, they are held to be descended from a Ṣúdra father and a Súnṛí mother. My own enquiries go to show that the sub-castes are now more numerous than they were in Dr. Wise's time.

The Magi or Maghaiya sub-caste of Central and Western Bengal seems to derive its name from some real or supposed connexion with Behar, and may possibly be composed mainly of immigrants from that province. In various parts of Eastern Bengal a Magí

Şreṇí, distinct from the Ráṛhí or Bárendra, and accounted fallen and outcaste, is to be met with. It is stated that in old days the Mags made marauding expeditions into this part of Bengal and outraged some Súnṛí women, whose offspring, defiled by the doubt as to their paternity, became the nucleus of a new sub-caste. The Súnṛí barber and washerman work for them, but they always have purohits of their own.

Sáha or Sháhá is the common title of the caste, but on becoming rich a merchant often adopts Dás as a surname by way of concealing the fact that he is a Sunri. Dr. Wise also mentions a case in which a well-known Sáha trader of Dacca selected Ráí Chaudharí as his family name. In the Maimansinh district a colony of Sáhas have taken the title of Pánjha, but can give no reason for doing so. They are chiefly talukdárs, writers, and shop-keepers, who eat and intermarry with Sáhas in other parts of Bengal.

Exogamy.

In Bengal Proper the sections are comparatively few, and the rule of exogamy seems to be gradually falling into disuse and giving way to the less archaic system of reckoning prohibited degrees from a common ancestor. The Sunris of Chota Nagpur observe the simple rule that a man may not marry a woman of his own section, and supplement this by a rather meagre table of prohibited degrees. In Behar marriage within the section denoted by the title is usually forbidden, but it sometimes happens that the group included under one title has split into two by reason of a quarrel or in consequence of the number of families in the group having increased so as to render the prohibition of marriage within the group unnecessary or inconvenient. In such cases one would *primâ facie* expect the newly-formed groups to adopt new titles or to qualify the original titles so as to indicate the change; but I am unable to quote instances where this has taken place. For reckoning prohibited degrees on the mother's side the standard formula in use is calculated to seven generations in the descending line. On the father's side the rule is said to be that a man may not marry any of his *Kes-Kátá* female relatives, that is to say, any of the women whose male relations would have to shave their heads if a death occurred in the family of the person whose marriage is in question.

Marriage.

The Sunris of Bengal marry their daughters as infants, and strictly prohibit widow-marriage and divorce. In Behar and Chota Nagpur adult-marriages occasionally take place when the parents of the girl are too poor to arrange for her marriage before the age of puberty. When both parties are children, the question of age is not minutely enquired into, and the essential point is that the bridegroom should be taller than the bride. This fact is ascertained by actual measurement—a method which commends itself to illiterate people, who keep no record of their children's ages. In the negotiations which precede the marriage, height of the parties is stated in *girahs*, and it is said to be the right thing for a girl to be married when she is from 12 to 14 *girahs* high and a boy when he is from 12 to 16 *girahs*. It is unusual for a girl to be unmarried at 16 *girahs* or a boy at 17.

When a girl is considered marriageable, one of her relatives or a professional marriage-broker is deputed to look out for a suitable bridegroom and to conduct the preliminary bargaining with his family. If the broker's overtures are favourably received, the bridegroom's father, accompanied by some of his relations, visits the bride's house and puts a garland of flowers (*hár*) on her neck. This ceremonial visit is returned by the bride's father, who also sends a present (*tilak*) of money, clothes, etc., to the bridegroom. According to the custom of the caste, the *tilak* must not exceed Rs. 101 or be less than Re. 1 or a pair of *dhotis*. When the *tilak* has been presented, a Brahman astrologer is called in to fix a lucky day for the wedding. This takes place in the bride's house. The ceremony is of the orthodox type, and *sindurdán*, or the smearing of vermilion on the bride's forehead and the parting of her hair, is believed to be its binding portion.

Polygamy is permitted, but it is unusual for a man to have more than two wives, and a second wife is usually only taken when the first wife is found to be barren. By all sub-castes except the Biyáhut, a widow is allowed to marry again by the *sagai* or *chumauná* ritual. As a rule this consists merely of *sindurdán*, but sometimes, when the parties are rich, the ceremony is amplified by introducing some of the forms used at the marriage of a virgin bride. In Chota Nagpur divorce is effected, with the sanction of the panchâyat, by tearing a *sál* leaf in two as a symbol of separation. Divorced wives may marry again within the caste. In Behar divorce is not recognized, and a woman taken in adultery is simply turned out of the caste, and probably ends by joining some of the less reputable religious sects or becoming a prostitute. The Bengal Sunris follow the same rule, but also hold that the husband is polluted by the sin of the wife. They therefore require him to perform an expiatory ceremony (*práyaschitta*), which consists, according to tradition, of giving from three to eleven (*káhans*) of cowries to a Brahman. At the present day, however, one four-anna bit is given for each *káhan*.

Religion.

According to Dr. Wise almost every member of the caste is a follower of Chaitanya, and the rich are celebrated for the ostentatious observance of the Sankirttana chants in honour of Krishna after the decease of any relative. The chief rites observed in Eastern Bengal are the worship of Ganesa on the 1st of Baisákh (April–May) and the 1st of Aghan (November–December); of Gandheswari on the 10th of Asín (September–October); of Durga at the time of the Durga Púja in October; and of Gangá whenever their boats are starting on a trading voyage. The majority being Vaishnavas, animals are rarely offered to any deity, but when this is done the victim is afterwards released. Sháhás are very fond of pigeons, and in the courtyard of almost every house a dovecot is fixed, as they believe that the air fanned by pigeons' wings wafts them luck. They are also devoted worshippers of Kártikeya, the Hindu god of war, constructing annually in November a life-size effigy of the god, and keeping it within the female enclosure for a year. Other Hindu castes throw the image into the river immediately after the Kártik Puja, but the Sháhás allege that their special veneration of the god is often rewarded, the barren rejoicing and the husband becoming the joyful father of children. It is easy to understand in what way this figure gives rise to scandalous stories among Bengalis, and how the Sáha becomes a butt for the wit and sarcasm of his neighbours.

The Behar Sunris follow the average Hinduism of that part of the country, and worship most of the regular gods as occasion offers. Their minor gods are very numerous—Dharam Raj, Bandi, Goraiya, Govindji, Hanumán, Kari Panjiár, Joti Panjiar, Apurba Panjiarin, Mirá, Saiyad, Jalpá, Sokhá, Hasankhán, and the Panch Pir. Rice cooked in milk and sugar (*khir*), cakes of ghí (*puri*), and various kinds of fruit, are offered to them and afterwards eaten by the worshippers. Kids are sacrificed to Bandi. On Sundays milk and flowers are offered to the sun. In Bengal, says Dr. Wise, the Brahman, peculiar to the caste, boasts that he never accepts alms from any one not a Súnrí, but it is quite certain that none of the clean castes would present him with charity. These Brahmans, who assume the bombastic titles of Vidyáságer, Vidyálankár, Chakravarttí, and Páṭhak, like the purohits of other low castes, read the funeral service at the burning ghât, and are looked down upon by other members of the sacred order. The Súnrís of Behar are served by a low class of Maithil Brahmans, who also minister to the religious necessities of the Teli caste. No other Brahmans will eat and drink with these men, who are known by the contemptuous epithet of Teliá Bábhan. In Chota Nagpur the Brahmans who serve the Súnrís call themselves Kanaujiás, but they have no right to the name, and no other Brahmans will have anything to do with them.

Disposal of the dead.

Súnris burn their dead and perform the regular *sráddh* ceremony in Bengal on the thirtieth, and in Behar on the thirteenth day after death. The usual periodical oblations for the benefit of departed ancestors are poured forth on the new moon of Kártik (October-November).

Social status in Bengal.

Dr. Wise gives the following account of the social status of Súnrís in Eastern Bengal:—

"The Súnrí is a very degraded individual, indulging freely in intoxicating liquors. A Brahman may not utter his name before noon. The majority of the workmen in the Government Abkári, or Excise Department, are Súnrís, and most of the gánja shops are owned by them. The Hindustani distiller (Kalár, Kalwár) has nothing in common with the Súnrí, as he only manufactures spirit, and will not vend it—an occupation carried on by Kurmís, or Baniyas.

"The Sáha, again, is perhaps the most enterprising and prosperous community in Bengal, comprising a large number of the cloth merchants, salt-traders, wood-dealers, and bankers. They are usually known as *Amda-wálá*, or traders who import goods wholesale and sell them to petty dealers by retail. Mahájan, Goladár, and Aṛhatdár, or broker, are also common designations. Notwithstanding their improved position of late years, they are still utterly abandoned in the eyes of the Hindus. Even the Bhúinmáli, who works for them, will not touch their food, and a Chaṇḍál loses caste if he lays his hand on the stool on which one of them is sitting. There is a saying among Bengalís that if a Ṣúdra be walking down a narrow lane with only Súnrí houses on each side, and an elephant approaches, he ought to allow the elephant to trample him under foot rather than take refuge in a house of the accursed. The Dhobá and Nápit are members of the Súnrí caste, the Ṣúdra washerman and barber declining to work for them. Although the Ṣúdra Nápit occasionally shaves the Sáhas, he will not attend at any of their religious ceremonies. When a member of the caste has to be employed. A Súnrí will not cultivate the soil, although he does so in Central Bengal, nor will he ply as a boatman unless the boat belongs to his caste and is entirely manned by Súnrís. He is also prohibited from becoming a fisherman and from selling fish in the market." Some of the lower classes of Súnris have taken to working as carpenters and thatchers of houses.

In Behar.

In Behar the Darchúa Sunris, who manufacture, and the Ganjwár, Dhakankorá, Sikhariá, and Chaurthán Sunris, who deal in country liquor, are considered lower in point of social standing than Kul-Sunri, Sagáhut, and Biahut sub-castes, the members of which are usually shop-keepers or dealers in grain. The entire caste, however, occupies a low position in the Hindu social system, and Telis are the highest caste which will take water from their hands. As a rule they affect to observe the restrictions in matters of diet which are characteristic of the Vaishnava sect, but the Kul-Sunris of Bhagalpur admit that they eat mutton, goat flesh, all kinds of fish, and even field-rats. Most of them indulge pretty freely in strong drink. Many Sunris have taken to cultivation, but comparatively few appear to have risen above the grade of tenure-holder or raiyat with occupancy rights.

The following statement shows the number and distribution of Sunris in 1872 and 1881. In the former year the figures of the districts in Behar and Chota Nagpur include those of Kalwárs and Kaláls.

District.	1872.	1881.	District.	1872.	1881.
Bardwan	22,259	19,688	Chittagong	1,742	2,152
Bankura	12,657	21,155	Noakhali	5,895	5,961
Birbhum	21,173	15,841	Patna	16,666	7,899
Midnapur	3,084	7,666	Gya	9,246	6,643
Hughli	} 6,509	{ 3,560	Shahabad	20,596	4,409
Howrah		1,771	Tirhut { Mozufferpur ...	} 94,180	{ 22,656
24-Parganás	13,272	5,270	Tirhut { Darbhanga ...		25,440
Nadiya	10,188	9,495	Saran	23,533	1,163
Khulna	......	9,998	Champaran	32,566	422
Murshedabad	16,411	13,039	Monghyr	26,703	8,982
Jessore	34,146	17,170	Bhagalpur	36,851	12,102
Dinajpur	6,685	4,498	Purniah	18,724	14,139
Rajshahye	8,228	6,871	Maldah	4,792	7,253
Rangpur	7,692	4,939	Santál Parganás	18,242	20,304
Bogra	6,683	5,775	Cuttack	3,246	4,261
Pabna	29,728	25,319	Puri	1,976	1,769
Darjiling	466	84	Balasore	1,757	1,588
Jalpigori	1,116	1,447	Tributary States	8,465	9,383
Kuch Behar	......	647	Hazaribagh	13,277	17,576
Dacca	63,511	58,299	Lohardagá	9,944	9,312
Faridpur	26,677	34,491	Singhbhum	3,274	2,611
Bakarganj	26,160	16,845	Manbhum	19,080	18,346
Maimansinh	35,982	44,308	Tributary States	1,858	2,834
Tipperah	35,323	32,749			

Sunri Dhánuk, a sub-caste of Dhánuks in Behar.

Sunriet, a *mul* or section of the Ghosin sub-caste of Goálás in Behar.

Sunriwár-Solhni, a *mul* of the Parásara section of Maithil Brahmans in Behar.

Sunuwár, *Sonwár*, a cultivating tribe of Nepal, forming with the Mangar Gurung and Khas the class known as Mukhya or chief. Although in theory the Sunuwárs are a strictly endogamous group, intermarriage with Mangars and Gurungs is tacitly recognized. The ceremony cannot be performed in public, but such unions are admitted to be valid, and the children are counted in all respects as Sunuwárs, except that during the first generation Sunuwárs of the whole blood may not take rice or *dál* from their hands. In the second generation this disability ceases to have effect. Sunuwárs say that they came originally from Simungarh near Bara Chhatri in Western Nepal, and that wandering east they came to Chuplu on the Likhukhola river and took possession of it. Makwani Raja was then ruler of Eastern Nepal. Likhukhola and Khuntikhola are now the main settlements of the tribe.

Origin.

The internal structure of the tribe is shown in Appendix I. There are no sub-tribes. All the names of the septs end in *cha*, which is conjectured by Babu Sarat Chandra Dás, C.I.E., to be a corruption of the Sanskrit *ja*, born of. Presumably, therefore, they have reference to descent, and further analysis may show that they preserve the names or nicknames of the first founders of the septs. For the following derivations and explanations I am indebted to Babu Sarat Chandra Dás:—Jespucha means 'born of the Jespu,' a tree, called Kairal by the Khas of Nepal Proper, the flowers of which are eaten by the hill people. Káticha-Káti is the name of a place. Jirel is supposed to be a mixed sept arising from a cross with some tribe not belonging to the Mukhya group. Although it is reckoned as a sept or *thar*, pure Sunuwárs do not intermarry with its members, nor will they eat *dál* or rice cooked by them. For all that the Jirel have not become endogamous, but marry with half-bred Sunuwárs and other tribes of the Mukhya and Kiránti groups. In Nepal tribal distinctions are not so sharply drawn as in India, and the offspring of mixed marriages find plenty of people in much the same position as themselves. The Wángdecha sept is considered in some sense inferior to the rest. Although they are admitted to marry with the other septs, *dál* and rice are not taken from their hands. Wandeh is said to be a Tibetan word, and it may be that this sept immigrated from Tibet after the others had become familiar with Hindu ideas. Kyahbohcha means 'born from a Kyahboh' (Tibetan *Kyahpo*), a rope ladder used by the hillmen for descending the face of a cliff to get wild honey, of which they are very fond. The fact that the two septs, Leokicha and Jespucha, are both called Preticha or earth-born, and may not intermarry, does not suggest any inference as to the affinities of the tribe.

Internal structure.

In most cases girls are married after they are grown up to men of their own choice, and sexual intercourse before marriage is tacitly recognized on the

Marriage.

understanding that in the event of the girl becoming pregnant she will be married without delay. Infant-marriage, however, is sometimes resorted to by well-to-do families which have been infected by Hindu ideas. Polygamy is allowed, but is not largely resorted to. If a man's first wife has no children, he is held to be justified in taking a second, and the matter is often arranged by his marrying his first wife's younger sister—an arrangement which is naturally more conducive to domestic peace than the selection of an outsider. The marriage ceremony consists for the most part of ritual borrowed from the Hindus, and *sindurdán*, or the smearing of vermilion on the bride's forehead and the parting of her hair, is the essential and binding portion. In addition to the standard forms, we find the peculiar usage that the bride's parents wash her feet when they give her to the bridegroom and splash the water over their own heads. By doing this they believe that they wash from her, and as it were take back, the quality of membership of her original sept, and transfer her to the sept of the bridegroom. On the next morning the bride washes the bridegroom's feet, and drinks the water, saying at the time that she does this as a sign that she has entered his sept and is truly his wife. After this has been done, she is considered competent to cook rice and *dál* for her husband and the members of his sept. The Nepalese regard it as characteristic of the Mukhya group that they treat the son-in-law as a very important personage and in a way worship him ; while the Kirántis look upon him rather in the light of a servant. By Kiránti custom, if a young man runs away with a girl and is unable to pay the fine which is appointed for such cases, his children by her are regarded and may be claimed as slaves by her parents. It is curious to find that the girl's *maternal* uncle is deemed the proper person to demand payment of the fine. The explanation of the difference of the Mukhya and Kiránti points of view is probably to be found in the fact that the former have been more affected than the latter by Hindu ideas, which tend always to exaggerate the value of men and to depreciate women.

A widow may not marry again by the standard ritual ordained for the marriage of a spinster, but she may live with a man without going through any ceremony at all, and in such cases public opinion recognizes her as his wife. Her children are deemed legitimate, and their status is in no way inferior to that of children born from a woman married by the full ceremony. If the deceased husband leaves a younger brother, married or unmarried, he is held to have a prior claim on the person of the widow, and she may not take up with another man until he has decided not to exercise his rights. Divorce is permitted on the ground of the adultery or misconduct of the wife. Divorced women may marry again in the same manner as widows, and their children by second husbands are deemed legitimate. Usually the first husband keeps his own children, but if the divorced wife is allowed to take them with her, as sometimes happens, they are treated as the children of her second husband.

Religion.

In point of religion the Sunuwárs may be described as undeveloped Hindus, still retaining many traces of an earlier animistic faith. They offer rice, flowers, sandal wood and vermilion to Siva, and sacrifice goats to

Káli, when sickness or domestic trouble afflicts them. Bhim Sen, the second of the Pándava brethren, is worshipped with sacrifices of he-goats, buffaloes, ducks, fowls and pigeons; but buffaloes are offered only on rare occasions, and the minor victims are usually thought sufficient. Tuesdays and Saturdays are the auspicious days. Offerings of rice, flowers and *sital-patti* leaves are also made to the rivers and mountain torrents and to the main peaks of the Himalayas visible from Nepal. Upádhya Brahmans serve them as priests and are received on equal terms by other members of the sacred order in Nepal. Among the minor religious observances of the tribe may be mentioned their solemn worship of the cow under the name of Lakshmi on the new moon of the month of Kartik, and their practice of marrying banyan and the pipul when found growing side by side.

Disposal of the dead.

Most Sunuwárs bury their dead and observe the same funeral ceremonies as the Mangars; but some well-to-do people have of late years taken to the Hindu practice of cremation, and perform a regular *sráddh* on the tenth or twelfth day after death.

Occupation.

The tribe believe hunting to have been their original occupation, and many of them are still strongly addicted to the chase. The bulk of the tribe, however, live by agriculture and pastoral pursuits.

Supáhá, a section of Kanaujiá Lohárs in Behar.

Supahran, a *mul* or section of the Kanaujiá sub-caste of Sonárs in Behar.

Supá-Parghá, a sub-caste of Parghás in Behar.

Supárá, a sub-caste of Doms in Behar.

Supat, a section of the Chhajáti sub-caste of Khatris in Bengal.

Suphar, a section of Kaserás in Behar.

Supolia, a title of Doms who make *sup*, a bamboo work for separating the chaff from the grain.

Sur, a title of Dakshin-Rárhi and Bangaja Káyasths and of Sánkháris and Sadgops in Bengal.

Surabani, a section of Kumhárs in Singbhum.

Origin.

Surahiyá, *Suraiyá, Sorahaiyá, Kalwat-Mallàh*, a boating, fishing, cultivating, and labouring caste of Behar. According to Dr. Wise their origin, like that of other boatmen, is traced to the fabulous hero Nikhád. There is a shadowy connexion between the Surahiyá and Cháin. The former use the water vessels and hookahs of the latter; but the Cháin, assuming a higher rank, will smoke, but will neither eat nor intermarry with Surahiyá. The Surahiyás have no traditions of their own, except the common one that their ancestors came 'from the west.'

Marriage.

Both infant and adult-marriage are in vogue, but the former is deemed more respectable. The marriage ceremony is the same as is used by most of the lower castes, *sindurdán* being the binding portion. Polygamy is allowed, but is not practised on a large scale. A widow may marry a second time. It is thought right for her to marry her late husband's younger brother if there is one, but she is not positively obliged to do so. Divorce is not recognized.

Religion.

In matters of religion the Surahiyás profess to be orthodox Hindus, and employ Maithil Brahmans for religious and ceremonial purposes. In practice, however, the greater gods of the Hindu Pantheon receive only occasional worship, and the working religion of the caste is concerned rather with the mysterious group known as the Pánch Piur, Koil Bába, the boatman's deity, and Amar Singh, a canonised Surahiyá, who seems to be their special patron. In his honour a part of the house is daubed with cow-dung on stated days in every month of the year except Paus (December–January) and Chait (March–April), and goats, rice, sweetmeats, ghi, etc., offered, and incense burned, the worshippers afterwards partaking of the offerings themselves.

Social status and occupation.

In point of social standing the Surahiyás rank immediately below the group of castes from whose hands Brahmans will take water. Thus Koiris, Barais, Gangotás, who belong to that group, will accept sweetmeats from Surahiyás, but will not eat boiled rice in their houses. The characteristic occupation of the caste is boating and fishing. Dr. Wise describes them as enterprising and hardy sailors often met with in Eastern Bengal during the cold season in large trading vessels laden with grain, pulse, or fuller's earth, which is sold to *mahájans* and a cargo of rice shipped for the return voyage. They are very muscular and large-boned, and their physique offers a striking contrast to that of the average Bengali boatman. Some Surahiyás have taken to cultivation, and hold land as occupancy and non-occupancy raiyats. Their number, however, is comparatively small, and there are at present no signs of their developing into a sub-caste: in fact, even cultivating Surahiyás are ready to engage themselves as boatmen.

The following statement shows the number and distribution of Surahiyás in 1881. The figures of 1872 were returned among those of 'others' of the Boating and Fishing castes.

District.	1881.	District.	1881.
Birbhum	105	Darbhanga	43
24-Parganás	24	Mozufferpur	44
Murshedabad	390	Champaran	3
Dinajpur	973	Monghyr	2,863
Rajshahye	163	Bhagalpur	2,199
Rangpur	3	Purniah	496
Maimansinh	4	Maldah	586
Patna	19	Santál Parganás	139
Shahabad	1,844	Singbhum	16

Surái, a *mel* or hypergamous sub-group of Rárhi Brahmans in Bengal.

Suraiyá, a synonym for Surahiyá.

Surajbansi, Surjabansi, a sub-caste of Tiyars; a synonym for Rajwár; a title of the Kochh tribe in Northern Bengal; a division of Rájputs; a sub-caste of Goálás in the North-Western Provinces and Behar. See **Suryabansi**.

Ṣuraj-bansi. This title, properly denoting one of the two main stocks of Rájputs, has been assumed within comparatively recent times by a hybrid Mongoloid caste claiming to be the aborigines of Kamrup and now inhabiting the jungly tracts of Bhowál in Eastern Bengal. According to Dr. Wise, from whose notes this article is condensed, the Súraj-bansís were formerly regarded as akin to the Kochh-mandái, but the Brahmans taking advantage of their credulity and ignorance, led them to believe that they were descendants of the Chhatrí who, by throwing away their sacred thread, escaped the axe of Parasuráma. Accordingly, in 1871, a body of representative Suraj-bansís went to the house of their zamíndár, Kálí Náráyana Rái, Rái Bahádur, a Ṣrotriyá Brahman, and requested him to reinvest them with the sacred cord. An offer of five hundred rupees was made, but declined. Disappointed at this unexpected rebuff, they retired to consult, and afterwards raised their offer to two thousand. This sum allayed the scruples of the Brahman, the sacred cord was with due solemnity presented, and ever since the Suraj-bansí have assumed the high rank of Chhatrí, to the great disgust of the Hindus of those parts.

The Kochh-mandái, who reside in the same jungle, assert that a few years ago the Suraj-bansí were known as Kochh-mandái, and even at present Bansí is their ordinary appellation. The Suraj-bansí are peculiar to Bhowál, and are not met with beyond the limits of the Dacca district. They are certainly allied to the Kochh-mandái, but have modified the Mongoloid type by marrying with low Bengali castes. Their original language, probably a dialect of Garo, has been forgotten, and Bengali is universally spoken. The Suraj-bansí is generally a darker and taller, but less muscular man, than the Kochh-mandái. Certain of them still retain the peculiar Mongoloid cast of features, with oblique eyelids and scanty growth of hair; but the majority have the common Bengali countenance, with bushy moustaches and voluminous cues, for they have adopted the Vaishnava fashion of wearing the hair. They already call themselves worshippers of Vishnu, and have engaged the services of a Patit-Brahman as purohit. Twice a year, in Phalgun and Baisákh, they worship under a *sál* tree Kamakha Devi, the tutelary goddess of Kamrup. Durga, Manasa Devi, and Bura-Buri are invoked in seasons of sickness and domestic trouble, and especial honour is paid to the sun as the reputed ancestor and eponym of the caste. They have borrowed three *gotras*, Kasyapa, Aliman, and Madhu-Kuliyá, and marriages into the same *gotra* are strictly forbidden. Widow-marriage has been abandoned; divorce is prohibited, and the Hindu system of marrying girls before puberty adopted. Furthermore, having assumed the sacred thread of the Chhatrís, they imitate them in observing the *sráddha* on the nineteenth day after death.

By Hindus they are not admitted to belong to a clean caste, but the Súdra servants are beginning to work for them, and in a few years they will doubtless have secured an established position. The Kochh-mandái affirm that the Suraj-bansí secretly indulge in the forbidden luxury of pork, although to curious strangers the fact is stoutly denied. It is a familiar experience that this taste survives in many tribes long after they have adopted the external observances of Hinduism. Almost all Suraj-bansís are cultivators, growing rice, pulse, tobacco, mustard and cotton on clearings in the jungle. Fishing is deemed dishonourable. A few who have acquired a slight knowledge of Bengali are employed as traders or servants to landholders.

Surajdhaj, a sub-caste of Káyasths in Behar.

Suran, a section of Rautiás in Chota Nagpur.

Suraniá, a section of Khariás in Chota Nagpur.

Surat, a section of the Ghosin sub-caste of Goálás in Behar.

Suratwalá, 'a good looking man,' a synonym for Barnasankar. In Gyá an ironical designation of the illegitimate descendants of Gyawals by women of the Rájput, Bábhan, and Bhát castes, but not of lower castes.

Surává, a sub-caste of Malláhs in Behar.

Suren, a section of Turis in Chota Nagpur.

Sureswari, a *gotra* or section of Subarnabaniks in Bengal.

Suret, a *mul* or section of the Kanaujiá sub-caste of Sonárs in Behar.

Surgane, a *mul* of the Parásara section of Maithil Brahmans in Behar.

Surgriá, a section of Bábhans in Behar.

Surhi, a wild cow, a totemistic sept of Mundas in Chota Nagpur.

Suri, fly, a totemistic sept of Mundas in Chota Nagpur; a section of the Bahánnajáti sub-caste of Khatris in Bengal; a synonym for Sunri.

Surijhabu, a sept of Chiks in Chota Nagpur.

Suril, a totemistic sept of Mundas who do not propitiate the 'Churin Deota.'

Surin, a sept of Mundas in Chota Nagpur.

Surinwár, a section of Turis in Chota Nagpur.

Surjáhá, a section of the Biyáhut and Kharidáhá Kalwárs in Behar.

Surkhi, a sept of the Suryabansi sub-tribe of Rájputs in Behar.

Surnair, a sept of Rájputs in Behar.

Suruan, a sept of Páns in Chota Nagpur.

Surunia, neck ornament, a sept of Kharwars in Chota Nagpur.

Surwár, a sept of the Suryabansi Rájputs in Behar.

Suryabansi, *Surji*, 'descendant of the sun,' an honorific title assumed by many castes, particularly the Rájputs, and castes which, like the Dravidian Rájbansi Kochh of Northern Bengal, attempt to affiliate themselves to the Rájputs; a sub-tribe of Rájputs in Behar; a *thar* or sept of Mangars in Darjiling.

Suryabansi Láma, a *thar* or sept of Gurungs in Darjiling.

Surya-dwija, a sub-caste of Támbulis in Behar.

Susan, a sept of Mundas in Chota Nagpur.

Suswár, *Suswári*, a title given by the former Rajas of Rámgarh to some of their servants of the Hajjám or Kahár caste, whose duty was to superintend their master's stores of provision and edibles.

Suta, a sub-caste of Águris in Western Bengal.

Suthrá Sahi, *Sutrasáhi*, certain sect of mendicants said to be worshippers of Nirgun—God, void of qualities. They attract notice when soliciting alms by beating two sticks together.

Sutihar, a low caste who spin cotton thread.

Sutihár, a synonym for Barhi in Behar.

Sutradhar, *Chhutár*, the carpenter caste of Bengal, named thread-holder, from the Sanskrit *sútra*, the thread, with which the course of the saw is marked. Sútradhars claim descent from Viswakarmá, or, according to others, from Karna, son of Kunti by the sun-god before her marriage to Pándu. Karna, as is stated in the Mahábhárata, was exposed by his mother on the banks of the Jumna, where he was found by Adhiratha, the charioteer of Dhritaráshtra. The Sútradhars seem to have adroitly taken advantage of the resemblance between the words *súta*, a charioteer, and *chhutár* or *sutár*, a carpenter, to equip themselves with a mythological pedigree of undoubted respectability. Their ingenuity, however, has availed them little. That shrewd observer Dr. Wise describes them as a very low caste, recruited from one of the aboriginal races of Eastern Bengal, and largely employed in boat-building. He also quotes the story that in the time of Ballál Sen the Sútradhars lodged a complaint against the Brahmans for not performing religious ceremonies for them until all other castes had been served, whereupon the king, to prevent all further controversy, enrolled them among the *nicha* or low castes, and gave them a special Brahman of their own. Another legend says that they were degraded for delay in supplying the wood required by the Brahmans for certain sacrifices.

Traditions of origin.

The internal structure is rather intricate, and they furnish a good instance of the tendency to multiply sub-castes, which has already been noticed as characteristic of the lower social groups in the Hindu system. No less than twenty-five sub-castes are shown in Appendix I, and though the materials at my disposal were fairly ample, I am by no means confident that the enumeration is exhaustive. Of these groups some are local, others occupational, while for many of the names no explanation at all is forthcoming. Thus the Western Bengal sub-castes are based on distinctions of locality, except the **Goálá-Bhuiyá**,

Internal structure.

a group of uncertain origin. In Dacca the **Chhutár** sub-caste make boats, household furniture, beams, wheels, and ploughs; the **Chúrá-Kutí** parch and husk rice, make wooden necklaces, and burn shells for lime; the **Káthuriá** make ploughs, tubs, platters, and wooden agricultural implements.

The Chhutárs claim, and are admitted to have, precedence of the other two divisions. They are all included in one *gotra*, the Alamyan, and invariably belong to the Vaishnava creed. The caste has a panchâyat, but no union (*dal*), and their headman, styled *Parámánik*, settles disputes between members. It is derogatory for a Chhutár to fell a tree, which is done by a class of Chandáls called *Karátí*, from the Sanskrit Kara-patra, a saw. Turning (*kund-kári*), however, is the legitimate occupation of a carpenter, and he is permitted to make moulds used by confectioners for preparing fancy sweetmeats, and by plasterers for ornamenting cornices and roofs. Chhutárs never cultivate the soil, but frequently carry on business as maháјans or wholesale traders. Muhamadan carpenters, unknown in Dacca, are common in Chittagong, where they are employed as shipwrights.

The members of the Churákuti sub-caste are gradually relinquishing their ancestral trade, and of late years have taken Muhamadan servants to husk rice, while they themselves act as grocers, selling pulse, grain, and oils. or as writers, servants, and shop-keepers. The only wooden article now made by them is the sandal wood necklace worn by all Hindus The Purohit is distinct from the family priest of the other subdivisions. The headman is styled Pradhán, and the only gotra is Alamyan. The Chúrákuti are all Vaishnavas in creed, the guru being the Farídábád Gosáín. Their principal festivities are the Gandheswarí on the 10th Aswin (September), and New Year's day, on the 1st of Baisákh.

The Káthuriá subdivision, scattered throughout the Dacca district, is engaged in cultivating the soil, building boats, and manufacturing lime with the fresh water shells dredged from the extensive *jhils*, or marshes, in the interior of Bikrampur, being for this reason often confounded with the Báiti or Chunari caste, a perfectly distinct community.' The Brahman of this sub-caste is an Achárji, who performs the same religious ceremonies as the priest of the other two. The headman is known as Sardár.

Similar distinctions appear under different names in the Santál Parganás, where the **Ket Chhutár** are ordinary carpenters working only in wood and making household furniture, palanquins, and the like; the **Páturá** are stone-cutters; the **Nagare** practise turning; and the **Bhar-Chhutár** parch and pound rice into *churá*.

Exogamy and hypergamy.

The sections have been borrowed from the Brahmanical system, and give no clue to the origin of the caste. They are not invariably exogamous, and the tendency seems to be for the Sútradhars of Eastern Bengal to regard the *gotra* as a sort of titular distinction and to regulate their marriages by the more modern system of counting prohibited degrees. This at least is the case with two out of the three sub-castes found in Dacca, while in Noakháli the caste is stated to have no sections at all. In Western Bengal, on the other hand, the sections are still intact, and three of them—Alamrishi, Bánrishi, and Kásyapa—appear in that district to be clearly totemistic. The Alamrishi will not eat, and even pay some sort of reverence to the eel (*áind*), while members of the Bánrishi and Kásyapa sections observe a similar taboo in respect of the *bán* fish and the water-tortoise. This curious survival of primitive usage lends important confirmation to Dr. Wise's opinion that the caste is really of non-Aryan descent. No regular system of hypergamy has yet been developed among them, but the beginnings of one may perhaps be discerned in the fact that families bearing the title of Parámánik are held in special esteem, and are usually spoken of as Kulins. Such families have not as yet reached the point of refusing to give their daughters in marriage to persons who are not Kulins, but a higher bride-price is paid for Parámánik girls, and members of Parámánik families are treated with special consideration at wedding and funeral feasts. In Dacca the Sútradhars of Bikrampur affect a high degree of ceremonial purity, and demand a special bride-price on giving their daughters in marriage to Sútradhars coming from other places. In the Bishanpur estate in Bankura the superior families of Sútradhar pay a small fee to the Raja of Bishanpur for the privilege of calling themselves Kulins, and the Raja is supposed to have the power of punishing a breach of caste custom by depriving the offender of this coveted distinction. No instance has come to my notice of this power being exercised in recent times, and the fee still paid is doubtless a survival from days when the Bishanpur family possessed considerable authority in Western Bengal.

Marriage.

Sútradhars marry their daughters as infants by the standard Hindu ceremony, of which *sátpák*, or the carrying of the bride seven times round the bridegroom, is deemed to be the binding portion. A bride-price is paid, which varies with the rank of the families concerned. Polygamy is permitted, and there appear to be no theoretical objections to a man having as many wives as he can afford to maintain. Widows are not allowed to marry again, nor is divorce recognized. Sexual indiscretions are usually hushed up within the circle of the family in which they occur; but a woman whose infidelity gives rise to public scandal is summarily turned out of the caste, and ceases thenceforth to be a member of respectable society.

Religion.

The great majority of the caste belong to the Vaishnava sect, but worshippers of the Saktis are also found among them. Viswakarmá is regarded as their patron deity, and sacrifices are offered to him on the last day of Bhádra and in Mágh Panchami. Images of the god are sometimes made in the likeness of a white man with three eyes, wearing a crown, and bearing a club in his right hand; but usually he is represented by the tools which the worshipper uses in his trade. These are set up inside the house and decorated with flowers, and offerings are placed before them, while the god is besought to favour his votaries on their profession during the ensuing year. Sútradhars employ Brahmans for religious and ceremonial purposes, but these Brahmans belong to the *Barna* class, and are not received on equal terms by other members of the sacred order. The dead are burned, and the ordinary *sráddh* ceremony is performed on the thirty-first day after death.

Social status.

The social rank of the Sútradhar is low. Brahmans will not take water from their hands, and they may be said to occupy much the same position as the Jugi, Sunri, and Dhobá. In Western Bengal the village barber has no objection to shaving them, but he marks his sense of their inferior status by declining to cut their toe nails or touch their feet.

Occupation.

Carpentry is believed to be their original and characteristic profession, but besides the occupations already enumerated, Sútradhars are employed in cutting conch shells into bracelets, in making images of the gods, and in painting religious pictures. In Murshedabad, indeed, this last occupation seems likely to form the basis of a new sub-caste, for I am informed that painters (Chitrakár) do not intermarry with the members of the caste who work as carpenters and shell-cutters. In Noakháli some Sútradhars work as goldsmiths. Cultivating Sútradhars are usually occupancy or non-occupancy raiyats. None of them appear to have risen to be zamindars or tenure-holders: on the other hand, very few have sunk to the position of landless day-labourers.

The following statement shows the number and distribution of Sútradhars in 1872 and 1881 :—

District.	1872.	1881.	District.	1872.	1881.
Bardwan	15,973	10,131	Jalpigori	73	831
Bankura	4,610	6,471	Kuch Behar	......	138
Birbhum	7,747	8,900	Dacca	15,907	15,295
Midnapur	10,586	14,784	Faridpur	5,086	5,200
Hughli	5,108	4,667	Bakarganj	2,081	1,151
Howrah		1,794	Maimansinh	21,479	27,488
24-Parganás	8,274	1,467	Tipperah	11,804	1,526
Nadiya	9,126	9,420	Chittagong	1,328	2,454
Khulna	......	1,632	Noakhali	2,768	3,554
Jessore	10,544	12,071	Maldah	2,189	2,757
Murshedabad	10,070	9,673	Singbhum	342	381
Dinajpur	678	1,019	Manbhum	2,027	1,927
Rajshahye	4,558	1,066	Tributary States	112	39
Rangpur	2,326	2,220	Cuttack	......	210
Bogra	1,569	1,567	Balasore	......	19
Pabna	10,282	12,714	Tributary States	......	1
Darjiling	159	106			

Sutrasáhi, a class of Baniyás in Behar. See *Suthrá Sahi*.

Suwahong, the mendicant, a sept of the Yangorup sub-tribe of Limbus in Darjiling.

Suyál, a *thar* or sept of Mangars in Darjiling.

Swáin, a title of Chásás in Orissa.

Swarna-kausik, a section of the Uttar-Bárendra Brahmans in Bengal.

Swártha, self-absorbed, a title of Brahmans and Vaishnavas.

Swarupsing, a group of the Fatehsing Telis in Murshedabad.

Swetbhadra, a *pur* or section of Sákadwipi Brahmans in Behar.

Swiri, a synonym for Savar.

T

Tabkáhila, a section of the Biyáhut and Kharidáhá Kalwárs in Behar.

Tabkar, a section of the Dhaprá sub-caste of Doms in Behar.

Tábria, a section of Mahesris in Behar.

Tag-tog-pá, *tag* or *brag*, a rock—a dweller on cliffs, a sub-sept of the Nah-pá sept of Sherpa Bhotias.

Tahalkiá, a setion of Goálás in the North-Western Provinces and Behar.

Taiá, a sept of Rájputs in Behar.

Taijaung, a sept of Limbus in Darjiling.

Tailakár, a synonym for Teli.

Tailangi or **Andhra**, a territorial division of the Pancha Drávira Brahmans who live in the south of the Vindhya range, a country of the Telugu language.

Taili, a synonym for Teli.

Taingchait, a sept of Maghs in the Hill Tracts of Chittagong.

Taipál, a synonym for Teli.

Tairan, a *gotra* or section of Agarwáls.

Taitia, a sept of Nágeswars in Chota Nagpur.

Taitum, a sept of Mundas in Chota Nagpur.

Taiyá, a title of Hindu Joláhás in Behar.

Tajna, name of a river, a totemistic sept of Chiks in Chota Nagpur.

Takware-Ankusi, a *mul* of the Bátsya section of Maithil Brahmans in Behar.

Takware-Nimá, a *mul* of the Bátsa section of Maithil Brahmans in Behar.

Talabáti, a *gáin* of the Kásyapa *gotra* of Rárhi Brahmans in Bengal.

Talahadába, palm-tree, a totemistic sept of Juángs in Orissa.

Táláiboná, a sub-caste of Doms in Bengal who make palm-leaf mats.

Talápátra, bottom of a pot, a title of Bárendra Brahmans in Bengal.

Tálkátá, a sub-caste of Háris in Bengal who extract the juice from *tál* trees.

Tálu, a *thar* or sept of Mangars in Darjiling.

Tamág, a *thar* or sept of Murmis in Darjiling. The term is sometimes used to denote the whole caste.

Tamagandiyá, a section of Turis in Behar.

Támár, a sept of Rájputs in Behar.

Tamáriya, *Murá*, or *Mánki-Murá*, a sub-tribe of Bhumijs originally settled in parganá Tamár of Lohardagá.

Támbá, copper, a sept of Kharwars and Mundas in Chota Nagpur.

Támberá, a sub-caste of Kaserás, braziers in Behar.

Támboli, a group of the Sri-Gaura sub-caste of Gaura Brahmans.

Támbrakhola, a sub-tribe of Limbus in Darjiling.

Támbuli, *Támuli*, *Támli*, a respectable trading caste of Bengal, Behar, and Orissa, whose original occupation is supposed to have been the selling of betel-leaf, Sanskrit *támbúla*. Tradition represents them as the descendants of a Vaisya father and a Brahman mother, but this legend clearly throws no light upon the true origin. It is possible that they may be an offshoot from one of the trading castes, whose usages have been transformed by contact with Brahmanical influences. The Támbulis of Behar have no sections, and regulate their marriages by the standard formula for reckoning prohibited degrees calculated to six generations in the descending line for *dhianiá* relations and fourteen for *deádi*. In Bengal and Orissa the Brahmanical *gotras* are in use, Vyása being included among them. Instead, however, of following the ordinary law of exogamy, the Támbuli have a peculiar system of their own, which depends partly on the *gotra* and partly on the family name. Persons who belong to the same *gotra* are allowed to marry provided they do not bear the same family name, and persons of the same family name may marry if they belong to different *gotras*. Where, however, both family name and *gotra* are the same, the prohibition on intermarriage is absolute. Marriage between *sapindas* and *samánodakas* is also forbidden.

Origin.

The Támbulis of Bengal are divided into five sub-castes or *tháks* —Saptagrámi or Kusadâye, Ashtagrámi or Kataki, Chauddagrámi, Biyállisgrámi, and Bardhamáni. The first-named say that they came from Northern India, and that their chief settlement was at Saptagrám or Sátgáon, where they numbered about 1,400 families. An outrage committed on one of their maidens by the Mahomedan Governor of the place induced them to leave Sátgáon in a body and settle at Kusadáhá, in the 24-Parganás, which they now regard as their head-quarters in Bengal. A similar origin is claimed for the Biyállis-grámi, the largest of the five sub-castes, who are supposed to have entered Bengal at a still earlier date. The Chauddagrámi, which is now reckoned the highest in rank, is said to owe its origin to one Sashthibar Singh, a member of the Biyállisgrámi group, who being turned out of his father's house for marrying the daughter of Srimanta Pál, a Támuli of the Bardhamáni sub-caste, took refuge with his father-in-law at Bainchi, in Hughli, and headed a faction of his own. Being a man of wealth and influence, he gained over to his side several leading families, and thus formed the nucleus of a new sub-caste, which comprised the Támulis of fourteen villages (*chauddagrám*). Some clue to the time when this took place is given by the inscription on a temple at Bainchi, which shows it to have been built by Gokul, the son of Sashthibar, in the Saka year 1504 = A.D. 1582. We may place the formation of the Chaudda-grámi sub-caste some fifty years earlier. The Bardhamáni sub-caste are supposed to have had their earliest settlement in the Bardwan district, but they are now most numerous in Birbhum. The Ashta-grámi profess to have come from Upper India at the same time as the Saptagrámi, but residence in Orissa has cut them off from the rest of the caste, and their social rank is now comparatively low. The

Internal structure.

Behar sub-castes are shown in Appendix I, and demand no special notice here.

Marriage.

Támbulis marry their daughters as infants. The Ásura form of marriage is in vogue, and the parents of the bridegroom pay a bride-price, which varies according to the status of the bride's family. *Kusandiká* forms part of the ritual, but the essential and binding portion is believed to be the formal gift of the bride and acceptance of her by the bridegroom. Yellow silk is the proper bridal dress, but should the family be poor a girl may be married in cotton dyed with turmeric. Polygamy is permitted, and in theory a man may have as many wives as he can afford to maintain. Such indulgence, however, is rare, and I understand that few Támbulis have more than one wife. A man may marry two sisters, but he must follow the order of age, and may not marry his wife's elder sister. Divorce is not recognized, and on the rare occasions when a public scandal occurs within the caste the offending wife is turned out to shift for herself. Widows are forbidden to marry again, and the custom of the caste compels them to lead a more strictly ascetic life than is usual among the other castes of the Navasákha. They are allowed only one meal a day, of which neither flesh nor fish may form part, and they must fast entirely twice a month. A Támuli widow indeed is subject to as severe ordinances of self-denial as a Brahman widow. These ascetic doctrines, however, hold good only in Bengal and Orissa. In Behar a widow may marry again, and is tied down by no special restrictions in her choice of a second husband, although it is deemed right and proper for her to marry her deceased husband's younger brother should such a relative exist. It deserves notice that among the Behar Támulis the ceremony used at the marriage of a widow, though called *sagai*, does not differ materially from that which is performed when a virgin is married. In most cases where widow-marriage is permitted, the ritual is extremely meagre, and usually consists of little more than the smearing of red lead on the bride's forehead. Divorce is effected with the sanction of the pancháyat, but divorced wives may not marry again.

Religion.

The religion of the Támbulis presents no features of special interest. Most members of the caste are Vaishnavas, and comparatively few worshippers of the Saktis are found among them. They employ Brahmans for religious and ceremonial purposes, who are received on equal terms by other members of the sacred order. Among the minor gods recognized by the caste in Bengal may be mentioned the sun and moon, to whom rice, plantains, etc., are offered occasionally; Chandi, Lakshmi, Sashthi, and Manasá. In Behar Bandi and Nar Singh are the favourite deities. The offerings presented to them are wheaten cakes, sweetmeats, curds, and plantains, which are afterwards eaten by the members of the household. On the Purnimá or full moon of Baisákh some Támbulis set up inside their houses a vessel of lime, some betel-leaves, and areca nut, with the scissors (*katári* and *jánti*) used for cutting the leaf and nut, and worship these as the emblems of their trade. The dead are burned, and the *ádya* or principal *sráddhá* performed on the thirty-first day after death. Those who are well off make a point of taking some of the ashes to the Ganges, but the poor merely throw them into the nearest stream or tank.

Occupation.

To prepare and sell betel-leaf, which they buy from the cultivators, is believed to be the original occupation of the caste, which they still adhere to in Behar and Upper India, often adding thereto the business of a *pansári* or druggist. In Bengal, however, the Támbulis have long since abandoned this special business, and taken to dealing in grain and petty shop-keeping. Some sell lime, others are employed as *gomáshtas* in large shops, a certain number hold land, and a few are Government servants, pleaders, *mukhtiárs*, doctors, clerks in merchants' offices, and schoolmasters. No Támbuli will hold the plough himself, and those members of the caste who have taken to agriculture are zamindárs, tenure-holders, and occupancy raiyats cultivating their lands by means of hired labour.

Social status.

The social rank of the caste is respectable. They are usually classed among the Nabasákha, and in most districts of Bengal Brahmans will take water from their hands. On this point, however, there seems to be some conflict both of ancient authority and of modern usage. The couplet of Parásara, which is usually cited as the *locus classicus* defining the Nabasákh or Nava-Sáyaka group, makes no mention of the Támbuli; and although it is alleged that the caste is included under the Teli, who also are descended from a Vaisya father and a Brahman mother, this seems rather a forced interpretation. On the other hand the Brahma Vaivarta Purána omits the Teli and gives the Támbuli a prominent place among the Sat-Sudras. So the Brahmans of Bengal, while usually according to the Támbuli a place among the Navasákha, do not invariably allow them the privileges attaching to this position; and a Támbuli gentleman,[1] to whom I am indebted for an excellent series of notes on the caste, informs me that neither Brahmans nor Rajputs will take water from their hands. Támbulis will partake of cooked food with none but members of their own sub-caste. Thus a Chauddagrámi will eat boiled rice only with a Chauddagrámi, and so on. Some, howevert will eat the leavings of Brahmans. Their own rules regarding die, are the same as are followed by most orthodox Hindus. Among lawful animal food they admit goat's flesh, venison, and all kinds of fish ordinarily sold except the scaleless varieties known as *pángás*, *gorchá*, and *etá*. Some also drink wine, but those who abstain from both animal food and strong drink are deemed to follow a more excellent path. In Behar, where less attention seems to be paid to the dicta of writers of the Pauranic age, the Támbuli rank with the Koiri, and no question has arisen as to the propriety of Brahmans taking water from their hands.

The following statement shows the number and distribution of Támbulis in Bengal Proper in 1872 and 1881. The figures for

---

[1] Babu Shambu Chandra Dé, of Hughli, a member of the Chaudda-grámi sub-caste.

Behar, Orissa, and Chota Nagpur are included in the table on Barais.

District.	1872.	1881.	District.	1872.	1881.
Bardwan	14,428	6,311	Rangpur	319	378
Bankura	12,034	16,097	Bogra	399	37
Birbhum	2,962	3,554	Pabna	290	130
Midnapur	9,869	11,682	Darjiling	181	7
Hughli	} 5,325	{ 8,457	Jalpigori	1	242
Howrah		1,896	Dacca	200	328
24-Parganás	6,043	1,651	Faridpur	236	2
Nadiya	1,683	1,802	Bakarganj	68	511
Jessore	136	444	Maimansinh...	38	251
Khulna	......	281	Chittagong	1,116	138
Murshedabad...	1,172	732	Noakhali	29	1
Dinajpur	13	648	Tipperah	322	1
Rajshahye	410	201			

Támgáin, a section of the Biyáhut and Kharidáhá Kalwárs in Behar.

Tamgarihar, a sept of Mundas in Chota Nagpur.

Tamghuria, a sept of Mundas in Chota Nagpur.

Támi, a synonym for Dámi.

Támli, a synonym for Támbuli.

Támrá, a sub-caste of Kámárs in Midnapur.

Támuli, a synonym for Támbuli.

Tandan, a section of the Bárajáti sub-caste of Khatris in Bengal.

Tángbuáh, a *thar* or sept of Khambus in Darjiling.

Tángi, axe, a totemistic section of Rautiás in Chota Nagpur.

Tankol, a *mul* or section of the Naomuliá or Goriá sub-caste of Goálás in Behar.

Tannahpurái-Solhni, a *mul* of the Kásyap section of Maithil Brahmans in Behar.

Tannán, a sept of Rájputs in Behar.

Tánti. *Tantrabáya, Tantubáya, Tatwá, Tantwá*, the weaver caste of Bengal and Behar, probably a functional group developed under the pressure of the natural demand for woven cloth. A common tradition represents them as descended from Siva Dás or Ghám Dás, who was born from the sweat (*ghám*) that fell from Siva while he was dancing, and his wife Kusbati, who was created by Siva from a blade of *kusa* grass. Siva Dás had four sons—Balarám, Uddhab, Purandar, and Madhukar, who were the ancestors of the four sub-castes bearing those names. Another story recounted in the Játi Kaumudi makes the caste the offspring of a Manibandha father and a Manikár mother; while a third supposes that the Tántis, in common with all the artisan castes, were begotten on a Sudra woman by the celestial artificer Viswakarmá.

Origin.

The internal divisions of the caste are shown in a tabular form in Appendix I, and need only a brief notice here. In Western Bengal the **Áswini** or **Ásan-Tánti** claim to be the original stock, from

Internal structure. — Bengal.

which the other sub-castes have diverged. The women of this group do not wear nose-rings, and this is regarded as a badge of social distinction. The Áswini sub-caste is very numerous, and has broken up into five subordinate endogamous groups, which appear to derive their names from particular localities. In the city of Dacca, says Dr. Wise, the Tántis have separated into two *sreni* or sub-castes, called **Bará-bhagiyá** or **Jhámpániya,** from the *jhámpán* or sedan chair in which the bridegroom sits when going to fetch the bride, and **Chhotá-bhagiyá,** consisting of Káyasths who on becoming weavers were expelled from their caste. The former are about ten times as numerous. They assume the title Basák, which was originally taken by rich persons who had given up weaving and become cloth merchants. A few titles inherited from their forefathers, who were employed as weavers in the East India Company's factory (*aurang*), are still preserved. Among these **Jáchandár,** appraiser; **Muhkim,** supervisor; **Dalál,** broker; and **Sardár,** head of a gang of workmen, are the most common. Family nicknames are believed to be commoner among the Tántis than in any other caste, and certain households are called **Mesha,** sheep, and **Chhagri,** goat. The popular explanation of the names is that the ancestors of the families accidentally killed these animals; but it seems at least equally likely that they are totems, which have survived as family titles. This view derives some support from the fact that among the Tántis of the Santál Parganás the titles **Lu, Chandra, Pál, Sil, Dás, Datta, Nandi, Bit,** and **De,** serve to denote exogamous groups. In Mag Bazár, a suburb of Dacca, there reside a peculiar subdivision of outcaste Tántis belonging to a Magi Sreni who, though excommunicated for the same reasons as the Magi Kumhars, conform to all the customs of the Súdra Tánti.

According to Dr. Wise, the Chhotá-bhagiyá, or Káyath-Tántis, formerly goldsmiths, took to weaving as a more profitable trade, and now eat with and visit the Basáks, although the latter do not reciprocate the politeness. The richer families, having always adopted the prerogatives of the Káyasths, have been recognized, and if wealthy receive wives from them. At present only from twenty to twenty-five houses in Dacca are occupied by them, and several households work as goldsmiths, bankers, and engravers (Naqqásh).

Dr. Wise mentions another class of Tántis, called **Bangá-Tántis,** settled in Eastern Bengal. These are quite distinct from the city weavers, and claim to be the descendants of the original Tántis of Bengal, who supplied the people with cotton fabrics for ages before the reign of Jahángír. Although the superiority which they claim over the Basáks is not conceded, there can be little doubt that these Bangá Tántis were earlier settlers in Bengal than their rivals. The Bangá Tántis are chiefly settled at Dhámrái, an old town about twenty miles north of Dacca, where they occupy about two hundred and fifty houses. Their bridal dresses are white, and not of red or other coloured silk, as is the case with the Dacca weavers. They manufacture the native *sári* and *chadar*, as well as *doriyá* and *nau-batti* muslins, which are sent to Dacca to be embroidered. At Dhámrái the famous female spinners (*Kátani*), who used to wind the fine native thread, were still to be found in 1873; but in 1885, when Dr. Wise revisited Dacca, the art had died out. In illustration of the delicate touch of these spinners, the story is told that one of them wound eighty-eight yards of thread on a reel which only weighed one *rati* or two grains. Now-a-days a *rati* of the finest thread equals seventy yards, which proves that either a coarser cotton is grown, or that the women have lost their delicate sensibility of touch.

Behar.

The Behar sub-castes of Tatwás, as the caste is generally called in that province, need little comment. We find among them the common territorial groups **Kanaujiá** and **Tirhutiá**. The names **Baiswárá** and **Uttarhá** seem also to have reference to locality. **Banaudhiá** occurs among some of the Baniyá castes; **Jaiswár** is a common sub-caste of the Kurmis, while the names **Chamár-Tántí** and **Kahár-Tántí** suggest, what is in itself by no means improbable, that some members of the Chamár and Kahár castes may have taken to the profession of weaving, and thus formed new endogamous groups loosely affiliated to the Tántis. In Orissa there appear to be three sub-castes. The **Mátibans-Tánti** weave coarse cloth from thread of English or native manufacture. Many of them have deserted their characteristic profession and become teachers in village schools, assuming therewith the titles **Abadhán** and **Khetiputra**. The **Gálá-Tánti** weave fine cloth, and the Hansi-Tántí make coloured cloth of various patterns.

Dr. Wise has the following remarks on the Behar Tántis settled in Dacca:—

"The Hindustání, or Mungírya, weavers are very common in Dacca, where they comprehend a large proportion of the 'Moṭhiás,' or coolies, street porters, pankha-pullers, gardeners, and packers of jute; while at home they are weavers and cultivators. Two divisions are met with—the Kanaujiyá and Tirhutiyá; the former, the more numerous, being of higher rank than the latter, who are despised and shut out from all social intercourse. The Tirhutiyá, degraded by carrying palanquins and by acting as musicians at their homes, collect in Dacca during the jute season, and are remarkable for their squalor and stupidity. They also work as syces, gardeners, boatmen, and musicians."

The exogamous sections of the Tántis are comparatively few in number, and throw no light upon the origin of the caste. In Bengal the Brahmanical *gotras* have been adopted; while in Behar only three sections are known, and those do not appear to be necessarily exogamous. In Western Bengal prohibited degrees are reckoned by the standard formula to three generations in the descending line except where *bhayádi*, or mutual recognition of family events, is kept up. In that case the prohibition extends to seven generations.

Marriage.

Except in Behar, where adult-marriage is still practised by the poorer members of the caste, Tántis marry their daughters before they have attained the age of puberty. The bride-price usually demanded for a girl does not exceed from Rs. 50 to Rs. 60, but it is deemed more respectable for a man to give his daughter free of price. The marriage ceremony is of the ordinary type. Polygamy is recognized to the extent that a man may take a second wife if the first proves barren. Tántis are usually too poor to regard plurality of wives as a luxury. Widow-marriage and divorce are forbidden in Bengal, while in Behar widows may certainly marry again without any restrictions being imposed on their choice, and the balance of authority seems on the whole to incline to the opinion that divorced wives may marry again by the *sagai* form, which is used at the second marriage of a widow. Others, again, say that divorce is not recognized: if a woman goes wrong with an outsider, she is turned out of the caste; but if she has an intrigue with a Tánti, her fault is condoned by the headmen and her husband is compelled to take her back. If the bridegroom—elect of a widow has not been married before, he must perform the ceremony of *matkorwa* in his own house, and must smear vermilion on a sword or a piece of iron before going to take his bride.

It should be mentioned here that instances are said to have occurred of women belonging to lower castes, such as Teli, Turha, and Gonrhi, being formally admitted into the Tánti caste. These women had become the mistresses of Tánti men, and the latter, having been excommunicated on account of this discreditable *liaison*, had afterwards prevailed on the *panchâyat* of the caste to admit them and their mistresses to social rights on the condition that a feast was given to the caste and substantial presents offered to the members of the panchâyat. Men of other castes can on no account be received in this fashion. In matters of inheritance, a daughter's son is excluded by the nearest male relative of the same *kul*.

The Tántis of Eastern Bengal are, says Dr. Wise—

Religion.

"With few exceptions, Vaishnavas, being probably the most obsequious disciples of the Khardah Gosáins. They have no *panchâit* and no headman, but the rich guide and instruct their poorer brethren, while the trade interests of the caste are secured by the supervision of powerful Dals, or guilds, presided over by a Dalpatí, or director.

"The Dacca Tántís have always been celebrated for the magnificent procession which parades the streets of the city on the Janmáshtamí, or birthday of their god Kṛishna, in Bhádra (August–September). As long as a Nawáb lived at Dacca, his troopers and band led the pageant, and at the present day, though divested of many of its attractions, it is still the most popular exhibition in Eastern Bengal. For many generations the Dacca weavers have resided in two quarters of the city, Tántí Bazár and Nawábpúr, and on the day following the birthday of Kṛishna a procession issues from each of these quarters and perambulates the streets. In 1853 the processions met, and a faction fight ensued. In 1855 the Government ordered that for the future they should never be permitted to come out on the same day, and each quarter, therefore, takes precedence on alternate years, the peace of the city having been so far assured. Kṛishna is worshipped by the Tántí Bazár section under the form of Muralí Mohan; by the Nawábpúr as the Sáligrám, or Lakshí Náráyana. At the present day the processions are preceded by a string of elephants, and a "Panja," or model of a hand, presented by a former Nawáb, is borne aloft, as at the Muharram pageant. The peculiar part of the cavalcade, however, are the "Misls," or raised platforms, carried on men's shoulders. On these are placed images of Hindu gods, figures, and often caricatures of local celebrities. On others are Nách girls and buffoons reciting comic songs and bandying chaff with the crowd. In fact, the anniversary and the show have come to be regarded as the occasion of a holiday, when thousands of villagers throng the city bent on pleasure and amusement, which are more considered than the deity in whose honour it is held.

"The Banga Tántís observe with especial pomp the Kámadeva Púja, or worship of the Indian Cupid, which, though generally neglected in Bengal and entirely omitted by the Jhámpániya Tántís, is still kept up in Bhowál, Kámrúp, and the districts bordering on that country. It is undoubtedly a worship of earlier origin than that of Kṛishna. On the Madana Chaturdaṣí, or fourteenth day of the waxing moon of Chait (March–April), the festival is held, but it does not last for seven days as formerly. The purohit officiates, no victims being sacrificed. The Banga Tántís, moreover, celebrate the Janmáshṭamí, but in a different way from the Basák. Two boys gorgeously dressed, representing Kṛishna and his foster-father, Nanda Gopa, are carried about in great state and with much discordant noise. The Viṣvakarma worship is observed on the usual day, and, as with the Basáks, the loom, shuttle, and other implements of weaving are adored."

In Western Bengal Vaishnavism is the characteristic belief of the caste. Lakshinarayan-Chakra and Rádhá Kṛishna Bigraha seem to be the commonest objects of worship. Reverence is also paid to Durgá and Siva, but no sacrifices involving the taking of animal life are offered to them. Viswakarmá is looked upon as the tutelary deity of the caste, and is worshipped twice a year with offerings of flowers, rice, molasses, etc., under the supervision of a *purohit*, who recites appropriate texts. Images are sometimes made, but more commonly the weaver's loom or some of the tools of the craft is regarded as the dwelling place or symbol of the god. In the Santál Parganás Rangadhári and Jaikhá are mentioned among the minor gods of the caste, but I have been unable to ascertain their precise functions.

Among the Tatwás of Behar Vaishnavism appears to have made but little way, and the majority of the caste are addicted to the grosser cult of the Saktis, or female forms of the great gods. Thus the Kanaujiá sub-caste worship Mahá-máyá, or Durgá, and those settled in Bengal keep the ninth and tenth days of the Durgá Púјah as holidays consecrated to her. On a certain date in Kártik they proceed to an open plain and sacrifice a male goat to Káli, a *khasi*, or castrated goat, to Madhu Kunwár, who, they say, was a Tánti. On the sixth day after a birth the *chhaṭhi* is held, and on the twelfth the mother goes to the well, smears red lead on the edge in the name of Kamalá (Lakshmí), then draws water and carries it within doors, when she is pronounced clean.

Káli, Durgá, and Mahádeva are worshipped by the Tírhutiá sub-caste, but the majority follow the teaching of one Buddh Rám, a Mochí of Tírhut, who founded a sect, differing in some slight respects from that of Nának Sháh. They observe few caste usages, but many superstitious rites, such as burning *ghi* in a lamp and adding resin, in execution of vows. Besides the regular minor gods of Behar—Bandi Goraiyá, Dharamraj, and the rest—Tatwás worship Saisyár and Káruchar, departed members of the caste, with sacrifices of sheep and goats on Wednesdays and Saturdays in the month of Sráwan. Brahmans do not preside at these animisitic rites, which are performed by the male members of the household, with the object of protecting themselves, their families, and cattle against the ill-will of powerful spirits.

Priests.

The Tántis of Bengal are served in religious and ceremonial matters by the Brahmans, who minister to the spiritual wants of the Nava-Sákha group. These Brahmans occupy at the present day a highly respectable position, and although some of the most select Brahmans affect to look down upon them as *Sudra-jájak*, high caste Kulins are willing to marry their daughters; and it may be affirmed on the whole that they are received on equal terms by other members of the sacred order.

In Behar a very different state of things prevails, which seems to indicate that the caste may have been developed locally at a comparatively later date, and may be composed to a great extent of non-Aryan elements. In many places Tatwas have no Brahmans at all, and their place is supplied either by members of the caste who have joined some religious order, or by the sister's son (*bhánjá*) of the person at whose instance, or for whose benefit, a particular religious office is performed. In either case, notwithstanding the ignorance of the person selected as priest, the title of Brahman is conferred upon him, and he is treated with extreme deference. These primitive methods of satisfying the religious needs of the caste seem, however, to be tending to die out, and Tatwas, like other low castes, are beginning to set up Brahmans of their own, usually low Kanaujiás or Maithils, who are not looked upon as a credit to the priestly order. Both in Bengal and Behar the caste burn their dead and perform a funeral ceremony modelled more or less on the observances of the higher castes. But by the Tatwas of Behar this ceremony is performed on the thirteenth day after death, while the Bengal Tántis, following orthodox Sudra usage, observe the thirty-first day.

Social status.

Although the caste holds a degraded position in Behar, and Brahmans will not take water from their hands, the Tántis have had sufficient influence in Bengal to raise themselves to the grade of clean Súdras, and take undisputed rank in the Nava-sákha group. The purity of a Tánti depends on the quality of the starch used in weaving. The Súdra weaver prepares starch from parched rice boiled in water, or *kái*, which is not, according to Hindu ideas, *ento* or, as it is called in Behar, *jhúthá*, leavings. Impure weavers, as the Jugís, make starch (*már*) by merely boiling rice—a process which is considered utterly abominable. The rules observed in matters of diet bear, as is usual, some relation to the social status of the caste. The Bengal Tántis abstain, or affect to abstain, from flesh and strong drink, and claim to be superior in these respects to other Nava-sákha castes. In Behar flesh and wine are deemed lawful for Tatwas, and whenever spirits are drunk a few drops are poured forth as an offering to Mahadeva. Tatwas, again, take both *kachhi* and *pakki* articles of food from the Gangota, the Barai, and generally the entire group of castes from whose hands a Brahman can take water.

Occupation.

Although Tántis admit weaving to be their immemorial profession, many of them have of late years been driven by the influx of cheap machine-made goods to betake themselves to agriculture. These cultivating Tántis are for the most part occupancy raiyats, or small tenure-holders, but in the Murshedabad district a member of the caste owns the zamindari right in a large property. It is difficult or impossible to say with any approach to accuracy what proportion of the caste have abandoned their original craft in favour of trade or agriculture. The Uttarkul Tántis of Western Bengal have on the whole adhered to weaving, and it is popularly believed that their comparative poverty is mainly due to their attachment to the traditional occupation of the caste. Among the Aswini and Máriáli about one-third are supposed to have given up weaving and settled down as regular cultivators. Some minor differences among weaving Tántis deserve a passing notice. The Uttarkul sub-caste weave only cotton cloth, and the Máriáli only silk, while the Aswini make either cotton or silk goods.

According to Dr. Wise, five different sorts of cloth were manufactured by the Dacca Tántis in their palmy days, but the art of making the finer qualities has been lost. The five varieties were—

1. *Malmal*. Muslins of the first quality included the *Abrawán*,[1] *Tanzib*, and *Malmal* made of Desí (country) cotton or Kapás; of the second quality were the *Shabnam*, *Khasah*, *Jhúna*, *Sarkár 'Ali*, *Ganga Jal*, and *Terindam*;[2] of the third were the coarser muslins, collectively called *Báfftah*, comprising *Hammám*, *Dimti* (? *Dimyáti*), *San*, *Jangal Khasah*, and *Galá-band*.
2. *Doriyá*, striped and ribbed muslin, such as Ráj-kot, Dakhan, Pádsháhi-dár, Kunti-dár, Kághazí, and Kelápáṭ.

---

[1] Abrawán, literally running water, was solely made for the Delhi zanánah, and the following stories regarding its gossamer-like texture are still told by the natives. A daughter of Aurangzíb, one day on entering the room, was rebuked for wearing immodest drapery, but justified her conduct on the plea that she was wearing seven suits (Jámá). Again, in the reign of 'Alí Vardí Khán (1742—56), a Dacca Tántí was flogged and banished from the city for not preventing his cow from eating up a web of Abrawán which had been laid out to bleach on the grass.

[2] Probably from Arabic *tarah*, 'mode,' and Persian *andám*, 'figure.'

3. *Char-Khanah*, checkered muslins, such as *Nandanshâhi, Anâr-dâna, Kabûtar-khopi, Sâ-Kuttâ, Bachhâ-dâr*, and *Kunti-dâr.*
4. *Jâmdâni*, by the early European traders called *Nain-sukah*,[1] or embroidered muslins. The different sorts are distinguished by the coloured flowers, sprigs, *búti*, or network pattern on them. The commonest are *Shâhbarga-búti, Chawal, Mel, Tirchhâ*, and *Dubliját.*
5. *Kashida*, or *Chikan*, muslins embroidered with Múgá, or Tasar silk ,generally dyed red, blue, or yellow. The commoner ones are *Katâw-Rúmi, Naubatti* or *Naubati, Yahúdi, Azizullah*, and *Samundar Lahar.*

The common Dhotí, Chadar, and Oṛhní, or wrapper with a coloured or embroidered end, were always regarded as distinct from the foregoing, being woven at their homes by weavers of various castes.

On glancing over the preceding list one is struck by the predominance of Arabic, Persian, and Hindi words, and the rarity of Sanskrit and Bengali. That weaving, like other Native arts, was known in Hindustán prior to the foundation of the Bengal kingdom is beyond a doubt,[2] and that the earlier settlers brought it with them into the Delta is likely; but it would seem that either the names given by the dominant Muhamadans displaced the native ones, or that the liberal Mussulmán rulers stimulated—it may be developed—the manufacture of the finer sorts of muslins. That the inhabitants of Bengal at an early period made cotton cloth of wondrous fineness is undoubted, for the two Muhamadan travellers of the ninth century mention that in an Indian country called Rahmi[3] were woven cotton garments "so fine that they may be drawn through a ring of middling size." Unfortunately we possess no further evidence until A.D. 1506, three hundred years after the Muhamadan conquest, when the Roman Vartomannus[4] visited the fabled city of Bengalla, where the finest cotton and silk in all the world were produced, and whence yearly sailed fifty ships laden with cotton and silk goods. The earliest traveller, however, who gives us the names of the fine cotton fabrics of Bengal is the Arab author of the "Muhít," written in 1554.[5] He mentions among the goods exported from Chittagong by his countrymen a fine cloth (*Chautár*), muslin sashes called *Malmal*, the finest being known as Malmalí Sháhí, terms which are Hindi and Persian. Furthermore, when Cæsar Frederick visited Chittagong (1563–81), "bombast cloth of every sort" was exported thence. After his day the authorities

---

[1] Nayana-sukha, pleasing to the eye.

[2] It is referred to in the *Rig* and *Atharva Vedas.* See *Zimmer Altind. Leben*, p. 254.—H. H. R.

[3] Rahmi, however, may not be Bengal, but as it was the country of elephants, of a shell currency, and of the "Karkandan," or unicorn (rhinoceros), the assumption is not altogether groundless.—Elliot's *History of India*, vol. i, 361.

[4] *Ludovici Vartomanni Navigatio*, p. 259.

[5] *Journal A. S. of Bengal*, vol. v, 467.

are numerous, and names identical with those in use in the present day are cited.

The conjecture that the Muhamadans merely developed an already flourishing trade is strengthened by the fact that the terms in use by the Dacca weavers for the warp, woof, shuttle, and loom generally are Sanskrit, while later improvements, such as the shána or reed, the charkhá or spinning wheel, and the daftí or reed frame, are Persian.

The decline of the cotton trade of Eastern Bengal has been sketched by a former resident of Dacca, Mr. James Taylor,[1] while much curious information is contained in Mr. Bolts' *Considerations* and in the works of Edmund Burke. Under the Mughal Government, and even as late as the Nawábship of 'Alí Vardí Khán (1742–56), the weavers manufactured in perfect liberty, and the enterprising among them advanced money to promote the trade, but with Siráj-ud-daulah (1756-7) the decadence began, and during his eventful reign seven hundred families of weavers left their homes at Jangalbári, in Maimansinh, owing to oppression, and emigrated to other districts. Before 1765, when the English obtained the Díwání of Bengal, bullion was regularly imported from Europe to meet the requirements of the traders, but after that day advances were made from the provincial treasuries to buy the annual stock or "investment." This gave a new and unprecedented stimulus to weaving, and in 1787, the most prosperous year on record, the estimated prime cost of the cloths entered at the custom house of Dacca amounted to fifty lakhs of rupees, or 625,000*l*. This prosperity, however, was very deceptive, being founded on injustice and intolerable oppression. The first decline may be traced to the rapacity of the "banyans" and gomastas, who arbitrarily decided the quantity of goods each weaver was to deliver, the prices he was to receive, while his name being entered on a register, he was not permitted to work for any one but his own gomasta. When the annual supply was ready the gomasta held a bazár, at which the jáchandár, or appraiser, fixed the price of the goods, but the rascality, Mr. Bolts says,[2] was beyond imagination, and the prices were often fifteen per cent., often forty, below the market rate.

The deplorable condition of the weavers in 1773 is depicted in the following extract from a letter written by Mr. Rouse, the Chief of Dacca[3]: —"The weavers are in general a timid, helpless people, many of them poor to the utmost degree of wretchedness, incapable of keeping accounts, industrious as it were by instinct, unable to defend themselves if oppressed, and satisfied if with continual labour they derive from the fair dealing and humanity of their employer a moderate subsistence for their families."

The following incident that occurred in 1767 gives a vivid idea of the state of matters in Dacca at that period. Mr. Thomas Kelsall,

---

[1] *A Descriptive and Historical Account of the Cotton Manufacture of Dacca, in Bengal.* By A Former Resident of Dacca. London. 1851.

[2] *Considerations*, part i, 193.

[3] *Burke's Works*, Bohn's edition, iv, 73.

Chief of Dacca, being informed that a certain weaver, Krishna Pál Kumár, was suspected of selling muslins to the French factory, ordered him to be seized, but he found shelter with the French. His relatives, however, were imprisoned and beaten, and their houses pillaged. Upon this the weaver gave himself up to the Díwán, Bhikam Lál Thákur, who ordered him to be flogged, after which he was confined in the factory for eleven days, during which time the peons fleeced him of forty-nine rupees and two pieces of cloth. By Mr. Kelsall's order his head was shaved, his face blackened "with lime and ink," and being mounted on an ox, he was paraded through Nawábpúr, where the brokers and Paikárs lived. After three more days the accused was forwarded to the Nawáb for trial, who, finding no fault, discharged him.

This hateful system was at last swept away, and the weavers for a short time enjoyed comparative freedom of trade and unusual prosperity; but in 1769 Arkwright obtained his patent, in 1779 Crompton invented the mule, and the cotton manufactures of Lancashire have gradually driven the finer and less durable fabrics of the Bengali weavers out of the market, and all but annihilated the trade."

The following statement shows the number and distribution of Tántis in 1872 and 1881 :—

DISTRICT.	1872.	1881.	DISTRICT.	1872.	1881.
Bardwan	46,647	20,913	Chittagong	2,799	4,894
Bankura	16,510	29,304	Noakhali	1,273	1,326
Birbhum	16,761	15,962	Patna	12,958	18,802
Midnapur	106,317	97,720	Gya	6,894	5,744
Hughli	39,079	29,647	Shahabad	8,156	10,388
Howrah		14,250	Tirhut { Mozaffarpur	82,496	56,656
24-Parganás	19,576	8,129	Tirhut { Darbhanga		90,913
Nadiya	9,416	6,806	Saran	4,806	10,826
Khulna	......	2,594	Champaran	11,496	21,186
Jessore	10,760	10,349	Monghyr	86,202	87,268
Murshedabad	17,409	19,814	Bhagalpur	63,037	58,884
Dinajpur	12,800	9,093	Purniah	35,307	29,273
Rajshahye	822	1,515	Maldah	16,360	6,503
Rangpur	3,235	4,553	Santál Parganás	4,656	10,949
Bogra	1,801	1,660	Cuttack	37,822	38,790
Pabna	4,059	4,110	Puri	14,154	14,215
Darjiling	644	428	Balasore	38,460	40,046
Jalpigori	4,034	5,453	Tributary States	13,706	19,947
Kuch Behar	......	1,437	Hazaribagh	641	854
Dacca	8,906	10,587	Lohardagá	5,837	11,340
Faridpur	3,410	3,304	Singbhum	20,758	21,260
Bakarganj	1,875	1,327	Manbhum	13,961	12,243
Maimansinh	7,392	8,430	Tributary States	......	5,121
Tipperah	1,792	1,540			

Tánti, a synonym for Jolhá and Pán.

Tánti-Mahili, a sub-caste of Máhilis in Manbhum who carry palanquins.

Tántiá, a section of Goálás in the North-Western Provinces and Behar.

Tantrabái, a synonym for Tánti.

Tantrabáya, a synonym for Tánti.

Tantubáya, a synonym for Tánti.

Tánuri, a *gáin* of the Bátsya *gotra* of Bárendra Brahmans in Bengal.

Tapaer, a section of Mahilis in Chota Nagpur.

Tapaspati, "Master of Penance," a title of religious mendicants.

Tarah, *Terri*, an up-country caste.

Tarat, a sub-section of the Bharadwája section of Utkal Brahmans.

Tári, a *mul* or section of the Chhamuliá Madhesiá sub-caste of Halwáis in Behar.

Táriál, a *gáin* of the Bátsya *gotra* of Bárendra Brahmans in Bengal.

Tariyá, a section of Saraogis in Behar.

Tarkanyark, a *pur* or section of Sákadwipi Brahmans in Behar.

Tároálá Bisi, a *gáin* of the Sándilya *gotra* of Bárendra Brahmans in Bengal.

Társi, a *mul* or section of Kasarwáni Baniyás in Behar.

Társuriya, a sub-caste of Pásis in Behar.

Tártar ke khirpuri, a section of the Biyáhut and Kharidáhá Kalwárs in Behar.

Tarwár, a sept of the Suryabansi sub-tribe of Rájputs in Behar; a totemistic sept of Mundas in Chota Nagpur who cannot touch a sword.

Tárzukmung, a sept of Lepchas in Darjiling.

Tatia, a kind of bird, a totemistic sept of Mundas in Chota Nagpur.

Tátoár, a *gáin* of the Sábarna *gotra* of Bárendra Brahmans in Bengal.

Tatwá, a synonym for Jolhá and Tánti.

Tatwa, a weaving caste in Behar, who apply caterpillars to trees for cocoons from which *tasar* silk is made. See *Tánti*.

Taulika, a synonym for Teli.

Taulo, earthen-pot, a title of Bárendra Brahmans in Bengal.

Taunr, a sept of Rájputs in Behar.

Taw, a sept of the Patar sub-tribe of Mahilis in Chota Nagpur.

Táyal, a *gotra* or section of Agarwáls.

Tej, a title of Dakshin-Rárhi and Bangaja Káyasths.

Tejaniá, a section of Sonárs in Behar.

Tek Bárá, a sub-caste of Gaura Brahmans.

Tekhá, a sept of the Chandrabansi division of Rájputs in Behar.

Tela, a section of Mahesris in Behar.

Telgá, a section of Khariás in Chota Nagpur.

Telhá, a sept of Binjhiás in Chota Nagpur who use oil at marriage.

Telhari, a group of Maghaiya Telis in Behar.

Teli, *Taili*, *Tailika*, *Tailakár*, *Tailpal*, *Kalu*, a large oil-pressing and trading caste of Bengal, Behar, and Orissa. Their original profession was probably oil-pressing, and the caste may be regarded as a functional group recruited from the respectable middle class of Hindu society. Oil is used by all Hindus for domestic and ceremonial purposes, and its manufacture could only be carried on by men whose social purity was beyond dispute.

Traditions of origin.

The Telis of Bengal have a variety of traditions, mostly of the mythological type, which are interesting for their attempt to account for the origin and comparative status of some of the main divisions of the caste. The creation of the first Teli is ascribed to the god Siva, who, being of a mind to rub himself after bathing with oil instead of with the wood ashes, which he generally used, made from the sweat of his arm a man named Rupnáráyan Teli or Manohar Pál, and inspired him with the idea of an oil-mill (*ghání*). Some say that the original oil-mill was turned by two bullocks without blinkers, and that the Kalus were degraded for using one bullock only and blinding its eyes with blinkers. Another legend bearing on the same point is the following:—In the beginning of time the goddess Bhagavati made two men out of turmeric paste and ordered them to bring her oil. One came back very soon with a pot of oil; the other took much longer. When the goddess asked the reason of the delay, the latter explained that he had to soak up the oil with a bit of rag and squeeze it into a pot, while the former had stolen a march on him by using a mill with a hole at the bottom, through which the oil trickled out. On hearing this the goddess was much offended at the idea that she had used oil procured by a process resembling one of the baser functions of the human body, and condemned the more inventive of the two oilmen to pay the penalty of his ingenuity by being degraded to a lower caste. It would be quite in keeping with other cases of the growth of sub-castes that the Kalus should have been separated from the parent caste by reason of their having introduced an improvement in the primitive oil-mill; and the myth of Bhagavati's anger may well have arisen to account for their separation and for the lower social status assigned to them. There are, for example, two outcaste classes of oilmen in Eastern Bengal, who have been excommunicated because they manufacture oil in a novel manner: the first, or Gáchhuá Teli, express the oil by crushing the seed between wooden rollers; the second, or Bhúnjá Telí, parch the seed and then extract the oil. I do not know whether these groups have as yet started myths connecting their degradation with the displeasure of a god; but it is reasonable to expect that some such legend should in course of time be evolved.

Internal structure.

Concerning the origin of the sub-castes which bear the curious names of Ekádas and Dwádas Teli an interesting legend is current. The father of all the Telis, it is said, was Manohar Pál, a *beopári* or hawker who travelled about selling various wares. He had two wives. While he was away on a journey, a rumour reached his home that he was dead. Thereupon the elder wife broke her ornaments and performed the rites appointed for a widow, but the younger wife disbelieved the tale. In fact Manohar Pál was not dead, and returned home after a few days. From the two wives sprang the two sub-castes in question. The Ekádas Teli are the descendants of the elder wife, and the Dwádas Teli of the younger. In memory of the elder wife breaking her ornaments on hearing of her husband's death, the Ekádas women do not wear nose-rings and do not tattoo their foreheads and arms. Each group claims precedence over the other. The Ekádas are of course the elder branch, and it is alleged that they represent the original stock of the Teli caste, which is stated in the list given in the Brahma-Vaivartta Purána to be derived from a Kumhár (potter) father and a mother of the builder caste, Kotak or Gharámi. It stands eleventh on the list, and this is the reason for the name Ekádas. The Dwádas Teli in their turn, while admitting the descent of the Ekádas from the elder wife of the founder of the caste, alleged that they have forfeited the precedence they might otherwise claim by submitting to be governed by Parámániks in all matters relating to caste, and by sending women of the bride's family to accompany her on her first visit after marriage to her husband's house. Another queer custom of the Ekádas group forbids them to wear moustaches, but English education is said to be breaking this down.

The **Ghaná, Ghání,** or **Gáchhuá** Telis work an oil-mill of primitive pattern. This machine has no hole for the removal of the oil, which has to be soaked up with a bit of rag tied on to a stick The **Kalu,** as has been explained above, use a mill with a hole to let out the oil. The status of the latter is very low, and their separation from the main body of the Telis is so complete that many regard them as a separate caste.

In Eastern Bengal, according to Dr. Wise, there are two great subdivisions of this caste: the **Tail-pál,** or **Manohar Pál,** and the **Teli,** the former being the richer and more numerous. The Tail-pál arefrequently distinguished by the epithet Do-paṭṭí, from having adopted the Súdra marriage custom of carrying the bride and bridegroom on stools. The Telí, again, are known as Ekgáchhí, from their planting a champa-tree, on which the bridegroom sits while the bride is carried round him several times, as is the custom with the Gandhabaniks.

Originally, it is said there were no divisions, and all oilmen belonged to one caste, but in course of time, as wealth accumulated in their hands, the richer families, ashamed of their ancestral occupation, have adopted a new name to conceal their parentage. Thus in the district of Central Bengal Telis who have grown rich call themselves **Tilís,** and affect to be of a higher lineage than the Telis, although they still retain the old family titles. Wealth and prosperity have made them give up the manufacture of oil, and led them to become Amdawáláh, or traders buying goods wholesale and selling them by retail. Some go the length of saying that Tili is a caste wholly distinct from Telí, but I doubt whether the process of separation has as yet gone so far as this.

In the northern parts of the Dacca district, beyond the limits of the country affected by the reforms of Ballál Sen, the oilman caste has hypergamous divisions, which are said to vary in almost every parganá. In Ráipúra, for example, there are four classes of this sort—

the Satrah, or seventeen families; the Báís, or twenty-two; the Chaubís, or twenty-four; and the Chár, or four—each taking rank in the order named. These differ from the standard Kulin grouping in that the competition is for wives, not husbands. Girls may marry in a class below their own, and large dowries are given by the three lower groups for wives belonging to the first class.

Marriage.

In Dacca city at the time of Dr. Wise's researches the Tail-páls and Telís used to intermarry, and were regarded as clean Súdras. The *gotras* common to both were Aliman, Şáṇḍilyá, and Kásyapa. In addition to the well-known Padavís, or family surnames, of Pál, Nandí, Dé, and Kúndu, Chaudharí, and Shikdar, honorary titles bestowed by the native government were common among them, while the headman was styled Mandal. In former days their unions (*dals*) were notorious for the faction fights which broke out whenever differences of opinion were expressed. No *dal* existed in Dr. Wise's time, but the Mandal used to summon a pancháyat when required.

The marriage arrangements of the Telis of Bengal are cast in the orthodox mould, and the attempt is to approach as closely as possibie to the example furnished by the higher castes. The sections which regulate marriage are of the eponymous type; infant-marriage is fully established, and the marriage ceremony is in general conformity with the ritual prescribed in the Hindu scriptures. Widows may not marry again, and divorce is not recognized.

In other parts of the country the influence of orthodox tradition has been less powerful, and the aspirations of the caste are more modest. In Behar their sections belong to the titular or territorial types, while among the Telis of Chota Nagpur and Orissa totems are still held in reverence and regulate the intermarriage of members of the caste. Infant-marriage, though more usual than adult-marriage, is not reckoned absolutely essential; widow-marriage is permitted, the widow being usually expected to marry her deceased husband's younger brother. Divorce is recognized, and divorced women are permitted to marry again.

Religion.

In Bengal almost all Telis are Vaishnavas. Their principal festivals are those in honour of Lakshmi, Saraswati, and Gandheswari, the last being celebrated at the Dasahara in Áswin (September–October) and not on the full moon of Baisákh (April–May), as is the custom of the Gandhabanik caste. They employ as their priests Rárhi Brahmans, who are received on terms of equality by the Brahmans who minister to the spiritual wants of the higher castes. The Brahmans who serve the Kalus, on the other hand, are generally looked down upon, and occupy a position hardly higher than that of the degraded Brahmans who are the priests of the Kaibartta caste.

In Behar the worship of Vishnu does not appear to be a special characteristic of the Telis, and the worship of the minor deities seems to hold a more prominent position than is the case in Bengal. Among these the Kanaujia Telis pay especial reverence to the Panch Pir and Goraya, while the Magahiyá sub-caste is more addicted to the cult of Kalihandi, Jalpait, and Dharam Ráj. To these rural divinities the former offer *khirpuri* sweetmeats and bread made of seven kinds of grain on Wednesdays during the light half of the month of Asin, while the latter observe a similar ritual on the same day during the light half of Sáwan and Mágh. If a vow is made or a special boon solicited from the god, a more sumptuous offering is needed, and in such cases the Maghayá Telis usually sacrifice a goat. On Tuesdays during the light half of Sáwan, the Kanaujiá Telis offer a sucking pig to Goraya. After the blood of the victim has been poured forth on the ground before the lump of dried mud which symbolises the presence of the god, the body is either buried under ground or given to a Dosádh, whose religious scruples do not deter him from a savoury meal. The practice may also be accounted for by the supposition, in itself by no means improbable, that the Dosádhs, like the Layas and Bhuiyas in Western Bengal, were generally recognized as the hereditary priests of the more primitive deities, and in that capacity were entitled to claim the offerings as their legitimate perquisite. An inferior class of Brahmans, spoken of contemptuously as "Tel-Bábhan," serve the Telí as priests.

In Eastern Bengal, according to Dr. Wise, the pure Telís only extract *til* oil from the sesamum seed, and caste is forfeited if any other oil be manufactured. The *ghání*, or oil-mill driven by bullocks, is never used, the oil being prepared in the following manner: The seeds are boiled and given to the Muhamadan Kútí to husk. After being sifted, the Telí puts them into large vats (*jálá*), boiling water being poured in, and the seeds allowed to soak for twelve hours. In the morning the liquid is beaten with bamboo paddles (*ghotná*) and left to settle, when the oil floating on the surface is skimmed off and stored, no attempts to purify it being made. The refuse (*khali*) is given to cattle.

Social status.

The social standing of the Telís differs in different parts of the country and for different sub-castes. In Bengal, for example, the higher sub-castes of Telís, who have abandoned the oil trade and become bankers, money-lenders, cloth-dealers, and shop-keepers, take rank among the Nava-Sákha, or nine castes (now in fact fourteen) from whose hands a Brahman may take water, while the Kalus, or working oil-men, are included in a lower group along with the Sutradhar, the Sundi, and the Kapáli. In Behar the entire caste seems to stand on this lower level, and no Brahman will take water from their hands.

Dr. Wise mentions that Krishna Kánta Nandí, better known as Kánta Babu, the banyan of Warren Hastings, was a Telí by caste, and did much to raise its position among the Hindus. On visiting Jagganáth he offered to provide an *atka* or assignment of land for the maintenance of the poor, but the *Pandá*, or presiding priest, refused to accept it from the hands of such an unworthy person. Against this decision Kánta Babu successfully appealed to the Pandits of Nadiyá and Hughli, who held that the Telí, by using the balance *Tula* in his trade, must necessarily belong to the Baniá, a clean Súdra caste. Kánta Babu died in 1780. He is said to have introduced the *nath*, or nose-ring, among the females of his caste, an ornament previously worn only by Brahmans and the higher Súdras. The present representative of his family, Mahárání Sarnamayí of Kásimbázár, is renowned for her munificent support of public and private charities, and her zealous efforts to further the intellectual advance of her countrymen and countrywomen.

The following statement shows the number and distribution of Telis in 1872 and 1881:—

District.	1872.	1881.	District.	1872.	1881.
Bardwan	123,276	61,199	Noakhali	2,954	4,469
Bankura	54,386	95,435	Tipperah	4,914	6,698
Birbhum	30,867	27,926	Chittagong Hill Tracts ...	......	8
Midnapur	76,240	77,339	Patna	47,509	52,880
Hughli	} 39,956	47,038	Gya	59,701	57,379
Howrah		15,492	Shahabad	41,440	47,836
24-Parganás	32,903	29,896	Mozaffarpur	} 136,206	82,856
Nadiya	30,119	32,335	Darbhanga		79,444
Jessore	21,443	14,280	Saran	55,138	63,087
Khulna	......	7,742	Champaran	42,916	52,842
Murshedabad	39,189	20,730	Monghyr	52,765	56,632
Dinajpur	6,955	6,044	Bhágalpur	64,103	66,946
Rajshahye	8,060	6,929	Purniah	38,701	38,156
Rangpur	3,262	3,379	Maldah	17,949	11,374
Bogra	1,946	2,740	Santál Parganás	27,954	36,915
Pabna	10,604	10,273	Cuttack	52,173	58,559
Darjiling	412	903	Puri	36,839	38,916
Jalpigori	2,728	2,471	Balasore	37,749	43,200
Kuch Behar	......	504	Tributary States	42,476	50,283
Dacca	13,711	16,201	Hazaribagh	29,876	42,319
Faridpur	7,818	14,490	Lohardagá	24,427	32,835
Bakarganj	12,184	7,280	Singbhum	3,904	4,110
Maimansinh	7,814	9,713	Manbhum	33,072	32,382
Chittagong	4,063	4,031	Tributary States	3,026	6,227

Telia, a tree, a totemistic sept of Mundas in Chota Nagpur.

Teliá-Nagasiá, a sub-tribe of Nageswars who use oil instead of *sindur* at marriage.

Teli Baniyá, a sub-caste of Baniyás in Behar.

Teligámia, a group of the Mihtar sub-caste of Telis in Behar.

Teliha, a section of Kamárkolla Sonárs in Behar.

Teling, the worker in cane, a sept of the Chhothar sub-tribe of Limbus in Darjiling.

Telinga, a small caste found in Bankura and believed to be the descendants of certain sepoys imported from Madras in the last century by one of the Rajas of Bishenpur. Curiously enough, they have adopted the totemistic sections used by the Bagdis and Bauris of Western Bengal.

Temdih, a *mul* or section of the Naomalia or Majraut sub-caste of Goálás in Behar.

Temrakoti, a *thar* or section of Nepáli Brahmans.

Tendun, a sept of Rájputs in Behar.

Tengrá, a section of Binjhiás in Chota Nagpur.

Tenshába, a bird, a totemistic sept of Juángs in Orissa.

Tentuliá, a section of Pátnis in Behar.

Tentuliá, *Tetuli*, a sub-caste of Bágdis in Bengal, named after the tamarind tree, and apparently totemistic.

Teor, a sub-caste of Bágdis in Bengal and of Kaibarttas who still serve as fishermen and boatmen.

Tera-Hazár or **Birbandhi**, a sub-caste of Cheros in Palámau.

Terahghariá, a sub-caste of Kurmis in Behar.

Tesá, a sept of Bhumijs in Chota Nagpur.

Tesong, a synonym for Limbu.

Teswár, a section of Doms in Behar.

Tetenga, bloodsucker, a totemistic sept of Parhaiyas.

Teteteyin or *Bagiár*, a section of Khariás in Chota Nagpur.

Tetiá, a sept of the Chandrabansi division of Rájputs in Behar.

Tetihá, a *kul* or section of Bábhans in Behar.

Tetong, a *thar* or sept of Murmis in Darjiling.

Teva Pánya, a *thar* or section of Nepáli Brahmans.

Tewan Raja, a kind of bird, a totemistic sept of Mundas in Chota Nagpur.

Tewári, **Tiwári**, a title of Kámárs in Bengal; of Brahmans and Bábhans in Behar; a section of Sribástab Káyasths and of Magahiyá Doms in Behar.

Tháda, a *thar* or sept of Mangars in Darjiling.

Thahráit, a section of the Kamár sub-caste of Dosádhs in Behar.

Thaini, a small labouring caste of Nepal.

Thákur, a synonym for Brahman; a section of the Sribástab sub-caste of Káyasths in Behar; a hypergamous division of the Maghayá sub-caste of Barhis; a title of Kanaujiá Lohárs, Bábhans, Brahmans, Rájputs, Kámárs, and of Hajjáms or barbers in Behar; a title of a respectable class of Tipperahs in Hill Tipperah.

Thákurmairar, a *pur* or section of Sákadwipi Brahmans in Behar.

Thákurta, an honorary title of Káyasths in Bengal.

Thambden, the stay-at-home, a sept of the Phedáb sub-tribe of Limbus in Darjiling.

Thampái-Mech, a sub-tribe of Meches in the Darjiling Terai.

Thamsong, a sub-sept of the Thekim sept of Limbus in Darjiling.

Thándár, a title of Haris and Chandáls in Bengal who serve as a village watch.

Thápa, a title of Mangars in Darjiling.

Thápángi, a section of Kámis in Darjiling.

Tharait, a section of Maghaya Kumhárs in Behar.

Tháriáme-Tháriám, a *mul* of the Kásyapa section of Maithil Brahmans in Behar.

Tharmáit, a *dih* or local section of the Maghayá sub-caste of Telis in Behar. The system of exogamy among this sub-caste of Telis seems, however, either to be dying out or to be of recent introduction, for some of the Maghayás say they have no *dihs*, but merely prohibit marriage within nine *pirhis* or degrees of relationship.

Thâru, a non-Aryan tribe of Behar and Upper India, whose scattered settlements are met with all along the Himalayan terai, from the Kosi river in Purniah to the Sárda between Kumáon and Nepal. In an exhaustive account of the tribe published in the *Calcutta Review*,[1] Mr. Nesfield has the following remarks on their name:—

"Absurd etymologies have been given for the name *Thâru*, some deriving it from *tahre*, "they halted" (after their alleged flight into the forest), others from *tar hua*, "wet," in allusion to the swampy nature of the tract they live in. One writer derives it from *áthwáru*, 'an eighth-day serf.'[2] But this implies what is not true. The Thârus are remarkable for their indolence, aversion to service, and incapacity for sustained field labour; and they have never been in the position of serfs to any landlords. Had this been the case, they would have sunk long ago into the ranks of Arakhs, Pâsis, Chamârs, Koris, and other Hindu castes of the lowest rank, who serve as field labourers or bond slaves to landlords in the open plain, and have lost the free life of the forest, which Thârus still enjoy. Another etymology suggested is from *thár*, which in the colloquial dialect of the lowest classes, but not in the language of books, signifies forest; and thus *thâru* would mean 'man of the forest,' a name which correctly describes the status of the tribe. On the whole, however, it is safer not to seek for any Hindi etymology, but to consider the name as sprung from the language of the tribe itself, which is now for the most part obsolete. An aboriginal name, underived from any Sanskrit or neo-Sanskrit source, is the fit appellative to an aboriginal, casteless, and un-Brahmanised tribe, whose customs have been only slightly modified by contact with those of the Aryan invader."

Traditions of origin.

The origin of the Thârus has formed the subject of much controversy. The Rautár sub-tribe claim to be the descendants of certain Rájputs of Chittor, who quarrelled with their chief after his defeat by the Mahomedans, divested themselves of the sacred thread, and took to agricultural

[1] *Description of the Manners, Industries, and Religion of the Thâru and Bogsha Tribes of Upper India.* By John C. Nesfield, M.A., Oxon. January 1885.

[2] The first etymology is alluded to in *Oudh Gazetteer*, 1877, vol. ii, p. 126; the second, in *North-West Census Report*, 1867, vol. i, p. 61; the third (the author of which is Raja Siva Prasad, C.S.I.), in *North-West Provinces Gazetteer*, 1881, vol. vi, p. 358.

pursuits. Mr. Nesfield, however, points out that—"Some Thárus know nothing about this tradition, and those who do are not able to tell you whether it was the sack by Alaudin (A.D. 1303), or that by Bahâdur Shah (A.D. 1533), or that by Akbar (A.D. 1567). The story is absurd on the face of it. Not the slightest allusion to Thârus in connection with any of these events is made by the Mahommedan historians. The fiction of having come from Rajputâna was invented by some of the clans merely to raise themselves in their own and their neighbours' estimation. There is scarcely any hunting tribe or caste in Upper India which has not set up a similar claim."

Putting aside the hypothesis of Rájput descent as wholly untenable, we may, I think, conclude from the physical appearance of the tribe that they are simply an aboriginal race, whose ancestors bore rule at one time in the valley of the Ganges, and were gradually driven up into the sub-Himalayan forests by the expansion of the Aryan community. Thus within the last two or three centuries they have been brought into contact with the Nepalese, and their physiognomy "has acquired in some instances a slightly Mongolian cast, which shows itself chiefly, but not to a striking degree, in slanting eyes and high cheek-bones. In other respects their physical characteristics are of the strictly Indian type. They have long, wavy hair; a dark, almost a black, complexion; and as much hair on the face and body as is usual with other natives of India.[1] In stature, build, and gait they are distinctly Indian, and not Mongolian; nor have they any traditions whatever which connect their origin with Nepal. A century's intercourse with the people of the hills is more than sufficient to account for the slight Mongolian cast which some members of the tribe have acquired." They belong, in fact, to the large group of aboriginal races who are classed as Dravidian or Kolarian, according to the character of the language which they speak. The Thárus having lost their language cannot be affiliated to one or other of these linguistic families; but Mr. Nesfield's description of their appearance, which agrees substantially with the accounts given by other observers, leaves little room for doubting their non-Aryan descent. The relations said to have sprung up in comparatively recent times between the Thárus and the Nepalese find a tolerably complete parallel in the intermixture which has taken place between the Dhimáls of the Darjiling Terai and some of the lower castes of Nepal.

Internal structure.

The internal structure of the tribe, so far as I have been able to work it out, is shown in Appendix I. My own researches, however, extend only to Behar, and the enumeration of sub-tribes and septs is probably not complete even for that province. The nomadic habits of the Thárus, and the great extent of forest-clad area over which their settlements are scattered, must in the long run tend to promote the formation of sub-castes, and at the same time to make it difficult for the most careful

[1] A Native correspondent, to whom I am indebted for some interesting notes on the Thárus of Champáran, remarks on the scantiness of their beards and moustaches, but this peculiarity may have been due to crossing with Nepalese or Mech.

inquirer to give an absolutely correct account of the internal divisions of the community, which in all likelihood are liable to continual variations.

In Gorakpur, according to Mr. Nesfield, the Thárus divide themselves into two classes,—the **Purabi** or eastern, and the **Pachhami** or western, the latter of whom call themselves Chattris, and refuse to eat with members of the eastern branch. The western Thárus again are broken up into an upper (*barka*) and lower (*Chhotka*) division. Further west, in the Gonda district of Oudh, we find the **Dangaria** sub-tribe, who eat pork, and the **Kathàriá**, who affect to abstain from it. In Behar the **Rautár** rank the highest, owing possibly to the belief, which their name may have helped to encourage, that they are somehow connected with the Rájputs. Rautárs will not eat food cooked by members of the other sub-castes. **Chitwaniá** or **Chitauniá** Thárus follow the profession of weavers, and say that their ancestors were Joláhás, who gave water to the Raja of Chittor when he was out shooting, and obtained from him the boon that good Hindus should ever afterwards take water from their hands. This sub-tribe is more common in Nepal than in British territory. Its members have certain peculiar usages, the reasons for which I cannot ascertain. They perform no *sráddh* after a death, nor do their women go through any purificatory ceremony after child-birth. The bridal procession (*barát*) is limited to four or five persons, who go on their way in silence and employ no musicians to proclaim their errand. Among their minor deities they worship the Raja of Chittor, to whom they owe their promotion from the comparatively low status of Joláhá.

The septs appear to be either titular or territorial, and throw no light upon the early affinities. The rule of exogamy followed is the simple one that a man may not marry a woman belonging to the same sept (*bán*) as himself. The standard formula for reckoning prohibited degrees is also observed to four generations in the descending line on either side.

Marriage.

Both infant and adult-marriage are in force, and sexual intercourse before marriage is said to be tolerated by the Chitwaniá Thárus. The traditional amount of the bride-price is supposed to be Rs. 9, but this is liable to vary according to the circumstances of the family. The marriage ceremony is modelled on the ritual in vogue among the lower Hindu castes. Slight traces of the form of capture may perhaps be discerned in it, but these are not very marked among the Thárus of Behar. Brahmans officiate as priests, and the brother-in-law (*ganjuá*) of the bride usually takes a prominent part in the proceedings. In the Mardaniá and Chitwaniá sub-tribes the bridegroom's party, instead of being entertained by the bride's people, are expected to feast the latter for three days before the bride is produced. No second ceremony (*gauná*) is performed when the bride goes finally to live with her husband. When she is married as an adult, she goes to her husband at once, and in all cases I understand it is deemed proper for her to spend one night at her husband's house immediately after marriage. On the occasion of this visit she and the relations who accompany her are entertained at a feast called *dulhi bhatáwan*, 'giving rice to the bride,' which celebrates her formal admission into the sept to which her husband belongs. If she is still an infant, she is taken back next day to her parent's house by her brother-in-law, and remains there until she has attained sexual maturity.

Polygamy is permitted, and there appears to be no definite rule limiting the number of wives a man may have. Widows may marry again, and are subject to no special restrictions in their selection of a second husband. Divorce is allowed, and appears to be extremely common. The bond of wedlock is held in light esteem among the Thárus, who countenance a degree of sexual laxity analogous to that which prevails among many of the Nepalese castes, and generally among the sub-Himalayan races. Divorced women may marry again by the same ceremony as widows, and both classes are distinguished by the designation *urari*, or 'selected,' from women who were married as virgins by the full ritual. The social status of an *urari* wife is respectable, though slightly inferior to that of a *byáhi* wife. Even this position, however, is not accorded to her unless she is married with the consent of the relatives of her second husband, which is signified by the ceremony of *bhatáná*, or formally admitting her to the *jus cibi* of the household. Unless this is done she is called a *suraitin*, or concubine, and her husband cannot take water or cooked food from her hands without endangering his own standing in the family. *Bhatáná* is also necessary when any one has been debarred from social intercourse for an offence against the customs of the tribe. There seems to be some difference of practice among the Tháru sub-tribes in respect of the admission of women from a different sub-tribe. Some groups receive women from any other group, others only from certain specified groups, while Rautárs decline to admit any outsiders to the privilege of *bhatáná*, although they allow a woman of another sub-tribe to be kept by a Rautár man as a *suraitin*. Such women, however, have no rights as members of the family, and their children belong to their mother's sub-tribe.

Religion.

The religion of the Thárus is a compound of the mingled animism and Nature-worship characteristic of the aboriginal races and of elements borrowed from popular Hinduism. A prominent place in their pantheon is taken by the hero Rikheswar, whom I suspect to be identical with the Rikhmun of the Musahar-Bhuiyas. According to the legend in vogue among the Thárus of Kheri, this deified founder was a son of the renowned aboriginal King Raja Ben, whose fame is still rife in many of the oldest cities of Upper India and Behar as one who held the rank and title of *Chakravarti*, or universal emperor, in the olden time. Rikheshwar or Raksha was banished, it is said, from his father's court, and ordered with his band of male followers to seek for a new home in the north, from which they were never to return. Setting out on their wanderings, they took as wives any women whom they could steal or capture on the road, and in this way the Tháru tribe was founded. It was not till they had reached the sub-Himalayan forest in which they still dwell that they decided to rest and settle. The soul of Raksha is still believed to hover among the people of his tribe. Just as in ancient days he led them safely through the wide wilderness into a new and distant settlement, so in the present day he is said to be the guardian and guide of men travelling on a distant journey. No Tháru ever sets out from his village for such a purpose without first propitiating him with gifts and promising him a sumptuous feast of flesh, milk, and wine on his return. His presence is represented by a mound of mud, with a stone fixed in the middle; and he delights in seeing the head of a live capon dashed against this stone, and to feel its blood trickling down the side. One peculiarity of this god is that he is deaf,—an emblem of his antiquity; and hence vows and prayers are addressed to him in a stentorian tone of voice. The title *gurua*, which is generally prefixed to his name, implies that during his residence on earth he was famous as a wizard or medicine-man, and acquired through this means the kingship or leadership of his tribe.

The animistic element in the Tháru faith being represented by Rikheswar, we may perhaps trace a mangled survival of Nature-worship in two other deities of some importance, to whom Thárus address their vows. One is Madadeo, the god of intoxicating liquor, especially of the rice-wine made by themselves; the other is Dharchandi, the patroness of cattle, though her name would imply that she was at first intended to impersonate the earth. Her shrine, like those of the other deities already named, is a mound of clay. The mound dedicated to Dharchandi is studded with short wooden crosses, on which rice, pulse, and other produce of the fields are offered, and always on plates of leaf. Her shrine is so placed that all the cattle of the village, together with the swine, sheep, and goats, pass it on going out to graze, and repass it on their return. When the cattle sicken or die, larger and more valuable offerings are made. Neither of these deities is known or worshipped by other natives of Upper India.

Fowls are offered to Dharchandi; he-goats to Mari, the patron goddess of Kanjars and, according to Mr. Nesfield, identical with Káli. This, however, seems not to be the case in Behar. In Champáran Kua is worshipped as a village deity by casting sweetmeats down a well (*kuá*) and smearing vermilion on its rim. All these primitive deities, however, are rapidly losing ground in the estimation of the people, and giving way to the more popular worship of Siva and his consort Káli. It is likely enough that both of these are themselves merely elaborated forms of aboriginal objects of worship, which may well have been familiar to an earlier generation of Thárus. But Siva and Kali, as now revered by the tribe, have clearly been borrowed at quite a recent date from the Hindus, and cannot be regarded as indigenous deities.

The goddess who presides over life and death, and whom the Thárus believe to be the supreme power in the universe, is Kâlikâ,—one of the numerous forms of Devi, Durgâ, or Kâli, at whose name all India trembles, especially the low castes and the casteless tribes, amongst whom she originally sprung. Medicine-men look to Kâlikâ as the special patroness of their art. To the fair sex she is the goddess of parturition, and her aid is especially invoked by women who have had no children. All classes combine to give her a periodical ovation, accompanied with much dancing, banqueting, and drinking of wine at about the middle of October. Thárus also take part in the huge animal sacrifice performed at her celebrated altar in Devi Patan (Gonda district). Such is her thirst for blood, that at this time 20 buffaloes, 250 goats, and 250 pigs are slaughtered daily for ten days continuously. The sacrifice is vicarious, the blood of buffaloes, etc., being intended as a substitute for that of human victims. This loathsome festival is thronged with visitors from the plains of India and from the hills of Nepal, Sikkim, and Bhotan.

"Another deity revered by Thârus, and, like Kâlikâ, of indigenous or non-Aryan origin, is her consort Siva, known chiefly amongst Thârus by the name of Bhairava, the Terrible, or Thakur, the Lord, and amongst Hindus by that of Mahadev, the great god. He, like his spouse, is a god of destruction, and thirsts for blood; but he is chiefly worshipped by Thârus as the author of reproduction, of which a stone lingam, as amongst Hindus, is sometimes made the symbol. It is more usual, however, for a Thâru to erect a mud mound in front of his house and fix an upright pole in its centre to represent the presence of this phallic divinity."

Although modern Hinduism is fast displacing the earlier gods of the Tháru religion, it seems probable that the principles of their primitive belief will long survive in the strong fear of evil spirits which continually haunts the tribe. It is to the action of these spirits that fever, ague, cough, dysentery, fainting, headache, madness, bad dreams, and pain of all kinds are ascribed. In fact, the Thárus have no conception of natural disease, and no belief in natural death, except what is faintly conceived to be the result of natural decay. Their state, therefore, would be one of utter helplessness were it not for the reputed skill of medicine-men or sorcerers, who profess to have the power to control the spirits of the air or to interpret their grievances and wants. In the Tháru language these men are called *bararar;* but the titles of Guru, Guruâ, Bhagat, Nyotya, Ojhait, all of which are borrowed from Hindi, are now in common use, though even of these the last two are probably of aboriginal or non-Sanskrit origin. The power of the medicine-man is tremendous. He has a host of liege spirits at his command. Not only can he expel a fiend from the body of the sufferer, but he can produce suffering or death by driving a malignant spirit into the body of his foe. In order to exorcise an evil spirit, he holds in his left hand some ashes of cowdung, or grains of mustard seed, or wild nuts, and after breathing some mystical virtue into them by the utterance of a spell, he causes the patient to eat them, or has them attached to his arm. One of the spells uttered at such times is as follows. It is addressed to Kâlikâ, the Tháru goddess of death and patroness of the magical art:—

Gur hai gur sair Gur tantra mantra Gur: Lakhai niranjan; toka sohai phulka bhâr; Hamka sohai gun vidyâ kai bhâr: Yahân kai vidyâ nahin, Kamru Kâm kai vidyâ. Jaise vidyâ Kamru Kâm kai lâgai, waise vidyâ lâgai mor.

The language is that of bad and scarcely intelligible Hindi, and might be rendered thus :—

"The Guru (Kâlikâ) is great, she is everything, she is *tantra* "(magic by deeds), she is *mantra* (magic by words). She points out "the way to relief. Thou (oh Kâlikâ) deservest to be heaped with "flowers. I too deserve to be heaped with secret wisdom,—the wisdom "of Kamru Kâm, not the wisdom of this country. Whatever "effects the knowledge of Kamru Kâm produces, such effects let my "knowledge produce also."

Disposal of the dead.

"The burial rites of Thárus are of various kinds. Sepulture or earth-burial seems to have been the original custom; but the Hindu rite of cremation has now become common in many clans, except in the case of persons who have died of cholera or small-pox; and these are invariably buried in the earth. After cremation the ashes are scattered on the nearest river. Before, however, the corpse has been disposed of by either rite, it is usual to paint it with vermilion and expose it for one night on a mound outside the house. From this mound, as from a stronghold, the spirit of the dead is supposed to scare away wild animals from the corpse. Whether the body is buried or burnt, the ceremony is always performed on the southern side of the village—a notion probably borrowed from Hindus, who consider that the north is the region commonly frequented by divine spirits, and the south by human souls. The man who puts the first fire to the funeral pyre is considered to be unclean, from having brought himself within dangerous reach of the contagion of death. He is therefore kept at a distance for ten days after cremation, and compelled to live entirely alone.". . . . ." On the expiry of the tenth day (or the thirteenth, as some Thârus relate), the friends of the deceased meet at the house where he died, and after undergoing the ceremony of shaving they hold 'a feast of the dead.' The banquet prepared for this purpose consists of cooked flesh and wine, the scent and smoke of which are intended to refresh the departed soul: the solid parts—that is, the flesh and wine themselves—are consumed by the living."

"In certain rare cases the burial rite is performed in a manner distinct from either of those already described. A man noted above his fellows for wisdom in counsel, bravery in the chase, or knowledge of the magical and medicinal arts, is buried under the floor of the house in which he was living before his spirit departed. The house thenceforth becomes a temple, and ceases to be used as a dwelling place for man. The soul of the dead becomes its occupant, and it lives there to bless those whom it has left behind. At periods of three or six months after the death, the friends and neighbours of the deceased assemble around his grave or temple and make an effigy in clay, parts of which are painted in various colours, intended to reproduce the appearance of resuscitated life. His worshippers fall down weeping and wailing before the image, and place offerings of cooked flesh and wine at its feet. Presently, at a given signal, as soon as the soul of the dead is believed to have been propitiated by the scent of roast meat and the fumes of wine, they commence to dance and sing with every demonstration of joy; and the proceedings of the day are closed with consuming the solid parts of the offerings."

Social status.

The Thárus stand wholly outside of the Hindu caste organization, and their social status cannot be defined by any of the ordinary standards. No orthodox Hindu will eat with a Tháru or take water from his hands, and by the higher castes his mere touch would be deemed pollution. This comparatively degraded position is, however, due in great measure to the nomadic habits of the tribe, and to the fact that they come very little into contact with settled Hindu communities. Thárus follow the forest; their typical village is a line of huts in the middle of a clearing, and their favourite mode of husbandry was until lately the *jhum* method of burning the jungle and planting a crop in the ashes. The scanty crops obtained in this fashion are eked out by hunting and fishing, by gathering forest fruits and vegetables, and by grazing cows and buffaloes. Avoiding the larger villages of the plains, they live their own life on the outskirts of Hindu civilization, and no place has as yet been allotted in the Hindu social system. "Every little village," says Mr. Nesfield, "is a self-governing community. Disputes are decided by a council of elders; and this is sometimes presided over by a headman, who in the Tháru language was formerly called *barwaik*, but who is now dubbed even by themselves with the ordinary Hindi title of *chaudhari*. The office of headman is not hereditary. The man selected is one whose age, experience, and knowledge of the magical and medicinal arts entitle him to more respect than the rest; and he acquires the status of headman by tacit consent, and not by formal election. The decisions of the council or the headman are obeyed unreservedly, and there is no such thing known as a Tháru taking a fellow tribesman before a tribunal outside his own community. Litigation between Thárus and Hindus is equally unknown. Among themselves the Thárus are for the most part a peaceful and good-natured race, following without question, as if by a law of nature, the customs and maxims of their ancestors." Notwithstanding their comparative isolation, their customs show many signs of the influence of Hindu example. Their religious observances tend unmistakeably towards Sivaism; their marriage ceremony is framed on a Hindu model; they revere the cow, and scrupulously abstain from eating beef. Their ultimate reception into the standard social system seems therefore merely to be a question of time. In other respects their practice in matters of food falls short of the orthodox standard. They eat pigs and fowls, and make no distinction between the clean and unclean species of fish. Field-rats they will cook when pressed for food, and the porcupine (*sáhi*) is thought a delicacy, because his flesh resembles that of the pig. Mr. Nesfield mentions that when their stock of meat becomes larger than they can consume at once, they preserve it by cutting it into strips and drying it in the sun.

Occupation.

As agriculturists they are still for the most part in the migratory stage, cultivating the land on which they have put up their temporary houses till it has given proof of exhaustion, and then moving off to fresh grounds to make a new clearance. Formerly it was their custom not to crop the same land for more than two years together. But this is now no longer the case. The Government conservancy laws, which have come into force of late, have interfered very seriously with their freedom in the selection of new sites; and hence the present tendency of the tribe is either to move up into Nepal territory or to remain below for a longer period in the same place. The crop in which Thárus chiefly delight is rice—the grain best suited to the swampy nature of their fields and to the heavy rainfall of the months between June and October. The coarse red rice called *sáthi* is the quality preferred. In the rainless months they chiefly grow peas, a small black grain called *kodo*, and the pulse called *arhar*. Such crops require occasional irrigation; and this is effected, not by drawing water from wells or from tanks and marshes and conveying it into the fields through artificial channels, as is the custom of Hindu cultivators, but by the rough-and-ready process of damming up the nearest rivulet and thus inundating the crop.

The women do the largest share of the sowing, weeding, and harvesting, while the men engage in hunting, fishing, etc., which they consider the proper calling of their sex. Such has been the invariable instinct of savage tribes both in India and elsewhere. The men have an intense repugnance to regular manual labour, and nothing will induce them to hire themselves out as labourers to Hindu landlords. The only kind of service which a Tháru will undertake is that of elephant-driver to some neighbouring princelet or râja. Their skill as elephant-drivers is admitted everywhere; and latterly they have acquired the art of catching wild elephants from the forest and taming them for the prince who employs them.

The only kinds of art or manufacture which Thárus can be said to possess are the manipulation of leaves, reeds, and fibres, and a rude kind of carpentry. The latter is exemplified in making the wooden part of the plough, in shaping the handles of tools, dove-tailing the corners of wells, and in fixing up the sides and roofs and floors of their houses. The former is an accomplishment common to backward races in every part of the world, wherever the materials exist; and here in India it is practised by all the low castes of Hindus (Bhars, Pâsis, Bhangis, Bâris, Dharkars, etc.) whose stage of culture is scarcely, if at all, raised above that of the casteless tribes. The Thárus make strong and durable mats out of the fine *bankas* grass, which they gather in large quantities from the lower ranges of the hills in the first quarter of the year. Excellent twine and rope are made from the same material; and such twine is used for the manufacture of fishing nets, nooses, and snares, for drawing water from the well, for tethering cattle, and many other purposes. Not less skilled are they in making the funnel-shaped baskets in which fish are caught, or in thatching the roofs of their houses. They have even invented a kind of umbrella made of cane and mat work; so great is their aversion to the sun and to the open plains. For plates and drinking cups they skewer large leaves together to the shape required for either purpose; and for drawing and keeping water they use a hollowed gourd or tomri. Some who are better off than others use vessels made of clay or brass; but these can only be obtained from Kumhârs (potters) and Thateras (braziers), both of whom are Hindu castes; for there is no such thing as home-made pottery or brass work amongst the Thâru tribe.

The following statement shows the number and distribution of Thárus in 1872 and 1881:—

District.	1872.	1881.	District.	1872.	1881.
Darjiling	......	118	Champaran	21,450	18,896
Darbhanga	320	915	Bhágalpur	48	112
Saran	......	2	Purniah	46	1,510

Thâther or *Thathera*, a sub-caste of Kándus in Behar; a section of the Banodhiá and Jaiswár Halwáis in Behar.

Thatherá, *Thatheri*, a brazier; in Shahabad also called Kaserá, which properly means a brass founder. See **Kaserá**.

Tháthung, a *thar* or sept of Gurungs in Darjiling.

Thawai, a synonyn for *raj mistiri* or mason, in use in Saran and South Champaran.

Thazœpá, a *rui* or sept of the Ruichhung sub-tribe of Dejong Lhoris or Bhotias of the south.

Theguba, the son of the cliff, a sept of the Phedáb sub-tribe of Limbus in Darjiling.

Thehbeh, a sept of the Yangorup sub-tribe of Limbus. This is an eponymous *thar* named after Thehbeh, son of Srijanga, the powerful chief of the tribe, since deified, who fought against Prithi Náráyan, the founder of the present ruling dynasty of Nepal.

Thek, a synonym for Chakmá.

Thekim, he who works in wicker, including the sub-septs (*a*) Meongba, (*b*) Thamsong, (*c*) Chobegu, (*d*) Petehhimba, (*e*) Angbu, the forest-dweller, (*f*) Yakten, formerly doctors—a sept of the Pánthar sub-tribe of Limbus in Darjiling.

Thekra, a section of Binjhiás in Chota Nagpur.

Themjáni, a *thar* or sept of Gurungs in Darjiling.

Thengáit, a section of the Dhusiá sub-caste of Chamárs in Behar.

Thenglahbo, the native of Thenglah, a sept of the Ahtharai sub-tribe of Limbus in Darjiling.

Theni, a section of Utkal or Orissa Brahmans.

Thero, *Tharua*, a sub-tribe of Santáls in the south of Manbhum who employ Brahmans and have adopted portions of the Hindu ritual.

Theya, a sept of Chakmás in the Hill Tracts of Chittagong.

Thholáchá, a *thar* or sept of Sunuwárs in Darjiling.

Thing, a section of Murmis in Darjiling.

Thingal, a *gotra* or section of Agarwáls.

Thithio, a bird with long legs, a totemistic sept of Mundas in Chota Nagpur.

Thobukya, he who has skin disease, a sept of the Phedáb sub-tribe of Limbus in Darjiling.

Thogleng, the suicide, a sept of the Chhothar sub-tribe of Limbus in Darjiling.

Thogphelagu, he who wears the rhododendron flower, a sept of the Charkhola sub-tribe of Limbus in Darjiling.

Thokar, a section of Murmis in Darjiling.

Thokcháki, a *thar* or sept of Mangars in Darjiling.

Thollong, the ragged one, a sept of the Miákhola sub-tribe of Limbus in Darjiling.

Tholochá, a *thar* or sept of Sunuwárs in Darjiling.

Thomi, a synonym for Mangar.

Thongtha, *Thongcha*, or *Jumiá Magh*, a sub-tribe of Maghs in the Hill Tracts of Chittagong.

Thoreliá, a section of the Banodhiá and Jaiswár Kalwárs in Behar.

Thukrán, a section of Goálás in the North-Western Provinces and Behar.

Thulung, a *thar* or sept of Khambus in Darjiling.

Thumuchá, a *thar* or sept of Sunuwárs in Darjiling.

Thungong-hepta, a sept of the Phágu sub-tribe of Yakhas in Darjiling.

Thupra, a sept of the Phágu sub-tribe of Yakhas in Darjiling.

Thupuku, a sept of the Yangorup sub-tribe of Limbus in Darjiling.

Thup-yumah, name of a place, a sept of the Tambrkhola sub-tribe of Limbus in Darjiling.

Tiar, a synonym for Tiyar a sub-caste of Kewats in Orissa.

Tiár, a sept of Rájputs in Behar.

Tiar, *Teor*, a sub-caste of Malláhs in Behar.

Tiar or Dalal, a group of the Rájbansi sub-caste of Kochhs in Northern Bengal.

Tig, a monkey, which is the totem of a section of Oraon-Dhángars settled for several generations in North Bhagalpur.

Tihu, a sept of Hos in Singbhum.

Tijra, a synonym for Mirshikár.

Tikaur, a sub-caste of Brahmans in Behar.

Tikká, a sub-sept of the Murmu sept of Santáls.

Tiklihár, *Trijattá*, or *Maghaiya Brahman*, a caste employed in making *tiklis*, the spangles, wafers, or glass patches worn upon the forehead by women. They permit widow-marriage and rank socially among the serving castes, such as Kahárs. In Patna the term *tiklihár* denotes merely the occupation described above, which is followed by Mahomedans.

Tilachhwar, a section of Bábhans in Behar.

Tiláiwár, a *mul* of the Sándil section of Maithil Brahmans in Behar.

Tilakchandi, a sept of Rájputs in Behar.

Tilak Dás, a sub-caste of Tiyars in Eastern Bengal; a sect of Vaishnavs who follow the tenets of Tilak-dás.

Tilatwár, a *mul* or section of the Naomulia or Majraut sub-caste of Goálás in Behar.

Tilautá, a sept of the Suryabansi sub-tribe of Rájputs in Behar.

Tilding, a sept of Limbus in Darjiling.

Tili, a worker in *til* (*sesamum orientale*), a synonym for Teli.

Tiliá, a section of the Baranwár sub-caste of Baniyás in Behar.

Timilsiná, a *thar* of the Mautkaha *gotra* of Nepáli Brahmans.

Tin, a sept of Hos in Singbhum.

Tinai Prabarái, a *thar* of the Basishtha *gotra* of Nepáli Brahmans.

Tindiha, a section of Bantariá Kándus in Behar.

Tingal, a *gotra* or section of Agarwáls.

Tingilmung, a sept of Lepchas in Darjiling.

Tinmuliá Madhesia, a sub-caste of Halwáis in Behar.

Tinriár, a section of the Amashta sub-caste of Káyasths in Behar.

Tior, a synonym for Tiyar.

Tipperah, *Tiprá*, *Mrung*, a wandering tribe of Hill Tipperah and the Chittagong Hill Tracts, who live by the *jhúm* cultivation described in the article on the Magh tribe. Lewin identifies them with the Mrungs of Arrakan, who, according to Colonel Phayre, believe themselves to be the descendants of persons carried away from Tipperah by the Arrakan kings. The Maghs speak of the entire tribe by the name Mrung, and do not use the Bengali word Tipperah. Members of the Tipperah tribe have no general name for their race, and when speaking his own language a man describes himself by mentioning the sept to which he belongs. When speaking Bengali, however, he would say he was a Tipperah. It seems to follow from this that the term Tipperah is not a genuine tribal name, but a designation conferred by outsiders by reason of the tribe being specially numerous in Hill Tipperah. Whether this was their original habitat or not is uncertain, and some have supposed that they came from Manipur. To attempt to trace the earliest home of a wandering tribe who live by *jhúm* cultivation and have neither written records nor definite oral traditions must always be a somewhat hopeless task, and the most reasonable view of the matter seems to be that taken by Friedrich Müller and other German ethnologists, who class all the wild tribes of the Chittagong and Tipperah Hills under the head Lohitic, a word which denotes some sort of connexion with the Brahmaputra river, and describe them in general terms as standing in the same ethnic relation to the Burmese as the Himalayan

Origin.

races do to the Tibetans.[1] The classification into Toungtha and Khyoungtha, hill-people and river-people, adopted by Captain Lewin, however convenient for local use, fails, as Professor Virchow[2] has observed, to bring out the true racial affinities of the various tribes.

Internal structure.

The Tipperahs are described in a survey report by Mr. H. J. Reynolds as having strongly-marked Mongolian features, with flat faces and thick lips. They are of much the same stature as Bengalis, but their frames are far more muscular and strongly made. Many of them have fair complexions, scarcely darker than a swarthy European. The tribe is divided into a number of septs, which are shown in the Appendix. They appear to be exogamous, but on this point there is some difference of opinion. I have only been able to discover the meaning of one sept name, Kákulu, a kind of gourd, and with regard to this no one could tell me whether the members of the Kákulu sept were forbidden to eat this gourd or were subject to any kind of taboo in respect of it. The point seems to demand further inquiry in the Hill Tracts by some one thoroughly acquainted with the language of the tribe. The Riáng sept serve as palanquin-bearers, and are said to be looked down upon by the others; but it does not appear that they have on this account been excluded from the right of intermarriage with other septs. The Mahárájas of Hill Tipperah, who now put forward an untenable claim to be Rájputs, are believed to belong to the Áfang and Jumátya septs, the members of which frequently call themselves Rájbansi by way of recalling their relationship to the royal family. The Káli sept furnish the guards of the chief.

Intermarriage.

Tipperahs admit into their tribe Lushais, Maghs, and Hindus. The ceremony of admission consists simply of a feast given by the new member, at which a pig is served up and a huge quantity of drink consumed. The proselyte declares himself to have entered the tribe, and is treated thenceforth as if he had been a Tipperah by birth. The liquors drunk on these and similar occasions are *khung* (ferment from rice), *sipá* (fermented from *birni*), and arrack (distilled from rice).

Marriage.

Adult-marriage is the universal rule, and "great freedom of intercourse is allowed between the sexes, but a Tipperah girl is never known to go astray out of her own clan. An illegitimate birth, also, is hardly known among them, for the simple reason that should a girl become *enciente* her lover has to marry her. The girls are totally free from the prudery that distinguishes Mahomedan and Hindu women, and they have an open, frank manner, combined with a womanly modesty that is attractive. At a marriage there is no particular ceremony, but a great deal of drinking and dancing. A pig is killed as a sacrifice to the deities of the wood and stream, the crowning point of the affair being this: the girl's mother pours out a glass of

---

[1] F. Müller, *Allgemeine Ethnographie*, p. 405

[2] Riebeck's *Chittagong Hill-Tribes, Anthropological Remarks.*

liquor and gives it to her daughter, who goes and sits on her lover's knee, drinks half, and gives him the other half; they afterwards crook together their little fingers. If a match be made with the consent of the parents, the young man has to serve three years in his father-in-law's house before he obtains his wife or is formally married. During the period of probation his sweetheart is to all intents and purposes a wife to him. On the wedding night, however, the bridegroom has to sleep with his wife surreptitiously, entering the house by stealth and leaving it before dawn. He then absents himself for four days, during which time he makes a round of visits among all his friends. On the fourth day he is escorted back with great ceremony, and has to give another feast to his *cortége*. A Tipperah widow may remarry if it so seems good to her. Every lad before marriage has his sweetheart, and he cohabits with her whenever opportunity serves. This, however, is without the knowledge of the elders.

"Divorce," says Major Lewin, "can be obtained among the Tipperahs, as among all the hill tribes, on the adjudication of a jury of village elders. One such case I remember to have seen. The divorce was sued for by the wife on the grounds of habitual cruelty. The jury deliberated and found that the cruelty was proved, and that the divorce should be granted. Some check, however, they determined, must be put upon the woman, or otherwise every wife would complain if her husband raised his little finger at her. Accordingly they gave sentence that the divorce was granted, but that as the woman was wrong to insist upon abandoning her lawful husband, she should give up all her silver ornaments to him, pay a fine of thirty rupees, and provide a pig with trimmings, in the shape of ardent spirits, to be discussed by the jury."

Religion.

The religion of the Tipperahs is a debased form of Hinduism. They offer to Káli black goats, rice, plantains, sweetmeats, areca nut, curds, red lead, etc. The goddess has no image, but is represented for sacrificial purposes by a round lump of clay, the edges of which are drawn out into four points or legs, so that the whole, seen from above, bears a rough resemblance to sea-urchin with four arms. Satya-Náráyan is also worshipped, but in his case the offerings consist only of fruits or flowers. The tribe do not employ Brahmans, but have priests, or rather exorcists, of their own, called *Auchái*, whose office is hereditary.

Disposal of the dead.

"When a Tipperah dies, his body is immediately removed from within the house to the open air. A fowl is killed and placed with some rice at the dead man's feet. The body is burnt at the water side. At the spot where the body was first laid out, the deceased's relatives kill a cock every morning for seven days, and leave it there with some rice as an offering to the manes of the dead. A month after death a like offering is made at the place of cremation, and this is occasionally repeated for a year. The ashes are deposited on a hill in a small hut built for the purpose, in which are also placed the dead man's weapons,—a spear, *dáos* of two sorts (one his fighting *dáo*, the other his every-day bread-winner), arrow heads, his metal-stemmed pipe, earrings, and ornaments. The place is held sacred."

In connection with the beliefs of the Tipperahs regarding the spirits of the dead, Major Lewin speaks of a curious practice. He says:—"We were travelling once through the jungles, and the path led across a small streamlet. Here I observed a white thread stretched from one side to the other, bridging the stream. On inquiring the reason of this it appeared that a man had died away from his home in a distant village; his friends had gone thither and performed his obsequies, after which it was supposed that the dead man's spirit would accompany them back to his former abode. Without assistance, however, spirits are unable to cross running water; therefore the stream here had been bridged in the manner aforesaid."

Another use of the white thread mentioned by Lewin as practised by the Tipperahs and most of the hill races seems to be a survival of the primitive animistic belief which attributes all disease to the action of malevolent spirits, who nevertheless can be propitiated by the exorcist who knows the proper means of turning away their wrath. When an epidemic breaks out in a village, the Tipperahs and many other hill tribes call in an *Áuchâi* to appease the demon of sickness by a sacrifice. The entire village is encircled with a newly-spun white thread, and the blood of the animal sacrificed is freely sprinkled about. This is followed by careful sweeping and cleansing, and the houses and gates are decorated with green boughs. For three days afterwards the thread is maintained unbroken, and no one is allowed to enter or leave the village. The theory seems to be that if the demon who presides over the malady can be kept at bay for that time, he will go away disappointed, while a breach of the quarantine or *khang* would lead to a renewal of the outbreak.

Dress.

"The dress of the Tipperahs," says Lewin, "is of the simplest description. Among the men a thick turban is worn, and a narrow piece of home-spun cloth, with a fringed end hanging down in front and rear, passes once round the waist and between the legs. In the cold season they wear a rudely-sewn jacket. The males wear silver earrings, crescent-shaped, with little silver pendants on the outer edge. The dress of the women is equally unornate. The petticoat is short, reaching a little below the knee, and made of very coarse cotton stuff of their own manufacture. It is striped in colours of red and blue. If the woman be married, this petticoat will form her whole costume; but the unmarried girls cover the breast with a gaily-dyed cloth with fringed ends. The women never cover their heads; they wear earrings like the men; but in addition to this ornament they distend the lobe of the ear to the size of half a crown by the insertion of a concave-edged ring of silver, placed, not through, but in, the lobe. Both sexes have long, black, abundant hair, which is worn in a knot at the back of the head. The use of false hair is common among them, especially the women. The meshes of false hair are woven in among the back hair to make the knot look larger."

The following statement shows the number and distribution of the Tipperah tribe in 1872 and 1881 :—

District.	1872.	1881.	District.	1872.	1881.
Kuch Behar	......	1,126	Chittagong	45	225
Dacca	88	47	Noakhali	232	16
Faridpur	......	101	Tipperah	3,004	1,896
Bakarganj	217	45	Hill Tracts	11,800	15,954

Tipperah-Suryabansi, also called Rajbansi—a mixed class of Bengalis and Tipperahs.

Tipriati, a section of the Maghayá sub-caste of Barhis in Behar.

Tirango, a wild bird, a totemistic sept of Mundas in Chota Nagpur.

Tirhutiá, a sub-caste of barbers; of Hindu Joláhás (Tatwa or Tánti); and of Kumhárs in Behar, who say they can intermarry with the Maghayá and Desi sub-castes. The Maghayás, however, allege that all the sub-castes are strictly endogamous; a sub-caste of Thatherá or brass-chaser and of Láheris, Telis, and Támbulis in Behar.

Tirhutiá or *Chiraut*, a sub-caste of Dhánuks, Doms, and Hajjáms in Behar.

Tirhutiá or **Maithil,** a territorial division of Brahmans in Behar.

Tirkar, a maker of bows and arrows; a title of Doms; a title of Byádhs who originally killed birds and beasts and lived on meat obtained by chase, at present most of them have taken to agriculture.

Tirki, bull, a totemistic sept of Goálás, Asuras, Chamárs, Kharwars, Lohars, Mundas, Oraons, and Nágeswars in Chota Nagpur who cannot touch any cattle after eyes open; a section of Ghásis and Goráits; a totemistic section of Doms and Turis implying a mouse.

Tirkiar, tree-mice, a totemistic sept of Mundas in Chota Nagpur.

Tirkoár, a section of Khariás in Chota Nagpur.

Tirkuar, fruit, a totemistic sept of Oraons and Turis in Chota Nagpur.

Tiro, a small bird, a totemistic sept of Mundas in Chota Nagpur.

Tirsuliá, a sub-caste of Pásis in Behar.

Tirtha, a sect of Dasnámi Sannyásis.

Tirthjátri, a pilgrim.

Tirtia, a bird, a totemistic sept of Mundas and Oraons in Chota Nagpur.

Tiru, a kind of bird or fish, a totemistic sept of Mundas and Oraons in Chota Nagpur.

Tiruá, a section of Kámis in Darjiling.

Tiruar, arrow, a sept of Kharwars in Chota Nagpur; a section of Kurmis in Behar.

Tiruhar, a bird, a totemistic sept of Mundas in Chota Nagpur

Tirusiá, a *mul* or section of Kasarwáni Baniyás in Behar.

Tisbaryá or *Teswár*, a section of the Pachainyá sub-caste of Doms in Behar.

Tisor, a section of the Sátmuliá Maghayá sub-caste of Kándus in Behar.

Tiswar, a *mul* or section of the Maghayá sub-caste of Koiris in Behar.

Titehiá, a section of Bábhans in Behar.

Tithi, a bird, a totemistic sept of Oraons in Chota Nagpur.

Titiá Bámbár, a *mul* or section of the Naomuliá or Majraut sub-caste of Goálás in Behar.

Titipi, a totemistic sept of Bediás in Chota Nagpur, signifying a night bird.

Tititihu, a section of Khariás in Chota Nagpur.

Tittal, a *gotra* or section of Agarwáls.

Titung, a section of Murmis in Darjiling.

Tiwári, see **Tewári**.

Tiyar, *Tiar*, *Tior*, *Rájbansi*, *Machhuá*, a Dravidian boating and fishing caste of Bengal and Behar, whom Mr. Beames seems disposed to identify with the Dhimar, a sub-caste of the Káhárs. It may be doubted, however, whether this opinion rests upon any surer basis than similarity of name and occupation; and the names appear to be distinct, Tiyar being a corruption of the Sanskrit *tivara*, 'a hunter,' while Dhimar is derived from Sanskrit *dhivara*, 'a fisherman.' The two groups, moreover, show marked differences of complexion and physical type. The Dhimar have a light-brown skin and fairly well-cut features, and are not noticeably below the average stature of Hindus of the middle class. The Tiyars, on the other hand, according to Dr. Wise, who had special opportunities of observing them, are short and muscular, with prominent cheek-bones, dark-brown—almost black—complexions, thick and generally projecting lips, and long coarse hair, worn in a cue, which has often a reddish tinge towards the tip—a peculiarity common to them and other low castes, which, although in the first instance produced by exposure, is now, if not hereditary, at least characteristic. In Eastern Bengal, where no subdivisions exist, the Tiyars call themselves **Ráj-bansi**, or sometimes, as in Maimansinh, **Tilak Dás**, while those living on the Ganges lay claim to the title of **Suraj-bansi**. According to Buchanan, the Tiyars of Bhagalpur are divided into **Báman-jagya**, who are cultivators and clean Sudrás, and **Govaríya**, who fish, eat pork, drink spirits, and are outcastes. Wherever they are regarded as pure, a Dasnámi ascetic acts as guru and a Maithil Brahman as purohit; when impure, a Gosáin of Bengal is guru, and a Patit or degraded Brahman is purohit.

Origin.

Internal structure.

The sections of the Tiyars shown in the Appendix throw no light on the origin of the caste. It is indeed doubtful whether the section-names are in general use for the purpose of enforcing the practice of exogamy; and I believe that practice, at least in its primitive form, to have been abandoned in favour of the more modern system of simply specifying the relations whom a man or woman may not marry. For this purpose they make use of the standard formula *mamerá*, *chacherá*, etc., calculated to five generations in the descending line on the male side and three generations on the female.

Marriage.

Girls are usually married as infants, but cases sometimes occur in which, owing to the poverty of her parents, a girl's marriage is deferred until she has passed the age of puberty. Polygamy is permitted, and in theory at least there are no restrictions on the number of wives a man may have. In Behar a widow may marry a second time. She is not obliged to marry her late husband's younger brother, if such a relative exist, but it is considered a very proper thing for her to do so; and the fact that he has a right to the custody of the children by the first husband tends as a rule to induce the widow to agree to the arrangement. In Bengal widows never marry, but earn a livelihood by selling fish, by manufacturing string, and such like petty industries. Those who find such an existence too monotonous, and desire a change of life and scene, usually join one of the mendicant orders of the Vaishnava sect. In the matter of divorce the practice of the caste seems to vary. Bengal Tiyars do not recognize it at all, while in Behar it is permitted only with the sanction of the caste pancháyat, a well-organized body presided over by a headman (*manjhan*), whose jurisdiction is supposed to comprise the traditional number of twenty-two villages. Each *manjhan* has under him a *chharidár* or stick-bearer, whose business it is to procure the attendance of persons summoned to appear before the pancháyat, and generally to carry out the orders of the *manjhan*.

Among the Tiyars of Bengal three hypergamous groups are recognized, the highest being the Pradhán, or chief families; next the Parámániks; while the rest go to form the Gana, or lower orders. The last can only intermarry with the higher by paying a large sum of money, the father receiving in all cases money for his daughter, so that female children are more valued than among the true Hindus. Widows never marry, but either earn a livelihood by selling fish, by manufacturing string, or, if desirous of change of life and scene, by becoming Boistubis (Vaishnavis).

Religion.

Tiyars are almost to a man Vaishnava in creed, their religious ceremonies being always held beneath trees. The seorhá (*Trophis aspera*), a very common scrubby plant, is held in especial veneration by them, and its shade is usually selected as the scene of their worship; but should this tree be not at hand, the nim, bel, or gujáli (*Shorea robusta*) forms an efficient substitute. Hindustáni Tiyars sacrifice a goat to Káli on the Diwáli, but the animal, instead of being decapitated in the orthodox Hindu way, is stabbed with a sharp-pointed piece of wood —a practice universal among the aboriginal races of India, after which, as with the Dosádhs, the flesh is eaten by the worshippers. Bengali Tiyars, on the other hand, sacrifice a swine to Bura-Buri on the Paus (December–January) Sankránti, slaughtering it in the same way as their Hindustani brethren. They do not, however, eat the flesh. At the Gangá festival in Jeth (May) they offer a white kid, pigeon and milk to the spirit of the river, and adore with great solemnity Manasá Devi in the month of Srávan (July-August).

As was natural, the Tiyars have peopled the waters and streams with beneficent and wicked spirits, whose friendship is to be secured, and enmity averted, by various religious rites. Along the banks of the river Lakhya they worship Pir Badr, Khwajah Khizr, and, in fulfilment of vows, offer through any Musalmán a goat to Madár, whom they regard as a water god, but who may be identified with Sháh Madár Badi'uddin. In stormy weather and in bad fishing seasons they invoke Khala-Kumári, a naiad, to whom the first fruits are presented, in the same way as Hindus do to Lakshmi. In Behar Mangal Chandi, Jai Singh, and Lál are their chief minor gods.

In Purniah Tiyars worship a peculiar deity called Prem Rája or Pamiráj, who, they say, belonged to their tribe and was a celebrated brigand residing at Bahurágar, in Tirhut. Having been on many occasions favoured by the deity, he was translated (Aprakása), and disappeared along with his boat. In 1864 one Baijua Tiyar gave out that Pamiráj had appeared to him in a vision and ordained that the Tiyars should cease to be fishermen and devote themselves instead to certain religious rites, which would procure general prosperity. Great excitement ensued, and in February 1865 about four thousand Tiyars from Gházipúr, Benares, and the adjoining districts assembled at Gogra, in Purniah, and after offering holy water to a private idol belonging to Baijua, which he said came to him out of a bamboo post, 3,000 goats were sacrificed. Shortly afterwards another meeting of the tribe was held in the Benares district, at which a murder was committed. This movement was a repetition of a precisely similar one among the Dosádhs of Behar in 1863, and, like it, was short-lived and unsuccessful.

As is done by all Bengali fishermen, the Jal Pálani, on the "Tilwá" Sankránti in Mágh (January-February), when the sun enters Capricorn, is observed by the Tiyars. The close time lasts from two to fifteen days, but the demand for fish being steady, they catch on the eve of the festival an extra supply and keep them alive for purposes of sale, there being no offence in selling, although there is in catching, fish at that period, when prices being high profits are unusually good.

Social status and occupation.

In Behar and Bengal generally Tiyars are reckoned impure, and along the northern bank of the Ganges Tiyars employed in manufacturing mats of the *nal* reed, and known as Nal Tiyars, are considered so utterly vile that the fisher Tiyars repudiate any fellowship with them.

In Dacca the Tiyars occupy an uncertain position, in one part of the district being pure and Pancha-varta, having the five Sudra servants working for them, while in another, being unclean, these servants are members of their own caste. Tiyars in Eastern Bengal are usually fishermen, but where the fishery has become unproductive, or the river has silted up, they are found cultivating the soil, keeping shops, and acting as boatmen. They manufacture their own nets, but their long narrow boats, called "Jalká," are made by Chandáls.

The following statement shows the number and distribution of Tiyars in 1872 and 1881:—

District.	1872.	1881.	District.	1872.	1881.
Bardwan	3,631	3,369	Tipperah	379	98
Bankura	62	866	Chittagong	1,128	......
Birbhum	307	1,775	Noakhali	190	......
Midnapur	16,304	14,099	Patna	1,185	1,036
Hughli	23,051	6,687	Gya	162	......
Howrah		18,623	Shahabad	242	16
24-Parganás	46,709	37,171	Tirhut { Mozaffarpur ...	873	130
Nadiya	12,423	2,362	Tirhut { Darbhanga ...		190
Khulna	......	3,823	Saran	1,513	2,609
Jessore	4,565	239	Champaran	10	434
Murshedabad...	12,033	7,735	Monghyr	18,014	19,163
Dinajpur	17,364	2,224	Bhagalpur	6,678	4,296
Rajshahye	2,249	2,016	Purniah	18,203	16,040
Rangpur	141,213	92,790	Maldah	13,717	15,736
Bogra	5,539	298	Santál Parganás	2,887	2,381
Pabna	2,786	1,253	Cuttack	541	889
Darjiling	1	......	Puri	907	876
Jalpigori	......	35,896	Balasore	682	688
Kuch Behar	......	54,152	Tributary States	1,613	1,615
Dacca	7,968	6,654	Hazaribagh	77	96
Faridpur	866	1,374	Lohardagá	761	126
Bakarganj	896	68	Singbhum	......	123
Maimansinh	14,461	15,069	Manbhum	256	493
			Tributary States	......	153

Tiyar, a sub-caste of Malláhs in Behar.

Toeba, flower of *parás* tree, a totemistic sept of Mundas in Chota Nagpur.

Toewa, a kind of bird, a totemistic sept of Mundas in Chota Nagpur.

Toinya, a sept of Chakmás in the Hill Tracts of Chittagong.

Toipá, a *rui* or sept of Dejong Lhoris whose ancestor had emigrated from South Bhotan.

Toktiham, a sept of the Pánthar sub-tribe of Limbus in Darjiling.

Tolángi, a *thar* or sept of Gurungs in Darjiling.

Tolwar, a section of the Chhajáti sub-caste of Khatris in Bengal.

Tongar, a sept of Surajbansi Rájputs in Behar.

Tongbángboha, a sept of Limbus in Darjiling.

Tongdu-Ruishi, the most respectable sub-tribe of Dejong Lhoris or Bhotias of the south.

Tongsi, a bird, a totemistic sept of Mundas in Chota Nagpur.

Tono, a big tree-ant, a totemistic sept of Mundas in Chota Nagpur.

Topna, a tree, a totemistic sept of Mundas in Chota Nagpur.

Topo, a sept of Asuras; a section of Khariás in Chota Nagpur.

Topoar, a bird with a long tail, body mottled black and white, a totemistic sept of Mundas, Oraons, and Lohárs and a section of Goraits in Chota Nagpur.

Toppo, a totemistic section of Turis in Chota Nagpur denoting a bird.

Toril, a section of the Sátmuliá Maghayá sub-caste of Kándus in Behar.

Toringtapá, a *thar* or sept of Mangars in Darjiling.

Tormeg, a *thar* or sept of Murmis in Darjiling.

Totábari, a section of Páns in Chota Nagpur.

Totaka, a *gáin* of the Sándilya *gotra* of Bárendra Brahmans in Bengal.

Tow, a kind of bird, a totemistic sept of Mundas in Chota Nagpur.

Trayodás, a sub-caste of Bágdis found in the 24-Parganás, said to have come from Bankura.

Tribedi, a title of Kanaujiá Brahmans in Behar.

Trikoniá, a title of low castes of the North-Western Provinces and Panjáb.

Trilokpuria, a section of the Banodhiá and Jaiswár Kalwárs in Behar.

Tripáthi, a title of the Dákshinátya Baidik Brahmans in Bengal.

Tripáti, a section of Utkal or Orissa Brahmans.

Triprá, a synonym for Tipperah.

Tsak, a synonym for Chakmá.

Tsakma, a synonym for Chakmá.

Tsègkhim-pá, *tseg*, 'a wall,' and *khim*, 'a house'—a dweller in a stone or walled house, a sub-sept of the Nah-pa sept of Sherpa Bhotias.

Tshe-gyu-thah, the family which sprang from the Buddha of life, a *rui* or sept of the Tongdu sub-tribe of Dejong Lhoris or Bhotias of the south.

Tshendangkya, he who lives apart, a sept of the Ahtharai sub-tribe of Limbus in Darjiling.

Tsonbang, he who listens and profits, a sept of the Miákhola sub-tribe of Limbus in Darjiling.

Tsong, a synonym for Limbu.

Tsong-zubo, a *rui* or sept of Dejong Lhoris, the members of which are the decendants of emigrants from Bhotan and Nepal.

Tubká, a section of the Tirhutiyá sub-caste of Doms in Behar.

Tudi, Tudu, a sept of Hos and Santáls.

Tuduar, hen, a totemistic sept of Kharwars in Chota Nagpur.

Tukipitá dumuriá, *dumur* fig, a totemistic section of Kurmis in Chota Nagpur and Orissa.

Tulatiá, a sub-caste of Telis in Orissa.

Tulsi, a group of Maghaiya Telis in Behar.

Tulsiar, a kind of flower, a totemistic sept of Mundas in Chota Nagpur.

Tumaliá, a section of Kumhárs in Singbhum.

Tumárung, a totemistic sept of the Bhumij tribe in Manbhum.

Tumbangphe, the earth-born or *Bhuiphutá*, a sept of the Phedáb sub-tribe of Limbus in Darjiling. This *thar* claim to be *terræ filii*, and point out a huge rock which covers the spot where their founder sprang from the earth.

Tumbapo, the eldest, a sept of the Pánthar sub-tribe of Limbus in Darjiling.

Tumbli, a red flying ant, a totemistic sept of Mundas and Kumhárs in Chota Nagpur.

Tumbli, Berni, a section of Kumhars in Lohardagá.

Tumbrok, born of a step-mother, a sept of the Pánthar sub-tribe of Limbus in Darjiling.

Tumkohong, a sept of Limbus in Darjiling.

Tumling, a sept of the Yangorup sub-tribe of Limbus in Darjiling.

Tundak, a section of Goálás in the North-Western Provinces and Behar.

Tundal, a *gotra* or section of Agarwáls.

Tunduár, a tree, a totemistic sept of Kharwars and Mundas; a section of Kurmis and Mahilis in Chota Nagpur and Orissa.

Tungá, a sub-caste of Karangás and of Máls in Midnapur and Manbhum.

Tungbai, a sept of Tipperahs in the Hill Tracts of Chittagong.

Tungjainya, a sub-tribe of Chakmás in the Hill Tracts of Chittagong.

Tungohong, the discontented, a sept of the Chhothar sub-tribe of Limbus in Darjiling.

Tunru, a totemistic section of Máhilis in Manbhum, the members of which will not touch or cut the grass which the name denotes.

Tuntiá Kaibartta, a sub-caste of Kaibarttas in Bengal who cultivate mulberry and rear silk cocoons, and produce all sorts of vegetables which their women sell in the market.

Tura, a sept of Bairágis in Chota Nagpur.

Turáha, a low caste who blow horns and play on flutes.

Turáhá, *Turhá*, a sub-caste of Káhárs who carry palanquins, sell fish and fresh fruit and cultivate; a sub-caste of Nuniás.

Turania, a sept of Mundas in Chota Nagpur.

Turhá, players on the wind instrument called *turhi*.

Turi, a non-Aryan caste of cultivators, workers in bamboo, and basket-makers in Chota Nagpur. The physical type of the Turis, their language, and their religion, place it beyond doubt that they are a Hinduised offshoot of the Mundas. In Lohardagá, where the caste is most numerous, it is divided into four sub-castes—**Turi** or **Kisán-Turi, Or, Dom,** and **Domrá**—distinguished by the particular modes of basket and bamboo-work which they practise. Thus the Turi or Kisán-Turi, who are also cultivators and hold *bhuinhári* land, make the *sup*, a winnowing sieve made of *sirki*, the upper joint of *Saccharum procerum*; the *tokri* or *tokiyá*, a large open basket of split bamboo twigs woven up with the fibre of the leaves of the *tál* palm; the *sair* and *nadud*, used for catching fish. The Ors are said to take their name from the *oriyá* basket used by the sower, and made of split bamboo sometimes helped out with *tál* fibre. They

Internal structure.

also make umbrellas, and the *chhotka dáli* or *dálá*, a flat basket with vertical sides used for handling grain in small quantities. Doms make the *harka* and scale-pans (*taráju*). Domrás make the *peti* and fans. Turis frequently reckon in as a fifth sub-caste the Birhors, who cut bamboos and make the *sikás* used for carrying loads slung on a shoulder-yoke (*bahangi*), and a kind of basket called *phanda*. Doms and Domrás speak Hindi; Turis, Ors, and Birhors use among themselves a dialect of Mundári. All these sub-castes profess to be strictly endogamous; but a Turi can marry the daughter of an Or provided that she is formally admitted into the Turi sub-caste. This is effected by her lover giving a feast to the leading men of the local caste community. Members of other castes who have taken to themselves Turi women and have been ejected from their own group may be admitted on similar terms.

Marriage.

The sections of the Turis shown in Appendix are for the most part totemistic, and correspond closely with those in force among the Mundás. The rule of exogamy extends only to a man's own section, and is supplemented by the standard table of prohibited degrees. Except in Hinduised and comparatively wealthy families, whose tendency is to affect infant-marriage, girls usually marry as adults. Free courtship is recognized, and sexual license before marriage tolerated. Both youths and maidens are said, however, to lead purer lives than the Oraons, owing, it is suggested, to the fact that they do not frequent the dancing ground (*ákhrá*), and are thus less exposed to the temptations of the flesh. Before a marriage can be celebrated the consent of the heads of the Mádalwár and Surinwár sections, who are known respectively as Rájá and Thákur, is obtained, and a bride-price of Rs. 2-8 is paid. The village *páhan* attends, and the head of the Charchágiyá section officiates as priest. *Sindurdán* is the binding portion of the ceremony. Polygamy is permitted, the only limit to the number of wives a man may have being his ability to maintain them. A widow may marry again by the *sagai* form, and it is usual for her to marry her husband's younger brother if there is one. *Sindur* is not used in the *sagai* ceremony as practised by the Turis. The essential points are the consent of the chief relatives and the presentation to the bride of a new cloth and a lac armlet. Divorce is allowed, and divorced women may marry again.

Religion.

The original religion of the Turis is beyond doubt closely akin to the form of animism current among the Mundás and described at length in the article on that tribe. In many villages, indeed, they hold the office of *páhan*. Baranda Bhut and Bura-Buri are held in special reverence. Of late years large numbers of Turis have embraced the tenets of the deistic sect, known to its members as Sri-Náráyani, from the name of God, and to outsiders as Siva-Náráyani, from the name of its founder, a Rájput of Gházipur, who lived early in the eighteenth century. These, however, who call themselves Sri-Náráyan Panthis, have by no means broken with the animistic faith of their ancestors, and in cases of illness have recourse to the regular aboriginal methods on propitiating the spirit who is believed to be afflicting them.

Turis will eat cooked food with Mundás and Oraons, take sweetmeats from Ahirs and Telis, and water from the Or sub-caste. They will smoke only with members of their own sub-caste. For the rest they are as lax in matters of diet as the Mundás and Oraons. Sri-Naráyanis abstain from beef, from the flesh of animals which have died a natural death, and from spirituous liquors.

Social status.

The following statement shows the number and distribution of Turis in 1872 and 1881:—

DISTRICT.	1872.	1881.	DISTRICT.	1872.	1881
Bardwan	47	44	Rangpur	......	91
Birbhum	65	3	Bogra	......	171
Midnapur	4	......	Pabna	407	125
Hughli	46	2	Faridpur	......	4
Howrah		51	Maimansinh	33	84
24-Parganás	98	1,854	Chittagong	......	4
Nadiya	336	447	Hazaribagh	11,136	17,529
Jessore	86	78	Lohardagá	4,778	6,530
Murshedabad...	473	17	Singbhum	251	255
Dinajpur	66	493	Manbhum	......	75
Rajshahye	......	43	Tributary States	1,330	1,465

Turi or *Dakhiná*, a sub-caste of Doms in Behar.

Turiar, a sept of Agariás in Chota Nagpur.

Turk-Bhát, a sub-caste of Bháts.

Turkia, a sub-caste of Telis in Behar, who are Mahomedans.

Turkiá or **Shekh**, a sub-caste of Mahomedan Dhobis in Behar.

Turk-Kumhár, a class of Mahomedan Kumhárs in Behar.

Turk-Nauwá, a class of Mahomedan barbers in Behar.

Turk Pási, a sub-caste of Pásis in Behar who are Mahomedan by religion.

Turku, a sub-sept of the Saren sept of Santáls.

Turman, a section of the Chhajáti sub-caste of Khatris in Bengal.

Tursia, a sept of Mundas in Chota Nagpur.

Turu, squirrel, a totemistic sept of Mundas and Bediás in Chota Nagpur; a section of Mahilis.

Turuar, *pákur* fruit, a totemistic sept of Kharwars and Mundas in Chota Nagpur.

Turuwar, a section of Cheros in Palamau.

Tuti, a bird, a totemistic sept of Bhumijs, Mundas, and Kharwars in Chota Nagpur; a section of Khariás.

Tutiear, a section of Mahilis in Chota Nagpur.

U

Uber, a *mul* or section of the Maghayá sub-caste of Kándus in Behar.

Ubhar, a *mul* or section of the Chhamuliá Madhesiá sub-caste of Halwáis in Behar.

Uchchharakhi, a *gáin* of the Bharadwája *gotra* of Bárendra Brahmans in Bengal.

Uchring, an insect, a totemistic sept of Mundas in Chota Nagpur.

Udadhi, a section of Málos in Eastern Bengal.

Udaniyár, a *pur* or section of Sákadwipi Brahmans in Behar.

Udási, *Udásin*, a religious mendicant; a title of Brahmans and Sannyásis; an indifferent person; a stranger. In Census papers may either be a variant for Udásin, or may merely mean that the persons enumerated under this title described themselves as strangers (udásin), and the word was taken to be a caste designation.

Udbaru, a tree, a totemistic sept of Mundas in Chota Nagpur.

Uddhabi, a sub-caste of Tántis in Bengal.

Udhmatiá, a section of Kanaujiá Lohárs in Behar.

Udwar, water cat, a totemistic sept of Lohárs in Chota Nagpur.

Uengsa, a sept of Maghs in the Hill Tracts of Chittagong.

Ugahar, a *mul* or section of the Chhamuliá Madhesiá sub-caste of Halwáis in Behar.

Ugrakhatri, a synonym for Aguri.

Uh, a sub sept of the Hemrom sept of Santáls.

Ujáin, a sept of the Surajbansi division of Rájputs in Behar.

Ujalá, a *gáin* or sub-section of Saptasati Brahmans in Bengal.

Ujhá or *Ojhá*, a sub-caste of Bágdis in Western Bengal, probably descended from the priests of the tribal gods, who would naturally tend to form themselves into a sub-caste.

Ujhá, Ojhá, or **Jhá**, a title of Maithil Brahmans in Behar.

Ujini, a group of the Fatehsing Telis in Murshedabad.

Ujli, a synonym for Dhobi in Behar.

Ukhar, a group of the Aoghár sect of Saiva ascetics founded in Guzerat by a Dasnámi mendicant named Brahmagiri. For a fuller account of the sect. see **Aoghar**.

Ukniyál, a *thar* or section of Nepáli Brahmans.

Uksarri, a sept of Chakmás in the Hill Tracts of Chittagong.

Ulárk, a *pur* or section of Sákadwipi Brahmans in Behar.

Ulit, a sept of Rájputs in Behar.

Ulluk, a *gáin* or sub-section of Saptasati Brahmans in Bengal.

Ulwár, a *mul* or section of the Naomuliá or Majraut sub-caste of Goálás in Behar.

Umatwár, a section of Bábhans in Behar.

Umethwár, a *mul* or section of the Naomuliá or Majraut sub-caste of Goálás in Behar.

Unain, a *mul* or section of the Ayodhiá sub-caste of Hajjáms in Behar.

Undhil, a section of Goálás in Behar.

Undhuri, a *gáin* of the Sábarna *gotra* of Bárendra Brahmans in Bengal.

Upádhyáya, a sub-caste of Utkal Brahmans in Orissa; an endogamous division of Nepáli Brahmans; a title of Kanaujiá and Saraswat Brahmans and of Bábhans in Behar.

Upamanya, a section of Brahmans.

Uphaltopi, a *thar* or section of Nepáli Brahmans.

Uranga, ? Uraun, a synonym for Oraon.

Urdágainhi, a section of the Biyáhut and Kharidáhá Kalwárs in Behar.

Urdwar, a sept of Mundas in Chota Nagpur.

Uriar, a sept of Kharwars in Chota Nagpur.

Uring, a wild bird, a totemistic sept of Mundas in Chota Nagpur.

Uriyá, a sub-caste of Pods.

Uriyá Dhobá, a sub-caste of Dhobás in Orissa.

Uriyá-Káet, a synonym for Karan.

Urmakhori, a sept of Páns in Chota Nagpur.

Urmakuli, a section of Páns in Chota Nagpur.

Urmi, a wave; a title of Jáliyas in Bengal.

Uruntá, a *thar* or sept of Gurungs in Darjiling who burn their dead on a hill top and then throw the ashes in the air.

Urwár, a *pur* or section of Sákadwipi Brahmans in Behar.

Usahiyárk, a *pur* or section of Sákadwipi Brahmans in Behar.

Usauth, a section of the Karan sub-caste of Káyasths in Behar.

Usrám, a *mul* or section of the Naomuliá or Majraut sub-caste of Goálás in Behar.

Utamapur, a section of the Karan Káyasths in Behar.

Utardáhá, a *mul* or section of the Maghayá sub-caste of Kándus in Behar.

Utkal, a territorial division of the Pancha Gaura Brahmans, deriving its name from the Province of Utkala or Odra (Orissa).

Utkuli, a *thar* or section of Nepáli Brahmans.

Uttara-Sreni, a territorial group of Brahmans in Orissa.

Uttar-Bárendra, an endogamous division of the Bárendra Brahmans in Bengal.

Uttardáhá, a section of the Sátmuliá Maghayá sub-caste of Kándus in Behar.

Uttarhá, a sub-caste of Tántis in Behar.

Uttariyá, a sub-caste of Doms in South Behar who work in *sirki*, and regard this as an important distinction between themselves and the Maghayá Doms who work with bamboos.

Uttar-Kabát, north gate, a title of Khandáits in Orissa.

Uttarkul, a group of the Áswini Tántis in Bengal.

Uttar-Rárhi, a sub-caste of Káyasths in Bengal; of Kámárs in the 24-Parganás; of Chásá-dhobás and Nápits; a group of the Hele Kaibarttas and of Bará-bhágiyá Muchis in Bengal.

V

Vaidika, one of the five main sub-castes of Bengal Brahmans; a group of the Srotriya sub-caste of Utkal Brahmans in Orissa.

Baishnaba, *Baishtab*, *Bairági*, a religious sect based upon the worship of Vishnu under the incarnations of Ráma and Krishna. Founded as a popular religion by Rámanuja in Madras, and developed in Northern India by Rámánand and Kabir, Vaishnavism owes its wide acceptance in Bengal to the teaching of Chaitanya, a Vaidik Brahman of Nadiya at the beginning of the 16th century. The contemplative devotion inculcated by this teacher as the ideal of the religious life was transformed by Vallabha-Swámi into emotional longings of a more sensuous type. The sects now included under the general name Vaishnava are the following :—

Rámánuja.

(1) **Rámánuja**, comprising three grades of disciples: the Brahmacharya, or novice; Upa Kurvvána, who lives as an udasi in the house of his guru; and the Naisthika, who practises a life-long asceticism. When undergoing the initiatory rite (tapta-mudrá), the disciple is marked with the *sankha* or conch-shell of Vishnu on the left shoulder and the *chakra* or wheel on the right, the stamp used being made of eight metals (ashta-dhátu), gold, silver, copper, brass, tin, lead, iron, and zinc. Rámánujas are most punctilious about the privacy of their meals, and should any one see or speak to them while they are eating, the food is either thrown away or buried. Silken or woollen garments, not cotton, must be worn at meals, and no one may taste food without permission of the guru. Rámánujas will only eat food cooked by a Brahman of their own sect, but they do not reject articles prepared with *ghi* by a Rámávat. They will not touch food cooked by a Kulin Brahman of Bengal, nor will they take water from the hands of a man of that caste.

Rámávat.

(2) **Rámávat**, a Hindustani sect, recruited mainly from among Kanaujiyá Brahmans, though persons of other castes are occasionally received on the understanding that it is open to any member of the sect to decline to eat with them. Vishnu or Ráma-Chandra is the patron god of the community, but in some cases his worship has been supplanted by that of Hari, who is identified with Krishna. Brindában is the head-quarters of those who revere the latter, and Ajodhyá of those who adhere to the worship of Ráma. Their sacred books are the Rámáyana, the Sri Bhágavat, and the Bhágavat-Gitá. Most of them, however, are very illiterate, and of those who can blunder through a Nagari book, few understand what they read. Pilgrimage is believed to be the chief duty of the sect. The Tápasi or penitential order of Rámávats, erroneously styled Jogis, a term properly reserved for Saiva ascetics, wander through India almost naked, smeared over with ashes and stupefied with ganja, living on alms, but lodging with no one and taking shelter under trees, in ruins, or among tombs

in preference to entering a human habitation. A rope round the waist and a scanty cloth round the loins form their sole attire. A few shave the head and beard, but most allow their hair to grow, and twist their matted locks round the head like a turban, or roll them into coils terminating in a large knot or chignon over the left ear. They wear necklaces of rudráksha wood (*Elæocarpus gianitrus*) containing seventeen, nineteen, twenty-one, fifty-four or a hundred and eight beads, and when indulging in long fits of abstraction, they support themselves with a bamboo crutch. At initiation a new convert is enrolled in a so-called 'gotra,' bearing the name Aichittra; but as all Rámávats belong to this, and in theory celibacy is strictly enjoined, the procedure is a mere form, and has no bearing on marriage or the relations of the sexes. Rámávat Sádhus are notorious for their dissolute and licentious character, and for their excessive indulgence in gánja, a drug which they smoke systematically in order to induce the dreamy sensual reverie regarded by them as the highest manifestation of religious sentiment. All forms of worship, except the unceasing repetition of the name Ráma or Hari, are deemed useless, but in every ákhárá or monastery of the sect an idol is tended at regular hours to the sound of *sankh* shells and gongs, while offerings of flowers and fruit are presented by the laity. A *tulsi* plant in the courtyard and a Sálagram in the shrine complete the religious furniture of the establishment.

Nimavat.

(3) **Nimavat,** recruited from among Hindustani Brahmans or members of those castes from whose hands a Brahman can take water. The mark of a Nimavat is a circular black patch on the forehead between two parallel yellow streaks. Mathurá and Jaipur are their most sacred places of pilgrimage, and the Bhágavat-Gitá is their chief religious book. The chief duty of the Biraktas or monastic members of the sect is to prepare and offer to the idols kept in the ákhárá *bhog* or food consisting of rice and pulse boiled together. Four times a day this compound is laid before the god, and is then eaten by the mahant and his disciples. The idols usually worshipped by Nimavats are Jagannáth, Madan-Gopál, Rádhá-Krishna, Balarám, and Subhadrá, the sister of Krishna.

Baishtam.

(4) **Vaishnava,** colloquially **Baishtam,** of Bengal, a class not very easy to define precisely, as the name Vaishnava includes (*a*) ordinary Hindus who, with out deserting their original caste, worship Vishnu in preference to other gods, (*b*) ascetic members of the Vaishnava sect, commonly called Bairági, (*c*) Ját-Baishtam, Samyogi, or Bántási, an endogamous group formed by the conversion to Vaishnavism of members of many different castes. It will be convenient here to treat first of the last-mentioned group. The Baishtam caste includes members of several Vaishnava sects, and in theory intermarriage between these sects is prohibited. But if a man of one sect wishes to marry a woman of another sect, he has only to convert her by a simple ritual to his own sect, and the obstacles to their union are removed. Baishtams have no *gotras*, but they are divided into fifteen sections (*paribár*), supposed to be descended from the principal

disciples of Chaitanya, such as Adwaita-Paribár, Nityánanda-Paribár, Achárya-Paribár, Syám Chánd, Jagadish Pandit, Gadádhar Pandit, Bakkeswar Pandit, Adhirám Gopál, etc. Although these groups are supposed to stand to the Baishtams in the place of *gotras*, marriage between persons belonging to the same *paribár* is not forbidden, and the grouping has no more effect on marriage than the *quasi*-endogamous division into sects referred to above. Outsiders are freely admitted into the community, however low their caste may be, provided only that they are Hindus. Chaitanya is said to have extended this privilege even to Mahomedans, but since his time the tendency has been rather to contract the limits of the society, and no guru or mathdhári (superintendent of a monastery) would now venture on such an act. The ceremony of initiation is simple. The guru or mathdhári, known on this occasion by the title of Bhek-gosain, 'the ascetic of alms,' after worshipping Chaitanya, gives to the convert a string (*dori*), a piece of cloth (*kaupin*) just sufficient to cover his nakedness, and a *báhirbásh*, a larger cloth, to wear round his loins over the *kaupin*. At the same time he whispers in his ear the *mantra* or sacred word, usually a monosyllable, indicating a name or attribute of a god or goddess, which is to guide him through life and must never be divulged to any one. The novice then bows down, and a small necklace of wooden beads is hung round his neck, and a *karanga* or cocoanut shell given him for the purpose of collecting alms.

Marriage.

Baistams profess to marry their daughters as infants, and this may be taken to be the rule of the caste, although in many instances it is departed from, as might be expected in a community comprising so many heterogeneous elements. Sexual intercourse before marriage is not visited by any social penalties, nor are girls who have led an immoral life turned out of the caste. Only before they can be formally married, they must again pass through the ceremony of initiation described above. The standard Hindu ritual is not observed in marriage. A guru or gosain presents to Chaitanya flowers and sandal wood paste, and lays before him offerings of *málsábhog*, a compound of rice, fruits and other articles. Hymns (*sankirtan*) in honour of Krishna and Chaitanya are then sung to an accompaniment of the *mridanga*, an elongated drum, tapering towards the ends, and the *kartál* or brass cymbal. The guardian of the girl takes her right hand in his and gives it to the bridegroom, and the couple exchange small garlands of flowers and necklaces of beads. Sankirtan is sung once more, and the ceremony is over. Its essential and binding portion is the exchange of flowers or beads, technically known as *kanthi-badal*. Widows may marry again (*sangá*), and are in no way restricted in the selection of their second husband, except that they may not marry within the prohibited degrees originally forbidden to them. The ritual is the same as that described above, except that no one gives away the bride. For a widow, as for a virgin, *kanthi-badal* is held to be the binding portion of the ceremony. Divorce is permitted at the option of either party, and divorced persons of either sex may marry again

Krishna is the tutelary deity of the caste, and most Baishtams worship him exclusively and disregard the other gods of the Hindu system. They also worship Chaitanya as the latest incarnation of Vishnu, Nityánanda as Balarám, and Adwaita as an incarnation of Siva. The following gurus rank as patron saints:—Swarup Goswámi, Sanátan, Bhatta Raghunáth, Srijiba, Gopal Bhatta, and Dás Raghunáth. To them are presented flowers of any colour but red, paste of sandal wood, *tulsi* leaves, *málsábhog*, parched rice, curds, sugar, cakes and sweetmeats of various kinds. Boiled rice and vegetable curry are sometimes offered. Báuls offer fish, and members of the Nerá-neri sect *masur dál* seasoned with onion. The twelfth day of every month and *janmashtami*, the birthday of Krishna, are the proper times for such offerings. The Kartá Bhajás, however, hold Friday to be especially sacred. After being laid before the god, the offerings are distributed among the worshippers present on the occasion. Although Baishtams do not consider it necessary to employ Brahmans for religious or ceremonial purposes, the gurus and goswámis who look after the religion of the caste are in fact usually members of the sacred order. But as their spiritual disciples come from low castes, and they themselves eat in their disciples' houses and take water from their hands, it follows that Baishtam Brahmans are not received on equal terms by the Brahmans who serve the higher castes, and the latter would as a rule decline to eat cooked food which had been touched by a Baishtam Brahman.

Religion.

Baishtams bury their dead in a sitting posture. Each of the several sects included in the caste is supposed to have a separate burial ground of its own; but it is not an uncommon practice to bury the dead within the precincts of the homestead. No regular *sráddh* is performed; Chaitanya is worshipped, and *málsábhog* is offered seven or eight days after death, and the relations of the deceased then indulge in a feast to show that the time of mourning is over.

Burial.

Baishtams eat cooked food only with people of their own caste; but they take water and sweetmeats from, and smoke out of the same hookah with, men of almost all castes except Muchis and sweepers. Their social standing is low, as the caste is recruited from among all classes of society, and large numbers of prostitutes and people who have got into trouble in consequence of sexual irregularities are found among their ranks. They have no characteristic occupation, and follow all professions deemed respectable by middle class Hindus.

Social status.

In the district of Midnapore the organization of the Baishtam caste seems to differ in some points from that described above. Two endogamous classes are recognized—(1) Játi-Baishnab, consisting of those whose conversion to Vaishnavism dates back beyond living memory, and (2) ordinary Baishnabs, called also Bhekdhári or 'wearers of the garb,' who are supposed to have adopted Vaishnavism at a recent date. The former are men of substance, who have conformed to ordinary Hinduism to such an extent that they are now Baishnabs in little more than name. In the matter of marriage they follow the usages of the Nabasákha; they burn their dead; mourn for thirty days; celebrate the *sráddh*, and employ high caste Brahmans to officiate for them for religious and ceremonial purposes. They do not intermarry or eat with the Baishnabs who have been recently converted. The latter are described to me by a correspondent as "the scum of the population. Those who are guilty of adultery or incest, and in consequence find it inconvenient to live as members of the castes to which they belong, embrace Vaishnavism, first, because they can by so doing place themselves beyond the pale of the influence of the headmen of their castes, and secondly, because their conversion removes all obstacles to the continuance of the illicit or incestuous connexions which they have formed."

Gosains.

With this attempt to define the extent to which Vaishnavism has developed into a caste, we may pass on to notice the more purely religious aspects of the Vaishnava community. Tradition has it that when Chaitanya died, his most zealous disciples formed a society consisting of six Gosains, eight Kabirajs, and sixty-four Mahants to organize the new teaching and to make proselytes throughout Bengal. In course of time there arose three great centres of the faith—Khardaha, between Calcutta and Barrackpur, the home of the Gosains or religious mendicants who traced their descent from Nityánanda, a devoted disciple of Chaitanya; Sántipur, on the river Bhágirathi in Nadiya, where Adwaitánanda or Adwaita, another zealous disciple, had settled; and Saidabad, in Murshedabad, the residence of Birbhadra, the son of Nityánanda. The Gosains or "Gentoo bishops," as they were called by Mr. Holwell, have now become the hereditary leaders of the sect. Most of them are prosperous traders and money-lenders, enriched by the gifts of the laity and by the inheritance of all property left by Bairágis. They marry the daughters of Srotriya and Bansaja Brahmans, and give their daughters to Kulins, who, however, deem it a dishonour to marry one of their girls to a Gosain. As a rule, they are tall and well-made men, of light complexion, fair specimens of the Aryan type as found in Bengal. The Adwaitánanda Gosains admit to the Vaishnava community only Brahmans, Baidyas, and members of those castes from whose hands a Brahman may take water. The Nityánanda, on the other hand, maintain that any such limitation is opposed to the teaching of Chaitanya, and open the door of fellowship to all sorts and conditions of men, be they Brahmans or Chandáls, high caste widows or common prostitutes. The Nityánanda are very popular among the lower castes, and hold a leading position among Vaishnavas. A *panjah* or silver hand is the badge of the family. The Gosains themselves worship Durgá, but their disciples do not follow them in this. They observe the birthday of Chaitanya on the 13th Phálgun, the Govardhan Pujá on the first day of the new moon in Kártik, and the Diwali on the night of the Káli Pujá. The Adwaitánanda Gosains are highly esteemed by the upper classes of Bengal, and it is very unusual for a Brahman or Baidya to enrol himself in the ranks of the other branch. They are said to be more sincere and more open to religious motives than the Nityánanda, and they avoid much scandal by refusing to initiate women.

For the purpose of making proselytes and governing the Vaishnava church, Bengal is divided into circles, each circle having its own Gosain with whose jurisdiction no other Gosain is supposed to interfere. Under the Gosain is the *adhikári* or superintendent, who acts as deputy, initiates disciples within a certain area, and collects fees. Under him again is the *faujdár*, called also *khuro* or uncle (the Gosain being the father), whose business it is to beat up proselytes, and whose activity is stimulated by a percentage of the fees. Lastly comes the *chharidár*, or usher of the rod, who is merely the messenger of the *faujdár*. Persons who join the Vaishnava communion pay a fee of twenty annas, sixteen of which go to the Gosain and four to the *faujdár*.

Mendicant Vaishnavas.

The mendicant members of the Vaishnava community, as distinguished from the Ját-Baishnabs or Gribi-Baishnabs on the one hand and the governing body of Gosains on the other, are, says Dr. Wise, "of evil repute, their ranks being recruited by those who have no relatives, by widows, by individuals too idle or depraved to lead a steady working life, and by prostitutes. Vaishnavi, or Baishtabi according to the vulgar pronunciation, has come to mean a courtesan. A few undoubtedly join from sincere and worthy motives, but their numbers are too small to produce any appreciable effect on the behaviour of their comrades. The habits of these beggars are very unsettled. They wander from village to village, and from one ákhára to another, fleecing the frugal and industrious peasantry on the plea of religion, and singing songs in praise of Hari beneath the village tree, or shrine. Mendicants of both sexes smoke Indian hemp (*ganjá*), and although living as brothers and sisters, are notorious for licentiousness. There is every reason for suspecting that infanticide is common, as children are never seen. In the course of their wanderings they entice away unmarried girls, widows, and even married women, on the pretext of visiting Sri Kshetra (Jagannáth), Brindaban, or Benares, for which reason they are shunned by all respectable natives, who gladly give charity to be rid of them.

The following account of an annual religious gathering in Bengal discloses the true character of these disreputable mendicants. Amid the ruins of ancient Gaur are large reservoirs of water, called Rupa and Sanátan, after the two distinguished Mahomedans converted by Chaitanya, on the banks of which the 'Rás Melá,' or 'Prem tal[á],' *i.e.*, real love, festival is held in the month of June. Crowds of Bairágis and Bairágins resort to this fair from all parts of Bengal, the latter being seated in long rows with their faces covered. Should a Bairági be in search of a companion, he pays the customary fee to the *faujdár* and a selection is made. He leads the female aside, raises her veil, and if satisfied takes her away, otherwise he refuses to allow another choice, unless the twenty-annas fee is again paid. It is a law with these licentious Bairágis that a man cannot put away the woman selected, even for adultery, until the next year's gathering comes round."

Báyán-Káupína.

(5) **Báyán-Káupína**, a sect of Vaishnavas, so called because, contrary to the usual custom, they wear the *kaupin* or loin cloth fastened on the left side

instead of on the right. The story goes that a guru while initiating a disciple tied the *kaupin* on the left side by mistake. He was about to change it when the novice insisted that Krishna himself must have pre-ordained the error, refused to have it corrected, and, going forth as he was, founded the Báyán-Káupíni sect. The members worship Rádhá-Krishna, but they are said to abstain from the immoral practices usually laid to the charge of those who worship this union of the male and female principles. Báyán-Káupínas abstain from flesh, fish and intoxicants, and only women of moral character are allowed to be initiated.

Kisori-Bhajana.

(6) Kisori-Bhajana, 'maiden-worshippers,' or Sáhuja, a sect of Vaishnavas concerning whose beliefs and ritual it is difficult to get any very precise information. The members seem to be aware that the equivocal name of their community lays them open to the suspicion of sexual immorality, and they are said to ward off curious inquiries by placing a book or an article of common use in a conspicuous part of the house and worshipping it as a symbol of their faith. The sect is supposed to be an offshoot of the Rádhá-Ballabhi, or, according to another account, of the Spashta-Dáyaka. The latter view is improbable. A Spashta-Dáyaka will not look upon a woman or take food from her; while the Kisori-Bhajana makes woman the chief object of worship. The sect is peculiar in having no Udási or mendicant class. The guru or pradhán initiates neophytes and conducts all religious services. The cult is said to be popular, especially with women and with the Sunri caste, and to have a large number of adherents. No distinctions of rank are recognized, and all converts, whether Brahmans or Chandáls, enter upon a footing of entire equality.

According to Dr. Wise, "at the initiation of a disciple a *mantra*, consisting of the word 'Hang-sha,' is whispered into his ear, and is believed to possess a certain mystical meaning, the first syllable typifying the air breathed, the latter the air expired. An indecent scene, in which a naked woman sits on the knee of the neophyte, is then rehearsed, as a crucial test of his having mortified the flesh and its lusts, and of his having become a worthy candidate for admission.

"The chief ceremony resembling the Rásmandalis of the Mahárájas of Bombay, which they have styled 'carnal love meetings,' is celebrated in a suitable room, where a long strip of white cloth is spread on the floor with plantain leaves laden with fish and rice, while flesh and spirits never appear.

"The feast being over, songs in honour of Rádhá-Krishna are chanted with the effect of often causing extravagant and violent excitement, terminating in hysterical weeping and convulsions. The pradhán then selects a woman, possibly the prettiest; the pair are dusted with sandal wood powder, crowned with flowers, and the company make adoration to them as the personations of Rádhá and her lover Krishna. Each man present then decorates himself with garlands, perfect silence being observed, and is presumed to fall into a dreamy sensuous condition, with mind abstracted and absorbed in the contemplation of the semblance of Rádhá at his side."

(7) **Jagat-Mohani**, an obscure sect founded about two centuries ago by one Jagat-Mohan of Mashulia in Silhet. The morals of its members are said to be exemplary. Women are not allowed to live in the monasteries, and the men are expelled on second conviction of immorality. As in most Vaishnava sects, there are two classes of votaries—the Grihi and Bairági, the former being house-holders, and the latter wandering about the country as beggars. The latter may not eat fish or flesh, and may not smoke ganja or tobacco or drink spirits. Corpses are usually thrown into a river, not burned, and burial is only resorted to at the express wish of a dying mahant. In such cases the patient is lowered into the grave before he actually dies, as it is considered lucky for him to die *in situ*.

Jagat-Mohani.

(8) **Spashta Dáyaka**, said to have been founded by one Rup Rám Kabiráj, a disciple of Krishna Chandra Chakravartti of Saidabad. Although Rádhá Krishna is the principal object of worship, the members of the sect affect a high standard of morality, and decline to take food that has been cooked by a woman. Women are admitted to the *mantra*, but not to the *bhek*. All castes including Chandáls are enrolled, but a preference is shown for the pure Sudras, from whose hands a Brahman may take water. The Spashta Dáyaka take alms from any Hindus, and even from Mahomedans, but reject the offerings of prostitutes and of Chamárs. They may not touch flesh or fish, or eat with any one not a member of their communion. They will not eat with Bairági Vaishnavas, but in this case the objections are said to be mutual. Their sectarian mark is a smear of ochre (*Gopi Chandan*) on the nose with two narrow lines drawn upwards to the roots of the hair. The sacred name of Hari is stamped on the temples, arms, chest, and shoulders. The dead are buried in a sitting posture, with a cloth (*námá-bali*) stamped with the name Hari wrapped round the head : the arms are folded across the chest, a necklace is hung round the neck, and a cocoanut shell (*karanka*), a wallet and a staff (*danda*) are placed by the side. If the dead man has had influence in the sect, and has left behind him many disciples, an ákhárá is built over his grave, religious rites are performed at his tomb, and his spirit is invoked for aid on occasions of trouble.

Spashta Dáyaka.

(9) **Kavi-Indra Paribár**, a small Vaishnava sect, claiming to be the Paribár or attendants of Vishnu Dás Kavi Indra, one of the original sixty-four mahants who went out into the world to teach the doctrines of Chaitanya. The story is that this Vishnu Dás affected great humility and made a point of eating the leavings of Chaitanya's food. One day the teacher left nothing on his plate, and the disciple seeking to abase himself had to make the best of a grain of rice which Chaitanya had spat out. This he swallowed without noticing that it was tinged with blood. A rival observed this, and seeing his opportunity put to Chaitanya the question what should be done to a disciple who tasted the blood of his guru. Chaitanya unwarily answered that he should be excommunicated, and as the judgment could not be recalled, Vishnu Dás had to leave the original community and set

Kavi-Indra Paribár.

up a dissenting society of his own. The doctrines of the Kavi Indra are much the same as those of the Vaishnavas. The office of mahant, however, is elective, not hereditary, and can only be held by a Sudra. There is no Bairági or Udási grade, and all the members are family men. All castes are admitted into the sect, and even Srotriya Brahmans are said to be occasionally enrolled as members.

Báola.

(10) **Báola** (*Sansk.* Váyula, crazed or inspired), a generic term including a number of disreputable mendicant orders which have separated from the main body of Vaishnavas, and are recruited mainly from among the lower castes. They call themselves Nitya, Chaitanya, and Hari Dás Báolas, after the great Vaishnava teachers. Differing from each other in minute points of ceremonial and social observance, the Báola sects agree in regarding pilgrimage to Vaishnava shrines as a sacred duty, and reverence the Gosains as their spiritual leaders. Flesh and strong drink are forbidden, but fish is deemed lawful food, and ganjá is freely indulged in. Báolas never shave or cut their hair, and filthiness of person ranks as a virtue among them. Ládu-Gopál, or the child Krishna, is the favourite object of worship; but in most ákháras the *charan* or wooden pattens of the founder are also worshipped. Báolas as a class are believed to be grossly immoral, and are held in very low estimation by respectable Hindus.

Darwesh-Faqir.

(11) **Darwesh-Faqir**, a recent and corrupt Vaishnava sect, founded in 1850 by Udaya Chánd Karmakár of Dacca. They worship Krishna, and distinguish their creed by the term Brahmadharma. When a novice is admitted, he receives a *kaupin* or loin cloth, a *khirka* or gown reaching to the ankles, and a cocoanut shell (*kishti*) in which he is to collect alms. Like the Aghoris and some of the Báola sects, he is required to taste various disgusting substances in order to show his superiority to ordinary prejudices. Darwesh-Faqirs never cut their hair or shave, and instead of washing with water, smear themselves and their clothes with mustard oil. Celibacy is professed, but not practised, and every ákhára or community of ascetics has several women attached to it, ostensibly to keep the place in order and cook the food. Nevertheless they affect great austerity and pretend to be the strictest of the Vaishnava sects. Animal life is never taken, and it is deemed sinful to break off the branches or even the leaves of a tree. Before the tombs of the founders, and on receiving a present, a very elaborate obeisance is made by kneeling, touching the ground with the forehead, and smearing the chest and face with dust.

Kartabhaja.

(12) **Kartabhaja**, an obscure sect believed to have been founded early in the eighteenth century by one Aul Chand, who was considered by his followers to be an incarnation of Chaitanya. Aul Chand observed no distinction of caste, and taught the worship of one god and certain moral precepts of a negative type. As Kartá or spiritual head of the caste, Aul Chand was succeeded by Ram Smaran Pal of Ghoshpára in Nadiyá, and the office is still held by members of the Pál family. Next in rank to the *Kartá* are the *Mahásays* or Deputies, of whom one acts as leader to every village congregration, his duty being to

collect the dues for the support of the Kartá, and to transmit or account for all amounts so received at stated dates. The religious ceremonies of the sect are kept secret and performed in private.

The following statement shows the number and distribution of Vaishnavas in 1872 and 1881:—

District.	1872.	1881.	District.	1872.	1881.
Bardwan	37,363	28,653	Noakhali	2,131	2,963
Bankura	10,250	20,325	Tipperah	5,847	6,164
Birbhum	23,243	21,411	Hill Tracts of Chittagong	......	5
Midnapur	26,178	21,858	Patna	2,082	717
Hughli	20,378	12,107	Gya	1,395	2,757
Howrah		15,284	Shahabad	1,070	1,842
24-Parganás	36,563	33,768	Mozaffarpur	6,726	4,744
Nadiya	16,885	21,330	Darbhanga		1,917
Jessore	13,039	14,841	Saran	3,777	2,320
Khulna	......	12,939	Champaran	2,666	3,345
Murshedabad	21,464	25,054	Mongbyr	3,184	2,759
Dinajpur	16,710	19,349	Bhagalpur	18,196	3,763
Rajshahye	14,268	17,061	Purniah	1,809	3,412
Rangpur	24,541	26,974	Maldah	6,030	9,569
Bogra	8,013	11,111	Santál Parganás	6,400	6,348
Pabna	8,726	13,157	Cuttack	24,339	29,614
Darjiling	222	567	Puri	6,770	7,273
Jalpigori	1,877	3,490	Balasore	18,651	23,057
Kuch Behar	......	1,210	Tributary States	6,410	7,681
Dacca	11,886	17,239	Hazaribagh	799	441
Faridpur	5,204	7,658	Lohardagá	4,459	2,579
Bakarganj	5,799	6,149	Sinhbhum	2,733	2,868
Maimansinh	11,991	18,098	Manbhum	12,768	11,948
Chittagong	894	2,035	Tributary States	808	1,640

Vaisya, a caste of Eastern Bengal claiming to be the modern representatives of the Vaiśyas of classical tradition. According to Dr. Wise, upon whose notes this article is based, they are most numerous in the Bhowal parganá of Dacca, and at Jahángirpur in Maimansinh. They can give no account of themselves, nor do they possess any traditions of their original home. They deny that Ballál Sen ruled over or reorganized them, and boast that no honorary titles inherited from ancestors serving the Muhamadan Government survive. For these reasons they regard themselves as exceptionally pure, having lived uncontaminated amid the changes of the country. The Vaiśyas are generally short and squat, some having fine aquiline noses and prominent superciliary ridges, while others have broad cheek-bones, badly formed chins and lower jaws. Their physiognomy suggests cunning combined with intelligence, but many exhibit the inanimate vacant expression so common among Bengali low castes. The Vaiśyas have relinquished many of the peculiar duties enjoined by Manu, though still wearing the sacred cord, composed of three strands knotted together, and another disconnected one of three threads, called Utarí. The ceremony of tonsure, Chúrá Karan, is observed before the thirteenth year, not postponed to the twenty-fourth, and on this occasion the youth is invested with the Brahmanical cord. Vaiśyas profess to repeat the whole of the Gáyatrí, but the Brahmans assert that at the present day few know more than three-fourths of it, and not having full permission to bestow a blessing on the Śúdras, they twist the *Paitá* round the right thumb, and holding the right hand on a level with the navel confer the usual benediction. Vaíşyas are permitted to read one of the four Vedas, and that always followed is the Yajur-veda. Each household celebrates by itself the Sáligrám, Chakra, and Vishnu Pújas, although Brahmans dispute their right to do so without requiring the services of the guru, or purohit, who are Şrotriyá Brahmans. In creed the caste is a Vaishnava one, yet a few Şákta worshippers are met with. The Vaíşyas formerly committed the sin of marrying in their own *gotra*, or exogamous group, but of late years, in order to stay the scandal, new *gotras* have been formed.

They have no peculiar titles, but Gupta is often adde to their names, while individuals employed as assistants to merchants frequently assume the surname of Biswas, literally a holder of one-fourth share. Manu says that the first part of a Vaíşya name should indicate wealth, the second prosperity; but the Bengali Vaíşyas have ceased conforming to this rule, and the names ordinarily met with are Rám Kamár, Dev Náráyana, Şítala Chandra, or Rám Gopála, to which the surname Vaíşya is always appended. Baidyás and Káyasths residing within the Ballálí country refuse to touch food prepared by the Vaíşyas, but those living beyond those limits readily do so.

The Vaíşya is generally a tolerable Bengali scholar, but few learn English, as it entails expense and delays the young from starting in life. In Maimansinh a few enter Government employ, but the majority are pleaders, mukhtárs, rent collectors and land surveyors. Formerly the cultivation of the soil was general, but now-a-days holding a plough is considered dishonourable, while managing a harrow is admissible. When a Vaíşya meets a Brahman he does not, like other Hindus, make the salutation Praṇáma, as the Brahman bestows his benediction without it. Among Vaíşyas the period of impurity after a death is fifteen days. All the Hindu festivals are observed by them, but the favourite one is that in honour of Lakhami, the goddess of wealth.

Vakat, a variant of Bhakat.

Vasta Gáin, a *thar* or section of Nepáli Brahmans.

Vátsa, see **Bátsya**.

Vedánta, he who knows the Vedas, a title of Brahmans.

Veni, a variant of Beni, a synonym for Baniyá.

Vidyádhara, a title of Kawális in Eastern Bengal.

Vishnu, see **Bishnu**.

Vishnumási, a section of Báruis in Bengal.

Vishnuswámi, a sect of Vaishnavs.

Viswál, a title of Chásás in Orissa.

Vumik, a variant for Bhaumik, a title of Kaibarttas.

Vyása, a section of Kaibarttas, Támbulis, Subarnabaniks, and Tántis in Bengal; of Gaura Brahmans in Behar.

Vyásokta, a title of those Rárhi Brahmans who perform religious offices for the Kaibarttas.

W

Wadsuesa, a sept of Maghs in the Hill Tracts of Chittagong.

Wahe, a section of the Panch-játi sub-caste of Khatris in Bengal.

Wáhsali, a *thar* or sept of Khambus in Darjiling.

Waientsa, a sept of Maghs in the Hill Tracts of Chittagong.

Wangdehchá, a *thar* or sept of Sunuwárs in Darjiling.

Warggu, a sept of Chakmás in the Hill Tracts of Chittagong.

Weh-ba, a *rui* or sept of Sherpa Bhotias of Nepal.

Winih, a section of Barhis in Behar.

Y

Yahián, a section of Naiyás.

Yakhá, a small agricultural caste of Nepal belonging to the Kiranti group.

Yak-kyukpa, a sept of the Phágu sub-tribe of Yakhás in Darjiling.

Yakpangden, the dweller on the pass, a sept of the Yangorup sub-tribe of Limbus in Darjiling.

Yakshoma, the guardian of the fort, a sept of the Ahtharai sub-tribe of Limbus in Darjiling.

Yaktachá, a *thar* or sept of Sunuwárs in Darjiling.

Yakten, formerly doctors, a sub-sept of the Thekim sept of Limbus in Darjiling.

Yakthumba, a synonym for Limbu.

Yamphu, a sub-tribe of Yakhás in Darjiling.

Yangdenba, he who paid his footing, a sept of the Pánthar sub-tribe of Limbus in Darjiling, said to be descended from a Mech, who got admission into the Limbu tribe by bribing the heads of the *thum-thum*.

Yángdi, a *thar* or sept of Mangars in Darjiling.

Yángmi, a *thar* or sept of Mangars in Darjiling.

Yangorup, a sub-tribe of Limbus in Darjiling.

Yangsoba or **Namlagpa**, the chief of the tribe, a sept of the Pánthar sub-tribe of Limbus in Darjiling.

Yeti, a *thar* or sept of Sunuwárs in Darjiling.

Yijám, the wanderer or eater, a sept of the Yangorup sub-tribe of Limbus in Darjiling.

Yithingu, the huntsman, a sept of the Yangorup sub-tribe of Limbus in Darjiling.

Yo-chang, a sub-sept of the Pon-po sept of Dejong Lhoris or Bhotias of the south.

Yoksuma, a sept of the Phágu sub-tribe of Yakhás in Darjiling.

Yong-tong-ba, a *rui* or sept of Dejong Lhoris, the members of which are the descendants of emigrants from Bhotan and Nepal.

Yongyah, a sept of Limbus in Darjiling.

Yongyahang, the son of a chief, a sept of the Yangorup and Charkhola sub-tribes of Limbus in Darjiling.

Yulsahb, a *rui* or sept of Dejong Lhoris, the members of which are the descendants of emigrants from Bhotan and Nepal.

Yul-then-bo, a *rui* or sept of the Tongdu sub-tribe of Dejong Lhoris whose ancestor was turned out of his fatherland.

Yungmá, the idler, a sept of the Yangorup sub-tribe of Limbus in Darjiling.

Yurumbang, they of the central village, a sept of the Phedáb sub-tribe of Limbus in Darjiling.

Z

Zamindár, a synonym for Bábhan.

Zamindár Brahman, a synonym for Bábhan.

Zargar, a synonym for Sonár.

Zargar, *Zardozi*, a maker of cloth of gold.

Zatti, a title of Kewats and Mallas in Behar.

ETHNOGRAPHIC GLOSSARY.

VOL. II.

APPENDIX I.

APPENDIX II.

APPENDIX III.

APPENDIX IV.

APPENDIX I.

LIST OF TRIBES AND CASTES WITH THEIR TITLES, SUB-CASTES AND SUB-TRIBES, SECTIONS AND SEPTS.

Agariá.

Titles :—Dhángar, Parja.

Sub-tribes.	Septs.
Paháriá-Agaria.	Baheroar, a jungle fruit.
Brijia-Agaria.	Mahatoar, a title.
Assur-Agaria.	Samduar.
Lohar-Agaria.	Sonoar, gold.
	Turiar.

Agarwál, *Ágarwálá.*

Sub-castes.	Sections.	
Pachhainya.	Airan.	Mangal.
Purbiya.	Bátsil.	Mittal.
Dasá.	Bhaddal.	Singhal.
Bisa or Birádari Rájá.	Garg.	Tairan.
	Gáwál.	Táyal.
	Gobhil.	Thingal.
	Goil.	Tingal.
	Goin.	Tittal.
	Kásil.	Tundal.

Aguri, *Ugra Kshatri.*

Titles :—Kesh, Pai, Pál, Sámanta, Syám.

Sub-castes.	Sections.
Bághá.	Bharadwája.
Bardwániyá.	Gautam.
Chágnáya or Chánga.	Kásyapa.
Jáná.	Sándilya.
Kásipuriá.	
Sátsaikiyá.	
Suta.	

NOTE.—In order to facilitate reference to these lists, the names of endogamous groups are printed in red ink.

Amát.

Titles :—Ghibihár, Khawás, Saghár.

Sub-castes.

Gharbáit or Raut.
Bahiot.

Sections.

Larwár.
Narhan.
Parabwár.
Pataiwár.

Asura, *Agoria*, *Lohrá.*

Titles :—Májhi, Parjá.

Sub-tribes.

Agariá.
Birjiá.
Kolh-Asur.
Lohra-Asur.
Pahária-Asur.

Septs.

Aind, an eel.
Baroa, a wild cat.
Basriár, bamboo.
Beliár, *bel* fruit.
Kachua, a tortoise.
Kaitháwar, *kaithá* or *chichinga* fruit.
Kerketa, a bird.
Mukruár, spider.
Nág, a snake.
Rote, frog.
Siar, jackal.
Tirki, a bird.
Topo, a bird.

Bábhan.

Synonyms :—*Ajagyak Bráhman*, *Bhuinhár*, *Chaudhriji*, *Grihasth Bráhman*, *Maghayá Bráhman*, *Pachhimá Bráhman*, *Zamindár*, *Zamindár Bráhman.*

Titles :—Arápe, Bharsi-Misr, Chaube, Chaudriji, Dikshit, Dube, Mawár, Misr, Ojhá, Panchobe, Pánde, Páthak, Rái, Singh, Sotri, Thákur, Tiwári, Upadhiyá.

SECTIONS.

(*a*) *Territorial.*

Abkáhon.
Aggechal.
Agnidhaut.
Ailwár.
Ajaitiá.
Ambariá.
Anarai.
Anwár.
Araich.
Arait.
Arewar.
Arnwait.
Aswariá.
Atrab.
Auigh baid.
Badoniá.
Badramiá.
Bagauchiá.

(a) *Territorial*—concluded.

Bagri.
Balaiár.
Bandihá.
Banriá.
Barhambiá.
Barhampuriá.
Barnait.
Basmait.
Baswait.
Baurihá.
Begampuriá.
Belkuár.
Belonchá.
Bemwár.
Bhadsuhiá.
Bhaju Chakwar.
Bhalrait.
Bhatan.
Bheloriá.
Bhomápoli.
Bhunasware.
Bigahiá.
Bijalpuriá.
Bilkhari.
Chaksiár.
Chakwár.
Chandráwat.
Chasiwar.
Chauriár.
Chausá.
Chesiá.
Chiksoria.
Chilimár.
Chiwár.
Dabhinchhwár, Dabhauchwar.
Dalihare, Dullihará.
Darihare.
Dhakáit.
Dhanichhwár.
Dharan.
Dharwár.
Dhauráni.
Dighwait.
Dighwe.
Dipár.
Domkatár.
Donwár.
Dudhnait.
Dumráit.
Dundwar.
Gambhariá.
Gangtiait.
Garhiá.
Gaur.
Ghatait.
Goait.
Harariá, foundling.
Hariambá.
Hartakia.
Hastgame.
Indrawar.
Jaitharia.
Jáji.
Jajim.
Jamraián.
Janwár.
Jesiwár.
Jethuliar.
Kadarai.
Kalemniá.
Kanchanbhár.
Karmuá.
Karnautiá.
Karnáyati.
Kestwár.
Katauniá.
Katewar.
Katiáin.
Kathautiá.
Kathwait.
Katthawa.
Kausonjhiá.
Kinwár.
Korache.
Koránch.
Kulhá.
Kumedwár.
Kunjalwár.
Ladilá.
Lamgoriá.
Larwariá.
Mahbariá.
Mahuari.
Mairiá.
Malikauliá.
Malitwár.
Manaria.
Manchia.
Mandra.
Mangrauni.
Manikshariá.
Nanjorá.
Naradwár.
Niktawár.
Nonaitwár.
Okinwár.
Onwár.
Pachbhajuá.
Pachgotya.
Panchobe.
Parhape.
Parsaria.
Pilchwar.
Piliksawár.
Pilkhait.
Raini.
Ramayá.
Rampai.
Ransadiyá.
Sahasnanghiá.
Sahdaulia.
Sakarwár.
Sakhwait.
Sakmait.
Salhariyá.
Sandaliá.
Sapdohá.
Sarwe.
Saubarniá.
Semraián.
Sihogiá.
Sihoriá.
Sihujiá.
Siriár.
Sirsait.
Sonbhadriá, living on the banks of the Sone.
Sonewár.
Sorawár.
Suargane.
Surgriá.
Tetihá.
Tetihia.
Tilachhwar.
Umatwár.

(b) *Functional* or *Personal.*

Bhusbarát, husk-gatherer.	Eksariá, born of one brother.	Kodáriá, worker with the spade.
Chaubhaiá, born of four brothers.	Jalewár, holder of fisihng nets.	Panchbhaiá, born of five brothers.

(c) *Brahmanical.*

Agnihotra.	Gautam.	Parásar.
Atharb.	Hárit.	Sábarna.
Basisht.	Kásyapa.	Sándil.
Bharadwáj.	Kaundin.	Vátsa.
Garg.	Kausik.	

Bágdi, *Bâgtit.*

Titles :—Bágh, Dhárá, Khán, Mánjhi, Masálchi, Mudi, Palankhái, Parámanik, Pherká, Puilá, Rái, Sántrá, Sardár.

Sub-castes.

1. Bájándáriá, found in Jessore.
2. Dandamánjhi.
3. Darátiá, found in Nuddea.
4. Duliá, a palanquin-bearing sub-caste.
5. Gulimánjni.
6. Kasái kuliá, said to live along the banks of the Kasái river in Manbhum and Midnapur.
7. Kusmetia, Kusmátiá, or Kusputra, said to be named after the *kusá* grass, and apparently totemistic.
8. Let, found in Murshedabad.
9. Máchhuá, Mechhuá, or Mecho, a fishing sub-caste.
10. Malla metiá, Mátiá, or Mátiál, fishermen and earth-workers.
11. Nodá, found in the 24-Parganás, said to have come from Bankura.
12. Tentuliá, named after the tamarind tree, and apparently totemistic.
13. Trayodás, found in the 24-Parganás, said to have come from Bankura.
14. Ujha or Ojha, probably descended from the priests of the tribal gods, who would naturally tend to form themselves into a sub-caste. For a parallel case, see Mallik.

SECTIONS.

(a) *Totemistic*—	(b) *Eponymous*—
Ardi, fish.	Alamyán.
Bághrishi, the tiger.	Kásyapa.
Kachcháp, the tortoise.	
Kásbak, heron.	(c) *Uncertain*—
Pákbasanta, bird.	Bágri.
Pátrishi, the bean.	Dásya.
Ponkrishi, jungle cock.	Gadibhárat.
Sálrishi or Sálmachh, the *sál* fish.	Kál.
	Ráncho.

Baidya, *Vaidya, Ambastha, Bhisak, Chikitsak.*

Sub-castes (Endogamous).	Sections (Exogamous).
Rárhi.	Ádya.
Banga, *Bangaja.*	Alamalaka.
Barendra, *Varendra.*	Angira.
Panchakoti.	Atreya.
	Baisvánara.
	Basishtha.
	Bátsya.
	Bharadwája.
	Dhanvantari.
	Dhruba.
	Gautama.
	Ghritakausika.
	Hingu.
	Kásyapa.
	Kausika.
	Krishnátreya.
	Madhukuliya.
	Márkandeya.
	Maudgalya.
	Sábarna.
	Saktri.
	Salankayana.
	Sándilya.
	Vishnu.

Hypergamous groups.

Kulin.
Bangsaja.
Maulik.

Family titles (padabis).

Titles	Group	Titles	Group
Dás	Siddha.	Chandra	Kashta.
Gupta	Siddha.	Kundu	Kashta.
Sen	Siddha.	Nág	Kashta.
Datta	Sádhya.	Nandi	Kashta.
Deb	Sádhya.	Raja	Kashta.
Dhar	Sádhya.	Rakshit	Kashta.
Kar	Sádhya.	Soma	Kashta.

Titles or popular designations of Baidyas practising medicine.

Used by themselves. Baidya-nidhi.
Kabi-ballabh.
Kabi-bhushan.
Kabi-indra.
Kabiráj.
Kabiranjan.
Kabi-ratna.

Used by outsiders.

Atai Baidya, doctor who defrauds the ignorant.
Chásá Baidya, plough doctor.
Deháti Baidya, village doctor.
Haturiá Baidya, a doctor who attends market, or, according to Wise, a quack, a meddlesome fellow.
Nári-tepá, pulse-feeler.

Bairági, *Jogi, Gosáin.*

Sub-tribes.	Septs in Chota Nagpur.
Nil.	Achut.
	Anaet.
	Anchit, tiger.
	Barandia.
	Bishnu.
	Dhobdhar, can't wash their clothes in child's birth ceremonies.
	Gobans, cow.
	Idri, a jungle fruit.
	Kansi, a kind of grass.
	Karanjea, an oil-seed.
	Nág, cobra.
	Ramgharia, a place.
	Sonar, can't wear gold.
	Tura.

Báiti, *Báoli, Chunári, Chuniyá, Barnak-Támuli.*

Titles:—Bhulyá, Rái, Sen.

Sub-castes.	Sections.
1. Báití of Dacca and Central Bengal.	Aliman.
2. Magi of Fáridpur.	Bághrishi.
	Kasyapa.
	Tilalochan.

Barhi, *Barhai.*

Titles:—Manjhan, Maraiya, Mistri, Rái, Sátun, Thákur.

Sub-castes.		Sections.
1. Kanaujiá	(Work only in wood.)	(*a*) *Territorial*—
2. Kokás		Bachberáit.
3. Maghayá.	(Work in wood and iron.)	Balbheráit.
		Bánsdih.

Sub-castes.	Sections.
	(a) *Territorial*—concluded.
4. Lohar. (Found in Bhágalpur. Work only in iron.)	Barhioth.
5. Kamár-Kallá.	Barnált.
6. Mathuriá.	Balhátt.
	Bharáii.
	Charwa.
	Chaudhrána.
	Dasáonth.
	Dobháit.
	Gritári.
	Háthián.
	Kápri.
	Kharáit.
	Lakwár.
	Mukund.
	Parus.
	Pipriáti.
	Sikalgar.
	Winih.
	(b) *Eponymous*—
	Biskarma.
	Sándilya.
	Kásyapa.

Hypergamous divisions of the Maghayá sub-caste.

Thákur.
Rái.
Kuar.

IN BENGAL.

Bárui, *Barai, Baraji, Bárajibi, Latá-baidya.*

Titles:—Ain, Ash, Bawál, Bhadra, Bhaumik, Bhawal, Biswás, Chánd, Chaudhri, Dám, Dás, Deo, Datta, Dhar, Guha, Háldár, Hor, Kar, Khán, Khor, Kundu, Láhá, Majumdár, Mallik, Mandal, Mantrini, Mánná, Márik, Mitra, Náha, Nág, Nandan, Nandi, Pál, Rakhit, Rudra, Sarkár, Sen.

Sub-castes.	Sections.	
1. Rárhi.	Aliman.	Kanwamaharsi.
2. Bárendra.	Batsya.	Kásyapa.
3. Náthán.	Bharadwáj.	Madhukuliya.
4. Kotá.	Chandramaharsi.	Sándilya.
	Gautama.	Vishnumaharsi.
	Jaimini.	Vyása.

IN BEHAR.

Barai, *Mistri*.

Title :—Ráut.

Sub-castes.	Sections.
1. Maghaya.	Kásyapa.
2. Jaiswár.	Nág.
3. Chaurasiá.	
4. Semerya.	
5. Sokhwá.	

Bauri, *Buno*.

Titles :—Digha, Mandal, Manjhi, Maulavi, Parámanik.

Sub-castes.	Sections.
1. Dhuliá or Dhulo.	Aliman.
2. Jhátiá or Jhetiá.	Kásyapa.
3. Káthuriá.	Madhukulya.
4. Mallabhumiá.	Májhi.
5. Maluá or Máluá.	
6. Mola.	
7. Panchakoti.	
8. Páturia.	
9. Sikhariá or Gobariá.	

Bediá, *Bedeá*, *Bejeá*.

Title :—Mahto.

Sub-tribes.	Septs.
Nil.	Bar, the banyan tree.
	Biha or Binjhá, a fish.
	Chidra or Cherrá, squirrel.
	Dhechua, a black bird.
	Dian, a kind of fish.
	Kachua or Kachchh, tortoise.
	Khopchá, an owl.
	Mahanadi, name of a river.
	Mahua, *bassia latifolia*.
	Mahukal, a bird with long tail.
	Maina, a bird.
	Nág, a cobra.
	Parewá, a pigeon.
	Pechâ, an owl.
	Suiá, a bird.
	Sulankhi, a bird.
	Sundi, mahua flower.
	Titipi, a night bird.
	Turu, a bird.

Beldár.

Titles :—Gadahya, Marár, Ráut.

Sub-castes.	Section.
Bhojpuriá.	Kasyapa.
Chauhán.	
Kathautiá or Katháwá.	

Bhandári, *Nápit*, *Hajjám*.

Titles :—Bárik, Kshuri.

Sub-castes.	Section.
Bangáli.	
Dakhini.	
Desi.	
Khariá.	
Khurdá.	
Gola.	
Hatuá.	

Bhar.

Title :—Ráná.

Sub-castes.	Sections.
	(*a*) *Totemistic*—
1. Bangáli.	Bánsrishi, bamboo.
2. Maghayá.	Bel, *bel* fruit.
	Kachhap, tortoise.
	Mayur, peacock.
	(*b*) *Eponymous*—
	Agni.
	Brahmarishi.
	Rishi.

Bhát.

Titles:—Bhárata, Dasaundhi, Kabiji, Rái.

Sub-castes.	Sections.
Baram-Bhát.	Anal.
Ráj-Bhát.	Antahriá.
Turk-Bhát (Mahomedan).	Balbandhiá.
	Bharadwája.
	Gaighatiá.
	Kailiá.
	Kásyapa.
	Kunwar.
	Lakhsariá.
	Lohárkoriyá.
	Mahrajiá.
	Menwár.
	Sahar.
	Sándilya.
	Sanhakiá.
	Sindhwatiá.
	Suarait.

Atselá, Baruá, Bhatara, Chaurási, Chúngele, Dasaundhi, Gujriwálá, Jangira, Kailiá, Maháputra, Nagauri, Sikatpúrea, are mentioned by Sir Henry Elliot as subdivisions of Bháts, but it is not stated whether these names denote sub-castes, sections, or merely titles.

Bhuinmáli, *Bhusundar, Siddhi-putra, Hári.*

Sub-castes.		Sections.
1. Bara-bhágiyá.		Parásara.
2. Mitra Seni Behará.		Aliman.
3. Chhota-bhágiyá.		
4. Amarábádi	Found in Noakhali, and apparently peculiar to that district.	
5. Sáráliá		
6. Hátiá		
7. Bhuluá		

Bhuiyá, *Bhuinyá, Bhuiyán, Bhuinhár, Bhumiyá, Musahar, Náik Khandáyat, Khandáyat-Páik, Ghatwál, Ghatwár, Tikáyat, Rajwár, Rái-Bhuiyá, Ber-Bhuiyá, Sardár, Puran.*

Titles:—Bhogta, Chharidár, Kopát, Mahton, Mánjhi, Náik, Rái Singh, Thákur, Tikáyat.

Sub-tribes.	Septs.
In Lohardagá—	Asura.
Bichwár.	Bagáli.
Deswáli.	Baliar.
Dundwár.	Banini.
Junwár.	Banka.
Khandait.	Bankiar.
Maghaiyá.	Banui.
Mahtwár.	Champiar.
Marheriá.	Chirra or Rikhiasan, squirrel.
Rajwár.	Golari.
Rikhiásan.	Jagdâ.
Tirwár.	Jagorari.
	Kach, tortoise.
In Keonjhar—	Kaliar.
Mál or Desh-Bhuiyá.	Kandni.
Dandsena.	Kanrui.
Khatti.	Kenduari.
Rájkuli.	Keruri.
	Kihar.
In Manbhum—	Kussum, a tree.
Dhorá.	Kutar.
Kátrás.	Lota.
Musahar.	Nág.
	Naragi.
In Hazaribagh—	Narari.
Ghátwár.	Noah.
Tikáyat.	Pachoar.
	Pansi.
	Rái.
	Ranangi.
	Sani.
	Satadi.
	Sinhi.

Bhumij.

Titles:—Mánki,[1] Matkum,[2] Mura,[3] Sardár.[4]

Sub-tribes.	Septs.
Desi.	Baddá Kurkutiá, a kind of worm.
Tamáriá, Murá, or Mánki-Mura.[5]	Bárdá.
Sikhariyá or Meno.[6]	Bhuiyá, fish.
Pátkumiá [7]	Chandil.
Shelo, iron-smelters.	Gulgu, fish.
Barábhumiá, zamindar Bhumij.[8]	Hánsdá, wild goose.
	Hemrong, betel palm.
	Járu, a bird.
	Kásyab, tortoise.
	Leng, mushroom.
	Nág, snake.
	Obársári, a bird.
	Pilá.
	Ságmá.
	Sálrishi, *sal* fish.
	Sándilya, a bird.
	Sáolá.
	Tesá, bird.
	Tumárung, pumpkin.
	Tuti, a sort of vegetable.

---

1 This title is common among the Mundas.
2 Applied to the Bhumij of Dhalbhum.
3 Mura is the common form of Munda in Manbhum.
4 Possibly borrowed from the *ghatwali* system, the leading executive unit of which is the *sardár* or head of the subordinate *ghatwals* (*tabidars*) of a village.
5 The two latter appellations clearly suggest Munda descent.
6 This group is supposed to come from Manbhum.
7 The Patkumiá and Tamáriá sub-tribes occasionally intermarry.
8 Probably descended from members of the Barabhum zamindari family.

Bind.

Titles:—Chaudhri, Mahto, Mukhiá, Ráut.

Sub-castes.		Sections.
Khariát	In Behar.	(*a*) *Territorial*—
Awadhiyá		Jarhuáit.
Lodhiyá		Jhauáit.
Gondh		Odaniá.
Jutaut Bind	In Eastern Bengal.	(*b*) *Eponymous*—
Nun Bind		Kásyapa.
Bin		

Binjhiá, *Birjiá, Brijiá, Binjhwár.*

Titles :—**Baráik, Dandlá, Gaunjhu, Kárji, Mánjhi, Mirdáhá, Náik, Náth, Parja, Pradhán.**

Sub-tribes.	Septs.
Pahári ya-Binjhiá.	**Bair**, *zisyphus jujuba.*
Dand-Binjhiá.	**Bansetti**, don't touch bamboo at a wedding.
Agaria-Binjhiá.	**Bhair.**
	Cheruka, fish.
	Chidra, squirrel.
	Chingri, a river-fish.
	Chorka, a pond-fish.
	Chutia, rat.
	Dádul, bull-frog.
	Garai, a river-fish.
	Huru, paddy-bird.
	Kachua, tortoise.
	Kási, a kind of grass (*saccharum spontaneum*).
	Kuns, grass.
	Mangar, crocodile.
	Murgi, hen.
	Nág, serpent.
	Pusway, a river-fish.
	Sinduria, use *sindur*, a red paint, at marriage.
	Telha, use oil at marriage.
	Tengra, a river-fish.
	Thekra, a river-fish.

Birhor.

Title :—**Birhor.**

Sub-tribes.	Septs.
Nil.	**Hemrom**, a kind of fish.
	Jagsaria.
	Liluai.
	Mahli.
	Nág, cobra.
	Nagpuria.
	Singpuria.
	Siruar.

Bráhman, *Báman, Bipra, Dwija, Thákur, Sarmá, Deva-Sarmá, Bhudeva, Bhusur, Agraja, Mahárájji, Bábáji, Gosáinji.*

Main divisions. *Territorial divisions.*

Pancha Gauriya—Sáraswat, Kányakubja, Gaura, Utkal, Maithil.

Pancha Drávira—Karnáti, Tailangi or Andhra, Gujráti or Gurjjara, Dráviri, Maháráshtriya.

Miscellaneous—Nepali, Vyásokta, Sákadwipi, Kraunchdwipi (including Jausi, Jotkhi or Jyotshi, Dákantiá, Bhadariá or Bhareri, Jadwá, Saguniá, Sanicherá), Mágadha, Bandijan or Suta, Atharva, Máthur, Mahá Bráhman otherwise called Mahápátra or Kantáha, Lakhauria, Belontiá, Kathak, Kaláwat, Tikaur, Sakuntalá, Sawálákhi, Kashmiri, Kámrupi.

Tirtha Purohits, Debal or Pandá:—Gayáwál, Prayágwal, Gangáputra, Dhámin, etc.

Sáraswat.

Sub-castes.	Sections.			
In the Panjáb.				
Four local divisions, divided into high, middle, and low endogamous groups.	1st division	High	... 50	The *gotras* are common to all Bráhmans.
		Low	... 172	
	2nd "	High	... 12	
		Low	... 23	
	3rd "	High	... 9	
		Low	... 48	
	4th "	High	... 11	
		Middle	... 20	
		Low	... 124	
		Total	... 469	

In Behar they have the following titles, which are endogamous:—Misra, Sukul, Dube or Dobe, Tiwári, Páthak, Pánde, Upádhyáya, Chaube or Chobe, Bájapeyi, Pandit.

Kánya Kubja, Kanaujiá.

Titles (*in Behar*):—Misr or Misra, Sukul, Tiwári, Dube or Dobe, Páthak, Pánre, Upádhyáya, Chaube or Chobe, Dichhit or Dikshit, Lakhnau or Bájapeyi, Sarwariyá or Saryupári.

Titles (*in Bengal*) :—Bhattáchárji, Ghatak, Chakrabartti, Bandya, Chattu, Mukhati, Rái, Munshi, Chaudhri, Sarkár, Majumdár, Háldár, Bidyáratna, Bidyábágis, Smritiratna.

Sub-castes.

In Bengal.

Rárhi.
 Piráli.
Bárendra.
 Uttar Bárendra.
 Pánchuriá.
Madhyasreni or Madyadoshi.
Barna or Patita Bráhman.
Agradáni.
A'chárji, Daibajna, Ganaka.
Bhát or Bhatta.
Maruiporá.
Saptasati or Sátsati.
Vaidik.
 Páschátya.
 Dákshinátya.

Sections or *gotras* common to all Bráhmans.

Abya.
Agastya.
A'lamyán.
Anábrikáksha.
A'ngirasa.
A'treya.
Atri.
Baijáhmapadya.
Baiyághrapadya.
Basishtha.
Básuki.
Bátsya.
Bharadwája.
Bhárgava.
Bishnu.
Biswámitra.
Briddha.
Brihaspati.
Garga.
Gautama.
Ghritakausika.
Gotama.
Jábáli.
Jaimini.
Jájnabalkya.
Jámadagnya.
Kalvisha.
Kánchan.
Kanwa or Kánna.
Kásyapa.
Kátyáyan.
Kaundilya.
Kausika.
Kaustav.
Krishnátreya.
Kusal.
Maudgalya.
Maunas.
Parásara.
Paulastya.
Rikhab.
Rohita.
Sábarna.
Saktri.
Sándilya.
Sánkriti.
Saukálin.
Saupáyan.
Sunaka.
Upamanya.

Sections of Uttar Bárendras according to "Laghu Bhárat" and "Sambandhanirnaya."

Swarna-Kausik.
Rajata-Kausik.
Ghrita-Kausik.
Kaundilya-Kausik.
Kausika.

Kshatrapeta or hybrid gotras.

Saunaka.
Kánwáyan.
Rathitara.
Agnibesma.

1. The Rárhi and Bárendra sub-castes have the following five *gotras* :—Kásyapa, Sándilya, Sábarna, Bátsya, and Bharadwája.

2. The Sátsatis have some of the *gotras* or exogamous sections in use among Baidik Brahmans.

3. There can be no intermarriage amongst persons of the following five *gotras* :—Jámadagnya, Bátsya, Sábarna, Maudgalya, Saupáyana, which are supposed to be of common ancestry and are therefore reckoned as one exogamous section.

4. The Madhyasreni or Madyadoshi Bráhmans of Western Bengal have the following *gotras* :—Sándilya, Bátsyaba, Kásyapa, Bharadwája, Sábarnya, Parásara, Gautma, Ghrita-Kausika.

5. The Bháts or Bhattas have the following *gotras* :—Kásyapa, Bharadwája, Sándilya, Ghrita-Kausika, Aurbba Rishi, Bátsya, Alimyán.

6. Each *gotra* has its *pravaras*, *i.e.*, a group of from three to five Rishis belonging to the same *gotra*. Intermarriage between persons having the same *pravaras* is in theory prohibited, but this rule is not now strictly observed.

Gáin or Grámin (56 or 59) of the Rárhi sub-caste under the five *gotras* :—

Sándilya Gotra (16).

Bandya.
Gargari.
Kesarkuni.
Kusumkali.
Párihál.
Kulabhi.

Ghoshli.
Sejagá.
Máschatak.
Barál.
Basuári.

Kadál.
Kusári.
Kulisá or Kulkuli.
Akás.
Dirgháti.

Kásyapa Gotra (16).

Gur.
Ambuli.
Bhuri.
Talabáti.
Pitamundi.
Chatta.

Palsái.
Har.
Porári.
Páladhi.
Koári.

Pákrási.
Simlái.
Pushali, Pushilál.
Bhatta.
Mul.

Bharadwája Gotra (4).

Mukhaiti.
Dingsáin.

Sáharik.
Ráyi.

Sábarna Gotra (12).

Gánguli.
Kundalál.
Siddhal.
Dáyi.

Nandi.
Báli.
Siárik.
Pungsika.

Sáteswari.
Páriál.
Ghanteswari.
Náyári.

Bátsya Gotra (8 or 11).

Mahintá.
Ghoshál.
Simlái.
Bápuli.

Pippalái.
Putitunda.
Purbba.
Kánjilál.

Kánjiári.
Chautkhandi.
Dighál.

The Gáins whom Rájá Ballál Sen made—*Kulin*, *Gauna Kulin*, and *Srotriya*:—

Kulin (8).

Bandya.	Ghoshál.	Kánjilál.
Chatta.	Putitunda.	Kundalál.
Mukhaiti.	Gánguli.	

Gauna Kulin (14).

Ráyi.	Pippalái.	Párihál.
Gur.	Gargari.	Har.
Mahintá.	Ghanteswari.	Pitamundi.
Kulabhi.	Kesarkuni.	Dirgháti.
Chautkhandi.	Dingsái.	

The remaining 34 or 37 are **Srotriyas.**

Those Ghataks who reckon 56 Gains, include Porári among Gauna Kulins and exclude Dighal, Chautkhandi, and Purbba. Those who reckon 59, exclude Porári, Dighal, and Purbba from Gauna Kulin, and show 34 Srotriyas.

Hypergamous groups *bháha* and sub-groups *mel* of Rárhis formed by the famous social reformer Devibar Ghatak:—

Groups.	Mels or sub-groups, mostly endogamous.	
Kulin.	Phuliá.	Sribarddhani.
Bhanga Kulin.	Khardaha.	Satánandkháni.
Srotriya { Suddha.	Ballabhi.	Chhayi.
Srotriya { Sádhya.	Sarbbánandi.	Kohambitá.
Srotriya { Kashta.	Panditratni.	Dasarath Ghataki.
Bansaja.	Bángál.	Subharájkháni.
	Surái.	Máládharkháni.
	Achárjya Sekhari.	Rághab Ghosháli.
	Gopálghataki.	Denáti.
	Chatta Rághabi.	Nariyá.
	Bijayapanditi.	Kákusthi.
	Mádhái.	Dharáduari.
	Bidyádhari.	Ráyi.
	Párihál.	Bhairab Ghataki.
	Sriangabhatti.	Parmánanda Misra.
	Pramodni.	Sunga Sarbbánandi.
	Báli.	Hari Majumdári.
	Chandrapati.	Chándái.

Gain or *Grámin* (100) of the Bárendra sub-caste under the five *gotras* : —

Kásyapa gotra (18).

Maitra.	Moáli.	Madhyagrámi.
Bháduri.	Kiral.	Mathgrámi.
Karanja.	Bijkunja.	Gangágrámi.
Bálayashthi.	Sargrámi.	Belgrámi.
Modhágrámi.	Sahagrámi.	Chamagrámi.
Balihári.	Katigrámi.	Asrukoti.

Sándilya gotra (14).

Rudrabágchhi.	Kámendra.	Subarna.
Láheri.	Sihari.	Totaka.
Sádhubágchhi.	Tároálá Bisi.	Pushána.
Champati.	Matasyási.	Beluri.
Nandanábási.	Champa.	

Bátsya gotra (24).

Sánnyál.	Simli.	Srutabati.
Bhimkáli.	Dhosáli.	Akshagrámi.
Bhattasáli.	Tánuri.	Sáhari.
Kámkáli.	Batsagrámi.	Káligrámi.
Kurmuri.	Deuli.	Kálihái.
Bháriál.	Nidráli.	Paundrakáli.
Laksha.	Kukkuti.	Kálindi.
Jámrukhi.	Borhgrámi.	Chaturábandi.

Bharadwája gotra (24).

Bhádar.	Bála.	Káchhati.
Láruli.	Sákati.	Nandigrámi.
Jhámál, Jhampati.	Simbi.	Gográmi.
Áturthi.	Bahál.	Nikhati.
Rái.	Sariyál.	Pippali.
Ratnábali.	Kshetragrámi.	Sringa.
Uchchharakhi.	Dadhiyál.	Khorjár.
Gochchhási.	Puti.	Goswálambi.

Sábarna gotra (20).

Singdiár.	Tátoár.	Khandabati.
Pákari.	Setu.	Nikari.
Dadhi.	Naigrámi.	Samudra.
Sringi.	Nedhuri.	Ketugrámi.
Medari.	Kapáli.	Jasográmi.
Undhuri.	Tuttari.	Sitali.
Dhundhuri.	Panchabati.	

Gáin of Uttar-Barendras according to "Gaure Brahman":—

Sándilya.	Kásyapa.	Bátsya.
Champati.	Bháduri.	Káláyi.
Bágchhi.	Karanjá.	Grihasodhani.
Lábar.	Simbi.	Madhugrámi.
Nandanábási.		
Sihari.		

Bharadwája.	Sábarna.
Rái.	Annásani.
Gopurbba.	
Sirasinthi.	
Jhámál.	

Kulins made by Ballál Sen:—

Láheri.	Maitra.	Kálihái.
Bágchhi.	Sannyál.	Bhádar.
Bháduri.	Misra.	

Srotriyas divided by Rájá Kansa Náráyan:—

(*a*) *Siddha Srotriya.*

Karanja.	Laruli.	Áturthi.
Nandanábási.	Champati.	Kálihái.
Bhattasáli.	Jhampati.	

(*b*) *Sádhya Srotriya.*

Uchchharakhi.	Sihari.	Bisi.
Jámrukhi.	Rái.	Karjjuri.
Ratnábali.	Goswálambi.	

(*c*) The rest are *Kashta Srotriyas.*

Hypergamous groups *bhába* and sub-groups *pathi* of Bárendras formed by the learned social reformer Udayanácharya Bháduri:—

Groups.	Sub-groups.
Kulin.	Jonáli.
Srotriya { Siddha.	Nirábil.
Srotriya { Sádhya.	Bhushná.
Srotriya { Kashta.	Rohilá.
Kápa, Chhaghariá.	Kutabkháni.
	Áliákháni.
	Bhabánipuri.
	Beni.

Bárendra titles:—

Bágh, tiger.	**Pánjá**, heap of bricks.
Bherá, sheep.	**Páthá**, goat.
Dhol, drum.	**Prachanda**, furious.
Gappi, tell-tale.	**Talápátra**, bottom of a pot.
Gonj, peg.	**Taulo**, earthen pot.

Gáin of **Saptasatis** :—Árath, Báguri, Bálthubi, Bhágái, Dháin, Dhardhar, Hálui, Háturi, Jabagrámi, Jagái, Kálui, Kándare, Kánthará, Kanyá, Kátádi, Kátáni, Káturi, Kusalá, Mulukjuri, Nálsi, Nánaksái, Pátári, Pharphar, Pithári, Ságáin, Sáin, Sugáin, Ujalá, Ulluk, etc.

Vaidik.

Sub-castes.	Sections (*gotras*).	Groups, *samáj*.
Páschátya Vaidik. { **Jonári.** **Konári.**	**Sándilya** ...	**Ákhará.** **Madhyabhág.** **Pánkunda.**
	Basishtha ...	**Joári.** **Gauráli.** **Aládhi.** **Dadhichi.**
	Sábarna ...	**Sántaru.** **Brahmapur.** **Marichi Grám.**
	Bharadwája ...	**Chandradwip.** **Navadwip.** **Kotálipárá.**
	Saunaka ...	**Sámantasár.**
	Local groups—	**Purbbasthálí.** **Bishnupur.** **Bhátpárá.** **Purbba Banga.**

Bráhmans of the following *gotras* came later on (1102 Sak or 1180 A.D.) and mixed up with the Páschátya Vaidiks :—Krishnátreya, Gautama, Rathitara, Kásyapa, Bátsya, Sunak; and still later on (1403 Sak or 1481 A.D.) came Bráhmans of the Ghrita-Kausika, Kausika, Átreya, Sankarshan, Parásara, Agnibesma, Maudgalya, Hárita, and Upamanyu *gotras*.

		Hypergamous groups.
Dákshinátya Vaidik.	**Kásyapa.**	**Kulin.**
	Gautama.	**Bansaja.**
	Bátsya.	**Maulik.**
	Kánwáyan.	
	Kausika.	Local groups or *samáj*.
	Ghrita-Kausika.	
	Játukarna.	**Majilpur.**
	Sábarna.	**Rájpur.**

The Dákshinátya Vaidiks have the following titles :—

Tripáthi, Misra, Páthak, Chakrabartti.

Gaura.

Sub-castes.		Titles.
Kevala Gaura.		Sukul.
Ádi Gaura	Sukalvála.	Pánde.
	Joshi.	Misra.
	Ojhá.	Joshi.
Sanádhya	Chingala.	Dube.
	Dáymia.	Tiwári.
	Khandelvála.	Chaube.
Hariyána.		Vyása.
Sri-Gaura	Támboli.	
	Ádi Sri-Gaura.	
Gurjar Gaura.		
Tek Bárá.		
Chamár Gaura.		
Kritanay.		

Maithil or Tirhutiá.

Titles :—Majhrote, Misir or Misra including Chaudhari, Ráya, Parihasta, Khána and Kumára, Ojhá, Ujha or Jhá, Páthu, Pura including Bakriyár and Charviyár, Thákur, Pádri.

Hypergamous groups.	Sections. *Gotra.*	Sections. *Dih or Mul.*
Srotriya or Srotri.	Bátsa	1. Karmahe-Majhaurá.
Jog.	Bátsa	2. Karmahe-Tarauni.
Panjibaddh.	Bátsa	3. Karmahe-Naruái.
Nágar.	Bátsa	4. Karmahe-Behat.
Jaiwár.	Bátsa	5. Karmahe-Majhiám.
	Bátsa	6. Karmahe-Alanpur.
	Bátsa	7. Karmahe-Baghát.
	Bátsa	8. Karmahe-Urará.
	Sándil ...	9. Karmahe-Ahpur.
	Bharadwája	10. Belaunche-Káko.
	Bharadwája	11. Belaunche-Ojhaul.
	Bharadwája	12. Belaunche-Sudai.
	Bharadwája	13. Belaunche-Ratpár.
	Bharadwája	14. Belaunche-Garh.
	Bharadwája	15. Belaunche-Dih.

Gotra.	*Dih* or *Mul.*
Bátsa ...	16. Hariáme-Rakhwári. 17. Hariáme-Sibá. 18. Hariáme-Balirájpur. 19. Hariáme-Katmá. 20. Hariáme-Ahil.
Bátsa ...	21. Paliwár-Mangrauni. 22. Paliwár-Mahesi. 23. Paliwár-Dibra. 24. Paliwár-Sakuri. 25. Paliwár-Haripur. 26. Paliwár-Samaul. 27. Paliwár-Kachhra. 28. Paliwár-Phuldáha. 29. Paliwár-Mahendra. 30. Paliwár-Jarhatyá.
Bátsa ...	31. Budhwáre-Mahesi. 32. Budhwáre-Sakuri. 33. Budhwáre-Dumrá. 34. Budhwáre-Balha.
Sándil ...	35. Saudarpurái-Mahiá. 36. Saudarpurái-Katka. 37. Saudarpurái-Jagaur. 38. Saudarpurái-Sarso. 39. Saudarpurai-Suket. 40. Saudarpurái-Hansauli. 41. Saudarpurái-Khoir. 42. Saudarpurái-Digaun. 43. Saudarpurái-Kanhauli. 44. Saudarpurái-Mánik. 45. Saudarpurái-Rohár. 46. Saudarpurái-Sundar. 47. Saudarpurái-Dhaul. 48. Saudarpurái-Baghát. 49. Saudarpurái-Gaul.
Kásyap ...	50. Darihare-Dih. 51. Darihare-Rájanpurá. 52. Darihare-Bargamiá. 53. Darihare-Ratauli. 54. Darihare-Sahasrám.
Bátsa ...	55. Anraiwár-Anrai. 56. Anraiwár-Usrauli. 57. Anraiwár-Jauá. 58. Anraiwár-Baingni.

Gotra.	*Dih or Mul.*
Kásyap ...	59. Baliáse-Narsam. 60. Baliáse-Balha. 61. Baliáse-A'si. 62. Baliáse-Sakuri. 63. Baliáse-Dharaurá. 64. Baliáse-Suket. 65. Baliáse-Baghánt.
Kásyap ...	66. Tannahpurái-Solhni.
Bátsa ...	67. Takwáre-Ankusi. 68. Takwáre-Nima.
Kásyap ...	69. Khowáre-Nahás. 70. Khowáre-Mahuá. 71. Khowáre-Mahnaurá. 72. Khowáre-Kokrahi. 73. Khowáre-Khari. 74. Khowáre-Murájpur.
Kásyap ...	75. Satlakhe-Sataur. 76. Satlakhe-Satlakha.
Kátyáyan ...	77. Kunjilwár-Malangiá. 78. Kunjilwár-Sater. 79. Kunjilwár-Ullu. 80. Kunjilwár-Bhakhren. 81. Kunjilwár-Digaun. 82. Kunjilwár-Bhakhrauli.
Sándil ...	83. Khanraure-Bhaur. 84. Khanraure-Khutti. 85. Khanraure-Gurdi. 86. Khanraure-Ekmá.
Kásyap ...	87. Sakariwár-Harari. 88. Sakariwár-Tatail. 89. Sakariwár-Chhámu.
Sándil ...	90. Pagulwár-Barhiám. 91. Pagulwár-Tarálohi. 92. Pagulwár-Dhen.
Kásyap ...	93. Maráre-Sihol. 94. Marare-Jagaul. 95. Marare-Ukki. 96. Marare-Barhampur. 97. Marare-Adauri. 98. Marare-Misrauli. 99. Marare-Rajaurá. 100. Marare-Jagatpur.
Sándil ...	101. Dighwe-Tipri. 102. Dighwe-Nagar. 103. Dighwe-Kankaurá. 104. Dighwe-Sannahpur. 105. Dighwe-Sakarpurá.

Gotra.		*Dih* or *Mul.*
Bátsa	...	106. Bahirarwár-Parhat. 107. Bahirarwár-Punách. 108. Bahirarwár-Párkhand. 109. Bahirarwár-Kasiám.
Kásyap	...	110. Bisaiwár-Nanhpur. 111. Bisaiwár-Bisphi.
Bharadwáj		112. Ekahre-Orá. 113. Ekahre-Ruchaul. 114. Ekahre-Kanhauli. 115. Ekahre-Sagrám. 116. Ekahre-Torne.
Sándil	...	117. Gangulwár-Sakuri. 118. Gangulwár-Dumrá.
Kásyap	...	119. Kataiwár-Andhrá. 120. Kataiwár-Phet. 121. Kataiwár-Malangia. 122. Kataiwár-Loám. 123. Kataiwár-Maráchi.
Sándil	...	124. Sariswe-Khangor. 125. Sariswe-Sakuri.
Bátsa	...	126. Ghusaute-Nagwár.
Bátsa	...	127. Babhanyáme-Katma. 128. Babhanyáme-Karrain.
Kásyap	...	129. Kusmáre-Sabás. 130. Kusmáre-Dhanauli.
Kásyap	...	131. Narwáre-Rámpur.
Gautama	...	132. Barhampurái-Barhampur.
Kásyap	...	133. Purue-Mahendra.
Sándil	...	134. Andarái-Nehra. 135. Andarái-Laguniá. 136. Andarái-Pirápur.
Sábarna	...	137. Panchaubhe-Khajuli. 138. Panchaubhe-Jhauá. 139. Panchaubhe-Birpur. 140. Panchaubhe-Barhmaul. 141. Panchaubhe-Bhithi. 142. Panchaubhe-Dadri. 143. Panchaubhe-Kariaun.
Bátsa	...	144. Jalaiwár-Jale. 145. Jalaiwár-Maranchi. 146. Jalaiwár-Ganraul. 147. Jalaiwár-Máli.
Sándil	...	148. Jajwáre-Bharám. 149. Jajwáre-Udanpur. 150. Jajwáre-Jamuni. 151. Jajwáre-Pachahi.

Gotra.		*Dih* or *Mul.*
Kásyap	...	152. Pakaráe-Mahesi.
Kásyap	...	153. Budhaure.
Kásyap	...	154. Bharhe.
Sándil	...	155. Gángaure.
Sándil	...	156. Bhatore.
Sándil	...	157. Sakarghore.
Parásar	...	158. Surganai.
Parásar	...	159. Sugarganai-Loám.
Kausika	...	160. Nekutwár-Barahi.
Sándil	...	161. Nonaitwár.
Sándil	...	162. Talaiwár.
Sándil	...	163. Sihásme-Khor. 164. Sihásme-Sihásam.
Bátsa	...	165. Kaiáre.
Kásyap	...	166. Ainwár.
Bharadwáj		167. Domtakarái.
Bharadwáj		168. Kanigáme Kanigám.
Kásyap	...	169. Bhandwál.
Kásyap	...	170. Thariáme-Thariam.
Garg	...	171. Basahe.
Parásar	...	172. Sunriwár-Solhni.
Parásar	...	173. Naraune Teghrá. 174. Naraune Saktárápur.
Sándil	...	175. Chhatimane-Chhatman.
Sándil	...	176. Kodarie.
Krishnán	...	177. Bhusware.

Utkal.

Titles :—Nanda, Pate, Kara, Achárya, Satpathi, Bedi, Senápati, Panigrahi, Nisank, Bainipati, Pandá, Padahári, Murhiá or Sebaka, Ghátiyá, Dája, Paya, Baghi, Muosi, Devatá, Dandapat, Mahanti, Dharsarmákar, Tripáti, Mahápátra, Misra, Rath, Dás, Sarangi, Sámágrahi, Hotá, Náth, Cheni, Pátra, Láik, Bahali, Pati, Pádhá Sálu, Páthak, Páni, Fakir, Feringi, Lau, Malo, Ghási, Ladu, Basu, Pakharpaila, Kantaru, Gorea, Tarat, Jayi, Karpur, Kandarpa, Parhatiá, Phunknali.

Sub-castes.	*Gotra* or sections.
Srotriya or Sásani— Sámanta.	Batsas. Kausika. Átreya. Kásyapa.
Bhatta Misra.	Kautsasa. Bharadwája. Átreya. Dattátreya. Krishnátreya.

Sub-castes.	Gotra or sections.
Vaidika.	Átreya. Kautsasa. Hárita. Kausika. Katyáyana. Maudgal. Sándil. Kaundinya. Gautam. Kásyapa. Bharadwája. Kapinja'a. Sábarnika. Játukarna. Parásara.
Upádhyáya.	*Gotras* are all the same as in Sásani, except Batsas and Kausika.
Asrotriya —	
Sarua Pandá =Bardhusika or Paniár.	Bharadwája.
Murhiá Pandá or Debalaka.	*Gotras as of* Vaidiks.
Grám Jáchaka.	Ditto.
Mahasthán, Mastán, Saraibaliá or Háliá.	Balarám or Balabhadriá.
Jhárua.	
Dakshiná Uriyá or Dákhinátya.	
Jájpuriá or Uttar-Sreni.	
Raghunáthiá.	
Jaiá or Purbiyá.	

Besides those mentioned above, the following *gotras* or sections are found among Utkal Bráhmans :—

Ángirasa.
Autathya.
Baikháyana.
Basishtha.
Biswámitra.
Garga.
Jaimini.
Jámadagna.
Kaphalya.
Kámakáyan.
Kauchha.
Paithinasa.
Pautimanna.
Sánkriti.
Saunaka.
Taittiriya.
Uddalaka.
Upamanna.

Mr. John Beames gives the following scheme of the subdivisions of the Brahman caste in Northern Orissa,—first, according to the Veda, whose ritual they profess to observe, and secondly into *gotras* or families:—

I.—Dákhinátya Sreni or Southern Line.

1. *Rig-Veda.*

Gotra or Sections.	*Upádhi* or Titles.
Basishtha.	Sárangi.
"	Mahápátra.

2. *Sáma-Veda.*

Kásyapa.	Nanda.
Dharagautama.	Tripáthi.
Gautama.	Udgátá, *vulgo* Utá.
Parásara.	Dibedi, *vulgo* Dube.
Kaundinya.	Tripáthi, *vulgo* Tíhári.

3. *Yajur-Veda.*

Bharadwája—	
a. Bharadwája.	Sárangi.
b. Sambhukar.	Misra.
c. Lándi.	Nanda.
Átreya—	
a. Dattátreya.	Ratha.
b. Krishnátreya.	"
Haritasa.	Mahápátra.
"	Dása.
Káuchhasa.	"
Ghritakauchhasa.	"
Mudgala.	Satpathi, *vulgo* Pathi, also Satpasti.
Batsasa.	Dása, Áchárya, Misra.
Kátyáyana.	Sárangi.
Kapinjala.	Dása.

II.—Uttara Sreni or Northern Line.

1. *Rig-Veda.*

Not represented.

2. *Yajur-Veda.*

Gotra or Sections.	*Upádhi* or Titles.
Kátyáyana.	Pandá.
Sándilya.	„
Krishnátreya.	„ and Dása.
Bharadwája.	„
Barshagana.	Misra.
Kaphalya.	„
Gautama.	Kara.

3. *Atharva-Veda.*

Ángirasa.	Upadhyáya, *vulgo* Upadhya.

Of lower branches, and considered inferior to the above, are—

Sánkhyáyana.	Mahanti.
Nágasa.	Dasa, Mahanti.

Sákadwípí, *Bhojyak*, *Bhuist*.

Their *gotras* are the same as in the other sub-castes of Bráhmans.

Pur or sections.

Adriár.	Deorahiár.
Ahilásariár.	Dewárk.
Aiyár.	Dihwár.
Áwadhiár.	Dumariár.
Baghwár.	Gadahpurná.
Bariswár.	Gadrahá.
Barsái.	Gandark.
Barwár.	Gochhpuriá.
Batsauriark.	Gorhárk.
Batwákariyár.	Gunsaiyá.
Bhalauniár.	Hadauriár.
Bhedbakárár.	Hemriárk.
Bherápákri.	Jamuár.
Bholárk.	Jurhá.
Binsaiyá.	Juthibariár.
Budhwárk.	Karaiárk.
Chadchák.	Kausikárak.
Chandratiár.	Khajurák.
Chandrorh.	Khandarp.
Chhariyár.	Khantwár.
Chhathwark.	Khatsopárk.
Chhatrawár.	Konárk.
Chitauriár.	Korankárk.
Chonchwár.	Kukurbandhá.
Dadhpuriárk.	Kundárk.
Dakráhi.	Kurái.
Debkuliár.	Lokárk.
Dehlásariár.	Madhubaniá.
Deodhiár.	Madhurasiárk.

Pur or sections.

Mahdauriár.	Pundárk.
Maheswar.	Punrakhiá.
Mahrasiá.	Rahdauriár.
Makhaiwár.	Sabhaiyár.
Mákhpawár.	Saphárk.
Malauriár.	Senduriár.
Márkandárk.	Sikauriár.
Mauriyár.	Sirmauriár.
Nandark.	Soniyár.
Osiár.	Soriyár.
Pachhwár.	Sukhsárá.
Panchbatiar.	Swetbhadra.
Panchhai.	Tarkanyark.
Panchkanthi.	Thakurmairar.
Pandiár.	Udaniyár.
Pariár.	Ulárk.
Pathaiár.	Urwár.
Patiyár.	Usahiyárk.
Pawaiyár.	

Nepáli Brahmans.

Endogamous divisions.	*Gotra* or sections.	*Thar* or sub-sections.
Upádhyáya. Kamiya. Purabi.	Básishta ...	Bhatta Rái. Dawári. Chálisa, Chelisya. Bharári. Bisishta Sakti. Páráswar. Tinai Prabarái. Brahmimá Dhán.
	Dhánjaya ...	Rijál. Gura Gáin. Homya Gáin.
	Átrái ...	Parel, Pondyál. Arjel.
	Kausika ...	Regmi. Soberi.
	Kaundin ...	Ácharjya. Párájuli. Neopáni, Nivipánya.
	Dhartá Kausik ...	Nepaliyá. Barál. Khodál or Khandyál.

Endogamous divisions.	*Gotra* or sections.	*Thar* or sub-sections.
	Bharadwája ...	Suberi. Jámár Katyál. Bagalya.
	Bachh ...	Dohál. Langsál or Lamsál.
	Atri ...	Gautam. Khatiwára. Misra. Champágáin. Archnáni.
	Kásyap ...	Dhimire.
	Kasya ...	Adhikári.
	Agasti ...	Dhungiál.
	Mautkaha ...	Timilsiná. Kainrála.
	Upamanya ...	Dhákal.
	Kanniá ...	Sapankotyá.
	Gargya ...	Murtel. Pyakarel or Pokharyál.

In addition to the above, Hodgson's list contains the following *thars*:—

Khanál.
Nirola.
Maháráshtra.
Pakonyal.
Sattyal.
Rimál.
Devakotya.
Parbatya.
Kaikyal.
Rupakheti.
Desjá.
Rukái.
Saival.
Laiyál.
Dotiyál.
Danjál.
Singyál.
Bikrál.
Ukniyál.
Bhattvál.
Gajniyál.
Chavala Gáin.
Vasta Gáin.
Banjára.
Dáji.
Soti.
Osti.
Utkuli.
Kandaria.
Ghartmel.
Ghartyál.
Temrakoti.
Uphaltopi.
Párijai Kavala.
Pandit.
Teva Pánya.
Kaphalya.
Gaithaula.
Gairaha Pipli.
Ghimirya.
Simkhárá.
Phuuvál.
Chámkasaini.
Purásaini.
Dhurári.
Bhurtyál.
Paneru.
Loityal.
Sidhyál.
Gotanya.
Ghorasaine.
Risyál.
Dhongán.
Dulál.
Bajgáin.
Satola.
Ghurcholi.
Kelatoni.
Gilal.
Lahoni.
Muthbári.

Buná, *Banuá, Buno.*

Cháin, *Barcháin.*

Sub-castes.	Sections.
Nil.	Bharadwáji. Charanbansi. Kásyapa. Sándil.

Chakmá, *Tsakmá, Tsak, Thek* (Burm).

Sub-tribes.	Septs.
1. Chakmá. 2. Doingnak. 3. Tungjainya. Septs of the Chakmá sub-tribe.	Amu. Bámu, named after rivers. Barbora. Baruwa. Batalya, a chisel. Boga. Borsege. Bung. Bungza. Darjea. Dawin. Dhaona, he of the mended cloth. Dhurjya, the wearer of *bhimráj* feathers. Durjea. Ichapocha, the eater of rotten shrimps. Kalá, a plantain tree. Kengragati,[1] the giver of the big crab. Khambe. Khiongje. Kurá, named after rivers. Kurjya, the idle one. Kutua. Larma. Leba. Loskra. Molima, named after rivers.

[1] The progenitor of this section is said to have presented to the head of the tribe a crab so large that a pig could cross the river Kanguli on its back.

Sub-tribes.	Septs.
Septs of the Chakmá sub-tribe—*concluded.*	Molima-Sege. Phaksa. Phe-dang-sirri. Phedungsa. Phema. Pirabhanga, the fat man who broke the stool. Poa. Poma. Rangyacelunya, the lover of shells or mother-of-pearl. Ranyin. Sadonga. Sege. Sekowa. Shoályiá, the jester. Theya. Toinya. Uksarri. Warggu, name of a river.
Septs of the Tung-jainya sub-tribe.	Aruyái, the man as thin as a skeleton. Bádál, a chisel. Bangál, descended from a Bengali father. Bhumar, he of high back ribs. Bolá, he whose family was as numerous as the wasps. Dunyá. Fariansa, he who excelled in wickedness. Gochalya, the strong man. Ichá, he who was too fond of shrimps. Kachui, they who built their houses in a row. Karuá. Lambacha. Lulang,[1] the devil. Millong. Monglá. Mo-u. Ongyo. Pumá.

[1] A girl became pregnant, but would not name her lover. She was severely beaten, and was rescued by a devil, who was supposed to be the father of the child.

Chamár, *Chámár, Charmakár, Rabi-Dás.*

Titles:—**Beár, Bohit, Chunipárá, Kápri, Mahaldár, Mahará, Marar, Mehtariá, Náik, Panarha, Pradhán, Ráut.**

Sub-castes.

Chamár-Tánti.
Dhárh.
Dhusiá.
Dohar.
Goria.
Jaiswara.
Janakpuri.
Jaunpuri.
Kháti-Mahará.
Korár.
Larkor.
Magahia.
Pachhián.

Sections.

Of the Dhusiá sub-caste.

Hondagiá.
Joriáhá.
Moghaliá.
Sonpursa.
Thengáit.

Septs in Chota Nagpur.

Azghalla.
Dhusiá.
Harbans, cannot wear bones in any shape.
Kachuá, tortoise.
Karwa.
Kerketa, a bird.
Mahuá, *bassia latifolia.*
Mus, rat.
Nág, cobra.
Ráot.
Sándh, bull.
Saur, a fish.
Tirki.

Sub-castes enumerated by Mr. Sherring.

Jaiswara, servants.
Mangatiwa, professional beggars.
Dhusia or **Jhusia,** shoe-makers and harness-makers.
Katua, leather-cutters.
Kori, weavers, grooms, field-labourers.
Kuril, workers in leather.
Rangiya, leather-dyers.
Jatua, labourers.
Tantua, maker of leather strings.

Aharwar, Azimgarhia or **Birheria, Dakshinia, Dohar, Garaiya, Jaiswara, Jatlot, Jatua, Kaiyan, Kanaujia, Kuril, Kori** or **Korchamra,** are mentioned by Sir Henry Elliot and Mr. Beames.

Chandál, *Nama-Sudra, Nama, Changa, Chánrál, Kotál* or *Kotwál, Pratham-bákya, Swapacha, Nishád, Antebási.*

Titles:—**Bágh,** tiger, **Bhála, Biswás, Dás, Dáuk,** bird, **Dháli, Dule, Háit, Hajrá, Háldár, Háthi,** elephant, **Háuikar, Khán, Laskar, Mahará, Majumdár, Mandal, Mánjhi, Mirdada, Mistri, Namadháni, Padhwán** or **Pradhán, Pandit, Parámánik, Pátra, Phaliyá,** fish, **Rái, Sántrá, Sená, Seuli, Shumardar, Singh, Tengrá,** fish.

	Sub-castes.	Sections.
In Eastern Bengal.	Halwah.	
	Ghási.	
	Kandho or Behará.	
	Karrál, Keral.	
	Bári.	Kásyapa.
	Beruá.	
	Pod.	
	Baqqál.	
	Sarálya.	
	Amarábádi.	
	Báchhár.	
	Sandwipá.	
In Central Bengal.	Dháni.	
	Jáliá.	
	Jiáni, Jiuni.	
	Kárál.	
	Nuniá.	
	Siáli.	
In Western Bengal.	Chási.	Bharadwája.
	Helo.	Lomasa.
	Jelo.	Sándilya.
	Kesarkalo.	
	Kotál.	
	Májilá.	
	Nalo.	
	Nuniá.	
	Pánphule.	
	Saro.	
	Siule.	

Chásá.

Titles:—Lenká, Puhár, Muduli, Swáin, Paridá, Padhán, Viswál, Náik, Raut, Jená, Sámal, Mahanti.

Sub-castes.	Sections.
Orhchásá or Mundi-chásá.	
Benátiyá.	Kásyapa.
Chukuliyá.	Sál-rishi.
Sukuliyá.	

Chásádhobá, *Chásádhopá.*

Titles:—Rái, Páik, Haladhar, Ballava, Sán, Samaddar, Biswás, Háldár, Házará, Mistri, Ráj-Mistri.

Hypergamous Groups.

Kulin. | Maulik.

Sub-castes.	Sections.
Uttar-Rárhi.	Alimán.
Dakhin-Rárhi.	Atulrishi.
Bárendra.	Bághrishi.
	Brihatbat.
	Dhabalrishi.
	Kásyapa.
	Sándilya.

Chero.

Titles:—Bábuán, Kanwár, Manjhi, Manár, Rautiá, Sánwát.

Sub-castes.	Sections.
Bára-Hazár.	(*a*) *Totemistic*—
Tera-Hazár or Birbandhi.	Besrá, hawk.
	Kachchhuá, tortoise.
	Kunwardár.
	Mahto.
	Mailwár.
	Sonwani.
	Soraniá.
	Turuwár.
	(*b*) *Brahmanical*—
	Kásyapa, etc.

Chik. *See* Pán.

Titles:—Baraik, Mahato.

Sub-tribes.	Septs.
	Aujana.
	Baghail, tiger.
	Bagti.
	Bajarpuriji.
	Bakura, paddy-bird.
	Balbandhiya, are bound to tie up their hair.
	Banichar.
	Bar, *Ficus Indica.*
	Bara.
	Barabhaia, ship.
	Bati.
	Bhengraj, kingcrow.
	Bhojraj, a kind of medicine.
	Bichwar, a centipede.
	Borá, a kind of snake.
	Chachet, a small bird.
	Chaenchair, a bird.
	Chand, moon.
	Chikanjari.
	Darká, born out of a crack in the earth.
	Dhan, paddy or rice soup.
	Dhandh, plum bushes.
	Dihbans.
	Dip, may not eat after lights have been lit.
	Dundoar, an owl.
	Gandha, flying bug.
	Gandhi.
	Ghatoar.
	Goherwar.
	Hanuman, monkey.
	Harin, deer.
	Induar, a kind of eel.
	Janamkiar.
	Kachua, tortoise.
	Kaita, curry vegetable.
	Kansi, field grass.
	Kara.
	Karhar, a fruit.
	Katri, subject to fits.
	Kechengia.
	Keora, a flower.
	Khambha, fork of a tree.
	Khukri.
	Korla, fig.

Sub-tribe.	Septs.
	Kotri, a small deer.
	Kowriar.
	Kulhai, a tiger.
	Kumharia, a tribe.
	Kusumni, a tree or its fruit.
	Loharbans, iron.
	Loyna.
	Maghi.
	Mahabaar, may not kill or chase the wild boar.
	Mahanadi, name of a river.
	Mahtoar, a title.
	Malta.
	Maria.
	Malua.
	Mawar, peacock.
	Munjaniar, a fruit from which oil is extracted.
	Mus, field-rat.
	Nág, cobra.
	Newra, mongoose.
	Nikharbans.
	Nimuani.
	Phul, flower.
	Phungune.
	Rikhiasan, may not eat beef or pork.
	Ság, vegetable.
	Samjhar.
	Saur, a fish.
	Singi, horn.
	Sinjikuria.
	Sonmanik.
	Sonwasi.
	Surijhabu.
	Tajna, name of a river.

Dámi, *Dam-yi, Támi, Kotwál, Nágarchi, Darji.*

Thars or Septs.

Bhusuwal.	Kala Kháti.	Panchkuti.
Burdewá.	Kurki Dholiar.	Shewa.
Damma Parriwár.	Kurno Beheri.	Sunam.
Darnal.	Mohara.	Sundas.
Dhuli.	Mutai.	Sungaru.

Dejong Lhori (Dejong Sikhim), *Lhopa Bhotia* or Tibetans of the south.

Sub-tribes.	*Rui, Thar* or septs.
Tongdu Rui shi. Bed (*d* silent) or Beh tshan-gye. Ruichhung.	
Of the Tongdu Rui shi sub-tribe	Guru Táshi, the blessed *rui*, of which Guru Pema was guide. Shang-dah-bo, ancestor born at his maternal uncle's when some tutelary deities were being propitiated. Tshe-gyu-thah, the family which sprang from the Buddha of life. Yui-then-bo, ancestor turned out of his fatherland.
Of the Bed tshan gye sub-tribe	Bangrongpá. Bhadpá. Dokhangpá. Ghingpá. Gnyambipá. Gyon-sah-pá, he of the new monastery. Khyung-toipá. Lagdingpá. Lin-dseh-bo. Nam-tsang-koba. Pon-po: Chhungpá. / Lhasung, domestic priest of all the *ruis*. / Nah-dik. / Nambon. / Yo-chang. Pu-tsho-bo, a mixed progeny of Lepcha mother and Tibetan father.
Mixed septs of low origin[1] ...	Assampá. Chungyepá. Kah-tsho-bo. Mang-beh-pá. Namang-po.
Lowest septs of Bhotias[1] ...	Doh-rúhb-pn̥, one dwelling under the feet. Doh-zepá, living in rough and craggy rocks. Gangye-pa, dwelling behind a hill. Shyag-tsangpá.
Septs which emigrated from Tibet and North Bhotan[1] ...	Chhumbipá. Hah-po. Koyungpo. Shyah-pá. Toipá.

[1] These groups of septs form in each case endogamous aggregates, the members of which do not intermarry with the other sub-tribes.

Sub-tribes.	*Rai, Thar* or septs.
Septs which emigrated from Bhotan and Nepal[1] ...	Bendah. Bindumbo. Gah-oh, blacksmiths. Gurumbo, Gyu-rumbo. Ling-tamba. Ongdáhba. Parubo. Phensa-pá. Pu-tsibo. Pyo-chhembo. Sang-behbo. Shyag-chom-bo. Tsong-zubo. Yong-tong-ba. Yulsahb, of new country.
Of the Ruichhung sub-tribe ...	Dorompá. Khol. Lah-ogpá, dwelling below *la* or mountain-top or pass. Mang-tshang-wa. Nahmah-pá. Shyag-ding-pá or Shyag-tshang-pa. Thazoepá.

[1] These groups of septs form in each case endogamous aggregates, the members of which do not intermarry with the other sub-tribes.

Dhánuk.

Titles:—Mandar, Raut, Rai, Mahato, Kámatl, Khawás, Ghibihár, Saghár, Bahíá, Bahiot, Sankatwár.

Sub-castes.[1]	Sections.
Chhilatiá or Silhotiá.	Kásyapa.
Magahyá.	Nág.
Banodhiá.	
Tirhutiá or Chiraut.	
Jaiswár.	
Kanaujia.	
Kahpariyá.	
Dudhwár or Dojwár.	
Sunri-Dhánuk.	
Kathautiá.	
Khawásiá, Mandal, Gharbeta or Gharbait — In Purniah.	

[1] Longbasta, Mathuriá, Katharia, Jaiswár, Magahyá, Dojwár, and Chhilatiya are given by Sir H. Elliot; Yasawar (Jaiswár), Magahi, Dojwar, Chhilatiyá are mentioned by Buchanan.

Dhenuar.

Sub-tribes.	Septs.
Nil.	Baiga, a tribe.
	Bard.
	Karwar, a tribe.
	Sanuani, can't wear gold.
	Sumai, a kind of fish.

Dhimál, *Dhemál, Maulik.*

Sub-tribes.[1]	Septs.
Agniá.	Chongá.
Láter.	Dauwá.
Dungiá.	Kauwá.
	Rángá.

[1] It is convenient to describe these groups as sub-tribes. They are not, however, strictly endogamous, as has been mentioned in the article on Dhimál.

IN BENGAL AND ORISSA.

Dhobá, *Dhopa, Dhupi, Dhávaka.*

Title:—Dás, Mistri, Rajak, Sabhá-Sundar, Sákalya.

Sub-castes.		Sections.
1. Rámer Dhobá	Eastern Bengal.	(*a*) *Totemistic*—
2. Sitár Dhobá		Nágasa (Orissa).
3. Sátisá	Central Bengal.	(*b*) *Eponymous*—
4. Athisá		Alamyán.
5. Hájará-Samáj		Kásyapa.
6. Niti Siná		Sándilya.
7. Bara-Samáj	Hughli.	
8. Chhota-Samáj		
9. Dhobá-Samáj		
10. Rárhiya-Samáj		
11. Bangali	Manbhum.	
12. Goriá		
13. Maghayá		
14. Khottá		
15. Bhuluá	Noakhali.	
16. Jugidiá		
17. Sundip		
18. Uriyá Dhobá ...	Orissa.	

IN BEHAR AND CHOTA NAGPUR, EXCEPT MANBHUM.

Dhobi, Ujli, Baithá, Sáfi.

Titles:—**Gozar, Mahto, Ráut.**

Sub-castes.	Section.
1. Kanaujiá.	Kásyapa.
2. Maghaya.	
3. Belwár.	
4. Awadhiyá.	
5. Bátham.	
6. Gorsár.	
7. Gadhayá, keep donkeys.	
8. Banglá, immigrants from Bengal.	
Turkia or Shekh, Mahomedan.	

Dom, *Doi, Chalanta, Baidya, Lakhiputra, Pátia Dás.*

Dom, *Domrá*, sometimes called *Chandál* by outsiders.

Titles:—**Malik, Marar, Mehalo, Mihtár, Marik, Mirdáhá, Raut.**

Sub-castes.

In Behar—

Bánsphor or Bánsbakurá, basket-makers: have nothing to do with funerals, and do not eat beef.
Chapariyá, make baskets and build the bamboo framework which supports the thatched roof of a house.
Dakhiná or Turi { Angwár. / Deswár. }
Dháprá, sweepers.
Dharkár, workers in cane.
Gadahiá, breeders of donkeys.
Hári or Bangali, probably immigrants from Bengal.
Harkár, scavengers.
Larhorá or Purbál-Mihtár, scavengers and basket-makers.
Magahiyá, in North Behar cultivators and thieves; in Gya basket-makers.
Pachainyá.
Raut-Mihtar { Bhojpuriá / Ghar-Raut / Gházipuriá } sweepers.
Supárá.
Tirhutiyá.
Uttariyá, workers in *sirki* basket and mat-makers.

Sub-castes.

In Bengal—

Ankuriá or **A'nkhuti**, basket-makers.
Bájuniá, musicians.
Bánukiá, breed silkworms and work in silk filatures in Murshedabad and Rajshahye.
Bisdeliá, make baskets and palm-leaf mats.
Dai-Dom, the men are day-labourers and the women serve as midwives.
Dhesiá Dhákál or **Tapaspuriá**, remove dead bodies, etc.
Dholá, supposed to come from Dhalbhum.
Ghaserá, cut grass for sale.
Kálindi, cultivators and basket-makers.
Kaurá, breed pigs and act as scavengers.
Magahiyá, musicians and basket-makers.
Mándároná.
Murdafarásh, remove dead bodies.
Sánchi.
Táláiboná, make palm-leaf mats.

In Behar—

	Sections.
Of the Bánsphor or Bánsbakurá sub-caste.	**Baithá. Chiranjiá. Dágri. Darbe. Gáin. Hát. Isar. Kotwal. Lakrihár. Mánjhi. Marar. Marik. Masrakhiyá. Nauriyá. Sakráit. Saunt. Sikrar. Sipahiyá.**
Of the Dakhiná or Turi sub-caste	**Angwár. Deswár.**
Of the Dhäprá sub-caste ...	**Hári. Mukariá. Parwariá. Pusaitá. Rosráit.**
Of the Dharkár sub-caste ...	**Káibtár. Mánjhi. Mehtar. Ráut. Sarin.**

Sub-castes.	Sections.
In Behar—	
Of the Tirhutiyá sub-caste ...	Barbattá. Belsandi. Chanauli. Hánsá. Hár. Maggah. Mahwá. Murwá. Pusadih. Sirpur. Sonpur. Teswár. Tubká.
Of the Magahiyá sub-caste ...	Akhauri. Belsandi. Chaudhri. Chauhán. Hánsá. Jádu. Mánjhi. Mirdaha. Rájá. Ráná. Santari. Sáwant. Teswár. Tewari.
Of the Pachainyá sub-caste ...	Adhárpur. Barabatiá. Bargamáet. Belsandi. Bhojpuri. Bikrampur. Chahraitá. Chandaulyár. Dholi. Hánsá. Hansotá. Kanauli. Kolandh. Mohbaita. Murba. Pahasrait. Pohobait. Pusá. Pusetá. Sansáit. Sirwár. Sonpuryá. Tabkar. Tibaryá or Teswar.

Sub-castes.	Septs.
In South Manbhum—	Azghala.
	Dhusia.
Aturá.	Harbans, bones can't wear in any shape.
Molá.	Kachua, tortoise.
Sikhariá.	Karwa.
	Kerketa, a bird.
	Mahua, a tree; wine is made from its flower.
	Mus, rat.
	Nâg, cobra.
	Raot.
	Sândh, bull.
	Saur, a fish.
	Tirki.

Dosádh, *Dusadh*.

Titles:—Chaukidár, Gorait, Hájará or Házará, Máhato, Mánjhi, Pásbán, Rái, Rám.

Sub-castes.

Magahiyá.
Bhojpuriá.
Kanaujiá.
Pailwár.
Kámar or Kánwar.
Kurin, Kuri, or Kurmá.
Dhár or Dhárhi.
Silhotia or Sirotiá.
Báhaliá.

Sections.

Of the Magahiyá sub-caste.

Agiyári.
Barbáik.
Bárik.
Beár.
Bhadáiyá.
Bhunsi Kurtho.
Darbe.
Fotadár.
Hát.
Hazári.
Isar.
Khankarárá.
Kotwál.
Kumarsan Bakri.
Mahrána.
Mahton.
Málti.
Mandar.
Mánjhi.
Marik.
Mirdahá.
Parbe.
Patwe.
Rái.
Rána.
Ráut.
Sanda.

Of the Pailwár sub-caste.

Bádsháhi.
Bára Kharak.
Panjiar.

Of the Kámar sub-caste.

Aghráit.
Amam.
Amol.
Assiswar.
Bhabániswar.
Busgarait.
Kamláit.
Kariont.
Lab Nagariá.
Madhupuriá.
Mahabbat.
Mahesbaráit.
Mainkisrár.
Nabanápuriá.
Purukhinu Naráin.
Rájáisur.
Thahrait.

Gandhabanik, *Gandhabaniyá, Baniyá, Putuli.*

Titles:—Of the Desá sub-caste—Sáhá, Sádhu, Láhá, Khán; of the Ǎut sub-caste—Datta, Dé, Dhar, Dhár, Kar, Nág.

Sub-castes.	Sections.
Ǎut-Ǎsram.	Ǎlamyán.
Chhatris-Ǎsram.	Bharadwája.
Desá-Ǎsram.	Kásyapa.
Sankha-Ǎsram.	Krishnátreya.
	Modgalya.
	Nrisingha.
	Ras-rishi.
	Sábarna.
	Sándilya.

Gangotá, *Gangautá.*

Title:—Mandar.

Sub-castes.	Sections.
1. Jethkar.	Gangájhl.
2. Maghaya.	Jáhnavi.

Ganrár.

Sub-castes.	Section.
Nil.	Aliman.

Gareri, *Gadariya, Bhenrihar.*

Titles:—Kambliá, Kammall, Marar, Raut.

Sub-castes.		Sections.
1. Dhengar.	Of the Dhengar sub-caste.	Chandel.
2. Farakhábádi.		Chaudhuriá.
3. Gangájali.		Kásyapa.
4. Nikhar.		Nánkar.
		Chak, Chikwá (Mahomedan).

Ghási.

Sub-castes.	Sections.
Hári.	**Ahir**, a tribe.
Simarloká.	**Air**, a kind of fish.
Sonaáti.	**Badhiria**, bats.
	Bágh, tiger.
	Bhat, a tribe. Degraded.
	Bhuana, a tribe. Bhuiya.
	Bhuinkora, hog.
	Bhurungia, a kind of tree.
	Bunduar, a tribe.
	Chahubar.
	Chinear.
	Daspuria.
	Desoar, a tribe.
	Dhamna sap, a red snake, poisonless snake.
	Dowalbandhi.
	Golvar.
	Kachua, tortoise.
	Kalhia, Lohar.
	Kasiár, corruption of Kásyapa?
	Kewat.
	Loharbans, iron-worker.
	Malar, a tribe.
	Mohdiar, honey-bee.
	Mukhi, Mukhi is a person, one of five, who can reinstate outcastes by eating first with them. Mukhi can lose his own jat. Mukhi only wear pagri.
	Pandki, dove.
	Phansia.
	Rajbandh.
	Rajput, a tribe.
	Sakri.
	Sanukra, shell.
	Sanwasi, cobra.
	Simarlásá, gum.
	Simarloka, a tree.
	Sonwan, cannot wear gold.
	Tirki.
	Uraon, a tribe.

Goálá, *Goál, Goár, Gopa, Gopál, Pallab-Gopa, Áhir, Ábhir.*

Titles:—*In Bengal*—Bárik, Chomar, Dháli, Ghosh, Jana, Mandal, Parámánik.

In Behar—Bharari, Bhogta, Chaudhri, Ghoraila, Khirahá, Mahato, Mandar, Mánjhi, Marik, Panjiara, Rái, Rást, Saonra, Singh.

Sub-castes.	Sections.
In Bengal—	
Pallab or Ballabh.	Almasi or Alamyán.
Gaura or Go-baidya.	Bharadwája.
Gop or Ghosh Goálá.	Gautama.
Karanjá.	Kásyapa.
Kajol.	Madrisi or Madhukulya.
Bágre or Ujaini.	Sándilya.
Madhu Goálá.	
Rárhi.	
Gumia.	
Áhir or Mahishá Goálá.	
Magai or Mágadhi.	
Bárendra: Pallal.	
Bárendra: Láheri.	
Bárendra: Mula.	
Bárendra: Gáwá.	
Bárendra: Dágániá.	
Bhogá: Sádá Goálá (Hypergamous)	
Bhogá: Lál Goálá. (Hypergamous)	
In Orissa—	
Dumala Jadupuria Goárá.	
Gaura or Gopopuria.	
Magadha Goárá.	
Mathurá or Mathurábási.	
In Behar—	
Goriá or Dahiára.	Bhadráj.
	Bhátásan.
	Chalasinghi.
	Chalasan.
	Dasil.
	Dhenu.
	Gaudhal.
	Jaliásinghi.
	Jethautlá.
	Kálásan.
	Láhágot.
	Mahraul.
	Nágásan.
	Nágráj.
	Pakra.
	Sakraul.
	Singhror.
	Tanokl.

Sub-castes.	Sections.
Majraut or Naomuliá.	Abhepur.
	Aganpuriá.
	Anrhráhi.
	Aunriá.
	Báergoá.
	Baini (Mhádes).
	Bájitpur.
	Bálágáchhpokrám.
	Bálgách.
	Barsám.
	Básáithi.
	Basárh.
	Bástiburhoná.
	Baurám.
	Belwár.
	Bháonroá.
	Bheludih.
	Bhotieth.
	Chámuár.
	Chámuk-Sháhpur.
	Chánchar.
	Chándkatorá.
	Chaumukhdih.
	Chiksári.
	Dabhrait.
	Dahiet.
	Dháman.
	Dharampuria.
	Doálak.
	Dudhpuriet.
	Gángthaiá.
	Ghiuádhár.
	Gobargárhá.
	Golrám.
	Gotsobhni.
	Guábári.
	Habibpur-Phupidih.
	Hansi.
	Jagatpur.
	Jailok.
	Jháj.
	Kabái.
	Kailwár.
	Kámrám.
	Kánháiwár.
	Kátaiyá.
	Káthádularpur.
	Khájuri.
	Khánrsimáriá.
	Kherho.
	Khuthá-Bhagwánpur.

Sub-castes.	Sections.
	Kirtoliá.
	Kotsobhni.
	Labnagar-Kumet.
	Lágmetá.
	Lakshanpuriá.
	Láwápur.
	Lepuriet.
	Levátiá { Barar. Chhalor. Dámu.
	Lohár.
	Madhepuriet.
	Mahárano.
	Mahisirupján.
	Mailidhurlak.
	Mailwár.
	Mánickhak-dudhpuriá.
	Meghalbariárpur.
	Mehdipur.
	Mehmánpur.
	Mithoriá.
	Mogalkáchá.
	Nimáchandpurá.
	Pachhiparganá.
	Pátori.
	Pipret.
	Rághopurdih.
	Raghunathpurdiár.
	Rájápákur.
	Rájápatischhni.
	Rasákmárhe.
	Sahasradih.
	Sahrwár.
	Sakarpuriet.
	Sálkhini.
	Samastipur.
	Sankarpur.
	Sánrári (Jaideb).
	Saresparganá-Dádádih.
	Sáthiet.
	Silotháer.
	Sobhádih.
	Sobhni-Tájpur.
	Somnidih.
	Sonám.
	Temdih.
	Tilatwár.
	Titiábámbár.
	Ulwár.
	Umethwár.
	Usrám.

Sub-castes.	Sections.
Kanaujiá.	Chaudhri.
	Gopa.
	Kaksa.
	Kásyapa.
	Khirahá.
	Mandar.
	Raksa.
	Raut.
Kishnaut or Sátmuliá.	Álakjaridárhuá.
	Banikarnauti.
	Bharduár.
	Chalasínghi.
	Dadhraut.
	Deseriet.
	Dhanu.
	Jeseriet.
	Kachásimar.
	Kátkiphulberiá.
	Kheláut.
	Laungijarhuá.
	Magháchewár.
	Májháliár.
	Málkarnauti.
	Málkiá.
	Nágrá.
	Páli.
	Rájápáker.
	Saudábáek.
	Sonápur-Sakarwár.
	Sundar.
	In general—
Bargowár.	Áindwár.
Dhanroár.	Baghwár.
Chauánlá.	Barhadagiá.
Chauthá.	Bella.
Goit.	Bhainsu.
Kantitáhá.	Bhant.
Puhoá.	Cher.
Sepári.	Dhokasan.
Banpar.	Dumar.
Gujiár or Godágá.	Hát.
	Kachhuá.
	Kási.
	Khanduár.
	Kurji.
	Kutár.
	Lauriá.
	Lukhasan.

Sub-castes.	Sections.
	In general—
	Mahar.
	Mahtwár.
	Mongar.
	Muntri.
	Nág.
	Nagar.
	Pur.
	Sahbar.
	Sanuár.
	Sáu.
	Saur.
	Suá.
	Sundi.
	Tirki.
	Undhil.
Gáddi, Ghosi or Ghosin.	Argariá.
	Banrait.
	Barbariá.
	Bhádiswár.
	Bhindwár.
	Bhuskuliá.
	Biráji.
	Dárkhuriá.
	Dhurjhár.
	Goit.
	Káiwár.
	Kusieth.
	Lohutiá.
	Mádowán.
	Máhátmá.
	Marik.
	Mukhiá.
	Nágh.
	Parselá.
	Sádhak.
	Santu-Kusáet.
	Sunreit.
	Surat.
Ját.	Chitosiá.
	Gadhuál.

	Septs.
In Chota Nagpur—	
Bhogta.	Aind, a kind of eel.
Chauániá.	Am, mango.
Goro.	Bacha, calf.
Kishnaut.	Bág, tiger.
Lari.	Bar, *Ficus Indicus*.

Sub-castes.	Septs.
In Chota Nagpur—concld.	
Majhwat.	Chownia, field-rat.
Sáonrá.	Demta, red tree-ant.
Sabor.	Diller.
	Gaegoal, *pakar* fruit forbidden.
	Garaur.
	Hasa, earth.
	Kachua, tortoise.
	Kaita, curry vegetable.
	Kamal, lotus.
	Kanojia, a tribe.
	Karam, a tree.
	Karsal.
	Karthia, a kind of grain or *dál*.
	Kasail, deer.
	Kasi, a grass.
	Maina, bird.
	Markam.
	Morpachi.
	Mus, rat.
	Nág, cobra.
	Phulwar.
	Rajhans, swan.
	Sir, arrow.
	Sona, can't wear gold.
	Sonwani.
	Tirki, can't touch any cattle after eyes open.

In the North-Western Provinces—

Sub-castes.	Sections.	
Desi.	Apharlá.	Bhánsriá.
Nandbansi.	Bachás.	Chabdiá.
Jadubansi.	Bachhwallá.	Charkhiá.
Surajbansi.	Badgar.	Chikaná.
Goálbansi.	Badhwadiá.	Chitosiá.
Áhar.	Bághiá.	Chorá.
Kátha.	Bálwán.	Dágar.
	Bámboriá.	Dahmá.
	Bán.	Dámboriá.
	Báthotiá.	Deswál.
	Bháklun.	Dhaiá.
	Bhálkiá.	Dhorán.
	Bhámbasrá.	Dhundhiá.
	Bhángar.	Dhundhlá.

Sub-castes.	Sections.	
In the North-Western Provinces—concld.	Diá.	Kharsán.
	Dohán.	Khátádiá.
	Dudhliá.	Kheswá.
	Dumániá.	Khodiá.
	Dumdoliá.	Khosá.
	Dusád.	Kidat.
	Gadháriá.	Kosliá.
	Gadhojiá.	Lahaniá.
	Gahalá.	Lámbá.
	Garwál.	Lohchab.
	Ghumlá.	Luniwál.
	Gidad.	Máhakarlá.
	Gigániá.	Mahalá.
	Gothwál.	Mahtá.
	Gumi.	Makadá.
	Guráh.	Mándhayá.
	Hádá.	Molán.
	Hadkwál.	Moldhiá.
	Hardá.	Motliá.
	Hudinwál.	Nadhiá.
	Jádu.	Nahadiá.
	Jadwál.	Nániá.
	Jánjdiá.	Nigániá.
	Jhádadiá.	Nikum.
	Jhagdoliá.	Nirbán.
	Kadayán.	Pacheriá.
	Kadián.	Padhániá.
	Kákas.	Parhar.
	Kakroliá.	Puhániá.
	Kaláliá.	Rábad.
	Kalganiá.	Ráriá.
	Kalinwál.	Sáhjáwán.
	Kaiot.	Sálangiá.
	Kalwadiá.	Sálodiá.
	Karirá.	Sámp.
	Kátha.	Sátoriá.
	Kátniá.	Sigadiá.
	Keswál.	Sikhwád.
	Khadoliá.	Simalwál.
	Khadotiá.	Sisodiá.
	Khadumiá.	Sunáriá.
	Khairwál.	Tahalkiá.
	Khalhad.	Tántlá.
	Khámtá.	Thukrán.
	Kharniá.	Tundak.

Gond.

Title :—Gaunjhu.

Sub-tribes.	Septs.
Gond.	Bágh, tiger.
Ráj-Gond.	Baghel, tiger.
Dhokar-Gond.[1]	Besrá, hawk.
Doroá-Gond or Náik.[2]	Bhainsá, buffalo.
Jhorá.	Bod, a big river-fish.
	Gaek, a kind of fish.
	Ganga, sea.
	Ghora, horse.
	Goh.
	Hansa, geese.
	Honti, a kind of fish.
	Jagaha, buffalo.
	Jagat.
	Jaipuria, name of a city.
	Kachhuá, tortoise.
	Káná Machhri, fish.
	Karma, a tree.
	Koput.
	Kusro.
	Loha, iron.
	Mahanadia, name of a river.
	Marai.
	Moti, a bead.
	Nág, snake.
	Naitam, tortoise.
	Pachia.
	Phaguahi.
	Poia.
	Poiti.
	Porri, a kind of hawk.
	Sawani.
	Sribakaria.

---

1 Also called Mángan-Gond from their begging habits.

2 Colonel Dalton suggests that these may be the same as the Náik or Dhurwe Gonds of the Central Provinces.

Gonrhi, Malláh, Machhuá.

Titles:—Chaudhhri, Jethman, Mandar, Mukhiár, Nákhudá, Sahni.

Sub-castes.	Sections.
Banpar.	Bánt.
Cháb or Chábi.	Goráit.
Dhoár.	Jathot.
Khunaut or Khulaut.	Kásyapa.
Kolh.	Mandar.
Kurin.	Marar.
Parbatti-Kurin.	Mukhiyá.
Semári.	Pandit.
	Pánre.
	Parihár.
	Ráut.

Goráit, *Kordit*, *Baikar*.

Sub-caste.	Sections.
Nil.	Adra.
	Aindowár.
	Bagh, tiger.
	Baghuár.
	Bar, *Ficus Indicus*.
	Baroár.
	Induar, a kind of eel.
	Káchhuá.
	Kerketá.
	Khalkho, a fish.
	Kujri, a fruit, makes oil.
	Kujur.
	Nonoár.
	Pithoár.
	Sándh, bullock.
	Sontirki, gold.
	Tirki, cannot eat birds born blind, nor deep-setting eggs.
	Topoar, a kind of bird.

Gulguliá.

Sub-castes.	Section.
Bantari.	*Nil.*
Pachpaniá.	
Sukwár.	

Gurung, *Gurum, Gurungá, Gurungáh.*

Sub-tribes.

Das-Gurung or Chár-Gotra.
Bárah-Gurung.

***Thars* or septs.**

Bagálya.
Baráhi.
Bhumjan.
Bulung.
Byápri.
Chandu.
Chárki.
Dah Láma.
Dhakaren.
Dháren.
Ghárti.
Ghundáne.
Gohori.
Golángya.
Gonduk.
Gosti.
Gothi.
Guáburi.
Jimel.
Karámati.
Khangbha.
Khaptari.

Of the Das-Gurung sub-tribe:
Chheni-lama.
Ghaleh.
Ghoneh.
Kohli.
Korángi.
Lamsani Tongi.
Lhebo Lamsani.
Poinju-lama.
Pungi-lama.
Ráhul.
Ráná Lamsani.

Kháti.
Khulál.
Koki.
Láma.
Lámi Chhanya.
Leh Láma.
Lopáte.
Lotháng.
Madán.
Meghi.
Mengi.
Paindi.
Palámi.
Pengi.
Shakya Láma.
Siddh.
Suryabansi Láma.
Tháthung.
Themjáni.
Tolángi.
Uruntá.

Of the Bárah Gurung sub-tribe:
Buthuja.
Ghybrim.
Jhagreb.
Satal.
Segmang.

Hajjám, *Nái, Náu, Nauá.*

Titles:—Naheri, Ostá, Thákur.

Sub-castes.

Awadhiá.
Bangáli.
Kanaujiá or Biáhut.
Magahiyá.
Sribástab or Bástar.
Tirhutiá.
Musalmániá or Turk-Nauá.

Sections.

Of Awadhiá Hajjáms—

Amraut.
Barthoár.
Beauran.
Beraut.
Bilsar.
Chausar.
Denrgamiá.
Dharmáhu.
Ekauniá.
Gaya.
Hargamiá.
Jainagariá.
Jaipur.
Janágadhiá.
Járdár.
Jaru.
Jaum.
Jurvaunt.
Kaisab.
Kalaen.
Kant.
Kapur.
Karaf.
Karaunti.
Katur.
Khavur.
Kopinyar.
Koránch.
Kujhariá.
Kumair.
Kundi.
Kurnat.
Mahrat.
Manerar.
Paithán.
Parurá.
Pauriár.
Puráin.
Rat.
Samaiyar.
Sansihar.
Sisah.
Telár.

Sub-castes. Sections.

Of Awadhiá Hajjáms—concld.

Unri.
Urkiser.
Utrauniá.

Of Kanaujiá Hajjáms—

Baksar-Chausá.
Kharpáik.
Maura.
Nipariá.
Satarwár.

Halwái, *Mithiyá.*

Titles:—Chaudhri, Dás, Modi, Sáhu.

Sub-castes.

Kanaujiá.
Magahiyá.
Bantiriá or Balamtiriá.
Pachhainya[1] Madesiá.
Purbiyá[2] Madesiá.
Bhojpuriá.
Koránch.
Maltariá.

Sections.

Sections of the Kanaujiá sub-caste.—Kachuá. Kusmauliá. Laskoriá. Lukáthiá. Santop Palwár.

Sections of the Bhojpuriá sub-caste.—Akhandhári. Amghát. Básáriá. Básdebpur. Bharsahar. Bijaibanáras. Dhakais. Dharkiá. Gauli. Gauthâhá. Jábáliá. Kandwár. Káro. Kotsá. Naorakhiá. Nárauni. Pacháttar. Pachopát. Pátor. Sákarwár.

Section of the Koránch sub-caste.—Pindwál.

---

[1] Also called Tinmuliá Madesiá.
[2] Also called Chhaumuliá Madesiá.

Sections of the Purbiyá Madesiá sub-caste.

Ájner.
Ákhanbári.
Ámi.
Ánar.
Ánokonwár.
Ánruá.
Ásármállá.
Bádábasti.
Bijái.
Baksár.
Bakulári.
Bánebanáras.
Baniápáthar.
Bansahar.
Bátor.
Chánwár.
Chausá.
Chilhár.
Dádukli.
Dáhárak.
Dariápár.
Dehádbanáras.
Deoghát.
Dhákais.
Dhákait.
Dhanej.
Dhemá.
Doem.
Don.
Gahunágáoná.
Gangápáli.
Hátser.
Indri.
Jewel.
Jirábasti.
Kádá.
Kalasdih.
Kándár.
Kángkol.
Kára.
Karar.
Kárkádo.
Kárni.
Kásiáon.
Kátári.
Káthej.
Kesaur.
Khontá.
Kotsá or Korsá.
Kurisár.
Kusarpákri.
Lakhansariá.
Larauni.
Lolutra.
Máhepurá.
Máil.
Manimanáras.
Márar.
Maruá.
Mohár.
Nágeswar.
Nagneswar.
Naknesá.
Ninghiám.
Pachauta.
Páchottar.
Paiharwáre.
Phuli.
Raksise.
Sahuri.
Sakarwár.
Sakin.
Sakrol.
Sarauli.
Sidhpur.
Sikiá.
Sinhagarh.
Sinharas.
Sisotar.
Sonhar.
Tári.
Ubhar.
Ughar.

Sections of the Pachhainyá Madesiá sub-caste.

Ákhanbári.
Básáriá.
Bhárauli.
Bijaibanáras.
Chauberiá.
Dhákáis.
Dhánautá.
Dhaneswar.
Dighwárá.
Dumri.
Gángauliá.
Gauángahunár.
Gureni.
Hánriáot.
Jawáliá.
Kachwár.
Káhinwár.
Kándeil.
Kánpákar.
Kárádhánauta.
Kárárihá.
Káru.
Kausár.
Khirkatorá.
Khoprihá.
Maruáhá.
Nárauni.
Páchottar.
Panthpákar.

Hári, *Mihtar*, *Harsantán*.

Sub-castes.	Section.
Bará-Bhágiya or Káorá-páik.	*Nil.*
Madhya-bhágiyá or Madhaukul.	
Khore or Khoriyá.	
Siuli.	
Mihtar.	
Bangáli.	
Maghaya.	
Karaiyá.	
Purandwár.	

Ho, *Larka Kolh.*

Sub-tribes.	Septs.	
None.	Alru.	Jámulu.
	Angariá.	Janku Samrai.
	Babangá.	Kalundiá.
	Bandi.	Kisku.[1]
	Bansa.	Korá.
	Barpai.	Kuntiá.
	Biruá.	Lagori.
	Bodru.	Lamamaka.
	Buriali Kálundiá.	Marli.[1]
	Buri Sámat.	Munduia.
	Cháki Dukri.	Murmu.[1]
	Champiá Tubir.	Naguriá.
	Chatra Tuiu.	Parayá.
	Chorái.[1]	Pata Sayá.
	Echaghatu.	Pinguá.
	Emboro.	Podoro.
	Gagriá.	Purthi.
	Gatsorá.	Sauiá.
	Haiboru Lángi.	Sinkoi.
	Hánsda.[1]	Sundi Deogam.
	Hembaran.	Tihu.
	Hesá.	Tin.
	Hone-hogá.	Tudi.[1]

[1] These septs are common to the Hos and the Santáls.

Jáliyá, *Jeliá, Jele, Jálo, Jaluá, Málá, Málo, Dhibar, Machhuá, Mahifurosh.*

Titles:—Árash, Bág, Barddhan, Bárik, Berá, Bidyánto, Bisoi, Biswás, Borál, Chaudhri, Dás, Gal Guriá, Háldár, Kundu, Láhá, Mandal, Mánjhi, Mauna, Pakre, Pálde, Párai, Pátra, Pradhán, Rojá, Sántrá, Sarkár, Sasmal, Sem.

Sub-castes.	Sections.
In Noakhali—	
Chátgáon.	Áliman.
Bhuluá.	
Jhálo.	
Kaibartta.	

Jolha, *Joláhá, Juláhá, Momin, Tánti, Tatwá.*

Titles:—**Lauki, Mahrano, Mahton, Mandar, Mandari, Manjhi, Marik, Mehter, Nuri, Pandit, Sanahiá, Taiyá.**

Sub-castes.		Sections.
Tirhutiá.		**Kachuá.**
Kanaujia.		**Parásar.**
Chapota, Chanpadda.	Of the Chapota sub-caste.	**Mánjhi.**
Khatwe.		**Marar.**
		Parimanik.
		Purbe.

Juáng.

Sub-tribes.	Septs.
Nil.	**Alemba**, hailstones.
	Baitiriba, buffalo.
	Bálimba, mosquito.
	Bánaiba, bear.
	Bárátaba, boar.
	Dumriába, a kind of tree.
	Gághraba, paddy.
	Hátisalaba, elephant.
	Jarigámba, *jari* tree.
	Kálimba, tobacco flower.
	Kánchaba, dog.
	Kelobo, bee.
	Kerálaba, pumpkin.
	Kotábándab.
	Lihimba, dove.
	Mundiba, *mahua* tree.
	Munduáb, small mushroom.
	Odhalaba, fox.
	Rangataba, a kind of yellow-coloured bird.
	Rásamba, mushrooms that grow on ant-hills.
	Sáramba, tigress.
	Sundriába, red mushroom.
	Talahadába, palm tree.
	Tenshába, a bird.

Jugi, *Jungi*, *Jogi* or *Yogi*, *Náth*.

Titles:—Adhikári, Biswás, Dalál, Goswámi, Jáchandár, Mahanta, Majumdár, Náthji, Pandit, Rái, Sarkár.

Sub-castes.

Rárhi.
Bárendra.
Baidik.
Bangaja.
Khelenda.
Bhuluá.
Sundipá.

Functional groups.

Hálwa.
Kambule.
Manihári.
Rangroz.
Grihasth { Dhanái Mandal. Jnánbar. Bhagan Bhájan. Paban. }
Ekádasi.
Másya.

Religious groups.

Bráhman.
Sannyási or Kánphát.
Dandi.
Dharmaghare.
Játh.
Kálipá.
Durihár.
Aghorpanthi.
Bhatrihari.
Sárangihár.

Hypergamous groups.

Kulin { Raghu. Mádhab. Nimái. Págmal. }
Madhyalá.
Bángál.

Sections.

Kásyapa.
Siva.
Adi.
Alarishi (Allamyán ?).
Anádi.
Batuk.
Birbhairab.
Goraksha.
Matsendra, king of fish.
Min, fish.
Satya, truth.

Kádar, *Bhuiyá.*

Sub-castes.	Sections.	
Kádar.	Báre.[1]	Mánjhi.
Naiyá.	Bárik.[2]	Maraiá.
	Darbe.[3]	Marik.[5]
	Hazári.	Mirdáha.[6]
	Kampti.[4]	Naiyá.[7]
	Kápari.	Raut.
	Mandar.	Rikhiásan.
	Mandri.	

[1] Will marry only with Mirdáha, Kampti, and Raut.
[2] Will not marry with Mandar, Mirdáha, Raut, and Báre.
[3] Will not marry with Marik and Báre.
[4] Will marry only with Bárik, Kápari, Marik, Darbe, Mánjhi, and Báre.
[5] Will only marry with Bárik, Kápari, Mánjhi, Mandar, and Naiyá.
[6] Will marry only with Darbe, Mánjhi, Kampti, and Báre.
[7] Will not marry with Marik, Hazári, Naiyá, Kampti, and Báre.

Kahár.

Titles :—Behará, Bhandári, Kamkar, Mahara, Mahato, Ráut, Sardár.

Sub-castes.	Sections.
Rawáni or Ramáni.	Alimán.
Dhuriá.	Bando, a small wild cat.
Dhimar.	Kanda, sweet potato.
Kharwárá.	Kansi, a kind of grass.
Turhá.	Kásyapa.
Jaswár.	Nág.
Garhuk or Garauwá.	Rawanpur.
Bisariá.	Suar, a pig.
Magahiyá.	

Kaibartta, *Kaibartta-Dás, Chási-Dás, Háliá-Dás, Parásar-Dás, Dhivara, Khyán.*

Titles :—*In Bengal*—Adaki, Arash, Bág, Bardhan, Bárik, Berá, Biswás, Borál, Chaudhri, Dás, Gharui, Giri, Haladhar, Háldár, Jáná, Kundu, Láhá, Máiti, Mallik, Mandal, Mánji, Mánná, Mete, Naskar, Pare, Patnáik, Pátra, Pradhán, Rojá, Sarkár, Sen, Sántrá, Sasmal.

In Orissa—Behará, Bhuiá, Dalái, Dás, Malhá, Mátiál, Náik, Sáhu.

Sub-castes.	Sections.
In Murshedabad—	
Pánchsata Baháttarghar.	Aládasi.
Chauddapárá Rárhibindus.	Almisi.
Rárhi.	Alamyán.
Bágri.	Kásyapa.
Bárendra.	Majlisi (Maudgalya).
Dakshini.	

Sub-castes.	Sections.
In Midnapur—	
Hele-Kaibartta { Uttar-Rárhi. Dakshin-Rárhi.	{ Lál-Chátái. Ekside. Doside. Mákunda. Almál. Kástu-Rishi. Kásyapa. Madhukulya. Sándilya. Vyás.
In Hughli—	
{ Uttar-Rárhi. Dakhin-Rárhi or Marwar. Tutiya. Jeliya, Málá or Jaliyá.	
In Jessore—	
Málo or Málá. Rájbansi. Mecho } Hypergamous. Helo }	Amrita-Rási. Kásyap-Rási. Mesh-Rási. Padma-Rási.
In 24-Parganás—	
Kaibartta. Dás.	
In Central Bengal—	
Chásá or Halwáha Kaibartta. Tutiyá Kaibartta.	
In Maldah—	
{ Hálik. Jálik.	
In Noakhali—	
{ Bhuluái. Sundipe. Karalái. Dántrái. Pátuá. Phirti.	Kásyapa.
In Dacca—	
Dás, Jalwah Kaibartta.	
In Bakarganj—	
Háliá Dás, Parásar Dás, or Chási Kaibartta.	Kálá Ráy Háliá Bálái Jádab Ráy Bhuban Kuri Mánji Samaddár Charmanái Ráy Majumdár Bángál } Hypergamous. Alamyán. Bharadváj. Ghrita-Kausik. Kásyap. Parásar.

In Bakarganj—

Sub-castes.	Sections.	
Kaibartta, Chandradwip.	Káwár	Hypergamous.
	Mandal	Hypergamous.
	Manjhi	Hypergamous.
	Páthar	Hypergamous.
	Sikdár	Hypergamous.
	Bángál.	
Bára-Hazári.		

In Orissa—

Sub-castes.	Sections.
Orh.	Dhamdi.
Rárhi.	Khauniá.
	Ghani.
	Gundi.
	Niáli.

In Behar—

Jethaut.
Garbetá.
Desi.
Semári.
Bangáli.

Kalwár.

Titles:—Abkár, Bhakat, Bhatthidár, Chaudhri, Goldár, Lála, Modi, Sáhu.

Sub-castes.	Sections of the Banodhia and Jaiswár sub-castes.	
Banodhiá.	Arddhálakhiá.	Kumhariá.
Biyáhut or Bhojpuri.	Bachhraián.	Lakhnauá.
Deswár.	Baniyá.	Mahátmá.
Jaiswár or Ajodhiábási.	Bardarhá.	Maurhiá.
Jasár.	Barpaserá.	Modi.
Khálsá.	Behnáhán.	Motrihá.
Kharidáhá.	Bhaiskayári.	Nagariá.
Ránki or Kalál (Mahomedan).	Chailáha.	Nikthá.
	Chamrauliá.	Rámi dhámi ke asámi.
	Chaubhaiá.	Rámpuriá.
	Chaurahá.	Sadábarti.
	Dewán ke asámi.	Senpuriá.
	Gadahiá.	Seth.
	Gaudanhá.	Slárahá.
	Ghorcharhá.	Srimaurhá.
	Harchanpuriá.	Tháther.
	Hosainpuriá.	Thoreliá.
	Karaiáchor.	Trilokpuriá.
	Khalrihá.	

Sections of the Biyáhut and Kharidáhá sub-castes.

Abkahilá.
Ami.
Bakat pánre ke pánre.
Baksariá.
Banárasiá.
Banráhá.
Báráha ke Máhto.
Barhariá ke pánre.
Baruár.
Básundár.
Bathuáke Máhto.
Bathuáke Ráut.
Battisi.
Beruke kisán.
Beruke Máhto.
Beruke pánre.
Bhádwariá.
Bhojpuriá.
Bhutáne.
Bihiá.
Chánre ke raut.
Chaugáin.
Chaugáinke pánre.
Chausá.
Datta ke ráut.
Daultá ke ráut.
Dhákáich.
Dhankháriá.
Dhobáhá.
Dhurfandá.
Ekauná.
Gádheyiá.
Gámel.
Gángdahiá.
Gareyiá.
Gharikárak.
Goá.
Gonr.
Hardwár.
Harnátar.
Hazári pánre.
Jagmanrá.
Jaintpur.
Jamuáon.
Kaithar.
Kálánuá.
Kamalsar.
Kámsar ke Máhto.
Kándh pákar.
Kaneil.
Kante ke rakmal.
Kante ke ras.
Karjáhá.
Kasarbáni.
Kasmal.
Kates.
Kateswar.
Kathariá.
Katherá.
Katsarwá.
Khan.
Khápráhá.
Kharknáke ke raut.
Khataiá.
Khereswarke pánre.
Krishán.
Laksham Seriá.
Lakshneswar.
Lamgariá.
Máhará.
Mahuári.
Májhaurá.
Mallik.
Maneriá.
Mángaf.
Masáre ke raut.
Mujniá.
Mulmaháli.
Nalakhiá.
Nunáon.
Nuneswar.
Nunhar.
Nunkhariá.
Osái.
Otoniá.
Pábai ke kisan.
Páchhnariá.
Pailáhá.
Pánihá chaur.
Pánkharayá.
Pánre ke Pánre.
Panthpákar.
Pariharbári.
Parlak Pánre.
Prási.
Rámkisán.
Rangpiár.
Sahadar.
Sáhál.
Sáhan.
Sanhá.
Sanichrá.
Sárgátiá.
Sohanpur.
Sonákánt.
Sonhar.
Sugardhar.
Surjáhá.
Tabkáhila.
Támgáin.
Tártar ke khir puri.
Urdágáinhi.

Kámár, *Kumár, Karmakár* (Bengal), *Lohár* (Behar), *Bhindhini* (Singbhum).

Titles:—In Bengal—Ari, Dás, De, Tewári: in Behar—Karuná, Mistri, Thákur.

Sub-castes.

In Bardwan—

Belási.
Máhmudpuriá.
Kámlá-Kámár.

Sections.

In Behar—

Bathuait.
Darsuriá.
Garbariá.

Sub-castes.	Sections.
In Midnapur—	*In Behar*—concld.
Lohár-Kámár } These two intermarry.	Godhanpurá.
Pitule-Kámár }	Harsariá.
Kánsari.	Hasanpuriá.
Sarna-Kámár.	Jakhalpuriá.
Ghatra-Kámár.	Jarangait.
Chánd-Kámár.	Jasiám.
Dhokrá.	Kalait.
Támrá.	Katosiá.
	Marturiá.
In 24-Parganás—	Pokharmiá.
Uttar-Rárhi.	Ratwariá.
Dakhin-Rárhi.	Sági.
Anarpuri.	Sonpuriá.
	Sothiwár.
In Eastern Bengal—	*In Bengal*—
Bhusnápati.	Alamyán.
Dhákái.	Bharadwáj.
Paschimá.	Kásyapa.
In Murshedabad—	Maudgalya.
Rárhi.	Sándilya.
Bárendra.	*In Singbhum and the Santál Parganás*—
Dhákáwál.	Alam-rishi.
Khottá.	Bágh-rishi.
In Pabna—	Bámuniá.
Rárhi or Dás-Samáj.	Kachhuá.
Bárendra or Panch-Samáj.	Khujiriá.
In Noakhali—	Manjari.
Játi-Karmakár.	Nág.
Shikhu-Karmakár.	Netriá.
In Manbhum—	Potá.
Magahiyá.	Puraliá.
Dhokrá.	
Lohsá.	
Básuná.	
In Santál Parganás—	
Ashtalai.	
Belálai.	
Churálai.	
Sankhalai.	

Kámi, *Kámiá.*

Sections.

Baráili.	Lohágun.
Darnál.	Lohár.
Devápáthi.	Lokándri.
Diáli.	Mangráti.
Dudhráj.	Parbaté.
Durál.	Pokhrel.
Gadáili.	Portel.
Gadál.	Rahapál.
Gahatráj.	Rámudán.
Gajmér.	Rasáili.
Ghám-ghotlé.	Rijál.
Gharti-ghauré.	Rujál.
Ghatáni.	Sápkotá.
Jár-Kámi.	Sásankhar.
Kairálá.	Setu-Suruál.
Kati-chioré.	Sin-chiori.
Kharkábáyu.	Singá-oré.
Kháti.	Thápángi.
Lámgádé.	Tiruá.

Kandh, *Kand, Kondh, Khond, Kui-loka, Kui-enju, Skandhasura.*

Titles :—Abbaye, Desauri, Jhankai or Jani, Máji, Málik, Muthá.

Sub-castes.	*Gochi* or septs.	*Klambu* or sub-septs.
Malua or Arria Kandh.	1. Besringia ...	1. Besera.
Orh or Uriya Kandh.		2. Masara.
Beniah-Kandh.		3. Boboto.
Betiah-Kandh.		4. Binjarra.
Nikitia-Kandh.		5. Suna.
Sauntia-Kandh.		6. Motaro.
		7. Mallika.
		8. Murkuri.
		9. Moku.
		10. Dokeri.
	2. Bhetumendi.	
	3. Rasimendi.	
	4. Sagormendi.	
	5. Bankamendi.	
	6. Bidumendi.	
	7. Baloskuppa.	
	8. Grandimendi.	
	9. Gumalmendi.	
	10. Dutimendi.	
	11. Sandumendi.	

Sub-castes.	*Gochi* or septs.	*Klambu* or sub-septs.
	12. Tuniamendi.	
	13. Bhetimendi.	
	14. Sidupari.	
	15. Delapari.	
	16. Kaliapari.	
	17. Rakodmoska.	
	18. Pundilkia.	
	19. Bogalkia.	
	20. Teridikia.	
	21. Koskirabi.	
	22. Domsing.	
	23. Kalabag.	
	24. Kutrengia ...	1. Kotringa. 2. Bisunga. 3. Damlunga. 4. Somanga. 5. Mongalka.
	25. Jehilingia.	
	26. Petingia.	
	27. Kerlingia.	
	28. Bakolmendi.	
	29. Dopsingia.	
	30. Sehelengia.	
	31. Dangnikia.	
	32. Adgirkia ...	1. Koskigan. 2. Panjurika. 3. Surumanega. 4. Pandega. 5. Sarenga. 6. Neringa. 7. Damanga.
	33. Lotpongia.	
	34. Danikia.	
	35. Robingia.	
	36. Mutungia.	
	37. Ganingia.	
	38. Behingia.	
	39. Dubosingia.	
	40. Dondikia.	
	41. Bhusangia.	
	42. Koinjabari.	
	43. Suramendi.	
	44. Bhursamendi.	
	45. Pobingia.	
	46. Gopingia.	
	47. Saitingia.	
	48. Pheringia.	
	49. Jorapongia.	
	50. Bobdengia.	

Kándu, *Kánu, Bharbhunjá, Bhunjá, Bhujári, Bhurji.*

Title :—Sáhu.

Sub-castes.	Sections of the Madhesiá sub-caste.	Sections of the Magahiyá sub-caste.	
Madhesiá.	Baniápáthar.	Akán.	Khádhnu.
Magahiyá.	Bijaibanáras.	Akhgáon.	Kokras.
Bantariá or Bharbhunjá.	Dhanutá.	Ankuri.	Mahuli.
Kanaujiá.	Háthsukhá.	Aráp.	Máldhiá.
Gonr.	Kotá.	Bághákol.	Maner.
Koránch.	Pachtar.	Barhi.	Másaur.
Dhuriá.	Sribitiá.	Bere.	Mehaus.
Rawáni.		Bhárath.	Murti.
Bállamtiriá.		Bháter.	Nenijor.
Thather or Thatherá.		Bireri.	Neprá.
		Chhitni.	Páli.
		Datiyán.	Parsautiá.
		Gáger.	Pilich.
		Gánrol.	Rájgiri.
		Háthiákán.	Rauniá.
		Ichbariá.	Saráihát.
		Jiárwár.	Saursambár.
		Kánáp.	Sirá.
		Káneil.	Tisor.
		Kárián.	Toril.
		Kásiam.	Uttardáhá.
		Káteár.	

Sections of the Bantariá sub-caste. { Tindiha. Chaudihá.

Sections of the Koránch sub-caste. { Chási. Dehri. Háthiá Kándhá. Koriár. Muthá.

Kapáli.

Titles :—Bhuiya, Rai, Háldár, Málá, Mandal, Mánjhi, Mutabar (headman of *pancháyat*), Shikdár.

Sub-caste.	Sections.
Nil.	Kásyapa.
	Siva.

Karan, *Katki-Káet, Uriyá-Káet.*

Titles:—Dás, Mahanti, Mahápátra.

Sub-castes.	Sections.
Karan, Nauli-Karan.	Atreya.
Srishti-Karan, Bhatuntara.	Bharadwája.
	Kantsasa.
Hypergamous groups.	Kásyapa.
	Mudgul.
Khará.	Nágása.
Purá.	Parásara.
Chaián.	Sankha.
Kulina.	

Karangá, *Mistri.*

Titles:—Bishoi, Dalui, Kaur, Khán.

Sub-castes.	Sections.
Dhaluá.	Sálmách.
Máluá.	Kachchhap.
Sikhariá.	
Tungá.	

Kaserá, *Kanserá, Tamherá, Thatherá.*

Sub-caste.	Sections.
None.[1]	Banaudhiyá.
	Basaiyá.
	Chauarsá.
	Chaughará.
	Hariharno.
	Lakar-Mahauliyá.
	Machhuá.
	Mahauliyá.
	Mauhariyá.
	Suariyá.
	Suppar.

---

[1] Mr. Sherring enumerates seven sub-castes—Purbiyá, Pachhawán, Gorakhpuri, Tank Tánchara, Bhariyá, Golar—none of which appear to be known in Behar.

Kástha.

Sub-castes.	Sections.
Madhyasreni-Káyastha.	Same as of Kayasths.
Kastha.	

Kaur.

Sub-tribes.	Septs.
Chánti.	Bambai, a kind of eel.
Cherwa.	Banjar.
Dudh-Kaur.	Bhainsa, buffalo.
Paikará.	Chalenga, a kind of vegetable.
Rathiyá.	Kariar.
	Kolkatári.
	Motiomán.
	Pakar, a fruit.
	Pharsádhenti.
	Rankankar.
	Sanwáni.
	Sarjál.
	Singar.

Kawáli.

Titles :—Dháli, Háldár, Mála, Mánjhi, Vidyádhara.

Sub-caste.	Section.
Nil.	Aliman.

Káyasth, *Káet, Lálá.*

Titles :—Dás, Lál, Rái, Singh.

Sub-castes.		Sections.
Aithána.	In general ...	Kásyapa.
Amashta.		Dedhgawe.
Bálmik.		Kableár.
Bhatnágar.		Katariyár.
Gaur.		Katháutiár.
Karan.		Lakhauriár.
Kulsreshta.		Nandkiriár.
Máthur.		Narhatiár.
Nigam.		Nimandih.
Saksená.		Nuniyár.
Sribástab { Khare. Dusre.		Samaiár.
Surajdhwaj.		Saraiyár.
		Sonkhare.

Sub-castes.	Sections.
Of the Amashta sub-caste.	Baidsáin.
	Bardiár.
	Bilwár.
	Birnáwar.
	Datkiliár.
	Dharkiliár.
	Gaprai.
	Gyásáin.
	Hargambai.
	Jaipuria.
	Jamuár.
	Kachgawai.
	Karpatne.
	Mahtha.
	Mandilwár.
	Pansain.
	Rukhiár.
	Sandhawár.
	Tinriár.
Of the Karan sub-caste.	Ajaidápál.
	Ambahlá.
	Atari.
	Badisámá.
	Bakholá.
	Baláin.
	Barhari.
	Battikbál.
	Benk.
	Garhbiwar.
	Ikahan.
	Kachhrá.
	Kánchanpur.
	Kothipál.
	Munga.
	Narangbali.
	Oari.
	Pakli.
	Sisab.
	Usauth.
	Utamapur.
Of the Sribástab sub-caste.	Kásyapa.
	Akhauri.
	Bakshi.
	Misir.
	Pánde.
	Rái.
	Sahuliar.
	Singh.
	Tewári.
	Thákur.

Káyastha, *Káet, Kait, Káyath.*

Sub-castes.	Sections.	
Uttar-Rárhi.	Agnibesya.	Kalvisa.
Dakshin-Rárhi.	Alambyán.	Kásyapa.
Bangaja.	Ari.	Kausika.
Bárendra.	Atreya.	Krishnátreya.
Madhya-sreni.	Baiyágrahapadya.	Kusik.
	Basishtha.	Maudgalya.
	Básuki.	Parásara.
	Bátsya.	Rohita.
	Bharadwája.	Sábarna.
	Biswámitra.	Sándilya.
	Gautama.	Saukálin.
	Ghritakausik.	Saupáyan.
	Jámadagnya.	

Titles arranged in Hypergamous Groups.

Dakshin Rárhi.

Kulin.—Basu, Ghosh, Mitra.

Siddha Maulik.—Dás, Datta, De, Guha, Kar, Pálit, Sen, Sinha.

Sádhya-Maulik or *Bahátture.*—Aditya, Aich, Ankur, Arnab, As, Baittash, Bal, Bán, Bandhur, Barddhan, Barmá, Bhadra, Bhanja, Bhui, Bhut, Bid, Bindu, Bishnu, Brahma, Chandra, Dáhá, Dáná, Dhanu, Dhar, Dharani, Gan, Ganda, Ghar, Guha, Gui, Guna, Gupta, Guta, Hem, Hes, Hor, Hui, Indra, Jas, Khil, Kirtti, Ksháni, Kshem, Kshom, Kunda, Lodh, Mana, Nág, Nandi, Náth, Om, Pál, Pil, Ráhá, Ráhut, Rája, Rakshit, Ráná, Ranga, Rudra, Sáin, Sakti, Sál, Sám, Sáná, Sarmá, Sil, Som, Sur, Swar, Tej, Upamán.

Bangaja.

Kulin.—Basu, Ghosh, Guha, Mitra.

Madhyalya.—Datta, Nág, Nath.

Mahápátra.—Adhya, Ankur, Bhadra, Bishnu, Chandra, Dás, Deb, Dhar, Kar, Kundu, Nandan, Nandi, Pál, Pálit, Ráhá, Rakshit, Sen, Sinha, Som.

Achal.—Abasakti, Aditya, Aich, Apa, Arnab, Baitosh, Bal, Bán, Bandhu, Barddhan, Barmá, Bed, Bhanja, Bhuin, Bhumik, Bhut, Bindu, Brahma, Chain, Chaki, Dáhá, Dám, Dáná, Dánri, Dhanu, Dharani, Dhol, Dhum, Dut, Gan, Gandak, Ghaniá, Ghár, Guna, Gupta, Háthi, Hem, Hes, Hom, Hor, Hui, Indra, Jas, Kachu, Karáiyá, Khil, Kirtti, Kshám, Kshem, Kshom, Lodh, Maguri, Mán, Mana, Nád, Náhá, Nalu, Pai, Pil, Pipi, Puin, Ráhut, Rája, Răná, Ranga, Riti, Roi, Rudra, Sáin, Sanga, Sarmá, Sil, Smár, Son, Suman, Sur, Syám, Tej.

Uttar-Rárhi.

Kulin.—Ghosh, Sinha.

Sanmaulik.—Dás, Datta, Mitra.

Sámánya Maulik.—Dás,[1] Ghosh, Kar,[1] Sinha.

Bárendra.[2]

Siddha.—Cháki, Dás, Nandi.

Sádhya.—Datta, Deb, Nág, Sinha.

Hej.—Dám, Dhar, Gun, Kar.

Honorary titles:—Bakshi, Bhándári, Biswás, Chaudhri, Dastá-dár, Dháli, Kánungo, Mahallanavis, Majumdár, Mallik, Munsif, Mushrif, Mustaufi, Neogi, Pattadár, Rái, Sarkár, Shikdár, Thákurta.

---

[1] These two families are considered a quarter each, so the Uttar-Rárhis reckon 7½ out of 9 families.

[2] Originally the Bárendras had seven families, but now they count 7½ by adding the descendants of one Saramá, a Nápit, as a half family, besides many immigrant families from other parts of the country which go to swell the Hej group.

Kewat, *Kiot, Kaibartta.*

Titles:—*In Behar*—Bhandári, Cháudhri, Deradár, Jándár, Kámat, Kápar, Khawás, Mahto, Mandar, Marar.

Sub-castes.	Sections.
In Behar—	
Bahiáwak, Bahiot, or Ghibihár.	Bhadauriá.
Garbháit, Gorwáit, or Sághár.	Biswás.
Ajudhiábási.	Házará.
Játhot.	Itwár.
Machhuá.	Kápar.
Mahádanda.	Kásyapa.
	Maharná.
	Marar.
	Mukhiá.

Khambu, *Nau-lákh Khambu.*

Titles:—Dhan, Jimdár, Kiráti, Mandal, Mukhiá, Rái, Sing.

Thars or septs.

Bábhaunchhá.
Bángdel.
Barlos.
Bokhime.
Bonthárua.
Boyong.
Bumákámchhá.
Butepáchhá.
Chamlingeh.
Chaurási.
Chuiráchhá.
Dilpáli.
Dungmáli.
Haidibuthá.
Hatuwáli.
Homodimchhá.
Horongpáchhá.
Jubhingeh.
Kási.
Kháling.
Kheresanchhá.
Kuásanchhá.
Kulung.
Láphaunchhá.
Maiduchhá.
Maikam.
Male Kumchhá.
Mayáháng.
Mukáranchhá.
Mulukuas.
Námbochhá.
Námdung.
Nardauchhá.
Necháhli.
Nimámbaunchhá.
Ninauchhá.
Nomahang.
Paderáchhá.
Phlumáchhá.
Phulehli.
Phurkeli.
Plembochhá.
Rabchháli.
Rajabin.
Rákháli.
Ránauchhá.
Rápungchhá.
Regálaunchhá.
Rimching.
Rochingáchhá
Sángpáng.
Silongchhá.
Sotháングeh.
Sungdele.
Tángbuáh.
Thulung.
Wáhsali.

Khandáit, *Khandait-Páik, Khandáyat, Bhuiyá-Páik.*

Titles:

In Chota Nagpur:—Amáut, Arhá, Baráik, Behará, Gaunjhu, Kotwár, Mahápátra, Mánjhi, Mirdáhá, Náik, Ohdár, Pátra, Pradhán, Ráut.

In Orissa.

Bághá, tiger.
Báhubalendra, like the god Indra in strength of arm.
Dakhin-Kabát, south gate.
Daubárik, messenger or sentinel.
Garh-Náik or Sinha, leader or lion of the fort.
Háti, elephant.
Jená.
Maharath or Mahárathi, great charioteer.
Malla, wrestlers.
Mangaráj.
Náik, leader.
Paschim-Kabát, west gate.
Praharáj.
Ranasinha or Samarsinha, lion of the fight.
Raut, horseman.
Rui.
Sámanta, officer.
Senápati, general.
Sinha, lion.
Uttar-Kabát, north gate.

Sub-castes.	Sections.
	(a) *Totemistic*—
Bar-gohri. Das-ghariá, in Saranda of Singbhum.	Kachhuá, tortoise.
Bar-gohri. Pachâs-ghariá, in Chota Nagpur.	Kadam, *nauclea grandifolia.*
Bar-gohri. Pânchsau-ghariá, in Gángpur.	Mor, peacock.
Bar-gohri. Pandrasau-ghariá, in Gángpur, Bonai, Bámrá, and Sambalpur.	Nág, snake.
Chhot-gohri, in Chota Nagpur.	Sál, fish.
	(b) *Eponymous*—
	Bharadwája.
	Kaundilya.
	Nágasá, etc.

Chásá or Orh-Khandait ... }
Mahánáik or Sresta-Khandait } In Balasore and Cuttack.
Bhanja-Khandait ... }
Harichandan Khandait ... } In Puri.
Khandait-Paik ... }
Sresta-Khandait ... } In the Orissa Tributary States.

Khariá.

Titles :—Dhángar, Kisán, Kol, Parja.

Sub-castes.	Sections.
Berga-Khariá.	Bage, a bird.
Dhilki-Khariá.	Bar, *Ficus Indica.*
Dud-Khariá.	Bárlá.
Erenga-Khariá.	Baroá, an animal.
Munda-Khariá.	Bilung, Nun, or Noná Mailá, salt.
Oraon-Khariá.	Demtá, red ant.
	Dhân, paddy.
	Dhanuár, can't eat rice soup.
	Dhelki, a bird.
	Dungdung, Aind, or Indu, eel.
	Durang, a fish.
	Háthi, elephant.
	Kasi.
	Kerketá, a bird of that name.
	Kiro or Bágh, tiger.
	Kulu or Kachchhuá, tortoise.
	Mailwar.
	Murgear.

Sub-castes.	Sections.
	Nág, cobra.
	Naik.
	Naniár.
	Pardhan.
	Pathal.
	Purti.
	Sáhul.
	Samdiá.
	Saur, fish.
	Suraniá, a rock.
	Telga.
	Teteteyin or Bagiár, a bird of that name.
	Tirkoár.
	Tititihu, a bird.
	Topo, a bird.
	Tuti, vegetable.

The above groups are found among the settled Khariás. I have been unable to ascertain whether the wild Khariás, commonly known as Ban-Mánush, 'men of the woods,' have any similar divisions.

Kharwár, *Kherwár.*

Titles:—Bhakat, Bhogta, Dás, Gaunju, Kapri, Mahto, Mandar, Manjhi, Ohdár, Panjiárá, Pradhán.

Sub-tribes.	Septs.
In Palamau—	Aind, a kind of eel.
Pátbandh.	Bág, tiger.
Daulbandh.	Bahera, a jungle fruit.
Khairi.	Baherwar, a tree.
	Bail, a fruit.
	Bair, plum.
	Bamnia, salt.
	Bandhia.
	Bania, a caste.
	Bar, *Ficus Indica.*
	Bhogta.
In Southern Lohardagá—	Binjoar.
Deswári-Kharwár.	Biserwar.
Bhogtá.	Bisra, a hawk.
Raut.	Chardiar, pineapple.
Manjhiá.	Chirra, squirrel.
	Chorant, a grass.
	Chundiar, a top-knot.
	Chuniar, lime.
	Demta, red tree-ant.
	Dhobi, can't touch washerman.

Sub-tribes.	Septs.
	Dolbandhi.
	Dudul, a kind of bird.
	Gai, cow.
	Ghansi, a pond fish.
	Hans, swan.
	Hansarwar, duck.
	Hasdajiá, a duck.
	Hathi, elephant.
	Hemremina.
	Kachua, tortoise.
	Kans, a grass.
	Kanwad, a jungle fruit.
	Karhar, a jungle fruit like ' bel.
	Kerketa, a bird.
	Kesargia.
	Khapu, a bird.
	Khichengia, a fruit.
	Kowriar.
	Kuardar.
	Kurdur.
	Kussum, a fruit.
	Maderwar.
	Mahukal, a bird.
	Mailwar.
	Manjar.
	Manjhi, a title.
	Munga, coral.
	Murgi, hen.
	Murmurwar.
	Mus, rat.
	Nág, cobra.
	Pátmurmurárá.
	Radhar.
	Rikhiasan.
	Sai Sonarwar.
	Samudwar.
	Saras, a water-fowl.
	Sheor, a fish.
	Sonar, goldsmith.
	Sonarwar, gold.
	Suia, a kind of little bird.
	Sumedhiar, a tree.
	Surunia, neck ornament.
	Tamba, copper.
	Tirki, a bird.
	Tiruar, Tirkuár, an arrow.
	Tuduar, hen.
	Tunduar.
	Turuar, a fruit (*pakur*).
	Tuti, a kind of bird.
	Uriar.

Sub-tribes.		Septs.
	Septs of the Daulbandh sub-tribe.	Behroár. Kaunsiár. Kauriár. Mánriár. Pát-murmu. Ráj-murmu. Sonoroár.

Khatik.

Sub-castes.	Section.
Khatik. Dharamdási.	Kásyapa.

Khatri, *Purbiyá Khatri.*

Titles :—Barman, Lál, Máhátá, Sáhu.

Sub-castes.		Sections.
Chárjáti. Panchjáti. Chhajáti. Bárajáti. Bahánnajáti. Piruwal.	Of the Chárjáti sub-caste.	Kápur. Khánná. Meherá. Set or Set-tálwár.
	Of the Panchjáti sub-caste.	Beri. Birj. Saigal. Sarwál. Wahe.
	Of the Chhajáti sub-caste.	Bhale. Dhawan. Supat. Tolwar. Turman.
	Of the Bárajáti sub-caste.	Chaupre. Ghai. Kakkar. Meheden. Soni. Tandan.

[1] The Chárjáti sub-caste is again divided into Arhái-ghar and Chári-ghar, apparently hypergamous groups, the former of which is deemed superior to the latter. It seems probable that the first five sub-castes were originally hypergamous divisions, the order of precedence being that given above. Intermarriage between members of different sub-castes is not unknown at the present day, but it is considered right for a man to marry in his own group, and the sub-castes are practically endogamous. The Piruwál sub-caste has always been endogamous for the reasons explained in the text.

Sub-castes.		Sections.
	Of the Bahánnajáti sub-caste.	Behal. Chal-agge. Dhandhábe. Gayalpure. Handi. Keoli. Khosle. Kuchal. Marwáhe. Náiár. Nándi. Suri.

Brahmanical Gotras—

Angirasa.
Bátsya.
Bharadwája.
Hangsarishi.
Kásyapa.
Kausalya.
Lomasá.

Khatwe.

Title :—Mandar.

Sub-castes.	Section.
Bahio. Goro.	Kásyapa.

Khyán or Kolita.

Sub-castes.	Sections.
Nil.	Aladish. Alamyán. Agni batsya. Kánsári. Kasyapa. Kauchan rishi. Madhukulya. Mugrish.

Kochh, *Rájbansi, Sivabansi, Suryabansi, Mándái, Bhanga-Kshatri, Kshatri-Sankoch, Patita-Kshatri, Paliyá, Desi.*

Titles:—**Bhaumik, Chaudhri, Dás, Mahat, Májhi, Tánti, Báns-árá, Sagun-ure.**

Sub-castes. | Sections.

In Northern Bengal—

Paliyá. — Kásyapá.
- Sádhu.
- Bábu, Byábahári.

Rájbansi.
- Kántái.
- Desi.
- Tiar or Dalai.
- Modásí.
- Dobhásir.
- Jáluá or Jháluá.

Bodo.

Dugu or Sections.

Mekhun.	Darang-Chiachi.
Dásik.	Darang-Saudana.
Senel.	Darang-Dambuk.
Chisim.	Darang-Dakal.
Náphák.	Shaini.
Darang.	Doi.
Richil.	Durgu.
Parak.	Lori.

In Dacca—

Kochh-Mándál.

Koiri, *Muráo.*

Titles:—**Mahto, Muráo** (green-grocer), **Marar, Dhelphor** (clod-breaker).

Sub-castes.	Sections of the Banáphar sub-caste.
Barki-Dángi.	
Chhotki-Dángi.	Bagwe.
Banáphar, Banapár.	Darbe.
Jaruhár.	Káno.
Kanaujiá.	Kápri.
Magahiyá.	Mánjhi.
Tirhutiá.	Marár.
Chirmait.	Marik.
Kumárá.	Panjiárá.
Goita, Dhár — In Champaran.	
Reutiá, Pauriá, Barákar, Palmohá — In Chota Nagpur.	

Sub-castes.	Sections of the Magahiyá sub-caste.
	Amrot.
	Gamaīyá Parganá Kharakpur.
	Kargaha.
	Maiketári beguná bágh.
	Mál.
	Sais.
In Chota Nagpur	Kásyap.
	Nág.
	Mujni.

Korá, *Kaorá*, *Khaira*, *Khayrá*, *Hári* (used inaccurately by outsiders only).

Titles:—Mudi, Rái.

Sub-castes.	Sections.
Dhalo.	Alu.
Molo.	Bárdá.
Sikhariá.	Butku, pig.
Bádámiá.	Hansdá, wild goose.
Sonárekhá.	Kásyab, tortoise.
Jhetiá.	Kásibak, heron.
Guri-Báwá.	Sámá.
	Sál or Saulá, fish.
	Sánpu, bull.

Korwa.

Title:—Majhi.

Sub-tribes.	Septs.
Agaria-Korwa.	Ainduar, a kind of eel.
Dand-Korwa.	Amba, mango.
Dih Korwa.	Asotoar.
Paharia-Korwa.	Bagher, tiger.
	Dhan, unhusked rice.
	Ginmuar.
	Ginuar, a kind of eel.
	Har, plough.
	Harrá, myrabolam.
	Hasda, wild goose.
	Huruj.
	Kerketta, a bird.
	Mujaniar.
	Muri, ancestors made a *chulá* of four skulls and cooked their dinner.
	Pakhua.
	Samat, pestle.
	Samp, snake.
	Sarai, a jungle fruit.
	Silli, a kind of fish.
	Suga, parrot.

Koshtá, *Máhárá.*

Title :—Dás.

Sections.

Bagháł, tiger.
Bagutia.
Bhát, rice.
Bhatpáhári.
Chaudhri.
Chaur, yak's tail.
Gohi.
Khanda, sword.
Kurm, tortoise.
Mánik, gem.
Nág, snake.
Son.

Kotál, *Kotwál.*

Title :—Pradhán.

Sub-castes.	Sections.
Atpárá.	*Nil.*
Dhukursáni.	
Kutabpur.	
Manoharsáhi.	

Kumhár, *Kumár, Kumati, Kumbhakár, Kulál, Ghatakár, Ghatakárpur, Prajápati, Rudrabans, Rudrapál, Pandit.*

Titles :—Behárá, Biswás, Dás, Deuri, Kunkál, Máhato, Májhi, Marar, Marik, Mehrána, Pál, Ráná.

Sub-castes.	Sections.
In Jessore—	
Belgáchi.	Aladoshi.
Dáspárá.	Alamyán.
Nautana.	Hansa.
Bhushná.	Kanaka.
	Kásyapa.
	Rishi.
	Sándilya.
In Murshedabad and Hughli—	
Rárhi.	
Bárendra.	
Dáspári.	
Chaurási.	

Sub-castes.		Sections.
In Pabna—		
Sirasthán.		
Májhasthán.		
Chandan-sára.		
Chaurási.		
Daspárá { Prámánik. Pánpátra. Mujgarni.		
In Dacca—		
Bara-bhágiyá } Lál.		
Chhota-bhágiyá } Sádá.		
Khatya.		
Rájmahália.		
Magi.		
In Noakhali—		
Bhuláiyá.		
Saráliá.		
Chátgáinyá.		
Sandwipá.		
In Behar and Chota Nagpur—		
Maghaiyá.	Of the Magahiyá sub-caste.	Asmait.
Kanaujiá.		Baid.
Tirhutiá.		Bárik.
Desi, Deswár.		Biswás.
Bardhiá.		Chaudhrián.
Biáhut.		Gáim.
Ajodhyábási.		Jeruhet.
Ardhauti.		Kápar.
Godahiyá.		Kásyapa, Kaisab.
Chápuá.		Kathalmalet.
Banaudhiá.		Kheri.
Masawár.		Madhust.
Bangáli or Rárhi.		Maháthá.
Turk-Kumhár.		Mahátman.
		Maheswar.
		Mehtar.
		Mukh.
		Nág.
		Pachmait.
		Panjiár.
		Parrarit.
		Pharkiet.
		Ráut.
		Ráworh.
		Senápat.
		Sonmain.
		Tharait.

Sub-castes.		Sections.
	Sections found in Singbhum.	Chána. Kharuá. Maher. Mandap. Natanya. Ranubád. Sikári. Sinhi. Surabani. Tumaliá.
	In Manbhum	Báilhor. Kásyab. Min, fish. Nág, snake. Sándil.
	In Lohardagá	Bar, *Ficus Indica.* Garhatia. Hathi, elephant. Kansi, a grass. Parihar. Sisingi, a river-fish, has two thorns on its head. Tumbli, Berni.
	In the Santál Parganás.	Káchim, tortoise. Nág, serpent.
In Orissa—		
Jagannáthi or Uriya-Kumhár.		Bhad-bhadriá, sparrow. Goru, cow. Kaundinya, tiger. Kurma, tortoise. Mudir, frog. Neul, weasel. Sarpa, snake.
Khatya-Kumhár.		Kásyapa.

Kurmi, *Kunbi, Kurambi, Kurum, Kurumánik.*

Titles:—Chaudhri, Mahanta, Mahárái, Mahato, Mandal, Marár, Mukhya, Parámánik, Raut, Sarkár, Singh.

Sub-castes.	Sections.
(*a*) *In Behar—*	(*a*) *In Behar—*
Ayodhiyá or Awadhiyá.	Garain.
Chandel or Chandan.	Kásyapa.
Chanaur.	
Ghamela.	
Ghorcharhá.	

Sub-castes.

(a) *In Behar*—concld.

Jaiswár.
Kachaisá.
Katriár.
Kharchwár.
Rámaiyá.
Sainthwár.
Sanswár.
Sauchánd.
Terahghariá

(b) *In Chota Nagpur*—

Adh-Kurmi or Madhyam-Kurmi.
Bagsariá or Bágsariá.
Khoriá.
Kurum.
Magahiá.
Nich-Kurmi.
Sikhariá or Chhota-Kurmi.

(c) *In Orissa*—

Bagsari.
Gádásari.
Gáysari.
Maisásari.

Sections.

(b) *In Chota Nagpur and Orissa* —

Andhachábár.
Andhachipá panariá.
Bághbanuár, tiger.
Bághwár, tiger.
Bagsariá, tiger.
Baherwár, a fruit.
Báns, bamboo.
Bánsriár, will not play the *bánsi* or bamboo flute.
Banuár, hunter.
Bendiár.
Bhokwár.
Bilár, cat.
Chhonch Mutruár, spider.[1]
Chilbindhá panariá.
Chilbinuár, kite.
Chiluár, kite.
Chorharuá.
Dugriár.
Dumuriá, *dumur*, fig.
Goriár.
Hánsdá.
Hásdagiá, wild goose.
Hastowár, tortoise.
Hemramiá, betel palm.
Henduár.
Homwár.
Jálbanuár, net.
Jhápábasriár.
Jhátideká.
Juruár.
Juthasankhwár.
Káchiári.
Káchimár.
Kaiobanuár.
Kairawár, illegitimate issues.
Kánbindhá, pierced ears.
Kárákátá Karwár, buffalo.
Katiár, will not wear silk cloth.
Kesariá, *Kesar*, grass.
Khechá Kesria.
Kundiár.

---

[1] In Midnapur Kurmis say that once upon a time water being needed to clear a place for some religious ceremony, a Kurmi there present made use of his urine for the purpose, and his descendants were therefore called Chhonch-mutruár.

Sub-castes.	Sections.
	Mangar, crocodile.
	Mantrawár.
	Mathrwár.
	Murmu, nilgao.
	Mus, rat.
	Nág, snake.
	Nágbasriár.
	Nángtoyár, give children their first rice naked.
	Nauákhuri.
	Punriár.
	Rájmor.
	Rimrimiá.
	Sálbanwár, *sál* jungle.
	Sankhawár, will not wear shell ornaments.
	Siár, jackal.
	Sona, gold.
	Tiruár.
	Tukipitá dumuriá, *dumur*, fig.
	Tunduár.

Laheri, *Laherá.*

Title :—**Sahu.**

Sub-castes.	Sections.
Dakhinhá.	**Kási.**
Tirhutiá.	**Mahuriá.**
Nuri.	

Lepcha, *Mon.*

Sub-tribes.[1]	Septs.
Rong.	**Barphungpuso.**
Khamba.	**Adinpuso.**[2]
	Singdyang.
	Tingilmung.
	Rangomung.
	Tárzukmung.
	Sungutmung.
	Námzingmung.
	Luksom.
	Sangmi.

[1] As stated in the text, these groups are not now endogamous.
[2] As stated in the text, Adinpuso is the only one of these groups which is now exogamous.

Limbu, *Das Limbu, Yakthumba, Tsong, Chang.*

Title :—**Subha** or **Suffah** (chief).

Sub-tribes (*thum* or *thum-thum*).

Sub-tribe	Classification
1. Pánthar	Classed as Kási-gotra, supposed to have immigrated into Nepal from Benares.
2. Chhothar	
3. Ahtharai	
4. Yangorup	
5. Chaibisá	
6. Miákhola or Terothar ...	Classed as Lhásá-gotra, supposed to have come from Lhásá.
7. Charkhola	
8. Maikhola	
9. Phedáb or Bhuiphuta ...	
10. Tambrkhola ...	

Septs (*thar*).

Of the Pánthar sub-tribe.

- **Angdenba**, lord of the forest.
- **Chehmjom**, a native of Chehm.
- **Chikchábá.**
- **Chobegu.**
- **Hangsnemba.**
- **Ingmaba**, he who kept fowls.
- **Kerungma.**
- **Kokenamba**, he who rises with the sun.
- **Laoti**, he who was obeyed.
- **Luhá.**
- **Manglagpa**,[1] the dancer.
- **Mephagpa**, the butcher, literally, pig-roaster.
- **Phejom**, the *kukri*-bearer, including (*a*) Nembong, (*b*) Sardak-peapi.
- **Pheodan**, the water-carrier.
- **Phyagpa**, the knife-grinder.
- **Serma**, rent-collector.
- **Songbangphe**, the new settler.
- **Thekim**, he who works in wicker, including the following sub-septs :—(*a*) Meongba, (*b*) Thamsong, (*c*) Chobegu, (*d*) Petehhimba, (*e*) Angbu, the forest-dweller, (*f*) Yakten, formerly doctors.
- **Toktiham.**
- **Tumbapo**, the eldest.
- **Tumbrok**, born of a step-mother.
- **Yangdenba**,[2] he who paid his footing.
- **Yangsoba** or **Namlagpa**, the chief of the tribe.

---

[1] The ancestor of this *thar* was ridden (possessed?) by a god, and danced.

[2] Descended from a Mech who got admission into the Limbu tribe by bribing the heads of the *thum-thum*.

Of the Chhothar sub-tribe.

- **Bargharri**, the twelve brethren.
- **Khema**,[1] a pheasant. Apparently totemistic.
- **Khojom**, he who ate his earnings.
- **Kurumbhong**,[2] the divider of the village.
- **Legma**, the worker in mud.
- **Maden**, the son of his mother.
- **Sangma**,[3] a buffalo. Apparently totemistic.
- **Teling**, the worker in cane.
- **Thogleng**, the suicide.
- **Tungohong**, the discontented.

Of the Ahtharai sub-tribe.

- **Angbohang**, king of the fir wood.
- **Inglamphe**, the liar.
- **Kondongwa**, the vagabond.
- **Pomo**, the large family.
- **Thenglahbo**, the native of Thenglah.
- **Tshendangkya**, he who lives apart.
- **Yakshoma**, the guardian of the fort.

Of the Yango rup sub-tribe.

- **Ingyaromba**.
- **Khebangba**, the native of Khebang.
- **Khingba**, branch of the same sept may not intermarry.
- **Lechenche**, the dissolute one.
- **Lekhogma**, he with swollen testes.
- **Lingden**, **Loksohm** } Admitted from the Lepchas.
- **Mahbho**, branch of the same sept may not intermarry.
- **Mangmu**.
- **Menyangbo**, the unsuccessful one.
- **Mongtupo**.
- **Phawahong**, the name of a village.
- **Pondha**, the wanderer.
- **Puktebu**.
- **Serling**, the thief.
- **Suwahong**, the mendicant.
- **Thehbeh**.[4]
- **Thupuku**.
- **Tumling**.
- **Yakpangden**, the dweller on the pass.

---

[1] This *thar* will not eat a pheasant or fowl or any bird of that class. The story is that the founder went out to shoot pheasants in a fir copse, but found none, and vowed never to eat a pheasant again.

[2] The founder of this *thar* is said, for reasons not stated, to have divided his village into two parts by drawing a line down the middle.

[3] The buffalo is taboo to this *thar*: the legend is the same as that of the Khema *thar*.

[4] An eponymous *thar*, named after Thehbeh, son of Srijanga, the powerful chief of the Limbus, since deified, who fought against Prithi Náráyan, the founder of the present ruling dynasty of Nepal.

Of the Yangorup sub-tribe—*concluded.*
- **Yíjám**, the wanderer, or eater.
- **Yithingu**, the huntsman.
- **Yongyahang**, the son of a chief.
- **Yungmá**, the idler.

Of the Chaibisa sub-tribe.
- **Lhoringten**,[1] the chief of Morrung.
- **Memophagpa.**
- **Papson**, the adopted one.
- **Pichagma**,[2] the son of the monkey.
- **Sonyokpa**, the guardian of the new fort.

Of the Miákhola or Terothar sub-tribe.
- **Hangam**, the king's officer.
- **Líbang**, the archer.
- **Nahlibo**,[3] he who chased his wife.
- **Thoilong**, the ragged one.
- **Tsonbang**, he who listens and profits.

Of the Charkhola sub-tribe.
- **Aktenhang**, name of a domestic demi-god.
- **Lingdam**, admitted from the Lepchas.
- **Mahbu**,[4] the physician.
- **Nembang**, the swollen one.
- **Photro.**
- **Thogphelagu**, he who wears the rhododendron flower.
- **Yongyahung**, the aristocrat.

Of the Phedáb sub-tribe.
- **Chikkophung**, he who planted the *brihati*.[5]
- **Hupachongbang**, he who was blessed and prospered.
- **Isbo**, name of a village.
- **Khamapong**, the dweller under the *bar* (*Ficus religiosa*) tree.
- **Lokmahung.**
- **Lumphongma**, those who shared the land.
- **Maden.**
- **Musuhang**, the lowland chief.
- **Ninglehku**, one who cuts poisonous plants.
- **Obung-gyakpa**, the dweller above the fountain.
- **Phehim**, the singer.
- **Pho-omphu**, the hangman.
- **Phungthag**, he who stole to order.
- **Pongyangu**, he who carries his goods on his back.
- **Senihang**, sons of the snow-chief.

---

[1] This *thar* was formerly under the Morrung Raja.

[2] This *thar* is said to have formerly worshipped the monkey.

[3] The story is that the wife of the founder of the *thar* ran away from him, but he caught her and brought her back, and afterwards had a large family by her.

[4] Literally a shaker; one who being ridden by ghosts or devils shakes himself free: hence a physician.

[5] A thorny plant with a bitter berry used for medical purposes.

Of the Phedáb sub-tribe—*concld.*

- Singogpa.
- Sodemba, the spy.
- Songbangphe, the dweller in the valley.
- So-onkobu, a resident of So-onko.
- Sothung, name of a village.
- Thambden, the stay-at-home.
- Theguba, the son of the cliff.
- Thobukya, he who has skin disease.
- Tumbangphe,[1] the earth-born or *Bhuiphuta*.
- Yurumbang, they of the central village.

Of the Tambrkhola sub-tribe.

- Legbahang.
- Lingkhim.
- On-chhombo, the horse-seller.
- Phenduá,[2] the hammerer of iron.
- Sahmbahang.
- Ssahoden, born in famine time.
- Thup-yumah, name of a place.

Septs.

Angláh.	Nagen.
Anlábáng.	Nermáh.
Baidohang.	Nogo.
Bákhim.	Pálu.
Chempajong.	Párkhari.
Chungbáng.	Patálang.
Hemphá.	Pekhá.
Hukpáh.	Petungbah.
Ichommah.	Phalechhuah.
Ikteh.	Pheyak.
Ilámháng.	Ponthák.
Imsong.	Samwah.
Ithinku.	Sángbah.
Kámbáháng.	Sanjokmah.
Kámbáng.	Sátling.
Kephuk.	Seduah.
Khámthák.	Sekwahdeng.
Khobaipong.	Sene.
Khuadang.	Singjangkuk.
Kunbáhong.	Singjuk.
Laktomáháng.	Sukhong.
Lingdenbeh.	Sukwabah.
Linglámphen.	Taijaung.
Lugumah.	Tilding.
Mangoyak.	Tongbángboha.
Mangyong.	Tumkohong.
Muromah.	Yongyah.

[1] This *thar* claims to be *terræ filii*, and point out a huge rock which covers the spot where their founder sprang from the earth.

[2] This *thar* was formerly the blacksmiths of the tribe.

Lohár, *Kamár.*

Titles:—Mistri, Ráut, Thákur.

Sub-castes.

In Behar—

Kanaujiá.
Kokás.
Maghaya.
Kamár Kallá.
Mahur or Mahuliyá.
Mathuriyá.
Kamiá, immigrants from Nepal.

In Santál Parganás—

Birbhumiá.
Govindpuriá.
Shergarhiá.

In Lohardagá—

Manjhal-Turiyá.
Munda-Lohár.
Sad-Lohár.
Sisutbansi Loharia, Lohondia.

In Bankura—

Angariá.
Gobrá.
Jhetiá.
Pánsili.

Sections.

Of the Kanaujiá sub-caste:

Asesmeghrám.
Baswariá.
Begsariá.
Bermán.
Bhákur.
Biskarmá.
Bunichhor.
Chausáhá.
Damdariá.
Dhakaniá.
Gungambhir.
Kamtariá.
Kantithiá.
Kásyapa.
Kathár.
Kathautiá.
Kissauriá.
Kukurjhampar.
Kulthari Mallik
Pahlampuri.
Pánre.
Ráne.
Sabri.
Sámil Thákur.
Sangiri Thákur.
Sarwat.
Sonaman.
Supáhá.
Udhmatiá.
Sálrishi, *sál* fish.

Sub-castes.	Sections.
In Manbhum—	
Lohár-Mánjhi.	
Danda-Mánjhi.	
Bágdi-Lohár.	

Sub-tribes.	Totemistic septs in Chota Nagpur.
	Bagh, tiger.
	Bán, a kind of eel.
	Bando, wild cat, makes a loud noise at night.
	Báns, bamboo.
	Baroha.
	Beloar, fruit.
	Besra, a hawk.
	Bhengraj, kingcrow.
	Bhutkuar.
	Bodrâ.
	Bukru.
	Chouria.
	Churuar.
	Demta, red tree-ant.
	Dhan, rice soup forbidden.
	Dumria, fig.
	Gaintwar.
	Goloar, sweet potato.
	Gunj, a kind of fruit.
	Hardi, turmeric.
	Hastuar.
	Hatti, elephant.
	Hemrom.
	Induar, a kind of eel.
	Jalwar, net.
	Kachua, tortoise.
	Kaethoar, a curry vegetable.
	Kaisale.
	Kamal, lotus.
	Kanda, sweet potato.
	Kanojia, a tribe.
	Karhar, a jungle fruit.
	Karkosa, cow.
	Karkusa, a bird.
	Kaua, crow.
	Kerketta, a bird.

Sub-tribes.	Totemistic septs in Chota Nagpur.
	Kisnot, a tribe.
	Koeá, a wild beast.
	Kons, grass.
	Kusuar, a river-fish.
	Lalihar, a bird.
	Lumria, a fox.
	Maelwar.
	Maghaia, a place.
	Maghnia.
	Mahili Munda, a tribe.
	Mahili, a tribe.
	Mormu, deer.
	Mutriar.
	Nág, cobra.
	Pánru, a snake.
	Phutka, vegetable.
	Purti.
	Retha, fruit.
	Runda, a wild cat.
	San, heron.
	Sándh, bullock.
	Sangalwar.
	Saur, a fish.
	Semanohangiar.
	Sonaome.
	Sonbesra, a bird.
	Son Maghia.
	Son Tirki.
	Suia, a small bird.
	Tirki, can't touch any animals after their eyes open.
	Topoar, a bird.
	Udwar, a water-cat.

Madhunápit, *Madak.*

Sub-castes	Sections.
Biswás-Madak.	Alamyán.
Játi-Madak.	Bharadwája.
Madhu-Madak.	Kásyapa.
Reláti-Madak.	Maudgalya.
	Parásara.
	Sándilya.

Magh, *Mag.*

Sub-tribes.

Thongtha, Thongcha or Jumiá Magh.
Marmá, Myammá or Roáng Magh.
Maramagri, Rájbansi, Baruá or Bhuiyá Magh.

Septs.

Cherengtsa.
Chingrisa.
Hroimajusa.
Kaukdaintsa.
Keophasa.
Kogdengsa.
Kolasa.
Krong Khyungtsa.
Kwinjusa.
Kyaukmatsa.
Kyaukpiatsa.
Mahlaingtsa.
Marotsa.
Orá.
Palainggritsa.
Palaingtsa.
Palása.
Phrangroatsa.
Rigretsa.
Saboktsa.
Taingchait.
Uengsa.
Wadsuesa.
Walentsa.

Mahesri.

Sub-caste.

Dasa.

Sections.

Sabu.
Mundra.
Rauti.
Sowáni.
Málpáni.
Lakhotia.
Palaur.
Janwár.
Kábra.
Baoti.
Millak.
Sadra.
Gatáni.
Tela.
Loyá.
Tábria.
Murkia.
Kalláni.

Mahili, *Mahali.*

Titles:—Mánjhi, Mahoto.

Sub-castes.

Bansphor-Mahili.
Mahili-Mundá.
Pátar-Mahili.
Sulunkhi-Mahili.
Tánti-Mahili.

Sections.

Chardhagia.
Chardhiár.
Charhar, a tree.
Dhilki.
Dumriár or Dungri, wild fig.

Sub-castes.	Sections.
	Goondli, a kind of grain, forbidden.
	Hánsdá or Hasdagiár, wild goose.
	Hemron.
	Induar, a kind of eel.
	Kantuár or Kánti, ear.[1]
	Karkusá.
	Khangar.
	Khariár.
	Kathargách, jack fruit tree.
	Kerketa, a kind of bird.
	Kundiar.
	Mahukal, a bird; its long tail.
	Mandriár.
	Marri.[2]
	Murmuár, nilgáo.
	Patariar.
	Pilua, a caterpillar.
	Rondiar.
	Sarihin.
	Silli.
	Tapaer, a bird.
	Taw.
	Tirki, bull.
	Tunduar.
	Turu, grass, cotton, fruit or seed.
	Tutiear.
Sections of the Mahili-Mundá sub-caste.	Bhuktuár.
	Láng Chenre.
	Sángá.

[1] Members of the Kantuár section may not eat the ear of any animal.
[2] Members of the Marri section do not allow their married daughters to enter their houses.

Mál.

Titles:—Háldár, Khámid, Machhuá, Mánjhi.

Sub-castes.		Sections.
Dhaliá	In Bankura.	Fenga, a bird.
Gobrá		Garur, adjutant.
Kherá		Ghátu, a bird.
Rájbansi		Kachhap, tortoise.
Sánágánthá		Nág, snake.
Dhunakátá	In Midnapur and Manbhum.	Pátrishi, bird.
Rájbansi		Penkál-máchh, fish.
Sápuryá or Bediya-Mál.		Sál-máchh, fish.
Tungá		

Sub-castes.		Sections.
Khuturiá Mallik Rájbansi	In Birbhum.	
Deswár Magahiyá Rajbansi or Rájá-Mál. Rarhi-Mál Sindurá	In the Santál Parganás.	

Málé, *Samariá-Málé, Sauriá, Savar Pahária, Sámil Pahária, Asal Pahária, Sangi.*

Máli, *Málákár, Phulmáli.*

Title :—Ráut (in Behar).

Sub-castes.		Sections.
(*a*) *In Bengal*—		(*a*) *In Bengal*—
Phulkátá-Máli	1. Rárhi. 2. Bárendra. 3. Athghariá.	Alamyán. Kásyapa. Maudgalya. Sándilya.
Dokáne-Máli.		
(*b*) *In Behar*—		(*b*) *In Behar*—
None.		Bhandári. Mallik.

Málo, *Málo-Pátni.*

Titles :—Bepári, Jáliyá, Jálo, Jalwá, Mánjhi, Pátra.

Sub-caste.	Sections.
None.	Alimán. Bánarási. Bángas-rási. Bharan-rási. Khonrá-rási. Kártik-rási. Kulin-rási. Mesh-rási. Padma-rási. Puyi-rási. Singh-rási. Sib-rási. Udadhi.

Mál Pahária.

Titles :—Mánjhi, Náik, Sardár.

Sub-tribes.	Septs.[1]
Kumár or Komar-Bhág.	Ahriti, hunters.
Mál Pahária proper.	Dehriti, priests.
	Grihi, householders.
	Mánjhi, village headman.
	Pátra.
	Pujhor, priests.
	Sikdár.

[1] The names of the septs are said to denote the original occupations of their members at the time when exogamy was introduced. The Male tribe, of which, according to Buchanan, the Mál Paháriás are an offshoot, have no exogamous divisions.

Mangar, *Magar*, *Thomi*.

Titles :—Ráná, Sing, Thápa.

Sub-tribes.	*Thars* or septs.	
Atháráh Panth.	Achámi.[1]	Ghatani.
Buráthoki.	Agri.	Ghatráj.
Gharti.	Aleh, Alliá.[1]	Gonda.
Sakhali.	Arghaunle (?).	Gránjá.
	Bareya.	Gurmáchhan.
	Bhujál.	Gyángmi.
	Braili.	Haio.
	Brangplagi.[1]	Jhángdi.
	Byángnási.	Jhári (?).
	Charmi, Chermi (?).	Kairálá.
	Chitauriá (?).	Kalalohár.
	Chumi.	Keli.
	Darnal.	Khápangi.
	Darrá Lámi.	Khaptari.
	Datt.	Khati.
	Devapáti.	Khulál.
	Dhamala.	Krubchhági.[1]
	Dhanuki.	Kyágchhági.[1]
	Dukhcháki.	Lahakpá.
	Gácha.	Lakándri.
	Gadaili.	Lamgadeh.
	Gadál.	Lámichánya.
	Gajamer.	Lamjál.
	Gandharma (?).	Lha-yo.[1]
	Geláng.	Loháguri.
	Gháli.	Lungyeli.[1]

[1] These seven *thars*, besides one not known, are called the Bára Mangar, and hold the title of Thápa.

Sub-tribes.	*Thars* or septs.	
	Magrathi.[1]	Sadásankar.
	Marsyángdi.	Sarángi.
	Máski.	Sáru.
	Meng.	Setisurwál.
	Namjáli.	Sheo.
	Pacháin (?).	Sijapati (?).
	Pánthi.	Sincheuli.
	Parbateh.	Singauri.
	Phyuyáli.	Sinjali.
	Pithákoteh.[1]	Sithung.
	Pongwar.[1]	Sripáli.
	Pulámi.[1]	Sunári.
	Pun.	Surya Vansi.
	Pung.	Suyál.
	Pusál.	Tálu.
	Rahapál.	Tháda.
	Rakhál.	Thokcháki.
	Rasaili.	Toringrapá.
	Rijal.	Yángdi.
	Sabkota.	Yángmi.

[1] These four *thars*, besides one not known, are called the Bára Mangar, and hold the title of Thápa.

Már, *Málwe Rájput.*

Sub-caste.	Sections.
Nil.	Aind, eel.
	Gandharb.
	Kási.
	Parás.

Maulik, *Láyá, Náyá.*

Title :—Bhumphor, peculiar to the Mál sub-caste.

Sub-castes.	Sections.
Chandana.	Belawahari, tree-rat.
Hariyán or Jehariyá.	Boro Sámp, rock-snake.
Mál or Már.	Dudhiá, snake.
Sauriyá.	Rikhiásan or Pátrisi, described as a small red bird with a long tail.
Rájbansi } Call themselves Hindus.	
Deobansi } Call themselves Hindus.	

Mayará, *Modak, Mairá, Kuri.*

Titles:—Ash, Chandra, Datta, Barát, De, Dán, Gul, Indl, Láhá, Nág, Nandi, Rakhit, Ráj.

Sub-castes.	Sections.
In Central Bengal—	
Rárh-ásram.	Alamyán.
Mayur-ásram.	Bharadwája.
Ajá-ásram.	Chandrarishi
Dharm-ásram or Dharm-Sut.	Debrishi.
	Madhurishi.
In Dacca—	Kasyapa.
	Gautam.
Ekpátiá.	Majurrishi.
Dopátiá.	Ganesrishi.
	Nágrishi.
	Sándilya.
	Somrishi.

Mech, *Mechi.*

Sub-tribes.	Septs of the Agniá sub-tribe.
(*a*) *In Darjiling—*	
Agniá-Mech.	Bamodá.
Játi-Mech.	Bosmáthá.
	Chhongphtháng.
(*b*) *In Assam—*	Chongphrán.
	Isáre.
Agniá-Mech.	Kuktáiáre.
Assam-Mech.	Mochháre.
Kachrá-Mech.	Narjenáre.
Thampái-Mech.	Nobáiáre.
	Phádám.
	Sabáiáre.
	Sibingáre.

Muchi, *Rishi, Rishiputra, Nishi.*

Titles:—Darshan, Muchiram Dás, Patradás, Ruidás, Sparshan.

Sub-castes.	Sections.[1]
Bará-bhágiyá { Uttar-rárhi. / Dakhin-rárhi.	Kásyapa.
Chhota-bhágiyá.	Sándilya.
Chásá-Kurur or Chásá-Kolai.	
Betuá.	
Jugi-Muchi or Korá.	
Baitál.	
Kurur.	
Málabhumiá.	
Sabarkárá.	
Sánki.	

[1] These are not exogamous, and no sub-caste appears to have more than one section, Kásyapa or Sándilya, as the case may be.

Munda, *Mura, Horo-hon.*

Titles:—Bhuinhar, Dhangar, Kol, Konkpat, Mahato, Manki, Nagbansi.

Sub-tribes.	Septs.
Bhuinhár-Munda.	Aind, a kind of eel.
Karangá-Munda.	Amba, mango.
Khangar-Munda.	Ambras, a fruit.
Khariá-Munda.	Area, a kind of fish.
Kol-Munda.	Aru, yam.
Konkpát-Munda.	Arul.
Mahali-Munda.	Ashár, a month—June.
Mánki-Munda.	Asur Lohara.
Munda-Mánjhi.	Aura, fruit.
Nágbansi-Munda.	Baba, rice.
Oraon-Munda.	Bage, anything forbidden.
Sad-Munda.	Bagear, tiger.
Savar-Munda.	Baghela, quail.
	Baghtuar, a devotee.
	Bahera, a fruit.
	Bahomar.
	Balamdár, spearman.
	Balmus, a kind of insect which is found in the sand of rivers.

Sub-tribes. Septs.

Balum, salt.
Baman, may not touch or be touched by a member of the Brahman caste.
Banda, a kind of leaf.
Bando, small jackal.
Bar, *Ficus Indica.*
Barabhaiá, the twelve brothers' sept.
Barha, hog.
Bari, flower.
Barjo, name of an ancestor's village some miles south of Ranchi.
Barjoki, fig tree root.
Barla, a fruit.
Barukandal, the kussum tree.
Barunda, a big frog.
Barupendil, kussum tree.
Barwa, small cocoon.
Basaroar, a kind of small hawk.
Batkuar, a bird.
Beng, frog.
Besra, small hawk.
Bhaji Ság, vegetable.
Bhaonra, a large black bee or hornet.
Bhengra, a horse.
Bhingraj, kingcrow.
Bhinjo, a yellow bird.
Bhuina.
Bhutkuar.
Bihan, seed.
Binha.
Binjuar, a kind of eel.
Bisrot.
Bisru, a kind of bird.
Bocho, a bird.
Bodra, the ancestors of this sept did not wash their mouths after eating.
Bojra, a kind of grass.
Budh or Budhwar, Wednesday.
Buim, a worm.
Bukru, a kind of bird.
Chadil, place of worship of a headman.
Chadu, a kind of bird.
Chali, rice soup.
Champia, a bird.
Chata, umbrella.
Chauria, rats.
Chelekchela, a small bird.
Chilhia, kite.
Chirko, mushroom.

Sub-tribes.	Septs.
	Chitti, a kind of snake.
	Chocha, a bird.
	Chota, a kind of bird.
	Chutia, a small rat.
	Dáng, a big stick.
	Dahanga, torch-bearer.
	Dangarwar.
	Dauru.
	Demta, red tree-ant.
	Dhan, paddy. To this sept rice and rice soup are forbidden; they eat only *gondli* or millet.
	Dhechua, a kind of black bird.
	Dhelakata, a kind of tree.
	Dirwar, a wood fruit.
	Dobongwar.
	Dodrai, a kind of bird.
	Dub Sag, vegetable.
	Dumrfar, figs.
	Dundu, a kind of eel.
	Dungdung, a river-fish.
	Dura, a fruit.
	Ergat, a kind of mouse which lives in plum bushes.
	Gandura, a big bird.
	Garabing, a big river-snake.
	Gari, a monkey.
	Garria, a kind of bird.
	Ghager, field bird.
	Ghi, clarified butter.
	Ghunri, a kind of fruit.
	Gidh, a vulture.
	Gobolachan, may not eat beef.
	Gondli, a kind of grain.
	Goria, red earth.
	Gua, areca nut.
	Gundki, a kind of wood.
	Gundri, a bird.
	Gurni, a kind of vegetable.
	Guru, may not eat beef.
	Habin, a tree.
	Hadung, big black tree-ant.
	Hajeri, a kind of tree or bush.
	Haluman, monkey.
	Han, nest of ants.
	Hanjait, a wild fruit.
	Hanre, a bird.
	Hansa, swan.
	Hanthi, elephant.
	Hardwar.

Sub-tribes. Septs.

Hargurra, bone.
Hari, ancestors did not wash their mouths after eating.
Harin, deer.
Hasada.
Hasará.
Hassa ara, a kind of vegetable.
Hausakar.
Heding, a bird.
Hembowar, ancestor.
Hemram, a kind of fish.
Hemromi, ashes.
Heride, a bird.
Herung, a kind of bird.
Hoduar, a bird.
Homjah.
Hong, a kind of bird with a long tail.
Horia, a wood bush.
Horo, a red ant on tree.
Hularbaha, a flower used to flavour curry.
Hundar, wolf.
Huni, mouse.
Hutar.
Imli, tamarind.
Indur katea, house-rat.
Ingaria, moonlight.
Jagdar.
Jago, tamarind.
Jamtuti, a kind of grain or vegetable.
Jangatras, the bone of a cow.
Jatrama.
Jatria.
Jhuri, dried bushes.
Jia, a river-fish.
Jirhul, a flower, used for curry.
Jitiapipar, a kind of fruit.
Jonk Haper, leech.
Kachhuá, tortoise.
Kakin, aunt.
Kamal, lotus.
Kanda, a kind of sweet potato.
Kandir, a bird.
Kandru, fish.
Kandurua, a fruit.
Karania, a kussum tree.
Karma, a tree.
Katea, a field-mouse.
Kaua, crow.
Kawnria, a water-snake.

Sub-tribes. Septs.

Kera, plantain.
Kerketa, a bird.
Khandania.
Khondua.
Khoyea, a wild dog with a long tail.
Khukri, a kind of mushroom.
Kiri, rice weevil.
Kissi.
Koá, cocoon.
Kodoság, a kind of water vegetable.
Kongaddi, crow.
Kotah kaisi, a small vulture.
Kujri, a fruit from which oil is made.
Kukur, dog.
Kukura.
Kundula.
Kurkuti, red ant.
Kursi, fruit.
Kusumbaha, kussum flower.
Lang, a kind of bird.
Lápung, a small bird.
Larapa, monkey-eater
Larsunar.
Lenda, earthworm.
Lilla, a wild cow.
Lipo, a tree.
Litiya, a bird.
Logna Kotra, small deer.
Logo, a kind of animal.
Lohrakhukhri, a kind of mushroom.
Longa, a bird with a long tail.
Lugniar, rabbit.
Lugum, a tree.
Lugun, a tree.
Lugunki.
Lupu, paddy husks.
Lutl, small black fly.
Machli, fish.
Madhuras, honey.
Mahukal, a bird.
Maina, a bird.
Mar, new rice soup.
Marmu.
Matha Ság, a kind of vegetable.
Mathia, brass bracelet.
Maugh, fish.
Mind.
Minjur, peacock.
Mowl.
Muduk.

Sub-tribes. Septs.

Mundoraj, a tree.
Mundri, quail.
Munga Ság, a kind of vegetable.
Munri, fried rice.
Murum, stag.
Muri, a wild fowl.
Musa or **Musu**, mouse.
Mutri.
Nadi Samp, a river-snake.
Nág, cobra.
Nagduar, a water-insect.
Nagrua, a kind of mud.
Nimak, salt.
Nois.
Oaria, verandah.
Orea, basket-maker.
Pakhora.
Pamia, a tree.
Pandar, a tree.
Panduchone.
Panduki, dove.
Pankhi, a bird.
Panr, a tribe.
Pardhiel kokaw.
Parsi, a tree.
Parsu, a bush.
Peo, a bird.
Peroan, pigeon.
Phurti.
Phuti, a rainbow.
Pikord, a bird.
Porti, crocodile.
Pussi, cat.
Putam, dove.
Raja, a bird.
Ramgharia.
Rani Poka, a red worm.
Raut, the Rautia caste.
Rugri, a kind of mushroom.
Rukhi, squirrel.
Runda, leopard.
Rutá, a tree.
Sadom, horse.
Sailum, porcupine.
Saisarunduar.
Sal, a big pond-fish.
Salkar, a kind of potato.
Salu, a root in pond.
Samal or **Samar**, deer.
Samdoar.

Sub-tribes.	Septs.
	Sandi, plough.
	Sandiguria, black monkey.
	Sandil, full moon.
	Sandipurti, cock.
	Sandi Sarin, fowl.
	Sanga, sweet potato.
	Sang Chiria, a kind of bird.
	Sangoar, sweet potato.
	Sankura, kingcrow.
	Sanpuri, a resident of Sanpur.
	Sarai, a tree.
	Sarnar, a curry vegetable.
	Semarkanda, root.
	Sengra, horse.
	Seornlá.
	Serhar, a kind of bird.
	Setampa, dog-eater.
	Sewar, moss.
	Siar Tuyio, jackal.
	Sikcharo, a bird.
	Sikra, hawk.
	Sindur, vermilion.
	Singh, horn.
	Sisungi, a kind of fish.
	Soa, a kind of vegetable.
	Soai, a bird.
	Sobarnarekha, name of a river three miles east from Ranchi.
	Soeka, a wood bush.
	Sohek, a kind of fish.
	Soi, spring.
	Sokoe, a kind of fruit.
	Solai, fish.
	Sonarwa, a bird.
	Sone, may not wear gold.
	Sonkharihan, a place where they worship before cutting grain.
	Son Maghia.
	Soso bheloa, a fruit.
	Suga, parrot.
	Sukru, potato.
	Sulankhi, a kind of bird.
	Surhi, a wood-cow.
	Suri, fly.
	Suril, do not propitiate the Churin Deota.
	Surin.
	Susan.
	Taitum.
	Támbá, copper.

Sub-tribes.	Septs.
	Tamgarihar.
	Tamghuria.
	Tarwar, may not touch a sword.
	Tatia, a kind of bird.
	Telia, a tree.
	Tewan raja, a kind of bird.
	Thithio, a bird with long legs.
	Tirango, a wood-bird.
	Tirki, a bird.
	Tirkiar, tree-mice.
	Tiro, a small bird.
	Tirtia, a bird.
	Tiru, a kind of bird.
	Tiruhar, a kind of bird.
	Toeba, flower of *paráe* tree.
	Toewa, a kind of bird.
	Tongsi, a bird.
	Tono, a big tree-ant.
	Topna, tree.
	Topoar, a bird.
	Tow, a kind of bird.
	Tulsiar, a kind of flower.
	Tumbli, a red flying-ant.
	Tunduar, a tree.
	Turania.
	Tursia.
	Turu, squirrel.
	Turuar, a fruit—kussum.
	Tuti, a kind of vegetable.
	Uchring, an insect.
	Udbarn, a tree, the oil of which is not used by members of the sept.
	Urdwar.
	Uring, a wild bird.

Murmi, *Tamang, Isháng, Sain.*

Sub-caste.	Sections.	
Nil.	**Báibá.**	**Gábag.**
	Baju.	**Galan.**
	Bal.	**Gánthen.**
	Baltong.	**Ghale.**
	Bomjan.	**Ghising.**
	Bulun.	**Gole.**
	Chapen Khor.	**Gomdan.**
	Chumi.	**Gongbá.**
	Dumjan.	**Gothar.**

Sub-caste.	Sections.	
	Grandan.	Neki.
	Hopthen.	Nesur.
	Jimbá.	Pakhrin.
	Jongan.	Rumbá.
	Kháni Khor.	Sángbá.
	Kitung.	Sángdan.
	Khungbá.	Sherbá Khor.
	Kulden.	Singar.
	Lámá Khor.	Singden.
	Lo.	Songden.
	Lopchan.	Thing.
	Mármunba.	Thokar.
	Mekchan.	Titung.
	Moktán.	Tubah.
	Nárbá.	

Musáhar, *Mushar, Bhuiyá.*

Titles :— Mánjhi, Sádá.

Sub-castes.		Sections.
Bahtawár.	Of the Chanrwar sub-caste.	Ghurmutná.
Chanrwár.	Of the Chiksauriá sub-caste.	Giári.
Chiksauriá.		Kanghattá.
Dhár.		Kosilwár.
Kanaujiá.		Mahatwár.
Maghaiyá or Deswár.		Patwári.
Nathuá.		Phulwár.
Pachhmá.		Sonwahi.
Surajiá.	Of the Magahiyá sub-caste.	Bálakmuni.
Tirhutiá.		Daitiniá.
		Gohlaut.
		Pail.
		Rikh-mun, Rishi-muni.
		Tisbariá.
	Of the Tirhutia sub-caste.	Bánsghát Pahadi-nagar.
		Dhanháriá.
		Sarpurkhá—Chakbariá.
		Kasmetá.
		Mártariá.

Sub-castes.	Sections.
	Baiyár.
	Balgachhiá.
	Batwar or Batwári.
	Bhachhuár.
	Bhakhiásin.
	Bhuiyár.
	Churihár.
	Dhangpatiá.
	Diár.
	Dodhuár or Dodwár.
	Gáuriá.
	Genduá.
	Gibhári.
	Kásyap.
	Khatdhár.
	Mehári yá.
	Mandwár.
	Sandhoá.
	Sondhuár.
	Suruar.
	Tikait Bhogtá.
	Ulauriá.
	Upwariyá.

Nágar.

Titles :—Biswás, Chaudhri, Langi, Mahárání, Panjiár, Panch-námá-Mandar, Ráut.

Sub-castes.	Section.
Jethaut.	Kásyapa.
Pulauns.	
Nágbansi.	
Káthautiá.	
Bhátnágar.	

Nagesar, *Nágasiá, Kisán.*

Title :—Ban-Ganjhu.

Sub-tribes.	Septs.
Sendara-Nagasia, use sindur at marriage.	Amba, mango.
Telia-Nagasia, use oil instead of sindur at marriages.	Barla, *Ficus Indica.*
	Dhanki.
	Induar, a kind of eel.
	Mahto, a kind of eel.
	Manjhi, a title.
	Nág, cobra.
	Sonwani, can't wear gold.
	Taitia.
	Tirki, a bull.

Naiyá.

Title :—Pujáhá.

Sub-caste.	Sections.
Nil.	Bhulá.
	Chilkhor.
	Dhankoi.
	Kulkhwár.
	Yahián.

Nápit, *Nái Nauá.*

Titles :—Bárik, Bhandári, Baidya,[1] Chandra-baidya,[1] Dás, Khyaurakár, Khán, Nara-Sundar, Nandi, Parámánik, Síl, Biswás, Mazumdár, Mandal, Sháhá, Sarkár, Shikdár, Járdár.

Sub-castes.	Sections.
Anarpuriá.[2]	Alamyán.
Bámanbane.	Gargrishi.
Bárendra.	Kásyapa.
Uttar-rárhi.	Madhukuliya.
Dakshin-rárhi.	Maudgalya.
Paschim-rárhi.	Sándilya.
Mahmudábáz[2]	Sections of the Mahmudábáz sub-caste: Bhagabán.
Saptagrám.	Daibaki.
Sátghariá.	Jádab-Mádhab.
Phul-Nápit.	Kánái-Madan.
In Noakhali—	Mahámandá.
Bhuluá-Nápit.	Rám.
Sundipá-Nápit.	Rághab.
In the 24-Parganás—	Rájib.
Háldar-Parámánik.	Siva.
Kola-Parámánik.	
Hansadáhá-Parámánik.	
Mujganji-Parámánik.	
Khottá.[3]	

[1] These titles are borne only by Napits who practise medicine.

[2] A few cases have occurred of marriages between members of these groups, but the breach of rule had in each instance to be expiated by giving a feast to the community.

[3] A designation of up-country barbers who have settled in Bengal. Such persons practically form a separate sub-caste, as Bengali barbers will not intermarry with them, and they are regarded as impure by the barbers of Upper India and Behar by reason of their having taken up their residence in Bengal.

Nuniá, *Luniá, Noniyán, Núngoliá.*

Titles:—Beldár, Cháimarár, Chaudhri, Jamadár, Mahátmá, Mahton, Mandar, Marár, Mihtar, Ráut.

Sub-castes.

1. Awadhiá or Ayodhiábási.
2. Bhojpuriá.
3. Kharáont.
4. Maghayá.
5. Orh.
6. Pachainyá or Chauhán.
7. Semarwár.

Sections.

(*a*) *Totemistic*—

Andhigot.
Jamgot.
Nág.
Pechgot.
Phulgot.

(*b*) *Eponymous*—

Bachgot.
Bághgot.
Káchhgot.
Kásyapa.

Oraon, *Kurunkh.*

Titles:—Dhangar, Kol, Parjá.

Sub-tribes.

Berga-Oraon.
Dhanka-Oraon.
Kharia-Oraon.
Khendro-Oraon.
Munda-Oraon.

Septs.

Amri, rice soup.
Bagh, tiger.
Bandh.
Bando, a wild cat which barks at night.
Bakula, paddy-bird.
Bar, *Ficus Indica.*
Barwa, a wild dog.
Basa, a tree.
Bekh, salt.
Beanh, a large fish with thorns on its back.
Bhakla.
Chigah, a jackal.
Chirra, a squirrel.
Chouria Musa, field-rat.
Dhan, rice soup forbidden.
Dhechua, kingcrow.
Dirra, a kind of eel.
Dom Khakha, a raven.
Ekka, tortoise.
Ergo, a rat.
Gari, monkey.
Garwe, a stork.
Gede, a duck.
Gidhi, a vulture.
Gislihi, a bird.
Godo, crocodile.

Sub-tribes. Septs.

Golala.
Gondrari, a tree.
Induar, a kind of eel.
Kachua, tortoise.
Kaith, curry vegetable.
Kanda, sweet potato.
Kaua, crow.
Kendi, a tree.
Kenu, a fish.
Keond, a fruit.
Kerketa, a bird which makes a noise like "ket ket."
Khalkhoa, cannot eat fish caught by baling water out of a tank or pool.
Kheksa, curry vegetable.
Khes, cannot eat plants that grow in ponds.
Khetta, a cobra.
Khoepa, a wild dog.
Kinda, a date palm.
Kispotta, pig's entrails.
Kosuar, a kind of fish.
Kujur, a fruit used to stain the horns of cattle at the Sohrai festival.
Kundri, curry vegetable.
Kusuwa, a fish.
Lakra, a hyena.
Lila, a kind of fish.
Linda, an eel.
Loha, iron.
Mahato, a title.
Minji, a kind of eel.
Munjniar, a wild creeper.
Murga, cock.
Nagbans, cobra.
Orgonra, a hawk.
Pusra, fruit of kusum tree.
Putri, a tree.
Rori, a fruit or tree.
Runda, a fox.
Sâl, fish.
Sarno.
Suar, hog.
Tig Hanuman, monkey.
Tirki, young mice.
Tirkuar, fruit.
Tirtia.
Tiru, a kind of fish.
Topoar, a bird with a long tail, and body mottled black and white.

Oswál, *Uswál.*

Titles:—Chánd, Dás, Dosi, Láb, Singh.

Sub-castes.	Sections.
Oswál proper.	Baid.
Dasá.	Baidmota.
	Chajla.
	Chaudalla.
	Chopra.
	Churáliye.
	Dháriwár.
	Gelra.
	Golchiá.
	Hinga.
	Jambar.
	Málkas.
	Methi.
	Nakat.
	Nolka.
	Ranka.
	Saitiya.
	Set or Seth.
	Sil.
	Singhi.
	Soni.
	Srimal.
	Srisrimal.
	Suchait.

Pán, *Pánwa, Pánr, Pab, Pánika, Chik, Chik-Baráik, Baráik, Mahato, Ganda, Sawási, Tánti.*

Sub-castes.	Sections.
In Manbhum—	Aind, a kind of eel.
Baráik.	Babunhathia.
	Bagh, Baghel } a tiger.
In Lohardagá and Sarguja—	Bagti.
Chik or Chik-Baráik.	Bail.
Sawási or Tánti.	Bajar.
Ganda.	Balbandhi.
	Baleswar or Balasore.
	Bando, small wild cat.
In Orissa—	Banjor.
Orh-Pán or Uriya-Pán.	Bar, *Ficus Indica.*
Buna-Pán.	Barabihá.
Betra-Pán or Ráj-Pán.	Bardi.
Patradiá.	Bariaro.

Sections.

Bel, a fruit.
Beniaro, frog.
Benkurá.
Besrá, a small hawk.
Bhaisa, buffalo.
Bhanjor.
Bhata, brinjal.
Birár, a cat.
Bordi.
Buru.
Cherabesari.
Cherchete, a shrub jungle.
Chik, a tribe.
Chownr, yak's tail.
Dandpati.
Dásabigha.
Dasbihá.
Daskaria, wild fowl.
Dernta, a red tree-ant.
Dhondh, a water-snake.
Dhunkro.
Dond-Chatra.
Gajbaniá.
Ghogor.
Ghorábach.
Goal, cow.
Hekoria, tomato.
Hunjar.
Hurjor.
Jia.
Kachua, tortoise.
Kansi, a grass.
Karunjua, a big black bird.
Kaua, crow.
Kesarari.
Kesrá, *rahar dál.*
Khechinjiá.
Khutibaran.
Kirki.
Kukuria.
Kulhai.
Kulhasia.
Kunjakuli.
Kunjasiri.
Kurai.
Kusum, a fruit.
Kutunjiá.
Loha, iron.
Lowa.
Machiwar.

Sections.

Mahánadia, name of a river.
Mahatoar, a title.
Mahua, *bassia latifolia*.
Malua.
Marai, wood-louse.
Mayur, peacock.
Mechari.
Mongri.
Mudu.
Mul.
Murchulia.
Mus, Musa, rat.
Nág, cobra.
Padowar.
Panchbiha, Panchbhia.
Panchhiah.
Purti.
Rájbansia.
Rajhasia, swan.
Raotia, crab.
Renta.
Saonsia.
Saruan.
Saul, a fish.
Sikra, hawk.
Silli, a place.
Sindhikuria, bull's horn.
Sing, horn.
Singhi, fish.
Sinjhikaria.
Sonamati.
Sonkharika.
Sonkoko.
Totabari.
Urmakhori.
Urmakuli.

Parghá, *Parighá*.

Sub-castes.	Sections.	
1. Supá-Parghá.	Kumár.	Pátar.
2. Paliyár-Parghá.	Mánjhi.	Rái.
	Marar.	Raut.
	Marik.	Siyar.
	Ojhá.	

Parhaiya.

Titles :—Kheroar, Gánju, Manjhi.

Sub-tribe.	Septs.
Nil.	**Bâg**, tiger.
	Gachai.
	Gidh, vulture.
	Fanigâ, grasshopper.
	Kauá, crow.
	Mainá, a bird.
	Nâg, cobra.
	Ophia.
	Tetenga, bloodsucker.

Pási.

Title :—Mahato.

Sub-castes.	Section.
1. Byádhá.	**Kásyapa.**
2. Gaiduhá.	
3. Kámáni.	
4. Tirsuliá.	
Turk (Mahomedan).	

Pátni, *Pátuni, Patauni, Dom-Pátni.*

Titles :—Gangáputra, Ghát-Mánjhi, Mánjhi, Pradhán.

Sub-castes.	Sections.
1. Ját-Pátni.	(*a*) *Territorial—*
2. Ghát-Pátni, Balami or Ghátwál.	**Bhadraghát.**
3. Dom-Pátni, Machhwá or Nagárchi.	**Jhiniá.**
4. Bánsphor.	**Kálágáchi.**
5. Dágará.	**Káliwálá.**
	Naskarpurá.
	Parámánik.
	Práchir.
	Ráipur.
	Saidábád.
	Sáttá.
	Tentuliá.
	(*b*) *Eponymous—*
	Alyamán.

Pator.

Title :—Mahto.

Sub-tribe.	Septs.
Nil.	**Bhengraj**, kingcrow.
	Charak, a festival.
	Kachua, tortoise.
	Katun.
	Kerwári, a tribe.

Sub-tribe.	Septs.
	Maitbukru, place where he buries his bones, being his ancestral birthplace.
	Nág, cobra.
	Samatti.
	Sandilai.
	Sarihin.
	Silli, place where he buries his bones, being his ancestral birthplace.
	Taw.

Pod, *Padmaráj*, *Chási*.

Titles:—Baidya, Biswás, Háldár, Kayál, Laskar, Mandal, Mistri, Páik, Pátra, Pundari Kákhya, Sapui, Sarkár.

Sub-castes.	Sections.
Bágande.	Alamyán.
Banglá.	Dhánesri.
Chási-Pod.	Kásyapa.
Khottá or Mauná.	Maudgalya or Madhu Kulya.
Uriyá.	

Rájput, *Kshatriya*, *Chhatri* or *Chhetri*, *Báhuja*, *Bhupál*, *Bhupati*, *Bhusur*.

Titles:—Bábu, Baraik, Barman, Khán, Malik, Mandal, Rái, Ráut, Sámant, Singh, Sipáhi, Thákur.

Sub-tribes.	Septs.	
In Behar—		
Suryabansi, Surajbansi.	Amaithiá.	Chaubariá.
	Baghail or Baghel.	Chaubnán.[1]
	Baráhi.	Dandwár.
	Baraiá.	Gaharwár.
	Bargáir.	Gautam.
	Besáin.[1]	Harihobans.
	Bhadariá.	Jasatbár.
	Bharsuriá.	Kachhwáh.
	Birwá.	Kákan.
	Chandail.	Kanwar.

[1] Besáin, Chaubhán, and Mahraur cannot intermarry, being supposed to be descended from the same ancestor.

Sub-tribes.	Septs.	
	Karnwár.	Ranauni.
	Kháti.	Sángir.
	Kinwár.	Sarniá.
	Kulchuliá.	Sirnait.
	Kulhariá.	Sirniá.
	Kurminiá.	Sisodhiá.
	Maulwar.	Somwár.
	Nikumbh.	Sukalnaki.
	Nimundih.	Sukarbár.
	Pamár.	Surkhi.
	Parihar.	Surwár.
	Raghubansi.	Tarwár.
	Ráhtaur.	Tilautá.
	Raksáin.	Tongar.
	Ráná.	Ujain.
Chandrabansi.		Bais.
Sombansi.		Banaudhiá.
		Barnár.
		Budhbansi.
		Damarwár.
		Dangar.
		Eh-Ár.
		Gahlaut.
		Kailwár.
		Kapur.
		Kausik.
		Kusbansi.
		Mahraur.[1]
		Narauni.
		Nauthni or Lautni.
		Nisán.
		Oh-Ár.
		Sabarniá.
		Sakarwár.
		Sengar.
		Subansi.
		Sulankhi.
		Tekha.
		Tetiá.
Agnikul.		
Bhojpuriá.		
Jadubansi.		
In Chota Nagpur—		
Malwe or Már-Rájput.		Chaudhriá.
		Mahto.
		Máli.

[1] Besáin, Chaubhán, and Mahraur cannot intermarry, being supposed to be descended from the same ancestor.

Sub-tribes. Septs.

In Bardwan Division—

Bálgori.
Baradai.
Mulki.

The following septs are common to all the sub-tribes of Rájputs in Behar:—

Ahir-Páik.
Ataiá.
Athral.
Báchhil.
Banámpur.
Banáphar.
Bardhiá.
Bardiá.
Barhwatiá.
Barniá.
Basbariá.
Bashariá.
Beruár.
Bhadaniá.
Bhalesultán.
Bhandári.
Bharchuihá.
Bhatgáiná.
Bhora.
Bhuthá.
Bichila.
Bijhuniá.
Binriá.
Bisokiá.
Bundelá.
Chakwán.
Chalhuk.
Dhán.
Dhaul.
Dhekhá.
Dhor.
Dikshit.
Donwár.
Dorowár.
Durgbansi.
Gáigwár.
Gáin.
Gajkesar.
Gandhauriá.
Ganhwariá.
Gargbansi.
Garhwár.
Gaudhaniá.
Gauláni.
Gaura.
Gehuaná.
Hárá.
Huddá.
Jádan.
Jádawár.
Jadubansi.
Kachnariá.
Kakir.
Kálhans.
Kámar.
Kanakwár.
Kandwár.
Karangarhyá.
Karcholiá.
Karjhuliá.
Karmwár.
Karsá.
Khánná.
Kharbahiá.
Khát.
Khechar.
Korwár.
Kuchhainá.
Kuká.
Kukurbans.
Kundail.
Kusbhabáni.
Lahtaur.
Láhuliá.
Lákat.
Lohtamiá.
Lukum.
Madhwál.
Mahuár.
Mándiár.
Maralbai.
Marhwár.
Mariár.
Maunachh.
Maunas.
Mehrá.
Mehri.
Mendru.
Nágbansi.
Nimri.
Pachhaniá.
Pachtariá.
Pailwár.
Pálki.
Phetiá.
Pundul.
Purubansi.
Rachhuáni.
Raikwár.
Rájkuar.
Rajwár.
Rekhaur.
Raksel.
Rankwár.
Rorah.
Sankarwár.
Segul.
Sihoglá.
Silewár.
Sinduriá.
Singhiniá.
Sirmaur.
Sirnet.
Sisoniá.
Sombansi.
Sukulbans.
Surnair.
Taiá.
Támár.
Tannán.
Taunr.
Tendun.
Tiár.
Tilakchandi.
Ulit.

The Rájputs also use the Brahmanical *gotras* or sections, of which the following are generally found in the caste:—

Baiághrapad.	Kásyapa.	Parásara.
Bátsya.	Kausika.	Prasidha.
Bharadwája.	Nág.	Sándilya.

Ráju.

Title:—Sinha.

Sub-castes.	Sections.
Dáiná or Chauán.	*Nil.*
Bainá.	
Sár.	
Bághál or Bághál.	

Rajwár, *Rájbansi.*

Title:—Máhato.

Sub-castes.	Sections.
Angrok or Angwár.	Bhogtá.
Chapwár.	Chápá.
Sikhariá.	Chirra, squirrel.
Sukulkárá.	Dorihár-jogi.
Bar-Gohri } In Lohardagá.	Karhar, a fruit.
Majhal-Turiyá } In Lohardagá.	Kásyapa.
Berrá-Rajwár } In Lohardagá.	Katwár.
	Kharakwár.
	Lathaur.
	Loharátengi.
	Majhiya.
	Marrik.
	Matwárá.
	Nág, cobra.
	Rikhi.
	Sankwá.
	Singh.

Rautia, *Raut.*

Titles:—Baráik, Gaunjhu, Kotwár.

Sub-caste.	Sections (*paris* or *got*).
1. Bar-Gohri.	(*a*) *Totemistic*—
2. Chhot-Gohri.	Aind, the eel.
	Karsul.
	Káshib, tortoise.
	Kási, a kind of grass (*Saccharum spontaneum ?*).
	Kátoár or Garur, vulture.
	Kharak, sword.
	Khariá, blade of grass.
	Koyá, the wild dog.
	Manjar, cat.
	Nág, snake.
	Rukhi, squirrel.
	Sanwani.
	Tángi, an axe.
	(*b*) *Eponymous*—
	Básudeo.
	Chandramani.
	Jogi.
	Kumár.
	Mánjhi.
	Sándilya.
	Siva.
	(*c*) *Territorial*—
	Baghel.
	Kanthwár.
	Kharakwár.
	(*d*) *Uncertain*—
	Chatgohri.
	Kabar.
	Kherkoar.
	Kum.
	Kundil.
	Lachh.
	Láthaur.
	Suran.

Sadgop, *Satgop, Chásá.*

Titles:—**Bákundi, Biswás, Dás, Ghosh, Konr, Neogy, Pál, Sarkár, Sur.**

Sub-castes.	Sections.
	(Of Paschim Kuliyá.)
Paschim Kuliyá.	Alamyán.
Purbba Kuliyá { Ghosh.	Kásyapa.
Purbba Kuliyá { Sarbesia.	Maudgalya.
	Sándilya.

Hypergamous Divisions.

(*a*) *Of the Paschim Kuliyá sub-caste.*

Kulin (Bhálki, Kánkshe, Praharáj, Siur).
Somaj.
Pratihár (Bangram and Gográm).
Maulik.

(*b*) *Of the Purbba Kuliyá sub-caste in Midnapur.*

Kulin (Biswás, Neogi, Sur).
Maulik.

(*c*) *Of the Purbba Kuliyá sub-caste in Murshedabad.*

Konr-Gop, who take their wives from other Sadgops, but give their daughters only in their own group.

Sánkhári, *Sankhakár, Sankhabanik.*

Titles:—**Bandhu, Bhadra, Chandra, Das, Datta, Dhar, Kar, Kundu, Nág, Nandi, Sen, Sur.**

Sub-castes.	Sections.
Bara-Bhágiya or Bikrampur Sánkharí.	Alyamán.
Chota-Bhágiya or Sunargaon Sánkharí.	Brahmarishi.
	Gautama.
	Gárgya.
	Kásyapa.
	Madhukulya.
	Mobrishya.
	Parásara.
	Sándilya.

Santál, *Sáontár*, *Kharwár* or *Safá-Hor.*

Titles:—Buná, Mandal, Mánjhi, Pradhán, Sardár.

Sub-tribes:—Deswáli Santál, Kharwár or Safá-Hor.

Septs.	Sub-septs.
Báski	Nij. Sádá.
Bediyá (sheep?)	*Nil.*
Besrá, hawk	Bundra. Kahu, crow. Kárá, buffalo. Nij. Sádá. Sibala. Son. Sung.
Chonre	*Nil.*
Hansda, Hasdak, wild goose.	Barwár. Chilbindhá, eagle-slayer. Jihu, a bird. Kerwar. Mánjhi-Khil. Niáki-Khil. Nij. Roh-Lutur, ear-pierced. Sádá.
Hemrom, Hembaram, betel palm.	Dántela, so called from their breeding pigs with very large tusks for sacrificial purposes. Guá, areca nut. Jahur. Kumár. Laher. Náiká-Khil. Nij. Roh-Lutur, ear-pierced. Uh.
Kisku	Abar. Ah. Kachuá, tortoise. Lát, bake meat in a leaf-platter. Nág, cobra. Nij. Roh-Lutur. Sádá. Somal, deer.

Septs.	Sub-septs.
Márndi, grass ...	Buru-birit, of the hills.
	Kekra, crab.
	Laher.
	Mánjhi-Khil.
	Niaki-Khil.
	Nij.
	Roht, *pánjaun* tree.
	Sádá.
Murmu, nilgái ...	Bitál.
	Boar, fish.
	Chopeár.
	Gánr, fort.
	Hándi, earthen vessel.
	Muro.
	Nij.
	Sádá.
	Sangda.
	Sikiyá, a chain.
	Tikká.
Paurlá or Pauliá ...	*Nil.*
Saren, the constellation Pleiades.	Barchi, spearmen.
	Hát.
	Jogi.
	Lát.
	Mál.
	Mundu or Badar, a dense jungle.
	Nij.
	Sánkh, conch shell.
	Sidup or Siduk, a bundle of straw.
	Turku.
Tudu	Agariá, charcoal-burners.
	Chigi, Chiki, impale.
	Dántela, breed pigs with very large tusks for sacrificial purposes.
	Lát, bake meat in a leaf-platter.
	Manjhi-Khil.
	Naiki-Khil.
	Nij.
	Roh-Lutur, ear-pierced.
	Sádá.
	Sung.

Septs.	Sub-septs.
Adeb.	
Aind, a kind of eel.	
Bansdeo.	

Sárák, *Sráwak*, *Srávaka*.

Sub-caste.	Sections.
Nil.	Adyeb.
	Ananta.
	Machli, fish.
	Sándilya.

Saraogi.

Sub-caste.	Sections.
Nil.	Kastuwál.
	Sogani.
	Kodar.
	Pátni.
	Bhainsá.
	Chaunrá.
	Soni.
	Gadiyá.
	Dosi.
	Bakliwál.
	Koteri.
	Pátodi.
	Pándrá.
	Sáh.
	Kálá.
	Barjátya.
	Bilálá.
	Tariyá.
	Pápriwál.
	Chariwál.
	Jánjhri.
	Paháriá.

Sarnakar, *Sekrá, Sarna-Kámár.*

Titles :—

Sub-castes.	Sections.
Bráhmandesi.	Bharadwája.
Dakhin-Rárhi.	Kásyap.
Khatangi.	Sabanta-Rishi.
Uttar-Rárhi.	Sándilya.
	Sarishi.

Sabar, *Sabar, Saur, Sar, Sayar, Suir, Sewri.*

Sub-tribes.	Septs.
Bendkar.	(*a*) *Totemistic*—
Jharuá.	Kásibak, heron.
Palli.	Sálmáchh, fish.
Parirá.	(*b*) *Eponymous*—
	Gargarishi.
	Sándilya.

Sherpa-Bhotia of Nepal, *Kham, Sálákhá, Nag-Chhang Shakzang.*

Rui, Thar or Septs.

Chah-ba.
Dong-ba.
Jing-ba.
Minag-pá.
Nah-pá ...
- Bhinásá, S. *Binása,* destroyed ; occupier of a deserted village.
- Goleg-pá, *Go,* a head, and *leg,* good ; the peaceful.
- Manding, *Man,* medicine ; a practiser of medicine.
- Pang-Karmo, *Pang,* pasture, and *Karmo,* white ; a dweller on pasture table lands.
- Sálák-khá, a merchant carrying on trade.
- Tag-tog-pá, *Tag* or *brag,* a rock ; a dweller on cliffs.
- Tsegkhim-pá, *Tseg,* a wall, and *Khim,* a house ; a dweller in stone or walled house.

Non-pá.
Shyang-ba.
Sser-Gomba.
Sser-Lungchan.
Sserpa.
Sser-Phen-zangná.
Weh-ba.

Sonár, *Káin, Rangdhárià, Zargar.*

Titles :—Chaudhri, Poddár, Sáhu.

Sub-castes.	Sections.	
Ajodhyábási.	Ainiá.	Janakpuri.
Ajodhyápuri.	Aminápur.	Josiám.
Bais.	Anril.	Karbhalá.
Bhojpuriá.	Aswaria.	Kastuár.
Gaur.	Báguan.	Kási.
Kamarkalla.	Barmáit.	Kásyab.
Kanaujiá.	Barni.	Katalpuri.
Máir.	Bathuet.	Kokarsá.
Oriá.	Belhá.	Kothádomar.
	Bhaunrájpuri.	Lohatiá.
	Bhekh.	Machhilhá.
	Bibarhiá.	Machi.
	Bihári.	Makundpuri.
	Bilar.	Marich-bhuswal.
	Bilauriá.	Marj-bhuswal.
	Borhá.	Mirchwan.
	Chalhaká.	Musamlá.
	Chauswár.	Noinjorá.
	Chithá.	Pachpákar.
	Chonrhá.	Parián.
	Dánrsuriá.	Prohá-Kerautá.
	Dhakaichhá.	Rájgrihl.
	Dhaundriá.	Rámpuri.
	Dubaithiá.	Rautar.
	Dumrahar.	Saharwár.
	Fatehpuri.	Sakaddi.
	Ganesiá.	Samundar-Khorá.
	Ganet.	Silaichiá.
	Garahlá.	Simar.
	Gehani.	Sisaundiá.
	Ghiohaddá.	Sochari.
	Hamdábádi.	Soncheri.
	Hanumán.	Sonpuriá.
	Hardiwál.	Sultánpuriá.
	Jakhalpuriá.	Tejaniá.
	Jamálpuri.	Telihá.

Subarnabanik, *Baniá, Banika, Sarnabanik, Sonárbaniá.*

Titles :—Adhya, Barál, Barddhan, Chandra, Dán, Dás, Datta, De, Dhar, Láhá, Mallik, Mandal, Nandi, Náth, Pál, Poddár, Rái, Sen, Sil, Sinha.

Sub-castes.	Sections.
Bangaja.	Aliman.
Dakhin-Rárhi.	Bharadwája.
Uttar-Rárhi.	Brahma-Rishi.
Saptagrámi or Nadiyá.	Gautama.

Sub-castes.	Sections.
	Kásyapa.
	Madhukulya.
Hypergamous groups—	Maudgalya.
	Nágrishi.
Kulin.	Parásara.
Maulik.	Sábarna.
	Sándilya.
	Sureswari.
	Vyása.

Sudhá.

Titles:—Amáyat, Beherá, Dehuri.

Sub-castes.	Sections.
Bara-Sudhá.	*Nil.*
Sáno or Kabátkoniá Sudhá.	
Pailá-Sudhá.	
Butká-Sudhá.	

Sudra, *Ghulám-Káyasth.*

Titles:—Bhandári, Shikdár.

Sub-caste.	Sections.
None.	Alimmán.
	Maudgalya.
	Vasishtha.

Sukli.

Sub-castes.	Sections.
Barabháiyá.	Alyamán.
Báhattarghari.	Kásyapa.
Dasasai.	Sándilya.

Sunri, *Hunri, Suri, Sundi, Saundika, Shaha, Chalita-Sau.*

Titles:—*In Bengal*—Bhakta, Bhuiyá, Chaudhri, Dás, Deori, Duryodhan, Kirttan, Majumdár, Mandal, Nirbhaya, Poddár, Pradhán, Rái.

In Behar—Bhandári, Chaudhri, Lál, Mandar, Mánjhi, Modi, Mohásib, Saho.

Sub-castes.	Sections.
In Bankura—	
Mandárane.	
Singhazári.	Kásyapa.
Jaibele.	
Dholo.	

Sub-castes.	Sections.
In Bardwan and Murshedabad—	
Sau or Chalita-Sau { Bárendra. / Rárhi.	Aládasi.
Sundi ... { Bich, distillers. / Palásram.	Bámrási. / Gágarish.
Chaturásrám or Chaturthan, vegetable-sellers.	Sándilya.
Barnakule.	
In Maldah—	
Mani.	
Shirashina.	Alamyán.
Jogidasi.	
Duarbandha.	
In Eastern Bengal—	
Rárhi.	
Banga.	
Banger Rárhi.	
Rárher Rárhi.	Aliman.
Bárendra ... { Phul. / Kul. / Aichá. / Panchsamáj. / Mahendra Khyáni. / Maughá.	Gautama. / Kásyapa. / Maudgalya.
Majlishi.	
In Tipperah—	
Rarhi, Panchasiá.	
Barendra ... { Athárachurá. / Chhaphuliá.	
In Noakhali—	
Rárhi ... { Mul. / Phul.	
Bárendra ... { Mul. / Phul.	
In Santál Parganás—	
Bich.	Gágrish.
Bárendra.	Andrish.
Chaturthán.	Madrish.
Paripál.	Sándilya.
Kulsunri.	
In Monghyr—	
Sagáhut.	
Biyáhut.	
Gaunjhu.	

Sub-castes.	Sections.	
In Bhagalpur—		
Kulsunri.	Bharwe.	Maháset.
Ganjwar.	Bichhu.	Mahton.
Dhukankorá.	Biár.	Mandar.
Barpárá.	Chaudhri.	Marar.
Sagáhut.	Dobar.	Mehran.
Biyáhut.	Gáin.	Náik.
Bitwár.	Gárá.	Panjiára.
Maghaiyá.	Garain.	Pardhán.
Banglá.	Háthi.	Parihár.
Darchuá.	Kapri.	Purbe.
Purbiya.	Kárak.	Ráut.
Sikhoria.	Kásyapa.	Sadá.
	Khán.	Satrá.
	Khárgá.	
	Of the Kulsunri sub-caste	Kámti. Mandar. Mánjhi. Mehtar. Sahu.
In Tirhut—		
Maghaiyá.		
Sagahut.		
Biyáhut.		
Darchuá.		
Kalwár.		
Sokiriá.		
Chaurthán.		
In Patna—		
Biyáhut.		
Sagáhut.		
Khajkaliá.		
Bishtwár.		
Bhangerá.		
In Manbhum—		
Biyáhut.		Kásyapa.
Lakargarhá.	Of the Paripál sub-caste.	Andrishi, a rope of untanned hide, with which the yoke is fastened to the plough.
Ariyár.		Kách, crab.
Maghaiyá.		Madrishi, honey-bee.
Sikhariyá.		Bandrisi, fish.
Chaturthán.		Nágrishi, snake.
Sagáhut.		Sándil or Sánrishi, a bull. The members of the section do not castrate their own cattle, but purchase bullocks and sell their own bulls.
Paripál.		
Holongwár.		

Sunu-wár, *Sonwár.*

Thars or septs.

Bráhmilchá.
Chhápátichá.
Durbichá.
Jeshkuchá.
Jespuchá.
Jijicha.
Jirel.
Kátichá.
Khyongpotichá.
Kintichá.
Kyahbohchá.
Liokichá.
Párgáchá.
Rahpáchá.
Rujichá.
Shushichá.
Thholáchá.
Tholochá.
Thumuchá.
Wangdehchá.
Yaktachá.
Yeti.

Surahiyá, *Suraiyá, Sorahaiyá, Kalwat-Malláh.*

Titles:—Jal Chhatri, Marar.

Section.

Kásyapa.

Sutradhar, *Chhutár.*

Titles:—Datta, De, Kar, Mistri, Kundu, Pál.

Sub-castes.		Sections.
Akrur-Paramánanda	In Murshedabad.	Alamrishi.
Chaturan-Khán ...	In Murshedabad.	Alamyán.
Mán-Gauránga ...	In Murshedabad.	Kásyapa.
Gopál-Kárikar ...	In Murshedabad.	Sándilya.
		Bánrishi.
		Kanakrishi.
		Madhukulya.
Ket-Chhutár ...	In the Santál Parganás.	
Paturá-Chhutár ...	In the Santál Parganás.	
Nagare-Chhutár ...	In the Santál Parganás.	
Bhar-Chhutar ...	In the Santál Parganás.	

Sub-castes.		Sections.
Chhutár ...	In Noakhali.[1]	
Sáitghariá ...		
Challisghariá		
Sri ...		
Srikrishna ...		
Sáini ...		
Dáturiá ...		
Báni ...		
Duman ...		
Ari ...	In Western Bengal.	
Mandaráná ...		
Bardwániyá[2] ..		
Kharipárá ...		
Goalabhuiyá[2]		
Chhutár ...	In Dacca.	
Churá-Kuti ...		
Káturiá ...		

[1] The Chhutár appear to be carpenters properly so called, while the other eight groups are endogamous subdivisions of the Churá-Kuti sub-caste found in Dacca.

[2] Of late years these two groups have begun to intermarry.

Támbuli, *Támuli*, *Támli*.

Titles :— Chaudhri, Chail, Datta, De, Khur, Pál, Pánti, Rakshit, Sen, Singh (*in Bengal*). Bhakat, Khili-wálá, Nágbansi, Paiti (*in Behar*).

Sub-castes.	Sections.
(a) *In Bengal—*	(a) *In Bengal—*
Saptagrámi or Kusadáye.	Kásyapa.
Biyállisgrámi.	Parásara.
Chauddagrámi.	Sándilya.
Bardhamáni.	Vyása.
Ashtagrámi or Kataki.	
(b) *In Behar—*	(d) *In Behar—*
Magahiyá.	None.
Tirhutiá.	
Bhojpuriá.	
Kanaujiá.	
Kurram.	
Karan.	
Surya-dvija.	

Tánti, *Tantrabáya, Tantubáya, Tatwá.*

Titles:—*In Bengal*—Barásh, Basák, Bhádya-bau, Bit, Chand, Chhagri (goat), Dalál (broker), Dás, Datta, De, Gui, Hansi, Jáchandár (appraiser), Kar, Lu, Mandal, Mesha (sheep), Muhkim (supervisor), Nandi, Pál, Prámánik, Sádhu, Sardár, Sarkár, Sil.

In Behar—Dás, Mahto, Manjhi, Marar, Marik.

Sub-castes.	Sections.
In Bengal—	
Aswini or Asan-Tanti. { Bardwáná.	Agastya Rishi.
Barna-kul.	Aladáshi.
Madhyakul.	Alamyán.
Mándároná.	Attri-rishi.
Uttarkul.	Bararási.
Balarámi.	Bátsya.
Banga.	Bharadwáj.
Bará-bhágiyá or Jhámpániyá.	Biswámitra.
	Brahmárishi.
Bárendra.	Garga-rishi.
Chhota-bhágiyá or Káyath-Tánti.	Gautam.
	Janaráshi.
Káture.	Kásyapa.
Korá.	Kulyá Rishi.
Kshir.	Madhukulya.
Madhukari.	Parásara.
Magi.	Sándilya.
Mariáli.	Sábarna.
Nir.	Vyása.
Páttar.	
Purandari.	
Purbbakul.	
Rárhi.	
Uddhabi.	
In Behar—	
Baiswara.	
Banaudhia.	Chamártali.
Chamár.	Hinduá.
Jaiswár.	Kasyab.
Kahár.	
Kanaujiá.	
Tirhutia.	
Uttarhá.	
In Orissa—	
Mátibans-Tánti.	
Gálá-Tánti.	
Hansi-Tánti.	

Teli, *Tili, Chakri, Garai, Kalu, Rausan, Tailakár, Taili, Tailika, Tail-Pál.*

Titles:—*In Bengal*—Chaudhri, De, Dhabal, Kundu, Koleman, Mandal, Masanta, Nandi, Pál, Parámánik, Parihara, Sádkhán, Sháhá, Sit.

In Behar—Behara, Chaudhri, Dafádár, Gorai, Kapri, Náik, Poddár, Sáhu, Sháhá, Tálukdár.

Sub-castes.		Sections.
		Aliman.
		Chandrarishi.
		Káchim.
		Kalmi.
		Kásyap.
		Madhukulya.
In Bengal—		
Anwarpuri.		Maudgalya.
Bárendra.	Bikrampur.	Nág.
	Chandradwip.	Niskalanka.
	Gangabisayi.	Niyárishi.
	Subarnabisayi.	Sándilya.
	Tulatia.	
	In Pabna—	
	Barapatti.	Sindhurishi.
	Chhotapatti.	
	Dáspárá.	
	Govindpuriá.	
Bhunjá Teli.		
Dwádas.	Bárahazári.	
	Bardwaná.	
	Chhága̍liá.	
	Mándaraná.	
	Maureswari.	
	Singhazári.	
Ekádas.	Chinpuriá.	
	Haludboná.	
Fatehsing.	Manoharsháhi.	
	Swarupsing.	
Gáchhuá or Kalu.	Ghaná Teli.	
	Desle.	
	Másle.	
	Pishle.	
Kutabpuri.		
Maghad Khandi.		
Rárhi.		
Saptagrámi.		
Senbhumiá.		
Sikhariá or Sindurtopá.		

Sub-castes.		*Bán* or sections.
In Orissa—		
Abhirám.		
Ekádas.		
Gáudá.		
Haldiá.		
Kalu.		
Tulatia.		
In Behar—		*In Shahabad*—
Aráiyá.		Demahá.
Barhäriá.		Dhobahá.
Biáhut.		Jhagaráhá.
Desi.		Rath-charh-bagh-marwá.
Hermaniá.		
Janakpuri.		
Jaunpuri.		
Kanaujiá.		
Khuskhelia.		
Lathaur.		
Maghaiyá.	Sahu.	
	Naik.	Boria.
		Hárpati, 'plough-owner.'
		Khargpur.
		Musipur.
		Telhari.
		Tulsi.
	Kapri.	Bhusiwar.
		Kapri.
		Pata-Ratnauli.
	Gáim.	
	Garain.	
	Indrabárá.	
	Maháseth.	
	Mihtar.	Lálgámia.
		Mihtar.
		Pata-Ratnauli.
		Teligamia.
	Malik.	
	Mandar.	
	Mahto.	
	Panjiár.	
	Sangwe.	
	Tharmait.	
Masnath.		
Sarwariá.		
Tirhutiá.		
Turkiá.		

Sub-castes.	Sections.
In Chota Nagpur—	*In Lohardagá—*
Dakhini.	Kárak.
Haldia.	Kásyapa.
Hiapela.	Pándiáin.
Kanaujia.	*In Singbhum—*
Maghaya.	Nágasya.
Mathuria.	Pakhichátá.
	Barharoa, a fruit.
	Kachuá, tortoise.
	Kansi, a kind of grass.
	Nág, cobra.
	Pandki, dove.

Hypergamous groups in Bengal—

Parámánik.
Koleman or Kalu.

Thárú.

Titles:—Barwáik, Khán, Mahto, Rái.

Sub-tribes.		Septs.
In Behar—	Of Thárus in general.	Chaudhri.
Rautár.		Dahait.
Gaurihár.		Dás.
Marichwár.		Gauro.
Khawásiyá, including—		Guro.
Bábhan-Khawásiyá.		Káji.
Donrehá-Khawásiyá.		Khatait.
Dhotiyá-Khawásiyá.		Khojwár.
Khatkalá.		Mahaut.
Bantar, including—		Mahto.
Dhelphorwá-Bantar.		Patwári.
Kath Katwá-Bantar.		Rái.
Bot.		Raut.
Batewár.		
In Nepal—	Of the Rautár sub-tribe.	Bánth.
Chitwaniá or Chitauniá.		Bhánr.
Belwadhiya.		Chautariá.
Kuchila.		Chitauniha.[1]
Iswájitauni.		Dahait.

[1] They are notorious for charms and spells.

Sub-tribes.		Septs.
In Nepal—concluded.		
Nauá.		
Purbiyá.		
	Of the Rautár sub-tribe—*concluded.*	Dangwaria. Danrehá or Gaunhá. Donwár. Gaharbári. Gaharwár. Gauro. Kachhriyá.[1] Káji.[2] Kanphatá. Kathariá. Khon. Kochilá. Konhar. Lampochhá. Mahto.[2] Majhiaur. Mardaniá, barber. Nawalpuriá.[1] Ojhaiyá. Patwári.[2] Rai. Senthá. Sokhait.

[1] They are notorious for charms and spells.
[2] These groups are said to have recently become endogamous.

Tipperah, *Triprá, Mrung.*

Sub-tribes.	Septs.
Nil.	Afang. Aialong. Fadung. Gaibing. Garjang. Harbang. Husoi. Jumátya. Kákulu. Káli. Keoya. Mising. Mongbai. Naithung. Nowattiá. Osui. Puran. Riáng. Tungbai.

Tiyar, *Tiar*, *Tior*, *Rájbansi*, *Machhuá*.

Titles:—Chaudhri, Chharidár, Malláh, Manjhan, Marar, Mukhíar.

Sub-castes.	Sections.
Rájbansi or Tilak Dás.	Itbál or Itbár.
Surajbansi.	Kásyapa.
Nal Tiyar.	Jai Singh.

Found by Buchanan in Bhagalpur—

Bámanjagya.
Govariyá.

Hypergamous Divisions—

Pradhán.
Parámánik.
Gana.

Turi, *Tori*.

Sub-castes.

Turi or Kisán-Turi.
Or.
Dom.
Domrá.

Sections.

(*a*) *Totemistic*—

Bar, *Ficus Indica*.
Charhad, tiger.
Hansdá, wild goose.
Hastaddá, eel.
Induar, a kind of eel.
Jariár, lizard.
Kachhuá, tortoise.
Kerketa, a kind of bird.
Samp, snake.
Saur, fish.
Sumat, deer.
Suren, a kind of fish.
Tirki, mouse.
Toppo, bird.

(*b*) *Uncertain*—

Bagehár.
Charchágiya.
Mádalwar.
Mal.
Panchbhaia.
Surinwár.
Tamagandiyá.
Tirkuar.

Vaisya.

Titles:—Arya, Bhumisprik, Bhumijivi, Dwija, Panik, Banik, Byanaharta, Uravya, Uruja.

Sub-caste.	Sections.
Nil.	Aliman.
	Kasyapa.
	Kátyáyana.
	Madhukuliya.
	Sándilya.

Yákha.

Sub-tribes.		Septs.
Phágu.	Of the Phágu sub-tribe.	Manem-ma.
Lhorong.		Mangthog.
Yamphu.		Okrabo.
		Sing-yangma.
		Songyokpa.
		Thungong-hehta.
		Thupra.
		Yak-kyukpa.
		Yoksuma.

APPENDIX II.

PROCEEDINGS OF CONFERENCE ON ETHNOGRAPHY OF NORTHERN INDIA, HELD AT LAHORE ON THE 18TH TO 22ND MARCH 1885.

Present:

MR. D. C. J. IBBETSON,
Director of Public Instruction, Panjáb.

" J. C. NESFIELD,
Inspector of Schools, Oudh.

" H. H. RISLEY,
On Special Duty, Bengal.

THE members of the Conference met at Mr. Ibbetson's office. Mr. Risley explained that he had come to Lahore, with the permission of the Government of Bengal, to consult Messrs. Ibbetson and Nesfield in consequence of certain demi-official suggestions received from Mr. FitzPatrick, Secretary to the Government of India in the Home Department. He stated that the Government of Bengal had decided to make an exhaustive enquiry into the castes and occupation of the people of these provinces, based upon the statistics recorded in the census of 1881, and had placed him on special duty for two years for that purpose. He laid before the meeting (*i*) a draft note setting forth the objects to be aimed at in the enquiry and the means to be adopted to obtain those objects, consistently with giving the minimum of trouble to the regular administrative staff; (*ii*) a set of ethnographic questions framed so as to facilitate the collection of fresh data in a systematic form through the agency of district officers, and of such private individuals as might be willing to give assistance in the matter. He asked the other members to assist him with such criticism as their experience of ethnographic enquiries might suggest. Messrs. Ibbetson and Nesfield, while ready and willing to assist to the best of their ability in discussing the papers in question, felt unable, without due leisure for consideration, to commit themselves to any final opinion as to the form that would be best suited for adoption in their respective provinces, should it eventually be decided to set such an enquiry on foot in those provinces.

In the absence of precise official instructions as to their functions, it appeared to the officers present that all they could usefully do was to indicate, with as much completeness as the circumstances under which they were called together admitted of, the direction in which ethnographic enquiries of the kind under description might best be pursued by any Local Government which might think it desirable to undertake them. With this view the members of the Conference prepared a note on certain difficult points of ethnographic terminology, a series of general questions calculated to elicit the salient characteristics of the several castes, and a set of special questions dealing with caste customs in greater detail, to be used by those whom inclination might lead to pursue the subject further. These papers form annexures A, B and C to these proceedings. It would remain for the Local Governments and Administrations concerned to determine in what manner the suggestions contained in them should be utilized.

At the present stage of the proceedings, and while the data have still to be collected, the members of the Conference did not feel prepared to consider the form in which the final results should be arranged and recorded.

DENZIL C. J. IBBETSON.
JOHN C. NESFIELD.
H. H. RISLEY.

A.

Suggestions regarding some doubtful points of Ethnographic nomenclature.

MUCH confusion is often caused by the indeterminate use of the various terms applied to the divisions upon which society in India is based. It seems that some attempt to define more precisely the nature of the groups to which these terms should respectively be applied might usefully be made, and the following is set forth as a suggestion.

The group organization commonly follows one of two main types—(1) the caste, (2) the tribe. The former may be defined as the largest group based upon community of occupation; the latter as the largest group based upon real or fictitious community of descent, or upon common occupation of territory.

Within the caste we find the *sub-caste*, and within the *sub-caste* the *section*. The *sub-caste* may be defined as the smallest *endogamous* group, and the *section* as the largest exogamous group, within the caste. No lower unit than the *section* need be regarded. The limits of the caste and *sub-caste* will occasionally be identical, there being no smaller endogamous groups included under a common caste name based on occupation.

Within the tribe we find many subdivisions. The smallest endogamous group within the tribe may be called the *sub-tribe*, which, as before, will occasionally coincide with the tribe. The largest exogamous group within the tribe may be called the *sept*, and no lower unit than this need be considered. Divisions intermediate between the sub-tribe and *sept* may, where they exist, be termed clans and sub-clans.

Some cases will occur in which the two types will run into each other, the caste based upon occupation being made up of tribes or tribal fragments based upon community of descent. In these cases the terminology of each type will be followed so far as the organization stands upon the same basis as the type, and no further.

It might be explained that the Brahmanical *gotras* have, in many cases, been adopted by or imposed upon castes and tribes in addition to their proper caste or tribal divisions. In such cases the *gotras* are not what is wanted : what is wanted is the organic divisions and subdivisions of the caste and tribe, not unusually called *got* by the people themselves, as distinguished from *gotra* in the strict Brahmanical sense. Occasionally these organic divisions and the *gotras* are identical ; but where the latter are distinct from, and have been superimposed upon, the former, the *gotras* run through the divisions, the same division often, though not always, including several *gotras*, while, on the other hand, the same *gotra* is found in several divisions. The Brahmanical *gotras* are chiefly used by the officiating priest at marriage and the ceremony of *sankalp*, and are often unknown to the people themselves without reference to their priests.

DENZIL C. J. IBBETSON.
JOHN C. NESFIELD.
H. H. RISLEY.

B.

ETHNOGRAPHIC QUESTIONS.

General Series.

1. Write in English and vernacular the name of the caste with synonyms, if any, noting if any of these are used only by outsiders.

2. Write in English and vernacular the names of the exogamous subdivisions of the caste, if such subdivisions exist.

N.B.—By the term exogamous subdivision is meant a group from within which its male members cannot take their wives.

3. Show the endogamous divisions of the caste, if such divisions exist. If these divisions consist of groups of the subdivisions mentioned in question 2, show the grouping. If they are distinguished by separate names, write the names in English and vernacular.

N.B.—By the term endogamous division is meant a group from outside of which its male members cannot take their wives.

4. State the limits within or beyond which marriage prohibited, *e.g.*, that a man must marry within the caste, but must not marry into his own or certain other subdivisions, or within certain degrees of relationship, or may not marry two sisters.

5. Name any prohibitions on inter-marriage based upon (*a*) social status, (*b*) geographical or local position, (*c*) differences of religious belief or practice, (*d*) differences or changes of occupation.

6. State the popular tradition, if any exists, as to the origin of the caste, naming the common ancestor, if any, the part of the country from which the caste is supposed to have come, and the approximate time of its emigration, as marked by the reign of any particular king, or the occurrence of any historical event, together with the number of generations supposed to have intervened.

7. Is the habit of the caste settled or wandering? Have they any recognized head-quarters in the province? If wandering, over what tract of country do they wander? Are their migrations periodical or irregular, and what are the shape and material of their dwellings?

8. Do they admit outsiders into the caste? If so, from what classes, by what forms, and under what conditions?

9. Is marriage infant or adult? If the latter, is sexual license before marriage recognized or tolerated?

10. Is (*a*) polygamy, (*b*) polyandry, permitted; if so, under what conditions and within what limits? In the case of polyandry, must all the husbands be brothers?

11. What form of marriage ceremony is in ordinary use? Name the forms and state the essential and binding portion of the ceremony.

12. Is the remarriage of widows permitted? If so, is the widow obliged or expected to marry her husband's elder or younger brother? If she does not marry a brother, within what limits may she marry? What form of marriage ceremony is used, and what is the essential and binding portion of it?

13. Under what circumstances is divorce permitted, and by what form is it effected? May wives who have been divorced marry again?

14. Do the members of the caste follow the Hindu or Mahomedan law of inheritance, or a tribal custom of their own?

15. To what religion and to what sect within the religion do the caste belong? If Hindus, do they by preference worship any special one of the regular Hindu deities, and are there any reasons for this preference?

16. Name any minor gods or patron saints specially worshipped by the caste. State what offerings are made, on what days of the week, and what class of people receive them? Is the worship of any of these gods or saints confined to women and children?

17. Do the caste employ Brahmans for religious and ceremonial purposes? If so, are these Brahmans received on terms of equality by other Brahmans? If they do not employ Brahmans, what class of people serve them as priests?

18. Do the caste burn, bury, or expose their dead? If buried, in what position? Where are the bodies or ashes finally disposed of?

19. Are any ceremonies performed for the propitiation of (*a*) ancestors in general, (*b*) childless ancestors, (*c*) men who have died

a violent death; and if so, of what nature and at what seasons? Is the ceremony of *sráddh* performed or not?

20. Is the caste, or any of its subdivisions, named after any animal, plant, weapon or implement? Do they show their reverence for any such object either by special worship, or by abstaining from killing, eating, cutting, burning, using, or naming it?

21. What do the caste believe to have been their original occupation or group of occupations? To what extent have they or any sections of them departed from it? Describe their present occupation.

22. If they are agriculturists, state what position they usually occupy in the agricultural system, *i.e.*, are they—

(1) Zamindars;
(2) Tenure-holders, specifying the kind of tenures they hold;
(3) Occupancy or non-occupancy raiyats, stating whether they have or claim any privileges in respect of rent;
(4) Nomadic cultivators, specifying the mode of cultivation they follow;
(5) Landless day-labourers, stating the manner in which they are paid?

23. If their occupation is that of—

(*a*) *Artizans*, what is their industry, and in what special material do they work, or abstain from working;
(*b*) *Hunters*, do they catch game or vermin;
(*c*) *Fishermen*, do they catch fish only or also crocodiles and tortoises?
(*d*) *Sweepers*, do they remove night-soil or not?

24. Name any implement or mode of working which is characteristic of the caste, and also note whether there is any form or detail of their main occupation by abstaining from which they believe themselves to be raised above others of the same craft?

25. Do they habitually prostitute their (1) unmarried, (2) married women?

26. Which of the following articles of food do the caste eat or abstain from eating:—flesh, wine, monkeys, beef, pork, the flesh of cloven-footed or uncloven-footed animals, fowls, scaly or scaleless fish, crocodiles, snakes, lizards, jackals, rats, other vermin, the leavings of other people? Is there any special article of food their abstaining from which tends in their opinion to raise them above some other caste which does not abstain from it?

27. Name the lowest well-known caste with which the caste will—

(*a*) Eat pakki.	(*c*) Drink.
(*b*) Eat kachhi.	(*d*) Smoke.

Name the highest well-known caste which will eat, etc. (as above), with the caste.

Sources of information.—Here should be noted the names, residence (village and thana), profession, caste, sub-caste, and section of the persons who answered the question. If any of them are *ghataks*, genealogists, heads of caste *panchayat*, or occupy any hereditary official position in relation to the caste, the fact should be stated. If the answers to the questions have been derived from any source other than personal enquiry addressed to members of the caste concerned, the source should be stated, and such references given as may enable the officer in charge of the enquiry to test the correctness of the answers.

DENZIL C. J. IBBETSON.
JOHN C. NESFIELD.
H. H. RISLEY.

C.

ETHNOGRAPHIC QUESTIONS.

Special Series.

INTRODUCTORY REMARKS.

The following questions have been drawn up in order to suggest lines of enquiry likely to prove interesting. They do not claim to be exhaustive, nor is it necessary that all of them should be answered. Some, for instance, will apply only to Mahomedans, others only to Hindus, and others again only to aboriginal tribes. In making use of them various forms of bias on the part of the person questioned will have to be guarded against, such as—

(*a*) The wish to exalt his own caste or subdivision of his caste at the expense of other castes.

(*b*) The tendency to give ideal or book explanations of facts.

Care must also be taken not to tire the persons questioned by asking too many questions at a time and to check their statements occasionally by asking for actual instances of any specially remarkable custom. Questions should be put in as concrete a form as possible, in order to avoid the danger of people assenting out of laziness in order to save the labour of thinking.

It will be found in the case of many—perhaps of most—castes that there is a primary division into what may be called sub-castes, each of which is again divided into sections. Where several of these sub-castes are present side by side in the locality, their names will probably be given. But where all the local representatives of the caste belong to the same sub-caste, there is a danger of the sub-caste name being taken for granted and only the sections being named. Both groupings are required, the sub-castes being, if anything, the more important of the two.

I.—Constitution.

1. *Origin and internal organization.*—Write in English and vernacular the name of the caste, with synonyms, if any, giving its derivation if known.

2. If the caste has more names than one, explain their meaning and state which are used by the members of the caste, and which by other people.

3. Are any distinctions between the synonyms based upon the occupations of those to whom they are respectively applied, their place of origin, habitat, religion, or the like?

4. Is there any name used only by members of the caste?

5. State in detail any tradition that may exist as to the origin or foundation of the caste, the place from which they came, and their subsequent migrations.

6. Do they believe themselves indigenous in the district or to have come from elsewhere?

7. If from elsewhere, note any king's reign or historical occurrence contemporary with their migration, and how many generations are believed or ascertained from genealogical lists to have intervened.

8. Is there any place which they consider their head-quarters in Bengal?

9. Note particularly the name of the place from which they or their ancestors are believed to have come direct to their present locality.

10. Are any pilgrimages undertaken by the caste to places which purport to be their original habitat or serve to suggest its locality?

11. Is there any place in which the members of the caste are or should be buried?

12. Do they draw their priests, barbers, or genealogists rfom that place?

13. Do they trace their descent from a first ancestor or chief, and does he appear to have actually existed or to have been an eponymic personage invented to account for the existence of the tribe?

14. If any genealogical tree exists, trace the descent of the founders of the existing subdivisions from the common ancestor. Is there a shrine to him in the village or neighbourhood, and is it built on a brick or stone brought from elsewhere? If so, from where?

15. Do they consider any other castes to have branched off from them, or that they and others have come from the same national source?

16. Have they any tradition regarding changes of religion, introduction of new ceremonies, etc.?

17. Are there any local legends connecting them with any monuments, such as old tombs, mounds, forts, sites of villages, etc. in the district?

18. Is any light thrown upon the former movements of the tribe by the names of villages or by the existence of monumental stones? For instance, the Mundas of the Chota Nagpur plateau can be traced to places far distant from their present settlements by these

places bearing Mundari names and containing Mundari grave-stones, which are now worshipped by low-caste Hindus.

19. Write in English and vernacular the names of the exogamous subdivisions of the caste, if such subdivisions exist.

N.B.—By the term exogamous subdivision is meant a group from within which its male members cannot take their wives.

20. Write in English and vernacular the names of the endogamous divisions of the caste, if such divisions exist. If these divisions consist of groups of the subdivisions mentioned in question 19, show the grouping.

N.B.—By the term endogamous subdivision is meant a group from outside of which its male members cannot take their wives.

21. In the caste of both classes of divisions and sections explain the meaning of each name, and if the name denotes animals or edible substances, state whether the members of the subdivision bearing that name are prohibited from naming, eating, killing, cutting, burning or otherwise using the animal or substance denoted?

22. Cases may also occur in which the name of the subdivision is the name of an instrument which its members are prohibited from using; or conversely, where the caste is one of occupation, of a particular instrument or mode of working to which the members of the subdivision are hereditarily addicted.

23. Are particular subdivisions bound to observe or refrain from particular actions, such as the eating or burning of certain plants, the worshipping of certain trees, etc.?

24. Do the names of the subdivisions correspond with those of the subdivisions of any other caste, and if so, how is the correspondence explained?

25. Have, for instance, the members of the lower caste done service to the higher caste and adopted their subdivisions?

26. If so, is there any trace of their having had different subdivisions of their own, and are there any reasons for supposing that these were aboriginal and were abandoned in favour of a Brahmanical classification?

27. Have they any representative assembly or governing body?

28. What is it called?

29. How is it constituted?

30. What are its functions?

31. Who presides at its meetings?

32. How are its orders enforced?

33. Is there a permanent president?

34. If so, by what title is he called, and is the office hereditary?

35. If the hereditary president happens to be a minor, by whom are his duties carried on?

36. In the case of the trading and artisan castes the functions of the *panchayat* of the caste are of special interest and should be carefully ascertained, most of all where the occupation is followed by members of distinct castes united in a sort of trades guild, in which case the connexions and cases of conflict between the *panchayats* of the caste and guild should be investigated

37. *Rules of Intermarriage.*—State the limits within or beyond which marriage is prohibited, *e.g.*, that a man must marry within the caste, but must not marry into his own or certain other subdivisions or within certain degrees of relationship, or may not marry two sisters.

38. Give the formula (if any) defining the prohibited degrees of relationship.

39. Name any prohibitions on intermarriage based upon (*a*) social status, (*b*) geographical or local position, (*c*) differences of religious belief or practice, (*d*) differences or changes of occupation.

40. How far are differences of religion or sect a bar to marriage?

41. Can persons of different castes intermarry?

42. If so, of what castes, and by what form of marriage?

43. Note cases in which wives will be received from another subdivision or caste, but daughters will not be given in marriage to members of that subdivision.

44. Is the distinction referred to in the last question based mainly on social status or on what?

45. Is there any formal ceremony of admitting the bride into the husband's house, village or family by payment, after a mimic struggle, by eating together, or otherwise?

46. How many wives are allowed?

47. If more than one, is there any head wife, and what are her privileges?

48. Do the wives live together, or do they have separate dwellings?

49. Is concubinage permitted?

50. Is polyandry permitted?

51. If so, how are the husbands selected?

52. Must they all be brothers?

53. Are the women allowed much freedom before marriage?

54. Are they prostituted before marriage, or are some prostituted and others reserved for marriage?

55. In the case of a girl who has been prostituted, is any payment made to the parents or the community, or is any special feast given by the bridegroom?

56. At what age may marriage take place?

57. Is an infant marriage voidable, if not actually consummated?

58. Who arranges the marriage?

59. Are there professional marriage-brokers?

60. Whose consent is necessary to the validity of marriage (1) if both parties are minors, (2) if both are of full age?

61. Is there any freedom of choice on the part of the persons marrying?

62. Is any price paid (*a*) by the bridegroom's family for the bride, (*b*) by the bride's family for the bridegroom?

63. How is such price determined?

64. Does it or any part of it become the special property of either bride or bridegroom, and does it devolve by any particular rule of succession?

65. What physical defects will be sufficient ground for the annulment of a marriage which has actually taken place?

66. State whether idiocy or lunacy, impotence or mutilation are such sufficient grounds.

67. Is any distinction made if the party seeking annulment knew of the defect at the time of the marriage, or if the defect has arisen after the marriage was consummated?

68. Under what circumstances is divorce permitted?

69. What form of divorce is in use?

70. May wives who have been divorced marry again?

71. How are the offspring of (1) first marriages, (2) marriages of widows or divorced persons, (3) illicit connexions between parents of different tribes, castes, or religions now classed?

72. Do all inherit on the same terms, or are any excluded?

73. Do they follow the tribe and caste of the father or of the mother, or are they known by an entirely new name?

74. Is there any distinction between them and others born into the tribe or caste in a more usual or legitimate manner?

75. Are there any cases in which members of one subdivision cannot marry into another subdivision as being of common origin with themselves?

76. Do illicit connexions ever entail a change of caste on either of the parents?

77. Are there any caste or subdivisions of castes the origin of which is ascribed to connexions between members of two different castes?

78. Give particulars, and state the evidence on which the tradition is based.

79. Is it admitted by the members of the caste or subdivision in question?

80. May widows remarry?

81. If so, by what form of marriage ceremony?

82. Must the widow of an elder brother marry the younger brother, and may the widow of a younger brother marry an elder brother?

83. May the widow marry outside her husband's family?

84. If so, has her husband's brother a right to the custody of her children, and does the same rule apply to both male and female children?

85. If she marries an outsider, what rights in her husband's property accrue to—

(1) The widow,
(2) Her children by her first husband,
(3) Her husband's brother?

86. If she marries a brother, what rule of succession applies to her husband's property, *e.g.*, what right in it accrues to—

(1) The widow,
(2) The brother whom she marries,
(3) Her children by her first husband,
(4) Her children by her second husband?

87. Are children begotten of the widow by the brother of the deceased considered to be the children of her first or of her second husband?

N.B.—In illustration of the last eight questions, it may be noted that among the Jeswar Kurmis the widow of an elder brother usually marries a younger brother by the *sagai* form, but may marry an outsider. If she marries the younger brother, she gets half of her deceased husband's property. If she marries an outsider, she forfeits all claim not only to her husband's property, but to the custody of her children, except in the case of daughters, who stay with her till of a marriageable age, when she is bound to bring them back to be married from her husband's brother's house. The widow of a younger brother cannot marry an elder brother.

88. *Adoption.*—Is it necessary that the adopter should be destitute of a son, a son's son, and a son's grandson?

89. Must he obtain the consent of his heirs?

90. Is a daughter's son a bar to the right of adoption?

91. May a man adopt who has male issue, if such issue be disqualified by any legal impediment (such as loss of caste) from performing the exequial rites?

92. Can a man who had already adopted a son adopt another during the lifetime of the first?

93. Can the following persons adopt—

(1) A bachelor,
(2) A man blind, impotent, or lame,
(3) A widower,
(4) An ascetic who has renounced the world?

94. Can a woman adopt?

95. State whether it is necessary to the validity of an adoption by a widow that she should adopt with the permission, written or verbal, of her deceased husband, or with the consent of his kindred.

96. Can a widow adopt a son *as her own* without thereby making him a member of her late husband's family?

97. Can she adopt a son as her own in addition to a son adopted as the representative of her deceased husband?

98. In the event of the death of a son adopted by a widow with the sanction of her husband, may the widow adopt another person without permission of her husband to that effect?

99. May a man give in adoption—

(1) His only son,
(2) His eldest son,
(3) His brother?

100. Must the person adopted be less than any specific age?

101. If so, up to what age may a person be adopted?

102. In the case of the higher castes, can a person be adopted after tonsure or investiture with the sacred cord in his own family?

103. Can girls be adopted?

104. Is there any rule by which it is required that the person adopted should be related to the person adopting ?

105. If so, what relatives may be adopted ?

106. Is any preference required to be shown to particular relatives ?

107. If so, enumerate them in order of preference.

108. Is it necessary that the adopted son and his adoptive father should be (1) of the same caste of tribe, (2) of the same *got* ?

109. Is there any rule prohibiting the adoption of the son of a woman whom the adopter could not have married, such as his sister's son or his daughter's son ?

110. Does an adopted son retain his right to inherit from his natural father ?

111. Can he inherit from his natural father if the natural father die without other sons ?

112. Describe the rights of an adopted son to inherit from his adoptive father.

113. What is the effect of the subsequent birth of natural legitimate sons to the adoptive father ?

114. Will the adopted son take equal shares with them ?

115. When a son-in-law leaving his own family takes up his residence permanently with his father-in-law as *ghar jamai*, what will be the effect on the rights of such son-in-law to inherit (1) from his father, (2) from his father-in-law.

116. *Succession.*—If a man die leaving a widow or widows, a son or sons, a daughter or daughters, brothers, and other relatives, upon whom will the inheritance devolve ?

117. If there be more sons than one, will they take equal shares ?

118. If the sons do not take equal shares, state upon what principle the shares are regulated.

(1) Is any regard had to uterine descent ? Are the shares in the inheritance distributed according to the number of mothers ?

(2) Is any regard had to the caste or tribe of the mothers, so that the sons by a wife of a high caste, or of the same caste, or tribe with the father take larger shares than the sons by the wife of a low caste, or of a different caste or tribe ?

(3) Is any regard had to the age of the sons, so that (1) the eldest son, (2) the youngest son, would take a greater or less share than his brethren ?

119. Can a father in his lifetime nominate a particular son as the fit person to take a larger share than his brethren after the father's decease ?

120. When an estate has been held jointly by a father and his sons, and is distributed amongst them upon his decease, are acquisitions made by the sons exempt from distribution; or will all the sons share in all the joint estate, moveable or immoveable,

ancestral or acquired, whether or no any part of such estate have been acquired by any one or more of the sons, by gift or succession from a maternal grandfather or father-in-law, or other relative through a female?

121. Where there are male descendants who do not all stand in the same degree of kindred to the deceased, and the persons through whom the more remote are descended from him are dead, will the nearer descendants exclude the more remote, or are the more remote descendants entitled to succeed simultaneously with the nearer descendants?

122. If in the case stated in question 121 the more remote descendants succeed simultaneously with the nearer descendants, how is the estate to be divided?

Is it to be divided in equal shares amongst all the heirs; or is it to be divided into such a number of equal shares as may correspond with the number of the male lineal descendants of the deceased, who either stood in the nearest degree of kindred to him at his decease, or, having been of the like degree of kindred to him, died before him, leaving male lineal descendants who survived him?

123. Where there is no son, but where the male lineal descendants are all grandsons or all great-grandsons, will the estate be divided equally amongst all such grandsons or great-grandsons, as the case may be, or will the shares be allotted to the grandsons proportionately to the shares which the sons would have taken had they been living, or to the great-grandsons proportionately to the shares which the grandsons would have taken had they survived the deceased?

124. Do the principles stated in the replies to questions 121 and 122 apply to every case of the distribution of an inheritance; or is there any distinction when collaterals inherit; that is to say, does a son or grandson always take the share his father or grandfather would have taken, if such father or grandfather had survived the deceased, whether or no the share descend lineally or through a collateral relative?

125. Does the inheritance successively devolve upon all male lineal descendants, how low so ever; or is there any degree fixed in the descending line within which, if there be no male lineal descendants, the inheritance will devolve on other relatives. If so, state what that degree is?

126. If a man die leaving a widow or widows, and either a daughter or daughters, or brother or their descendants, or uncles or their descendants, or great-uncles or their descendants, but no male lineal descendants, within three generations, upon whom will the inheritance devolve?

127. If the estate devolve upon the widow, define her interest therein?

128. What rights has the widow to alienate by sale, gift, mortgage, or bequest?

(1) Are there any special circumstances or expenses under, or on account of, which alienation is permissible? If so, what are these?

(2) Is there any distinction in respect of moveable or immoveable, ancestral or acquired property, or in respect of alienation to the kindred of the deceased husband?

(3) Supposing alienation to be permissible, whose consent is necessary to make it valid?

129. As regards the right of a Mahomedan widow to alienate, is any distinction taken in respect of her legal share?

130. If there be several widows, do they take in equal shares?

131. Is any distinction made in respect of the rights of widows who are not of the same family with their deceased husband?

132. Is there any distinction in the rights of widows based upon the circumstance whether the husband was or was not associated with his brethren?

133. What is the effect of unchastity upon the right of a widow in respect of the estate of her deceased husband?

134. In the case of widows who are not Hindus, what is the effect of their remarriage?

135. Under what circumstances are daughters entitled to inherit? Are they excluded by the sons or by the widow, or by the near male kindred of the deceased? If they are excluded by the near male kindred, is there any fixed limit of relationship within which such near kindred must stand towards the deceased in order to exclude his daughters? If so, how is the limit ascertained? If it depends on descent from a common ancestor, state within how many generations relatively to the deceased such common ancestor must come.

136. Is there any distinction as to the rights of daughters to inherit (1) the immoveable or ancestral, (2) the moveable or acquired, property of their father?

137. (1) Under what circumstances are daughters entitled to be maintained out of the estate of their deceased father?

(2) What is the effect of (*a*) marriage, (*b*) residence in a strange village, upon the right of the daughter to inherit, or to be maintained?

(3) If a married daughter with her husband live with the father up to his decease, can the daughter inherit?

(4) Can daughters who are married and barren, or widowed, and without male issue, or mothers of daughters only, inherit the father's estate?

138. What is the nature of the interest taken by a daughter in the property she inherits? Define her rights of alienation, if any, by sale, gift, mortgage, or bequest.

139. After daughters, do daughters' sons succeed? If so, is the property equally divided amongst all the sons of several daughters, or are the shares proportioned to the number of daughters who leave sons?

140. When a man dies leaving no male lineal descendants, no widow, and no daughters or daughters' sons, upon whom will the inheritance successively devolve?

141. When the estate devolves upon the mother of the deceased, what is the nature of the interest she acquires?

142. Define her powers of alienation.

143. On the death of the mother, will the property devolve on the heirs of the son, or on her heirs?

144. When the property devolves on brethren, what, if any, regard is paid (1) to uterine descent, (2) to association? Do uterine associated brethren exclude all others? In what order succeed—

(*i*) Unassociated brethren of the whole blood?
(*ii*) Associated brethren of the half-blood?
(*iii*) Unassociated brethren of half-blood?

If a man die leaving a uterine brother separated and a half-brother associated, how will these two inherit?

145. When a man dies leaving associated brethren and unassociated brethren, and the property devolves on his brethren, have the associated brethren any preferential claim to acquired property, moveable or immoveable property, or to ancestral moveable property?

146. In default of brethren, does the property devolve upon their sons?

147. Does the property ever devolve upon sisters, or upon sisters' sons. If upon sisters' sons, how are their shares computed?

148. Where a wife dies holding property in her own right, is the husband entitled to succeed to such property, or any part of it?

149. Can the son by a former marriage of a woman who contracts a second marriage inherit from (1) his natural father, (2) his stepfather? If from his stepfather, is her share equal to, or less than that of, his stepfather's own sons?

150. Is any distinction taken as regards the stepson (*i*) if he be not born till after the second marriage of his mother, (*ii*) if the stepfather in his lifetime assign him a share by deed?

151. Are stepsons entitled to be maintained by their stepfather? If so, till what age?

152. Enumerate in the order of their succession the persons entitled to the estate of a man who dies intestate leaving no relations.

153. If a person voluntarily retires from the world and becomes a member of a religious order, what is the effect upon (*i*) his right to retain his property, (*ii*) his right to acquire property by inheritance? Upon whom will devolve property which he would have inherited if he had not retired from the world?

154. State any rules recognized by the caste governing the succession to—

(*a*) Zamindaries.
(*b*) Service tenures.
(*c*) Headships of villages.

155. In the case of tribes practising polyandry, state carefully the rules of inheritance, *e.g.*, does a man's property devolve upon his brother, his sister, or his sister's son?

156. *System of Relationships.*—Are any persons considered to be relations besides those who are descended from a common ancestor?

157. Are all or any of the kindred of the wife considered to be the relations of—

(1) the husband,
(2) the husband's relatives or children?

158. If so, state the persons who are relatives, with the names of the relationships.

159. How are generations reckoned?

160. Give a table of kindred with the local names of the generations up to the third degree in both the ascending and descending line.

161. By how many generations are the following persons said to be related to the person whose relatives are to be reckoned?

(1) Brother.
(2) Father.
(3) Uncle.
(4) Cousin-german, *i.e.*, uncle's son.
(5) Brother's grandson.
(6) Great-grandson.
(7) Great-grandfather.

162. Fill in the following tables with the local names of the relations.

A.—Relations, through the Father, whether of man or woman.

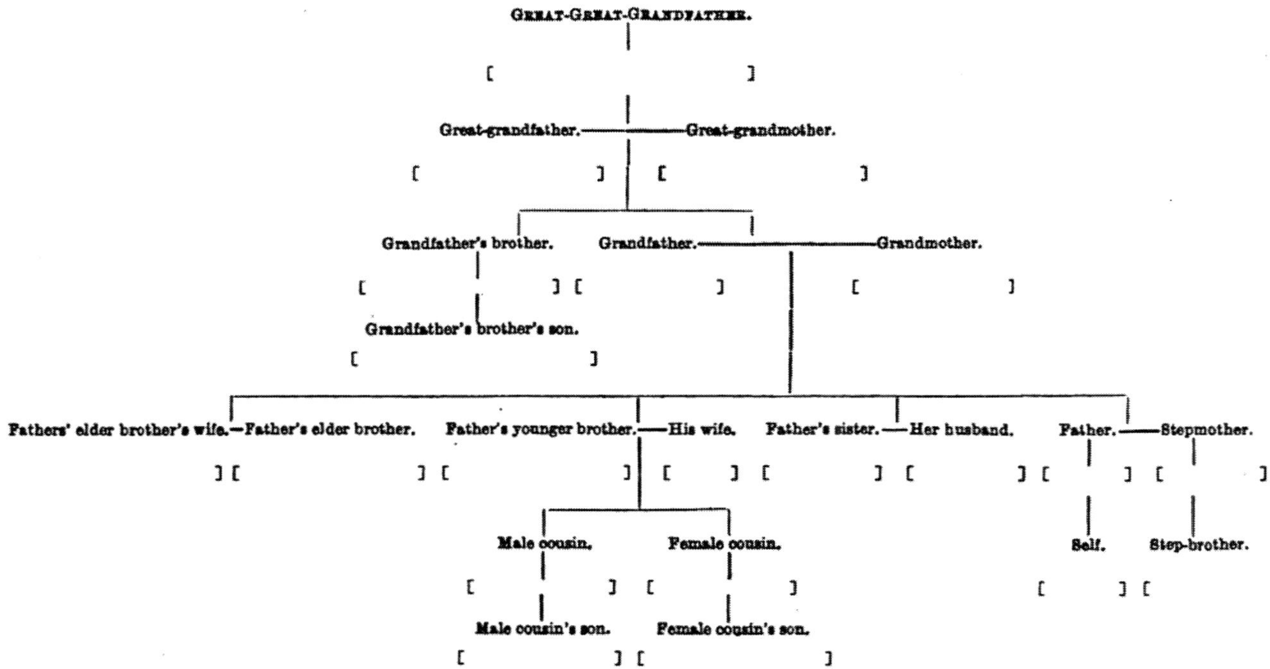

B.—Relations, through the Mother, whether of man or woman.

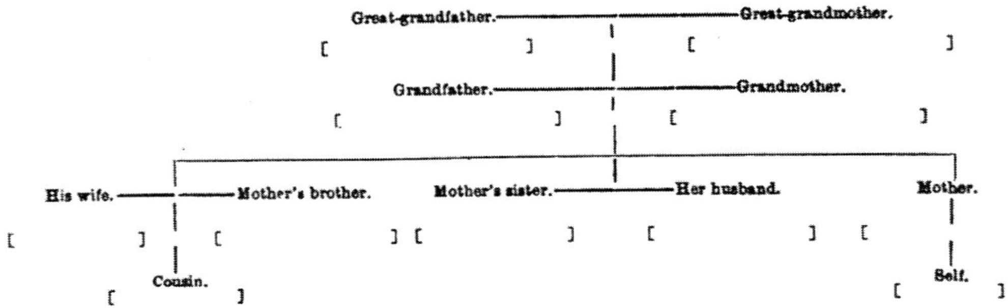

C.—Relations, through the Brother and Sister, whether of man or woman.

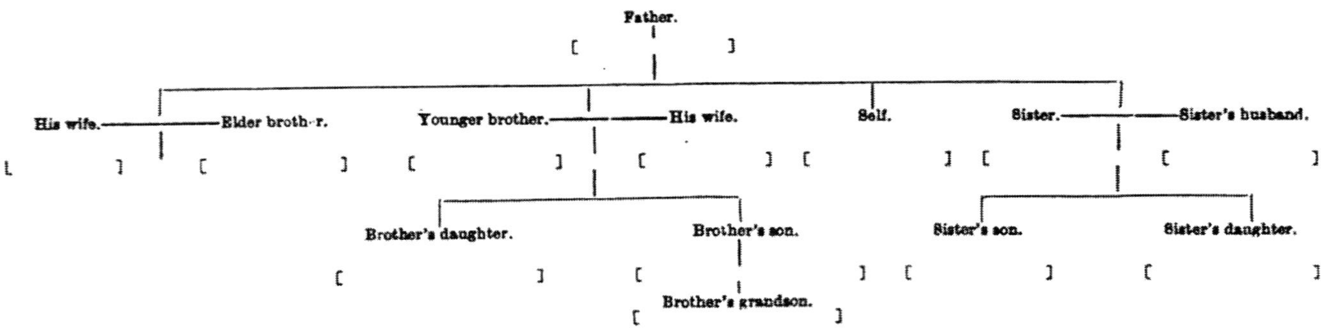

D (1).—*Relations, through the Wife, of a man.*

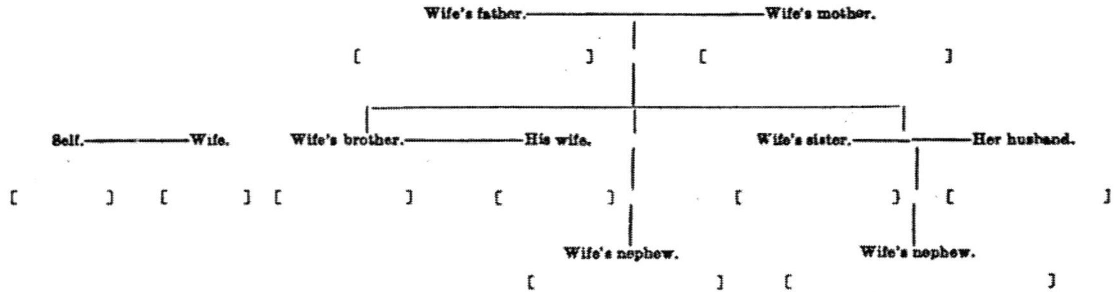

D (2).—*Relations, through the Husband, of a woman.*

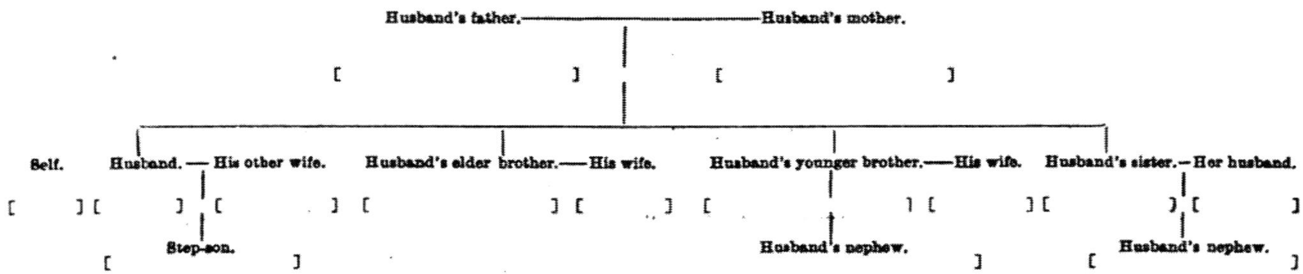

E (1).—*Relations, through the Son, whether of man or woman.*

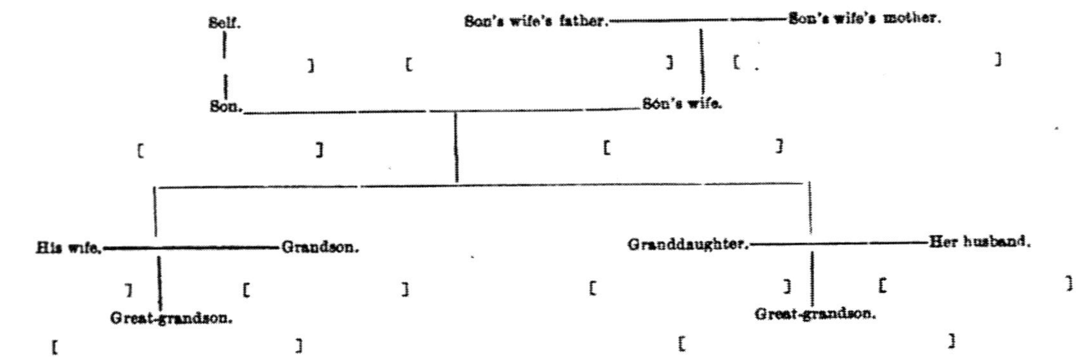

E (2).—*Relations, through the Daughter, whether of man or woman.*

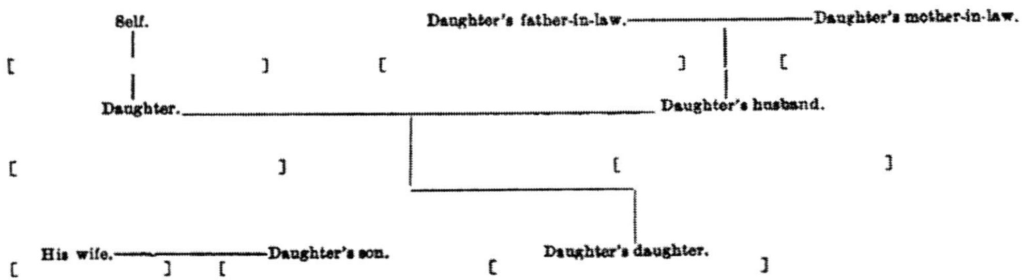

163. How is each group spoken of collectively by a man and by a woman?

164. Add any relationships not included in these groups for which there are special names.

165. Is a great-uncle distinguished from a grandfather's and a parent's cousin from a man's own cousin?

166. Into what classes are relations distributed?

167. Specify each class and the relations included in it.

168. Give the distinctions, if any—

(i) between sapindas, sakulyas, samanodakas, bandhus, and gotrajas.

(ii) between personal, paternal, and maternal kindred.

(iii) between legal sharers and residuaries, near and distant kindred, lineal and collateral relations.

169. State the various modes of addressing and speaking of particular relatives, *e.g.*, how do men and women address and speak of their husbands and wives respectively?

170. How does a man address and speak of his brother-in-law?

171. Are there any cases in which names originally denoting particular relationships are used in addressing or speaking of persons not related in the manner the name denotes? *e.g.*, a man sometimes speaks of another man as his *bhai*, when in fact he merely means that the other is a member of his own caste.

172. Are genealogies carefully kept?

173. Do they include the names of females?

174. Note any forms of adoptive relationships based upon friendship or on land (*e.g.*, *phulbahin* and *bhumbhai*), and state what consequences and obligations are annexed to them.

II.—Domestic Ceremonies.

175. *Birth and Pregnancy.*—Describe any ceremonies performed during pregnancy, and state what effect, if any, they are believed to have upon the mother or child.

176. What posture is adopted in accouchement?

177. Who attends on the mother (*a*) during her confinement, (*b*) after the confinement is over?

178. What ceremonies are performed on the birth of a child?

179. Are the ordinary occupations of the father given up or interrupted in any way in consequence of the birth of a child?

180. What reasons, if any, are assigned for such interruption?

181. Are there any special customs with reference to twins?

182. *Adoption.*—Describe the different ceremonies in use for adoption.

183. Does the validity of the adoption depend upon the performance of the customary ceremony?

184. Does the status of the person adopted depend upon the form of ceremony used?

185. If so, what is the effect of each of the different forms?

186. *Puberty or Adolescence.*—What ceremonies are performed when (*a*) a son, (*b*) a daughter, attains puberty?

187. In the case of a son, is there any ceremony purporting to admit him among the grown men of the caste?

188. *Betrothal.*—Describe the ceremony of betrothal.

189. What is considered the binding portion of the ceremony?

190. Is there any distinction between formalities after which the betrothal is reversible and formalities which are absolutely binding?

191. At what age does betrothal take place?

192. Whose consent is necessary?

193. If a betrothal be annulled, is there any custom as to the repayment of the expenses incurred?

194. *Marriage.*—Describe in detail the various kinds of marriage ceremonies in use, distinguishing between superior and inferior kinds?

195. What is considered to be the essential or binding part of each kind of ceremony?

196. In the marriage ceremony is there any pretence of capturing the bride, or does any part of the ceremony or of the previous or subsequent proceedings suggest that marriage by capture was formerly in vogue.

197. In the marriage ceremony is there any symbol of a previous marriage to any deity, *e.g.*, is the bride first married to a tree or to any natural object?

198. *Death and Burial.*—Do the caste burn, bury, or expose their dead?

199. If buried, in what position?

200. Where are the bodies or ashes finally disposed of?

201. Describe the ceremonies performed at the burning or burying of a corpse?

202. Are any ceremonies performed for the propitiation of (*a*) ancestors in general, (*b*) childless ancestors, (*c*) men who have died a violent death; and if so, of what nature and at what seasons?

203. Describe the ceremony of *sraddh*, and state whether the caste perform it or not?

204. Who officiates as priest at the funeral ceremonies and repeats formulæ of prayer (mantras, etc.)?

205. In the case of castes which do not employ Brahmans it should be enquired whether the sister's son or other relative on the female side officiates in the place of the Brahman.

206. *Purification.*—Are ceremonial purifications practised?

207. Are any persons at any time impure or unclean and requiring purification, as after child-birth, during menstruation, after funerals, etc.?

208. For how long does the ceremonial impurity last?

209. How are they purified?

III.—Religion.

210. *Worship, Priests, and Temples.*—To what religion, and to what sect within the religion, do the caste belong?

211. If Hindus, do they by preference worship any special one of the regular Hindu deities, and are there any reasons for this preference?

212. Have its members always professed that religion, or were they converted to it *en masse*, or gradually?

213. How did their conversion take place, and when—before their migration to their present abode or after?

214. Are members of the caste found in the neighbourhood professing the tenets of different religions or sects?

215. Do they affect a peculiar saint or shrine?

216. State the names, origin, and attributes of the minor village deities and local or patron saints whom they worship, describing, if possible, the shape and aspect of the shrine, the ceremonies observed in worship, the nature of the offerings made, the times, days, or seasons when they are made, the caste and subdivision of the officiating priests and of the persons who take the offerings.

217. Are any of these deities peculiar to women and children?

218. State any indications of ancestor worship, snake or tree worship, sun, moon, fire, or devil worship, which the religious practice of the caste suggests.

219. Is there any special shrine to which pilgrimages are made, and at what seasons?

220. Has any great religious teacher arisen in the caste? Give his name and state his peculiar tenets.

221. Is the caste, though nominally belonging to one of the main religions, excluded from any of the rites and ceremonies practised by other castes belonging to the same denomination, and is any specific reason assigned for this exclusion?

222. All cases of left-handed sect and worship of sexual principles, orgies, etc., should be noted.

223. Have they any ceremony of admission into the religious body corresponding to baptism or circumcision?

224. All cases of Hindus and Mahomedans, or their women and children, worshipping the same deities or saints, or frequenting the same shrines, should be carefully noted.

225. Do the caste employ Brahmans for religious and ceremonial purposes?

226. If so, to what caste or section of Brahmans do they belong, and are they received on terms of equality by other Brahmans?

227. If they do not employ Brahmans, what class of people serve them as priests?

228. Are there any family priests who perform ceremonial functions not connected with any particular deity?

229. Are particular persons or clans set apart as priests?

230. Is the same person often both priest and chief?

231. Do they practice austerities, observe chastity, etc.?

232. Is any special building set apart for worship?

233. Is it built in a particular position, as facing the east, etc.?

234. Has it any special shape, and is it called by a special name?

235. Are idols kept there?

236. What rites are performed?

237. Are all the rites public, or are any of the nature of mysteries or orgies?

238. *Sacrifice.*—Is sacrifice offered, to what deities, and of what animals?

239. May any one or only priests offer sacrifice?

240. Where is sacrifice offered?

241. After sacrifice, do the priests or worshippers consume or remove the objects offered?

242. Are substitutes used in sacrifice, such as part of an animal, an effigy or imitation?

243. Do worshippers sacrifice parts of themselves, such as hair, nails, drops of blood, etc.?

244. Is there any tradition of men, women, or children having been sacrified in former times to any deity?

245. If so, name the deity, and state all you can learn about the tradition.

246. Whence and in what manner was the victim obtained?

247. Enquire why the custom of human sacrifice was discontinued, how long ago, and what was substituted in its place?

248. *Festivals.*—Give a list of the festivals observed, stating the dates when each is celebrated.

249. What do they consist in—processions, games, dances, banquets, etc.?

250. Which are at regular periods and which occasional?

251. Are there annual religious festivals marking the months, seasons, equinoxes, solstices, seed-time, first fruits, harvest, etc.?

252. Is there an annual feast of the dead?

253. To what extent does the caste observe the great Hindu festivals?

254. Is there any great festival observed by the caste, but not observed by Hindus generally?

255. Are there festivals at which marriageable youths and girls mix, and matches are made?

256. Are any festivals specially connected with sexual relations?

257. Is drunkenness common on these occasions, and is the use of any particular intoxicating drink regarded as part of the festival.

258. *Fetichism.*—Do spirits or deities enter into or attach themselves to objects, such as sticks, bones, ornaments, etc.?

259. Are such objects kept sacred and believed to contain supernatural power?

260. Are blocks of wood, stones, etc., believed to be inhabited by deities, and worshipped accordingly?

261. *Worship of natural spirits, plants, and animals.*—Are there spirits especially attached to natural objects, such as rivers, springs, wells, rocks, trees, animals, etc.?

262. How are they worshipped?

263. Are fields believed to be haunted, and by whom?

264. Are groves and woods favourite places of worship or sacrifice?

265. If so, explain what gods are worshipped there, and note if the wood or grove is or is supposed to be part of a large forest which has been cleared, a portion being left as a refuge for the forest gods.

266. Are any beasts worshipped as gods? If so, describe the mode of worship.

267. *Ancestor worship.*—Are the souls of ancestors worshipped with prayers and sacrifices?

268. Describe briefly the ceremony in vogue?

269. Is the supposed primitive ancestor of the caste worshipped under the form of, or in connexion with, some sacred animal, plant or other object as a totem or clan deity?

270. Are animals sacrified at funerals; if so, with what object?

271. Are any funeral offerings given, so that the souls of the dead may become possessed of objects or their phantoms?

272. Are food, money, ornaments, etc., placed near the corpse, burnt or buried with it, or offered periodically at the place of burial?

273. Are the survivors in fear of the ghosts of the dead?

274. Do they attribute dreams to their influence, and do they take any means to get rid of them, or keep them off?

275. Do ghosts of the dead haunt houses or burial-places, and if so in what forms?

276. Does their doing so indicate that their bodies have not been properly buried?

277. How are ghosts propitiated?

278. Are there several kinds of them; if so, state the names, characteristics, and attributes of each?

279. Are any days sacred to ancestors, and what is done on these days?

280. Do the caste go to Gya or to any other well-known place of pilgrimage to perform the *sraddh* of their ancestors?

281. *Totems.*—Is the caste or any of its subdivisions named after any animal, plant, weapon, or implement?

282. Do they show their reverence for any such object either by special worship or by abstaining from killing, eating, cutting, burning, using or naming it?

283. Are there any cases of the object which the caste reverence being tattooed or painted on the body, possibly in a very conventionalised form, or of its representation being always carried about on the person?

284. If so, how do the members of the caste explain the practice?

285. Do the women of the caste pay special reverence to certain trees, by veiling their faces before them as if in presence of an elder relative, or worship them in the hope of getting children in the belief that the spirit of the ancestor inhabits them?

286. Are any trees or plants used or worshipped at weddings and similar ceremonies, and are children named after them?

IV.—Superstitions.

287. *Omens, etc.*—Do any superstitions prevail as to lucky and unlucky days, numbers, animals, places, houses, points of the compass, roads, physical functions, such as sneezing, spitting, etc., natural events, or calamities?

288. Are there any superstitions connected with stars, and may they be got over by burying a picture or rude representation of the star?

289. Is there any objection to crossing water under certain conditions? Is meeting a particular animal regarded as ominous, and does the character of the omen depend upon the direction in which the animal is seen? Are omens taken from accidents, such as stumbling, etc.?

290. Are there any peculiar customs as to wearing or abstaining from wearing particular kinds of dress, jewels, ornaments, etc.; as to using particular kinds of cooking vessels; or as to eating or growing particular plants or drugs?

291. In the case of plants, notice whether the name of the plant affected by the superstition corresponds with the name of a subdivision of the tribe?

292. Are there any superstitions as to the naming of children, *e.g.*, are two names given, one for every-day purposes and one for ceremonial use, or is a son whose elder brother has died given an approbrious name?

293. Do these practices apply to girls as well as to boys?

294. *Oaths and ordeals.*—Are any forms of oath in common use, and are they accompanied by any symbolic forms, such as swearing on a tiger's skin?

295. What consequences are supposed to be entailed by breaking an oath?

296. Are any ordeals in use, such as plunging into water, passing through fire, eating food under special conditions, etc.?

297. Are they used merely for the decision of personal disputes or for questions affecting the community, such as the boundaries of villages, etc.?

298. *Magic and witchcraft.*—Is the practice of magic arts confined to special sorcerers, witches, etc.?

299. Are these priests, etc., connected with religion, or is there jealousy or hostility between the priest and the sorcerer?

300. What are the functions of sorcerers and witches, and how are they generally regarded?

301. Are there any supposed arts by which it can be determined whether a particular individual is a witch or sorcerer or not?

302. Are spirits or demons called upon to give oracles, disclose secrets, do good or harm?

303. Is demoniacal possession believed in, and what remedies are resorted to in order to cure persons supposed to be possessed?

304. Is such possession regarded as a valuable quality; if so, how is it acquired; is it confined to particular castes or clans?

305. Are dreams regarded? Do they give information of the past and prophecy or omens for the future.

306. Are any special persons called upon to interpret them, and is there any recognized system of interpretation?

307. Are they ascribed to visits or communications from spirits, as, for instance, to persons recently deceased in the family of the person who has the dream?

308. Is there any mode of propitiating the spirits of persons recently dead so as to prevent them from causing dreams?

309. Is the effect of the evil eye believed in?

310. To what is it attributed?

311. How is it obviated?

312. Are sorcerers and witches supposed to act on their victims by objects belonging to them or intimately connected with them, such as cut hair or nails, or by making effigies or pictures of them and wounding the pictures in order that the victims may be affected?

313. Is special care therefore taken to destroy cuttings of hair or nails?

314. Is any kind of divination or astrology practised?

315. Who are its professors?

316. Describe the modes of divination and exorcism in use, and state what class of persons are resorted to as exorcisers.

317. Is disease attributed to the influence of spirits?

318. How is the particular spirit at work detected and how appeased?

Ceremonial Prohibition or Taboo.

319. Is any particular food, animal or vegetable forbidden, though obtainable and wholesome?

320. Do the whole caste abstain from it, or only certain families or individuals, or persons under some special circumstances?

321. Is the prohibition religious?

322. Is the animal or plant abstained from regarded as in any way divine, as a tribe fetish, the incarnation of a local deity, or personal guardian spirit or the soil of some ancestor?

323. Is it the animal or plant from which the caste or sub-division derives its name?

324. Give any explanation that may be current of the prohibition in question.

325. Do any members of the caste object to eating with, touching, speaking to, looking at, or calling by name other persons?

326. Do these prohibitions apply to persons of different rank, occupation, or caste?

327. Is any particular caste held in peculiar abhorrence, and if so, why? A good instance of what is meant is afforded by the fact that the Doms hold the Dhobis in special detestation. It is believed that other low castes have similar eccentric prejudices.

328. Are women and children specially prohibited from doing any particular religious acts, entering particular temples, performing particular acts of worship, etc.?

329. Do similar prohibitions apply between relations? And specially between relations by marriage, *e.g.*, does the husband's father avoid the wife's relations, etc.?

330. What appears to be the motive?

331. Is the person whose name may not be mentioned supposed to be holier than the other?

332. Is there an idea of magical harm, or is it merely a question of social separation?

333. Are the names of chiefs, dead persons, etc., avoided in conversation?

334. Are any special words or subjects considered improper?

335. Are there any cases in which gods, persons, or subjects whose mention by name is prohibited are spoken of under some honorific title?

336. *Agricultural Superstitions.*—Mention any remarkable superstitious beliefs connected with agriculture, such as the days on which ploughing, sowing, reaping, etc., must be begun, intermitted, or finished; the periods within which a shower of rain is specially lucky or unlucky; the customary number of times agricultural operations should be performed; the objects set up in the fields to avert injury to the crops, to frighten away demons, etc.?

337. Is any propitiatory or quasi-religious ceremony observed before the commencement or after the completion of any agricultural operations, such as the sinking of a well, sowing, reaping, or the like?

338. What times and seasons are lucky or unlucky for the commencement or completion of the various agricultural operations?

339. Are there any gods specially connected with particular crops?

340. If any of these are peculiar to the caste, the fact should be noted.

V.—Social Customs.

341. *Food and drink.*—Which of the following articles of food do the caste eat or abstain from eating:—flesh, wine, monkeys, beef, pork, the flesh of cloven-footed or uncloven-footed animals, fowls, scaly or scaleless fish, crocodiles, snakes, lizards, jackals, rats, other vermin, the leavings of other people?

342. Are there any seasons during which the use of special articles of food is forbidden?

343. Are such restrictions due to the desire to increase the stock of such article of food or to superstitious or sanitary causes?

344. Is the use of certain articles of food restricted to women or children, or to chiefs and persons of rank?

345. Are individuals or families prevented from eating certain animals and plants for superstitious reasons, such, for instance, as their being the totems of the individuals or family?

346. Does all the household eat together, or each person separately, or is there a distinction of ranks, sexes, or ages?

347. Do men and women eat together?

348. Are there any ceremonies used at the commencement of meals, such as offerings to the divinities, etc., or any religious rites connected with them?

349. Are there any marked peculiarities in the mode of eating and drinking of the caste, and how are these peculiarities explained?

350. State what spirituous liquors, drugs, and narcotics are in ordinary use.

351. Are any of them connected with particular religious ceremonies or festivals?

352. Are any of them supposed to have the effect of keeping off malaria?

353. How is the use of spirituous liquors and drugs regarded by the caste—for instance, is (*a*) drunkenness, (*b*) habitual indulgence in opium or ganja looked upon as disreputable?

354. *Customs of social intercourse.*—What customs prevails as to salutation?

355. Do they differ according to rank and relationship?

356. How do members of a family, friends and relations, and strangers greet one another?

357. What special processes of compliment and rules of precedence are in vogue?

358. How are guests, women, and aged or infirm persons treated?

359. What are the rules of hospitality as recognized between kinsfolk, neighbours, and strangers?

360. Are peculiar forms of language in use?

361. Are certain words or forms of address used or avoided in addressing certain people?

362. *Customs bearing on social status.*—Name the lowest well-known caste with which the caste will (*a*) eat paki, (*b*) eat kachhi, (*c*) drink, (*d*) smoke.

363. Name the highest well-known caste which will eat, etc., as in the last question with the caste.

364. Is there any special article of food their abstaining from which tends in their opinion to raise them above some other caste which does not abstain from it?

365. Mention any remarkable customs of the caste regarding dress, ornaments, implements of handicrafts, fishing or hunting, distinguishing marks, cutting of hair and beard, musical instruments, dances, etc., which affect their social status in relation to their neighbours.

VI.—Occupations.

366. What do the caste believe to have been their original occupation or group of occupations?

367. To what extent have they or any sections of them departed from it?

368. Describe their present occupation?

369. If their occupation is that of—

(*a*) *Artisans*—What is their industry and in what special material do they work, or abstain from working?

(*b*) *Hunters.*—Do they catch game or vermin?
(*c*) *Fishermen.*—Do they catch fish only or also crocodiles and tortoises?
(*d*) *Sweepers.*—Do they remove night-soil or not?

370. Name any implement or mode of working which is characteristic of the caste, and also note whether there is any form or detail of their main occupation by abstaining from which they believe themselves to be raised above others of the same craft?

371. Do they habitually prostitute their (1) unmarried, (2) married women?

372. Does a change of religion, such as conversion to Mahomedanism, or a joining a special sect of Hindus, usually involve a change or modification of occupation on the part of the convert?

373. In cases where an hereditary occupation is abandoned, do the persons changing their occupation change or modify their caste name, and are their ties with those members who adhere to their original occupation in any way broken or relaxed?

VII.—Relations to Land.

374. To what class of agriculturists do the caste or tribe usually belong, *e.g.*, are they—

(1) Zamindars;
(2) Tenure-holders, specifying the kind of tenures they hold;
(3) Occupancy or non-occupancy raiyats, stating whether they have or claim any privileges in respect of rent;
(4) Nomadic cultivators, specifying the mode of cultivation they follow;
(5) Landless day-labourers, stating the manner in which they are paid?

375. Have they any legend or tradition accounting for the position they occupy?

376. Have the caste any privileges in respect of land, *e.g.*, do they—

(*a*) hold at lower rates of rent than their neighbours;
(*b*) hold a certain proportion of their holdings rent-free;
(*c*) receive a certain proportion of the produce of each field or of particular crops in consideration of any kind of service?

377. Do they hold any peculiar kinds of tenures?

378. If so, have they any tradition accounting for the fact, such as that they are the descendants of the first clearers of the soil, of a former dominant race, or the like?

379. Do they claim special privileges in respect of land on the strength of traditional affinity to, or supposed contact with, the ancestors of the local zamindars?

380. Have they any hereditary right to perform certain services or receive certain fees?

381. Is it supposed that the ancestors of the local zamindars were members of the caste or tribe, and do they now admit this, or deny it?

382. Are there any traces among the caste or tribe of village communities, or of a communal organization embracing groups of villages?

383. Give all details that can be ascertained on this subject, or if the organization has already been described in print, quote the reference.

384. Does the system preserve its vitality, or is it dying out?

385. If the latter, state from what cause.

386. Are there any traces of the periodical redistribution of common arable land among the members of sections of the community?

387. If the communal organization has now fallen into disuse, can any trace of its previous existence be found in the character of distribution of the tenures now held by the caste or tribe?

388. Are there any restrictions upon the order in which certain fields are to be cultivated or certain crops sown?

389. Do communal rights of pasturage exist, or are they asserted over land which is private property?

390. Among hunting, fishing or wandering tribes does any apportionment of land or water exist between the divisions of the tribe, each division confining its operations to the tract allotted to it, and does the apportionment extend to the individual members of the division?

391. Does this custom obtain even where the land or water apportioned is not the property of the tribe?

Sources of information.—Here should be noted the names, residence (village and thana), profession, caste, sub-caste, and section of the persons who answered the questions. If any of them are *ghataks*, genealogists, heads of caste *panchayat*, or occupy any hereditary official position in relation to the caste, the fact should be stated. If the answers to the questions have been derived from any source other than personal enquiry addressed to members of the caste concerned, the source should be stated, and such references given as may enable the officer in charge of the enquiry to test the correctness of the answers.

DENZIL C. J. IBBETSON.
JOHN C. NESFIELD.
H. H. RISLEY.

APPENDIX III.

MR. DENZIL IBBETSON'S MEMORANDUM ON ETHNOLOGICAL INQUIRY IN THE PANJÁB.

1882.

*Memorandum for guidance in collecting Ethnological Notes.**

N.B.—Proper names and vernacular words should be very clearly and correctly written, and in vernacular as well as in English characters, if possible.

1. *Caste or Tribe—Clan—Locality—Tahsil—District.*—This information should always be given at the head of the note regarding the people from whose statements the note is compiled; and if they belong to a single village, it should be named in case of further inquiry being needed.

It is often difficult to decide what should be entered as the caste. Many clans, for instance, are called Jats in some districts and Rájpúts in others. A mere tradition of Rájpút origin, even though admitted by the Rájpúts of the neighbourhood, is not enough to warrant their being entered as Rájpúts, though the tradition and the fact of its admission should of course be stated; for a caste will often claim Rájpút origin, while readily admitting that they have lost the status which their ancestors enjoyed.

The real question is *whether they are, for practical purposes, looked upon and treated as Rájpúts at the present time by admitted Rájpúts of the neighbourhood.* The same test applies to claims to be classed as Patháns, Qoreshís, &c., &c. The claim, however, should always be noted, together with the considerations which may lead you to hold that it is inadmissible.

In any case the name by which the people are best known and most commonly spoken of among their neighbours, generally that of their clan, should always be prominently noted.

2. *Distribution.*—It is useful to state whether the particular caste or clan is numerous in the tahsíl; where their local head-quarters are; and if few, where they are to be found in larger numbers. The provincial head-quarters, if any, should be named. The people will often tell you that they hold 27 villages in this and 84 in that tahsíl, and so on, giving the old traditional number of villages rather than the number as they now stand. Such statements should be recorded.

3. *Subdivisions.*—The various grades of tribal subdivision to which the people belong should always be stated: for instance, they

* I need hardly say that I am indebted for many of the notes in this memorandum to the suggestions of friends who have been kind enough to help me in its compilation.

should be described as belonging to the A family of the B clan of the C tribe of the D race or caste. And especially it will be useful to give the traditional number of subdivisions of the tribe or clan under discussion, and to detail the names of as many of them as possible, as these names often appear in the census papers with nothing to indicate to what tribe they belong, and in such cases the barest list of names would be most valuable to me.

A tree showing the local subdivisions of a caste or tribe is always exceedingly useful, and should be accompanied by a detail of the vernacular terms used to denote the various degrees of subdivision; such as *zát, got, al, jad, pál, múhín, thok, movi, sútan, kuldevi, carri, bolak, tuman, páro, phalli, zai, khel, &c., &c.*

In the case of menial castes, it should be noted whether the name of their subdivision is the same as the clan name of the villagers whom they serve, or of the prevailing agricultural clan in the neighbourhood, or in the part of the country whence they came.

4. *Synonyms*—

(*a*) If the caste or clan is known by more thano ne name, all should be given; as *Jhínwar* and *Kahár*, *Juláha* and *Páoli.* So, too, if the name varies with the religion; as *Chúhrá* for Hindu, *Musallí* for Musalmán; and *Mazbi* for Sikh sweepers; *Mahra* for Hindu and Sikh, and *Jhínwar* for Musalmán *Kahárs; Rángar* for Musalmán Rájpúts, and so on. It should always be noted whether the synonyms are co-extensive or not; whether, for instance, the term Rángar is applied to all Musalmán Rájpúts, and to them only, or not.

(*b*) Too great caution cannot be exercised in accepting synonyms. To the educated and twice-born Native, every vagrant is a *Nat*, every outcast a *Chúhrá* or *Dúm*, and so on. The real test is whether, for instance, the same individual will call himself *Jhínwar* and *Kahár* indifferently; whether a Hindu *Chúhrá* would be called on conversion a *Musallí;* whether a *Juláha* from the east would, on settling in the west, be recognized as a *Páoli;* whether the people themselves accept and recognize the identity. Mere identity of *origin* is not sufficient. For instance, *Parāchas* are said to be converted *Banyas;* but no *Banya* could now become a *Parácha* by conversion; the caste is closed to outsiders, and has become separate and distinct.

(*c*) Names of occupations often give rise to most difficult questions of this sort. For instance, some say that *Jhínwar* and *Máchhi* are identical; and that all *Malláhs*, *Bhatyáras, Barbhúnjas*, and *Dáyás* are *Jhínwar* by caste, these words being the names of occupations only, and not of castes. Taking *Malláhs* only, the test questions would be something of this sort. Are there any *Malláhs* who never were *Jhínwars;* would a *Jhínwar*, on first taking to work as a boatman, call himself *Jhínwar*, or

Malláh, or both indifferently? What would his son call himself? What would he call himself if he reverted to working as a porter or village water-carrier or cook? Would he ordinarily marry a *Malláh* woman (1) while still working as a porter, (2) while working as a boatman, and *vice versâ*?

(*d*) Where the custom of the neighbourhood forbids marriage out of the caste, freedom of intermarriage is the best possible test of identity. But this is often not available. As to the general question, see section 21 below. Questions of this sort are the most difficult which have arisen in the classification of census figures, and a thorough examination of them is much needed.

5. *Origin or foundation of caste.*—The tradition as to the origin or foundation of the caste or clan, though often absurd, should always be given, together with any facts which may seem to bear upon its probable truth.

6. *Place of origin and course of migration.*—The ultimate place of origin, as stated by the people, should be recorded, together with such account as they may give of their subsequent stages. But especially the name of the village or neighbourhood from which their ancestors came direct to their present locality should always be stated, as this last can generally be relied upon, and enables us to trace them back, step by step, in their wanderings. It will often be found that they still make periodical pilgrimages to a place of origin, there to worship at a *satti*, or at the shrine (*jathera*) of their common ancestor.

The place of origin of their *Parohits* and *Náis* will often be a guide; and it is useful to know where their family genealogists (*Bhát, Jága, Cháran, Mirási*) live, and to what caste and religion they belong. These men should always be got hold of and examined if possible, as they are the repositories of all the traditions of the tribe.

The number of generations since immigration is often known, or can be got from the genealogical tree, and is useful as approximately fixing the date of arrival.

The people generally have a tradition as to who held the village or locality before their coming. These traditions often throw light on past movements of tribes, and should be examined into and recorded over as wide an area as possible.

7. *Religion*—

(*a*) Should be stated; and whether the same caste or clan is found of more than one religion in the neighbourhood. Original Musalmáns, who came into India as such, should be distinguished from those whose ancestors have been converted from Hindúism. The latter can often state who converted them, and when and where. [It is important to ascertain whether their conversion took place before or after their settlement in their present homes.]

(*b*) The sect, where it can be discovered, should also be stated. Whole villages of nominal Hindús or Musalmáns are sometimes adherents of a sect which practically eclipses the parent religion. It will often be found that the people affect a particular *gurú* or *pír* or *gurúdwára*, and will be of the sect to which he or it belongs (*see* further, section 20 *infra*); especially weavers, water-carriers, and other village menials are often devotees of some saint or shrine, local or distant; and in such cases the fact should be noted.

(*c*) It will generally be found that the peasantry worship minor village deities and local saints far more than the recognized gods of the Hindu Pantheon. Particulars regarding worship of this sort are especially valuable. The names, origin, and attributes of the deity, the shape and aspect of the shrine, the days of the week or year consecrated to him or her, the ceremonies observed in worship, the nature of the offerings made, and the class of people by whom they are taken, should be given.

(*d*) It should be especially noted whether any of these deities are peculiar to any particular sex, age, class, caste or clan, or their worship specially affected by them, or in any given locality.

(*e*) It is not impossible that the minor deities may be distributable into two classes, Aryan and Aboriginal, the former being worshipped by all, and the offerings made to them being pure and taken by Bráhmans, while the worship of the latter is often largely confined to women and children, and the offerings consist of fowls, pigs, *churmas*, and other impure things, and are taken by Jogis, Faqírs, Chúhras, and the like. The latter class are perhaps more often malevolent than the former.

(*f*) It should also be stated whether Sikhs or Hindús worship the same deities at the same shrines or not; and it will often be found that Musalmáns still worship these minor deities of the neighbourhood, *especially their women and children.*

(*g*) Customs forbidden, or not authorized by the nominal religion, are of special importance, as, for example, the worship of saints by Musalmáns, and of Musalmán saints by Hindús, the circumcision of females, and the like.

(*h*) It is particularly important to note the cases where a caste, though nominally Hindu, Sikh or Musalmán, is not recognized as such, and not admitted to a religious equality, or to a participation in public rites and ceremonies by others of the same denomination.

(*i*) Information regarding the religion and worship of the outcast and vagrant castes, such as sweepers and the various kinds of gipsies, is much needed.

Snake-worship and tree-worship will be found in full vitality in many parts of the province, and traces of fire-worship and devil-worship should be carefully looked for.

8. *Fairs, Fasts, and Festivals.*—These almost always have a semi-religious significance, and are of great sociological interest. The places at which they are held, and the fixed dates on which they fall, should be noted; and the name, history, and attributes of the saint or deity, if any, in whose honour they are instituted given; if none, the origin and significance attached to them by the people. It should be stated what sex and age, what castes or clans of people, and of what sect or religion, principally attend or observe them; what is the nature of the offerings made, and who takes these offerings. A rough estimate of the numbers usually attending a fair will be useful. Any tradition connected with the occasion should be narrated, and all rites and ceremonies observed should be minutely described.

9. *Omens and Superstitions.*—These are often peculiar to a clan or a locality, and are always interesting for comparison with those of other races. Divination; sooth-sayers (*bhagat syána, &c.*); witch-craft; the evil eye; the release of animals or scapegoats during epidemics; [the use and nature of charms, especially against small-pox and cattle-plague]; the sanctity of certain days, especially in connection with horned cattle; auspicious and inauspicious days, numbers, sights and events; and belief in and propitiations of ghosts (*bhút, paret, chhurel*) and fairies (*nári sháhpuri*) are some of the points on which information is needed; as also the worship of ancestors and the propitiation of those who die by violence (*upgat*) or childless (*gyál*), the custom of building little platforms with cup-marks (*bhorka*) for their worship, the custom of heaping up earth (*cf.* the cairns of Europe) in their honour, or in honour of some of the minor deities.

There is a large mass of superstitious custom connected with agriculture, such as the days on which ploughing, sowing, reaping, &c., must be begun, intermitted or finished; the rites observed or invocations employed at their commencement or completion; the ceremonies attending cotton-picking, cane-crushing, winnowing and division of grain, and commencement and completion of a well; the customary number of times which weeding should or should not be performed; the dimensions of wells and well-gear being measured in so many *and three quarter* hands, and the like.

The number 5 and its aliquot parts, as 1¼, 2½, will be found to run through many of the superstitious, and even of the religious, customs of the people.

10. *Use of Bráhmans.*—Musulmáns often still retain and fee the family Bráhmans, employing them especially at betrothals and weddings, in casting horoscopes and fixing lucky names and dates, and the like. This is valuable, as indicating Hindú origin. The *class* of Bráhman so employed should always be ascertained.

Some of the lower castes have a sort of outcast Bráhmans who minister to them only; and I understand that there are Musalmán Bráhmans (called Huseni) who perform hereditary offices for their converted clients. Any special order of priesthood of this sort should be described. Most of the frontier tribes include Levitical clans, who have the monopoly of priestly functions, and occupy a position somewhat similar to that of Bráhmans among Hindús.

More information is needed about the different classes of Bráhmans, as the *Achárj*, *Dákaut*, *Gújráti*, *&c.*, what position they hold in the sacerdotal ranks, what offerings they accept, what functions they perform, and what is the origin of the distinction into classes.

11. *Totemism.*—Signs of reverence for some animal or plant peculiar to the caste or clan will often be met with. Thus, some clans will not eat or burn certain plants; the women of others veil their faces before certain trees, as if in presence of an elder relative, or worship them in hope of getting children, in the belief that the spirit of the ancestor inhabits them; others use or worship certain plants at weddings and similar ceremonies; and some castes call all their sons after plants. A clandestine marriage round a fire made of certain wild plants, even though performed without the usual ceremonial, is sometimes considered to be of a peculiary binding nature. The clan name is sometimes derived from that of a plant or animal; and there is often a tradition connecting it with the clan and accounting for the reverence shown it. The people's explanation of the clan name, though often apparently absurd, should always be given.

12. *Social Customs.*—All social customs are exceedingly useful in tracing ethnic affinities, as they are marvellously persistent. The simplest method of recording them probably is to describe minutely any set of customs or ceremonies as practised by the principal tribe of the neighbourhood; and, taking that as a standard, to note the points in which the practice of other tribes departs from it—

(*a*) *Differential* customs, which are special to one tribe, and differ from the custom of other tribes in the neighbourhood, are most important of all.

(*b*) Birth customs; the giving two names, one for every-day wear, and one for ceremonial use; the meanings of names, often intended to deceive or frighten the small-pox goddess by depreciating or exalting the qualities of the child; name-jingles or rhymes within the family, perhaps marking the paternity in polyandrous families; the rites connected with the scalplock, puberty, and cuttings and offerings of hair in general, are all interesting and often important. The period of ceremonial impurity after birth and death (*sútak* and *pátak*) should always be given, as they vary with the caste.

(*c*) Marriage and betrothal customs are especially valuable. It will often be found that a Musalmán tribe will have identical marriage ceremonies with those of its Hindu neighbours, with the single exception of the substitution of the *nikáh* for the *pherá*, or even the addition of the former to the latter.

(*d*) Polyandry is practised, in a sort of half-recognized manner, far more generally throughout the Panjáb than is usually supposed. It may always be suspected where the custom is for the eldest only of a family of brothers to marry. Other curious forms of marriage will also be found in certain parts, such as the infant son marrying an adult woman who cohabits with the nominal father

(e) It should always be stated whether the people burn or bury their dead; if the former, where the bones and ashes are finally bestowed; if the latter, whether they are buried lying or sitting, on the face or on the back, in a graveyard or at home; in both cases, in which direction graves or shrines face. In the case of menials, it should be noted whether they have a distinct custom proper to their caste, or whether they merely follow the custom of the village to which they are attached, which will vary with the religion of the villagers.

(f) All customs of committing corpses or ashes to local streams or tanks should be noted, and the origin and nature of the virtue these possess should be recorded. This practice is believed to be dying out in favour of the more orthodox localities.

13. *Karewá.*—It is of capital importance to know whether a tribe practises *karewá*, or the remarriage of the widow, as the existence of this custom helps to fix both origin and social status. The custom exists in two forms, which must be carefully distinguished:—

(1) The Levirate, in which the eldest surviving brother of the deceased takes the widow: this is either a remnant of past or a token of existing polyandry.

(2) Where the existing restrictions upon marriage out of the caste, &c., are relaxed in the case of widows, a marriage with almost *any* widow being permitted.

It should be noted which of these forms is practised; [and further, what rule of inheritance is observed, especially under the Levirate: whether, for instance, the son begotten of the widow by the younger brother of the deceased inherits as the son of the elder or of the younger brother.]

14. *Inheritance*—

(a) Minute details of the rules of inheritance do not generally bear upon our subject. But it is important to know whether the tribe follows the strict Islamic law of succession, or whether their rules, by denying rights of succession to females, tend to keep property in the clan.

(b) Primogeniture; equal division between sons; *Págband* and *Chúndaband*; succession of sons during the father's lifetime; distinctions between whole and half-brothers on the father's and mother's side respectively; succession of daughters; and inheritance by the son-in-law of a sonless father (*gharjawái*), are all points which may be usefully noticed, more especially when customs are found to differ on any of them.

(c) Any traces of inheritance through the female line, such as inheritance by brothers or sisters, or by sister's sons, should be carefully recorded.

(d) Traces of *vesh*, or the periodical redistribution by lot of common arable land among the households or adults of the community, are interesting.

15. *Relationship and its incidents.*—A table showing the terms used for the various kinds and degrees of relationship, and the people who are included under each, will often throw valuable light upon the ancient constitution of the family. It should be stated what relations may not be mentioned either by name, or by the term for the relationship; as for instance, that a woman may not name her husband, and that a man will not describe his brother-in-law (*sála*) as such.

The admission of strangers to inherit, the manner of and restrictions upon adoption, the relations arising from and destroyed by adoption, *gharjawái*, and foster kinship, and by the custom of making *bhúmbhai*, should all be noted.

Especially the relations which are created by marriage—(1) between the woman and the members of the family she marries into, (2) between the two families, are important. In the west of the Panjáb a woman changes her clan (*got*) by marriage; in the east she does not. It would be interesting to discover where the custom changes, and to note any facts bearing upon it; as, for instance, the custom of formal admission of the bride into her husband's clan. The functions which custom assigns to sisters' sons and husbands, brothers' wives, sister-in-laws' mothers and similar relations, in social ceremonials, such as marriage rites, are exceedingly interesting and instructive, and need further examination.

Further facts bearing upon the importance of eating together (*confarreatio*) in ceremonies where a new relationship is created, are needed. The custom often takes the form of a distribution of *gur* or sweetmeats.

16. *Intermarriage.*

(a) It is specially important to discover the limits within or beyond which marriage is forbidden; for instance, that a man must marry, in the first instance at any rate, within the caste; but must not marry into his own, his mother's or his paternal or maternal grandmother's clan, nor a girl, of whatever clan, who lives in a village marching with his own, and must not marry two sisters; or whether the prohibited degrees of Islám are the only limitations observed. It is important to know how far differences of religion or sect are a bar to marriage.

(b) It is also of great importance [as throwing light upon the possible mixed origin of some of our tribes and clans] to know how the offspring of—(1) first marriage, (2) *karewá* marriages, (3) illicit connexions between parents of different tribes, castes or religions are now classed; whether they follow the tribe and clan of the father or of the mother, or are known by an entirely new name; and what distinction, if any, is made between them and others who are born into the tribe and clan in a more usual or legitimate manner.

(c) Clans often cannot intermarry with certain other clans as being of common origin with themselves; for instance, the *Deswál*, *Mán*, and *Dalál* Jats, the *Mandhár*, *Kandhár* and *Bargújar* Rájputs, and so on. Ties of this sort should be carefully sought for and recorded.

(d) Castes and clans often refuse to, or are not allowed to, intermarry with certain others on the score of social status. In some cases wives will be received, but daughters will not be given in marriage. It is useful to give these particulars, as helping to fix the social standing.

17. *Social status.*—This is denoted in three ways:—

(a) by the customs regarding intermarriage just referred to;

(b) by the standing of the castes which will—(1) eat, (2) drink, (3) smoke with them, the Brahmanical distinction between *pakki roti*, or dry food cooked in ghi, and *kachhi roti* or food not so cooked, being noticed where it exists. Thus, in some parts of the province a *Gaur* Bráhman will eat *pakki roti* from the hands of a Hindu Jat, while he will not eat *kachhi roti* even from the hands of a *Sársút* Bráhman;

(c) by the general custom of the neighbourhood, which condemns certain castes to live in separate quarters, drink from separate wells, and so on.

18. *Occupation.*—The principal local occupations of the caste should be specified. It will often be found that change of religion affects the occupation. Thus a sweeper converted to Islám usually ceases to remove night-soil, while a Sikh Chamár will often leave leather work and take to weaving. It is often the case, moreover, that different clans pursue different branches of the occupation hereditary to the caste. Thus some Ghosi clans keep cattle and sell milk only; others buy milk and sell butter.

Instances of abandonment of hereditary occupation should be noticed, and whether in such cases the caste name is abandoned or altered, and the ties with the original caste broken or relaxed (*see* section 21 below).

19. *Minor peculiarities.*

(a) Customs prohibiting or enjoining the eating or growing of certain plants, as onions, turnips, indigo, &c., the eating of flesh, drinking of wine, smoking, and use of drugs, the use of vessels made of a particular metal or of earth, or ornamented with stripes or otherwise, often afford useful indications.

(*b*) It will generally be found that the dress and jewels vary with the religion, caste, clan and conjugal condition; especially as to the colour of the clothes, red, blue, whole or party-coloured; the use of drawers or petticoats, *dhotis* or *tahmans;* the use of boddices; of nose-rings, small or large, of gold or of silver; the use of bracelets of silver or lac; the colour of the wrap and of the head-dress; and the general method of shaping and wearing the garments and jewels. Customs regulating personal adornment, such as tattooing, ornamenting the teeth with gold, compressing the skull, &c., &c., are always valuable.

(*c*) Honorific titles peculiar to castes or clans should be noted.

(*d*) Peculiarities of language will often point to place of origin, and peculiarities of physique betray ethnic descent; but these two are very difficult to detect.

(*e*) Local songs, proverbs, and folk-lore often afford curious and useful hints about custom, and are always interesting and valuable. They should be taken down exactly as spoken or sung, and not doctored to make them conform with grammatical rule or theory.

19*a*. *Tribal and Village Organization.*—Traces of tribal organization will generally be found, even where the tribe is now least prominent. Some of the points to be noted are—the tract, often called *Thapa* or *Thamba*, held, now or formerly, by the tribe or clan; the existence and organization of a tribal assembly or *pancháyat;* how it is convened, and what questions it deals with; whether its constitution involves any rudimentary idea of representation, either hereditary or elective; the mode of selection of a tribal chief or *Sarpanch;* whether he must necessarily belong to the head (*thíka*) village or family; how that village or family is determined, and the privileges it enjoys; how far the assembly or chief represents the body, so that the latter is bound by its or his acts, and how its or his decisions are enforced; what privileges the chief enjoys; what dues he receives; what power he possesses over the land of the tribe, and what share he owns in it, or whether he is the one tribesman who has no share at all. The organization within the village should be similarly described.

Relics of a now extinct tribal organization will sometimes be found in the titles or social privileges accorded to members of a certain family; and it is often the case that the organization which has almost wholly died out among the land-owning communities, survives in comparative integrity among their priests and menials, whose *pancháyats* are organized upon the basis of the land-owing tribe to which they are attached, while those who come from the *thíka* village enjoy certain rights and privileges.

20. *Sects and Ascetic Orders.*—Sects are exceedingly numerous, especially among Hindús; and new ones are constantly springing into existence. The various orders of faqírs are numbered by hundreds, while the census papers show many such of which little

or nothing appears to be known. The points most worthy of record are—the name, date, and life history of the founder of the sect or order; where its head-quarters are situated; peculiar tenets and ceremonial practices which distinguish it from other sects or orders; what deities or saints are specially venerated; peculiarities of dress, if any; what castes are admitted, what chiefly enter, and whether caste names, rules, and distinctions are recognized after entry; the rites used in admission; whether any special occupations, colours, dress, food, &c., are encouraged, prescribed, prohibited or discountenanced. In the case of a new sect, the estimated number of followers, where they most abound, to what classes they belong, and whether it is spreading or dying out. In the case of an order, whether the faqírs are celibate or not; whether they are wholly wandering and independent, or are attached to monasteries and have a system of internal government; what is their general character; and what functions, if any, they perform in the life of the people.

21. *Trade-guilds.*—These guilds appear to assume every form intermediate between castes proper and the European trades-union. Even true castes, such as that of the sweepers, where the occupation is prescribed by birth, are, where they follow a trade, handicraft, or menial occupation, generally governed by an elaborate *pancháyat* organization. And this is almost always the case where the guild, like, for instance, that of tailors, includes men of very different castes.

In these cases the nature of the organization should be described, the degree of control which it exercises over the members of the guild, and the method in which it enforces its decisions. Points worthy of note are—whether they admit men of all castes and religions, and what castes and religions usually enter the guild; whether the caste name is abandoned for that of the occupation, either in the first instance or in the second generation, and whether it is resumed again if the occupation is abandoned; whether the different castes within the guild intermarry with each other, with their own castes within the guild, or with their own castes outside the guild; how far the occupation tends to becom hereditary; in what degree the rules of the guild supersede or override those of the caste, and what happens when the two conflict. The titles of the heads of the various guilds should always be given, as *Mahtar*, *Ráj*, *Khalífah*, as they explain the mode of addressing followers of the trade or occupation.

22. *Formation of new castes.*—Any facts bearing upon the origin or growth of new castes should be carefully watched for and noted. It will sometimes be found that a tribe or family has lately begun to affect a religious sanctity or a social exclusiveness beyond that of its fellows, has changed or abandoned its former occupation in whole or in part, has adopted or relinquished the custom of widow-marriage, has excluded from or admitted to matrimonial alliance clans with which it formerly did or did not intermarry, and so on. It is believed that instances of a clan or family which, a very few generations ago, was undoubtedly classed as Jat, being now generally admitted as Rájput, and *vice versâ*, or of the descendants of

a Jat grandfather having now, by virtue of mere change of occupation, become Náís or Lohárs, and been admitted to caste privileges by the other Náís or Lohárs of the neighbourhood, are more common than is generally supposed. Nothing can be more important than a careful record of the actual facts in such cases; whether the people in question have risen or fallen in the social scale; how their position in respect of intermarriage with other sections of the community has been affected; whether they have adopted a new or are still known by the old name, and so on.

23. *Boundaries.*—It is important to define, as far as possible, the boundary which marks any change in religion, language, custom, or tribal distribution or nomenclature; such as the line at which Khatrís supersede Banyas or Aroras Khatrís, at which Bágri take the place of Dese Jats, Kutánas and Musallis of Chúhras, or Charhoas of Dhobis and Chhímpis, at which Juláha yields to Páoli, Ját to Jat, Hindi to Panjábí, Hinduism to Sikhism, at which the custom changes as to marriage within the caste but outside the clan, as to the hereditary nature of occupations, or as to the change of a bride's clan. The limits within which dialects are spoken also stand in great need of definition, though they are often by no means clearly marked. There is very generally an intermediate or neutral zone, within which the distinct dialects, tribes, or customs which prevail on either side of it are to be found in a state of intermixture or transition. Such zones should be defined as accurately aspossible.

24. *Tracts.*—It is useful to define the exact limits of the many local tracts into which the people themselves have divided the province; such as the Bágar, the Nardak, Hariána, Bhattíána, the Málwa, the Mánjha, the Pawád, the Bajwát, the Rohi, the Jangal-des, the Dogar-des, the Dáman, the Pachhád, and a hundred others. These divisions are permanent; and, unlike our artificially formed districts and subdivisions, represent natural features, either physical or ethnographical.

Information is also much needed regarding the limits of the old *parganahs*, *sarkárs*, *súbahs* and other ancient administrative divisions of the country; as in the absence of such information we cannot fully understand the statements of the old historians which refer to these divisions. The Sikhs often altered considerably the old units of Mughal administration; and it should always be stated to which of these two dynasties the facts given refer.

25. *Bibliography.*—Much information on the subject of the divisions of the people will be found in all the various Settlement Reports; while their religious and social customs are treated of in Mr. Lyall's Report on Kángra, paragraphs 66, 72 to 74, 112 to 119, 154, 160 to 169, in Mr. Barnes' Report on Kángra, paragraphs 253 to 294, in Captain Waterfield's Report on Gujrát, paragraphs 121 to 164, in Mr. Maconachie's Report on Delhi, paragraphs 143 to 150, in Mr. Channing's Report on Gurgaon, pages 34 to 37, and in my Report on Karnál (now passing through the Press), Chapters VI, VIII, IX, and part of VII. Elliot's Races of the North-West Provinces of India, edited by Beames (London, Trübner, 1869, two vols., 8vo., price 36*s*.), is a store-house of valuable information; as

are a little book on the Domestic Manners and Customs of the Hindús of Northern India by the Rev. Ishuree Dass (Benares, Lazarus, and London, Trübner, 1866), Wilson's Sketch of the Religious Sects of the Hindús (Calcutta, Bishop's College Press, 1846, cost about 5*s*.), and some of Colebrooke's Miscellaneous Essays (reprint of 1858, cost 6*s*.)

The constitution of the tribe and family can be studied in pages *i* to *c* of vol. II of Mr. Tupper's work on Panjab Customary Law; and in the earlier pages of Mr. Wilson's Code of Tribal Customs in the Gurgaon District (reprinted in the volume just mentioned).

The learner who is anxious to acquaint himself with some of the published results of sociological research cannot do better than begin with Sir John Lubbock's Origin of Civilisation (London, Longman, 1870, one vol., 8vo., price 16*s*.); while the following are a few less elementary works on the same and cognate subjects:—Tylor's Early History of Mankind (London, Murray, 1870, one vol., 8vo., price 12*s*.); Tyler's Primitive Culture (London, Murray, 1871, two vols., 8vo., price 24*s*.); MacLennan's Primitive Marriage (London, Quaritch, 1876, one vol., small 8vo., price 16*s*.); Morgan's Ancient Society (London, MacMillan, 1877, one vol., 8vo., price 16*s*.); Maine's Village Communities (London, Murray, 1872, one vol., 8vo., price 12*s*.); Maine's Early History of Institutions (London, Murray, 1875, one vol., 8vo., price 12*s*.)

26. *Finally*, I would remind you that *no notes can possibly be too fragmentary or too trivial to be worth sending me*. Incomplete as this memorandum is, a complete examination of even a single caste in a single district with regard to all the points noted would be a very serious undertaking. But it is only meant to suggest lines of inquiry, some of which will interest one person and some another. Even bare lists of clans and subdivisions, or a note that a certain single clan belongs to such a tribe, will be most useful. And *all* details regarding the customs of the people, however minute or apparently uninteresting, possess great ethnological value; and *especially points in which the customs of one people differ from those of another*. For instance, a statement which I have just seen that the temporary huts which the *Báwarias* build for themselves are circular in plan, at once suggests the inquiry where the pattern was brought from, and invites comparison with the bee-hive shaped tent of the nomad Mongols. It is always well to test and confirm any information which has been collected by inquiries from fresh individuals. But where this cannot be done, the information will still be of great value; for it can be tested by comparison or by subsequent inquiry, whic, if not noted at once, it is lost. It is as well, however, in sending notes, to state how far the information has been tested and supported by repeated inquiry.

The primary distribution of the Panjab peoples among the aboriginal inhabitants, and the several great waves of immigration which have at different times swept into the country, can only be arrived at by a minute comparison of their various social and religious customs; and the immense question of the growth and nature of caste can only be elucidated by a study of the internal relations and economy of existing castes. The habits of the vagrant and outcast classes afford an almost untrodden field for the one inquiry; the exceedingly interesting and elaborate caste-organization of the menial castes, and of those numerous trade-guilds of which it is often so difficult to say whether they are castes or only occupations, affords equally unexplored material for the other. Work in either field, or indeed in any cognate direction, will help on the inquiry into the early history of social institutions which has lately assumed such great interest and importance. We in India have an inexhaustible store-house of facts at our very doors, and unequalled facilities for ascertaining and recording them. Every year sees some of the existing material disappear under the powerful solvent of contact with European thought and the appliances of civilization. We are probably too near our subject to generalise with success; but we, and we alone, can obtain the facts from which generalisations can be made.

APPENDIX IV.

LIST OF CORRESPONDENTS SELECTED TO TAKE PART IN THE ETHNOGRAPHIC SURVEY OF BENGAL.

Division.	District.	Names of correspondents.
Bardwan	Midnapur	Baboo Bisseswar Banerji. „ Kali Narayan Roy. The Deputy Inspector of Schools. K. C. Ghosh, Esq. Baboo Rajendra Lal Gupta. The Executive Engineer, Cossye Division.
	Bardwan	W. B. Oldham, Esq. Baboo Tara Prosad Chatterji. The Subdivisional Officer, Culna. Ditto ditto, Cutwa. Ditto ditto, Raniganj. Baboo Jaga Mohan Bhattacharji.
	Hughli	B. N. De, Esq. Baboo Kedar Nath Dutt. The Subdivisional Officer, Jehanabad. Baboo Aswini Kumar Bose.
	Howrah	Baboo Bankim Chandra Chatterji. „ Prasanna Kumar Bose.
	Birbhum	Baboo Bhuban Mohan Raha. N. Warde-Jones, Esq.
	Bankura	Baboo Atul Chandra Chatterji. „ Guru Das Barman. The Sub-Registrar of Khattra. Ditto of Kotalpur. Baboo Haris Chandra Rai.
Presidency	24-Parganás	Baboo Hem Chandra Kar. Kumar Gopendra Krishna Deb. Pandit Hara Prasad Sastri. Baboo Ranga Lal Mukharji.
	Calcutta	Dr. Rajendra Lal Mitra, C.I.E. Jagannath Khanna, Esq. Baboo Protab Chandra Ghosh. „ Adya Nath Banerji. T. N. Mukharji, Esq. Baboo Protab Chandra Roy.

Division.	District.	Names of correspondents.
Presidency—*concluded.*	Nadiya ...	Baboo Tarini Kumar Ghosh. „ Ishan Chandra Ghosh.
	Jessore ...	Baboo Krishna Kali Mukharji. „ Kedar Nath Biswas. „ Bankim Chandra Chatterji. „ Chandi Das Ghose. „ Troylakya Nath Sen. „ Annada Prasad Sen. „ Kali Prasanna Sarkar.
	Khulna ...	Baboo Khagendra Nath Mitter. „ Bhubaneswar Sing. „ Narendra Nath Roy Chowdri.
	Murshedabad ...	Baboo Bansidhar Roy. „ Pran Kumar Das. „ Bipin Bihari Mukerji. „ Bijoy Krishna Bose. „ Srinath Gupta.
Rajshahye ...	Rajshahye ...	Baboo Mahendra Nath Bhattacharji.
	Dinajpur ...	Dr. U. C. Mukerji. Baboo Sarat Chandra Chatterji.
	Rangpur ...	Moulvi Abdul Khaleque. H. E. Ransom, Esq. J. T. Mackay, Esq. Baboo Sarada Prasad Chatterji. „ Kumud Bihari Samanta.
	Bogra ...	Baboo Bhubaneswar Gupta.
	Pabna ...	E. F. Growse, Esq. Baboo Barada Churn Mitter. „ Purna Chandra Gupta.
	Jalpigori ...	Baboo Priya Nath Mukerji. H. H. Heard, Esq. D. Sunder, Esq.
	Darjiling ...	Baboo Parbati Charan Roy. „ Sarat Chandra Das, C.I.E. Raja Tenduk Palgar. Baboo Mari Das Pradhan. „ Hathura Nath Chatterji. „ Gelong Nimsring.
	Kuch Behar ...	Baboo Calica Das Dutt.
Dacca ...	Dacca ...	Baboo Mati Lal Sarkar. „ Rajani Nath Ghosh. „ Syam Kishore Bose. „ Aswini Kumar Bose. „ Aditya Chandra Chakrabarti. „ Ram Chandra Dhar.

Division.	District.	Names of correspondents.
Dacca—concld.	Dacca—concld.	Maulvi Mazharal Anwar. Baboo Nalini Nath Mitra. " Gopal Chandra Bose. E. B. Harris, Esq. Baboo Bagala Prasanna Mazumdar. " Raj Kumar Sen. " Dina Nath Dhar.
	Faridpur ...	Baboo Khetra Gopal Roy. " Girindra Nath Chatterji.
	Bakarganj ...	Maulvi Syed Obedulla. Baboo Jogadish Chandra Roy. " Umakishore Roy. " Sasi Sekhar Dutt. F. Wilcox, Esq. Baboo Pitambar Sing. " Aswini Kumar Dutt. " Parbatti Nath Ghose.
	Maimansinh ...	Maulvi Mohamed. Baboo Jogendra Nath Banerji. Mr. Ellison (missionary).
Chittagong ...	Chittagong ...	Baboo Gaur Mohan Basak. " Radha Kishore Chakrabati.
	Noakhali ...	Baboo Jogendra Nath Chakrabati. " Satis Chandra Bose. The District Magistrate.
	Tipperah ...	Dr. J. ffrench-Mullen. Baboo Tarak Chandra Gupta.
	Hill Tipperah ...	Baboo Uma Kanta Das.
	Chittagong Hill Tracts.	Baboo Braja NathShaha. " Hari Pada Ghosh.
Bhagalpur ...	Bhagalpur ...	A. H. Giles, Esq. Baboo Ram Narain Banerji. " Mathura Nath Mukerji.
	Purniah ...	Baboo Karunamaya Banerji. Surji Kumar Agasti, Esq. Baboo Kastori Lal.
	Monghyr ...	Baboo Debi Prasad. The Subdivisional Officer, Begusarai. Ditto ditto, Jamui.
	Maldah ...	Baboo Shib Chandra Nag. Maulvi Zakir Hossein. H. R. Reily, Esq.

Division.	District.	Names of correspondents.
Bhagalpur—*concluded.*	Santál Parganás	Baboo C. N. Gupta. " N. C. Banerji. A. W. Stark, Esq. Syed Nejabat Hossein. Rev. L. O. Skrefsrud.
Patna ...	Patna ...	The District Superintendent of Police. Maulvi Majibar Rahman. Syed Zahiruddin. Baboo Bemala Charan Bhattacharji. " Sheo Nandan Lal Roy. C. N. Banerji, Esq. Maulvi Wahed Uddin.
	Gya ...	Dr. R. Macleod. Baboo Rajkishore Narain. " Radha Lal. " Sarada Prasad Ganguli.
	Shahabad ...	The District Superintendent of Police. " Subdivisional Officer, Buxar. J. R. Hand, Esq. The Subdivisional Officer, Bhabua.
	Darbhanga ...	The District Magistrate. " Subdivisional Officer, Tajpur. " ditto ditto, Madhubani. " Sub-Registrar, ditto. Maulvi Gowhar Ali. Baboo Dwarka Prasad. " Pramath Nath Chaterji. " Okhoy Kumar Chaterji.
	Mozufferpur ...	Baboo Ram Prakas Lal. H. W. C. Carnduff, Esq.
	Saran ...	The Deputy Inspector of Schools. A. Tytler, Esq. Baboo Raghunath Sahai. R. F. H. Pughe, Esq.
	Champaran ...	The Deputy Inspector of Schools. " Sub-Inspector of Schools. " Canungo at Sudder Station. W. R. Bright, Esq. The Sub-Deputy Collector, Bettiah. " Canungo at Bettiah.
Chota Nagpur	Hazaribagh ...	Baboo Girendra Nath Mitra. Rai Jadu Nath Mukerji.
	Lohardagá ...	Baboo Girindra Chandra Banerji. " Gagan Chandra Banerji. F. A. Slack, Esq. Baboo Rakhal Das Haldar. C. A. G. Lillingston, Esq. The Munsif of Palamow.

Division.	District.	Names of correspondents.
Chota Nagpur—*concld.*	Manbhum ...	Baboo Surya Kumar Guha. „ Paresh Nath Ghosh. „ Atal Bihari Moitra. Rev. A. Campbell. The Munsif of Bara Bazar.
	Singbhum ...	The Deputy Commissioner, Singbhum.
	Tributary States	The Commissioner of Chota Nagpur.
Orissa ...	Cuttack ...	Baboo Ramakhoy Chatterji.
	Puri ...	The Senior Deputy Collector at head-quarters.
	Balasore ...	Baboo Rash Behari Naik. „ Akhoy Kumar Chatterji. Hon'ble Kumar Baikant Nath De.
	Tributary States	The Tehsildar of Khandmals. „ Manager of Nilgiri. „ „ of Dhenkanal. „ „ of Mohurbhanj. Rev. Father Schaff. Srinath Dutt, Esq.

W. J.—Reg. No. 4044J—120—11-12-91